AUSTRALIA
HANDBOOK

AUSTRALIA
HANDBOOK
FIRST EDITION

MARAEL JOHNSON,
NADINA PURDON & ANDREW HEMPSTEAD

MOON
PUBLICATIONS INC.

AUSTRALIA HANDBOOK
FIRST EDITION

Published by
Moon Publications, Inc.
P.O. Box 3040
Chico, California 95927-3040, USA

Printed by
Colorcraft Ltd., Hong Kong

Please send all comments,
corrections, additions,
amendments, and critiques to:

**AUSTRALIA HANDBOOK
MOON PUBLICATIONS, INC.
P.O. BOX 3040
CHICO, CA 95927-3040, USA
e-mail: travel@moon.com**

Printing History
1st edition — January 1997

ISBN: 1-56691-072-2

ISSN: 1088-6427

Editor: Michael Raymond Greer
Assistant Editor: Lisa Stowell
Copy Editor: Deana Corbitt Shields
Production & Design: Carey Wilson
Cartographers: Bob Race, Brian Bardwell, Rob Warner, Chris Folks, Jason Sadler
Index: Nicole Revere

Frontispiece: red kangaroo by Bob Race

Front cover photo: savannah grasslands with snappy gums and termite mounds, near Normanton,
Queensland, by Bill Bachman
All photos by Bill Bachman unless otherwise noted.

Distributed in the U.S.A. and Canada by Publishers Group West
Printed in Hong Kong

CONTENTS

TIME'S WINGÉD CHARIOT

Though we strive to be as accurate and current as possible, alas—
things change. If you discover an error, or something new and
exciting (a walking trail, dinosaur footprint, cache of diamonds, a reflection of the man in the moon), please let us know.

Australia Handbook
c/o Moon Publications, Inc.
P.O. Box 3040
Chico, CA 95927 USA
e-mail: travel@moon.com

MAPS

MAP SYMBOLS

HIGHWAY

MAIN ROAD

OTHER ROAD

- - - - TRACK

BRIDGE

· — · · — · STATE BORDER

+ + + RAILROAD

· — · · — · PATH

NOTE: NOT ALL ROADS INDICATED BY A
  SOLID LINE ARE PAVED. CONDITION OF
  UNPAVED ROADS OR TRACKS MAY VARY.

O CITY

O TOWN

■ POINT OF INTEREST

● ACCOMMODATIONS/CARAVAN PARKS

C. P. = CONSERVATION PARK

N. P. = NATIONAL PARK

♪ GOLF COURSE

NATIONAL HIGHWAY

STATE HIGHWAY

DRY LAKE

WATER

MOUNTAIN

CAMPING

SHIPWRECK

AIRPORT

ABORIGINAL ROCK ART

CHARTS AND SPECIAL TOPICS

ABBREVIATIONS

ACT—Australian Capital Territory

B&B—bed and breakfast

BHP—Broken Hill Proprietary

C—Celsius

CWA—Country Women's Association

d—double

DC&NR—Department of Conservation and Natural Resources

F—Fahrenheit

4WD—four-wheel drive

NPWS—National Parks and Wildlife Service

NSW—New South Wales

NT—Northern Territory

P.O.—post office

pp—per person

RAA or **RAC**—Royal Automobile Association or Royal Automobile Club

QLD—Queensland

s—single

SA—South Australia

STA—State Transit Authority (South Australia) or Student Travel Association

TAS—Tasmania

tel.—telephone

VIC—Victoria

WA—Western Australia

YHA—Youth Hostel Association

YMCA/YWCA—Young Men's/Women's Christian Association

ACKNOWLEDGMENTS

Thanks to everyone for helping me pull this masterpiece together: Cheryl Grant and Garuda Indonesia for generous help and support; my sister, Susan (a.k.a. The Good One), for her crackerjack contract negotiations; Taran March, saintly editoress and all-around fall guy; guru Bill Dalton, for inspiring me to be a travel writer in the first place; Hamish Trumble and Macro The Wonder Dog for their contribution to this book's Introduction; Mike Greer, editor and Volvo mechanic; Bill Bachman, heaven-sent outback photographer; Michael, for sorting countless illustrations of boomerangs, koalas, and big rocks; Moon computer whiz Asha Johnson, *artistes* Bob Race and Dave Hurst, all the other Moon Beams; and all my mates down under and my pals up top who put up with my bad moods and midnight appetites during this intense project, ESPECIALLY the Argyle Street gang (happy now?).

— MARAEL JOHNSON

Thanks to our friends and relatives in the eastern states who contributed their local knowledge to help make this book more complete. Those with the most comfortable lounges, state by state, included Tony Williams in Ballina (NSW), Clayton Barr in Torquay (Victoria), and Matt and Lindy in Bundaberg (Queensland). Tony Williams' presence was also appreciated on a couple of research trips, including one through the New South Wales outback and to the far reaches of Victoria. The Tasmanian chapter of the book was researched by Jane King and we thank her, along with Pete Lingard and Donna Lee Young for an insight to the island they call home.

At Moon Publications, thanks to those who had the faith to offer us the project. Thanks to Michael Greer, our editor, for ironing out the rough spots, and to his able assistant Lisa Stowell, who now both have a better appreciation of the Australian language.

— NADINA PURDON AND ANDREW HEMPSTEAD

BOB RACE

INTRODUCTION

Waltzing Matilda through Australia will take you to more places than the Great Barrier Reef and the outback. The Great Southern Land is massive and, if you have a true swagman's spirit, limitless. Australia comprises six states and two territories, with Canberra, ACT, being the national capital and Sydney, NSW, the largest city (pop. four million). Well over half of Australia's total population of 18 million lives within 100 km of the Pacific shore, a 4,000-km stretch of beaches, harbors, and rivers. The Great Barrier Reef, 2,000 kilometers of reef dotted with islands, and one of the world's greatest wonders, protects the northern half of Australia's east coast. Rural Australia and the outback lie west of the Great Diving Range, a spine of mountains that runs the entire length of the east coast. The outback sprawls across five states, with the Northern Territory, Western Australia, and South Australia almost entirely desert. Along the coasts of these states cling their three capitals—Darwin, Perth, and Adelaide, respectively—each with a distinctive charm not found in the main eastern population centers. The Northern Territory's Uluru (Ayers Rock), the world's largest mono-

lith, rises from the heart of Australia. Australia is by no means just beaches and desert; at the southern end of the Great Dividing Range vast areas of high country are blanketed in snow

AUSTRALIA COMPARED TO NORTH AMERICA

0   1,000 km

© MOON PUBLICATIONS, INC.

each winter, offering Aussie-style alpine experiences. Different from anywhere else in the country, Tasmania, a 68,000-square-km island off the southeast coast of the mainland, is often missed by travelers down under, and even by many Aussies themselves. As well as having some of Australia's best-preserved convict-era villages, Tasmania, with its hiking, climbing, and sea-kayaking opportunities, is a mecca for zealots of the outdoors.

THE LAND

Australia is made of contradictions and conundrums. Is it the smallest continent or the biggest island on earth? Is it the oldest place in the world? Indeed it is, and you can stroll over rocks that were formed four billion years ago. But geologists will remind you that Australia didn't separate from the Asian landmass to become its own continent until recent, almost modern times—a mere 50 million years ago.

Its isolation in the remote southern ocean meant that Australia, aside from Antarctica, was the last continent to succumb to human occupancy (Aborigines arrived about 40,000 years ago); but long before Europeans arrived, philosophers from Athens to Alexandria postulated the existence of the "antipodes" on the theory that symmetry demanded a southern continent to balance the known world in the north.

Australia is a fragment of the ancient supercontinent Pangaea. Six hundred million years ago, South America, Africa, Antarctica, Australasia, and the Indian subcontinent were all hooked together. Over the millennia since, they have been drifting apart, as the massive tectonic plates float across the earth's mantle. Australia is riding in the middle of a plate whose leading edge in northern India is relentlessly smashing into central Asia, piling up the Himalayas. The eastern edge of the same plate runs alongside New Zealand, which experiences the volcanic consequences of two unimaginably vast slabs of rock grinding away at each other.

Being in the middle of this enormous plate has meant that the Australian continent has been comparatively free of volcanic and other cataclysmic upheavals. Consequently, Australia is the flattest of the continents; time and weather have eroded mountain ranges that once would have dwarfed Mt. Everest. Mount Kosciusko in New South Wales, Australia's highest mountain (2,228 meters above sea level), would barely pass muster as a respectable foothill elsewhere in the world. Australia has an average height of only 200 meters, and one of the most powerful impressions the traveler experiences in Australia is of awesome, mind-numbing flatness.

Another impression is dryness. Australia is the driest of the continents; some areas are subject to more evaporation than precipitation. While 40% of its landmass lies in the tropics, almost 70% is arid, with an annual rainfall below 25 centimeters. These parched conditions are accompanied by a *big* load of sand; some of the longest sand dunes in the world run parallel for up to 200 kilometers in the Simpson Desert. Where the sandy deserts give out, they are replaced by stony "gibber" deserts, relics of an ancient inland sea.

PROTECTING THE LAND

Land Protection Programs

The Register of the National Estate, compiled by the Australian Heritage Commission, provides annual grants for more than 200 projects within all states and territories. The 1990s have been dedicated the "Decade of Landcare" by the federal government, which has established environmental and conservation protection programs throughout the country—with all levels of government participating. This is a feather in the Green caps of the estimated 800,000 members of Australia's conservation societies (numbering nearly 1,000—up from 50 in the '50s).

In 1974, Australia became one of the first signatories to the UNESCO World Heritage convention—signers and members are committed to identify, protect, and promote World Heritage properties. Australia's list consists of: the Great Barrier Reef, Kakadu National Park, the Willandra Lakes Region, the Tasmanian Wilderness, Lord Howe Island Group, the Australian East Coast Temperate and Sub-tropical Rainforest Parks, Uluru National Park, Wet Tropics of Queensland, Shark Bay in Western Australia, and Fraser Island in Queensland. State and territorial governments join with the federal entity to protect these ecologically diverse and magnificent regions.

Pollution-wise, the feds control dumping of waste in the sea, as well as imports and exports of hazardous waste, while state and territory governments hold main responsibility for pollution controls (though guidelines for permitted levels of pollution are a collaborative effort with the federal government). As for industrial pollution, the federal government offers "encouragement" for cleaner methods.

State and territory governments are accountable for native wildlife within their respective boundaries, with the federal government taking over for the critters inhabiting federal territories. The federal level also has the say-so regarding international import and export of wildlife, and holds the pen when it comes to international treaties and conventions dealing with nature conservation.

Conservation Organizations

Greenies and other concerned travelers have several ways to join or support Australia's environmental consciousness.

The **Australian Conservation Foundation** (ACF) is the country's largest private conservation organization. Often working in coalition with the Wilderness Society and other action groups, the ACF is concerned with ozone depletion and the greenhouse effect, rainforest preservation, logging, and land abuse. It even casts its (save-the) eagle eye on the fragile Antarctic region. Memberships, subscriptions, and individual donations constitute most of their funding (the government contributes only about

10%). For more information, contact ACF, 340 Gore St., Fitzroy (Melbourne), VIC 3065 (tel. 03-9416-1455).

The **Wilderness Society**, which began as the Tasmanian Wilderness Society in response to the forthcoming *damning* of the Franklin River, has expanded its causes to encompass the entire country. You can support their positions by purchasing goods such as T-shirts, posters, books, and postcards from shops in all states except the Northern Territory. For more information, contact the main office at 130 Davey St., Hobart, TAS 7000 (tel. 03-6234-9366).

National Parks

For information on Australia's more than 2,000 national parks, wildlife sanctuaries, and nature reserves, contact the following organizations.

Australian Capital Territory, Parks and Conservation Service, G.P.O. Box 1119, Tuggeranong, ACT 2901 (tel. 06-237-5222)

New South Wales, National Parks and Wildlife Service, 43 Bridge St., Hurstville, NSW 2220;

NATIONAL PARK CODE

The Australian Nature Conservation Agency (formerly the National Parks and Wildlife Service) asks you to follow a number of simple rules to protect both you and the parks.

· Guard against fire. Use fireplaces where provided. Native timber is the home of small animals, so please preserve it by using a portable stove. No fires, including gas barbecues and stoves, may be lit when a fire ban is in force.

· Do not disturb, collect, or damage animals, wildflowers, vegetation, or earth or rock formations.

· Do not disturb or collect artifacts from Aboriginal sites. Sites and items may have sacred, ceremonial, mythological, and historical significance to Aboriginal people, and have scientific value.

· Firearms are not permitted.

· Do not litter. Carry your rubbish out of the park when you leave, or use a litter bin.

· Leave your pets at home. Dogs and cats are not allowed in parks, as they disturb both native animals and park visitors.

· Drive carefully and observe all notices.

· Use of registered off-road vehicles is restricted to existing designated roads and tracks.

· Contact local rangers for camping permits and for information on local conditions for bushwalking.

G.P.O. Box 1967, Hurstville, NSW 2220 (tel. 02-9585-6444)

Northern Territory, Conservation Commission of the Northern Territory, P.O. Box 496, Palmerston, Darwin, NT 0831 (tel. 08-8999-5511); or Australian Nature Conservation Agency, Smith St., Darwin, NT 0800; G.P.O. Box 1260, Darwin, NT 0801 (tel. 08-8981-5299)

Queensland, Queensland Department of Environment and Heritage, 160 Ann St., Brisbane, QLD 4000; P.O. Box 155, North Quay, Brisbane, QLD 4002 (tel. 07-3227-7111)

South Australia, Department of Environment and Natural Resources, 77 Grenfell St., Adelaide, SA 5001; G.P.O. Box 667, Adelaide, SA 5001 (tel. 08-8204-1910)

Victoria, Department of Conservation and Natural Resources (DC&NR), 240 Victoria Parade, East Melbourne, VIC 3002; P.O. Box 41, East Melbourne, VIC 3002 (tel. 03-9412-4011)

Tasmania, Department of Environment and Land Management, 134 Macquarie St., Hobart, TAS 7000; P.O. Box 44a, Hobart, TAS 7001 (tel. 03-6230-8011)

Western Australia, Department of Conservation and Land Management, 50 Hayman Rd., Como, WA 6152 (tel. 09-334-0333)

For countrywide information, contact the **Australian Nature Conservation Agency,** G.P.O. Box 636, Canberra, ACT 2601 (tel. 06-250-0200).

CLIMATE

The Seasons

Visitors from the Northern Hemisphere will immediately be struck by Australia's topsy-turvy seasons: summer officially begins on 1 December and winter on 1 June. This means that the academic and calendar years coincide, and both end with the summer holidays, in December. It also means you may experience the novelty of sitting down to a piping-hot Christmas dinner, perhaps of roast turkey or baked ham with all the trimmings, in the sweltering heat of high summer. And don't forget—here the sun rides across the northern sky and new rules apply. If you get lost and look for the mossy side of trees, just remember you're pointed south instead of north.

Most of the country doesn't experience the climatic extremes of, say, North America, but, still, choosing the correct time of year to travel is important. For those planning an extended trip around the country, try to spend spring, summer, or autumn in the south and leave the outback and the tropical areas of Queensland and the Northern Territory for the cooler months.

Australia straddles the Tropic of Capricorn, and climatic conditions range from temperate in the south to tropical in the north. Sydney enjoys a climate similar to Southern California, with mild winters and summer heat tempered by cooling sea breezes. Heading north, the year-round temperature increases, and while summers in Brisbane are pleasant, after crossing the Tropic of Capricorn (at Rockhampton) the summer heat can become unbearable for those unaccustomed to it. Being the tropics, summer in northern Queensland is the Wet (Aussie for the wet season), when torrential downpours are part of life, and travel up Cape York and in the Gulf Country is almost impossible. This far north, winters are comfortable, particularly near the coast, with dazzling days and dreamy nights. However, summer brings tropical rains and cyclones, some of which have been devilishly savage. In 1974, Cyclone Tracy—like a lover on a rampage—destroyed Darwin overnight, and most other coastal cities have suffered extensive damage from cyclones in the past. While traveling in these regions during the summer cyclone season, keep your ears open for radio weather reports, which give frequent updates on the movements of cyclones as they develop. Perth's weather is some of the best: sunny, mild, and not too humid (conditions are mild by run-for-the-thermal-undies standards). Adelaide enjoys a mild, almost Mediterranean climate, with moderate winters and dry summers. Summer is the best season to travel through Victoria and Tasmania, although spring and autumn can be pleasant (and less crowded).

The Aboriginal Seasons

The Aborigines who live around Kakadu National Park recognize six annual seasons rather than the "usual" four. The terms come from the

Gundjeidmi (Maiili) language. *Gunumeleng,* the early storm season, is marked by hot, increasingly humid weather, along with building thunderstorms and scattered showers; *gudjewg,* the early monsoon season (known as the Wet), is usually a time of thunder and lightning, heat and humidity, and blossoming plant and animal life; *bangereng* is late monsoon season (also referred to as "knock 'em down" season) with violent storms, intense humidity, and a riot of flora and fauna; *yegge,* late storm season, brings early morning mists and water lilies, as well as strong winds and the first fires; *wurrgeng,* the cool, dry season, sees continuing burning, drying billabongs, dewy nights, and the relatively low humidity and temperatures that bring prolific bird- and wildlife as well as flocks of tourists; *gurrung,* the hot dry season, is *very* hot with some wind, rapidly traveling fires, and building thunderheads, which signal the return of *gunumeleng.*

Droughts, Fires, and Floods

The vast interior is arid; this makes for clear skies, warm to hot days, and chilly (and amazingly starry) nights. Rain west of the Great Dividing Range is a hit-and-miss affair, and rarely

The Aborigines who live around Kakadu National Park recognize six annual seasons rather than the usual four.

falls in the outback, but when it does the landscape responds spectacularly as dormant vegetation bursts into life. Australia's aridity is such that many areas are subject to drought, and it is common for some regions to struggle for as much as seven years without a drop of rain. Even the wetter coastal areas are not immune to occasional droughts, and water restrictions are something that most Australians are familiar with. In 1994, the weather reversed its geographical pattern, bringing bizarre summer rains to the Red Centre and South Australia and devasting drought (the worst in Australian history) to the east coast. The farming community was hard hit as cattle, crops, and wildlife bit the dust and farmers were forced both to slaughter livestock early and refrain from planting summer crops.

In the normally dry summer months in the south, bushfires are an annual danger, and the consequences of uncontrollable outbreaks have been devastating for some time. In 1982, incalculable damage was caused by the terrible fires that broke out, ironically enough, on Ash Wednesday of that year, in Victoria and South Australia. And, certainly, few Australians will forget 1994's out-of-control wildfires (the worst since European colonization 200 years ago), which snuffed out more than 400,000 hectares of bush and grasslands, destroyed 100-or-so homes, and roared within a few kilometers of central Sydney. Ash and haze left the city's famous opera house a shade of dismal orange rather than its customary blinding white—but at least it was spared.

The flip side of the drought-and-fire coin is flood. Many agonizingly long droughts have been broken by catastrophic floods that can isolate outlying communities for weeks.

Australia's highest recorded temperature was a brain-frying 53.1° C (127.6° F) in Cloncurry, Queensland, in 1889, while Marble Bar, in Western Australia, had 160 sweltering days over 37° C (99° F) in 1923-24, still a world record. The highest rainfall in a 24-hour period was 108 cm in 1979 at Bellenden, Queensland, which also holds the Australian record for the highest annual rainfall—over 10 meters.

Sunshine and Ozone

Australia is exposed to more hours of sunshine than most countries. This has two important consequences. First, the anxiously observed hole in the protective ozone layer over the South Pole has extended at times to expose southern parts of the continent, and it is expected that the hole will only enlarge further. Scientific opinion about the negative effects of this startling development are divided. There is no doubt, however, about the consequences of exposure to high levels of sunshine on humans. Even before the rent in the ozone layer became a concern, Australia's rate of skin-cancer cases was abnormally high. The combination of a fashion for bronze suntans, an addiction to sunbathing, a beach culture, and a love of outdoor activities has led to a national health problem of major proportions. It is worth remembering the simple creed propounded in a recent public health campaign: Slip, Slop, Slap (slip on a shirt, slop on some sunscreen, and slap on a hat).

Harsh climatic conditions have helped to shape the national character, and, far from resenting the forces of nature that so often blight the lives of Australians, especially in the bush, many people have a strangely sentimental attachment to this rigorous and inhospitable land. The words of Dorothy Mackellar in this poem, which most Australians learn at school, sum up their ambivalent affection:

> *I love a sunburnt country,*
> *A land of sweeping plains,*
> *Of rugged mountain ranges,*
> *Of droughts, and flooding rains.*
> *I love her far horizons.*
> *I love her jewelled sea.*
> *Her beauty and her terror;*
> *A wide brown land for me.*

FLORA AND FAUNA

In wilderness is the preservation of the world. We need the tonic of wilderness, to wade sometimes in the marshes . . . we can never have enough of nature.

—Henry David Thoreau

Australia's 50 million years of geographic isolation has led to the evolution of a bewildering array of indigenous plant and animal life that has little in common with life-forms in relatively nearby parts of the world. It is one of the fascinations of travel in the outback to be continually confronted with animals and plants that might easily spring from the fevered brains of science fiction writers.

FLORA

"The great quantity of plants Mr. Banks and Dr. Solander found in this place occasioned my giving it the name of Botany Bay." This brief entry in Captain Cook's 1770 journal does little justice to the excitement the two botanical gentlemen in his company must have experienced. The flora they collected was certainly novel and was the subject of lively academic interest in Europe. The following overview highlights some of the botanic marvels that Banks and Solander probably observed.

The Bush

The term "bush," which Australians bandy about so loosely, covers a variety of terrains and broad vegetation types, including rainforests, both temperate and tropical, mangrove swamps, savannahs, rolling scrub-covered hills, forests of eucalypt or conifer, grasslands, and deserts. Australian plants and trees are generally nondeciduous, and many species bear fragrant blossoms. After a desert rainstorm, the air is cloyingly sweet, and sailors say they can smell the sharp medicinal scent of gums (eucalypts) far out to sea.

Myrtles and Gums

The largest and most famous of Australian plant groups is the myrtle family. It contains over 1,000 native species, from the ground-hugging heathlike kunzeas to the 500-odd species of eucalypt. It includes the tea-tree (so named by Captain Cook's crew, who made a tea-colored drink from its leaves), the picturesque paperbark with its white papery trunk, and the brilliantly colored bottlebrush. The hundreds of species of eucalypt, or gum tree, many with colorful scarlet, coral, and white blossoms, are now the most transplanted trees in the world. More than 100 years ago these fast growers, well-suited to arid climates, were planted in California and Arizona as windbreaks, and you can find Australian eucalypts in well over 70 countries, a tribute to their hardy adaptability.

Fewer than 100 species of eucalypt are found in the country's arid climes, many of them shorter and squatter than their relatives living in the bush, highlands, or coastal regions. These varieties have developed an ability to resist heat and preserve moisture. Many gum trees have leaves that turn their edges to the sun's rays to reduce evaporation, which, incidentally, makes them poor shade trees on scorching afternoons. Gum leaves are generally thick-skinned and equipped with oil glands to provide an oily film to resist the heat.

Commonly sighted eucalypts include: the snow gum, with a distinctive gnarled look, found in alpine regions; the ghost gum with sheeny, bleached-out bark and vibrant green leaves, a haunting vision around central Australia and the tropical north; the river (or "red") gum, a large-limbed giant of a tree with slick bark tattooed in tans and grays, found rooted in waterways;

KAREN MCKINLEY

ANDREW HEMPSTEAD

snow gum

good Aussie football player, the wattle is extremely hardy and fast growing, and can thrive in the arid, bare interior where even eucalypts cannot compete, but its career is not long-lived. Some species have adapted to sand dunes drenched with salt spray, some to soggy ill-drained swamps, and others to stony exposed ridges. And like many Australian plants, they have adapted to fire.

The bushfire did not come to Australia with the Europeans. Since ancient times, lightning has started many a blazing inferno, and Aborigines used fire to flush animals out of dense foliage. Many species of Australian plants have developed a remarkable resistance to fire. Eucalypts have dormant buds beneath their bark that open immediately after a bushfire to restore foliage to a burnt tree. The seeds of other plant species do not readily germinate until the first rains after a fire, when great quantities of acacia seedlings spring up from the charred earth. The woody fruits of hakeas and banksias actually require the heat of fire before they will burst open and release the seeds.

The ubiquitous banksia trees and shrubs are named after Sir Joseph Banks, and they have a special place in the nightmares of Australian children after the artist May Gibbs created the wicked Banksia men for her popular bush fairy tales. Banksias belong to the Protaceae family, which has developed most abundantly in Australia. It is named after Proteus, the shape-changing Old Man of the Sea in Greek mythology, and it points to the enormous diversity of the family. Some banksias, for instance, grow half submerged in the sand, while others grow into trees 15 meters tall. Leaves and flowers of this family vary tremendously from the so-called spider flowers of the *Grevillea* genus to the dense heads of the waratahs. The most commercially valuable members of the family are the macadamia, which are grown in Queensland for their rich, yummy nut, and the silky oak, which produces a fine cabinet wood.

And yet there are still more wildly beautiful, utterly strange trees and shrubs to stumble across: spinifex, a hardy, prickly, spiky plant—and favorite reptilian hiding place—that blankets much of central Australia; some 30 varieties of saltbrush, a staple in the diets of outback livestock that has a special fondness for the Birdsville

coolabahs, another water- and swamp-dweller, recognizable by its gnarly shape, lackluster leaves, and tough bark; the Darwin woollybutt, a tall lumbering tree with a two-toned, dual-textured trunk and seasonal orange blossoms, scattered coast-to-coast across the Top End; and mallee, a stunted eucalypt that thrives in the desertlike conditions of, appropriately enough, the Mallee in northwestern Victoria.

Other Plants and Shrubs

The wattle, Australia's floral emblem, belongs to the acacia family, which is represented by some 600 species across Australia. Mulgas, the most common arid-zone wattle, can grow in sparse clumps or thick groupings and look somewhat like scrawny eucalypts. In early days, colonists made wattle-and-daub huts, an ancient building technique involving interwoven saplings covered with mud, and the name "wattle" was attached to this profusely blooming species with its either spikey or rounded yellow flowers. Like a and Oodnadatta Tracks; the boab tree, a squatty, gnarly-branched oddity with a bloated, water-retaining trunk, and a relative of the African baobab, expat-ing it in the northeastern Northern Territory and the southwestern Kimberley; the desert oak, a tall, shady drama queen of a breed prevalent around arid spots like Ayers Rock and King Canyon; and a species of red cabbage palms, known as *Livistona mariae,* which has not been identified any place else on the planet! Groves of the palms as well as cycads—all left over from prehistoric times—are alive and well in the Northern Territory.

Late and Early Bloomers
Australia's native plants include profuse bloomers. Sturt's desert pea stretches like a red carpet across vast tracts of inland desert. More than 600 varieties of orchids, including the only two underground species in the world, lend their sensuous beauty to the steamy rain-forests of the north, while water lilies float gently and dreamily atop Top End lagoons.

Western Australia alone grows more than 6,000 species of wildflowers and flowering shrubs and trees. For many eons, the south-

grass tree

west corner of Australia was virtually a floral island, isolated from the world by the Indian Ocean and the deserts to its north and east. Among the most colorful of Western Australia's flowers are the kangaroo paw, the Gerald-ton wax flower, the scarlet coc-cinea, the exquisitely scented boro-nias, and the pine grevillea with its enormous deep orange spikes that grow to six meters. Australia's Christmas tree is not a conifer, but a relative of the mistletoe, a parasite that blooms at Christmas in masses of orange balloon-like blossoms.

One reason for the very different configurations of Australian flowers, in which petals are often tiny or nonexistent while stamens and pistils are prominent, is that many have evolved in isolation where they are pollinated by birds, not bees, and have had to adapt to the demands of a host of honey-eaters' beaks.

The sight of Western Australian wildflowers, covering the earth as far as the eye can see, like the prolific blue leschenaultia (which Aborigines called "the floor of the sky"), is worth the cost of a dozen trips there. But there are fantastic botanical eye-poppers to be found elsewhere: the stately kauri and jarrah forests; the majestic mountain ash and beech myrtle of the temperate rainforests; ghost gums silhouetted against the setting sun; grass trees spiked with flowers; primitive tree ferns slowly inching their way up from the mossy, mist-shrouded forest floor; the sparse but fascinating vegetation of the Nullarbor Plain—so inhospitable but so alive; and for the ghoulish, two carnivorous species, the pitcher plant and the rainbow plant. The isolation and stress of a harsh climate have created plantlife in Australia that is unique, extraordinary, and well worth investigating.

FAUNA

The Extinct
Carnivorous lizards standing nine meters tall, eight-meter ichthyosaurs (or fish lizards), and three-meter labyrinthodonts (or frog lizards) in-

FOSSILS, FOOTPRINTS, AND OLD BONES

The land of Oz was home to some of the earth's earliest life-forms, many of them uncovered in the outback (and probably more waiting to be discovered). These are some discoveries and their finding spots.

TYPE OF FIND IN: NEW SOUTH WALES	WHERE FOUND
Cretaceous-period carnivorous theropod	Lightning Ridge
a monotreme—the country's oldest fossil of a mammal	Lightning Ridge

NORTHERN TERRITORY	
Ordovician-period vertebrate fish	Amadeus Basin
Miocene-period fossils including enormous flightless birds, meat-eating thylacinids, a huge diprotodontid, and a marsupial lion	Alcoota Station, near Alice Springs
extinct marsupials	Bullock Creek

QUEENSLAND	
Permian-period fish.	Blackwater
Australia's first theraspid	Carnarvon Gorge
the sauropod, Australia's first Jurassic-period discovery	near Roma
Jurassic-period pliosaurs	Mount Morgan area
plesiosaurs	north of Wandoan
"Mutta," an Ornithopoda-period dinosaur— unalive and well in Queensland Museum	Thomson River near Muttaburra
possibly the largest known marine reptile, from the Cretaceous period	near Hughenden
Cretaceous-period ichthyosaurs	Richmond
many dinosaur footprints	Lark Quarry, south of Winton
pterosaurs	near Boulia and Richmond
extinct marsupials, kangaroos, and other mammals	Riversleigh

habited prehistoric Australia. These creatures died out in the cataclysmic worldwide extinction of the dinosaurs, long before humans arrived. Their most dangerous descendants are the saltwater crocodile, the great white shark, and a gallery of the world's deadliest snakes. A class of creature known as megafauna, however, still roamed the land when the first Aborigines came ashore. The bones of gigantic wombats bigger than buffalos, huge saber-toothed marsupial lions, and outsized kangaroos that would dwarf their puny descendants have been found, and some of these creatures

may well have entered the racial memory of the Aborigines, in the form of Dreamtime myths.

The Extraordinary
Some of Australia's native fauna are candidates for *Ripley's Believe It or Not!*. The silver barramundi, found in the Northern Territory's Kakadu National Park, spends the first six years of its life as a male and the rest as a female. Australia has the world's largest and most ferociously destructive termites, some of which build nests as high as six meters. The grand champion of termite mounds is near Hayes Creek in the

TYPE OF FIND IN: SOUTH AUSTRALIA	WHERE FOUND
"Eric," a Cretaceous-period opalized pliosaur— usually on tour	Coober Pedy
carnivorous theropod of the Cretaceous period	Andamooka
Miocene-period river dolphins	Lake Frome region
extinct marsupials	Lake Eyre basin
Pleistocene-period wombats	Cooper Creek, Lake Eyre, and Lake Callabonna

WESTERN AUSTRALIA	
Archaean-era stromatolites, the planet's oldest life form	Shark Bay
Devonian-period fish	The Kimberley
Devonian-period placoderms	Gogo Station, near Fitzroy Crossing
Triassic-period fish predators	Erskine Range, between Derby and Fitzroy Crossing
dinosaur footprints	Gantheaume Point, near Broome

Northern Territory, and others are scattered about the central deserts. The world's most venomous snake is the taipan, and its kissing cousin, which inhabits northeastern South Australia and southwestern Queensland, carries enough venom to kill more than 200,000 mice.

The rather unsavory platypus frog deserves a mention; the female carries her young in her stomach and gives birth by regurgitating them. Personally, this seems like a much more humane method than the labor-and-delivery hell that most women go through! Hmpf, Mother Nature must never have been pregnant.

Marsupials

The most famous of Australian animals are the marsupials—mammals that lack a placenta, give birth to offspring still in the gestative stage, and carry them in a pouch. Almost all the 150-odd marsupial species—most notably kangaroos, wallabies, possums, koalas, and wombats—are found in Australia.

Kangaroos, or "'roos," the largest of the marsupials, are the country's national symbol. They are also the most widespread; since the arrival of Europeans, their numbers have increased as pastoralists cleared land and drilled water bores for sheep and cattle. Australians now resort to "culling," a euphemism for massacring large numbers of native animals that interfere with graziers' interests and thereby earn the title of pest.

Despite the increasing numbers of some kangaroo species, it is a misconception that kangaroos can be seen loping down the main street of any town in Australia. In fact, they are timid creatures—usually hiding in forests—often most active at night, and they are seen about as often as a deer is in North America.

Kangaroos are hunted for their skins and meat by Aborigines, for whom they form an important food source. It used to be that most culled kangaroos would end up as dog food, but recent initiatives have allowed kangaroo steaks and burgers onto the menus of sophisticated (and some not-so-sophisticated) city restaurants. Reputedly, kangaroo meat is highly nutritious, containing no cholesterol and very little fat. So, dear travelers, you and your canine mates can now feast on the same chow.

The largest recorded kangaroo was 3.2 meters tall and weighed nearly 100 kilograms. Far from being the harmless, inoffensive creature gazing doe-eyed from a glossy tourist brochure, kangaroos are ready and able to defend themselves. When attacked, by dingoes or a rival kangaroo, they use their fore-paws to immobilize their opponent and, rearing up on their powerful tail, they attempt to rip open their adversary's belly with knifelike hind claws.

The kangaroo has evolved a remarkably efficient means of locomotion: jumping. It cannot walk or run, though it can swim surprisingly well, but it can achieve speeds of up to 50 km per hour by just hopping along. The sight of a group of kangaroos loping across an open field in full flight is exquisite.

Kangaroos' powerful hind legs are cunningly structured with a system of counter-weighted tendons and muscles that conserve the energy expended in motion, thus enabling the animal to travel at high speeds for prolonged periods. Some rural race-tracks have stories to tell about kangaroos bounding onto the track and beating a field of thoroughbred race horses.

The female kangaroo, like some other marsupials, is able to control her reproductive cycle depending on the availability of food and water. A female can carry a "joey," or immature kangaroo, in her pouch and one in her uterus. Should conditions become unfavorable, she will terminate her unborn joey in utero. The joey at birth is about one inch long and must drag itself from the birth canal to the mammary gland in the pouch, a perilous journey during which the mother offers no assistance. Hairs on the mother's belly grow in a pattern that gives the joey directional aid, but should the joey fall off the mother, she will abandon it. Once the joey puts its mouth to the mammary gland, the nipple swells up and effectively locks the joey onto the teat until it has grown sufficiently to suck for itself. The joey will stay in the pouch for six to eight months until it is weaned, but it will continue to use its mother's pouch for safety and transportation until it is almost ridiculously big—a big, old pouch potato.

Kangaroo species range in size from the five-centimeter dusky hopping mouse to the giant

koala

two-meter red kangaroo. "Wallaby" usually denotes smaller kangaroos, while "wallaroo" usually denotes kangaroos that prefer a rocky or densely wooded habitat.

The sleepy, cuddlesome **koala,** beloved star of so many Australian tourist promotions, is not a bear but another marsupial. Despite its endearing good looks, koalas prefer not to be handled by kootchy-kooing humans, and they frequently outrage distinguished visitors, who pose for photo opportunities, by piddling on them. They are also equipped with formidable claws and are really much better left dozing in the trees where they belong, well-hidden atop a gum tree.

Koalas rarely drink water; they obtain their moisture from the 37 species of eucalypt leaves that form their sole diet. Their sleepy attitude is due in part to the sedative and hypnotic effect of a naturally occurring barbiturate in the eucalypt leaves. Koala numbers have rapidly declined since European settlement, and now they are a protected species. No longer hunted for their pelts, they are still under threat from loss of habitat and a venereal disease similar to chlamydia. Needless to say, that stuffed bear you take home will—hopefully—be a fake.

Wombats are stocky, thickset marsupials slightly bigger than the koala. They make their home in burrows on the forest floor. They are nocturnal animals, and consequently the headlights of cars upset their night vision.

Other marsupials include the tree kangaroo, the monkeylike cuscus, batlike flying foxes, a host of tree-dwelling possums (which are really the only marsupial to have adapted to city life), marsupial rats and mice.

One disturbing sight for drivers on rural roads is passing countless carcasses of wombats and other native animals. Road signs warn motorists of frequent crossing points, and not just for the animals' protection. Many drivers have cracked a radiator—or worse—in a collision with a kangaroo.

Monotremes

Monotremes are egg-laying mammals. There are only two in the world and they are both in Australia: the platypus and the echidna.

The **duck-billed platypus** is perhaps the most intriguing of all Australia's odd creatures. The first specimens sent to the British Museum were dismissed as a hoax. Scientists thought that the web-footed, duck-billed creature with fur and claws had been intricately stitched together from the various parts of several animals, like so-called mermaids made of monkey heads attached to fish bodies that travelers brought back from time to time from the East. However, the platypus is genuinely odd. It represents a possible link in the evolutionary chain between reptiles and mammals, since it both lays eggs and suckles its young. Its choice of home is also peculiar. The platypus, living within the confines of eastern Australia and Tasmania, seems equally happy whether basking in a tropical river or freezing its bill off in a nippy mountain stream. It lives in burrows in the banks of streams and feeds off the streambed. The platypus must close its eyes and ears under water and uses a mysterious electric sense to locate food. For protection against natural predators, the adult male has venomous spurs on its hind legs. The platypus is extremely shy and sensitive to pollution or any disturbance to its habitat. Naturally, since European settlement, its numbers are well down; so, now it is a protected species. It's not too likely that you'll see a platypus in the wild (Eungella National Park, Queensland, offers the best opportunity), but if you do, remember that these creatures are enormously sensitive and their existence is utterly dependent on being left alone.

The other monotreme, the **echidna,** or spiny anteater, is much more accessible and a reasonably common sight in the bush, deserts, and mountains. It is named after Echidna, a monster of Greek mythology—part beautiful woman, part voracious serpent—whose offspring were even more monstrous than her own sweet self. The echidna resembles a North American porcupine, with a spine-covered body, a protruding snout, and a distinctive waddling gait, as it rolls along on its knuckles. It also

The echidna, or spiny anteater, is a common sight in the bush, deserts, and mountains.

has sharp claws, but its usual response to disturbance is to roll into a ball with its quills flexed.

Dingoes, Bats, and Bandicoots

Australia's native dog is the dingo, which was actually introduced from Southeast Asia about 6,000 years ago, well after the Aborigines arrived. Traditionally, Aborigines used dingoes for several activities, including sleeping beside them for warmth on cold nights—hence the expression "a three-dog night" for a particularly cold night. Nowadays the dingo roams the outback in packs, and it is a difficult, though not impossible, animal to domesticate. The dingo earned worldwide notoriety through the Azaria Chamberlain case (wherein a dingo allegedly snatched—and, later, gnawed to death—baby Azaria from her family's Ayers Rock campsite), which only reinforced the need to take precautions when traveling in the more remote regions of the outback. (Those dark-of-night dingo howls hardly inspire dreamy-bye lullabies.) Actually, sheep have more to worry about than newborn babes. Dingoes are known to wreak havoc (i.e. feast upon) whole flocks of sheep, inspiring a "shoot-to-kill" stance among many graziers. The famous Dingo Fence—the world's longest fence—stretches from the bottom of South Australia up to northwest Queensland. Inspectors regularly patrol about one-half of the

platypus

dingo

fenceline, mending holes and setting traps, keeping the dingoes to the north and west of the barrier and out of southeastern Australia.

Australia is home to about 50 species of bats, including the colossal fruit bat. These large bats congregate in huge colonies, often in the tops of trees, and feed at night. Watching a colony wake up at sunset is a spectacle not to be missed: there is an all-pervading batty smell, and the sound of their bat cries as they fly in bat formation round the treetops is quite eerie. Gradually they disperse in search of fruit. Many species can be found grouped inside caves, and the rare golden horseshoe bat can be viewed at the Cutta Cutta Caves south of Katherine in the Northern Territory.

Both feral and domestic cats, unfortunately, have taken a vampire-ish liking to the rare— and getting rarer—rat-ish little bandicoot. The mostly nocturnal bandicoots, however, prefer a diet of insects with perhaps a bit of plant fiber to aid digestion. The short-nosed bandicoot, found around both eastern and western Australia, is the most common breed, while the rabbit-eared is a scarce sight in the Northern Territory.

Introduced Species
These are "the animals that ate Australia." Feral dogs, cats, pigs, goats, rabbits, and a host of other nonnative species, introduced by a series of intentional and accidental blunders, have brought with them economic and environmental devastation and a wave of extinctions unparalleled in the 50 million years since Australian life was cut off from outside influence by plate tectonics. Scores of native animals have been driven to near or complete extinction by competition with or attack from introduced species. Unique and irreplaceable creatures like the eastern hare-wallaby, the golden bandicoot, and the short-tailed hopping mouse have disappeared forever.

With today's population into the hundred millions, Australia's rabbits were first introduced by English colonists soon after settlement for the purpose of sport. The spry hippity-hops adapted marvelously to the semiarid areas that were cleared for pasture, and they soon out-ate the resident animals. Now, rabbit infestations regularly break out, producing tens of millions of rabbits at a time. Huge amounts of money and effort have been poured into the control and eradication of the rabbit, most notably for the construction of the "rabbit-proof fence," which extended for thousands of miles across the continent, and for the hideous virus myxomatosis, which wiped out millions of rabbits in the 1930s. These days rabbits are largely immune to myxomatosis and vast research programs seek new and more virulent solutions to the rabbit problem. In late 1995 a virus being tested on a small rabbit population on an island off the South Australian coast "escaped" to the mainland. In the ensuing months, the virus slowly spread in ever increasing arcs across the country.

An estimated 10 million feral pigs cause in excess of $100 million worth of damage annually and pose a nightmarish threat to Australia's lucrative livestock industry should they contract and spread diseases like foot-and-mouth disease or rinderpest.

Feral cats and dogs create havoc in national parks. In the trees, gorgeously colored native parrots, parakeets, and lorikeets are fighting a losing battle against introduced sparrows and starlings (the sparrows and starlings, however, have not yet made it into Western Australia, thanks to the sharpshooters on watch at the state's borders). Wild horses and feral goats roam at will, ravaging remote areas of

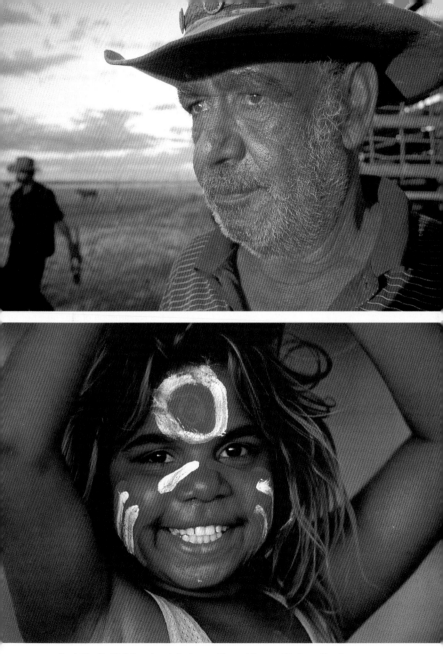

(top) Charlie McAdam, head stockman, Tanami Downs, Northern Territory
(bottom) North Tanami Aboriginal child

(top left) Sturt's desert pea; (top right) the kangaroo paw;
(bottom) Hollows and holes in trees are favorite nesting sites for the budgerigar.

wilderness. More than 70,000 feral donkeys are shot each year. Foxes—also introduced deliberately for sport—are a pest for farmers, but they are steadily wiping out native species as well.

In the arid zones, wild camels—one-hump dromedaries, descendants of animals brought here for cartage purposes—are actually captured for export to the Middle East; Australia now has the dubious distinction of being home to the last wild camels (approximately 100,000 of them) on earth.

Until the arrival of Europeans, Australia had never known a cloven-hoofed beast; the hard impact of hoofs breaks up the dry crusted earth in the arid regions so that annually millions of tons of topsoil simply blow away. In the Northern Territory, herds of wild buffalo and semiwild cattle roam across a fragile landscape that struggles to recover from the devastation.

Where feral animals encroach on the interests of agriculture, enormous efforts are made to control the situation. But where human population is thin, and livestock (and, consequently, livelihoods) are not affected, feral animal populations are quite literally out of control. Paradoxically, in areas that are declared national parks—and there are more than 500 of them—feral animals often thrive because they are no longer subject to the control mechanisms of agriculture, and park authorities rarely have sufficient resources to take over.

kookaburra

Birds

Australia's birds are a wonderful and unexpected surprise for many visitors—about 700 species, of which approximately 500 are endemic and 200 migrate to all parts of the world.

One of Australia's most distinctive birds is the flightless emu, which roams the open plains, often inside the Dingo Fence. It's slightly smaller than the ostrich. The male emu has sole responsibility in child-rearing from the time the eggs are laid. Most recently, the emu—part of the country's coat-of-arms, along with the kangaroo—is becoming trendy in the skin/feather/nouvelle cuisine arena.

Birdwatchers throughout the country will spot a large and exotic assortment of multicolored parrots (including the raucous cockatoo), budgerigars, and galahs. If you're hanging around the termite mounds you might glimpse the rare hooded parrot. Of the kingfishers, the largest is the kookaburra, found near permanent water sources. Its infectious laughing cry has earned it the nickname "the laughing jackass."

Most of Australia's 18 types of finch inhabit the tropic regions, but two renegades, the painted fireball and the zebra finch, have managed to adapt in the arid zone, usually close to permanent water sources. (Hint to outback travelers: zebra finches = nearby water.) The exquisitely colorful Gouldian finch, once a common sight across the Top End, is now almost extinct.

Common thoughout Australia are swans, ducks, geese, and pelicans, but they are most spectacular when rain falls in the interior and long-dry watercourses and lakes fill for a few months; millions of birds appear, feeding on the long-dormant creatures that have lain for years under the scorched clay.

Curvy-billed honeyeaters—67 species that range from small and colorful to big and drab—not only frequent the watercourses but are regulars around scrub, plains, and woodlands.

Around the coast, seabirds congregate in large numbers. Gulls and terns, the fairy penguins of Adelaide, Kangaroo Island, Phillip Island, and Tasmania, the muttonbird, and even the lonely albatross all may be seen in the southern oceans.

The bowerbird constructs an elaborate "bower" or display for mating purposes. It collects all manner of shiny and colorful objects for inclusion in its display, from flowers and berries to jewelry stolen from campsites. Some bowerbirds mix various substances into a form of paint to enhance their overall concept of interior decorating. The females select their mates from the most resourceful and tasteful males.

The lyrebird, so named after the fabulous lyre-shaped display feathers of the male, is a great mimic and will deliver prolonged concerts imitating the sounds of the forest, other bird-calls, and even a tractor or a chainsaw. A single concert may contain up to 40 different calls.

The stately brolga (a large crane) is famous for its courtship dance, a spectacle of immense beauty.

Of the birds of prey, the keen-sighted, wedge-tailed eagle is the largest, and hawks and kites are a common sight, hovering motionlessly above their intended victims or wheeling in pairs high over their territory. White-bellied sea eagles and ospreys do their preying along the remote coasts.

A fashion for native gardens that swept Australia in the '60s has meant that many species of native birds have returned to the suburbs of cities to feed on the flowering shrubs that replaced the hedges and annuals imported from Europe. Many previously unsighted species of native birds are now common in suburbs that once knew only sparrows and pigeons.

Unfortunately, many of Australia's exotic birds are highly prized by collectors overseas and, since the birds are protected, a cruel and illicit smuggling industry has developed. Snaring threatens to wipe out some species, especially of parrots, and the smuggling process itself kills more of these sensitive creatures than can satisfy this objectionable market.

Reptiles and Amphibians

Love lizards and snakes? Then you've come to the right place. Select from about 230 species of lizard, from the extraordinary frill-necked lizard to the lethargic two-meter-long goanna, plus 140 species of snake and two species of crocodile. Relatively few people are killed annually by snake bites, and occasionally an incautious swimmer is taken by a crocodile—sometimes beside a sign warning against swimming (or, worse, beside a sign that *used* to be there but was pinched by a thoughtless tourist!).

Fewer than 20 species of Australian **snakes** have the potential to kill humans. The taipan is the deadliest, although its bite is not necessarily fatal if an antivenin is administered soon enough. Other snakes to be wary of include the tiger snake, the copperhead, the death adder,

the brown, and the red-bellied black snakes. Additionally, more than 30 species of poisonous sea snakes frequent coastal waters, though they are rarely encountered by humans. Remember that snakes are no more delighted to meet you than you are to meet them. Most snake bites are the result of humans trying to kill the snake, or stumbling across one suddenly and startling it into attack. When hiking it's sensible to wear boots, thick socks, and long pants. Never stick your fingers into holes and be especially careful when poking around wood or rocks (obviously). Tromp and stomp and any nearby snakes should sense your approach well in advance; most will simply move—hopefully in the opposite direction.

The two types of **crocodiles** found in Australia, freshwater and saltwater (or "salties"), are now protected since hunting severely depleted their numbers. The salties, inhabitants of tidal estuaries along Australia's northern coastline, occasionally creep into freshwater territory and are *extremely dangerous*. Big and bulky, and growing up to seven meters long, salties viciously attack and kill humans. And make no mistake—they move fast! More finely built, shorter in length (three to four meters), and with smaller teeth, the freshwater croc usually sticks to a diet of fish and frogs. It has, however, been known to attack humans, especially to defend its nests.

Good advice: No matter how inviting the river or pool, and no matter how tantalizing the prospect of diving into its limpid depths, if there are crocodile warning signs, *always* resist the temptation to swim there. Most victims of crocodile attacks have ignored the warnings. It is worth going out of your way to see these magnificent creatures, but always treat them with the greatest respect and give them a wide berth!

Lizards are harmless to humans, but you might not believe that when you look at them. The very size of the giant perentie goanna, almost 2.5 meters long, is enough to keep most of its foes at bay. The goanna inhabiting central Australia is a sleek-appearing critter with distinctive yellow spots on its back; its large gray cousin hangs out around northern riverbanks.

Lazing about the western arid zone, the fierce-looking thorny, or mountain devil, dragon can change color to a limited extent and is covered with spines so sharp that no predator would contemplate eating it. *It,* on the other hand, has a fetish for eating nothing except heaps of black ants. The Top End's frill-necked lizard is another whose hiss is worse than its bite; when threatened, it unfurls a vividly colored ruff of membrane, which makes it appear much larger, and sways menacingly from side to side, spitting and hissing with gusto. The bearded dragon has the ability to flatten its body while sunbathing in its favorite arid-zone turf.

Giant leatherback turtles (one of Australia's dozen or so species of freshwater tortoise and five types of marine turtle) breed on some northern beaches, but they are under threat from driftnet fishing and suffocation from floating plastic bags that impersonate their favorite kind of jellyfish. One of Australia's premier turtle-viewing spots is Mon Repos Environmental Park, east of Bundaberg (Queensland), where four species of turtles nest through the months of summer.

You can pick out 130 species of **frogs**. In the arid claypans where rains come only once every few years, some croakers survive by filling their bladders with water and burrowing into the mud just before it dries. There they coat their bodies with a mucilaginous secretion that seals in their juices for the next few years until rain falls again. In this way they might live for 40 years—unless they are dug up by Aborigines who use them as a source of fresh water.

Insects and Arachnids

Just as there are numerous bird species across Australia, there are some 50,000 insect species for them to feed on. These include 350 species of butterflies, 7,600 varieties of moths, and 18,000 types of beetles. New insect species are discovered with almost monotonous regularity.

Australia's 9,000 kinds of ants make it the mecca for ant scientists around the world. In some arid areas of Western Australia, there are more ant species in half a hectare than there are in the rest of the world.

Termites, also called "white ants" though they are not ants at all, are hard to miss; their humongous mounds, some in the shapes of pillars or tombstones (actually the topsides of nests), are eye-popping sights in the tropical north.

The various types of flies will soon become all too familiar to visitors with no interest in natural history, as will the staggering array of mosquitoes, midges, and other biting mites. Native bees and wasps are present as are the generally larger and more vicious European varieties. And, if the human race were to die out, cockroaches are already established in Australia, poised to take our place.

Mosquitoes cause the usual grief and are most bothersome in tropical areas. Ward them off with your choice of poisons, keep skin well covered, and sleep beneath netting; mosquito coils may or may not work. The rare but potentially fatal Ross River fever is a mosquito-induced malady with mononucleosis-like symptoms.

Thousands of spider species reside here, many of them large and hairy enough to feature in the most horrific Hollywood fantasy, but the only two posing a threat to life and limb are the infamous red-back (kin to the black widow) and funnel-web spiders. Popular mythology places the red-back squarely under the seats of outdoor lavatories so that uneasy thoughts of tiny red spiders haunt many Australians' more intimate moments. Scientists tell us that only the female red-back is venomous, but it is hard to tell the difference in a creature so small. The funnel-web spider is the most toxic in the world and is confined to Sydney and its environs. Still, very few people in Australia have died from spider bites in the last two decades. Other species to watch out for are the three varieties of scorpion, which like to hide inside shoes and clothing (clean or not), and the trap-door spider, which lives in underground holes.

The most ubiquitous, infuriating, and unsavory creature in the Australian biosphere is without a doubt the fly. In hotter months or after rains, flies descend like a nightmarish scene out of a Hitchcock film. They are relentless: they want your sweat, they want your tears, they want your moistest orifice, and they live for the moment you drop your drawers. They will irritate you into resorting to the most ridiculous contrivance of a hat fitted with dangling corks, or covering your head with a fly net, drawstring tied snugly around your neck (it's amazing how the sadistic creatures know exactly when you're going to sneak a bite of food or sip a drink!). Repellents, such as Aerogard, are moderately effective. Or simply resort instead to waving your hand constantly in front of your face, like

OFFICIAL FLORA AND FAUNA EMBLEMS

FLORA

The golden wattle *(Acacia pycnantha)* is Australia's national floral emblem. Individual state emblems are:

New South Wales; waratah *(Telopea speciosissima)*
Northern Territory; Sturt's desert rose *(Gossypium sturtianum)*
Queensland; Cooktown orchid *(Dendrobium bigibbum)*
South Australia; Sturt's desert pea *(Clianthus formosus)*
Tasmania; Tasmanian blue gum *(Eucalyptus globulus)*
Victoria; common heath *(Epacris impressa)*
Western Australia; kangaroo paw *(Anigozanthos manglesii)*

FAUNA

New South Wales; platypus *(Ornithorhynchus anatinus);* laughing kookaburra *(Dacelo novaeguineae)*
Northern Territory; red kangaroo *(Macropus rufus);* wedge-tailed eagle *(Aquila audax)*
Queensland; koala *(Phascolarctos cinereus)*
South Australia; hairy-nosed wombat *(Lasiorhinus latifrons)*
Tasmania; none (not even the Tasmanian tiger or devil)
Victoria; helmeted honeyeater *(Meliphaga cassidix)*
Western Australia; numbat *(Myrmecobius fasciatus);* black swan *(Cygnus atratus)*

Marinelife

Australia's seas are filled with such diversity and abundance that this topic deserves its own book. The first sea creature that most Aussies would think of is the **shark.** Australians love the beach and the danger of shark attack is instilled into all swimmers from a tender age. Consequently, the shark has been hunted mercilessly and undeservedly, without regard to the vital part it plays in the overall marine ecology. As a result, the existence of some shark species is threatened. The largest sharks inhabit southern waters, the home of the white pointer that starred in *Jaws.* The best place to ogle these monsters is Dangerous Reef (hence the name) on South Australia's Eyre Peninsula. By the way, smaller sharks are the staple fish in fish and chips shops, where they are called "flake."

Swimmers should also beware of the deadly **box jellyfish** (a.k.a. sea wasp or stinger), prevalent along tropical coastal waters and estuaries between late October and May. Unfortunately these are the exact spots and months when the beach looks oh-so-inviting. Steer clear! The translucent box jellyfish is very difficult to see and its potentially fatal bite elicits horrific pain, red welts, possible collapse, and the need for emergency medical help. Why do you think the locals stay away?

Fishing addicts, don't worry that Australia's aridity will prevent you from finding a catch of the day (or year). Whether your taste runs to game fishing a la Hemingway or dropping a line off the end of a pier, a fish waits for you! Surfing beaches usually provide space enough for surf fishing, and the reefs, bays, estuaries, and outback rivers and pools are full of fish. Among the most sought-after catches is the barramundi in northern Australia; abalone, crayfish, oysters, and prawns are also delicious and lucrative resources. Arid-zone fish are plentiful, though generally on the small side. The yellowbelly, or golden perch, found in Cooper Creek and the Diamantina River, defies the norm by growing as large as 20 kilograms. The spangled perch, a common catch throughout most of the country's coastal waters and inland streams as well as central Australia's Finke River, is one of the largest of its kind, growing up to one-half kilogram. Three other species of perch are found at Dalhousie Springs, near the Simpson Desert.

Most coastal areas of Australia are visited by **dolphins,** and surfers often tell of schools of dolphins frolicking with them while they surf. An isolated beach in Western Australia called Monkey Mia has become quite famous for the intimacy of its regularly visiting dolphins. Humans flock to this remote spot in such droves that there is a danger of the dolphins being frightened away or getting sick from too much human contact.

From June through October **southern right whales** can be seen during their annual breeding migration along the coastline between Yalata and the border. (See "Crossing the Nullarbor" in the South Australia chapter.)

HISTORY

Australian history . . . does not read like history, but like the most beautiful lies. And all of a fresh sort, no mouldy old stale ones. It is full of surprises and adventures and incongruities, and contradictions and incredibilities; but they are all true, and they happened.

—MARK TWAIN

FIRST SETTLERS

Contrary to the assertion of most Australian school textbooks published before 1980, Australia was not discovered by Europeans, and certainly not by the intrepid Captain Cook. Australia's first settlers were the Aborigines, who arrived from Asia at least 40,000 years ago, and possibly as early as 100,000 years ago.

At that time the sea levels were very much lower than they are today, and the Australian landmass was connected to Papua New Guinea in the north and Tasmania in the south. Nevertheless, the water distance separating what was then Asia from this extended Australian continent was 100 km at its very shortest. The sea journey necessary to reach and colonize Australia was a remarkable achievement, especially when you consider that early Europeans had not yet reached some Mediterranean islands where the distances involved were a lot shorter. Aborigines had arrived and populated the entire continent millennia before the great expansionary movements of either the Europeans or the Polynesians.

At least 1,800 generations of Aborigines have lived in Australia with a simple but appropriate technology—a stark contrast to the eight or nine generations of Europeans with their highly inappropriate mechanical and agricultural technologies.

Early Aboriginal Society

Much of the archaeological evidence revealing Aboriginal history comes from places like Lake Mungo, an ongoing living excavation in southwest New South Wales. Sites like this are natural treasures because their remoteness and aridity has left the fossil record undisturbed. Lake Mungo used to lie on the edge of a vast inland sea, even at the time of the earliest Aboriginal relics, and huge piles of discarded bones and seashells (known as "middens") found there provide a fairly detailed peek into the daily life of the Aborigines.

Aborigines dwelt in hunter-gatherer societies, following the kangaroos, wallabies, goannas, and fish and collecting "bush food" like witchetty grubs, roots, seeds, honey, nuts, and berries. Conditions in Australia seem to have been so favorable and the bounties of nature so prolific that Aborigines never developed permanent agricultural settlements as their cousins in Papua New Guinea did. Their main tools were spears, three types of boomerang, sharpened stones for digging and shaping wood, and a spear-thrower called a woomera. They fished with nets, traps, and hooks. Controlled fires were started to flush game and, it has been suggested, as a land-management practice, since some forests have adapted to periodic bushfires. The remnants of elaborate stone weirs designed to trap fish can be seen in parts of Victoria and New South Wales. In northern Australia's wetlands bamboo-and-cord nets trapped end-of-wet-season fish, while woven nets were employed to snag wallabies and 'roos galavanting the Queensland tablelands.

Aborigines were split up into clans—a practice that still occurs today. Clan members were considered to be descendants of a common ancestor, bound by ritual, tradition, law, and—most importantly—to designated spiritual sites. Their religious belief decrees that, after death, clan members' spirits will return to these sites. Consequently, clan rituals to honor their Dreamtime creators and ancestral spirits are supremely important events, as are their spiritual links to the land. Designated members of the clan are responsible for keeping the ancestral spirits

DREAMTIME

Aborigines were telling stories about the land and animals around them long before the ancient Egyptians built the pyramids. Cave paintings of animals and spirits in Australia are at least as old as the earliest example in Europe. The paintings and stories tell how the great spirits made the land, animals, and plants, and how they taught the people to find food, perform ceremonies, dance, sing, paint, and keep the laws.

The spiritual interconnectedness of all living things is very powerful for Aborigines. For example, among some central Australian tribes, the Kadaitja, an elder sorcerer who wears boots of emu feathers that leave no tracks, enforces the decisions of the community. He has only to take a certain bone and point it at a miscreant to punish him. "Pointing the bone" will cause an offender to withdraw from the tribe, pine away, and eventually die. In other examples, certain painted images are invested with such power that their misuse can result in the deaths of those to whom the paintings are sacred. Disputes have arisen as recently as 1989, when some sacrosanct tribal designs were incorporated in the decor of the new Parliament in Canberra.

Dreamtime, not merely the ancient period of creation but an ongoing relationship between the land, Aborigines, and all living creatures, is essential to Aboriginal spirituality.

In the Dreamtime, animal spirits exist in human form, and eventually turn into the various animals that we know as kangaroo, snake, and so forth, while the spirits of their human kin remain related to them totemically. To the Aborigine, the Dreamtime is to be acknowledged, honored, and fortified with ritual.

Family groups or individual Aborigines have their own Dreaming, which can be a particular plant, animal, place, or natural force. Significant places where Dreamtime spirits lived or played out their destiny are marked by physical formations such as rocks, waterholes, trees, or the shape of the land. These are sacred sites, and recently some of these places have been protected from mining or other development by legislation.

An Aboriginal leader, Pat Dodson, describes the Dreaming this way:

Our dreaming in this country travels thousands of kilometres. It comes from the sea in the north to Uluru in the centre, and it spreads out in all directions, east, north, south and west. We relate to other people through the Dreaming tracks which form paths among the sacred places, and there is not just one Dreaming line, there are many.

happy by protecting the sacred sites (hardly an easy task with white settlers and, later, tourists trampling upon them) or else risk traditional punishments and/or the wrath of the ancestral ones—disasters, sicknesses, and droughts are often signs that the spirits are mighty annoyed.

Parts of Australia contain the harshest and most inhospitable environments on the planet, yet the Aborigines developed an affinity with the land that is a testament to their knowledge and skill. As recently as the mid-1980s, an Aboriginal family arrived at a remote outback station, never before having had contact with whites. Their only possessions were two stone knives, two rubbing sticks to make fire, a container of dried worms, a boomerang, a spear, a woomera, and a dingo. In contrast, automobile clubs today advise travelers in the same terrain to carry the following equipment in their 4WD ve-

hicles: long-range fuel tanks, water tanks, food for twice the expected stay, two spare wheels and tires, spare battery, tools, medicine, cooking gear, mosquito nets, blankets, maps, compass, and a radio!

Long before Captain Cook sailed into Botany Bay and formally "took possession" of their land on behalf of the British Crown, there were 700 Aboriginal tribal groups using some 300 different languages. Their population then is estimated at anywhere up to a million people, distributed in subgroups of up to 40. By that time theirs was an ancient, complex culture, rich and finely tuned to the environment. Like their American Indian counterparts, the Aborigines lived in a spiritual communion with the land. Concepts of land ownership (like that icon of European social order—the fence) implicit in Captain Cook's first act of possession, are alien to Aborigines: "We serpent, and the Milky Way is the river of the sky where, after the rainbow serpent has swallowed the sun, people fish for stingrays and turtles, and the stars are their campfires.

The Southern Cross is an especially significant constellation for all Australians. One Dreamtime myth gives this account of its creation: A father had four daughters. When he was old, he told his daughters that they had no one else to protect them and that when he died they might have to marry men they did not like. They agreed to meet him in the sky after he was dead. With the aid of a sorcerer, he spun a silver rope from the strands of his hair, and when he died, his four daughters climbed the rope to take up their positions as the four bright points of the Southern Cross. Their father is the brightest of the nearby pointers, Alpha Centauri, still watching over them.

The complexity of the Dreamtime for most non-Aborigines is not simply that it is obscure. Many aspects of the culture are accessible only by initiation, and taboos forbid some ceremonial and spiritual practices to be even discussed. Men and women often have separate and exclusive ceremonies. Non-Aborigines often can only guess at the real significance and experience that underlies the Dreamtime stories. Here is a world where giant marsupials carve out the hills, the hills themselves are age-old marsupials frozen in moments of significance, the rivers are the tracks of the rainbow don't own the land," says Aboriginal poet Oodgeroo. "The land owns us."

European Contact

Like white Americans, European Australians have historically accorded the native culture and heritage little or no value. This attitude was encapsulated in the earliest recorded commentary on the Aborigines by a European, the gentleman pirate William Dampier, when he wrote in 1688: "The Inhabitants of this country are the Miserablest People in the World . . . they are long visaged and of very unpleasing Aspect, having no one graceful Feature in their Faces."

The balance and harmony that Aborigines had developed and refined in their world was doomed to destruction with the first contact with land-owning Europeans who quickly "pioneered" beyond their first few coastal settlements. They brought in sheep and cattle, subsequently annihilating the waterholes that for millennia had supported many plants and animals—staples of the Aboriginal diet. Those sheep and cattle started looking mighty tempting to Aborigines, empty bellies growling with hunger. Thus the spears went a-flying, the cow pies hit the fan, and savage retaliation by the settlers left many Aborigines dead. The dispossession of the Aborigines came with brutal suddenness and more from epidemics of introduced diseases to which they had no immunity than from gunfire and violence. Aborigines died by the thousands from smallpox, sexually transmitted diseases, tuberculosis, measles, and influenza, all of which spread rapidly through the nonresistant native community. In addition there was a policy of "dispersal," in which Aborigines were cynically cleared like any other pest from areas valuable to the pastoralists—a sickening practice tantamount to massacre. Aborigines were even hunted "for sport"—an unofficial sport, of course—as recently as the 1950s in isolated parts of Australia.

The Tasmanian example illustrates the deliberate policy of genocide instigated by the invading Europeans. Aborigines were either killed or simply rounded up and shipped to small island colonies "for their protection," where they died of disease, malnutrition, and mistreatment. Tasmania's Aboriginal population declined from an estimated 4,000 to fewer than 500 between 1800 and 1830. By 1847 only 40 remained.

Truganini, the last Tasmanian, died in 1876. Her body was preserved and displayed in a museum. Hers was not the only body to receive such ignominious treatment. Scientists in the learned universities of Europe were excited by the search for a "missing link" to demonstrate Darwin's novel theories of evolution, and thought that the Tasmanian Aborigines might prove to be that link. Bodies were purloined from burial sites to enhance the anthropological collections of faculties from Dublin to Leipzig. In 1803, the governor of New South Wales presented the preserved head of the Aboriginal warrior Pemulwoy to botanist Sir Joseph Banks, who wrote that the head "caused some comical consequences when opened at the Customs House but when brought home was very acceptable to our anthropological collections." Today, the remains of some 3,000 Aborigines, together with objects of immense cultural value, lie moldering in British museums; Aboriginal groups have been negotiating for some time, with little success, to retrieve the bodies for proper burial.

Not everybody contributed to this genocide. There were well-meaning, sometimes enlightened, but usually ineffectual efforts to help. Reservations were created, rations issued, and religious missions established, many of which are still the focus of Aboriginal settlements today. However, by the beginning of the 20th century, most Aborigines were beggars in their own country, dependent on handouts of food and clothing (without the latter they were not allowed in the white settlers' towns), or they worked for white bosses without pay. (Not too long ago, a newspaper photo of several Aboriginal entertainers on tour in America showed them posing in costume, i.e., nearly naked, while being presented with brand-new suitcases.)

White society, if it thought at all about Aborigines, took a paternalistic approach, which resulted in legislation aimed at the "benevolent" protection of an inferior race for its own good. Aborigines were under the control of official guardians in the bureaucracy until very recent times. Children were sometimes taken from their families to be raised within the "civilizing" influence of urban, Christian folk. A form of segregation, with limits to movement, property restrictions, separate employment conditions, and regulated marriage, has existed in different forms from state to state until the last few decades. In fact, the infamous South African apartheid laws grew in part from the observations of a delegation, early this century, to Queensland, where the treatment of Aborigines was at its worst.

Up until 1939, official policy was still predicated upon the inhuman thesis that the Aborigines were a self-solving problem, meaning they would eventually die out. It was not until 1967 that Aborigines were granted the vote and the Department of Aboriginal Affairs was created by the government to legislate their needs. Australians are traditionally suspicious of attempts to alter the Constitution by referendum, and most referenda fail. So it is to Australia's credit that one of the very few to succeed was this landmark 1967 vote to grant Aborigines the same status as the rest of the community. Too bad it had to take so long. The full horror of the dispossession of the Aborigines is difficult for many Australians to grasp, and there is still an enormous gulf that separates the lives of white Australians from the ugly realities that Aborigines are laboring under even today.

ABORIGINES TODAY

Why change our sacred myths for your sacred myths?

—OODGEROO

Of the 18 million people who live in Australia today, fewer than two percent are Aborigines. The largest population of Aborigines (about 40,000) is in the Northern Territory where the first land-rights legislation returned some lands to their original owners. Altogether there are some 300 Aboriginal reserves totaling about 286,000 square kilometers.

Most Australians seldom ever see an Aborigine, but political pressure from Aboriginal groups means that they are no longer psychologically invisible. Issues like land rights, unlawful discrimination, and Aboriginal deaths in cus-

ABORIGINAL ARCHAEOLOGICAL SITES

Lake Mungo, a World Heritage site in the Willandra Lakes region of southwestern New South Wales, is the undisputed badass of Aboriginal archaeological discoveries. Though the lake has been dried up for about 20,000 years, the site itself is an active excavation. Muddy, sandy embankments have eroded with time and weather, unearthing a treasure trove of human and animal remains that date back about 38,000 years. Other relics, such as fireplaces, tools, and leftover food (!) provide a good glimpse into the Aborigines' daily life. One extraordinary find was the 25,000-year-old cremated remains of a young woman—the world's first recorded cremation.

Northern Victoria's Kow Swamp has yielded a bounty of 10,000-12,000-year-old remains, while Keilor (near Melbourne and the international airport) has uncovered evidence of human occupation 40,000 years back. A relative baby (maybe 7,000 years old) was dredged up around Lake Nitchie in western New South Wales.

Tools and other artifacts, 20,000-40,000 years old, have been plucked from rock shelters at Miriwun on the Kimberley's Ord River, Mt. Newman in the Pilbara, and Malangangerr in Arnhem Land. Significant sites in southwestern Australia are the Swan Valley, where the oldest implements have been found, and Devil's Lair, near Cape Leeuwin in the very southwesternmost corner (near good surfing and vineyards).

Some of the oldest petroglyphs (Ice Age rock engravings) are located on the Nullarbor in South Australia's Koonside Cave. Other petroglyph-viewing spots include the Lightning Brothers locale (Delamere, Northern Territory), Early Man shelter (Laura, Queensland), Mootwingee National Park (far western New South Wales), and Burrup Peninsula (Damper, Western Australia).

Terra nullius, anyone?

tody are much more likely to gain media attention today than just 10 years ago. Hand in hand with increased political struggle is a renaissance of Aboriginal identity through art, dance, and music. The 1988 Bicentennial celebrations, which marked two hundred years since the establishment of the first penal colony, saw protests and demonstrations from highly visible and vocal Aboriginal groups who tried to point out that the country was a bit older than that. Still, there's a long struggle ahead.

In most states Aborigines make up 25-40% of prison populations; infant mortality among Aborigines is twice the national average; Aboriginal children are affected by serious diseases like trachoma and hepatitis B at rates well above the national average; Aborigines are still more vulnerable to sexually transmitted disease; Aborigines have a life expectancy 20 years below the national average; unemployment among Aborigines is four times the national average; access to education and health services in remote areas, where most Aborigines live, is minimal; racial discrimination, while outlawed theoretically, is a constant reality for many Aborigines. Under these demoralizing conditions many (especially young and middle-aged men) are vulnerable to alcohol abuse or, worse, petrol-sniffing. Not surprisingly, domestic violence follows in the heavy footsteps of substance abuse.

But thanks largely to Aboriginal women who have been victimized, many communities now ban booze, and rehab programs have been implemented. Inroads have also been made by the Royal Commission into Aboriginal Deaths in Custody which, in its report to the federal Parliament, acknowledged the need for big changes in police practice and the justice system as they pertain to Aborigines. The Aboriginal and Torres Strait Islanders Commission (ATSIC), created in 1990, authorizes elected Aboriginal representatives to give input and exercise some control over a number of federally funded employment and social-works programs.

Land Rights

Advances on the land-rights issue are slow but have gained momentum since the '60s when the Yolngu people of Yirrkala in northeastern Arnhem Land had the audacity to present a petition (on a sheet of bark, no less) to the federal government, demanding recognition of their original ownership. As you might imagine, that action was dismissed quickly. But the Yolngu people—a tough-nut bunch—fought the matter all the way to court where (surprise) it was quashed in the Yirrkala Land Case of 1971, wherein the courts upheld the Australian government's credo of *terra nullius,* i.e., no one had lived in the island-continent before 1788. This outrageously racist stance eventually pressured the government into passing the Northern Territory Aboriginal Land Rights Act of 1976.

Three Aboriginal Land Councils were established to reclaim Aboriginal lands; however, the act applied only to the dregs of the Territory, deserts or semideserts, nothing within town boundaries or owned or leased by anyone else, i.e., *anyone* else. Even Kakadu and Uluru-Kata Tjuta (Ayers Rock and the Olgas) were declared exceptions, albeit *big* exceptions, because the land fell within boundaries already designated as conservation reserves. Thus the lands were handed over with the provision that they were to be leased back to the Australian Nature Conservation Agency. The Aborigines do, however, constitute a majority of the management board and hold 99-year leases that are renegotiated in five-year increments. The co-managers, intrinsically knowledgeable about the delicate ecology and precious conservation of their formerly sacred sites, are snappy in their ranger uniforms as they give directions to ogling tourists.

The complex rules and regulations of the claiming process have meant years of haggles and hassles butting against the Territorial government, mining companies, and the federal conservation agency. Still, about one-half of the Northern Territory has been or is being "processed." Some enterprising Aborigines have started small businesses and, as for those mining rights, the Aboriginal owners have accepted the majority of the mining companies' proposals. This is progress, no?

In South Australia, the semi-obscure Aboriginal Land Trust Act of 1966 established small reserves with but few rights. More far-reaching was the Pitjantjatjara Land Rights Act of 1981, which bestowed the Anangu Pitjantjatjara and Yankunytjatjara people with title to the Anangu Pitjantjatjara Lands in the far north, about 10% of the state's area. This was followed by the Maralinga Tjarutja Land Rights Act of 1984, which returned another eight percent of the state known as the Maralinga Lands to the Anangu people. This parcel, though conveniently located just south of the designated Anangu Pitjantjatjara Lands, is hardly choice property; it was widely contaminated in the 1950s and '60s by British nuclear testing. The Anangu retain the right to regulate liquor availability as well as access to their land. Mining is another story: an arbitrator makes the ultimate decision in any dispute between the Anangu people and the mining companies.

Land rights in the rest of Australia are still very limited. In Western Australia, where Aboriginal land constitutes about 13% of the state, the Aboriginal Affairs Planning Authority exercises dominion over only two-thirds of the Aboriginal reserves; they are granted 99-year leases for the remainder. Queensland allots less than two percent of that state to Aborigines, many of whom, because of the Queensland Aboriginal Land Act of 1991, are unable to claim their land. The Queensland Nature Conservation Act of 1992 commands that, should a claim to one of that state's parks prove successful, the Aboriginal owners must immediately lease it right back to the government—no future lease negotiations, no majority representation on the park management team, pretty much no nothing. New South Wales is not much better. That state's Aboriginal Land Rights Act of 1983 merely turned over the titles to already established Aboriginal reserves, with the possibility to claim a few other clumps of land as well as receiving some piddling privileges to the national parks. Provisions for land rights in Tasmania and Victoria are minuscule. (There *are* no Aborigines in Tasmania, you say? Guess what? They're back—well at least about 6,000 descendants are—and they're pushing to reclaim their land and heritage.)

On the national level, however, recent measures have been taken, if not to actually bond the Aborigines and the white folk, to at least reconcile them to one another's presence on the same land. A legal battle initiated in 1982 by Eddie Mabo and four other Torres Islanders over Queensland's Murray Islands culminated 10 years later with the groundbreaking Mabo Decision in which the High Court of Australia actually rejected *terra nullius.* This effectively acknowledged that Aborigines were the original owners of the land—yes, *before* the British!

Nothing of the kind was ever done in the past. Despite adverse hoopla from pastoralists, mining companies, and other "special interest" groups, the Native Title Act was passed by federal Parliament in 1993 and implemented in 1994, paving the way for Aborigines to claim their rightful title. Sounds good, doesn't it? Don't kid yourself. There are so many limitations and complexities surrounding this law that claims will no doubt be tangled up in legal mumbo jumbo far into the future. And somehow those mining companies (and "significant others") don't seem to be whining as much; maybe because the small print reads that existing leases and ownership supersede Aboriginal land claims.

If the Aborigines believe the Australian government will truly return their land—well, they'd better keep on dreaming.

EUROPEAN SETTLEMENT

The ancient Greeks, who were quite comfortable with the notion that the earth was round, proposed without any concrete evidence that a large southern continent was necessary to preserve the earth's equilibrium. In the 2nd century A.D., the mathematician Ptolemy, conjecturing, mapped the "Terra Incognita," the Unknown Land. It was not until the great age of European exploration, more than a thousand years later, that these intuitions were confirmed. Following the sea routes opened up by Magellan, who entered the Pacific while exploring South America, Portuguese navigator Cristoval de Mendonca made an unauthorized trip to map much of the north and east coasts of Australia. This expedition violated the treaty between Spain and Portugal, which gave Spain all the lands west of Brazil, and so the discovery was kept hush-hush. As a result no European saw the east coast of Australia until Cook's expedition 240 years later.

As early as 1606, the Spanish navigator Torres, approaching from the west around southern Africa, sailed through the straits that separate Australia from Papua New Guinea and now bear his name. Willem Janzoon followed in the same year and entered the Gulf of Carpentaria. Seventeen years later, Jan Carstensz followed Janzoon's route and mapped the western coast of Cape York. In 1642, the Dutch almost completed the coastal surveillance of Australia when Abel Tasman circumnavigated Tasmania, calling it "Van Diemen's Land," but he could see little potential for the mercantile interests that he largely represented.

By the end of the 17th century, the Dutch had poked about every part of Australia but the east coast. This was partly because they caught the prevailing westerlies as they rounded Cape Horn in Africa, sweeping them on to the lucrative markets of the East Indies. Interestingly enough, many of the Europeans who found their way to Australia had simply overshot their mark on the way to the Spice Islands to the north.

The first Englishman to visit Australia, William Dampier, landed near King Sound on the northwest coast in 1688 with a rather disreputable company that had lost its way and needed to stop for repairs. He was so unimpressed with the desolate country that he could see no reason to return or to encourage his countrymen to do so.

It was not until 82 years later that the celebrated navigator Capt. James Cook visited Australia and dragged it into the modern world. Cook had been sent to the South Pacific primarily to make astronomical observations of Venus and, while he was about it, to explore a region that was receiving more and more attention from the great powers of the day. After accomplishing his scientific mission, he returned, circumnavigating New Zealand. On 20 April 1770, he sighted the southeast coast of Australia. He turned north and charted the length of the east coast. His first landfall was "a fine bay," which Cook later called "Botany Bay" because of the numerous botanical specimens they were able to collect there.

Cook continued north for 3,000 kilometers until his ship *Endeavor* ran aground on a coral reef near what is now Cooktown in north Queensland. It took his crew two months to repair the damage before they sailed north through Torres Strait. On an island three kilometers off Cape York, which he named Possession Island, Cook raised the Union Jack and formally took possession of the eastern part of the continent. British law enabled him to do this as long as the land was regarded as *terra nullius* or unoccupied. This legalistic form of finders-keepers could only be sustained subsequently if the Ab-

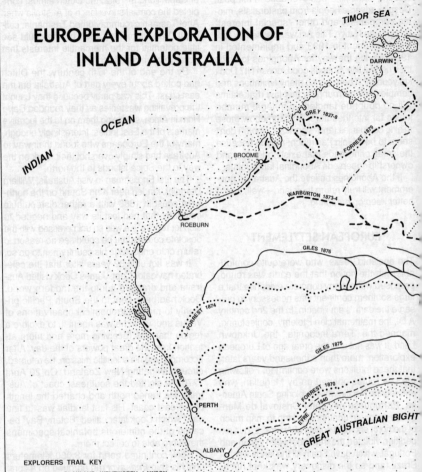

EUROPEAN EXPLORATION OF INLAND AUSTRALIA

TIMOR SEA

DARWIN

INDIAN OCEAN

GREY 1837-8

A. FORREST 1879

BROOME

WARBURTON 1873-4

ROEBURN

GILES 1876

GILES 1874

J. FORREST 1874

GILES 1875

GREY 1839

J. FORREST 1870

PERTH

J. FORREST 1870

EYRE 1840

ALBANY

GREAT AUSTRALIAN BIGHT

EXPLORERS TRAIL KEY

xxxxxxxx	BLAXLAND, WENTWORTH, LAWSON
············	EVANS
▬ ▬ ▬	OXLEY
·▬·▬·▬·	CUNNINGHAM
▬ · ▬ · ▬	STURT
▬·· ▬·· ▬	MITCHELL
/////////	McMILLAN
·· ▬ ·· ▬	STRZELECKI
▬ ▬ ▬	EYRE
▬ ▬ ▬	LEICHHARDT
·▬··▬·	KENNEDY
···········	STUART
▬ ·· ▬ ··	BURKE & WILLS
▬ · ▬ · ▬	GREY
▬·· ▬··	A.C. GREGORY
·▬·▬·▬	J. FORREST
·········	A. FORREST
▬ ▬ ▬ ▬	GILES
▬ ▬ ▬	WARBURTON

ARAFURA SEA

CORAL SEA

A.C. GREGORY 1855-6

LEICHHARDT 1844-5

KENNEDY 1848

ALICE SPRINGS

BURKE & WILLS 1860-1

STURT 1844-5

STURT 1862

KENNEDY 1847

BOURKE

STURT 1835

MITCHELL 1845-6

BRISBANE

CUNNINGHAM
1823, 1827, 1828

OXLEY
1818

MITCHELL 1835

BATHURST

OXLEY 1817

NEW CASTLE

PORT AUGUSTA

ADELAIDE

STURT 1829-30

YASS

SYDNEY

BLAXLAND, WENTWORTH,
LAWSON 1813

EVANS 1813-1815

MITCHELL 1836

MELBOURNE

STRZELECKI 1840

McMILLAN 1839-41

0   400 km

TASMANIA

© MOON PUBLICATIONS, INC.

origines were ignored or, worse, considered as less than human. And so it was all the way up to 1992, when the High Court of Australia finally rejected *terra nullius* and acknowledged that the Aborigines were the original title-holders. (See "Land Rights," above.)

Colonization

Cook's discovery of Australia was timely for British interests in more than one way. Cook was excited by the tall straight trunks of the Norfolk pine that grew in this new land, thinking they would make excellent masts for the expanding British navy. As it turned out they were not suitable, but Britain had recently lost its colonies in the American War of Independence, and so with them went a cheap and easy way of disposing of the convicts that were clogging British jails. Voila! Australia was the perfect spot for a brand-new penal colony. On 18 January 1788, a fleet of 11 ships arrived at Botany Bay. On board were 1,044 people, 730 of them convicts, under the command of Captain (later Governor) Phillip. The convicts were a mixed bunch—murderers, petty thieves, political radicals, hardened criminals thrown together with mere children convicted of stealing a loaf of bread. Their sentences varied from seven years to life, and they must have contemplated their new life in this strange and thankless land with dismay.

Indeed, the survival of the infant colony was by no means assured, and the inverted seasons, the unfamiliar flora and fauna, and the isolation conspired to make the first few years precarious to say the least. The colonists relied on food supplies shipped from Britain, and even when their crops failed in the unsuitable soil, they insisted on ignoring the veritable feast of native food that surrounded them, to the point of near starvation.

As for Australia's west coast, a.k.a. New Holland, the British showed little interest until 1802 when Matthew Flinders, on his sail-around-Australia, concluded that both coasts were part of the same continent. And then of course there was that nasty rumor that the French were preparing to colonize. So—up went the Union Jack.

Expansion

Lady Luck certainly did not grace those first colonists, who barely survived from one supply ship's arrival to the next. However, while they did not prosper, they did cling to the settlement at Sydney Cove, and gradually established a permanent presence.

Eventually the time came to spread out. In 1802 Matthew Flinders, captain of the intrepid *Investigator,* circumnavigated the continent, with Phillip Parker King treading behind in 1817 and 1822. A bevy of big name explorers such as John Oxley, Sir Thomas Mitchell, Charles Sturt, Hamilton Hume, and William Hovell were blazing trails. Before long other settlements sprang up: Hobart in 1803, Brisbane in 1824, King George Sound (now Albany) in 1826, and Perth and Fremantle in 1829. Melbourne, established in 1835, and Adelaide, in 1836, were Australia's first nonconvict colonies. In 1838, Charles Grey and friends made a stab at settling Hanover Bay in the Kimberley, but were driven away by the exhausting terrain.

The Blue Mountains to the west of Sydney presented an impenetrable barrier to inland expansion, until 1813 when a passage was found that opened the way for a great western push into the plains of central Australia. Land was granted to graziers and pastoralists who could use the labor of convicts to clear the forests, build the fences, and generally "improve" the land.

John MacArthur, a wealthy landowner, imported some fine-fleeced merino sheep from Spain and embarked on a breeding program that was to profoundly influence the subsequent course of Australia's development. The wool industry has transformed the face of Australia, placed its stamp on Australia's culture, and shepherded the nation to prosperity over and over again.

Searching for the Centre

Despite the burgeoning townships and rural ranches, it was the vast interior that represented the prize petunia to most explorers. Talk of a huge inland sea prompted a sort of magnetic pull to find the something; nothing; everything— somewhere in there!

Rummaging around the Flinders Ranges in South Australia in 1840, Edward John Eyre found not a big sea but an enormous salt lake. The lake, which he named "Torrens," prevented him from getting to his goal: Australia's center. So he had to trek south to Port Lincoln, then cross the continent to Albany in Western Australia. (Lake Torrens is actually only one in a group of lakes that includes Lakes Eyre and Frome.)

Taking up the challenge in 1844, Charles Sturt embarked on an 18-month odyssey that took him from lovely Adelaide, along the Murray and Darling Rivers, then northwest to Sturt Stony Desert where inferno-like heat, scurvy, and a variety of other horrific conditions drove him back to the city. Poor Charles never was the same, but he did end up with a forboding desert named after him.

Enter Prussian doctor Ludwig Leichhardt. Departing from Brisbane in 1844, Leichhardt and his men made a historic 14-month crossing between Darling Downs and Port Essington, near Darwin, and were credited with finding potential farmlands for pastoralist expansion. Unfortunately, the heroic Leichhardt vanished two years later while attempting another crossing. In the same year that Leichardt went poof, the Edmund Kennedy Expedition also met a dismal demise. Trekking from Rockingham Bay, south of Cairns, to Cape York in northern Queensland, a combination of bad strategy, illness, and Aboriginal attack wiped out Kennedy and most of his men.

In 1860 the Burke and Wills Expedition was running neck-in-neck with that of John McDouall Stuart, as they raced to conquer Australia's mysterious center and to forge the best route for the overland telegraph line soon to begin in Darwin.

Explorers Robert O'Hara Burke and William John Wills had money, men, and equipment aplenty, but still they did not fare very well. Departing Melbourne, Burke and Wills left most of their men at Menindee, southeast of Broken Hill. After establishing a depot at Coopers Creek, only four members of the expedition headed any farther: Burke, Wills, John King, and Charles Grey.

Summer. Ah, a marvelous time for a 1,100 kilometer stroll through central Australia up to the Gulf of Carpentaria. They eventually achieved their goal—it was the return journey that was the killer. Grey bit the dust first, followed by Burke and Wills, who actually made it back to the Coopers Creek depot only to find their loyal mates had split back to Menindee that same morning. You can still visit the Dig Tree with its carved message on the Cooper Creek banks.

John King, however, survived, thanks to nursing by local Aborigines.

Meanwhile, John McDouall Stuart turned out (in some ways) the big winner. A much better planner, Stuart had traveled round-trip from Adelaide to Chambers Bay on the north coast, east of Darwin—a route eventually mimicked by the original road, railway, and overland telegraph lines. He went down in history as the first explorer to reach Australia's geographical center, but then he just went down, period, losing his vision, memory, and his life soon after his journey.

As for that big inland sea, it turned out to be the vast, dry outback interior. No oasis, just a *big* mirage.

Western Exploration

Except for settlements at Perth and Fremantle, the western half of Australia remained virtually unexplored by Europeans until the latter part of the nineteenth century, when a handful of intrepid explorers ventured into the region: William Gosse, aiming west from the Alice Springs telegraph station, stumbled upon Uluru (Ayers Rock); Ernest Giles bumped into Kata Tjuta (the Olgas) on his crossing attempt, then made a later expedition from between the Gascoyne River to Kata Tjuta and the telegraph line; Major John Warburton, also trying to locate a westward route from Alice Springs, eventually forged his way to the Oakover River; from the west coast, John Forrest made expeditions from Geraldton to the Overland Telegraph Line, and from Perth to Fowlers Bay in South Australia.

The 1890s brought a series of scientific expeditions into the region to check out flora and fauna, rocks and minerals, and lifestyles of the local Aborigines. Explorations were conducted northeast of Coolgardie by David Lindsay (in charge of the Elder Scientific Exploring Expedition), while the territory west and south of Alice Springs was covered by the Horn Expedition. Prospector David Carnegie staked a route from Coolgardie to Halls Creek while, around the same time, the Calvert Expedition did not survive its foray around Western Australia's Great Sandy Desert.

It was Alfred Canning, in 1906, who mapped out his famous Canning Stock Route southwest from Halls Creek to Wiluna in Western Australia—a barren, treacherous track through the

Great Sandy and Gibson Deserts and a thumbs-up favorite with diehard four-wheel-drivers.

Gold and the Australian Psyche

The discovery of gold in the 1850s sparked a gold rush that brought huge numbers of hopeful prospectors from around the world.

Edward Hargraves began the fury in 1851. The news of even his relatively small find at Ophir, near Bathurst in New South Wales, was all it took to start the fever. Diggers came flocking, first to Ophir, and then to Turon. The Victorian government, none too happy with the migration to its neighboring state, offered a reward for gold discovery closer to, say, their own Melbourne. Within a month gold was discovered at Clunes, followed by the extraordinary finds at Ballarat, Castlemaine, and Bendigo, thereby establishing Victoria as a center of wealth and influence.

Spawned by an 1887 find in Southern Cross, Western Australia, the rush rushed westward. Five years later, Arthur Bayley staked an astoundingly huge claim near Coolgardie; then came an even larger find by three Irish prospectors at neighboring Kalgoorlie. This so-called "Golden Mile" is supposedly the world's richest area of gold-bearing earth. Once the country's poorest and most undeveloped state, Western Australia's population soared; the place was on the map—even European opera stars traveled to the wild mining settlements to have gold nuggets thrown at their feet. Even today, Western Australia is the country's richest state.

The opulence and grandeur of Melbourne and the cities that grew up around the gold mines were the exuberant expressions of an unprecedented boom. Vast fortunes were made and Australian society was transformed almost overnight. Gold fever brought Prussians, Americans, Italians, Chinese, and—of course—more English, Irish, Scottish, and Welsh. Today, Darwin's mix of over 50 ethnic groups reflects the demographic wealth brought about by the gold rush. A tiny provincial society was inundated with intellectuals, merchants, entrepreneurs, professionals, artists, and adventurers ready to take advantage of new opportunities that seemed to be opening up everywhere.

Economic and social consequences aside, the gold rush gave birth to a peculiarly Australian ethos, that of "mateship." In many other parts of the English-speaking world, "mate" means a marriage partner; in Australia it also means a friend, and as a form of address, it carries an unspoken appeal to deep levels of devotion, loyalty, and affection that come from a tradition of interdependence that was born in the crucible of the goldfields. This fraternal tradition remains deeply entrenched in the Australian psyche.

It was on the goldfields near Ballarat that the Eureka Stockade incident took place. With easily extractable ore already mined, the "diggers" were forced to sink deeper and more elaborate shafts, causing mining costs to increase. As a result the gold miners' license fee became the subject of outraged protest. The dispute between the miners and the government agents became so heated that a group of diggers who refused to pay the fee built a stockade at a place called Eureka, and fought government troops on 3 December 1854. Thirty diggers died and the incipient rebellion was quashed, but the event remains significant as an expression of what author Thomas Keneally calls "that most Australian of birthrights, the Fair Go." This is a central concept for Australians, involving a sense of natural justice based on common sense, equality, and a healthy disregard for authority and ideology.

The Bushrangers

A passion for the "fair go" flows on as a sympathy for the underdog, the "battler." This accounts for the affection—almost reverence—rogues and outlaws command in the popular imagination, particularly the 19th-century bushrangers. The most famous of them was Ned Kelly, whose distinctive homemade helmet and suit of armor have become icons of Australian culture. Kelly came from an Irish family of small selectors (cockatoo farmers, or "cockies") whose frequent conflict with wealthy pastoralists, or "squatters," and the authorities led them into a miniature revolt. After seeing their mother imprisoned and serving time themselves for uncommitted crimes, the Kelly brothers took to the bush and began a brief but spectacular career as bank robbers. Ned Kelly often brazenly and single-handedly captured entire townships for days at a time. His reputation grew until he was captured after a siege at Glenrowan in which he received 28 gunshot wounds. He was taken to Beechworth where a sensational trial took place, then transported to Melbourne to be hanged. "Tell them I died game," he said, awaiting execution. On the gallows his last words summed up the battler's philosophy: "Such is life."

There were many other bushrangers—Bold Ben Hall, Mad Dog Morgan, Frank Gardiner, Martin Cash (who was one of only a few to escape the infamous Port Arthur penal colony in Tasmania), Bogong Jack, Captain Midnight—and it is interesting to note that much of the mythology about them centers around the unfair and treacherous circumstances of their captures and deaths. Traditionally, Australians have tolerated almost every kind of social aberration, but they draw the line at the arbitrary exercise of power and privilege by the strong over the weak.

Social Reform

By the end of the 19th century the scene was set for further social upheaval. Labor was organizing itself and leading the world in a militant struggle for workers' rights. The Australian Labor Party was founded over 100 years ago in 1891, and that same year a wave of strikes for better wages and conditions culminated in the famous Shearers' Strike, which was ruthlessly put down by the wealthy landowners who employed scabs, or "blacklegs," to bring in the all-important wool clip (crop). Labor leaders were imprisoned, which led to the cry: "If they jail a man for striking, it's a rich man's country yet." If the cardinal virtue in Australia is mateship, the two deadly sins are scabbing and dobbing—informing against one's mates.

On 1 January 1901, after a decade of debate and negotiation, the six Australian colonies were joined in a federation of states with the passage of the Constitution by the British Parliament. The new federal government met in Melbourne until moving to the new capital, Canberra (designed by the fashionable architect Walter Burley Griffin), in 1927. Australia continued to pioneer policies of social reform that did not go unnoticed elsewhere in the world. For example, Australia was the first country to elect Labor representatives and the first country to elect a Labor government. It was one of the first countries to grant women the vote.

These notable developments came to the attention of Lenin, who wrote a tract on the Australian Labor Party. He concluded that it was a tool of the bourgeoisie. Nevertheless, a number of progressive developments were enshrined in Australian legislation long before they were achieved elsewhere. The old-age pension, the eight-hour workday, the right to strike—all these became realities in Australia when other nations would not even tolerate their advocacy.

While Australia achieved its independence from Britain without bloodshed, it still remained emotionally and psychically bound to the mother country. Britain remained Australia's chief trading partner and military ally through two world wars. The decline of the British Empire and the emergence of the United States as a world power meant merely that dependence was transferred from one to the other. More recently, however, talk of breaking with the monarchy and creating a brand-new Republic of Australia is rife in the air from outback pubs to city clubs. Many Australians would like to see this change instigated by the year 2000—possibly as an Olympic event?

World Wars

The first world war terribly scarred the generation that took part in it. Australia's first action was at Gallipoli in the Dardanelles, where, hopelessly outnumbered and outpositioned by a firmly entrenched Turkish army, thousands of young Australians were slaughtered. The incident was so profoundly shocking to a young nation that the sacrifice and suffering of those Anzacs (Australia and New Zealand Army Corps) has never been forgotten.

Perhaps the most moving story of that conflict concerns a young soldier, Simpson, who with his donkey rescued the injured and dying without regard for his own safety. Eventually he fell to a sniper's bullet, but Simpson and his donkey have an honored place in the national consciousness.

Australians went on to fight on the battlefields of Europe, and, if nothing else, their experiences helped to open the eyes of an insular and isolated community to the wider world. This process was terribly gradual, and despite its proximity to Asia Australia for years regarded itself as an outpost of the British Empire.

The 1920s brought increased prosperity, largely through the export of primary produce. Refrigeration had made possible the shipment of frozen meat over the enormous distances necessary to reach markets in Europe; Australia was said to ride once again on the sheep's back. Unable to avoid the worldwide depression of the 1930s, Australians suffered all the hardships that were familiar to people in America and Europe, and—with the outbreak of WW II—once again took up arms for king and country. This time, however, there was a direct threat from Japan and, while Australians fought in Europe and Africa, they also had to defend their own land. An air raid on Darwin by Japanese bombers created an unprecedented response and helped cement a military alliance with the United States that continues today. General Douglas MacArthur's proud boast that he would return to the Philippines was made possible in part by retreating and regrouping on the Australian mainland.

Changing Times

After the war, social change picked up tempo. A positive immigration drive replaced the infamous White Australia Policy, which had restricted entry to Australia largely to white Anglo-Saxons. Displaced refugees from Europe were recruited to come for a new start in the land of opportunity. For many, the realities did not measure up to the promise, but, nevertheless, ever-increasing numbers of Italians, Greeks, Hungarians, Yugoslavs, and peoples from a host of other countries began to make their presence felt.

It is often hard now for Australians to appreciate just how staid, unimaginative, and limited their society was only a few decades ago. The isolated outback, as might be expected, has almost always possessed a typically anarchic "we make our own rules" nature, while the Western Australians are plain and simply "laid-back," like their Southern California geographic counterparts. Other parts of the country, particularly the east coast, were slightly on the uptight side. In Melbourne, for example, no alcohol could be sold after six o'clock, which led to the degrading "six o'clock swill," as patrons rushed into hotels after work and downed as many beers as quickly as they could. "Wowserism," or puritanism, ensured that virtually no activity of any kind, except church-going, could take place on Sunday. A combination of the influx of more sophisticated migrants and the liberating influence of the youth culture of the '60s has irreversibly transformed the face of Australian society over the past two or three decades.

During the same period, Australia's traditional allegiance to Britain became more and more irrelevant. Meanwhile, Britain has gradually divested itself of its colonial heritage and turned more and more toward a future in Europe. With Britain's entry into the Common Market, Australia lost automatic access to its traditional markets and was forced to face the reality of its location on the edge of Asia. The increasing numbers of European and, later, Asian migrants felt no sentimental attachment to the British institutions that had figured so largely in the minds of Anglo-Saxon Australians.

Finally, Australia's strategic position in the South Pacific brought it into the sphere of American influence. Since the 1950s, Australian troops have answered the call from Washington, not London, first in the Korean War and more disastrously in the Vietnam War. Australia's longest-serving prime minister, Sir Robert Menzies, once said of Queen Elizabeth, "I did but see her passing by, and yet I love her till I die," much to the dismay of independence-minded Australians. Nothing could better illustrate the dramatic shift in cultural focus that has taken place in Australia than the words of his successor, Harold Holt, at the height of the Vietnam War: "All the way with L.B.J."

AUSTRALIA TODAY

Australia describes itself as a multicultural society, and it is perhaps the most cosmopolitan society in the world, with almost one-quarter of its present population having been born elsewhere. The benefits of such a wide mix of ethnic, cultural, and religious backgrounds are immense and, although the potential for social discord undoubtedly exists, somehow the friction that characterizes similarly heterogeneous communities has rarely occurred in Australia. Whether this is due to a tradition of easygoing tolerance, or to an ambience of apathy which infects all new arrivals, Australia's numerous ethnic communities have achieved a harmony that would be unthinkable in many parts of the world.

That is not to say that discrimination and prejudice do not exist, but most Australians have grown to appreciate the differences that succeeding waves of migrants bring to their society—from the novelty of new foods (Australia boasts some fabulous—and tony—ethnic restaurants) to the challenge of learning new languages, customs, and ways of thinking.

But beneath the gloss of tourist promotions is a dark side—Australians consume more alcohol and pain killers per capita than any other English-speaking country. Like other developed countries, Australia is plagued by recession, unemployment, a blowout of foreign debt, natural disasters, and pressing environmental degradation. Having a small population, and a tax base that is minuscule compared to that of larger industrialized countries, Australia is helpless in the face of international economic developments. For decades, the country has relied on the export of primary produce and now finds that its markets are increasingly unreliable, while prices are out of control. A new drive to turn the "Lucky Country" into the "Clever Country" has been launched to stop the flight of its scientists and technicians to the universities and research companies of America and Europe, and at the same time develop the "sunrise" industries necessary for a high-technology future. New high-technology cities, or the "Multi-function Polis," are planned in partnership with the Japanese, the first having already been approved at a site near Adelaide.

Aborigines have made strides because of the Native Titles Act, and through international recognition of their art, music, and culture. The harsh outback has become romanticized through films and books—and the more far-fetched the better.

Australians have developed a unique laissez-faire attitude, embodied in the expressions "no worries" and "she'll be right," and it seems difficult to rouse them to action. The advantage of this approach is that life in Australia is remarkably relaxed and stress-free, even in the cities. Violence and the social blight of drug abuse have not quite reached the heights that most Americans would consider normal. Access to a comfortable standard of living is easier in Australia than almost anywhere else on earth. The price for such a self-satisfied lifestyle is indolence, apathy, and procrastination, and Australians are only just beginning to realize how precarious their delightful existence is.

Australia is changing, and never more so than now. The past has forced Australians to be innovative and adaptable because of their extreme isolation. Air travel, which so many Australians helped to pioneer, and the information superhighway have meant that Australia no longer must labor under the "tyranny of distance."

Despite its very real problems, Australia still has a refreshing, overriding sense of optimism—hey, South Australia still has its festivals; Northern Territory and outback, their mystique; Queensland, the reef; New South Wales, its harbor; Victoria, her restaurants; Tasmania, its wild beauty; and Western Australia, the surfers and prospects of gold. So, what's the problem, mate?

GOVERNMENT

For a country of only 18 million people, Australia has an awful lot of government. It is a measure of Australians' political apathy that they have allowed themselves to become, according to some commentators, one of the most over-governed peoples in the free world. Australians labor under three tiers of government—federal, state, and shire or municipal. There are six state governments, two assemblies for the territories, and 900 local government bodies. All are accompanied by the appropriate bureaucracies, red tape, and seals of approval (or disapproval).

STRUCTURE

Australia follows the American example in the separation of powers, whereby the executive, legislative, and judiciary are independent. The federal government is an odd mix of the British Westminster system and the American congressional system. Australia's Constitution is an Act of the British Parliament, passed in 1901, which provides for a House of Representatives, whose 147 members (divided on the basis of population) are elected every four years, and an upper house, the Senate, whose function is to act as a house of review and provide equal representation for each state, thereby preserving state rights. The political party with most members in the House of Representatives becomes the governing party and the prime minister is elected from within that majority. Regional breakdowns for house members are: New South Wales, 50; Victoria, 38; Queensland, 25; Western Australia, 14; South Australia, 12; Tasmania, 5; Australian Capital Territory, 2; and Northern Territory, 1. On 2 March 1996 the Liberal Party, under the leadership of John Howard, swept into power after more than a decade of Labor majority.

Canberra (Australian Capital Territory, or ACT) is home to the federal Parliament and other government agencies, as well as foreign embassies. Surrounded on all sides by New South Wales and on its own piece of land, Canberra resembles Washington, D.C., but it's not nearly as exciting.

The formal head of state is still the Queen of England, although her powers are vested in the governor-general, who is nominated by the Australian government of the day. With all the current buzz about ditching the monarchy, however, the title Governor-General may soon transmute into President of the Republic of Australia. Under the Australian Constitution, the governor-general, being the chief executive, has the power to dissolve Parliament, ratify legislation, appoint ministers of the government, command the armed forces, and appoint judges to the high court. Under an unwritten convention, the governor-general acts, in a mainly titular capacity, under the instructions and advice of the prime minister, as does the queen.

Many Australians remember with outrage the events of 11 November 1975, when Governor-General Sir John Kerr dismissed the Labor government of Prime Minister Gough Whitlam, thus bucking the customary hierarchy. Right before a general election Whitlam couldn't pass supply bills through the hostile Senate, agitated by the governor-general. The intricacies and implications of that decision still reverberate in the corridors of Parliament House and the case is still a hotly debated point for many Australians.

The Senate is made up of 12 senators from each state and two from each territory. State senators are elected for six years, but only half the Senate faces the electorate every three years. Territory senators serve a maximum of three years, their terms coinciding with those of House members. Because the popular mandate only affects those senators who stand for reelection, this has often led to the situation in which the House of Representatives faces a hostile Senate. The Senate, while theoretically a house of review, is able to block legislation—as it did in the crisis of 1975.

State governments are microcosms of the federal structure and are bicameral, with the exception of Queensland, which disbanded its upper house as soon as it could. Numerous attempts in other states to follow that example have all been

met with the in-built suspicion with which Australians treat politicians who start tinkering around with the system: it is axiomatic that politicians are not to be trusted, so if they want to do something it is much safer not to let them do it. Consequently, most states are lumbered with unwieldy edifices of government. With the exception of the Northern Territory, which is governed by a chief minister, the states are run by individual premiers. Aside from renegade Queensland and the Northern Territory, upper houses in the states are known as the Legislative Council; lower houses in New South Wales, Victoria, and Western Australia are the Legislative Assembly; lower houses in South Australia and Tasmania are the House of Assembly. The state governments are based in each capital city.

The struggle between the state and federal governments is ongoing. The Constitution gave the states considerable powers, many of which have been whittled away by the federal government over the years. States have responsibilities for health, housing, education, justice, and transport, but they have lost much of their power to raise revenue and must receive grants from Canberra, which controls the power of taxation. The control of natural resources is under the jurisdiction of the states, but the federal government has used its powers to make foreign policy (particularly by entering the World Heritage Treaty) to block development in environmentally sensitive areas of Tasmania and Queensland. Other federal controls consist of the usual matters concerning defense, foreign policy, immigration, the economy, and the postal service.

Australia has a plethora of local governments, responsible for collecting rubbish, mending holes in the road, giving out parking tickets, and holding up homeowners' plans to renovate their kitchens. Councilors are mostly unpaid, except for the widely publicized case of the mayor of Brisbane who, it turned out, was earning more than the prime minister.

POLITICS

Parties

Historically, Australian politics has been effectively dominated by a two-party system. The Australian Labor Party (ALP) has traditionally drawn its support from the union movement but in recent times has extended its base to white-collar workers and liberals. The Liberal Party (LP), drawing its support from private enterprise, small business, and the professions, is the principal partner in a conservative coalition with the rural-based National Party. Recently, the Australian Democrats (AD), a centrist party with a strong environmental platform, and various Green Independent parties have made inroads into the two-party system. In 1996 the Australian Labor Party and the Liberal Party were running neck-in-neck in Senate representation, while in the House of Representatives the ALP had stretched way ahead. The Australian Democrats currently hold seven Senate seats.

The drive to make the final break with Britain and declare Australia a republic has recently intensified. Former Prime Minister Paul Keating pushed hard for it, and the Queen didn't object! (Is this good or bad?) A government-established Republic Advisory Committee is advising details on the changes involved, including the flag (currently with the Union Jack in one corner) and the national anthem. The turnover, which will require a referendum, is poised to become reality by the year 2000 when the Olympic athletes flame their way into Sydney.

Voting

Because of the huge variations in population density across Australia, it has never been possible to achieve "one vote, one value." Rural electorates can be quite enormous in area but still have fewer electors than inner-city seats, so there is an inevitable gerrymander that favors rural communities, traditionally the most conservative voting block.

Voting is mandatory for all citizens over 18; electors who fail to vote are liable for a fine. Voluntary voting was tried in the '20s, but the turnout was so abysmally low that it was abandoned. Voting is preferential and candidates on the ballot must be numbered in order of the elector's preference. This has made it necessary for political parties to produce "how to vote" cards and hand them out at polling booths, to instruct their supporters in the best manner of distributing their preferences. Some Senate ballot papers have had over 60 candidates, and voters have had to number each one for

their vote to be valid. This system has given rise to the "donkey vote" in which a lazy, bored, or hurried voter will simply number the candidates in order down the page. So widespread did this practice become that it has decided the outcomes of several close ballots, and candidates with names at the beginning of the alphabet enjoyed such an advantage that they have been known to change their names to secure the donkey vote. To counter this practice, candidates' positions on the ballot are now determined by random selection.

International Relations

The Australian government is signatory to a number of international treaties including ANZUS, a joint-defense pact between Australia, New Zealand, and the United States. Recently, New Zealand was suspended from this arrangement because of its refusal to allow nuclear-armed ships into its ports; still the Aussies haven't abandoned the Kiwis—they have other agreements. Strategic commitments are also active in Papua New Guinea and nearby southwest Pacific islands.

The United States maintains three top-secret military bases in Australia—at Pine Gap, the North West Cape, and Narrungar. No rental is charged for these facilities (unlike U.S. bases in the Philippines); while they are described as joint facilities, access for Australians is limited. Many Australians believe these bases are first-strike targets and have lobbied for their removal. The North West Cape facility has currently been turned over to the Australians.

Australia is one of the senior members of the Commonwealth of Nations and has a long history of concerned involvement in international affairs through the United Nations and, more recently, the South Pacific Forum. The country

lays claim to the largest area of the Antarctic and has been instrumental in ensuring that Antarctic Treaty nations agree to prevent mining and damaging development of the continent. Australia has also campaigned vigorously against French nuclear testing in the Pacific.

Acknowledging its identity as Asia-Pacific (and not part of the United States or Europe), Australia is taking steps to build relations with its northern neighbors. One example is dispassionate work for a solution to the terrible problems that beset Cambodia; e.g., the Khmer Rouge. Australia's "good guy" reputation for being the first country to recognize the early 1970s Beijing government has been used to persuade the Chinese government to improve civil rights for its people. Similarly, relations with close neighbor Indonesia have been helped through two 1992 events: the creation of the Australia-Indonesia Ministerial Forum and the signing of the Timor Gap Treaty, which recognizes Timor's sovereignty and legitimacy as an Indonesian country. The government is also increasing dialogue regarding security and defense with important nations such as Malaysia, Singapore, and Indonesia, and continues to pursue mutual arrangements and agreements with Japan, China, the Republic of Korea, and Vietnam.

Relations with independent African nations are relatively friendly, as they are in parts of Latin America and the Carribean, and of course Europe. Australia is a supporter both of peace negotiations in the Middle East and the Israeli-Palestine Liberation Organization peace accord.

But don't think for a minute that Australia has softened its allegiance with the United States, despite occasional tensions over wheat subsidies and airline routes. Australia sent a battalion to join the U.S.-guided task force in Somalia and was also the first country to back the Gulf War.

ECONOMY

Official embassy statistics peg Australia twelfth from the top of the world's economies, with a GDP (Gross Domestic Product) around 70% that of the United States. Agriculture and mining still account for much of Australia's wealth, but, increasingly, other sectors such as tourism, manufacturing, and service industries have shown big promise as "econo-boosters."

Life wasn't looking so rosy during the world recession of the early 1990s, which dragged Australia down with it. The usual greed, corruption, and rah-rah investments of the booming 1980s—most of them instigated by a few megarich Western Australian tycoons—lost big bucks for many—trusting senior citizens and hyped-up spendthrift yuppies alike. Few went unscathed. The result of those high-profile entrepreneurs shuffling worthless pieces of paper back and forth was the same: huge stock market losses, wiped-out savings accounts, building societies and banking institutions gone belly-up.

Times were tough on the farm those days—not just because of the recession but because of an international trade war with potentially disastrous consequences for the land of Oz. Even rural Australia, while it might seem removed from the rest of the planet's concerns, gets heavily spun up in the buy-and-sell trade-war web. Cattle, wool, and mining (and now tourism) are major rural commodities, and rural Australia comprises a big chunk of the country, which relies heavily on global trade.

Australia has been working diligently to establish an internationally competitive economy, enabling it to compete with the United States and Europe, but most particularly with the rapidly exploding Asia-Pacific markets (Japan, which purchases more than one-fourth of the country's merchandise exports, remains the largest single export market). To enable primary export commodities to compete, Australia has greatly reduced tariffs on once heavily protected industries.

Overall, the increased-trade plan seems to be working and, happily, the country is pitting its growth against that of the top industrialized nations. In 1995 the economy grew by four percent,

and, with the change in government in 1996, it is expected to jump another one-half percent. The knocking-down of the high tariff walls means that Australian manufacturers, production having increased about 25%, now compete with traditional commodities to bring export revenue into the country. Latest statistics show that manufacturing and services exports have increased threefold, while overall exports have doubled.

An annual average inflation rate that hovered at about eight percent in the 1980s has slid to about three percent in the mid-1990s, equal to or below that of most of the country's largest trading partners. Interest rates have dropped considerably in the last decade. Official short-term rates plunged from about 18% in 1989 to about seven percent in mid-1996; long-term rates of about eight percent are at their lowest since the early 1970s. This is certainly good news in a country that boasts one of the highest levels of home ownership in the world.

Unemployment, however, has not fared too well in the numbers game. And, while a substantial number of jobs were created in the manufacturing and services sectors (1.4 million 1983-1990), the traditional arena saw massive layoffs and cutbacks. Optimists point to signs of a strengthening job market with the change of government, but the reality is that unemployment, which ranked a whopping 11% in late 1992, still occasionally drifts within the double-digit range. At the change of government, in March 1996, just over six million people worked full-time, with women making up 41% of the labor force. Most employment fell within manufacturing, construction, community services, and wholesale and retail trade.

The pressure of international competition has inevitably eroded the hard-won conditions that a century of union activity had established. At one time more than 50% of the labor force belonged to one of 227 unions, affiliates under the umbrella of the national Australian Council of Trade Unions (ACTU). And even though membership has dropped some 10%, industrial relations—and the ubiquitous strikes—continue to be a thorny issue in Australian politics.

Employment discrimination because of race, color, sex, marital status, pregnancy, descent, or national or ethnic origin is illegal throughout Australia, and age discrimination is now squeaking its way onto the list as well. The average work week is 38 hours and almost every employee is entitled to four weeks per year of paid holiday time. But, how about wage discrimination? Women's average weekly earnings equal a whopping two-thirds of men's earnings. As for the Aborigines—do you even have to ask?

In rural Australia, as well as throughout much of Australia, volatile prices have alternately wreaked havoc and created glory with the economy. The massive mining and agricultural enterprises usually get by nicely while the "independent" gold and opal miners, small-scale ranchers ("cockies"), and burgeoning Aboriginal-owned businesses struggle for survival.

Bear in mind that the picture presented by government stats on laser-printed spread sheets may appear much brighter than the black-and-white images of battlers barely scraping by and the all-too-invisible Aborigines focused in the corners of a harsh, shadowy landscape.

Major Trade Agreements

GATT (General Agreement on Tariffs and Trade): Australia has been a GATT member since the organization's inception in 1948 as a vehicle for strengthening international trade and resolving related disputes. When the Uruguay Round met in 1991, Australia lobbied heavily for the removal of all agricultural trade barriers. It is allied in this endeavor with the Cairns Group—named for its initial 1986 meeting in North Queensland. The Cairns Group, chaired by Australia, includes Argentina, Brazil, Canada, Chile, Colombia, Fiji, Hungary, Indonesia, Malaysia, New Zealand, the Philippines, Thailand, and Uruguay, and altogether these nations provide about 20% of the world's agricultural exports. The group aims to reduce protection and subsidy practices by the big industrialized nations, including those granted under the U.S. Export Enhancement Program (i.e., recall the sale of subsidized wheat by the United States to China and Yemen).

APEC (Asia Pacific Economic Cooperation): Initiated by Australia to facilitate economic cooperation within the region, a group of 12

ministers representing Australia, New Zealand, the United States, the Philippines, Singapore, Thailand, Indonesia, Japan, Canada, Brunei, and the Republic of Korea met in Canberra in 1989; two years later China, Hong Kong, and Taipei joined the group. In 1992 APEC positioned a secretariat in Singapore and has become a high-level forum for dialogue and consultation on regional economies and trade policies.

ASEAN (Association of South East Asian Nations): Though most economic matters with the member nations are conducted through APEC, Australia still keeps its foot in the door of this group. Mutual trade issues negotiated at the Uruguay Round, particularly those regarding agriculture, have established a strong link (let's not forget that Indonesia, Malaysia, the Philippines, and Thailand are part of the Cairns Group). At the regularly held ASEAN-Australia Forum, senior officials put their heads together on matters of education, trade, science, technology, and telecommunications.

ANZCERTA or CER (Australia New Zealand Closer Economic Relations Trade Agreement): This 1983 pact between neighbors opened the way for important trade and investment expansion when all restrictions were abolished, enabling each country to open up service operations and manufacturing concerns on each other's turf.

Papua New Guinea: Papua New Guinea, recipient of an estimated 2,500 Australian products, relies heavily on Australian trade, services, and foreign investment funds. The Joint Declaration of Principles of 1987 is the umbrella under which a number of bilateral agreements fall, including those ensuring duty-free and unrestricted access for most PNG exports, investment protection, and development cooperation.

Japan: As the country's strongest single export market, Japan is accorded most-favored-nation status. Formal arrangements between the two countries date back to the Agreement on Commerce signed in 1957 and renegotiated in 1963. Double taxation agreements hold as do those with shipping, air services, and investment.

Indochina: The dramatic rise in petroleum imports from Vietnam was the major factor behind Australia's almost $400 million worth of trade with Indochina during 1994-95; other large imports from the area are coffee and seafood.

Australia provides crude petroleum, ore processing machinery, zinc, wheat, and telecommunications equipment to Indochina. Power generating machinery is targeted for Cambodia and nonmonetary silver and gold head to Laos.

SPARTECA (South Pacific Regional Trade and Economic Cooperation Agreement): This agreement comprises individual trade agreements between Australia and the South Pacific Forum countries of New Zealand, Fiji, Federated States of Micronesia, Cook Islands, Solomon Islands, Papua New Guinea, Republic of the Marshall Islands, Kiribati, Nauru, Niue, Tuvalu, Tonga, Vanuatu, and Western Samoa.

Women: Finally, women are trading instead of *being* traded! In 1994 a delegation of almost 100 Australian female executives journeyed to Singapore to join 130 other women from 14 Asian countries in the Australia/ASEAN Women Leaders conference. Supported by the Australian government's Office of the Status of Women and the Department of Foreign Affairs and Trade, the groundbreaking mission finally allowed businesswomen entree into the male-dominated South East Asia trade arena. For three days the Australian women liaised and networked—the outcome being an invitation to establish a branch of the Women for Women support group, the creation of a women's investment fund for small-business start-up costs, and the decision to build a joint-venture cosmetics factory in Vietnam. (I said *entree,* not *equality.*)

AGRICULTURE

Just two percent of Australia's workforce is involved in agriculture, and yet agricultural products account for nearly one-fourth of Australia's export revenue—as well as feeding the other 98% of Australians. Not too bad, considering that only about two-thirds of the country is suitable for any kind of agricultural or ranching enterprise, and half of *that* area can only handle pastoral activities. Nevertheless, advanced know-how in crop yields, pastoral output, and soil fertility, along with the related equipment and machinery, have inaugurated and/or boosted cultivation at many desert and semidesert stations (rural ranches). And, of course, Australia's so-called "cattle kings" of the late 1800s were instrumental to the in-

land's pastoral development; Sir Sidney Kidman, Nat Buchanan, the Durack family—all of them were successful cattle-station pioneers.

Stations are enormous. Numbering about 125,000, they encompass 60% of the country's total land area and are the breeding grounds for most of the cattle and sheep. South Australia's Anna Creek Station, for example, totals 31,000 square kilometers and is the size of some European countries. Typically each station has a homestead, or headquarters, where the owners, managers, and other staff tend to their livestock. (Overnight station-stays have also become de rigueur on some tourist circuits.)

Australia is the world leader in wool production and, with the majority of its sheep being that fine merino breed, most of that wool eventually threads its way into (warm) apparel, while skins off the sheeps' rears often end up cozying those of humans riding in cars or sprawled in front of a fireplace. Australia's major wool markets are Germany, Italy, France, Japan, and China.

In case any of you thought we were entering some sort of "cut your cholesterol, curtail your meat intake" era—forget it. As of the 1990s, Australia knocked out the entire European Community as the largest international exporter of veal and beef, with mutton and lamb following behind. And although exports are sent to more than 100 countries, guess who's stuffing down the most? Yes, the new "fat-free" United States. Skinny Japan, however, is the biggest spender. (Some consolation: Japan and the United States are also the main export markets for fish and seafood.) The Aussies, coming in third as the world's biggest meat-eaters, support their own country by consuming approximately 100 kilograms per person annually of beef, veal, chicken, lamb, mutton, and pork.

Dairy concerns, situated mainly around the high-rainfall southwestern and southeastern mainland coasts and northern Tasmania, pump out billions of liters of whole milk; two-thirds are made into cheese, butter, milk powders, and other related products.

Australia's massive wheatbelt, stretching across all five mainland states, produces more than 15 million tons of the grain, with nearly two-thirds exported to big buyers like India, Egypt, Japan, Korea, and China. Wheat production accounts for almost half of farmers' total income from field crops, but also important are rice, cotton, barley, sugarcane, oats, oilseeds, and field peas.

Fruit and vegetables are practically devotional commodities in Australia, and the country enshrines approximately 125,000 hectares of vegetables and 25 million fruit trees. Vineyards, planted on 65,000 hectares, produce millions of liters of wine annually and are receiving recognition—and occasional raves—from rapidly growing export markets in the United States, United Kingdom, New Zealand, Canada, Japan, and Sweden. Major winegrowing regions are in South Australia and New South Wales, but Victoria and Western Australia each have noteworthy cellars. Australian beer has also been hopping.

Forestry, as in many other parts of the world, is a touchy subject. Three-quarters of Australia's native forests (mainly eucalypt forests, but significant areas of rainforest as well) have disappeared since the arrival of Europeans. Some have been destroyed by fire, but the majority have—as elsewhere—simply been logged. Parts of Tasmania look positively ravaged. Plantation forests are usually pine, which offer no food or habitat to native bird and animal life. Logging in native forests and reserves, the "national estate," has been increasingly opposed by environmental groups on the grounds that such activities are unsustainable, and bitter disputes rage between the Greens and proponents of the timber industry, who see their jobs and livelihoods threatened.

The government has ostensibly recognized the environmental concerns and designated the 1990s the "Decade of Landcare." National programs include rainforest and soil conservation, biodiversity, and the reversal of tree decline by planting an estimated one *billion* trees.

MINING

You name it, Australia probably mines it—the country has been mined for well over a century.

Once the only mineral of any interest to the prospector was gold, gold, and more gold; this is still one of the principal targets of the mining industry (after all, Australia is still the world's third-largest producer), and gold miners have tax-exempt status. There's still gold lurking (and

a man and his monster—symbol of the rich Pilbara district

luring) in the hills; every now and again some lucky fossicker trips over a nugget and sells it to a Las Vegas casino for a million dollars.

Now miners have turned their attention to the host of other valuable minerals still underground. Prices fluctuate and mining has its slumps and booms, but the only check on mining activities for the past decade has been the combination of environmental and Aboriginal land-rights issues.

Australia is the world's largest producer of bauxite, which is mined mostly at Weipa, on Queensland's Cape York. The principal source of aluminum, bauxite is also a major player in the iron ore business, of which Australia, along with Brazil, is the world's largest exporter. Much of Australia's iron ore is mined from the remote Pilbara region of Western Australia and is a big reason for the state's wealth. Iron ore launched BHP (Broken Hill Proprietary) on the path that has made it Australia's largest company and a multinational corporation.

Australia has some of the world's largest reserves of black coal, most of it mined in Queensland and New South Wales where it was discovered in 1791. It's an energy source that becomes more significant as global supplies of oil are depleted. Like so many of Australia's raw materials, minerals are generally shipped offshore to the industrial powerhouses of Europe, Japan, and other Asian countries to be turned into consumer products like cars, television sets, and computers, and sold back to Australia, aggravating the problems of foreign debt and balance of trade. The government's "Buy Australian" admonishment is taken quite seriously by citizens.

Australia is a major producer of copper, which is mined in all states except Victoria. The largest deposits are at Queensland's Mount Isa and

South Australia's Olympic Dam, with refineries in South Australia, Queensland, and New South Wales.

Nickel, another huge output, is mined largely in Western Australia, followed by Queensland. Groote Eylandt, in the Northern Territory, is home to one of the world's largest manganese mines, while Kunwarara in Queensland is a major cryptocrystalline magnesite reserve.

More megaproducers are the wealth of mineral sands that contain titanium minerals and byproducts such as zircon and monazite, minerals important in the development of new technology ceramics. These sands have traditionally been found and mined on the nation's beaches, and pristine areas of environmental importance have been ravaged in the past. Public pressure has resulted in the preservation of Fraser Island, Moreton Island, and other sensitive areas, while places like the Shelbourne Bay wilderness in Cape York, where mineral sands have been identified, are the subject of ongoing disputes.

Australia contains an estimated one-third of the world's known uranium ore, with the major deposits situated in South Australia, Western Australia, and the Northern Territory. The government allows the mining and export of uranium from Northern Territory's Ranger Mine and South Australia's Olympic Dam—export conditions being that the raw "yellowcake" is to be used for peaceful purposes only. Further exploration for uranium threatens parts of Kakadu National Park in the Northern Territory, where environmentalists and Aboriginal activists have joined to oppose development.

Other mining activities bring much happier thoughts of future use: Australia is the world's leading producer of diamonds, sapphires, and opals. Sparkly, happy things!

ENERGY

Australia is ideally situated to take advantage of the development of solar energy, although progress in this field is slow; fewer than 10% of Australian homes are equipped with solar hot-water units, but the figure is growing. In the Northern Territory and Western Australia, where cloudless days are as numerous as anywhere on earth, the figure is much higher. Locally developed silicon solar cells power remote railway crossings. Telstra, the national telephone authority, has installed solar-powered telephones in isolated communities in the outback. Interest in solar power is getting stronger in Australia, which is running low on traditional energy sources. In 1993, Perth (Western Australia) was designated the first United Nations Centre for Applications of Solar Energy, giving it a leading edge in international research.

Wind provides another environment-friendly energy option, particularly in the high-wind coastal areas of South Australia, Western Australia, Tasmania, and the Bass Strait. Its main uses are to power windmills and small turbine generators, and it is now the preferred choice over diesel at outback homesteads.

Most of Australia's energy requirements are still supplied by coal, which is also exported in the millions of tons along with large quantities of liquefied natural gas and light crude oil. Australia is roughly two-thirds self-sufficient in oil and produces plenty of natural gas. Most petroleum comes from the Bass Strait and Timor Sea regions, while Western Australia's North West Shelf—Australia's largest development project—is pumping out millions of tons of liquefied natural gas (LNG). (More areas, showing potential for large gas and oil discoveries, have yet to be fully explored.) Light crude oil as well as LNG represent increasingly significant exports, most of it slicking toward the South Pacific and Japan. Heavy crude, however, is still on the import list, supplied by the Middle East but refined domestically.

Huge, easy-access coal reserves give Australia the benefit of substantial, low-cost electricity, most of it produced by coal-fired power plants bolstered by hydroelectric systems and natural gas-fired units. State public utilities have been the suppliers for most of the country's electricity; however, the federal government is geared up for a soon-to-come national electricity grid to provide a competitive market for business consumers.

Gas is becoming increasingly more important as a power source in Australia. The federal government's National Gas Strategy is encouraging free and fair trade between states, the dismissal of a lot of red-tape approvals, and a "casual" approach to pipeline regulations. Natural gas is supplied to all mainland capital cities via pipelines from producing fields.

Environmental Concerns

The looming greenhouse effect from carbon gas emission is becoming more critical, even to the normally apathetic Australian public. Several neighboring nations in the South Pacific face the prospect of literally sinking beneath the waves should global warming cause sea levels to rise even a meter or two.

Substantial hydroelectric systems operate in Tasmania and the Snowy Mountains between New South Wales and Victoria, but it is unlikely that further development of this energy source will be acceptable to a public that, thankfully, is growing more environmentally aware. It was the planned flooding of the Gordon River for hydroelectricity that placed environmental issues firmly on the agenda of every political party in Australia early in the 1980s.

And, remember that little problem with the ozone layer . . .

The good news is the politicians have been listening and maybe even *care* (at least about reelection). Concerned Greenies, innocent islanders, gasping asthmatics—help may be on the way!

In 1994 the Commonwealth Environment Protection Agency in Australia signed an agreement with the United States Environmental Protection Agency to help each other with mutual environmental concerns. This global stance will encourage joint research-and-development projects and an information-and-personnel network that will benefit both countries and thereby extend to the rest of the world, hopefully. Both countries are part of the Montreal Protocol on Substances that Deplete the Ozone Layer, which regulates trade in, and production of, ozone-depleting substances. Also, Australia is a signatory to the Climate Change Convention. Too, the federal government has developed a National Greenhouse Response Strategy and is preparing a National Strategy for the Conservation of Biological Diversity (for preservation of ecosystems, plants, and animals).

Ocean Rescue 2000, a 10-year program (due to end . . . guess when?) promotes conservation and sustainable use of Australia's marine environment; the Antarctica Treaty protects that region's fragile environment; and—hang on you sinking South Pacific islands—Australia is a spirited member of the South Pacific Regional Environment Program, which hopes to promote conservation, protection, and sustainable development in the South Pacific countries.

TOURISM

Beloved travelers, *you* are the brightest stars in Australia's economic Southern Cross. Over the past decade, tourism has boomed, driven by the success of Big Croc Dundee and an aggressive marketing campaign in which juicy shrimp were tossed on the barbies of Europe, Japan, and the United States. Also helpful were the 1987 America's Cup Challenge at Fremantle (near Perth) and Expo 88 in Brisbane, both of which brought large numbers of tourists—and their large wallets—streaming into the country. And, though Paul Hogan's overused shrimp have been replaced by the Olympics 2000 in Sydney, Australia is still cookin'.

Tourism has consistently been the highest growth sector of the economy, and tourist dollars promise to be the country's largest source of foreign income. The setbacks of a crippling pilots' strike, which adversely affected many resorts in the late 1980s and nearly devastated Tasmania tourism, thankfully are over.

The Australian Tourist Commission (ATC), tourism-marketing arm of the government, has offices throughout the world from which it promotes Australia's glories as a tourist destination. Marketing endeavors have been particularly successful in Asia and Europe, with North Asia accounting for nearly one-third of short-term visitors. And Sydney's successful bid for the summer Olympics in 2000 is certain to bring a soar of inbound tourists.

The ATC hardly has a tough job—the land of Oz is an easy sell. It's safe, healthy, friendly, and full of spectacular scenery, fabulous beaches, and natural wonders.

The federal government, in fact, is aiming to promote the country's unique natural sites, and yet wants to ensure manageable ecotourism. Substantial funds have already been committed to spur regional tourism and expand opportunities for the rural and backpacker markets.

prompting the Bureau of Tourism Research to project accommodation shortages by the late 1990s in the outback areas of the Northern Territory, Perth, Brisbane, Far North Queensland, and the Gold Coast.

Australians are an amiable people and easygoing, but they've had to learn the rudiments of a service industry like tourism from the ground up—trying to master the "art" of commercial hospitality in a culture that does not readily distinguish between service and servility. So don't always expect them to do a kangaroo hop whenever a demanding tourist snaps his fingers. For the most part, tourists are treated with great openness and friendliness, and the delight that visitors generally take in Australia has stimulated the Aussies to take new interest in the natural wonders of their own country—wonders that had previously been taken for granted in a country that's a mix of Stone Age, New Age, and the year 2000.

MANUFACTURING

Australia's manufacturing industry has boomed during the past decade, since trade barriers and economic regulations have been dropped to make the country a more productive and competitive exporter. Manufacturing, which has seen a rapid rise of about 16% per year, now composes about 15% of the country's GDP (Gross Domestic Product), with about one-fifth of the goods being exported, mainly to Asian countries.

The broad range of manufactured items includes iron and steel products (BHP, the predominant producer, is Australia's largest company); engineering equipment and tools; telecommunications and electronic equipment; small- to medium-sized ships and vessels; chemicals and plastics; aerospace equipment; information technology; motor vehicles; processed foods; paper and woodchips; and aluminum.

Australia would like you to know that it is behind the scenes where least expected. The Swiss Stock Exchange and Frankfurt-based Lufthansa's ticketing system use Australian software; Aussie software also manages Heathrow, Schipol, and Manchester airports. Many BMW gearboxes are Australian-made, as are most of Europe's high-speed ferries and all of the public transport "smart cards" in Scandinavia and the United Kingdom.

Smaller entrepreneurs are cashing in also. One fast-growing company ships large cryogenic gas storage tanks to Thailand and other Asian markets, another supplies "Ronald on a Park Bench" figures to McDonald's outlets around the globe, and one outfit sends off hundreds of thousands of individually wrapped cheesecake slices to Japan every year.

Increasing numbers of international companies already active in, or about to pounce upon, the booming Asian markets have already set up regional headquarters in Australia. Two such companies are Mars and Kellogg Australia. (Lifesaving Tip: Down under, your Mars and Snickers bars remain the same, but your Rice Krispies and Raisin Bran masquerade as Rice Bubbles and Sultana Bran.)

THE PEOPLE

Australia's population is about the same as Texas, and would fit between Los Angeles and San Diego, except it is spread over a continent roughly the size of the United States. Mostly the people are concentrated along the two widely separated coastal regions: the eastern coastal area between Cairns and Adelaide and Western Australia's "high-density" corner from Perth down to the southwest coast.

Almost the entire population lives in six or seven cities, most of them congested enough you'd scarcely sense that vast emptiness outside the urban limits. The current population breakdown is as follows: 6,008,000 in New South Wales; 4,465,000 in Victoria; 3,116,000 in Queensland; 1,677,000 in South Australia; 1,676,000 in Western Australia; 471,000 in Tasmania; 299,000 in Australian Capital Territory; and 169,000 in the Northern Territory. Aborigines and Torres Strait Islanders make up about 1.6% of the total population, with the majority residing in the Northern Territory.

Before World War II, the majority of Australians were of British and Irish origin. That mix, however, has changed drastically. After the war, migrants came in droves and the island continent soon included significant numbers of Italians, Greeks, Yugoslavs, Dutch, Germans, Lebanese, Turks, and Maltese. Melbourne is said to be the second-largest Greek city in the world, after Athens, and has the largest population of Italians outside Italy, with Sydney having the second-largest; Germans made stakes in the Barossa Valley; Chinese pearled around Broome; and Darwin is just one big cosmopolitan city, with people from just about everywhere.

Waves of migration occurred in the 1850s, 1880s, early 1900s, and 1920s. The Great Depression and World War II restricted immigration, and a low birthrate made necessary a renewed migration drive in the 1950s. This campaign brought three million people to Australia (mostly to the major cities) between 1947 and 1974.

The scrapping of the White Australia Policy along with Australia's humanitarian refugee program after the Vietnam War has brought a steady increase in Asian immigration, particularly Vietnamese refugees. Also, Hong Kong's reversion to China in 1997 is looming and many Hong Kong nationals are looking to Australia for possible emigration.

Presently, as home to almost five million immigrants from approximately 160 countries, Australia is rich in cultural and ethnic diversity. Nearly 13% of Australians have parents who were both born in another country; four out of 10 Australians are first-generation children of migrants—or migrants themselves—and many come from non-English speaking households. Southeast and Northeast Asia contributed 41% of new immigrant arrivals in the early 1990s and thousands more resettlement places have been allotted to refugees and displaced persons throughout the decade.

THE OUTBACK DWELLERS

Outback residents *are* rugged individualists taming a savage wilderness, *and* they are a unique breed. Hey, life in the middle of nowhere isn't especially easy—most residents live 500 kilometers or more from the nearest corner store, and even farther from a school or physician.

BIG STUFF

Size *does* make a difference—well, they must think so in big ol' Oz. Travelers will find a kitschy array of humongous "Big Things" popping up in various towns and cities throughout the country. Most are mega-life-sized replicas of fruits or creatures that house, or sit in front of, souvenir shops or tourist offices. Some notable examples are the Big Lobster, Big Orange, Big Pineapple, Big Banana, Big Penguin, Big Cow, Big Gold Panner, and Big Apple (move over, New York City). Whatever your proclivity, you'll undoubtedly find yourself trampling over others to snap some photo of a regular-sized human snuggling up to a big hunk of fiberglass.

In general, outback men are very brusque and very strong, with too many tattoos and too few teeth. They sweat, drink, sweat again, and drink some more. They work in the mines, operate big rigs and heavy equipment, tend to heated beasts (who sweat and drink), and they party hard—usually in the remote pubs where they spin dubious tales until they pass out. The outback women are saints.

Outback Health and Education

Medical care is provided by the Royal Flying Doctor Service (RFDS), which, since the 1920s, has been coming to the rescue of the outback's sick and injured in an area equal to about two-thirds of the United States. Established by John Flynn in Cloncurry, Queensland, in 1912, the service is now a sophisticated network of 15 bases with twin-engine aircraft and a large staff of doctors, nurses, radio operators, pilots, aircraft engineers, and other personnel, with the capacity to arrive on the scene within a few hours. Funded by donations and government subsidies, the RFDS does not charge patients unless they have workers' compensation or accident insurance coverage. About 40% of RFDS patients are Aborigines.

High-frequency radio networks enable outback residents to be in contact with doctors around the clock. Besides fly-in-and-out emergency evacuations to base hospitals, the RFDS also supervises small nurse-run hospitals and community clinics and provides remote clinics, reserves, and homesteads with comprehensive first-aid and medicine chests. (Ah, how comforting to know a friend or relative could perform emergency surgery while getting radio instructions!)

Since 1951, when the first facility opened in Alice Springs, School of the Air has been educating school-age children living on outback stations or in other remote parts of Australia. Lessons are a combination of high-frequency radio transmissions, correspondence courses (including audio and video materials), once-a-week "private" radio sessions, and at least one annual personal visit—when teachers swoop in via light planes or heavy vehicles.

The Royal Flying Doctor Service high-frequency radio network also provides an important social forum. Regular open broadcasts, called "galah sessions," allow far-apart residents to gab and gossip, share information, keep up on events, and send or receive telegrams.

ABORIGINES AND TORRES STRAIT ISLANDERS

Though white Australians often refer to themselves as the "world's newest people," the Aborigines who began living there at least 50,000-60,000 years ago (and maybe as far back as 100,000 years ago) are surely the world's oldest people. The most current census shows that Aborigines and Torres Strait Islanders number 265,459, or about 1.6% of Australia's total population. The majority are concentrated in the remote outback, many still living (or trying to live) according to their traditional ways; even Aborigines living in or near towns hang out primarily with their own people.

There is dispute among anthropologists over the exact number of Aboriginal cultural groups: it could have been 11, it could have been twice that. Basically, groups were linked by common language, tools, art forms, social structure, and their environment—most of them lived in the desert or its fringes, along the coast or down in Tasmania. Political activism over the last two decades has inspired a cultural revival among surviving groups with a renewed commitment to those traditional common links. Consequently, these days many Aborigines prefer to be called by their self-designated names: Kooris (Victoria and New South Wales); Murris (Queensland); Anangu (western desert); Yappa (Warlpiris); Nunga (coastal South Australia); Nyoongah (southwest Australia); and Yolngu (northeast Arnhem Land). If you have any doubts about correct affiliation, it's probably best to simply refer to the traditional people as "Aborigines"—and that goes for those of mixed descent, as well. The terms "abo" and "coon" are hideously derogatory and unacceptable.

Though often lumped together with the Aboriginal people, the estimated 10,000 Torres Strait Islanders are mainly Melanesian and represent a separate cultural group with two distinct languages. Residing on the islands separating New Guinea and Cape York, the eastern islanders work the rich soil while the a a regularly scheduled ferry ride from Queensland's Cape York, is administrative center of Torres Strait. The gone but never-to-be-forgotten Eddie Mabo neoned the speck-size islands on the map when he had the gumption to suggest the Australian government acknowledge the Merriam people as rightful, traditional owners of Murray Island, sparking the landmark Mabo Decision and Native Title Act.

The Aboriginal and Torres Strait Islander Commission (ATSIC), established in 1990, is the major policy-making agency that allows indigenous people to make decisions about important matters such as education, housing, and employment; the ATSIC is also responsible for administering federal government programs. (See "Aborigines Today" in the "History" section, above.)

RELIGION

The First Fleet brought to Australia the alien concept of the separation of church and state in the form of an Anglican minister to service the religious needs of the convicts and their keepers. It was well over a week after their arrival before the immigrants got around to performing their first religious ceremony, however, and religion seems to have been consigned to the backseat

of Australian life ever since. In this regard, Australia offers a curious contrast to America's pilgrim fathers, who knelt in prayer as soon as they stepped ashore.

This is not to say that religion doesn't play any part at all in Australian life—it's just not a starring role. Adherents of every major world religion practice their faith in an environment of freedom and tolerance. Not surprisingly, Christianity in all its variants and deviants is the principal religion. The largest group belongs to the Roman Catholic Church, followed by the Anglican. Anglicans have declined in number, possibly because the days when the establishment and Anglican Church went hand-in-hand are over. The Uniting Church now encompasses most of the Protestant sects. Roman Catholic numbers have been boosted since the war, with the arrival of Catholic migrants from Europe. However, the overall membership of any formal religious group is in decline in Australia, due in part to a secular, almost hedonistic, culture. Nevertheless, visitors who want to practice their religion and contact the Big Boss up top from the land down under will find plenty of opportunity.

Australia's major non-Christian faiths are Judaism, Buddhism, and Islam, but there are growing leagues of just about every California-meets-The East, New Age religion—replete with channelers, UFO-watchers, and surfing nudists.

Aboriginal Religion

To cast off the Aborigines' religion in a paragraph or two (or a century or two) is a real sacrilege. The early Christian missionaries couldn't fathom their beliefs at all; they simply assumed the Aborigines, without any seeming belief in a white God and his crucified son, were Judgment Day goners.

Australia's first inhabitants, in isolation, had a spirituality that was inseparable from their way of life. In a sense their religion was and is an all-encompassing experience in which their life, their tribe, the land, the plants and animals around them, the past, and the great Dreamtime legends are inextricably interwoven. (See the special topic "Dreamtime.")

(above) rainbow bee-eaters
(following page) water tank at Quamby Hotel, Queensland

(previous page) man and machine at Argyle Diamond Mine, East Kimberley, Western Australia (top) mating season in the caravan park; (bottom) deep-water jetty, Broome, Western Australia

LANGUAGE

English, with its distinct Australian accent and vocabulary, is the predominant language spoken throughout Australia. Of course, that's aside from hundreds of Aboriginal languages and dozens of other languages—Italian, Greek, Vietnamese, Turkish, you name it!—spoken within various immigrant communities.

One advantage to visitors is that regional variants are very subtle, so if you can understand someone in Perth, you can understand someone in Cairns or Melbourne. Class-linked distinctions are more noticeable than regional ones; the upper middle classes affect a plummier accent closer to their English cousins, while the working classes are prone to exaggerate the idiosyncratic earthy tones that distinguish the Australian accent. But even these distinctions are much less dramatic than those that Americans are used to amongst themselves.

However, be warned. The Australian accent can be tricky for American or British visitors, at least at first. Australians love to tell stories about their compatriots traveling overseas and failing to make themselves understood; tales of Australians trying to explain to bewildered American barkeepers that all they want is a beer, or British hotel receptionists calling for the house translator to cope with Australian tourists.

One common misconception is that all Australians use a profusion of colorful idiomatic words and phrases, such as those that are regularly listed in travel books. Such words are well known to all Australians, but have a currency that may exist solely in the minds of the compilers of Australian slang dictionaries. Some Australians will live their whole lives without ever saying "fair dinkum" or "chunder," even though they know perfectly well what these terms mean. Treat such words with caution! People using them may be doing so facetiously or ironically. "Bastard," for example, can mean several different things, depending on context: a bad bastard is someone who's bigger than you; good bastard, someone who's lent you money; lucky bastard, someone who has a better job than you; and a greedy bastard, someone with a better

house. "Mate" may be the cheery greeting of long-lost chums *or* the signal for a barroom brawl. With the proviso that the words are often the fossilized relics of an Australia that may never have existed, and that they can sound quite peculiar in an American accent, refer to this book's glossary (but don't write us if you're laughed at).

You *won't* go wrong, however, if you shorten just about any word to one- or two-syllables and then add a "y," "ie," or "o" to the end. Examples: "television" becomes "telly"; "journalist," "journo"; and "surfers," "surfies."

Transatlantic variations that exist between English and American usage often occur in Australia, where generally the English version is preferred. However, from being regularly bombarded by American film, music, and television, Australians are familiar with all things American, and most people will understand that when you say "cookie" you really mean biscuit, and so on.

In some parts of Australia a variant of the Cockney rhyming slang is used and this can lead to profound confusion for the visitor. Often the rhyming part of the expression is left out altogether, which confounds the uninitiated even more. Examples are far too numerous to give more than a few of the most common and relevant instances:

> Arra—Aristotle, bottle (of beer)
> Captain Cook—a look
> china—china plate, mate
> rubbity—rubbity dub, pub
> septic tank—Yank

If it seems from these examples that Australians use only the most insulting and derogatory terms for almost everything except alcohol and for everyone except themselves, be assured that for most Australians the use of many of these expressions would be unthinkable. The visitor to Australia will find a language with its own unique flavor that is riddled with delightful idioms while remaining basically English.

Aboriginal Languages

If you thought the shortening and rhyming and unique idioms discussed above were confusing, just wait! Aboriginal languages number at least 100 and have many dialects. This isn't quite so overwhelming when you realize that before the Europeans barged in the number was in the ballpark of 250 languages and 700 dialects—all thought to stem from just one language that changed and expanded as the traditional people broke off into groups and spread around the continent. Most languages were exclusively oral, not written, and subsequently died out along with their speakers. Others, such as Pitjantjatjara—the most common dialect of the western desert language group—were painstakingly transcribed. Pitjantjatjara (also known as Pitjantjara) is spoken in Uluru National Park (where visitors find it written phonetically on park signs), in Aboriginal communities from the Northern Territory/Western Australia border to the Simpson Desert's eastern border, and within the Anangu Pitjantjatjara traditional lands in South Australia. Pitjantjatjara contains three vowels (each having an additional long form) and 17 consonants, some of which require some tricky curling-tongue action.

Most Aboriginal languages contain about 10,000 words and some of these have also merged with Australian English: dingo, boomerang, kangaroo, kookaburra, barramundi, galah, mulga, mallee, and wallaby should be recognizable to most readers. Conversely, some English has found its way into Aboriginal speech, particularly in the relatively new Aboriginal Kriol, the "adopted" language of a growing contingency of younger people.

Many outback Aborigines speak little or no English—they don't learn it in their communities, nor do they need to. Even on shopping trips to town, the Aborigines seem to get by, communicating adequately via fistfuls of money. Nonetheless, when speaking to Aborigines, use your normal English words and voice tones. The Aborigines will probably do the same for you—in their own language. Hopefully, someone will understand.

By the way, most Aboriginal languages do not contain words that mean "hello," "please," or "thank you," but if you need any kind of plant or animal, are looking for water, or want to say "sorry," you're in business.

ON THE ROAD
SPORTS AND RECREATION

Australians love sport. They love it so much that it's tempting to include this section under the "Religion" heading. They have a tradition of competitive sport that goes back to the earliest days of colonization, and they'll travel anywhere on earth if there's someone willing to play against them. Australia is one of the few countries to have been represented at every modern Olympiad. The Olympic Games were held in Melbourne in 1956, where Australians won the third-most medals, an extraordinary feat for a nation with such a tiny population. Yet that is a measure of how seriously Australians treat athletic achievement. Australian champions regularly crop up in sports as diverse as golf, tennis, weightlifting, squash, yachting, cycling, and swimming.

A significant number of champion athletes enter public office after their sporting career is over, and political leaders of all persuasions find it necessary to publicize their allegiance to particular sporting clubs. Personal appearances at matches are a prerequisite to a successful career in politics. Australians can name past or present world champions in almost every sport, a phenomenon that causes their chests to swell with pride, even though sporting involvement for many Australians is confined to watching their idols on the telly.

Water Sports

Swimming is particularly important in a land where so much social activity takes place on the beach, and most Australian children are taught to swim very early. Let's face it—the country is filled with spectacular beaches. And, while the beaches are deserted and beautiful, the water may be dangerous. In surf areas, strong "rips" can sweep an unwary swimmer out to sea. Most popular beaches are patrolled by Surf Life Saving Clubs, which post flags to indicate safe swimming areas. (Swim between the flags.) Large swells often curtail swimming at the ocean beaches, but there are many other options, ranging from the clear blue water of Sydney Harbour to thermal hot springs bubbling out of the ground in the outback town of Lightning Ridge.

Once the Hawaiians introduced the surfboard to Australia, it was hang-ten fever, and surfies soon made their own innovations to the Malibu, creating more maneuverable short boards suited to Australian conditions. Superb surfing beaches surround the country; most renowned are the beaches of the Gold and Sunshine Coasts in Queensland, the east coast of New South Wales, along Victoria's Great Ocean Road, and around Margaret River south of Perth.

Australians are equally at home in boats, and the America's Cup created national heroes out of the team that wrested it briefly from the grip of the New York Yacht Club. Most water-lovers have their sights set a bit lower than 12-meter racing, however, and are content to go fishing, skin diving, and waterskiing on the country's bountiful oceans, rivers, lakes, and streams.

Barramundi Fishing

Fishing for the highly prized barramundi (or "barra") seems to reel in all types—from local pros and holiday-making Aussies to big-shot Hollywood celebrities and international politicians; catching it is a challenge and eating it is a treat. The barra teases fishers in coastal and river waters of the Top End, Kimberley region (Northern Territory), Cape York, and Gulf Country (Queensland). Enthusiasts seem to have very individual ideas regarding method, timing, and season—which is just as well or they'd be trampling over each other. Both novices and pros will find a myriad of organized fishing trips (see "Tours," later in this chapter). For information regarding bag and size limits, permits, seasonal and other restrictions, contact: Amateur Fishermen's Association of the Northern Territory, P.O. Box 41512, Casuarina, NT 0810 (tel. 08-8999-5096); Fisheries Service of the Queensland Department of Primary Industry, Cairns, QLD (tel. 070-35-1580); Northern Territory Game Fishing Association, G.P.O. Box 128, Darwin, NT 0801 (tel. 08-8999-5605); or Western Australia Department of Fisheries, 108 Adelaide Terrace, East Perth, WA (tel. 09-220-5333).

Spectator Sports

Australians love and excel at many competitive sports and flock in droves to watch their favorites. So important is sport in Australia that federal and state governments appoint quite senior ministers to Departments of Sport. The federal government sponsors a kind of athletic university in Canberra, called the Institute of Sport, where promising atheletes are coached. Tennis, golf, basketball, and soccer are all played and followed with keen interest, and the feats of champions are heralded on the television and analyzed in the press.

Australians are very patriotic to their favorite code of football, and while the three main codes—**Australian Rules** (best known as Aussie Rules or footy), **Rugby League** (also known as footy), and **Rugby Union** (best known as, simply, rugby)—are played throughout the country, each code has a stronghold on particular parts of the country. In Victoria the most important game—and one which visitors must not miss—is Australian Rules. Developed on the goldfields of central Victoria well over a century ago, it is Australia's gift to the world.

Visitors can look forward to witnessing the game being played at the very highest levels

---

SYDNEY 2000

Word came in September 1993 that Sydney had been chosen to host the Summer Olympic Games in the year 2000, and Sydneysiders have been celebrating—and preparing—ever since. (Talk about optimism—some 65% of competition sites had already been constructed, or were underway, when the announcement was made!)

With the exception of four of the 25 Olympic sports, all games (with about 85% of athletes participating) will take place in two areas, just 14 km apart.

Sydney Olympic Park, within 30 minutes' travel of all game venues, will actually become a new Sydney "suburb." The estimated 15,000 athletes will be housed in one village—a "first" in modern Olympic Games history.

The games will take place from 16 September until 1 October. Mark your calendars. The year is 2000.

DO-IT-YOURSELF MINING

Fossicking is a favorite Australian adventure. Seek your pot of gold or cache of gems in river deposits, rock bars, along the bases of rock outcrops, or around old mine dumps. Stay out of old or abandoned mines!

Basic tools will suffice: pick and shovel, prospecting dish, small crowbar, sledgehammer, a gravel-washing container, and varied aluminum sieves.

All fossickers must have a fossicking permit or miner's right from either the state or territorial government, or, on private land, permission must be obtained from the landowner or leaseholder.

The following agencies will provide you with specific info on mining laws and can point you to fossicking guides and geological maps:

New South Wales, Dept. of Mineral Resources, P.O. Box 536, St. Leonards, NSW 2065 (tel. 02-9901-8888)

Northern Territory, Dept. of Mines and Energy, P.O. Box 2901, Darwin, NT 0800 (tel. 08-8999-5511)

Queensland, Dept. of Minerals and Energy, 61 Mary St., Brisbane, QLD 4000 (tel. 07-3237-1435)

South Australia, Dept. of Mines and Energy, P.O. Box 151, Eastwood, SA 5063 (tel. 08-8274-7500)

Victoria, Dept. of Energy and Minerals, P.O. Box 98, East Melbourne, VIC 3002 (tel. 03-9651-7799)

Western Australia, Dept. of Minerals and Energy, 100 Plain St., East Perth, WA 6004 (tel. 09-222-3333)

many Americans might be surprised to learn that the U.S. even has a national team and that the West Indies have in the past been formidable cricketers, it is today strongest in England and those Commonwealth countries like India, New Zealand, South Africa (current World Champions), Sri Lanka, and Pakistan, as well as Australia, which left the British Empire only this century.

A leisurely and cerebral sport, important games last five days, and to the novice whole days may pass with very little actually happening. This provides the spectator with ample time to chat (and drink) with a neighbor and discuss the Byzantine intricacies of past controversies. A livelier version of the game takes place in one day and is guaranteed to end in a result; this provides a more suitable introduction to the game.

Other Sports
The natural beauties of the Australian bush make bushwalking (or hiking) a popular activity for anyone who wants to see the wildlife up close. City and country cycling is another favorite pursuit, and Australia has a history of producing champions in world competitions (see "Cycling" under "Getting Around," later in this chapter). Golf, tennis, horseback riding, camel trekking, hot-air ballooning, hang gliding, lawn bowls, downhill skiing, even baseball and basketball all have their adherents.

at grounds throughout Melbourne each Saturday through winter. Of the other two codes, Rugby League is most widespread, with most teams in the national competition based in New South Wales and southern Queensland.

Unfortunately, footy is only played in the winter months, and Australians turn their attention in summer to their other great passion—cricket. Cricket is a relic of a colonial past and, although

ENTERTAINMENT AND EVENTS

Like other Western industrialized nations, Australia is replete with the wonders of modern technology: television, films, popular music, and so on. Americans will find that much of their culture has preceded them and taken root to the point that Australia is beginning to export its own version of America's late-20th-century global techno-culture back to the United States—with the exception of film.

Filmmakers Peter Weir, Gillian Armstrong, Paul Cox, Jocelyn Moorehouse, Bruce Beresford, Baz Luhrmann, and P.J. Hogan, along with film stars Errol Flynn, Mel Gibson, Paul Mercurio, Judy Davis, Bryan Brown, Nicole Kidman, and Toni Collette lead a coterie of Australian artists who have dazzled star-bright Hollywood. They learned their craft in the domestic Australian industry, offering entertainment with not merely an Australian accent but with some fabulously quirky characters and fresh, innovative themes. Thankfully, in this respect, Australia does not lean heavily on the traditional box-office, crass-market models (*Crocodile Dundee* excepted) normally provided by the U.S. film industry. Some of the many well-known films include not only *Crocodile Dundee,* but *Mad Max I, II,* and *III, My Brilliant Career, Evil Angels (A Cry in the Dark), Breaker Morant, Walkabout, Chant of Jimmie Blacksmith, Strictly Ballroom, Romper Stomper, Muriel's Wedding,* the delightfully fashionable *Priscilla, Queen of the Desert,* and the 1996 smash hit *Babe,* about a talking pig.

Australia also has a vital and dynamic music industry, very much in evidence in the major cities and towns throughout the country. Hundreds of hopeful young musicians play nightly in every style you can name—and some you can't. Not long ago it was possible to see bands like Midnight Oil, AC/DC, Men at Work, and INXS playing in small suburban pubs, and you can bet the bands that play there now have big ambitions. Australian contemporary music embraces a dynamic diversity from jazz to hip-hop, rock to heavy metal. Other international headliners include Sexing the Cherry, Single Gun Theory, My Friend the Chocolate Cake, Trout Fishing in Quebec, silverchair, and Vince Jones. Melbourne, Adelaide, and Perth have major international arts festivals (see "Holidays and Festivals," below).

Aboriginal Music and Dance

Aboriginal music—an inspiring mix of political and racial statements, contemporary electronics, and traditional didgeridoo (a large wooden trumpet)—has been garnering international acclaim in recent years. Two of the best-known Aboriginal entertainment troupes are Tjapukai Aboriginal Dance Theatre (performing daily outside of Cairns) and the rock band Yothu Yindi (lead singer Mandawuy Yunupingu was named 1993 Australian of the Year). Both groups were part of 1994's Festival Australia, a 12-day performance and cultural extravaganza held at the Kennedy Center in Washington D.C.

Aboriginal dance is another resurgent art form, and new performances of established companies are eagerly awaited—particularly those of the Tjapukai company. Corroborees are ceremonial dances accompanied by the unearthly music of the didgeridoo. Non-Aborigines are rarely invited to authentic corroborees, but you can catch tourist versions at Darwin and a few other spots.

Finally, Australia offers one superb entertainment that you won't see in the Northern Hemisphere—the brilliant glow of a million stars lighting up the unfamiliar constellations of a strange southern sky, an impossibly classy act to follow.

Gambling

Australians love to gamble—you can bet on it. Each of the major cities has its glitter-and-flash gambling mecca: the Harbourside Casino in Sydney, Casino Canberra, Brisbane's Conrad Treasury Casino, Townsville's Sheraton Breakwater Casino, the Reef Hotel Casino in Cairns, the Diamond Beach Hotel Casino in Darwin, Perth's Burswood Island Resort, the Adelaide Casino, the Melbourne Casino, and Wrest Point Hotel Casino in Hobart.

A huge industry has also grown up around horse racing, harness racing (pacing or trotting), and greyhound racing. Billions of dollars are invested annually either with trackside bookmakers or off-course government-run totalizators. Champion thoroughbred horses occupy as exalted a position in the galaxy of Australian sporting heroes as champion human athletes, and a racing subculture has long been established in which the uninitiated quickly find themselves lost in a strange land. The passion for horses culminates in the fabulous Melbourne Spring Carnival; the prized petunia of that meet is the Melbourne Cup, a race that few Australians fail to bet on—and a declared local holiday.

HOLIDAYS AND FESTIVALS

Australia is partyland, folks, and *any* excuse for a long weekend or a raucous rage is welcomed. Most public holidays fall on Monday, allowing for what is called a "long weekend." You can pretty much count on everything being closed for all three (or, in some instances, four) days.

Major National Holidays
New Year's Day: 1 January

Australia Day: 26 January

Good Friday, Easter Saturday, Easter Sunday, and Easter Monday: varies

Anzac Day: 25 April

Queen's Birthday: second Monday in June (Western Australia celebrates in late September/early October)

Melbourne Cup Day: first Tuesday in November (the whole country stops in its hooves for this all-important race—Melbourne stops for the entire day!)

Christmas Day: 25 December

Boxing Day: 26 December

Regional Holidays
Labour Day: first or second Monday in March (Victoria)

Labour Day: first Monday in March (Western Australia and Tasmania)

Labour Day: first Monday in May (Queensland)

May Day: 1 May (Northern Territory)

Adelaide Cup Day: third Monday in May (South Australia)

Foundation Day: first Monday in June (Western Australia)

Show Days: four days throughout July (Northern Territory)

Bank Holiday: first Monday in August (New South Wales)

Picnic Day: first Monday in August (Northern Territory)

Labour Day: first Monday in October (South Australia, New South Wales, and Australia Capital Territory)

School Holidays
These are scheduled four times a year and fall on different dates throughout all the states and territories. Basically they run mid-December to early February, mid-April to mid-May, late June to late July, and mid-September to mid-October. It is especially important to book transport and accommodations ahead during school holiday periods, as that's when most Aussies hit the road or take to the skies.

Festivals and Seasonal Events
January: The **Schützenfest** goes full guns in Hahndorf, South Australia's German community. At Lake Jabiru, in the Northern Territory, the **Jabiru Regatta** features offbeat games and races.

February: The two-day **Kangaroo Island Racing Carnival** comes to Kangaroo Island's Kingscote (South Australia). In the Northern Territory, **race meetings and rodeos** take place at Alice Springs, Tennant Creek, and Darwin.

March: The **Australian Formula One Grand Prix** burns rubber through Melbourne streets for four days (the race is on the last day). South Australia's famed **Adelaide Festival of the Arts** (even-numbered years) offers three weeks of premier theater, music, dance, arts exhibitions, and fringe events. The **Festival of Perth** is a similar cultural extravaganza in Western Australia, beginning the end of February and lasting a month. Also in Western Australia, at Bindoon, is the **Bindoon Rock Festival,** a Woodstock-wannabe music fest.

April: In odd-numbered years, South Australia's **Barossa Valley Vintage Festival** is a major weeklong taste-till-you-waste celebration in honor of the local grapes and vintners. Also in April Coober Pedy hosts its **Opal and Outback Festival.**

May: In the Northern Territory, Alice Springs' **Bangtail Muster** features a float parade and other events. Other Alice Springs festivals include the **Alice Springs Cup** annual horse race and the **Lions Camel Cup** with races, fireworks, and—of course—camel races. **May Day** in Darwin signals the end of those treacherous box jellyfish and the beginning of beach parties.

June: Darwin's **Bougainvillea Festival** offers two weeks of flowery events. The **Katherine Gorge Canoe Marathon** (Northern Territory) is a 100-km race along the Katherine River, organized by the Red Cross. Grab the opportunity to celebrate (non-alcoholically) with the traditional people at **Barunga Festival,** at the Northern Territory's Beswick Aboriginal Land Trust.

July: Darwin is at the forefront again with its **Beer Can Regatta,** featuring sailing "craft" constructed entirely from empty beer cans. Almond-lovers will want to attend the **Almond Blossom Festival,** in Willunga, South Australia, with assorted nutty activities.

August: Shinju Matsuri ("Festival of the Pearl") is a weeklong Asian-theme event held in Broome, Western Australia's old pearling port. The **Darwin Rodeo** is a well-attended international competition. And Darwin's **Mud Crab Tying Competiton** is another must on the cultural calendar.

September: The tiny outback community at Birdsville, Queensland, hosts the hot-to-trot **Birdsville Races.** The **AFL Grand Final,** Australian football's final game, is in Melbourne but religiously followed by almost everyone in the

country. Watch it on the telly from your favorite pub. Also, Perth blossoms over its **Western Australia Wildflower Festival.**

October: The **Henley-on-Todd Regatta** in Alice Springs (late August or early September) features bizarre and creative mock-ups of boats propelled by the racers' feet as they run along the dry Todd River bed. South Australia's **McLaren Vale Bushing Festival** commemorates the release of a new vintage with a variety of events including the crowning of a Bushing King and Queen. The **Kalgoorlie Cup** horse race is held in Western Australia's eponymous mining town.

December: And all's right with the world.

Bush Bashes

Rodeos are favorite rural and outback entertainments. You'll see stockmen who are dead ringers for cowboys, Americano-style—10-gallon hats, chaps, spurs, struts, the whole she-bang. Flies, dust, *lots* of beer, and monstrous steak sandwiches lend that unique Aussie flavor. The range of events includes calf roping, steer wrestling, bull riding, and saddle- and bareback broncing.

The other live-to-die-for event is the **B&S Ball.** The B&S have nothing to do with what's left after the rodeo—it actually stands for "bachelor and spinster," though the event is no longer confined to just single folk. The balls are grand social occasions where rural dwellers can socialize, renew old aquaintances, and kick up their dusty heels. In true Aussie style, the balls are one big, long party, with lots of drinking, eating, and carousing. Despite the fact they're held in big barns or open fields, ball-goers dress to the hilt.

ARTS AND CRAFTS

Australians have long been noted for a "cultural cringe," meaning they look to London and New York in matters of taste and style, slavishly following their lead. Although this attitude dies hard, Australians are making real advances in the creation of a national culture. Bolstered by the success of expatriates in all artistic endeavors (Dame Joan Sutherland, Nobel Laureate Patrick White, artist Sir Sydney Nolan—not to mention the Bee Gees and INXS), artsy Aussies are growing more confident and ready to take their work to the outside world.

Each state capital has its own symphony orchestra, opera company, ballet company, theater, and art gallery, which are recipients of generous arts funding. Lovers of traditional Western art forms will be happily surprised at the high standards and support from a quite sophisticated public at the end of the earth.

Australia also is home to a lively "fringe" arts scene, mainly centered in the bohemian suburbs of Sydney, Melbourne, and Adelaide. Adelaide's Fringe Festival, which runs concurrently with the city's renowned and highbrow Festival of the Arts, honors the more avant-garde contributions to theater, music, art, and literature. And while it isn't Times Square or Haight-Ashbury, the low-key local color can be a lot of fun. The cultural melting pot of Australia's cities has meant that artists no longer need to travel to

Europe or America to eke out a penurious living in a squalid garret; they can do it here!

The "Heidelberg School" of young artists who resided near Melbourne in the 1930s, along with a group of artists living up around Sydney Harbour, established the first uniquely Australian painting style. Working in oils and watercolors, using natural light to its full advantage, the painters captured the magic, starkness, and intensity of Australian life and landscape. Notable artists of that period were Julian Ashton, Louis Abrahams, Charles Conder, Frederick McCubbin, Tom Roberts, and Arthur Streeton. A later revolution in the 1940s brought fame and acclaim to Sir Sidney Nolan and Arthur Boyd—probably Australia's most well-known painters—and a bevy of other talents, including Pro Hart, who still strokes outback images from his Broken Hill studio.

Aboriginal Art

Aboriginal art has its own aesthetics, which reflect the profound experience of life in Australia. Recently "discovered" by the West, Aboriginal paintings can command substantial prices on the world market.

Most Aboriginal art forms are spiritually based and concerned with the myths and totemic beliefs of the Dreamtime. Painting on bark and, more recently, canvas, Aboriginal artists em-

Aboriginal rock art can be found in all corners of rural Australia.

ploy a decorative dot technique that to Western eyes appears quite abstract, and representational images of animals and spirits are painted in the style of an X-ray, revealing internal organs. These techniques are incredibly ancient. Extremely old examples are found on the walls of caves in Arnhem Land. Often the actual rendering of these works is accompanied by songs that instruct the artist in the progress of the work and invest him with spiritual power. The full significance of such works is sacred and available only to the initiated. Aborigines also craft exquisite implements, from the aerodynamically perfect boomerang to ceremonial belts and headdresses.

Australia's most famous Aboriginal artist, Albert Namatjira (1902-59), hailed from Hermannsburg Lutheran Mission, west of Alice Springs. Learning European-style watercolor techniques from a non-Aboriginal painter, Namatjira became comparatively successful for what were considered to be European-style, central Australian landscapes; eventually he became the first Aborigine to "achieve" Australian citizenship. This achievement, however, did not accord him blanket privileges. Just one year later, in 1958, Namatjira was arrested for buying alcohol for other Aborigines; one year after that, he died. Still, he inspired other would-be artists with his technique, use of color, imagery—and his image.

The 1970s weren't exclusively prime time for American and European artists—the creative renaissance of that period also surfaced at Papunya, a tiny impoverished Aboriginal community northwest of Alice Springs. There, the painting of a mural—a children's school project—turned into a cross-generational creation when elders (with mixed feelings about their traditional symbols being splattered across a public wall) joined in and helped complete the piece. The result, *Honey Ant Dreaming,* became the first art piece in which traditional images were displayed on something other than a rock or human body. Pretty soon the community was passionately painting away and, though more murals were produced, acrylic paints on canvas eventually became the preferred medium. Central Australian painting has since evolved as an important source of religious and traditional instruction for Aboriginal children.

Other distinctive contemporary Aboriginal arts and crafts include: batiks, pottery, wooden sculptures and carvings in central Australia; bark paintings, painted log coffins, fiber art, Ngukurr acrylics on canvas in Arnhem Land; paintings and engraved pearl-shell pendants in the Kimberley; spears, bark baskets, carved and painted burial poles, sculptures, and bark paintings on the Tiwi Islands.

As some of us might expect, the works of city-dwelling Aboriginal artists tend to reflect either European influences or deep, raging, racially themed anger. In fact, the beginnings of Aboriginal urban art can be traced to the land-rights issues of the 1970s.

If you'd rather view Aboriginal art from earlier times, drawn or engraved on rocks rather than hanging on gallery walls, significant sites open to visitors are: Mootwingee National Park (New South Wales); Ewaninga (Northern Territory); Chambers Gorge and Cooper Creek (South Australia); The Grampians (Victoria); and Mersey Bluff near Devonport (Tasmania). Both the Australian Museum, in Sydney, and the South Australian Museum, in Adelaide, have outstanding collections of Aboriginal artifacts.

SHOPPING

It is possible to buy Aboriginal art from cooperatives run by local communities; these are often the best sources. Much of what is passed off as Aboriginal art in the cities is worthless imitation and souvenir schlock. Some excellent Aboriginal-owned or -managed shops and galleries are the Papunya Tula Artists in Alice Springs, Maruka Arts and Crafts Centre in Uluru National Park, and Mt. Ebenezer Roadhouse on the Lasseter Highway, en route to Uluru. In major cities, recommended outlets for authentic Aboriginal artworks are: Sydney's Aboriginal Art Centre, Queensland Aboriginal Creations in Brisbane, and Aboriginal Handcrafts in Melbourne. Most buyers will be able to take home a print, small carving, or T-shirt, but be prepared to pay dearly for gallery originals.

Aside from Aboriginal arts and crafts, Australia is *not* shop-till-you-drop territory. In all the cities and most smaller towns, you will find everything you need, from flyscreens to condoms. You'll find necessary and desired gear and clothing in most cities around Australia. Prices for most items are higher than in the U.S., and books and records are *much* more expensive. Either bring books with you or buy them secondhand.

Distinctly Australian items include Blundstone boots (elastic sides; Aussie Doc Marten's), Akubra hats, and Driza-bone overcoats. You will just have to purchase at least one sheepskin item, a bottle of Australian wine, and an opal (or 10). One of the largest concentrations of down under souvenir shops is in the historic Rocks area of Sydney, where you'll find the colorful artwork of Ken Done and the distinctive landscape photography of Ken Duncan.

Be cautious when buying opals; try to get recommendations from tourist bureaus, and definitely comparison-shop. The three types of solid opal are: black opal, the most valuable, found at Lightning Ridge, New South Wales, and Mintabie, South Australia; white opal, also called "light" or "fire" opal, found at Coober Pedy and Andamooka, South Australia; and boulder opal, found at Quilpie in southwestern Queensland. All major cities have shops specializing in opals (and selling them to tourists with too much money), but you're better off buying them at their source. A "triplet" is a thin slice of opal layered between a clear dome capping of dark opal potch and crystal quartz.

A not-to-be-missed shopping experience is at the mostly outdoor, sometimes indoor markets held almost everywhere in the country. In Melbourne, Queen Victoria Market north of downtown is a prime example, as is Paddy's Market in Sydney, Adelaide's Central Market near Victoria Square, and Darwin's Big Flea Market, the city's oldest. These usually take place on weekends, though some city markets are open during the week. Depending on where you are and the type of market it is, you'll be able to pick up bargains on fruits and veggies, furniture, secondhand clothing, used tools, camping gear, and various bric-a-brac, like the ubiquitous plastic fish and fake handcuffs from Asia.

Normal shopping hours are Mon.-Fri. 9 a.m.-5 p.m., Saturday 9 a.m.-noon, but most of the major shopping centers stay open all day Saturday as well as Sunday. One night a week—either Thursday or Friday—is designated "late shopping night" with doors staying open until 9 p.m. In the outback and in rural towns, shops basically open and close whenever.

ACCOMMODATIONS

Australian lodging is well represented by the cliche, "myriad of possibilities." Choices range from backpacker dorms to penthouse suites in luxury hotels—with motels, pubs, guesthouses, bed and breakfasts, holiday flats, caravan parks, and outback stations tossed in between. You can get accommodation guides with up-to-date prices at branches of the automobile clubs or, often, at state tourist bureaus. It is advisable to book ahead during public and school holidays. (See "Tourist Information" under "Maps and Tourist Information," later in this chapter.)

Hotels

These come in a few varieties—the big Hyatt-type places, older-style pubs, and private hotels. Worldwide, national, and regional hotel chains and resorts are of international standard and feature all the requisite luxuries and amenities—pools, saunas, spas, room service, complimentary toiletries, phones next to the toilet. Pubs are called "hotels" because originally they were required to provide lodging for travelers. Thus they are usually rather old (and, in some cases, magnificent), with simple rooms and "facilities" down the hall. The private hotel (versus the licensed hotel) does not serve alcohol and is more like a guesthouse.

Motels

As in the U.S., motels are prevalent throughout Australia, owned either by independent operators or chain establishments (Flag, Budget, Country Comfort, and Golden Chain are the biggies). Rooms—usually doubles—are serviced daily and have private bathrooms, radios, televisions, refrigerators, and the ubiquitous electric jug accompanied by packets of instant coffee and tea bags. Motels often have a swimming pool and attached restaurant, and some have family suites with cooking facilities.

Serviced Apartments and Holiday Flats

Serviced apartments are usually found in the cities, while holiday flats (or units) are in resort or vacation areas. They range from basic motel-style rooms with kitchenettes to full-on posh apartments with several rooms. Cutlery, dishes, and cooking utensils are provided but, unless you're staying in one of the upmarket pads with daily or weekly maid service, plan on doing the cleaning yourself. Rented by the week or month, they cater mainly to those who plan an extended stay in one place, and can be an exceptionally good value for a group traveling together.

Guesthouses

Guesthouses, bed and breakfasts, and private hotels are all basically the same—small establishments with shared facilities and "brekkie" thrown into the deal. Other meals can often be arranged. Again, these can be anything from simple residences to elegant mansions. This style isn't for everyone—for instance, if you're secretive or reclusive. Be prepared to hear the other guests'

life stories or have your own dragged out of you over the morning's bacon and eggs.

Backpacker Accommodations and Ys

Until recently, the only accommodations in Australia designed specifically for budget travelers were Youth Hostels, run by the YHA, an Australian arm of Hostelling International. The last few years have seen backpacker accommodations spring up around the country. Standards vary considerably; some are old downtown hotels with noisy bars downstairs, some are tacked onto the back of motels, and others are filled with seasonal workers, but for the most part they are excellent, with locations as diverse as the country. They are the ultimate for budget travelers (about $10-18 per night), to say nothing of a superb clearinghouse for local information, job possibilities, ride-sharing, juicy gossip, et cetera. Accommodations are in dormitories or bunkrooms (though often double rooms are available to couples), and usually offer communal cooking and laundry facilities. "Extras" might include bicycle, surfboard, and equipment rentals, as well as organized excursions and tour bookings.

Increased competition in the budget travel market has seen the **YHA** change direction in recent years, ridding itself of the "youth" image, along with the need for guests to do chores. You can rely on YHAs to be well organized, efficiently run, and, best of all, inexpensive (about $10-18 per night). They can be found throughout the country, including all major cities, ski resorts, national parks, and the outback, and operate from an incredible variety of locations, including tiny shelters, railway cars, suburban mansions, and country churches. Unlike some countries, which impose lockouts and curfews, all Australian YHA hostels provide 24-hour access. Even membership of the YHA ($24 per year, plus $16 to join) isn't compulsory anymore, although it only takes a few nights of dis-

---

HOME AND FARM STAYS

It's easy—you stay with Aussies in their homes or on their farms. In homes, you're treated like one of the family. You'll have a private bedroom, though you'll probably share bathroom facilities with your Aussie parents and siblings. Breakfast is almost always included, and other meals can often be arranged.

Farm stays (usually on very large sheep or cattle stations) can mean anything and—if you're fussy—should be checked out thoroughly in advance. You might be lodged in the bunkhouse or shearers' quarters and expected to work alongside the jack-and-jilleroos. Particularly on outback stations, life is simple and often tough. Then again, you might arrange a motel-style farm stay, where you sit back on the veranda with a cold beer (probably *many* cold beers) and breathe in the scent of fresh cow and sheep dung. Ah, nature!

Book home and farm stays through state tourist centers or the following North American representatives: **Bed and Breakfast Australia** (Adventure Center, tel. 800-227-8747 U.S.); **Farmstays** (Sprint Australia, tel. 800-423-2880 U.S.); **Inta-Aussie Accommodation Service** (Inta-Aussie Tours, tel. 800-531-9222 U.S.); **Austravel** (tel. 800-633-3404 U.S.); **Goway Travel** (tel. 800-387-8850 Canada); and **SoPac** (tel. 800-551-2012 or 213-871-0747 U.S. and Canada).

counted lodging to make up the difference. If you're a YHA member in your home country, it will entitle you to reciprocal rights in Australia. Pick up the handy booklet *YHA Accommodation Guide* at any YHA office in Australia.

For more information, contact: YHA, 422 Kent St., Sydney, NSW 2000 (tel. 02-9261-1111); YHA, 154 Roma St., Brisbane, QLD 4000 (tel. 07-3236-1680); YHA, Darwin Hostel Complex, 69A Mitchell St., Darwin, NT 0821 (tel. 08-8981-3995); YHA, 65 Francis St., Northbridge, WA 6003 (tel. 09-227-5122); YHA, 38 Sturt St., Adelaide, SA 5000 (tel. 08-8231-5583); YHA, 205 King St., Melbourne, VIC 3000 (tel. 03-9670-9611); or YHA, 28 Criterion St., Hobart, TAS 7000 (tel. 03-6234-9617).

In the United States, contact **American International Hostels,** 133 1st St. NW, Suite 800, Washington, D.C. 20005 (tel. 202-783-6161). In Canada, contact Hostelling International—Canada, 333 River Rd., Vanier City, ONT K1L 8B9 (tel. 800-668-4487). In the U.K., contact **Youth Hostel Association,** Trevelyan House, St. Stephen's Hill, St. Albans, Herts. AL1 2DY (tel. 0171-836-1036). In New Zealand, contact **Youth Hostels Association of New Zealand,** P.O. Box 436, Christchurch 1 (tel. 03-79-9970).

The **YMCA** and **YWCA** offer good-value city residences with plain rooms and shared bathrooms. Some Ys have dorm rooms for travelers; others are occupied mainly by permanent residents. You don't need to be a member to stay. The **CWA** (Country Women's Association), somewhat akin to the Y, has both city and country locations, and sometimes allows men and couples.

Camping and Caravanning

Australia has plentiful caravan (trailer) parks, which offer powered and unpowered camp-sites ($8-18 s or d per night), on-site vans (a caravan that stays on its site; $20-45), and cabins ($25-70). Parks are located along highways, near beaches and rivers, in country towns, and on the city fringes. Basic facilities include showers, toilets, hot and cold water; fancier parks might have swimming pools, playgrounds, and recreation rooms, and some even feature bathrooms for each site. Most of Australia's many national parks have campgrounds; facilities range enormously—from having to bring your own drinking water to those with hot showers and a laundry. In all cases a fee applies, either payable upon arrival or collected by the ranger in the evening. Camping is permitted on some islands of the Great Barrier Reef. This entails being totally self-sufficent, and often requires an expensive drop-off charge, but the thrill of being alone on a tropical isle is priceless. In Queensland, camping is permitted at designated rest areas along all major highways. There are no fees involved, bathroom facilities are offered, and at busy times of the year volunteers are on hand to serve up tea and coffee each morning.

Other Accommodations

During academic holidays (usually November through February, plus May and August), you might try scoring a room at one of the universities or colleges. It isn't that easy—you must book in advance and most of the places are inconveniently located. Students are given first preference and cheaper rates (about $20 for B&B, double for nonstudents).

For longer stays, check bulletin boards at hostels, bookshops, and cafes, as well as the local newspaper's classified ads.

FOOD AND DRINK

TUCKER

With the exception of major cities, tucker (food) is basic meat and potatoes fare. Just keep in mind that the "meat" may be crocodile, kangaroo, emu, camel, or buffalo! Seafood, especially the prized barramundi, John Dory, yabbies (freshwater crayfish), and Moreton Bay bugs (a local crustacean), is popular around the coastal areas. Though most supermarkets are well stocked, don't expect to find very fresh fruits and veggies in Australia's Red Centre.

Breakfast is an all-important meal down under, and Vegemite, a dark yeast mixture, is the national spread. Whatever you do, don't malign Vegemite in Australia—it's worse than desecrating the flag.

Although some progress has been made in recent years, this is *not* an easy country for cholesterol watchers—many foods are fried, breaded, cheesed, and buttered. Food labeling is not very detailed. For example, a label may proclaim "100% vegetable oil" but does not elaborate on what kind of vegetable.

The bigger cities have supermarkets that rival even those in the United States, and even smaller communities have a passable assortment of shops. It's a very good idea to stock up before you go bush or outback; otherwise you'll be at the mercy of roadhouses—far apart and high-priced. Don't forget that quarantine regulations prohibit fruits, veggies, plants, and some other agricultural products from crossing state lines—eat them, plant them, or prepare to relinquish them at each border.

Favorite takeaway items include roast chicken, fish and chips, chips with gravy, meat pies, pasties, sausage rolls, and hamburgers with "the lot" (meaning with egg, bacon, pineapple, cheese, lettuce, tomato, and a slice of red beet). And, thanks to the ethnic population, you'll find a large number of luscious Italian, Greek, Lebanese, Turkish, and Asian establishments for sit-down meals or takeaways.

Takeaways are cheap, pub meals are cheap to moderate ($4-9), and restaurant meals run the price gamut ($10 and *way* up).

FOOD AND DRINK GLOSSARY

You say toe-mate-oh and I say toe-motto! Here are some common Aussie words, translated for your dining pleasure:

barbie—barbecue
billy tea—bush tea boiled in a tin container
biscuit—cookie
brekkie—breakfast
BYO—Bring Your Own (booze)
chips—French fries
chook—chicken
cuppa—tea or coffee
damper—bush bread
Darwin stubby—Darwin's two-liter beer bottle (mainly a tourist item)
flagon—two-liter wine bottle
flake—shark meat (usually the fish that goes with your chips)
floater—meat pie floating in pea soup

lollies—candy
middy—medium-size beer glass
milk bar—local convenience shop
pavlova—traditional cream-and-meringue dessert
piss—booze
pissed—drunk
plonk—wine, especially rotgut
pot—large mug of beer
schooner—large beer glass
serviette—napkin
slab—four six-packs of tinnies/stubbies
snag—sausage
takeaway—takeout
tea—evening meal
tinny—can of beer
tomato sauce—ketchup
tucker—food

Restaurants

One of the best things about Australian dining is this: when you book a table in a restaurant, it's yours for the whole night. No one hovers vulture-like, intimidating you to gulp your meal so the table can be turned over to other diners. That's where the no-tipping stance really shines—no tips involved, no need to hurry the patrons. Consequently, dining out is popular entertainment for most Aussies.

Other things to know: A licensed restaurant serves alcohol (though sometimes only beer and wine), while a BYO restaurant, though unlicensed, allows you to bring your own bottle; dinner is often called "tea"; entree means appetizer; pub counter meals (commonly veal, chicken, steak, or sausages, with salad and chips) are normally available noon-2 p.m. and 6-8 p.m., and can be eaten either at the counter or at a table in the adjoining lounge (if there is one); many pubs now have attached "bistros"—but be aware that the word "bistro" will probably add an extra digit to the tab!

DRINK

Australians love to drink. Walk into someone's house and the kettle is instantly put on the stove; make a deal and you'll invariably seal it at the local pub. Favorite nonalcoholic drinks include mineral waters, Coca-Cola, fresh juices, flavored milk, tea, and *lots* of coffee. "White" tea or coffee has milk in it; "flat white" or "flat black" coffee has milk in it, but no froth, as opposed to a cappuccino. Despite the ubiquitousness of the almighty espresso machine, out in the bush tea- and coffee-drinkers may have to resort to the trusty tea bag and instant coffee powder.

Australian Beer

Ice cold and plenty of it! Aussies love their beer, and each state and territory has its favorite brand, though Foster's is the best known worldwide. In addition, boutique breweries have popped up in the major cities, but you'll only be able to taste their efforts at the hotel where they're made. Beer comes in a dizzying variety of containers—tinnies, twisties, stubbies, mid-

dies, pots, schooners, ponies, goblets, and plain old glasses. The containers and glasses vary by location, so it's best to ask advice from the publican or a friendly local.

Each state or territory has its own special brew, though most are available Australia-wide: **Swan** and **Emu** (Western Australia), **Coopers** (South Australia), **XXXX** (pronounced "FOUR-ex") and **Powers** (Queensland), **Tooheys** (New South Wales), **Victoria Bitter** (Victoria), and **Brogues** (Tasmania). Some of the best-known boutique varieties are: **Redback** (Western Australia), **Eumundi** and **Cairn's Draught** (Queensland), and **Cascade** (Tasmania). Try 'em all.

Locals prefer draught (draft) beer straight from the tap. Keep in mind that Australian beer is higher in alcohol content than American varieties (even the Foster's you buy in the U.S. has been watered down), so gauge your consumption accordingly.

"Drink-driving" laws are tough in Australia; on-the-spot sobriety checks and booze buses (Breathalyzer vans) are common in urban areas. (See "Laws and Licenses" under "Getting Around," below.)

Australian Wine

Australia's premier wine-producing areas are South Australia's McLaren Vale, Barossa and Clare Valleys, and in New South Wales the Hunter Valley. Domestic wines are produced in many other parts of Australia, including Western Australia's Swan and Margaret River Valleys and throughout Victoria, which has well over 100 vineyards. Australian champagne (oops—*methode champenois*) is widely imbibed and a good value. Tour the vineyards for free tastings, then buy a bottle or two of your favorite wine or bubbly. Less expensive wines can be purchased in two- or four-liter casks.

Spirits

If you're on a budget, you'd best stick to beer and wine—spirits down here are expensive, at least compared to prices in the Unites States. If money is no object, you'll find most of your favorite brands readily available at bottle shops and bars. Australia also produces port, brandy, and sherry, as well as two types of Queensland rum (but beware of the alcohol content, which could be considerably more than the normal 33%).

Drinking Laws

You must be 18 or older to buy or consume alcohol. Liquor licenses vary from state to state (and territory). Pubs normally stay open for 12 hours (10 a.m.-10 p.m., or variations thereof)

seven days a week. Other bars, clubs, and restaurants can offer alcohol until 2 or 3 a.m. Some establishments can serve you only if you're eating food, or else they are designated BYO (Bring Your Own). Beer, wine, and spirits can be purchased at bottle shops (often attached to a pub) or liquor stores. It is illegal to bring alcohol into an Aboriginal community or reserve.

GETTING THERE

Fly. It's the only way to get down under, unless you opt for an expensive cruise with a couple of one- or two-day port stops. Most international airlines operate wide-body aircraft to Australia. The main gateway cities are on the east coast, with Sydney (from North and South America, throughout the Pacific, Asia, and Europe) handling the majority of passengers. Other major gateways are Brisbane and Cairns (from throughout the Pacific and Asia), Darwin (from Asia), Perth (from Asia and Africa), and Melbourne (from North America, the Pacific, Asia, and Europe).

Other cities with international airports are Port Headland (from Indonesia), Adelaide (from Asia), and Hobart (from New Zealand). If you can avoid flying in over Christmas, Easter, or

STUDENT TRAVEL ASSOCIATION OFFICES

IN THE UNITED STATES

Berkeley, 2nd Floor, ASUC Building, UC Berkeley, Telegraph at Bancroft Way, Berkeley, CA 94720 (tel. 510-642-3000)

Boston, 297 Newbury St., Boston, MA 02115 (tel. 617-266-6014)

Cambridge, 65 Mt. Auburn St., Cambridge, MA 02138 (tel. 617-576-4623)

Chicago, 429 S. Dearborn St., Chicago, IL 60605 (tel. 312-786-9050)

Los Angeles, 7202 Melrose Ave., Los Angeles, CA 90046 (tel. 213-934-8722); 920 Westwood Blvd., Los Angeles, CA 90024 (tel. 310-824-1574); 120 Broadway #108, Santa Monica, CA 90401 (tel. 310-394-5126)

New York, 10 Downing St., New York, NY 10014 (tel. 212-627-3111); 103 Ferris Booth Hall, Columbia University, New York, NY 10027 (tel. 212-854-2224)

Philadelphia, 3730 Walnut St., Philadelphia, PA 19104 (tel. 215-382-2928)

San Francisco, 51 Grant Ave., San Francisco, CA 94108 (tel. 415-391-8407)

Seattle, 4341 University Way NE, Seattle, WA 98105 (tel. 206-633-5000)

Washington, D.C., 2401 Pennsylvania Ave., Suite G, Washington, D.C. 20037 (tel. 202-887-0912)

IN AUSTRALIA

Adelaide, 235 Rundle St., Adelaide, SA 5000 (tel. 08-8233-2426)

Brisbane, Shop 25, Brisbane Arcade, 111-117 Adelaide St., Brisbane, QLD 4000 (tel. 07-3221-9388)

Cairns, Shop 2, Central Court, 43 Lake St., Cairns, QLD 4870 (tel. 070-31-4199)

Canberra, Ground Floor, 13-15 Garema Pl., Canberra, ACT 2601 (tel. 06-247-8633)

Darwin, Darwin Transit Centre, 69 Mitchell St., Darwin, N.T. 0800 (tel. 08-8941-2955)

Melbourne, 222 Faraday St., Carlton, VIC 3053 (tel. 03-9349-2411)

Sydney, First Floor, 732 Harris St., Ultimo, Sydney, NSW 2007 (tel. 02-9281-2604)

Perth, 100 James St., Northbridge, Perth, WA 6003 (tel. 09-227-7569)

ELSEWHERE

Germany, Leipzigerstrasse 17a, 60487 Frankfurt/Main (tel. 069-979-0760)

Japan, 7th Floor, 1-16-20 Minami-Ikebukuro, Toshima-Ku, Tokyo 171 (tel. 03-5391-2889)

Netherlands, Schipholweg 101, 2316 XC Leiden (tel. 071-68-8888)

New Zealand, 10 High St., Auckland (tel. 09-309-9723)

Singapore, 02-17 Orchard Parade Hotel, 1 Tanglin Rd., Singapore 1024 (tel. 734-5681)

Thailand, 14th Floor, room 1406, 33 Surawong Rd., Bangrak, Bangkok 10500 (tel. 02-233-2582)

U.K., 6 Wrights Lane, London W8 6TA (tel. 071-938-4711)

COUNCIL TRAVEL OFFICES

IN THE UNITED STATES

Austin, 2000 Guadalupe St., Austin, TX 78705 (tel. 512-472-4931)

Berkeley, 2486 Channing Way, Berkeley, CA 94704 (tel. 510-848-8604)

Boston, 729 Boylston St., Suite 201, Boston, MA 02116 (tel. 617-266-1926)

Chicago, 1153 N. Dearborn St., 2nd Fl., Chicago, IL 60610 (tel. 312-951-0585)

Los Angeles, 10904 Lindbrook Dr., Los Angeles, CA 90024 (tel. 310-208-3551)

New Orleans, Joseph A. Danna Center, Loyola University, 6363 St. Charles Ave., New Orleans, LA 70118 (tel. 504-866-1767)

New York, 205 E. 42nd St., New York, NY 10017 (tel. 212-661-1450); New York Student Center, 895 Amsterdam Ave., New York, NY 10025 (tel. 212-666-4177); 148 West 4th St., New York, NY 10012 (tel. 212-254-2525)

Portland, 7155 W. Morrison, Suite 600, Portland, OR 97205 (tel. 503-228-1900)

San Diego, 953 Garnet Ave., San Diego, CA 92109 (tel. 619-270-6401); UCSD Price Center, 9500 Gilman Dr., La Jolla, CA 92093 (tel. 619-452-0630)

San Francisco, 530 Bush St., San Francisco, CA 94108 (tel. 415-421-3473); Suite 102, 919 Irving St., San Francisco, CA 94122 (tel. 415-566-6222)

Seattle, 1314 N.E. 43rd St., Suite 210, Seattle, WA 98105 (tel. 206-632-2448); 219 Broadway Ave. East, the Alley Building, Suite 17, Seattle, WA 98102 (tel. 206-329-4567)

Washington, D.C., 3300 M St. NW, 2nd Fl., Washington, D.C. 20007 (tel. 202-337-6464)

For other U.S. cities, phone (800) 226-8624.

ELSEWHERE

France, 22, rue des Pyramides, 75001 Paris (tel. 1-44-55-55-65); 16, rue de Vaugirard, 75006 Paris (tel. 1-46-34-02-90)

Germany, Düsseldorf (tel. 211-36-30-30); Munich (tel. 089-39-50-22)

Japan, Tokyo (tel. 3-3581-5517)

Singapore (tel. 65-738-7066)

Thailand, Bangkok (tel. 66-2-282-7705)

U.K., 28A Poland St., London W1V (tel. 0171-437-7767)

---

the middle of Australia's summer or school holiday periods, do so. Otherwise book well ahead as these are Australia's heaviest travel periods. Also, try to avoid weekend arrivals.

Travel Agents

If you're looking for the most economical fare, make sure you have a travel agent who doesn't mind doing a little work on your behalf. **Council Travel** and **STA** (Student Travel Association)—both student-oriented agencies, often with university locations—usually offer the cheapest deals with the fewest restrictions, and student status is not a prerequisite for many of their fares. In London, bucket shops (advertised in *Time Out, City Limits* and *TNT*) offer discounted fares; reliable agencies include: **Campus Travel,** 52 Grosvenor Gardens, London SW1 (tel. 071-730-8111); **Quest Worldwide,** 29 Castle St., Kingston, Surrey KT1 (tel. 081-547-3322) and **Trailfinders,** 42-50 Earls Court Rd., London W8 (tel. 071-938-3366). Before contemplating which travel agent to use, call individual airlines yourself and do the comparison-shop routine. That way, when you talk to an agent you'll have a good idea of the route options and fares available. Important questions to ask include applicable standby fares, accommodation packages, special promotions, allowed stopovers, and restrictions and penalties.

If you're not fussy about travel dates, say so. You can save plenty of bucks by traveling in the low or shoulder season instead of sky-high peak time. **Fare seasons** from the Northern Hemisphere are: 1 May-31 August, low; 1 December-28 February, high; everything else, shoulder. Some airlines vary these periods by a few weeks.

APEX, Round-the-World, And Circle-Pacific Fares

Scads of fares are available—from rock-bottom, off-season economy to super-luxe, super-bucks first class. Business class, an upgraded economy and downgraded first class, is available on most airlines. Advance-purchase excursion (APEX) fares are usually the best value, though some (and, occasionally, many) restrictions apply. These might include minimum and maximum stays, and nonchangeable itineraries (or hefty penalties for changes); tickets may also be nonrefundable, once purchased—and most airlines are not buying the "medical excuse" bit anymore.

Other travel options to consider are Round-the-World or Circle-Pacific fares. Round-the-World tickets—usually combining two airlines—allow travel in the same direction (with no backtracking) around the world anywhere on their combined route systems. Tickets ordinarily require that the first sector be booked in advance and that travel be completed within one year. The number of stops permitted may vary, and cancellation penalties may apply. Circle-Pacific tickets work pretty much the same as round-the-worlders except that they circle only the Pacific rather than the whole world. A sample itinerary might encompass San Francisco, Honolulu, Auckland, Sydney, Singapore, Bangkok, Hong Kong, Tokyo, then back to San Francisco. Contact travel agents for participating airlines and current fares; both types of tickets can be an exceptionally good value.

At the time of this writing, the average low-season, round-trip APEX fare from either Los Angeles or San Francisco—with one stopover allowed—is $1100 to Sydney and $1770 to Perth; high season is $1100 to Sydney and $1838 to Perth.

AIRLINES

From North America

Direct nonstop flights (15-16 hours) between North America and Australia are offered by Air New Zealand, Qantas Airways, and United Airlines, which each have daily services between Los Angeles or San Francisco and Sydney. Qantas and Air New Zealand also offer a staggering variety of stopover possibilities, such as Honolulu/Tahiti/Fiji Islands with Qantas; and Honolulu/Western Samoa/Tahiti/Fiji Islands/Cook Islands/ Tonga/Auckland with Air New Zealand.

From Canada: Air Canada and Canadian Airlines have a code-sharing agreement with Air New Zealand and Qantas, which entails a change of carrier in Honolulu. Another option to consider from Canada's west coast is to fly Malaysian Air Systems via Singapore. Be forewarned: Fares, airlines, and routes are continually changing. Call your travel agent or the individual airlines for up-to-date info and fares.

Garuda Indonesia

An exotic way to enter Australia is to hop over to Darwin from Bali with Garuda Indonesia. From North America, Garuda flies out of Los Angeles, via Honolulu, to Bali and Jakarta. From these cities connections can be made to Sydney, Brisbane, Cairns, Darwin, Perth, Adelaide, and Melbourne. From Europe, Garuda takes off from London, Amsterdam, and a host of other major capitals as well as the Asian cities of Tokyo, Beijing, Seoul, Hong Kong, Bangkok, Singapore, Kuala Lumpur, and Manila. For **Circle-Pacific** ticket holders, Garuda's partners are Delta and Cathay Pacific. (If traveling through the Indonesian archipelago, you will want to explore the country with Moon's *Indonesia Handbook*—Bill Dalton's bible to the country—or with *Bali Handbook,* Dalton's smaller epistle.) For Garuda Indonesia reservations in the United States, phone (800) 342-7832; in Canada, phone (800) 663-2254; and, in London, phone (071) 486-2644 or 486-3011.

Other International Carriers

From Asia: Air France, Air India, Air New Zealand, Air Niugini, All Nippon Airways, Ansett Australia, British Airways, Cathay Pacific Airways, Garuda Indonesia, Japan Airlines, KLM Royal Dutch Airlines, Malaysian Air System, Philippine Airlines, Qantas Airways, Singapore Airlines, and Thai International.

From Europe and the United Kingdom: Air France, Air India, Air New Zealand, Alitalia, British Airways, Cathay Pacific Airways, Garuda Indonesia, Japan Air Lines, KLM Royal Dutch

AIR ROUTES
TO AUSTRALIA

ROUTES ARE SUBJECT TO CHANGE
WITHOUT PRIOR NOTICE

0   1,000 km

PACIFIC
OCEAN

INDIAN
OCEAN

TO TORONTO

VANCOUVER

SAN FRANCISCO
LOS ANGELES

TO CHICAGO,
BOSTON, NEW YORK,
AND WASHINGTON

HONOLULU

PAPEETE

NORFOLK ISLAND

NADI

NOUMEA

AUCKLAND

WELLINGTON

CHRISTCHURCH

HONIARA

PORT MORESBY

CAIRNS

BRISBANE

SYDNEY

MELBOURNE

HOBART

ADELAIDE

PORT
HEDLAND

DARWIN

DENPASAR

PERTH

JAKARTA

SINGAPORE

KUALA LUMPUR

MANILA

HONG KONG

BANGKOK

PHUKET

FUKUOKA

NAGOYA

TOKYO

TO BUENOS AIRES

TO HARARE

TO LONDON AND MANCHESTER
TO FRANKFURT AND LONDON
TO ROME
TO LONDON AND MANCHESTER
TO LONDON AND MANCHESTER

Airlines, Lauda Air, Malaysian Air System, Qantas Airways, Scandinavian Airlines, Singapore Airlines, and Thai International.

From South America: Lan Chile (via Easter Island and Tahiti) and Aerolineas Argentinas (via Auckland) in conjunction with Ansett Australia.

From Africa: Qantas (from Harare, Zimbabwe, and Johannesburg, South Africa).

GETTING AROUND

Australia is enormous. Distances between places are vast and destinations often completely isolated—don't try to see the whole continent on a 10-day tour. Australia is also not a dollar-a-day country, nor an especially good one for hitchhiking. Allow yourself plenty of time, plan at least a tentative itinerary, and budget your funds accordingly.

Travel Times Australia is a comprehensive transport timetable with rail, coach, and ferry schedules, as well as reservation numbers, addresses, and maps. Purchase it from newsagents, or get a copy in advance by sending $7.95 (which includes airmail postage) to Traveltime Publishing, 3 Goodwin St., Glen Iris, VIC 3146 (tel. 03-9889-3344).

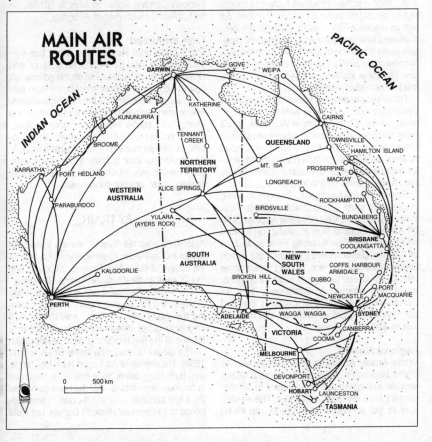

MAIN AIR ROUTES

BY AIR

The main domestic carriers are **Ansett Australia** (tel. 13-1300) and **Qantas** (tel. 13-1313). To book from North America, call (800) 366-1300 and (800) 227-4500 respectively. These two giants of Australian air travel have undergone massive upheavals since deregulation, taking many smaller regional airlines under their wing and blasting upstarts, such as ill-fated Compass Airlines, out of the sky. The bottom line for travelers is that the price of flying within Australia has dropped considerably in the last few years. The days of paying $1200 to fly across the continent are long gone; today the round-trip between Sydney and Perth is about $500 and the airlines will throw in a couple nights' accommodation as part of the deal. As well as regular APEX fares (the cheapest tickets available), both airlines offer some excellent package deals (most travel agents will have details), such as under $300 pp for travel between Sydney and Tasmania inclusive of three nights' accommodations and a rental car.

Domestic passes don't offer the exceptional value they once did, what with the advent of deregulation. Once you're in Australia, you'll most likely see a number of advertised special fares and promotions. Also, international ticket holders are eligible for 40% discounts off regular economy fares on domestic routes anyway (you have to show your ticket).

Passes worth investigating before you leave home (they must be purchased outside Australia) are Ansett's Visit Australia Airpass, 55% off full fare, Special See Australia, up to 40% off full fare, and See Australia Fare, up to 25% off full fare; Qantas offers Explorer Pass, which averages 50% off full fare. Some passes come with an exhausting barrage of segment coupons, travel zone separations, directions-of-flight, regional and other restrictions. Check dos and don'ts thoroughly before purchase. You might do just as well without them.

Regional Airlines

While Ansett Australia and Qantas handle flights between major centers, about a dozen smaller airlines shuttle passengers to smaller centers from the main gateways. The easiest way to get schedule information and make reservations is through the central booking services of Ansett Australia (tel. 13-1300) and Qantas (tel. 13-1313). The major regional carriers are: **Eastern Australia** (book through Qantas); **Hazelton,** serving central and outback New South Wales (book through Ansett); **Sunstate,** serving coastal Queensland (Qantas); **Flightwest,** serving Queenland's outback and far north (call 13-2392 or Qantas); **Airnorth,** serving the Northern Territory (Ansett); **Skywest,** serving Western Australia (Ansett); **Southern Australia,** serving South Australia (Qantas); **Kendell Airlines,** serving Victoria and southern New South Wales (Ansett); and **Airlines of Tasmania** (call 1800-03-0550). Flights to Lord Howe Island can be booked through Qantas; flights to Norfolk Island can be booked through Ansett Australia.

From the Airport

Major cities offer inexpensive public bus service to, from, and between international and domestic airports. A variety of shuttle companies operate convenient door-to-door minivan service, usually operating till the last flight arrives. These are cheaper than taxis if you're traveling alone, but if you're with one or more companions, a taxi is probably better value. Larger hotels, as well as many motels, provide free pickup service for their guests. In smaller towns, you'll have to rely on whatever you can—a taxi, passing local, or your good looks.

BY TRAIN

Australia's main rail "events" are the transcontinental Indian-Pacific (Sydney-Perth, 65 hours), the Ghan (Adelaide-Alice Springs, 20 hours), and the Queenslander (Brisbane-Cairns, 32 hours).

The **Indian-Pacific** spans 4,350 kilometers between the Pacific and Indian Oceans, crossing the vast Nullarbor Plain and the world's longest length of straight railway track (478 km). It's one of the few remaining great rail journeys.

The **Ghan** is, alas, the "new Ghan" of the 1980s. The original Ghan, begun in the late 1800s, was built along creek beds that were assumed to be bone-dry—that is, until the rains came and the route became regularly flooded. It was supposed to run from Adelaide to Darwin, but it still

RAIL AUSTRALIA ~ MAJOR SERVICES

TIMOR SEA

CORAL SEA

DARWIN

NORTHERN TERRITORY

CAIRNS

NORMANTON   CROYDEN

TOWNSVILLE

MOUNT ISA

PROSERPINE

ALICE SPRINGS

WINTON

MACKAY

ROCKHAMPTON

WESTERN AUSTRALIA

BUNDABERG

QUEENSLAND

QUILPIE

SOUTH   AUSTRALIA

CUNNAMULLA

BRISBANE

DIRRANBANDI

KALGOORLIE

PORT AUGUSTA

BROKEN HILL

NEW SOUTH WALES

PERTH

GREAT AUSTRALIAN BIGHT

ORANGE

NEWCASTLE

BUNBURY

MILDURA

ADELAIDE

SWAN HILL

SYDNEY

CANBERRA

INDIAN OCEAN

BAIRNSDALE

MELBOURNE

VICTORIA

TASMANIA

0   500 km

hasn't made it beyond Alice Springs. The original broad-gauge line went only to Marree, becoming a narrow-gauge all the way to Oodnadatta, where passengers were escorted to Alice Springs via Afghani-guided camel trains, thus the name "Ghan." By the late 1920s the railway was extended to the Alice—but the rains still flooded the original lines. Often the train was left stranded, and supplies had to be parachuted down to waiting travelers. The old Ghan was rarely used after its film scene in *Mad Max III*. The new Ghan is still a good trip, but without the risk and romance.

The **Queenslander** is a luxurious, yuppy-ish scoot up the coast from Brisbane to Cairns (1,680

km). You can get off at Proserpine (gateway to the Whitsundays) or go to the end of the line. You'll be pampered with great views, gourmet cuisine, and sophisticated entertainment.

Other rail services include the **Sunlander** (Brisbane-Cairns, 32 hours), the **Spirit of the Tropics** (Brisbane-Cairns, 32 hours), the **Spirit of the Outback** (Brisbane-Longreach, 24 hours), the **Westlander** (Brisbane-Cunnamulla-Quilpie, 22 hours), the **Inlander** (Townsville-Mount Isa, 19 hours), the **XPT** (Sydney-Brisbane, 14 and one-half hours), the **Overland** (Adelaide-Melbourne, 12 hours), the **XPT** (Sydney-Melbourne, 10 and one-half hours), the

Xplorer (Sydney-Canberra, four and one-half hours), the **Prospector** (Perth-Kalgoorlie, eight hours), and the **Silver City Link** (Melbourne-Mildura, Broken Hill, 13 hours).

First- and economy-class seats and berths are available on all long-distance services and must be booked in advance. First-class twinette cabins have seats that turn into two sleeping berths; most have private shower, toilet, wash basin with hot and cold water, and electric shaver outlet. First-class single cabins only have toilets and basins—showers are down the hall. Economy-class sleepers in Queensland accommodate three people, with toilets and showers available in each car. Available on the Ghan and Indian-Pacific only, "holiday class" offers two-berth cabins with economy sleepers. Coach-class cars feature reclining seats and, on many hauls, also provide showers. Meals are included with first-class accommodation fares. All long-distance trains have dining cars, bars, buffet cars, and lounges with a variety of entertainment.

For all scheduling and ticketing information call 13-2232 toll-free anywhere in Australia. The same information is available by calling Countrylink (New South Wales, tel. 02-9217-8812); Queensland Rail (tel. 07-3235-1122); Westrail (Western Australia, tel. 09-326-2813); Australian National (South Australia, tel. 08-8231-7699); or V/Line (Victoria, tel. 03-9619-5000).

Rail Passes

Austrailpasses allow unlimited rail travel, including metropolitan trains, and are good deals if you plan to do a lot of rail travel. They must be purchased outside Australia. Costs in Australian dollars are: 14 days, $725 first class, $435 economy; 21 days, $895/$565; 30 days, $1100/$685; 60 days, $1535/$980; 90 days, $1765/$1125. The **Austrail Flexi-Pass** allows limited travel within a six-month period. Costs are: eight days, $560 first class, $340 economy; 15 days, $790/$500; 22 days, $1100/$700; 29 days, $1400/$900. The eight-day pass does not allow travel on the Ghan or Indian-Pacific from Adelaide to Perth. Passes do not cover charges for sleeping berths or meals. For more information or reservations, phone **Rail Australia** (tel. 800-423-2880 U.S. or 800-387-8850 Canada).

If you want to catch a train but don't have a rail pass, inquire about **Caper Fares.** If booked seven days ahead, they can save you some 30% off regular rail fares.

BY COACH

Modern air-conditioned coaches (buses) are an easy and comfortable way to see the country. Most of them have bathroom facilities, overhead video monitors, piped-in music, on-board hostesses, and drivers who double as tour guides. Buses are usually the cheapest way to travel *and* they go to a far wider range of places than trains and planes—to all capital cities, country towns, provincial centers, and most outback regions. If there's a place they don't travel, they can usually hook up with a local bus system (which might be a mail truck) that will get you where you're going.

Greyhound Pioneer (tel. 13-2030) has Australia's most extensive network of routes, serving all mainland capitals and just about everywhere in between. Other large companies are **McCafferty's** (tel. 07-3236-3033), based in Brisbane, traveling the east coast, Townsville, Darwin, Alice Springs, and Adelaide; **Premier Roadlines/Stateliner** (tel. 08-8415-5544), offering Adelaide regional service, including the Flinders Ranges; **Westrail** (tel. 09-326-2813 or 13-2232 toll-free), operating within the Western Australia region; and **Tasmanian Redline Coaches** (tel. 03-6334-4442), which traverses most of that state. A plethora of small local companies venture just about everywhere else.

Coach travel is a good way to kick back and relax, see the countryside, and meet other Aussie and international travelers. On the downside, you might find yourself locked up with some madding crowd.

Daily express routes include: Sydney-Adelaide (24 hours, $95); Sydney-Canberra (four and one-half hours, $28); Sydney-Melbourne (14 and one-half hours, $61); Canberra-Melbourne (nine and one-half hours, $55); Melbourne-Adelaide (nine and one-half hours, $55); Adelaide-Alice Springs (20 hours, $142); Adelaide-Perth (35 hours, $189); Adelaide-Brisbane (33 and one-half hours, $155); Darwin-Alice Springs (19 hours, $142); Darwin-Kakadu (three and one-half hours, $155); Alice Springs-Ayers Rock (six hours, $77); Cairns-Brisbane

(25 hours, $137); Cairns-Darwin (42 hours, $261); Brisbane-Sydney (17 hours, $73); Brisbane-Melbourne (25 hours, $129); Perth-Darwin (33.5 hours, $347).

Bus Passes

Again, you have an almost infinite assortment of bus passes—local, regional, national, and bus and train combination passes—explorer passes, backpacker discounts, bargain fares, etc. Some you have to buy outside Australia; others you can only buy once you're there.

Aussie Passes offer unlimited travel on the Greyhound Pioneer national network, using the "flexi-pass system." Travel days consist of 24-hour periods. Costs are: seven days in one month, $380; 10 days in one month, $540; 15 days in one month, $635; 21 days in two months, $890; 30 days in two months, $1080; 60 days in three months, $1610; 90 days in six months, $2225.

For more information for both Greyhound Pioneer and McCafferty's, phone (800) 531-9222 (U.S. and Canada).

Alternative Buses

A new breed of "adventure" buses has spawned within Australia. They head off the beaten path, carry small groups, and ease—rather than rush—you along. For more information, contact: **Oz Experience,** Sydney-Cairns via Alice Springs adventure travel (tel. 02-9907-0522); **Straycat,** Melbourne-Sydney high country adventure (tel. 1800-80-0840); or **Wayward Bus,** with a range of city, Centre, and transcontinental journeys (tel. 1800-88-2823). **Tasmanian Wilderness Transport** (tel. 03-6334-4442) offers transport between that state's cities and national parks and major trailheads.

BY BOAT

The *Spirit of Tasmania* links Port Melbourne, Victoria, and Devonport, Tasmania, three times weekly. The 14-hour overnight trip offers everything from hostel-style dormitories to private cabins, but even the basic bed sometimes costs more than an airline flight. The ferry does take vehicles, but unless you own one, this isn't very practical as most rental agencies prohibit sea

transport of their fleet. Also, be forewarned, the Bass Strait can be a very rough ride!

The **Kangaroo Island Sealink** operates two roll-on roll-off ferries daily between Cape Jervis, South Australia, to Kangaroo Island.

Western Australia's Rottnest Island is serviced daily by **Boat Torque.**

BY CAR

Car Rental

Outside the major cities, cars are about the only practical way to go. Rentals are not cheap, but if you're with a group the cost can work out more favorably. Avis, Budget, Hertz, and Thrifty are well represented and can be booked ahead from North America, but you'll often get a better deal from smaller, independent concerns after you've arrived. One advantage of the big conglomerates is that you can pick up and return your car at the airport and, in many cases, drop your car off at a destination other than your pick-up place (one-way rentals are not usually available in Western Australia, the Northern Territory, or other remote locations).

Before renting a car, find out if it includes unlimited kilometers. Daily rates range from about $75 for a small car (Toyota Corolla, Ford Laser), $90 for a medium size (Toyota Camry, Holden Camira), and $105-plus for a larger vehicle like the Holden Commodore. These rates include insurance, but if you're paying by credit card, check with your company to see if you qualify for CDW (Collision Damage Waiver), which can save you considerable money. For U.S. residents, your regular auto insurance policy also might cover this charge. For more information, contact: Avis (tel. 800-831-2847 U.S.); Budget (tel. 800-283-4382 U.S.); or Hertz (tel. 800-654-3001 U.S.). Territory Rent-A-Car, with six Northern Territory branches, can now be booked from the U.S. (tel. 800-423-2880).

Four-wheel-drive vehicles are available for more adventurous travel, but they are costlier than conventional cars ($100-150 daily, many with limited kilometers). Also, insurance can add considerably to the cost. When tallying up the cost and equipment of a 4WD journey, travelers may find that organized tours are more economical and less stressful. Reputable rental

ROAD WARNING SIGNS

CROSSING HERE

NEXT 15 km

WARNING SIGNS

SPEED LIMIT ENDS

agencies include: Brits: Australia (tel. 800-641-8772, U.S.); Oz Rentals (tel. 03-9877-2986, Victoria); Cairns Rent-a-Car (tel. 070-51-6077); and South Perth 4WD Rentals (tel. 09-362-5444, Western Australia).

Campervan and Caravan Rental
Campervans (two to three berths) and caravans (four to six berths) range in price from $900 to $1400 per week, with unlimited mileage. Most come equipped with refrigerator, sink, gas stove, and water tank, and some have showers and toilets. **Maui Campervans** (tel. 02-9597-6155 or 1800-22-7279) has depots in all major cities and often offers special deals to get vans back from certain centers. For example, most people travel up the east coast from Sydney or Melbourne to Cairns, leaving a surplus of vans in Cairns. At last report, the rental rate for all size of campervan from Cairns to just about anywhere in Australia was $85 per day inclusive of unlimited mileage and insurance. Other camper rental agencies include: Apollo Motorhome Holidays (tel. 800-286-2147 U.S.); Inta-Aussie RV Campavans (tel. 800-531-9222 U.S.); and Koala Camper Rentals (tel. 800-423-2880 U.S.).

Purchasing a Car
Buying a car, especially for the short-term visitor, can be a pain—an *expensive* pain. New ones, whether locally manufactured or imported, are not cheap; used ones can turn out to be unreliable lemons. This is not like going to Sweden or Germany to pick up a shiny new Saab or Porsche and drive off into the sunset. Buying a car, particularly a used one, can be the same kind of arduous, time-consuming hell in Sydney or Perth as it is in Los Angeles or Detroit. And, as you ride off into that central Australian sunset, and the car blows its head gasket or cracks the

block, your salty tears will do nothing more than blur your written guarantee.

The **buy-back** plan is another option: you buy a car (or motorcycle) at a fixed rate, put down a deposit equal to the vehicle's value, return it after a specified period, and get your money back, less the agreed-upon fee. Most prices include a set number of kilometers, limited warranties, and short-term insurance. One company that specializes in both car and motorcycle buy-backs is **Car Connection Australia,** RSD Lot 8, Vaughan Springs Rd., Glenluce, VIC 3451 (tel. 03-5473-4469, fax 5473-4520).

Highways and Byways
City expressways and thoroughfares are just about as hectic and expletive-inspiring as those in any other first world metropolis and come complete with rush-hour (peak) traffic, which, increasingly, seems to last early morning until late at night. The major highways are sealed (called "bitumen") with asphalt or tar and well-maintained—though they are often only two-lane affairs (in the outback, bitumen roads can barely accommodate even one vehicle). Only since the 1980s have Highway 1 (the around-Australia road) and the Stuart Highway (up the center) been completely surfaced.

Filling stations are plentiful in cities, suburbs, and townships, but can be few and far between in the outback. Petrol, sold by the liter, comes in leaded and unleaded grades and works out to $3-3.50 per gallon, though in desolate areas prices can go much higher (what are you going to do, shop around?). Diesel and leaded premium are usually available, but remote service stations may not have unleaded in stock—and, occasionally, they have *no* stock. Distances between petrol pumps can be considerable; check with each roadhouse and service station before assuming a fill-up will be available at your next stop when traveling in outback regions.

Laws and Licenses
First rule to remember: Drive on the left side of the road! (And for you four-on-the-floorers, this means you shift with your *left* hand.) Second rule: The vehicle on your right has right-of-way, though there are some variations to this rule

that seem to confuse locals and tourists alike. Play it safe and watch carefully.

The maximum **speed limit** in cities and towns is 50-80 kph, increasing to 100-110 km/h on country roads and highways, unless signs say otherwise. **Seat belts** are mandatory and must be worn by the driver and all passengers; small children must be harnessed into a safety seat. **Motorcyclists** need a special license, as well as a helmet (check with state automobile clubs). **"Drink-driving" laws** are strict and spot checks, including Breathalyzer tests, are commonplace. Drivers having blood-alcohol levels 0.05 percent or higher (0.08 percent in the Northern Territory) will incur large fines, a court appearance, and loss of driving privileges.

Tourists can get away with using their valid overseas driver's license (along with a passport) if driving the same class of vehicle. International Driver's Licenses are only recognized if used in conjunction with a valid driver's permit (so, why bother?).

If you're a member of an official Automobile Club in your home country, bring your membership card to receive reciprocal rights from Australian automobile clubs.

CYCLING

Both long-distance and round-the-city cycling are popular in Australia. Most cities have designated bike routes, and flat country roads can be sheer heaven. Remote areas and outback tracks require careful planning, extra equipment, and excellent health—always check with locals and notify police or park rangers before venturing into desolate regions. Make certain to drink heaps of water, wear plenty of sunscreen, and use a bicycle helmet (mandatory). You can bring your own bike from overseas (check with your airline regarding packing and costs) or buy a touring or mountain bike once you get to Australia.

For route maps, trail suggestions, and information on bicycle touring, contact **Pedal Power ACT,** P.O. Box 581, Canberra, ACT 2601 (tel. 06-248-7995); **Bicycle Institute of New South Wales,** 82 Campbell St., Surry Hills, NSW 2010 (tel. 02-9212-5628); **Bicycle Institute of Queensland,** The Web, 142 Agnew St., Norman Park, QLD 4101 (tel. 07-3899-2988); **Bicycle Institute of South Australia,** 11 Church Rd., Mitcham, SA 5062 (tel. 08-8271-5824); **Pedal Power Tasmania,** c/o Environment Centre, 102 Bathurst St., Hobart, TAS 7000 (tel. 03-6234-5566); **Bicycle Victoria,** 29 Somerset Pl., Melbourne, VIC 3000 (tel. 03-9328-3000); **Cycle Touring Association,** P.O. Box 174, Wembley, WA 6014 (tel. 09-349-2310).

OTHER OPTIONS

Motorcycles

Read the info above regarding car purchases; the same applies to motorcycles. You can ship your own over (special permit necessary, and expensive) or buy one out of the classifieds—April or May, the beginning of the Australian winter, is a good time to shop. Rentals are usually available only in the cities, but the same buy-back scheme for cars (see above) can be had for motorcycles. A favorite is the Yamaha Ténéré, a long-distance cruiser and off-road beauty.

ROAD SIGNS

NATIONAL HIGHWAY   NATIONAL ROUTE   STATE ROUTE   TOURIST DRIVE

It is *not* recommended that bikers solo into the outback. Tag-along tours, similar to those for 4WD vehicles (see "By Car and Caravan," above) are also available for motorcylists. Rates for motorcycles range $60-95 per day and $300-500 per week, depending on engine size; a refundable deposit—around $500—is required.

Hitchhiking

Hitchhiking is illegal in most states and strongly discouraged throughout Australia. Check the bulletin boards at YHA hostels and other backpacker lodges for rides, though this, too, has its risks.

Mail Trucks and Planes

Outback mail runs, whether by truck or plane, are one of Australia's most enduring traditions. The weekly runs—covering hundreds or thousands of kilometers—often provide the only outside human contact for outback dwellers. Besides being a reliable source for important information and juicy gossip—and, of course, the mail—the service also delivers everything from Vegemite to spark plugs.

Travelers can ride the mail truck every Monday and Thursday for its 600-kilometer route around Coober Pedy, Oodnadatta, and William Creek. Fare is $50-60. For information, call (1800) 80-2074 (toll-free), or contact Underground Books, 1 Post Office Hill Rd., Coober Pedy (tel. 08-8672-5558). Mail planes are costlier ($140-300). For information, contact Cape York Air Services, Cairns, QLD (tel. 070-35-9399), which operates the world's longest mail run; Air Mount Isa, QLD (tel. 077-43-2844), or Augusta Airways, Port Augusta, SA (tel. 08-8642-3100).

TOURS

The range of tours available in Australia is as vast as the country, as wild as your imagination, as extravagant or economical as you wish, and as environmentally conscious or politically correct as you choose. The place to begin is at each state or territory's government tourist office (see "Maps and Tourist Information," later in this chapter). These offices are glorious resources for all kinds of information, and will not only recommend and seek out a suitable tour for you, but will book it as well. Major cities offer the usual tourist-friendly range of commercial "city sights," "by day," and "by night" tours, either in a big bus, minivan, or hop-on-and-off shuttle.

Recommended tour operators in North America are: **Inta-Aussie Tours,** an Australian-owned concern with a vast range of outback, value, wilderness, and coach expeditions, as well as city, coastal, reef, and island adventures (tel. 800-531-9222 U.S. and Canada) and **Globus,** dating from 1928, specializing in escorted and independent first-class tours to Australia (tel. 800-221-0090 U.S. or 800-268-1639 Canada). Or try **Adventure Express** (tel. 800-443-0799 U.S.) and **American Wilderness Experience** (tel. 800-444-0099 U.S.) for adventure holidays. Other tour operators specializing in a broad spectrum of Australian tours include: **ATS Tours** (tel. 800-423-2880 U.S.), **SoPac** (tel. 800-551-2012 U.S. and Canada), and **Swain Australia** (tel. 800-227-9246 U.S. and Canada). **Rascals in Paradise** (tel. 800-872-7225 U.S.) organizes Australian adventures geared to the whole family. YHA travel offices are also excellent sources for inbound tours, including 4WD and motorcycle outback tag-alongs.

Aerial Tours

From the comfort of a six- or 10-seater Piper, fly high above the parched land, peering down at the ant-like climbers at Uluru or the Bungle Bungles. Tours from a few days to a few weeks can be arranged through the state tourist offices, **Air Adventure Australia** (tel. 1800-03-3160), **Aircruising Australia** (tel. 02-9693-2233), **Aviatour** (tel. 03-9589-4097), or **Outback NT Air Safaris** (tel. 08-8979-2411). Also see "Mail Trucks and Planes" under "Getting Around," earlier in this chapter.

Cruises, Riverboats
Camel Treks, and Greased Lightning

Many of the Great Barrier Reef islands can be accessed by day cruises, ranging from a simple shuttle service (from $15 round-trip) to a full day of island activities, scuba diving, and meals (from $98). The *Kangaroo Explorer* cruises between Cairns and Thursday Island on a five-day adventure that takes in a remote section of the coast. **Captain Cook Cruises** (tel. 02-9206-1144) and **Proud Australia Holidays** (tel. 08-8231-9472) will cruise you along the Murray River. **Frontier Camel Tours** (tel. 08-8953-0444) will take you for a day's outing near Alice Springs, or a longer trek; **Frontier Outback** (tel. 800-227-8747) also offers extended safaris. Explore the Alice Springs area with **Harley Davidson Scenic Tours** (tel. 08-8953-4755).

Fishing Tours

Catch the big one with **Angling Adventures Australia** (tel. 800-356-6982 U.S.) or **Fishing International** (tel. 800-950-4242 U.S.). For more specialized fishing tours, contact **Lizard Island Lodge** (tel. 070-60-3999 or from the U.S. 800-551-2012) for details of the game-fishing season north of Cairns; **Arafura Safaris** (tel. 08-8927-2372 Northern Territory) for barramundi fishing; or **London Lakes Fly-fishing Lodge** (tel. 03-6289-1159), Australia's premier fly-fishing accommodation.

Volunteer Programs and "Green" Tours

WWOOF (Willing Workers On Organic Farms), will trade you bed and board in exchange for several hours' daily work. The farms, numbering more than 300, are not always organic, nor are they always farms; an occasional pottery or other enterprise might sneak in there. Some farms are in outback areas, though most are in more built-up regions. Membership ($25 outside Australia, $20 within the country) is required. Send the fee and you'll receive a membership number and WWOOF directory in re-

ABORIGINAL TOURS

Certainly one of the most rewarding opportunities of outback travel is to visit one or more of the Aboriginal lands. As in all of Australia, tourism plays an important economical role for the Aborigines. The tour companies listed below are owned, managed, and/or led by the traditional people. Focus might be on religion, the rudiments of "Dreaming," art and culture, the use of plants and animals, or bush tucker. Be prepared to abide by special customs and rules of behavior (e.g., do not spit out the food—unless you're *supposed* to).

NORTHERN TERRITORY

Ipolera Community (tel. 08-8956-2299): short culture-oriented walks and talks

Kurkara Tours (tel. 08-8956-7442): tours of Watarrka (Kings Canyon) National Park

Ntaria Aboriginal Community (tel. 08-8956-7402): self-guided tours of historical Hermannsburg

Oak Valley Day Tours (tel. 08-8956-0959): day tours to areas south of Alice Springs

Walala Bush Tucker Tour (tel. 08-8962-3388 or 62-1353): Aboriginal women led, March-November, in Tennant Creek

Wallace Rockhole Aboriginal Community (tel. 08-8956-7415): short walks and talks about culture and rock art

NORTHERN TERRITORY—TOP END

Aussie Safaris (tel. 08-8981-1633): day tours of Peppimenarti Aboriginal Community

Manyallaluk and Travel North (tel. 08-8972-1044): tours and meetings with Jawoyn traditional owners, leaving from Katherine

Tiwi Tours (tel. 08-8981-5144): trips to Vathurst and Melville Islands, off of Darwin

Umorrduk Aboriginal Safaris (tel. 08-8948-1306): flying and driving art-and-culture tours of northwest Arnhem Land and Kakadu National Park

Wilderness Experience (tel. 08-8941-2899): Aboriginal guided tours, leaving from Katherine

QUEENSLAND

AngGnarra Aboriginal Corporation (tel. 070-60-3214): guided tours of Split Rock Gallery and other rock sites, departing from Laura

Munbah Aboriginal Culture tour (tel. 070-60-9173): north of Cooktown, Hopevale Aboriginal community will give you a tour and let you bed down in a traditional hut

SOUTH AUSTRALIA

Desert Tracks (tel. 08-8956-2144): excellent—but costly—cultural tours of Anangu-Pitjantjatjara Lands, departing from Uluru (Ayers Rock) Resort

WESTERN AUSTRALIA

Derby Tourist Bureau (tel. 091-91-1426): arrangements can be made to cruise Geikie Gorge with Bunuba traditional people

Karijini Walkabouts (tel. 09-309-1395): backpacking trips in the Pilbara's Karijini National Park.

Flack Track Tours (tel. 091-92-1487): Aboriginal community visits departing from Broome

Point Inbound Tours (tel. 09-388-2210): Aboriginal artist, Shane Pickett, will accompany you to the Kimberley or Pilbara

---

turn. For more information, contact WWOOF, Mt. Murrindal Co-op, Buchan, VIC 3885 (tel. 03-5155-0218).

Volunteer conservation projects are available through **ATCV** (Australian Trust for Conservation Volunteers). This is a wonderful opportunity for travelers to do something constructive for the environment, meet other like-minded souls, and visit some roads less traveled. Projects are often situated in the outback and can include track construction, tree planting, and cataloging natural habitation. Volunteers make a contribution to help cover costs and, in return, are supplied with transportation, accommodations, and food. You can join for a week, weekend, or several weeks. For more information, contact ATCV, P.O. Box 423, Ballarat, VIC 3350 (tel. 03-5333-1483).

Volunteers can also help out the **ANZSES** (Australian and New Zealand Scientific Exploration Society). One hundred or so assistants are sent annually with an experienced guide into remote parts of the country, usually to collect flora and fauna specimens. For more information, contact ANZSES, P.O. Box 174, Albert Park, VIC 3206 (tel. 03-9690-5455).

Operators specializing in organized ecotours include **Ecotour Travel Agency** (tel. 02-9223-2811) and **Eco-Adventures Australia** (tel. 800-724-4880 U.S.). **Tailored Tours** (tel. 08-8363-0068) and **Wait-A-While Rainforest Wildlife Tours** (tel. 070-33-1153) take small groups on wildlife safaris.

VISAS AND OFFICIALDOM

Keep up to date on current red tape by contacting the nearest embassy or consulate, as well as your country's customs service. See "Australian Embassies and Consulates," below, for addresses.

PASSPORTS AND VISAS

Every visitor must have a valid passport for entry into Australia. In addition, visas are required for everyone except holders of Australian and New Zealand passports.

Tourist visas are issued free of charge, for stays of three months or less, at Australian consulates and embassies and, for U.S. and Canadian citizens, are generally valid for one year. For a US$24 fee, you can request an additional three months or multiple entries for a period of four years (or the life of your passport, if it is less than four years)—if you're planning more than one trip to Australia, this can cut down considerably on bureaucracy and keep your passport updated for spontaneous travel.

If applying in person, a visa will probably be issued on the spot; if applying by mail, be sure to enclose the completed application, any necessary fees, and a stamped, self-addressed envelope large enough to accommodate your passport. Also, allow at least 21 days for processing. If you want special services, such as your documents returned via first-class, certified, registered, or express mail, enclose the appropriate forms and postage. Mail that is marked "insufficient postage" will be returned, unprocessed.

Whether applying in person or by mail, you must present your passport and a signed application form (they don't seem to want your photograph anymore).

Within Australia, visas can be extended (often on the whim of the official you approach) at Department of Immigration and Ethnic Affairs offices in major cities. Do this well ahead of your visa expiration date, as the process can be lengthy. The application fee for the further extension of either a three-month (short-stay) or six-month (long-stay) visa is $135. These fees are *not* returned should your extension be denied. You may be required to have a personal interview and produce bank statements and other proof of financial solvency, including medical insurance and an onward ticket. The maximum stay, including extensions, is one year.

The tourist visa, no matter how long it's good for, does not allow you to be employed or take formal study in Australia. If you want to reapply as a resident, you'll probably have to go home and do it—the old pay-someone-to-marry-you-and-stay-forever technique is pretty much a thing of the past.

Visitors from Britain, Ireland, Canada, Japan, or the Netherlands, aged 18 to 26 (sometimes a bit older), may be eligible for a **working holiday visa.** This visa, which should be applied for in the applicant's home country, allows casual employment for a period of three months, though the visa is good for up to 12 months. **Student visas** entitle the holders to study full-time and work part-time, up to 20 hours per week. Application must be made in person—and in advance—at an Australian consulate or overseas

Australian Education Centre. Individuals who have approved sponsorship from an employer or organization in Australia can apply for a **temporary working visa** at their nearest Australian consulate—be forewarned, the requirements are stringent.

WORK

Regular tourist visas clearly state that *no* employment of *any* kind is allowed during your stay. A lot of travelers used to think, "sure, sure—I'll just work 'under the table.'" Unfortunately, with Australia's high unemployment rate, this is no longer a reliable option—there are too many "legit" citizens looking for jobs. Also, it is now required that workers have a "Tax File Number" (i.e., a Social Security card) in order to receive earnings; forms are available at the Taxation Department office or post office (be prepared to show your passport and visa).

Holders of working holiday visas are officially allowed to work for three out of 12 months, and can take advantage of the CES (Commonwealth Employment Service), the government employment agency that has branches or representatives in virtually every city and town. Casual labor is what you'll probably be offered—possibilities are fruit-picking, bar and restaurant work, ski resorts jobs, nannying, as well as some skilled positions for carpenters, electricians, plumbers, mechanics, and such. Check bulletin boards at hostels and cafes, and also ask around.

Harvesting is the best possibility. Opportunities are: South Australia—Barossa Valley grapes (Feb.-April), Riverlands citrus and soft fruits (all year); Western Australia—west coast seafoods (March-Nov.), Kununurra-area fruits and vegetables (May-Oct.), southwest-region grapes (Oct.-June); Queensland—central coast fruits and vegetables (May-Dec.), New South Wales border area grapes and orchard fruits (Dec.-March), Bundaberg-area fruits and vegetables (all year), northern coast bananas, tobacco, and sugarcane; New South Wales—northern coast bananas (all year), central eastern-area asparagus, cottons, onions, orchard and other fruits (Nov.-April); Victoria—Shepparton-area orchard and soft fruits, grapes, tobacco, and

PERMITS

You may need special permits to enter, pass through, or camp in certain areas of Australia.

Aboriginal Lands

The laws vary—on some lands you can pass through on "main roads" or stop in a community for fuel, on others you need a permit just to put your little toe on the land. If you're on an organized tour, the operator or guide will probably have taken care of all the red tape, otherwise apply well in advance (allow a couple of months) to the following land councils (you must apply to each state or territory that you wish to visit): Permits Officer, Aboriginal Affairs Planning Authority, P.O. Box 628, West Perth, WA 60005 (tel. 09-483-1222, fax 321-0990); Administration Officer, Maralinga-Tjarutja Inc., P.O. Box 435, Ceduna, SA 5435 (tel. 08-8625-2946); Permits Officer, Central Land Council, P.O. Box 3321, Alice Springs, NT 0871 (tel. 08-8951-6320, fax 8953-4345), for central and southern areas; Permits Officer, Northern Land Council, P.O. Box 42921, Casuarina, NT 0811 (tel. 08-8920-5172,

fax 8945-2633), for northern areas and Arnhem Land; Aboriginal Coordinating Council, P.O. Box 6512, Cairns Mall Centre, QLD 4870 (tel. 070-31-2623); Permits Officer, Tiwi Land Council, Ngulu, Bathurst Island via Darwin, NT 0822 (tel. 08-8978-3966), for Melville and Bathurst Islands.

National Parks and Desert Parks

Obtain camping and visitor permits in advance (see destination chapters for more info). If you're planning a visit to Simpson Desert Conservation Park, Simpson Desert Regional Reserve, Lake Eyre National Park, Innamincka Regional Reserve, and/or Witjira National Park in South Australia, you'll require a Desert Parks Pass. The pass, which costs around $50 per vehicle, includes camping and visiting permits, essential maps, and mini-travel guides. Purchase one at various shops in the northern part of the state, or through Flinders Ranges-based South Australian National Parks and Wildlife Service, Far Northern Region (tel. 08-8648-4244).

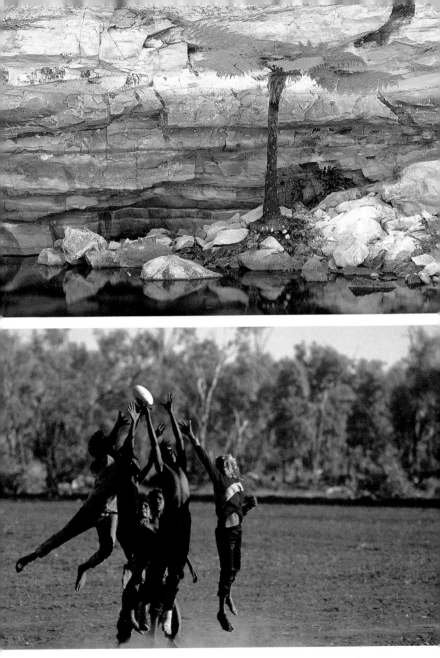

(top) tree fern and precipice sandstone along Carnarvon Creek, Queensland
(bottom) Aboriginal kids playing football

(top) emus among the mulga scrub and wildflowers of Mt. Augustus National Park, Western Australia
(bottom) high stakes in Western Australia

tomatoes (Nov.-April); Tasmania—grapes, hops, orchard and soft fruits (Dec.-March).

AUSTRALIAN CONSULATES AND EMBASSIES

United States
The **Australian Embassy** is at 1601 Massachusetts Ave. NW, Washington, D.C. 20036 (tel. 202-797-3000). You'll find Australian consulates in the following cities:

Atlanta, Suite 2920, 303 Peachtree St. NE, Atlanta, GA 30308 (tel. 404-880-1700)

Honolulu, 1000 Bishop St., Penthouse, Honolulu, HI 96813 (tel. 808-524-5050)

Houston, Suite 800, 1990 Post Oak Blvd., Houston, TX 77056 (tel. 713-629-9131)

Los Angeles, Century Plaza Towers, 2049 Century Park East, 19th floor, Los Angeles, CA 90067 (tel. 310-229-4800)

New York, Suite 420, 630 5th Ave., New York, NY 10111 (tel. 212-408-8400)

San Francisco, 7th floor, 1 Bush St., San Francisco, CA 94108 (tel. 415-362-6160)

Canada
Ottawa, Suite 710, 50 O'Connor St., Ottawa, ONT K1P 6L2 (tel. 613-236-0841)

Toronto, Suite 314, 175 Bloor St. East, Toronto, ONT M4W 3R8 (tel. 416-323-1155)

Vancouver, Suite 602, 999 Canada Place, Vancouver, BC V6C 3E1 (tel. 604-684-1177)

New Zealand
Auckland, 32-38 Quay St., Auckland 1 (tel. 09-32-4291)

Wellington, 72-78 Hobson St., Thorndon, Wellington (tel. 04-73-6411)

Asia
China, 21 Dongzhimenwai Dajie, San Li Tun, Beijing (tel. 10-532-2331)

Indonesia, Bali, Jl. Prof. Moh Yamin 51, Renon (tel. 0361-235-092); Jakarta, Kav. c 15-16; Jl. H.R. Rasuna Said, Jakarta Selatan (tel. 021-522-7111)

Hong Kong, 25 Harbour Rd., Wanchai (tel. 2827-8881)

India, No. 1/50-G Shantipath, Chanakyapuri, New Delhi 110021 (tel. 011-688-8223)

Japan, Osaka, 2-1-61 Shiromi, Chuo-ku 540 (tel. 06-941-9271); Tokyo, 2-1-14 Mita, Minato-ku (tel. 03-5232-4111)

Malaysia, 6 Jalan Yap, Kwan Seng, Kuala Lumpur 50450 (tel. 03-242-3122)

Papua New Guinea, Independence Dr., Waigani, Port Moresby (tel. 675-325-9333)

Philippines, 104 Paseo de Roxas, Makati, Metro Manila (tel. 02-817-7911)

Singapore, 25 Napier Rd., Singapore 1025 (tel. 737-9311)

Thailand, 37 S. Sathorn Rd., Bangkok 10120 (tel. 02-287-2680)

Europe
Denmark, Kristianagade 21, 2100 Copenhagen (tel. 035-26-2244)

France, 4 rue Jean Rey, Paris 15 (tel. 01-40-59-33-00)

Germany, Godesberger Allee 107, 5300 Bonn 1 (tel. 0228-81-030)

Greece, 37 Dimitriou Soutsou St., Ambelokipi, Athens 11521 (tel. 01-644-7303)

Ireland, Fitzwilton House, Wilton Terrace, Dublin 2 (tel. 01-676-1517)

Italy, Via Alessandria 215, Rome 00198 (tel. 06-85-2721)

Netherlands, Carnegielaan 14, 2517 KH The Hague (tel. 070-310-8200)

Sweden, Sergels Torg 12, Stockholm (tel. 08-613-2900)

Switzerland, 29 Alpenstrasse, Berne (tel. 031-351-0143)

United Kingdom
Edinburgh, 25 Bernard St., Leith EH6 6SH (tel. 0131-555-4500)

London, Australia House, The Strand, London WC2B 4LA (tel. 171-379-4334)

Manchester, Chatsworth House, Lever St., Manchester M1 2DL (tel. 161-228-1344)

South Africa

Pretoria, 292 Orient St., Arcadia, Pretoria 0083 (tel. 012-342-3740)

FOREIGN CONSULATES AND EMBASSIES

Canberra (Australian Capital Territory), Australia's equivalent to Washington, D.C., is where you'll find the foreign embassies. Wieldy connections such as New Zealand, the United Kingdom, the United States, and significant others, maintain consulates in other capital cities such as Sydney and Melbourne; an Indonesian consulate resides in Darwin. Canberra offices include:

Austria, 12 Talbot St., Forrest (tel. 06-295-1533)

Canada, Commonwealth Ave., Canberra (tel. 06-273-3844)

Germany, 119 Empire Circuit, Yarralumla (tel. 06-270-1951)

India, 3 Moonah Pl., Yarralumla (tel. 06-273-3999)

Indonesia, 8 Darwin Ave., Yarralumla (tel. 06-250-8600)

Ireland, 20 Arkana St., Yarralumla (tel. 06-273-3022)

Japan, 112 Empire Circuit, Yarralumla (tel. 06-273-3244)

Malaysia, 7 Perth Ave., Yarralumla (tel. 06-273-1543)

Netherlands, 120 Empire Circuit, Yarralumla (tel. 06-273-3111)

New Zealand, Commonwealth Ave., Yarralumla (tel. 06-270-4211)

Norway, 17 Hunter St., Yarralumla (tel. 06-273-3444)

Papua New Guinea, Forster Crescent, Yarralumla (tel. 06-273-3322)

Singapore, 17 Forster Crescent, Yarralumla (tel. 06-273-3944)

South Africa, State Circle, Yarralumla (tel. 06-273-2424)

Sweden, 5 Turrana St., Yarralumla (tel. 06-273-3033)

Switzerland, 7 Melbourne Ave., Forrest (tel. 06-273-3977)

Thailand, 111 Empire Circuit, Yarralumla (tel. 06-273-1149)

United Kingdom, Commonwealth Ave., Yarralumla (tel. 06-270-6666)

CUSTOMS

Australian Customs

Visitors may bring personal clothing and effects into Australia duty-free. If you're over 18 years old, you're also allowed 250 cigarettes or 250 grams of cigars or tobacco, in addition to one liter of wine, beer, or spirits (you must carry these items on you to qualify). Other taxable goods (up to $400 worth per adult and $200 per child under 18 years old) may be admitted duty-free if included inside personal baggage.

Drugs, weapons, and firearms are prohibited or restricted in Australia. Eager (and possibly kinky) German shepherds will be sniffing you as you wait to clear immigration. Drug laws are strictly enforced. Also, certain quarantined items such as meats (including dried meats), vegetables, honey, fruit, and flowers will be confiscated. Forget about bringing in items made from endangered species (an ivory mojo man in a polar bear fur pouch, for example), live animals (endangered or not), and certain types of nonapproved telecommunication devices. If you're not sure of something, *don't* try to smuggle it in—ask a customs agent. And if that doesn't suit you, drop the questionable article in the amnesty box.

Since you will probably not want to drop cash into the amnesty box, you should also know that persons carrying or sending cash and coins valuing A$5000 or more (in *any* country's currency) into or out of Australia must declare the money and fill out a report with the Australian Customs Service at the airport. Traveler's checks in any amount of Australian or foreign currency are exempt from this rule.

Aside from international customs, quarantines on fresh fruit, vegetables, and plants are in effect between states and territories. Eat everything up before you reach the state line.

International Customs

Each family member is allowed to bring back into the U.S. up to US$400 in duty-free goods; that is, if you're out of the U.S. for a minimum of 48 hours and haven't taken any other international journey in 30 days. Family members may combine their exemptions. Goods between $400 and $1400 are assessed at a flat 10% rate. If you're at least 21 years old, your allowance may include 100 cigars (no Cuban brands), 200 cigarettes, and one liter of wine, beer, or spirits. You may mail gifts, valued under $50, duty-free to friends or relatives—but don't send more than one package per day to any one person.

Canadians who have been abroad for less than eight days may bring back up to C$100 of goods duty-free. Those who have been away for eight days or more are allowed up to C$300 in merchandise. The duty-free allowance for Canadians includes up to 1.1 liter of spirits, one carton of cigarettes, and fifty cigars. Tax rates vary by item.

Travelers from the United Kingdom may bring home up to £32 of goods duty-free. In addition, goods such as wine, tobacco, and perfume are duty-free, and so is anything you've owned for longer than six months. The same regulations apply to items that are mailed home. The standard value-added tax rate for the U.K. is 17.5%.

Departure Tax

Unless you're a transit passenger who's been in the country less than 24 hours (in which case you probably wouldn't be reading this book), every person 12 years and older must pay a $27 departure tax when leaving Australia. To offset the cost of insulating houses under a new flight path, all passengers departing from Sydney must also pay an Airport Noise Levy of $3.40. In most cases, departure tax for all countries that you visit is added, or hidden, in the cost of your ticket.

DISTINCT INTERESTS

WOMEN

Most Aussie men come off as being pretty brusque and gruff—though they're not always that way deep under down under. In the outback—too few teeth, too many tattoos, remember?—they are macho and oftentimes big, mean, and hard-drinking. City men are easier to deal with but, in the end, women still must endure the usual cat-call and sexually explicit verbal assault. And worse—*much worse.*

Aussie men still consider their mates, cars, and sports atop the pecking order, with the women coming in last. The men are usually anything but gallant, but the Aussie women seem to take this in stride.

Always exercise common sense: don't walk alone late at night in the city (also city trains at night are not particularly safe); try to avoid bars and pubs—particularly outback pubs; don't hitchhike alone.

Conditions for women are slowly improving: less sexism in the media, more career opportunities, et al. There are women's resource centers, health clinics, and hotlines in every major city for help and assistance.

GAY AND LESBIAN

Well, *Priscilla, Queen of the Desert,* managed quite well, thank you, in her outback travels. But, will *you* if you're gay or lesbian?

Oddly enough, despite all of Australia's machismo, Sydney enjoys one of the world's largest and most active gay and (lipstick) lesbian scenes. Other cities and many country areas have gay-and-lesbian havens. Parades, gatherings, networks, and club-life are all part of the open lifestyle.

The outback, however, is not quite so accepting—those miners, ranchers, and truckers have been known to be a wee bit intolerant. Consequently, it might be best to keep your sexual preference under wraps in those circumstances.

Monthly gay and lesbian mags such as *Outrage* and *Campaign* provide current information as well as lists of services and resources. The Australian Gay and Lesbian Tourism Association, P.O. Box 429, North Sydney, NSW 2060 (tel. 02-9957-3811), publishes a homosexual-friendly accommodation guide.

TRAVELERS WITH DISABILITIES

Many of Australia's accommodations, restaurants, cinemas, and tourist attractions provide facilities and access for travelers with disabilities. Most newer buildings are equipped with wheel-chair access. Guides and booklets for travelers with disabilities, which include state and local organizations and travel specialists, can be obtained from **National Information Communication Awareness Network** (NICAN), P.O. Box 407, Curtin, ACT 2605 (tel. 06-285-3713, fax 285-3717).

HEALTH AND SAFETY

Yes, you can drink the water and eat your fruit unpeeled—Australian hygiene standards are high. Most city hospitals are well equipped, though you might run into problems in country towns, particularly on weekends, when some hospital laboratories are closed. If you're in the middle of the outback, you can have the well-trained Royal Flying Doctor Service soar to your aid (see "Outback Health and Education" under "The People" in the Introduction chapter).

Pharmacies (chemists) are readily available and stock most drugs, though often by their generic name. If you're taking medication, bring a supply and duplicate prescriptions with generic equivalents with you—and that goes for eyeglasses, too.

Take it easy until you get acclimated, especially if the weather is hot or humid, if you're traveling into the outback, or if you're planning any strenuous physical activities. Go slow, and work up to a pace you're comfortable with. Always carry a good first-aid kit and handbook (auto clubs and St. John ambulance service sell a selection of kits; and consider taking Moon Publications' *Staying Healthy in Asia, Africa, and Latin America*, an informative, practical first-aid handbook). In Sydney the **Traveller's Medical & Vaccination Centre,** Level 7, 428 George St. (tel. 02-9221-7133), is a good source of local medical information and sells a range of medical kits to suit all purposes.

The **International Association for Medical Assistance to Travellers** (IAMAT) provides a list of doctors worldwide with U.S. standards of medical training. For more information, contact IAMAT, 417 Center St., Lewiston, NY 14092 (tel. 716-754-4883). If you find yourself in a real medical nightmare, contact your country's consulate or embassy for emergency help.

Vaccinations

Vaccinations are not necessary if you're traveling from the United States, Canada, or the United Kingdom. If you've visited a yellow fever-infected country within six days of your arrival in Australia, you'll need appropriate inoculations.

Health Hazards

This is a country with one of the highest rates of skin cancer in the world. The sun is intense and the hole in the ozone layer is *wide*—wear sunblock and a hat whenever you're outdoors. Also, drink plenty of fluids to ward off possible dehydration. When traveling in outback areas, check in first with the automobile club, local police, or park rangers.

Other potential dangers include Australia's infamous poisonous snakes, those faster-than-you'd-care-to-imagine saltwater crocs, a few poisonous spiders, and the box jellyfish (see "Flora and Fauna" in the Introduction chapter). Obey all warning signs and, when in doubt, ask the locals.

Animals on the road, particularly at night, can also be deadly. When walking on coral reef, protect your feet with sturdy shoes. Seek prompt medical treatment for any coral cuts.

Health Insurance

Though a visit to the doctor's office might only cost $35 or so, other medical expenses can be quite hefty (for example, if you need an ambulance or search-and-rescue team). Make sure you have health insurance to adequately cover possible accidents and illness before you leave home; if you plan to take part in any dangerous sport or activity, make sure the policy covers it. Both Council Travel Services and STA offices, as well as most travel agents, can recommend reliable insurance companies. Cov-

FIRST AID

For expert first-aid information, see Moon Publications' *Staying Healthy in Asia, Africa, and Latin America,* by Dirk G. Schroeder, ScD, MPH.

Prevention
Be sensible! The ultraviolet rays are intense, the ozone hole wide, and the skin cancer rate very high. Even cloudy skies can cause a bad burn and—as for the super-bright outback—wow! Wear a hat and sunblock, drink plenty of water to avoid dehydration, go easy on booze and cigarettes, and you should be right, mates.

Exhaustion and Heat Exposure
It's *hot* in the outback. Keep a slow pace until you get acclimated. Get lots of rest, fill up on water, make sure you have enough salt in your diet, and avoid overexposure to the harsh sun. Wear loose, cotton clothing and your hat, of course. Beware of heatstroke. Symptoms include increased body temperature, a reduction in sweat, and occasional vomiting or nausea. Heatstroke is an emergency situation: the victim should be taken to a cool place, then doused, fanned, and sponged with cold water until body temperature drops to at least 39° C (102° F).

Traveler's Diarrhea
It doesn't matter how clean the place is, unfamiliar foods, overeating, too much drinking, and a variety of other factors can cause the runs. Again, be sensible until you get used to your new environment. If you do come down with Bali Belly or Montezuma's Revenge, ward off dehydration by drinking lots of fluids such as clear broth or soup, weak tea, or juice (*no* alcohol or coffee). Gradually add bland and boiled grub to your diet—rice, biscuits, bread, bananas.

Stings and Bites, Snakes and Beasties
Oz is renowned for its numerous evil snakes. Most won't attack unless provoked, but exceptions are the "fierce" tiger and taipan snakes (the most dangerous). For bites, apply a pressure bandage and splint, keep the victim calm and immobilized, and get medical help fast. Don't move the victim if at all possible; make sure someone stays behind in case artificial respiration is required.

Spiders to watch out for are the red-back (usually found in dunnies and toilets), the trap-doors (usually lurking in holes, with or without trap-door lids), and the funnel-web (only in Sydney!). Place ice on the affected area and seek prompt medical attention.

Know your nasty sea critters before you wiggle your toes in the water. The box jellyfish can inflict a fatal sting. Douse the area with vinegar, pull out tentacles, and procure immediate medical attention. Some other poisonous marine dwellers are the sea snake, the blue-ringed octopus, the scorpion fish, and the stonefish (which masquerades as a harmless piece of rock). Treat stings as for snake bites.

Finally, if you're attacked by a saltwater croc, well . . . *adios.*

Sexually Transmitted Diseases
There is AIDS in Oz. Use condoms. Period.

Help!
To summon emergency help, dial 000 (a free call) from any telephone. The Royal Flying Doctors can be contacted any time, any day, via HF (high-frequency) radios. These units can and should be rented by anyone venturing into very remote areas.

erage can also be obtained for emergency transportation, lost luggage, and trip cancellation. Holders of International Student Identity Cards receive automatic coverage up to certain limits. In any case, be sure to read all fine print.

Travel insurers include: **Travel Assistance International,** Suite 400, 1133 15th St. NW, Washington, D.C. 20005 (tel. 202-347-2025 or 800-821-2828); and **TravelGuard International,** 1145 Clark St., Stevens Point, WI 54481 (tel. 715-345-0505 or 800-782-5151).

MONEY

Note: All prices quoted in this guide are in Australian dollars (A$) unless otherwise noted.

Currency

Australian currency is based on the dollars-and-cents decimal system (100 cents equal one dollar). Notes, of different colors, come in denominations of $5, $10, $20, $50, and $100. Unfortunately the majority of $5, $10, $20, and $50 notes are new and improved, i.e., plasticky and indestructible; the paper notes are rapidly disappearing. Coins are in denominations of 5 cents, 10 cents, 20 cents, 50 cents, $1, and $2.

You may bring in or take out any amount of personal funds; however, if you're carrying or sending $5000 or more in Australian or foreign currency, you must file a form with the Australian Customs Service. You may also be required to furnish a report with customs agents in other countries.

Changing Money

Currency exchange facilities are available at all international airports, though many open only for incoming and outgoing flights. Larger hotels and most banks will also exchange foreign cash and traveler's checks (traveler's checks fetch a slightly higher exchange rate). Traveler's checks are easily cashed in the city (have identification with you) but can be a pain in rural communities.

Outback areas and smaller towns may only deal in hard cash; have a good stash of it before you head outback.

Banking hours are generally Mon.-Thurs. 9:30 a.m.-4 p.m., Friday 9 a.m.-5 p.m. A few of the larger city banks are open on Saturday morning—but don't count on it.

Credit Cards

The most commonly accepted credit cards are American Express, Bankcard, MasterCard, and Visa, and it shouldn't be a problem using them anywhere in Australia (but always carry some cash to be safe). Also, many rental agencies will only rent vehicles to customers with recognized credit cards.

Another advantage to the credit card is the ability to pull cash advances from ATMs (automatic teller machines), which are prevalent throughout Australian cities and towns.

Bank and Passbook Accounts

Another way to handle your funds (and to ensure easy access) is to open a local bank account, especially if you'll be in the country for several months. Commonwealth, National, ANZ, and Westpac are located nationwide. If you're a foreigner, you can open an account within six weeks of arrival in Australia, using just your passport for identification. After that the ante is upped—you'll need your passport, birth certificate, driver's license, credit cards, etc. Make sure to apply for an ATM (or cash) card. It takes about a week (you'll need an Australian address for delivery). Many of the banks accept each other's cards, so you'll have access to plenty of ATM machines across the country. Also, as in the U.S., many establishments such as petrol stations and supermarkets accept cash cards for payment.

Your home ATM card should work in Australia if it is designated for one of the following systems: Star, Cirrus, or Plus. Check with your issuing bank regarding use and service charges.

You can also open a passbook account at

CURRENCY EXCHANGE

As of April 1996, the Aussie dollar was trading at about US78 cents per A$1 (exchanging at about A$1.26 per US$1). Travelers with currency other than the almighty greenback should be able to exchange funds at most banks and airport money-changing facilities without problem. Current exchange rates (into A$) for other major currencies are:

C$1 = 93 cents
DM1 = 84 cents
HK$10 = $1.63
NZ$1 = 85 cents
UK£ = $1.91
¥100 = $1.16

the Commonwealth Bank. They'll give you a funky little booklet that you can use at all Australian post offices or post office agencies (as well as the Commonwealth Bank). A passbook with a blacklight signature is important, as some offices may require it. Also, the account normally has to be closed at the same branch where it was opened (if you're not planning to return to Australia for a long time, just use up the money in the account).

Costs

You've probably guessed, transport is the most expensive. The country is huge and transportation costs are comparatively high. Buying a rail, air, or coach pass, or going in on a car with others can be a real money saver. Fuel is more expensive than in the U.S. and Canada, but cheaper than in Europe; however, you'll probably use large quantities of it. Clothing is also fairly expensive. On the other hand, food and accommodations are both relatively cheap.

Tipping and Bargaining

Tipping is not mandatory in Australia. Your waitperson will not follow you into the street, meat cleaver in hand, for the extra 15-20%. Normally, tipping is done only in an expensive restaurant, or when service has been extra good—and then 10% will suffice. Leave taxi drivers the extra change to make the tab an even amount and they'll be happy.

Bargaining is confined to flea markets and some of the larger secondhand shops. It is downright offensive to do so with Aborigines for their arts and crafts.

Student and Senior Discounts

Students and seniors with proper photo identification (such as an International Student Identity Card) are eligible for "Concession" rates on many transportation services and at attractions, cinemas, and entertainment venues.

Check with the ticket office before you purchase your ticket.

COMMUNICATIONS AND MEDIA

COMMUNICATIONS

Postal Services

The mail averages a whopping seven to 10 days or longer between Australia and North America or Europe—going either direction. Domestic service, however, is relatively efficient (barring postal strikes).

General post offices and branches will hang onto your mail, free of charge, for up to a month. Alternatively, American Express cardholders can have mail sent to city American Express offices, to be held for later pick-up.

Post office hours are Mon.-Fri. 9 a.m.-5 p.m. There is no Saturday mail delivery. Stamps can also be purchased at some hotels, motels, and from newsagents. A domestic stamp costs 45 cents; to the U.S. and Canada, stamps are 95 cents for postcards and $1.05 for letters.

Main post offices have philatelic desks, which sell sets of souvenir stamps ranging from poignant and historical to political and colorful.

Outback mail runs operate weekly via truck or plane (see "Getting Around," earlier).

Telephone

Telstra (formerly Telecom Australia) has followed the deregulation path of AT&T. A second company, Optus, now offers alternative service—on long-distance and international calls—in the big-user cities. The result is the same kind of confusion, special access codes, varying rates, and endless advertising perks and bribes that occurred after U.S. telephone deregulation.

Basically, if you're not a player in the Telstra/Optus game, the telephone system is easy to master and efficiently operated.

Local calls from pay phones (i.e., coin boxes) cost 40 cents. Telstra phone cards can also be purchased in $2, $5, and $10 amounts from chemists (pharmacies), newsagents, and other shops. Some phones accept only credit or bank cash cards and, though convenient, are more expensive.

Almost all public phones are equipped for STD (subscriber trunk dialing) and ISD (international subscriber dialing). Just keep feeding coins into the slots (you can use one-dollar pieces, if you like). There is no three-minute

TELEPHONE ALERT

As of this writing, Austel (Australian Telecommunications Authority) is in the process of changing the country's telephone-number system. The restructuring process, begun in 1994 and due for completion by 1999, will shrink Australia's previous 54 area codes down to a paltry four: New South Wales and Australian Capital Territory, 02; Victoria and Tasmania, 03; Queensland, 07; South Australia, Western Australia, and the Northern Territory, 08. Ultimately all telephone numbers will consist of eight digits. In larger cities, where numbers are currently seven digits, an additional digit will be attached to the front. In country and rural regions, existing six-digit numbers will receive two extra digits (probably the last two digits of what was the previous area code). The point of this is to make more telephone numbers available. (For what, the exploding population???) Anyway, for six months callers will be able to reach both old and new numbers; for another few months, a recorded message will inform callers to "let their fingers do the walking."

minimum and unused change will be returned when you hang up.

When placing international calls, dial 0011 (the international access code), the country code, the city code, and then the desired phone number. From private phones it's about $1.50 per minute to the U.S. or U.K. (discounted midnight-8 a.m. and on Sunday); on pay phones it's much more.

Operator-assisted calls can be placed from any phone, though fees for reverse-charge (collect) and person-to-person calls run $6-8. Credit card phones are now installed in many airports, hotels, and post offices. Refer to the front pages of the local telephone book for dialing information and charges. Try not to make any long-distance calls from big hotels—the surcharges are usually astronomical and can double or triple the actual cost of the call.

Country Direct allows travelers to access operators in their home countries (more than 40 countries are hooked up to the service) for easier, and maybe cheaper, credit card, calling card, or collect calls. To the U.S. operator, call (1800) 88-1011 (AT&T), (1800) 88-1877 (Sprint), or (1800) 88-1100 (MCI). To Canada, call (1800) 88-1150. For other countries, refer to the local telephone book or call the international operator.

Toll free numbers have the prefix 1800; companies such as airlines and other transport ser-

vices often have six-digit numbers beginning with 13, meaning it is charged as a local call even if it's cross-country; the prefix 018 is an example designation for mobile phones; and nine-digit numbers, beginning with 0055, are usually psychic, sex, lonely-hearts, or do-it-yourself lines.

In this land of few and far between, **fax** machines are used everywhere, including the outback. Almost every post office provides a fax calling and receiving service.

In remote outback locations, both CB and HF (high-frequency) radios play an important part in communications. CBs are used mainly for vehicles to keep in contact with each other, while HF radios are used to summon medical help, provide education, spread community information—and gossip. Licenses are necessary for both types of radio. Telstra (OTC), with government-controlled frequencies, will most likely take over future communications for the Royal Flying Doctor Service.

In **emergencies,** dial 000 to summon help.

MEDIA

Newspapers and Magazines

The most respected daily newspapers are *Sydney Morning Herald* and Melbourne's *Age.* Ordinarily available in the major cities and many small towns (even if a day or so old), they might not hit the outback stands at all. Other city newspapers are Brisbane's *Courier Mail,* Adelaide's *Advertiser,* Darwin's *Northern Territory News,* and Perth's *West Australian.* The monthly *Adelaide Review* lists theater, gallery, and restaurant reviews while *Rip it Up* and *dB* are free music and street-happening mags available at bars, clubs, and record shops. For entertainment news in Perth, pick up a free copy of *X-Press,* Australia's biggest weekly music magazine, also available at record shops as well as many other locations. Australia has two national dailies: the

Australian and the *Australian Financial Review.*

Australian editions of *Time, Vogue, Cosmopolitan,* and other international magazines, plus worldwide newspapers (like *USA Today*) and foreign-language press are sold at many news agencies. Most newsagents, in fact, stock an astonishing array of specialty magazines. Two "women's mags," *New Idea* and *Woman's Weekly,* will assure that you never are out-of-touch with the U.K.'s latest royal scandals.

Radio and Television

The independent, government-funded ABC (Australian Broadcasting Corporation) is the national television and radio network. Often its programs are all you will hear or see in rural areas, though the major cities and towns will feature two or three regionally based commercial stations. Stations frequently televise nearly-first-run movies, as well as some excellent foreign films. The government-sponsored SBS beams excellent multicultural news and entertainment, along with uncensored films, to all state capitals.

American look-alike programming includes the *Today Show, 60 Minutes,* and several genre dating game, newlywed, quiz, and love connection shows—plus MTV. You can also catch the U.S. *Today Show, Oprah, Entertainment Tonight,* and *Late Show with David Letterman* in many locales, and—never fear—*Roseanne* is part of the regular programming (although it's about a year or so behind).

Alice Springs-based Imparja is an Aboriginal-run station that broadcasts many types of programs, including some produced by and for Aborigines, over about one-third of Australia.

The ABC, which operates radio stations in many of the cities, can be picked up in all parts of Australia. Other listening options (AM and FM) include everything from rock and Muzak to talk shows and community services.

MAPS AND TOURIST INFORMATION

MAPS

Tourist offices and automobile clubs are gold mines for free and cheap maps. Rand McNally, with several locations, is an excellent supplier: 595 Market St., San Francisco, CA 94105 (tel. 415-777-3131); 150 E. 52nd St., New York City, NY 10022 (tel. 212-758-7488); 444 N. Michigan Ave., Chicago, IL 60611 (tel. 312-321-1751). Also try Eliot Bay Book Company, 101 S. Main St., Seattle, WA 98104 (tel. 206-624-6600). Other good sources are Magellan Travel Books (tel. 800-303-0011 U.S.) and South Pacific Travelers Boursource (tel. 800-234-4552 U.S.)

For outback travel, you might want to obtain topographic sheets from AUSLIG (Australian Surveying & Land Information Group), the country's mapping agency. For information or a catalog, contact AUSLIG, Department of Administrative Services, P.O. Box 2, Belconnen, ACT 2616 (tel. 06-201-4300).

TOURIST INFORMATION

Tourist Offices

There's no lack of Tourist Information Centres in Australia. All of the states and territories have branch offices in major city centers—veritable treasure troves of details on tours, attractions, sports, accommodations, package deals, car and campervan rentals, and local and interstate transportation. Most of these centers will make bookings for you, and all will load you with brochures. Additionally, almost every country town has an information center—albeit an office, petrol station, or museum—marked by the international "I" sign. Hours are usually Mon.-Fri. 9 a.m.-5 p.m., Saturday 9 a.m.-1 p.m. Centers in heavily touristed areas are often open on Sunday as well.

Main **state tourist offices** are:

Canberra Tourist Bureau, Northbourne Ave., Canberra, ACT 2601 (tel. 1800-02-6166 toll-free)

Darwin Regional Tourism Association Information Centre, 33 Smith St., Darwin, NT 0800 (tel. 08-8981-4300)

Central Australian Tourism Industry Association, Ford Plaza Building, Todd Mall, Alice Springs, NT 0871 (tel. 08-8952-5199)

Queensland Government Travel Centre, 196 Adelaide St., Brisbane, QLD 4000 (tel. 07-3221-6111)

Far North Queensland Promotion Bureau, corner of Grafton and Hartley Streets, Cairns, QLD 4870 (tel. 070-51-3588)

South Australian Tourism Commission Travel Centre, 1 King William St., Adelaide, SA 5000 (tel. 08-8212-1505)

Tasmanian Travel Centre, 80 Elizabeth St., Hobart, TAS 7000 (tel. 03-6230-0250)

RACV Victorian Tourism Centre, 230 Collins St., Melbourne, VIC 3000 (tel. 03-9650-1522)

Western Australia Tourist Centre, corner Forrest Place and Wellington St., Perth, WA 6000 (tel. 09-483-1111)

Overseas Tourist Offices

For information on travel to Australia *before* your trip, contact the nearest office of the **Australian Tourist Commission.**

United States, Suite 1200, 2121 Avenue of the Stars, Los Angeles, CA 90067 (tel. 310-552-1988); 31st floor, 489 5th Ave., New York, NY 10017 (tel. 212-687-6300)

United Kingdom, Gemini House, 10-18 Putney Hill, London, England SW15 6AA (tel. 081-780-2227)

Germany, Neue Mainzerstrasse 22, D60311 Frankfurt am Main (tel. 069-274-0060)

New Zealand, Level 13, 44-48 Emily Place, Auckland 1, New Zealand (tel. 09-379-9594)

Hong Kong, Suite 1006, Central Plaza, 18 Harbour Rd., Wanchai, Hong Kong (tel. 802-7700)

Singapore, Suite 1703, 17th floor, United Square, 101 Thomson Rd., Singapore 1130 (tel. 255-4555)

Osaka, 4th floor, Yuki Building, 3-3-9 Hiranomachi, Chuo-ku, Osaka 541, Japan (tel. 06-229-3601)

Tokyo, 8th floor, Sankaido Building, 1-9-13 Akasaka, Minato-ku, Tokyo, 107 Japan (tel. 03-3582-2191)

For the **head office** of the Australian Tourist Commission, contact: Level 3, 80 William St., Woolloomooloo (Sydney), NSW 2011 (tel. 02-9360-1111).

The tourist commission also produces *Destination Australia,* a free, magazine-format guide with tempting photos, sample itineraries, and listings of transport companies and tour operators. To order, phone (800) 333-0262 (U.S.).

Aussie Helplines

Aussie Helplines work in conjunction with the Australian Tourist Commission to answer questions, offer travel tips, assist with itinerary planning, and mail out brochures. Free travel information sheets are available on many aspects of Australia, including sports, beaches, diving, Aboriginal Australia, nightlife, backpacking, surfing, etc. For more information in the U.S. and Canada, phone (708) 296-4900, Mon.-Fri. 8 a.m.-7 p.m. central standard time.

Other Helpful Information

Hostels, airports, and coach depots carry quite a few free publications and brochures for travelers—everything from fruit-picking information to accommodation options. Especially useful are *For Backpacker By Backpackers, Aussie Backpacker, Backpacker's Guide,* and *Go Oz YHA Magazine.*

Available for purchase at newsagents is *Travel Times,* an inexpensive timetable of all coach, train, and ferry schedules throughout Australia.

Automobile Associations

Australian automobile clubs offer reciprocal rights to members of the American Automobile Club and the United Kingdom's RAC and AA (bring your membership card with you). The **Australian Automobile Association**'s services include free roadside emergency breakdown service (within certain city limits), route maps, touring information, discounted travel guides, and accommodation and camping directories. Many offices will make tour and accommodations reservations for you.

The **main state offices** are: **Australian Automobile Association** (AAA Head Office), G.P.C

Box 1555, Canberra, ACT 2601 (tel. 06-247-7311); **National Roads and Motorists Association** (NRMA), 151 Clarence St., Sydney, NSW 2000 (tel. 02-9260-9222), or 92 Northbourne Ave., Canberra, ACT 2601 (tel. 06-243-8826); **Automobile Association of the Northern Territory** (AANT), 79-81 Smith St., Darwin, NT 0800 (tel. 08 8981-3837); **Royal Automobile Club of Queensland** (RACQ), 300 St. Pauls Terrace, Fortitude Valley, QLD 4006 (tel. 07-3361-2444); **Royal Automobile Association of South Australia** (RAA), 41 Hindmarsh Square, Adelaide, SA 5000 (tel. 08-8223-4500); **Royal Automobile Club of Tasmania** (RACT), corner Patrick and Murray Streets, Hobart, TAS 7001 (tel. 03-6238-2200); **Royal Automobile Club of Victoria** (RACV), 550 Princes Highway, Noble Park, VIC 3174 (tel. 03-9790-2627); **Royal Automobile Club of Western Australia** (RACWA), 228 Adelaide Terrace, Perth, WA 6000 (tel. 09-421-4444).

WHAT TO TAKE

Clothing

Australians are casual dressers. Follow the old, basic rule: Dress for comfort and climate. If you're going to the tropical north, take lightweight cottons, which are suitable year-round. (Shorts are okay most places.) The southern temperate regions also call for cottons and other natural fibers during summer months; winters can be very cold there, so pack a heavy sweater and jacket. The outback will be searing during the summer, giving way to chilly nights in winter. And rain can drop any time, unexpectedly, and in great torrents; you might want to include a light raincoat and an umbrella in your suitcase. It's always well advised to dress in layers, particularly due to rapidly changing weather conditions in many regions.

Outback Clothing

For the authentic outback Aussie look in warmer months, outfit yourself in a singlet (sleeveless T-shirt), a pair of shorts (Stubbies are the Oz favorite), heavy socks, and Blundstone boots (they have elastic sides, last forever, but are somewhat costly). You'll definitely need a hat, so, if you still have some clothing budget left, pick up an Akubra (the Aussie working-bloke's Stetson).

Et Cetera

Other articles to bring along are a sunhat, sunglasses, sunscreen, sturdy walking shoes (again, broken-in *before* arrival), and waterproof sneakers for coral reef-walking. You might also want to pack a voltage converter, adapter plugs, insect repellent, prescription medications, and an extra pair of eyeglasses or contact lenses. Most brands of cosmetics, toiletries, and over-the-counter medications are readily available at chemist shops (pharmacies).

Et Cetera Et Cetera

Pack light. Leave room in your backpack or luggage for necessities (and souvenirs) that you'll collect along the way. Bring a sheet sack if you'll be doing the hostel routine, as well as your usual camping gear. Don't forget any required permits (which you should have obtained beforehand), maps, and a good, ahem, *guidebook*. Special equipment, swags or other camp bedding, cooking equipment, first-aid kits and such, can all be purchased in Australia—and may be better suited to the unique environment than the closer-to-civilization gear you may be used to. Often you can pick up good deals on used equipment from departing travelers at hostels. If you sign up for an organized tour, many operators provide many needed items. You can pick up the fly net to wear over your face after you arrive in Australia.

FILM AND PHOTOGRAPHY

Film and Processing

Film, processing labs, and photo equipment are easy finds in Australian cities. Bring your own 35mm camera and lenses. Unless you're coming in via Singapore or Hong Kong, it's unnecessary to stock up on film beforehand; Australian film costs about the same as in North America or Europe. You'll also find many "one-hour" photo shops with speedy processing for those on the move.

Photo Tips

Special conditions to be aware of are: intensity of light, particularly in the outback; temperature extremes (try to keep film cool and dry); outback dust; and, in the country's far north, tropical humidity.

Best times for taking photos are early morning and late afternoon. A polarizing filter will help minimize washout.

As for those airport X-ray machines—if you're worried about your film (especially any over 400 ASA), carry it in a lead-lined bag and/or request hand inspection.

Photo Etiquette

Do not photograph Aboriginals without their permission—which you probably won't get. They do not like having their photos taken—and that includes crowd and distance shots.

WEIGHTS AND MEASURES

Measurements

Australia uses the metric system, like almost every other country in the world. Temperatures are in Celsius (C). (See the conversion tables at the back of this book.)

Electrical Voltage

Australia's electrical current is 240/250 volts, 50Hz AC. You'll need a **three-pin adapter plug** (different from the British three-pronger) for any 110-volt appliances you intend to bring, as well as the appropriate **voltage converter.** It's best to purchase adapter plugs and converters before arrival, though both are available in the larger cities. If you're bringing a computer or other specialized equipment, be sure to check with the manufacturer for exact requirements.

Time Zones

Australia has three time zones. New South Wales, Australian Capital Territory, Victoria, Tasmania, and Queensland operate on **eastern standard time** (EST); South Australia and the Northern Territory use **central standard time** (CST); and Western Australia has its very own **western standard time** (WST).

Here is the confusing part: central standard time is half an hour behind eastern standard

time, while western standard time is two hours behind eastern standard time. And all of the states except Western Australia, Queensland, and the Northern Territory go on **summer time** (daylight saving time) from October to March, when clocks are set ahead one hour. And Tasmania keeps to daylight saving time one month longer than the others. It's no wonder the Aborigines keep to Dreamtime!

TIME ZONES
(EAST OF GREENWICH)

NEW SOUTH WALES
INTRODUCTION

Although New South Wales is the most populous of Australia's six states and two territories, in many places it's remarkably remote, especially west of the Great Dividing Range, a ridge of ancient mountains that parallels Australia's entire east coast. Because of New South Wales's relatively small size (10% of the continent's total area), most destinations are within one day's drive of the state capital, Sydney. The beaches are one of New South Wales's best-known features, but the state boasts more than sun, sand, and surf. Whether it be schussing down snow-covered slopes, fishing and boating on magnificent river systems, exploring ghost towns, sampling world-class wines, or hiking through lush rainforests, New South Wales has something for everyone.

LAND

New South Wales, on the east coast of Australia, is bordered by Queensland to the north,

Victoria to the south, and South Australia to the west, with the eastern border a 1,400-km stretch of magnificent coastline. Most of the state's residents live along the coast, with over half of the population living in Sydney, the birthplace of modern Australia and Australia's largest city. Sydney lies on a convoluted harbor, with downtown concentrated around Sydney Cove, and it's surrounded on three sides by land set aside as national park. South of Sydney are long stretches of unspoilt and uncrowded beaches and small seaside communities. The Australian Capital Territory, home to the national capital Canberra, 250 km southwest of Sydney, boasts many fine civic buildings. Beyond Canberra are the Snowy Mountains, including Mt. Kosciusko, Australia's highest point, and a winter playground of ski resorts. West of Sydney are the Blue Mountains, a vast expanse of spectacular wilderness right on Sydney's back doorstep. Beyond the mountains is the Golden West, an area of stately old towns dating from successive gold rushes. Much of western New South

© MOON PUBLICATIONS, INC.

Wales is outback and the entire western portion of the state comprises a flat, dry, and barren land dominated by sheep farms and the odd town or settlement. Immediately north of Sydney is the industrial city of Newcastle, gateway to a string of beautiful beaches and the wine-producing Hunter Valley. From Newcastle there are two routes north to Queensland. The inland route, the New England Highway, passes through north-central New South Wales and the country music capital of Australia, Tamworth. The Pacific Highway, the coastal route, extends the entire length of the north coast, along a seemingly endless stretch of seaside towns, national parks, and long strips of sand. Few travelers on the route between Sydney and Brisbane fail to stop at Byron Bay, a melting pot of Australian cultures backed by a beautiful hinterland of rainforested national parks.

Climate

Temperatures in Sydney are pleasant year-round, but the city is far enough south to get reasonably cold in winter. During the months of summer, the climate can be very humid, especially along the coast north of Sydney. West of the Great Dividing Range summer temperatures can be unbearably hot, making travel unpleasant and, in the extreme west, dangerous. Spring and fall are pleasant throughout the state, and these are probably the best times of year to travel (and you'll miss the maddening summer crowds). Winter on the far north coast, with daytime temperatures averaging 15° C (59° F), is pleasant, while in the mountainous region in the state's south, a blanket of snow extends thousands of square kilometers. Snow occasionally falls as far north as Armidale.

HISTORY

Archaeological finds in Mungo National Park, in the southwest of the state, point to human habitation up to 30,000 years ago. Aboriginals probably lived throughout the state during this time, their nomadic lifestyle changing with long-term weather patterns, such as successive ice ages. The Aboriginals' first contact with Europeans came in 1770, when Capt. James Cook landed at Botany Bay, claiming possession of the east coast for England. A few years later, with British jails overcrowded, the British government decided to send prisoners to the unknown continent down under. The First Fleet, of which over half the people were convicts, found life at Sydney Cove difficult. Crops failed, more and more convicts arrived, and a succession of governors was unable to control the rebellious officers. Expansion was at first slow, and by the early 1800s, the only other settlements were a few penal colonies along the coast north of Sydney Town; inland exploration had been nonexistent. That all changed in 1813, when three landowners crossed the Blue Mountains in search of greener pastures. Settlers streamed

New South Wales is dotted with historic sandstone buildings from the convict era, including this one, the Surveyor General Inn, Berrima.

westward, clearing the land and establishing the crops that were so important to Australia's self-sufficiency. The next mass exodus inland from Sydney occurred within weeks of the discovery of gold near Bathurst in 1851.

At the turn of the 20th century, the six colonies scattered in all corners of the continent federated to form the Commonwealth of Australia. Sydney and Melbourne both had strong claims as the new national capital, so as a compromise, a site for the Australian Capital Territory was chosen halfway between the two and the modern city of Canberra was built. Since that time, while Sydney has evolved into one of the world's great multicultural cities, the face of coastal and rural New South Wales has changed little.

SYDNEY

In a little over 200 years since the first shiploads of convicts landed in Port Jackson, Sydney has grown to become one of the world's great cities. Sydney's dominant feature is magnificent **Sydney Harbour,** a waterway that often draws comparisons between Sydney and San Francisco. The harbor's shoreline extends over 300 km. Around the outer heads, the coastline is protected by national park and reserves. Farther into the bay, the houses that reflect the trappings and wealth of the Lucky Country are

Bondi Beach

perched on the rocky shoreline, which is broken occasionally by slivers of sand. The city center lies on the southern side of the harbor, a few km from the open ocean. This collection of high-rises is surrounded by inner-city suburbs such as The Rocks, birthplace of modern Australia, and the famous red-light district Kings Cross. On the north side of the harbor, linked to downtown by Sydney Harbour Bridge, are the affluent northern suburbs, and the coastline along which Sydney lies boasts 32 sandy beaches, with famous Bondi Beach closest to downtown.

Sydney has never had long-term development plans. Instead, it's seen 200 years of expansion in ever-increasing circles from the original colony at Sydney Cove (now Circular Quay). City limits extend south to Port Hacking, north to the Hawkesbury River, and west to the Blue Mountains, well over 5,000 square km in total. Don't underestimate Sydney's size. It's the world's largest city in area (officially, Mt. Isa in Queensland is larger in area, but this is only through a quirk of town planning), so plan any sightseeing carefully or you may spend half the day just getting to your destination. Within this massive urban sprawl, over 750 suburbs house 3,460,000 residents (20% of Australia's total population).

HISTORY

The First Fleet
Throughout the 1700s Britain had been selling their unwanted criminals to the colonies of North America, but after the War of Independence they had to find somewhere else to dump them. The massive continent down under was first suggested in 1783. And four years later the First Fleet left England. The fleet, led by Capt.

SYDNEY

TO NEWCASTLE

HAWKESBURY RIVER

PACIFIC HWY

BROKEN BAY
BARRENJOEY HEAD
PALM BEACH

BEROWRA

KU-RING-GAI

AKUNA BAY

CHASE

PITTWATER

AVALON

NEWPORT

WARATAH PARK

N. P.

MONA VALE

WINDSOR

HAWKESBURY RIVER

RIVERSTONE

DURAL

HORNSBY

TURRAMURRA

ST. IVES

NARRABEEN

KOALA PARK SANCTUARY

PENNANT HILLS

GARIGAL N.P.

FEATHERDALE WILDLIFE PARK

CASTLE HILL

ROSEVILLE

ST. MARYS

LANE COVE N.P.

SEE "SYDNEY HARBOUR AND ENVIRONS" MAP

BLACKTOWN

PARRAMATTA

CHATSWOOD

MANLY

WESTERN

EASTERN CREEK

MOTORWAY

NORTH SYDNEY

TO BLUE MOUNTAINS AND GOLDEN WEST

SYDNEY OLYMPIC PARK

CONCORD

VAUCLUSE

STRATHFIELD

(M4)

BADGERYS CREEK

LIDCOMBE

FAIRFIELD

ENFIELD

SYDNEY

CABRAMATTA

BANKSTOWN

CANTERBURY

BONDI

0   10 km

RANDWICK

MASCOT

PAGEWOOD

COOGEE

GEORGES RIVER N.P.

HURSTVILLE

SYDNEY AIRPORT

MAROUBRA

LITTLE BAY

LA PEROUSE

OCEAN

HUME HWY.

BOTANY BAY

CAMPBELLTOWN

31

BOTANY BAY N.P.

TO SOUTHERN HIGHLANDS AND CANBERRA

SUTHERLAND

CRONULLA

PACIFIC

HEATHCOTE

BUNDEENA

PRINCES HWY.

TO WOLLONGONG AND SOUTH COAST

ROYAL N.P.

SOUTH

Arthur Phillip, comprised 11 ships and 1,044 people. Of the ships, six were filled with convicts (numbering around 730), three with enough supplies to last the new colony for two years, and two warships for protection. The fleet was bound for Botany Bay, south of present-day downtown Sydney. This waterway had been explored by Capt. James Cook in 1770, at the same time he took possession of the east coast for England. Captain Phillip found it unsuitable for settlement and headed north to Port Jackson (best known as Sydney Harbour), named by Cook but not explored. They dropped anchor on 26 January 1788 with Phillip noting in his diary that it was "the finest natural harbor in the world."

Early Settlement

Phillip's site for settlement, on land dense with trees, sloping gently to the harbor, and with fresh water provided by the Tank Stream, was named **Sydney Cove** for Secretary of State of the colonies, Lord Sydney.

The new colony experienced problems from day one. From early writings, it seems the first arrivals were impressed by the beauty of Sydney Harbour, but the task of becoming self-sufficient was beyond them. They found the soil parched and barren, unlike anything they knew in England. The idea was to put the convicts to work clearing land, establishing crops, and building permanent structures. But most convicts were city born and bred: petty thiefs, pick-pockets, prostitutes, and cardsharps that had never done a day's manual labor in their lives. The marines sent to guard them were also of city stock, unfamiliar with toiling on the land. Living on the rim of an unknown continent (that no one even knew was an island) was tough for everyone. Floggings and hangings were part of everyday life, crops failed, and seasons were reversed.

While the settlers appealed to the British Government for more supplies, exploration parties found suitable pastoral land west of Sydney Cove at Parramatta and along the Hawkesbury River. In early 1790, the *Lady Juliana* dropped anchor in Sydney Cove. She carried supplies, 225 female convicts, and the first news from the outside world in two years.

Formulative Years

In the first decades, with the population slowly increasing, the area of the colony expanded rapidly. After Captain Phillip returned to England in 1792, conditions in Sydney Town deteriorated as the power of officers increased. Morale was reflected in the comments of one respected member of the community, who stated that there was "not a single article in the whole country that in the nature of things could prove of the smallest use or advantage to the mother country or the commercial world." A succession of governors—first Hunter, then King and Bligh—tried to strip the officers of power that they had slowly developed, but to no avail. Cap-

St. Mary's, one of many cathedrals in Sydney

tain Bligh, best known for being mutineered on his ship the *Bounty,* was a strict disciplinarian. Led by one of the colony's richest landowners, John MacArthur, a group of officers marched on Government House and arrested Bligh as being unfit to hold office. The next governor was Colonel Lachlan Macquarie. Upon arrival in Sydney Town in 1809 with his own regiment of officers, he set about securing the long-term future of the colony, building the first paved roads, erecting public buildings, and setting aside Hyde Park for public recreation. In 1840, transportation of convicts was abolished. By this time over 100,000 wretched souls had been exiled to Australia.

20th Century

The allure of a new and exciting life down under had seen thousands of Anglo-Saxons stream into Sydney and other major Australian ports through the second half of the 1800s. By the time of Federation in 1901, Sydney was a thriving city of 500,000 people. By the time the Sydney Harbour Bridge had been built, 30 short years later, the population had topped one million.

Apart from a few thousand Chinese who had remained after coming to Australia seeking their fortune on the goldfields, Sydney's population at the time of WW II was made up almost entirely of Brits. After the war, the Australian government began paying the passage of other Europeans to immigrate. Within a decade, Sydney had changed from an Anglo-Irish enclave to one of the world's most cosmopolitan cities. And in this same decade the population doubled again. During the Vietnam War, Sydney became a favorite haunt of U.S. servicemen on R&R. Thousands of them descended on Kings Cross, then a quiet suburban neighborhood, turning it into a 24-hour party zone of strip joints, bars, and brothels. In this same period, a building boom saw the construction of many downtown high-rise buildings, and the urban sprawl continued marching westward. By the time the 1980s had rolled around, Sydney had grown to become one of the world's great cities. The city, and Australia, celebrated its bicentenary in 1988 with much fanfare, an event that will surely be equaled in 2000 when Sydney hosts the Summer Olympic Games.

CITY CENTER SIGHTS

Downtown extends from Central Station in the south to Circular Quay in the north and is bounded by Hyde Park and Macquarie St. to the east and Chinatown and Darling Harbour to the west. The city has no real "center," but Martin Place, a five-block-long pedestrian mall, is pretty central and a popular meeting place. The business district, where the head offices of many major banks and insurance offices lie, is between King St. and Circular Quay. The original Government House, now long gone, was at the junction of Bridge and Phillip Streets, with the original layout of streets leading like spokes to the center of a wheel. Some of the "spokes" remain, now leading nowhere. **George St.,** the city center's main thoroughfare, was originally a track used by convicts hauling bricks along the west bank of the Tank Stream. This street runs the entire length of downtown. Halfway along is the French Renaissance-style **Town Hall** (1889), which hous-

Queen Victoria Building

es one of the world's largest pipe organs. Adjacent, the magnificent **Queen Victoria Building,** originally the city markets, was restored to its former glory in the mid-1980s. From Town Hall, Park St. leads east through Hyde Park to William St., which is lined with car showrooms and car rental outlets, to Kings Cross. Apart from the bustle of Chinatown, the area south of Park St. is uninspiring, an area where future urban planners have their work cut out.

Sydney Tower

On top of the Centrepoint complex, in the heart of the city, is Sydney Tower, the Southern Hemisphere's highest public building. This distinctive 300-meter-high landmark is topped by a massive viewing gallery and two revolving restaurants. At street level, high-speed elevators whisk visitors from the Centrepoint complex (easiest entrance is from Market St.) to the Podium Level, then it's all aboard double-decker lifts to the Observation Level. Needless to say, views from the top are magnificent, extending west to the Blue Mountains, east over the Pacific Ocean, and south to Wollongong. The Observation Level (tel. 02-9229-7444) is open Sun.-Fri. 9:30 a.m.-9:30 p.m., Saturday 9:30 a.m.-11:30 p.m. On the other levels of Sydney Tower are Australia's highest coffee lounge and two other restaurants (see "Harbor Views" under "Downtown Dining," below).

Australian Museum

Recognized as one of the world's best natural history museums, the Australian Museum's impressive displays of Aboriginal culture, the Pacific Islands, minerals, and massive whale skeletons, various models of marine mammals, and a collection of Australian flora and fauna make it well worth visiting. Admission is adult $5, child $2. Open daily 9:30 a.m.-5 p.m. It's at 6 College St. (tel. 02-9320-6000). The closest railway station is Museum, from where the museum is a short walk across Hyde Park.

MACQUARIE STREET

After coming to power in 1809, Governor Macquarie began Sydney's first building program, putting an end to the maze of twisting streets and the haphazard array of structures around Sydney Cove. His vision of wide streets and large areas of public parkland was implemented with the laying out of Macquarie St. and the commissioning of Francis Greenway to design a row of important civic buildings along its eastern flank. Greenway, interestingly enough, was a convict who had been sent to Australia for fraud.

Parliament House

Parliament House, seat of the New South Wales state legislature, is a grand old colonial building that was Sydney's first hospital. Originally known as the Rum Hospital (contractors were given a monopoly on the rum trade for their labor), parts of the building date from 1811. It was first used as a parliamentary building in 1829.

On days that parliament is sitting, visitors can view proceedings from the public gallery after 9:30 a.m. On other days, free tours are offered Mon.-Fri. 10 a.m.-4 p.m. For further details, call (02) 9230-2111. The nearest railway station is St. James.

Sydney Mint Museum

Another wing of the Rum Hospital, used for a time to mint coins, is a museum dedicated to the work of the goldsmiths and silversmiths who, through Australia's short history, created an astonishing array of jewelry and ornaments from the precious gems upon which much of Australia's early wealth was created. Admission is adult $5, child $2. Open daily 10 a.m.-5 p.m. (tel. 02-9217-0311).

Hyde Park Barracks

Designed by Francis Greenway, this Georgian-style building was originally constructed in 1819 as accommodations for convicts. Today it houses a small museum that catalogs the social history of Australia from the First Settlement to the European immigration of the 1950s. Admission is adult $5, child $3. Open daily 10 a.m.-5 p.m. It's on Queen's Square (tel. 02-9223-8922).

Art Gallery of New South Wales

A short walk through Hyde Park's Domain from Macquarie St. is the Art Gallery of New South Wales on Art Gallery Rd. (tel. 02-9225-1744). For recorded gallery information, call (02) 9225-1790. The complex consists of two wings. The earlier one, built at the turn of the century, hous-

ROYAL BOTANIC GARDENS

STATE LIBRARY

SYDNEY HOSPITAL
SYDNEY MINT MUSEUM
HYDE PARK BARRACKS

COLLEGE ST.

HYDE PARK

RITZ-CARLTON SYDNEY
HOTEL INTER-CONTINENTAL SYDNEY

MacQUARIE ST.

PHILLIP ST.

CHIFLEY PLAZA

PARLIAMENT HOUSE

PLACE

ST. JAMES STATION

LOFTUS

ELIZABETH
CASTLEREAGH

SKYGARDEN
IMPERIAL ARCADE
CENTREPOINT/ SYDNEY TOWER

SHERATON ON THE PARK
CRITERION HOTEL

REGENT OF SYDNEY

TRAVEL BOOKSHOP

BRIDGE ST.

PHILLIP ST.

HUNTER

AMERICAN EXPRESS

MLC CENTRE

PITT

POST OFFICE

MARTIN

ST.

PITT ST.

MALL

STRAND ARCADE

STATE THEATRE

SYDNEY HILTON

PARK ST.

PAXTON'S
AUSTRALIA SQUARE TOWER
ALL SEASONS PREMIER MENZIES

GEORGE

ST.

QUEEN VICTORIA BUILDING

JAMISON ST.

WYNYARD PARK

KENT STREET THEATRE

DYMOCKS & TRAVELLER'S MEDICAL CENTRE/ CONTACT POINT

JADON COLOR

DARLING PARK

HARRINGTON ST.

YORK

WYNYARD STATION

WYNYARD HOTEL

CLARENCE

ST.

ST.

DISTRIBUTOR

ERSKINE

MACHIAVELLI

NRMA

KENT

KING

MARKET

SUSSEX

WESTERN

DOWNTOWN SYDNEY

DARLING HARBOUR

SYDNEY AQUARIUM

PYRMONT BRIDGE

AUSTRALIAN NATIONAL MARITIME MUSEUM

HARBOURSIDE

NOVOTEL SYDNEY

PYRMONT

© MOON PUBLICATIONS, INC.

150 m

Sydney Opera House

es European and Australian art from the early 1900s and Aboriginal art and artifacts. The new wing contains contemporary art, including works by Sidney Nolan, Russell Drysdale, and William Dobell. A small theater screens art films, and a cafe overlooks Sydney Harbour; you can pick up gifts at the souvenir shop. Admission to the gallery is free. It's open Mon.-Sat. 10 a.m.-5 p.m., Sunday noon-5 p.m.

Royal Botanic Gardens
When the First Fleet arrived at Sydney Cove in 1788 the convicts were put to work planting vegetable gardens, but the important project met with little success. The gardens were moved west, to Parramatta, and in 1816 the original site was set aside as a botanic garden. Popular with workers at lunchtime, the gardens are home to 400 species of plants from around the world. Within the park is the Conservatorium of Music, originally built as horse stables, and Government House. The main road through the park is Mrs Macquarie's Rd., which ends at **Mrs Macquarie's Chair,** cut into a rocky outcrop nearly two centuries ago for the governor's wife to watch for incoming ships. The park is open between 8 a.m. and dusk.

CIRCULAR QUAY

Circular Quay, transportation hub of Sydney Harbour, sits at the head of Sydney Cove and at the north end of the City Circle rail line. The Quay is always busy, with tourists and workers boarding and alighting from a seemingly never-ending parade of ferries, trains, and buses. There, you are also in sight of Sydney's two most famous landmarks, the Opera House and the Bridge.

Sydney Opera House
Described by many as "the most beautiful building of the 20th century," this architectural masterpiece is one of the few buildings worldwide that immediately identifies a city. It lies east of Circular Quay on Bennelong Point, named by Governor Phillip for an Aboriginal he had befriended and taken back to England. Danish architect John Utzon won an international competition to design a building for the site, which had been used as a tram depot until 1956. His design was imaginative and unique: "I had white in mind when I designed the Opera House. And the roof, like sails, white in the strong day, the whole thing slowly coming to life as the sun shone from the east and lifted overhead. In the hot sun of the day it will be a beautiful, white shimmering thing—as alive to the eyes as architecture can make anything, set in the blue-green waters of the harbour. And at night the floodlit shells will be equally vibrant—but in a softer, more majestic way." But troubles started early when the old two-hectare tram site was deemed unstable. Costs blew out considerably, and to fund the massive project a lottery was set up (the winner of the first lottery had his son

kidnapped then murdered before a ransom could be paid).

The Opera House's shell had been completed by 1966, when because of contention with the actors and artists over the interior's furnishings and the cladding, John Utzon went home, leaving the project only half-finished. Even the name, "Opera House," was settled upon to appease factions—the main hall had always been planned as a venue for orchestras. The Opera House was finally completed in 1973, but with a budget that had blown to over 1,000% of the original.

The Opera House is most spectacular from the outside, viewed from the promenade that surrounds it or, better still, from a harbor ferry. Inside is the main auditorium, which is capable of seating 2,800, and three performance halls. Guided tours are offered daily 9:15 a.m.-4 p.m.; adult $9, child $4. For bookings, call (02) 9250-7250. On Sunday jazz is performed free outside, and craft markets are at the front entrance. The closest railway station is Circular Quay.

Coca-Cola Quayside

Between the Opera House and Circular Quay Ferry Terminal is this small museum cataloging the history of the world's best-known soft drink. As well as displays of advertising paraphernalia dating from the 1920s, there's a booth to make your own Coca-Cola advertisement and a Coca-Cola retail shop. Admission adult $4, child $2. It's open daily 10 a.m.-5 p.m. For further information, call (02) 9259-6700.

THE ROCKS AND VICINITY

The Rocks are both picturesque and of historical importance. In 1788 Captain Phillip came ashore with a few hundred marines and 736 convicts and set up a shanty town on the slopes of a rocky sandstone outcrop overlooking the bay Phillip had named Sydney Cove. As development spread slowly inland, The Rocks evolved into an area of disrepute, known to seamen around the world for the brothels, rowdy taverns, and cheap liquor. The area later became a port facility, with many large warehouses. When bubonic plague broke out in 1900 many original buildings were demolished, and in later years the construction of the Sydney Harbour Bridge saw entire streets disappear under tons of concrete. In the early 1970s, preservation began, with the oldest buildings restored and innumerable cafes and tourist shops opened.

Historic Buildings

Beside the Rocks Visitor Centre on George St. is **Cadman's Cottage,** built in 1816 for former convict John Cadman, who was superintendent of the governor's boats. At the time of construction, the cottage stood on a small sandy beach, but the land in front has since been reclaimed. The house now serves as an office of the National Parks and Wildlife Service (tel. 02-9247-8861). Open daily. The center of The Rocks is the junction of Argyle and George

Cadman's Cottage

THE ROCKS AND CIRCULAR QUAY

SYDNEY HARBOUR

SYDNEY HARBOUR BRIDGE

PIER ONE

PIER FOUR

PYLON LOOKOUT

HICKSON RD

LOWER FORT ST.

BRADFIELD HWY.

PARK HYATT SYDNEY

BENNELONG POINT

SYDNEY OPERA HOUSE

EARTH EXCHANGE

CAMPBELLS COVE

MERCANTILE HOTEL

WESTPAC MUSEUM

HERO OF WATERLOO

CUMBERLAND ST.

PLAYFAIR ST.

SYDNEY COVE

CIRCULAR QUAY WEST

OVERSEAS PASSENGER TERMINAL

ROYAL

LORD NELSON HOTEL

ARGYLE CENTRE/ ARGYLE TAVERN

GUMNUT TEA GARDEN

ARGYLE

ARGYLE PLACE LAUNDRY

SYDNEY OBSERVATORY

KENT ST.

NURSES WALK

SUSANNAH PLACE

THE STAFFORD

GEORGE ST.

HARRINGTON ST.

SEE DETAIL

CIRCULAR QUAY EAST

BOTANIC

6 5 4 3 2

COCA-COLA QUAYSIDE

GARDENS

CAHILL EXPRESSWAY

CIRCULAR QUAY

NOT TO SCALE

ALFRED ST.

DETAIL

ROCKS VISITOR CENTRE ■

CADMAN'S COTTAGE ■
ORIENT HOTEL ■

ARGYLE ST.

ZIA PINA ■

ROCKS CAFE ■

PHILLIP'S FOOTE ■

MUSEUM OF CONTEMPORARY ART ■

DORIAN SCOTT ■

ABORIGINAL ART CENTRE ■

SYDNEY HARBOUR SHOP ■

AUSTRALIAN CRAFTWORKS ■

THE RUSSELL ■

GEORGE ST.

Streets. On this corner is the **Orient Hotel,** built in 1844 and operating as a hotel since 1851. Uphill from the Orient are many more historic buildings. Along Nurses Walk is a narrow lane known as **Suez Canal,** one-time haunt of the "Rocks Push," a gang of notorious thugs who terrorized passersby late last century. The **Argyle Centre,** farther up Argyle St., is a series of warehouses dating from as early as 1840. Today they house shops selling arts, crafts, and souvenirs. At the top of the street is **Argyle Cut,** an excavation through a massive slab of sandstone that convicts cut by hand to connect Sydney Cove with what is now known as Darling Harbour. Immediately south of the Cut, at 58

Gloucester St. (tel. 02-9241-1893), is **Susannah Place,** a small terrace built for a working-class family back in 1844. It's open for inspection Sat.-Sun. 10 a.m.-5 p.m. At the end of Playfair Street, a cobbled pedestrian mall, is the **Westpac Museum** (tel. 02-9251-1419). The museum, in an old bank building, features the story of Australian currency. It's open daily noon-4 p.m. One block north, at 77 George St., is the **Earth Exchange** (tel. 02-9251-2422). This interesting museum features three floors of displays that catalog the geology of the planet we live on and various mining processes used to extract minerals. It's open daily noon-4 p.m., and admission is $7.

Museum of Contemporary Art

This museum at 132 George St. (tel. 02-9252-4033) is contained in a large art deco building overlooking Circular Quay (walk around to the back entrance to appreciate its size). Displays include anything from today's world of art, from modern Aboriginal works to the art of Andy Warhol to computer-created art. Admission is adult $6, child $4. It's open daily 10 a.m.-6 p.m.

Sydney Observatory

On Observatory Hill, reached by passing through the Argyle Cut and climbing a steep flight of stairs, this observatory is an old graystone structure dating from 1857. Part of the observatory's original function was as a timekeeper for the new colony. Daily at 1 p.m. the ball at the top of the weather vane was dropped simultaneously with the firing of a gun on Fort Denison, allowing settlers on land and sailors on ships out on the harbor to check their timepieces. The observatory is open daily for tours 2-5 p.m. (free) and nightly except Wednesday for telescope viewing at 8:30 p.m. (adult $5, child $2). For further information, call (02) 9217-0485.

Sydney Harbour Bridge

This bridge, linking the city center to the northern suburbs, is, along with Opera House, a symbol of Sydney. Known locally as the "Coathanger," it today looks old-fashioned, with the four massive stone pylons built purely for decoration not the least bit decorative. A bridge for the harbor was talked about for much of the second half of the 19th century, but it wasn't until 1932 that one was completed. The bridge spans 550 meters (one of the world's longest single-span bridges), rises 120 meters above the harbor, weighs over 50,000 tons, and is supported entirely by the distinctive span girders.

Walking across the bridge takes about 20 minutes (the east side of the bridge has a pedestrian walkway while along the west side is a cycleway). Pedestrian access is from Cumber-

land St. in The Rocks. The pylon closest to The Rocks is open to the public daily 10 a.m.-5 p.m. Inside, a 200-step stairway ends at a lookout. Admission is $1.

Since the bridge's opening in 1932, traffic across the harbor has increased dramatically. For many decades various proposals to ease bridge congestion were put forward, including building a brand-new bridge and adding an additional level to the existing bridge. Least popular of options, increasing the bridge toll from 20 cents to $2 overnight, was implemented, but it had little long-term effect on the problem. Money collected from the toll helped pay for a tunnel, which opened in 1992.

DARLING HARBOUR

Originally a shipping and storage area for the city, Darling Harbour, a narrow inlet immediately west of downtown, was an eyesore for decades until a massive redevelopment program in the 1980s saw the birth of a stylish waterfront shopping and entertainment complex. The centerpiece is **Harbourside Festival Marketplace,** a massive complex of 200 shops, restaurants, and bars, alive with color of clowns, musicians, dancers, and mime artists. On the harborfront are long promenades, gardens, and parkland as well as a variety of other attractions. Access from downtown is at the end of Market St. over the Pyrmont Bridge (pedestrians only). Another option is the **monorail,** which circles Darling Harbour and links it to the city center. The one-way fare is $2.50, or ride it all day for $6. Beside Harbourside is the Exhibition Centre, a massive expanse of space protected by a suspended roof canopy seven stories high. The Darling Harbour Superticket ($35.50), valid for three months, includes the monorail, aquarium admission, lunch at the Craig Brewery, Chinese Garden admission, and discounts at selected stores.

Sydney Aquarium

Located on the city side of Darling Harbour, this aquarium complex is the largest in the Southern Hemisphere. It contains 5,000 Australian specimens, including one of the world's largest collections of sharks, as well as Barrier Reef fish and crocodiles. Other features are the mock river system and a touch pool where visitors are encouraged to get their hands wet. Two massive tanks moored in the harbor contain larger species, such as sharks and rays, while other tanks contain marinelife found in Sydney Harbour. Admission adult $14, child $7. Open daily 9:30 a.m.-9 p.m. For more information call (02) 9262-2300.

Australian National Maritime Museum

This museum catalogs Australia's shipping history and the influence the ocean has had on the country. Displays include the relationship between Australian and North American marine history, Aboriginal canoes, the victorious 1983 America's Cup wing-keeled yacht *Aus-*

One of the highlights of the National Maritime Museum is the display of boats tied up at the wharf.

tralia II, the role of lifesavers, beach culture through the years, the world's fastest boat *Spirit of Australia,* and the anchor from the *Sirius,* wrecked on Norfolk Island in 1790.

Tied up at the museum's docks are a number of vessels, including a navy submarine, the destroyer HMAS *Vampire,* a Vietnamese refugee boat, a tug boat, and a couple of old racing yachts. Admission is adult $7, child $3.50; tours of the museum are free. For more information, call (02) 9552-7777. Tours of the historic waterfront suburb of Pyrmont depart the museum at 10:30 a.m. on the first Tuesday of every month; $10 pp.

Powerhouse Museum

Housed in an enormous building that once generated power for Sydney trams, this, Sydney's most spectacular museum, definitely shouldn't be missed. Displays encompass Australia's entire social history, and it's easy to spend an entire day wandering through the building, large enough to house entire airplanes, trains, and houses. Exhibitions are expertly displayed, with many interactive displays encouraging visitors to push buttons and pull levers. As well as the science and technology upon which the country has been built, displays show an old settler's hut, an old arena, and a suburban grocery store. Admission is a worthwhile adult $5, child $2. Open daily 10 a.m.-5 p.m. It's at 500 Harris St., Ultimo, immediately south of Darling Harbour (tel. 02-9217-0111).

Harris Street Motor Museum

Behind Darling Harbour, at 320 Harris St. (tel. 02-9552-1210), this museum is devoted entirely to the automobile, with around 160 machines on display. Classic cars are exhibited, along with motorcycles, vans, and vehicles with famous former owners. Also in the museum is a two-km-long slot-car track for enthusiasts to test their skills. Admission is adult $8, child $4. Open daily 10 a.m.-5 p.m. Easiest access is from the Convention Centre monorail station.

SIGHTS AND SUBURBS
EAST OF DOWNTOWN

Kings Cross

Sleaze. Porn. Drugs. The Underworld. You name it, Australia's best-known suburb, "The Cross," has it. Located immediately east of the

SYDNEY HARBOUR AND ENVIRONS

PACIFIC OCEAN

PORT JACKSON (SYDNEY HARBOUR)

0   1 km

Domain, this famous red-light district is Australia's answer to London's Soho. The main drag is Darlinghurst Rd., a continuous stretch of strip joints, porn shops, nightclubs, and late-night restaurants. Although things are seedy and sleazy after dark, it's a lively place 24 hours a day. Darlinghurst Rd. is reasonably safe, but you definitely wouldn't want to wander down too many dark alleys. The Cross attracts a great array of people, from overseas tourists to drugged-out teenage hookers. It is a popular travelers' center and has Australia's largest concentration of backpacker accommodations. **El Alamein Fountain,** a local landmark and popular meeting place, is on the corner of Darlinghurst Rd. and MacLeay Street.

Darlinghurst

Southeast of downtown along Oxford St., this old suburb features restaurants, lively nightlife, and many restored Victorian-era terraces. The main attraction is **Sydney Jewish Museum** at 148 Darlinghurst Rd. (tel. 02-9360-7999). Jews were among the first fleet of convicts to land on Australian soil. While telling the history of these people, the museum also functions as a memorial to Jews who died in the Holocaust. Their story, depicted through interactive displays and stunning photographic images, is particularly moving. Admission adult $5, child $2. Open Mon.-Thurs. 10 a.m.-4 p.m. and Sunday noon-5 p.m. From downtown take bus no. 373 or 374.

Paddington

South of Kings Cross, this suburb, very run-down as recently as the 1970s, is now one of the inner city's most desirable areas to live. The streets are hilly and twisted, lined with narrow Victorian-era terraces featuring ornamental plasterwork and balconies decorated with cast-iron lace work. The heart of "Paddo" is Oxford St., dominated by fashionable boutiques, antique shops, art galleries, cafes, and bric-a-brac stores. The downtown end of Oxford St., around the corner of Flinders St., is the gay center of Sydney. **Paddington Village Bazaar** is held in the church on the corner of Newcombe and Oxford Streets every Saturday. Also of interest is **Victoria Barracks,** Oxford St. (tel. 02-9339-3445). The barracks, finished in 1848, were built using convict labor. Australian forces currently occupy the bar-

racks, and every Tuesday at 10 a.m. there is a ceremonial changing of the guard. After this weekly event, tours of a small military museum are offered. Admission to the barracks is free.

South of Paddo is Sydney's largest stretch of parkland, 200-hectare **Centennial Park,** opened to commemorate Australia's 1888 centenary. Also south of Paddington is the **Royal Agricultural Society Showground,** parts of which are currently being transformed into a Foxtel movie studio. The north end of the showground is taken up by the **Sydney Cricket Ground** and **Sydney Football Stadium,** premier venues for cricket and rugby league respectively. **Sportspace** (tel. 02-9380-0383) is a tour that takes in both grounds, dressing rooms, players' tunnel, security control center, 1886 Member's Stand, and a cricket museum. Tours depart from the Club Lounge in the Sydney Football Stadium on non-match days at 10 a.m., 1 p.m., and 3 p.m. The cost is adult $18, child $12.

Double Bay and Vaucluse

The harborside suburbs east of Kings Cross, including Double Bay, Rose Bay, Vaucluse, and Watsons Bay, are all upmarket and very expensive to live and shop in. Double Bay, especially, boasts shops representing some of the world's top fashion designers as well as many trendy cafes and restaurants. Ferries leave Circular Quay every 20 minutes for Double Bay; for details call 13-1500.

Toward the headlands is the swank suburb Vaucluse, where **Vaucluse House** lies. This imposing mansion was built for William Charles Wentworth, who in 1813 was a member of the first party of Europeans to cross the Blue Mountains. The house, set on 11 magnificent harborside hectares, is furnished from that period, with original outbuildings and stables still in place. Admission is adult $5, child $3. It's open Tues.-Sun. 10 a.m.-4:30 p.m., with afternoon tea served daily. It's located on Wentworth Rd. (tel. 02-9337-1957). Take bus no. 325 from downtown.

PARRAMATTA AND VICINITY

When the First Fleet arrived at Sydney Cove, they had enough supplies to last two years. This made becoming self-sufficient a top priority.

When the first crops failed, search parties sent out from the colony discovered a fertile area 30 km inland on the bank of the Parramatta River. Many buildings from the town that developed around the gardens have been preserved, and the site of the gardens is now a pleasant strip of parkland along the river. (What was then a wild, unknown area a day's ride from the coast is now *east* of Sydney's geographical center.)

The most enjoyable way to travel to Parramatta is aboard the *RiverCat* ($4.20 each way), which departs regularly from Circular Quay (tel. 3-1500). You can also catch a train from either Central or Wynyard Stations. Once in Parramatta, head to **Parramatta Visitors Centre,** corner Market and Church Streets (tel. 02-9630-8703). Open daily.

Old Government House

What is now Parramatta Park was the original plot chosen by Governor Phillip for farming. In 1790 Phillip had a residence built on the site, with major additions made by Governor Macquarie in 1815. Many governors lived in the residence, the intricate paneling, handcrafted furniture, and expensive furnishings attesting to their grand tastes. On the western side of the house are fruit trees and grapevines dating to the era of Phillip's reign as governor. Admission to the house is adult $4, child $1. It's open Tues.-Thurs. and Sunday 10 a.m.-4 p.m. (tel. 02-9635-8149).

Elizabeth Farm

Built in 1793 as a home for John MacArthur, founder of the merino wool industry, this is the oldest existing house in Australia. Featuring wide verandas, it's typical of Australian homestead construction. Restored, and decorated with many pieces of original furniture, the house is open for inspection Tues.-Sun. 10 a.m.-4:30 p.m. Admission adult $5, child $3. It's at 70 Alice St. (tel. 02-9635-9488).

Australia's Wonderland

This, Australia's largest theme park, is west of Parramatta on Wallgrove Rd., Eastern Creek (tel. 02-9830-9100). Set on over 200 hectares (that's larger than Disneyland), it has six themed areas, including one containing cartoon charcters, an International Village, fun park, water slides, and wildlife park. Admission is adult $26.95, child $19.95. Open Sat.-Sun. 10 a.m.-5 p.m. The nearest railway station is Rooty Hill, from where buses run to Wonderland every half hour.

Sydney Olympic Park

Upon arriving in Sydney, and seeing all the bumper stickers, flags, and T-shirts, you'll quickly understand that it's no secret that Sydney is hosting the 2000 Summer Olympic Games. Homebush Bay, a disused industrial site between the city center and Parramatta, is currently being transformed into the Sydney Olympic Park, a sporting and residential complex for the games. Construction will continue right until the commencement of the games. Tours of the partly built park take around 45 minutes. They leave from the north side of Strathfield Railway Station Mon.-Fri. at 9:30 a.m., 10:30 a.m., and 12:30 p.m. Tour cost is $5. Call (02) 9735-4860 for further information.

SIGHTS NORTH OF THE HARBOR

Taronga Zoo

Overlooking the harbor and a short ferry ride across the harbor from Circular Quay, this is Australia's premier zoological garden, having what is often described as the best setting of any zoo in the world. Across 30 hectares are 4,000 animals from around the world. Highlights include the seal pool, underwater platypus house, noctarium, Friendship Farm, and, yes, they have all the usual lions, tigers, bears, elephants, giraffes, and monkeys. Admission is adult $13.50, child $6. A Zoo Pass, available at Circular Quay, includes ferry transfers, the Aerial Safari, and zoo admission for adult $17, child $8.70. Road access is from Bradleys Head Rd. off Military Rd., Mosman (tel. 02-9969-2777).

Oceanworld

In the bustling seaside suburb of Manly, this four-million-liter aquarium features a unique moving walkway that runs underneath the main tank. This allows visitors the unusual angle of looking *up* at large sharks and stingrays. Other tanks contain reef fish, octopuses, eels, lobsters, crabs, and poisonous dwellers of the deep.

A highlight of Oceanworld is the daily shark feeding at 12:15 and 2:30 p.m. Admission is adult $11, child $4.40. Open daily 10 a.m.-5:30 p.m. It's on West Esplanade, Manly Cove (tel. 02-9949-2644). The most enjoyable way to get there is aboard a ferry from Circular Quay.

Other Manly Sights

Manly is almost a self-contained resort rather than a suburb, and boasts one of Sydney's most popular beaches. Access from Circular Quay is easy aboard ferries, which dock at Manly Wharf, Manly Cove. From there a 500-meter-walk extends along the **Corso,** a pedestrian mall, to the oceanfront. On West Esplanade is **Manly Art Gallery and Museum** (tel. 02-9949-2435), with local memorabilia and photographs of the beaches' earliest swimmers and surfers. Admission is adult $2 (free with an Oceanworld ticket). It's open Tues.-Fri. 10 a.m.-4 p.m., Sat.-Sun. noon-5 p.m. Darley Road through Manly leads to **North Head,** at the entrance to Sydney Harbour and within Sydney Harbour National Park. On the headland is the **Royal Australian Artillery Museum** (tel. 02-9976-1138), displaying guns and cannons used by Australian forces in colonial times. Admission adult $3, child $1. It's open on weekends only 10 a.m.-4 p.m.

NATIONAL PARKS

Not only is Sydney blessed with one of the world's great harbors, but within the city limits are no less than seven national parks. Combined with the six national parks along the city limits, well over 800,000 hectares of native bushland are protected in the Sydney area. The best source of information about all parks is the National Parks and Wildlife Service office in **Cadman's Cottage,** 110 George St., The Rocks (tel. 02-9247-8861).

Sydney Harbour National Park

This, the closest national park to downtown, protects various sections of undeveloped coastline around Sydney Heads, including **Gap Bluff** at Watsons Bay; **Shark** and **Clarke Islands; Bradleys** and **Middle Heads** near Mosman; **Dobroyd Head** at Balgowlah Heights; and **North Head,** south of Manly.

Ku-ring-gai Chase National Park

When residents of Sydney's northern suburbs feel like escaping the crush of city living, they needn't travel far, for this 14,840-hectare national park is right on their back door (in some cases, literally). The park extends from the leafy outlying suburbs of the North Shore to the Hawkesbury River and east from the Pacific Highway to Pittwater. It's part of an area known geographically as the Sydney Basin, once part of the ocean floor until uplift created the high plateau through which watercourses have carved deep valleys. Many of these valleys have flooded to become part of Broken Bay. Most larger species of mammals are long gone (although gray kangaroos are often seen at dawn and dusk along Bobbin Head Rd.), but possums, gliders, echidnas, and bandicoots are present. Three main access roads lead into the park, but they are not linked. Bobbin Head Rd begins at Mt. Colah, descending to the far reaches of Cowan Creek, where the Halverson Boat Sheds are located. Beyond the boat sheds, toward Terrey Hills, is the **Visitors Centre** (tel. 02-9457-9322), with displays of park fauna and an audiovisual. The other park access is north off Mona Vale Rd. to West Head, from where views extend across Broken Bay to Lion Island and across Pittwater to the narrow spit of sand joining Barrenjoey Head to Palm Beach. From West Head, the 3.5-km Garigal Aboriginal Heritage Walk passes various sites sacred to Australia's first inhabitants. Camping is possible at the Basin on Pittwater, accessible on foot from West Head Rd. or water taxi from Palm Beach.

Royal National Park

Disastrous fires in January 1994 left this 15,000 hectare park a charred wasteland. Human intervention in the natural cycle of fires—as was the case in the U.S.'s Yellowstone Park a few years earlier—encouraged the park to become overly dense, making it susceptible quick spreading fires. First gazetted (proclaimed) in 1879, Royal National Park is the world's second-oldest national park. The early preservation of this coastal landscape allows visitors the unique chance to explore the same environment that early European visitors did. The park extends between the Princes Highway and the Pacific Ocean and south from Port Hacking to

Wollongong's northern suburbs. For 8,000 years before the arrival of Europeans, the Dharawa tribe lived around the bays of Port Hacking, fishing and collecting shellfish. Piles of empty shells (known as middens), a burial site, and rock art are reminders of their presence.

One of the most enjoyable ways to reach the park is on the regular ferry service between Cronulla and **Bundeena,** a small town at the southern entrance to Port Hacking and surrounded by the park. From Bundeena, the Coast Track leads 28 km south to Otford, on the main southern rail line. The trail passes many delightful bays and beaches and is easily completed in two days. For day-trippers, Marley Headland and Big Marley Beach (three km one-way) are popular destinations from Bundeena, as is Jibbon Point (one km one-way), where Koori rock art is carved into a rock platform. The main road into the park passes Audley Weir (boat rentals and picnic areas), then divides: one fork ends at Bundeena, the other winds through the park's southern reaches. Side roads access the coastline at Wattamolla Beach and Garie, both popular picnic and bushwalking spots.

Other Parks

Garigal National Park extends from the lower reaches of Middle Harbour north to the suburb of St. Ives. The park has boat rentals near Roseville Bridge and over 100 km of hiking trails, including one along Middle Harbour Creek.

Smallest of the city parks, at just 327 hectares, is **Lane Cove National Park,** which protects an area of bushland west of Chatswood. Trails lead along Lane Cove River, and over 30 picnic areas dot the park.

South of Bankstown, 328-hectare **Georges River National Park** features riverside hiking trails and picnic areas.

Botany Bay National Park protects the tip of Kurnell Peninsula as well as a small section of coastline at the north entrance to Botany Bay. The park is best known as the landing place of Captain Cook.

WILDLIFE PARKS

One of the world's great zoos is Taronga Zoo (see above), with many displays of animals from around the world, but Sydney has three other wildlife parks. These specialize in the unique fauna of the Australian continent.

Waratah Park

More of a nature reserve than a park, this place is good for viewing kangaroos, wallabies, emus, and wombats as they wander around freely in their natural environment. Other native species, such as Tasmanian devils and dingos, are caged. The 10-hectare site is adjacent to Kuring-gai Chase National Park. Cuddle the koalas in the Koala House, and take the Bush Railway, which winds through eucalypts and bushland typical of the area. The park also has a cook-your-own steak bistro, a restaurant, and souvenir shop. Admission is adult $11.60, child $5.80, and it's open daily 10 a.m.-5 p.m. Waratah Park is on Namba Rd., Duffys Forest (tel. 02-9450-2377). Many city day tours include the park on their itinerary. Otherwise take a train to Chatswood in time to meet the 11:45 a.m. Forest Coach Lines bus.

Koala Park Sanctuary

For over 65 years Koala Park has helped preserve Australia's favorite native animal. It was the state's first such sanctuary and has been instrumental in the species' survival. As well, the park houses kangaroos, wallabies, wombats, dingoes, and colorful birds. Attend one of their knowledgable talks about the koalas. Admission to the sanctuary is a reasonable adult $7, child $4. Open daily 9 a.m.-5 p.m. Located at 84 Castle Hill Rd., West Pennant Hills (tel. 02-9484-3141). By public transportation take the train to Pennant Hills (via Strathfield), then bus no. 651 or 655 to the park entrance.

Featherdale Wildlife Park

Although farther from the city, this park has Australia's largest collection of native fauna. Large enclosures containing all the usual species are spread through extensive native bushland. Highlights are the native-bird aviaries, koala-cuddling, crocodile-feeding (daily at 3:30 p.m.), fairy penguins, and a large collection of raptors. Admission to the park is adult $8.50, child $4.25. It's open daily 9 a.m.-5 p.m. The park is on Kildare Rd., Doonside (tel. 02-9622-1644). By public transportation, take the train from Central Station to Blacktown and jump aboard bus no. 725.

OUTDOOR ACTIVITIES AND SPECTATOR SPORTS

Boating and Fishing

"Heading out on the harbor" is a favorite Sydneysider pastime and on any given weekend, Sydney Harbour is alive with sea craft of all shapes and sizes, from colorful windsurfers to speeding 18-footers to luxurious motor cruisers.

Northside Sailing School, at the southern end of the Spit Bridge, Mosman (tel. 02-9969-3972), rents small boats and sailboards from $15 an hour. They offer sailing lessons in all manner of craft, including racing yachts. At the same location is **It's a Breeze Yacht Charter** (tel. 02-9960-3999). Up in Ku-ring-gai Chase National Park, various places rent boats, including **Skipper a Clipper,** at Akuna Bay (tel. 02-9979-6188). This operation rents large cruisers, complete with kitchen, electric anchor, radios, linen, fuel, and a dinghy, for $40-110 pp per day. These boats are perfect for exploring the many estuaries and coves of the Hawkesbury River and busy Pittwater. At Brooklyn, **Bait n' Boats** (tel. 02-9455-1206) rents small aluminum boats with fishing gear for around $50 a day.

Swimming

No city in the world has a string of ocean beaches as beautiful as Sydney does, extending from Cronulla in the south to Palm Beach in the north. All major beaches have shark nets (the last recorded shark attack on a Sydney beach was 30 years ago), and volunteer lifesavers patrol beaches all summer and weekends year-round. Within the harbor are good beaches, including **Nielsen Park** and **Watsons Bay,** and on the north side of the harbor, **Balmoral** and **Reef Beaches.**

The closest swimming pools to the city are **Andrew Boy Charlton Pool,** in the Domain, Woolloomooloo (tel. 02-9358-6686); **Prince Alfred Park Swimming Pool,** Chalmers St., Surry Hills (tel. 02-9319-7045); and **North Sydney Olympic Pool,** Alfred St., Milsons Point (tel. 02-9955-2309).

Scuba Diving

Water in Sydney Harbour is remarkably clear and many hundreds of established dive sites exist. The best way to arrange a dive trip and equipment rental is through one of the following operators: **Dive 2000,** 2 Military Rd., Neutral Bay (tel. 02-9953-7783); **Pro Dive,** 227 Victoria Rd., Drummoyne (tel. 02-9819-7711); or **Pro Dive,** 39 Old Pittwater Rd., Manly (tel. 02-9976-3499).

SAFETY AT THE BEACH

Australia's infamous wild animals should be the least of your worries when heading down to the beach. Sharks are occasionally present, but attacks off Sydney beaches are rare, as offshore meshing and regular aerial patrols protect the masses from the marauding monsters of the deep. In fact, sunburn (Australians have the world's highest incidence of skin cancer) presents much more of a threat than sharks, especially for visitors who have fled a Northern Hemisphere winter. Most of the popular beaches have nearby kiosks and general stores selling sunscreen (ask for one with a 15+ rating), but even with this protection, a wide-brimmed hat or beach umbrella is recommended.

In the water, **bluebottles** are the biggest danger. Known locally as "stingers," they are often confused with box jellyfish. These annoying critters float in with summer's northeasterly breezes, en masse, and are easily recognizable as bright blue sacks with tentacles trailing up to two meters. Stings are not fatal but can involve intense local pain, lasting 10-15 minutes, and will leave long red welts where the tentacles touched you. Rubbing the affected area with wet sand removes many of the unbroken stinging sacks, but the poison that's already been discharged will run its course. Dousing the wound with Methylated Spirits or vinegar may ease the pain (surf clubs always have a supply).

Most Sydney beaches are patroled between October and Easter by volunteer **surf lifesavers.** Distinctive red-and-yellow flags are set up on the beach to indicate safe swimming areas.

SYDNEY BEACHES

Visitors to Australia usually need little prompting to "head down the beach," and with 32 beaches at Sydney's doorstep, there is no better place to experience distinctive Aussie culture. Sydney's beaches can get very crowded, especially on weekends, but this disadvantage is far outweighed by the advantages—golden sand, clear and warm water, and accessibility to the city itself. You can swim in the ocean year-round, but it's most pleasant Dec.-April, when water temperatures rise as high as 21° C. Sydney has three distinct groups of beaches—within the harbor, south of the harbor, and north of the harbor—extending 60 km from Cronulla in the south to Palm Beach in the north. And while at the beach, you may notice you feel overdressed. At many of the area's beaches, topless sunbathing is both legal and accepted—but make sure that's the case where you are before tossing that top.

Harbor Beaches

A number of remarkably beautiful beaches lie within the harbor, with some, such as **Nielson Park** at Vaucluse, just minutes from downtown yet surrounded by native forest. Nielson Park is protected by netting and has change sheds, lockers, and a kiosk. East, toward the heads, is **Watsons Bay**, where a small area of beach is netted. Immediately north, around a rocky headland, is **Camp Cove**, a trendy little spot popular with families. Busy **Balmoral Beach**, east of Mosman, on the north shore of the harbor, has two netted sections and plenty of parking.

Beaches South of the Harbor

The coastline between Sydney Harbour and Botany Bay is dotted with beautiful stretches of beach, but high cliffs and rugged headlands prevent extensive coastal views. Development is extensive and haphazard, with no decent road linking the beaches.

Australia's best-known beach, and closest to downtown, is **Bondi**. Like other beaches south of the harbor, it's surrounded by ugly high-rise development in various states of disrepair, though it's popular with travelers, and many New Zealanders and Brits live in the area. South of Bondi are two small beaches, **Tamarama** and **Bronte;** the former is often plagued by strong currents that make swimming unadvisable. Farther south, **Coogee** is another popular beach, with a large pub on the foreshore. All the above southern beaches can be reached by bus from Circular Quay.

Within Botany Bay lies a long stretch of beach at **Brighton Le Sands,** with netted swimming areas making it perfect for families. Southernmost of Sydney's beaches is **Cronulla,** a magnificent stretch of sand backed by pristine sand dunes that stretch from a developed area in the south along a narrow peninsula to Kurnell, landing site of Captain Cook in 1770. Cronulla is Sydney's only beach accessible by train; these depart Central Station every half-hour.

Beaches North of the Harbor

The 30 km of coastline north of the harbor is less developed but no more beautiful than that south of the harbor. **Manly,** reached by ferry from Circular Quay, has a real seaside resort atmosphere, with its tree-lined foreshore and many outdoor cafes and restaurants. From Manly a crescent of sand extends two km to **Queenscliff Beach.** Beyond Queenscliff is **Curl Curl,** a popular family spot, then **Dee Why,** which is backed by a large lagoon and wildlife reserve. The crescent ends in the north at **Long Reef Point,** which has a spectacular oceanfront golf course.

Beyond is **Narrabeen,** a legendary surf spot (and the only Australian beach mentioned in a Beach Boys' song). Farther north is another excellent surfing beach, **Newport,** which has some of Sydney's most consistent surf—and you may even find yourself sharing a wave with former world surfing champion Tom Carroll, a longtime resident. Newport lies at the southern end of a narrow peninsula that ends at Barrenjoey Heads. Along the peninsula are **Bilgola, Avalon, Whale,** and **Palm Beaches,** all backed by the calm waters of Pittwater, an arm of the Hawkesbury River.

Golfing

Sydney is blessed with fine golf courses, including a string of famous courses immediately south of downtown. Some of the better courses that allow visitors are: **Moore Park Golf Club,** corner Cleveland St. and Anzac Parade (tel. 02-9663-4966), green fees $15-18; **The Lakes,** King St., Mascot (tel. 02-9667-3558), $60-90; **Concord Golf Club,** Majors Bay Rd., Concord (tel. 02-9743-0265), $50; **Bonnie Doon Golf**

*the clear water of
Sydney Harbour at
Nielson Park*

Club, Banks Ave., Pagewood (tel. 02-9344-5835), $50; **St. Michael's,** Little Bay (tel. 02-9661-7549), $60; and **Bondi Golf Club,** 5 Military Rd., North Bondi (tel. 02-9130-3170), $8.

Rugby League

Sydney is a stronghold of rugby league, hosting many competitions with teams across Australia and New Zealand. Crowds are never as large as those at Aussie Rules matches in Melbourne, but are no less fanatic. Closest of the grounds to downtown is the Sydney Football Stadium, which hosts the Grand Final every September. The main season runs March-Sept., with most games on Sunday afternoon. Contact the individual clubs for tickets.

Cricket

With Australia heading toward becoming a republic, the leisurely paced game of cricket may soon be the country's strongest link to England. During summer, cricket is played across the country, from kids playing on quiet backstreets to Internationals at the Sydney Cricket Ground. For match information at this and other major venues, contact the New South Wales Cricket Association at (02) 9127-4053.

Horse Racing

Sydney has four racecourses. They are: **Royal Randwick Racecourse,** Alison Rd., Randwick (tel. 02-9663-8400); **Canterbury Park Racecourse,** King St., Canterbury (tel. 02-9930-4000); **Rosehill Racecourse,** Grand Ave., Rosehill, near Parramatta (tel. 02-9682-1000); and **Warwick Farm Racecourse,** Hume Hwy., Warwick Farm (tel. 02-9602-6199). Races are held at one of these venues every Wednesday and Saturday year-round. Racing starts at 12:30 p.m. (in summer at 2:30 p.m.), with the last race run around 5 p.m. Each course offers a Tote, or a bookmaker, through whom you can bet, as well as restaurants, bars, and plenty of parking. Another good place to bet on the horses (via a television screen), as well as see a cross-section of Sydneysiders, is at one to the many licensed clubs throughout the city.

ARTS AND ENTERTAINMENT

Art Galleries

Along with large public galleries, such as the Art Gallery of New South Wales and the Museum of Contemporary Art, Sydney has dozens of commercial galleries, many concentrated in Paddington and The Rocks. The **Aboriginal Art Centre,** 117 George St., The Rocks (tel. 02-9247-9625), sells native artifacts, ranging from traditional art to contemporary paintings. Open daily 10 a.m.-5 p.m. Also in The Rocks is **Australian Craftworks,** 127 George St. (tel. 02-9147-7156) housed in an old police station from the Colonial era. It features arts and crafts for sale in all mediums. Australia's largest private art gallery is **Holdsworth Galleries,** 86 Holdsworth St.

Woollahra (tel. 02-9363-1364), showcasing all the best that contemporary Australian artists have to offer. Open Mon.-Sat. 10 a.m.-5 p.m., Sunday noon-5 p.m. More good Australian art is for sale at **Watters Gallery,** 109 Riley St., East Sydney (tel. 02-9331-2556), which is open Tues.-Sat. 10 a.m.-5 p.m. For a bizarre range of glass sculptures, head to **Glass Artists' Gallery,** 70 Glebe Point Rd., Glebe (tel. 02-9552-1552).

Theater

In Sydney, live theater has never reached the heights of popularity it enjoys in Melbourne, and it didn't really catch on at all until the 1960s. Also, Sydney has no "theater district," and many of the old playhouses have been bulldozed. That said, Sydney now has 27 theater companies, which perform over 200 plays and musicals annually. Downtown theaters include: **Her Majesty's,** 107 Quay St. (tel. 02-9212-3411), a large theater, seating 1,500, that features musicals, Christmas pantomimes, and historical productions; **Kent Street Theatre,** 420 Kent St. (tel. 02-9529-5333), an old church featuring Australian and British productions; and **Opera House Drama Theatre** (tel. 02-9250-7111), home to the Sydney Theatre Company, which puts on a broad spectrum of productions. This theater company also has its own theater on Pier Four, Hickson Rd., Millers Point (tel. 02-9250-1700). **Theatre Royal,** MLC Centre, King St. (tel. 02-9231-6111), is a large and lavish venue featuring international musicals; tickets range $34-39.

For regular drama, comedy, and modern dance, head to the **Seymour Theatre Centre,** corner City Rd. and Cleveland St., Chippendale (tel. 02-9364-9444). Tickets range $15-20. The **Footbridge Theatre** (tel. 02-9320-9000) is named for a footbridge that spans Parramatta Rd., Glebe. It's on the University of Sydney campus, catering mostly to the student crowd through comedy and a cynical look at the establishment. The **Belvoir Street Theatre,** 25 Belvoir St., Surry Hills (tel. 02-9699-3444), features a wide range of Australian productions, from Aboriginal themes to children's shows; tickets are $15-20.

Dinner Theater

Harbourside Brasserie, Pier 1, Hickson Rd., Millers Point (tel. 02-9252-3000), is an upmarket dinner theater overlooking the harbor. Dinner,

which is excellent, is followed by theater or cabaret, then dancing until the early hours. Open Tues.-Saturday. Prices range $15-40.

Music and Dance

Sydney's premier music venue is also its most recognizable, the **Sydney Opera House,** on Bennelong Point near Circular Quay. It hosts a broad range of productions, including those performed by the Australian Opera, Australian Ballet, Sydney Dance Company, and Sydney Symphony Orchestra. For bookings, call (02) 9250-7250. The **State Theatre,** 49 Market St. (tel. 02-9373-6655), built as a grand picture palace in the 1930s, has been restored to its former glory and now hosts visiting dance groups, musicals, and movies.

Cinemas

The main concentration of movie houses is at the southern end of George St., between Bathurst and Liverpool Streets. Here you'll find **Village** (tel. 02-9264-6701), **Greater Union** (tel. 02-9267-8666), and **Hoyts** (tel. 02-9267-9877). Ticket prices at these mainstream cinemas ranges $9-12, with Tuesday night generally half price. **AFI Cinema,** corner Oatley Rd. and Oxford St., Paddington (tel. 02-9361-5398), screens works produced by the Australian Film Institute as well as some unforgettable (and forgettable) Australian classics. A center of alternative movies, the **Valhalla,** 166 Glebe Point Rd., Glebe (tel. 02-9660-8050), is a social center for fans of all movie genres including comedy, science fiction, and animation.

Hotels and Bars

Sydney has literally hundreds of hotels and bars, many with high-quality live music performed nightly. The best source of entertainment information is the Metro pull-out in Friday's *Sydney Morning Herald.*

For a quiet drink downtown, there are a few options, including the longtime favorite **King George Tavern,** corner King and George Streets (tel. 02-9232-3144), an upmarket drinking hole that attracts local white-collar workers. It's open from noon daily. Another stylish place is **Marble Bar** in the Sydney Hilton at 259 Pitt St. (tel. 02-9266-0610).

The **Lord Nelson Hotel,** corner Argyle and Kent Streets, The Rocks (tel. 02-9251-4044), brews its own beer, while the Mercantile Hotel, George St. (tel. 02-9247-3570), is the best place to head for a pint of Guiness.

At Darling Harbour *the* place for a drink is the **Pumphouse Tavern,** 17 Little Pier St. (tel. 02-9281-3967), with beer brewed on site and served in old-style pint glasses. The tavern is built around an old water-pumping station that dates from 1891. The old cast-iron water tank remains, with a beer garden built around it. Also at Darling Harbour, the **Craig Brewery** (tel. 02-9281-3922) is a popular hangout, especially Thursday night when a schooner of beer is just $1.

Friend in Hand Hotel, 58 Cowper St., Glebe (tel. 02-9660-2326), has cheap beer nights and a packed entertainment program. Also in Glebe is the **Nag's Head,** 162 St. Johns Rd. (tel. 02-9660-1591), with lots of British beers and live entertainment Wed.-Sunday.

It's after dark when Kings Cross really comes alive, with streets bustling through the night. Crowds make the main streets relatively safe, but still be careful. Before disappearing into a crowded and smoky bar, check out El Alamein Fountain, which is beautifully floodlit after dark. For a cheap beer head to the **Darlo Bar,** on the corner of Darlinghurst and Liverpool Streets. For something with a bit more style, the **Civic Club,** 44 Macleay St., Potts Point (tel. 02-9358-4347), sells drinks at bar prices and has live entertainment; open daily 10 a.m.-5 a.m.

Nightclubs

Most downtown nightclubs cater to the upmarket or over-30 crowd, providing an enjoyable but often expensive night out. One exception is **Deja Vu Nitespot,** 252 Pitt St. (tel. 02-9261-8899), which plays the hippest dance and techno music until dawn. **Juliana's,** Sydney Hilton, Pitt St. (tel. 02-9266-0610), is the place to be seen, with international acts followed by dancing until about 3 a.m. Cover charge is $10. Trendy **Riva,** Sheraton on the Park, Castlereagh St. (tel. 02-9286-6666), is a dressy nightclub with ultramodern decor and the latest dance and jazz music. It opens Wed.-Sat. 10 p.m.-5 a.m. Cover charge $12. **Rokoko** is a popular place with tourists. The great variety of entertainment includes jazz, comedy, raffles, and plenty of dancing. Admission is free before 9 p.m. and varies after. It's at 16 Argyle St., The Rocks (tel. 02-9251-1579).

Kinsela's, 383 Bourke St., Darlinghurst (tel. 02-9331-6200), a renovated funeral parlor, has entertainment on three floors. Dancing is on the third-floor disco; the second floor has a cocktail bar and the ground floor features pool tables. Disco admission is $10. The **Metropolis,** 99 Walker St., North Sydney (tel. 02-9929-8222), is the spot for those on the North Shore. In Kings Cross, **Joe's Garage,** popular with backpackers, has a happy hour, bar games, and plenty of entertainment. The **Colosseum,** 54 Darlinghurst Rd. (tel. 02-9357-3800), gets pretty rowdy, especially Friday and Saturday, but it's all good fun. Drinks are half price 5-8 p.m., and admission is $5. For serious dancers, **Sight/Soho,** 171 Victoria St. (tel. 02-9358-4221), is the place to go for a scene similar to an English rave party. **Studebaker's,** 33 Bayswater Rd., Kings Cross (tel. 02-9358-5656), has a '60s theme, serves dinner, and provides a good atmosphere.

Rock

Sydney has some legendary rock venues, mostly large pubs with an auditorium out back. Admission varies with the act but is rarely more than $10-15, even for international performers. The biggest big-name acts perform at the **Sydney Entertainment Centre** or **State Theatre. Selina's,** in the Coogee Bay Hotel, 253 Coogee Bay Rd., Coogee (tel. 02-9665-0000), is a classic Aussie rock venue, with big-name acts every Friday and Saturday, with the action usually ending around 3 a.m. This venue also has six bars and a disco capable of holding 3,000 people. The **Bridge Hotel,** 135 Victoria Rd., Rozelle (tel. 02-9810-1260), is a little more upmarket, but no less rowdy, and often attracts international rock acts. Bands play nightly with cover charges ranging $3-15. The **Hard Rock Café** is at 121 Crown St., Darlinghurst (tel. 02-9331-1116). This shrine to music memorabilia has happy hour 5-7 p.m. with rock bands kicking off around 8 p.m.

Jazz, Blues, Folk, and Country

The **Real Ale Cafe,** 66 King St. (tel. 02-9262-3277), is one of Sydney's premier jazz venues with local and international acts performing Tues.-Saturday. Happy hour (5-7 p.m.) features half-price drinks; jazz starts at 8 p.m. and the action continues to as late as 4 a.m. on weekends. **Strawberry Hills Hotel,** 453 Elizabeth

St., Surry Hills (tel. 02-9698-2997), features contemporary jazz in fine surroundings with performances nightly as well as weekend afternoons. The **Basement,** 29 Reiby Place, Circular Quay (tel. 02-9251-2797), hosts many international jazz and blues acts, usually kicking off at 8:30 p.m. Admission is from $5. Folk fans flock to the **Rose, Shamrock, and Thistle Hotel** (known locally as "The Three Weeds"), an old pub with a pleasant atmosphere and live folk, reggae, or blues most nights. Admission ranges $5-16, and the action runs 8-11 p.m. It's at 193 Evans St., Rozelle (tel. 02-9555-7755). Sydney's main venue for country music is **The Shed** in the Brookvale Hotel, 509 Pittwater Rd., Brookvale (tel. 02-9905-0217).

Comedy

The **Harold Park Hotel,** 115 Wigram Rd., Glebe (tel. 02-9692-0564), is a great entertainment venue with stand-up comedians performing Mon.-Fri.; admission $8. The **Comedy Store,** corner Crystal St. and Parramatta Rd., Petersham (tel. 02-9564-3900), presents a smorgasbord of comedy talent ranging from local amateurs, overseas acts, and all-female shows (Thursday night). Admission averages $10. In Kings Cross, the **Comedy Club,** Hyatt Kingsgate Hotel (tel. 02-9268-4800), is a stylish setting with comedy performances Tues.-Sun. at 8 p.m. and 10 p.m.

SHOPPING

The three main strips of retail shops in downtown Sydney are along George, Pitt, and Castlereagh Streets (but for touristy souvenirs you're better off heading to Darling Harbour or The Rocks). For overseas visitors, the only real bargain shopping will be at duty-free stores along these streets, including **Downtown Duty Free** at 84 Pitt St. (tel. 02-9221-4444). Sydney's largest and most fashionable department store is **David Jones,** on the corner of Elizabeth and Market Streets. It features a wide range of retail items, with this store containing a travel agency, food court, restaurant, and beauty parlor. Down-market from David Jones is **Grace Bros.,** at 436 George Street. Sydney has many fine shopping arcades but, by far, the most magnificent is the

Queen Victoria Building (QVB) on George Street. Built in 1898, it has been restored and now contains a stylish food court, fashion boutiques, and specialty shops. The **Strand Arcade,** built in 1892, connects Pitt and George Streets. It features 82 distinctive shops and is a pleasant escape from the busy footpaths. Worth visiting for the stylish decor is **Skygarden,** connecting Pitt St. Mall to Castlereagh Street, where a massive glass dome covers upmarket specialty shops and a trendy mix of cafes and restaurants. **Harbourside Festival Marketplace** is a bright, colorful complex at Darling Harbour with around 200 shops selling all sorts of items from tacky souvenirs to designer-label fashion accessories. It's open daily until 9 p.m.

Markets

After a few years' absence, **Paddy's Markets** have returned to their former home of 150 years adjacent to Chinatown. These markets attract both locals and tourists with over 1,000 stalls selling just about everything you could imagine. The markets operate Sat.-Sun. 9 a.m.-4:30 p.m. **Paddington Village Bazaar,** held in the church grounds on the corner of Oxford and Newcombe Streets every Saturday, has a great atmosphere with locally crafted works, books, handmade toys, and clothing by young designers for sale. The buskers are the other attraction of these markets. A similar atmosphere prevails at **Glebe Sunday Market,** held on the corner of Glebe Point Rd. and Derby Place every Sunday. There's also a market at the top end of George St. in The Rocks every Saturday and Sunday.

Australiana

Sydney has several Aboriginal galleries. The biggest and best is the **Aboriginal Art Centre,** 117 George St., The Rocks (tel. 02-9247-9625). It features a wide range of authentic Aboriginal and Melanesian artifacts including weaponry, jewelry, clothing, carvings, and paintings.

R.M. Williams, 389 George St. (tel. 02-9262-2228), is a legendary Aussie bush wear shop selling oilskins, hats, boots, and belts. Closed Sunday. This company has another outlet down at the airport on the Departure Level of the International Terminal. **Sydney Harbour Shop,** 125 George St. (tel. 02-9247-2740), sells the work of Ken Done, whose colorful designs appear on just about everything. A few doors away, at 105 George St., is **Dorian Scott,** whose colorful clothing is a great Australian souvenir.

If you're after opals, there are plenty of duty-free jewelers around The Rocks and Circular Quay. A better option if you have the time is **Costello's** at 280 George St. (tel. 02-9221-1770).

FESTIVALS AND EVENTS

The entire month of January is taken up by the **Festival of Sydney,** featuring open-air concerts in the Domain, contemporary music at Hyde Park, a variety of performances at the Opera House, and outdoor movies in Hyde Park. The month-long **Gay and Lesbian Mardi Gras** culminates in a colorful parade along Oxford St. with all manner of floats on the first Saturday night in March.

The most eagerly awaited of Sydney's festivals is the **Royal Easter Show,** a 12-day agricultural extravaganza. The show provides an opportunity for the bush to come to the big smoke, and for city folk to experience life on the farm. The agricultural society was formed in 1822. Its chief goal was to ensure that levels of stock and produce resources were sufficient to support the fledgling colony. The first show put on by the society was held out at Parramatta in 1823. The venue is the Royal Agricultural Society Showground, south of Paddington, and the show has been held annually at this site

since 1882. Originally showcasing livestock and agricultural machinery, the show now also features a fun park, polo, rodeo, cooking competitions, wood chopping, and a pavilion full of showbags. Show attendance averages around 850,000 over the 12 days, so try to plan your visit on a weekday. Entry is adult $13, child $10. For details call (02) 9331-9111. Future dates are: 1997, 21 March-1 April; 1998, 3-14 April.

The **Biennale of Sydney,** held every two years (even-numbered years), brings together the world's leading artists with lectures, workshops, and lectures.

Held in theaters throughout the city, the **Sydney Film Festival** brings together filmmakers for two weeks through June.

Each Boxing Day dozens of yachts flanked by hundreds of spectator craft assemble in the harbor for the **Sydney-Hobart Yacht Race,** a spectacular event that sees the harbor foreshore lined with Sydneysiders.

HOTEL AND MOTEL ACCOMMODATIONS

Downtown—Budget

Sydney has no budget accommodations right downtown, but south of the city center, around Central Station, are several old pubs offering accommodations. In this category is **George Street Private Hotel,** 700 George St. (tel. 02-9211-1800), a rambling old place with basic but

Sydney skyline

clean rooms, a laundry, and a kitchen. Rates are $30 s, $44 d, with shared facilities. In the same area is **CB Private Hotel,** 417 Pitt St. (tel. 02-9211-5115), with over 200 rooms; $30 s, $49 d. Across the road is **Westend Hotel,** 412 Pitt St. (tel. 02-9211-4822), of a higher standard and with rooms with private facilities; $55 s, $65 d. At the north end of downtown, and one block from Wynyard Station, **Wynyard Hotel,** corner Clarence and Erskine Streets (tel. 02-9299-1330), has a reasonable standard of rooms with shared facilities for $45 s, $55 d.

Downtown—Moderate

Best value in this price range is **Sydney Travellers Rest Hotel,** 37 Ultimo St. (tel. 02-9281-5555), close to Darling Harbour and Chinatown. Rooms are small but well-furnished and all have bathrooms; $75 s, $84 d. Opposite Central Station and a short walk to Darling Harbour is **Country Comfort Sydney Central Hotel,** corner George and Quay Streets (tel. 02-9212-2544). Facilities are good and parking is free; $120 s or d. Directly opposite the Sydney Entertainment Centre and close to a monorail station is **Furama Hotel Sydney,** 68 Harbour St. (tel. 02-9281-0400), with all the facilities you'd expect of a four-star hostelry; $120-175 s or d. **Park Regis Hotel,** 27 Park St. (tel. 02-9267-6511), has a central location and has recently been refurbished, making it good value at $118 s or d. It also features a pool and free parking. **All Seasons Premier Menzies,** 14 Carrington S (tel. 02-9299-1000), is in the heart of the city center, one block from Wynyard Station, Facilities include an indoor pool, gym, laundry, restaurant, and bar; $162 s or d.

East of Hyde Park, but still well within walking distance of downtown, are a number of moderately priced accommodations. Best-value of these is **Oxford Koala Hotel,** corner Oxford and Pelican Streets (tel. 02-9269-0645), comprising motel-style rooms and self-contained apartments for $99-140 s or d. All rooms are well-furnished, air-conditioned, and have hair dryers. On the 13th floor is a pool. A little farther out is **Cambridge Hotel,** 212 Riley St. (tel. 02-9212-1111), three blocks east of Hyde Park. It has a pool, spa, sauna, and secure parking as well as a few rooms with kitchenettes. Rates are $105-115 s or d, including breakfast.

Downtown—Expensive

Most guests of the hotels in this category survive on business expense accounts and pre-booked accommodation packages, but often reduced rates and weekend packages are offered, reducing costs considerably. Least expensive of Sydney's nine five-star accommodations is the **Sydney Marriott,** 36 College St. (tel. 02-9361-8400), which overlooks the southeast corner of Hyde Park. Rooms are spacious and well-furnished, and each has a large bathtub. On the top floor is a pool and a sundeck with city views. Rates start at $185 s or d. Farther north, overlooking the Royal Botanic Gardens and 200 meters from Circular Quay, is the **Hotel Inter-Continental Sydney,** 117 Macquarie St. (tel. 02-9230-0200; call 800-332-4246 to book from North America), a 31-story hotel that incorporates the old 1849 Treasury building. Rooms are large and well-furnished, and many have views. Rates in standard rooms range $205-245 s or d. Open since 1990, the elegant **Ritz-Carlton Sydney,** 93 Macquarie St. (tel. 02-9252-4600), overlooks the same gardens. Rates start at $219 s or d, but good weekend packages are offered. The **Regent of Sydney,** 199 George St. (tel. 02-9238-0000; call 800-545-4000 to book from North America), is a luxurious hostelry featuring king beds, marble bathrooms, and oak furnishings in every room. It is also home to Kable's, one of Sydney's best restaurants. Rates start at $270 s or d. **Novotel Sydney on Darling Harbour,** 100 Murray St. (tel. 02-9934-0000), 100 meters from the attractions of Darling Harbour and with a monorail station on the doorstep, has comfortable rooms (request city views), a large pool area, gym, restaurant serving a high-quality buffet breakfast and a la carte dinner, and free guest parking. Rooms start at $195 s or d.

The Rocks

A continuation of downtown, the historic Rocks area is close to many sights and the public transportation hub of Circular Quay, making it an ideal alternative to staying in the city center. The **Lord Nelson Hotel,** 19 Kent St. (tel. 02-9251-4044), Sydney's oldest licensed hotel, has six rooms above a popular bar. Each has a private bathroom and is decorated with antiques. Guests have use of communal tea- and coffee-

*Lord Nelson Hotel
is an inexpensive
accommodation just
a five-minute walk
from the heart
of The Rocks.*

making facilities. Rates range $60-100, depending on room size, and include a continental breakfast. In the heart of The Rocks is **The Russell,** 143A George St. (tel. 02-9241-3543), not luxurious but oozing Victorian charm with bright furnishings, antique iron beds, and a roof-top garden with views over Circular Quay. Rates are $95-220 s, $105-230 d, depending on room size and facilities. All rates include a daily newspaper and light breakfast in the downstairs cafe. **The Stafford,** 75 Harrington St. (tel. 02-9251-6711), comprises 54 apartments spread through six floors and seven renovated 100-year-old terraces. All units are well furnished and self-contained with kitchens. Some rooms have balconies. The complex also boasts a laundry, outdoor pool, spa, and gym. Rates are $170 for a studio, rising to $185-195 for a one-bedroom apartment or a Terrace Room. **Park Hyatt Sydney,** 7 Hickson Rd. (tel. 02-9241-1234), on Campbells Cove, is absolute waterfront. It's a low-rise development in the heart of The Rocks, with most rooms having water views. Rooms are luxurious and start at $440 s or d, rising to $3000 for the Governor Suite, which boasts no less than six private balconies.

Kings Cross and Vicinity
As well as being home to many backpacker lodges, Kings Cross has a range of accommodations for those who like to be in the center of a lively nightlife. Immediately north, and just a short walk from the action, is the suburb of Potts

Point. **Kingsview Motel,** 30 Darlinghurst Rd. (tel. 02-9358-5599), is a good-value choice in the heart of the action. Rooms are of a high standard and range $68-105 s or d. Top of the range in Kings Cross is the **Hyatt Kingsgate Sydney,** William St. (tel. 02-9356-1234), with rooms for $230.

In Potts Point, **Challis Lodge,** 21 Challis Ave. (tel. 02-9358-5422), is two adjacent terraces offering basic but clean rooms. Rates are $28 s, $34 d with shared facilities; $36 s, $42 d with private facilities. Weekly rates start at $154 for a double. Similarly priced is **Bernly Private Hotel,** 15 Springfield Ave. (tel. 02-9358-3122). The friendly **De Vere Hotel,** 46 Macleay St. (tel. 02-9358-1211), is a good choice for overseas visitors as staff are more than happy to make tour arrangements. Rates are $79 s, $89 d. **Victoria Court Hotel,** 122 Victoria St. (tel. 02-9357-3200), is a boutique hotel of two adjoining terraces dating from 1881. Each room has its own character, and all rooms are decorated in Victorian style. Guests have use of a cozy sitting room where daily papers are supplied and a conservatory where tea- and coffee-making facilities are provided. Rates start at $60 s, $75 d, rising to $165 in a suite with a four-poster bed and private balcony. All rates include a continental buffet breakfast.

Elizabeth Bay
Northeast of Kings Cross, this upmarket suburb is a good choice for those who don't mind a

short cab ride into the city. **Roslyn Gardens Motor Inn,** 4 Roslyn Gardens (tel. 02-9358-1944), comprises 29 rooms, each air-conditioned and with a fully equipped kitchen; from $49 s, $59 d. On a residential backstreet is the art-deco **Manhattan Hotel,** 8 Greenknowe Ave. (tel. 02-9358-1288), a large accommodation dating from the 1940s but renovated and having a modern feel. Rooms are comfortable, and some have harbor views. Rates are $65-85 s or d. Overlooking busy Rushcutters Bay Marina is the **Sebel Town House,** 23 Elizabeth Bay Rd. (tel. 02-9358-3244), reasonably priced but long the choice of theater and showbiz personalities. Standard rooms are spacious and well furnished; $129-149 depending on the view. Suites have spectacular water views, kitchens, and are luxuriously outfitted; these rooms start at $195 (these rates on weekends include breakfast and dinner).

Bondi

The old **Hotel Bondi,** 178 Campbell Parade (tel. 02-9130-3271), has been extensively renovated on the outside and in the downstairs bar and restaurant areas, and although the rooms have seen better days, they are comfortable and clean. Standard pub-style rooms are $30 s or d; $35 for a room with a private bathroom. Rooms with beach views start at $50, while the best rooms are $95. Also overlooking the beach is **Bondi Beachside Inn,** 152 Campbell Parade (tel. 02-9130-5311), where basic rooms are $50 s, $60 d. Bondi's most luxurious accommodation is **Swiss Grand,** corner Campbell Parade and Beach Rd. (tel. 02-9365-5666), where self-contained apartments start at $180 s or d. **City Beach Motor Inn,** 99 Curlewis St. (tel. 02-9365-3100), with a tropical-looking facade a five-minute walk from famous Bondi Beach, has rooms of a good standard for $95 s or d.

Glebe

Glebe is a leafy suburb immediately west of downtown and with regular bus links to all the sights of downtown. Among the rows of cafes and restaurants are a couple of good-value accommodations. **Alishan International,** 100 Glebe Point Rd. (tel. 02-9566-4048), set back slightly from busy Glebe Point Rd., features 19 rooms, some with bathrooms, a recreation room,

barbecue area, communal kitchen, and laundry; $50-65 s, $65-85 d. **Rooftop Motel,** 146 Glebe Point Rd. (tel. 02-9660-7777), has a pool, barbecue, and large rooms for $75 s, $85 d.

Airport and Vicinity

Airport Sydney International Motor Inn, 35 Levey St. (tel. 02-9556-1555), within easy walking distance of the International Terminal, has comfortable rooms for a reasonable $99 s or d, and offers a day rate (6 a.m.-6 p.m.) for $60 s or d. Rates include airport transfers. Directly opposite is **Sydney Airport Hilton,** 20 Levey St. (tel. 02-9597-0122), with all the facilities expected of this international chain. Rates start at $150 s or d. To book from the United States, call (212) 697-9730. A few km east of the airport is **Tradewinds Travel Inn,** 200 Maroubra Rd., Maroubra (tel. 02-9344-5555), an elegantly furnished accommodation, with a pool, security parking, and airport transfers; $90-115 s or d.

North Shore

Centra North Sydney, Blue St. (tel. 02-9955-0499), has spectacular harbor and city views and is in the perfect location for a walk over the Bridge to begin a day's sightseeing. Rates start at $155 s or d, but good weekend packages are offered. Immediately west of North Sydney is **Harbourside Apartments,** which comprise 82 fully self-contained luxurious units right on Sydney Harbour. The main feature is a harborside pool with sundeck. The complex also features a private jetty served by regular ferry services. Rates begin at $116 s or d, rising to $198 for two-bedroom units. It's at 2 Henry Lawson Ave., McMahons Point (tel. 02-9963-4300).

Heading north on the Pacific Highway through the North Shore, most suburbs have motels. Pick of the bunch is **Killara Inn,** corner Pacific Hwy. and Commonwealth Rd., Killara (tel. 02-9416-1344), which has a wide range of facilities and comfortable rooms; $90-130 s or d.

Manly and the Northern Beaches

Manly Paradise Motel, 54 North Steyne (tel. 02-9977-5799), is a stone's throw from the beach and is the best choice for mid-priced accommodation north of the harbor. Motel-style units are well equipped, and guests have use of a rooftop pool and sundeck. Rates are $75-95. Facing the beach are huge two-bedroom fully self-contained apartments for $170 s or d. Similarly priced and 50 meters from the beach is **Manly Beach Resort,** 6 Carlton St. (tel. 02-9977-4188). Overlooking the beach is **Manly Pacific Parkroyal,** 55 North Steyne (tel. 02-9977-7666), an upmarket establishment with a resort feel about it. Rates start at $155 s or d. **Periwinkle-Manly Cove Guest House,** 18 East Esplanade (tel. 02-9977-4668), is a small privately owned accommodation on the harbor side of Manly. Rooms are clean, comfortable, and large, and some have harbor views. Guests have use of a communal kitchen, lounge room, and barbecue area in a central courtyard. Rates are $70 s, $80 d, which includes a continental breakfast. All of the above accommodations are within walking distance of both the beach and Manly Wharf.

Newport Mirage, corner Queens Parade and Kalinya Streets, Newport (tel. 02-9997-7011), is on the quiet waters of Pittwater yet just minutes from famous Newport Beach. A large pool, barbecue area, and sundeck right on the harbor are the main features, while rooms are bright and airy. Rates start at $110, with waterfront rooms for $150.

BACKPACKER ACCOMMODATIONS

The largest concentration of backpacker lodges is in Kings Cross, a couple of km east of downtown. Staying in one of the world's most infamous red-light districts isn't to everyone's liking; other choices are inner city Glebe, west of the city center, and the suburbs scattered along the beachside where the pace is slower.

Downtown
The **YWCA,** 5 Wentworth Ave. (tel. 02-9264-2451), offers safe, clean, and convenient accommodations for both men and women. Rooms are spartan but the location and price are right, and guests have use of a communal TV lounge and laundry. Rates with shared bathrooms are $52 s, $60 d; with private facilities $60 s, $85 d.

Kings Cross
With no less than 20 backpacker lodges, you'll always be able to find a bed in this lively part of the city. Most lodges are along Victoria St., but on the main drag are another couple of choices. **Highfield House Private Hotel,** 166 Victoria St. (tel. 02-9358-1552), is a popular choice with overseas visitors. Dorms are $12-15, and private rooms (shared facilities) $25 s, $40 d. Heading north, next door but one, is **Original Backpackers,** 162 Victoria St. (tel. 02-9356-3232), with a friendly atmosphere and reasonable facilities; dorms $10-13, $20 s, $28 d. Farther down the street is **Travellers Rest,** 156 Victoria St. (tel. 02-9358-4606), one of Kings Cross's best hostels. Facilities are excellent and some rooms have balconies opening to leafy Victoria Street. Dorms are $15 and private rooms are $22 s, $32 d. **Sydney Central Backpackers** (also known as Jolly Swagman) is another good choice. Facilities are modern, beds comfortable, and on the roof is a sundeck and barbecue area with city views. Dorm beds are $18, and there are a few private rooms for $42. It's at 144 Victoria St. (tel. 02-9368-1332).

Backpackers Connection, 2 Roslyn St. (tel. 02-9358-4844), an old motel off Darlinghurst Rd., has a modern kitchen, rooftop sundeck, and large rooms each with a bathroom and television; some are even air-conditioned. Rates start at $15 pp, with singles and doubles for $45. Of an equal standard is the **Pink House,** 6 Barncleuth Square (tel. 02-9358-1689), in a quiet location adjacent to the Travellers Car Market. Dorms are $14, private rooms $30 s or d.

Newtown
Newtown, an old suburb south of the city center, is home to **Billabong Gardens,** 11 Egan St. (tel. 02-9550-3236), one of Sydney's best budget accommodations. It's just off busy King St., home to lively pubs, cafes, and many alternative-fashion boutiques. Facilities include indoor and outdoor dining areas, laundry, modern kitchen, comfortable TV lounge, pool, spa, and barbecue area. Each room has a private bathroom. Dorms are $16, doubles $35.

Glebe
This historic suburb west of downtown features many cafes and restaurants, plenty of nightlife, and two of Sydney's three YHA hostels. **Glebe Point YHA Hostel,** 262 Glebe Point Rd. (tel. 02-9692-8418), has a rooftop sundeck, lounge

and TV rooms, laundry, and lots of organized activities. Rates in four- and six-bed dorms are $15 and $16 pp, respectively, and a bed in a twin room is $20 pp. **Hereford Lodge,** the other YHA hostel, has rooms with private bathrooms and a small rooftop pool. Rates are $15-22 pp depending on the number of beds in each room. This hostel is at 51 Hereford St. (tel. 02-9660-5577). From downtown, along George St., buses no. 431 and no. 433 pass both hostels. From the airport, catch the Kingsford Smith Transport bus and the hostels will deduct the fare from your room cost. Across the road from Hereford Lodge is **Wattle House,** 44 Hereford St. (tel. 02-9552-4997), with beds from $15 pp.

Bondi and the Southern Beaches

Bondi Beach Guesthouse, 11 Consett Ave. (tel. 02-9389-8309), just two blocks from the beach, is very central to Bondi attractions. Each room has a TV and fridge, and the communal kitchen is spotlessly clean. Dorm beds are $15 and doubles $35. A little closer to the beach is **Lamrock Hostel,** 7 Lamrock Ave. (tel. 02-9365-0221), basic but clean and with beds from $15 pp and good discounts for longer stays.

The best backpacker accommodation along the southern beaches is **Surfside Backpackers,** 186 Arden St., Coogee (tel. 02-9315-7888), right by the beach. Rates are $16 in dorms and $36 for a double. Up the hill from the beach is **Coogee Beach Backpackers,** 94 Beach St. (tel. 02-9665-7735), also of a high standard and similarly priced.

Cremorne Point

Harbourside Hotel, 41 Cremorne Rd. (tel. 02-9953-7977), is in leafy Cremorne Point, north of the harbor and east of North Sydney. It's right on the harbor, and popular with those who don't need a raging nightlife. Rates start at $15 pp, mostly in twins, and include a light breakfast. The easiest access by public transport is to get a ferry from Circular Quay to Cremorne Wharf and walk up the hill.

Manly and the Northern Beaches

Manly Beach Resort Backpackers, 6 Carlton St. (tel. 02-9977-4188), is part of the large and modern Manly Beach Resort, 50 meters from the beach. Facilities are good value at $16 for a

dorm and $32 d. Of a similar standard, in an anonymous red brick building, is **Manly Backpackers Beachside,** 28 Raglan St. (tel. 02-9977-3411).

Avalon Beach Backpackers Hostel, 59 Avalon Parade, Avalon (tel. 02-9918-9709), has a relaxed atmosphere and is a short walk to Avalon Beach. The hostel has all the usual facilities as well as surfboard and mountain bike rentals. Dorm beds are $14-16, doubles $36.

Sydney's most unique hostel is **Pittwater YHA Hostel** (tel. 02-9999-2196). It's at Morning Bay, in the heart of Ku-ring-gai Chase National Park, and accessible only by boat from Church Point, at the southern end of Pittwater. The lodge is rustic but comfortable. Rates are $14-18 pp. Call ahead for transportation details.

CAMPGROUNDS

North

The closest campground to the city center is **East's Lane Cove River Van Village,** Plassey Rd., North Ryde (tel. 02-9805-0500), set among eucalypts adjacent to Lane Cove National Park. Facilities are excellent and include a pool, laundry, kiosk, and barbecue area. Unpowered sites are $15.50-17.50, powered sites $16.50-18.50, on-site vans $48, and air-conditioned fully self-contained cabins go for $48-68. To get there take Delhi Rd. off Epping Rd. immediately west of the Lane Cove River, then take the second left.

West of Pacific Highway, in the rural area of Dural, is **Dural Village Caravan Park,** 269 New Line Rd. (tel. 02-9651-2555), with similar rates and facilities (as well as a tennis court), but is unsuitable for tent camping.

Just 400 meters from North Narrabeen Beach is **Lakeside Caravan Park,** Lake Park Rd. (tel. 02-9913-7845). Facilities are modern. Sites are $15-20, while comfortable cabins range $58-88.

South

At Lady Robinsons Beach (safe swimming) on Botany Bay is **Grand Pines Caravan Park.** Facilities are good and there's a city bus stop just around the corner. Sites are $19 (no tents), on-site vans $30, and cabins $40-65. It's at 289 Grand Parade, which runs along Botany Bay, but access is one block west on Alfred St. (tel.

02-9529-7329). From the Princes Highway in Blakehurst, Ramsgate Rd. passes the park.

Farther south, in the picturesque township of Bundeena, is **Bundeena Caravan Park** (tel. 02-9523-9520), in a quiet location a few blocks from the beach. Sites are $12-17, and cabins are $35-55. The road to Bundeena passes through Royal National Park, where camping is at Bonnie Vale, two km from Bundeena. Facilities here include toilets, showers, and a laundry. For bookings, call (02) 9521-2230.

DOWNTOWN DINING

Cafes

The old officer's mess of **Hyde Park Barracks** (tel. 02-9223-1155) has been converted to a pleasant cafe with tables tucked into a sunny corner of a large courtyard. Lunch averages around $10-12. As the name suggests, **Uptown Brasserie, Bar, & Cafe,** Level 3, Skygarden, Pitt St. Mall (tel. 02-9223-4211), has a section for all occasions. The cafe features strikingly innovative furniture that's worth a look even if you don't plan on eating. The cafe is good for those in a hurry, with fast efficient service and all the usual cafe fare (try for one of the tables overlooking busy Castlereagh Street). Also on Pitt St. Mall is the Strand Arcade, filled with stylish boutiques and a couple of cafes, including the old-fashioned **Miss Sippy's,** serving Devonshire teas for $5. Across the arcade is **Old Sydney Coffee Shop,** where coffee is ground on the premises.

Paradisio Cafes are dotted through the city; two of these outlets are within the Darling Park complex on Sussex Street. One, near the main entrance, features indoor cafe-style seating as well as comfortable lounges, coffee tables, and outdoor seating overlooking a small chunk of parkland.

Food Courts and Other Cheap Eats

These popular eating spots are the best places in the city for quick and inexpensive meals, and there are generally enough choices to suit all tastes. One of the best food courts is on the ground floor of the Queen Victoria Building on George Street. While most food courts are buried in the lower floors of large complexes,

Skygarden, on Pitt St. Mall, is in a stylish setting on the top floor. Outlets serve food from four continents, and there's even a bar serving champagne. In Chinatown, at the corner of Dixon and Goulburn Streets, is the **Chinatown Centre,** with a wide range of eateries; most dishes are under $6. It's open daily 10 a.m.-10 p.m. Another Chinatown food court is in the **Sussex Centre,** between Dixon and Sussex Streets.

The **YWCA,** 5-11 Wentworth Ave. (tel. 02-9264-2451), has a small inexpensive cafe. The setting is plain, but no dish costs over $7.50. Open daily 7:30 a.m.-7 p.m. With similar prices and atmosphere is the cafeteria in **Woolworths,** on the corner of George and Park Streets. Down Park St. one block is the **Criterion Hotel** (tel. 02-9264-3093), with lunchtime counter meals from $4.50 and steak and salad for $7. **Bar Ace,** 624 George St. (tel. 02-9264-6946), has a friendly atmosphere, pastas from $5, and steaks from $10. Opposite the Strand Arcade is **Soup Plus,** 383 George St. (tel. 02-9299-7728), where four different soups are offered daily along with a blackboard menu with lunch dishes, including soup and lasagna for $5. Most dinner dishes are $7-12. The decor is plain, but the atmosphere is good. Open Mon.-Sat. noon-late. Live jazz is performed nightly. **Sketches Bar & Bistro,** Hotel Inter-Continental, 117 Macquarie St. (tel. 02-9230-0200), is a stylish self-service pasta bar. The atmosphere is casual: pay the cashier, then choose from a dozen-odd choices at the self-service salad bar. All pastas are under $10, and two-course specials are around $14.

For vegetarian meals, head to **Bodhi,** 436 Sussex St. (tel. 02-9281-9918), where dishes such as eggplant fritters start at $2.50 and main dishes range $5-10. It's open daily 11 a.m.-3 p.m. and 5-10 p.m. Slightly more expensive is **Minar,** 16 Wentworth Ave. (tel. 02-9283-4634), toward Darlinghurst, which offers a wide variety of vegetarian and Indian cuisine. It's best known for tandoori dishes ($10-13), but there are plenty of other choices.

Steak

For reasonably priced steaks cooked to perfection head to **Daniel's Steakhouse,** 1 Bent St. (tel. 02-9251-6977). The beef is all grain-fed, raised on the rich pastures of Queensland's Darling Downs. It's open weekdays only for lunch and dinner. Built as a candle factory in the 1830s, **Kingsley's,** 29 King St. (tel. 02-9262-4155), features exposed sandstone blocks decorated with prints of Australian folk heroes, such as Captain Cook and Ned Kelly, and polished wooden floors. Steaks are thick and juicy and cooked to perfection. Expect to pay from $18 for a main meal. Steaks come no better than those cooked at **Kable's** in the Regent of Sydney, 199 George St. (tel. 02-9238-0000). The setting is a long art deco room with tables set as if for royalty, including crystalware and silverware. As well as steak, the menu includes such delicacies as lobster from Tasmania and lamb from the Victorian Gippsland; main dishes range $24-40. Desserts are delicious and begin at $8. Open Mon.-Fri. noon-2:30 p.m. and Tues.-Sat. 6:30-10:30 p.m.

Australian

Few countries in the world encourage the consumption of their national emblem, but in Australia kangaroo and emu appear on many restaurant menus. **Il Edna's Table,** Lobby Level, MLC Centre, Martin Place (tel. 02-9231-1400), features decor that reflects the stunning ochre colors of the outback and cool colors of the ocean, with grass trees decorating the room. The menu reflects typical bush tucker, cooked using native herbs. Open Mon.-Fri. for lunch and Mon.-Sat. for dinner.

Harbor Views

Harbour Take-out is on the west side of the Opera House (past the entrance to the Drama Theatre) with seating both under cover and out on the promenade. It's a good place for inexpensive seafood. Fish and chips starts at $5.50 and the filling Seafood Box is $9.50. Otherwise, cake and coffee is $3.50. It's open daily 10 a.m.-5:30 p.m. Also on the promenade is **Bennelong** (tel. 02-9250-7300). This restaurant attracts a wide variety of diners but is most popular with tourists, mostly because of its location at Sydney's top tourist attraction. The atmosphere is casual yet smart, with seating inside or out, and some of the best harbor views; the outside tables are protected from the elements by massive white umbrellas. The menu is eclectic, suiting the tastes of as many cultures as possible. Main dishes range $15-28, and wine can be

dining in the shadow of the Opera House

bought by the glass. It's open Mon.-Sat. 10 a.m.-11 p.m., Sunday 10 a.m.-5 p.m.

Sydney has three revolving restaurants. Two of these are on the top of Sydney Tower. The **International Restaurant,** on Level One 85 stories above the city streets, has (for a revolving restaurant) excellent food. The same menu is offered at lunch and dinner, with the former less expensive. On Level Two is a less-expensive restaurant with the same spectacular views. This eatery is self-service, with a large buffet that includes over a dozen main courses, including a carvery, grills, seafood, and Asian dishes. Lunch is a reasonable $27.50 ($32.50 on Sunday) and dinner is $32.50 ($35 Saturday and Sunday). For bookings at either restaurant, call (02) 9233-3722. The world's largest revolving restaurant is the **Summit,** on the 47th floor of Australia Square Tower, George St. (tel. 02-9247-9777). Needless to say, the views are stunning. Food is a little more expensive than the other two revolving restaurants, but there's also a buffet. Open daily for lunch and dinner.

Chinatown

For inexpensive no-frills Chinese food, try **Hingara Restaurant,** 82 Dixon St. (tel. 02-9212-2169), where the menu is pretty standard—dozens of soups and sweet and sour everything—but portions are good and the service is efficient. For similarly priced Cantonese-style Chinese head to **New Tai Yuen,** 31 Dixon St. (tel. 02-9212-5244). A longtime Chinatown favorite is **BBQ King,** 18 Goulburn St. (tel. 02-9267-2433), which, as the name suggests, specializes in barbecued meats. The atmosphere and decor are nothing special, but this restaurant is a good spot for a quick meal. The **Lantern Restaurant,** 515 Kent St. (tel. 02-9267-1153), has a lunchtime buffet for $7.90. **Marigold,** 683 George St. (tel. 02-9281-3388), an upmarket restaurant that wouldn't be out of place in Hong Kong, occupies two floors and seats around 700 diners at one sitting. It's the place to come for *yum cha,* a traditional form of eating small courses wheeled around from table to table on a trolley. Open Mon.-Sat. 10 a.m.-3 p.m. and daily from 6 p.m. for dinner. Popular with locals is the bright and breezy **Emperor Garden,** 213 Thomas St. (tel. 02-9281-9899). Around the corner is **House of Guang Zhou,** 76 Ultimo St. (tel. 02-9281-2205), a well-established restaurant famed for its local seafood cooked Chinese-style.

Other Asian Restaurants

The streets around Chinatown are dotted with many Asian restaurants. **Minh-Hai,** 615 George St. (tel. 02-9281-1875), is a Vietnamese restaurant in the heart of Chinatown. Aside from garish lighting and plain decor, the food is delicious and very inexpensive. Most meals are around $7 (adventurous diners may want to try the fish porridge). It's open Mon.-Sat. 10 a.m.-9:30 p.m. **Malaya,** 761 George St. (tel. 02-9211-0946), offers the choice of cuisine from China, Malaysia, and Indonesia.

Matsukaze, Level 1, Chifley Plaza, Chifley Square (tel. 02-9229-0191), specializes in tempura, a traditional method of deep-frying all manner of meats and vegetables in special oils. The lunch menu is simple and inexpensive, but it's

the dinner that most people come for. Open weekdays only.

Greek

Diethnes, 336 Pitt St. (tel. 02-9267-8956), is an old favorite that has been serving up delicious Greek salads, calamari, moussaka, and lamb dishes for over 40 years. Service is fast and friendly and the food reasonably priced. Closed Sunday. The **Hellenic Club,** 251 Elizabeth St. (tel. 02-9261-4910), is a staid, old restaurant, good for souvlaki. The dining room has unimpeded views across Hyde Park.

Italian

A Sydney institution is **Machiavelli,** 123 Clarence St. (tel. 02-9299-3748). This well-patronized restaurant is cavernous, with hanging sausages and hams adding a delicate touch. Lunch's main dishes average $18 (the antipasto is delicious), but there are a couple of offerings for around $12. Open for lunch Mon.-Fri. and for dinner Wed.-Friday. Another good choice for a casual Italian meal is **Primo's,** Queen Victoria Building (tel. 02-9283-5093), decorated in mellow green and white with a few tables looking down on the bustle of shoppers. Light lunches are priced from $6 with more filling Italian specialties from $11.

If you've spent the morning exploring the Australian Museum, a great place for lunch is **Beppi's,** corner Stanley and Yurong Streets (tel. 02-9360-4558), which celebrated 40 years of service in 1996.

French

Claudine's, 151 Macquarie St. (tel. 02-9241-1749), has a stunning blue and gold interior with a very modern finish. As well as the elegant setting, food is exquisite, prepared with a touch of Asian style. At lunch this restaurant fills with the business crowd while in the evening the atmosphere is more intimate. Plenty of seafood is offered. Main dishes start at $15.50. Open Mon.-Fri. for lunch and dinner.

Spanish

Around the intersection of Liverpool and Kent Streets is a small enclave of Spanish cafes, restaurants, and tapas bars. **Casa Asturiana,** 77 Liverpool St. (tel. 02-9264-1010), is a dimly-lit, always-crowded restaurant with rows of solid wooden tables that draw diners to indulge in tapas, a Spanish specialty of small servings (two to three tapas with a salad will fill most stomachs). The 30-odd different tapas are priced $4.50, $5.50, and $6.50, making keeping to a budget easy. Open for lunch Tues.-Fri. and dinner Tues.-Sunday. A couple of doors away is **Capitan Torres,** 73 Liverpool St. (tel. 02-9264-5574), formerly one of Sydney's great cheap eats. Prices have risen over the last few years, but it's still good value. Seafood is the specialty, with portions generous. The mixed grill of seafood is especially good. Open daily for lunch and dinner.

The Rocks

This historic area west of Circular Quay has Sydney's largest concentration of cafes and restaurants but, unlike those in inner-city suburbs, they are geared mostly to tourists, and there are no real dining bargains. The **Rocks Cafe,** 99 George St. (tel. 02-9247-3089), is a cozy little place with breakfasts that are surprisingly cheap for this popular tourist area. Next door is **Phillip's Foote,** 101 George St. (tel. 02-9241-1485), an English-style restaurant featuring a barbecue with grill-your-own steak, and a salad, for $16. Smaller meals are available in the cafe section from $6. It's open between noon and midnight. In an 1830s convict-built cottage with sloping wooden floors and crooked walls, the **Gumnut Tea Garden** (28 Harrington St. (tel. 02-9247-9591), has an authentic atmosphere. Seating is in one of many small rooms or outside along a wide veranda. This is a great place for breakfast ($4-10), and it gets crowded at lunchtime, especially on weekends. For a no-frills pub-style meal head to **Orient Hotel,** at 89 George St. (tel. 02-9251-1255). Typical Aussie fare, such as meat pies, is on the menu, and no meal is over $12. The most-pleasant eating area is a courtyard out the back of the pub.

In the Argyle Centre is the **Argyle Tavern** (tel. 02-9247-7782). The original structure, dating from 1828, remains, a good surrounding for the nightly "Jolly Swagman Show," which includes a three-course meal, sing-along, and sheep-shearing demonstration for adult $49.50, child $25. **Zia Pina,** 93 George St. (tel. 02-9247-2255), is a small restaurant that seems continuously full. The menu consists of two sizes of pizza, but a staggering variety of toppings are offered, with the most expensive $18. It's open for lunch and dinner daily.

Originally built as a jail, **Hero of Waterloo,** 81 Lower Fort St. (tel. 02-9252-4553), has been a licensed hotel since 1815. In its earlier days it was a rough-and-tough hangout, and while the look remains, today it's a lot tamer. Off the main bar is the Duke's Room, an old-world restaurant with lots of polished brass, old wooden tables, and gas lamps hanging from the rafters. The menu is varied and the food good. Expect to pay around $12 for a main meal. Friday-Sun. nights, folk musicians entertain diners.

Probably the best-placed of Sydney's restaurants is **Bilson's,** in the Overseas Passenger Terminal at Circular Quay West (tel. 02-9251-5600). Harbor views are stunning from all tables, with large wraparound glass windows. Apart from the views, friendly staff, and efficient service, we recommend it for the consistently good food upon which the restaurant has built its reputation. Specializing in modern Australian cuisine, the steak is the major drawcard, but the menu changes regularly and features cuisine from any of a dozen countries. Dinner has a set price ($50-60 pp), but lunch is markedly less expensive.

Darling Harbour Dining

Along the promenade of Harbourside Festival Marketplace is a string of restaurants with seating inside and out, but the prime location means prices are high. Best of the bunch is **Jordon's** (tel. 02-9281-3711), offering fish and chips from $17.50. **Bobby McGee's,** Level 2, South Pavilion (tel. 02-9281-3944), is a unique dining experience where waitpersons run around in far-out costumes singing and dancing while serving up wholesome American-style food such as Southern-fried chicken and gourmet cheeseburgers; there's also a great salad bar. It's open daily from noon till late. Near the Chinese Garden is the **Pumphouse Tavern** (tel. 02-9281-3967), best-known for its in-house brewery, but it also serves up good counter meals ranging $8.50-16.

Sydney Showboat

A luxurious replica of the old paddlewheelers that operated on the harbor, this floating restaurant cruises around the harbor nightly. The boat features a large outdoor platform designed especially for viewing the sights and lights of Sydney. It departs daily at 12:30 p.m. for a 90-minute Jazz Luncheon Cruise, when a massive buffet feast is laid out and diners eat to the music of jazz performers; adult $40, child $32. The evening Cabaret Cruise departs at 7:30 p.m. Dinner is a la carte, with cabaret performances after dinner; $95 pp. Both cruises depart from Campbells Cove, The Rocks. For bookings, call (02) 9552-2722.

RESTAURANTS IN OTHER PARTS OF THE CITY

East Sydney

Within this old suburb east of Hyde Park is an enclave of bistro-style restaurants that come alive each lunchtime with the business crowd. **The Edge,** 60 Riley St. (tel. 02-9360-1372), is a large, noisy eatery best-known for delicious pizza (from $12), but also for offering crisp salads and a great variety of pastas. The desserts are especially delicious. No reservations are taken, but there's a bar where you can wait for a table. Across the road, in a converted warehouse, is **Atlas Bistro & Bar,** 95 Riley St. (tel. 02-9360-3811), with a similar atmosphere as the Edge's, and busy every lunch and dinner. Around the corner, on Stanley St., is a string of small restaurants. **Two Chefs,** 115 Riley St. (tel. 02-9331-1559), is a stylish eatery with large windows overlooking the leafy streets. The emphasis is on good food, and best value is the fixed-price lunch for $18.50. It's also open for dinner. Vegetarians can head to **3 Frogs,** 66 Stanley St. (tel. 02-9361-3370), a vegan restaurant with an upstairs balcony. **No Name,** 2 Chapel St. (tel. 02-9360-4711), which can be entered from Stanley St. through the Arch Cafe, is the ultimate no-frills restaurant. No reservations are taken, and there's basically no decor, but the food is surprisingly good, and most meals are under $8. Open daily for lunch and dinner.

Darlinghurst

Silver Spoon, 203 Oxford St. (tel. 02-9360-4669), is a great little restaurant serving up the gently spiced food of Thailand, much of it prepared using local seafood. Expect to pay around $12 for a main meal. It's open daily for lunch and dinner. One of the best-value inner-city Indian restaurants is **Bombay Tandoori,** 231 Oxford St. (tel. 02-9361-3014), a colorful place with walls decorated with colorful murals. As the name suggests, most dishes are cooked tandoori-style, but they also serve some mixed platters and vegetarian dishes. It's open Mon.-Fri. for lunch and daily for dinner. **Kim's,** 235 Oxford St. (tel. 02-9357-5429), is a very small two-story Vietnamese restaurant where the food and atmosphere are surprisingly good for the price you pay—$8-10 for a main meal. It's open for dinner only and closed Tuesday.

Oh Calcutta, 251 Victoria St. (tel. 02-9360-3650), which features dishes from across the subcontinent, has some very hot tandoori choices. Main dishes are from $8. Open for dinner daily. In the same part of Darlinghurst is **Dov,** corner Forbes and Burton Streets (tel. 02-9360-9594), a small, stylishly decorated place serving a wide range of dishes, but all well-prepared and inexpensive. Most dishes are about $12. Open Mon.-Sat. 6:30 a.m.-10 p.m.

Kings Cross

The **Astoria Restaurant,** 7 Darlinghurst Rd. (tel. 02-9358-6327), is a no-frills place with roast dinners for around $5, and desserts, such as canned fruit with a dollop of ice cream, from $1. It's open Mon.-Sat. 10:30 a.m.-2:30 p.m. and for dinner 4-8:30 p.m. Developed to suit the demands of U.S. servicemen on R&R in the 1960s, the **Bourbon and Beefsteak Bar,** 24 Darlinghurst Rd. (tel. 02-9358-1144), still rages 24 hours a day. The breakfast menu could be right out of a U.S. roadside diner—hash browns, pancakes, and omelettes—while the rest of the day dishes such as Son-of-a-bitch Cowpoke Stew are offered. The **Last Aussie Fishcaf,** 24 Bayswater Rd. (tel. 02-9356-2911), is a 1950s-style seafood joint where staff lead sing-alongs and party games. It's not cheap, and not the place for a quiet night; from $10 for a main meal and $31 for the weekend fixed-price three-course dinner.

The casual **Bayswater Brasserie,** 32 Bayswater Rd. (tel. 02-9357-2177), is a popular spot, considered by many to be the best bar/

bistro in the city. Food is reasonably priced, service friendly, and it's one place that retains its popularity through the years. It's possible to just drop by for a cappuccino. The Sunday brunch (10 a.m.-5 p.m.) is very popular, while the rest of the week it's open for lunch and dinner. Tiny **Cafe Pralinka,** 4 Roslyn St. (tel. 02-9358-1553), is an inexpensive spot with just five tables. The fare is pretty standard but portions are good, and no dish costs over $8. Open Tues.-Sat. 11 a.m.-9 p.m. Next door is **Kings Cross Steak House,** 2 Roslyn St. (tel. 02-9358-5639), a little more expensive and, as the name suggests, specializing in steaks.

At the south end of Kings Cross is **Sirocco,** 23 Craigend St. (tel. 02-9332-4495), a wide-open restaurant with an open kitchen and a hint of Mediterranean style. The setting is stylish and the food modern Australian, which usually means local ingredients cooked in a style from overseas. Open daily except Monday for lunch and dinner.

Along Kellett St. are nightspots and late-night restaurants. Pick of the bunch is **Lime and Lemongrass,** 42 Kellett St. (tel. 02-9358-5577), a Thai restaurant and cocktail bar open daily 6 p.m.-4 a.m. Tables are inside and out and the food is very good. Main meals are a reasonable $10-16.

Woolloomooloo

One of Sydney's legendary eating spots, **Harry's Cafe de Wheels,** on Cowper Wharf Rd., has no tables and doesn't even open until 9 p.m. But for decades this pie wagon has been serving pies and hot drinks to regular clientele that vary from shift workers to visiting celebrities. Once the haunt of only thirsty wharfies, the **Woolloomooloo Bay Hotel,** 2 Bourke St. (tel. 02-9357-1177), now has a stylish bistro with an interesting blackboard menu and a pianist tickling the keys every evening. Open daily 11 a.m.-9 p.m.

Surry Hills

This revitalized suburb extends from the back streets around Central Station through leafy streets lined with terraces to a large Lebanese community centered on the junction of Cleveland and Elizabeth Streets. The Lebanese restaurants in this area differ greatly in quality. **Gazal**

Restaurant, 286 Cleveland St. (tel. 02-9318-1982), is one of the best, with a great variety of dips for about $5 and main meals about $8. For takeaway, try **Abdul's,** across the road.

One block up Crown St. from the Lebanese restaurants, at Devonshire St. (tel. 02-9318-1034), is **Rustic Cafe,** a popular spot (with a distinctive bright yellow exterior) where the coffee is ground on the premises daily and they serve tasty pastries. One block to the east, at 633 Bourke St. (tel. 02-9690-1894), is **La Passion Du Fruit,** a great little cafe with a few tables on the sidewalk and plenty of reading material inside. As well as serving great coffee, they serve light snacks, with the emphasis on healthy eating. Soups are $5, and other dishes average $10. Desserts range $3-5. Open Tues.-Sat. 8 a.m.-10:30 p.m., Sunday 11 a.m.-4 p.m. **Dolphin Hotel,** 412 Crown St. (tel. 02-9331-4800), has fantastic pub food and a good beer garden. The T-bone steaks are particularly good, and for an extra $7 you can have unlimited servings of salad. Open daily for lunch noon-2 p.m., dinner 6-9 p.m. **Strelitzia,** 26 Buckingham St. (tel. 02-9698-3349), is a terrace dating to early this century that has been transformed into a cozy restaurant with an open fire and balcony. Some of the best dishes are char-grilled, including chicken breast and kangaroo. All main dishes are $15 and desserts are $8. Open weekdays for lunch and Tues.-Sat. for dinner.

Glebe

In recent times, the main street of this old inner-city suburb has been transformed to a trendy cafe and restaurant precinct. Many places cater to the university folks who hang out at cafes like **Well Connected,** which allows coffee-guzzlers to surf the Internet. **Rose Blue Cafe,** 23 Glebe Point Rd. (tel. 02-9552-2105), is seemingly out of place in Glebe, with a relaxed atmosphere and plenty of room between tables. Out back is a large courtyard terrace, the perfect place to relax with a slab of one of many delicious cakes and a strong coffee ($6.50). Other meals are available, including breakfasts from $2, with many American-style choices such as eggs Benedict and omelettes from $7. The rest of the day a wide variety of dishes are offered, with the Caesar salad ($10.50) especially good.

Yak and Yeti, 41 Glebe Point Rd. (tel. 02-

9552-1220), is a small eatery serving up the traditional Nepalese cuisine in a simple yet stylish setting. Open daily 6-10:30 p.m. Next door is **Paganini,** 43 Glebe Point Rd. (tel. 02-9552-1541), named for the famous violinist. This restaurant is tastefully decorated with memorabilia from his concerts and interesting oil jars set into whitewashed walls. Main dishes are about $20. Open for lunch and dinner daily except Sunday.

Eastern Suburbs

Large **Pepper's Bayside,** 22 Knox St., Double Bay (tel. 02-9363-0100), is a sophisticated cafe with tables inside and out. It attracts locals but is mainly the haunt of better-dressed overseas visitors. Open daily from 8 a.m. until late. Also in Double Bay is **The Cleveland,** 63 Bay St. (tel. 02-9327-6877), one of Sydney's most stylish Chinese restaurants. The restaurant is divided in two sections—downstairs is Bhuddist-style vegetarian and upstairs is Sichuan. Open daily for lunch and dinner.

In Nielson Park, Vaucluse, opposite a beautiful little beach, an old kiosk has been converted to a stylish Italian restaurant with a casual atmosphere. Open for a hot or cold buffet breakfast on Saturday and Sunday and lunch Tues.-Sunday. Located on Graycliffe Ave. (tel. 02-9337-1574).

Doyle's on the Beach

Eating at this famous restaurant is a Sydney dining experience you shouldn't miss. The restaurant, overlooking Watsons Bay, is a hive of activity in summer and a peaceful retreat the rest of the year. The best way to arrive is by water taxi from Circular Quay (last one departs at 3 p.m.). Seafood is what draws the crowds, and they rarely leave disappointed. The selection is varied, ranging from grilled fish to a mixed seafood platter. Desserts are also good. It's open daily noon-3 p.m. and 6-9:30 p.m. Located at 11 Marine Parade (tel. 02-9337-2007).

Bondi

The year-round summer atmosphere of Bondi makes this seaside suburb a good place for outdoor dining. If you're staying at the Alice Motel (or even if you're not) don't miss breakfast in the small restaurant overlooking Tamarama Bay. Located at 30 Fletcher St. (tel. 02-9130-5231).

Lunch in Bondi is typically fish and chips. For this, head to **Bondi Surf Seafoods** at 128 Campbell Parade, where it'll cost from $3.50. One of Bondi's original cafes is **Bates Milk Bar,** at 126 Campbell Parade, with surf murals on the walls, chrome chairs, and speckled laminex tables. Service is friendly and efficient, and the burgers are as good as they get for under $5. At the opposite end of the to-be-seen-at scale are the cafes clustered around the corner of Campbell Parade and Lamrock Avenue. Right on the corner of these streets is trendy **Le Crepe Cafe,** while next door is a similar set-up, **Hugo's.** On the other side is tiny **Dip,** 10 Lamrock Ave. (tel. 02-9130-8075), open all day. Don't come here for bacon and eggs though; dishes such as scrambled tofu are the order of the day. Another good cafe is **Bondi Aquabar,** 266 Campbell Parade (tel. 02-9130-6070), toward North Bondi and overlooking the beach. This place is bright, casual, and has a large menu.

Right on busy Campbell Parade is a string of restaurants of very different standards. Pick of the bunch is **Beechwood,** 100 Campbell Parade (tel. 02-9365-5986), a large, dimly lit restaurant where it's possible to escape the crowds. Meals are well-priced, with most main dishes under $10.

Away from the beach, nearly opposite City Beach Motor Inn, is **Intra Thai,** 90 Curlewis St. (tel. 02-9130-3342), a budget restaurant with surprising style, right down to white tablecloths and attentive waiters. Expect to pay less than $30 for a filling meal for two. In the same area is **Little Snail,** 96 Curlewis St. (tel. 02-9365-4847), an inexpensive French restaurant open Mon.-Fri. for lunch and nightly for dinner. The best deal is the fixed-price three-course dinner for $20.

Southern Beaches

Coogee isn't exactly the culinary center of Sydney, but **Barzura,** 62 Carr St. (tel. 02-9665-5546), has plenty of choices, is licensed, and, best of all, has great ocean views. **Boatshed Cafe** is exactly that—an old boatshed overlooking Botany Bay. It's right on the beach at La Perouse (tel. 02-9661-9315).

North Shore

Since being bypassed by the freeway a few years back, Crows Nest, immediately north of North Sydney, has become a lot quieter. But that hasn't changed the brisk trade at **Eric's Seafood Cafe,** 316 Pacific Hwy. (tel. 02-9436-

4906), which has been serving fish and chips since the 1920s. Surprisingly, one of Sydney's best-loved Chinese restaurants is in the commercial area of Crows Nest, well away from Chinatown. It's **Peacock Gardens,** 100 Alexander St. (tel. 02-9439-8786), where the local specialty is *sang choy bow* with seafood substituted for the usual generic meat.

For an intriguing mix of cuisine from Morocco and Sri Lanka, head to **Mosquito Bar,** 142 Spit Rd. (tel. 02-9968-1801). Main meals are a reasonable $8-14. Open for dinner Mon.-Sat. 6-10 p.m.

Manly and the Northern Beaches

For inexpensive fish and chips, deep-fried to perfection in olive oil, head to **Manly Fish Market and Cafe,** on Wentworth St.; fish, chips, and a salad is around $8. Along the Corso are other casual seafood joints, including **Cristals,** 90 the Corso (tel. 02-9977-3758), with tables spread around the Corso. Seafood dishes start at $11 and it's also open for breakfast (croissants here are delicious). Along the Steyne, either side of the Corso, are trendy cafes and restaurants. South of the Corso is the large **Cafe Rimini,** 35 South Steyne (tel. 02-9977-3880), with tiered levels of tables opening to ocean views. Diners have a choice of Land or Ocean menus, with the Grilled Barramundi especially good for $17.50. It's open daily for all meals. Farther along, at 25 South Steyne, is **Cafe Nice** (tel. 02-9976-3658), serving up good coffee and with daily newspapers to read. On North Steyne are more eateries, including **Wi Marn,** 47 North Steyne (tel. 02-9976-2995), specializing in seafood cooked in Thai style. **Manly Pier Seafood Restaurant,** Commonwealth Ave. (tel. 02-9949-1994), is a stylish and simply furnished restaurant where the main feature is the view across Manly Cove through massive glass windows. Seafood is the specialty, with most main meals about $20 and all desserts $8.50.

Traditionally, meat pies have been a staple at breakfast for many Australians. But, the pies at **Sylvia and Fran's Upper Crust,** at 1003 Pittwater Rd., Collaroy, deserve better. They are very popular and many varieties are offered. **Surfside Pie Shop,** 383 Barrenjoey Rd., Newport, is equally good, and the cooks use real cream in their cream buns. Farther north, at 231 Whale Beach Rd., Whale Beach, is **Whaley's** (tel. 02-9974-4121), a good place for a healthy burger.

A great luncheon spot on Sydney's northernmost beach, Palm Beach, is **La Palma,** 1108 Barrenjoey Rd. (tel. 02-9974-4001), which has a lovely outdoor eating area. The food is well-prepared and the freshest of ingredients are used. Dinner main dishes average $18-20, with lunchtime prices considerably lower. Open daily for lunch and dinner.

GETTING THERE

Air

Sydney Airport (officially known as **Kingsford Smith,** but also called Mascot, for the suburb it's in) is on Botany Bay, surrounded by urban sprawl 15 km south of the city center. More passengers pass through this gateway than any other Australian airport, and for over a decade there has been talk of developing a brand-new airport. A site, 40 km west of downtown at Badgerys Creek, has been decided upon, but, in the meantime, a third runway has been developed at Sydney to handle ever-increasing passenger numbers.

In the International Terminal you'll find car rental companies, the **Travellers Information Centre** (open daily 6 a.m. until the arrival of the last flight; ask for hotel discounts), a post office, currency exchange, lockers, duty-free shops, showers, restaurants, and bars.

The best way to arrive in Sydney is aboard the flying kangaroo, **Qantas** (tel. 02-9957-0111 or, from North America 800-227-4500). Qantas flights originate from major centers around the world, providing a little Aussie culture before arriving down under. Other international carriers arriving in Sydney are: **Air Italia, Air New Zealand, Ansett Australia, British Airways, Canadian Airlines, Japan Air Lines, Lauda Air, Malaysian Air System, Singapore Airlines,** and **United Airlines,** as well as many Pacific Island airlines. Around a dozen domestic carriers serve Sydney Airport, but, with the exception of **Impulse** (tel. 13-1381), flying to rural and coastal New South Wales, flights to all centers can be booked through **Ansett Australia** (tel. 13-1300) or **Qantas** (tel. 13-1313). To call these airlines from North America, call (800) 366-1300 and (800) 227-4500, respectively.

The **Airport Express** (tel. 02-9669-1118) operates a regular service between both airport terminals and downtown (Route 300) and Kings Cross (Route 350), stopping at points throughout the city. Departures are every 10-20 minutes between 6 a.m. and 1 p.m. The fare is $5 one-way, $8 round-trip. A transfer between the two terminals is $2.50. **Kingsford Smith Transport** (tel. 02-9667-3221) operates from both terminals, dropping passengers right at the door of all city and inner suburban accommodations. The fare is $5 each way. A cab between the airport and downtown runs about $18.

Rail

Countrylink (tel. 13-2232) operates an extensive rail service throughout the state, with bus connections to smaller centers. **Central Station,** at the south end of downtown, is the main interstate and intrastate terminal. Fares are comparable to traveling by bus, with transport and accommodation packages often making rail travel even cheaper. Standard fares between Sydney and other state capitals are: Canberra, economy $35, first class $48; Melbourne, economy $49, sleeper $135; Adelaide, economy $104, sleeper $317; Perth, a 65-hour trip aboard the Indian-Pacific, economy $495, first class $850; and Brisbane, economy $98, first class $142. Within New South Wales, rail services run along the north coast, west to Bathurst and Dubbo, and south through Canberra to Albury.

Bus

Greyhound Pioneer (tel. 13-2030) operates the most extensive network of bus services with daily services from Sydney to all state capitals as well as most major towns throughout the country. The Sydney terminal is at the corner of Oxford and Riley Streets. The other major carrier is **McCafferty's** (tel. 02-9212-3433), which also runs Australia-wide. Buses terminate at the Sydney Coach Terminal on the corner of Eddy Ave. and Pitt Street. Standard one-way fares with both companies from Sydney are: Canberra $28 (Greyhound Pioneer runs directly between Sydney Airport and Canberra; $32), Melbourne $40, Adelaide $70-90, Perth $245, Alice Springs $211, Brisbane $73, and Cairns $185. McCafferty's offers over a dozen different Travel Aus-

tralia Passes with the most comprehensive being 12 months unlimited travel on the entire route network for $1160.

Oz Experience (tel. 02-9907-0522) operates an alternative bus service along the east coast, with stops made at points of interest en route and nights spent at backpacker lodges. The trip between Sydney and Cairns takes nine days. The fare is $295, with the ticket valid for six months. A ticket for travel between Sydney and Melbourne via Canberra is $110 one-way, $220 round-trip. From Sydney to Darwin via Cairns and Alice Springs is $609 one-way and is valid for 12 months. Within North America bookings can be made through any STA agent.

GETTING AROUND

Transport around Sydney is provided by **CityRail,** which operates train services, and **State Transit,** which operates buses and ferries. The best deal for extensive sightseeing is a **SydneyPass,** which allows unlimited travel on buses, ferries, the *RiverCat* to Parramatta, Airport Express services, some harbor cruises, and the Sydney Explorer bus. The cost is three days $60, five days $80, and seven days $90. Call 13-1500 for details. The passes can be purchased from both airport terminals, Circular Quay booking agents, and all Tourist Information Centres.

Rail

The suburban rail service covers most parts of the city (except the northern beaches), and, because of heavy road traffic, it's often quicker than bus travel. The City Circle line runs underground, linking Central Station to Town Hall, Wynyard, Circular Quay, and Hyde Park; $1.20 per sector. Other main routes from Central are to Bondi, Cronulla, Parramatta, and across the Harbour Bridge to North Sydney and the North Shore. A City Hopper ticket ($2.20) allows one day's unlimited train travel Mon.-Fri. after 9 a.m. and all weekend. For all local rail travel, call 13-1500.

Bus

State Transit buses run throughout the city but travel is slow compared to trains, especially during peak hours. The main downtown bus stops are at Circular Quay, Railway Square

(Central Station), and Wynyard Park. The best source of bus information is the kiosk on Alfred St., Circular Quay. Fares start at $1.20 per sector (about four km), with the maximum you'll pay $3.80 for the 44-km trip between downtown and Palm Beach. Buses run daily 4:30 a.m.-11:30 p.m., with less-frequent weekend services.

The easy-to-recognize red **Sydney Explorer**, operated by State Transit, runs every 20 minutes between 26 of the city's top attractions. The ticket price of $20 (included in the SydneyPass; see above) includes discounts at many attractions. They can be bought onboard the bus or at any State Transit office. The service runs daily 9 a.m.-7 p.m. The blue **Bondi & Bay Explorer** has a similar format, running from Circular Quay through Kings Cross, Double Bay, and Watsons Bay to famous Bondi Beach. Tickets are $20.

Monorail

The state-of-the-art monorail connects Darling Harbour with Chinatown, George St., and Pitt St. (travel is counterclockwise), whisking passengers along high above the congested streets below. It operates Mon.-Wed. 7 a.m.-10 p.m., Thurs.-Fri. 7 a.m.-midnight, Saturday 8 a.m.-midnight, Sunday 9 a.m.-8 p.m. Tickets cost $2.50 each way.

Ferry

The ferries of Sydney Harbour are the most scenic way to travel around the city. From Circular Quay Ferry Terminal ferries run to Balmain, Sydney Aquarium, Darling Harbour, McMahons Point, Kirribilli, Cremorne Point, Mosman, Taronga Zoo, Manly, Rose Bay, and Watsons Bay. Fares range $2.60 for the trip to Darling Harbour to $3.40 for the 35-minute trip across to Manly. Another way to get to Manly is aboard the high-speed **JetCat;** $4.60 each way. The high-speed **RiverCat** runs up the Parramatta River to Parramatta, passing Sydney Olympic Park. All the above services are covered on the SydneyPass. Ferries run daily 5:30 a.m.-midnight. For further ferry information, head to the small information center behind Wharf 4 at Circular Quay or call 13-1500.

Taxi

Cabs run throughout the city 24 hours a day. Flag charge is $1.80, then $1.75 per km. Taxi ranks are throughout the city, but the best places to look for a cab are outside railway stations and major downtown hotels. Otherwise, call: **Legion Cabs** (tel. 13-1451), **RSL Taxis** (tel. 02-9581-1111), or **Taxis Combined** (tel. 02-9332-8888).

Water taxis run around the harbor but are expensive. Sample fares from Circular Quay are Kirribilli $8 pp, Darling Harbour $10, Watsons Bay $40. For bookings, call **Taxis Afloat** at (02) 9955-3222.

Car

The major car rental companies have desks at both the International and Domestic Terminals of Sydney Airport. Otherwise call: **Avis** (tel. 02-9353-9000), **Budget** (tel. 13-2727), **Dollar** (tel.

Circular Quay is the terminus of all manner of boats, from cruise ships to commuter ferries.

ANDREW HEMPSTEAD

Pyrmont Bridge

02-9223-1444), **Hertz** (tel. 13-3039), or **Thrifty** (tel. 02-9380-5399). Rates from these companies range $75-105 per day depending on car size, kilometer allowances, and insurance inclusions, but rates are often lower. With branches throughout the city, **Ascot** (tel. 02-9317-2111) is a lot cheaper, with new cars for $30 a day and $36 for medium-sized cars. A number of companies rent secondhand cars, including **Down Under Rent-a-car** (tel. 02-9971-8447). **Maui** (tel. 1800-22-7279) operates a massive fleet of campervans that can be rented from $85 per day.

If you plan a long stay in Australia, buying a car is the best option. **Mach 1 Autos,** 495 New Canterbury Rd., Dulwich Hill (tel. 02-9569-3374), will sell you a car, with the guarantee of buying it back at a pre-agreed price, depending on how long you want it for. A car market popular with travelers is on the corner of Ward Ave. and Elizabeth Bay Rd., Kings Cross. Sellers are charged $35 per week to display their vehicles there; open daily. On a Sunday, Flemington Car Market, right by Flemington Railway Station, is a good bet for a wide range of vehicles.

Bicycle
Sydney certainly isn't the best city in the world for cycling, but there are a few interesting routes around the inner city. **Rockcycle Tours,** Circular Quay West (tel. 02-9247-7777), rents mountain bikes for $9 an hour and $39 for a full day and have put together itineraries for cycling around The Rocks area. **Inner City Cycles,** 31 Glebe Point Rd., Glebe (tel. 02-9660-6605), has good bikes for $30 a day, $45 for a weekend, and $100 a week. On the north side of harbor, **Manly Cycle Centre,** 36 Pittwater Rd., Manly (tel. 02-9977-1189), is well priced with bikes for $5 an hour and $60 a week.

The publication *Cycling around Sydney* ($10.50), published by the Bicycle Institute of NSW (tel. 02-9212-5628), details all routes around the city.

Tours
Apart from the Sydney Explorer (see "Bus," above), many private operators offer tours of the city and its surrounds. The main companies are **Clipper Gray Line Tours** (tel. 02-9319-4666 or 1800-22-6086), **Murray's** (tel. 02-9252-3590), and **Australian Pacific Tours** (tel. 13-1304). Typically, a tour of the city and Northern Beaches is $38-48, of the city and Bondi is $32, and a full-day tour including lunch and a harbor cruise is $78-92. These companies also offer night tours that take in various lookouts with the option of dinner or a visit to Harbourside Casino. Look for their brochures at all information centers and pick an itinerary that best suits your needs. **Australian Pacific Tours** (tel. 13-1304) has a popular Night Lights and Sights tour in a double-decker bus for $34 and the famous After Dark Tour, which includes dining in Sydney Tower Restaurant, viewing Les Girls Revue, and visiting Kings Cross; $97 pp.

Harbor Cruises
Captain Cook Cruises, based at Wharf 6, Circular Quay (tel. 02-9206-1111), offers a great variety of cruises to destinations around the harbor. The Coffee Cruise passes all the major points of interest, departing daily at 10 a.m. and 2:15 p.m.; adult $30, child $18. The Harbour High-

ights Cruise is shorter, passing sights around the Harbour Bridge. Departures are five times daily; adult $16, child $11. Other tours include Fort Denison (departs 10 a.m., noon, and 2 p.m.; adult $8.50, child $6), a Luncheon Cruise (departs 12:30 p.m.; adult $42, child $32), which features fresh seafood, and the Showtime Dinner Cruise (departs 7:30 p.m.; adult $79, child $44). This company also operates the hourly **Sydney Harbour Explorer,** which stops at six major harbor attractions between 9 a.m. and 5 p.m.; adult $19, child $11.

SERVICES

Sydney's **general post office** is in Martin Place, between Pitt and George Streets. It's open Mon.-Fri. 8:15 a.m.-5:30 p.m., Saturday 8:30 a.m.-noon. **Travelex Australia** has eight foreign money exchange outlets throughout the city, including at both airport terminals, in Martin Place at 37 Pitt St. and 182 George St., and in Kings Cross at 48 Darlinghurst Road. **American Express** is at 92 Pitt St. (tel. 02-9239-0666). All major banks will also cash traveler's checks; those in a foreign currency often entail a fee.

One-hour photo developing shops are scattered throughout the city, but one that we've found to be very professional is **Jadon Color** on Level 6, 89 York St. (tel. 02-9262-1114). For purchasing photographic equipment, **Paxton's,** 285 George St. (tel. 02-9299-2999), is well priced, with some good duty-free buys.

Along Kent St., behind Town Hall, are shops specializing in adventure travel. This is also the location of YHA offices.

The **Flight Centre** is the best place to search out inexpensive tickets for onward travel. The branch at 580 George St. (tel. 02-9267-2999) is central, or call 13-1600 for quotes over the phone. The folks at **Surf Travel Co.,** 2/25 Cronulla Plaza (tel. 02-9527-4722), specializing in travel for surfers and snowboarders, are experts in onward travel through Indonesia and the Pacific Ocean, as well as adventure tours through New Zealand. The airfares they offer are also competitive.

Most better accommodations and backpacker lodges have a laundry for guest use. Otherwise, try: **Tina Co-op Laundry,** 148 Glenayr Ave., Bondi; **Soap Sud City,** 56 Bayswater Rd., Kings Cross; **St. Johns Laundromat,** 176 St. Johns Rd., Glebe; **Pacific Laundrette,** 10 Campbell Parade, Bondi Beach; **Manly Beach Laundry,** 28 Darley Rd., Manly; **Argyle Place Laundry,** 9 Argyle Place, The Rocks.

Emergency Services
Sydney's main hospitals are: **Sydney Hospital,** Macquarie St., Sydney (tel. 02-9228-2111); **St. Vincents Hospital,** corner Victoria and Burton Streets, Darlinghurst (tel. 02-9339-1111); **Royal Prince Alfred Hospital,** Missenden Rd., Camperdown (tel. 02-9515-6111); and **New Children's Hospital,** Hawkesbury Rd., Westmead (tel. 02-9845-0000). The **Traveller's Medical & Vaccination Centre** is on Level 7, 428 George St. (tel. 02-9221-7133). It's open Mon.-Fri. 9 a.m.-5 p.m., Saturday 9 a.m.-noon.

INFORMATION

State Library of New South Wales
This magnificent library faces Macquarie St. (tel. 02-9230-1414) and is sandwiched between a line of colonial-era buildings. The original library, now known as the **Mitchell Wing,** is a cavernous room housing rare and antiquarian books on shelves around a three-story-high atrium that's lit by a massive skylight. On this wing's lobby floor is a mosaic reproduction of Abel Tasman's map of Australia. Through a walkway and past the library cafe is the modern wing, with the main collection, audiovisuals, and newspapers and magazines from around the world. The library is open Mon.-Fri. 9 a.m.-9 p.m., Sat.-Sun. 11 a.m.-5 p.m.

Bookstores
The **Travel Bookshop,** 20 Bridge St. (tel. 02-9241-3554), has an extensive range of books to all Australian destinations, including cycling, hiking, climbing, and cruising guides. It's open daily. **Angus and Robertson** has a bookshop in the Imperial Arcade, 174-186 Pitt St. (tel. 02-9235-1188), and **Dymocks** is at 428 George St. (tel. 02-9235-0155). Specializing in rare and antiquarian books is **Berkelouw Book Sellers,** 19 Oxford St., Paddington (tel. 02-9360-3200). If you're heading south on the Hume Highway, it's

Mitchell Wing,
State Library

worth stopping at their main shop, **Berkelouw Messrs** in Berrima (tel. 048-77-1370).

Information Centers
Coming off an international flight, the first place you should stop is the **Travellers Information Centre,** in the International Terminal. It's open every day of the year from 6 a.m. until the arrival of the day's last flight. The **Rocks Visitor Centre,** 106 George St. (tel. 02-9255-1788), in a building dating from the 1860s, has lots of brochures as well as books and maps for sale; open daily 9 a.m.-5 p.m. Out in beachside Manly is **Manly Visitors Information Bureau,** South Steyne St. (tel. 02-9977-1088), open daily 10 a.m.-4 p.m. The New South Wales automobile

club is the **National Roads and Motorists Association** (NRMA), with an office at 151 Clarence St. (tel. 02-9260-9222). For members of affiliated clubs, maps and accommodation guides are free. This office is open Mon.-Fri. 8:30 a.m.-5 p.m., Saturday 8:30 a.m.-11:30 a.m. **Travellers Contact Point,** Suite 11-15, 7th Floor, 428 George St. (tel. 02-9221-8744), deals with all travel questions, including accommodations, employment, Sydney tourist information, travel insurance, visa and immigration information, tips on buying and registering a car, and mail holding service. They're also an agent for adventure tour operators, major bus companies, and New Zealand tour operators. They are open Mon.-Fri. 9 a.m.-6 p.m., Saturday 10 a.m.-2 p.m.

SOUTH COAST

Two main roads connect Melbourne and Sydney: the Hume Highway, which is the most direct, and the Princes Highway, which follows the coast. Along the Hume Highway, the trip between the two cities can be done in one day, while the Princes Highway takes longer, passing small seaside towns, glorious stretches of beach, and many coastal national parks. A good compromise is to take the Hume Highway through the southern highlands, before crossing to the coast at Kiama. As you get farther from Sydney, crowds become nonexistent (except in summer) and the beaches more appealing. Some of the better spots are the holiday towns of Kiama, Merimbula, Tathra, and Eden, while the national parks of Jervis Bay, Murramarang, and Ben Boyd protect long stretches of spectacular coastline.

Sydney to Wollongong

Southbound travelers are presented with two very different options for the short drive to Wollongong. The Princes Highway follows the ridge of the Illawarra Escarpment, with panoramic views of the coast at places like Stanwell Tops (a favorite spot for hang-gliding enthusiasts). The other option is a winding road that passes through a string of coastal communities sandwiched between the ocean and escarpment. Northernmost of these communities is **Stanwell Park,** which lies behind a sandy beach where offshore sandbars create waves popular with surfers.

WOLLONGONG

Located 80 km south of Sydney, Wollongong (pop. 220,000) is Australia's seventh-largest city.

On 1 August 1997 all telephone numbers in this section will change. To dial the new number, simply add the last two digits of the existing area code to the old number. As an example, (042) 12-3456 becomes 4212-3456. The new area code will be (02).

Port Kembla, Wollongong's industrial heart, has never really been seen as a tourist attraction, but the newly opened **Australia's Industry World** makes a visit worthwhile.

Wollongong's main thoroughfare is **Crown St.,** part of which is a pedestrian mall. In the mall is an information center, which has walking tour maps outlining the many historic buildings around downtown. On Market St., one block from Crown St., is a small **museum.** Before Port Kembla was developed, coal was shipped from a small harbor at the end of Marine Drive. Out on the point stands a lighthouse built in 1872; open for inspection Sat.-Sun. noon-4 p.m.

Accommodations and Food

Beach Park Motor Inn, 10 Pleasant Ave. (tel. 042-26-1577), overlooks the beach at North Wollongong; $50 s, $55 d. If you must stay close to the city center, try **Downtown Motel,** 76 Crown St. (tel. 042-29-8344), where rooms are small but clean; $55 s, $65 d. North from Wollongong, Corrimal and Bulli have council-run campgrounds, with sites for $12 and cabins from $45. Another option is **Wollongong Surf Leisure Resort,** Pioneer Rd. (tel. 042-83-6999), right on the beach at Fairy Meadow. Facilities include an indoor heated pool, tennis court, spa, sauna, and laundry. Sites are $15-25, cabins $50-60.

At the east end of Bourke St. is a bunch of cafes and restaurants. The casual **North Beach Gourmet Food** (tel. 042-28-6824) opens around 8 a.m. for breakfast. Just around the corner is **Beach House Seafood Restaurant,** 16 Cliff Rd. (tel. 042-28-5410), overlooking North Beach. The menu features seafood, but meat and chicken dishes are also offered; lunch starts at $10, dinner from $13.

Transportation, Services, and Information

State Rail (tel. 13-1500) runs trains regularly between Sydney and Wollongong; $8.60 round-trip, or take a day return with unlimited stops for $10.60. **Greyhound Pioneer** (tel. 042-29-7233) runs a coastal route between Sydney and Melbourne, stopping at Wollongong ($15 one-way);

the terminal is on the corner of Keira and Campbell Streets.

Just east of the pedestrian mall, at the corner of Crown and Kembla Streets, is the **Tourist Information Centre** (tel. 042-28-0300); open daily 9 a.m.-5 p.m.

KIAMA AND VICINITY

Kiama's biggest attraction is a **blowhole,** but it hasn't been performing that well in recent years. When a heavy southerly is running and the tide is right, water is sucked under a ledge, exploding through a narrow crevice high into the air (up to 50 meters when conditions are right). Much of the blowhole's force has been lost in the last 20 years as water action has enlarged the crevice. The town's commercial center is within walking distance of the blowhole, while immediately south are small beaches protected from wave action by deeply indented bays.

Practicalities

Kiama appeals mainly to holidaying families and is especially busy in January and during Easter week. At other times of the year, the town reverts to its sleepy self, and getting a room or campsite is no problem. Rooms at **Briggdale Seaside Motel,** 18 Hothersall St. (tel. 042-32-1767), on Bombo Beach one km north of town, all have beach views; $35 s, $40 d. **Easts Beach Caravan Park,** south of Kiama (tel. 042-32-2124), has excellent facilities and is right on the beach. Sites are $14-18, on-site vans $32, and cabins $38.

Built in 1885 to house mining families, The Terraces are a row of weatherboard houses on Collins St. that have been restored and now contain boutiques and restaurants. One of these is **Ritzy Gritz** (tel. 042-32-1853), a small, casual restaurant specializing in modern Mexican dishes at good prices. Also at The Terraces is **Chachi's** (tel. 042-33-1144), an Italian restaurant, where a few outside tables catch the sun at lunchtime.

Kiama Visitors Centre is out on Blowhole Point; open daily 9 a.m.-5 p.m. (tel. 042-32-3446).

Budderoo National Park

West of Kiama, beyond the small town of Jamberoo in the Jamberoo Valley, is 5,746-hectare Budderoo National Park. The highlight is **Minnamurra Rainforest,** with its fern-filled gullies, a spectacular waterfall, and giant fig and cedar trees. The 1.6-km Rainforest Walk leads through this subtropical environment, across an elevated boardwalk that leads into the canopy and over a couple of suspension bridges. Beyond the boardwalk is **Minnamurra Falls** (the track to the falls is steep in places, so take care after rain), a four-km round-trip from the parking lot. The Rainforest Centre is open daily 9 a.m.-5 p.m. (tel. 042-36-0469).

SHOALHAVEN

These 150 km of coastline extend south from Gerringong. It's a stretch of sleepy seaside villages backed by dairy farms and the Illawarra Escarpment.

Gerringong

With a population of 2,800, Gerringong is a picturesque village spread along a beach of golden sand surrounded by pastures. At the south end of the beach is **Ourie Park,** a campground with sites for $11-13 and a few on-site vans for $35 (tel. 042-34-1285).

Berry and Vicinity

The town of Berry has streets lined with oaks and elms planted by early settlers, and a variety of buildings, including a courthouse, post office, and a couple of banks, dating to last century. It's a great little spot to stop and stretch your legs and have a meal in one of its many cafes. Breakfast is particularly popular, especially on Sunday.

West of Berry, and hidden from the coast by a high ridge, is **Kangaroo Valley,** an area of land cleared for farming by early timber cutters. The valley has an interesting suspension bridge. Built in 1898, it's the oldest such structure in the country. Farther west are the rainforested slopes of the Great Dividing Range, protected by Morton National Park (see "Moss Vale and Vicinity" under "Southern Highlands and Goulburn," later in this chapter).

Jervis Bay

Bigger than Sydney Harbour and largely undeveloped, Jervis Bay is one of the safest anchorages on the east coast. The bay is divided in two by **Currumbene Creek.** The north section of the bay is accessible from Nowra, along a road that leads out to the sleepy seaside village of **Currarong** and spectacular **Point Perpendicular,** on Beecroft Peninsula.

Huskisson is south of Currumbene Creek. Protected by long headlands, the beaches here provide safe swimming, and farther around the bay at Hyams Beach the sand is as white as any beach in the world—or so the brochures claim.

Jervis Bay National Park encompasses the broad headland forming the southern boundary of the bay. The park was set aside in 1915 to provide port facilities for the Australian Capital Territory, but in late 1995 it was handed back to the local Koori of Wreck Bay, in much the same way Uluru (Ayers Rock) was a few years previous. A small naval college, **HMAS Creswell,** is the only sign of the base's stalled development. **Greenpatch** is one of the nicest beaches on the south coast. Protected from the elements, it has a picnic area, with hundreds of tame rosellas, and a popular campground. To the east is **Murray's Beach,** another pretty spot.

On the south side of the headland is the wild surf of Wreck Bay and nearby Summercloud Beach, which has a good picnic area and some rocky headlands, while offshore is a legendary surf break.

Ulladulla and Vicinity

At Ulladulla a colorful fleet of fishing boats bob around in a manmade harbor flanked by undeveloped headlands. On the Princes Highway south of town is **Beach Haven Tourist Park Resort** (tel. 044-55-2110), right on the beach and with a heated pool, spa, tennis court, and barbecue area. Rates are $12.60-23, on-site vans $25-30, and cabins from $47.

Farther south is **Burrill Lake,** a small community sandwiched between the lake's outlet and the ocean. The lake is particularly picturesque; easiest access is Kings Point (turn off 500 meters north of Burrill Lake township), where watercraft can be rented.

Murramarang National Park

Extending along the coast between Bawley Point and Batemans Bay, this 1,757-hectare park is of exceptional beauty, featuring beaches, rugged headlands, tidal platforms, and extensive warm-temperate rainforest. Six access points lie between Termeil and Cullendulla on the Princes Highway. From Kioloa a road leads to **Pebbly Beach,** where kangaroos feed on the beach. This beach has a campground with sites costing $10 per night; call (044) 78-6006 for bookings. **Depot Beach,** to the south, is another good camping spot.

EUROBODALLA COAST

The Eurobodalla Coast, extending from Batemans Bay to Narooma, has more of those great south coast beaches, and, chances are, outside of the summer school holidays you'll have them to yourself. The Princes Highway runs through the area about four km from the coast, but access to the many beaches is easy. West of the highway is 81,820-hectare **Deua National Park,** which protects remote forested valleys, high ridges, limestone outcrops, and limestone caves. Access is from Moruya.

Batemans Bay

Batemans Bay is a fishing port at the mouth of the Clyde River, which starts high in the Budawang National Park to the north. The town is popular with people from Canberra, who regularly make the two-hour run over the Great Dividing Range from the landlocked national capital. Batemans Bay itself has little of interest, but swimming, surfing, fishing, boating, and golfing are all popular. Southeast of town, **Obser-**

vation Head has a lookout where panoramic views extend across the bay to offshore rock stacks.

Mariners Lodge, Orient St. (tel. 044-72-6222), is right in town and overlooks Clyde River, with many rooms having ocean views; $50 s, $60 d. **Lincoln Downs,** Princes Hwy. (tel. 044-72-6388), one km north of downtown, is a stylish retreat boasting the best of everything in a magnificent country-style setting—landscaped gardens run down to a lagoon alive with waterbirds, and pathways link rooms to the main lodge with a restaurant, lounge, cocktail bar, and billiards room. Rates are $150 s or d. Campers have many choices along the coast south from Batemans Bay; best of the bunch is **Coachhouse Tourist Van Park,** on a beach and across from the golf course at the south end of town (tel. 044-72-5187). All facilities are excellent and a grassed area is set aside for tents; sites are $14-18, on-site vans $25-40, and cabins $45-80.

On the main drag through town is the **Tourist Information Centre** (tel. 044-72-6900); open daily 8:30 a.m.-4:30 p.m.

Braidwood

Braidwood, located on the highway linking Canberra to the coast 63 km northwest of Batemans Bay, was founded in the mid-1830s. Many buildings from this era remain, including **Doncaster Inn,** which dates from 1837. After functioning as a nunnery for many years, it was recently restored and now operates as a guesthouse. Rooms have been furnished with iron four-posters, and each opens to a veranda. Rates are $55-65 s, $85-100 d, which includes a hearty cooked breakfast. For bookings, call (048) 42-2356.

Broulee

Broulee is southernmost of a string of small townships along George Bass Dr., which branches off the Princes Hwy. at Batemans Bay. Broulee itself is bordered to the north by Tomaga River and to the south by a stumpy headland, which at low tide is linked to **Broulee Island.** Before a port at Batemans Bay was established, shipping docked at a jetty on the north side of the island; all that remains are foundations of a hotel and a lone grave.

Narooma

Narooma is a small seaside town of 3,300 at the mouth of Wagonga River, 350 km south of Sydney. Like so many other towns on the south coast it comes alive in summer, while the rest of the year it's a sleepy seaside village. North of the river are several short beaches, and snorkeling at the headland is excellent in calm weather. Above the high cliffs east of downtown is Narooma's golf course, which has many difficult holes, including one which requires a very accurate shot over a deep chasm.

Amooran Court, 30 Montague St. (tel. 044-76-2198), is a small motel opposite the golf course and has views of the ocean; $43 s, $45 d. Facilities at **Surf Beach Caravan Park,** Ballangalla St. (tel. 044-76-2275), aren't anything special, but the location is excellent; sites are $12-19, cabins $30.

Montague Island

Located nine km east of Narooma, this 82-hectare island is a nesting site for crested terns, shearwaters (muttonbirds), silver gulls, and around 20,000 little penguins. Before Europeans, Koori often visited the island to collect bird eggs. In 1881 a lighthouse was built there to allow shipping a safer passage up the treacherous coast. Visiting the island is possible on a tour operated by the National Parks and Wildlife Service; the office is on the corner of Princes Hwy. and Field St., Narooma (tel. 044-76-2888).

SAPPHIRE COAST

At Narooma the Princes Highway heads inland to **Bega**, rejoining the coast at Merimbula. A pleasant alternative to the inland route is along the Sapphire Coast, passing three national parks and a number of picturesque towns.

Wallaga Lake

The coastal road south from Narooma crosses an outlet channel of Wallaga Lake. The lake, which formed when a wide valley flooded at the end of the last ice age, is deeply indented, its shoreline stretching over 100 km. Access to the lake is possible from the east and north.

Part of the shoreline through here is protected by 1,237-hectare **Wallaga Lake National Park,** which has a high concentration of wildlife, including koalas, swamp wallabies, and lyrebirds, and is dotted with Koori middens. Access to the park is on foot from Regatta Point or by boat.

Bermagui

The picturesque fishing village of Bermagui (pop. 1,000) is fronted by an area of parkland that separates the main street from the quiet waters of **Horseshoe Bay.** The Continental Shelf, off which the ocean floor drops dramatically, is closest to mainland Australia east of Bermagui.

Bermagui's manmade harbor is home to a large commercial fishing fleet and a number of game-fishing boats, including many for charter (if you're interested, contact the Tourist Information Centre for charter details). Marine Dr., running east from the main street to a high headland and out of town to the south, passes **Blue Pool,** an ocean-fed swimming pool, **Beares Beach,** and several rocky headlands. Other activities in town include fishing, golf (call 064-93-4340 for tee times), and scuba diving. Held over Easter weekend, **Four Winds Easter Concert** is a unique combination of classical and Aboriginal music. For details call (064) 93-4105.

Beachview Motel, 12 Lamont St. (tel. 064-93-4155), is close to everything and has modern facilities; rates are $50 s, $60 d, except in holiday periods when they rise markedly. **Zane Grey Caravan Park,** Lamont St. (tel. 064-93-4382), overlooks the bay and is within easy walking distance of town. Sites are $16.50-19 in summer holidays, and $5 less the rest of the year. Cabins here are excellent, and each has a TV and microwave. Other facilities include free gas barbecues and a laundry.

The fish shop on the harbor should have great fish and chips. But it doesn't. And unfortunately, in a town so famous for its seafood, there's really nowhere else to recommend for inexpensive seafood. For somewhere more formal, head to **Roly's Wharf Restaurant,** Lamont St. (tel. 064-93-4328), for seafood; open daily for lunch and dinner. **Whispers,** 2 Wallaga St. (tel. 064-93-4377), is a pleasant cafe open from 7 a.m. daily, with breakfasts ranging $3-8.50 and lunch around $6. For Chinese, head to the Country Club on Tuross St. (tel. 064-93-4177).

Mimosa Rocks National Park

A 17-km stretch of coastline between Bermagui and Tathra is protected by this 5,230-hectare park, which also extends eight km inland from Nelson Lagoon. The Tathra-Bermagui Road passes through only a small section of the park, but the coast can be accessed in many places. Northernmost of these, Aragunnu Rd., 20 km south of Bermagui, leads to a sandy beach surrounded by dark volcanic rock and the deep blue of the Pacific Ocean. From the campground at the end of this road, it's easy to scramble around a rocky bay to the stack of volcanic rock for which the park is named. At the end of Wapengo Lake Rd., the next access road, is a campground, picnic area, and trail leading to a headland. The next two roads off the Tathra-Bermagui Road lead to Middle Beach and Gillards Beach, both of which have camping. At the park's southern end is **Nelson Lagoon,** and at the end of Nelson Lakes Rd. trails lead to pleasant sandy beaches at the lagoon's outlet. None of the park's camping areas have drinking water. For further park details, call (044) 76-2888.

Tathra

Flanked by two national parks and nestled in the protected northeast corner of a long headland, Tathra is one of the south coast's most picturesque villages. Out on the headland is **Tathra Wharf;** dating to 1862, it's the oldest sea wharf on the east coast. It has been extensively restored, with the two-story storehouse given a coat of red paint to spruce it up. The storehouse is open as a general store selling everything from fishing gear to fresh prawns. Views from the wharf extend across the bay to Tathra and around a beautiful sandy beach to the mouth of the Bega River.

Tathra Hotel Motel, Bega St. (tel. 064-94-1101), is on Tathra Head, and every room has panoramic ocean views; $55 s, $65 d. **Tathra Beach Tourist Park,** between the beach and Andy Poole Dr., is spread along the foreshore near the surf club. Rates are $10-12 for camping and $32 for on-site vans; call (064) 94-1302 for bookings.

Opposite the caravan park is **King Parrot Cafe,** 61 Andy Poole Dr. (tel. 064-94-1483),

Tathra Wharf

which serves light lunches daily 10 a.m.-4:30 p.m. and dinner (seafood dishes are especially good) daily 6-10 p.m. Up on the headland in a residence dating from 1906 is **Harbourmaster Restaurant.** The elegant setting and fine food combine to make it an excellent choice for dinner. It's located at 15 Bega St. (tel. 064-94-1344).

Bournda National Park

This 2,305-hectare park extends from south of Tathra to Tura Beach, north of Merimbula, and encompasses wetland areas around **Wallagoot Lake.** In the north of the park, forests of eucalypt extend to the deeply indented coastline, accessible along a gravel track leading south of Tathra

Hobart Beach, near the south end of Wallagoot Lake, has a picnic area and campground (bring drinking water). This part of the park is crisscrossed with hiking trails, including one around Bondi Lake.

SAPPHIRE COAST HINTERLAND

Early settlers found the narrow strip of land wedged below the foothills of the Great Dividing Range ideal for running cattle, and for over 150 years the land has provided its farmers with a healthy living.

Tilba Tilba

In the shadow of **Mt. Dromedary** (860 meters), this historic town boomed during an 1852 gold rush and is today a picturesque village, home to many artisans who sell their wares in period-style buildings along the main street. The village boasts a cobbler, wood-turner, leadlight artist, leatherman, and small cheese factory. Behind the cheese factory is **Wirrina** (tel. 044-73-7279), a small B&B where rates are $45 s, $68 d.

Cobargo

Cobargo developed as a dairy town in the 1860s, and with the abundance of wattle a prosperous tanning industry thrived. Today this charming town's main street is lined with buildings from all eras of Cobargo's history, including a bakery, pharmacy, saddlery, grain store, and newsagency.

Wadbilliga National Park

Primarily protecting Wadbilliga Plateau, this large 79,000-hectare park is in a remote part of the Great Dividing Range west of Cobargo. From the plateau's highest reaches flow the Wadbilliga, Tuross, and Brogo Rivers. Each of these has carved a deep gorge, with that of the Tuross being the most accessible. Elevation changes in the park provide habitat for a variety of vegetation—from temperate rainforests on the valley floor to subalpine forests of snow gum at higher elevations. The only two-wheel drive access is west from Cobargo, along a road that ends at Wadbilliga Crossing, where there's a picnic area and basic campground.

Bega

Bega is synonymous with cheese, an industry upon which the town has grown into the largest commercial center between Wollongong and the Victorian border. The highlight of a visit to the town is **Bega Cheese Factory** on Lagoon St. (tel. 064-92-1444). Cheese tastings are offered Mon.-Fri. 9 a.m.-5 p.m. and Sat.-Sun. 10 a.m.-4 p.m. On the outskirts of town is **Grevillea Estate Wines,** also open for tasting and home to a fair-sized herd of dairy cows milked daily at 3 p.m. Located on Buckajo Rd. (tel. 064-92-3006).

MERIMBULA AND VICINITY

Merimbula is a popular holiday town set around the sparkling waters of a narrow channel that drains Merimbula Lake into the ocean. Jutting out from the township are Short and Merimbula Points, ochre-colored headlands that drop vertically into the ocean. Merimbula grew as a private port for the Twofold Bay Pastoral Association, and boomed when gold was discovered in the Snowy Mountains.

On the headland at the lake's entrance is a wharf, which is a good fishing spot and home to **Merimbula Aquarium** (a bit much at adult $6, child $4); open daily 10 a.m.-5 p.m. (tel. 064-95-3227). To get out to the headland, follow Main St. out of town to Lake Street. The surrounding national parks offer many hiking opportunities, but the town itself is the starting point for many walks. One leads along the western shore of Merimbula Lake to a beach where Boggy Creek drains into the lake. Birdlife abounds in this area, and around dusk kangaroos and wallabies feed in the open. Merimbula is known for its beaches; the best of these are either side of Short Point and **Bar Beach,** a protected spot along Lake St. facing the channel and backed by a grassed picnic area.

Recreation

The least expensive way to get out on the lake is a cruise on the glass-bottomed *Merimbula Princess,* departing from the jetty daily 2 p.m.; adult $12, child $8. *Seafari* departs daily 9 a.m. and 2:30 p.m. for a half day of fishing and a short bushwalk; adult $25, child $12, including lunch. **Sapphire Coast Canoe Tours** operates on the Pambula, Brogo, and Bega Rivers, with full-day trips for all abilities; $40 pp.

Yellow Pinch Wildlife Park is set in native bushland nine km west of Merimbula. Apart from the usual array of Australian animals, there

MERIMBULA

are rides for the kids and a cafe with picnic area. Admission is adult $7.50, child $4.50. Open Wed.-Sun. 10 a.m.-5 p.m. (tel. 064-94-9225).

Pambula-Merimbula Golf Club has one of the best courses on the south coast and is open to the public most days (tel. 064-95-6280). North of town is **Mandeni Resort** (tel. 064-95-9644), featuring a nine-hole golf course (green fees $5) and a unique deepwater driving range, where balls are hit into a lake.

Accommodations and Food

Merimbula Motor Lodge is one of the town's better motels; rates start at a reasonable $45 s, $50 d; located at 131 Princes Hwy. (tel. 064-95-1748). **Fairway Motor Inn,** 386 Princes Hwy. (tel. 064-95-6000), is, as the name suggests, right opposite the golf course. Rooms are large with modern facilities, and rates are $54 s, $58 d. **Wandarrah YHA Lodge** is a purpose-built

backpacker accommodation one block from the beach and a 10-minute walk from downtown Rates are $15 pp for a dorm, and $24 s, $36 d located at 18 Marine Parade (tel. 064-95-3503) A good accommodation deal is **Mandeni Resort,** eight km north of town on Sapphire Coast Dr. (tel. 064-95-9644). Rooms are self-contained; each has two bedrooms, a kitchen, wood heater, TV, and laundry. The complex also has a swimming pool, barbecue area, nine-hole golf course, and tennis courts. Rates start at $55 s o d in the off season, rising to $140 midsummer **Sapphire Valley Caravan Park,** Sapphire Coast Dr. (tel. 064-95-1746), is within walking distance of town and has excellent facilities Rates are $14-20 per site, and self-contained cabins are $30-85.

Merimbula RSL Club, corner Market and Main Streets (tel. 064-95-1502), has hot lunches for $4 and a restaurant that opens nightly at 6 p.m. **Black Dolphin Bar & Grill,** Princes Hwy. (tel. 064-95-1500), is a stylish restaurant overlooking Merimbula Lake; much of the food served is locally produced, and meals are well priced.

Information

Merimbula Tourist Information Centre is on Beach St. (tel. 064-95-1129); open daily 9 a.m.-5 p.m.

Pambula

Pambula is a charming town nine km south of Merimbula. The townsite was originally laid out along **Pambula River** but was moved to higher ground after repeated flooding. Some buildings date to the 1860s (grab a *Historic Pambula* brochure from the newsagency if you'd like to find them all), and many have been restored to their former grandeur. Down on the river, **Sinbad River Cruises** has daily cruises to Pambula Lake. Prices range $15-24 (tel. 064-95-2037). **Pambula Beach,** at the mouth of Pambula River two km east of Pambula, is at the end of a beach stretching north to Merimbula.

Merimbula has a better range of accommodations than Pambula, although Pambula Beach has a caravan park. As for food, though, Pambula excels, with excellent restaurants. The elegant **Retreat Restaurant,** 26 Quondola St. (tel. 064-95-6674), is a historic inn dating from 1850. Open for breakfast, lunch, and dinner daily (except Tuesday). **The Grange** on the road out to Wyndham (tel. 064-95-6169), was built in 1844 and is open for lunch and dinner. Closed Monday.

EDEN AND VICINITY

The sparkling blue waters of Twofold Bay and the dense forests that flank the town are Eden's major tourist drawcard and also the lifeblood of the area's sometimes-grisly past as well as present economy. The town itself, 490 km south of Sydney and 50 km north of the Victorian border, is spread over a narrow spit of land extending into Twofold Bay, a deep body of water lined by beaches and rocky headlands.

The first in a long line of entrepreneurs who tried to make their fortunes from Eden's bountiful natural resources was Englishman Ben Boyd,

whose ambitious plan to build a city rivaling Sydney in importance began in 1843 with the construction of an inn, a church, and houses at the southern corner of Twofold Bay. But by 1849 Boyd was broke. Farther around the bay, **Davidson Whaling Station** was faring much better, landing around a dozen whales each season. They operated until 1929, by which time whale numbers had been decimated and the station had become uneconomical to run. The station has been partially restored, with interpretive panels describing the "processing" of the whales. On the road out to the old station, it's impossible

EDEN

TO MERIMBULA

GOLF VIEW MOTEL

LAKE CURALO

PRINCES HWY

BARCLAY ST.

ASLINGS BEACH RD

ASLINGS BEACH

TWOFOLD BAY

BUNGO ST.

INLAY ST.

MITCHELL ST.

CATTLE BAY

BASS ST.

EDEN TOURIST INFORMATION CENTRE

HOTEL AUSTRALASIAN
TWOFOLD ARCADE
TWOFOLD BAY MOTOR INN
EDEN FISHERMAN'S RECREATION CLUB
ALBERT TERRACE
KILLER WHALE MUSEUM
GREENSEAS CANNERY
COCORA ST.

TO SHADRACK RESORT, SEAHORSE INN, BEN BOYD NATIONAL PARK, AND IMLAY NATIONAL PARK

SNUG COVE
EDEN WHARF

INLAY ST.
BRAMBLE ST.

ROTARY PARK
LOOKOUT POINT

NOT TO SCALE

© MOON PUBLICATIONS, INC.

to miss **Harris Daishowa Mill,** where trees are wood-chipped for export. If scrambling around piles of woodchips sounds enticing, tours are offered on Thursday; book through the Tourist Information Centre. The other mainstay of Eden's economy is fishing, and there can be few sights as peaceful as watching the fleet of boats bobbing around the wharf. Commercial fishing is a dangerous, year-round operation, as the **Seamen's Memorial Wall** in Rotary Park will attest. Most of the fish are transported to Sydney or processed at the **Greenseas Cannery,** down on the harbor.

Killer Whale Museum and Whalewatching

Whaling has long since ended in Australia, and this museum catalogs its history. The main feature is a skeleton of Old Tom, a killer whale that hunted in Twofold Bay. Also on display is a whaleboat, and in the Viewing Gallery descriptions of today's fishing industry adorn a room overlooking the bay. You'll find displays of seashells and the Koori, and an audiovisual in other galleries. The museum is open Mon.-Fri. 10:15 a.m.-3:45 p.m., Sat.-Sun. 11:15 a.m.-3:45 p.m. It's at 94 Imlay St. (tel. 064-96-2094).

Whalewatching has really caught on in the last few years, but the season runs only two months—October and November. The humpback whales can be seen from *Cat Balou* but often come right into the bay where they can be watched from vantage points around town. During the season, the boat departs daily at 7 a.m. for a five-hour cruise. The boat is not allowed within 100 meters of whales, but the whales, disregarding the rules, often surface alongside the boat. Cruise cost is adult $45, child $30; book through the Tourist Information Centre (tel. 064-96-2027) or call direct at (015) 26-0489.

Accommodations

The **Seahorse Inn,** built by Ben Boyd in 1840, is a Tudor-style mansion overlooking Twofold Bay. Although rooms are fairly basic, its historic charm and beachfront location make it the best place in Eden to stay. Rooms are $70 s, $85 d, including breakfast. It's at Boydtown Park, eight km south of Eden (tel. 064-96-1361).

Golf View Motel, Princes Hwy. (tel. 064-96-1601), is one km north of downtown Eden and has the least expensive rooms in town; $35 s, $40 d. Of a higher standard, and overlooking the bay, is **Twofold Bay Motor Inn,** 164 Imlay St. (tel. 064-96-3111), which has an indoor pool and spa; rates are from $55 s, $60 d.

Eden Tourist Park, Aslings Beach Rd. (tel. 064-96-1139), fronts both the beach and lake. Sites are $11-17, basic on-site vans are $28-40, and cabins are $52. **Shadrack Resort,** south of Eden, is one of three campgrounds on the shore of Twofold Bay. This large park has all the facilities you'll need. Sites are $15, and those with bathrooms are $20. The cabins are excellent and start at $40 d (tel. 064-96-1651).

Seahorse Inn, Boydtown Park

Food

Although Eden is one of the state's largest fishing towns, most of the catch is transported to markets in Sydney. Still, if it's seafood you want, Eden excels. Down on Eden Wharf, **The Wharf Fish Shop** has a selection of battered and grilled fish from $3 and prawns for $15-20 per kilogram; open daily 8 a.m.-5 p.m. **Wheelhouse Restaurant,** also on the Wharf (tel. 064-96-3392), is a more formal joint, with views of all the activity and generous portions of the freshest seafood from $11 for dinner. The **Hotel Australasian,** 60 Imlay St. (tel. 064-96-1600), has good bar meals for $4-7 and is least rowdy of the town's many pubs. **Eden Fishermen's Recreation Club,** Imlay St. (tel. 064-96-1577), has a popular bistro and restaurant with higher-than-usual club prices.

Transportation, Services, and Information

Edward's Bus Service (tel. 064-96-1422) runs between Merimbula and Eden Mon.-Sat., with some services via Bega and others along the coast; buses stop outside Twofold Arcade on Imlay Street.

Eden **Tourist Information Centre** is on the corner of Imlay and Mitchell Streets (tel. 064-96-1953); open daily 9 a.m.-5 p.m. At the back of Twofold Arcade on Imlay St. is an **NPWS** office (tel. 064-96-1434) and an **Eden Forestry Office** (tel. 064-96-1500), a good information source on the many interesting forest drives between the south coast and Snowy Mountains.

Ben Boyd National Park

This 9,455-hectare park extends along 40 km of coastline from Pambula in the north to Disaster Bay in the south and is divided in two by Twofold Bay. This stretch of coastline is nothing less than spectacular, with folding and faulting of the bedrock creating a rugged shoreline. The main feature of the park's north section is **The Pinnacles. Haycock Point,** at the park's northern tip, has a picnic area protected from prevailing nor'easters. The park's most recognizable feature is **Boyd Tower,** in the southern section. The tower was built in the 1840s for spotting whales, and was later used mostly as a lighthouse. The main access to the tower, and other features of this part of the park, is Edrom Rd., spurring east from the Princes Hwy. 18 km south of Eden. Campgrounds at **Saltwater Creek** and **Bittangabee** are reached off this road. For more information on the park, head to the NPWS office in Twofold Arcade on Imlay St. (tel. 064-96-1434).

Mount Imlay National Park

The 886-meter peak for which this park is named rises high above the surrounding forests and provides an excellent vantage point. Changes in elevation create habitat for a wide variety of vegetation within the park, including the newly discovered *Eucalypt imlayensis*. For most people, the main purpose of a visit to the park is climbing Mt. Imlay. The climb is only three km each way, with an elevation gain of 600 meters, but it's a hard slog, with the final ascent along an exposed ridge. The summit track trailhead is at the park's only facilities—a picnic area—located at the end of Burrawang Rd., which spurs off the Princes Hwy. 19 km south of Eden.

SOUTHERN HIGHLANDS AND GOULBURN

The original Hume Highway, the main route between Sydney and Melbourne, has been re-routed in many places, bypassing towns established to serve early travelers. Immediately south of Sydney's southwestern suburbs, a turnoff to Mittagong signals the old highway, which passes through a string of charming towns, offering the chance to browse antique shops, eat in historic cafes, and stay overnight in luxurious guest-houses. **Morton National Park,** south of these towns, is a rugged and remote wilderness with some spectacular waterfalls and a good range of hiking for all levels of fitness.

Wombeyan Caves

Jenolan Caves may be Australia's best-known cave system, but there are others of equal beauty, the difference being that access is more difficult. Wombeyan Caves, 65 km northwest of Mittagong, is one such system. The final 40-km stretch is along a rough gravel road that passes through a convict-built sandstone tunnel. Almost 230 caves make up the system, of which five are open to the public. **Fig Tree Cave** has a self-guided trail through it, with buttons to press for commentary and, more importantly, light. Of the other four, **Wollondilly Cave,** featuring a 25-meter-high cathedral, is regarded as the most spectacular. Admission to self-guided caves is $4, guided caves $6.

At the caves' entrance is a wide open area (*wombeyan* is Aboriginal for "grassy flat between two mountains") with a campground that features a camp kitchen, hot showers, kiosk, and laundry. Unpowered sites are $10, powered sites $15, on-site vans $40 s or d. For campground bookings and cave tour information, call (048) 43-5976.

> On 1 August 1997 all telephone numbers in this section will change. To dial the new number, simply add the last two digits of the existing area code to the old number. As an example, (048) 12-3456 becomes 4812-3456. The new area code will be (02).

BERRIMA

Berrima lies beside a sweeping bend of the Wingecarribee River, 120 km southwest of Sydney. Established in 1828 to serve travelers, the township developed with the construction of a stone courthouse, post office, and a number of inns. In 1850, when the rail line between Sydney and Bowral bypassed Berrima, the town's prosperity came to an abrupt end. Since that time, Berrima has become a popular getaway for Sydneysiders, but has changed little. A certain amount of peace came to the streets in the late 1980s when the Hume Highway was diverted north of town, leaving the sleepy village almost traffic free.

Sights

Berrima is one of Australia's best remaining examples of a 19th-century town, remarkably unchanged since the 1840s. The town's most impressive building is the **courthouse,** which dates to 1838. Within the grand sandstone structure are displays explaining court proceedings in colonial Australia. Behind the courthouse is Australia's oldest remaining jail (now a minimum-security prison). For most of last century it was among the most dreaded of all jails, mainly for the fact that for the first nine months of his sentence a prisoner wasn't allowed to talk to anyone, lest he be flogged. On the south side of the jail is **Bull's Head Fountain,** designed to catch runoff from the roof. Down the hill is the **Surveyor General Inn.** Open since 1835, it is Australia's oldest continually licensed hotel. **Harper's Mansion,** on Wilkinson St., is a fine example of a large Australian home from early last century; open Sat.-Mon. 11 a.m.-4 p.m. At least 20 other buildings of historic significance are detailed in the *Two Foot Walking Tour* brochure, available from the courthouse.

Berkelouw Book Barn, three km north of Berrima (tel. 048-77-1370), has over 200,000 books, including many rare early Australian works; open daily 8:30 a.m.-3 p.m.

Accommodations and Food

Walden Wood, Old Mandemar Rd. (tel. 048-77-1164), is an 1860 sandstone cottage set on three hectares. Two rooms, each with private bathroom, are offered, and the lounge area has an open fire. Rates are $65 s, $85 d, which includes a cooked breakfast. A little less expensive is **Berrima Bakehouse Motel,** right in the heart of town (tel. 048-77-1381); $50 s, $60 d.

Cottage Kitchen is open daily 9 a.m.-5 p.m. for light lunches and Devonshire teas in a country atmosphere. For something a bit more formal, head to **Colonial Inn** (tel. 048-77-1389), a sandstone structure dating to 1842 and built by convict labor. Tables are set in five rooms, four with fireplaces. Main dishes start at $13 (less at lunch). Open daily noon-3 p.m. and 6-9:30 p.m. **Surveyor General Inn** (tel. 048-77-1226) is worth visiting, if only to have a beer in Australia's oldest pub. Meals are served at lunch and dinner, with a wide choice of steaks for $10-13.

BOWRAL

While Berrima is noted for its historic charm, Bowral (pop. 5,500), 10 km east, is renowned for magnificent gardens, tree-lined avenues, and as the childhood home of the world's best-known cricketer, Sir Donald Bradman. The population of Bowral is markedly different from almost all other country towns in that almost all residents are wealthy or retired, giving the town an air of pomp. Bowral grew from a subdivision of land owned by Australia's first Surveyor General, John Oxley. By the 1920s the town had become a popular getaway for Sydneysiders, and to cater to them guesthouses and inns were established.

Sights

Bowral is a fitting site for the **Bradman Museum,** St. Jude St. (tel. 048-62-1247), dedicated to, arguably, the finest cricketer the world had ever seen. Overlooking the town's main cricket ground and across the road from Bradman's childhood home, the museum catalogs not just his career but development of cricket through Australia, and is filled with memorabilia from all eras—from a 1750s cricket bat to the modern equipment used by today's test cricketers. Admission is adult $3, child $1. The museum is

ANDREW HEMPSTEAD

Sir Donald Bradman grew up in Bowral, playing cricket on this ground that now has a museum in his honor.

open daily 10 a.m.-4 p.m. Bradman lived opposite the oval, at 20 Glebe Rd., as well as two blocks east, at 52 Shepard Street. Back near the center of town, on the corner of Boolwey and Bendooley Streets, is **Bowral Schoolhouse Museum,** set up as a mid-1800s school room. On Bendooley St. are many other historic buildings, including a courthouse, police station, and rectory. Bowral has many fine shops, most around the town center and in **Grand Arcade.** For views over town and surrounding rolling farmland, head to 980-meter **Mt. Gibraltar,** a rocky outcrop accessible along Oxley Dr., off Mittagong Road.

Tulip Time Country Fair, the first weekend of October, attracts thousands of visitors to Bowral. The highlight is 60,000 blooming tulips in Corbett Gardens, but many private gardens are also open for inspection, and musicians play in various venues through town; call (048) 61-3133 for details.

Accommodations

Port O'Call Motor Inn, corner Bong Bong and Bundaroo Streets (tel. 048-61-1779), is the least expensive motel in town; rooms start at $40 s or d midweek. **Links House,** 17 Links Rd. (tel. 048-61-1977), is a small, colorful hotel in a lovely setting of landscaped gardens. Each room has a private bathroom and costs $85-115 pp, including dinner and breakfast. Built in 1925, **Berida Manor,** 6 David St. (tel. 048-61-1177), is a large boutique hotel surrounded in gardens on the edge of the golf course and is a five-minute walk from downtown Bowral. Rooms are well-furnished, and guest facilities include a pool, spa, sauna, gym, tennis courts, snooker rooms, and mountain bikes. Rates are $100 s, $139 d.

Food

Bowral Cafe, 336 Bong Bong St. (tel. 048-61-1568), has an old-world atmosphere but, more importantly, a delicious array of cakes, pastries, and ice cream; closed Tuesday. At 326 Bong Bong St. is **Bowral Country Kitchen** (tel. 048-61-4560), a casual restaurant with coffee and cake around $5. On Friday and Saturday nights a three-course dinner is offered for $15 pp. **Truffles,** Highlands Arcade, Bong Bong St. (tel. 048-61-1257), is a small, casual restaurant, with breakfast $6-10, lunch $6-12, and dinner $11-15.

MOSS VALE AND VICINITY

Moss Vale

Moss Vale, a thriving country town, lacks the pretensions of Bowral and Berrima, but with tree-lined streets and many historic buildings, it's still a pleasant place to stop. **Cecil Hoskins Nature Reserve,** along the Wingecarribee River, two km northeast of Moss Vale, is home to waterbirds and platypuses.

Bundanoon

Bundanoon (pop. 1,500), 26 km south of Moss Vale, is a sleepy southern highlands village where two lookouts provide spectacular views across Morton National Park. To the east is a **glowworm cave,** well signposted from town. Early this century, Bundanoon was a popular mountain getaway, and many sandstone buildings remain from that era.

Brigadoon Highland Gathering, in mid-April, celebrates the coming of autumn with pipe bands, a street parade, haggis hurling, and other traditional highland games.

Mildenhall Guesthouse, 10 Anzac Parade (tel. 048-83-6643), dates from the 1920s and is just 500 meters from the center of town. Rates are $50-75 pp for bed and breakfast; dinner is an additional $25-35 pp.

Morton National Park

This little-known park occupies 162,000 hectares of a rugged and almost inaccessible section of the southern highlands. Access is from the Illawarra Highway, which links the southern highlands to the south coast, or from **Bundanoon,** south of Moss Vale. Dominant geological features are the deep gorges around the headwaters of the Shoalhaven River and its tributaries and a large plateau in the center of the park. **Fitzroy Falls,** a 250-meter walk from Nowra Rd., is a park highlight, plunging 81 meters. From the same parking lot, trails lead along the East and West Rims to lookouts above the falls; the 3.5-km East Rim trail is the easier of the two routes. **Fitzroy Falls Visitors Centre** (tel. 048-87-7270) is open daily 9 a.m.-5 p.m. Also at the center is a general store and campground.

The park's remote southern section protects the ancient **Budawang Range,** providing the opportunity for experienced hikers to explore an area of extraordinary sandstone formations and long, forested valleys. In the far south is 719-meter **Pigeon House Mountain,** a volcanic plug towering high above surrounding forest.

GOULBURN

Located 190 km south of Sydney, this large inland city of 24,000 is the center of a rich wool-growing area—but you won't need anyone to tell you that after seeing the massive fiberglass sheep beside the main drag though town.

Goulburn was gazetted in 1833, and for years it was base for large numbers of police hunting for bushrangers. By the early 1860s free settlers from Sydney were moving to the area, and as early as 1885 Goulburn had been proclaimed

Big Merino

a city. Many buildings from that era remain, including the courthouse (1887), surrounded by the landscaped gardens of Belmore Park.

Goulburn's major attraction is, undoubtedly, the **Big Merino** (tel. 048-21-8800), a grotesque monument to the lifeblood of the city. Inside its fiberglass hulk are displays describing the wool-growing process, and part of the same complex is an agridome, where several times daily sheep shows are conducted, which include a shearing exhibition; admission adult $6, child $3.

Practicalities

Along freeway access roads north and south of Goulburn is a variety of accommodations. **Lilac** City Motor Inn, Hume Hwy. (tel. 048-21-5000), has rooms of a good standard, with all the expected services for $45 s, $48 d; it's two km north of downtown. **Centretown Lagoon Motel** is on the opposite side of the Hume Hwy. and closer to downtown (tel. 048-21-2422). Facilities include an indoor pool, restaurant, and bar; $60 s, $68 d.

South of Goulburn, in the historic village of Bungendore, is **The Carrington** (tel. 06-238-1044 or 1800-04-6079). Built in 1885 as a stopping point for coaches traveling between Sydney and Melbourne, the inn has been totally restored with luxurious rooms for $105 s, $120 d. Meal packages in their renowned restaurant are also available.

CANBERRA AND THE AUSTRALIAN CAPITAL TERRITORY

Midway between Sydney and Melbourne is the Australian Capital Territory, home to the country's capital, Canberra. The site was a compromise between the powers of Sydney and Melbourne, who, after Australia's federation in 1901, both claimed their city as the rightful capital. Today, Canberra, which lies away from the ocean (Canberra is Australia's largest inland city), away from a major river, and away from mineral deposits, exists for no other reason than to serve the politicians and bureaucrats running Australia, but don't let that put you off visiting— it's a unique and oddly beautiful city with many fine museums and attractions.

Canberra is a planned city. From the original plans submitted by architect Walter Burley

On 1 August 1997 all telephone numbers in this section will change. To dial the new number, simply add "6" to all existing numbers. As an example, (06) 212-3456 becomes 6212-3456. The new area code will be (02).

TO DUNTROON HOUSE AND AIRPORT

DR. MOLONGLO RIVER

MORSHEAD WAY

KINGS AVE.

ASPEN ISLAND

CARILLON

KINGS PARK

NATIONAL OF AUSTRALIA

QUESTACON

HIGH COURT OF AUSTRALIA

KING EDWARD TERRACE

KING GEORGE TERRACE

OLD PARLIAMENT HOUSE

QUEEN VICTORIA TERRACE

PARLIAMENT HOUSE

CAPITAL HILL

CAPITAL CIRCLE

STATE CIRCLE

THE LODGE

FLYNN DR.

HYATT HOTEL CANBERRA

CORONATION DR.

CORONATION PARK

STIRLING

WENTWORTH AVE.

PARK

KINGS AVE.

BRISBANE AVE.

CANBERRA AVE.

CIRCUIT

TELOPEA

NATIONAL

ADELAIDE AVE.

MELBOURNE AVE.

YARRALUMLA

DEAKIN

RAILWAY STATION

CANBERRA AVE.

TO QUEANBEYAN AND COOMA

DIPLOMAT BOUTIQUE HOTEL

KINGSTON

VICTOR LODGE MOTEL MONARO

ST. DAWES

KENNEDY ST.

EYRE ST.

GILES ST.

OXLEY ST.

KINGSTON COURT

MANUKA PARK SERVICED APARTMENTS

MANUKA

TO ROYAL AUSTRALIAN MINT, WESTON, AND TUGGERANONG

0   500 m

© MOON PUBLICATIONS, INC.

Griffin to the newest row of trees, nothing is out of place. Arterial roads bypass all political, commercial, and residential areas, which, in turn, are separate from each other. It's possible to drive through the city's heart without spotting a petrol station, shopping mall, fast food outlet, or neon sign. Political buildings such as the High Court, National Gallery, and National Library are within the **Parliamentary Triangle,** bordered by Parkes Way, Kings Way, and Commonwealth Ave., the latter two forming and an apex at Capital Hill, site of Parliament House. The city proper surrounds the triangle. To the north, across manmade **Lake Burley Griffin,** lies **Civic,** Canberra's commercial heart. The city's 300,000 or so residents live in decentralized suburbs, each with its own commercial center and completely bypassed by arterial roads. All suburbs have blocks of land varying in size, and therefore, in theory, there are no "rich" or "poor" suburbs.

Through all this, politicians are only small in number, and are only in town when parliament is sitting. Most of the population consists of public servants, who serve the large infrastructure of government and related services.

History
At federation in 1901, and until a permanent site had been decided upon, Melbourne was deemed temporary capital of Australia. Various existing towns through the southeast were considered, but eventually it was decided to build the capital from scratch. The site chosen, a wide floodplain on the Molonglo River, was halfway between Sydney and Melbourne, the two cities most vocal about becoming the nation's capital. The land, granted to a free settler as a reward for helping with the capture of a bushranger, was bought by the Commonwealth and named Canberra, Aboriginal for "Meeting Place." The creation of the new capital began in 1911 with an international design competition. American architect Walter Burley Griffin was declared the winner, but it would be half a century before his original plan was fully implemented.

To coincide with the 9 May 1927 opening of a temporary parliament, 1,000 families were moved to Canberra. But Canberra was no boomtown; it wasn't until after WW II that the city took the form it does today, and in 1960 the population was only 50,000. And the temporary Parliament House? It wasn't until 1988 that the permanent structure was completed.

PARLIAMENTARY TRIANGLE SIGHTS

Within the Parliamentary Triangle, bounded by Commonwealth Ave., Parkes Way, and Kings Ave., lie the federal buildings. Parliament House, on Capital Hill, forms the triangle's apex. Across Lake Burley Griffin, and beyond the base of the triangle, is Anzac Parade, which ends at the Australian War Memorial. Scattered around the leafy streets west of Capital Hill are the embassies of many countries. **The Lodge,** on Adelaide Ave., is the official residence of Australia's prime minister.

Parliament House
After eight years of construction and $1 billion of taxpayers' money, Australia's Parliament House, the culmination of Walter Burley Griffin's city plan, opened in 1988. The building is very distinctive, sitting at the apex of the Parliamentary Triangle and half-underground, its roofline following the natural slope of Capital Hill. Part of the design plan was that the building be accessible to the public, and this is definitely the case. From the main entrance, submerged into the hill, two massive granite walls radiate to the base of the hill, from where grassed banks lead up and over the roof to a massive 81-meter-high flagpole. The main foyer, dominated by 48 marble columns, is flanked by grand marble staircases leading to the House of Representatives and the Senate. Beyond the foyer is the Great Hall, housing a 20-meter-long tapestry based on a painting by Australian artist Arthur Boyd. On the first floor of the foyer is a collection of Australian landscape paintings, a small part of the 3,000 pieces of artwork throughout the building. Beyond the Great Hall important historical documents are displayed, including the original Act of Constitution and one of only four known copies of the 1297 Magna Carta.

When Parliament is not sitting, guided tours take place every half hour 9 a.m.-5 p.m. When parliament is sitting, tickets for the House of Representatives (3 p.m.) and Senate (2 p.m.) are available from the ticket office in the Members Hall (tel. 06-277-4889). Other facilities open to the public include a cafeteria with city views, and an audiovisual display. The main building is open daily 9 a.m.-5 p.m.

Old Parliament House

Below Capital Hill, on King George Terrace, this building was the seat of Australian Government between 1927 and 1988. It's now home to the **National Portrait Gallery** (tel. 06-273-4723), which is open daily 9 a.m.-4 p.m. Admission is $2, which includes a guided tour of the building and a glimpse of the Prime Ministerial suite.

National Library of Australia

Overlooking Lake Burley Griffin, this elegant five-story building has over five million books, as well as newspapers, maps, pictures, prints, films, videos, periodicals, and oral history tapes. The library opened in 1968 and was renovated in 1991 to include an Exhibition Gallery where various collections of the library material previously in storage are displayed; this area is open Mon.-Thurs. 9 a.m.-9 p.m., Fri.-Sun. 9 a.m.-4:45 p.m. The main reading rooms are open similar hours, with the exception of Sunday, when the Newspaper Room is closed. Tours are offered weekdays. For general library information, call (06) 262-1111.

Questacon—The National Science and Technology Centre

This museum, on King Edward Terrace between the National Library and High Court, features over 200 hands-on exhibits spread through six galleries. The aim is to give everyone a basic understanding of scientific concepts through pushing buttons, pulling levers, and pressing knobs. Admission is adult $6, child $3. Open daily 10 a.m.-5 p.m. For further information, call (06) 270-2800.

High Court of Australia

Opened in 1980, this uniquely shaped 40-meter-high concrete-and-glass structure overlooking Lake Burley Griffin is home to the highest court in Australia. The main feature is a seven-story public hall that is linked to the National Gallery by an overpass. Each of the three courtrooms features elegant woodwork, and in Courtroom One a large tapestry is displayed. The building is open daily 10 a.m.-4 p.m. If court is sitting you must stay in the courtrooms at least 10 minutes. The cafeteria here is excellent and has good views. For High Court information, call (06) 270-6811.

National Gallery of Australia

Within the triangle, the only other federal building open to the public is the National Gallery. It displays the world's largest collection of Australian art, as well as featuring permanent and temporary exhibitions of art from around the world. The Australian collection includes Aboriginal art and works by 20th-century artists such as Arthur Boyd and Sidney Nolan (look for his distinctive Ned Kelly works). Photographs, sculptures, prints, drawings, and fashions are also displayed. For details on the program of regular lectures and film screenings, call (06) 271-2502. The gallery is open daily 10 a.m.-5 p.m., with guided tours at 11 a.m. and 2 p.m. Admission is $3 pp.

ANDREW HEMPSTEAD

High Court of Australia

National Capital Exhibition and Vicinity

This small center at Regatta Point on the north side of the lake (signposted from Commonwealth Ave.) tells the story of Canberra's development through photographs, models, and an audiovisual display. It's open daily 9 a.m.-5 p.m., and admission is free.

Along the lakefront west of the center is **Terrestrial Globe,** where Captain Cook's three world journeys are traced. In front of the globe is the **Captain Cook Memorial Water Jet,** which throws water a spectacular 140 meters in the air. It operates daily 10 a.m.-noon, 2-4 p.m., and during summer 7-9 p.m. **Blundell's Farmhouse,** 800 meters east of the National Capital Exhibition, dates to 1860 and was moved to the site and restored in 1964. It's open daily 10 a.m.-4 p.m., and admission is $1. Farther around the lake, on Aspen Island, is the **Carillon,** a three-column bell tower. Comprising 53 bells, including one weighing six tons, they are rung Wednesday 12:45-1:30 p.m. and Sat.-Sun. 2:45-3:30 p.m.

OTHER SIGHTS

Royal Australian Mint

This is where Australia's coinage is minted, and, naturally, you're not free to wander round the place or collect free samples. The closest you'll get to the coins is looking through a plate-glass window to the area where the minting process takes place. In the foyer are displays cataloging the development of Australian currency, including the story of Governor Macquarie who, in 1813, punched out the center of coins to create double the currency. Admission is free. Open Mon.-Fri. 9 a.m.-4 p.m., Sat.-Sun. 10 a.m.-3 p.m. The mint has an interesting gift shop and a cafe. It's southwest of Capital Hill on Denison St. (tel. 06-202-6999).

Australian Federal Police Museum

Through displays of badges, uniforms, vehicles, and memorabilia from well-known police operations, this small museum catalogs the history of the Federal Police Force through a dozen-odd name changes. It's open Mon.-Fri. 9 a.m.-3 p.m., and admission is free. Located in the Police Services and Training Centre off Unwin Pl. in Weston, southwest of downtown (tel. 06-287-0618).

Australian National University

The grounds of this university sprawl over 130 hectares between City Hill and Black Mountain. The information center at Balmain Crescent (tel. 06-249-0794) has maps and entertainment programs. The grounds themselves are pleasant to wander through, and there are a couple of art galleries, restaurants, and cafes. On McCoy Circuit is the **National Film and Sound Archive,** a collection of Australia's cinematographic and audio history. Old movie house equipment is on display, and old news bulletins run in a small theater. Open daily 9:30 a.m.-4 p.m. Admission is free.

Australian National Botanic Gardens

These gardens, on the lower slopes of Black Mountain west of the university, cover 50 hectares and are devoted entirely to the unique flora of Australia. Features include 600 species of eucalypts and a garden planted with species used by the Aborigines. Guided tours depart from the gardens' Visitor Information Centre (tel. 06-250-9540) Wednesday, Friday, and Sunday at 11 a.m. and Sat.-Sun. at 2 p.m. The center is open daily 9:30 a.m.-3:30 p.m. To get there, take bus no. 904 to Clunes Ross Street.

Black Mountain

The best place for city views is 812-meter Black Mountain, immediately west of Civic. A sealed road leads to the summit and to **Telecom Tower,** which features displays of Australia's telecommunications history and has a revolving restaurant. Admission is $3, and it's open daily 9 a.m.-10 p.m. (tel. 06-248-1911). Access is off Clunes Ross St., or take bus no. 904.

Australian War Memorial

This in one of Canberra's top attractions, housing an impressive collection of wartime memorabilia, photographs, and exhibitions as a tribute to the wars in which Australians have been involved, including Gallipoli, where thousands of Anzacs were killed, and the wars in which Australians have fought alongside Americans, such as WW II in the Pacific Ocean. The memorial is on the north side of Lake Burley Griffin, at the foot of Mt. Ainslie at the top end of Anzac Parade, looking down to Parliament House.

Australian War Memorial

Another part of the memorial is the Hall of Memory, where the body of the unknown Australian soldier, symbolizing all those Australians lost in action, lies. Admission is free, and the museum is open daily 10 a.m.-5 p.m. Tours are held regularly. To get there take bus no. 901 or 302 from the city. Call (06) 243-4211 to contact the memorial.

Duntroon House
This was the home of the first settler along the Molonglo River, and it is now part of the **Royal Military College.** Parts of the stone house date from the 1830s. For tour details, call (06) 275-9545. To get there from Civic, take Parkes Way southeast to Morshead Drive and turn onto Jubilee Avenue.

Australian Institute of Sport
This facility provides the training facilities for the cream of Australia's athletes. The indoor and outdoor training facilities and stadiums are of the highest standard and include swimming pools and tennis courts. Athletes in training lead tours daily at 11 a.m. and 2 p.m. for $2 pp. For bookings, call (06) 252-1444. Located five km northeast of City Hill on Leverrier Crescent. Get there on bus no. 431 from downtown.

Australian Heritage Village
North of Canberra, on the corner of the Federal Hwy. and Antill St., this place is a re-creation of a rural Australian village of late last century. With cobbled roads linking stone and timber buildings around a small lagoon, the village also boasts a large collection of buggies, carts, and carriages. On the grounds are various Australiana shops, galleries, a tavern, cafe, restaurant, and antique shops. Admission is free. Open daily 9 a.m.-5 p.m.

National Dinosaur Museum
Australia's only museum dedicated only to the prehistoric animals that once roamed the earth, this private collection includes 300 exhibits including nine full-size dinosaur replicas. Mike Durrant, the founder, has collected specimens from around the world for display, with many bones and other fossils displayed to illustrate this period of the earth's history. Admission is $5. Open daily 10 a.m.-5 p.m. Located 11 km north of downtown on Gold Creek Rd., off Barton Hwy. (tel. 06-230-2655).

OUTDOOR ACTIVITIES AND SPECTATOR SPORTS

Biking
Canberra is probably Australia's best city for biking, with over 120 km of cycleways winding through the city and around Lake Burley Griffin. The best map for biking is *Canberra Cycleways* ($2.50), available from the main Tourist Information Centre and many bookshops.

Mr Spokes Bike Hire, in Acton Park (tel. 06-257-1188), rents mountain bikes for $6 an hour and $20 a day. Helmets are an extra $1.

Canoeing and Boating
At the Acton Park Ferry Terminal, on the north shore of Lake Burley Griffin and immediately west of Commonwealth Ave., is **Dobel Boat Hire** (tel. 06-249-6861), which rents canoes and surf-

skis for $10 an hour and catamarans for $20 an hour. Motorized craft are banned on the lake.

Swimming
The **Australian Institute of Sport** (see above) has a 50-meter heated pool open to the public; call for times; $3.50 per session; located eight km northwest of Civic on Leverrier Crescent (tel. 06-252-1111).

Rugby League
The **Canberra Raiders** have been Australia's most successful rugby league team this decade. They play home games every second week March-Sept. at Bruce Stadium, Battye St., Bruce. Call (06) 253-2111 for ticketing information.

ARTS AND ENTERTAINMENT

Theater
The **Canberra Theatre Centre,** London Circuit, Civic (tel. 06-257-1077), is the city's main venue for performing arts. The large theater seats around 1,200, and performances range from Shakespeare to international rock acts. Tickets range $30-55. **Gorman House Arts Centre,** Ainslie Ave., Braddon, occasionally has theater and dance performances. For ticketing details, call (06) 249-7377.

Cinemas
A few cinemas are scattered around Civic Square, and the **National Library of Australia** screens films Tuesday and Thursday at lunchtime.

Casino
Casino Canberra is on Constitution Ave. (tel. 1800-80-6833). Games played are baccarat, blackjack, keno, pai gow, roulette, and sic bo. Dress regulations include no denim jeans or sports shoes, and blokes must wear a jacket and tie after 7 p.m. It's open weekends 24 hours, weekdays 10 a.m.-4 a.m.

Bars and Nightclubs
The **Canberra Tradesmen's Union Club,** 2 Badham St., Dickson (tel. 06-248-0999), is a workingman's club four km north of downtown. It has rows and rows of pokies (slot machines),

regular bingo sessions, a snooker room, and, best of all, beer for just $2 a schooner. The club also boasts a large collection of historic bicycles. **Dorette's Bistro,** 17 Garema Place, Civic (tel. 06-247-4946), is a popular and stylish place overlooking a pedestrian plaza. Jazz is performed during the week, blues on weekends, but it is a pleasant place for a drink or light meal at any time. Happy hour is 5:30-6:30 p.m. **Pandora's,** on the corner of Alinga and Mort Streets (tel. 06-248-7405), is a large dance club. Another nightclub, **Private Bin,** 50 Northbourne Ave. (tel. 06-247-3030), is popular with the younger set.

Festivals and Events
The 10-day **Canberra Festival** each March celebrates the city's birth. The festival opens with a colorful street party, while other features include an outdoor film festival, a nighttime street parade, fireworks display, hot-air balloon competition, entertainment in Glebe Park, and an evocative nighttime reading of Canberra's history. **Floriade,** in September, is a spectacular collection of springtime flowers.

SHOPPING

The **Canberra Centre** encompasses four blocks between City Walk, Ballumbir St., Petrie St., and Akuna Street in Civic. It has over 150 shops, all surrounding a three-story glass-roofed atrium. In the **City Market** section, you'll find fresh produce and a food court. On the first floor is **Craftsman's Collection** (tel. 06-257-4733), crammed with Australiana, including pottery, glasswork, woodcarving, and jewelry.

ACCOMMODATIONS

Getting a motel room close to the city center can be difficult midweek, so you should try to make advance reservations. On weekends the city is deserted and most motels offer reduced rates.

Hotels and Motels
You'll find several hotels and motels in and around Civic. Least expensive of the downtown motels is **Acacia Motor Lodge,** 65 Ainslie Ave.

DOWNTOWN CANBERRA

(tel. 06-249-6955), a five-minute walk from the city center. Rates are $66 s, $72 d, which includes a continental breakfast. Moderately priced motels are on Northbourne Ave., immediately north of downtown. **Down Town Spero's Motel,** 82 Northbourne Ave. (tel. 06-249-1388), is best value at $68 s, $75 d. **Olims Canberra,** corner Ainslie and Limestone Avenues (tel. 06-248-5511), first opened its doors in 1927 and is as close as you'll get to a historical accommodation in the capital. It's been totally renovated, and many rooms overlook a landscaped courtyard. Rates are $95 s or d, but on weekends rates drop to $60. Other more expensive options are: **Canberra Travelodge,** 150 Northbourne Ave. (tel. 06-248-5311), where rooms are $100-125 s or d, and **Country Comfort**

Inn, 102 Northbourne Ave. (tel. 06-249-1411), with large rooms and a range of facilities, $129 s or d.

Moving away from the city, **Hyatt Hotel Canberra,** Commonwealth Ave., Yarralumla (tel. 06-270-1234), adjacent to the Parliamentary Triangle and Lake Burley Griffin, is the city's most luxurious hotel; rooms are $290 s or d.

Victor Lodge, 29 Dawes St., Kingston (tel. 06-295-7777), is a small place two km from Parliament House. Meals are available, and guests can rent bikes. Rooms, with shared bathrooms, are $35 s $40 d. Next door is **Motel Monaro,** 27 Dawes St. (tel. 06-295-2111), with large rooms and modern facilities for $62 s, $72 d. **Kingston Court,** 4 Tench St. (tel. 06-295-2244), has 36 self-contained apartments each measuring close to 100 square meters and with a modern kitchen, balcony or courtyard, and laundry facility. The pool, half tennis court, and barbecue are for communal use. Rates are $95 s, $100 d. **Diplomat Boutique Hotel,** corner Canberra Ave. and Hely St. (tel. 06-295-2277), is just south of Kingston. Rooms are large and well-decorated and most face inward to a tropical atrium. Rates are $115 s or d.

The modern and stylish **Manuka Park Serviced Apartments** is set around a large pool. Each unit has a well-equipped kitchen, laundry, and separate bedroom area. Rates are $95 s or d. It's at 1 Oxley St., Manuka (tel. 06-285-1175).

Backpacker Accommodations

Canberra YHA Hostel, Dryandra St., O'Connor (tel. 06-248-9155), is a beautiful hostel six km northwest of Civic. All facilities are modern and well kept. Bikes can be rented, and there's a travel desk. Dorm beds are $15 pp, $18-23 in a twin room, and it's $5 pp extra for nonmembers. The office is open daily 7:30 a.m.-10:30 p.m.

The **Australian National University,** west of Civic, has colleges where rooms are available during holiday breaks, including all summer. Rates range $15-48 pp per night depending on facilities and meals offered. Call (06) 267-4333 or (06) 267-5222 for bookings.

Campgrounds

North of Civic, in the suburb of O'Connor, is **Canberra Motor Village,** Kunzea St. (tel. 06-247-5466), set among natural bushland. All sites are powered and $18, while on-site vans are $39 and cabins $65.

Another option is **Riverside Caravan Park,** 12 km southeast of Canberra in Queanbeyan. Facilities are great, and it's a few dollars cheaper than the one above. Unpowered sites are $9, powered sites $12, and cabins $38. Located on Morisset St. (tel. 06-297-4749).

FOOD

Civic

A great place for breakfast is **Waffles,** a casual restaurant serving delicious waffles as well as bacon and eggs, and cakes and pastries to go.

It's at 46 Northbourne Ave. (tel. 06-247-2913); open daily 8 a.m.-midnight. Another popular breakfast hangout is **Tu Tu Tango's,** 124 Bunda St. (tel. 06-257-7100), a modern cafe with tables inside and out and a wide variety of breakfast dishes. Also try **Gus's Coffee Lounge,** Bunda St. (tel. 06-248-8118), in the Garema Arcade, which is busy at lunch, when locals in the know come to feast on focaccia and other European delights as well as a wide variety of desserts. Prices are excellent, with soup for $4.50 and most main dishes $4-8. Open daily 7 a.m.-midnight.

One of Canberra's busiest cafes is **Caffe Della Piazza,** on Garema Place (tel. 06-248-9711). Tables are spread around the cobbled square and are perpetually filled with coffee-drinking locals. Across the mall is **Pizza Cafe** (tel. 06-248-9131), where a slice of pizza is $3 and a full pizza ranges $10-20. Another good pizza joint, this one on the corner of East Row and London Circuit, is **Australian Pizza Kitchen** (tel. 06-257-2727), featuring pizza from a wood-fired oven.

In the Sydney Building, at 27 East Row, is **Thai Lotus** (tel. 06-249-6507), serving Thai cuisine from Thailand at lunch Tues.-Fri. and dinner nightly. At 21 East Row (and up a narrow staircase) is **Canberra Vietnamese Restaurant** (tel. 06-247-4840), where all main meals are under $10. Away from the crowds of Garema Place is **Anatolia,** corner Mort and Bunda Streets (tel. 06-257-1100), open daily 7 a.m.-4 p.m. for cafe-style fare at good prices. At the opposite end of the scale is **Antigo,** a trendy cafe offering fairly standard dishes on their set menu for $22-26; or just drop by to enjoy an atmosphere a world away from the mall out front. It's at 143 London Circuit (tel. 06-249-8080).

La Scala, Cinema Centre, Bunda St. (tel. 06-248-8338), is a small and elegant Italian restaurant with comfortable seating in an formal atmosphere. A good choice for an appetizer is three pastas for $11.50 pp, while main dishes average $16. They have an extensive wine list. It's open Mon.-Fri. for lunch and daily for dinner. **Charcoal Restaurant,** 61 London Circuit (tel. 06-248-8015), specializes in juicy steaks but also offers chicken and seafood. Main dishes are $15-27. Open for lunch Mon.-Fri., dinner Mon.-Saturday.

Parliamentary Triangle Dining

The **Public Dining Room** in Parliament House has surprisingly good food, including all the usual Aussie fare, at reasonable prices. It's open daily 9 a.m.-5 p.m. (between 11 a.m. and 2 p.m. a $7.50 carvery is offered). The **High Court Cafe** has similar choices, as well as inexpensive afternoon teas. A popular politician hangout is **The Lobby Restaurant,** King George Terrace (tel. 06-273-1563). It's only open for lunch weekdays and dinner Tues.-Saturday.

Manuka

Manuka is a suburb south of Lake Burley Griffin, with services for politicians, bureaucrats, and embassy staff from around the world. On Franklin St. is **My Cafe** (tel. 06-295-6632), a quiet place with healthy snacks around $7. **La Grange** (tel. 06-295-8866), also on Franklin St., is a stylish bistro with main dishes $10-17. In Style Arcade is **Chez Daniel** (tel. 06-295-7122), with main dishes from $18.

Black Mountain

Apart from an inexpensive cafe with excellent views, Telecom Tower boasts **The Tower Restaurant** (tel. 06-248-6162), a revolving restaurant with spectacular views, especially at sunset. At lunch an extensive buffet is offered for $24.50, while in the evening dinner plates average $20.

GETTING THERE

Air

Canberra Airport is on Pialligo Ave., 12 km east of downtown. **Ansett Australia** (tel. 13-1300) and **Qantas** (tel. 13-1313) have regular flights between Canberra and all major Australian cities. A taxi to downtown runs $12-15, or catch an **Airport Shuttle** (tel. 06-291-4592); $5-8.

Rail

The **Countrylink Xplorer** operates daily between Sydney and Canberra; four hours one-way. The fare is economy $35, first class $48; call 13-2232 for bookings. **Canberra Link** is a combined rail/bus service from Melbourne. The fare is $59.50 one-way, and for details you should call V/Line at (03) 9619-5000 or 13-2232. The railway station is on Wentworth Ave., Kingston, three km southeast of Capital Hill.

Bus

Long-distance buses arrive and depart from the **Jolimont Centre,** on the corner of Northbourne Ave. and Alinga St., Civic. **Greyhound Pioneer** (tel. 13-2030) has regular services between Sydney and Canberra for $35 one-way (some services depart from Sydney Airport). **Murray's** (tel. 06-295-3611) offers a quicker service (four hours) for a few bucks less and also runs east to the south coast town of Batemans Bay ($21).

GETTING AROUND

Bus

Canberra's local bus service, **Action,** runs throughout the city and suburbs Mon.-Sat. 7 a.m.-11 p.m. and Sunday 8:30 a.m.-6 p.m. The main terminal is at the west end of Garema Place on the corner of Alinga St. and East Row. The basic sector fare is $2, and day-tripper tickets are $4.80. For further information, call (06) 207-7611.

Taxi

The city has just one taxi company, **Aerial.** Call (06) 285-9222 for pick-ups.

Car Rental

Canberra has a good public transportation system, and tours (see below) cover most popular sights, but if you need to rent a car, call: **Avis** (tel. 06-249-6088), **Budget** (tel. 06-257-2200), **Hertz** (tel. 06-257-4877), **National** (tel. 06-247-8888), or **Thrifty** (tel. 06-247-7422). For something cheaper, try **Rumbles** (tel. 06-280-7444), where cars are $35 per day and $200 per week.

Tours

The **Canberra Explorer** (tel. 06-295-3611) makes 19 stops around a 25-km circuit, and there's a commentary along the way. **Greyhound Pioneer** (tel. 13-2030) also runs tours.

The fare is adult $15, child $8. From the main terminal, bus no. 901 runs to sights around the Parliamentary Triangle.

SERVICES

The main **post office** is on Alinga St., Civic; it's open Mon.-Fri. 9 a.m.-5 p.m. **60 Minute Cleaners** is on Bailey's Corner, Civic (tel. 06-248-0521).

Emergency Services
Woden Valley Hospital is on Yamba Dr., Garran (tel. 06-244-2222). For medical emergencies, call (06) 244-2611. **Capital Medical Centre** looks after nonurgent cases; it's at 2 Mort St., Civic (tel. 06-257-3766); open Mon.-Fri. 8:30 a.m.-5 p.m. **Canberra City Pharmacy** is on the corner of Alinga St. and East Row (tel. 06-248-5469).

INFORMATION

Books
The **National Library of Australia** (see "Parliamentary Triangle Sights," above) has over five million books. It's open Mon.-Thurs. 9 a.m.-9 p.m., Fri.-Sat. 9 a.m.-4:30 p.m., and Sunday 1:30-4:30 p.m. Call (06) 262-1111 for more information.

The **Commonwealth Government Bookshop,** Melbourne Building (tel. 06-247-7211), has many coffee table books and other Australiana. **Dalton's,** in the Capital Centre (tel. 06-249-1844), is another good choice.

Information Centers
The **Visitor Information Centre** is on Northbourne Ave., the main road into the city from the north. Staff are helpful and friendly and offer good advice on accommodations. It's open daily 9 a.m.-5 p.m. (tel. 06-205-0044 or 1800-02-6166).

SNOWY MOUNTAINS

While Australia is best known for its red center, endless beaches, and the Great Barrier Reef, there is another side to this land of extremes, an area of alpine country that extends across the far south of New South Wales into Victoria. Many visitors from the Northern Hemisphere are surprised to find that many thousands of square kilometers of Australia are blanketed in snow for part of the year. But unlike the European Alps or North America's Rocky Mountains, there are no dominant peaks. Instead, Australia's Snowy Mountains are a high plateau, with only 10 peaks higher than 2,000 meters, and the highest, **Mt. Kosciusko** (pronounced "koz-ee-OS-ko"), rising to just 2,228 meters. The entire area is protected by 690,000-hectare **Kosciusko National Park.**

The mountains may not have the height of ranges on other continents, but in their own distinct way they are spectacular, an ancient landscape of alpine meadows, alive each spring with a carpet of wildflowers, providing almost unlimited opportunities for hiking in summer, while in winter lifts crank up on four ski resorts, including **Perisher-Blue,** whose network of lifts serves an area larger than any North American ski resort.

The Land

Volcanic activity deep below the earth's surface began pushing the Great Dividing Range upward around 350 million years ago. Around 20 million years ago, further uplift occurred, and the high plateau of today took shape. This final uplift pushed the plateau to elevations double those of today. Erosion from wind, rain, and snow saw the range slowly breaking down to its present height, while also forming its rugged topography.

On 1 August 1997 all telephone numbers in this section will change. To dial the new number, simply add the last two digits of the existing area code to the old number. As an example, (064) 12-3456 becomes 6412-3456. The new area code will be (02).

During two successive ice ages, beginning 50,000 years ago, the area was covered in a deep sheet of ice. The last ice age was less severe, with glaciers confined to a combined total of less than 40 square km at the heads of the highest valleys. A number of lakes around Mt. Kosciusko were gouged out by glaciers, with moraines of rock blocking the flow of water. These lakes provide the only clearly visible signs of glaciation on the Australian mainland.

Flora and Fauna

The most identifiable feature of the Snowy Mountains is the gnarled **snow gum,** but this is only one of 700 flora species in the park. While much of the Monaro region has been cleared for pastoral use, within the boundaries of Kosciusko National Park many east-facing valleys are naturally devoid of trees. On the opposite side of the range, where rainfall is high, forests of towering mountain ash, stands of stringybark, and even a small area of rainforest are able to be supported. At higher elevations, between 1,500 and 1,800 meters, dense forest gives way to open forests of alpine ash and snow gum. Above 1,800 meters, treeless alpine meadows are dominated by heathlands, and grasslands of snow grasses, daisies, grand orchids, and violets are found, broken only by ferns and sphagnum bogs.

The great diversity of vegetation provides ideal habitat for many species of fauna. Gray kangaroos, red-neck wallabies, wombats, koalas, and the rare tiger quoll live at lower elevations. Only small rodents and marsupials such as the rare mountain pygmy possum, which lives in scree-covered slopes, live above the treeline.

HISTORY

The First Visitors

Around 15,000 years ago, as Australia's climate warmed, the mountains became habitable for humans year-round. For thousands of years, Aboriginal people living in the valleys would head for the high country to feast on **bogong moths,** a great delicacy rich in protein.

Exploration, Gold, and Settlement

Explorers Hume and Hovell were the first Europeans to visit the mountains. Paul Edmond Strzelecki later surveyed much of the high country, naming Mt. Kosciusko for the patriot of his Polish homeland. The talk of all Australian colonies in the 1850s was gold, and many a high-country stockman kept his eyes peeled for the precious metal. The first gold strike in the mountains was made by the Pollock brothers in November 1859. The area experienced no sudden rush, but as finds in neighboring Victoria declined, thousands of diggers crossed the mountains to try their luck at the field that became known as **Kiandra.** A year later, at the height of the rush, 10,000 diggers lived in the shantytown. As finds were made elsewhere and the harsh winter climate came upon them, the diggers moved on.

With the diggers gone, the pastoral service towns of Cooma, Jindabyne, and Adaminaby continued to grow. The rail line reached Cooma in 1889, opening up the mountains to tourists who came to hike in summer and ski in winter. A small area of the mountains was set aside for public recreation in 1906, but it was not until 1944 that the foundation of the national park as it is today was proclaimed.

AUSTRALIA'S EARLIEST SKIERS

For early residents of the gold-rush town of Kiandra, skiing was a great way to break up the long, cold winter. Skis were made from alpine ash and, although ski poles weren't used, a single sapling was pushed into the snow to propel the skier forward, then straddled to control braking. In 1878 a skiing carnival was held at Kiandra, an event that is claimed to make Australia the birthplace of competitive downhill skiing.

Snowy Mountains Scheme

Best known through the poetry of Banjo Patterson, the Snowy River is much altered from its original state, especially its upper reaches, which have been diverted to form an important part of the Snowy Mountains Scheme, which harnesses the river's hydroelectric power as well as providing water for inland irrigation in one of Australia's greatest engineering feats.

As early as the 1880s, plans were being made to change the river's direction to divert its waters to what was then an agricultural wasteland in southwestern New South Wales. These plans became financially viable in the 1920s, when the river's hydroelectric power was harnessed to supply electricity to Canberra, the nation's new capital. The scheme was launched on 17 October 1949 with the first stage, a five-km tunnel completed to Guthega

Dam. A 60,000-kilowatt power station was constructed at the dam. Eucumbene Dam was completed in 1958, along with another power station, and on 1 April 1966 the Snowy River finally flowed westward, changing the face of Australian agriculture forever.

COOMA

Descending into Cooma (pop. 8,000), in the heart of the Monaro, your first impression will be the profusion of ski shops and billboards advertising the ski resorts a farther 80 km away. Cooma itself rarely gets snow, but for four months each year, tens of thousands of snowbound Sydneysiders pass through town.

The Monaro's first permanent settlers were squatters who had secured massive cattle runs in the region. Cooma was the name of one of these original runs and has grown from a small village. After the Snowy Mountains Authority established its headquarters there, the population boomed, rising for a time to above 15,000.

Sights

Construction of the Snowy Mountains Scheme may have finished 20 years ago, but day-to-day operations employ over 600 people. Many of these are based at the scheme's headquarters on Cooma's northern outskirts. A modern complex replaced the old in 1987, and within its walls is an information center (tel. 064-53-2004)

Cooma Courthouse

NEW SOUTH WALES SKI RESORTS

Skiing in Australia is like no place in the world. Australian skiers are unbelievably keen; most travel great distances to reach the mountains, prices are high, and the slopes crowded in even the most atrocious conditions. That said, after a fresh fall of snow, skiing through massive granite boulders and stands of gnarled snowy gums on a cloudless day is an unforgettable experience. Heading to the mountains is known, simply, as "going to the snow," and when fresh snow has fallen and the weekend forecast is good, Friday night sees cars bumper to bumper from Sydney's southwestern suburbs to Jindabyne. On-snow accommodations are at a premium all winter and need to be booked well in advance. The opening of the ski season, the first weekend of June, is infamous for a lack of snow, but no-one seems to mind too much, especially the publicans, who do a roaring trade. Generally, good snow conditions can be relied on July to mid-Sept., while snow-making allows skiing a month either side of these dates.

The four ski areas are **Thredbo,** a stylish European-style village with mostly intermediate terrain and some of Australia's longest runs; **Perisher-Blue,** a conglomeration of four ski areas that combined in 1995 to form Australia's largest resort; **Charlotte Pass,** accessible only by snowcat; and **Mt. Selwyn,** popular with families and beginners. New South Wales is not the only state with skiing; Victoria has five resorts with a great variety of skiing, and Tasmania has two small ski areas.

Thredbo

Thredbo is considered the most upmarket of Australia's ski resorts, mainly for the self-contained European-style village overlooking the lower slopes. Twelve lifts access 175 hectares of skiing for all levels of expertise. Karel's T-bar rises to 2,037 meters, making it the highest lift point in Australia. From the summit, trails up to five km long descend to the valley floor. Thredbo is also the only Australian resort to host a World Cup Event (1989 World Cup Giant Slalom and Slalom). Although Thredbo's season runs early June to early Oct., it's generally only July to mid-Sept. that all lifts are operational. Lift tickets are adult $56, child $30, with five-day passes adult $245, child $130. Thredbo is also a good resort for seniors; those over 65 pay only $8 for a day pass. Other costs to budget for are park entry ($14 per car) and rental equipment ($20-50 per day). For further resort information, call (064) 59-4100; for snow reports call (0055) 34-320.

Perisher-Blue

In 1995 the combining of four existing ski resorts to create Perisher-Blue was the ski news of the decade, creating a megaresort of over 50 lifts spanning seven mountains and 1,605 hectares. The original resorts (Perisher Valley, Smiggin Holes, Blue Cow, and Guthega) are linked by lifts and trails, but it's most practical to ski in just one area. One of the great advantages of Perisher-Blue is **Skitube,** an underground rail service linking Bul-

with models of the scheme's various aspects and display boards detailing its workings; open Mon.-Fri. 8 a.m.-4:30 p.m.

The streets of Cooma are dotted with historic buildings, many of which are along the main drag. On the corner of Sharp and Lambie Streets is the **Royal Hotel,** a sandstone structure dating to 1858. Lambie Street boasts a number of Victorian-era terraces, while Barrack St., parallel to Lambie, has several civic buildings, including a post office (1877), courthouse (1879), and jail (1867).

Accommodations and Food

Except for winter weekends, accommodation in Cooma is easy to come by. **Dodd's Hotel,** Commissioner St. (tel. 064-52-2011), has rooms for $20 s, $36 d, including breakfast. A better deal is the **Family Motel,** 32 Massie St. (tel. 064-52-1414), where rooms with private bathrooms are $20 s, $30 d in summer, and $30 s $40 d in winter. Rates include breakfast. Another budget place is **Bunkhouse Motel,** 28-30 Soho St. (tel. 064-52-2983), featuring self-contained units and a laundry for $25 s, $40 d. The **Swiss Motel,** 34 Massie St. (tel. 064-52-1950), has rooms of a reasonable standard for $30 s, $37 d. **Nebula Motel,** 42 Bombala St. (tel. 064-52-4133), is a well-kept accommodation with modern rooms and a range of handy facilities; rates are $50 s, $57 d and slightly higher in winter.

powder day at Thredbo

ing below the snowline. Perisher Valley is the heart of the ski area, with Front Valley suited to beginners and Mt. Perisher to intermediates. Smiggin Holes and Guthega are also well suited for beginners, while Blue Cow has runs for all abilities, including Kamikaze, claimed to be Australia's steepest run. Lift tickets are priced the same as Thredbo, with the Skitube an extra $6 pp.

Charlotte Pass
Australia's oldest ski area, Charlotte Pass sits well above the treeline at the end of Kosciusko Road. Slopes are not extensive or particularly steep, but they are uncrowded and the scenery is beautiful. The resort road is snowed over for most of the winter; access is by snowcat and is limited to those staying at the resort's two lodges. Rates at **Stillwell Lodge** (tel. 064-57-5073) are $120 pp per night, including meals, and at **Kosciusko Chalet** (tel. 064-57-5245) it is $139 pp. For general resort information, call (064) 57-5247.

Mount Selwyn
Skiing in Australia began just around the corner from this small day-use resort along the Snowy Mountains Hwy. west of Kiandra. Cooma is 100 km to the southeast and the closest accommodation is 50 km away at Adaminaby. Twelve lifts access 45 hectares of beginner and easy-intermediate skiing. The day lodge has ski rentals, a ski school, and a restaurant. But probably the best aspect of skiing at Mt. Selwyn is the cost—day tickets are only adult $29, child $20. For resort information, call (064) 54-9488.

locks Flat, along Alpine Way, to Perisher Valley and Blue Cow. This allows skiers to avoid paying the national park entrance fee ($14 per car) while parking below the snowline.

The Monaro Highway through town is lined with roadhouses and cafes and, although parking is often difficult in the center of town, that is where the best eateries are. **Cafe Upstairs,** at 21 Sharp St. (tel. 064-52-4488), serves lunches for $6-8 and dinners under $14. This place gets crowded at lunch. Across the road are two bakeries; try **Rolf's** for the best meat pies. **Cooma Ex-serviceman's Club,** 106 Vale St. tel. 064-52-1144), serves bistro meals from $4-8 and has a more formal restaurant open Fri.-Sun. 6-9 p.m. Cooma has a couple of good Asian restaurants, including **Grand Court Chinese Restaurant,** Snowstop Village, Sharp St. tel. 064-52-4525).

Transportation, Services, and Information
Getting to the mountains by air is not very practical. Cooma has the closest airport taking scheduled flights, but there is no scheduled bus service into the mountains from this airport. **Eastern Australia** (tel. 13-1313) flies daily between Sydney and Cooma ($162 one-way), and **Kendell** (tel. 13-1300) flies into Cooma from Melbourne ($150 one-way). **Greyhound Pioneer** (tel. 13-2030) operates services between Cooma and: Sydney ($36 one-way), Canberra ($14), Jindabyne ($15).

Cooma Visitors Centre is in the center of town on Sharp St. (tel. 064-50-1742); open daily 9 a.m.-5 p.m.

THREDBO ALPINE VILLAGE

JINDABYNE

The service town of Jindabyne is 65 km west of Cooma and a 30-minute drive from the major ski areas. It's not a pretty town, nor is the surrounding scarred landscape anything to write home about, but it provides an excellent off-mountain base during the ski season. The town's official name is New Jindabyne. The original Jindabyne was in a valley that flooded when a dam for the Snowy Mountains Scheme was built nearby. Residents were moved to a planned town at a higher elevation, overlooking the lake that was their nemesis.

Eucumbene Trout Farm, on the road out to Lake Eucumbene (tel. 064-56-8866), is a commercial operation open to the public for trout fishing. Two trout ponds are open for fishing. One is large and requires some fishing expertise, while in the small one you can't miss. Either way, you'll end up with a juicy trout to be cooked on the spot or prepared to take away. Also at the trout farm is a horseback riding center. Both are open daily 9 a.m.-6 p.m.

Accommodations

Winter is high season in all parts of the Snowy Mountains. Rather than offer greatly reduced rates in non-skiing months, most accommodations offer packages, which are a good deal if you want to spend three or four days in the mountains. That said, summer rates at the ski areas themselves are an even better deal and are closer to the action. Bookings in the ski season are essential, especially during school holidays and on weekends. The easiest way to secure a room during this period is through a booking agent, while the rest of the year you should contact the accommodations directly.

Since being refurbished in 1994, **Lazy Harry's Lodge,** 18 Clyde St. (tel. 064-56-1957), is the best of the budget accommodations in town. Each room has private facilities, and many have lake views. The communal kitchen is large and modern. Other facilities include a drying room and lounge area with a log fire. Rates in summer are $40 s or d, while in winter they start at $70 s or d. Four-share dorms are $15 pp in summer, $25 pp in winter. Another budget accommodation is **Aspen Chalet,** Kosciusko Rd. (tel. 064-

56-2372), where summer rates are $35-60 s o d, and double in winter.

Lake Jindabyne Hotel, Kosciusko Rd. (tel 064-56-2203), best known as Jindabyne's fa vorite drinking hole, has basic motel units or the lake side of the complex. Summer rates are $50 s, $70 d, including breakfast, but they dou ble and even triple in winter. **Nettin Chalet,** 2 Nettin Circuit (tel. 064-56-2692), has excellen summer rates; $39 pp, with most rooms hav ing balconies and lake or mountain views, and guest facilities including a spa, sauna, game room, bar, and bistro. **Enzian Lodge,** 42 Gipp sland St. (tel. 064-56-2038), is a pleasant guest house within walking distance of all services With just eight rooms, the atmosphere is per sonal and relaxed. Summer rates are $35 s $55 d, rising to $85 s, $130 d in winter. All rate include breakfast.

On the road out to Dalgety, six km south o Jindabyne, is **The Station Resort** (tel. 064-56 2895 or 1800-02-0808), a sprawling comple× under the same ownership as Perisher-Blue sk area. Accommodation is sparse; most room are six- to 10-bed dorms, but there are also a few doubles available. The resort is best suite for those looking for a cheap place to sleep and a raging nightlife. Other features include a bistr and restaurant, bar, nightclub, and laundry Summer rates are $58 s or d, while in winte packages for two days' accommodation, break fasts, and skiing start at around $140.

Snowline Caravan Park is on Kosciusk Rd. two km southwest of Jindabyne (tel. 064-56 2099). Grassed tent sites are spread amon trees and overlook the lake ($12-22), and whil basic cabins are $32, there are some new one up by the road for $65.

Food

Restaurants are in some motels, but most are i **Jindabyne Shopping Centre,** overlooking th lake, and **Nugget's Crossing,** toward the moun tains. A great place for breakfast is **Sundanc Bakehouse,** in Nugget's Crossing (tel. 064-56 2951). **Mario's Mineshaft Restaurant,** Lake view Plaza Motel, 2 Snowy River Restaurar (tel. 064-56-2134), is the place to head for pizza Other Italian dishes are offered and tables ar set around a log fire. The **Brumby Bar,** Jind abyne Shopping Centre (tel. 064-56-2526), i a popular steakhouse, where you choose a steak and cook it on a central chargrill. A restaurant in the Station Resort has a similar setup.

Information
Snowy River Information Centre is at the far end of Jindabyne Shopping Centre (tel. 064-56-2444).

JINDABYNE TO CHARLOTTE PASS

Beyond Jindabyne, Kosciusko Rd. passes the Kosciusko National Park gate, where an entrance fee of $14 per vehicle will be collected, and climbs steadily to a lookout over Lake Jindabyne, then continues into the park's interior.

Sawpit Creek
Sawpit Creek, 15 km from Jindabyne along Kosciusko Rd., is home to **Park Headquarters** (tel. 064-56-1700). The center has displays on the park's natural wonders and an audiovisual. It's open daily 8:30 a.m.-4:30 p.m. Beyond the center is a pleasant picnic area with barbecues and the trailhead for a 1.6-km hike through a subalpine environment.

Adjoining park headquarters is **Kosciusko Mountain Retreat** (tel. 064-56-2224), a large national park campground set among eucalypts. Unpowered sites are $17, powered sites $26, and cabins range $53-130 depending on the season.

Blue Cow
Blue Cow, part of the massive Perisher-Blue ski area, is accessible only by Skitube, a rail system built to transport skiers from below the snowline to Blue Cow. The Skitube begins from Bullocks Flat, on the Alpine Way, and reaches a depth of up to 550 meters under the ground as it makes its six-km trek to Blue Cow. At Blue Cow you'll find many hiking opportunities, and mountain bikes can be rented for $12 per hour. The half-day ($32) and full-day ($42) bike rental rates include travel on the Skitube. A bistro at Blue Cow is open daily 10 a.m.-4 p.m. Outside of the ski season, Skitube operates between Christmas and May (closed February for maintenance) four to six times daily. The round-trip fare from Bullock's Flat to Blue Cow is adult

$18, child $10. From Perisher, the fare is adult $12, child $7.

Charlotte Pass and Nearby Hiking
Kosciusko Road ends on a high ridge overlooking the alpine village of Charlotte Pass. In winter, the road is snowed over and village access is by snowcat from Perisher Valley. In summer, Charlotte Pass becomes a popular staging area for hikes, including to the summit of Mt. Kosciusko. This part of the national park has a complex trail system, and because of the high elevation of the road, most of the hard work has been done. The main trails are the **Main Range Track** and **Summit Walk.** Both end at the summit of Australia's highest peak, **Mt. Kosciusko.** The Main Range Track descends to the headwaters of the famous Snowy River before climbing to a lookout over Blue Lake, one of five glacial features around the peak. This lookout is five km from Charlotte Pass, with Kosciusko's summit a farther seven km. The Summit Walk is a more direct route, following an old four-wheel drive track to the summit; eight km one-way.

In Charlotte Pass village is **Kosciusko Chalet** (tel. 064-57-5245), a relaxed accommodation where summer rates are $79 pp, including meals.

THREDBO

Thredbo is the only New South Wales ski area actively promoting summer activities, but with Australia's beach-loving population, it's a hard task, and outside of winter, the village is quiet. Thredbo lies on the Alpine Way 36 km southwest of Jindabyne, spread along a steep north-facing hill, overlooking the valley floor and ski area.

Sights and Recreation
The **Crackenback Chairlift** rises from the village to an elevation of 1,930 meters, providing an excellent starting point for hiking through the high country. The most popular trail is to the summit of Mt. Kosciusko (seven km one-way). The summit trek is steep, but can be done by anyone with a reasonable level of fitness. Another good hike is the 10-km **Dead Horse Gap/Thredbo River Track,** which follows a

ridge from the top of the chairlift to the summit of the Alpine Way, returning to the village along the Thredbo River.

A great variety of activities are possible in the village; most can be booked through the **Thredbo Centre** (tel. 064-57-6275). One of the most popular is the **Alpine Slide**, a twisting 700-meter slide on which speeds of 50 kph can be reached. A single ride is $4, three rides $9, and 10 rides $20; book through the Thredbo Centre. Other resort facilities include a nine-hole golf course (green fees $10), tennis, guided walks, horseback riding, whitewater rafting, mountain biking, and fishing.

Events

A packed schedule of events takes place each summer, commencing with the Summer Cup, the weekend after Christmas—if there's any snow left. **Thredbo Country and Blues Festival**, in mid-January, is a weekend of music and entertainment. The last weekend of January is the **Thredbo Mountain Challenge**, combining the disciplines of running, mountain biking, kayaking, and swimming. The first weekend of February the **Alpine Wildflower Festival** features guided walks, a photographic display, and painting workshop. Events thin out after this, with the **Australian Mountain Bike Championships** held mid-March, a golf tournament early April, and the **Thredbo Jazz Festival** the first weekend of May.

Accommodations

During the ski season accommodations in Thredbo are at a premium. In summer, things are very different and some excellent packages are offered. For bookings and current rates, either contact the accommodations direct or call Thredbo Resort Centre at (1800) 02-0589.

Thredbo YHA Lodge, Jack Adams Path (tel. 064-57-6376), is the cheapest lodging option in the village. The hostel was purpose-built, with a modern kitchen, lounge area, laundry, and drying room. Summer rates are $12 pp in a dorm or $16 pp twin. In the ski season rates rise to $37 pp per night or $170 for six nights. During this time a ballot (lottery) system is in place, with reservations needed months in advance.

Thredbo Alpine Hotel (tel. 064-57-6333) is a three-story complex in the heart of the village.

Rooms are spacious and comfortable. Summer rates are $110 s, $135 d, or $99 pp, including meals and a chairlift ride.

Many of Thredbo's most-popular accommodations are European-style ski lodges. **Bernti's** (tel. 064-57-6332 or 1800-50-0105) is a central lodge with a relaxed atmosphere and a real mountain charm. Facilities include a cafe, bar, restaurant, sauna, spa, and large lounge area. Summer rates are $60 s, $70 d, including breakfast, but their various packages, from $90 pp, are a better deal.

All rates quoted below are for high season (August); rates in July and September will be markedly lower (around 25%)—and in June up to 50% lower.

One of the best deals is **Riverside Cabins** (tel. 064-57-6700), set alongside Thredbo River away from the village. Each unit is fully self contained. Rates are $499-799 pp for five nights accommodation and a corresponding five-day lift pass.

Thredbo's many self-contained apartments come into their own during the ski season when rates in the village are phenomenally high, ranging $300-1200 per night. In the heart of the village and also self-contained is **Thredbo Alpine Apartments,** Friday Dr. (tel. 064-57-6414) $549-849 pp for five nights with ski passes.

Between Thredbo and Bullocks Flat is Thredbo Diggings, site of a short-lived gold rush and now a small riverside campground.

Transportation

In winter, **Greyhound Pioneer** (tel. 13-2030) operates daily services between Sydney and Thredbo; $125 round-trip.

WEST FROM THREDBO ON THE ALPINE WAY

From Thredbo, the Alpine Way climbs steadily through the Thredbo Valley to Dead Horse Gap atop the Great Dividing Range, before descending into a remote part of the national park that was only opened up with the construction of the Snowy Mountains Scheme. The road then changes direction sharply to the north and descends into the rugged hill country around Khancoban.

A long stretch of road beyond the pass is unsealed and can be rough going in a two-wheel drive. This section of road is closed in winter, reopening when the snow melts (usually October).

Khancoban

Khancoban, 113 km northwest of Jindabyne along the Alpine Way, is a small high country town that exists to serve workers on the Snowy Mountains Scheme. Water from the upper reaches of the Snowy River is pumped westward to two massive power stations near Khancoban, before being discharged into the Murray River. Part of this system, **Murray One Power Station,** is open for tours Mon.-Fri. 10 a.m.-2 p.m. Book through the Snowy Mountains Hydro-electric Authority Information Centre in Cooma (tel. 064-53-2004). Khancoban's proximity to some of the country's best trout fishing makes it an excellent base for anglers. The town also has a nine-hole golf course, tennis courts, and horseback riding operations.

Khancoban Alpine Inn (tel. 060-76-9471) is the town's only motel and has a bar and restaurant; rooms are $50 s, $60 d. Camping is through town to the west at **Murray Gates Caravan Park** (tel. 060-76-9488), where sites are $9-10, on-site vans $22-28, and cabins $35-45.

SOUTHWEST SLOPES

The southwest slopes, as they are called, encompass the northern end of Kosciusko National Park as well as the **Tumut Valley,** an important link in the Snowy Mountains Scheme. From Cooma, access to the region is along the **Snowy Mountains Highway.** From Jindabyne, you can take the Alpine Way (see "West from Thredbo on the Alpine Way," above), a longer yet more scenic alternative.

Kiandra

The ghost town of Kiandra, in the north end of Kosciusko National Park, is 90 km northwest of Cooma and at the junction of a road through the mountains to Khancoban. Kiandra provides a graphic reminder of gold-rush days, when thousands of diggers would converge on a newly discovered field and just as quickly move to the next. In Kiandra's case, the year was 1859, and

it was around 16,000 diggers who came to try their luck. Through pastoral use and the Snowy Mountains Scheme, the landscape surrounding Kiandra has changed considerably in the last 100 years, but buildings in varying degrees of disrepair remain. **Kiandra Heritage Trail** leads through the once-thriving town, with boards describing the original purpose of each building.

Yarrangobilly Caves

This extensive system of limestone caves is at the floor of the Yarrangobilly River Valley, 20 km north of Kiandra. The cave system extends over an area of 12 square km and includes over 200 caves. The limestone that the caves are in is estimated to be up to 450 million years old, and during all that time, spectacular formations have developed. The **Glory Hole Cave** is open for self-guiding tours daily 10 a.m.-4 p.m. ($4 pp), while tours of the other caves are offered weekdays at 11 a.m. and weekends at 11 a.m., 1 p.m., and 3 p.m. ($8-12 pp). For details, call (064) 54-9597.

Tumut

Tumut (meaning "Quiet Resting Place by the River") boomed with construction of the Snowy Mountains Scheme, although it was the hard work of settlers from as early as the 1820s that cleared the vast tracts of land along the valley floor. Two of the scheme's largest dams are close to town, and **Tumut Three Power Station,** boasting the largest generating capacity of all the power stations, is open for tours 10 a.m.-2:30 p.m.

Fishing in lakes and streams around Tumut is legendary. The most accessible spots are along the Tumut River, where experienced fly fishermen rate this river as among the best in the country. **Blowering Dam,** 10 km north of Tumut, is stocked with trout, cod, and perch. **Baker's Sports Store,** 44 Russell St. (tel. 069-47-1243), has all the fishing gear you'll need and sells relevant licenses.

Around town are interesting cottage industries worth visiting. Locally grown millet is prepared and processed at **Tumut Broom Co.,** 30 Adelong Rd. (tel. 069-47-2804); open Mon.-Fri. 9 a.m.-4 p.m. for factory tours. Stock whips are made at **Tumut Valley Whipworks and Saddlery,** 139 Wynyard St. (tel. 069-47-3889), and you can try cracking a whip yourself; open Mon.-Fri. 9 a.m.-5 p.m., Saturday 9 a.m.-3 p.m. Locally excavated marble, which is renowned for its amazing colors, is cut and polished at a factory on Adelong Road; it's open to the public Mon.-Fri. 3-4 p.m.

The **Commercial Hotel,** 103 Wynyard St. (tel. 069-47-1040), has high-standard rooms, each with private facilities, for $40-50 s, $55-65 d, including breakfast. None of the town's half dozen motels are inexpensive, although standards are generally good. Try **Ashton Motel,** 124 Wynyard St. (tel. 069-47-1043), where facilities include a pool; $50 s, $55 d. **Riverglade Caravan Park** is spread along the Tumut River. Unpowered sites are $11, powered sites $13. It's right in town on the main highway through town (tel. 069-47-2528).

Tumut has a surprisingly large number of cafes and quality restaurants. One of the best cafes is **Matinies,** 27 Russell St. (tel. 069-47-3056). Hearty breakfasts there range $5.50-9, and everything seems remarkably fresh. Lunch is more of the same delicious home-style cooking, and picnic baskets can be ordered in advance. **Brooklyn on Fitzroy,** 10-12 Fitzroy St. (tel. 069-47-4022), is an old homestead restored to an upmarket restaurant, elegantly decorated in turn-of-the-century style. Main meals start at $12, or for $15 you get the three-course Squatters Meal. Open Tues.-Sat. for lunch and dinner.

Tumut Tourist Information Centre is on Fitzroy St. (tel. 069-47-1849); open daily 9 a.m.-5 p.m.

Adelong

With a population that hovers around 1,000, Adelong is a far cry from the 1860s when 20,000 diggers lived on surrounding goldfields. Like most other fields, miners left as quickly as they arrived, but, in Adelong's case, the town had already gained an air of permanency. These prosperous beginnings can be seen along the main drag, where many National Trust-classified buildings have been restored. During the original rush, claims were made on every stream and gully in the region; at Adelong Falls traces of the diggers' frantic activities can be seen. **The Old Pharmacy,** 88 Tumut St (tel. 069-46-2263), offers accommodations with shared facilities, and meals are served in a cafe downstairs.

Batlow

If you like apples and apple cider, you'll love Batlow, a small town of 1,500 in the Tumut Valley surrounded by Australia's largest concentration of apple orchards. Thousands of tons of apples are processed into apple juice and canned for apple pie each year by the local Letona company, famous for the Mountain Maid brand. Tours are arranged through **Granny Smith's Country Cottage,** Pioneer St. (tel. 069-49-1447), which also acts as the local information center. To sample the apples and see the packing complex, head to **Batlow Fruit Co-op,** Forest Rd. (tel. 069-49-1408), weekdays 9 a.m.-4 p.m.

SOUTH-CENTRAL NEW SOUTH WALES

In 1817, while exploring west of the Snowy Mountains, John Oxley planted a couple of oak and apricot trees to commemorate the king's birthday and noted in his diary that the trees would "serve to commemorate the day and situation, should these desolate plains ever again be visited by civilised man of which, however, I think there is little probability." But how wrong he was. As traffic on the Sydney-Melbourne route increased, towns such as **Yass, Gundagai,** and **Albury** thrived. In later years, the untapped potential of the vast, empty tracts of land along the **Murray** and **Murrumbidgee Rivers** was realized as modern technology developed a complex irrigation system that transformed the countryside. The **Murrumbidgee Irrigation Area** became among the most intensely farmed regions of the country, with crops including over 90% of Australia's rice, 80% of the state's wine grapes, and every single gherkin you'll ever eat at an Australian McDonalds.

GOULBURN TO WAGGA WAGGA

Yass

The area around Yass was opened up to settlers after the explorers Hume and Hovell returned to Sydney with reports of land suitable for grazing. Hume ended up settling in Yass. His home, one of the oldest houses still standing in this part of the state, has been restored to its 1870s colonial glory and is open daily except Tuesday 10 a.m.-4 p.m. Admission is $4, and about that amount

On 1 August 1997 all telephone numbers in this section will change. For numbers with the area code (06) simply add "6" to the existing number. As an example, (06) 212-3456 becomes 6212-3456. For all other numbers in this section add the last two digits of the existing area code to the old number. As an example, (069) 12-3456 becomes 6912-3456. The new area code for all numbers in this section will be (02).

again will get you tea and scones in the tearooms. The house is five km east of Yass along the Hume Hwy. (tel. 06-226-1470). **Hamilton Hume Museum,** Comur St. (tel. 06-226-2557), which has displays on the explorer and his expeditions through New South Wales, is open daily except Tuesday and Thursday 10 a.m.-3 p.m.

Thunderbird Motel, on the north side of town (tel. 06-226-1158), has modern rooms, a swimming pool, and restaurant; $59 s, $72 d. In Coronation Park, along the main drag, is the **Tourist Information Centre** (tel. 06-226-2557).

Vicinity of Yass

Much of the water used on farms in the Murrumbidgee Irrigation Area is stored at **Burrinjuck Dam,** southwest of Yass. At the time of construction, in 1927, it was one of the world's largest dams, capable of storing over one million megaliters and with a shoreline of around 500 km. **Burrinjuck State Recreation Area,** on a southeastern arm of the lake, is one of the few areas of natural bushland around the lake. It has a number of bushwalks and is the departure point for lake cruises (tel. 06-227-7270). **Lake Burrinjuck Leisure Resort,** along the same access road, features a swimming pool, boat rentals, and excellent facilities for campers. Tent sites are $12, on-site vans $25, and cabins $35; call (06) 227-7271 for bookings.

Wee Jasper is a town of 150 in a wooded valley 54 km southwest of Yass along the road to Tumut. Apart from the tranquil surroundings, **Carey's Caves** make the detour worthwhile. These deep limestone caves are open to the public Sat.-Sun. 1-4 p.m. Admission is $6 pp (tel. 06-227-9622). Accommodation is available in the rustic **Shearer's Quarters** (tel. 06-227-9642) for $15 pp. Formerly the police station, **Stables Tavern** (tel. 06-227-9619), a classic limestone building, serves meals and beer.

Back on the Hume Highway, 12 km west of Yass, is **Bowning,** a small hamlet where the original Cobb and Co. Coaching Station still stands. In **Binalong,** a charming town of 250 northwest of Bowning, is **The Black Swan,** which has an excellent reputation for food. Open

ALONG THE ROAD TO GUNDAGAI

There's a track winding back to an old-fashioned shack,
Along the road to Gundagai;
Where the blue gums are growing and the Murrumbidgee's
Flowing beneath that sunny sky,
Where my daddy and mummy are waiting for me
And the pals of my childhood once more will I see;
Then no more will I roam when I'm heading right for home,
Along the road to Gundagai

The little town of Gundagai has been immortalized in verse like no other place in Australia; this is the chorus of the most famous song. Written by local poet Jack O'Hagan, it has become part of Australian legend.

Also at Gundagai is one of Australia's best-known monuments, the **Dog on the Tuckerbox,** which,

as every Australian knows, sits "five miles from Gundagai." Its origins were also in a poem, penned from an old yarn about a bullock-driver who got bogged by Five Mile Creek. Then, to top his troubles off, his "dog sat on the tuckerbox, five miles from Gundagai," although, in the original version, the bullocky's dog did a lot more than *sit* on his tuckerbox.

Wed.-Sun. 7 p.m.-midnight and for lunch on Sunday; call (06) 227-4236 for bookings.

Gundagai

Originating as a crossing point of the Murrumbidgee River, Gundagai has seen few changes in the last 100 years. Drovers, and in later years diggers, rested on the riverbank before crossing and heading into the frontier farther south. The river was also the settlement's downfall—on 23 June 1852 the river flooded the town, destroying most buildings and killing 89 people, almost a third of the population. A gravel road leads to the summit of **Mount Pernassus,** from where the layout of the town and area of the disastrous flood can be clearly seen.

Gundagai's best-known attraction, the **Dog on the Tuckerbox** is, as every Australian knows, five miles from Gundagai. At the same site is a statue of **Dad and Dave,** fictional bush characters immortalized in a series of Australian pre-WW II films, which later turned into a radio serial that still runs in some parts of the country today.

WAGGA WAGGA

Straddling the Murrumbidgee River 478 km southwest of Sydney and 48 km west of the Hume Highway, Wagga Wagga (pronounced

"WO-ga WO-ga") is the hub of southern New South Wales, and with a population of 54,000 it's one of Australia's largest inland cities. The area was first inhabited by the Wiradjuri, the state's largest tribe. After exploration by Capt Charles Sturt, settlers streamed into the region looking for prime pastoral land, and by the 1850s hundreds of farms had been established with Wagga Wagga, originally a river crossing point, growing into the region's transportation and service hub.

Sights

You won't need to spend long in Wagga to see why it's called the "Garden City." The largest formal garden is **Wagga Wagga Botanic Gardens,** set on nine hectares at the base of Williams Hill, south of town. Trails lead through the gardens to an open-air chapel, traditional Japanese chapel, cafe, petting zoo for kids (free admission), and an area of rainforest. At the top of the gardens is the **Historical Society Museum** (tel. 069-25-2934), with indoor and outdoor displays; open Tuesday, Wednesday, Saturday, and Sunday 2-5 p.m. Admission is adult $2, child 50 cents.

Wagga Wagga City Art Gallery, Gurwood St. (tel. 069-23-5419), is worth visiting to view a large collection of contemporary glass sculpture and the Carnegie Print Collection. Open

Tues.-Fri. 11 a.m.-5 p.m., Saturday 10 a.m.-5 p.m., and Sunday 2-5 p.m.; admission is free. For history buffs, three walking trail brochures, available from the Tourist Information Centre, detail buildings of historical importance.

Murray Cod Hatcheries and Fauna Park (tel. 069-22-7360) is a 10-minute drive east of Wagga along the Sturt Highway. Murray cod grow to legendary sizes, and a couple of fine specimens are displayed, along with a variety of other Australian freshwater fish. The fauna park boasts koalas, kangaroos, wombats, and dingos. A small fossil museum displays the fossilized remains of a four-meter fish. Admission adult $6, child $3. Open daily 9 a.m.-5 p.m.

Accommodations

Most of the hotels along Baylis and Fitzmaurice Streets have rooms, but most are a bit rough around the edges. Try **Romano's Hotel,** corner Fitzmaurice and Sturt Streets (tel. 069-21-2013), which has been restored; $40 s, $58 d. Motels are located on all the main routes into town. One of the least expensive is **Club Motel,** 73 Morgan St. (tel. 069-21-6966), just north of downtown; $41 s, $52 d. **Centralpoint Motel,** 164 Tarcutta St. (tel. 069-21-7272), is another good option. It has a handy location, across from the Tourist Information Centre and one block from the main commercial strip. Each room has cooking facilities; $54 s, $65 d. One of the nicest places to stay is **Country House Motor Lodge,** five km east of town on the Sturt Hwy. (tel. 069-22-7256). Set among two hectares of gardens, it features a pool and spa, laundry, and restaurant, and rooms are furnished with handcrafted heritage-style furniture; $72 s, $78 d.

Crepe Myrtle Bed and Breakfast, 102 Kincaid St. (tel. 069-21-4757), retains much of its original 1870s charm. The four rooms have period furniture and shared facilities; $70 s, $90 d.

Riverview Caravan Park, two km east of town on the Sturt Hwy. (tel. 069-21-4287), is adjacent to the Murrumbidgee River and has excellent facilities. Shaded sites range $8-14, basic on-site vans are $34, and great little cabins are $45 d.

Food

Of the many downtown cafes, **Street Cafe,** 32 Fitzmaurice St. (tel. 069-21-7360), has the most character. It's open weekdays from 7:30 a.m., weekends from 9 a.m. **Ginger's Cafe,** 35 Gurwood St. (tel. 069-21-9621), is another good choice—the food is always fresh and a light lunch costs just $5.

For a more substantial meal, head to **Baylis Street Bistro,** in the Victoria Hotel (tel. 069-21-5233), or **Golden Grill Family Restaurant,** in the Wagga RSL Club on Kincaid Street. **Pavilion Garden Restaurant,** Kincaid St. (tel. 069-21-6411), is an upmarket dining room in a garden atrium. Breakfast is served daily from 7 a.m., lunch daily except Sunday, and each evening the good cutlery comes out with an a la carte menu. For something more exotic, try **Bahn Thai Restaurant,** 73 Morgan St. (tel. 069-21-4177).

North of town, over the Murrumbidgee River toward Junee, is **Wagga Wagga Winery,** 427 Oura Rd. (tel. 069-22-1221). As well as daily winetasting, a restaurant serves lunch and dinner daily with an excellent steak and salad deal for only $10 pp.

Information

The **Tourist Information Centre** is in a pleasant area of parkland on Tarcutta St. (tel. 069-23-5402).

WHY THE DOUBLE-BARRELED NAMES?

Wagga Wagga is one of many Australian towns and landmarks with double-barreled names. As the Aboriginal language had no plurals, words were repeated to convey quantity or size, hence Wagga Wagga, meaning lots of crows.

SOUTH FROM WAGGA WAGGA

The quickest route south from Wagga is back out on the Hume Highway, from where it's 140 km to the Victorian border. Just over halfway is **Holbrook.** In town is **Woolpack Inn Museum** (tel. 060-36-2131), a two-story hotel on the main drag with displays depicting life in the late 1800s; open daily 10 a.m.-4:30 p.m.

ANDREW HEMPSTEAD

Ettamogah Pub

Ettamogah Pub, 50 km south of Holbrook and 15 km north of Albury (tel. 060-26-2366), is arguably Australia's most famous hotel. To appreciate just why, pick up a copy of *Post* magazine (from any newsagency), where the Ettamogah Pub cartoon has been featured for decades. Originally the figment of a cartoonist's imagination, the cartoon has been converted to reality, leaning walls and all.

Morgan Country
The alternative route south from Wagga is Highway 41 (Olympic Way), which passes through the heart of a territory once roamed by the notorious bushranger Dan "Mad Dog" Morgan.

For three days each September, the small town of Henty comes alive for **Henty Machinery Field Days.** The event began with a few equipment salesmen displaying machinery to local farmers, and has now grown into one of Australia's largest agricultural events. Every-

one's welcome, and non-farmers will find plenty of interest on the 150-hectare site, with machinery trials, animal judging, and displays of historic equipment. For details, call (069) 29-3305.

Culcairn, 18 km south of Henty, is the region's largest town. The sprawling redbrick **Culcairn Hotel,** opposite the railway station, was the largest hotel between Sydney and Melbourne for many years after its construction in 1891. Nearby **Morgan's Lookout** was used by the infamous bushranger. Access to the lookout is from Walbundrie, west of Culcairn.

ALBURY

On the northern bank of the Murray River, 559 km southwest of Sydney and 310 km northeast of Melbourne, Albury is the largest center on the Hume Highway. Explorers Hume and Hovell, the first Europeans to travel overland from Sydney to Port Phillip Bay, crossed the Murray River in 1824, where Albury now lies. Within a few years a settlement first known as the Crossing Place had become established.

Sights
Much of the floodplain between the commercial center of Albury and the Murray River is open parkland, with river red gums lining the riverbank and a few picturesque barbecue areas spread around. The *Cumberoona,* a replica of a wood-fired paddlesteamer, once the main form of river transport, cruises the river a couple of times daily; for departure times, call (060) 21-1113. Where the highway parallels the river through town, you'll find **Albury Regional Museum** (tel. 060-21-4550), occupying the old Turks Head Hotel on Wodonga Place. It features an interesting collection of locally collected memorabilia; open daily 10:30 a.m.-4:30 p.m.

Monument Hill, off Memorial Drive west of downtown, provides views of the city and sweeping bends of the Murray River.

Accommodations
Motels line either side of the Hume Hwy. north of town, including **Sodens Australia Hotel/Motel,** corner David and Wilson Streets (tel. 060-21-

2400). It has pub rooms with shared facilities for $22 s, $36 d, which includes breakfast, and motel units (no breakfast) for $38 s, $45 d. Off the main drag is **Albury Golf Club Motor Inn,** 530 North St. (tel. 060-41-1211). The motel is set in a quiet area, with rooms overlooking the pool and an 18-hole golf course. Rooms are large and of a high standard, each with coffee-making facilities and a fridge; $62, $72 d.

Albury Central Caravan Park has a pool, tennis court, and shop, but sites are small; sites $10-12, cabins $30-43 d. It's on North St. (tel. 060-21-8420). As an overnight stop, this place is fine, but for a nicer environment, it's worth the 32-km drive out to **The Great Aussie Resort,** on Jingellic Rd. east of Bowna (on the Hume Hwy. north of Albury, tel. 060-20-3236). This large park is spread around the shore of Lake Hume and has enough facilities to keep you busy for days—from golf to grass skiing and boat hire to bingo games. Sites are $14-20, depending on the season; basic cabins start at $40, and on-site tents, complete with cooking facilities, are $50.

Food

There are a few **Matilda's Family Steakhouses** spread around this part of the country, and wherever you see one, you'll get a decent meal at a good price. A lunch buffet is $7.95, and a steak dinner, with all-you-can-eat soup, salad, and dessert, is $11.25-16. In Albury, Matilda's is at the corner of the Hume Hwy. and David St. (tel. 060-41-4400). **Cultura Cafe & Restaurant,** 515 Kiewa St. (tel. 060-41-3884), has a trendy interior with a variety of dishes from around the world. Each dish is offered in varying sizes, with large portions running $14.50-18.50 and desserts around $6 (including an excellent Mississippi Mudcake).

Transportation, Services, and Information

Mylon Motorways (tel. 060-56-3100) operates a different tour every day of the week. For example, the Friday tour visits historical areas north of Albury ($38 pp), and the Sunday tour takes in town sights ($24). Book through the information center.

Albury Information Centre is located Wodonga Place (Hume Hwy.) west of town (tel. 060-21-2655). Open daily 9 a.m.-5 p.m.

WEST OF ALBURY ALONG THE MURRAY RIVER

Corowa

Corowa (pop. 5,500) is a quiet town 52 km west of Albury. Popular as an inland holiday destination, it boasts a challenging 27-hole golf course, and just across the river is the Rutherglen, one of Australia's premier wine producing areas (see "Along the Murray from Echuca to Wodonga" under "Central Victoria: Melbourne to the Murray," in the Victoria chapter). Fans of lawn bowling may want to visit **Corowa Bowling Club** in Ball Park. It has 54 rinks on seven greens, the world's largest such complex.

Tocumwal

Tocumwal is a sleepy little town where the Newell Highway crosses the Murray River, with a picturesque park between the river and the main street. Many shops date from the late 1800s, including one that has been restored to an antique emporium and tearoom. Next door to this store is the sprawling **Tocumwal Hotel,** 121 Deniliquin St. (tel. 03-5874-2025), where rooms are $30 s, $40 d, which includes a light breakfast.

Jerilderie

A small article published in an 1868 edition of the *Jerilderie and Urana Gazette* about a shortage of police did little to prompt government action, but news of the police shortage filtered through to Ned Kelly. On 8 February 1869 the infamous Victorian bushranger and his gang rode into town. They locked the town's two policemen in their own cells and spent the day walking around town in police uniforms, even helping a policeman's wife to set the church for Sunday service. On that Monday morning they bailed up staff of the Royal Mail Hotel, shooting drinks at the bar while two gang members emptied the coffers of the bank next door. Thumbing their noses at authority, the gang rode out of town, raising their hats to the cheers of those they'd held hostage in the hotel. Before the gang left town, they visited the Telegraph Office to cut telegraph wires; that building, on Powell St., still stands, and is open daily 9:30 a.m.-4:30 p.m.

Next door is **The Willows** (tel. 03-5886-1666), a historic home serving lunch and Devonshire teas.

Deniliquin

Straddling the Edward River, at the junction of the Cobb and Riverina Highways and 204 km west of Albury, this town of 8,000 is in the heart of a rich rice- and wool-growing area. **Deniliquin Rice Mill** is the largest such mill in the Southern Hemisphere, with 750,000 tons of rice milled annually. A visitor center at the mill features an audiovisual and cooking demonstrations; open daily 9 a.m.-5 p.m. It's south of town, off the road to Barmah (tel. 03-5881-2477). The **merino** breed of sheep, resilient to the harsh and dry conditions of Australia and now the backbone of the country's rural economy, was pioneered by the Deniliquin-based Peppin family. **Peppin Heritage Centre** catalogs the family and their successful breeding program, which literally changed the face of Australia. Displays are housed in an old school building, while, outside, the grounds are stocked with those famous merinos. The center is open daily 10 a.m.-4 p.m.; located on George St. (tel. 03-5881-4150).

Globe Hotel, 280 Cressy St. (tel. 03-5881-2030), has basic but clean rooms for $25 s, $30 d. The nicest place in town is **Deniliquin Country Club Motor Inn,** 68 Crispe St. (tel. 03-5881-5299), which is close to the golf course and clubs and has large rooms with king-size beds; $55 s, $66 d. Camping is at **Pioneer Tourist Park,** north of town (tel. 03-5881-5066), or at **McLean Beach Caravan Park** Butler St. (tel. 03-5881-2448).

MURRUMBIDGEE IRRIGATION AREA

Known as the **Riverina,** the region west of Wagga Wagga is able to sustain high yields of a great variety of crops through the workings of the massive Murrumbidgee Irrigation Area (M.I.A.), named for the river that is central to its success. The first stage of the project was the construction of Burrinjuck Dam, on the higher reaches of the Murrumbidgee River. Once this dam was completed, a complex system of over 3,500 km of canals was dug. This opened up a huge tract of land west of Narrandera and north

of the Murrumbidgee River for farming. Today, over 500,000 hectares are irrigated, transforming the once-dry land to one of Australia's richest food-producing regions. The main crops are rice, a variety of fruits, and cereals.

Narrandera

Narrandera is a midsized town of 5,000 on the north bank of the Murrumbidgee River, 95 km west of Wagga Wagga. Within the grounds of **Narrandera Park,** in the heart of town, is an information center housing the world's largest playable guitar. **Parkside Cottage Museum,** Twynam St. (tel. 069-59-1372), is a two-story building with a variety of local relics; open Mon.-Tues. 2-5 p.m., Wed.-Sun. 11 a.m.-5 p.m. Admission is $2. Along Lake Dr., off the main drag through town, is **Lake Talbot Complex** (tel. 069-59-1211), comprising swimming pools, water slides, a picnic area, and a small colony of koalas. Near the complex entrance is **Bundidgerry Walking Track,** which winds around a lake and down to the Murrumbidgee River. **John Lake Centre,** five km east of town toward Wagga (tel. 069-59-1488), carries out research on various species of freshwater fish found in local rivers; open Mon.-Fri. 9 a.m.-4 p.m. with tours ($5 pp) at 10:30 a.m.

Historic Star Lodge, corner Newell Hwy. and Arthur St. (tel. 069-59-1768), is a classic Aussie hotel with well-furnished pub rooms for $15 s, $30 d, and breakfast an extra $5 pp. This place is also an associate YHA, with dorms for $12. **Country Roads Motor Inn,** Newell Hwy. and East St. (tel. 069-59-3244), features modern rooms and is within walking distance of town; $48 s, $55 d. **Lake Talbot Caravan Park,** Broad St. (tel. 069-59-1302), has unpowered sites for $10, powered sites for $13, and on-site vans for $24-29.

For an inexpensive feed, head to **Narrandera Hotel** at 183 East St. (tel. 069-59-2057), or **Polo Dining Room** in the Murrumbidgee Club at 43 Douglas St. (tel. 069-59-3832), where a juicy T-bone steak with vegetables or salad is $8.

Narrandera Tourist Information Centre is in Narrandera Park on the Newell Hwy. (tel. 069-59-1766); open Mon.-Fri. 9 a.m.-5 p.m., Sat.-Sun. 10 a.m.-4 p.m.

Leeton

Laid out in the early 1900s as part of the Murrumbidgee Irrigation Area project, this town of

Historic Star Lodge, Narrandera

6,000, 24 km northwest of Narrandera, is home to a number of large food-processing companies. Those that conduct tours (Mon.-Fri. only) are: **Sunwhite Rice Mill** (Calrose St.), between 9:30 a.m. and 2:45 p.m.; **Quelch Juice Factory** (Brady Way), at 10:45 a.m.; and **Letona Fruit Cannery** (Wamoon Ave.), at 10:30 a.m. and 1:30 p.m. Tours through **Historic Hydro Motor Inn,** Chelmsford Place, are offered daily at 2 p.m. Book all tours through **Leeton Visitor's Centre,** Chelmsford Place (tel. 069-53-2832). One of many wineries in the M.I.A. is **Lillypilly Estate,** out on Lillypilly Rd. (tel. 069-53-4069). Guided tours of the vineyard are conducted Mon.-Fri. at 4 p.m., with the winery open for tastings Mon.-Sat. 10 a.m.-5:30 p.m.

Leeton Visitors Centre, Chelmsford Place (tel. 069-53-2832), is open Mon.-Fri. 9 a.m.-5 p.m., Sat.-Sun. 9:30 a.m.-12:30 p.m.

Griffith

This, the largest town of the M.I.A. (pop. 22,000), should be best known for colorful gardens and surrounding rich agricultural land; but that is not the case. Most Australians know Griffith as "Drug Capital of Australia" and "Chicago of the Outback," long after the 1970s when the waters of the Murrumbidgee River were irrigating crops a lot different than those the founders intended.

Pioneer Park Museum, a large area of native bushland north of town, is dotted with 40 historic buildings dating from the late 1800s. Although the buildings have been relocated to the site, together they create an authentic reproduction of what an early Riverina town would have looked like. The complex is open daily 8:30 a.m.-5 p.m. and admission is a worthwhile $5; it's two km north of town on Airport Rd. (tel. 069-62-4196).

The area's many wineries are also a major attraction. **McWilliam's Wines** offers tours Friday at 2 p.m. This winery also has a barrel-shaped tasting room open Mon.-Sat. 9 a.m.-5 p.m. Located eight km south of Griffith (tel. 069-63-1001). (The unusual smell often hovering around the winery will horrify vegetarian wine-tasters—it comes from nearby Barter Enterprises, Australia's largest egg producers and supplier of 60,000 chickens a week). **Cranswick Estate,** Walla Ave. (tel. 069-62-4133), produces wine purely for export, with the colorful labels and "Barramundi" name synonymous with Australian wine overseas; tastings are Mon.-Fri. 9 a.m.-4:30 p.m.

Held over Easter, the **Griffith Wine & Food Festival** celebrates the popularity of the area's wineries with activities throughout town and at the wineries, including "grape-treading" at McWilliam's Wines. Another big event is the **Festival of Gardens,** held in mid-October, when many local families open their gardens to the public.

Motel accommodation in Griffith isn't particularly cheap, with **A-line Motel,** 187 Wakaden St. (tel. 069-62-1922), having rooms for $50 s, $60 d. If you want to spend a little extra, the

Acacia Motel, 923 Irrigation Way (tel. 069-62-4422), is of a higher standard. **Griffith Caravan Village,** on the road out to Leeton (tel. 069-62-3785), has tent sites for $10, on-site vans for $25, and a swimming pool, barbecue area, and laundry.

Pasticceria Bassano, 449 Banna Ave., is open daily 8 a.m.-5:30 p.m., serving a variety of coffees, great bowls of pasta, and healthy sandwiches. Also try the bread—it's baked daily in the wood-fired oven. **La Scala,** 455 Banna Ave. (tel. 069-62-4322), is a pizzeria, with most pizzas costing $12-18.

Griffith Visitors Centre is at the eastern entrance to town on the corner of Banna and Jondaryan Avenues. (tel. 069-62-4145). Available here are wine-tour maps and information on the far southwest of the state. Open Mon.-Fri. 9 a.m.-5 p.m., Saturday 9 a.m.-3 p.m., Sunday 10 a.m.-2 p.m.

Cocoparra National Park

This 8,358-hectare park northeast of Griffith protects a section of the ancient Cocoparra Range. The range comprises sediments laid down on the ocean floor 400 million years ago and uplifted by movements beneath the earth's surface in the ensuing years, with erosion sculpting the present landscape. Cliffs and gullies along the park's western border are great for exploring, with the trail through **Ladysmith Glen** among the most accessible.

The first European to penetrate the range, John Oxley, had scant appreciation for the area's flora and fauna, commenting in his diary that the mountains had been "abandoned by every living creature capable of getting out of them." The main access is from Yenda north to a stock route along the park's western boundary. This road leads to Mt. Bingar, Woolshed Flat Camping Area, and a number of shaded picnic areas. In the park's southeast corner an access road leads to **Spring Hill Picnic Area,** from where a 1.2-km trail leads into a canyon and Falcon Falls.

WEST FROM GRIFFITH

The Sturt Highway passes 32 km south of Griffith before passing through Hay and Balranald; then it crosses the Murray River at Mildura and continues to Adelaide. The highway was named for Capt. Charles Sturt, who followed much the same route on his 1829-30 expedition tracking the Murrumbidgee River to the Murray River and following it to the Great Australian Bight.

Hay

Hay (pop. 3,000) is at the junction of three main highways midway between Sydney and Adelaide. Unlike other river towns, Hay is set back a few blocks from the waterway, and wandering around town there's little indication that the Murrumbidgee River flows so close. The town has a colorful history—from its early days as a river crossing, then as a major Cobb and Co. coach stop, and during WW II as home to 20,000 prisoners of war. One of many historic buildings on the main street is **Hay Gaol,** an imposing structure dating to 1878.

BLUE MOUNTAINS AND VICINITY

The Blue Mountains might not have the height of the North American Rockies or the tradition of the European Alps, but in their own rugged way they're awe-inspiring and one of Australia's great natural wonders. Named for a blue haze caused by sunlight reflecting from evaporating eucalyptus oil, they are part of the Great Dividing Range that runs along Australia's east coast. Although most areas of the mountains can be reached in under two hours' driving time, much of the area is rugged and remote. Over 200,000 hectares are protected by Blue Mountains National Park, and the only development is along the Great Western Highway, constructed along a high ridge linking Sydney to the western plains. Along this 70-km stretch of road are 26 towns and villages, the largest being Katoomba, just two km from Echo Point, vantage point for viewing the Three Sisters and trailhead for a number of hikes leading into the vast valley below. Wentworth Falls, Leura, and Mt. Victoria are other picturesque Blue Mountains villages, and each has a wide range of historic guesthouses, charming restaurants, and plenty of nearby hiking.

For a country addicted to the coastline, it's surprising how busy the Blue Mountains can get, especially on weekends; try to plan your visit midweek, and apart from more room to move, you'll benefit from good deals on accommodation packages.

SYDNEY TO WENTWORTH FALLS

The most direct route from Sydney to the Blue Mountains is the Great Western Highway, which bypasses the sprawl of Sydney's western suburbs before crossing the Nepean River and

On 1 August 1997 all telephone numbers in this section will change. To dial the new number, simply add the last two digits of the existing area code to the old number. As an example, (047) 12-3456 becomes 4712-3456. The new area code will be (02).

climbing steadily to Glenbrook, easternmost of the Blue Mountains' communities.

Glenbrook
Glenbrook provides a gateway to the middle section of Blue Mountains National Park. Immediately south of town an access road leads into the park, passing a **park information center** (open Sat.-Sun. and school holidays 11 a.m.-4 p.m.). Along this road are a variety of picnic areas, bush camping at **Euroka Clearing,** Koori hand stencils at **Red Hands Cave,** and a couple of lookouts.

Norman Lindsay Gallery and Museum
Norman Lindsay was an imaginative artist and author who spent much of his life in the Blue Mountains. He died in 1969 at the age of 90, his infamous lifestyle portrayed in the 1994 movie *Sirens.* Lindsay's former home is classified by the National Trust and is open for inspection Fri.-Sun. 11 a.m.-5 p.m.; admission is adult $5, child $1. On display are many of his works as well as a display of his best-known writing, *The Magic Pudding,* and many of his sculptures are scattered around the landscaped gardens. It's located on Chapman Crescent, north of Faulconbridge (tel. 047-51-1067).

WENTWORTH FALLS

Named for the youngest member of the successful expedition across the Great Dividing Range, the falls tumble 300 meters from a high escarpment into a remote valley. The town Wentworth Falls (pop. 5,000) is less commercialized than those farther west and is the starting point for some excellent hikes.

Yester Grange
Nestled in beautiful landscaped gardens above Wentworth Falls, Yester Grange is one of the finest Victorian-era houses in the Blue Mountains. Dating to the 1870s, it has been restored to its former glory. It now combines an art gallery, museum, and tearooms in a setting with glori-

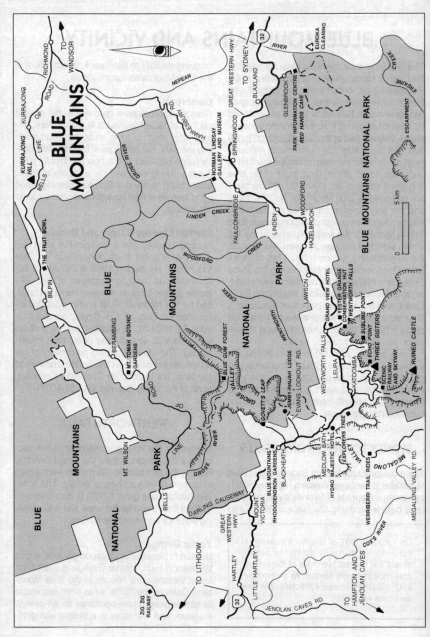

CROSSING THE WESTERN BORDER

Hemmed in by the ocean to the east and mountains to the west, Sydney Town struggled to expand for the first 25 years of its existence. Many attempts were made at crossing the Great Dividing Range, but it wasn't until 1813 that the crossing of what Governor King described as "a formidable barrier impassable for man" was successful.

Gregory Blaxland, William Lawson, and William Charles Wentworth, landowners at the base of the mountains, had a desire to find better pastures and set out westward on 11 May 1813 with the idea of following ridges rather than valleys, which had been the downfall of earlier expeditions. Each man brought a different talent to the expedition, and together they crossed the Great Dividing Range in less than two months.

Just six months after the official route had been mapped, a gang of 30 convicts was put to work constructing a track over the mountains. Within six months a trail was completed, the convicts had been pardoned for their good work, and settlers were streaming west.

ous views over the Jamison Valley. Morning and afternoon teas are served in a former ballroom, and in summer tables are set around the veranda. Admission to the gardens and house is $5 pp; open Wed.-Sun. 10 a.m.-4:30 p.m. Located on Yester Rd., off Tableland Rd. (tel. 047-57-1110).

Hiking

Conservation Hut, on Fletcher St., is the main trailhead, with trails leading east along the escarpment to the end of Falls Rd., west to Inspiration Point, and south into the valley below. From Falls Rd. a short trail leads to various lookouts, with a one-km trail crossing Jamison Creek and ending at Rocket Point Lookout. From Conservation Hut the shortest route into the valley is two km one-way, but it's a *very* strenuous return climb, so allow three hours' round-trip. Another option is to descend from the hut to **National Pass,** below the main ridge, and follow it beyond Wentworth Falls, returning along the top of the escarpment (six-km round-trip, allow four hours).

Accommodations and Food

Grand View Hotel, on the Great Western Hwy. (tel. 047-57-1001), is in the heart of Wentworth Falls, right opposite the railway station and shopping area. It dates from last century; its solid mass and distinctive pink color make it a Blue Mountains landmark. Rooms are $55 pp and have private facilities.

Grand View Hotel has a bistro open daily and a restaurant open Saturday night. **Conservation Hut Cafe,** Fletcher St. (tel. 047-57-3827), is an informal place, perfect for relaxing after a hike into the valley below. Back in town, at 30 Station St., is **Conditorei Patisserie,** baker of fine cakes and pastries.

LEURA

Leura, five km west of Wentworth Falls, is arguably the mountains' most charming town. Spread between the Great Western Highway and the escarpment, its tree-lined streets are dotted with fine examples of early Australian architecture, and spectacular **Cliff Drive** provides access to picnic areas and hiking trails. The highlight of Leura is **Leura Mall,** directly south of the railway station, lined with tearooms, boutiques, cafes, and gift shops—the largest concentration of such shops in the Blue Mountains.

Lookouts and Hiking Trails

One of the best viewpoints is **Sublime Point,** south of the golf course and signposted from town. The panorama extends 270 degrees, from Wentworth Falls in the east, to remote stretches of Warragamba Dam in the south, and Echo Point and the Three Sisters in the west. West of Sublime Point, at the end of Olympian Parade, is **Gordon Falls Lookout** and a shaded picnic area. **Prince Henry Cliff Walk** leads from here to Echo Point; it's about four km one-way and passes numerous lookouts. For the keen, it's possible to return on the valley floor along **Dardanelles Pass** (nine km round-trip; allow four hours). East from Gordon Falls Lookout a trail leads up Gordon Creek to **Lyrebird Dell;** two km round-trip.

Accommodations

Historic guesthouses dot the streets of Leura, and although weekend rates are high, midweek packages are a good deal. **Leura House,** 7 Britain St. (tel. 047-84-2035), is a three-story Victorian-era guesthouse faithfully restored and set among rambling landscaped gardens. Rooms are furnished with antiques, and many have views. On the first floor is an enormous lounge area and dining room. Rates Sun.-Thurs. are $125 pp for two nights, including breakfast, and from $226 pp weekends, which includes breakfast and dinner. **Little Company Guest House,** 2 Eastview Ave. (tel. 047-82-4023), is a series of small cottages set on a two-hectare property and centered around The Nunnery, a rambling old house with 12 large rooms of the highest standard. Rates of $120 pp per night include breakfast and dinner.

For those who like the flexibility of preparing their own meals, **Jack's House** is a good option. It's a restored two-bedroom cottage with a comfortable lounge area and fully equipped kitchen. Rates are $70 per night for the entire house or $280 for a three-night weekend; located between Leura and Katoomba; for bookings and directions, call (02) 9368-1047.

Fairmont Resort, overlooking the valley on the road out to Sublime Point (tel. 047-82-5222), is the only resort-style development in the mountains. It boasts all modern conveniences, including a health club and 18-hole golf course; rates start at $155 s or d.

Food

The Ferns, 130 Megalong St. (tel. 047-84-3256), is a federation-style restaurant specializing in international cuisine in an elegant atmosphere. Open daily except Wednesday for lunch and dinner.

KATOOMBA

Katoomba is the largest tourist and commercial center in the Blue Mountains, and although it lacks the charm of Leura, it has many of the best-known sights, including the **Three Sisters,** an impressive rock formation floodlit daily until 10 p.m. Echo Point is the best place to start a visit to the area, not only for the information center, but for the variety of hiking in the immediate vicinity.

Scenic Railway and Skyway

Although not designed as such, these two commercial attractions give an adrenalin rush as well as any fun park can. Originally built in the 1880s to haul coal and shale from the valley floor, the Scenic Railway is claimed to be the steepest railway in the world, operating on an incline of 45 degrees. Mine management began giving early tourists the ride of their lives in sooty coal skips; mining has long since ceased, and the coal skips have been replaced by more comfortable cars. The fare is $3.80 round-trip, but the one-way fare ($2) allows you to descend to the valley floor on foot and catch the train back up to Katoomba. Starting from the same complex is the Skyway (tel. 047-82-2699), an aerial cable car that glides horizontally over a 280-meter-deep valley. The fare for each ride is $3.80 round-trip. The Scenic Railway provides access to a variety of hiking on the valley floor; the one-way fare is $2. Both operate daily 9 a.m.-4:50 p.m. Also at the complex is a large, tacky souvenir shop and a revolving restaurant.

the Three Sisters

Skyway

Hiking
Views of the Three Sisters are best from the parking lot at Echo Point; to get a closer look, take the 500-meter trail around the back of the information center to another lookout. This trail is also the beginning of **Prince Henry Cliff Walk,** which follows the escarpment to Leura Falls and Gordon Falls Lookout in Leura (four km one-way). From Echo Point, the **Giant Stairway** accesses the valley floor from where Federal Pass Walk leads to the base of the Scenic Railway and the Dardanelles Pass Walk heads northeast toward Leura. Also from Echo Point, a trail leads westward to **Katoomba Falls** (two km one-way) and around to the Skyway and Scenic Railway. For experienced hikers, the six-km (one-way) trail from the base of the Scenic Railway to a rocky outcrop known as **Ruined Castle** is a good way to escape the crowds.

One of the most interesting overnight hikes is the 45-km **Six Foot Track** linking Katoomba and Jenolan Caves. Four campgrounds are located along the trail, but it can easily be completed in three days. **Country Walks** (tel. 047-84-3266) operates a guided walk along its entire length; $195-275 pp, including meals and transportation.

Other Outdoor Activities
A number of mountain climbing and abseiling (rappelling) companies based in Katoomba offer full-day adventure-packed activities as well as a variety of training courses. The **Australian School of Mountaineering,** 182 Katoomba St. (tel. 047-82-2014), offers a beginners abseiling course, which includes an 80-meter jump, lunch, and transport; $69 pp. A two-day rock climbing course is $160, and you can then advance to a climb of the Three Sisters; $95. Thursday and Saturday Oct.-March, the company offers a canyoning experience, abseiling into a water-filled canyon and swimming/scrambling out; $59 pp.

Nalara Adventure Treks (tel. 047-57-3149) operates day and overnight mountain-bike treks through Blue Mountains National Park; from $70 pp per day.

A great way to explore the more remote portions of the Mountains is on a 4WD safari with **Cox's River Escapes** (tel. 047-84-1621). They offer full-day trips (eight to 10 hours) four-wheel driving in Megalong Valley, combined with easy bushwalking, lunch and a light snack, and swimming in the clear water of Cox's River; $95-120 pp. Other options are a half-day tour ($65) and a Twilight Tour, which includes dinner and spotlighting animals ($95).

Yulefest
For those from the Northern Hemisphere, celebrating Christmas in the middle of summer probably doesn't seem right, so each winter (June-Aug.) up in the Blue Mountains, Yulefest celebrations make up for Australia's climatic reversal. No official celebrations are held, but many accommodations offer special packages that include Christmas dinners, a visit by Santa, and, you never know, it may even snow.

Historic Guesthouses
Along the Great Western Highway are a few motels, but these are generally expensive, and for the same price you can stay at a historic guesthouse or B&B. The least expensive of these is **Katoomba Mountain Lodge,** 31 Lurline St. (tel. 047-82-3933), close to the town and

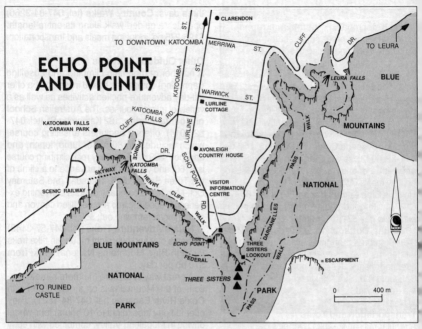

ECHO POINT AND VICINITY

with basic but adequate facilities, including a large lounge area, free tea and coffee, and game room. Rates are $28 pp for bed and breakfast midweek, $66 for a two-night weekend package, and a three-course dinner is an extra $15 pp. Dating from 1876, **Balmoral House,** 196 Bathurst Rd. (tel. 047-82-2264), has 10 basic rooms, a dining area, and small lounge furnished with antiques. Rates are $65 pp Mon.-Fri., $85 weekends, which includes breakfast and dinner. **Megalong Lodge,** 40 Acacia St. (tel. 047-82-2036), has a real homey feel and is set in a large property, right by Katoomba Golf Course. Rates are $45 pp for bed and breakfast. The **Clarendon,** 68 Lurline St. (tel. 047-82-1322), is a small boutique hotel with plain but elegant rooms for $44 pp midweek. Weekend rates of $165 pp include two nights' accommodation, breakfast, and dinner with theater performance. **Avonleigh Country House,** 174 Lurline St. (tel. 047-82-1534), dates to the turn of the century and has been restored to its former glory, yet retains a homey ambience. Rates are $95 pp midweek, which includes a delicious three-course dinner and cooked breakfast. **Mountain Heritage Country House Retreat,** corner Apex and Lovel Streets (tel. 047-82-2155), is 100 meters from Katoomba's main street; rooms are large and furnished to the highest standard. Rates for bed and breakfast are $86 s, $135 d.

Budget Accommodations

What **Blue Mountains YHA Hostel** lacks in historic grandeur it makes up for in location, halfway between town and Echo Point and within walking distance of both. Facilities include a communal kitchen, game room, lounge area with log fire, and bike rental. Rates are $13 in dorms and $17 pp twin or d. It's located at 66 Lurline St. (tel. 047-82-1416).

Katoomba Falls Caravan Park, Katoomba Falls Rd. (tel. 047-82-1835), has a laundry and barbecues. Sites are $7 pp and on-site vans $35 d. Another option for budget travelers is **Nomads Gearins Hotel,** right opposite the railway station (tel. 047-82-6028), where dorms are $12-14 and doubles are $38.

Food

Along Katoomba St., the main drag through town, are some great cafes scattered among an otherwise ordinary strip of shops. One of the most interesting is **The Paragon,** 65 Katoomba St. (tel. 047-82-2928), an art-deco masterpiece with wood-paneled booths for privacy; open daily 10 a.m.-5 p.m. Funky **Parakeet Cafe,** 195 Katoomba St. (tel. 047-82-1815), is a popular hangout for local artisans with sandwiches from $5 and pasta from $7.80; open daily 8 a.m.-6 p.m. **Poppyseeds Cafe,** 179 Katoomba St. (tel. 047-82-6043), is another modern place, this one with a country feel and the emphasis on healthy meals. At the top end of town, in Gearins Hotel, is **Blue Cactus Bar and Grill** (tel. 047-82-6127), with good-quality meals at pub prices; expect to pay $7-10 for dinner.

Lurline Cottage (132 Lurline St., 047-82-2281) features that great Swiss invention, the fondue, as well as a variety of other Swiss-influenced dishes. It's only open for dinner Fri.-Sat., but Wed.-Sun. light lunches and afternoon tea are served.

Transportation and Tours

A regular rail service links Sydney's Central Station and Katoomba ($8.80 one-way), or purchase a combined rail ticket/bus tour ($40); call 13-2232 for details. All major tour companies offer day trips from Sydney to the Blue Mountains from $50 pp.

Katoomba's **Fantastic Aussie Tours** offers a three-hour tour of all major sights for adult $28, child $14, as well as a full-day tour for adult $55, child $45. They also operate the **Blue Mountains Explorer Bus,** which runs daily 9:30 a.m.-5 p.m. between 17 major sights around Katoomba and Leura for $15 pp. If you just want to get from one point to another **Katoomba Leura Bus Service** (tel. 047-82-3333) runs regular weekday services. **Blue Mountains Adventure Company** (tel. 047-87-1233) rents mountain bikes for $30 a day. If you're staying there, Katoomba Hostel also has a few bikes. **Katoomba Radio Cabs** can be reached at (047) 82-1311.

Services and Information

The **post office** is at 95 Katoomba Street. **Blue Mountains District Hospital** is up on the Great Western Hwy. (tel. 047-82-2111). Camping gear is available at **Rockcraft Outdoor Shop,** 182 Katoomba St. (tel. 047-82-2014). Head to **Katoomba Washing Well,** Pioneer Place (near Kmart), for laundry services; open daily 7 a.m.-7 p.m.

If you visit just one bookstore in Australia, make it **Brian's Books,** 44 Katoomba St. (tel. 047-82-5115). Apart from two floors of second-hand books on every subject imaginable, you'll often have background ambience of Brian tapping away at his piano or giving lessons in one of many ancient languages; after hours scrabble games are often held. **Blue Mountains Visitor Information Centre** is at Echo Point (tel. 047-82-0756); open daily 9 a.m.-5 p.m.

KATOOMBA TO HARTLEY

Immediately west of Katoomba is **Explorers Tree,** engraved by Blaxland, Wentworth, and Lawson. It is, in fact, less interesting than you may think. A wall built around the tree killed it, so the dead trunk was removed, leaving a stump, from which the explorers' initials have long since rotted away. Near the tree are sandstone headstones on graves of convicts who died during construction of the road.

Hydro Majestic Hotel

The community of **Medlow Bath,** six km northwest of Katoomba, consists of a cluster of houses that would be inconspicuous if it wasn't for the Hydro Majestic Hotel, an ochre-colored Edwardian monolith set in 80 hectares of landscaped garden right on the escarpment. Built late last century as a luxurious health resort, it features a cavernous lounge, dining room, two bars, swimming pool, and tennis courts. Rates are $87 pp midweek, $110 pp weekends, which includes breakfast and dinner. For bookings, call (047) 88-1002.

Blackheath

The natural beauty of the Blue Mountains certainly doesn't end at Katoomba, for Blackheath (pop. 4,000), 14 km farther northwest, is gateway to the glorious **Grose Valley** to the north and **Megalong Valley** to the south. The town itself is a good base for exploring these areas, has a great number of historic buildings, and is noted for rhododendron gardens, many planted in private residences. **Blue Mountains Rhododendron Garden,** north of the highway off Sturt St., features 18 hectares of landscaped gardens; open daily 9 a.m.-5 p.m.

Norwood Guesthouse, 209 Great Western Highway (tel. 047-87-8568), is a small B&B dating from 1888. Rates are $65 s or d midweek, $80 weekends. **Rowan Brae Guesthouse,** 284 Great Western Hwy. (tel. 047-87-8296), is a romantic getaway surrounded in English-style gardens just a short walk from town; $105 pp Mon.-Fri., $125 pp weekends, which includes breakfast and a delicious three-course dinner. **Jemby-Rinjah Lodge,** 336 Evans Lookout Rd. (tel. 047-87-7622), is a series of log cabins set in native bushland, each with a kitchen and bathroom, and the complex has a laundry, lounge area with log fire, and plenty of native animals. It's only a short walk from Govett's Leap (see "Grose Valley," below). Cabins are $80 Mon.-Thurs., $105 Fri.-Sunday. **Blackheath Caravan Park,** Prince Edward Rd. (tel. 047-87-8101), has sites for $8 pp and on-site vans for $35.

Grose Valley

The northern section of Blue Mountains National Park encompasses spectacular Grose Valley, a deep box canyon carved through millions of years of erosion by the Grose River and its tributaries. The valley has no railway accessing the valley floor, and no famous landmark such as the Three Sisters, but views from various lookouts at the top of the escarpment are nothing short of breathtaking. The main lookout is **Govett's Leap,** at the end of Govett's Leap Road. The story behind the leap is that a bushranger pursued by troopers chose death rather than capture and spurred his horse over the 450-meter cliffs. From the lookout, trails lead north to Horseshoe Falls (800 meters one-way) and Pulpit Rock (2.5 km one-way), and south past Bridal Veil Falls, which can be seen from Govett's Leap, to Evans Lookout (three km one-way). The trail down into the valley is extremely steep and in places narrow (one km each way, but allow two hours round-trip). If you are confident enough to negotiate this track, it would be a pity not to continue to Junction Rock, from where one trail branches south, climbing the

escarpment at Evans Lookout (nine km round-trip, allow five hours), and one branches north along Govett's Creek to the Blue Gum Forest (eight km one-way). Although not the valley proper, **Grand Canyon** is an interesting and moderately difficult five-km round-trip from Evan's Lookout, perfect if you're staying at Jemby-Rinjah Lodge.

Along Govett's Leap Rd. is **Blue Mountains Heritage Centre,** displaying different aspects of the mountain's human and natural history; open daily 9 a.m.-5 p.m. (tel. 047-87-8877).

Megalong Valley

The Megalong Valley, south of Blackheath, is not part of Blue Mountains National Park and is mostly cleared farmland, but driving into the valley allows a different perspective on the escarpment.

In the valley, **Werriberri Trail Rides** offers horseback riding for all levels of expertise, and charges $15 pp per hour or $70 for a full day. An overnight ride is $170 pp. Open only on weekends and school holidays (tel. 047-87-9171).

Mount Victoria

Westernmost village of the Blue Mountains, Mt. Victoria is a charming place with a small museum behind the railway station (open 2-5 p.m. Sat.-Sun.) and a few grand buildings along the main street. On the eastern outskirts of the town is the **Toll Keepers Cottage,** built in 1849 to collect one shilling six pence from every coach—heavy vehicles (those without springs) were not required to pay the toll as they helped crush the stones and form the road. Built in 1878, the **Imperial Hotel** (tel. 047-87-1233) has rooms with shared facilities for $40 pp, private facilities for $50 pp, including breakfast, with weekend packages only slightly higher. Also offered are a few dorm beds for $20 pp.

From Mt. Victoria, the Great Western Highway continues to Lithgow and Bushranger Country, or you can return to Sydney along the Bells Line of Road (see below) or head to Jenolan Caves, south of Hartley.

Hartley

On the western slopes of the Blue Mountains, and beyond Little Hartley, Hartley, totally devoid of 20th century development, is one of Australia's best examples of an early 1800s town. Established in 1815 as a stopping point for travelers heading to the newly opened western plains, Hartley thrived within 20 years, with a courthouse, police station, hotels, and churches constructed. The town's fate was reversed in 1869 when it was bypassed in favor of a northern route for the rail line. Today, 17 buildings remain as a symbol of the town's short but prosperous past. The most impressive is the **courthouse,** completed in 1837. Many notorious bushrangers were sentenced here, and the graffiti-lined walls of the cells allow an insight of early guests. Across the road is a well-preserved church, sandstone hotels, a post office, and other residences. The post office operates as an information center (open daily 10 a.m.-5 p.m.), and the courthouse is open for inspection, with tours daily 10 a.m., 11 a.m., noon, 2:15 p.m., and 3:30 p.m.

JENOLAN CAVES AND VICINITY

These caverns, nestled in a valley on the western slopes of the Blue Mountains 160 km west of Sydney, are among the most spectacular cave systems in Australia. They're especially popular because a couple are floodlit and have stairs leading through them. A bushranger was the first to discover the caves, and by 1866 the government had opened them to visitors, who made an arduous three-day trek on horseback from Katoomba.

From the Western Highway, the final descent to the main caves complex is through **Grand Arch,** an impressive open-ended cave over 100 meters long and 20 meters high. Parts of the cave system are still unexplored, and of the 22 main caves, 12 are open for inspection—nine on a guided tour, three on a self-guided basis. The caves themselves are magical, with all the formations associated with limestone caverns. Tours run every 15-30 minutes (9:15 a.m.-5 p.m.) and last up to 90 minutes; $10-12 pp. Entry to self-guided caves is $6-8 pp.

Accommodations

Open for visitors since 1906, **Jenolan Caves House** is a three-story guesthouse built of lo-

cally quarried sandstone. Although extensive renovations have been done, rooms are still fairly basic; $95 s, $148 d, including breakfast and dinner. A cheaper option, 24 km north of the caves at the small village of Hampton, is **Jenolan Halfway Motor Inn** (tel. 063-59-3302). Motel-style rooms are basic, and there's a restaurant and bar on the premises; $30 s, $55 d.

Kanangra Boyd National Park

An extension of Blue Mountains National Park, this 68,000-hectare park is a vast wilderness of sandstone cliffs, gorges, limestone caves, and the impressive **Kanangra Walls,** equal in beauty to areas around Katoomba but totally undeveloped. The walls are 33 km south of Jenolan Caves along a rough gravel road. A lookout here allows spectacular views across **Grand Gorge** and is the starting point of three short walks.

BELLS LINE OF ROAD

Originally built to provide a link between Windsor and the western plains, Bells Line of Road, north of the Great Western Highway, is an alternative route across the Blue Mountains.

Zig Zag Railway

The major problem engineers had with construction of a rail line across the Blue Mountains was the final descent into Lithgow. Eventually, a Z-shaped line, with two reverse stations, two tunnels, and three sandstone viaducts, was completed. The line operated 1869-1910, falling into disrepair after a 10-tunnel deviation of the main line was constructed. The original route has been restored, and steam trains run weekends and school holidays. For bookings and timetable information, call (063) 53-3061; for information on packages from Sydney and Katoomba, call State Rail at 13-1500.

Mount Wilson

In 1868 an area of crown land at the base of Mt. Wilson was subdivided and sold off to Sydneysiders who subsequently built cottages and planted extensive gardens reminiscent of England. Today the community remains a beautiful hideaway, different from anywhere else in the

Blue Mountains. Exotic trees line most avenues, with rows of elm, beech, liquid amber, and lime dominating Church and Queens Avenues. In spring and autumn many private gardens are open to the public. Many hiking trails begin from Mt. Wilson, including one-km Waterfall Creek Trail and, through town, the 400-meter Cathedral of Ferns Trail.

Mount Tomah Botanic Gardens

Maintained by the Sydney Royal Botanic Society, these gardens were developed on the site of a nursery once operational as a flower farm. Sections of the original garden remain, including a corner devoted to species of the Southern Hemisphere, but the highlight is the view from the Visitor Centre, which extends right across Sydney. The gardens are open daily 10:30 a.m.-6 p.m. (tel. 045-67-2154).

Bilpin to Windsor

Bilpin is famous for its apples, or more precisely, its apple juice; both can be bought from the **Fruit Bowl,** a large fruit stall east of town. Farther east, on Kurrajong Hill, is a fabulous view across the city, and on a clear day the skyscrapers of downtown Sydney can be seen. **Kurrajong,** the last community before crossing the Nepean River eastbound for Windsor, has a main street lined with tearooms, antique emporiums, and a few craft shops.

HAWKESBURY RIVER

The Hawkesbury is the largest river system draining into the Pacific Ocean from the Great Dividing Range. The eastern slopes of the Blue Mountains are its watershed, from where it flows northward along the base of the Great Dividing Range, looping around Sydney's outlying suburbs, flanked by a number of national parks, then draining into the ocean at **Broken Bay,** a wide body of water separating Sydney from the central coast.

Windsor

Windsor, located 56 km northwest of Sydney at the eastern end of Bells Line of Road, has seen much development in recent years, but the main street is lined with historic buildings. Windsor is one of five **Macquarie Towns** established along the Hawkesbury Valley by Governor Lachlan Macquarie in the late 1700s as a source of farmland for the new colony on Sydney Cove. Head first to the **Hawkesbury Museum,** in the old inn on Thompson Square (tel. 045-77-2310), which catalogs the history of the Macquarie Towns and has maps for exploring the whole area; open daily 9 a.m.-5 p.m. On nearby George St. is **Macquarie Arms Hotel,** which first opened in 1812. Farther along George St. is **St. Matthew's Anglican Church,** designed and built by convicts in 1822. On Palmer St. is **Tebbutt Observatory,** named for a keen astronomer who built an observatory on the site in 1879 (look for his face on the Australian $100 note).

North from Windsor

The **Australian Pioneer Village,** six km north of Windsor in the Macquarie Town of Wilberforce, is a re-creation of an early Hawkesbury Valley township. Many buildings are original, including an 1811 timber cottage, the oldest such structure in the country. The park is open Tues.-Thurs., Sat.-Sun. 9 a.m.-5:30 p.m. and admission is $8. Located on Buttsworth Lane (tel. 045-75-1457).

Wilberforce is on the west side of the Hawkesbury River, and if you continue north along Putty Rd., you'll finish at Singleton, in the Hunter Valley west of Newcastle. The alternative is to travel along the east bank of the Hawkesbury on Cattai Rd. to Wisemans Ferry through the delightful towns of **Pitt Town** and **Cattai.**

GOLDEN WEST

West of the Great Dividing Range are the western slopes, a rich agricultural land sandwiched between the mountains and the outback. European settlement west of the Great Divide was

On 1 August 1997 all telephone numbers in this section will change. To dial the new number, simply add the last two digits of the existing area code to the old number. As an example, (063) 12-3456 becomes 6312-3456. The new area code will be (02).

at first slow; townships developed up and down the coast from Sydney Town before any movement west was made. Three landowners from the base of the range, Wentworth, Blaxland, and Lawson, were the first to make the crossing. Within months convicts were put to work constructing a road, and upon completion settlers began streaming west. The new settlers cleared vast tracts of land, opening it up for cereal crops, cattle, and sheep. In 1851, when Edward Hargraves discovered gold on Lewis Ponds Creek, north of Bathurst, thousands more flowed west, seeking fame and fortune. As at other goldfields of the same era, only a few struck it rich, and within a few years, life in the Golden West returned to normal.

Bathurst, Australia's first inland city, is a fine example of an Australian country town, with impressive buildings lining wide streets. To the north is the best-preserved of the gold-mining towns, Hill End, while to the south is Carcoar, scene of many daring bushranging exploits. South of Carcoar is Cowra and the grand town of Forbes. The northernmost town of the Golden West is Dubbo, home to Australia's largest open range zoo.

Lithgow and Vicinity
The first town west of the Blue Mountains is Lithgow (pop. 12,000), once an important coal-mining town and now a large manufacturing and industrial center. First settled in 1824, coal mining commenced in 1869, peaking in 1980 when 240,000 tons per day were extracted. Relying on the coal supply, industries such as steel, copper, brickworks, and pottery were also established.

Built in 1864, **Eskbank House,** corner Bennett and Inch Streets (tel. 063-51-3557), the home of one of Lithgow's earliest settlers, still stands. As well as original furniture, the house contains a coal-mining exhibit, while other relics are scattered around the grounds. Open Thurs.-Mon. 10 a.m.-4 p.m.

North of Lithgow, in Wollemi National Park, is a **glowworm tunnel.** The tunnel itself is man-made, having been constructed for a rail line, but the glowing worms are completely natural. To get there take Inch Street out of Lithgow, turning onto Atkinson St. and following this road onto Newnes Plateau. From the parking area, it's five km to the tunnel, but it's possible to continue a farther four km by road. A trail through the tunnel continues 11 km to the former shale-mining town of Newnes.

BATHURST

Bathurst lies 200 km west of Sydney. It is Australia's oldest inland city, and while other population centers of the same era have slid into oblivion, Bathurst continues to thrive and is now an important rural center of 31,000.

History
Construction of a road west from Sydney began within months of the explorers Wentworth, Blax land, and Lawson's crossing the Blue Moun tains. By 1815, less than two years after the first crossing, a rough track had been completed over the mountains and as far west as the Mac quarie River, where the township of Bathurst developed. As a pastoral center, Bathurst grew steadily in its formulative years, but it wasn't until the 1850s, with nearby gold discoveries that the town boomed. Gold strikes to the north of Bathurst brought thousands of prospectors through the town, as well as a number of bushrangers. The rush for gold has long since ended, but Bathurst remains a thriving city, serv ing the large agricultural industry and becoming the focus of national attention for the running of Australia's most popular motor race.

Mt. Panorama Sights
A racing circuit was first developed on Mt Panorama, southwest of town, in the 1930s. It's Australia's only public road-racing circuit, mean ing you're free to drive around the 6.2-km circuit year-round. All normal road rules apply, so chances are you won't break the lap record of two minutes and 12 seconds.

On Murray's Corner is the **Motor Racing Hall of Fame** (tel. 063-32-1872), featuring bikes and cars dating from 1930, photographic displays of the track's winners and losers, and other rac ing memorabilia. It's open daily 9 a.m.-4:30 p.m Admission is adult $4, child $1.

At the top of Mt. Panorama is **Sir Joseph Banks Nature Park,** a 41-hectare enclosure of native bushland that's home to kangaroos, koalas, wombats, dingos, emus, quolls, and a variety of birds. Admission is free, and it's open daily 9 a.m.-4 p.m.

Off the Conrod Straight section of the motor racing circuit is **Bathurst Gold Diggings** (tel 063-32-2022), a replica of an 1850s goldfield All aspects of mining techniques have been reconstructed as well as a blacksmith's shop, ore stamper, and traditional miner's hut. Ad mission is adult $6, child $4, which includes gold panning. On Sunday at 11 a.m. and 2 p.m. guided tours are conducted for an addi tional $4 pp. The diggings are open Sun.-Fri. 10 a.m.-4 p.m.

BATHURST

The big race, the **Tooheys 1,000,** is a five-day extravaganza that culminates in the final 161-lap race on the first Sunday in October. A general admission ticket to the final day's racing is $30, $120 if you want to sit on Pit Straight. For tickting information, call (1800) 02-5496.

own Sights

Ben Chifley, one of Australia's great prime ministers, was born and raised in Bathurst. He ran the country between 1945 and 1949. His small, unpretentious Bathurst home is open to the public Mon.-Sat. 2-4 p.m. and Sunday 10 a.m.-noon. Admission is adult $2, child $1. It's on the corner of Busby and Bant Streets.

Bathurst's oldest building is **Old Government House,** at the northeast end of George St., which dates from 1820. Many of the city center's other buildings, including commercial, civic, and residential, date from the Victorian era (1840-1900). **Bathurst Courthouse,** Russell St., is the most impressive of these and is open Mon.-Fri. 9:30 a.m.-4 p.m. In the courthouse's east wing is **Bathurst and District Historical Museum** (tel. 063-32-4755). Open Saturday 9:30 a.m.-4:30 p.m. and Sunday 10 a.m.-4 p.m.; admission $1.

Many of Australia's greatest artists have drawn inspiration from Bathurst's natural surroundings and nearby ghost towns. Works displayed at **Bathurst Regional Art Gallery,** 70 Keppel St. (tel. 063-31-6066), depict this environment. It's open Mon.-Fri. 10 a.m.-4 p.m., Saturday 11 a.m.-3 p.m., Sunday 1-4 p.m.

Bathurst Courthouse

Accommodations

Central and inexpensive is **Park Hotel,** corner George and Keppel Streets (tel. 063-31-3399), where rooms with private facilities are $35 s, $55 d. Most motels are at least one km from downtown, including a few on the road out to Cowra. Of these, **Capri Bathurst Motel,** Mid Western Hwy. (tel. 063-31-2966), is least expensive, with basic rooms for $46 s, $56 d. One block east is **James Cook International Motor Inn** (tel. 063-32-1800), Bathurst's best motel. Rooms are of the highest standard, with an indoor pool, laundry, health club, and fine-dining restaurant. Rates are $110 s or d for a standard room, $135 with a private spa.

Built as a private residence in 1882, **Strathmore,** 202 Russell St. (tel. 063-32-3252), is one of Bathurst's many historic B&Bs. Each of the five refurbished rooms has a private bathroom. Guests have use of a comfortable lounge area and tea- and coffee-making facilities in the elegant dining room. Rates are $75 s, $100 d, including breakfast.

Bathurst Caravan Park is five km east of town on the Great Western Hwy. (tel. 063-31 8286). Facilities are excellent and include a game room, barbecue area, tennis court, and laundry. Sites are $10-12, and cabins range $32-45.

Food

A popular spot each morning is **Bernard's Bakery,** at 81 George Street. The choice of pies, pastries, and sandwiches is staggering, and food can be eaten in or taken out. **Terrace on William,** 164 William St. (tel. 063-31-1838), is a small cafe with a historic ambience. For something more modern, head to **Ziegler's Cafe,** 52 Keppel St. (tel. 063-32-1565), with a wide range of coffees and light meals from $5. Tables are set inside the simply decorated cafe and in a courtyard surrounded by greenery. **Lamplighter Restaurant,** William St. (tel. 063-31-1448), is in a building dating from 1890 in the commercial heart of the city. Lunches average $7, dinners start at $12. Open for lunch Mon.-Fri. and for dinner Mon.-Saturday. Claimed to be Australia's best Indian dining west of the Great Divide is **Tandoori House** at 94 Bentinck St. (tel. 063-32-3320). For Mexican, head to **Rio Grande,** at 159 George St. (tel. 063-31-9136).

Transportation, Services, and Information

Hazelton (tel. 13-1300), the main airline carrier west of the Great Divide, has daily flights between Sydney and major centers in the region. The flight between Sydney and Bathurst takes 40 minutes and costs $140 one-way. **Countrylink** (tel. 063-32-4844) runs the **XPT** between Sydney's Central Station and Bathurst Railway Station at the end of Keppel Street; $28 one-way. All long-distance buses stop in town.

Bathurst Visitors Centre is at 28 William St. (tel. 063-32-1444). Open daily 9 a.m.-5 p.m.

NORTH FROM BATHURST

The area north of Bathurst was the scene of frenzied gold rushes in the 1850s but is today a quiet destination, well off the beaten track. The first village north of Bathurst is **Sofala,** a picturesque settlement on the Turon River. At the height of the gold rush, in the late 1850s, 40,000 eople lived in Sofala. The town has aged naturally, with very little changing since late last entury. The main street, lined with buildings in arying states of disrepair, features a general tore, post office, small museum, and a couple f cafes.

ill End

Valking through the deserted streets of Hill End, bout 36 km west of Sofala, it's difficult to imagne the atmosphere that must have prevailed etween 1871 and 1874 when thousands of opeful diggers descended on the remote valley n hope of making their fortune. When gold was und at **Hawkins Hill** in 1871, word of the enormous amount of gold spread quickly around the orld. The reef of gold uncovered was 400 meters long, 100 meters wide, and 80 meters deep. brought fortune to those lucky enough to arrive arly, and as merchants, tradesmen, and miners stablished themselves, the town gained an air f permanence. Within two years, though, the upply of gold had dwindled, and the newly established town saw a mass exodus of diggers. hose who remained searched the mullock eaps for gold missed in the initial rush and anned for alluvial gold in the creek beds.

Where Hill End differs from other historic old-mining towns is that there has been virtually no development since the boom years. The treets are lined with buildings from the 1870s. ach is marked with a plaque describing its istory, while the sites of those demolished uildings are marked with photos of the original tructures. A two-km trail leads around Hawkins ill and to an old mine on Bald Hill. In the old ospital on Bathurst Rd., the NPWS, caretaker f the town, operates an excellent **museum** el. 063-37-8206). It's open daily 9:30 a.m.-:30 p.m.

Dating from 1872, the **Royal Hotel** (tel. 063-7-8261) sits atop a small rise overlooking town. ooms, with shared facilities, are of an excellent tandard and open to a wide balcony. Rates re $30 s, $45 d; $38 s, $60 d, with breakfast. he NPWS operates three campgrounds in wn, including one within walking distance of e pub and general store. Out back of the hotel s a bistro counter—either eat at tables set round the beer garden or in the small room off e main bar.

Mudgee

Farther north, the medium-sized country town of Mudgee lies in a shallow valley through which the Codgegong River flows. While it was gold that saw other towns thrive, Mudgee's wealth is centered on agriculture, in particular wine and honey. The wide main street, typical of country towns, features a number of impressive civic buildings, including a town hall dating from 1880. **Colonial Inn Museum,** 126 Market St., is in the old West End Hotel. Parts of the old hotel have been restored—including the bar, parlor, and a kitchen—using relics from a nearby inn. **Mudgee Honey Co.** is a good place to view the honey production process. Open daily 9 a.m.-5 p.m. It's at 28 Robertson St. (tel. 063-72-2359).

The **Paragon Hotel,** corner Gladstone and Perry Streets (tel. 063-72-1313), has a few basic rooms with shared facilities for $26-30 pp, including breakfast. The nicest place in town is **Country Comfort Inn Mudgee,** Cassilis Rd. (tel. 063-72-4500), with a bar, bistro, and restaurant; $88-108 s or d.

Mudgee Country Bakehouse, 79 Market St., has all the usual pies and pastries as well as healthy sandwiches. For a pub meal, head to **Lawson Park Hotel,** 1 Church St. (tel. 063-72-2183), where a good roast is offered Monday and Tuesday. For something a bit more formal, try **Augustine Vineyard Restaurant,** George Campbell Dr. (tel. 063-72-3880). Morning and afternoon teas ($5) are the highlight, with cheese plates ($5) also available. Lunch dishes are prepared using mostly local produce and range $12-15.

Mudgee Visitors Centre is at 84 Market St. (tel. 063-72-5875). It's open Mon.-Fri. 9 a.m.-5 p.m., Saturday 9 a.m.-3:30 p.m., Sunday 9:30 a.m.-2 p.m.

Gulgong

While most Australians took the recent introduction of plastic banknotes in stride, it was a sad time for Gulgong, the town on the old $10 note. Gold was discovered at nearby Red Hill in 1870, and a prosperous town soon developed. The streets of Gulgong, about 29 km north of Mudgee, are narrow and winding, lined with a variety of one-story buildings. **Gulgong Pioneer Museum,** 73 Herbert St. (tel. 063-74-1513), is one of the best small-town museums in the state. On display is a blacksmith's shop, settler's cottage, Cobb & Co. coach, and a collection of Aboriginal artifacts. It's open daily 9:30 a.m.-5 p.m.

Stables Guest Rooms, 149 Mayne St. (tel. 063-74-1668), is a late-Victorian accommodation, and while a couple of rooms are in the original stables others are in the main house. Rates are $50 s, $75 d.

Wellington

This medium-sized town of 5,000 is on the Macquarie River between Bathurst and Dubbo. The town's main drawcard is **Wellington Caves,** eight km south of town. The caves were discovered by Europeans in 1828 and for most of this century have been a popular tourist destination. Cathedral and Gaden Caves are lit for public inspection, while River Cave is only open to cave divers. Tours are conducted seven times daily (tel. 068-45-1733). Around the caves' entrance are tourist attractions, including a house made entirely from bottles, and a golf course. Also here is a campground with good grassy and shaded sites; $10-12 per night, and cabins are $40-50. For bookings, call (068) 45-2970.

DUBBO

Dubbo is a city of 28,000 on the Macquarie River, 400 km northwest of Sydney. It's the hub of western New South Wales and gateway to the outback. Dubbo, meaning "Red Earth" to the Aborigines, is an important wheat and wool center but is a transportation point for a great variety of other agricultural industries. Prior to European settlement, the region was inhabited by the Wiradhuri Aborigines. The first Europeans arrived in 1824, settling land along the Macquarie River. By 1840 a general store had opened, followed by a hotel and courthouse. A decade later the town had been surveyed and blocks of land were for sale.

Western Plains Zoo

Australia's largest open-range zoo, this facility features animals from six continents roaming over 300 hectares six km south of Dubbo. As well as over 1,000 Australian animals, there are lions, tigers, cheetahs, rhinos, a herd of ele-

phants, bison, oryx, monkeys, and giraffes None of the animals are caged; instead the are contained subtly—by moats, for example Kids can pet animals at the Friendship Farm Admission is adult $14.50, child $7.30. Because of the zoo's large area, you may want to rent a bike ($8 four hours) or mini-moke ($30 for three hours) to get around. For park information, ca (068) 82-5888.

Other Sights

Old Dubbo Gaol, right downtown between the Commonwealth and State Banks, has held some of Australia's most notorious bushrangers. Established in 1847, the jail was in use until 1966 Many of the cells have been restored, and along with gallows, padded cells for condemned prisoners, and a hangman's kit, the place makes for a grisly yet interesting attraction. Animated models of prisoners tell of their crimes and tragic endings. Admission is adult $3, child $1. It's open daily 9 a.m.-4:30 p.m. (tel. 068-82-8122).

In a sandstone building dating from 1876 is **Dubbo Museum** at 232 Macquarie St. (tel. 068 82-5359). It features a coach-building display Aboriginal relics, and memorabilia from early settlers. Admission is adult $3, child $1. Open daily 9 a.m.-4:30 p.m.

Accommodations and Food

Of the cheap hotels, **Castlereagh Hotel** is the best, with basic rooms for $25 pp, including breakfast. It's at the corner of Talbragar and Brisbane Streets (tel. 068-82-4877). Also basi is **Park Vue Motel,** 131 Bourke St. (tel. 068 82-4253), where rooms are $36 s, $42 d. Mos other motels are strung along Cobra St., south o downtown. Of these, one of the best values i **Golden West Motel,** 87 Cobra St. (tel. 068-82 2822), which has all the usual facilities, a poo spa, and barbecue area. Rates are $58 s, $66 d Similar in standard, and with an excellent poo area, is **Alexandra Palms Motor Inn,** 35 Cobra St. (tel. 068-81-8155); $58 s, $68 d. **Kurrajong House** is a YHA hostel on the north side of the rail line a short walk from downtown. Facilitie are fine, and dorm beds are $12 pp. Bikes ca also be rented. **Dubbo City Caravan Park** i across the river from town on Whylandra S (tel. 068-84-4820). Sites are $10-13, on-sit vans $28, and cabins $30-45.

Along Macquarie St. are good cafes, including the **Coffee Bean,** opposite the Old Dubbo Gaol t 43 Macquarie St., and **Grape Vine Cafe,** opposite the courthouse at 144 Brisbane Street. ule's Crepes, 213 Macquarie St. (tel. 068-82-300), is a heritage-style restaurant with an informal atmosphere. Savory crepes are a reasonable $10-13.50 pp, with the all-important essert crepes averaging $6. For an inexpensive heal head to **Dubbo RSL Memorial Club** on Vingewarra St. (tel. 068-82-4411).

Transportation, Services, and Information
Countrylink (tel. 13-2232) operates **XPT** rail ervices between Sydney and Dubbo; $52 each ay. Countrylink also offers packages, including avel from Sydney, one-night accommodations, heals, and entry to Western Plains Zoo, for 247 pp. Dubbo Railway Station is on Talbragar treet. The main bus depot is on Erskine Street. t is served by **Greyhound Pioneer** (tel. 13-030) and **McCafferty's** (tel. 068-84-4199). The are from Sydney is around $45 each way.

Dubbo Visitors Centre is on the corner of Macquarie and Erskine Streets (tel. 068-84-422). There's plenty of parking at the center, naking it a good place to base yourself for exploring downtown, a 400-meter walk away.

ORANGE AND VICINITY

)nce considered as the site of the national capital, Orange, 260 km west of Sydney, is a thriving fruit-growing center of 35,000. Orange's dominant natural feature is 1,395-meter **Mt. Canobolas,** one of the continent's highest peaks way from the Great Dividing Range. Oranges re not grown at Orange (the city is named for Villiam of Orange, former King of Holland); instead apples, pears, and cherries are the major rops, thriving in the rich volcanic soil. Australian oet Banjo Patterson was born in town.

The **Tourist Information Centre** is on Byng t. (tel. 063-61-5226).

)phir

When news of gold discoveries west of the Great Divide first filtered through to Sydney in ne late 1840s, the government tried to keep ne news quiet, afraid that settlers would desert their farms for the diggings. The situation changed dramatically when gold was discovered in California. Fearing a mass exodus across the Pacific, the government reversed its decision and offered a reward for the discovery of a payable goldfield. On 12 February 1851 Edward Hargraves found traces of gold on Lewis Ponds Creek, 20 km northwest of Orange. While he rushed off to Sydney to claim the reward, his partners, William Tom and John Lister, found the mother lode. This first rush was short and sweet. A few thousand diggers worked the creek and tributary, but within months they were lured away by finds elsewhere.

A few foundations and depressions at the junction of Lewis Ponds and Summer Hill Creeks are all that remain of the Ophir township. Walking tracks lead through the old workings, and a primitive campground has been developed above Fitzroy Bar, site of the original find.

Millthorpe
The historic village of Millthorpe, 25 km southeast of Orange, features numerous Victorian-era buildings and a small commercial center with cobbled sidewalks and winding streets. Buildings such as the school, a couple of hotels, and banks have changed little in over 100 years. At the top end of Victoria St. is **Rosebank Guesthouse** (tel. 063-66-3191). Built in 1902, it's one of Millthorpe's more-modern buildings, but it lacks nothing in grandeur, with spacious rooms, a cozy lounge area, and extensive gardens. Rates are $60-70 pp, including breakfast, and dinner is available for an extra $20-25 pp. The **Old Mill Cafe,** just down the hill from Rosebank at 32 Victoria St. (tel. 063-66-3188), is one of many restored buildings. It serves delicious morning and afternoon teas ($4-8) and is also open for lunch (closed Monday).

BATHURST TO COWRA

Abercrombie Caves
South from the Mid Western Highway, on a rough road linking Bathurst and Goulburn, is Abercrombie Caves. Koori were the first to explore the remote cave system, but it wasn't until bushrangers began using them as a hideout that they came to the attention of officialdom.

A massive limestone arch is the dominant aboveground feature of the cave system, and two caves are lit for public inspection. They are open daily 9 a.m.-4 p.m., with guided tours departing at 2 p.m. At the caves' entrance are campsites for $10 and cabins $40-45. Facilities include hot showers, a laundry, kiosk, and barbecue area. For tour information and campsite bookings, call (063) 68-8603.

Tuena

This small gold-mining village lies on the Tuena River 20 km south of Abercrombie Caves. Gold was discovered on the river in the mid-1850s, and although many permanent buildings were established, the field never amounted to much. **Parson's General Store,** dating from 1860, is Tuena's oldest building. It still operates as a general store and is good for supplies and hints on fossicking areas. Dating to 1866, the **Goldfields Inn** (tel. 048-34-5214) is an original wattle-and-daub building.

Carcoar

Straddling the Belubula River, 50 km southwest of Bathurst, this charming old village of 400 was at one time the second-largest town west of the Blue Mountains. Established in 1838 to curb the activity of bushrangers, it grew steadily in importance, but when gold was found to the north its population steadied. As transport links became better, the need for the local banks and the courthouse lessened.

The biggest concentration of historic buildings is along Belubula St., which slopes down to the river. The Commercial Bank (1862) was often the target of bushrangers. Other historic buildings are the courthouse (1882) and Royal Hotel (1891). On the opposite side of the river is **Stoke Stable,** dating from 1849. It's now a small but interesting museum open daily 10 a.m.- p.m. Admission $1.

Farther down Naylor St. is **Dalebrook Guest House** (tel. 063-67-3149). Facilities are shared $85 s, $95 d. On the north side of the river is **Bridges Tea Rooms,** serving good hamburgers and some light meals.

COWRA

Best known as site of the greatest prisoner escape in British military history, Cowra is a quiet country town on the Lachlan River, 300 km southwest of Sydney and 200 km north of Canberra. During WW II Cowra was the site of four prisoner-of-war camps. In the early hours of August 1944 a mass breakout took place from one of two camps holding Japanese prisoners. In the darkness, confusion reigned, and guards manning machine guns were helpless against hundreds of marauding Japanese. Of the 1,104 prisoners, 378 escaped. Many were killed on the spot, others escaped and committed suicide, and still others were recaptured. Four guards were killed. Although little remains of

Carcoar

he camp, photographs of the original com-
ounds and a few foundations make the site
vorth visiting. It's northeast of town on Sakura
venue. North of the camp, on Doncaster Dr.,
re the Cowra and Japanese War Cemeteries,
here victims of the breakout lie. At the southern
nd of Sakura Ave. is the **Japanese Garden**
el. 063-41-1890). The gardens have been de-
eloped through years of close ties between
apan and the people of Cowra, officially open-
g in 1979. The gardens include ponds, cas-
ading waterfalls, pathways, a cultural center, a
estaurant serving light meals, and a gift shop.
's open daily 8:30 a.m.-5 p.m.

Cowra also has a couple of museums, in-
uding **Cowra Military Museum,** on River Park
d. (tel. 063-42-1863), and **Mid State Rail Mu-
eum,** five km east of town (tel. 063-42-2666).
oth are open daily 9 a.m.-5 p.m.

While most of the land around Cowra has
een cleared for agriculture, 7,590 hectares
ithin **Conimbla National Park,** 27 km west,
re protected. Within the park, Ironbark Walking
rack leads to a lookout above the surround-
g open forests.

racticalities

labaster Motel, 20 Lynch St. (tel. 063-42-
133), has large modern units, a pool, spa, and
arbecue area; $49 s, $51 d. **Nandewah,** on
oorowa Rd. 11 km south of Cowra toward
anberra (tel. 063-45-3237), is a farmstay B&B
a 400-hectare property. Two rooms are of-
red in the 1920 homestead, and breakfast is
erved on the veranda. Rates are $50 s, $75
; $75 s, $95 d with a private spa. **Caravan
ity Holiday Resort** is five km east of Cowra to-
ard Bathurst (tel. 063-42-2666). It has all the
sual facilities and is adjacent to the rail muse-
m. Sites are $12-15, on-site vans $30, and
abins $40. The other alternative for campers is
onimbla National Park, 27 km west of Cowra.

Ilfracombe Restaurant, 127 Kendal St. (tel.
63-41-1511), in a private residence dating from
379, retains the authentic charm from the Vic-
rian era. A coffee house provides light snacks
hile the restaurant proper offers steak, chicken,
nd seafood from $15.50. Closed Sunday.

The **Tourist Information Centre,** on the Mid
Vestern Hwy. (tel. 063-42-4333), features
eakout memorabilia. Open daily 9 a.m.-5 p.m.

VICINITY OF COWRA

Grenfell, west of Cowra, grew from a gold rush
on nearby Emu Creek, and relics from this time
can be viewed at **Grenfell Museum** on Camp
Street. Australia's best-known poet, Henry Lawson, was born in his parents' canvas tent at the
Emu Creek goldfields. A cairn on Lawson St.
marks the site, and each June long weekend
the event is celebrated during the Henry Lawson
Festival, a gathering of poets and songwriters.

Weddin Mountains National Park
Protecting the rugged Weddin Range, this
8,360-hectare park was an ideal hideout for
bushrangers who took refuge in its dense cover
and many caves. The most famous of these
was Ben Hall, who with his gang often hid out at
a cave in the west of the park. A 500-meter trail
leads up to the cave from Nowlands Road. On
the range's eastern slopes, at the end of Holy
Camp Rd., is a campground.

West Wyalong
At the junction of the Newell and Mid Western
Highways, this small country town of 4,000 is
in the heart of a rich wool- and wheat-growing region. The town was never officially surveyed,
so early residents dug the main street around
tree stumps, and as a result West Wyalong's
main drag is strangely crooked. A small museum
downtown displays relics from the town's gold-
mining history. It's open daily 2:30-5 p.m. (tel.
069-72-2117). Southeast of town, toward Temo-
ra, is a mineral pool, good for a relaxing dip.
Lake Cowal, 47 km northeast of town, is a shallow body of water covering 200 square kilometers. Over 150 species of birds have been reported there. Access is from Clear Ridge Road.

Best value of the dozen motels in town is **Colonial Motor Inn,** on the Mid Western Hwy. 500
meters west of downtown (tel. 069-72-2611); $48
s, or d. The **Tourist Information Centre** is in a
train carriage in McCann Park, at the junction of
the Newell and Mid Western Highways (tel. 069-
72-3645). It's open daily 10 a.m.-4 p.m.

Forbes
Forbes, 90 km northwest of Cowra, is a stately
town of 8,000 on the Lachlan River. Having

been founded in the 1840s, many historic buildings line the streets, including the town hall, post office, courthouse, and a number of churches and hotels. Bushranger Ben Hall and his gang were active in the Forbes area, with Hall being brought down in a hail of bullets 20 km west of Forbes. He's buried in the cemetery northwest of town on Bogan Gate Road. **Lachlan Vintage Village,** one km south of town (tel. 068-52-2655), comprises historic buildings that have been moved to the site, as well as re-creations of Ben Hall's wattle-and-daub cottage. It's open daily 8 a.m.-5:30 p.m. On Cross St. is **Forbes Historical Society Museum,** with more Ben Hall relics. It's open 3-5 p.m.

The **Vandenberg Hotel,** Court St. (tel. 068-52-2015), has basic rooms with shared facilities for $22 s, $36 d, including breakfast. **Country Roads Motor Inn,** 14 Cross St. (tel. 068-52-4099), is the best motel in town; $60 s, $69 d. Campers should head to **Lachlan View Caravan Park,**

two km southeast of town toward Cowra (te068-52-1055). Facilities include a pool, laundrshop, and camp kitchen. Sites are $9-13, on-sivans $33, and cabins $33-50.

The **Tourist Information Centre** is in threailway station on Union St. (tel. 068-52-4155open daily 9 a.m.-5 p.m.

Parkes

The highlight of a visit to Parkes, 33 km north Forbes, is the **radio telescope,** 20 km north town. The telescope's massive 64-meter-widish collects radio waves from throughout thgalaxy and beyond, analyzing the signals oncomputer to produce images. This telescophas been involved in various international prjects, including the 1969 Moon Landing and thVoyager II journey to Neptune. A visitor center the telescope is open daily 8:30 a.m.-4:15 p.rwith the film *The Invisible Universe* shown hour(tel. 068-62-3677).

OUTBACK NEW SOUTH WALES

o the government, the outback of New South Wales is known by the rather uninspiring name **Western Division,** an area encompassing more an 40% of the state and with a population that overs around 50,000 (half of which live in Broen Hill). Although it is generally accepted that ne "real" outback lies west of the Darling River, which flows in a southwesterly direction from p near Lightning Ridge to the Murray River est of Mildura, the only official boundaries of utback New South Wales are the borders of ueensland to the north and South Australia o the west.

utback Tours

you only have a few days to spare, the best ay to cover the great distances of outback Iew South Wales would be to fly into Broken Iill and take a tour. Many companies offer ours taking in all the best features of this part of ne country. **Silver City Tours** (tel. 08-8087-956) operates day tours from Broken Hill out o Mootwingee and Kinchega National Parks nd White Cliffs. The six-day tour includes all ne above, plus it takes in sights closer to Broen Hill and provides basic motel accommoations for $478 pp. **Broken Hill's Outback ours** (tel. 08-8087-7800) is another option. four-day Outback National Parks tour dearts twice weekly and costs $615 pp. The ost comprehensive tour is offered by **Cenek Safaris** (tel. 03-9775-2211) and includes ne Dingo Fence and Cameron Corner in a even-day 4WD safari; $995 pp, including airre from Melbourne.

BARRIER HIGHWAY

he Barrier Highway heads west from Nyngan rough to Broken Hill and on to Adelaide and is ealed the entire way. The scenery is fairly munane, featuring low undulating scrub-covered ills until the highway crosses the Darling River t Wilcannia, where red soils, typical of the outack, dominate.

Nyngan

Nyngan, at the junction of the Mitchell and Barrier Highways 167 km northwest of Dubbo, is best-known to Australians for the disastrous floods in April 1990, when water from the usually dry **Bogan River** rose to such a height that the town all but disappeared and residents had to be airlifted by helicopter to Dubbo. During these same floods, an area larger than Great Britain was underwater north of Nyngan. The only reminders of the flooding are a sandbag levee constructed between the Bogan River and town and a helicopter in Vanges Park. A part of the railway station is a small museum, and the old stationmaster's cottage has been restored.

Country Manor Motor Inn, 145 Pangee St. (tel. 068-32-1447), is the best place to stay in town. Facilities include a saltwater pool, and across the road is the RSL Club, a good place for a meal; $46 s, $56 d.

Information about the town and other outback destinations is available from **Burn's Video and Gift Shop** at 105 Pangee St. (tel. 068-32-1155); open seven days.

Cobar and Vicinity

Cobar (pop. 6,000) thrives on its tremendous mineral wealth, and unlike other towns of outback NSW (except for Broken Hill) it's far away from any natural river source. The mineral outcrop around which the town was founded in 1871 is still being mined, with 920,000 tons of copper, lead, and zinc extracted annually. Tours of the mine are offered Friday at 2 p.m.; book ahead by calling (068) 36-2001. **Cobar Regional Museum**

> On 1 August 1997 telephone numbers in this section with the area code (068) will change. To dial the new number, simply add the last two digits of the existing area code to the old number. As an example, (068) 12-3456 becomes 6812-3456. The new area code for these numbers will be (02). The area code for existing eight-digit numbers in this section is (08).

OUTBACK NEW SOUTH WALES

as some excellent displays pertaining to the
history of the area and the people who settled in
this harsh part of the country. An Aboriginal display shows the various bush tucker to be found
in the outback, while upstairs is devoted to mining and the mineralogy of the land upon which
Cobar was built. The museum is on a rise overlooking the town, on the Barrier Hwy., and is
open daily 9 a.m.-5 p.m.

The **Great Western Hotel,** built in 1898,
has always been the grandest establishment in
town. Rooms have shared facilities and are
$25 s, $35 d, with breakfast $4-6 pp extra. Lo-
cated on the corner of Linsley and Marshall
Streets (tel. 068-36-2503). **Longworth Restaurant and Bar,** 55 Linsley St. (tel. 068-36-2611),
is a formal eatery in a house built in 1899 for
Thomas Longworth, one of the original directors
of the Great Cobar Copper Mine. The setting is
historically authentic, with pressed-metal ceilings and period furnishings. The menu features a wide variety of dishes ranging $13-21;
open daily 7 p.m.

If you are passing through Cobar in early August, the detour to **Louth,** 132 km northwest of
Cobar, is worthwhile. The first or second Saturday in August (call Louth Hotel at 068-74-7422
to check dates) is the annual Louth race meeting, which has grown in stature to boast over
$30,000 in prize money and live television cov-
erage across Australia. West of Cobar, 40 km
along the Barrier Highway, a 35-km road spurs
north to **Mt. Grenfell Historic Site,** where over
1,300 pieces of Koori rock art are scattered over
rock walls and overhangs. Toilets and water
are supplied for campers.

Wilcannia

Wilcannia, 265 km west of Cobar and 200 km
east of Broken Hill, spreads out along the west
bank of the Darling River. The town grew as a
staging point for wheat and wool transported
from outback stations and sent downriver on
massive barges. Today's 1,000 inhabitants still
rely heavily on the sheep and cattle industry,
along with the tourist trade, to make up the local
economy. The wharf used by paddlesteamers
still stands, as does a historic jail, courthouse,
and post office. The town has two motels and a
couple of hotels that offer meals.

White Cliffs

White Cliffs is as famous for its housing as for its
black opals. Most of the population lives underground, escaping the climatic extremes of
unbearably hot summers and near-freezing
nights during winter. The town is very remote,
100 km north of Wilcannia along a gravel road
that leads up to the northwestern corner of New
South Wales. The sign at the edge of town
records the population at 300, but, besides during the searing heat of summer, it's many times
this number as hopeful miners descend on the
town to find their fortune. The surrounding landscape is dotted with hundreds of mullock
heaps—the remains of small-scale opal mining operations that characterize the elusive nature of opal mining.

White Cliffs Underground Motel is just
that—underground, where temperatures remain
constant at 22° C (72° F), day and night, winter
and summer. Rooms are small but adequate
and have shared facilities; $34 pp. Located one
km south of town (tel. 08-8091-6677).

SOUTH OF THE BARRIER HIGHWAY

Menindee

Menindee is accessed by gravel road from
Wilcannia (160 km) or by sealed road from Broken Hill (110 km). The town has lost much of
its original charm, but one of its oldest features,
Maidens Menindee Hotel (tel. 08-8091-4208)
stands proudly on the main street. In 1860, explorers Burke and Wills arrived, resting in Maid-
en's Menindee Hotel for a few nights before
heading north on their ill-fated expedition across
the continent. Apart from the hotel and coal-
stained riverbanks, signs of the settlement's
earlier days have all but disappeared—so there's
nothing really to do except have a beer in the
pub or a meal in the historic dining room.

Menindee lies in an area surrounded by shallow lakes that act as an overflow when the Darling River floods. The flow of water is now controlled, creating a water supply for Broken Hill
and an ideal spot for water sports. Campsites
are spread out along the lakeshore north of
town, or head south into Kinchega National
Park.

Kinchega National Park

This 44,180-hectare park surrounds Menindee and Cawndilla Lakes, whose waters are regulated by a complex system of weirs. At one time, 140,000 sheep were run on the property that is now the park. The former woolshed and outbuildings are now a living museum. Apart from the lakes, the park's landscape consists of mostly sandy plains and black river soils, and although the park's eastern boundary, the Darling River, is lined with impressive river red gums, the vegetation is generally prickly wattle, bluebush, and canegrass. Waterfowl congregate around the lakes and, of course, 'roos are prevalent.

When you visit, take **River Drive,** a 16-km loop that follows the Darling River from west of Menindee; **Lake Drive** traverses sections of the two major lakes' shorelines. Campsites are spread along both roads, and the historic woolshed houses a park information center (tel. 08-8091-4214).

Mungo National Park

Little known outside the world of anthropology, the ancient landscape of this remote 27,840-hectare park seems, at first, uninspiring. But the geology and human history will fascinate even the most casual observer. Although the park is on the "wrong" side of the Darling River to be classed as the real outback, a sense of isolation prevails. From all directions it is a long, dry,

and dusty drive to the park—the closest town with more than a handful of people is Mildura, 110 km to the southwest, while Balranald, on the Sturt Highway, is 150 km south and Menindee 21? km north.

Around 35,000 years ago the Lachlan River brought so much water off the Great Dividing Range that it spilled into the **Willandra Lakes,** vast area of water and wetlands that remained for 15,000 years. The lakes, filled with fish and mollusks, attracted thousands of waterbirds and provided a food source for giant marsupials such as seven-meter-tall kangaroos. With dramatic climatic changes at the end of the last ice age, rainfall lessened, rivers changed course and over thousands of years the lakes dried up. **Lake Mungo,** once 200 square km in area, has been dry for 15,000 years. During that time prevailing southerly winds have blown sediments from the dry lakebed into crescent-shaped sand dunes, known as the **Walls of China,** extending for over 30 km along the eastern edge of dried-up Lake Mungo.

At the park entrance is an unmanned park information center (open daily 9 a.m.-5 p.m.) with panels showing the park's natural and human history, including life-size replicas of the gigantic mammals that once inhabited the Willandra Lakes. Beside the center is a woolshed dating from 1869. From the main facility area, road leads through the dry lakebed to the Walls of China. It's easy to spend a few hours in and around the dunes' bizarre landscape. A 60-km loop road leads over Lake Mungo, and along and over the Walls of China.

The main camping area, near the park information center, is spread through a cleared area with drinking water and basic facilities. Another camping area is along the loop road. The modern **Mungo Lodge,** a privately owned operation three km from the visitor center, has rooms for $55 s, $65 d, and self-contained cottages for $75. Also at the lodge is a restaurant; for reservations, call (03) 5029-7297.

BROKEN HILL

Once described as the city of "Silver, Sin, and Six-penny Ale," Broken Hill may have changed over the years, but this legendary outback city

---

MUNGO WOMAN

In 1968 a geologist stumbled upon ancient human bones in the sand dunes of Willandra Lakes, which led to some of the most important anthropological finds ever made, including the burnt bones of a young woman, dated at 26,000 years. Proof of early habitation was a sensation in itself, but the fact that the bones had been burnt and "buried" was of special significance, as it was the world's earliest known evidence of cremation, establishing that Mungo Woman lived in a society that had cultural and spiritual practices. Since that find, more than 100 others have been made, including a whole skeleton dated at 30,000 years.

BROKEN HILL

TO TIBOOBURRA

TO WILCANNIA AND SYDNEY

TO MULBERRY VALE CABINS AND MENINDEE

TO OUTDOOR SCULPTURE GALLERY

TO DAYDREAM MINE AND SILVERTON

TO MILDURA

DETAIL

MICA ST.
WOLFRAM ST.
COBALT ST.
OXIDE ST.
BERYL ST.
IODIDE ST.
SULPHIDE ST.
CHLORIDE ST.
BROMIDE ST.
BLENDE ST.
ARGENT ST.
CRYSTAL ST.

LAUNDROMAT
TRAVELAND
OCEANIA
CITY ART GALLERY
SILVER CITY TOURS
ASTRA HOUSE BACKPACKERS
POST OFFICE
N.P.W.S.
CRYSTAL MOTEL
RAILWAY, MINERAL, AND TRAIN MUSEUM
GRAND GUESTHOUSE
TOURIST INFORMATION CENTRE
RAILWAY STATION
GEOCENTRE
YHA TOURIST LODGE

McGILLVRAY DR.

KAOLIN ST.
WYMAN ST.
CHLORIDE ST.
ZEBINA ST.
BAGOT ST.
BLENDE ST.
ARGENT ST.

SCHOOL OF THE AIR

McCULLOCH ST.
BUCK ST.
RACECOURSE RD.

SILVER CITY HWY.

BARRIER HWY.

32

HOSPITAL
MORGAN ST.
THOMAS ST.
WILLIAMS ST.
SULPHIDE ST.
BROMIDE ST.
MICA ST.
GARNET ST.
IODIDE ST.
OXIDE ST.
BERYL ST.

THE HAVEN

HOLTEN DR.

MENINDEE RD.

HORSINGTON DR.
BROOKFIELD AVE.
GALENA ST.

BROKEN HILL CARAVAN PARK
STURT MOTEL

RAKOW ST.
NICHOLLS ST.
WILLS ST.
GYPSUM ST.
CREEDON ST.

CRYSTAL ST.

SEE DETAIL

DELPRATS MINE

BURKE WARD HALL

32

SOUTH RD.

EYRE ST.

KNOX ST.

SILVER CITY HWY.

BONANZA ST.

79

N

0   1 km

ROYAL FLYING DOCTOR SERVICE

the middle of nowhere typifies the hardships of life in Australia and, through a colorful past, boasts a distinctive Australian character. The extravagant civic buildings and tree-lined boulevards of Broken Hill are often a surprise to first-time visitors, but this belies a tumultuous history of the classic struggle between a large mining company and miners. With a population of 25,000, Broken Hill is the largest outback center and, in fact, in 1900 was Australia's sixth-largest city. The Silver City, as it's best known, is in the state's far west and is closer to Adelaide (510 km) and Melbourne (830 km) than Sydney (1,160 km).

In 1883, boundary rider Charles Rasp was prospecting in the Barrier Range when he found what he thought was tin. With capital of £70 he staked a claim. And, as they say, the rest is history. The ore turned out to be not tin, but silver, and within six years, original shares were worth one million pounds. Broken Hill Proprietary, as the company came to be known, grew quickly to become Australia's largest company, providing raw materials for Australia's processing and manufacturing industries, and later diversifying into iron, steel, and shipping. Soon after, they left town, leaving a legacy of environmental depredation and a hatred among workers that remains to this day.

Town Sights
The brochure *The Silver Trail—A Guide to the Heritage of Broken Hill,* available from the Tourist Information Centre, details the **Heritage Wa** and **Heritage Trail.** The two-km Heritage Wa winds through downtown, passing many buildin dating from the beginning of this century. Th Heritage Trail is a 40-km self-guided driving to taking in over 100 points of interest, includi mines, lookouts, and historic buildings.

The **Railway, Mineral, and Train Museu** opposite the Tourist Information Centre, boasts large collection of rolling stock and displays the area's mineralogy; open daily 10 a.m.-3 p. For a more detailed look at Broken Hill's geolog head to the **Geocentre** on Argent Street. Loca ed in a historic bond store, displays here catalo the mineralogy and metallurgy of the area throu working models and interactive displays; op daily 1-5 p.m. For a miner's perspective of t town, you can take a tour of Broken Hill's fi mine, **Delprats.** Tours depart Mon.-Fri. at 10:3 a.m. and Saturday at 2:30 p.m., and cost $18. F bookings, call (08) 8088-1604. **Daydream Min** off the road to Silverton, has tours daily 10 a.m 3:30 p.m. (tel. 08-8087-6077); $10. Neither is working mine, but these tours are a great wa to experience what a miner's work entails.

Out at the airport is a museum dedicated the work of the **Royal Flying Doctor Service** **Australia** (tel. 08-8088-0777). Admission is $ which includes a tour and audiovisual displa Book yourself for the tour at the Tourist Informatic Centre. Another outback institution is **School** **the Air,** a distance-education facility that broa

Broken Hill's Railway, Mineral, and Train Museum

TWO-UP

Two-up is a low-stakes Australian game that dates from WW I. It's often described as the country's national game—even though it's illegal on all but one day of the year. Punters bet on the fall of two coins tossed in the air; in professional games, a "spinner" (anyone in the crowd) tosses the coins high in the air after players have bet among each other as to the fall. If the result is one head and one tail, it's a "no throw," and the coins are tossed again until there's a uniform result to settle all bets.

The best time of year to play two-up is on Anzac Day (25 April), the only day of the year it's legal (usually played in the parking lot of licensed clubs). A two-up "school" in Burke Ward Hall on Wills St. operates through the year Friday and Saturday nights.

asts lessons to school-age children living in remote parts of the country. To sit in on "classes" contact the Tourist Information Centre.

Galleries

Some of Australia's most renowned contemporary artists call Broken Hill home. The most famous of these are Jack Absolum and Pro Hart, whose works command tens of thousands of dollars and are in demand around the world. The **Pro Hart Gallery** is at 108 Wyman St. (tel. 8-8087-2441); open Mon.-Sat. 9 a.m.-5 p.m., Sunday 1:30-5 p.m. **Ant Hill Gallery,** 24 Brohide St. (tel. 08-8087-2441), has works from the largest range of local artists. Includes interesting pottery; open Mon.-Sat. 9 a.m.-5 p.m., unday 1:30-5 p.m. The stunning outback landscapes of Eric and Roxanne Minchin are displayed at **Minchin Gallery,** 105 Morgan St. (tel. 8-8087-7446), open daily 9 a.m.-5 p.m. The only gallery with an admission charge is **Broken Hill City Art Gallery,** corner Blende and Chloride Streets (tel. 08-8088-9252), but it's only $2. The gallery has a huge collection of works, all by local artists, spread through three galleries. Open Mon.-Fri. 9 a.m.-4 p.m., Saturday 9 a.m.- p.m.

Broken Hill Outdoor Sculpture Gallery, five km north of town, comprises 12 large sculptures scattered on a rocky outcrop. They were created by sculptors during a 1993 symposium.

Silverton

Through the Barrier Range, 26 km northwest of Broken Hill, is Silverton. Promoted in tourist literature as a ghost town, there is in fact not an empty building in town. At its peak, in 1880, the town boasted a population in excess of 3,000, and hotels with names like Silver King and Nevada reflected the early dreams of entrepreneurs who came to make a fortune in this harsh country. The gold rush lasted less than a decade, with most miners moving back to Broken Hill. The only prospecting done around town today is for tourists. You can still get a beer in the sandstone and brick **Silverton Hotel,** and many of the other original buildings remain—making this photogenic town the perfect setting for movies, including *Mad Max II, A Town Like Alice, Razorback, Hostage,* and more recently *Race the Sun* starring James Belushi. The jail houses a small museum, an information center is in the school building (tel. 08-8088-5327), and three good art galleries are scattered along the main street.

Camel rides are offered by Bill Canard, who ties his beasts up by the hotel. A 15-minute ride is $5, a one-hour ride is $20, and overnight adventures are also offered; contact Bill at (08) 8091-4880 for details.

Accommodations

Grand Guesthouse, 313 Argent St. (tel. 08-8087-5305), has an excellent standard of pub-style rooms with shared facilities. Rates start at $42 s, $54 d, and rooms with private facilities are $80, including a continental breakfast. The least expensive motel in town is the **Sturt Motel,** 153 Rakow St. (tel. 08-8087-3558), but it's three km west of town; $41 s, $47 d. **Crystal Motel,** 328 Crystal St. (tel. 08-8088-2344), has the most comfortable rooms in town and a ton of facilities; rates of $69 s, $74 d, include a cooked breakfast. **Mulberry Vale Cabins,** Menindee Rd. (tel. 08-8088-1597), are located five km east of town. Set among native bushland, each cabin is self-contained with rates at $50-60, including a cooked breakfast. The **YHA Tourist Lodge,** 100 Argent St. (tel. 08-8088-2086), 100 meters from the bus depot and Tourist Information Centre, features a communal kitchen, lounge and recreation rooms, laundry, and shaded courtyard; rates are $10 for members, $13 non-members. **Astra House Backpackers,** 393 Argent St. (tel. 08-8087-7788), has facilities of a similar standard but is a little farther from town; $10 per night. **Broken Hill Caravan Park** is three km west of downtown on Rakow St. (tel. 08-8087-3841); sites are $10-13, and a few cabins go for $30-40.

Food
The clubs are the best place for an inexpensive meal. The **Musicians Club,** 276 Crystal St. (tel. 08-8088-1777), is open daily for lunch and dinner and most meals are under $10. The **Barrier Social and Democratic Club,** 218 Argent St. (tel. 08-8088-4477), is another good option. Of the hotels, **Black Lion Inn** has counter meal lunches for $5 and dinners for $8-10. **Oceania,** 423 Argent St. (tel. 08-8087-3695), is a Chinese joint open for lunch and dinner with specials starting at $6. **The Haven,** 577 Argent St. (tel. 08-8088-2888), is a casual seafood and steak restaurant open seven nights a week.

Transportation and Tours
Hazelton has daily flights between Sydney and Broken Hill ($337 one-way), and **Kendell** connects Broken Hill to Adelaide. **Traveland,** 350 Argent St. (tel. 08-8087-1969), is the Broken Hill agent for both these airlines. The **Indian-Pacific,** Australia's transcontinental train service, stops in town ($86 one-way from Sydney) twice weekly, departing Sydney Monday and Thursday. The railway station is on Crystal St. (tel. 08-8087-1400). All major bus companies stop at Broken Hill on the Sydney-Adelaide run. From Broken Hill, fares are: Sydney $80 one-way, to Adelaide $40.

Silver City Tours, 328 Argent St. (tel. 08-8087-6956), operates a dozen different tours around town (from $20), to Silverton, and out to nearby national parks.

The various car rental agencies are: **Avis** (tel. 08-8087-7532), **Hertz** (tel. 08-8087-2719), and **Thrifty** (tel. 08-8088-1928). As the name suggests, **Broken Hill 4WD Hire** (tel. 08-8087-2927) rents four-wheel drives, with rates starting at $80 per day. For a taxi, call **Yellow Radio Cabs** at (08) 8088-1144.

Services and Information
Broken Hill Base Hospital is at 174 Thomas St (tel. 08-8088-0333). A **laundromat,** at 400 Argent St., is open daily 7 a.m.-10 p.m. For camping gear, head to **Disposals of Broken Hill** a 55-57 Oxide St. (tel. 08-8088-5977). **Outback Books,** 309 Argent St. (tel. 08-8088-1177) stocks a lot of local and general outback literature. **Charles Rasp Memorial Library** is or Blende St. (tel. 08-8088-9291).

The **Tourist Information Centre** is located right downtown at the corner of Blende and Bromide Streets (tel. 08-8087-6077). As well as al the usual literature, there's a historic display and a cafe, and all long-distance buses use the center as a depot; open daily 9 a.m.-5 p.m. The **NPWS** has an office at 5 Oxide St. (tel. 08-8088-5933); open Mon.-Fri. 8:30 a.m.-4:30 p.m.

NORTHWEST CORNER

The northwest corner of New South Wales is the state's least visited and most remote region; an area larger than many European countries, ye with only a few towns where the population ex ceeds five. Only gravel roads lead into the area and although the main ones are passable in two wheel drives, travel after rain is impossible. From Broken Hill, **Silver City Highway** is the main ac cess with other two-wheel drive roads leading north from Wilcannia and west from Bourke. Like all outback areas, travel requires forward plan ning—spare tires, extra fuel, and water are the basic prerequisites for safe travel.

Mootwingee National Park
Dominated by the knobbed and broken **Byn guano Range** rising from the surrounding star landscape, this large 68,912-hectare park i dotted with Aboriginal rock art and intriguing geological formations. The Bynguano Range i a sloped layer of sedimentary rock, laid down i a seabed 400 million years ago. Over time, ero sion has gouged out gullies and cliffs and former contorted geological features. The Wilyaka people took shelter in the range, protectin themselves from the elements while feastin on the flora and fauna living around the roc pools that remained after other water source had dried up.

Over 300 Koori sites are scattered through the range—but vandalism has taken its toll and two of the most concentrated areas are accessible only on a ranger-led tour. The tour takes in **Snake Cave,** featuring an eight-meter serpent. Hiking through the magical Bynguano Range is a highlight of Mootwingee. One of the most interesting, yet easiest, hikes is through **Homestead Gorge,** on a loop track following a dry creek bed up through crumbling cliffs. Watch overhangs anywhere along the route for rock art. Up near the entrance to the gorge is rock art from a more recent time—the initials of William Wright, who guided Burke and Wills through the range. This trail begins north of the campground. On the opposite side of the access road is the **Western Ridge Trail,** which climbs to a low summit from where sunrise and sunset can be seen in all their glory. The return trip takes three hours. Another interesting area to explore is **Old Mootwingee Gorge,** south of the campground. This narrow gorge, one km from the carpark, marks the end of the marked trail, but if you want to take to the water, swimming up the gorge is a unique experience.

The campground is well equipped, with drinking water, showers (you'll need some outback common sense to operate them), and a handful of gas barbecues. Fees are $10 per night, plus a park-use fee of $7.50.

Ask at the Tourist Information Centre in Broken Hill about tours out to the park—apart from these, you're by yourself. The park is 130 km northeast of Broken Hill; turn off Silver City Highway 55 km north of the city.

Near the park entrance is a covered area with information boards and camping registration slips. Also look for details on tours into restricted areas (usually Wednesday and Saturday) or call (08) 8091-5937.

Milparinka
It is 296 km from Broken Hill to Milparinka along

petroglyph in Mootwingee National Park

the Silver City Highway. Gold was found in the Milparinka area in 1880; within a few years a minor gold rush had taken place and the township gained an air of permanence, with three hotels, a few stores, and a stone courthouse serving 3,000 miners. By the mid-1930s, the Albert Hotel was the only business still operating—and it's been open ever since. Rooms are $23 pp (call 08-8091-3963 for bookings), the beer is cold, and basic pub meals are inexpensive. If you'd like to have a look inside the courthouse, pick up the key at the hotel.

A worthwhile detour is northwest to **Depot Glen,** a waterhole where Capt. Charles Sturt and his party were forced to rest for six months in the summer of 1844-45. The area is a small oasis surrounded by dry plains—it is easy to see why Sturt chose it. A couple of km east of Depot Glen is a grevillea tree with "J.P. 1845" carved into its trunk, marking the resting place of James Poole, who died during the ordeal.

Tibooburra
Meaning "Place of Granite" in the language of local Koori, Tibooburra is New South Wales's most remote town, being 340 km north of Broken Hill and 1,500 km northwest of Sydney. It is also the state's hottest place, with summer temperatures occasionally topping 50° C (122° F). Tibooburra is in an area known as Corner Country, over a million hectares of sandhills and mulga. Tibooburra resembles a town of the U.S. Wild West, with a smattering of buildings along a small section of paved road.

Tibooburra grew from a gold rush in the 1890s, but the gold proved elusive, and after a couple of decades the population had dipped perilously low. The pastoral industry kept Tibooburra alive. Then, in the 1950s, the town served as a service center for natural gas exploration across the northeast part of South Australia.

Tibooburra's most famous buildings, and those that locals and tourists alike spend the most time in, are the two hotels. The **Family Hotel** (tel.

08-8091-3314) was the home of outback artist Clifton Pugh for most of the 1960s. He spent his time decorating the walls with his distinctive style of art for free beer. Across the road is the no-less-grand **Tibooburra Hotel** (tel. 08-8091-3310), known locally as the "two-story."

Both pubs have accommodations for about $25 s, $30 d, or you can stay in **Granites Motel** (tel. 08-8091-3305), which lacks atmosphere but has a pool; $36 s, $46 d. At the north end of town is **Dead Horse Gully Campground.** It is officially within the border of Sturt National Park (see below) and has toilets and a few broken tables in an area of unusual boulders.

Before leaving Tibooburra, visit Sturt National Park Visitor Centre, Briscoe St. (tel. 08-8091-3308), for road conditions, an excellent interpretive display, and park literature.

Sturt National Park

For many, the stark desert landscape of this 310,634-hectare park may be monotonous, but this is the outback at its best, with desolate gibber plains extending seemingly forever. The park is a conglomeration of six sheep stations, stretching for 80 km along the Queensland border from Cameron Corner. Since the removal of stock, the park has regenerated quickly, with native grasses covering much of the park, attracting large numbers of red kangaroos, flocks of emus, a variety of lizards, and other birds such as wedge-tailed eagles and kestrels. The park is divided into two halves by its most dominant geological feature, the **Grey Range,** bluffs of sandstone rising 150 meters above the red plains. For these rises, this area is known as "jump-up country," as the bluffs seem to jump up from the surrounding landscape.

The biggest attraction west of the jump-ups is the long dusty drive out to Cameron Corner, but in the east, the land is more varied and there are two interesting circuits to drive around. **Gorge Loop Road** begins in Tibooburra and heads west to Mt. Wood Homestead, where you'll find camping and a small **Pastoral Museum** featuring a whim, which is turned by horses to draw water from bores deep below. The road continues north to a spectacular gorge before rejoining Silver City Highway. From this junction, it's south to Tibooburra. But most people would want to drive the **Jump-up Loop**

Road; short interpretive trails start from a campground along the way.

Access to the western portion of the park from two km south of Tibooburra. It is 140 km from the Silver City Highway to Cameron Corner. **Fort Grey,** 30 km from the corner, is a camp set up by Charles Sturt in 1845 on his journey to find an inland sea. At this site is a seven-km trail and campground.

Cameron Corner

Cameron Corner, 140 km northwest of Tibooburra, is the spot where three states—New South Wales, Queensland, and South Australia—meet. It was surveyed by John Cameron in 1880. His unenviable task that year was to survey the entire border of NSW and Queensland (when resurveyed in 1969, his pegs were found to be accurate within the meter). Until 1990, the corner boasted only a marker peg, but in that year the **Corner Store,** transported from South Australia, opened for road-weary travelers to quench their thirst.

BOURKE AND VICINITY

You need only look at a map of New South Wales to understand how the saying "Back of Bourke" has come to mean a long way from anywhere. This remote town of 3,500 is on the eastern bank of the **Darling River,** 780 km northwest of Sydney. In the 1890s, when famous bush poet Henry Lawson lived in one of the town's 22 pubs, Bourke was a bleak frontier town, where locally grown wool was loaded onto barges for the long trip down the Darling River to Echuca and then on to England.

Bourke has changed little since Lawson's days, and many buildings remain from that era, including an impressive stone courthouse, built in 1899. The main drag is Mitchell Street, but service and civic buildings are scattered for four blocks between here and the Mitchell Highway. Many of the area's attractions are a fair drive from Bourke. **Mount Gunderbooka,** on Mulgowan Station, has Aboriginal rock art spread along a spectacular gorge, with three paintings in shallow caves directly across Mullareena Creek from the camping and picnic area. Up the gorge a couple of kilometers are a number of other paintings and from these it is possible to continue to the long ridge that forms the summit of the mountain. The mountain is signposted along the Bourke-Cobar road, but you'll need a mud map tours brochure (available from the information center) for details.

Rooms at the **Old Royal Hotel,** 32 Mitchell St. (tel. 068-72-2544), are $24 s, $30 d with shared facilities and $60 for the rooms with private facilities. **Darling River Motel,** 74 Mitchell St. (tel. 068-72-2288), has rooms of a reasonable standard and is only a short walk to the center of town; $38 s, $48 d. The flashiest place in town is **Major Mitchell Motel,** back out on the highway (tel. 068-72-2311). Facilities include a pool, laundry, and barbecue area; rates here start at $58 s, $66 d. **Mitchell Caravan Park** is one km east of town, along the road out to Brewarrina (tel. 068-72-2791). Sites are $10, and the on-site vans are $25 d. **Paddlewheel Caravan Park,** Mitchell St. (tel. 068-72-2277), is right in town and similarly priced.

All the hotels serve counter meals, with the atmosphere at the **Carrier Arms Hotel,** 71 Mitchell St. (tel. 068-72-2040), being the most authentic. The restaurant area looks much the same as the days when Henry Lawson lived upstairs. Service isn't that slick, but for $8-10 you won't go hungry.

Buses run four times daily between Bourke and Dubbo. From there trains make connections to Sydney ($70 one-way). The local agent is **Lachlan Travel** at 35 Oxley St. (tel. 068-72-2092).

The **Tourist Information Centre** is in the railway station on Mitchell St. (tel. 068-72-2280) and is open daily.

North from Bourke

From Bourke to the Queensland border is 138 km, but the first full-service town is **Cunnamulla,** 119 km north of the border. The only community before the border is **Enngonia,** a small settlement with a pub and a petrol pump. The grave of bushranger Midnight, whose "gentlemanly" conduct and dashing attire were the inspiration for the character Captain Starlight, of the book and movie *Robbery Under Arms,* is 35 km west of Enngonia.

CENTRAL COAST, NEWCASTLE, AND VICINITY

CENTRAL COAST

The Hawkesbury River is the official northern boundary of Sydney. What begins there is the central coast, a 50-km stretch of beautiful but developed beaches and large areas of rugged coastline protected as national parks. A freeway skirts the entire coast, ending west of Newcastle at the junction of the Pacific and New England Highways.

Brooklyn

On the southern bank of the Hawkesbury River is the small village of Brooklyn, a world away from city living, which is just a 20-minute drive away. Brooklyn was named after the hometown of American workers who built the adjacent railroad bridge. **Hawkesbury River Ferries** (tel. 2-9985-7566) delivers supplies and mail to families living at inaccessible locations along the river. They take passengers for $20 pp. Departures are Mon.-Fri. at 9:30 a.m., returning just after 1 p.m.

Old Sydney Town and Gosford

Take the first exit north of the Mooney Mooney River Bridge to find Old Sydney Town, an excellent attraction that re-creates Australia's original European settlement. The streets are lined with re-creations of early 1800s buildings, and dozens of people in period costume stroll the town, living life as they would have in the early

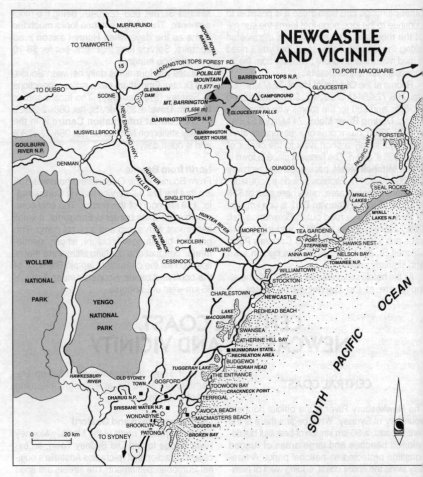

NEWCASTLE AND VICINITY

MURRURUNDI

TO TAMWORTH

MOUNT ROYAL RANGE

BARRINGTON TOPS FOREST RD.

POLBLUE MOUNTAIN (1,577 m)

BARRINGTON TOPS N.P.

TO PORT MACQUARIE

SCONE

GLENBAWN DAM

GLOUCESTER

TO DUBBO

MT. BARRINGTON (1,556 m)

BARRINGTON TOPS N.P.

CAMPGROUND

GLOUCESTER FALLS

MUSWELLBROOK

NEW ENGLAND HWY.

BARRINGTON GUEST HOUSE

FORSTER

GOULBURN RIVER N.P.

DENMAN

HUNTER VALLEY

DUNGOG

SEAL ROCKS

SINGLETON

HUNTER RIVER

MORPETH

MYALL LAKES

MYALL LAKES N.P.

BROKENBACK RANGE

POKOLBIN

MAITLAND

TEA GARDENS

PORT STEPHENS

HAWKS NEST

WOLLEMI

CESSNOCK

ANNA BAY

NELSON BAY

TOMAREE N.P.

WILLIAMTOWN

NATIONAL

STOCKTON

YENGO

CHARLESTOWN

NEWCASTLE

PARK

NATIONAL

LAKE MACQUARIE

REDHEAD BEACH

SOUTH PACIFIC OCEAN

PARK

SWANSEA

CATHERINE HILL BAY

HAWKESBURY RIVER

MUNMORAH STATE RECREATION AREA

BUDGEWOI

NORAH HEAD

OLD SYDNEY TOWN

TUGGERAH LAKE

THE ENTRANCE

GOSFORD

TOOWOON BAY

CRACKNECK POINT

DHARUG N.P.

TERRIGAL

BRISBANE WATER N.P.

AVOCA BEACH

WONDABYNE

MACMASTERS BEACH

BROOKLYN

BOUDDI N.P.

PATONGA

BROKEN BAY

TO SYDNEY

0   20 km

1800s. They encourage visitors to inquire about life in the old days. The most popular reenactments are floggings and hangings (even visitors may get flogged if they don't behave themselves), and there are wagon rides, bullock-driving, and a large sailing ship to explore. Also on site is a gift shop, bar, and restaurant. Admission is adult $14.50, child $8. It's open Wed.-Sun. 10 a.m.-4 p.m., daily during school holidays. Sydney tour operators include Old Sydney Town in their itinerary, or catch the train to Gosford and hop aboard a connecting bus service. Call (043) 40-

1104 for more information on Old Sydney Towr

Descending from the freeway to protecte **Brisbane Water,** you'll pass West Gosford an **Henry Kendall Cottage,** named for its one time resident, one of Australia's most prolifi poets. At the north end of Brisbane Water is th central coast's largest town, **Gosford.** On Th Entrance Rd., beyond the turnoff to Terrigal, i the rural hamlet of Matcham, home to **Ken Dun can Australia Wide Gallery,** displaying works c Australia's premier landscape photographe It's on Oak Rd. (tel. 043-67-6777).

Beaches and National Parks

Immediately north of the Hawkesbury River is 11,370-hectare **Brisbane Water National Park,** extending east from the freeway to Broken Bay and north to Somersby. The best way to experience the park is along a hiking trail linking **Wondabyne** (accessible only by train) to the coastal village of **Patonga** (10 km one-way). On a narrow finger of land between Brisbane Water and the ocean is **Bouddi National Park,** a long stretch of undeveloped coastline with hiking trails leading from Killcare to **Tallow Beach** and from park headquarters at Killcare Heights to picturesque **Maitland Bay,** named for a ship that wrecked on an offshore reef (look for wreckage around the northern headland).

North of the national park, high rocky headlands are linked by long stretches of golden sand; popular surfing and swimming spots include **MacMasters, Avoca,** and **Terrigal Beaches.** The latter is a resort town with trendy cafes and boutiques on a beach lined with stately Norfolk pines. Adjacent to the beach is the Haven, a protected bay backed by a grassed headland with panoramic views.

Continuing north is a string of beaches, including secluded **Spoon Bay** and long **Shelley Beach,** which is backed by a coastal golf course. **The Entrance,** immediately north of protected **Toowoon Bay,** is on a spit of land flanked by shallow **Tuggerah Lake** to the west and the ocean to the east. It is a popular holiday spot, especially for families. The main street

A pelican waits for the daily fish-feeding at The Entrance.

overlooks a grassed reserve where boats can be rented, lake cruises are offered, and hundreds of pelicans gather for a frenzied 3:30 p.m. fish-feeding session.

North of The Entrance, on a low sandy spit of land that extends to Norah Head, is 597-hectare **Wyrrabalong National Park,** which protects a stretch of undeveloped coastline and an impressive stand of red gums. Farther north is **Munmorah State Recreation Area,** a coastal reserve encompassing Birdie Beach and Frazer Park, both beautiful little spots with rocky headlands to explore, picnic areas, and camping. The north end of the central coast is timeless **Catherine Hill Bay,** dominated by coal-loading facilities at the southern end of the main beach. The south end of town has changed little this century, with old wooden cottages dotting the hill and a great pub overlooking the bay.

Accommodations

The central coast has long been a popular weekend getaway for jaded Sydneysiders, and it boasts a number of upmarket resorts, as well as accommodations to suit all other budgets.

Terrigal has a few choices. **Clan Motor Lodge,** 1 Ocean View Dr. (tel. 043-84-1566), overlooks Terrigal Lagoon and is just 100 meters from the beach; $75 s, $80 d. **Terrigal Pacific Motel,** 224 Terrigal Dr. (tel. 043-85-1555), a little farther from the beach, has modern facilities and a landscaped pool area; $90-100 s or d. Terrigal's premier accommodation is **Holiday Inn Crowne Plaza,** Esplanade (tel. 043-84-9111), an eight-story, five-star resort separated from the beach by a row of towering Norfolk pines. The resort is totally self-contained, with a pool, bar, nightclub, restaurants, gym, lounge, and staff to organize local activities. All but six rooms have ocean views, and all are large with private balconies. Rates start at $240 s or d, but look for off-season and midweek package deals. For those wishing to stay on Terrigal Beach for markedly less money, head to **Terrigal Beach Backpackers,** on Campbell Crescent, directly behind the main shopping precinct and 100 meters from the beach. Dorm beds are $14, doubles $35. For bookings, call (043) 85-3330; with advance notice, pick-ups can be arranged from Gosford railway station.

The Entrance also has a concentration of accommodations. Most have seen better days, but locations are generally excellent. **Pinehurst Caravillas,** 11 The Entrance Rd. (tel. 043-32-2002) offers self-contained units opposite the lake; rates are just $42 s, $46 d most of the year, rising to $75 in summer. **El Lago Waters Resort,** 41 The Entrance Rd. (tel. 043-32-3955), is one of the better motels; rooms here start at $60 s or d.

Kim's Retreat, at Toowoon Bay between The Entrance and Terrigal, is, without being pretentious, one of the state's most luxurious hideaways. It comprises 34 bungalows spread among lush vegetation on a beachfront property. Each room has a private balcony, most have spas, and some have fireplaces. Rates start at $180 pp (more on weekends), which includes all meals. For bookings, call (043) 32-1566.

Many coastal communities have caravan parks. From north to south, the best are: **Easts Ocean Beach Caravan Park,** Umina (tel. 043-41-1522); **Sun Valley Tourist Park,** Bateau Bay (tel. 043-32-1107); **Toowoon Bay Tourist Park,** overlooking North Shelly Beach (tel. 043-32-2834); **Dunleith Caravan Park,** at The Entrance (tel. 043-32-2172); and **Budgewoi Tourist Park,** Budgewoi (tel. 043-90-9019). All these parks are on or near the beach.

Food

Terrigal has two excellent takeaway fish and chip shops: the **Co-op** is above the boat ramp at Terrigal Haven and the **Snapper Spot** is on the Esplanade. Head to **Mouthfulls,** on Church St., for a wide variety of breakfast choices, healthy sandwiches, or coffee and cake on the sidewalk. Holiday Inn Crowne Plaza (tel. 043-84-9111) has a wide range of eateries, including **Point Break Cafe,** a casual place decorated in a beach theme; the **Conservatory,** serving buffet breakfast and lunch; and the formal **La Mer,** specializing in fresh seafood prepared with a French flair. On street level is a large beer garden. **The Galley,** in Terrigal Haven (tel. 043-85-3222), overlooks the beach and is renowned for excellent seafood.

At The Entrance, **La Terazza** (tel. 043-32-9082) is a stylish Italian restaurant with main dishes from $12 and seafood dishes from $16. Open daily from 6 p.m.

Transportation, Services, and Information

State Rail (tel. 13-1500) operates hourly services from Sydney's Central Station to Gosford, from where **Busways** (tel. 043-92-6666) operates regular bus services to Terrigal and **Entrance Red Bus Services** (tel. 043-32-8655) runs to The Entrance. This company also operates an **Airbus** between the domestic and international terminals of Sydney airport and the central coast.

In front of Gosford railway station, at 200 Mann St. (tel. 043-25-2835), is a **Tourist Information Centre.** Another is on Terrigal Dr., a short walk along the lagoon from Terrigal Beach (tel. 043-85-4431).

NEWCASTLE

Newcastle is best known as an industrial city, but away from the smelters and loading docks of Australia's second-largest port are some worthwhile attractions. It's the state's second-largest city (pop. 280,000), a massive sprawl of industry and residential suburbs centered at the mouth of.the Hunter River. Downtown is Newcastle's redeeming feature. Few cities in the world can boast a commercial and civic heart such as Newcastle's, right on the ocean, and with a main street and rail line ending a stone's throw from magnificent sandy beaches. A freeway bypasses the city completely, but the old Pacific Highway follows the coast north from the central coast through **Swansea** and **Redhead Beach** to Newcastle proper.

History

Massive seams of coal lie under the area, and although coal was was first mined in 1801, Newcastle, then known as Coal Harbour, was officially established in 1804 when the worst members of Sydney's ever-growing convict population were transported to the site. The government soon realized the wealth of the region's natural resources, so the convicts were transported farther north, and mining and settlement along the river began in earnest.

Newcastle's recent history has been almost as infamous. In late December 1989 residents were shaken by a massive earthquake. In a

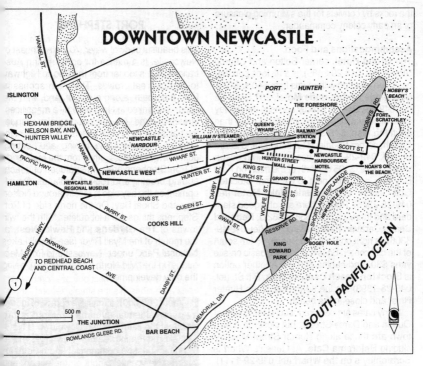

DOWNTOWN NEWCASTLE

country where fire and flood are a part of life, the shock of this type of natural disaster was hard to comprehend, especially as the epicenter was immediately west of downtown. As well as killing 12 people, the quake destroyed dozens of commercial buildings, damaged thousands of homes, and changed the face of the city forever.

Sights

An extensive redevelopment program along the mouth of the Hunter River has brought a much-needed boost to Newcastle's pride. Officially known as the Foreshore, it extends between the easternmost dockyards and the golden sands of **Nobby's Beach.** Along the Foreshore is a replica of *William IV,* the first steamer built in Australia. Toward the ocean is **Queen's Wharf,** combining a small marina, bar, restaurant, and a tower from where views extend along the river. Take a pleasant walk from here to **Nobby's**

Head. When Captain Cook first sailed up this way, Nobby's Head was an island; it was reduced to aid shipping and, in 1846, connected to the mainland by a breakwall as the Hunter River was developed as a port. At the southern end of Nobby's Beach is **Fort Scratchley.** Completed in 1886 as part of a defense system around Australia's coastline, it consists of various sandstone and brick structures and a system of underground tunnels. Originally built to repel a perceived Russian invasion (that never came), the guns were fired in 1942 when a Japanese submarine attacked Newcastle. The fort now houses **Newcastle Region Maritime Museum** (tel. 049-29-2588); open daily 10 a.m.-5 p.m. **Newcastle Regional Museum,** 787 Hunter St. (tel. 049-62-2001), has a supernova display and is open Tues.-Sun.; admission $4. Four blocks south of Hunter St. is **King Edward Park,** which overlooks the ocean, and the **Bogey Hole,** cut in

the rocks by convicts for the swimming pleasure
of an early colony commander.

Accommodations and Food

The **Grand Hotel,** corner Bolton and Church
Streets (tel. 049-29-3489), is a historic pub that
has been restored with rooms from $40 s, $42 d.
Newcastle Harbourside Motel, 107 Scott St.
(tel. 049-26-3244), is directly opposite the railway
station, but you're paying for position more than
anything else; $45 s, $50 d. **Noah's on the
Beach,** corner Shortland Esplanade and Zaara
St. (tel. 049-29-5181), has rooms with ocean
views; $95 s, $105 d. North of the river, on Fern
Bay Rd., and right next to excellent Stockton
Golf Course, is **Newcastle Links Motel** (tel.
049-28-2366). Rooms here are of a good standard and there's a pool; $58 s, $62 d. **Redhead
Beach Caravan Park,** Kallaroo Rd. (tel. 049-49-
8306), is right on Redhead Beach, 15 km south
of the city center. Sites are $12-15, basic on-site
vans $30, and cabins $40-60. Another option
is **Stockton Beach Caravan Park,** Pitt St. (tel.
049-28-1393), on the north side of the Hunter
River and close to the beach.

Many cafes are centered around the corner of
Queen and Darby Streets, but closer to downtown are those along Hunter Street Mall, including **Belorama Cafe.** At Queen's Wharf is
Scratchley's on the Wharf (tel. 049-29-1111),
a stylish restaurant featuring seafood; open daily
for lunch and dinner. For pizza and pasta, head
to **The Etna,** 115 King St. (tel. 049-26-1159),
open for lunch Wed.-Fri. and for dinner daily
from 6 p.m. For the best views in town, try a
meal at **Seaspray Terrace Restaurant,** at
Noah's on the Beach, corner Shortland Esplanade and Zaara St. (tel. 049-29-5181). It's
open all day, including for breakfast, and on
Sunday night there's a seafood buffet.

Transportation, Services, and Information

The most practical way to travel between Sydney and Newcastle is by train. **State Rail** (tel. 13-
1500) runs a regular service between the two
cities ($14 one-way), and once you're in New-
castle, the beach and other sights are all within
walking distance.

The **Tourist Information Centre** is at
Queen's Wharf on the Foreshore (tel. 049-29-
9299).

PORT STEPHENS

This beautiful body of water, 70 km northeast of
Newcastle, is a mecca for ocean-loving Australians, but is too far from the Pacific Highway
to attract great crowds. The main access is
from the south, along a spit of land, with the
ocean side linked to Newcastle by a magnificent
stretch of sand. As well as being picturesque
the bay's calm and clear waters are excellent for
scuba diving, swimming, fishing, and boating.
Just a few kilometers' drive from the main body
of Port Stephens are long stretches of beach,
surfing breaks, and rocky headlands. Development on the bay side is mostly around Nelson
Bay and Shoal Bay. On the north side of Port
Stephens things are a lot quieter, with the twin
towns of **Tea Gardens** and **Hawks Nest,** at
the mouth of the Myall River (see "Myall Lakes
National Park" under "Newcastle to Port Macquarie" in the "Mid-North Coast" section), being
the only development.

*Jewfish are highly sought after by anglers along
the New South Wales coast.*

Sights and Recreation

The largest settlement on the shores of Port Stephens is **Nelson Bay** (pop. 8,000), with a steep main street that ends at a large marina chock-full of fishing boats and pleasure cruisers. To the west is a string of protected sandy beaches, while to the east is **Halifax Point,** a popular scuba-diving spot. East of this point is **Shoal Bay,** a two-km stretch of golden sand where calm waters are dotted with catamarans and sailboards. At the eastern end of the beach is **Tomaree Head** and the mouth of Port Stephens. On the ocean side of this headland is a string of short beaches with often-rough waters. These beaches are separated by high headlands rising to 150 meters. The only official summit track is up Tomaree Head. **Fingal Bay,** farther south, is a long crescent-shaped beach ending at Point Stephens, where a lighthouse has been guiding ships since 1862. Access to the headland is only possible at low tide, when a finger of sand is exposed. Fingal Bay is part of **Tomaree National Park,** 900 hectares of coastal heathland extending south to **Anna Bay.**

The best way to get out on the water is aboard the *Tamboi Queen* (tel. 049-81-1959), which departs Nelson Bay daily at 10:30 a.m. for a two-hour dolphin-watching cruise, with swimming and snorkeling included in the cost; adult $9, child $7. Also departing from Nelson Bay is the **MV** *Dolphin,* which shuttles passengers across to Tea Gardens Mon.-Sat. 9 a.m., noon, and 3:45 p.m.; $15 round-trip. For bookings, call (049) 81-3798.

Accommodations

One of the best-value accommodations in Port Stephens is **Beaches Motel Apartments,** east of Nelson Bay at 12 Gowrie Ave. (tel. 049-84-3255). Each apartment has a large living area, separate bedroom, modern kitchen, laundry, and a private balcony overlooking a pool and landscaped gardens. Rates start at $85 per unit but rise dramatically on weekends and holidays. **Marina Resort,** 33 Magnus St. (tel. 049-81-4400), with panoramic water views, features rooms of high standard, but without kitchens; $52-120 s or d, depending on the season. **Santa Catalina Motel,** 9 Shoal Bay Rd. (tel. 049-81-1519), is an inexpensive place right on the beach; from $40 s or d.

Bardouroka Holiday Park (tel. 049-81-1473) is a sprawling campground opposite delightful Fingal Bay, offering long beach walks and protected swimming areas. Sites range $13-18.50, on-site vans $25-50, and cabins $28-80. Another good spot, and similarly priced, is **One Mile Beach Holiday Park** (tel. 049-82-1112), with a large tenting area and absolute beachfront.

BARRINGTON TOPS NATIONAL PARK

Protecting the highest peaks of the Mount Royal Range, this 39,121-hectare park northwest of Newcastle encompasses a large chunk of rainforest between the coast and the Hunter Valley. Standing apart from the Great Dividing Range, the range was formed through a combination of uplift and lava flows. But it is erosion, aided by an annual rainfall of over 2,000 millimeters, that has formed the deep gorges that are the park's most impressive features. The park's highest peak is **Polblue Mountain** (1,577 meters), at the north end of a high plateau.

The park's higher elevations are dominated by ancient Antarctic beech up to 2,000 years old. Other flora present in the subtropical rainforests include ferns, rosewood, corkwood, strangler figs, and palms.

A variety of access roads lead into the park, but none climb to the park's higher elevations. From Gloucester, a road leads to a facility area in the east of the park, while another loops around from the north to the main hiking area. From Dungog, a road leads north to Barrington Guest House.

Hiking

From the end of Gloucester Tops Rd., beyond the campground at Gloucester River, a short trail leads to Gloucester Falls and a spectacular lookout, while back at the campground, a five-km (one-way) trail leads upstream to a couple of swimming holes. The gravel track off Barrington Tops Forest Rd., linking Gloucester and Scone, winds past Mt. Barrington (1,556 meters) to an area with many hikes, including to Careys Peak and the 22-km Link Trail across Gloucester Tops.

Practicalities

Camping is at Gloucester River, 40 km west of Gloucester. Facilities are limited to toilets and fireplaces. At the south end of the park, 40 km northwest of Dungog, is **Barrington Guest House** (tel. 049-95-3212). This historic guesthouse has basic rooms and a few activities such as tennis. Rates are a reasonable $70 pp, including meals. For further park information, call (049) 87-3108.

HUNTER VALLEY

For thousands of years the Hunter River has washed rich soils down from the peaks of the Great Dividing Range, depositing them along its banks and creating the largest lowland plain on the NSW coast. The soil and a temperate climate provide the ideal conditions for growing grapes, which, in turn, has turned the valley into one of Australia's premier winemaking regions.

The valley's first grapevines were planted by the Tyrrell family over 150 years ago, but it's only since the 1950s, when wine became popular among Australians, that the industry has boomed. Although the valley produces less than five percent of Australia's wine, its reputation extends across the world. The valley itself is delightful to explore, with country lanes linking over 50 wineries, stylish accommodations, and a great variety of restaurants. In stark contrast to the rolling hills of the valley are three rugged and remote national parks that border it to the south.

Cessnock, a rural service center, is the valley's largest town. The other major town of the Lower Hunter is **Maitland,** established in 1818 and once destined to rival Sydney in importance. The largest concentration of wineries is west of Cessnock in the **Pokolbin** area. North of Pokolbin is the New England Highway, which passes through the Hunter Valley and Upper Hunter towns of **Singleton, Muswellbrook,** and **Scone.**

Maitland

Pardoned convicts and free settlers first arrived in the Lower Hunter Valley around 1818. The town of Maitland was established soon after, with its importance growing as traffic up the valley increased. Coal mining commenced late last

century and created much wealth. These early riches are reflected in many impressive civic buildings, including the post office (1889), which boasts an ornate clock tower, and the courthouse (1895). **Brough House,** on Church St., was built in 1870 by a local merchant and is today an art gallery. Other historic buildings are along **Maitland Heritage Mall.**

Windsor Castle Hotel, George St. (tel. 049-33-7276), is in East Maitland; rooms are very basic but are just $32 s, $45 d. The best place to stay is **Country Comfort Inn Hunter Valley,** just off the New England Hwy. two km north of downtown (tel. 049-32-5288), located in a building dating from the middle of the 19th century. Rooms have been renovated and are well-equipped, while facilities include a tennis court, pool, billiard room, lounge, bar, and restaurant. Rates are $83 s or d. For more of a personal touch, **Cintra,** at 34 Regent St. (tel. 049-32-8483), is an excellent place to stay. Built in 1878, five of 31 rooms have been converted for guest use, each distinctively furnished with individual character. Other features include a beautiful billiard room, lounge with open fire, and magnificent gardens.

One of the Hunter Valley's premier restaurants is the **Old George and Dragon,** 48 Melbourne St., East Maitland (tel. 049-33-7272), a historic hotel restored magnificently with three dining areas; open for lunch Tues.-Fri. and dinner Wed.-Saturday.

Maitland Tourist Information Centre is in King Edward Park, East Maitland (tel. 049-33-2611); open daily 9:30 a.m.-4 p.m.

Morpeth

Although the streetscape of Morpeth, eight km northeast of Maitland, hasn't changed for over 100 years, its vendors have; blacksmiths, bakeries, and leather merchants have been replaced by over 20 specialty craft shops, making it one of the state's premier towns for shopping.

Cessnock

South of the New England Highway, and gateway to the winegrowing Pokolbin region, Cessnock (pop. 16,000) was first settled in 1826 by Scottish settler John Campbell, who named the town after a castle in his homeland. The town grew as the coal-mining industry developed. I has little of interest to travelers, although the excellent **Cessnock Visitor Information Centre,** southeast of town on Aberdare Rd. (tel. 049-90-4477), is worth visiting. Cessnock is also an alternative to staying in the Pokolbin vineyards area; try **Hunter Valley Motel,** 30 Allandale Rd. (tel. 049-90-1722); $40 s, $50 d.

Pokolbin

As you approach Pokolbin from the south, the most noticeable sight is a distinct lack of vineyards. Even through the mining town of Cessnock, the cleared land is only partly planted, but once you have turned off the New England Highway onto Broke Rd. there's a sudden profusion of wineries, restaurants, and guesthouses; enough to warrant large maps and up to 40 confusing signs at each intersection.

Probably the best part of visiting the wineries of the Pokolbin area is that you don't need to be a wine snob to appreciate their products, and although winegrowers are in the business of selling wine, most appreciate that not everyone is an expert and are happy to help tasters make decisions. To encourage patronage, many wineries have picnic areas, and a couple offer tours or displays of winemaking equipment. Until recently, the wineries were mostly the destination for day-trippers, but in the last few years many accommodations have been developed, some within the vineyards themselves, and a whole range of other activities developed. Without a teetotaling driver, getting around the wineries can be a problem, because, although they are relatively close together, walking isn't practical. **Cessnock Radio Cabs** rents cabs by the hour, and **Grapemobile** (tel. 049-91-2339) has bike tours of the wineries.

At the south end of Pokolbin, on Marrowbone Rd., is **McWilliams Mt. Pleasant Winery** (tel. 049-98-7505), part of Australia's largest family-run wine company. Tours of the winery are offered daily 11 a.m. and 2 p.m., and, as well, there's winetasting. In the same area, **Lindemans Hunter River Winery** (tel. 049-98-7501), part of a winemaking empire known throughout the world, was started by Dr. Henry John Lindeman, who planted vines in the valley in 1843. A museum at the winery displays a large collection of winemaking equipment; it's open Mon.-Fri. 9 a.m.-4:30 p.m., Sat.-Sun. 10 a.m.-

4:30 p.m. Over the hill to the north is **Tulloch's Winery** (tel. 049-98-7503), also over 100 years old and open daily for tasting. **Tyrrell's** (tel. 049-98-7509), owned by the same family since 1858, has a great range of wines for all budgets and has tours of the winery daily at 1:30 p.m. Also on the grounds is the slab-hut family home of the founder, which dates to 1864, as well as a barbecue and picnic area with great views across vineyards to the distinctive Brokenback Range. The above wineries are only a sampling of the larger operations; others worth visiting are **Pepper Tree Wines,** Halls Rd. (tel. 049-98-7539), with a tasting area in a delightful barn surrounded by colorful gardens, and **Oakvale Winery,** Broke Rd. (tel. 049-98-7520), which has a bookshop featuring a great variety of wine-related literature.

Pokolbin Accommodations and Food

The best value accommodation in the Pokolbin area is **Grapeview Villas,** Thompsons Rd. (tel. 049-98-7630), set on 10 hectares of natural bushland, with views across the valley and west to the Brokenback Range. It is also central to all the wineries and the closest accommodation to Cypress Lakes Golf & Country Club. (The owners are keen golfers, so they'll give you the inside running on the course as well as organize a discount for green fees.) Each of the eight split-level villas is self-contained with a modern kitchen, private balcony with outdoor furniture, separate bedroom, and a small bathroom; other facilities include a pool and barbecue area. Midweek rates are $65 s, $70 d, rising to $120 weekends. A little cheaper, but more basic and farther from the action, is **Hunter Hideaway,** Tuckers Lane (tel. 049-38-2091); $30-40 s, $60-80 d. If you prefer the facilities of a small resort, including a restaurant, bar, and tennis court, **Tallawanta,** Broke Rd. (tel. 049-98-7854), is a good choice; $81-125 s or d. **Hunter Resort,** Hermitage Rd. (tel. 049-98-7777), is part of Hunter Estate, the Valley's largest winery. Rooms aren't huge, but are well-furnished and have a large sliding door opening to a balcony overlooking a small part of the vineyard. Rates are $95 s or d, rising to $130 weekends.

The Hunter Valley's wineries are complemented by a variety of restaurants, many within the larger winery complexes. **Blaxland's**

Restaurant, Broke Rd. (tel. 049-98-7550), built from sandstone blocks hand-hewn by convicts, has a colonial atmosphere. The menu changes daily, but the choice is always varied with main dishes generally under $20; open daily for lunch and dinner. **Arnold's,** Pokolbin Village, Broke Rd. (tel. 049-98-7619), is a little less expensive and serves a great rack of lamb ($17.50). **Hunter Coffee Lounge,** in Pokolbin Estate Vineyard on McDonalds Rd. (tel. 049-98-7828), has a small bistro serving healthy sandwiches and burgers; it's also open for breakfast.

National Parks

On the southern edge of the Hunter Valley, around the foothills of the Great Dividing Range, are three remote and almost inaccessible national parks that protect a landscape dominated by outcrops of sandstone. Extending between Blue Mountains National Park and the Hunter Valley is 488,000-hectare **Wollemi National Park,** the state's largest national park. To the east of Wollemi is 139,861-hectare **Yengo National Park,** featuring deep gorges among the sandstone. Smallest of the three parks, at 69,875 hectares, is **Goulburn River,** dissected by the river for which it's named. Wildlife such as gray kangaroos, wombats, and emus are prolific, while platypuses live in slow-flowing sections of the river.

The Upper Hunter

West of the historic New England Highway town of **Singleton,** the Hunter River flows through picturesque rolling hills backed by the wilderness of three remote national parks. The area features wineries that attract fewer crowds and are more casual than those downstream. The center of the area is the small town of **Denman.** Best known of the wineries is **Rosemount Estate,** dating from

WOLLEMI PINE

For scientists, the discovery of new species is always exciting, but not particularly unusual. But in 1995, when rangers exploring a remote gully within Wollemi National Park stumbled upon a stand of Wollemi pine, the find was of particular importance. For, like the coelacanth fish discovered off Madagascar earlier this century, the species was already known to scientists only through fossils, in this case fossils 150 million years old. Study of these ancient trees is only in its infancy, and, at the very least, the Wollemi pine allows us a glimpse of vegetation that was present when dinosaurs roamed the earth.

1864. Tastings are Mon.-Sat. 10 a.m.-4 p.m., Sunday 10:30 a.m.-4 p.m. It's on Rosemount Rd., west of Denman (tel. 065-47-2467). The only accommodation in town is **Denman Motor Inn,** at 8 Crinoline St. (tel. 065-47-2462); good value at $42 s, $48 d. **Denman Visitors Centre** is in a railway carriage in the center of town (tel. 065-47-2731).

The northern reaches of the Hunter River, around the towns of **Scone** and **Muswellbrook,** are the heartland of Australia's thoroughbred industry, with the scenery of green fields and white fences seemingly never-ending. Scone is known as "Horse Capital of Australia" and has a popular Horse Week each May. **Russley,** a charming B&B, was originally built as the manager's residence for Segenhoe Stud. Although the historic house has lost none of its original charm, rooms are decorated in a modern style; rates are $80-100 s or d. It's east of Scone, just off the road out to Glenbawn Dam (tel. 065-43-7230).

NORTH-CENTRAL NEW SOUTH WALES

In the north of the state, between the western slopes of the Great Dividing Range and endless plains to the west, is an area rich in mineral deposits and cleared for a thriving agricultural industry. The most interesting feature of this part of the state is the Warrumbungle Range, ancient mountains rising from surrounding plains in astounding formations. Farther west, along the Castlereagh Highway, is Lightning Ridge, a small town serving miners working the world's largest known concentration of black opal. From Sydney, the quickest way to access north-central New South Wales is through the Hunter Valley on the New England Highway or, from the south, the Newell Highway, the most direct route between Melbourne and Brisbane.

To the east is the New England region, a high plateau along the Great Dividing Range north of the Hunter Valley. On its eastern slopes are spectacular escarpments, waterfalls, and gorges, most of which are protected by national parks. The main route through the region is the New England Highway, which starts in Newcastle and runs north through the Hunter Valley to Queensland. Tamworth, largest of the New England towns, is the Australian capital of country music.

Beyond the Black Stump

The Black Stump Wine Saloon, named for a nearby creek, was one of many such watering holes scattered across the country in the days of horse travel. Located at the junction of trails leading west to Coonabarabran and north to Gunnedah, it traded for only 40 years, and today no sign of it remains, but, unwittingly, it has become one of Australia's best-known pubs. "Beyond the Black Stump," meaning beyond civi-

lization, has become part of the Australian language. The site of the saloon is marked with a black stump at a rest area 10 km north of the small agricultural town of **Coolah,** 159 km northwest of Muswellbrook.

Coolah Tops, east of Coolah, is worth exploring if you have the time and inclination. Linked geologically to the Warrumbungle Range to the west and the Great Dividing Range to the east, the area is a high ridge rising to an elevation of 1,240 meters. The main access is **Warung Forest Rd.;** it follows a north-facing escarpment and passes waterfalls, lookouts, two camping areas, and a forest of snow gums.

Coonabarabran

They say the night sky around Coonabarabran is bigger and blacker and the stars brighter than anywhere else in the country. And after camping out in the Warrumbungles, you'll probably agree. A low horizon and high percentage of cloudless nights combine to make Coonabarabran an ideal location for stargazing. The 17-story **Siding Spring Observatory,** housing Australia's largest optical telescope, is located on 610-meter Siding Spring Mountain from where it is claimed you can see one-sixth of the state. Tours of the complex are offered daily 9:30 a.m.-4 p.m.; $5 pp. It's located 15 km west of town on National Park Rd. (tel. 068-42-6211). **Skywatch Observatory** is a commercial operation taking advantage of the dark skies. Night viewing begins daily at 7:30 p.m., but the complex is open a couple of hours earlier for you to wander around various displays. Admission is adult $7.50, child $5. Located two km west of town (tel. 068-42-2506).

Imperial Hotel, 70 John St. (tel. 068-42-1023), has the least-expensive rooms in town; $26 s, $40 d, includes breakfast. **Amber Court Motel,** north of town (tel. 068-42-1188), and **El Paso Motel,** south of town (tel. 068-42-1722), both have double rooms under $50.

The **Tourist Information Centre** is on the south side of town and is open daily 9 a.m.-5 p.m. (tel. 068-42-1441).

On 1 August 1997 telephone numbers in this section with the area code (068) will change. To dial the new number, simply add the last two digits of the existing area code to the old number. As an example, (068) 12-3456 becomes 6812-3456. The new area code for these numbers will be (02).

NORTH-CENTRAL NEW SOUTH WALES

QUEENSLAND
NEW SOUTH WALES

TO ST. GEORGE

MACINTYRE RIVER

HWY 39

LIGHTNING RIDGE

CASTLEREAGH RIVER

GWYDIR RIVER

GWYDIR

MOREE

HWY 38

NEWELL RIVER

55

BARWON

WALGETT

55

NAMOI

PILLIGA

CUTTABRI

WEE WAA

AUSTRALIA
TELESCOPE

MT. KAPUTAR
(1,524 m) ▲

NARRABRI

MT. KAPUTAR
NATIONAL
PARK

39

37

BAAN BAA

CASTLEREAGH RIVER

BOGGABRI

39

NEWELL HWY

RIVER

COONAMBLE

GUNNEDAH

HWY 34

HWY

SIDING SPRING
OBSERVATORY

WARRUMBUNGLE
NATIONAL
PARK

COONABARABRAN

NEWELL

GULARGAMBONE

55

34 39

OXLEY

TO NYNGAN

34

GILGANDRA

TO DUBBO

RIVER

0   50 km

BLACK
STUMP

COOLAH
TOPS

COOLAH

WARRUMBUNGLE NATIONAL PARK

The Warrumbungle Range rises abruptly from the plains west of Coonabarabran in, as explorer John Oxley said in 1818, ". . . every variety of shape and form that the wildest imagination could ever paint." A 21,000-hectare park protects the most spectacular features of the range, including formations that can be reached only on foot.

The Land

Around 13 million years ago this part of the country was the center of much volcanic activity. As molten rock spewed from faults in the earth's crust, layers of lava built up, forming a mountain range. This period of activity ended when the volcanic vents became blocked with tough trachyte. Over time, as erosion wore away the crater, the plugs remained as spires of rock rising from the forest. The most spectacular of these is the 90-meter **Breadknife,** a cast of a massive crack that formed in the side of a main crater.

The harsh climate and lack of soil on the northern slopes create a very different environment than that of the southern slopes where rainfall is higher. In spring, flowering plants create a profusion of color around lower elevations, with 25 species of wattle alone. Gray kangaroos, red-necked wallabies, and possums are common around the campground. Around 175 species of birds have been recorded in the park.

Hiking

The park has 35 km of linked trails, allowing combinations that take in all the most spectacular geological features. The two main trails are **Grand High Tops** and the one to the summit of **Mt. Exmouth.** Grand High Tops crosses Spirey Creek 12 times before passing the base of the Breadknife and climbing a ridge to some fantastic views. This trail is 12.5 km round-trip, or 15 km if you take **Gould's Circuit** to the summit of Febar and Macha Tors, where good views extend across the valley. To get to the trailhead take the first left west of the Visitor Centre road.

The six-km (one-way) trail to Mt. Exmouth begins farther west, just beyond Camp Wambelong. Shorter trails lead around Camp Blackman and to Belougery Split Rock.

Practicalities

Camp Blackman, beyond the Visitor Centre, has semiprivate sites and excellent facilities, including showers and a laundry. Unpowered sites are $10, powered sites $15. **Camp Wambelong,** west of the Visitor Centre, and **Camp Pincham,** a short walk from Grand High Tops trailhead and drinking water. Along the hiking trails are five primitive campgrounds ($2 per night) and one hut.

The **Visitor Centre,** featuring an interesting audiovisual display, is open daily 8:30 a.m.-4 p.m. (tel. 068-25-4364).

WARRUMBUNGLE NATIONAL PARK: HIKING TRAILS AND FACILITY AREA

NORTH ALONG THE NEWELL HIGHWAY

The road between Coonabarabran and Narrabri passes through half a million hectares of pilliga scrub. The area was heavily grazed by cattle last century, stripping the land of the soil, encouraging the growth of a hardy cypress pine-like tree, and rendering the land useless.

Narrabri and Vicinity

This town of 7,500, 118 north of Coonabarabran, is in an area famed for cotton-growing. The cotton industry in the Narrabri region didn't begin until the 1960s but now dominates the landscape, and is especially picturesque in late fall when the cotton balls have opened.

The **Australia Telescope,** 20 km west of Narrabri on Yarrie Lake Rd. (tel. 067-90-4000), is the most powerful telescope in the country. It is a radio telescope, using images from radio signals received in six massive dishes that move along an eight-km rail line. The radio signals are processed by computers that translate them into visual pictures. An information center at the facility is open daily 8 a.m.-4 p.m.

At **Cuttabri,** beyond the telescope and along the road to Walgett, is Australia's only remaining wine shanty. Predating the era of beer in Australia, wine shanties were scattered along all major bush roads. This particular one served travelers on the road between Narrabri and Walgett and, unlike all others, is still operational. Drinkers have a choice of two drinks, Red Dog (port and Coke) or Brown Dog (muscat and Coke). It's open whenever the licensee has a customer to serve, which, more often than not, is most of the time.

Mount Kaputar National Park

Mt. Kaputar (1,524 meters), protected by a 36,800-hectare national park, is Australia's highest peak away from the Great Dividing Range—and you can drive right to the summit. The Nandewar Range, part of which the park encompasses, is an ancient volcano that has long since eroded, leaving only the layer of lava that spewed from its vents 18 million years ago. The main access road leads east from Narrabri, ending at the summit (53 km one-way) and **Dawsons Spring Campground,** which has hot showers. For bookings, call (067) 92-4724. At the north end of the park (access from the Newell Hwy. north of Narrabri) is **Sawn Rocks** a 40-meter-high basalt wall comprising octogonal rock columns that soar skyward.

Moree

Moree is a large agricultural service center straddling the Gwydir River 100 km north of Narrabri Artesian bores in town are tapped into baths for therapeutic bathing; $2.50. Open during daylight hours.

CASTLEREAGH HIGHWAY

Beginning at Dubbo, 410 km northwest of Sydney, the Castlereagh Highway heads in a northerly direction before turning into a dusty track somewhere near the Queensland border north of Lightning Ridge.

Gilgandra is a good starting point for traveling the Castlereagh Highway, as it's an easy day's drive from Sydney. The town's main attraction is **Gilgandra Observatory,** owned and operated by Jack Estens, a local resident whose zest for astronomy never seems to wane. The observatory is open for day viewing Thurs.-Mon. 2-4 p.m. and for night viewing Thurs.-Mon. dusk-10 p.m. It's on Wanboin Rd. (tel. 068-47-2646).

Walgett

Walgett is on the Barwon River, one of a dozen rivers that flow westward from the Darling Downs to the Darling River. Walgett was the birthplace of the **Wolseley Shearing Machine,** which radically changed the face of the shearing industry. Today, the town has 2,500 residents and is popular as a base for fishing the Barwon, Narran, Castlereagh, and Macquarie Rivers.

The pubs in town can't really be recommended for a quiet night's sleep; instead, stay at the **Walgett Motel,** 14 Fox St. (tel. 068-28-1355); $50 s or d. For town information, head to **Walgett Shire Council Chambers,** also on Fox St. (tel. 068-28-1399); open Mon.-Fri. 8:30-4:30 p.m.

LIGHTNING RIDGE

Lightning Ridge, a dry, dusty frontier town of 3,000, near the end of the Castlereagh Highway, 760 km northwest of Sydney, is synonynous with opal. Hundreds of small-scale mining operations around the area produce most of the world's black opal, Australia's national gemstone. Opal is found in varying qualities in the United States, Mexico, and Brazil, but the black opal of Lightning Ridge, reflecting all colors of the spectrum off the dark body of rock, has few equals in the world. Its name, Lightning Ridge, originated in the 1870s when a drover was killed by lightning while sheltering from a storm on a ridge.

Sights

Surrounding the town are an estimated 1,000 claims, each mined by small-time operators, hoping against hope for the same success that prospectors had at Nebea Hill in the 1970s when $3 million worth of opal was extracted from one mine in two years. You don't need a license to fossick on abandoned mullock heaps—they are strewn with chips of boulder opal, and there's always a chance of finding a good one. Stephen and Lesley Henley offer tours of their mine and a demonstration of opal cutting daily at 10 a.m.; the mine is on Three Mile Rd. (tel. 068-29-0247). **Walk-in Mine,** on Bald Hill (tel. 068-29-0473), is a similar setup, with tours departing at 9 a.m. and an audiovisual shown regularly. **Spectrum Opal Mine,** Bald Hill Rd. (tel. 068-29-0581), has an underground showroom chock-full of spectacular opals, including one worth over $80,000. They show a film here hourly, and aboveground is an area for fossicking and a picnic area with barbecues.

If you want to buy opal, Lightning Ridge is the place to do it, as prices often double by the time the opals reach the east coast. Opal shops line Opal and Manilla Streets. Often, cheaper opals are from other parts of Australia, so, if having an opal from Lightning Ridge is important to you, ask before you buy. You can buy good chunks of "solids" for under $100. Top-quality black opal sells for about $3000 per carat.

The Ridge is also known for artesian bores, bubbling out of the ground at around 40° C (104° F). The therapeutic powers of the water have soothed the muscles of work-weary miners for a hundred years, but also attract visitors whose arthritic conditions are claimed to improve in the water. The pools are open 24 hours; admission is free.

Accommodations and Food

Lightning Ridge Motor Village is a four-hectare complex with accommodation styles to suit all budgets. Motel rooms with private facilities are $50-59 s, $65-69 d; unpowered sites $9, powered sites $11. On-site is a bistro, bar, and restaurant, and a small area is set aside for fossicking. It's west of town on Onyx St. (tel. 068-29-0304). **Black Opal Motel,** Opal St. (tel. 068-29-0518), has basic rooms for $51 s, $59 d, each with a safe for those precious opals. Another inexpensive option is **Lightning Ridge Caravan Park,** Harlequin St. (tel. 068-29-0532), where basic on-site vans are $25, cabins are $42, and sites for tents and vans are $9-11.

Digger's Rest Hotel, Opal St. (tel. 068-29-0404), serves bistro meals noon-2 p.m. and 6-8 p.m. If you're after more than steak and mashed potatoes go to the **bowling club** on Morilla St. (tel. 068-29-0408), or, for Chinese, try **Miner's Mate Restaurant** on Opal St. (tel. 068-29-0215).

Transportation, Services, and Information

Log Cabin Opal Shoppe, 47 Morilla St. (tel. 068-29-0277), is the agent for long-distance bus companies serving the town, including Transcity, McCafferty's, and Sid Foggs, and rail bookings. A Countrylink bus/rail ticket between Sydney and Lightning Ridge is $67 one-way.

Apart from its remote location, Lightning Ridge is like any similar-sized town, with all expected services including a doctor (tel. 068-29-0416), post office, supermarket, bakery, banks, butchers, and gas stations (80-90 cents a liter for fuel). The **Tourist Information Centre** is on Fred Reece Way (tel. 068-29-0565); open Mon.-Fri. 8:30 a.m.-4:30 p.m.

TAMWORTH

This sprawling city of 35,000, 400 km northwest of Sydney, is Australia's country music capital. Country music in Australia doesn't have the following it does in the United States, but each January, when thousands of fans descend on Tamworth for the Australian Country Music Festival, the spirit is certainly there. For the other 51 weeks of the year, Tamworth uses its reputation as the home of country music to lure visitors off the highway.

TAMWORTH

TO MANILLA

TAMWORTH BASE HOSPITAL

OXLEY PARK

OXLEY SCENIC LOOKOUT

SEE DETAIL

RIVERSIDE

PARK

TAMWORTH WORKMEN'S CLUB

TAMWORTH CAFE

MATILDA'S FAMILY STEAKHOUSE

POWERHOUSE BOUTIQUE MOTOR INN

TAMWORTH VISITORS CENTRE AND BUS DEPOT

PARADISE CARAVAN PARK

TO AIRPORT AND COONABARABRAN

GOLF COURSE

COUNTRY CAPITAL MOTEL

TO MOONBI AND ARMIDALE

TO MOONBI AND ARMIDALE

RILEY'S MOTEL AUSTRALIA

COUNTRY COLLECTION AND LONGYARD HOTEL

GOLDEN GUITAR

ALANDALE FLAG INN

TO HUNTER VALLEY

0 ___ 1 km

DETAIL

POWER STATION MUSEUM

RIVERSIDE

OLD VIC CAFE

CENTRAL HOTEL

RAILWAY STATION

HANDS OF FAME

AUSTRALIAN COUNTRY MUSIC FOUNDATION

TAMWORTH CITY GALLERY

PARK

The Golden Guitar marks the southern gateway to Tamworth.

Country Music Sights

The names won't be familiar to overseas visitors and even most Australians), but the format will— a hall of fame, handprints in the footpath, and a museum full of music memorabilia. Coming into town from the south, it is impossible to miss Country Collection and the **Golden Guitar,** a 12-meter-high replica of the award handed out annually to Australia's best country musicians. Behind the guitar is **Gallery of Stars,** featuring wax models of various country music stars; admission adult $4, child $2. Open daily 9 a.m.-5 p.m. Back in town is **Hands of Fame,** on Kable Street. The **Australian Country Music Foundation,** 93 Brisbane St. (tel. 067-66-9696), has changing exhibitions in a historic building (adult $8, child $5) and is working toward establishing a museum in Tamworth dedicated to Australian country music. Tamworth's three major recording studios can be toured, but prior appointments must be made through the Visitors Centre.

Other Sights

Tamworth was the first town in Australia to have electric streetlights; the original power station has been restored as a museum, with a steam-powered generator displayed, along with a whole lot of other early memorabilia. It's open Tues.-Fri. 9 a.m.-1 p.m., and, best of all, admission is free; located at 216 Peel St. (tel. 067-64-1293). **Marsupial Park,** in Oxley Park, is an area of native bushland with kangaroos, wallabies, possums, and birds; open daily 8 a.m.-5 p.m., and admission is free. Located at the end of Brisbane Street. At the end of White St. is **Oxley Scenic Lookout,** which provides panoramic views of the city and surrounding plains. **Tamworth City Gallery,** 203 Marius St. (tel. 067-68-4459), has an excellent collection of Australian paintings; open Mon.-Fri. 10 a.m.-5 p.m., Saturday 9-11:30 a.m., Sunday 1-4 p.m. For a different type of art, head to **Fred Hillier's Ceramic Gallery,** 18 km north of Tamworth at Moonbi. Best known for his ceramic dunnies, all Hillier's work is unique and original.

Australian Country Music Festival

Every January, Tamworth's population doubles as country music fans descend on the city for 10 days of celebrations. The entire city comes alive with 800 events and nearly 6,000 hours of live music, and the best part of it is that most of it is free. The official reason for the festival is the annual **Australian Country Music Awards** (tickets needed), but most of the fun occurs outdoors—at the Star Makers Quest, Country Music Cavalcade, Poets Corner, Chute Out Rodeo, and duck races; hundreds of buskers perform on the streets. Make accommodation bookings well in advance for this weekend.

Accommodations

Central Hotel, corner Peel and Brisbane Streets (tel. 067-66-2160), has rooms with shared bathrooms for $20 s, $32 d. Tamworth has dozens of motels, and although none are cheap, the standard is generally high. **Riley's Motel Australia,** 354 New England Hwy. (tel. 067-65-9258), is a couple of km south of town but has reasonable rates at $35 s, $40 d. Farther south, beyond the Longyard Hotel, is **Alandale Flag Inn** (tel. 067-65-7922), famous for its guitar-shaped swimming pool; $63 s, $69 d. **Country Capital Motel,**

193 Goonoo Goonoo Rd. (tel. 067-65-5966), has excellent facilities and is only $45 s, $55 d. **Powerhouse Boutique Motor Inn,** on the New England Hwy. east of town (tel. 067-66-7000), is Tamworth's most luxurious accommodation. Rooms are large and elegantly furnished, many having a private spa; $85-100 s or d.

Paradise Caravan Park, Peel St. (tel. 067-66-3120), fronts the Peel River and has a pleasant area set aside for tents. All sites are $12, and basic on-site vans start at $26 per night.

Food

Many of Tamworth's eateries are on Peel St., while better restaurants are located in the motels. **Tamworth Cafe,** 282 Peel St. (tel. 067-66-4830), has fast efficient service and good food; open daily 9 a.m.-9 p.m. Farther along, at 261 Peel St. (tel. 067-66-3435), is **Old Vic Cafe,** serving healthy breakfasts ($5-9) and lunches ($6-11). **Matilda's Family Steakhouse,** corner Peel and Murray Streets (tel. 067-66-5133), is a great buffet restaurant with lunches starting at $8 and dinners at $10. Tamworth's many clubs offer some great dining bargains; try **Tamworth Workmen's Club,** Reserve Place, West Tamworth (tel. 067-65-9291).

South of town, behind the Golden Guitar, **Longyard Hotel** (tel. 067-65-3411) has a large beer garden and bistro that serves meals daily from 11 a.m. Of the motel restaurants, **Monty's,** in the Powerhouse Boutique Motor Inn, New England Hwy. (tel. 067-66-7000), is the pick of the bunch. The menu features mainly seafood, but steak and chicken dishes are also excellent and prices of main dishes run mostly $14-19; their breakfast is also good.

Transportation, Services, and Information

Eastern Australia (tel. 067-66-8400) and **Tamair** (tel. 067-61-5000) have regular services between Sydney and Tamworth. The airport is west of town (a $10 cab ride). The **bus depot** is part of a modern complex on the corner of Peel and Murray Streets. All major bus lines stop at Tamworth, each with at least one service daily. In addition, **Border Coaches** (tel. 1800-02-8937) runs daily services from Tamworth to Sydney and Melbourne, and **King's Bus Service** (tel. 1800-62-5587) runs

three times weekly between Tamworth and Port Macquarie via Armidale and Coffs Harbour. **Tamworth Railway Station** is on Bridge St. (tel. 067-66-2357) or 13-2232, with daily Xplorer service south to Sydney and north as far as Moree.

From the main bus depot, **Tamworth Coaches** (tel. 067-66-2840) runs around the city and to outlying towns. For a rental car, call **Avis** (tel. 067-65-2000) or **Budget** (tel. 067-66-7255).

Tamworth Base Hospital is on Dean St (tel. 067-66-1722). The excellent **Tamworth Visitors Centre** is at the corner of Peel and Murray Streets (tel. 067-66-9422); open daily 9 a.m.-5 p.m.

VICINITY OF TAMWORTH

Fossickers Way

The Fossickers Way, so named for a variety of gemstones that you can find en route, is a designated tourist route between Tamworth and Inverell, rejoining the New England Highway at Glen Innes. The information center at Barraba has details of all the best fossicking areas; 30 km west of this town is **Horton Falls.**

Bingara and the surrounding area are noted for diamonds. The town has some historic buildings along the main drag. At **Upper Bingara** to the south, once a thriving town of thousands of miners, gold can still be found.

Farther north, on the Gwydir Highway, is **Warialda,** where agate, jasper, and petrified wood are also found. **Cranky Rock,** eight km east of Warialda, is a group of massive granite boulders through which Reedy Creek flows. The unusual name is said to come from a cranky Chinese man who jumped to his death from one of the rocks.

The last town along the Fossickers Way, and also the largest, is **Inverell,** located in an area known for sapphires.

Oxley Wild Rivers National Park

This 90,276-hectare park encompasses a number of spectacular gorges and escarpments along the Great Dividing Range east of Tamworth. The park, a high plateau through which over 500 km of rivers flow, is divided into many sections, all accessible by regular vehicle.

TO BRISBANE

15 HWY.

TO GOLD COAST

NEW ENGLAND

BRUXNER

44

QUEENSLAND

NEW SOUTH WALES

BALD ROCK
NATIONAL PARK

BOONOO BOONOO
NATIONAL PARK

44

TO
BALLINA

MT. LINDESAY HWY.

TENTERFIELD

RANGE

WASHPOOL
NATIONAL PARK

TO
GRAFTON

MACINTYRE

WARIALDA

FOSSICKERS

DELUNGRA

38

WAY

GWYDIR

GIBRALTAR
RANGE
NATIONAL
PARK

38

HWY.

NEW ENGLAND HWY.

BINGARA

GWYDIR

INVERELL

RIVER

GLEN INNES

DIVIDING

GUY
FAWKES
RIVER
NATIONAL
PARK

TO
GRAFTON

FOSSICKERS

RIVER

BARRABA

HORNTON
FALLS

NEW

DUNDURRABIN

15

CATHEDRAL ROCK
NATIONAL PARK

EBOR

NEW
ENGLAND
NATIONAL
PARK

LAKE
KEEPIT

GREAT

ARMIDALE

WOLLOMOMBI
FALLS

OXLEY

WAY

URALLA

OXLEY WILD RIVERS
NATIONAL PARK

34

OXLEY

HWY.

ENGLAND

OXLEY

HWY.

TAMWORTH

WALCHA

OXLEY

BUDDS
MARE

WILD RIVERS

NEW

APSLEY
GORGE

NATIONAL

TIA
FALLS

50 km

PARK

34

TO
PORT
MACQUARIE

TO NEWCASTLE

15

HWY.

Apsley Gorge, 18 km east of Walcha, is one of the park's most spectacular features. Viewing platforms have been set up around a waterfall at the head of the gorge, and a teahouse is open daily 10 a.m.-5:30 p.m. Farther east is **Tia Falls. Budds Mare,** accessible on a gravel road from Walcha, provides more panoramic views and access to a remote part of the park. Some areas of the park extend north to Armidale, and include **Wollomombi Falls,** Australia's highest waterfall, located 40 km east of Armidale. Camping is permitted at all picnic areas.

Uralla

The rolling hills around Uralla were the stomping grounds for **Thunderbolt,** one of the Australia's most infamous bushrangers. His reign of terror through the New England region spanned two decades in the mid-1800s. His favorite haunt was a jumbled pile of granite boulders south of Uralla, from where he had views of approaching travelers and mail coaches. Now buried in Uralla Cemetery, he met his demise east of the rocks when he was brought down by gunfire from a plucky constable. **McCrossin's Mill,** a three-story building dating from 1870, houses memorabilia from Thunderbolt's era, including gold-mining and Aboriginal relics; open daily noon-5 p.m., and admission is $3.50.

Bushranger Motor Inn (tel. 067-78-3777) features large rooms with modern facilities; $57 s, $65 d. **Lindon House Antiques and Tea Rooms,** on the main drag, is open daily for Devonshire teas. **Uralla Tourist Information Centre,** in the center of town (tel. 067-78-4496), is open Mon.-Fri. 9 a.m.-6 p.m.

ARMIDALE

Armidale is a large educational and agricultural service center of 23,000 on the New England Highway 110 km north of Tamworth. Located at an altitude of 1,000 meters, summers are relatively cool. The town's main employer is the **University of New England,** established in 1938 and now with an enrollment of 14,500 students.

Sights

Within a dozen blocks of downtown are many historic buildings, most of which are seen on the **Armidale Heritage Drives;** a brochure available from the Tourist Information Centre details each one. **Saumarez Homestead,** southwest of town on Saumarez Rd. (tel. 067-72-3616), is an impressive home built late last century for a wealthy grazier family; open for tours daily at 2 p.m. and Sat.-Sun. 3 and 4 p.m. Back in town on the corner of Faulkner and Rusden Streets, is **Armidale Folk Museum** (tel. 067-73-8536) open daily 1-4 p.m. **New England Regional Art Museum,** Kentucky St. (tel. 067-72-5255) boasts an impressive collection of Australian artworks; open Mon.-Sat. 10 a.m.-5 p.m., Sunday 1-5 p.m., and admission is $5.

Accommodations and Food

Wicklow Hotel, corner Marsh and Dumaresc Streets (tel. 067-72-2421), is right opposite the bus station and near downtown. Basic rooms start at $18 s, $24 d, and there are a few dorm beds for $12 pp. Armidale has no really cheap motels; most start at around $50 d. **Cedar Lodge,** 119 Barney St. (tel. 067-72-9511), is right downtown, and rooms start at $48 s, $58 d. **Deer Park Motor Inn,** 2.6 km north of town on the New England Hwy. (tel. 067-72-9999), has large rooms of an excellent standard, a heated indoor pool, cocktail bar, and spa; $46 s, $54 d. **Pembroke Caravan and Leisure Park,** corner Grafton and Cooks Roads (tel. 067-72-6470) two km east of town, has facilities of an excellent standard; unpowered sites $12.50, powered sites $14.50, on-site vans $24-32, cabins $34-52. Another option for campers is to head east to the national parks detailed below.

Being a university town, there's a wide variety of inexpensive cafes and restaurants to choose from, many spread along Beardy St pedestrian mall. **QC's Tea & Coffee House,** Hanna's Arcade, Beardy St. (tel. 067-72-6266) a popular student hangout, has good inexpensive food; open daily 8:30 a.m.-5 p.m. **Chocolates and Fine Things,** 119 Beardy St. (tel. 067-71-2171), has a variety of coffees and mouthwatering homemade cakes and chocolates. For a casual lunch, head four km south of Armidale to **The Berry Best,** a cafe/restaurant on a berry farm. Everything is homemade, and if the tempting array of fruit pies isn't enough sandwiches and hot dishes are also offered (tel. 067-72-5974). **Jitterbug Mood,** 231

Beardy St. (tel. 067-72-3022), is one of Armidale's better restaurants; the setting is elegant, the food and service excellent, with choices ranging from Middle Eastern to vegetarian; open Tues-Sat. from 6:30 p.m.

Transportation, Services, and Information

All major bus lines stop at Armidale on the main Sydney-Brisbane route. **King's Bus Service** (tel. 1800-62-5587) links Armidale to Coffs Harbour ($18.30 one-way). The coach terminal is on the corner of Marsh and Dumaresq Streets (tel. 067-73-8527).

Armidale Visitor's Centre is in the coach terminal (tel. 067-73-8527 or 1800-62-7736). They have a ton of local information and a large parking area (a good place to leave your car if heading into town); open Mon.-Fri. 9 a.m.-5 p.m., Saturday 10 a.m.-5 p.m., Sunday 10 a.m.-4 p.m.

ARMIDALE TO THE COAST

From Armidale, a road winds eastward across the Great Dividing Range to the coast south of Coffs Harbour (172 km) or, spurring north beyond Ebor, to Grafton (205 km). Three very different national parks are accessed from this road, but the first stop should be **Wollomombi Falls,** 39 km east of Armidale. This waterfall, the highest in Australia, is in Oxley Wild Rivers National Park (see "Vicinity of Tamworth," above).

New England National Park

Often shrouded in mist and totally undeveloped, this 30,000-hectare park encompasses a vast tract of rainforest along the eastern extremity of the New England Plateau, and includes many peaks over 1,500 meters. Wildlife is varied and abundant, with 110 species of birds alone recorded. One of the most panoramic viewpoints is **Point Lookout,** at the end of the park access road, where the panorama extends to the Pacific Ocean. From its Banksia Point, seven-km **Lyrebird Walk** follows the escarpment through a fern-filled gully (with a chance to see lyrebirds) and returns along the ridge.

Near the park entrance is **Thungutti Campground;** facilities include cold showers and drinking water. Three rustic cabins are also available; call (066) 57-2309 for reservations.

Cathedral Rock National Park

The main features of this 6,529-hectare park are impressive granite tors for which the park is named. The easiest access to the tors is from Barokee Rest Area, at the end of a 10-km gravel road spurring north off the Armidale-Grafton Road. The 5.8-km summit-circuit trail crosses a wetland before climbing through a forest of eucalypts and banksias and emerging among the massive granite boulders. Camping is available at Barokee or on the other side of Cathedral Rock at Native Dog Rest Area.

Guy Fawkes River National Park

With road access from northwest of Dundurrabin ending at the park border, this is one of the least-visited of the New England national parks. Protecting the watershed of Guy Fawkes River, it is a favorite destination for wilderness whitewater canoe adventurers. From the headwaters, near Ebor, you can travel on the river for days, eventually flowing into the Nymboida then Clarence River. The only designated hiking trails begin from the end of the main access road, where a primitive campground is located. For canoeing information, contact the NPWS in Dorrigo (tel. 066-57-2309).

ARMIDALE TO QUEENSLAND

Glen Innes

As the name suggests, many of this town's earliest settlers were Scottish. They were attracted by the prospect of making their fortunes from the wealth of minerals in the area. Although agriculture keeps this town of 6,000 alive today, fossicking for gems is still productive, and a good reason to stop by. Sapphires are the region's best-known gemstone, but garnet, beryl, and topaz are all found in areas set aside for public use. If you don't have any luck, try the gem shops along Main Street.

Amber Motel, 135 Meade St. (tel. 067-32-2300), has rooms of a high standard for $37 s, $45 d, and **Poplar Caravan Park,** New England Hwy. (tel. 067-32-1514), has a covered kitchen area; powered sites $10, on-site vans $25.

Gibraltar Range and Washpool National Parks

These two parks straddle the Gwydir Highway east of Glen Innes. In 1967, soon after construction of the road between Glen Innes and Grafton, a 17,273-hectare chunk of land was set aside to protect the virgin forests of the Gibraltar Range. Rainforests of the Washpool Creek watershed were at the mercy of loggers until 1982 when a further 28,000 hectares were protected. Combined, these two parks protect the largest remaining area of rainforest in New South Wales. Plantlife in both parks is amazingly diverse, and includes sassafras, corkwood, lilly pilly, yello carabeens, strangler figs, and the largest stand of coachwood in the world. Many rare species of mammals live in the parks, including the long-nosed potoroo and the parma wallaby.

The five-km **Dandahra Falls Walk,** south of the highway, is the most interesting of the many hikes. It follows Surveyors Creek through a beautiful rainforest. On the north side of the highway is **Coombadjha Nature Walk,** beginning from Coachwood Picnic Area and passing through rainforest to a swimming hole.

Campgrounds are located north and south of the highway, and the **Visitor Centre,** at the parks' entrance, is open daily 8:30 a.m.-4 p.m. (tel. 067-32-1177).

Tenterfield

Tenterfield is a surprisingly pretty town, at the junction of the New England and Bruxner Highways. It was the birthplace of entertainer Peter Allen, and the saddlery, run by his grandfather for 50 years, was the source of inspiration for one of his best-known songs, "Tenterfield Saddler." The saddlery is open to the public Mon.-Fri. 9 a.m.-5 p.m.; it's on High St. (tel. 067-36-1478).

From Tenterfield the most direct route to Queensland is the New England Highway, but a more interesting route is Mt. Lindesay Highway (gravel), the original inland route between Sydney and Brisbane.

Boonoo Boonoo National Park

Located 25 km north of Tenterfield along Mt. Lindesay Highway, this 2,695-hectare park is in the heart of "Granite Country," an area of the northern tablelands strewn with granite boulders. Morgan's Gully, along the park access road, was site of a short-lived gold rush late last century, but the most spectacular feature of the park is the Boonoo Boonoo River, which cascades across dozens of granite rock pools (near Cypress Rest Area) before plunging 210 meters to the v\alley floor. At the very end of the access road, a 300-meter trail leads to a viewing platform over the falls and the spectacular gorge beyond, or you can continue along a steep and often slippery track to the valley floor. Camping is allowed at both rest areas.

Bald Rock National Park

West of Mt. Lindesay Highway, this little-known park contains one of the most impressive geological features of New England—Bald Rock. From the park access road, the massif is hidden by towering eucalypts; the only way to appreciate its size is by scrambling to the summit. Rising 200 meters above the surrounding forest, it is Australia's second-largest rock (behind Uluru), measuring 500 meters wide and nearly one km long. Two trails lead to the summit: the most direct route is, naturally, the steepest, and can be slippery early in the morning (follow the white dots); a longer trail climbs steadily but at an easier gradient. Both trails begin from the picnic area. Beyond the picnic area is a campground (bring drinking water).

MID-NORTH COAST

The drive between Sydney or Newcastle and the far north coast of New South Wales can be easily completed in one day, but the 600-odd kilometers of coastline in between offer a variety of national parks, beaches, and charming seaside towns, worthy of as much time as you can afford. The main route north, the **Pacific Highway,** takes a direct route, parallel to the Great Dividing Range and inland from the coast and most seaside towns.

Along the highway are dozens of roads spurring east to towns that come alive during January before reverting to their sleepy selves the other 11 months of the year. One of the least-developed towns is also the southernmost; Seal Rocks has changed little in 80 years. Others, such as Forster and Port Macquarie, are popular year-round. North from Port Macquarie the highway passes a string of picturesque coastal villages, including Crescent Head, Hat Head, and South West Rocks, before it descends to Coffs Harbour, halfway between Sydney and Brisbane and the largest town on the north coast. When the thrills of this activity-packed town wear off, continue north to the national parks of Yuraygir, Bundjalung, and Broadwater.

NEWCASTLE TO PORT MACQUARIE

Myall Lakes National Park

This 31,562-hectare park protects the state's largest coastal lagoon system, separated from the ocean by a sandy strip of beach extending between Port Stephens and the picturesque fishing village of **Seal Rocks.** Around 10,000 years ago the Pacific Ocean extended farther inland than today, and higher areas such as

On 1 August 1997 all telephone numbers in this section will change. To dial the new number, simply add the last two digits of the existing area code to the old number. As an example, (065) 12-3456 becomes 6512-3456. The new area code will be (02).

Seal Rocks, Bombah Point, and Violet Hill were islands. Wave action pushed sand around these islands, eventually creating the sand dunes that are such a dominant part of the park today. **Broughton Island,** two km offshore (one of the original islands that didn't become part of the mainland) is part of the park and a popular dive site. The lagoon system comprises three main lakes—Myall, Boolambayte, and Broadwater—linked by narrow inlets and forming the headwaters of the Myall River, which flows southward behind the dune system for many kilometers before draining into Port Stephens at Tea Gardens. Much of the dune system is covered in grasses, while lower elevations support forests of eucalypts, wattles, banksias, and paperbarks. Gray kangaroos, red-necked wallabies, koalas, and dingos call the park home. Birdlife is prolific, too, with waterbirds such as black swans, herons, egrets, cranes, and pelicans common.

Access to the park is from Hawks Nest, Seal Rocks, or Bulahdelah. An unsealed road traverses the length of the park, but it is generally in bad shape and not recommended for two-wheel drives. From Hawks Nest, a road leads to **Mungo Brush,** a popular camping area. At Mungo Brush, a 500-meter hiking trail leads through a littoral rainforest, and access to both the lake and beach is possible. From Seal Rocks, off the Forster Rd., an unsealed road leads south into the park to **Yagon,** where a great little campground is nestled behind the dunes. For more information on the park, call (049) 87-3108.

Forster

Forster (pop. 11,000) and the smaller town of **Tuncurry** straddle the outlet of **Wallis Lake,** 66 km northeast of the highway town of Bulahdelah. Holidaymakers flock to Forster for great fishing, surfing, and long sandy beaches. Wallis Lake is also famous for oysters, producing two million annually. Some of the best fishing is just meters from the main street. Another way to explore the lake is on the cruiser *Amaroo II;* call (065) 54-7743 to check departure times.

NEWCASTLE TO
PORT MACQUARIE

TO TAMWORTH

OXLEY HWY.

HASTINGS RIVER

TIMBERTOWN

WAUCHOPE

PORT MACQUARIE

KEW

LAKE CATHIE

LAURIETON

MANNING VALLEY RIVER

PACIFIC HWY.

DIAMOND HEAD

WINGHAM

COOPERNOOK

CROWDY BAY NATIONAL PARK

CROWDY HEAD

GLOUCESTER

TAREE

HARRINGTON

NABIAC

HALLIDAYS POINT

TUNCURRY

FORSTER

TO SINGLETON

WALLIS LAKE

DUNGOG

STROUD

BULAHDELAH

MYALL LAKES

SEAL ROCKS

YAGON

TO NEWCASTLE

PACIFIC HWY.

MYALL LAKES NATIONAL PARK

MUNGO BRUSH

TEA GARDENS

PORT STEPHENS

HAWKS NEST

BROUGHTON ISLAND

SOUTH PACIFIC OCEAN

0   20 km

Accommodation will be very difficult to find in summer and during school holidays, so make bookings well in advance. **Lakes and Ocean Hotel,** 10 Little St. (tel. 065-54-6005), has pub-style rooms of a good standard, most with a balcony, for $32 s, $48 d. **Great Lakes Motel,** 24 Head St. (tel. 065-54-6955), is right by the beach and has large comfortable rooms for just $40 s, $48 d. **Dolphin Lodge,** 43 Head St. (tel. 065-55-8155), is affiliated with the YHA; dorm beds are $12, doubles $25. Guests can rent bikes and surfboards.

Local prawns and oysters are sold at various outlets around town; for something casual head to **Little Shell Restaurant,** 6 Head St. (tel. 065-55-6890); open Tues.-Sun. from 6 p.m.

Taree and the Manning Valley

Taree is a busy service town on the banks of the Manning River. There's nothing to see in town but to the west, **Wingham** and other small Manning Valley towns are interesting. Many historic buildings line Wingham's streets, and a museum (tel. 065-53-5823) is on Farquhar St.; open daily 10 a.m.-4 p.m. Behind the town and alongside the Manning River is Wingham Brush, an area of old-growth subtropical rainforest that has escaped logging. Many thousands of gray-headed flying foxes live in the reserve and their call can be deafening, especially Sept.-April.

Immediately north of Taree is **Manning Valley Tourist Information Centre** (tel. 065-52-1900).

aree to Port Macquarie

t is only 85 km between these two towns, but in-
eresting detours abound. The first is at Cooper-
ook, 22 km north of Taree, where a road fol-
ows the north bank of the Manning River to the
oastal community of **Harrington.** Beyond Har-
ngton is **Crowdy Head,** named by Captain
Cook for a crowd of Aboriginals he sighted on
he headland. Views from this spot are spec-
acular, extending north along Crowdy Beach.
his beach is part of **Crowdy Bay National
Park.** Access to the park itself is from the Pacific
lighway eight km north of Coopernook. The
ark's main feature is a long beach of golden
and that ends in the north at **Diamond Head,** a
20-meter bluff that drops dramatically to the
cean. The park's 8,022 hectares encompass
oastal heath and wetlands where birdlife is
rolific. At the park's north end are three camp-
rounds with firewood supplied, but bring your
wn water. The NPWS, Lord St., Port Macquarie
el. 065-84-2203), has more park information.

PORT MACQUARIE

Port Macquarie (pop. 20,000) is a bustling holiday town at the mouth of the Hastings River,
20 km north of Sydney, where developed areas
prawl around rocky headlands linked by stretch-
s of beach, great for surfing and sunbaking.
land, the quieter waters of the river foster boat-
ng and fishing.

The river mouth was first surveyed in 1818.
Three years later, three ships chock-full of con-
icts and enough food for four months arrived
om Sydney Town. The convicts were put to
vork, and a small penal colony was soon es-
ablished. Once they had served their time,
nany convicts chose to remain in the region,
nd as the population of free settlers increased,
vord of its surrounding beauty spread. By the
urn of this century Port Macquarie had grown to
ecome Australia's first resort town, and has
ontinued to attract tourists for almost a century,
nostly families looking for a quiet getaway.

Sights and Recreation

Port Macquarie's commercial area is sand-
viched between Kooloonbung Creek and the
cean. The main drag, Clarence St., loops
around the mouth of the river, passing a grassy
headland with views northward and Town
Beach below. Overlooking Town Beach is an
old pilot's cottage that has been converted to a
small **maritime museum.** It's open daily 10
a.m.-4 p.m., and admission is $2. **Hastings
District Museum,** 22 Clarence St. (tel. 065-
83-1108), has interesting relics, some dating
to convict days.

One of Port Macquarie's oldest buildings,
Roto House, Lord St. (tel. 065-84-2203), dates
from 1890 and was built using local materials.
After falling into disrepair it was restored in the
1980s and now operates as an NPWS office. In
1966, 12 hectares around the house were set
aside as a reserve for injured koalas, which can
be seen convalescing in cages on the property.
Both are open daily 10 a.m.-4 p.m. Another
good place to view Australian wildlife is **Billabong Koala & Aussie Wildlife Park,** west of
town on the Oxley Hwy. (tel. 065-85-1060). The
koalas are favorites, but the park also has a
large number of kangaroos, wombats, and
emus. Admission is adult $5, child $3.

West from this wildlife park is **Timbertown**
(tel. 065-85-2322), one of the north coast's best-
loved attractions. It's a re-creation of a late 1800s
logging settlement, with a main street lined with
relevant businesses, including a blacksmith,
wood-turner, bakery, and hotel, while horse-
drawn vehicles and steam trains make regular
jaunts around town. Admission is adult $15,
child $6. Open daily 9:30 a.m.-3:30 p.m.

Sea Acres Rainforest Centre (tel. 065-82-
3355) is a 72-hectare reserve of littoral rainforest
south of downtown that extends down to the
beach. A raised boardwalk leads through the
forest, and there's also an audiovisual display
and ecology center. Admission is a steep $8.50.
Open daily 9 a.m.-4:30 p.m.

The **Water Bus Co.** (tel. 065-83-1293) offers Everglades Tours on the Hastings River
and its tributaries. Cruises depart from the west
end of Clarence St. daily at 2 p.m. for Oyster
World, an oyster farm ($15), and Monday,
Wednesday, Fri.-Sun. at 9:30 a.m. for a four-
hour trip ($30) farther upstream. Children are
half price. *Port Venture* (tel. 065-83-3058) also
has two-hour cruises up the river. Boats and
canoes can be rented from **Hastings River
Boat Hire** at Port Marina (tel. 065-83-8811).

PORT MACQUARIE

TO CRESCENT HEAD
(CHECK ROAD CONDITIONS)

SETTLEMENT POINT FERRY

SETTLEMENT POINT RD.

HASTINGS RIVER

PELICAN ISLAND

NORTH BEACH

SOUTH PACIFIC OCEAN

TO KEMPSEY AND PACIFIC HWY

HASTINGS RIVER

PARK ST.

BULLER ST.

Port Marina
Sails Resort

SEE DETAIL

TOWN BEACH

STEWART ST.

BIRD ROCK

HAY ST.

GRANT ST.

MARITIME MUSEUM
OXLEY BEACH
BEACHFRONT REGENCY

Lindel Travellers Hostel

GORDON ST.

LORD ST.

ROCKY BEACH

HILL ST.

ROTO HOUSE AND KOALA RESERVE

FLYNN'S BEACH

TO BILLABONG
WILDLIFE PARK,
WAUCHOPE,
TIMBERTOWN,
AND
PACIFIC HWY.

OXLEY HWY.

LAKE RD.

KOOLOONBUNG CREEK

PACIFIC DR.

NOBBY'S BEACH

KOALA ST.

SHELLY BEACH

SEA ACRES RAINFOREST CENTRE

MINERS BEACH

DETAIL

SUNDOWNER BREAKWALL TOURIST PARK

JETTY

PORT MACQUARIE HOTEL/MOTEL

AL DENTE AND CRAY'S RESTAURANT
INTERSECTION CAFE

MARGO'S CAFE

EL PASO MOTOR INN

CLARENCE ST.

0   1 km

FISHERMEN'S CO-OP

SHORT ST.

HORTON ST.

HAY ST.

MURRAY ST.

MUNSTER ST.

HASTINGS DISTRICT MUSEUM
TOURIST INFORMATION CENTRE

WILLIAM ST.

CHURCH ST.

BEACHSIDE BACKPACKERS

GORDON ST.

N

TO LAKE CATHIE AND KEW

ccommodations

ort Macquarie Hotel/Motel, Clarence St. (tel. 65-83-1011), is right downtown and close to he cruise docks. Pub-style rooms, basic and ith shared facilities, are $25 s, $35 d. Motel ooms are $45 s, $55 d.

The motels close to the beach are reasonably riced, but rooms must be booked in advance r all holiday periods. One of the best values nd a short walk to the beach is **Beachfront Re- ency,** 40 William St. (tel. 065-83-2244), set round a pool and barbecue area. Rooms are 55 s, $67 d. **El Paso Motor Inn,** 29 Clarence St. el. 065-83-1944), is right on the waterfront in wn. Facilities include a pool, spa, recreation om, and restaurant; rates are $65 s or d. The pmarket **Sails Resort** is on Park St. (tel. 065-83- 999), right on the Hastings River and beside e marina. Each room is well appointed and has private balcony. Facilities include a large river- ont pool, tennis courts, steam room, spa, and estaurant. Rates for standard rooms are $120, ose with kitchenettes $140, and executive ooms with water views are $240 s or d.

Beachside Backpackers, 40 Church St. (tel. 65-83-5512), is an associate YHA hostel with- easy walking distance of both the town and each. A variety of activities are organized there, nd it's clean and friendly. Dorms are $12 pp. indel Travellers Hostel, corner Hastings River r. and Gordon St. (tel. 065-83-1791), is away om the beach but has a pool, guests have use f bikes, and drop-offs to the bus depot and each are made. Dorms are $12, twins $24.

Sundowner Breakwall Tourist Park stretch- s along the Hastings River right across from own Beach. Facilities are excellent, and sites re $15-27, on-site vans $30, and cabins from 57. Located at 1 Munster St. (tel. 065-83-2755).

ood

long Clarence St. are cafes and restaurants, in- luding **Intersection Cafe,** 72 Clarence St. (tel. 65-83-5529), with outdoor and indoor tables; pen for breakfast, lunch, and dinner. Also at this nd of town is the **Fishermen's Co-op,** where sh is sold straight from the ocean. **Al Dente,** 74 larence St. (tel. 065-84-1422), an Italian restau- ant overlooking the river, features pastas from 11. In the same building is **Cray's** (tel. 065-83- 885), an upmarket seafood restaurant.

In the historic Garrison Building, opposite the information center, is **Margo's Cafe** (tel. 065-83- 5145). It's open daylight hours.

Transportation, Services, and Information
Port Macquarie is 20 km east of the Pacific High- way, and although buses make the detour, the closest railway station is at Wauchope. By bus, **Lindsay's** (tel. 1800-02-7944) runs daily be- tween Port Macquarie and Sydney ($36 one- way), Armidale ($35), Coffs Harbour ($30), and Brisbane ($45). **Eastern Australia** (tel. 13-1313) and **Impulse** (tel. 13-1381) have daily flights be- tween Port Macquarie and Sydney ($143 one- way), with Impulse continuing north to Brisbane.

Port Macquarie Bus Service (tel. 065-83- 2161) has a regular service around town. **Bud- get** (tel. 065-83-5144) rents cars and bikes.

The **Tourist Information Centre** is on the corner of Clarence and Hay Streets (tel. 065- 84-2987 or 1800-02-5935). The **NPWS** (see above) is based in Roto House (tel. 065-84- 2203).

PORT MACQUARIE
TO COFFS HARBOUR

The most direct route north from Port Macquar- ie is the Pacific Highway, but an interesting al- ternative, if you don't mind a rough road, is an unsealed coastal track that ends at Crescent Head. The road begins on the north side of the Hastings River, accessed by a ferry from Set- tlement Point.

Crescent Head

As the name suggests, this township is on a long sweeping beach. The magnificent beach continues unbroken for many kilometers to the north. When the swell is large, waves bend around the headland becoming near-perfect, often breaking all the way to the beach. The waves are ideal for longboards, and in the 1950s and '60s surfers on the long haul north would make a customary stop at Crescent Head to check out the waves. The town of 950 remains much as it was then, a sleepy holiday hideaway with a well-positioned nine-hole golf course, and a bowling club that comes alive whenever an out-of-town band plays.

Crescent Head Caravan Park (tel. 065-66-0261) is definitely *the* place to stay. Cabins with cooking facilities are $40 per night, and sites are $9-14 (advance bookings necessary in January). **Mediterranean Motel,** 35 Pacific Crescent (tel. 065-66-0303), has rooms for $40, rising to $80 in holidays.

Kempsey

Kempsey is a large town of 10,000 on the Pacific Highway, 50 km north of Port Macquarie. The town serves the farming communities of the rich Macleay Valley, but, for tourists, it has little of interest. **Macleay River Museum and Cultural Centre** is at the south end of town. Next door is **Kempsey Tourist Information Centre** (tel. 065-63-1555).

Hat Head National Park

This 6,448-hectare park stretches along a strip of undeveloped coast northeast of Kempsey. The park is rich with birdlife, which thrives in low coastal scrub, while inland are freshwater lagoons and thick tea tree forests. In the middle of the park is the small community of **Hat Head**, spread along a sandy peninsula, bordered on one side by the sparkling waters of the Pacific Ocean and on the other by the tea tree-stained waters of Korogoro Creek. A hiking trail out to the headland takes in a unique coastal rainforest and sea caves. The town has no motels, but **Hat Head Caravan Park** (tel. 065-65-7501) has on-site vans for $30 and camp sites for $9-13. Within the park, camping is at **Smoky Cape,** in the north end of the national park.

PORT MACQUARIE
TO COFFS HARBOUR

0   20 km

outh West Rocks

t the mouth of the Macleay River, overlooking orseshoe Bay, is this small holiday town of ,500. The first European visitors were convicts ho had mutinied on the ship *Trial* in Sydney arbour and sailed up the coast, smashing into ocks in Horseshoe Bay. The next visitors were so convicts, but these didn't arrive of their own ccord. They were the residents of Trial Bay aol, built on a headland overlooking the bay in 880. The idea was that prisoners would se- ure early release by working on a breakwater at e mouth of the Macleay River. Heavy waves ampered the prisoners' work, reducing the wall a pile of boulders. The prison closed in 1903, eopening during WW I to house German in- rnees. Prison walls still stand, and visitors can alk through the ruins and visit a small museum rammed with relics from the days of the penal olony. Admission is $3.

Below the jail is **Arakoon State Recreation rea** (tel. 065-66-6168), where camping is $10 nd on-site vans are $20 (prices double during chool holidays), with coin-operated showers. ack in South West Rocks is **Horseshoe Bay each Park,** slightly more expensive but with etter facilities and right in town (tel. 065-66- 370). Also in town are three motels, including ay Motel, on Livingstone Ave. (tel. 065-66- 909), where rooms are $45, and $80 in summer.

ambucca Heads

his small resort town of 4,000 is halfway be- ween Kempsey and Coffs Harbour and a cou- e of km off the Pacific Highway. It's one of the rettier spots along the north coast, and out- de of Christmas school holidays, things are etty quiet. The town is spread along the braid- d mouth of the **Nambucca River,** which drains to the ocean between the long sweep of orster Beach and the high bluffs of North Head. hifting sands made the river mouth difficult to ross for loggers in the 1840s, so a breakwater as constructed along the northern river bank. oday logs are transported by road, and the nly vessels using the river are pleasure craft. ishing for flathead, bream, and whiting is great nywhere along the breakwall, while the main urf beach is at the end of Liston Street. Golfers siting town can enjoy the unique opportunity of aying a course on an island in the river.

If all you're after is an inexpensive room for the night, the motels out on the highway will suffice. In the off season, rooms are around $30; try **Jabiru Motel** (tel. 065-68-6204), which has a laundry and pool. Best value of accom- modations in town is **Miramar Motel** (tel. 065- 68-7899). Rooms are $40 s, $49 d, and are of an excellent standard. **Nambucca Back- packers Hostel,** 3 Newman St. (tel. 065-68- 6360), has a relaxed atmosphere and good fa- cilities, and the managers can arrange white- water rafting trips. Beds are $13 pp, whether in a dorm or double. Caravan parks are strung out south of town, but the best and most central is **White Albatross Holiday Centre,** Welling- ton Dr. (tel. 065-68-6468). It can get crowded in summer holidays, but the rest of the year it's quiet. Facilities include barbecues, a kitchen, laundry, bistro, restaurant, tennis court, and car wash. Tent sites are $11, powered sites $13.50, on-site vans a reasonable $22, and cabins $35-38.

Nambucca is on the main rail line north, with the station three km west of town, out on Bowra Street; the fare from Sydney is $58. Long-dis- tance buses stop out on the highway; north- bound at Aukaka Motel and southbound at the Shell service station. The fare to Sydney is $42 and to Byron Bay $38.

The **Tourist Information Centre** is beside the post office on Ridge St. (tel. 065-68-6954); open daily 9 a.m.-5 p.m.

BELLINGEN AND VICINITY

Bellingen, a small town west of Urunga, is home to many alternative-lifestylers who've escaped mainstream living, though they aren't as radical as those farther north. Their arts and crafts, mostly displayed at the **Old Butter Factory,** definitely make a detour worthwhile. The town also has a museum open daily 2-4 p.m. **Oasis Cafe,** in the Old Butter Factory, rents canoes for $10 per hour or $32 per day. On the third Saturday of each month the town hosts a large market.

Dorrigo National Park

Well away from the coast, and west of Bellingen, this park of 7,800 hectares encompasses part of the Dorrigo Plateau and an escarpment that drops 900 meters into the Bellinger Valley. The steep-sided valleys off the plateau are covered in a lush subtropical rainforest, thriving in an area receiving 2,500 millimeters of rainfall annually. Dominant trees are strangler figs with chunky aboveground root systems, towering red cedars, and black booyangs, easily recognizable for their buttresses. Fauna is less diverse, and most species in the park are nocturnal; look for pademelons and gray kangaroos feeding in cleared areas at dusk.

Dorrigo Rainforest Centre (tel. 066-57-2309) has impressive displays explaining the various rainforest types. As well, an elevated boardwalk extends from the center above the rainforest canopy. The center is at the park entrance on the Dorrigo-Bellingen Road; open daily 8:30 a.m.-4:30 p.m.

The 5.8-km **Wonga Walk,** beginning from the rainforest center, passes waterfalls and a lookout before returning through a forest of towering eucalypts. At the end of the park access road is **Never Never Picnic Area** and more hiking opportunities, including the 6.4-km **Cedar Falls Trail.**

Camping is not allowed in the southern section of the park, although near the end of Slingsbys Rd., northeast of Dorrigo township, bush camping is possible. Between the park entrance and Dorrigo is **Dorrigo Mountain Resort** (tel. 066-57-2564), where powered sites are $12.50 and great little log cabins are $28-42.

COFFS HARBOUR

Coffs Harbour, 550 km north of Sydney, is large resort town of 53,000. It sprawls along 1 km of coastline, sandwiched between the Pacifi Highway and the Pacific Ocean. The man beaches along this stretch of coast coupled wit an ideal year-round climate have led to exter sive tourism development, including world-clas golf courses and big resorts.

The city was named for John Korff, an ear settler, and through time the present spellin has become dominant. Loggers were the area first permanent settlers, their job made easier 1892 when a jetty was constructed in front town. Banana plantations, first developed at th turn of the century, dominate the landscap around Coffs Harbour, and, with the develor ment of the industry, have made Coffs Harbou Australia's major banana-growing area.

Sights

With all the surrounding natural beauty, it's iror ic that Coffs Harbour's most recognizable featur is manmade. It's the **Big Banana,** recently vote one of the world's 10 grossest tourist attrac tions, a monument to the area's biggest industry What was once a convenient photo-session an banana-smoothie stop has grown into a sma theme park, with three different tours offered The basic tour includes a short bus ride to

Big Banana

COFFS HARBOUR

TO BIG BANANA, ZOO, GOOD BEACHES, BANANACOAST CARAVAN PARK, AND BALLINA

BRAY ST.
GREENHOUSE TAVERN

ROYAL PALMS MOTOR INN
COACHMENS INN
PARK
BEACH RD.
OCEAN PARADE MOTEL
PARK BEACH CARAVAN PARK
LITTLE MUTTONBIRD ISLAND

CATHOLIC CLUB
PLANTATION HOTEL
POST OFFICE
WHITEWATER RAFTING PROFESSIONALS
BUS STATION
TOURIST INFORMATION CENTRE

NORTH COAST BOTANIC GARDEN

PET PORPOISE POOL

WORLD OF WHEELS
FISHERMAN'S KATCH
JETTY DIVE CENTRE
PIER HOTEL
RAILWAY STATION

AZALEA ST.
ALBANY ST.
HIGH ST.
COFFS HARBOUR YHA
AUSSIETEL BACKPACKERS

MUTTONBIRD ISLAND

TO BOAMBEE BAY RESORT, BONVILLE GOLF COURSE, DORRIGO N.P., AND SYDNEY

TO AIRPORT

SOUTH
PACIFIC
OCEAN

0   700 m

lookout and a wander through the plantation ($4). The other tours take in a hydroponic glass house ($5) or, on the Grand Tour ($9), all of the above as well as a train ride. The complex is three km north of town on the Pacific Hwy. (tel. 066-52-4355).

Small islands immediately offshore from the city are the breeding grounds of shearwaters (called muttonbirds by hungry settlers). Spring is the main breeding season. The most accessible of the islands is **Muttonbird,** a nature reserve linked to the mainland by a breakwall. Birds remain on the island through April when parents and newly hatched chicks head north for the winter. North of Muttonbird Island is a string of beautiful beaches; head to **Park Beach** for proximity to the city and north to **Sapphire Beach, Emerald Beach,** and **Korora Bay** to escape the crowds.

On the same side of the city as the Big Banana is **Coffs Harbour Zoo** (tel. 066-56-1330), a large facility in a native bushland setting. Suited for kids, it features pony rides and animal petting. Right downtown, at the end of Hardacre St., is **North Coast Botanic Garden,** a pleasant place for a quiet walk or picnic lunch. **Pet Porpoise Pool** has shows daily at 10:30 a.m. and 2:15 p.m. ($9.50), with dolphins, seals, and penguins on display.

Recreation

Named by Captain Cook in 1770, the **Solitary Islands,** northeast of Coffs Harbour, provide an offshore playground for divers and anglers. **Jetty Dive Centre,** 398 High St. (tel. 066-51-1611), organizes dive trips out to the islands, as does **Dive Quest** (tel. 066-54-1930), which operates out of Mulloway, farther up the coast. At the harbor is **Coffs Harbour High Flyers** (tel. 066-51-5200), charging $50 for a half hour of parasailing.

Inland is the remote **Nymboida River,** New South Wales's premier whitewater rafting destination. Its rapids challenge all levels of expertise, but all guides are professionals and anyone with a sense of adventure will have the time of their lives. **Whitewater Rafting Professionals,** 20 Moonee St. (tel. 066-51-4066), operates half-day trips on the river for $95 pp, including transport from Coffs Harbour.

Golfers have the choice of a half dozen courses, with **Bonville International Golf and Country Club** (tel. 066-53-4544), the pick of the bunch.

Accommodations
A few years ago, the only choice was one of a dozen caravan parks or about 40 strip motels lining the Pacific Hwy., but today many world-class resorts have been constructed and two excellent backpacker lodges cater to budget travelers.

Pier Hotel, High St. (tel. 066-52-2110), has large rooms with shared facilities for $18 pp and is close to the harbor and shopping areas. Of the motels out on the highway, many offer advertised rates of $40 d most of the year, doubling in price during school holidays. Other motels are near Park Beach, including **Coachmens Inn,** 93 Park Beach Rd. (tel. 066-52-6044), with a high standard of rooms and a swimming pool and spa; $38 s, $40 d. In the same area is **Ocean Parade Motel,** 41 Ocean Parade (tel. 066-52-6733), right on the beach; $35 s, $38 d. **Royal Palms Motor Inn,** 87 Park Beach Rd. (tel. 066-52-4422), has large rooms for $40 s or d.

The large resorts are north and south of the city. They cater mostly to prebooked holidayers, although good standby rates are offered. **Boambee Bay Resort** (tel. 066-53-2700 or 1800-02-8907) is a 10-minute drive south of Coffs Harbour, but everything you need is here, so the distance from town doesn't really matter. Rooms are huge, and each has a balcony, TV and video, microwave, washing machine, and kitchen. Resort facilities include tennis and squash courts, gym, canoes, snooker rooms, coffee shop, bistro, and restaurant, and the beach is just a short walk away. Rates are $125 s or d.

Coffs Harbour YHA, 110 Albany St. (tel. 066-52-6462), is one km from the center of town

and has a laundry, game room, and lots of spor ing equipment for guest use; staff often arrang day trips to Dorrigo National Park. Dorm bed are $12 pp per night. **Aussietel Backpackers** 312 High St. (tel. 066-51-1871), has similar fa cilities, as well as a pool, and, although farthe from town, is closer to the harbor and beaches Dorms there are $13 pp, and there are a few doubles for $15 pp.

Caravan parks line the Pacific Hwy. sout and north of town, but the most central is **Par Beach Caravan Park,** Ocean Parade (tel. 066 52-3204), right opposite a great swimming an surfing beach. All sites are $12, on-site van $26, and basic cabins $35. **Bananacoast Car avan Park,** four km north on the Pacific Hwy (tel. 066-52-2868), has a pool and tennis cour sites are $12-16, cabins start at $30.

Food and Entertainment
Banana smoothies at the Big Banana are del cious, but mankind can not live on milk shake alone, so for something more substantial, you need to head into town. Along the mall at the to end of High St. are casual eateries, includin the **Short Black Coffee Shop** (Monterey A cade), which serves healthy lunches daily an often has live music Thursday and Friday. **Duc Cottage** (Commonwealth Bank Arcade) ha more of the same, as well as delicious cheese cake for $3.50 a slice. **Coffs Harbour Catholi Club,** 61 High St. (tel. 066-52-1477), has a bistr serving lunch and dinner for $4-8 and beer fo under $2.

Most of the seafood garnered from the ocea around Coffs Harbour finishes up in Sydney but there are still a number of good seafoo joints. The **Fisherman's Katch,** 386 High S (tel. 066-52-4372), is both a takeaway an restaurant. An order of fish and chips is $4-takeaway, while the restaurant boasts a wid variety of seafood with main dishes rangin $11-23. At this end of town are restaurants serv ing cuisine from France, China, and Thailand.

Each of the resorts has bars open t nonguests, but you should check dress regu lations before charging in with thongs and boar shorts on. **Greenhouse Tavern,** corner Pacifi Hwy. and Bray St. (tel. 066-51-5488), is a casu place with three eateries and three bars, in cluding one with a maritime theme, complet with a 12-meter yacht above the bar. Bands often play there weekends. Other places for live music are **Park Beach Hotel,** Ocean Parade (tel. 066-52-3833), and **Plantation Hotel,** Grafton St. (tel. 066-52-3855).

Transportation, Services, and Information

The airport is south of town on Hogbin Dr., a $5 cab ride from the town center. It is served by **Ansett Australia** (tel. 13-1300) and **Impulse** (tel. 13-1381), with regular services between major north coast centers and Sydney. Often no more expensive than the airfare, packages offered by Ansett start at $259 pp, including airfare from Sydney and three nights' accommodation.

Countrylink (tel. 13-2232) runs the **XPT** between Sydney and Coffs Harbour daily. The standard one-way fare is $62 pp, but a better deal is a package that includes round-trip fare and two nights' accommodation from $149 pp. In Coffs Harbour, the railway station is at the end of High St. (six blocks from Aussietel Backpackers).

All long-distance buses stop at Coffs Harbour, with **Lindsay's** (tel. 066-58-3232) heading over the Great Dividing Range to Armidale ($18.30). Sample one-way fares from Coffs Harbour are: Sydney $44, Port Macquarie $30, Nambucca Heads $10, Grafton $12, Byron Bay $32, and Brisbane $41. The main bus stop is on Moonee Street.

Bob Wallis World of Wheels, corner Collingwood and Orlando Streets (tel. 066-52-5102), rents bikes for $8 per hour and $20 per day. For a cab, call (066) 51-3944.

The **Tourist Information Centre** is in a small park on Grafton St. (tel. 066-52-8824); open daily 9 a.m.-5 p.m.

COFFS HARBOUR TO BALLINA

The first town north of Coffs Harbour is **Woolgoolga,** nestled around the southern corner of a sweeping beach, with the Solitary Islands clearly visible a few km offshore. This holiday town of 2,000 has a high population of East Indians, and the unmistakable onion-shaped dome of Guru Nanak Sikh Temple dominates the turn-off to town.

Immediately north are the quiet coastal villages of **Mulloway** and **Arrawarra,** perfect places to laze on the beach for a few days. **Arrawarra Caravan Park** (tel. 066-49-2753) has unpowered sites for $10-16, powered sites for $13-20, and basic cabins for $39-70; it's within walking distance of the beach and a small general store serving delicious fish and chips. Farther north, before the Pacific Highway heads inland to Grafton, is **Red Rock,** named for an abundance of jasper around a headland at the mouth of Corindi River.

Yuraygir National Park

From Red Rock, the Pacific Highway heads inland to Grafton, with the next main coastal access at Yamba, over 100 km to the north. The long stretch of undeveloped coastline in between is protected by Yuraygir National Park, broken by a few small holiday towns that provide basic services for holidaymakers and park visitors. The park currently encompasses 20,000 hectares of beaches, headlands, coastal heath, impenetrable forests of tea tree, and many areas of wetland, with plans to link the three existing sections. Birds such as emus, brolgas, storks, and lorikeets are present, as are gray kangaroos.

Access to the park's central section is along Wooli Rd., which branches off the Pacific Highway 32 km north of Red Rock and 14 km south of Grafton. Picnic and camping areas are available at Minnie Water. For details of the park's northern section, see "Yamba and Vicinity," below.

Grafton

Nestled in the Clarence Valley 85 km north of Coffs Harbour, this proud country town of 22,000 is dominated by streets lined with jacaranda trees. The mighty Clarence River makes a wide loop around town before emptying into the Pacific Ocean at Yamba, to the northeast. Many stately buildings stand around town in testimony to the wealth created by farming through the city's 140-year history. The jail and cathedral are both National Trust-classified and **Schaeffer House,** at 192 Fitzroy St. (tel. 066-42-5212), is open for inspection Tues.-Thurs. 1-4 p.m. and Sunday 2-4 p.m. **Grafton Art Gallery,** 158 Fitzroy St. (tel. 066-42-3177), is in 1880 Prentice

House. Each Spring, the jacarandas come alive with color, an annual event celebrated during the October **Jacaranda Festival.**

One of the least expensive places to stay is **Crown Hotel/Motel,** Prince St. (tel. 066-42-4000), where rooms are $20 s, $28 d; $28 s, $30 d with private bathrooms. Back out on the highway are a couple of cheap motels, including **Hi-way Motel** (tel. 066-42-1588), where rooms are just $32 s, $38 d.

Also on the Pacific Highway side of the river is **Clarence River Tourist Centre** (tel. 066-42-4677); open daily 9 a.m.-5 p.m.

Yamba and Vicinity

Located 14 km east of the Pacific Highway, this resort and fishing town may lack the hype of Coffs Harbour, but its picturesque setting makes it a worthwhile detour. The town is at the mouth of the Clarence River, one of New South Wales's largest waterways. While commercial fishermen use the river only as shelter for their boats, it's a prime fishing spot for amateurs who pull out flathead, flounder, and bream. Just $10 spent at a fishing store, along with some local advice, ensures a good day's fishing. For an extra $15-25 per hour, boats can be rented

COFFS HARBOUR TO BALLINA

from **BP Bait Place** on Yamba Road. Town beaches are partly protected by Yamba Point, especially Yamba Beach, which has a grassy picnic area overlooking it and a rock pool for safe swimming. In the river mouth is **Hickey Island,** which has a stretch of sandy beach.

A few km south of Yamba is **Angourie** and the northern section of Yuraygir National Park. At the very end of the road into Angourie Township is a parking lot overlooking **Angourie Point,** a legendary surf spot that has been drawing surfers with its steep long waves for over 30 years. As the road first enters town, a road forks left to **Blue** and **Green Pools.** Originally quarries for a breakwall at the mouth of the Clarence River, they have long since filled with water, creating safe swimming areas. Blue Pool is the larger of the two and has a natural platform for diving. South of Angourie is Yuraygir National Park (turn off one km before Angourie, then take the first left). The stretch of beach there is beautiful and generally uncrowded. A 10-km one-way trail traverses a spectacular section of coastline, taking in coastal heathland, deserted beaches, and rocky headlands, with back-country camping allowed at three spots en route.

Pacific Hotel, on the best chunk of real estate in town, is on a high bluff overlooking Yamba Beach. Rooms are $18 s, $25 d. It's at 18 Pilot St. (tel. 066-46-2466). **Surf Motel,** 2 Queen St. (tel. 066-46-2200), is also good value at $35 s, $40 d, although prices double during school holidays. **Calypso Caravan Park,** Harbour St. (tel. 066-46-2468), is right in town and on the river. Sites are $10-14, on-site vans $28, and cabins $32.

Iluka

Iluka, over the Clarence River from Yamba, is a small fishing town. An interesting way to travel between the two is on a ferry departing River St., Yamba, four times daily; $3 pp; call (018) 66-4556 for times. Of special interest in Iluka

(apart from a great pub overlooking the river) is the largest chunk of littoral rainforest in New South Wales. It's protected by Iluka Nature Reserve, which extends between town and Iluka Beach. **World Heritage Rainforest Walk** traverses a large section of it before ending at a rocky headland.

Bundjalung National Park

This 17,700-hectare park, extending between Iluka and Evans Head, features 40 km of unspoilt beach backed by coastal heathland and a dune system containing ancient Aboriginal campsites. The road into Iluka skirts the park's southern boundary and passes **Woody Head camping area,** where sites are spread out around a headland flanked by beaches. Facilities at the campground include a kiosk and hot showers. For reservations, call (066) 46-6134.

The main park access is farther north and is signposted from the Pacific Highway south of Woodburn. This road ends at **Black Rocks,** where outcrops of black rock rise from the beach.

Evans Head

Like so many small townships along this coast, fishing and tourism provide a thriving economy for Evans Head. Surfing on the tame beach breaks is popular with tourists, as is fishing in the Evans River. Of special significance to the local Koori is **Goanna Headland,** on the south side of the river. Legend has it that this is where their race first settled in Australia. Farther inland, at the end of Bundjalung Rd., a footbridge leads over Oyster Creek to an ancient Koori campsite with shell middens. Also at Oyster Creek is a kurrajong tree, of special significance to historians because this species is otherwise only found at high elevations of the Great Dividing Range, so it is thought local Koori accidently brought back the seed during a trip inland.

FAR NORTH COAST

Mother Nature has managed to cram some of the country's most spectacular and diverse scenery into a 100-km stretch of coastline in the far north of New South Wales. The southern gateway to the far north coast is Ballina, a popular seaside holiday destination. Immediately north is Byron Bay, where the cultural clash of mainstream dropouts, sunburnt tourists, and the wealthy creates a colorful atmosphere found nowhere else in the country. From Byron Bay to the border, the coast is dotted with small holiday villages, starkly different from the development of the Gold Coast immediately north of the border. Extending 80 km inland from the coast is the hinterland, a region of lush subtropical and temperate rainforests dominated by Mt. Warning, the magma vent of an enormous volcano that erupted over 20 million years ago.

BALLINA

This coastal city of 15,000 is concentrated on a low island at the mouth of the Richmond River. The island is almost entirely developed, but immediately north is a stretch of beautiful beaches rivaling any in the country.

A long breakwall was constructed at the mouth of the river in the 1880s, stabilizing its mouth, and allowing clear transit for shipping. Unintentionally, the wall created a protected swimming beach at **Shaws Bay** and a consistent surf break at **Lighthouse Beach.** The former outlet, under Ballina Head, is now a low-lying area where a deep tidal lagoon provides shark-free swimming and a pleasant shaded area with picnic tables.

Sights

Behind the Tourist Information Centre is **Ballina Naval and Maritime Museum,** featuring *La Balsa,* a small raft that made an epic journey from Ecuador to Ballina; open daily 9 a.m.-4 p.m. Admission by donation.

North of Ballina are two commercial attractions worth visiting. **Thursday Plantation,** four km north, is a tea-tree farm. Tea-tree oil was used by the Koori for its medicinal properties and is now a popular remedy for head colds, blocked sinus, ulcers, cuts, and even arthritis. An audiovisual explains the farming process, and tours of the farm and nursery are offered. Open daily 8:30 a.m.-4:30 p.m. (tel. 066-86-7273). Farther north is **Macadamia Land** (tel. 066-87-8432), with free nut tasting, a sanctuary for native animals, and a cafe.

Recreation

Ballina Quays Marina, west of Ballina near the Big Prawn, is the departure point for *River Princess* and *Richmond Princess,* which regularly cruise the Richmond River; call (066) 87-1216 for details. Also at the marina are rental boats. Rates start at $55 per day for a small runabout and $140 for a large riverboat; for bookings, call (066) 86-4289.

Bream and flathead are easily caught in the Richmond River (a favorite fishing spot is along North Creek between Worm's Place and Cherry St.), and North Wall is a good spot for deepwater fishing.

Ballina Golf Course, Jameson Ave. (tel. 066-86-2766), is open to the public during the week but is generally busy; $15 for 18 holes. **Royal Teven Golf Course** isn't really "royal," but that's the way it's known; green fees $12. Located at Teven, west of Ballina (tel. 066-87-8386).

Accommodations

Central to downtown is **Ballina Heritage Inn,** 229 River St. (tel. 066-86-0505). This place opened in 1993, so there isn't anything historic

---

On 1 August 1997 telephone numbers in this section with the area code (066) will change. To dial the new number, simply add the last two digits of the existing area code to the old number. As an example, (066) 12-3456 becomes 6612-3456. The new area code for these numbers will be (02). The area code for existing eight-digit numbers (Tweed Heads) is (07).

about it. Rooms are large and elegantly furnished, some with spas. Other facilities include a laundry and pool; $63 s, $68 d. Off the main road and just 200 meters from Lighthouse Beach is **Ballina Beach Resort,** Compton Dr. (tel. 066-86-8888), which has a swimming pool, tennis court, restaurant, and bar. Rates are at $68 s or d, rising to $120 during school holidays. Less expensive is the **Australian Hotel,** 103 River St. (tel. 066-86-2015), with pub-style rooms of a decent standard for $35 s, $40 d. Inexpensive motels are along the Pacific Hwy. west of downtown. **Ballina Motel** (tel. 066-86-2208) is the least expensive of these, with basic rooms for $30 s or d. **Ballina Centrepoint Motel,** 285 River St. (tel. 066-86-6877), is right downtown and has rooms from $38 s, $40 d.

Ballina Traveller's Lodge, 36 Tamar St. (tel. 066-86-6737), is a modern YHA hostel two blocks from downtown. All facilities are of a high standard, and bikes can be rented for $1 an hour. Dorm beds are $12 pp.

Shaws Bay Caravan Park, by Missingham Bridge, has tent sites for $10-12 and basic cabins for $25-45 (tel. 066-86-2326). Farther out, on the Pacific Hwy. north of town, is **Ballina Gardens Caravan Park** (tel. 066-86-2475). Although not suited to tents, facilities are excellent. Sites are $12-15 and cabins start at $24.

Food
Without a doubt, the best place for a casual meal is **Shelly's on the Beach** (tel. 066-86-9844). Tables are indoors and out and overlook Ballina Head and Shelly Beach; open daily 7:30 a.m.-3:30 p.m. Back in town, in the mall beside Woolworths, is **Natural Addiction,** River St. (tel. 066-86-5229), a popular cafe with a blackboard menu featuring healthy meals for $6-12. **Ballina RSL Club,** River St. (tel. 066-86-2544), has both an inexpensive bistro and the more formal **Spinnakers,** a seafood restaurant open daily 6-10 p.m. Lunch in the bistro is inexpensive, and Friday noon-2 p.m. fish and chips and dessert is just $2.

Transportation, Services, and Information
Ballina has no official bus depot, but all major bus lines stop at the Big Prawn, west of downtown. **Blanch's** (tel. 066-86-2144) serves Lennox Head ($2.80 one-way) and Byron Bay ($4.60). **Ballina Motel** (tel. 066-86-2208) has rental cars from $40 per day.

The **post office** is at 85 Tamar Street. **Ballina Public Library,** beside the Tourist Information Centre, is open Mon.-Fri. 10 a.m.-5 p.m., Saturday 9 a.m.-noon. **Ballina Tourist Information Centre** is a modern facility located at the east end of River St. on the corner of Norton St. (tel. 066-86-3484); open daily 9 a.m.-5 p.m.

North to Lennox Head
The most interesting route north from Ballina is along a coastal road through the picturesque village of Lennox Head, which overlooks a long grassy headland of the same name. The ceaseless motion of the ocean has pulled sand from the town's main beach, exposing long reefs of black rock. **Seven Mile Beach** extends north from Lennox Head and is backed by **Lake Ainsworth,** a freshwater lagoon.

The town has a couple of motels, but **Lennox Head Backpackers,** 3 Ross St. (tel. 066-87-7636), a purpose-built hostel, is the least expensive place to stay. Bikes, boats, and surfboards are available for guest use, and Lake Ainsworth is a short walk away. Dorm beds are $14, and the double room is $30.

The bakery on Ballina St. has great meat pies and pastries, and **Lennox Head Hotel** has live music on weekends.

North of Lennox Head is **Broken Head Nature Reserve,** an area of subtropical rainforest extending right to the ocean. At the north end of the reserve is a hiking trail leading along a cliff and descending to King's Beach.

BYRON BAY

A north coast sojourn wouldn't be complete without a stop at Byron Bay, 800 km north of Sydney and 100 km south of the Queensland border. "Byron," as it's best known, sprawls along a spectacular stretch of coastline dominated by **Cape Byron,** the easternmost point of mainland Australia. It's difficult to pinpoint exactly what makes the place so popular; originally it was the surf and setting, which is picture-postcard perfect—long sandy beaches flanked by a hinterland of rainforest. Today the town is a

BYRON BAY

LITTLE WATEGOS BEACH

TO JULIAN ROCKS

CAPE BYRON

WATEGOS BEACH

THE PASS
THE PASS CAFE

LIGHTHOUSE

CLARKS BEACH

LITTLE WATEGOS BEACH

BELONGIL BEACH

CHILDE ST.

BELONGIL BEACH HOUSE

THE WRECK

CAPTAIN COOK LOOKOUT

CAPE BYRON WALKING TRACK

EWINGSDALE RD.

BYRON BAY BACKPACKERS INN

HOSPITAL

WOLLONGBAR MOTOR INN

MAIN BEACH

BAY ST.

BYRON HIBISCUS COURT MOTEL

LAWSON ST.

LIGHTHOUSE RD.

BUTLER ST.

MIDDLETON ST.

MASSINGER ST.

BELONGIL CREEK

ARTS FACTORY LODGE

BURNS ST.

SEE DETAIL

THE PLAZA

BACKPACKERS HOLIDAY VILLAGE HOSTEL

BYRON BAY SERVICES CLUB

JONSON ST.

BROWNING ST.

BANGALOW RD.

TO TYAGARAH RIDING RANCH AND BRUNSWICK HEADS

SKINNERS SHOOT RD.

0   500 m

PACIFIC OCEAN

TALLOW BEACH

DETAIL

BAYMIST MOTEL

BAY ST.

BEACH HOTEL

BLUE IGUANA

FIRST SUN CARAVAN PARK

RAVING PRAWN

LAWSON ST.

EARTH 'N' SEA

CHARBONNADE ST.

CATALINA TAPAS BAR

RINGO'S

GREAT NORTHERN HOTEL

THE BYRONIAN

CAPE BYRON YHA HOSTEL

POST OFFICE

BYRON ST.

FLETCHER ST.

RAILWAY FRIENDLY BAR

JONSON ST.

MARVELL ST.

TOURIST INFORMATION CENTRE

CAPE BYRON LODGE

SCOTT ST.

THE OASIS

TO SUFFOLK PARK, BROKEN HEAD, AND LENNOX HEAD

MOON

unique blend of lifestyles, with drifters and dreamers mixing with celebrities and overseas tourists, and one of Australia's most expensive suburbs a stone's throw from fibro houses full of surf bums.

Byron wasn't seen as anything more than a working-class seaside village until the 1960s, when rapid development hit the Gold Coast to the north and jaded Queenslanders escaped by migrating south. This coupled with an influx of hippies during Nimbin's 1973 Aquarius Festival began a counterculture that continues to this day. Things remained relatively low-key until the mid-1980s, when developers began

investing in the town, a trend that has continued into the 1990s.

Cape Byron

The **lighthouse** on Cape Byron has been a landmark since its construction in 1901. A road leads right to the cape but **Cape Byron Walking Track** is a more interesting option. This trail begins at Captain Cook Lookout and follows the shoreline to The Pass and Wategos Beach before it climbs steeply to the lighthouse. Although the lighthouse compound is locked at dawn (open daily 8 a.m.-5:30 p.m.), the headland commands fantastic views of the sun rising over

he Pacific Ocean. The cape is also a good van-
age point for whalewatching.

Beaches

Main Beach extends along the front of down-
own and is a safe swimming area. To the north-
est is **Belongil Beach** and a favorite surfbreak
nown as **The Wreck,** named for the *Wollong-
ar,* which is partly visible beyond the breaking
aves. East of Main Beach is **Clarks Beach,**
where the sandy headland **The Pass** is a popu-
ar surf spot. Behind The Pass is **Wategos
Beach,** one of the few beaches on Australia's
ast coast that faces north. South of the cape is
Tallow Beach, accessible along a gravel track
ff Lighthouse Road. This stretch of beach is
pen to the fury of the ocean, and seas can be
ough. Farther south is a long stretch of beaches,
ncluding **Suffolk Park.**

Recreation

Julian Rocks, three km off Cape Byron, is a
opular diving spot. The area around the rocks

Cape Byron

has been declared a marine reserve, protecting a vast assortment of marine species. **Byron
Bay Dive Centre,** 9 Lawson St. (tel. 066-85-
7149), has been established the longest of the
five dive operators in town; two boat dives, including equipment rental, runs about $80 pp.
Cape Byron Marine Charter (tel. 066-85-6858)
and **Byron Boat Charter** (tel. 066-85-3399)
offer daylong fishing trips starting at $80 pp.

Hang gliders can often be seen soaring around
the cape, and the recent introduction of **tandem
hang gliding** has made this adventure sport
more accessible; for details, call **Flight Zone**
(tel. 066-85-3178). Instruction is included and
rates start at $70 per half hour. For the less ad-
venturous, kites can be hired at Byron Kites in
Cape Byron YHA Hostel (tel. 066-85-5299).

Tyagarah Riding Ranch is out by the airstrip
north of town (tel. 066-84-7499). A one-hour
ride is $18 and the two-hour Twilight Ride is
$32.

Not all recreation need cost a fortune; spend
your time swimming, surfing, snorkeling, sunbaking, and fishing, or, for the price of a beer at
the Beach Hotel or a coffee at Ringo's, watch the
world of Byron Bay go round.

Entertainment
Beach Hotel, corner Bay and Jonson Streets
(tel. 066-85-6402), is definitely *the* place for a
drink. In summer patrons spill out of the hotel
onto the lawn overlooking Main Beach. **Railway Friendly Bar,** at the railway station (tel.
066-85-7662), has live music most evenings,
but things generally wrap up early. **Catalina
Tapas Bar,** 32 Jonson St. (tel. 066-85-8493), is
a Spanish-style bistro with jazz, soul, and blue-
grass music Thurs.-Sat. from 10 p.m.

Hotels and Motels
The **Great Northern Hotel,** Jonson St. (tel. 066-
85-6454), has rooms for $50 s or d. **Byron Hi-
biscus Court Motel,** 33 Lawson St. (tel. 066-85-
6195), is the least expensive of the motels close
to downtown. Rooms are $55 s, $59 d, rising
to over $100 during school holidays. **Baymist
Motel,** 12 Bay St. (tel. 066-85-6121), is also
central; $69 s, $79 d. **Wollongbar Motor Inn,** 19
Shirley St. (tel. 066-85-8200), has a pool, barbecue, and rooms with basic cooking facilities;
from $60 s, $65 d.

The Oasis

South of town is The Oasis (24 Scott St. (tel. 066-85-7390)). It offers the choice of accommodation in fully self-contained two-bedroom apartments, with a massive pool, tennis courts, three-story game room, gym, spa and masseuse, and outdoor barbecue area. Rates for apartments range $525-609 per week, rising to $1295 during summer school holidays; the nightly rate is $95-105.

Magnificent cedar **Treetop Houses** are part of the same resort. Each gives you ocean views and three stories of casual luxury, including two bedrooms, two bathrooms, a private pool on the deck, large lounge area with television and VCR, and full kitchen. The minimum stay is seven nights; $980-1099 per unit, rising to $2205 during summer school holidays.

Backpacker Lodges

Byron Bay has an excellent selection of backpacker accommodations, many as good or better than motels twice their price. All hostels are busy year-round and bookings are essential in summer. **Cape Byron YHA Hostel** is a new place just 150 meters from Jonson St.; excellent facilities include a large modern kitchen area, lounge, outdoor deck, barbecue, laundry, shops, heated pool, and bikes and surfboards for rent. Dorms are $13-15 pp and double rooms $45. Located at the corner of Middleton and Byron Streets (tel. 066-85-8788). Also associated with the YHA is **Cape Byron Lodge,** 78 Bangalow Rd. (tel. 066-85-6445), two km south of town toward Suffolk Park and a short walk to Tallow Beach; dorm beds $12-15, doubles $45.

Backpackers Holiday Village Hostel, 116 Jonson St. (tel. 066-85-8888), is, in our opinion, the pick of the bunch. Facilities are of the highest standard, rooms are large and brightly decorated, and bikes, surfboards, and boogie boards are available for guest use. Rates are $15 pp, $38-45 d. **Byron Bay Backpackers Inn** is close to both the beach and downtown and has all the facilities of the above hostels. Rates are $14-16 in dorms and $35 d. Located at 29 Shirley St. (tel. 066-85-8231).

Belongil Beach House, Childe St. (tel. 066-85-7868), is a relaxed place a couple of km west of town and just across the road from Belongil Beach. All facilities are of a high standard,

and the cafe (open daily 8 a.m.-10 p.m.) serves healthy food at excellent prices. Rates are $12 in dorms, $25 s, $30 d, and rise a few dollars during school holidays.

Arts Factory Lodge is farthest from the beach, but the atmosphere is laid-back and guests have free use of bicycles to get into town. Dorms are $13, doubles $28, or you can camp for $8 pp. The newest hostel-style accommodation is offered by **Blue Iguana,** right opposite Main Beach at 14 Bay St. (tel. 066-85-5298). This is the smallest hostel, but facilities are adequate and views from the deck are nothing short of spectacular. Rates start at $15 pp in a four-share dorm.

Campgrounds

First Sun Caravan Park, Lawson St. (tel. 066-85-6544), is in a prime location on Main Beach, right downtown, with some unpowered sites on the absolute beachfront. Sites are $8-16.50 and small cabins are $31-73. Facilities at **Cape Byron Van Village** are of a higher standard, but this place is farther out—located 2.4 km northwest of town on Ewingsdale Rd. (tel. 066-85-7378)—and more suited to vans. Sites range $10-18, cabins $33-60. **Suffolk Park Caravan Park,** six km south of Byron (tel. 066-85-3353), is in a great spot surrounded by Broken Head Nature Reserve and fronting a long sandy beach; sites are $9.50-16, cabins $28-60.

Food

Byron has a huge choice of cafes and restaurants; some have been around for years and have become landmarks while others seem to come and go with the seasons. **Ringo's,** 29 Jonson St. (tel. 066-85-6433), is a cavernous place with poster-covered walls and an eclectic crowd. Open daily 8:30 a.m.-9 p.m. **The Byronian,** 58 Jonson St. (tel. 066-85-6754), is another casual place, with tables indoor and out. One of Byron's most relaxing and enjoyable places for a meal is **The Pass Cafe,** Brooke Dr. (tel. 066-85-6074), off Lighthouse Rd. and an easy half-hour walk from town along Main and Clarks Beaches. Breakfast is served in summer only and ranges $5-10, while lunch and dinner feature European cuisine and seafood. Back in town, the Great Northern and Beach Hotels serve counter meals, while the bistro in

Byron Bay Services Club, Jonson St. (tel. 066-85-6878), has a daily $3 lunch special (probably the best dining deal in town); open noon-2 p.m. or lunch and 6:30-9 p.m. for dinner, with other specials Tues.-Thursday.

The **Raving Prawn** is a casual seafood restaurant in Feros Arcade on Jonson St. (tel. 066-85-6737). Most main dishes are about $15, with appetizers and desserts $5-8; open Tues.-Sat. from 6 p.m. For the best pizza in town head to **Earth 'N' Sea,** Jonson St. (tel. 066-85-5011), with indoor/outdoor dining and large pizzas from $15. One of Byron's more formal restaurants is **Charbonnade,** Lawson Arcade, Lawson St. (tel. 066-85-5588), which serves French cuisine in an outdoor courtyard. Open for dinner Mon.-Sat. from 6:30 p.m.

Transportation, Services, and Information
Byron Bay is on the Sydney-Murwillumbah rail line. An XPT service departs Sydney daily at 7:05 a.m., arriving in Byron at 7:30 p.m. Byron is also a stopping point for all the major bus companies; fares to Sydney are $70 (one-way) and to Surfers Paradise $18. The departure point is the Tourist Information Centre on Jonson Street. **Kirklands** (tel. 066-85-6554) runs from Byron Bay to Lismore ($9 one-way) and north to Brisbane ($22.20) via Surfers Paradise ($17.80).

Cheap rental cars are available from **Earth Car Rental,** where rates start at $35 per day with 200 free km; book through any hostel or call (066) 85-7472. All hostels have bikes for guest use, or hire them from **Byron Bay Bicycles,** The Plaza, Jonson St. (tel. 066-85-6315), or $10-15 per day.

The **post office** is at 61 Jonson Street. **Byron District Hospital** is on Shirley St. (tel. 066-85-6200).

The **Tourist Information Centre** is at 80 Jonson St., beside the railway station (tel. 066-85-8050); open daily 8:30 a.m.-4:30 p.m.

BYRON TO THE BORDER

Brunswick Heads and the Tweed Coast
Colorful fishing boats at the mouth of the Brunswick River mark this small seaside town, a popular tourist stop 40 km north of Byron Bay. Immediately north is the sprawling residential estate of **Ocean Shores,** which has a challenging 18-hole resort-style golf course. Green fees are $20; call (066) 80-1247 for tee times.

A few km north of Brunswick Heads, the Pacific Highway heads inland. The coastal route (turn off north of Brunswick Heads on Wooyung Road) is more picturesque, passing numerous holiday towns and long sandy beaches. **Pottsville** and **Hastings Point** are low-key towns with good beaches, fishing, and a choice of accommodations. Heading north, the next township is **Cabarita Beach,** overlooking a rocky headland and a popular surf break. It was known as "Bogangar" until a developer decided he could sell more land by changing the town's name.

North of Cabarita Beach the road traverses a narrow strip of scrub-covered dunes, crossing Cudgen Creek at the resort town of **Kingscliff,** with an atmosphere so relaxed it is hard to believe the Gold Coast is a half hour's drive north. **Kingscliff Motel,** 80 Marine Parade (tel. 066-74-1780), opposite the beach, has rooms for $38 s, $45 d, rising to $65/$85 in summer. Along a narrow strip between the main road through town and the beach is **Kingscliff Beach Caravan Park** (tel. 066-74-1311), where sites are $9-17 and cabins are $45-70. The best place in town for a feed is **Sea Salt Restaurant,** 26 Marine Parade (tel. 066-74-4066), boasting ocean views and a menu featuring seafood, chicken, and meat dishes ranging $12-18; open for lunch and dinner Wed.-Sunday. **Kingscliff Bowls Club,** right on the beach (tel. 066-74-1404), has inexpensive food and beer.

Tweed Heads
Although the towns of Tweed Heads and Coolangatta merge to become one long residential strip, they are markedly different, courtesy of development restrictions on the New South Wales side of the border. Tweed Heads extends along the west bank of the Tweed River, much of it on reclaimed mangrove swamps. The state border hits the coast at **Point Danger,** a high bluff overlooking **Duranbah,** Tweed Heads's only beach, and where views extend north to Surfers Paradise. The point's dominant feature is an 18-meter-high monument to Captain Cook. At the monument's base is a replica of the capstan from the *Endeavour,* Cook's ship.

At South Tweed Heads is **Minjungbal Aboriginal Cultural Centre,** located in an area of historic importance to the Koori. The area provided ample food for generations of their people, and a sacred ceremonial site within the grounds remains. From the center, a two-km trail leads through native bushland and to a boardwalk out on a mangrove swamp; open daily 10 a.m.-4 p.m. Located at the end of Kirkwood Rd., off the Pacific Hwy. beside Tweed City Shopping Mall.

Tweed Heads has a few motels, but those in Coolangatta are much cheaper. On the other hand, campers are well catered to at **Border Caravan Park,** Boundary St. (tel. 07-5534-1266), which overlooks the Tweed River and is just two blocks from Coolangatta Beach. Sites are $15-19 and on-site vans $28-40.

The licensed clubs are a haven for budget-conscious diners, with each offering a variety of good deals. For example: **South Tweed Bowls Club,** Pacific Hwy. (tel. 07-5524-3655), has $2.50 lunches daily, and roast dinners are offered Sun.-Tues. for just $6.90; **Terranora Lakes Country Club,** Marana St. (tel. 07-5590-9223), offers $2.90 lunches and two-course dinners for $7.50 in the bistro. The club has a restaurant and Thurs.-Fri. $12.50 three-course meals are offered, and at Sunday lunch and dinner a $10 buffet is laid out. Both the above clubs have a courtesy bus from Gold Coast hotels.

The **Tourist Information Centre** is on the east side of the Pacific Hwy. in the middle of Tweed Heads and is open Mon.-Sat. 9 a.m.-5 p.m. (tel. 07-5536-4244).

HINTERLAND

The far north coast hinterland, extending from Lismore to the Queensland border and about 70 km west from the coast, is an area of unrivaled beauty, of lush subtropical forests and picturesque towns with high populations of those who have attempted to escape the boundaries of modern life. It all began with the 1973 Aquarius Festival at Nimbin, and while many of the original hippies still live in the area's many communes, they have been joined by many others, including people who like to be known as ferals—wanderers who make the remaining hippies look conservative, completely rejecting the outside world, moving around the hinterland worshipping the earth (and one plant in particular) in an almost primitive existence.

Colorful festivals such as the Growers Cup, Mardi Grass, and Pope of Dope, which take place throughout the year, are a highlight of life in the hinterland.

The Land

The dominant feature of the hinterland is **Mt. Warning,** the central magma vent of volcanic action 20 million years ago. The area was a shield volcano, twice as high as Mt. Warning and covering an area of 5,000 square km. Since the volcanic action ceased, wind and rain erosion have carved out an enormous caldera, with Mt. Warning rising to 1,156 meters in the center. This enormous basin is bordered by the **Nightcap Range** to the south and the **Tweed** and **McPherson Ranges** to the west, forming escarpments bordering high country beyond.

Lismore

Self-proclaimed capital of the far north, Lismore (pop. 40,000) is 35 km west of Ballina on the southern slopes of the caldera. Much of the town is subject to the flooding of the Wilson River, and many houses are raised to counteract this annual cycle. Down on the river the excellent **Lismore Information and Heritage Centre,** corner Bruxner Hwy. and Molesworth St. (tel. 066-22-0122), has an interesting rainforest display; admission $1. Just up the road, on Molesworth St., is **Richmond River Historical Society Museum,** and next door is a **regional art gallery.** The *Bennelong* cruises the Wilson and Richmond Rivers on a variety of itineraries including a lunch cruise (departs 11 a.m., $2? pp) and a full-day cruise from Lismore to Ballina with morning and afternoon teas, lunch, and return bus transport (departs 10 a.m., $50 pp). For details call (066) 21-7729, or book through the Tourist Information Centre. A worthwhile side trip from Lismore is to **Tucki Tucki Nature Reserve,** 16 km south of town, which protects a small colony of koalas.

Currendina Lodge, 14 Ewing St. (tel. 066-21-6118), is a good choice for budget travelers; dorm beds are $14, $18 s, and $32 d. The atmosphere is friendly and communal cooking and laundry facilities are offered. Best value of the area's many motels is **Arcadia Motel,** six km east of Lismore in the village of Goonellabah (tel. 066-24-1999); $42 s, $50 d. **Lismore Lake Caravan Park,** two km east of town on the road out to Ballina (tel. 066-21-2585), has excellent facilities; sites are $14, and small cabins start at $24 d.

Mecca Cafe, 80 Magellan St. (tel. 066-21-3901), is a 1950s-style diner; it was open before the '50s became a novelty. **Maggie Moore's Pub,** 29 Molesworth St. (tel. 066-22-1888), has inexpensive lunches from $3. **Honey's,** 48 Magellan St. (tel. 066-21-3174), is one of a number of vegetarian places in town; you'll find breakfasts from $4 and lunches from $6; open Mon.-Fri. 8 a.m.-5 p.m., Saturday 9 a.m.-2:30 p.m. **Boccaccio,** 55 Keen St. (tel. 066-22-0283), has lunchtime all-you-can-eat pasta for $7.50 and dinner main meals from $8.

Nimbin

Nimbin was a dairy town in decline when, in 1973, a group of students descended on the town and convinced the council to let them hold a festival. Little did locals realize that the **Aquarius Festival** would change the town forever and mark the beginning of a hinterland counterculture movement that continues to this day. The festival attracted about 5,000 people, young and old, who came to dance, listen to music, and discover themselves. Many festival-goers were so impressed with the beauty and peacefulness around Nimbin that they bought up cheap dairy farms and settled in communes where everything was shared and life made as simple as possible. Communes still exist, as such, scattered around the district in remote areas that casual visitors would be lucky to find.

Colorful murals along the main street are the dominant characteristic of Nimbin. **Nimbin Museum,** near the Rainbow Cafe (tel. 066-89-1123), is an eclectic collection of memorabilia from the Aquarius Festival, and with admission only $2 pp, it shouldn't be missed. Also on the main street, shops sell the weird and wonderful work of local artisans.

A good deal for accommodation is **The Old Rectory** next to the church on Cullen St. (tel. 066-89-1097); $30 s, $40 d. **Nimbin Motel,** four km north of town on Crofton Rd. (tel. 066-89-1420), has basic rooms for $25 s, $40 d.

Granny's Farm is a YHA hostel in a relaxed atmosphere, a 10-minute walk north of town (tel. 066-89-1333). Dorm beds are $13-15 pp, private rooms $25 s, $30 d. Behind the hotel is a council-operated caravan park with sites for $9 and on-site vans for $28 (tel. 066-89-1402).

The legendary **Rainbow Cafe** on Cullen St. has been around for years and is the most popular of a half dozen cafes in town. Healthy meals start at around $6; open daily at 9 a.m. Farther down the street is **Nimbin Rocks Cafe,** which is a little more mainstream.

Nightcap National Park

A long fight between environmentalists and the government was finally resolved in 1983, when this 4,950-hectare park, 15 km northeast of Nimbin, was proclaimed. The park encompasses the Nightcap Range, part of the southern rim of the Mt. Warning caldera. The main access road from Nimbin leads to the summit of **Mt. Nardi,** from where panoramic views extend over the park and valleys to the south. The other access is north from **The Channon,** along a gravel road that ends at Terania Creek Picnic Area, where a 500-meter trail leads through a lush rainforest to **Protestor's Falls.** Camping is allowed at the picnic area.

Mullumbimby

Although not as extreme as Nimbin, the alternative lifestyle of many of "Mullum's" 2,000 residents can be appreciated by spending time on the main street or lounging in the cafes. The forests around town are subtropical, with the most spectacular feature, **Minyon Falls,** dropping nearly 100 meters into a heavily forested gorge. A gravel track off the main Mullumbimby-Lismore Road (signposted) leads to within a few minutes' walk of the falls.

Mount Warning National Park

The summit climb of 1,156-meter Mt. Warning is a highlight of a trip to the far north coast, but, be warned, the final ascent is *very* steep. The summit trail is just five km one-way, but you should allow five hours for the return trip. If you leave early enough to watch the sun rise over the Pacific Ocean, you'll be the first to do so on mainland Australia. All flanks of Mt. Warning are covered in rainforests—subtropical at lower eleva-

AQUARIUS FESTIVAL
— 17-28 April 1973 —

Rumors had been circulating around the country for weeks about an arts festival in a small town called Nimbin in the hills of New South Wales. Communes, hippies, and travelers were converging on the site from all over Australia. Stuck in Cairns after seven years traveling to over 70 countries I hitched a ride south in a car that had **Nimbin or Bust** spelled out in dust on its rear window. Driving deep into the countryside, we at last arrived at Nimbin. A fountain of red paint spurted above a storefront, psychedelic motifs ran from building to building all along the main street, and outlandishly dressed people emerged barefoot from all manner of wheeled contraptions. As I surveyed the scene, I realized that I had happened upon an Australian Woodstock, a landmark event of the 1970s, a brilliant once-in-a-lifetime experience.

Nimbin was perched on top of a small hill. Below was a broad valley cut in two by a winding river. Scattered across the valley floor were hundreds of tepees, tents, multicolored domes, makeshift plastic shelters, vans, and RVs, all under tall bushy eucalyptus trees. I was invited to stay in a huge communal plastic orange igloo with a gang of bikers. Late into the first night, chillums sparked in the darkness as a New Zealand organist pierced the night air with Christian rock music. The next morning I woke to the sound of flutes and chanting Hare Krishnas. A heavy mist encircled the trees and drifted over a sea of bodies crashed everywhere on the damp grass. Smoke puffed above a small Aborigine tribe from central Australia camped on a nearby hill where they performed dances and told stories. The Aborigines considered Nimbin a holy place inhabited by departed spirits and refused to pay the entrance fee to land they felt had been stolen from them.

That day hundreds of celebrants—each one a character—arrived. Fred Robinson, an amazing white-haired 83-year-old Moses figure from Perth, gave talks on the Grand Order of the Universe, flying saucers, and Right Diet in order to save the world by 1978—which promised to be a very heavy year. In a nearby field, peddling furiously, a man attempted to get an absurd spiral-shaped flying machine off the ground. As the crowds swelled into a mushroom-eating greeter called out "Hello Bruce!" to everyone. Webster, a sexual activist, revolutionary, and spiritualist, enthused on his soapbox in his faultless British accent: "What we need is not a new Christ but a new Robin Hood! Not pie in the sky! Pie *now!*" A bedraggled band of crazy long-haired flautists and bongo drummers from Melbourne, who called themselves "The White Company," poured out of a long white bus. All shared food and whatever else they had; at the communal privies, guys and girls—complete strangers—shared the toilets and took showers together. Everyone was repeating "It's working, it's working!" Nimbin was to become a metaphor for a whole generation of Australians.

The hilltop was swarming with people and humming with activity. Rock concerts, be-ins, peak ex-

tions and temperate closer to the summit. Even if you aren't attempting a summit climb, the park is worth visiting for these rainforests, best appreciated along a short trail beginning at the end of the access road. Camping is not allowed within the park, but **Wollumbin Wildlife Refuge** (tel. 066-79-5120), along the park access road, has sites set among towering forests of eucalypts; park facilities are modern; tent sites $10, on-site vans $24, and cabins $30-38. Other accommodation is available at **Uki**, a historic and picturesque village spread along the Tweed River east of the park and nine km southwest of Murwillumbah. Located here is **Village Guest-**

house (tel. 066-79-5345), which has rooms for $55 s, $75 d.

No public transportation runs up to the park, but Mon.-Fri. **Beaumont's** (tel. 066-21-6231) runs a bus service between Murwillumbah and Lismore via Uki.

Murwillumbah
Largest of the Tweed Valley towns, Murwillumbah (pop. 8,000), out on the Pacific Hwy., is in an area of lush subtropical rainforests and many banana and sugar plantations. On Queensland Rd. is a small museum (open Wed.-Fri. 10 a.m.-3 p.m.), and at the east end of Murwillumbah

periences, spontaneous dances swirled around us. Shops sold oatmeal cookies and stir-fry veggies on paper plates (the locals called whole-wheat flour "hippie flour" and brown rice "hippie rice"). At the Learning Exchange were workshops on silversmithing, transcendental meditation, instrument- and batik-making, mime by the White Company, and others such as "Sex—The Virile Sport." A massage tent had opened up, and in the afternoon at the Butter Factory vehement diatribes were underway on racism, gay and feminist liberation, radical sociology, and anti-psychiatry. At the Nimbin Pub, packed with freaks and farmers 10 a.m.-10 p.m., the till was white hot. And the din! A few doors down, a poetry group was reading Yevtushenko by candlelight in the middle of the street. Dollar Brand, an African pianist, was playing a wild improvisation in Nimbin Hall, taking the audience to a crescendo then into the nadirs. In the Central Cafe, the New Zealand jug band Blertha sent a hundred people rockin' with their shivering electric guitars. It was a scene of mind-boggling freshness and innocence.

By the 10th day, the media got hold of the event and turned it into a real circus. Straight tourists walked down the main street warily like they were in a lion park. Keeping their kids close to their sides, they stood agape at the goings-on, laughing nervously. Plainclothesmen drove the dirt roads and notices circulated with their license plate numbers. Cameramen worked the throngs. An official-looking man asked me "Where's the main attraction?" Later that morning, news spread of an orgiastic be-in on the soccer field. It started as a snake-like procession winding in and out of all the tents—a freak parade with everyone singing and playing musical toys. In the center the crowd danced and gyrated, a naked free-spirited frenzy, while a shaggy bare-ass photographer with an oversized 16mm movie camera recorded the climax for posterity.

—Bill Dalton

While many festival-goers remained in the area after the Aquarius Festival ended, Bill Dalton headed to Sydney to self-publish in booklet form A Traveler's Notes: Indonesia, which he had been flogging on the streets of Nimbin. Little did he realize that in the ensuing years what had begun as six pages of mimeographed notes would grow into Moon Publications, a publishing organization with a series of 60 guidebooks covering Asia, the South Pacific, and the Americas.

St. on Tumbulgum Rd. is **Tweed River Regional Art Gallery** (hours same as museum).

A good place to stay is **Mt. Warning Backpackers,** 1 Tumbulgum Rd. (tel. 066-72-3763), where the managers organize hinterland tours. Basic dorm beds are $14, private rooms $18 s, $26-29 d.

Border Ranges National Park

Largest of the caldera national parks, this 31,508-hectare park encompasses part of the New South Wales side of the McPherson Range, the western rim of the caldera. Like other hinterland parks, subtropical and temperate rainforests dominate, with other features including spectacular escarpments, waterfalls, and deep gorges. The most easily accessible section of the park is the Tweed

Range, in the south of the park. **Tweed Range Scenic Drive,** which begins at Lillian Rock midway between Murwillumbah and Kyogle, follows the rim of the caldera on a 100-km loop. Along this route, lookouts provide panoramic views of the entire region and the many short walks are worthwhile. The park's dominant geological feature is **The Pinnacle,** a sheer-sided sliver of volcanic rock that towers above the rainforest. A lookout provides views of the rock, but those with a sense of adventure (and balance) will want to continue out to the pinnacle itself. Along the scenic drive are numerous picnic areas and camping at Forest Tops and Sheepstation Creek.

The rest of the park is remote; the only road access is Lions Road north from Kyogle. For further park information, call (066) 28-1177.

OFFSHORE ISLANDS

New South Wales may have nothing like the number of offshore islands that neighboring Queensland boasts, and apart from numerous uninhabited rocky outcrops close to the mainland, you have to travel a long way from the coast to find anything resembling an island paradise, but two such islands exist, very different from each other and little known outside of Australia. **Lord Howe Island,** 600 km from the mainland, a subtropical paradise surrounded by fringing reef, has a relaxed atmosphere unlike anything you'll find on the Great Barrier Reef. The other is **Norfolk Island,** a remote outpost where the worst of Sydney Town's convicts were once sent and where descendants of *Bounty* mutineers now live.

OFFSHORE ISLANDS

NEW CALEDONIA

NOUMEA

AUSTRALIA

BRISBANE

NORFOLK
ISLAND

■ LORD HOWE
ISLAND

SYDNEY

MELBOURNE

AUCKLAND

NEW ZEALAND

0   1,000 km

© MOON PUBLICATIONS, INC.

LORD HOWE ISLAND

Few people who have visited this unique subtropical island would argue that it lacks anything intrepid island-hoppers could ask for. It's a gem of composition, with towering peaks rising abruptly from the ocean, lush rainforests, a colorful coral lagoon, and a menagerie of birds, caged only by the island's location—all this condensed on an island of just 1,455 hectares and enjoyed by a permanent population of 280, plus a maximum of 400 visitors at any one time. The island is also popular for what it *doesn't* have: snakes, spiders, biting insects, crime, litter, poverty, or traffic jams. The island is linked to the mainland by daily flights from Australia's east coast and has a wide range of tourist facilities including accommodations (no camping), restaurants, and recreation as diverse as golfing and game fishing.

The Land and Climate

Lord Howe Island lies a little less than 600 km east of Port Macquarie, New South Wales, and 700 km northeast of Sydney. It's 1,455 hectares in area, 11 km long, and three km across at its widest point. The island formed around six million years ago when volcanic activity left a scattering of barren peaks in the middle of the ocean. Lord Howe's two highest points, **Mt. Lidgbird** (777 meters) and **Mt. Gower** (875 meters), were two such peaks. Since volcanic activity ceased, the actions of wind and water have laid alluvial sediments around these peaks, linking them to lower outcrops to the north. Over time, these materials compressed to form sedimentary rock and the low topography that dominates the center of the island today.

On 1 August 1997 Lord Howe Island telephone numbers will change. To dial the new number, simply add the last two digits of the existing area code to the old number. As an example, (065) 12-3456 becomes 6512-3456. The new area code will be (02).

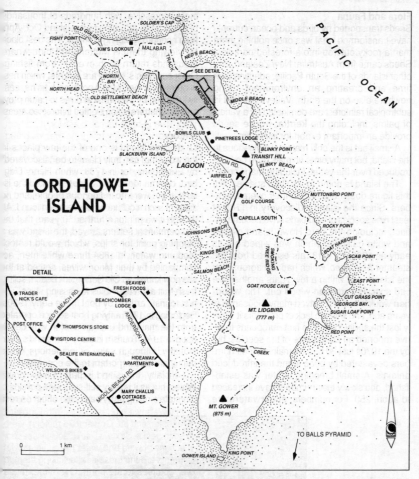

LORD HOWE ISLAND

DETAIL

- TRADER NICK'S CAFE
- POST OFFICE
- THOMPSON'S STORE
- VISITORS CENTRE
- SEALIFE INTERNATIONAL
- WILSON'S BIKES
- SEAVIEW FRESH FOODS
- BEACHCOMBER LODGE
- HIDEAWAY APARTMENTS
- MARY CHALLIS COTTAGES

NED'S BEACH RD.
ANDERSON RD.
MIDDLE BEACH RD.

0   1 km

Lord Howe Island has the world's southernmost coral reef. It survives at the southern latitude due to warm currents of water moving down the Queensland coast. A lagoon of fringing reef encloses a wide part of the island's west shore, which boasts a great variety of beaches; within the lagoon, coral debris has washed ashore to form beautiful sandy beaches. On the island's east coast, beaches are made up of small volcanic rocks and, in the case of Boat Harbour, large basalt boulders smoothed over by wave action.

The 551-meter **Balls Pyramid,** 23 km south of Lord Howe itself, is the most spectacular of the isolated outcrops of rock north and south of the island.

The island's climate is oceanic. Summer temperatures rarely exceed 30° C (86° F), while even in the dead of winter 15° C (59° F) is considered a cold day. The best time to visit the island is spring and fall—most rain falls in winter, and in summer moderate easterly winds blow almost unabated.

Flora and Fauna

Seeds transported by birds and ocean currents have transformed what was once nothing more than a rocky outcrop into a forested paradise. Seeds came from Australia, New Zealand, and other islands of the South Pacific, adapting over time and creating an environment found nowhere else on the earth. Valleys cloaked in subtropical rainforest are dominated by a variety of palms, including the **kentia,** whose seeds provide an important export for islanders.

A small bat is the only mammal indigenous to the island, but many other animals have been introduced over the years, including many cows.

The island is home to 130 bird species, but this figure does no justice to their overall numbers. Since the island's discovery in 1788 at least nine species of land birds have become extinct, including the Lord Howe Island pigeon and white gallinule, which was wiped out as early as 1830. In 1918 rats escaped from the steamer *Makambo,* which had run aground on the island, and within a few years another five bird species had been wiped out. The **woodhen** would have first arrived many thousands of years ago, and with the lack of predators it slowly lost the ability to fly. The first Europeans to arrive reported an abundance of the species, but by the 1970s just 30 birds remained, their numbers devastated by people and the introduced animals. A small breeding center was established, and slowly their numbers have increased to about 250. For numbers, **shearwaters** are

most impressive, with hundreds of thousands of these birds returning to the island Oct.-April from northern wintering grounds. The best place for viewing them is Muttonbird Point, where thousands return each evening from fishing. Other common seabirds are **petrels,** which nest in burrows at the island's north end; **terns,** easily identified by their vertical dives to catch prey; and **kingfishers,** often sighted in forested areas.

History

Lord Howe Island is one of the few places in the world that can truly claim to be "discovered" by Europeans, for in 1788, when Henry Lidgbird, commander of the *Supply,* sighted the island, there were no indigenous people, and no signs of such a culture have ever been found. Although it wasn't for a further 50 years that the first permanent settlers arrived, the island was a stopping point for ships, which would restock food and water. In 1834 three white men, accompanied by their Maori wives, settled at the site now known as Old Settlement Beach, selling fresh fruit and vegetables to passing ships. The first tourists arrived by boat in the early 1930s. Beginning in 1947 a flying boat service operated from the mainland until an airstrip was developed in 1974. Tourism is today the island's main industry, although sales of indigenous kentia palms are also important to the economy.

Officially, the island is part of New South Wales, but as it is fairly self-sufficient, policies of the state's ruling party have little effect on resi-

Lord Howe Island

lents. In 1953, the NSW parliament passed the **Lord Howe Island Act,** passing responsibility of the island's "care, control, and management" over to a Lord Howe Island Board. The board oversees management of health care, the airport, power supply, waste disposal, the palm-seed industry, and the environmental care of the island's delicate ecology. Funding comes from a levy placed on residents, revenue from exports, and a fee charged to all visitors.

Hiking

Hiking is by far the most popular activity on the island, with trails to the southern peaks testing the fittest hikers. An easy yet interesting trail is the four-km (round-trip) **Malabar Track.** Beginning near the end of Ned's Beach Rd., the trail climbs steadily through open pastures to a lookout on Malabar Ridge, before continuing along the headland to Kim's Lookout and descending back to Lagoon Road. The finish of the trail is the beginning of another, this one ending at North Bay, where you'll find a pleasant beach with picnic tables and good snorkeling offshore. From North Bay, it's 300 meters across a low ridge to **Old Gulch,** a narrow inlet backed by a boulder-strewn beach.

The longer and more difficult hiking is at the island's rugged southern end. Beginning from Kings Beach, the strenuous climb to **Goat House Cave,** perched high in the sheer eastern face of Mt. Lidgbird, is less than three km one-way, but is very steep. For the first one km the trail climbs steadily, branching south from a trail to Boat Harbour before climbing Smoking Tree Ridge. The final ascent is up a scree slope to a cave from where the spectacular view extends across the island and lagoon. If you found that the climb to Goat House Cave tested your stamina and stretched your fear of heights to the limits, read no further—the ascent of **Mt. Gower** is steeper, longer, and scarier, so much so that *must* be made with a guide (ask at your accommodation or the Island Administrative Office; $25 pp). The trail starts at Salmon Beach, skirting the ocean for 1.4 km before the first test of nerves, a narrow ledge with a 100-meter drop on one side and a rope for guidance on the other. The trail then ascends steadily through a thickly vegetated valley and climbs, climbs, and climbs an excruciatingly steep slope, almost

vertical in places (there's a rope for guidance), to the summit.

Other Outdoor Activities

With crystal-clear water, 100 species of coral, and 500 species of fish, the lagoon is fantastic for snorkeling. Rent gear from **Thompson's Store.** If you'd like to view life in the lagoon without getting wet, a glass-bottomed boat tour costs adult $12.50, child $7.50. **Sealife International** (tel. 02-9315-7699 or 1800-80-6820) operates scuba diving on the island, with an eight-meter dive boat to access all the best spots. They also offer PADI dive courses. Fish feeding takes place each afternoon at Ned's Beach. Fishing around the island can be very productive (it's prohibited in the lagoon); buy equipment at Thompson's Store. **Wilson's Bikes** rents bikes and paddle skis from $5 per day.

South of the airfield is a nine-hole **golf course.** Club rental and payment of green fees ($10) is on an honor system. A competition is conducted each Sunday from 1 p.m.; call (065) 63-2179 to book. The **bowls club** is open to the public and racquets for the **tennis court** can be rented from Thompson's Store.

Accommodations and Food

All island accommodations are operated by local families. They range from motel-style rooms to fully self-contained units. Central to all island services is **Hideaway Apartments** (tel. 065-63-2054), one of the least expensive options and with a kitchen in each unit. **Mary Challis Cottages** (tel. 065-63-2076), just 50 meters from the lagoon, features two large cottages surrounded in lush greenery. Each has a kitchen with microwave. Rates are similar to Hideaway Apartments. **Pinetrees Lodge** (tel. 065-63-2177), the island's largest accommodation, has been operating since 1900. Rooms lack cooking facilities, but rates include meals. The all-inclusive rate at **Beachcomber Lodge** (tel. 065-63-2032) is slightly lower.

The island has a couple of grocery stores and a bakery; groceries are more expensive here than on the mainland, but less expensive than eating at island restaurants. **Thompson's Store** sells pies, pastries, and cakes. Generally, accommodations without self-contained units have a restaurant. Of these, head to **Capella**

South (tel. 065-63-2008) for a huge breakfast layout ($15 pp) between 8 and 9 a.m. Lunches here average $6-8, and a three-course set menu is offered 6:30-8 p.m. for $35 pp. The Beachcomber Lodge (tel. 065-63-2032) has a restaurant open daily 7 a.m.-10 p.m. **Trader Nick's Cafe** (tel. 065-63-2002) is open Tues.-Sun. 10 a.m.-4:30 p.m. and has cappuccinos and all the typical big-city fare.

Booking a Trip to Lord Howe Island
Eastern Australia (tel. 13-1313) flies daily between Sydney and the island. The regular airfare is $660 round-trip in summer and $600 the rest of the year, but the smart way to visit the island is on a package. Rather than contacting the resorts directly, book through one of the following agents: **Fastbook Holidays** (tel. 02-9958-2799 or 1800-24-4336), **Pacific Island Travel Centre** (tel. 02-9262-6011 or 1800-22-1713), or **Pacific Unlimited Holidays** (tel. 02-9233-3311). In the high season (Dec.-Jan.) airfare from Sydney and five night's accommodation start at $1000 pp. With full board, rates start at $1400. Outside of summer holidays rates are markedly lower, with five-night packages from $650 (check the Travel Section in Thursday's *Sydney Morning Herald* for even cheaper deals). Departure tax is $10 pp.

Services and Information
The **post office** is on the corner of Ned's Beach and Lagoon Roads; open weekdays. The island has three banks; open varying hours Mon.-Friday. For a doctor, call (065) 63-2000. A bus service operates along the island's road system weekdays only; $8 for an all day ticket; call (065) 63-2120 for times.

The **Visitors Centre,** on the corner of Lagoon Rd. and Ned's Beach Rd., features displays of the island's geology and unique flora and fauna, as well as showing audiovisuals on request. It's open Mon.-Fri. 9 a.m.-12:30 p.m. A bulletin board outside the center has bus timetables, weather forecasts, and other island information.

NORFOLK ISLAND

An elevated plateau of lush green rolling hills encircled by steep cliffs that drop straight into the raging ocean and steeped in a tragic yet romantic history, Norfolk Island is like no other place in the world. Its tragic history and remote location alone make it an interesting destination, but the small things that visitors are left to discover for themselves make it all the more so: the annual horse race around the golf course, a phone book that lists nicknames, and unique cuisine developed over 100 years of isolation, just to name a few. Although the island attracts surprisingly few younger travelers (only newlyweds and nearly deads, the locals say) there is something to suit nearly everyone, including hiking, snorkeling, scuba diving, surfing, tours of the island's many convict-era buildings, and cheap booze. Most visitors arrive a part of a package and stay in self-contained units. While package cost is slightly higher than on Lord Howe Island, cost of living is generally less expensive. (The island is tax free, meaning inexpensive shopping.)

The Land
Norfolk Island is 1,600 km northeast of Sydney and on the same latitude as Byron Bay. About eight km long and up to five km wide with 32 km of coastline, the island is 3,455 hectares in area. Volcanic in origin, it is a high point along the Norfolk Ridge, a range of submerged mountains extending between New Zealand and New Caledonia. Norfolk is not your typical South Pacific paradise; its shoreline is dominated by high cliffs rising to a plateau of rolling hills and the peaks of **Mt. Bates** (321 meters) and **Mt. Pitt** (320 meters). The only section of the coastline without cliffs is at the island's southern end.

Nepean Island is a chunk of rock that rises to a massive plateau. It lies 800 meters from Norfolk's southern tip, and through the years there's been talk of constructing a breakwall linking it to the mainland to create a safe anchorage for visiting ships. Farther south is **Phillip Island.** Rugged and surrounded in precipitous cliffs, it is inhabited only by seabirds.

Flora and Fauna
After volcanic activity ended around 2.3 million years ago, forces of erosion began breaking down the island and creating a rich volcanic soil. Over time, seeds arrived on ocean currents and germinated. At the time of European

ettlement, in 1788, 178 species of plants had colonized the island, many of which had evolved o be better suited to the environment. Most ominant of endemic species is the **Norfolk Island pine,** a majestic tree that grows to a height f 50 meters. Dense stands of tree ferns and alms once covered most of the island but are ow restricted to Norfolk Island National Park, where a canopy of greenery and an understory f creepers, vines, and ferns thrive. Another endemic species of interest is the **sharkwood ee,** which gives off a rotten onion smell.

Only two animals are native to the island, geckos and skinks, and both are very rare. Birdlife is prolific, with 45 species nesting on Norfolk Island, including both sea- and land birds. Rarest of the land birds is the **green parrot,** which is endemic. At one time their population dipped to 20, but a breeding program is slowly increasing numbers. At one time even more endangered was the **Norfolk Island mopoke,** whose population numbered just one in 1987. A breeding program with a closely related species from New Zealand has been successful. Of the seabirds present, some live year-round along the coastline while others are migratory. **Gannets** are common on offshore rock stacks, and **terns,** a variety of **petrels, shearwaters,** and **noddies** are present.

Convict Settlement

In 1784 Captain Cook became the first European to record the presence of Norfolk Island. Although evidence of Polynesian settlement has been uncovered, at that time the island was uninhabited. On 6 March 1788, two months after settlement at Sydney Cove, the first settlers arrived aboard the *Supply.* There were 24 people in all, including 15 convicts sent to cultivate the land. They named their settlement King's town, after Australia's first governor. As more convicts were transported to the island, life for the settlers became tougher. Farming proved difficult, and as settlers were under orders not to allow vessels to land, there was no communication with the outside world. For season after season crops failed, troubles arose when convicts began distilling liquor, and the entire exercise was eventually deemed a failure. In 1806 the government began moving free settlers and convicts to Tasmania and by 1814 the island was once again uninhabited.

In 1825 it was decided to send the very worst convicts, those considered beyond reform, from mainland Australia to Norfolk Island. Unlike the first settlement, there were no free settlers. It was a hellhole of lashings, hangings, and murder, with convicts living under constant fear of punishment and guards wary of mutiny. The convicts were put to work clearing land, constructing roads, and building stone structures, which remain to this day. With pressure mounting from the mainland, prisoners were removed from the island in 1855, and it became uninhabited yet again. But not for long.

The Pitcairners

Most of today's islanders are descendants of *Bounty* mutineers, who set their captain, William Bligh, adrift on 28 April 1789, and under the leadership of 24-year-old Fletcher Christian sailed for the uninhabited island of Pitcairn, halfway between South America and New Zealand. Their life on Pitcairn Island was a violent one and within a decade only one of the

original mutineers was alive. But they ha brought a swag of Polynesian women with then and by 1854 the island's population had grow to nearly 200, putting pressure on food an water supplies. The British government decide to move them all to Norfolk Island. They cam ashore on Norfolk Island on 8 June 1856. Eac family was granted 50 acres and they soon se tled down to an easy-going lifestyle of fishin and farming and exchanging goods on the barte system with no real use for money.

Norfolk Island Today

In typical colonial fashion, the early New Sout Wales government considered the Pitcairner unable to look after themselves, and the islar was governed from the mainland. In 1914 the i land was declared an Australian territory an is today administered under the Norfolk Islar Act of 1979. Australia is represented by an a ministrator who lives at Government Hous And although officially under Australian autho ity, for all intents and purposes the island is se governed, receiving no government assistanc and surviving on a budget of just $8 million year. This revenue is raised through gover ment services such as electricity and telecon munications, customs duty, tourism, and a le placed on financial institutions. Income earne on the island is not taxed. The Norfolk Island 1,500 residents are divided as to their political f ture, and a lot will depend on if Australia is su cessful with its push to become a republic. D pending on the results, Norfolk will either re main under the wing of an Australian republic secede but remain under the Commonwealth

The island's official language is English, b locals also speak Norfolk, a delightful blend old English, Gaelic, and Tahitian.

Sights

Most of the 2,000 islanders live on the centr plateau away from the rugged and windswe coastline. Commercial development is confined **Middlegate** and **Burnt Pine,** in the center of th island. South of this area is **Kingston,** site settlement of the second wave of convicts. A v riety of stone structures from this era remai many along **Quality Row.** Some stone buildin have been restored and are open museums, i cluding the original storehouse, which house

Norfolk Island Museum (tel. 6723-23-088). It's open Mon.-Fri. 9 a.m.-4 p.m., Sat.-Sun. 10 a.m.- p.m. Open similar hours is **Sirius Maritime Museum,** housed in an old chapel. At the east end of Quality Row is a cemetery, with graves nearest to the ocean predating the arrival of the Pitcairners. **Emily Bay,** in front of Kingston, is backed by a crescent of golden sand. At low tide it's possible to walk from the beach onto the reef to view rock pools. The *Sirius* was wrecked on this reef in 1790; its anchor was salvaged and is now mounted in the New Military Barracks.

Beyond the airport, on Douglas Drive, is **St. Barnabas Chapel,** part of an 1866 Melanesian Mission established to train Melanesians in the ways of Christianity. This impressive church features intricate stonework, marble floors, kauri pews, and stained glass windows.

Norfolk Island National Park encompasses 460 hectares, the greater part of the island's north section. Hiking trails lead through the most interesting areas, including to Mt. Bates (500 meters each way) and a monument to Captain Cook's landing in 1774 (three km each way). At the park's southern end is a **botanic garden,** developed to ensure the future of the island's unique flora.

Recreation and Events

Fishing is a popular island pastime, with snapper and kingfish most sought after. Although the island is not renowned for waves, surfers occasionally arrive with their boards looking for surf; the most consistent breaks are in the south. The island has a large population of windsurfing enthusiasts, and although you can't rent boards, ask around and you should be able to borrow one. Waters away from Emily Bay are often rough, but good dive sites do exist; call **Bounty Divers** at 6723-22-751 for details. Bounty Divers also rents snorkeling gear for $7 per day. **Norfolk Island Golf Club** is down in Kingston, right on the oceanfront (tel. 6723-22-354). Green fees are $8 and club rentals are also $8. The clubhouse is the old magistrate's house. **Cheryl Tennis Club** is on Queen Elizabeth Ave., Midlegate (tel. 6723-22-966). A good way to see the island's north end is on horseback with **Silky Oaks Stables** (tel. 6723-22-291), where a two-and-a-half-hour ride with billy tea and damper is $25 pp.

Anniversary Day commemorates the Pitcairners' arrival on Norfolk Island. The 8 June celebrations include a re-creation of the landing at Kingston Jetty and a procession of islanders dressed in period costume to the cemetery where hymns and a prayer written by John Adams, one of the original mutineers, are read. Then everyone heads to the ruins of Quality Row for a picnic and game of cricket. Norfolk Island is the only place outside of the United States to officially celebrate **Thanksgiving Day,** a throwback to the days when a U.S. whaling station operated on the island.

Accommodations and Food

The island has dozens of accommodations. Most are motel-style units or self-contained apartments, and although none are luxurious all are adequate and comfortable. Bookings are best made in conjunction with an airfare (see "Transportation and Tours," below).

One of the least expensive places to stay is **Colony Lodge** (tel. 6723-22-256), where self-contained apartments are $64-90 per night. Similarly priced are the self-contained **Hibiscus Crown Apartments** (tel. 6723-22-235), featuring a tennis court. **Nuffka Holiday Apartments** (tel. 6723-22-615) is also good value at $75 pp. **Callum Court,** New Cascade Rd. (tel. 6723-22-850), comprises comfortable self-contained units with a wide range of facilities; $90 s or d. For more than two people, Callum House, on the same property, is an excellent deal. The luxurious three-bedroom house is $120 d plus $25 each extra person. For large self-contained units of a high standard and just a short walk from town stay at **Shiralee Executive Cottages,** on Taylors Rd. (tel. 6723-22-118). Rates are $130 s or d.

While most motels offer food service for guests, enjoying the over 20 restaurants is the best way to experience everyday island life. Both the bowling and golf clubs are open daily for lunch and are inexpensive (the bowling club has an $8 fish fry Sunday night). Another cheap choice is the bistro in the **South Pacific Resort Hotel,** Taylors Rd. (tel. 6723-23-154), which offers a $10 roast Monday, Tuesday, Thursday, and Saturday nights. Milk produced at the island's dairy is smooth, creamy, and delicious, but grocery stores generally sell out by lunchtime. Also look for locally made Cascade lemonade.

As well as locally grown fruit, the island special-ty is fish, and many restaurants have traditional fish fries once a week. **Christian's,** at the Cast-away Hotel (tel. 6723-22-625), has a fish fry Sat-urday night, a Pitcairn/Norfolk dinner Tuesday, and a roast dinner Sunday. **Bishop's Court** (tel. 6723-22-211) features a traditional dinner and live entertainment Monday night for $26 pp. **Branka House Restaurant** (tel. 6723-22-346) is in an old jail building, with foundations of cells below the main dining room. Main meals are well-priced at $13-15, but most people come for the Chicken Peba ($13).

Transportation and Tours
Ansett Australia flies to the island daily from Sydney ($700 round-trip) and Brisbane ($640). Four-night accommodation packages purchased in conjunction with these fares begin at $185 pp. Book packages through Ansett Australia (tel. 13-1344) or **Fastbook Holidays** (tel. 02-9958-2799 or 1800-24-4336).

Air New Zealand (tel. 1800-73-7767) has regular flights between Auckland and the is-land, but packages offered by the airline are a better deal than purchasing flights and accom-modations separately. Airport transfers are gen-erally included with accommodation packages. Airport departure tax is $25 pp.

Car rentals are surprisingly inexpensive; start-ing from $19 per day, plus $3 for insurance. Try **Aloha Rent-a-car** (tel. 6723-22-510). Many ac-commodation packages include a rental car. **Bill's Hire** (tel. 6723-22-139) rents bikes for $4 per day. For a cab, call **Pacific Taxi** at (6723) 22-182.

Pinetree Tours (tel. 6723-22-424) and **Cherie's Island Tours** (tel. 6723-22-269) offer a variety of island tours from $18 pp, a sound

and light show depicting the convict past fo $17, and dinner theater shows for $32. A scen flight over the island is $45 pp.

Services and Information
The island provides all services of a midsize Australian country town. The **post office** is op posite the police station in Burnt Pine. (Colorf stamps issued by Norfolk Island are prized b philatelists the world over.) The Commonwealt and Westpac Banks operate branches in Bur Pine; hours are Mon.-Thurs. 9:50 a.m.-4:3 p.m., Friday 9:30 a.m.-5 p.m.

As Norfolk Island has no import restrictions, a booze, electronic equipment, and other exot goods can be purchased duty-free. Duty-fre shops as such don't exist, but these items ca be purchased at discounted prices from shops i Burnt Pine. The maximum liquor allowance three bottles per person, but you must purchas them at one time.

Shops are generally closed Wednesday an Saturday afternoons and all day Sunday. **Aus tralian currency** is used, but most major cre it cards also accepted. Norfolk Island is on time zone 90 minutes ahead of Australian eas ern standard time and 18 hours ahead of Paci ic standard time. While on the island you do n need to dial the 6723 phone prefix.

A small **hospital** is off Grassy Rd. (tel. 672 22-091); it's open Mon.-Fri. 9 a.m.-5 p.m., b emergencies are seen to any time.

The **Tourist Information Centre** is besid the post office on Taylors Rd., Burnt Pine (te 6723-22-147); it's open Mon.-Fri. 9 a.m.-5 p.m Sat.-Sun. 9 a.m.-noon. For information before a riving, write Norfolk Island Government Touri Bureau, Box 211, Norfolk Island 2899 (tel. 672 22-147).

THE NORTHERN TERRITORY
INTRODUCTION

Ah, beware Australia's last frontier. Take just one look and it's likely to itch clear through your bones and sting your spirit, and not even those venerable Royal Flying Doctors will be able to cure you. Long after the red dust has settled and you've put Aboriginal myths to rest, your Dreamtime will be influenced forevermore by this superlative land with its big rocks, big crocs, and big thirst.

This barren-but-bewitching region, encompassing 1,346,200 square kilometers, is a veritable dynamo of contrasts—the tropical Top End and the arid Red Centre, sacred grounds and tourist meccas, Stone Age culture and Kmarts—inhabited by less than one percent of Australia's population (about 150,000); a quarter of the people are Aboriginal, and the remainder reside mainly in Darwin and Alice Springs.

Touring
Remote though the Territory is, you'll have no problem getting there on a number of sched-uled flights into Darwin (which is closer to Indonesia and the Philippines than it is to Melbourne or Sydney), the Alice (Alice Springs), and yes, even the Rock with its nearby airstrip. The Ghan will rail you from Adelaide to Alice Springs, while coaches, cars, caravans, and trucks can take the straight-as-an-arrow, bitumen Stuart Highway, a.k.a. the Track, all the way to Darwin. From Darwin, it's easy to rent a car or sign up for an organized tour to Top End sites (almost mandatory for Aboriginal lands), and from the Alice you have the option of humping round the Red Heart on a friendly camel or riding through the desert on a horse with no name.

Don't come here expecting to find an Aboriginal guru to take you under his wing and impart Stone Age-old knowledge while you're on holiday. But don't despair. Aboriginal-led tours and "experiences" are available at a variety of sites throughout the Territory.

And you can easily be your own guide—just find your way here, lose yourself immediately, and let your imagination run wild. You may find

QUEENSLAND

TO MOUNT ISA

TO MOUNT ISA

*Barkly
Tableland*

SEMI-DESERT

Tableland
HW

200 km

SOUTH AUSTRALIA

Barkly
HWY.

Barkly
Homestead

66

JERVOIS

PLENTY HWY.

SANDOVER HWY.

UTOPIA

TODD RIVER

FINKE R.

ROSS RIVER

CHAMBERS PILLAR

THREE WAYS

TENNANT CREEK

87

ALICE
SPRINGS

FINKE

TO ADELAIDE

STUART HWY.

SIMPSONS GAP
NATIONAL
PARK

MACDONNELL RANGES

FINKE GORGE
NATIONAL PARK

PALM VALLEY

ERLDUN-DA

DESERT

TANAMI

YUENDUMU

MOUNT
EBENEZER

LASSETER HWY.

MT. CONNER

TO ADELAIDE

ERNEST GILES RD.

WATARRKA
(KINGS CANYON)
NATIONAL
PARK

AYERS ROCK

YULARA

ULURU
NATIONAL
PARK

MT. OLGA

LAKE
AMADEUS

TANAMI TRACK

RABBIT FLAT

LAKE NEALE

DOCKER
RIVER

WESTERN AUSTRALIA

TO BROOME

TO PERTH

yourself in quite a state, but it goes with the Territory. Despite inevitable infiltration by the 20th century, the Northern Territory, with its ancient lands, eerie geological formations, and 40,000 years of Aboriginal history, ceremony, and tradition, is still the ultimate magical mystery tour.

THE LAND

Orient yourself by the Aussie buzzwords: the Top End, the Track, the Alice, the Rock, and the Red Centre. The Top End refers to the northern part of the Territory, comprising Darwin (the cosmopolitan gateway, with one of the world's highest consumptions of beer per capita), glorious Kakadu National Park (where *Crocodile Dundee* was born, or at least filmed, and real-life home to those man-eating saltwater crocs), the Aboriginals' Arnhem Land and Tiwi and Melville Islands, nature wonderland Litchfield Park, plus turquoise beaches, thick rainforests, profuse birdlife, raging waterfalls and jungle rivers, six-meter-high termite mounds, and scads of native rock and bark paintings dating from prehistory through the 1960s.

When you head down the Track—as the 3,188-kilometer Darwin-to-Adelaide Stuart Highway is called in these parts—you'll pass Katherine, a town with 13 nearby gorges, limestone Cutta Cutta Caves, the old gold-mining township Tennant Creek, the Devils Marbles (in case you wondered where he lost them), some rough pubs and petrol pumps, assorted outback characters, and a bunch of other travelers who'll want to know if you're "headin' up or down."

It should go without saying that the Rock is none other than Ayers Rock, the awesome 650-million-year-old monolith rising 348 meters out of the stark desert. It's a holy Aboriginal mythological site as well as visitors' pilgrimage spot and big-time photo op. The Red Centre, named for the color of the soil, and usually associated with the Rock, is really a blanket term for the whole vast area, which also encompasses a surreal, eyeball-popping collection of many more rocks, canyons, craters, chasms, gaps, pillars, and a strange, seemingly out-of-place valley of cabbage palms—a spectacular, inspiring, and

provocative region interchangeably known as Australia's Red Heart.

CLIMATE

The Northern Territory climate runs from subtropical sweat bath to dry-as-old-bones desert

The Top End
The Top End has two distinct seasons—the Wet and the dry season. The Wet, roughly October through April, brings months of oppressive heat (high 30° C, or 86° F), live-in-the-shower humidity, and monsoonal rains. Rain averages 150 cm per year and falls mainly from December through April, often causing roads plains, and rivers to flood. Swimmers and divers should remember that from October to May northern waters are rife with the dangerous box jellyfish.

The dry season is May through September which are probably the most comfortable months for travel, with only about 2.5 cm of rainfall and a lower daily temperature range, from the high 20s to low 30s C (high 70s to low 90s F).

The Centre
The Centre is a different story. Summer days are long and hot, from 35-40° C (95-104° F), with low humidity and warm nights. The Rock, the Olgas, and other heat-generating regions can reach 50° C (about 122° F), and strenuous treks (or even piggyback rides while twirling a parasol) should be avoided. Winter days are mild to warm, averaging 20° C (68° F), with plenty of clear skies and sunshine. Campers and bush walkers, particularly, should come prepared for freezing nights.

Rainfall, though erratic, usually hits during summer months, occasionally flooding creek beds and back roads, though normally the sealed Track stays open to motorists. The annual average downpour is 37 cm around Tennant Creek and 29 cm in the Alice area.

HISTORY

Prehistory
It's generally agreed that the Aborigines migrated from Indonesia at least 40,000 years

(previous page) Tiwi Islanders in ceremonial dress, Melville Island
(top) Aboriginal stockmen, Tanami Downs Station, Tanami Desert; (bottom) Ah, beware Australia's
last frontier . . . it's likely to itch clear through your bones and sting your spirit.

go, and some historians set the date even 0,000 years earlier, making the Aborigines uite possibly the world's oldest surviving race. Any way you look at it, they've been in Australia a long time, with Arnhem Land in the Territo-y's northeast corner marking the spot of tropical Australia's first human settlement.

For several centuries the Aborigines enjoyed a sort of love-hate relationship with Macas-arese fishermen from Indonesia who visited egularly in search of trepang (sea slugs) until he early 1900s, when the Australian govern-ment told them to scoot.

Exploration and Colonization

In 1623, the Dutch ship *Arnhem* became the rst recorded European contact, followed by Abel Tasman's exploration of the northern coast n 1644. Aside from naming some of the fea-ures, the Dutch didn't seem terribly interested in he region. Additional charting of the coast was undertaken by Matthew Flinders in 1803, and hen navigator Phillip King 14 years later.

The British began the old colonial ball rolling vhen, in 1824, Capt. Gordon Bremer—in the name of King George IV—claimed the land as part of New South Wales. After settlement at-empts failed at Melville Island, Raffles Bay, and Port Essington (lousy climate, no trade), he northern coast was left alone for about 15 years. In 1863, on the heels of John McDouall Stuart's groundbreaking south-north continen-al crossing, the Northern Territory became a vested interest of South Australia (called North-ern Territory of South Australia). Another set-lement was created by the territory's first gov-ernment resident, Col. Boyle Finniss, at Es-cape Cliffs near the Adelaide River mouth. An-other failure.

Finally, in 1869, Surveyor-General George Goyder decided to try out Darwin as a prospec-ive site. Bingo! Good choice, especially when shortly thereafter gold was discovered at near-y Pine Creek—bringing with it a railway line, ollowed by the Overland Telegraph Line and, subsequently, the predictable array of cattle anchers, Chinese laborers, pastoralists, and significant others. Additional mineral finds in he 1880s through the early 1900s cinched the area as "a go." The Track, lifeline between Alice Springs and Darwin, was not constructed until the 1930s and not sealed for about another 20 years.

Recent History

The Australian Commonwealth government took over control of the Territory in 1911, and though the Northern Territory became self-governing in 1978, it still remains economically dependent upon the commonwealth. Agriculture, cattle-raising, mining (gold, bauxite, uranium), and booming tourism are the region's major mon-eymakers.

The Aborigines

Wondering what happened to the Aborigines? Some tried to resist colonization of their land—in vain. The hunters and food gatherers who'd lived for so long in perfect harmony with the land were, by the early 1900s, herded onto gov-ernment reserves, introduced to Christian char-ities, forced into hard labor for low pay, left to rot on the fringes of towns, and given a taste of al-cohol. Only those few who lived in the most re-mote areas were left alone to practice their age-old traditions.

It took some time, but in the 1960s Northern Territory Aborigines began pressing for their rights—with various protests against mining, ranching, and other intrusions on their re-serves—culminating with the passage of the 1976 Aboriginal Land (NT) Act, giving them con-trol of their lands (i.e., designated reserves) and returning their sacred sites, including Kakadu and Uluru-Kata Tjuta (Ayers Rock and the Olgas). Currently the Aborigines compose a majority of the management board of these heavily touristed areas, and word has it that by the year 2000 visitors will be banned from climb-ing the spiritual sites. Instead, they will just have to walk around them, gazing in wonder. Stay tuned.

The act also allowed for the appointment of Aboriginal Land Commissioners and the cre-ation of administrative Aboriginal Land Coun-cils. Presently the Aborigines own about one-third of the Territory. Many have returned to their traditional ways and stay on the reserves, out of white reach; others live in squalid condi-tions around townships, ravaged by the effects of racism and alcohol; still others have turned militant or, worse, have become *capitalists*.

DARWIN

The Northern Territory's capital city was named for Charles Darwin, a shipmate of harbor discoverer John Lort Stokes, and the place has been in a state of evolution ever since.

Australians commonly joke about this Top End tropical city—with its difficult climate, transient population, and fabled thirst. Though true, those elements have also inspired a thriving frontier town, lively cosmopolitan center and, yes, lots of laughs as well as fisticuffs over that amazing intake of beer known worldwide as the Darwin Thirst. (Don't laugh—the Darwin stubby contains two liters of beer instead of the normal 375 milliliters; the average per person intake is 230 liters per year, and that's a *low* estimate.)

People don't stick around here long, that's a fact. The weather and the isolation take their toll. Heck, not even the city stays put! During WW II, more than 60 bomb attacks by the Japanese pretty much turned Darwin into a pile of rubble. Then, in 1974, Cyclone Tracy paid a surprise Christmas Day visit, leveling practically the entire city. With indomitable Territorian pull-together spirit (and no doubt *many* thirst-quenchers under their tool belts), Darwin was rebuilt into a durable, modern center, punctuated here and there by the few surviving historical structures, accented by flowering bougainvillea, frangipani blossoms, and swaying palms.

Today's Darwin, with a population of 68,000, is a conglomeration of 50 or so ethnic groups, including descendants of the Chinese miners, Japanese pearlers, Europeans who sought escape from postwar oppression, a relatively new onslaught of refugees from Southeast Asia, barramundi fishers, and a steady stream of travelers and backpackers headed to or from Asia, Top End attractions, or the rest of Australia. Most of the people who "do time" here work within some element of this Territorial administrative center's government, mining, or tourism sectors.

The city center, compactly situated on a peninsula looking toward Darwin Harbour, is easily explored on foot. The Stuart Highway becomes Daly Street as it enters the city, bisecting Smith Street. Head one km toward the harbor to Smith Street Mall, the main shopping district and location of the Darwin Regional Tourism Association Information Centre. The majority of central Darwin sites and services—including Darwin Transit Centre, the general post office and the Automobile Association of the Northern Territory—fall within a few blocks' radius of the mall. Noteworthy suburban attractions are mostly located at Larrakeyah, Palmerston, Fannie Bay, and East Point, all within 10 kilometers to the north and east of city center. Head back away from the harbor and take a right turn off Smith St. onto Gilruth Ave. (which becomes East Point Rd.) to access most of these areas.

And, though you won't find the flair and sophistication of a highfalutin metropolis like Melbourne or Sydney, easygoing and eclectic Darwin can hold its own. And it can *certainly* hold its beer.

THE HISTORICAL TOUR

Yes, acts of war and God aside, a few dead structures—or pieces thereof—still stand. *A Walk Through Historical Darwin*, a booklet published by the National Trust, is a good source of information. This particular stroll may move your spirit as well as your feet. It starts off at the Tree of Knowledge, on the east side of downtown, continues in a loop around the Esplanade, heads down Smith Street Mall, and winds up at the Chinese Temple.

Tree of Knowledge
The ancient banyan behind the Civic Centre on Harry Chan Ave. is a longtime city landmark. Heralded as the Tree of Knowledge by Buddhists (Gautama received enlightenment while sitting beneath a bodhi tree—same genus, different species), this particular tree, survivor of cyclone and bombings, is serenely and defiantly spreading with age.

Brown's Mart
Follow Henry Chan Ave. and turn left onto Smith Street. The stone cottage on your left is a building with a past. Originally constructed in 1885 as a mining exchange, it changed hats several

DARWIN

times to become a fruit and veggie market, a police station, and a brothel. The roof was blown off by two cyclones (though maybe from the action inside!). Today the reconstructed building—with exposed beams—is home to a well-regarded community theater. Hours are Mon.-Fri. 8:30 a.m.-5 p.m. For information, phone (08) 8981-5522.

Old Town Hall

The old town hall, across the street, didn't fare as well with Cyclone Tracy. The 1883 rectangular building, used during WW II for naval administration and later as an art gallery, was flattened by the cyclone. Its stone walls are all that remain, providing a memorable backdrop for outdoor theater performances.

Old Courthouse and Police Station

At the corner of Smith St. and the Esplanade, the old courthouse is a classic 1884 South Australian building, originally constructed to house that government's offices, with the police station and cellblock connected behind. Used by the navy from WW II through Cyclone Tracy, the reconstructed rubble retains its external charm and now serves as offices for the Northern Territory's Administrator.

Christ Church Cathedral

Set on the opposite corner, this post-Tracy modern Anglican church incorporates ruins from the 1902 original. The porch was part of a 1944 addition to the earlier building. Hours are daily 7 a.m.-6 p.m.

Government House

Farther south along the Esplanade, Government House (a.k.a. the Residency and House of the Seven Gables), first built in 1870, was a superb bit of colonial architecture ravaged first by white ants, then by two cyclones. Except for the white-ant demolition—after which timber was replaced with stone—the building and gardens have been continually restored to original splendor.

Hotel Darwin

Walk north along the Esplanade to Herbert St. and one of the city's oldest pubs. The original pub, known as the Palmerston, opened in 1883.

The post-Tracy rebuild included lots of wicker palms, and the tropically ubiquitous "just like a Somerset Maugham novel" slogan.

Old Admiralty House

Continuing up the Esplanade, at the corner of Knuckey St., Admiralty House, former home to North Australia's naval commander, is one of Darwin's last remaining 1920s tropical houses. Undamaged by Tracy, the cypress pine building, elevated on stilts, houses an arts-and-crafts gallery with works by Top End-ers, with an al fresco tearoom down below.

Lyons Cottage

The Georgian-revival-style bungalow across Knuckey St. was built in 1925 as a residence for the head honcho of the British Australia Telegraph Company (BAT), and later occupied by former Darwin mayor John Lyons. Now a BAT museum, the stone cottage features exhibits on Australia's history of telecommunications. Open daily 9:30 a.m.-3 p.m. Admission is free. For information, phone (08) 8981-3355.

Victoria Hotel

Take Knuckey St. to the Smith Street Mall and turn right. Occupying a prime position in the center of the mall, the Victoria Hotel (called the Vic, locally) was originally built in 1894 and painstakingly reconstructed after each cyclone and war. Still Darwin's premier pub, the Vic's Verandah Bar, overlooking the mall and busker action, is a top spot for that big thirst.

Star Village

Star Village, a shopping arcade across the mall from the Vic, was the site of The Star, Darwin's first open-air cinema. The original 1930s projection booth and entranceway have been incorporated within the arcade's facade.

Commercial Bank

At the mall's Bennett St. corner, only the Commercial Bank's 1884 stone colonnade was saved and restored when its 1981 counterpart was built.

Chinese Temple

Continue along Bennett St. to Woods St., site of the post-Tracy temple that serves Darwin's large

Chinese community. The original 1887 structure couldn't weather the storm, and only the door, altar masonry blocks, and stone lions were spared. The current temple, built in 1978, has taken care to blend the old ruins within its steel and concrete replacement. Open Mon.-Fri. 8 a.m.-4 p.m., Sat.-Sun. 8 a.m.-3 p.m. Admission is free. **Note:** Please do not take photos while people are praying. (Did I even have to tell you that?) For information, phone (08) 8981-3440.

OTHER CITY SIGHTS

Aquascene

Located on the Esplanade, at Doctors Gully, this is one of Darwin's best attractions. Almost every day at high tide, throngs of catfish, mullet, bream, milkfish, and others come along to nibble bread from the hands of knee-deep, wading tourists. This bizarre ritual began about 20 years ago when a local denizen tossed some scraps to passing mullet (who told their friends, who told their friends, who . . .). Anyway, talk about *wonder bread!* Open daily at high tide. Phone (08) 8981-7837 for each day's feeding time. Admission is $3.50.

Indo-Pacific Marine

This small aquarium, near the roundabout at Smith St. West and Gilruth Ave., is one of the few such facilities in the world with displays of isolated coral reef ecosystems. Other features include informative talks, a gift shop, and a small garden cafe. Open daily 10 a.m.-5 p.m. Admission is $10. For information, phone (08) 8981-1294.

National Trust

Consisting of four pre-WW II houses in the Myilly Point Heritage Precinct, just outside downtown, the National Trust buildings feature sideslung windows, louvers, feathered eaves, and other trappings of tropical architecture. Pick up booklets, brochures, good tips, and souvenirs at the information center and gift shop within. Open Mon.-Fri. 8:30 a.m.-4:30 p.m. Admission is free. For information, phone (08) 8981-2848.

Botanic Gardens

Just outside the city center on Gardens Rd. (off Gilruth Ave.), Darwin's botanic gardens, wiped out

by three cyclones and a fire since their creation in 1879, have returned to glory with collections of figs, palms (nearly 400 species), and other tropical flora. New additions include a rainforest and wetlands area, plus a greenhouse with ferns and orchids. The restored cottage of Dr. Maurice Holtze, the gardens' founder, houses a restaurant, and occasional live concerts are performed at the amphitheater. Open daily 8 a.m.-sunset. Admission is free.

Aviation Museum

View more war paraphernalia such as wreckage of the Japanese Zero (first enemy aircraft ever shot down over Australia), a Boeing B-52 bomber (a loan from the U.S. Air Force), Mirage and Sabre jets, and a host of other aviation memorabilia. The museum is on Gardens Hill Crescent, Stuart Park (back near the botanic gardens). Open Mon.-Fri. 10 a.m.-2 p.m., Sat.-Sun. 10 a.m.-5 p.m. Admission is $4. For information, phone (08) 8981-7617.

Northern Territory Museum of Arts and Sciences

The Territory's major museum, on Conacher St., Fannie Bay, features exceptional Aboriginal, Southeast Asian, and Oceanian galleries with arts and crafts, maps, photos, and artifacts (including a pearling lugger and Vietnamese refugee boat out front on the lawn). As a research and scientific institution responsible for cataloging plant and animal species, the museum also houses a comprehensive natural sciences section. One big attraction is Sweetheart, the five-meter, 780-kilogram saltwater crocodile that had terrorized trolling fishermen until its capture in the late 1970s.

The art gallery features works by important Australian artists such as Russell Drysdale, Sir Sidney Nolan, and Donald Friend, as well as touring exhibitions. The museum bookshop has a good selection of local lore as well as gift items. The Cornucopia Museum Café, set in tropical gardens, looking out at the Timor Sea, is a great spot for sunset-watching, contemporary cuisine, and good wines.

Open Mon.-Fri. 9 a.m.-5 p.m., Sat.-Sun. 10 a.m.-6 p.m. Closed Good Friday and Christmas Day. Admission is free. For information, phone (08) 8982-4211.

Fannie Bay Gaol

Farther along East Point Rd., Darwin's main prison from 1883 to 1979 is now a museum where visitors can reminisce about life in the cells and view the gallows where the last hanging took place in 1952. Comprehensive exhibitions devoted to Cyclone Tracy's devastation include newspaper clippings and videotaped news footage from that time. Open daily 10 a.m.-5 p.m. Admission is free. For information, phone (08) 8999-8211.

East Point

The north shore of Fannie Bay affords dramatic harbor, city, and sunset views. This peninsular reserve, with good bushwalking and cycling trails, is a popular spot at sunrise or twilight when wallabies frolic in the nearby field.

Check out heavy artillery, small arms, and other military memorabilia and relics of WW II at the **Royal Australian Military Museum,** a former coastal defense complex adjacent to the reserve. Open daily 9:30 a.m.-5 p.m., closed Christmas Day and Good Friday. Admission is $4. For information, phone (08) 8981-9702.

Wharf Precinct

Stokes Hill Wharf, transformed first by war, then by tourism, offers historic walking paths, a war-era tunnel and lookout, and tourist creations such as cheap restaurants, trendy bars, live entertainment, and sports, which include bungee jumping and parasailing.

BEACHES

Watch your tootsies October to May when it's the deadly box jellyfish season! Though you'll be tempted by Darwin's sparkling beaches (and the ever-present humidity)—*don't chance it.* Nightcliff Beach, off Casuarina Dr. in north Darwin, has a protective stinger net.

Nude bathing is allowed on a strip of beach at **Casuarina Coastal Reserve,** a 1,180-hectare area that also contains rainforests and WW II gun emplacements.

The first Sunday in May is the official opening of Darwin's beaches, and **Mindil Beach,** on Fannie Bay, is the place to be. Celebrations include rock bands, dancers, acrobats, foodstalls, fashion shows, and sandcastle-building contests. Mindil and nearby **Vesvey's** beaches stay crowded until the stingers return.

ACCOMMODATIONS

This gateway city with a frontier heart has accommodations to suit just about any lifestyle or pocketbook. The central city and surrounding suburbs feature a good selection of hostels, hotels, motels, and holiday flats, while most of the campgrounds and caravan parks are situated on the outskirts of town. If you're seeking a roommate, check out the downtown cafes or around the mall, where you're bound to meet other travelers.

Getting a room is usually not a problem, but advance bookings are a good idea if you plan to arrive during the more crowded dry season and at festival times. Rates during the Wet are usually cheaper or at least up for bargaining. The Northern Territory levies a 2.5% Tourism Marketing Duty on all accommodations, with the exception of caravan sites and campsites (on-site vans and cabins are taxed). Revenues are supposedly used to promote tourism to the Territory.

Inexpensive (Under $35)

Darwin Transit Centre, 69 Mitchell St., inside the coach transit center (tel. 08-8981-9733), is one of the best deals in town. It's not gorgeous but it's certainly convenient—the bus is practically at your bedside. This former workers' residence has been revived with refurbished rooms, cooking facilities, a pool, sauna, gym, laundry, and game room. Bathroom facilities are shared. Nearby **Larrakeyah Lodge,** 50 Mitchell St. (tel. 08-8981-2933), is a long-established place with air-conditioned rooms, shared facilities, a pool, laundry room, and coffee shop.

Park Lodge, 42 Coronation Dr., Stuart Park, two km north of city center (tel. 08-8981-5692) is a friendly 20-room guesthouse with four shared bathrooms, communal kitchen, dining room, TV room, laundry, pool, and spa.

Moderate ($35-70)

Coolibah Resort, 91 Aralia St., Nightcliff, about 12 km from city center (tel. 08-8985-4166), is in the moderate price range but has a cheap, air conditioned, six-bed bunkroom with communal facilities and kitchen. **Air Raid City Lodge** (comforting name, eh?), 35 Cavenagh St., close to the general post office (tel. 08-8981-9214), has plain but clean rooms, private facilities, air-conditioning, TVs, communal kitchen, and laundry room.

Hotel Darwin, 10 Herbert St. (tel. 08-8981-9211), near the post office, is the city's former grande dame. The colonial building is somewhat worn but still has some charm, as well as the requisite wicker and cane decor. Facilities include TVs, phones, pool, restaurant, pub, and laundry. **Asti Motel,** 7 Packard Pl. (tel. 08-8981-8200), with restaurant, pool, and spa, is large and comfortable.

Ponciana Inn, on the corner of Mitchell and McLachlan in the center of town (tel. 08-8981-8111), is a four-story motel with a pool. **Parvista,** 5 MacKillop St., Parap (tel. 08-8981-0200), near Fannie Bay attractions, also has a pool and barbecue area. Small and cozy **Palms Motel,** 100 McMinn St. (tel. 08-8981-4188), is about one km north of the post office.

Expensive ($70 and Way Up)

All of Darwin's top-notch hotels provide the usual luxury range of restaurants, bars, recreational facilities, and business services. **The Beaufort,** the Esplanade (tel. 08-8982-9911), has colorful desert architecture. The **All Seasons Atrium,** Peel St. and the Esplanade (tel. 08-8941-0755), features—natch—a beautiful seven-story, glass-roofed atrium. **Diamond Beach Hotel Casino,** Gilruth Ave., Mindil Beach (tel. 08-8946-2666), features interesting geometric shapes, beachfront accommodations and an action-packed casino. The newer **Melia Darwin,** 32 Mitchell St. (tel. 08-8982-0000), the city's highest rise, is near the business district.

Hostels

Darwin's hostels are perfect places to meet travelers from everywhere and pick up tips—and maybe a companion. Dorm beds average $10 per night.

Darwin's **YHA Hostel** (tel. 08-8981-3995), next to the Transit Centre on Mitchell St., features 182 beds in 90 rooms, shared bathroom and kitchen facilities, pool, courtyard, and friendly atmosphere. The convenient on-site travel office offers discounted tour and bus tickets.

Make sure you have your YHA membership card in hand.

Fawlty Towers, 88 Mitchell St. (tel. 08-8981-5385), down the street from the YHA, is smallish, with air-conditioned dorm rooms, two communal kitchens, pool, barbecue, TV, video, and a helpful staff. Popular **Frogshollow Lodge,** 27 Lindsay St. (tel. 08-8941-2600), is largish, with spa and continental breakfast included.

The popular **YWCA,** 119 Mitchell St. (tel. 08-8981-8644), accepts both women and men at its 42-room facility with clean rooms, communal bathrooms and kitchens, and TV lounges. Dorm beds and single or double rooms are available. Other hostels that draw crowds are **Elke's Inner City Backpackers,** 112 Mitchell St. (tel. 08-8981-8399), and **Ivan's Backpackers Hostel,** 97 Mitchell St. (tel. 08-8981-5385).

The **CWA Hostel** (Country Women's Association), 3 Packard Pl. (tel. 08-8941-1536), offers two four-bed rooms for both men and women and four two-bed rooms for women only. Facilities include a communal kitchen, TV lounge, and large garden area.

Camping

Unfortunately all of Darwin's campsites are about 10-15 km outside the city. The following parks allow tents as well as caravans: **The Overlander Caravan Park,** McMillans Rd., Berrimah, 13 km east (tel. 08-8984-3025); **The Palms Caravan Park,** Stuart Hwy., Berrimah, 17 km east (tel. 08-8932-2891); **Shady Glen Caravan Park,** Stuart Hwy. and Farrell Crescent, Winnellie, 10 km east (tel. 08-8984-3330).

For additional camping opportunities in the Howard Springs area, 26 km from the city, see "Vicinity of Darwin" under "The Top End," below.

Camping gear can be rented from U-Rent, 50 Mitchell St. (tel. 08-8941-1280).

FOOD

What's your favorite nosh—buffalo, crocodile, camel, or kangaroo? You'll find such territorial specialties listed alongside fish 'n' chips in some restaurants. Tasty barramundi, fresh from local waters, is plentiful also. And, as might be expected in this multinational city, ethnic foods are widely offered, with Asian cuisine ranking supreme. Supermarkets, small groceries, and takeaways are easy to spot throughout city and suburbs, and the Smith Street Mall area is full of coffee shops and lunch counters. Darwin's best dining value—and the most fun—is at the Asian-style markets held several times weekly.

Inexpensive

Head to Smith Street Mall, though keep in mind that most of the coffee shops shut down when the shops do, meaning 5 p.m. on weekdays (except for Thursday), Saturday afternoon, and Sunday. **Central City Café** is a popular breakfast and gathering spot. **Cosmopolitan Café**, in Anthony Plaza, serves up good breakfasts and lunches. Next door, the **French Bakehouse** is open daily for coffee and light meals. The historic **Victoria Hotel**, opposite Anthony Plaza, features a relatively cheap lunchtime carvery upstairs and good-value counter meals downstairs.

Toward the Knuckey St. end of the mall, **Darwin Plaza** houses a glut of Lebanese, Thai, Chinese, and health food counters. The **Taco House**, within that same plaza, is where you can sample croc, buffalo, and 'roo burgers, along with tacos, of course (watch that filling!). The **Sate House**, in Victoria Arcade, across from Anthony Plaza, has cheap Indonesian dishes.

Confetti's, 85 Mitchell St., is open late and serves homemade ice cream, cappuccino, pancakes, and a variety of smoothies, sundays, and snacks. Open daily 11 a.m.-late. **The Pancake Palace**, Cavenagh St., is also open late every day to please pancake-heads.

The Barra Bar, 15 Knuckey St., is a good, cheap, fish 'n' chippery. **Fisherman's Eatery**, on Fisherman's Wharf, specializes in takeaway barramundi 'n' chips, and you'll find many other inexpensive choices in the Wharf Precinct.

Hana Sushi Bar, 31 Knuckey St., will feed you traditional Japanese tidbits.

Moderate

Jade Gardens, on the mall, serves Chinese banquets and business lunches. Open Mon.-Fri. lunch, daily dinner. **Rendezvous Café**, on Smith Street Mall, offers hot and spicy Malaysian meals. Open Mon.-Sat. lunch, daily dinner. The **Maharajah**, 37 Knuckey St., features an extensive menu and excellent curries. Open Mon.-Sat. for lunch and dinner.

Lindsay Street Café, 2 Lindsay St., serves contemporary cuisine either inside its historical building or outside in the lush tropical gardens. Open Tues.-Fri. lunch, Tues.-Sat. dinner, and Sunday brunch.

Satisfy your pasta urge at **Guiseppe's**, Cavenagh St., with both regional and traditional Italian specialties. Open Mon.-Fri. lunch, Mon.-Sat. dinner. **Roma Bar Café**, 30 Cavenagh St., is a local favorite with an eclectic crowd, superb focaccias, pastas, and coffees. Open daily for breakfast and lunch. **Kafe Neon**, in the Wharf Precinct, is a casual eatery with superb Greek salads. Open daily for lunch and dinner.

Expensive

Christo's on the Wharf, in the Wharf Precinct (tel. 08-8981-8658), has fabulous seafood (try the garlic prawns) and is a splendid place to view the sunset. Open Tues-Fri. lunch, Tues.-Sun. dinner. **Hanuman Thai Restaurant**, 28 Mitchell St. (tel. 08-8941-3500), opened in 1992 but has already been declared one of the country's finest dining establishments. Heavenly prepared Thai and Nonya delicacies are placed before you with grace and style. Open Mon.-Fri. lunch, nightly dinner.

Siggi's, at the Beaufort Hotel (tel. 08-8999-1179), is the city's classical-French star. Intimate settings and a changing menu keep the fat wallets coming back for more, more, and still *beaucoup plus*. Open Tues.-Sat. for dinner.

Markets

Darwin's thriving, colorful markets can be categorized equally under Food, Shopping, and Entertainment listings.

The foodaholics come early to set up folding tables and chairs beachside, watch the sunset, socialize, then tease their taste buds at the **Mindil Beach Market**. Foodstalls serve up Thai, Indian, Malaysian, Chinese, Indonesian, South American, and other ethnic cuisine, as well as cakes, breads, fruits, and veggies at very reasonable prices. The market is held Thursday 6-10 p.m. during the dry season.

Other sniff-and-gobble markets are: **The Big Flea Market**, Darwin's oldest, held Sunday 8 a.m.-2 p.m. at Rapid Creek Shopping Centre; **The Parap Market**, held Saturday 8 a.m.-2 p.m. at Parap; and **Palmerston Markets**, held Friday

:30-9:30 p.m. at Frances Mall, Palmerston. Except for Mindil Beach, the markets are open year-round.

ENTERTAINMENT AND EVENTS

Don't expect big city culture, but there is a range of theaters, cinemas, pubs, clubs, and the casino for amusement. On the other hand, special events in this isolated region can be a whole lot of fun. The *Northern Territory News* provides listings of all the current doings. Again, if you're looking for companionship for a night on the own, scout around the Smith Street Mall, surrounding coffee shops, or the hostels. This is an easy town to meet people in.

Cinemas
You can catch the usual commercial showings (several months or so old) at **Cinema Darwin,** on Mitchell Street. **Darwin Film Society** (tel. 08-8981-2215) often hosts artier movies at the Museum Theatrette, Conacher St., Bullocky Point (tel. 08-8982-4211). Inquire at the Tourist information Centre about **Deck Chair Cinema,** an open-air cinema with artsy films, which are sometimes upstaged by a showy night sky.

Pubs and Clubs
The oldies are goodies. The **Vic,** on the mall, features live bands in the upstairs Verandah Bar, Wed.-Saturday. The **Darwin Hotel,** on Mitchell St., hosts live bands on Friday night, piano in the lounge Wed.-Sat., and a poolside jazz barbecue on Sunday. On Sunday afternoon and Fri.-Sat. nights you can alternate between indoor and outdoor bands at the **Beachfront Hotel,** Rapid Creek. Or get down and grungy at the infamous **Nightcliff Hotel,** corner of Bagot and Trower, about 10 km north of the city center. Depending on which night you visit, entertainment consists of live bands, wrestling females covered in a variety of cooking sauces, very thirsty men, and wild women. The Nightcliff is what's referred to as a Darwin "experience."

Favorite discos, most open nightly, are: upmarket **Circles,** at the Beaufort Hotel; **Dix,** 21 Cavenagh St. in the Hot Gossip Complex; and **Beachcombers,** corner Daly and Mitchell Streets. Trendies should check out the array of nightclubs, piano lounges, and discos in the chichi hotels. Neat, casual dress is required.

Expect to pay a cover charge of about $5-7 in the pubs (when bands are on), $8-10 in the discos, and $12 or more at the five-star spots.

For those of you in the "Blowin' in the Wind" mood, the **Top End Folk Club** holds sessions at the East Point Gun Turret on the second Sunday of each month, from 8 p.m. Visitors and musicians are encouraged to join in the hoot. Admission is $6. For information, phone (08) 8988-1301 or 8941-1699.

The Casino
Depending on your inclination, wardrobe, luck, and budget (or *non*-budget), the **Diamond Beach Hotel Casino** might be the only entertainment you need. All the games are represented, including the Aussie two-up. The 350-seat Cabaret Room hosts a variety of theatrical entertainment, along with bar service and elaborate buffets; a coffee shop is open round-the-clock. During the dry season, the casino puts on a Sunday afternoon poolside barbecue with live jazz.

Dress regulations are strict: neat, clean, tidy clothing at all times; no shorts, thongs, running shoes, or denim wear of any kind (not even your best hole-in-the-knee Levi's); and, it should go without saying—keep your shirt on your back, even if you lose it in the casino.

Diamond Beach is on Gilruth Ave., Mindil Beach. Casino hours are daily noon-4 a.m. For information, phone (08) 8946-2666.

Corroborees
You're in your own Dreamtime if you're waiting for an invite to an authentic Aboriginal corroboree. These sacred spiritual ceremonies are off-limits to the general public. You *will* be able to join tours that feature a kind of pseudo event, with traditional dancing, singing, and didgeridoo-ing.

Theater, Dance, and Concerts
The **Darwin Performing Arts Centre,** 93 Mitchell St., next to the Beaufort Hotel (tel. 08-8981-1222), regularly stages theater, musical, and dance performances. The playhouse (capacity 1,070) also houses a rehearsal room, exhibition gallery, and dance studio. Phone the

center, or check the daily newspaper. The center can also provide details of upcoming events at the botanic gardens outdoor amphitheater.

Events

This isolated laid-back city takes every opportunity to come together for just about any occasion. **The Northern Territory Barra Classic,** a premier "tag-and-release" tournament held by the Darwin Game Fishing Club, is held about the first of May. The **Mindil Beach Carnival** in May (see "Beaches," above) celebrates the departure of the box jellyfish and the opening of the beaches. More than a decade old, the **Bougainvillea Festival** is held for 18 days in late May or early June, the flower's peak blossoming time. Numerous festivities include a Mardi Gras, grand parade, concerts, photography contest, art exhibitions, music and film festivals, a food and wine fair, picnics, ethnic events, and daily doings on the mall. A weekend Festival Fringe Club produces alternative music, dance, theater, and literature events.

Darwin's famous **Beer Can Regatta** tailgates the Bougainvillea Festival in early June, and is certainly an event to inspire the Darwin Thirst. Empty beer cans are used to construct rafts and boats, which then "race" in the local sea. Using full cans of beer to build the craft is strictly *verboten!*

Other big-turnout annual events—all falling in August—are the barefoot **Mud Crab Tying Competition,** the **Darwin Cup** horse racing meet, and the internationally known **Darwin Rodeo.**

The **Marratjila Festival** is a nine-day celebration of Aboriginal heritage that draws participants from both tribal communities and urban areas to join in dance and theater performances, contemporary and traditional music, and arts and crafts exhibitions.

SPORTS AND RECREATION

You'll find a wide range of sports and recreation opportunities in the city and suburbs, but bear the heat and humidity in mind if you're not fit or not used to the climate. Joggers and cyclists will find plenty of good, scenic tracks. Best bets

DANGER !
BOX JELLYFISH CAN BE DEADLY

OCT. to MAY
DO NOT SWIM
JUNE to SEPT.
TAKE CARE SWIMMING

FIRST AID:
Resuscitation + Vinegar
(poured on affected area)
+Transport to Hospital = LIFE

NT DEPARTMENT OF HEALTH
AND COMMUNITY SERVICES

are the waterfront area that follows the Esplanade and the shoreline reserve from Fannie Bay to East Point.

Water sports and fishing are favorites here, but heed those box jellyfish and crocodile warnings! For information on any Darwin sport, phone the **Sports Hotline** (tel. 08-8981-4300).

Scuba Diving

Divers can explore the litter of WW II wrecks as well as the large coral reef off Darwin's shores. Good dive shops are **Fannie Bay Dive Centre,** 2 Fannie Bay Pl. (tel. 08-8981-3049) and **Sand Pebbles Dive Shop,** De Latour St., Coconut Grove (tel. 08-8985-1906).

Fishing

Top End waters are jumping with sport fish, particularly Australia's famous **barramundi.** The best time to score a catch is from Easter through May. The prime spots near Darwin are around the harbor arms, Leader's Creek, Bynoes Harbour, and in the creeks and estuaries of Shoal Bay. Other common species are queenfish, Spanish mackerel, longtail tuna, giant trevally, threadfin salmon, and barracuda. **Mud crabbing** in the estuaries is another favorite local activity.

For information on **licenses, regulations,** and **fishing tours,** contact the Department of Primary Industry and Fisheries, Bennett St. (tel. 08-8999-4821). For **tidal charts,** contact the Port Authority, Henry Chan Ave. (tel. 08-8981-6701).

Swimming Pools

Practically every hostel, motel, and hotel has its own pool. In addition, you'll find public pools at Darwin, Casuarina, Nightcliff, and Winnellie. One of the better locations is on Ross Smith Ave., Fannie Bay (tel. 08-8981-2662).

Sporting Facilities

Tennis: Four courts are available for public use at the **Darwin Tennis Centre,** Gilruth Ave., The Gardens (tel. 08-89 85-2844). Courts are also available outside the casino, near Mindil Beach. For information, phone (08) 8981-2181.

Golf: Darwin Golf Club, Links Rd., Marrara (tel. 08-8927-1015), has the only 18-hole course in town. Nine-hole courses are available at **Gardens Park Golf Links,** opposite the casino (tel. 08-8981-6365), and **Palmerston Golf Club,** Dwyer Crescent, Palmerston (tel. 08-8932-324). Equipment can be rented on-site.

For information on other sporting facilities, phone the Sports Hotline, above.

Other Sports

Sailboards are available for rent in front of the Diamond Beach Hotel Casino at Mindil Beach. For **sailboat** hire, contact the Darwin Sailing Club (tel. 08-8981-1700). For information about weekend **hiking** expeditions, contact Darwin Bushwalking Club (tel. 08-8985-1484). **Darwin Gym,** 78 the Esplanade (tel. 08-8941-0020), features workout and fitness equipment.

The most prominent spectator sport in Darwin is **horse racing,** with greyhounds placing, and an occasional touch football game making quite a show.

SHOPPING

Darwin's major shopping areas are **Smith Street Mall, Darwin Plaza, The Galleria,** and **Casuarina Shopping Square,** in the northern suburbs. Just about any creature comfort or service can be purchased at any of these places (and Casuarina has a Kmart, too). City shopping hours are Mon.-Fri. 9:30 a.m.-5:30 p.m., Saturday 8:30 a.m.-1 p.m., late-night trading Thursday until 9 p.m. Casuarina shopping hours are daily 9 a.m.-5:30 p.m., late-night trading Thursday and Friday until 9 p.m.

Markets

Darwin's markets have a lot more than just food-stalls. You can pick up crafts, books, plants, dolls, knickknacks, Indian and Balinese clothing, and other goodies (see "Markets" in the "Food" section, above).

Crafts

Aboriginal art collectors will find a large variety of arts and crafts in Darwin. **Framed: the Darwin Gallery,** 55 Stuart Hwy., is the place to pick up fine Top End and central Australian bark paintings, sand paintings, weavings, didgeridoos, baskets, and hand-blown glass. Open Mon.-Sat. 8:30 a.m.-5:30 p.m., Sunday 11 a.m.-5 p.m. The **Raintree Gallery,** 29 Knuckey St., sells similar wares, specializing in items made by the Tiwi people from Bathurst and Melville Islands.

Purchase T-shirts printed with Aboriginal designs, as well as Tiwi printed fabrics, at **Riji Dij-Australian and Original,** 11 Knuckey Street.

Weavers Workshop, Parap Pl., Parap, sells locally made handknits, pottery, natural soaps, and toiletries. **Shades of Ochre** (in the Old Admiralty House), 70 the Esplanade, displays and sells fine local arts and crafts.

Darwin Shipstores, Frances Bay Dr., sells flags from all over the world, including the Boxing Kangaroo and Northern Territory state flags.

Other Shops

Photo Supplies: You'll find camera houses at just about every turn in this photo-op territory. **Camera World,** in Darwin Plaza, Smith Street Mall, offers fast passport service, a good range of photo supplies, and one-hour film processing. **Palm Photographics Drive-in Transit Shop,** on Mitchell St., right next to the Transit Centre, provides film processing and sales daily 8:30 a.m.-10 p.m.

New Age: Center yourself at **Inner Dreams Book and Gift Shop,** Parap Shopping Village, with quartz crystals, incense, flower essences, oils, books, tapes, and videos.

Gear: Everything you need for going bush is stocked at the **Northern Territory General Store,** 42 Cavenagh St. (tel. 08-8981-8242). Inventory includes tents, boots, maps, compasses, knives, tarps, sleeping bags, mosquito nets, etc.

Surf Wear: Purchase top Australian brands at **Fannie Bay Beach Bums,** 2/5 Fannie Bay Pl., Fannie Bay. Open daily 10 a.m.-6 p.m.

Book Exchange: Nearly 20,000 books are stocked at **J.R. Book Exchange,** in Central Arcade, Smith Street Mall. You can also pick up good used clothing at this shop.

TRANSPORTATION

Getting There by Air
Airlines serving Darwin from North America are **Qantas** (tel. 13-1313 toll-free), with a change of plane in Cairns, and **Garuda Indonesia** (tel. 08-8981-6149), with a change of plane in Bali. Other international carriers are **Merpati**, from Indonesia, and **Singapore, Qantas**, and **Royal Brunei** from Asia.

From other Australian states, Darwin is easily reached on **Ansett**, Shop 14, Smith Street Mall (tel. 08-8980-3333, or 13-1300 toll-free), and **Qantas**, 16 Bennett St. (tel. 08-8982-3333, or 13-1313 toll-free).

All international and domestic flights arrive and depart from **Darwin Airport**, just eight km north of the city center. Services include rental car desks, money exchange, and a visitor center. **Darwin Airport Bus Service** (tel. 08-8941-1656) will shuttle you to or from the city for $6. Taxis are ready and waiting; fare to the city is about $12.

Getting There by Bus
Greyhound Pioneer Australia (tel. 13-2030 toll-free) offers the most frequent service to Darwin from Australia's capital cities and outback communities. The **three routes into the city** are: up the Track from Alice Springs, with stops at Tennant Creek and Katherine; the Barkly Highway from Townsville, Queensland, via Mt. Isa, joining the Track at Three Ways; and the Victoria Highway from Western Australia through Broome, Derby, and Kununurra. One or more of the coach companies make daily runs along all routes. On Queensland routes it's sometimes necessary to change coaches at Tennant Creek or Three Ways.

McCafferty's Coaches (tel. 08-8941-0911) provides service along and from the east coast, and closes a Townsville/Darwin/Alice Springs/Adelaide loop.

Fares vary little among the coach lines and they all offer stopovers and money-saving passes (some need to be purchased outside the country).

All intercity coaches arrive and depart at **Darwin Transit Centre,** 69 Mitchell Street.

Getting There by Car
See the "Getting There by Bus" section above for routes into the city. The main highways are sealed with asphalt and have roadhouse facilities. But remember—it's a long way to the Territory tip: 350 km from Katherine, 978 km from Tennant Creek, 1,482 km from Alice Springs, 3,215 km from Adelaide, 2,489 km from Townsville, and 4,430 km from Perth. Don't venture off the main roads without a good 4WD vehicle, emergency supplies, and a phone call to the nearest police facility.

Getting Around by Air
Due to airline deregulation, flying within the country has become much more affordable. Check with both the YHA and the visitor center as well as with **Ansett** and **Qantas**—both airlines are booking agents for the small commuter carriers, which seem to change with the seasons.

Getting Around by Bus
Darwin Bus Service operates weekdays and Saturday morning, entering the city along Mitchell St. and departing by way of Cavenagh Street. Routes no. 4 (to Fannie Bay, Nightcliff, Rapid Creek, and Casuarina) and no. 6 (to Fannie Bay, Parap, and Stuart Park) will take you to most of Darwin's attractions and other points of interest. Fares, based on zones, range from 70 cents to $2. The city terminal is on Harry Chan Ave., near Cavenagh Street. For information, phone (08) 8999-7513.

Getting Around by Car
Taxis are available at the airport, or phone **Darwin Radio Taxis** (tel. 08-8981-8777).

Major **car rental** firms such as **Budget, Hertz,** and **Thrifty** have airport and city locations. Better deals might be had at **Territory-Rent-a-Car** (tel. 08-8981-8400), **Rent a Rocket** (tel. 08-8981-6977), or **Rent a Dent** (tel. 08-8981-1411). Rates start at about $35 per day with 150 free km—20 cents to 30 cents per km after that. Rates are higher if you take the car more than about 70 km outside Darwin—which is probably just about everywhere you want to go. Be sure to inquire about weekend specials or extended-rental deals. Check with **Territory Rent-A-Car** or 4WDs (starting at $75 per day, plus km charges).

Getting Around by Bicycle

Check first with the backpacker hostels—either they'll have cheap deals or, if you're a guest, they might lend you one for free. Otherwise, try **U-Rent,** 50 Mitchell St. (tel. 08-8941-1280), or **Darwin Bike Rentals,** 57 Mitchell St. (tel. 08-89 41-0070). Rates are about $8 per half-day, $12 per 24 hours.

Getting Around by Boat

Take a ride across the harbor to Mandorah on **Darwin Harbour Ferries.** Service operates Mon.-Fri. year-round, from Stokes Hill Wharf. Fare is $18 round-trip, and the journey takes 30-40 minutes each way. Two-hour sunset and harbor cruises are also available. For information and schedules, phone (08) 8978-5094.

Tours

The organized tour offerings in and around Darwin are numerous—Litchfield Park, Kakadu Park, Cobourg Peninsula, Arnhem Land, Bathurst and Melville Islands, crocodile farms, and other destinations and activities can be explored by plane, boat, jeep, chopper, canoe, or foot, for one day or longer. The visitor center has reams of info describing tours and operators, including prices and departure days. The YHA travel office also makes recommendations and bookings. Some tours operate infrequently, or not at all, during the Wet.

Also see the chart "Aboriginal Tours," in the On the Road chapter.

Getting Away

Due to its close proximity, Darwin is a popular gateway to Indonesia. **Garuda Indonesia** flies twice weekly between Darwin, Denpasar, and Jakarta (about $600 round-trip to one or the other city). Garuda's city ticket office is at 9 Cavenagh St. (tel. 08-8981-6149).

Merpati, Indonesia's domestic carrier, flies twice weekly between Darwin and Denpasar and once a week between Darwin and Kupang, in Timor, with onward flights to many other Indonesian cities. Tickets can be purchased from the Indonesian government travel agency, **Natrabu,** 16 Westlane Arcade, beneath the Vic-

toria Hotel on Smith St. Mall (tel. 08-8981-3694). Sample fares are $240 one-way from Darwin, with stops in Kupang, Maumere, Ruteng, Labuhanbajo, Bima, and Ampenan; $200 one-way from Darwin to Kupang, a bargain for island-hoppers headed toward Bali. Scour the newspaper listings and check with travel agents about the many APEX and excursion fares and package deals available to Indonesia.

Also check out special deals with **Singapore Airlines,** 48 Smith Street Mall (tel. 08-8941-1799).

Unless you're in the big bucks, cruises are not a practical option.

Hitching

It's not so easy (and it's illegal, remember?). Track traffic is sparse outside cities and towns. Many hitchhikers report long waits at Three Ways, junction of the Track and the road to Mt. Isa.

SERVICES

Branches of national and territorial banks are located on and around the Smith Street Mall. Many have suburban offices and automatic teller machines. Banking hours are Mon.-Thurs. 9:30 a.m.-4 p.m., Friday until 5 p.m. Be sure to take your passport or other identification.

Darwin's glossy newer **general post office,** 48 Cavenagh St., has instigated computerized postal services, including self-selection service, electronic counters, and digital readouts. Postal officers stand by to assist with any problems. Operating hours are Mon.-Fri. 8:30 a.m.-5 p.m.

For visa and work permit inquiries, call on the **Department of Immigration,** 40 Cavenagh St. (tel. 08-8946-3100).

Casual labor opportunities fluctuate. Check with the hostels or other travelers for up-to-date info.

INFORMATION

The **Darwin Regional Tourism Association Information Centre,** 33 Smith Street Mall (tel. 08-8981-4300), will quite likely be your one-stop shop for any information about the Territory. The bureau also provides free maps and informative booklets, and arranges accommodations, car rentals, and tours to fit all budgets. Hours are Mon.-Fri. 8 a.m.-6 p.m., Saturday 9 a.m.-2 p.m., Sunday 10 a.m.-5 p.m. In addition, there's a visitor office at Darwin's airport.

The **Australian Nature Conservation Agency,** Smith St., between Lindsay and Whitefield (tel. 08-8981-5299), provides information about the Territory's parks, regulations, and required permits. Alternately, the **Conservation Commission of the Northern Territory** (tel. 08-8999-5511) is out in suburban Palmerston, about 20 km from the city center.

The **Disabled Persons Bureau,** Shop 7, Group floor, Casuarina Plaza, Casuarina (tel. 08-8922-7213), offers an information and referral service for disabled visitors.

Darwin Gay and Lesbian Society (tel. 08-8981-6812) offers info on social activities, counseling and health facilities, and other pertinent topics.

Maps, up-to-date road information, and camping and accommodation guides can be obtained from the **Automobile Association of the Northern Territory,** 79-81 Smith St. (tel. 08-8981-3837). The AANT has reciprocal arrangements with both Australian and overseas auto-mobile associations. Bring your membership card for free and discounted services.

Emergencies: Dial 000, or contact the **police** (tel. 08-8927-8888) or **ambulance** (tel. 08-8927-9000). **Royal Darwin Hospital,** Rocklands Dr. Casuarina (tel. 08-8920-7211), has a 24-hour accident and emergency center. **Central Darwin Dental Surgery,** 59 Smith St., CML Bldg. (tel. 08-8941-1899 or 8941-1717), also handles dental emergencies. For **Travel and Immunization Services,** phone 08-8981-7197.

More Information

The **State Reference Library of the Northern Territory,** 25 Cavenagh St. (tel. 08-8999-7177), has shelves full of books, photos, and other documents relating to the Territory. Interstate and international newspapers are available for browsing. Open Mon.-Sat. 10 a.m.-6 p.m. (come for free lunchtime entertainment Feb.-Nov.). The **city library** is in Paspalis Centrepoint arcade on Smith Street Mall.

Bookworld, 30 Smith Street Mall, is a good bookshop with regional literature, contemporary fiction, and an ample selection of everything else.

Darwin's local daily newspaper is the *Northern Territory News.*

THE TOP END

Keep your hat on and knock your socks off. Ever since ad-rep Paul Hogan was reincarnated as Crocodile Dundee, the Northern Territory's tip-top has become one of Australia's most popular tourist destinations. Most of the moviedom believers head straight for Kakadu National Park and its realer-than-film-reel glories, with the spillover forging onward, upward, and backward to Arnhem Land, the Cobourg Peninsula, Litchfield Park, and Bathurst and Melville Islands. Most of these spots can be visited on day trips from Darwin, but at some you'll no doubt want to stay longer. Make the most of your visit to this ancient and extraordinary region—there will be no sequel.

VICINITY OF DARWIN

Mandorah

Situated 10 km across the harbor from Darwin, this small resort on the northeast tip of Cox Peninsula is noted for its sandy beaches, superior fishing, and the tourist-oriented Aboriginal corroborees performed by the local Kenbi community and hosted by Mandorah Inn (tel. 08-8978-5044). Otherwise, hop on a Darwin Harbour ferry for an easy day trip from the city. If you're driving up the Cox Peninsula road, you'll encounter magnetic anthills on the way into town. (By the way, they're called "magnetic" because they point north.)

Howard Springs

This nature park, 27 km southeast of Darwin along the Stuart Hwy., features a refreshing spring-fed pool set amid lush rainforest and is often crowded with city escapers. Additional features include a fish-viewing area, short bushwalking tracks, birds and wildlife, a kiosk, and barbecue facilities. The facilities are open daily 7 a.m.-5 p.m. For information, phone (08) 8983-1001.

Campsites are available at **Coolalinga Caravan Park,** Stuart Hwy. (tel. 08-8983-1026), and **Howard Springs Caravan Park,** 290 Whitewood Rd. (tel. 08-8983-1169). **Nook Van-**

O-Tel, Morgan Rd. (tel. 08-8983-1048), has campsites and on-site vans.

Darwin Crocodile Farm

I hate to tell you—many of the thousands of saltwater and freshwater crocs you see here are annually killed. But don't despair! You'll soon be able to admire them on someone's designer feet, slung over a fashion-setting arm, or inside tomorrow's burger. Come at feeding time when these beasts display their feelings about the future! Located 40 km from Darwin, on the Stuart Hwy., the farm is open daily 9 a.m.-5 p.m., with tours at 11 a.m. and 2 p.m. Feeding time is daily at 2 p.m., with an extra one Sunday at 11 a.m. For information, phone (08) 8988-1450.

Berry Springs

Two top attractions make this spot worth the 56-km journey (take the turnoff from Stuart Hwy.). **Berry Springs Nature Park** offers spring-fed, croc-free swimming sites with fewer people than Howard Springs, plus rainforest, picnic areas, and barbecue facilities. The springs are open daily 8 a.m.-7 p.m. year-round, except after extremely heavy rains. For information, phone (08) 8988-6030.

Territory Wildlife Park, next door, is a 400-hectare open-range sanctuary housing kangaroos, wallabies, water buffalo, dingoes, and other Northern Territory species, as well as a 20-meter-high walk-through aviary, an aquarium, natural lagoon with waterbirds and a viewing blind, and a nocturnal house. A motor train transports visitors along a four-km link road. Open daily 8:30 a.m.-6 p.m. (no admittance after 4 p.m.), except Christmas Day and Good Friday. Admission is $10. For information, phone (08) 8988-6000.

Litchfield Park

Long overshadowed by Kakadu, this becoming-more-and-more-developed 65,700-hectare reserve, just a two-hour drive from Darwin, is now basking in the tourist limelight.

Dominated by the vast sandstone Tabletop Range and escarpment, some of the notable features of this awesome region include four major waterfalls cascading over the plateau (each with its own swimming pools and rainforest), creeks, caves, abundant flora, birds, and other wildlife, gigantic magnetic termite mounds, and numerous excellent bushwalking trails.

The **Lost City,** about six km east of Tolmer Falls, is a mysterious area of gigantic sandstone outcrops that resemble buildings, pillars, and humans. Adding to the mystique is the fact that no Aboriginal settlement has been traced here. The "city" is accessible by foot or 4WD.

Swimming is safe in the falls area of the park (i.e., no crocs), but saltwater crocs *do* inhabit

Surprise Falls and the Finniss and Reynolds Rivers, so watch your tail there. **Camping** is permitted at Florence Falls, Buley Rockhole, and Tjaynera Falls; bush campsites are available at Walker and Bamboo Creeks.

Privately owned **Petherick's Rainforest Reserve,** 10 km north of Wangi, features thick monsoon rainforest, waterfalls, rock pools, and wildlife. Marked walking trails include a special botanist trail where trees are identified. Entrance and camping fees total $5 pp. **The Drover's Rest,** just before Petherick's, offers a similar deal plus 15-minute helicopter rides ($55).

To reach Litchfield Park, take either the Cox Peninsula/Wangi Road (beyond Berry Springs) or the Stuart Hwy. to Batchelor and into the park. It's possible to make somewhat of a loop, entering at the northern boundary (which has a ranger station), continuing about 18 km to Wangi Falls, 10 km to Tolmer Falls, 20 km to Florence Falls on the eastern edge, and out through Batchelor to the Track. Conventional vehicles should have no problem on the ring road, but a 4WD is necessary for access to other areas.

For information, phone the **Conservation Commission** (tel. 08-8999-5511).

A plethora of tours operate out of Darwin to Litchfield Park.

BATHURST AND MELVILLE ISLANDS

These two flat islands (pop. 2,500), about 80 km north of Darwin and divided by narrow Apsley Strait, comprise 8,000 square km. As with much of the Top End, the seasons produce dramatic changes in this region. In the dry season, grass withers, turns to straw, and burns; the Wet brings monsoon rains and lush greenery.

History

Strange as it seems, these islands and their Tiwi owners not only had little contact with Europeans but, until the late 1800s, had limited dealings with mainland Aborigines. The British attempted to establish their first settlement on Melville Island in 1824, but disease, isolation, and the animosity of the Tiwis sent the new residents quickly packing. Other visits were made by Macassarese fishermen, possibly the Portuguese, and a Japanese pilot who crashed onto Melville during WW II. Nguiu, a Catholic mission begun in 1911 in Bathurst's southeast, is the main settlement, followed by Milikapiti and Pularumpi, both on Melville.

Crafts

Tiwi culture is particularly rich and relatively unscathed. Locally produced arts and crafts include unique carved totems and burial poles, screen printing, bark painting, pottery, and interesting ethnic clothing.

Tours

Permits are not given to independent tourists, so the only way to visit these islands is through an all-inclusive organized tour that will fly you over from Darwin. Other than watching the Tiwis create their art (with, of course, an opportunity to make purchases), many tours allow visitors to experience traditional Aboriginal living, including the preparation and ingestion of typical bush tucker (not for the dietarily squeamish). A swim and lunch stop at **Turacumbie Falls** is another recreational feature.

Tiwi Tours (tel. 08-8981-5144), the largest local operator, has a wide range of half- or full-day "Tiwi experience" excursions, costing $175-240; two- to three-day tours, $450-600, include accommodations at **Putjamirra Safari Camp** on the northwest tip of Melville Island, where guests are given the opportunity to really share in the Aboriginal lifestyle. **Australian Kakadu Tours** (tel. 08-8981-5144) offers two-, three-, and five-day Putjamirra stays, costing $550-1100.

It's best to bring necessities with you from Darwin. Stores stocking incidentals are located at Nguiu and at Barra Lodge at Port Hurd. Except for the bar at Barra Lodge, no alcohol is permitted on the islands.

ALONG ARNHEM HIGHWAY

The Arnhem Highway joins the Stuart Highway 34 km southeast of Darwin, traveling 217 km to Jabiru in the heart of Kakadu National Park. City buses go out as far as Humpty Doo, but you'll have to rely on the Kakadu-bound coaches or a car for other sites.

Humpty Doo

You can't miss this little service town (pop. 3,000) 10 km into this stretch—a massive replica of a croc decked out with red bulb-eyes and boxing gloves signals your arrival.

Turn west four km to **Graeme Gows Reptile World,** where you can see one of Australia's largest collections of snakes and lizards. Of special interest are Goddess Marael and Psycho, two of the world's deadliest snakes, and *Crocodile Dundee* python-stars Hoges and Strop. Informative talks are given each day.

Open daily 9 a.m.-5 p.m. Admission is $5. For information, phone (08) 8988-1661.

Stop in at **Humpty Doo Hotel,** home of the annual Darwin Stubby Drinking Competition (31 July). Any time of year this pub is full of local color, serves counter meals, has an occasional live band, and is adorned with Territorial memorabilia.

Fogg Dam

Once an experimental rice farm, this 1,569-hectare conservation reserve, 11 km east of Humpty Doo, is an important refuge for waterbirds such as magpie geese, herons, ducks, egrets, brolgas, and rainbow pitta. Other wildlife includes jabirus, wallabies, frilled-neck lizards, file snakes, and pythons. Dawn and dusk during the dry season are the best viewing times. Camping is not allowed.

Adelaide River Crossing

Another eight km along the Arnhem Highway, the *Adelaide River Queen* (tel. 08-8988-8144) departs from the western bank for 90-minute upstream cruises to view crocs (who leap for morsels being dangled from poles), buffalo, pigs, and birds. The two-story vessel has an air-conditioned lower deck and snack bar. Cruises operate Tues.-Sun. Feb.-Oct., less frequently Nov.-January. Cost is $45 from Darwin, $20 at the jetty. Two-hour excursions are conducted by **Frontier Jumping Crocodile Cruises** (tel. 08-8941-0744). Cost is $50 from Darwin, $25 at the jetty.

Leaning Tree Lagoon

Off the highway, some 13 km from the river crossing, Leaning Tree Lagoon Nature Park (101 hectares) is another waterbird refuge during the dry season. The locals come here to picnic, canoe, and camp (no facilities).

Mary River Crossing

Continue another 25 km to this 2,590-hectare reserve, shelter to barramundi, saltwater crocs, waterbirds during the dry season, and wallabies who peek from the granite outcrops. Boating, fishing, and camping are permitted.

Accommodations

Built in the 1970s, this favorite roadside pub, the **Bark Hut Inn** (two km beyond Mary River

Crossing), is the replica of a 1918 Annaburroo Station homestead and is decorated with all the Territorial trappings. An on-site wildlife enclosure houses dingoes, donkeys, kangaroos, wallabies, emus, buffalo, and pigs. Accommodations are in the moderate range, but campsites are also available. For information, phone (08) 8976-0185.

The **YHA Annaburroo Lodge and Backpackers Hostel,** off the Arnhem Hwy., lies in the wetlands on Annaburroo Billabong. Tours are available to Kakadu and Mary River, as are bushwalks to Aboriginal sites and wildlife areas. With prior arrangement, Greyhound Pioneer will drop you off at the hostel. For information, phone (08) 8978-8971, or inquire at the Darwin YHA hostel.

KAKADU NATIONAL PARK

Hallelujah—you've arrived at one of Australia's most majestic, mystical natural wonderlands, a tropical wilderness encompassing 1,307,300 hectares and six major topographical regions stretching some 100 km to the western border of Aboriginal-controlled Arnhem Land. Listed as a World Heritage site for its important wetlands and cultural significance, Kakadu's spectacles include a fortress-like sandstone escarpment, thick-as-thieves woodlands and forests, magnificent rock formations, lowland savannah, wide floodplains, amazing birds and wildlife, gorges, waterfalls, caves, lagoons, mangrove-covered tidal flats, plentiful fish, flowers, and crocs, and an exquisite collection of Aboriginal rock art—some dating back 20,000 years or more.

It is recommended that, if possible, visitors experience the park during both the Wet and the dry season as features undergo drastic metamorphoses. During the oppressively humid Wet, rain falls in thunderous sheets over the weathered Arnhem Land escarpment, causing floodplains to swell, landscapes to green, posies to blossom, birds to breed, fish to jump, and all the beasties of the jungle to send out invites to fertility rites. In the height of the dry season, however, the searing sun cracks the earth, plants wither away, the fish die off, the abundant birds fight over the last bit of feed. (Secret: Shaded gorges and billabongs off the main roads are still green and filled with wildlife.)

Nature lovers will have a hard time getting bored here at any time of year. Kakadu is home to a staggering variety of flora and fauna, with species numbering 1,000 plants, 50 mammals, 75 reptiles, 25 frogs, 275 birds (check out the massive flocks of magpie geese), 55 fish, and 10,000 insects (bring lots of repellent). Many are rare or endangered, and new species continue to be identified. One interesting fish is the silver barramundi, which makes a sex change from male to female at the age of about six.

Wanna-be croc hunters should have no problem spotting some of the thousands of freshwater and saltwater dinosaur cousins inhabiting the park. It's the saltwater croc ("saltie," in Aussie parlance) that's the big threat. **Be forewarned:** Salties do not live only in saltwater but wherever they damn well please, and are masters of camouflage. Also, do not ignore any crocodile-warning signs (don't steal them, either!), and don't leave food scraps anywhere near the water. A safe way to see these prehistoric descendants is on a Yellow Water or South Alligator River boat cruise.

Approximate distances to and through Kakadu are 120 km from the Arnhem and Stuart Highways junction to the park entrance, another 100 km east along sealed roadway to Jabiru. From Jabiru: The Ranger Uranium Mine is about 10 km southeast; Ubirr is 38 km north on mostly dirt road; and turn onto the sealed Kakadu Highway just west of Jabiru, going 21 km south and then another 12 km southeast, to arrive in Nourlangie. The sealed portion of the Kakadu Highway ends near Mardukal camping area, Cooinda, and Yellow Water; it's unsealed from there to Pine Creek and the Stuart Highway (about 160 km), and impassable during the Wet. It's 20 km along the Kakadu Highway from the Nourlangie turnoff to the Jim Jim Falls detour— 60 km of 4WD-only track.

History

Aboriginal settlement has been traced back at least 25,000 years. "Kakadu" derived from "Gagadju," the name of one of the area's first tribes; today the park is back under Aboriginal control, with many Aborigines serving on the staff and as park rangers.

Wouldn't you just know that the Kakadu lands hold about 10% of the whole world's top-grade uranium ore? Three major mine sites—Ranger, Jabiluka, and Koongarra—sitting near the eastern edge, were leased to outside companies before the establishment of either the park or Aboriginal land rights. Land rights granted in the 1970s did not include the yea or nay of mining on sacred territory, only leasing terms by which the independent mining companies would abide.

In 1978, the Aborigines cut a deal with the Ranger Mine that included a nice chunk of royalties. So nice, in fact, that many Aboriginal owners of Jabiluka and Koongarra now feel that a little uranium mining might well be worth the enormous royalties. Currently, only the Ranger Mine is in full swing, but future operations may still be in the offing.

A vast area of Kakadu, in what is known as "stage three," has been set aside as a protected conservation zone, with the exception of mineral rights—for now, that is. If no mining company comes forth with an acceptable plan in due course, then stage three will continue life as a national park. Naturally, environmentalists are extremely concerned over the destructive forces of the Ranger, as well as any additional pollution and defilement of the land and heritage sites. Who'll win? Protesting conservationists, powerful mining interests, kissy-assed politicians, sell-out Aborigines, or the almighty dollar? Care to lay odds?

Rock Art

The park's natural environment is of profound spiritual significance to Aborigines—just read the paintings on the walls. More than 5,000 archaeological sites within Kakadu's confines provide a rock-art record of Aboriginal culture and mythology, as well as a picture of changing environmental and historical conditions, spanning a period from 20,000 years ago up until the 1960s. Aborigines used their art forms and natural canvases to convey messages and myths, to link past centuries with the present day. And though you'll happen upon tours, pamphlets, and explanations galore, don't be surprised or disappointed if you feel like you're still missing something—many works communicate only to the Aboriginal heart.

Distinctive styles that evolved with the ages include hand and object imprints (the oldest), naturalistic outline drawings of stick-figure-like hunters and extinct animals (such as the Tasmanian tiger), dynamic "in motion"-type drawings with naked women and mythological beings, strange yam-shaped figures, and "X-ray" images showing skeletal structures and internal organs of mostly barramundi and crocs (the most recent at 1,000-9,000 years old).

More elaborate "X-ray" studies, produced within the last 1,000 years, convey the Aboriginal contact with Macassarese fishermen and European "discoverers." Yellow, red, and white powdered minerals, blended with water, are the predominant colors in all the works. Other artifacts include little odds and ends like 20,000-year-old edge-ground stone axes.

Though contemporary Aboriginal artists have pretty much abandoned rocks as a medium, opting to work on sand or bark commercial creations, the ancient sites are revered and carefully guarded. Visitors are allowed at three major locations: both Nangaloar and Anbangbang Galleries at Nourlangie, and Ubirr. A number of sacred sites are kept private and off-limits to the public. Visitors are asked to stay on marked paths, follow signs, and to refrain from touching or interfering with any site.

Kakadu Holiday Village

Set amid rainforest and bushland, this tourist complex features inexpensive and moderately priced motel accommodations, shady campsites, dining facilities, rainforest walking tracks, tennis courts and swimming pool (for paying guests only), souvenir shops, and petrol stations. For information and booking, phone (08) 8979-0166.

South Alligator River cruises depart daily from the nearby crossing. Popular two-hour tours depart daily during the dry season. Cost is $25. For information and bookings, phone (08) 8941-0800.

Jabiru

Jabiru (pop. 1,300) was established in 1982 to provide housing and services for the miners working at nearby Ranger. With the onslaught of tourism, however, the township now offers visitor facilities as well, including shops, a lake with sandy beach, picnic areas, golf, tennis, and car-rental agencies.

One-hour tours of the **Ranger Uranium Mine** depart three times daily from the Jabiru East Airport, six km east. Cost is $10. For schedules and bookings, phone Kakadu Air at (08) 8979-2411.

Jabiru is also the location of **Gagudju Crocodile Hotel Kakadu,** Flinders St. (tel. 08-8979-2800). This is the crocodile-shaped *expensive* hotel where guests enter through the "jaws" then pay through the nose to sleep and eat inside the belly and brains. The croc "head" houses shops, restaurants, and bars. It's definitely worth a look just for the reptilian kitsch angle.

Kakadu Frontier Lodge and Caravan Park (tel. 08-8979-2422) offers camping.

For emergencies, contact: **police** (tel. 08-8979-2122) or **medical aid** (tel. 08-8979-2018 or 8979-2102).

Ubirr

Also known as Obiri Rock, this major rock-art site is home of some of the country's most important works, which are contained within six different sheltered areas. A one-km path leads visitors to all of the sites, but most impressive is the main gallery with its exquisitely preserved "X-ray" paintings that depict jungle and sea wildlife, as well as several haughty white boys in a 15-meter frieze. Another path leads to the top of the rock and magnificent views of Kakadu and Arnhem Land (some *Crocodile Dundee* scenes were shot up there).

Facilities include picnic grounds and a park headquarters with interpretive display and informative brochures. Park rangers lead guided tours during the dry season. Near Ubirr sit a border store and 20-bed **Hostel Kakadu,** closed during the Wet. Beds are $12, and on Thursday evenings park rangers host a slide show. For information and opening dates, phone (08) 8979-2333. Keep in mind that the gravel road to Ubirr is impassable for conventional vehicles—and often 4WDs—during the Wet.

Nourlangie Rock

The other major art site, reached via a short jog off the Kakadu Highway, is open year-round. The Aborigines call this rock Burrung-gui, and the surrounding area Nawulandja, both of which somehow were bastardized into Nourlangie.

Rising from the Arnhem Land escarpment, this massive weathered sandstone, sheer-cliffed outcrop features several formidable areas: **Anbangbang,** an Aboriginal shelter for at least

20,000 years, where mythological figures such as Namarrgon, "Lightning Man," are friezed in time; **Anbangbang Gallery,** behind the shelter, with works created by Najombolmi (a.k.a. Barramundi Charlie) as recently as the 1960s; and **Nangaloar Gallery,** reached by a three- to four-km walk, with styles including "X-ray" paintings, hand stencils, and stick figures with subjects ranging from mythical beings and fish to European ships.

On the way back to the highway, a turnoff to the left leads a short walk's way to **Nawulandja lookout,** where park rangers will guide you to the only known blue paintings.

Facilities include interpretive displays, guided walks, and a picnic area.

Jim Jim Falls
You'll take a 4WD-only road, then walk one kilometer across boulders to reach these dramatic falls, which plunge 200 meters over the Arnhem Land escarpment, thundering during the Wet and, in comparison, trickling during the dry season.

Visitors trek here for the majestic scenery, deep-plunge pool, freshwater crocs, sandy beach with shallow swimming area, breathtaking bushwalks, and good camping.

Twin Falls
It's not quite so easy to reach Twin Falls, 10 km south of Jim Jim Falls, where access is gained by fording Jim Jim Creek. Take your choice of two double-dare routes: make a few short swims and rock climbs up the gorge and hope you don't run into any freshwater crocs (no one said they were *safe,* just *safer*); or scramble, climb, and walk your way across Jim Jim Creek. On arrival you'll be rewarded by the glorious vision of the crystal falls (yes, two of them), lush ferns and greenery, and a sandy palm-lined beach.

Yellow Water
No worries—despite its name, this billabong derives its color from an algae that, when concentrated, produces a distinctive yellow tinge. These wetlands are a sanctuary for a large number and variety of waterbirds (whistling ducks, jabiru, egrets, pelicans, magpie geese, spoonbills, etc.), as well as crocs, and boat trips on the

Twin Falls Gorge, Kakadu National Park

mangrove-lined billabong are one of the park's highlights.

Access to Yellow Water is through Cooinda, about four km off the Kakadu Hwy., 48 km from its junction with the Arnhem Highway. Accommodations at Cooinda are either at the expensive **Gagudju Lodge Cooinda** (tel. 08-8979-0145) or at the adjacent caravan park, which also has campsites and a bunkhouse section. Other facilities in the tourist complex include a restaurant, bistro, bar, takeaway, small supermarket, souvenir shop, petrol station, Tourist Information Centre, car rental agency, and airstrip.

Gagudju Lodge Cooinda Tours operates two-hour Yellow River cruises departing three times daily. Cost is $24. Twice-daily 90-minute tours are a few bucks less. If you can keep your eyes open early in the morning, shoot for the first trip (around 6:30 a.m.) when birdlife is most active (you know who catches the worm . . .). Advance bookings are essential for this popular outing. Phone the hotel for information, and don't forget to wear plenty of insect repellent.

To Pine Creek
Just past the Cooinda turnoff, the Kakadu Highway becomes mostly dirt for the 208-km, southwesterly "back way" to Pine Creek on the Stuart Highway. The road is often closed during the Wet; check with park rangers or police at either end for current status. **Barramundie Gorge,** about 35 km along the highway from Cooinda, then a 10-km turnoff on 4WD track, is lush with rainforest patches, gorge pools and beaches, freshwater crocs, and abundant birdlife. Camping is allowed.

Farther south and west, and often inaccessible during the Wet, **Waterfall Creek** (also known as Gunlom, and once known as Uranium Development Project Falls) is part of that iffy stage-three region, as well as another site locale for *Crocodile Dundee.* Features include a 100-meter waterfall, interesting flat rocks, a large pool bordered by paperbark and pandanus, freshwater crocs, aerobic bushwalks, camping, and picnic areas.

Camping
Aside from the privately run campgrounds mentioned above, Kakadu has a variety of campsites under jurisdiction of the Australian Nature Conservation Agency. Major sites with showers, flush toilets, hot water, and drinking water are at **Merl** (near the border store), **Muirella Park** (near Nourlangie Rock), and **Mardukal** (just south of the Cooinda turnoff). Other camping areas are Djaburluku, Gadjuduba, Melabanbandju, Burdulba, Jim Jim Falls, Barramundie Gorge, Gunlom (Waterfall Creek), Alligator Billabong, Black Jungle Spring, Two Mile Hole, and Four Mile Hole.

All of the campgrounds except Mardukal are subject to wet-season closures. Permits (get them at park headquarters) are required for bush camping outside of designated areas. Camping fees are $7 pp, per night, and are payable at the park information center. Bush camping is free.

Transportation and Tours
Kakadu Air (tel. 08-8979-2411) provides regular service between Darwin and Jabiru, as well as scenic flights over the park.

Greyhound Pioneer Australia travels daily between Darwin and Kakadu, stopping variously at Humpty Doo ($15), Bark Hut ($24), Kakadu Holiday Village ($35), Jabiru ($48), and Nourlangie Rock and Cooinda ($52). Service may be delayed or suspended during the Wet.

Rental cars and 4WD vehicles can be procured in Darwin or within the park from Territory Rent-A-Car, Gagudju Crocodile Hotel Kakadu (tel. 08-8979-2800).

Bushwalkers can choose from marked trails or isolated terrain. Contact Darwin Bushwalking Club (tel. 08-8985-1484) for information on Kakadu walks. **Willis's Walkabouts** (tel. 08-8985-2134) organizes two-day to two-week bushwalks.

For visitors arriving by bus or conventional vehicle, there are tour companies longing to take you around. Aboriginal-owned **Magela Tours** (tel. 08-8979-2227) conducts day tours around the park's lesser-traveled areas, but the price is a pretty hefty $200-plus (includes Jabiru pick-up). **Kakadu Gorge and Waterfall Tours** (tel. 08-8979-2025) offers 4WD jaunts from Jabiru or Cooinda to Jim Jim and Twin Falls for around $120 during the dry season.

Most tours depart Darwin, are of two-day duration (in the $180 range), and embrace the typical Nourlangie Rock, Jim Jim Falls, and Yellow River-cruise itinerary. Some respected companies include: **All Terrain** (tel. 08-8941-0070); **Hunter Safaris** (tel. 08-8981-2720); and **Saratoga** (tel. 08-8981-6473). **Australian Kakadu Tours** (tel. 08-8981-5144), for the less adventurous, does a one-day tour to Kakadu for about $90.

The **Darwin Regional Tourism Association Information Centre** in Darwin has an exhaustive listing of Kakadu tour operators. The Park Information Centre, Kakadu Holiday Village, Gagudju Lodge Cooinda, and Gagudju Crocodile Hotel Kakadu all book a number of excursions within the park.

For **boat trips,** see "Kakadu Holiday Village" and "Yellow Water," above.

Information
The **Kakadu National Park Information Centre** is a few kilometers south of Jabiru on the Kakadu Highway. The center provides extensive literature, guide maps, and tour info (particularly the ranger-led art and nature tours), as

CROCODILES

Know your crocs and take those warning signs seriously! There are two kinds: saltwater ("salties") and freshwater. The smaller freshwater croc is usually harmless unless provoked, while the larger saltie poses a definite danger. Worse, the saltie also inhabits freshwater! My opinion—don't trust either of 'em. They're smart and *fast*.

Aside from the obvious swimming hazards, you should avoid cleaning fish, leaving food waste, and hanging out near the water's edge. Also, crocs seem to get upset around dogs and teasing boaters.

well as audiovisual displays ($3 admission) and video screenings. The center is open daily 8 a.m.-5 p.m. For information, phone park headquarters at (08) 8979-2101.

Tourist information is also available at Jabiru Airport and the hotels. In Darwin, contact the **Australian Nature Conservation Agency,** Smith St., Darwin, or write G.P.O. Box 1260, Darwin, NT 0801 (tel. 08-8981-5299).

Entry fee to the park is $10 and is good for two weeks' stay. Impromptu checkpoints are set up throughout the park, so do the right thing.

ARNHEM LAND AND BEYOND

Within this huge region (pop. 5,000), comprising the entire eastern half of the Top End, scattered groups of Aborigines keep their traditional fires burning in a homeland filled with escarpments and plateaus, gorges and rivers, an abundance of rock-art sites and birdlife.

The district was named by Matthew Flinders in 1803 for one of the Dutch ships that "discovered" the coast in 1623—though earlier "discoverers" were most likely Malaccans, Indonesians, and Portuguese on a visit.

Don't even try to go onto these designated Aboriginal lands without the necessary permit—and don't count on getting one very easily either. Permits are seldom given to curious tourists, but several tour operators can take you up to the Cobourg Peninsula and to Bathurst and Melville Islands, and a couple of companies offer trips deep into Arnhem Land. (Stop in at the Darwin Regional Tourism Association Information Centre for tour info—also see the special topic "Permits" and the chart "Aboriginal Tours" in the On the Road chapter.)

If flying in, you won't need a permit to visit Gove Peninsula, at the northeast tip.

Gurig National Park

Isolated on the Cobourg Peninsula, 200 kilometers northeast of Darwin, Gurig National Park (220,700 hectares) embraces exquisite virgin wilderness, important wetlands, protected coral reefs and marinelife, vast numbers of migratory birds, relics of the Macassarese trading days, and, of course, rich Aboriginal culture. The park is operated by the Conservation Commission in conjunction with traditional owners (the Gurig people, made up of about 40 clans), many of whom live near Black Point and work within the tourist sector.

The Cobourg Peninsula was the location for several of those pre-Darwin, failed European settlements. Ruins of **Victoria Settlement,** the 1838 British garrison community at Port Essington, include building foundations, walls, stone chimneys, and a half-buried powder magazine. An interpretive walking track incorporates many sights; pick up informative pamphlets at the **Visitors Centre and Museum** at Black Point.

The British left more than just their ruins—imported livestock still roaming the peninsula include Indian sambar deer, Timorese ponies, Balinese banteng cattle, and Javanese buffalo and pigs. Saltwater crocs, turtles, sea cows, and numerous tropical fish inhabit the coastal waters (though I won't credit the Brits for those.) Along the sandy shores, beachcombers are apt to walk away with some primo shells for their collections. Fishing is idyllic year-round, but swimming is not recommended, unless you don't mind playing Russian roulette with the sharks, saltwater crocs, and box jellyfish.

A small **campground** near the shore at Smith Point has showers, toilets, a picnic and barbecue area, jetty, and nearby store with sporadic hours.

The peninsula is about a nine-hour drive from Darwin along the Arnhem Highway, turning northwest from Jabiru. It's 4WD only from East Alligator River to Gurig, and the road is closed during the Wet. Advance permits to enter Arnhem Land are mandatory. For information, contact the **Northern Territory Conservation Commission** (tel. 08-8999-5511). Be forewarned: Only 15 vehicles per week are allowed access, and bookings are now running one to two years behind (most of the permits are snatched up way in advance by fishers on their way to Smith Point).

If you have a fat wallet (or a gold card), indulge yourself at **Seven Spirit Bay,** a super-remote, super-luxurious eco-resort that's accessible by light aircraft or boat. Gourmet cuisine is part of the $400 pp double-deal, as are various eco-activities. This is a favorite hideaway for celebs and type-A's (who probably go nuts after half a day). For information and bookings, phone 08) 8979-0227.

An **organized tour,** all-inclusive of air or land transport, accommodations, and necessary permits, is really the easiest way to go. Again, check with the tourist center and YHA Travel Centre. "Mini-tours" into Arnhem Land from Kakadu are offered by **Kakadu Parklink** (tel. 08-8979-2411) and **Arnhemlander** (tel. 08-8979-2411).

Gove Peninsula

This remote region on Arnhem Land's very far away northeastern tip was first charted in 1803 by Matthew Flinders, but only settled at Nhulunbuy as late as 1969—when the bauxite mining began. The local Yirrkala Aborigines protested the intended rape of their traditional land and, though mining proceeded anyhow (surprise, surprise), a government inquiry and subsequent compensation award attracted national attention, planting a seed for the ongoing land-rights movement.

Visitors come to this balmy, tropical region expressly because it is so isolated and untouristy. White-sand beaches, wildlife, reef and big-game fishing, varied sports facilities, and saltwater croc and buffalo safaris are the big attractions. In addition, **Yirrkala,** a former mission, displays and sells art and artifacts produced by local Aborigines. Free half-day tours of the **Nabalco Mine** are given on Thursday mornings.

The only practical way to get up to Gove is by air. Ansett flies into Nhulunbuy, and no permit is necessary. The cheapest fares are in conjunction with land packages, which include accommodations and sightseeing. Driving up here is not practical because of the long distances (800 km of pretty lousy road from Katherine) and the number of complicated permits involved. Coastline explorers who fly in can rent cars in Nhulunbuy (see the special topic "Permits" in the On the Road chapter).

For information on tour operators to the peninsula, contact the **Darwin Regional Tourism Association Information Centre** (tel. 08-8981-4300). Most tours depart from Darwin or Jabiru.

DOWN THE TRACK

It's about 1,500 km from Darwin to Alice Springs on the Stuart Highway (National Route 87). Closely paralleling explorer John McDouall Stuart's path (its namesake) and the 1872 Overland Telegraph Line, the Track has grown from a pre-WW II dirt stretch to a two-lane, sealed, all-weather highway. Sights on or near the road add interest to the long drive.

DARWIN TO KATHERINE

See "Vicinity of Darwin," above for towns and attractions on the Track within about 50 kilometers south of Darwin.

Manton Dam

This huge reservoir, 42 km down the Track from Darwin and another few kilometers along the turnoff, was originally built for WW II military personnel stationed in the Territory. The 440-hectare recreation area features sailing, swimming, waterskiing, and barbecue facilities. Open Mon.-Fri. 9 a.m.-5 p.m., Sat.-Sun. 8 a.m.-7 p.m. For information, phone (08) 8999-5511.

Lake Bennett

Situated 80 km down the Track and then seven km east, this 404-hectare human-made lake provides a large range of water activities, including windsurfing, swimming, sailing, canoeing, and fishing. Other features include prolific birdlife, tropical wilderness areas, bushwalks, and barbecue facilities. Accommodations at **Lake Bennett Holiday Park** (tel. 08-8976-0960) consist of campsites or camp-o-tels (a combination tent and motel).

Batchelor

This Litchfield Park gateway (pop. 600) and former service town to the defunct Rum Jungle uranium and copper mine lies 84 km from Darwin and another 13 km to the west, in a lush forest setting with colorful birdlife. Nearby is an old airstrip, used from time to time by Gen. Douglas MacArthur during WW II, as well as other wartime memorabilia. **Karlstein Castle,** a miniature repli-

ca of a Bohemian castle, sits oddly out of place across from the police station. **Rum Jungle Lake,** six km from town, is a popular center for sailing, swimming, and canoeing. This town is also the site of an **Aboriginal Teacher Training College** and base for the **Top End Aerial Sports Association**'s parachuting and gliding activities.

Moderate to expensive accommodations are available at **Rum Jungle Motor Inn,** Rum Jungle Rd. (tel. 08-8976-0123). **Batchelor Cara-**

SECRET RECIPE FOR BILLY TEA

Brew your own "cuppa," just like the original outback pioneers. It's an easy picker-upper from the land down under. Here's how:

Equipment: one Billy can (a small metal bucket), a campfire, cups, one hand with a limber wrist

Ingredients: water, loose black tea, milk, sugar

La méthode: Fill the Billy can with cold water, allowing it to boil on the campfire; add a big old handful of tea (three to four heaping tablespoons); grab the Billy by its handle and swing that baby around and around to blend tea; place Billy back on campfire, allowing the tea leaves to settle and steep; pour tea into cups, adding lots of milk and sugar. Ah, you'll be ready to conquer the outback.

village, Rum Jungle Rd. (tel. 08-8976-0166), offers on-site vans and campsites, and also arranges tours of the Rum Jungle Mine.

Adelaide River

Located on the Adelaide River (but not the crossing on Arnhem Hwy.), 110 km south of Darwin, this tiny township (pop. 200) was a hub of WW II military activity, undoubtedly due to its railway depot and prime position. Relics and armaments still in evidence include the **Snake Creek Arsenal,** a major armaments depot and wartime military camp; **Adelaide River War Cemetery,** Australia's largest such graveyard where most of the Darwin dead have been laid to rest; and a host of old airstrips smattered around the Track. The restored **Railway Station** (built 1888-89) is a designated National Trust property, housing a **Tourist Information Centre** (tel. 08-8976-7010), open Wed.-Sun. 8:30 a.m.-5 p.m. The **Railway Bridge,** built the same year as the station, occasionally doubled as a road bridge during the Wet.

Adelaide River Inn, Stuart Hwy. (tel. 08-8976-7047), offers inexpensive rooms, and **Shady River View Caravan Park,** War Memorial Dr. (same phone), has campsites.

For emergencies, contact the **police** (tel. 08-8976-7042) or an **ambulance** (tel. 08-8927-0000).

The Scenic Route

From Adelaide River you can continue on the Track or take the scenic Old Stuart Highway, an extra 14-km jog slightly to the west, for a variety of interesting attractions—though during the Wet, access is sometimes impossible.

First stop is **Robin Falls,** 17 km southwest of Adelaide River and a short walk from the road. Aside from the 12-meter-high falls (which are but a few drips and trickles during the dry season), this spot features a monsoon-forested gorge, good swimming, and, for those up to the climb, excellent views from the top.

The **Daly River** area is a bit of a detour (109 km southwest of the highway at Adelaide River), but it's worth the drive for several attractions. The town of Daly River (pop. 250), an 1880s copper mine, was the scene of a bloody race riot between Aborigines, who opposed the mine, and white miners. Though the mine did not stick around for long, the Jesuit mission, established around the time of the conflict, did—today it is run by the local Aboriginal council. The town has a variety of services, including a supermarket, Aboriginal art center, roadside inn, takeaway food, and petrol and camping gas.

Nearby attractions are: **Daly River Nature Park** (tel. 08-8978-2347), a 60-hectare reserve with barramundi fishing, boating, picnic and camping facilities; **Bamboo Creek Rainforest Park** (tel. 08-8975-3410), 13 km from Daly River on Woolianna Track, featuring fishing, canoeing, guided motorbike and boat tours, camping, and moderately priced cottage accommodations; and **Daly River Mango Farm** (tel. 08-8978-2464), five km south of Daly River and another seven km from the turnoff, offering a variety of scenic, wildlife, croc-spotting, fishing, and hunting tours, plus safari tents, campsites, and moderately priced cabins. Be sure to inquire at the Aboriginal council office in Daly River as to travel on local tribal lands.

Travel back to the old highway and turn another 35 km southwest (just before the junction with the Track) to reach **Douglas Hot Springs Nature Park** (tel. 08-8973-8770). The top attraction of this 3,107-hectare park is the thermal pools, particularly **Hot Springs Lagoon,** with 40° C (104° F) bathtub water. Swimming, bushwalks, and camping are also popular here. **Butterfly Gorge Nature Park** (tel.

08-8989-5511), 17 km farther along a 4WD track, is a 104-hectare tranquil woodland reserve with swarming butterflies, deep rock pools, and a high-cliffed gorge ideal for bushwalking, fishing, and swimming. As crocs may be present, check first with the **ranger station,** located about five km from the park's turnoff. Next to the ranger station, **Corn Patch Riverside Holiday Park** (tel. 08-8975-3479) offers a variety of facilities including general store, petrol, bar, restaurant, takeaway, camping gas, and campsites.

Back on the Track, keep your eyes peeled for one of Australia's largest **termite mounds** (6.7 meters tall and 7.35 meters around the base) set in the bush near **Hayes Creek.**

Pine Creek
This historic township (pop. 500) 230 km south of Darwin was the site of a massive gold rush during the 1870s. Discovery of the precious metal during the building of the Overland Telegraph Line brought not merely an influx of gold diggers but the accoutrements that follow—Chinese coolies to do the hard labor, and lots of Chinese-run stores and butcheries. At one point the Chinese so outnumbered the Europeans that a law was passed in 1888 forbidding Chinese admittance to the Northern Territory. Originally named Playford in 1888, the town was renamed Pine Creek for—obviously—the pines that used to grow by the creek. Though Pine Creek was hardly even noticed during the world wars, the 1960s and '70s' uranium and iron ore mining brought renewed activity, followed by present gold-mining ventures and increased tourism.

Your first stop should be **Pine Creek Museum** in the old repeater station on Railway Terrace, the oldest surviving prefab building in the Territory. The National Trust, located within the museum, has identified approximately 140 historic sites in and around the town and provides visitor guides and heritage trail maps. Hours are daily April-Sept. 11 a.m.-1 p.m., closed Oct.-March. Admission is $2. For information, phone (08) 8976-1279.

Opened in 1889, **Playford Club Hotel** is the Territory's oldest surviving pub, now a private residence. Also located on Main Terrace is the 1888-89 **Railway Precinct,** including the station, weigh bridge, crane, water tank, sheds,

and employee housing. **Miners Park,** next door, features assorted mining relics.

Pine Creek Hotel/Motel, Moule St. (tel. 08-8976-1288), has moderately priced rooms. **Pine Creek Caravan Park,** Moule St. (tel. 08-8976-1217), features campsites as well as a fully equipped bunkhouse.

In case you forgot—or haven't read that part yet—Pine Creek is also the "back road" gateway to Kakadu Highway and Kakadu National Park. Pine Creekers fish for barramundi, black bream and catfish at Mary River, at the park's edge.

KATHERINE

This third-largest Northern Territory center, 350 km south of Darwin, has practically doubled in population, from 6,200 to about 10,000, with the 1988 opening of RAAF Tindal, Australia's largest air base. Other than military activities, Katherine is a booming tourist town renowned for nearby Katherine Gorge and Cutta Cutta Caves as well as being a service town and turnoff point for the Kimberley region in Western Australia.

Set amidst tropical woodland and along the Katherine River banks, the town grew up in conjunction with the installation of the Overland Telegraph Line and railway. World War I brought a number of airstrips to the area and more recently, regional administration, agriculture, cattle stations, and service facilities have added prosperity to this middle-of-nowhere tourist center.

Katherine Museum and Historical Park on Gorge Rd., opposite the hospital, features a variety of local history displays and architectural relics, in a former airport terminal building. Hours are Mon.-Fri. 10 a.m.-4 p.m., Saturday 10 a.m.-2 p.m., Sunday 2-5 p.m. Admission is $3. For information, phone (08) 8972-3945.

Katherine Railway Station, on Railway Terrace, houses railroad memorabilia and the local branch of the National Trust. Pick up a self-guided tour brochure to 10 heritage sites. Hours are Mon.-Fri. 1-3 p.m. late April-Sept., closed public holidays. For information, phone (08) 8972-3956.

Watch teachers in action with their outback students at **School of the Air,** Giles Street. Guided tours are available Mon.-Fri. 9 a.m.-5 p.m. Admission is $2. The **O'Keefe Residence,** on Riverbank Dr. across from Campbell Terrace, is an exceptional example of Territorial architecture, built of bush poles, corrugated iron, and asbestos(!). Hours are Mon.-Fri. 1-3 p.m. late April-Sept. Admission is $2. For information, phone (08) 8972-2204.

Katherine Low Level Nature Park, a 104-hectare section of the Katherine River, is a local favorite for fishing, swimming (safe mainly during the dry season), and picnicking. Check locally about the possibility of freshwater crocs.

Knotts Crossing marks the site of Katherine's beginnings. Accessed via a turnoff past the hospital, the original settlement included a pub, store, telegraph, and police station. The old pub, located at the top of the riverbank, is now a private residence.

Springvale Homestead

Located eight km southwest of Katherine, on Shadforth Rd., Springvale, established in 1878, is reputedly the Territory's oldest original station homestead. Now a tourist facility, the homestead's features include period-costumed staff, walking tours, canoeing, croc-spotting, swimming (in the dry season), fishing, and Aboriginal corroborees (in the evening). Free tours of the homestead are given daily during the dry season at 9 a.m. and 3 p.m. (historical reenactments coincide with the afternoon tour). Croc cruises and corroboree nights cost $35. Canoe hire is $5 per hour or $20 for the day. For information, phone (08) 8972-1044.

Lazy L Stables, at the homestead's entrance, offers trail rides and pony rides. For information, phone (08) 8972-2618.

Katherine Gorge National Park

This glorious park (180,352 hectares), 32 km northeast of Katherine township, ranks third—after Ayers Rock and Kakadu National Park—among the Territory's most visited attractions. Now returned to the Jawoyn Aborigines, its traditional owners, the park is administered jointly by the Conservation Commission and the Jawoyn people.

A total of 13 gorges, carved by the Katherine River through Arnhem Plateau sandstone merely 25 million years ago (though the base material is some 2.3 billion years old), are geological marvels with sheer rock faces rising 75 meters

high, exquisitely patterned stone floors, and weathered canyon walls adorned with Aboriginal paintings and engravings. Aside from the magnificent gorges, the landscape encompasses rugged escarpments and plateaus, and a superb variety of flora and fauna, especially birds and aquatic life. This is an area of mosses and ferns, pandanus and paperbark, freshwater crocs and long-necked tortoises, red-winged parrots and blue-winged kookaburras—and bat caves. Ten **bushwalks,** taking from two hours to several days, cover approximately 100 km of always scenic, sometimes rugged, track. The longest walk is the 76-km trek to **Edith Falls,** a series of low falls and cool rock pools at the extreme western edge of the park. In case you're contemplating a swim, be forewarned: freshwater crocs inhabit these waters. Katherine Gorge is another place that changes markedly with the seasons, becoming thunderous during the Wet, drying into deep pools as the rains subside.

The **visitor center,** near the park entrance, provides area and bushwalking maps, informative displays, and literature, and also issues the required permits for long-distance or wilderness hikes.

Cutta Cutta Caves

Situated west of the Track, 27 km south of Katherine, this series of limestone caverns dates back 500 million years, give or take a year or so. Classic stalactite and stalagmite formations and tower karsts are the primary characteristics of this protected nature park (1,499 hectares). Rare and strange cave dwellers include blind shrimp and the golden horseshoe bat. Though Katherine tour operators often include these caves in their excursions, if you come on your own you can sign up for an informative ranger-led tour (you can only enter the caves while on a guided tour). Ninety-minute ranger-led tours operate daily at 10:30 a.m., noon, and 1:30 p.m., except during the Wet, when caves are closed. Cost is $6. For information, phone (08) 8973-8770.

Accommodations

Springvale Homestead, Shadforth Rd. (tel. 08-8972-1355), offers inexpensive rooms in historic surroundings. For moderately priced accommodations, try **Kuringgai Motel,** Giles St. (tel. 08-8971-0266), or **Beagle Motor Inn,** cor-

THE EDIBLE DESERT

These notes (provided by the Northern Territory Conservation Commission) are a brief introduction to the traditional lifestyle and bush foods of central Australian Aborigines.

You should not eat any bush foods unless they have been positively identified as being edible. The desert areas contain many poisonous plants, some of which look just like their edible relatives.

Aboriginal Lifestyle

Aborigines have survived the harsh conditions of semiarid and desert lands for thousands of years. The secret to their survival lies in their detailed knowledge of the plants, animals, and water sources available in the country.

The women and children gathered fruits, roots, witchetty grubs, and small animals, while the men hunted larger game such as kangaroos and emus. Many of the traditional foods are still collected and eaten today.

cyclorana

Water

Knowledge of all available water sources is passed down from old to young. Water is not only found in local water holes and under the dry surface of creek beds, but also in a variety of plants and certain animals. The succulent leaves of the parakeelya plant can be eaten in time of emergency. The graceful desert oak tree holds a secret store of water in its roots and in hidden hollows amongst its upper branches.

The water-holding frog, **cyclorana,** burrows beneath the ground with an abdomen full of water and waits for the next heavy rains to fall. With their detailed knowledge of the land, the Aborigines can dig these frogs from their burrows and squeeze them for a thirst-quenching drink.

witchetty grub

Protein

Witchetty grubs live in the roots of certain acacia bushes. These grubs, the juvenile stage of a large moth, contain large amounts of protein and fat, and can be eaten either raw or cooked. When roasted, the grub has a pleasant nutty flavor.

Both the **perentie** and its eggs are valuable sources of protein. The perentie is roasted whole in

ner 4th and Lindsay St. (tel. 08-8972-3998). The **Palm Court Backpackers Lodge,** corner Giles and 3rd (tel. 08-8972-2722), charges $12 pp for shared rooms. **Kookaburra Lodge,** corner Lindsay and Third (tel. 08-8971-0257), features $12-per-night dorm rooms.

Campsites are available at **Katherine Gorge Caravan Park,** Katherine Gorge National Park (tel. 08-8972-1253), **Katherine Low Level Caravan Park,** Shadforth Rd. (tel. 08-8972-3962), and **Riverview Caravan Park,** 440 Victoria Hwy. (tel. 08-8972-1011).

Events

Though Aboriginal lands are normally off-limits to the public, everyone is invited to the big **Barunga Festival** at Beswick Aboriginal Land Trust, 130 km south of Katherine and an additional 29 km off the highway. Held over the Queen's Birthday weekend in June, it draws Aborigines from throughout the Territory for a four-day celebration of dancing, sports, arts and crafts, plus bush-tucker stalls. Sunday is the best day, with fire-lighting as well as boomerang and spear-throwing competitions.

hot coals with the eggs, which are pierced to remove the whites before cooking.

Flour

The seeds of the **woollybutt** grass and **hakea** tree are just two of the many seeds that can be mixed with water to make damper or seed cake. The seeds are dehusked, ground, mixed with water, and then baked on hot coals. The result is a highly nutritious seed cake.

Fruits and Vegetables

The arid lands of central Australia provide an abundant supply of native fruits. The **ruby saltbush** bears a small red berry that can be eaten.

The yellow **bush tomato** is very high in vitamin C and can be dried and stored for long periods. **Bush onions** can be peeled and roasted on hot

hakea

coals before being eaten, perhaps with seed cake or witchetty grubs.

Honey

There are many sources of honey in the bush. The tiny lac scale insects that live on the branches of the **mulga tree** appear as red bumps that exude sweet sticky honeydew. The dew is usually sucked directly from the mulga branch.

The flowers of the **honey grevillea** produce quantities of sweet nectar, which can be sucked straight from the flower or mixed with water in a *mimpu* (wooden bowl) to make a sweet drink.

A different source of honey comes from **honey ants.** These ants live in nests several meters underground and have honey-filled abdomens the size of small grapes. The honey can be eaten by biting off the honey pot or by mixing the whole ant with flour to make a sweet damper.

Transportation, Services, and Information

Regularly scheduled flights are operated between Katherine, Alice Springs, and Darwin. Check with **Ansett** (tel. 13-1300 toll-free) or **Qantas** (tel. 13-1313 toll-free).

Greyhound Pioneer Australia (tel. 13-2030 toll-free) and **McCafferty's** (tel. 08-212-5066) stop in Katherine on their Port Augusta-Darwin runs. Fare from Darwin is about \$48 one-way; from Alice Springs, \$125 one-way.

Rental cars are available from **Avis,** Hobbitt's Auto Electrical, 47 Victoria Hwy. (tel. 08-8972-1482), or **Freedom Hire,** Happy Corner Complex, 3rd St. (tel. 08-8971-1411).

Inquire at the tourist bureau for best local tours. **Travel North** (tel. 08-8972-1253) and **Frontier** (tel. 08-8971-1381) operate a variety of Katherine Gorge excursions, including river cruises (\$20-60); Frontier also runs 15-minute helicopter flights. Canoes can be rented from **Kookaburra Canoe Hire** (tel. 08-8972-3604).

Bill Harney's Jankangyina Tours (tel. 08-8972-2650) are excellent two-day, one-night Aboriginal adventures including rock-art sites, bush foods, and campfire stories. Prices range \$225-270.

Pick up heaps of local info and maps at the **Katherine Region Tourist Association,** Stuart Hwy. (tel. 08-8972-2650). Hours are Mon.-Fri. 9 a.m.-5 p.m.

For emergencies, contact the **police** (tel. 08-8972-0211) or **hospital** (tel. 08-8972-9211).

TO WESTERN AUSTRALIA

It's 513 km southwest from Katherine to the Western Australia border along the **Victoria Highway.** Though the road is bitumen all the way, it's extremely narrow and impassable during the Wet, when torrential rain causes rivers to flood bridges and roadways.

Note: Exercise caution when driving this route—if another vehicle approaches, so does an impending barrage of stones; slow down and pull as far off the road as possible.

It's 125 km along the Victoria Highway to the **Delamere Road** turnoff. **Top Springs** (pop. 15), 164 km south at the Buchanan Highway junction, features a popular beer-guzzler (an average of nine tons per week!) roadhouse, pools for swimming, moderately priced accommodations, campsites, and the usual range of services. For information, phone (08) 8975-0767. The Buchanan continues 170 km southwest to **Kalkaringi** (pop. 250), a service town for the Daguragu Aboriginal Land Trust, and another 222 km to the Western Australia border. Four-wheel-drives are recommended for this highway, which is often flooded during the Wet.

Back on Victoria Highway, **Victoria River Wayside Inn** (tel. 08-8975-0744), 196 km southwest of Katherine, sits at Victoria River Crossing, backed by smooth ranges and rugged cliffs. Known as the "friendliest pub in the scrub," facilities include a general store, supermarket, restaurant, pub, takeaway, petrol station, Tourist Information Centre, mechanic and towing service, campsites, and moderately priced motel rooms. **Red Valley boat tours** depart from here or Timber Creek three times daily (April-Oct.) on cruises of the scenic river and gorges. Cost is $10-20. Barramundi and bream fishing are good in these parts, but both freshwater crocs and salties live in the water as well, so stave off your temptation to swim.

Surrounding the Wayside Inn and Victoria River and stretching all the way to Timber Creek is more recently established **Gregory National Park** (10,000 square km), which encompasses much of the surrounding scenery, plus traces of Aboriginal and European presence, several historic homesteads, a few excellent camping spots (with no facilities), rare flora and fauna, abundant birdlife, and bushwalking trails. **Kuwang Lookout** offers spectacular views of Stokes Range. Access, at present, is mainly by 4WD. Park headquarters is in Timber Creek. For information, phone (08) 8975-0888.

Historic **Timber Creek** (pop. 100), 91 km from the Wayside Inn, was noteworthy for its Victoria River Depot and massive cattle stations. The old port, established in 1891, is now a historical reserve, located about eight km from town. The **Police Station Museum** presents displays, artifacts, and an occasional informal talk relating to police action and racial turmoil in the 1880s (tip: don't ask about those subjects *today!*). **Gregory's Tree Historical Reserve,** west of town, features a baobab tree carved with early explorers' initials.

Campsites and moderately priced accommodations are available at **Circle F Motel and Caravan Park,** Victoria Hwy. (tel. 08-8975-

0722). A 16-bed **youth hostel** is located behind the police station.

Most basic services are available at Timber Creek. For emergencies, contact the **police** (tel. 08-8975-0733).

Keep River National Park (59,700 hectares) is 190 km from Timber Creek, at the Western Australia border. The park, known for its extraordinary land formations and distinctive geology, also is characterized by tropical savannah, dramatic escarpments and plateaus, enormous baobab trees, Aboriginal art sites, volcanic rocks, and profuse plantlife, birds, and reptiles. Before embarking on bushwalks, make sure you are prepared for the searing heat and have plenty of water on hand. Check in with the park ranger located near the park entrance at Waters of Cockatoo Lagoon. **Camping areas,** with marked interpretive walking tracks, are located at **Gurrandalng** (15 km from Victoria Hwy.) and **Jarrnarm** (28 km within the park). Conventional vehicles can access the park, though roads may be closed during the Wet. For information, phone (091) 67-8827.

TO TENNANT CREEK

Mataranka

Heading south on the Track, Mataranka (pop. 150) is 109 km from Katherine. Tropical bushland, crystal-clear thermal pools, a *very* colorful pub, and a chunk of literary history are the celebrated characteristics of this small cattle and service community.

Historic **Mataranka Homestead,** nine km east of town, is a wooded tourist resort bordering Waterhouse River. Adjacent is **Mataranka Pool Nature Park,** a four-hectare reserve with relaxing thermal pools, plentiful birdlife, as well as palm, paperbark, pandanus, and passion fruit forest—and growing crowds of tourists.

Near the homestead stands a replica of **Elsey Station Homestead,** a set for the 1981 film *We of the Never Never,* based on the well-known outback novel of the same name in which author Jeannie Gunn relates the life and times at the remote station she managed for a brief time. **Elsey Cemetery,** 13 km south of Mataranka and eight km east of the Track, is the ashes-to-ashes, dust-to-dust home of *Never Never* characters in

(previous page) Station Track, Tanami Desert
(above) More than 5,000 archaeological sites within Kakadu's confines provide a rock-art record of Aboriginal culture and mythology.

Canoes can be rented ($6 per hour) at Waterhouse River jetty. Historic **homestead walking tours** are available daily at 11 a.m. **Brolga Tours** (tel. 08-8975-4538) offers a highly recommended four-hour tour of the Roper River, historic Elsey Station (the real one is at McMinns Bar on the Roper River), and Red Lily Lagoon ($60).

In emergencies, contact the **police** (tel. 08-8975-4511) or **ambulance** (tel. 08-8972-1200).

Roper Highway

The Roper Highway intersects the Track seven km south of Mataranka. Another 185 km east—on mostly sealed road—is **Roper Bar,** a small tropical outpost (pop. six) popular for boating and barramundi fishing (not swimming, though—both salties and freshwater crocs call this place home). Facilities at "The Roper" include general store, takeaway, picnic and barbecue area, visitor information, boat ramp, airstrip, petrol station, Aboriginal art tours, moderately priced rooms, and campsites. For information, phone (08) 8981-9455.

Private Aboriginal lands begin just past Roper Bar.

Larrimah

Lots of WW II activity took place in this former railhead township (pop. 25) 68 km south of Mataranka. Apart from being a supply base, a top-secret airfield was located here, from where Gen. Douglas MacArthur made some heavy-duty decisions. The original settlement was actually five km away at Birdum but, except for the 1920s Birdum Hotel which was moved to Larrimah, the rest of the town was abandoned after the war. The railway closed down in 1976, due to lack of funding and Cyclone Tracy's devastation, but its remains, as well as those of the Overland Telegraph Station and old post office, are near the hotel. **Larrimah Hotel,** another old bush pub, is not to be missed for its dining specialties—how do boar's tits on toast tickle your taste buds?

Campsites and cheap rooms are available at **Larrimah Wayside Inn,** Stuart Hwy. (tel. 08-8975-9931). **Green Park Tourist Complex,** Stuart Hwy. (tel. 08-8975-9937), offers campsites and is also a good clearinghouse for local information.

uding Jeannie and Aeneas Gunn, Fizzer the ailman, and Muluka.

Old Elsey Roadside Inn, the colorful pub n the Track (tel. 08-75-4512), features inexensive accommodations and counter meals. **lataranka Homestead** (tel. 08-8975-4544) ofrs moderately priced motel rooms, a **YHA ostel,** and campsites. Another choice in the oderate range is **Territory Manor,** Martin Rd. el. 08-8975-4516), with both motel rooms and ampsites, and a pool.

DALY WATERS PUB
Northern Territory

(ME - AN - U)

STAKE SAMIGE
AM BUGGERS
TOE STEAD SAMIGES
PLANE SAMIGES
STAKE-N-EGGS MATE
STAKE-N-VEGEES
QLD STOO (FROGS EXTRA) ALLOWS YOU TO
WALK ON WATER
TRANE SMASH (PIES & PEAS)
CURRY & RI (BURN THE BUM OFF A BOEING 747)
DINGO'S BREAKFAST A PEE & A LOOK AROUND
BUM NUTS ON TOEST
TE & KOFFY
BUSH CHAMPAGNE POA
WE DONT SERVE WOMEN BRING
YOUR OWN !
CREDIT GIVEN TO WOMEN OVER 80
ACCOMPANIED BY THEIR MOTHER
DALY WATERS PUB
EST 1893

some daily fare
at the Daly Waters Pub

Daly Waters

First stop is **Daly Waters Pub,** 89 km from Larrimah and another three km off the highway. It's known as one of the Territory's best and oldest outback pubs, and visitors are certain to soak up any color they desire amid a setting of Australian bush and traditional architecture, surrounded by tropical forest. The front bar "museum" displays pioneer and Aboriginal artifacts. A sign above the bar offers free credit to any 80-year-old woman who is with her mother. Inexpensive rooms and campsites are available. For information, phone (08) 8975-9927.

Daly Waters (pop. 20), two km beyond the pub, is a former campsite for Overland Telegraph Line workers and cattle drovers, as well as a refueling stop for Qantas Airways' first international route between Brisbane and Singapore in the 1930s.

Carpentaria Highway

Often mistaken for the real Daly Waters, **Daly Waters Junction** is another four km south, where the Stuart and Carpentaria Highways meet. The **Hi-Way Inn** roadhouse only dates back to 1974—thus many of us can well imagine both its history and the origins of its name. All the usual outback roadside facilities are offered, including inexpensive accommodations, campsites, restaurant, shop, pub, beer garden, and petrol station. For information, phone (08) 8975-9925.

From the junction, the bitumen Carpentaria Highway travels 391 km east to Borroloola with-

in the Narwinbi Aboriginal Land Trust, passing **Cape Crawford** (and the Heartbreak Hotel) 27¾ km along the way. The **Heartbreak** (tel. 08 8975-9928) offers moderately priced rooms campsites, restaurant, takeaway, shop, bar, picnic area, camping gas, and petrol station. From Cape Crawford, you can either turn south on the **Tablelands Highway** (also sealed) 378 km to Barkly Homestead on the Barkly Highway or continue on the Carpentaria Highway 11¾ km northeast to Borroloola.

Once a booming, colorful 1880s frontier town, today's **Borroloola,** set along the McArthur River, is a famous barramundi fishing hole and site of the Easter **Barra Classic** barramundi fishing competition. Some of the old building ruins, including the former police station, can still be seen. Inexpensive bunkhouse accommodations are available at **Borroloola Holiday Village** (tel. 08-8975-8742), and **McArthur River Caravan Park** (tel. 08-8975-8734) offers on-site vans and campsites. Camping along the riverbanks is not advisable due to croc danger.

Dunmarra

It's 36 km along the Track from Daly Waters Junction to the Buchanan Highway turnoff (another route to Top Springs), and another eight km to Dunmarra, a WW II staging camp for southbound convoys from Larrimah. **Shell Wayside Inn** (tel. 08-8975-9922) offers moderately priced accommodations, campsites, travelers services, and facilities.

Elliott

The landscape gets drier as you near this Darwin-Alice Springs near-halfway point, 120 km south of Dunmarra and 23 km beyond **Newcastle Waters** historic cattle station. Also a former WW II staging camp, Elliott (pop. 600) is a low-key regional service center for the surrounding cattle-raising community. **Elliott Hotel** (tel. 08-8969-2069) has moderately priced rooms. **Halfway Caravan Park** (tel. 08-8969-2025) offers campsites, and **Midland Caravan Park** (tel. 08-8969-2037) has campsites and an inexpensive bunkhouse.

For emergencies, contact the **police** (tel. 08-8969-2010) or **ambulance** (tel. 08-8969-2060).

Renner Springs

The pub building is a typical example of postwar roadhouse architecture, and the pub interior is a prime example of wayside ambience—a few growls and a few giggles. Moderately priced rooms, campsites, dining, takeaway, petrol, and mechanical services are offered. For information, phone (08) 8964-4505.

According to Aboriginal mythology, **Lubra Lookout,** a flat-topped mesa four km south, was the place where local women kept watch for visitors. It is also considered the borderline between the wet Top End and the dry Centre.

Three Ways

Marked by a large stone memorial to Rev. John Flynn, founder of the Royal Flying Doctor Service, Three Ways, 134 km south of Renner Springs, sits at the junction of the Track and the Barkly Highway. A fabled "getting stuck" place, this little hole in the Track is also known as hitchhiker hell. **Three Ways Roadhouse,** right at the crossroads (tel. 08-8962-2744), features inexpensive rooms and campsites, as well as a sign warning hitchhikers not to loiter.

Barkly Highway

From Three Ways, the Barkly Highway travels 643 east to Mt. Isa, in Queensland. **Barkly Homestead,** 185 km along the way, is a modern roadhouse that provides basic facilities, including moderately priced accommodations, a caravan park, campsites, and petrol. For information, phone (08) 8964-4549.

TENNANT CREEK

Other than Katherine, Tennant Creek (pop. 3,400) is the biggest town between Alice Springs and Darwin. Situated 675 km south of Katherine and 507 km north of Alice Springs, Tennant Creek is a modern outback cattle and tourist town as well as an important past and present gold-mining center.

According to legend, the town's location is attributed to the breakdown of a beer cart—instead of carting the beer and building materials back to the intended site, the camp was moved to where the beer had fallen! Another tribute to laziness is that the shops and pub were supposedly built closest to the creek because the miners didn't want to walk any farther than necessary.

After gold was discovered here in 1932, 100 mines sprang up before WW II (though most were small producers), followed by copper mining in the 1950s, which continues to the present day along with that of gold and silver. The Tennant Creek area, home to Warumungu Aborigines, who call the place Jurnkurakurr, features some interesting historic structures, working mines, and unique geological formations.

Sights

The **National Trust Museum,** Schmidt St., originally a WW II army hospital, features early memorabilia and historical displays. Open Mon.-Fri. 4-6 p.m. during the dry season.

Church of Christ the King, Windley St., a classified historic corrugated-iron and wood structure, was originally built in Pine Creek in 1904 and eventually moved to its present location.

The 1872 stone **telegraph station,** 10 km north of town, has been renovated as a museum. For information, phone (08) 8962-3388.

Artworks Gem and Mineral Display, Peko Rd. (tel. 08-8962-3388), exhibits regional gems and minerals as well as locally produced art. Hours are daily 9 a.m.-4 p.m.

Watch the ongoing action of gold-bearing ore being crushed and flushed at **Battery Hill,** about two km along Peko Road. Erected in 1939, it is one of Australia's few 10-head batteries still in operation. You can take a guided tour and nose

ROAD TRAINS
50 METRES LONG

Allow plenty of room to pass!

around the museum, which features historical displays and other artifacts. Tours are daily at 8 a.m., 9:30 a.m., and 4 p.m. Admission is $5. For information, phone (08) 8962-3388.

The **Dot Mine,** Warrego Rd., is one of Tennant Creek's oldest mines. Originally leased in 1936 to German-born Otto Wohnert, the mine was signed away to friends after war broke out and Otto was interned. While Otto was tucked away, malicious rumors spread that he had poisoned the local waterholes. It's no surprise that after the war Otto returned to a burnt-out mine and home and a lot of missing machinery. It is still possible to glimpse gold extraction by the old gravitation method. Tours are Mon.-Fri. at 9 a.m., 11 a.m., 2 p.m., and 4 p.m. For information, phone (08) 8962-2168.

One of Tennant Creek's best views is at **One Tank Hill Lookout,** two km east along Peko Road. Eleven significant local sites are depicted on plaques embedded in a semicircular wall. **Purkiss Reserve,** corner of Ambrose and Peko Roads, has a shady barbecue and playground area, plus a swimming pool. A better recreation spot is at **Mary Ann Dam,** six km north of town, with a lake perfect for swimming and boating. Bicycle and bushwalking tracks plus boat and sailboard rentals are also offered.

Devils Pebbles, 11 km north on the Track and another six km left on a dirt road, are rounded boulders—weathered from a 1.7-billion-year-old granite mass—heaped across the landscape. Come at sunset when the combination of minerals and evening sun produces exquisite colors. Camping is permitted, but there are no facilities.

Accommodations and Food

Moderate to expensive accommodations are available at **Eldorado Motor Lodge,** Paterson St. (tel. 08-8962-2402); **Goldfields Motor Hotel,** Paterson St. (tel. 08-8962-2030); **Bluestone**

Motor Inn, Paterson St. (tel. 08-896-2617); an **Safari Lodge,** Davidson St. (tel. 08-8962-2207). Safari Lodge has cheap bunkhouse beds.

Campsites and on-site vans can be rente at **Outback Caravan Park,** Peko Rd. (tel. 08 8962-2459), and **Tennant Creek Caravan Park** Paterson St. (tel. 08-8962-2325).

A 26-bed **YHA Hostel** is on Leichhardt S (tel. 08-8962-2719).

Most restaurants and takeaways are on o around Paterson Street. **The Dolly Pot Inn** Davidson St., a combination squash cour restaurant, is supposed to have the best food i town ($8-16). The **Coffee Place** and **Galler Restaurant,** 53 Paterson St. (in the Tavern) are the town's artsy/trendy attempts.

Tennant Creek's pubs beckon a heavy-dut drinking and fighting clientele. Unless you'r game for that kind of action, stick to the tame bars at the **Tavern, Swan,** and **Goldfields** Ho tels, all on Paterson Street.

Transportation, Services, and Information

Ansett (tel. 13-1300 toll-free) operates regula flights into Tennant Creek.

Greyhound Pioneer Australia (tel. 13-203 toll-free) and McCafferty's (tel. 08-212-5066 stop in Tennant Creek on daily services be tween Darwin and Alice Springs.

Rent cars from **Outback Caravan Park,** Pek Rd. (tel. 08-8962-2459), or **Ten Ant Tours,** 10 Paterson St. (tel. 08-8962-2358).

Ten Ant Tours also offers various local e> cursions, including a popular two-hour fossicke and plant-lover expedition to Kraut Downs. Cos is $22.

The **Tennant Creek Visitor Information Cen tre,** Paterson St., in the transit center, provides li erature and information and books tours an accommodations. Hours are Mon.-Fri. 9 a.m.- p.m. For information, phone (08) 8962-3388.

In emergencies, contact the **police** (tel. 08 8962-1211) or **hospital** (tel. 08-8962-4399).

TO ALICE

Devils Marbles Conservation Reserve (1,82 hectares), 104 km south of Tennant Creek, i situated on both sides of the Track. These mag nificent, precariously balanced granite boulders

TO ALICE SPRINGS

TENNANT CREEK

TO KATHERINE AND DARWIN

DEVILS MARBLES CONSERVATION RESERVE

WAUCHOPE

WYCLIFFE WELL

STUART HWY.

BARROW CREEK

CENTRAL MOUNT STUART HISTORICAL RESERVE

TI TREE

AILERON

PLENTY HWY.

TO RABBIT FLAT

TANAMI TRACK

SIMPSONS GAP NAT'L PARK

ALICE SPRINGS

MOON

TO AYERS ROCK AND ADELAIDE

0   50 km

spread across a wide shallow valley, were created from a single granite mass (similar to the Devils Pebbles). The Warumungu Aborigines believe the marbles are eggs that were laid by the Rainbow Serpent. Sunrise and sunset are the optimal visiting times to this Stonehenge-esque region. A short walking trail has signposts explaining the marbles' origins. Camping is allowed. For information, phone (08) 8951-8211.

Wauchope, 113 km south of Tennant Creek, is a 1938 characteristic bush pub, full of tall tales and imaginative stories. A one-time post office and store, Wauchope offers inexpensive rooms, campsites, and roadhouse facilities. For information, phone (08) 8964-1963.

Wycliffe Well (tel. 08-8964-1966), 18 km south of Wauchope, is another roadhouse rest, boasting one of Australia's largest selections of foreign beers.

The oldest roadhouse on the Track is **Barrow Creek** (tel. 08-8956-9753), another 88 km south. Its widely known "bush bank" is a wall covered with all types of notes and currency, signed by patrons to ensure they'll never go broke. (No withdrawal has ever made it beyond the bar.) This combination pub, art gallery, museum, and community center is definitely one spot where you'll meet some "real locals." Inexpensive accommodations, campsites, a restaurant, takeaway, tourist information, six-hole golf course, petrol, camping gas, and other necessary services are provided.

Barrow Creek was not always the site of jovial goings-on: in 1874 the old telegraph repeater station was attacked by local Aborigines, resulting in the deaths of the stationmaster and linesman (graves nearby the pub), as well as a number of Aborigines.

Ti Tree, 76 km from Barrow Creek, serves both the tourist sector and the surrounding Aboriginal community with a range of facilities including **Ti Tree Roadhouse** (tel. 08-8956-9741) and the adjacent **Aaki Gallery,** which sells locally produced arts and crafts.

Last roadhouse stop before Alice Springs is **Aileron** (tel. 08-8956-9703), which provides the necessary services.

Another 65 km farther, the Track meets the **Plenty Highway,** a part-sealed, part-gravel, and part-dirt track to the Queensland border and Mt. Isa. The first portion of the Plenty is a popular fossicking area. The **Sandover Highway** links up to the Plenty 27 km off the Track, heading farther north through Aboriginal land to a dirt track that eventually connects to the Barkly Highway.

The **Tanami Track** turnoff, 48 km past the Plenty Highway junction, travels 604 km northwest to Rabbit Flat in the Tanami Desert, near the Western Australia border. Fascinating plants and wildlife inhabit this region, but most of the area sits on Aboriginal lands. Check with the Central Australian Tourism Industry Association in Alice Springs regarding necessary permits and other preparation, including good maps. The Tanami Track, with only about the first 100 km sealed, is suitable only for 4WD vehicles.

ALICE SPRINGS

Welcome to Alice (the Alice, as it's also known), the Red Centre of Australia. The thought can send chills up the straightest spine even in the most brain-meltdown heat. But, if you're thinking of the frontiersy outback depicted in Neville Shute's slap-on-the-back novel *A Town Like Alice,* you'll be disappointed. However, the Alice isn't so bad, and, enclosed as it is within the MacDonnell Ranges, the surrounding area is downright astonishing. Just keep in mind that this is no longer an outback town but a convenient tourist center for exploring the real outback.

History

Originally "a town called Stuart" (after explorer John McDouall Stuart) and site of an important 1871 telegraph station built alongside normally dry Todd River (after telegraph superintendent Charles Todd) and its permanent spring (named Alice, after Todd's wife). When the repeater station was shifted into town in 1933, Stuart was renamed "Alice Springs." The town's growth was slow-going, particularly as supplies were delivered only once yearly by Afghan camel teams. Though the railway arrived in 1929, the European population was only about 250. Cattle and mining industries, as well as establishment of a government seat 1926-31, still barely doubled Alice's population.

It was war and the WW II Darwin bombing that created a comparable population explosion. As a major military base, postwar rumors about the area's attributes were leaked, creating tourist interest and subsequent development. Presently the Alice Springs area is home to approximately 20,000 inhabitants. Besides being a service center to the neighboring Aboriginal and pastoral communities, and its obvious importance as a tourist base, nearby Pine Gap is home to a major (and controversial) hush-hush U.S. communications base.

A WALKING TOUR

Alice proper is easily explored on foot. The city center (including most accommodations and restaurants) is bordered by the Track (Stuart Highway) on one side, the Todd River (creek bed) on the other, Anzac Hill on the north, and Stuart Terrace on the south—about a five-square-block grid. Todd Street, with its pedestrian mall between Wills and Gregory Terraces, is the main shopping street and site of the general post office. The bus terminal and Central Australian Tourism Industry Association are nearby.

Old Telegraph Station

The original settlement site is now a 570-hectare historical reserve, featuring *the* Alice spring (you can swim in it), a small museum, several restored buildings, a walking trail to Trig Hill Lookout, picnic areas, and a wildlife enclosure. The reserve is an easy walk from town center along the path on the western edge of the Todd River bank. Hours are daily 8 a.m.-9 p.m. Oct.-April, 8 a.m.-7 p.m. May-September. Free ranger-guided tours are given Sunday 10 a.m., but book ahead. Admission is $2.50. For information, phone (08) 8950-8211.

Anzac Hill

Just north of the town center, Anzac Hill provides superb views of Alice and the surrounding ranges. Sunset and sunrise are the best viewing times. Walk up via "Lions" walk opposite the Catholic church on Wills Terrace.

Spencer and Gillen Museum

On Todd Mall, at the corner of Parsons St., this museum of central Australia features natural history, Aboriginal culture, and early pioneering displays relating to the local region. Hours are Mon.-Fri. 9 a.m.-5 p.m., Sat.-Sun. 10 a.m.-5 p.m. Admission is $2. For information, phone (08) 8951-5335.

Adelaide House

On the mall, across Parsons St., Adelaide House operated 1920-26 as the first Alice Springs Hospital, later became a convalescent home, and in 1980 was declared a museum. Established by Rev. John Flynn (founder of the Royal Flying Doctor Service) and his Australian Inland Mis-

ALICE SPRINGS

TO TENNANT CREEK

87

DIXON RD.

STUART HWY

OLD TELEGRAPH
STATION

ALICE SPRINGS
TELEGRAPH STATION
HISTORICAL RESERVE

CHARLES RIVER

WOODS TERRACE

SMITH ST.

SCHWARZ CRESCENT

ANZAC HILL

WILLS TERRACE

PARSONS ST.

BATH ST.
HARTLEY ST.
TODD ST.

ST.

UNDOOLYA RD.

RAILWAY STATION

RAILWAY
TERRACE

POST OFFICE

GREGORY TERRACE

GEORGE

TOURIST
OFFICE

STOTT TERRACE

LARAPINTA DR.

ARALUEN
ARTS CENTRE

STREHLOW
RESEARCH
CENTRE

AVIATION MUSEUM

MEMORIAL DR.

BILLY GOAT HILL

Stuart Terrace

ROYAL FLYING
DOCTOR BASE

HOSPITAL

YOUTH HOSTEL

LEICHHARDT ST.

OLIVE
PINK
FLORA
RESERVE

TUNKS RD.

BRADSHAW DR.

TELEGRAPH TERRACE

GAP RD.

SOUTH TERRACE

BARRETT DR.

TODD RIVER

TODD RIVER

HEAVITREE GAP

87

TO AIRPORT,
AYERS ROCK,
AND ADELAIDE

TO ALICE SPRINGS SOUTH

0   500 m

sion, the stone radio hut behind the building marks the spot where Traeger and Flynn sent their first field transmission in 1926, prompting the invention of Traeger's Pedal Radio, which Flynn used for outback communication in his Flying Doctor service. The **Flynn Memorial Church,** next door, was built to honor the good doctor. Hours are Mon.-Fri. 10 a.m.-4 p.m., Sat.-Sun. 10 a.m.-noon, March-November. Admission $2.50. For information, phone (08) 8952-1856.

Old Government Homes

On Hartley St., between Stott and Stuart Terraces, these dwellings built for government officers in the 1930s were constructed of concrete blocks, timber, fly-wire verandas, and other architectural details indicative of that period. Hours are Mon.-Fri. 10 a.m.-4 p.m. For information, phone (08) 8952-6955.

Royal Flying Doctor Base

Straight ahead, across Stuart Terrace, this medical facility and lifeline to outback residents offers educational tours including an informative film, displays, memorabilia, and a gift shop. Hours are Mon.-Sat. 9 a.m.-4 p.m., Sunday 1-4 p.m. Tours are given every half hour. Admission $2.50. For information, phone (08) 8952-1129.

Olive Pink Flora Reserve

Behind the Flying Doctor Base, near the hospital, follow Tunks Rd. across the Todd River causeway to see this excellent collection of central Australian native plants. Founded by Olive Pink, who lived with the local Aborigines, this arid-zone botanical reserve also features a visitor center and several short walking trails. Hours are daily 10 a.m.-6 p.m. For information, phone (08) 8952-2154.

Billy Goat Hill

Back across Stuart Terrace (and the other side of the Royal Flying Doctor Base), Billy Goat Hill was an early goathering location with goat yards built around its base and Aboriginal shepherds leading their flocks to wells near the present expanse of lawns.

Panorama Guth

Heading back toward town, on Hartley, see *Panorama Guth,* a 360-degree realistic land-scape painting of the Centre created by Dutch artist Henk Guth. Viewers can check out the scene from an elevated platform. But wouldn't you rather see the real thing? An art gallery exhibits a range of works by Hermannsburg School watercolorists. Hours are Mon.-Sat. 9 a.m.-5 p.m., Sunday 2-5 p.m., closed Sunday and public holidays Dec.-February. Admission $3. For information, phone (08) 8952-2013.

Hartley Street School

Farther up the street, across Gregory Terrace, the first government school opened in 1929. Architectural contrasts between the original building and later octagonal addition depict typical Alice Springs '20s and '40s styles. The building houses the National Trust office. Hours are Mon.-Fri. 10:30 a.m.-1 p.m., closed public holidays. For information, phone (08) 8952-4516.

The Residency

On the other side of the post office, this 1927 stone structure, built for John Charles Cawood, Alice's first government resident, now serves as a museum with Territory history, Aboriginal art, and meteorite exhibits. Hours are Mon.-Fri. 9 a.m.-4 p.m., Sat.-Sun. 10 a.m.-4 p.m. For information, phone (08) 8951-5335.

Old Stuart Gaol

Across Hartley St., on Parsons St., the old jail was built in 1907-08 and is the oldest building in Alice, having housed offenders from horse thieves to railway stowaways until its closure in 1938. Hours are Tuesday and Thursday 10 a.m.-12:30 p.m., Saturday 9:30 a.m.-noon. Admission is $2.

Old Court House

Across Parsons St. diagonally from the jail, this courthouse served as Administrator's Council Rooms 1926-31, and operated as Alice Spring's primary court until 1980, when a new facility was constructed. Viewing is from the outside only.

Railway Terrace

Continue along Parsons St. to Railway Terrace. Toward your right, three 1920s concrete-brick **railway cottages** can be seen. Turn to the left to see the **Wild Dog** (Gnoilya Tmerga) sacred site, which depicts an Aboriginal legend about a great white Dog Man.

LARAPINTA DRIVE SIGHTS

Across the railway tracks from Billy Goat Hill, Stott Terrace becomes Larapinta Drive, a winding road with several additional attractions.

Pay your respects to some of the early pioneers at **Pioneer Cemetery,** the original Stuart Town graveyard on George Crescent, off Larapinta Drive.

The **Aviation Museum,** on Memorial Dr., just off Larapinta, is housed inside the former Connellan Hanger, site of Alice's first airport. Besides the predictable early aviation memorabilia, exhibits include a couple of (previously) missing aircraft and a road train. Open Mon.-Fri. 9 a.m.-4 p.m., Sat.-Sun. 10 a.m.-2 p.m. Free admission.

Next to the Aviation Museum, also on Memorial Dr., **Memorial Cemetery** contains a few more interesting graves—most notably those of Aboriginal artist Albert Namatjira and Harold Bell Lasseter. (Lasseter was the fellow who claimed to have found a gold reef near Docker River on the Northern Territory/Western Australia border. The resulting hoopla was astounding and has continued from the 1930s to the present day, with the gold reef being lost, found, and lost again, many times over. Lasseter's reef may be folly, but his grave is well marked.)

Back on Larapinta Drive, you'll find the multi-million-dollar **Strehlow Research Centre,** opened in 1992 to commemorate the work of anthropologist Theodor Strehlow. Professor Strehlow devoted much of his life to studying the Aranda traditional people, ultimately being honored with the designation *ingkata,* or ceremonial chief. Much of the hands-on collection is hands-off due to its religious significance, but the public exhibits are still quite informative, giving a unique glimpse into the Aranda people's lifestyle and belief system. Hours are daily 10 a.m.-5 p.m. Admission is $4. For information, phone (08) 8952-8000.

Next door, **Araluen Arts Centre** houses two art galleries (one with paintings by noted Aboriginal artist Albert Namatjira), a craft center, restaurant, and bar, and presents a variety o performances. Hours are Mon.-Fri. 9 a.m.-p.m., Sat.-Sun. 10-4 p.m. Admission is $2.5C For information, phone (08) 8952-5022.

Beyond the arts center, **Diorama Village** features gaudy displays of Aboriginal Dreamtim legends. Hours are daily 10 a.m.-5 p.m. Admission is $2. For information, phone (08) 8952 1884.

SOUTH ALICE SIGHTS

Yet another group of sights is clustered aroun the Stuart Highway, on Old South and Emil Gap Roads, south of the town center.

Pitchi Ritchi Aboriginal Experience
This open-air museum, south of the Heavitre Gap causeway, showcases a large collectio of vintage machinery and other early relics, a well as Aboriginal sculptures by noted Victoria artist William Ricketts (most of Ricketts's work i in his sanctuary, outside Melbourne). A kios on the premises sells souvenirs. Hours are dail 9 a.m.-2 p.m., and guided tours by local Ab origines are available. Admission $8. For infor mation, phone (08) 8952-1931.

Stuart Auto Museum
See restored vintage cars and motorcycles, a well as old phonographs, telephones, stean engines, and exhibits relating to Territorial mc toring history (including the saga of the first ca to cross the Territory back in 1907). A restaurar serves light meals and refreshments. Hours ar daily 9 a.m.-5 p.m. Admission $3.

Mecca Date Gardens
Australia's only commercial date farm feature more than 20 different varieties of this ancier tree crop, introduced to the area by the Afgha camel drivers. Dates are available for purchase and tours are given regularly. Hours are Mon Sat. 9 a.m.-5 p.m., Sunday 10 a.m.-4 p.m. Apri October. For information, phone (08) 8952-2425

Frontier Camel Farm
This strange site includes a camel museun camel rides and tours, and a big reptile hous filled with goannas, lizards, and desert snakes

The staff offers informal talks. Hours are daily 9 a.m.-5 p.m., camel rides at 10:30 a.m. and 2 p.m., closed Christmas Day to New Year's Day. Admission is $8, $5 without the camel ride. For information, phone (08) 8953-0444.

Old Timer's Folk Museum
If you haven't had enough pioneering-day reminders, then stop in, pay a buck, and get another fix. Hours are daily 2-4 p.m., except summer months. For information, phone (08) 8952-2844.

Ghan Preservation/MacDonnell Siding
Okay, now we're talking *my* fix—trains. Come join other railway aficionados at this MacDonnell Siding site (built to original design specs), with restored and preserved classic 1929 Ghan locomotives and carriages along a 26-km stretch of the old train track. The Old Ghan, named for the Afghan camel drivers, operated between Alice and Adelaide for 51 years, until it was replaced by the New Ghan in 1980. Open daily 9 a.m.-5 p.m. April-Oct., 10 a.m.-4 p.m. Nov.-March. Admission is $3. Guided train journeys are $15; in July, night tours, including dinner, cost $50. Daily one-way journeys are also offered, with return by coach. For information, phone (08) 8955-5047.

Chateau Hornsby Winery
Take the Colonel Rose Dr. turnoff from Stuart Highway, then hang a left at Petrick Rd., to visit central Australia's only winery, where you can sip and taste shiraz, cabernet sauvignon, riesling, semillon, and chardonnay. A restaurant is open for lunch (with wine, of course). Hours are daily 9 a.m.-5 p.m., closed Christmas Day. For information, phone (08) 8955-5133.

Next to the winery, a commercial carnation farm offers sales and tours on weekdays.

ACCOMMODATIONS

Most Alice accommodations are conveniently located smack-dab in the center of town, while campsites and caravan parks are scattered around the fringes. If possible, book ahead—especially at the most and least expensive places. Rates are usually somewhat lower during the hotter-than-hell summer months.

Inexpensive (Under $35)
The **Todd Tavern,** on Todd Mall (tel. 08-8952-1255), features simple accommodations with shared facilities and continental breakfast, but beware the noise from live bands playing in the pub most weekends. **Desert Rose Inn,** 15 Railway Terrace (tel. 08-8952-1411), has an inexpensive hotel section and a pricier motel with pool and spa. **Alice Lodge,** 4 Mueller St. (tel. 08-8953-1975), is a small seven-room establishment with weekly rates and a four-bed dorm. Facilities include a communal kitchen and laundry, plus pool and barbecue area.

Moderate ($35-70)
Alice Sundown Motel, 39 Gap Rd. (tel. 08-8952-8422), features modern rooms with TVs, pool, barbecue area, and courtesy coach. One of Alice's best values is **Desert Palms Resort,** Barrett Dr. (tel. 08-8952-5977), with large rooms, cooking facilities, pool, and half-court tennis. For longer stays, **Alice Tourist Apartments,** corner Gap Rd. and Gnoilya St. (tel. 08-8952-2788), is also a good value, with a variety of rooms particularly well suited to groups of travelers who pool their resources. Pool, laundry, cooking, and barbecue facilities are available.

Outback Motor Lodge, South Terrace (tel. 08-8952-3888), offers clean, simple rooms with kitchen facilities as well as a pool and barbecue area. A pool and fully equipped, self-contained units with TVs are available at **The Swagmans Rest,** 67 Gap Rd. (tel. 08-8953-1333). A good choice near Alice South attractions is **Sienna Apartments,** corner Palm Circuit and Ross Hwy. (tel. 08-8952-7655). TVs, pool, and cooking facilities are included.

Expensive ($70 and Up)
The top choice for big budgets is **Plaza Hotel,** Barrett Dr., about 1.5 km from town (tel. 08-8952-8000). This 243-room property with pastel decor and manicured grounds offers all the luxury comforts including TVs, videos, room service, pool, spa, sauna, tennis court, health club, restaurants, bars, live entertainment, and boutiques. **Vista Alice Springs,** Stephens Rd. (tel. 08-8952-6100), is about twice as far from town as the Plaza Hotel, half the size, but not quite half the price. Amenities include a pool, tennis court, rental bicycles, gift shop, restaurant, and

bar. **Lasseter's Hotel Casino,** 93 Barrett Dr. (tel. 08-8952-5066), reopened after a long hiatus, offers well-appointed rooms, tennis, pool, nightclub, and, of course, the casino.

Hostels

Backpackers will find plenty of options in Alice. Dorm beds average $10-14 per night and should be booked ahead during peak holiday periods. The **Pioneer YHA Hostel,** corner Parsons St. and Leichhardt Terrace (tel. 08-8952-8855), is a busy, centrally located operation, housed inside an old outdoor movie theater. Facilities include air-conditioned rooms, communal kitchen, recreation room, a laundry, and small food store. Travelers here will pick up all sorts of helpful information on the local scene.

Melanka Lodge, 94 Todd St. (tel. 1800-81-5066 toll-free), is another popular choice, offering a variety of accommodations from backpacker and dorm beds to guesthouse and motel rooms. **Toddy's Resort,** 41 Gap Rd. (tel. 08-8952-1322), also has a wide range of accommodations consisting of dorms, a bunkhouse, cabins, and double rooms with or without private baths.

The **YWCA Stuart Lodge,** Stuart Terrace (tel. 08-8952-1894), accepts both men and women, though many of the 31 rooms are occupied by permanent guests.

Dorm and bunkhouse beds are also available at **Gapview Resort Hotel,** corner Gap Rd. and South Terrace (tel. 08-8952-6611), with a pool, tennis courts, bar, and restaurant.

Camping

All of the following parks allow caravan and tent camping, and many rent on-site vans as well: **G'day Mate Tourist Park,** Palm Circuit (tel. 08-8952-9589), near South Alice sights; **Greenleaves Tourist Park,** Burke St. (tel. 08-8952-8645), two km northwest of Todd River causeway; **Stuart Caravan Park,** Larapinta Dr. (tel. 08-8952-2547), near the arts center; **Wintersun Gardens Caravan Park,** Stuart Hwy. (tel. 08-8952-4080), two km north of the post office; **Carmichael Tourist Park,** Tmara Mara St., off Larapinta Dr. (tel. 08-8952-1200); **Heavitree Gap Caravan Park,** Emily Gap Rd. (tel. 08-8952-2370), adjacent to the Todd River;

MacDonnell Range Tourist Park, Palm Pl. off Ross Hwy. (tel. 08-8952-6111), also nea Alice South attractions; and **Ross River Homestead** (tel. 08-8956-9711), at the end of Ross Highway.

FOOD

Foodies who'll die without nouvelle cuisine bet ter steer clear of Alice—'cause steer is exactly what you'll find on most menus, and well-done shoe leather steer at that. Along with the frozen barramundi and other occasional fish, it's good old meat and taters in mid-Oz—just like it is in middle America. (By the way, that Kentucky Fried Chicken place is at the corner of Todd St and Stott Terrace.)

Inexpensive

Todd Street Mall is lined with coffee shops and takeaways and most are open seven days a week. **Jolly Swagman,** opposite Flynn Church is open daily from 5:30 a.m. for breakfast, home made cakes and dampers, and vegetarian and Asian-style meals. **Thai Kitchen,** off the mall, of fers decent Asian food.

The **Fish and Chips** shop, on Lindsay Ave. near the corner of Undoolya Rd., is highly rec ommended by locals. **Eranova Cafeteria,** 72 Todd St., offers continental-style dining, a di verse selection, and good value. Open Mon. Sat. for breakfast, lunch, and dinner.

Alice Plaza lunch spots consist of **Fawlty's Red Centre Chinese,** and **Doctor Lunch;** al cheap and casual. For pub meals, try **Stuar Arms Bistro,** upstairs in the Alice Plaza or Todd Street Mall.

Moderate

Lilli's, at Heavitree Gap Motel, Ross Hwy. (tel 08-8952-2370), specializes in Australian deli cacies (watch out for that witchetty grub sauce) **La Casalinga,** 105 Gregory Terrace, is an Alice favorite for pizza and Italian specialties. Oper daily for dinner. **Camel's Crossing,** in Fan Ar cade, off Todd Mall (tel. 08-8952-5522), fea tures Mexican and vegetarian dishes. **Swinger's Café,** 71 Gregory Terrace, is a show-off place but with good pasta and curry.

For Chinese meals, try **Chopsticks**, in Yeperenye Shopping Centre on Hartley St. (tel. 08-8952-3873); **Oriental Gourmet**, 80 Hartley St. (tel. 08-8953-0888); or **Golden Inn**, 9 Undoolya Road. All are open daily.

Expensive

The **Overlanders Steakhouse**, 72 Hartley St. (tel. 08-8952-2159), serves up genuine Aussie tucker, including buffalo, camel, and kangaroo steaks, accompanied by live Australian folk entertainment.

Puccini's, corner Todd Mall and Parsons St. (tel. 08-8953-0935), offers fine Italian cuisine—surprisingly fine, in fact, for the Territory.

Rossini's, in the Diplomat Hotel (tel. 08-8952-8977), is another unique find with its continental cuisine and formal settings.

El Patio, in the Plaza Hotel (tel. 08-8952-8000), and **Kings**, in Lasseter's Hotel Casino (tel. 08-8952-5066), are other good choices.

ENTERTAINMENT AND EVENTS

Cinemas

Films screen regularly at **Araluen Arts Centre**, Larapinta Road. The **Alice Springs Film Society** presents cinema programs at Totem Theatre, Anzac Oval, on the second and fourth Tuesdays of each month. For information, phone (08) 8950-2383.

Pubs and Clubs

The pub scene is somewhat limited. The **Todd Tavern**, corner Todd St. and Wills Terrace, features live piano-bar entertainment Thurs.-Sat., disco Thurs.-Sat., Monday night jam sessions, and Sunday night folk concerts. **Stuart Arms Bistro**, Todd Mall, occasionally presents cabarets and live weekend entertainment.

Simpsons Gap Bar, in the Plaza Hotel, a popular hangout for travelers, offers live entertainment every night and a DJ Thurs.-Saturday. Hipper-than-hip **Uncles**, corner of Hartley St. and Gregory Terrace, buzzes every night, but Friday is the big scene. **Alice Junction Tavern** (AJ's), at Heavitree Gap Tourist Resort, off Ross Highway, features disco Fri.-Sat., and **Bojangles Restaurant and Nightclub**, Todd St., also has occasional late-night disco.

Bush Entertainment

Chateau Hornsby Winery presents the long-running **Ted Egan Outback Show**, with tall tales, bush lore, and outback songs. Performances are three times a week. Cost is $15, about twice that with dinner included. For bookings, phone (08) 8955-5133.

The **Overlanders Steakhouse**, 72 Harley St., features local entertainers nightly, including sing-alongs and bush bands.

Often the big hotels will host a **Bush Tucker Night**, which typically includes campfire meals and storytelling.

Theater and Music

Araluen Arts Centre, Larapinta Dr., is Alice's venue for cinema, musical and theatrical performances, and visual arts. For schedules and ticket information, phone (08) 8952-5022.

Events

Alice hosts a variety of strange and colorful events, usually during the cooler winter months.

The end of April or early May brings the **Camel Cup**, a series of camel roundups and races on the Todd River bed, commemorating the old Afghan camel train days. A **Food and Wine Festival** takes place the day after Camel Cup on the lawns of Verdi Club, Undoolya Road. The **Alice Springs Cup** annual horse race runs practically neck-in-neck with the camels.

The **Bangtail Muster**, held the first Monday in May, once glorified the cutting of horses' tails before they were shipped out, but today it's an excuse for a colorful and satirical parade.

In June, the **Finke Desert Race, Taps, Tubs and Tiles** is a 500-km, two-day endurance race for trail bikes and off-road vehicles.

Rodeo lovers will revel in August's weeklong **Alice Springs Rodeo**, with heaps of events, and cowboys and wanna-bes parading around town in full drag.

The **Henley-on-Todd Regatta**, in late September, is Alice's most famous event: competitors "race" along the dry riverbed in an amazing variety of bottomless boats, racers' legs poking out as they pick up their craft and speed along on foot. The series of peculiar events is followed the next day by the **Annual Beer Festival**, featuring live entertainment, children's activities, food, and many beer stalls.

SPORTS AND RECREATION

Swimming Pools
Almost every hotel and motel has its own pool. Alice Springs Swimming Centre, Speed St. (tel. 08-8952-3757), also has a water slide, trampoline, and aquarobics classes. Open daily mid-Sept. through April.

Sporting Facilities
Squash: Guests are welcome at Alice Springs Squash Centre, 13 Gap Rd. (tel. 08-8952-1179). Equipment is available for rent.

Tennis: Public courts and private coaching can be hired at Traeger Park, off Traeger Ave. (tel. 08-8952-4320).

Golf: Alice Springs Golf Club, Cromwell Dr. (tel. 08-8952-5440), welcomes visitors.

Gambling: Lasseter's Hotel Casino is the venue for gaming tables and pokeys. A dress code is enforced (decent, not dressy).

Spectator Sports
Australian Rules **football** and **baseball** are played at Traeger Park, Gap Road. **Rugby League** meets at Anzac Oval, and Larapinta Oval, Memorial Dr., is the **softball** venue. The season for most sports is April-September.

Bond Springs Airstrip, North Stuart Hwy. (tel. 08-8952-1417), is the site of weekend **gliding.**

SHOPPING

You've got a humongous Kmart, Woolworth, and a mall—those will take care of most immediate shopping needs. But Alice's big consumer draw, of course, is Aboriginal art. Alice is the place to pick up a didgeridoo or boomerang for that special someone. Distinctive works include Papunya sand paintings, batiks from the local Utopia settlement, as well as a good selection of weavings, carvings, and bark paintings.

Highly recommended outlets are **Jukurrpa Gallery and Artists**, 35 Gap Rd., both a gallery and working studio, and the **Original Dreamtime Gallery,** 63 Todd Mall, with an impressive range of Aboriginal arts and crafts. Other good shops are the **Papunya Tula Artists** shop, Todd St., south of the mall; **Gondwana Gallery,** on the mall; and the **Central Australian Aboriginal Media Association** shop, on Hartley Street.

Opal buyers might enjoy the gems and jewelry at the **Gem Cave**, 85 Todd Street Mall.

Camping supplies can be purchased or rented from **Alice Springs Disposals,** off the mall, on Reg Harris Lane (tel. 08-8952-5701). **Centre Canvas,** 9 Smith St. (tel. 08-8952-2453), manufactures quality swags (bed rolls).

TRANSPORTATION

Getting There by Air
Alice Springs Airport, 14 km southeast of town center, is served by **Ansett** (tel. 13-1300 toll-free) and **Qantas** (tel. 13-1313 toll-free) with daily scheduled flights from all capital cities. Offices are opposite each other at Todd and Parson Streets. In case you'd like to skip Alice and fly directly to the Rock, direct flights are available from both Sydney and Adelaide.

Alice Springs Airport Shuttle Service (tel. 08-8953-0310) meets all flights and provides transport to the city center for $9. Book ahead for service to the airport. **Taxis** into the city cost about two bucks more. Taxi ranks are located at the airport, or phone **Alice Springs Taxis** (tel. 08-8952-1877).

Left luggage lockers are available at the airport.

Getting There by Bus
Interstate coaches arrive and depart from the terminal on Hartley St., near Wills Terrace. Daily services between Alice, Darwin, and Adelaide are operated by **Greyhound Pioneer Australia** (tel. 13-2030 toll-free) and McCafferty's (tel. 08-212-5066 Adelaide, 08-8952-3952 Alice Springs). You can also pick up a daily connection to the Rock and the Olgas. Fares are approximately $175 from Darwin or Adelaide. Buses change at Three Ways Roadhouse for connections to Queensland, and at Katherine for the route to Western Australia.

Getting There by Train
The **Ghan** does not have quite the same flair and sense of adventure as its famous predecessor, but it's a terrific ride all the same. Half the fun of the original train was the dreadful track,

frequent flooding, and the good chance of being stuck in the middle of nowhere and having emergency supplies parachuted in!

These days, darn it, the new track is fairly flood-proof, the train carries twice as many passengers in half the time (20 hours from Adelaide, instead of 50), and probably nothing exciting will happen along the trip. The scenery, however, and the ability to take a shower while choo-chooing through the central Australian desert, make this one of the country's great rail journeys.

Trains depart Adelaide on Monday and Thursday, returning to Adelaide on Tuesday and Friday; one additional service runs April-January. If you purchase a rail pass, the Ghan journey is included. Otherwise, one-way fares run about $145 economy sitting, $249 holiday-class berth, or $456 first-class berth, with meals included. For information and bookings, phone **Rail Australia** (tel. 13-2232 toll-free).

Getting There by Car, Thumb, Hook, or Crook

Basically it's the straight and narrow Track all the way from Adelaide or Darwin. Be careful hitching; traffic is light. Many hitchikers report long waits at Three Ways. Women should not hitch around the outback without a male companion. Check the Alice YHA notice board for possible rides.

Getting Around

Other than taxis, Alice has no public transportation. **Alice Springs Taxis** (tel. 08-8952-1877) offers local transport.

Rental cars will cost $30-70 per day, plus insurance and per-km charges; a 4WD will run $85-160 per day, typically including 100 free km per day. Many vehicles cannot be taken outside a 50-km radius of town or on dirt roads without written permission—and extra fees. Read all fine print regarding insurance, as some coverages don't apply when vehicles leave paved roads (why else would you rent a 4WD in the outback?).

Rental companies include **Avis** (tel. 08-8952-3899), **Brits Rentals** (tel. 08-8952-8814), **Budget** (tel. 08-8952-8899), **Centre Car Rentals** (tel. 08-8952-1405), **Territory Rent-a-Car** (tel. 08-8952-9999), and **Thrifty** (tel. 08-8952-2400).

Most of the above offices are located on or near Todd Mall, and some have airport counters. Also inquire regarding moped, campervan, and motorhome rentals.

Rent **bicycles** (about $12 per day) from just about any of the backpacker hostels.

Tours

As with Darwin, you can choose from a seemingly endless array of organized tours to the Rock and other Red Centre sites, traveling by air-conditioned coach, 4WD, camel, balloon, or airplane. Call into the Central Australian Tourism Industry Association for advice and bookings, according to your specific interests. The Pioneer YHA also arranges tours.

Rod Steinert offers a variety of outings, including his ever-popular **Dreamtime Tour and Bushtucker Tour,** a half-day excursion that'll give you a taste of Aboriginal culture including bush food preparation, boomerang- and spear-throwing, and a "quickie" Dreamtime explanation. Cost is $45. For information, phone (08) 8955-5000.

Tourists also flock to Alice for camel treks—everything from a quick ride to breakfast and dinner outings (yes, *on* the camel), to treks of several days. The tourist bureau will provide details and bookings, or contact **Frontier Camel Farm** (tel. 08-8953-0444). Or saddle up on a horse with **Trail Rides** (tel. 08-8952-2308). *Or,* saddle up on a Harley with **Harley Davidson Scenic Tours** (tel. 08-8953-4755).

Other good all-around companies include **Trek About** (tel. 08-8953-0714) and **Tracks Outback Expeditions** (tel. 08-8995-30244).

Sunrise **hot-air balloon** rides are particularly mesmerizing over the Red Centre. Costs range $100-150 (including silver service breakfast) and are offered by **Outback Ballooning** (tel. 1800-80-9790 toll-free) and **Ballooning Downunder** (tel. 08-8952-8816).

The **Alice Wanderer** (tel. 08-8953-0310) operates daily, on hourly rounds to most tourist sites in town. For $18, passengers can get on and off the bus at whim. A running commentary explains each point of interest.

Also see the chart "Aboriginal Tours" in the On the Road chapter.

SERVICES

Branches of national **banks** and automatic teller machines are located on Todd Mall, Todd Street, and Parsons Street. Almost all banks will change overseas traveler's checks, usually for $2-3 per transaction.

The **general post office,** Hartley St., is open Mon.-Fri. 9 a.m.-5 p.m. For information, phone (08) 8952-1020.

The **Wash-house Launderette,** corner Stuart Hwy., Parsons St., and Railway Terrace, provides coin-op machines for do-it-yourself washing and ironing, daily 8 a.m.-8 p.m. Almost every hotel, motel, or hostel has laundry facilities.

INFORMATION

The **Central Australian Tourism Industry Association,** corner Hartley St. and Gregory Terrace (tel. 08-8952-5199), dispenses information, maps, and literature, and books tours and accommodations. Hours are Mon.-Fri. 9 a.m.-5 p.m., Sat.-Sun. and public holidays 10 a.m.-3 p.m. For information, phone (08) 8952-5199.

Pick up maps, books, and information on ranger-led tours at the **Conservation Commission of Northern Territory,** either at the

desk in the tourism office or at the main office, off the Stuart Hwy., several km south of town. For information, phone (08) 8951-8211.

In emergencies, dial 000, or contact the **police** (tel. 08-8951-8888) or **Alice Springs Hospital,** Gap Rd. (tel. 08-8951-7777). The hospital provides 24-hour emergency service, plus an outpatient walk-in clinic Mon.-Friday.

For details about local driving conditions (including those rough, unpaved "roads"), contact **Road Conditions Information** (tel. 08-8952-3833).

The **public library,** near the corner of Leichhardt and Gregory Terraces, is open Mon.-Fri. 9 a.m.-5:30 p.m., Saturday 9 a.m.-3:30 p.m.

A branch of the **Angus and Robertson** bookshop chain is in the Yeperenye Centre. Other good shops are the **Arunta Gallery,** Todd St. south of the mall, and **Dymocks** in the Alice Plaza.

Stock up on even more maps at the **Automobile Association of the Northern Territory,** Gregory Terrace (tel. 08-8953-1322), or at the **Department of Lands, Housing and Local Government,** also on Gregory Terrace (tel. 08-8951-5743).

Almost every newsagent stocks *The Centra Advocate,* Alice's local paper, which comes out on Wednesday and Friday, and many carry a large selection of air-freighted national dailies and mags.

VICINITY OF ALICE

Weathered gorges, rocky walls, and sheer cliffs of the ancient MacDonnell Ranges run east and west of Alice, with many of these scenic and mysterious spots an easy day trip or overnight away from the town center.

About the same age as Ayers Rock (650 million years old, give or take a few years), the mostly sandstone MacDonnells reach 400 km east to west and 160 km north to south. As babies, the ranges stood more than 3,000 meters above sea level, eroding over the millennia to an average height today of under 500 meters. The rocky crags, crevices, and chasms are variegated with ferrous red, olive, and forest green—striations made even more evident by sparse vegetation. In spring, wildflowers pro-

vide an even more spectacular sight, while shy wildlife, such as the black-flanked rock wallaby is a bit more difficult to spot (try early morning o late afternoon). Whichever direction you trave in this majestic and meditative region, you'l end up gorged and centered.

TO THE EAST

Emily and Jessie Gaps

These two gaps, just east of Alice on the Ross Highway, form a 695-hectare nature park noted for its scenic river red gums and waterholes The area was also significant to Aborigines, who have left rock paintings along the eastern face o

Emily Gap. The area is popular with picnickers. For information, phone (08) 8952-1013.

Corroboree Rock

Local Aborigines used this limestone rock outcrop, located 46 km east of Alice on the Ross Highway, for both manhood rituals and as a storage area for sacred stones used in Dreamtime storytelling. The seven-hectare conservation reserve features a short walking trail and picnic and barbecue facilities. Camping is allowed. For information, phone (08) 8956-9765.

Trephina Gorge Nature Park

A few km north of the Ross Highway, and 80 km east of Alice, this 1,770-hectare nature park features two contrasting gorges: scenic Trephina Gorge with its tall river gums, gentle pool, and wide sandy creek bed, and, a few kilometers

west, shady and secluded John Hayes Rockhole, an area especially rich in birdlife.

The park offers grand campsites and walking tracks (one leads to John Hayes Rockhole); access for conventional vehicles may be limited in some areas. For information, phone (08) 8956-9765.

Ross River Homestead

Situated about 12 km east of Trephina Gorge, this 1898 whitewashed homestead (the original headquarters of Loves Creek Station) features a variety of tourist pleasures including moderate to expensive accommodations, a budget bunkhouse, caravan park, country walking trails, horse and camel rides, a restaurant, and pub. Keep in mind that tour buses love it here also—even so, it's worth a stop. For information and bookings, phone (08) 8956-9711.

N'Dhala Gorge Nature Park

Continue about 10 km southeast of the homestead (4WD is necessary) to this 501-hectare park noted for the thousands of prehistoric rock carvings (at least 35,000 years old) decorating the gorge walls. Mystery fact: Present-day Aborigines have no inkling of what the designs mean or who the artists were! A short trail leads to the engravings. Picnic and barbecue facilities are available and camping is allowed, but you have to bring your own water. For information, phone (08) 8956-9765.

Arltunga Historical Reserve

Set along the eastern edge of the MacDonnells, 44 km northeast of Ross River Homestead, Arltunga preserves the remains of this particularly isolated gold-mining town, which was in operation 1887-1912 and held a population only of about 75 people during that period. Ruins within the 5,506-hectare reserve include mine offices, miners' graves, a police station, jail, assayer's residence, the old stamp batter and cyanide works, and many other sites. Walking tracks and picnic facilities are provided within the park. **Arltunga Tourist Park,** referred to as the "loneliest pub in the scrub," has a small campground and shop. The graded track to Arltunga is recommended for 4WD only, as is the 111-km northwest loop back to the Stuart Highway. For information, phone (08) 8956-9770.

Ruby Gap Nature Park

If you're in a 4WD, head 39 km southeast to Ruby Gap (also known as Ruby Gorge), an unusual geological site composed of ribbon-like quartz and limestone strata along glorious, rugged gorges that parallel the winding Hale River. Bush camping is allowed along the river, but take care of your own waste. For information, phone (08) 8956-9770.

TO THE WEST

Two different routes lead to sights in the western MacDonnell Ranges. You start off on Larapinta Drive and, about 54 km out of Alice (past Standley Chasm), either continue along Larapinta or turn onto Namatjira Drive. For information on any of the parks below, phone (08) 8950-8211.

John Flynn Historical Reserve

What historical reserve? It's a half-hectare grave site on Larapinta Drive, where rest the ashes of Rev. John Flynn, founder of the Royal Flying Doctor Service. One of the Devils Marbles was imported to the site for effect.

Simpsons Gap National Park

Conveniently located only 18 km west of Alice, this is a great spot to get your gap-and-gorge fi if you're short on time, money, or energy. Comprising purple-tinged mountains, steep ridges, huge white ghost gums, wooded creek beds, and colonies of rock wallabies, Simpsons Gap (30,950 hectares) is a favorite with tourists. Good walking tracks begin at the excellent visitor center (pick up maps and other literature) and include 20-km unmarked climbing treks, 18-km roundabout bushwalks, and short, easy trails to lookout points. The park has picnic facilities but camping is not allowed.

Standley Chasm

Photographers love to shoot this steep, rusty walled crevice, 50 km west of Alice, especially when the sun provides natural overhead lighting that turns the chasm fireball red. As you can probably imagine, it's not likely you'll be the only one clicking away. A kiosk sells snacks, refreshments, and souvenirs, and picnic facilities are available.

Namatjira Drive

Ellery Creek Big Hole Nature Park (1,766 hectares), 43 km beyond Standley Chasm, is another exquisite gorge with steep red cliffs and a large river-red-gum-shaded waterhole. This is an especially popular location for picnickers and energetic bushwalkers who climb to the ridge tops for majestic views.

Another 11 km west will bring you to narrow, winding **Serpentine Gorge Nature Park** (518 hectares), which is actually two gorges with high rock walls, waterholes, and palmlike cycad vegetation. Picnicking and camping are allowed.

Next stop, 28 km down the road, is **Ormiston Gorge and Pound Nature Park** (4,655 hectares). The dominant two-km-long red cliff, rugged wilderness, permanent waterhole, and towering ghost gum and cypress pine forests have earned Ormiston its reputation as one of the most scenic and colorful gorges in the western MacDonnells. Fea-ures include wonderful walking tracks (the seven-km trail through the pound area is reputedly one of the country's finest wilderness treks), a visitor center, and small campground.

Glen Helen Gorge, just one km farther, is a 386-hectare nature park where the Finke River (supposedly the world's oldest, having run this same course for 350 million years) begins its journey through the MacDonnells to the Simpson Desert. An interesting walking track follows along the riverbed. **Glen Helen Lodge,** a restored 1930s homestead, provides a range of accommodations including modern motel-style rooms, campsites, and a YHA-affiliated hostel. Other lodge facilities are a restaurant, bar, bistro, occasional live entertainment, takeaway, and petrol station. For bookings, phone (08) 8956-7489.

Redbank Gorge Nature Park (1,295 hectares) is situated 30 km west of Glen Helen; recommended for 4WD vehicles. Steep slopes with those mighty ghost gums hovering above this remote site provide the scenic beauty. If you intend to jump into one of the deep pools, be forewarned that the walls are slippery and the water is icy cold. Redbank also makes a good base for experienced climbers who wish to scale nearby **Mt. Sonder** (1,380 meters). Picnicking and camping are allowed.

Continuing along Larapinta Drive
The first sight you'll come to, about 100 km from Standley Chasm, is **Namatjira Monument,** which honors Albert Namatjira, one of Australia's most noted Aboriginal artists, famous for his central Australian landscape paintings.

Hermannsburg, another 30-40 km along, is the site of an 1880s mission brought to the Aranda people by Lutheran pastors. Though the Aranda own the mission now, this township still retains links with the Lutheran church. Historic buildings include the original church, Bethlehem church, schoolhouse, and smithy. A museum and tearooms are housed within two of the old residences, and a variety of local Aboriginal art and souvenirs can be purchased. The town also has a petrol station, garage, supermarket, and hardware store.

Finke Gorge National Park (36,000 hectares), 12 km south of Hermannsburg, can be reached only via 4WD vehicle. Within its protected wilderness, the park straddles the south-ward-bound Finke River and contains large waterholes, bird refuges, sculpted rock formations, more sandstone gorge, and a very comprehensive collection of central Australian plants. The park's most famous attraction, however, is **Palm Valley,** a strange and bizarre tropical area encompassing approximately 400 plant species, including the red cabbage palm *(Livistona mariae),* found nowhere else in the world. The valley is thought to be a remnant from the days (about 10,000 years ago) when the Centre supported a moister climate. An information and ranger station is near the entrance to Palm Creek. Picnicking and camping are allowed. For information, phone (08) 8951-8211.

TO THE ROCK

Back on the Track and aiming toward Ayers Rock, more fascinating sights await travelers willing to steer off the very well-beaten path. One route will take you along the Old South Road, which parallels the Old Ghan line shortly past the Ross Highway junction; the other is the Kings Canyon turnoff (Ernest Giles Road), a gravel road that cuts into the Track about 145 km south of Alice. (Be careful if driving this road during or after rains—it gets very slippery.) Or you can just keep on the Track all the way to Lasseter Highway (200 km south of Alice) and turn west 241 km to the Rock.

Along Old South Road
Ewaninga Rock Carvings are located within a six-hectare conservation reserve 39 km south of Alice. As with the N'Dhala Gorge site, these prehistoric engravings contain symbols so ancient that not even today's Aborigines can figure them out. Other features here include abundant plants, birds, and wildlife. Visitors are asked to not climb on the boulders.

With a 4WD you can access **Chambers Pillar Historical Reserve,** 104 km south of the carvings. This impressive sandstone pillar rises 58 meters out of the surrounding flat plain, casting a phenomenal glow at sunrise and sunset. Used as a landmark by early explorers, the pillar still bears the evidence of pioneers who scratched their names onto the surface. (Don't *you* do this!)

Still on Track

Virginia Camel Farm, 93 km south of Alice along the Stuart Hwy., is run by breeder Noel Fullerton, founder—and ofttimes winner—of the Camel Cup. Noel runs the outfit that can take you humping through the center on short rides or long safaris. He even arranges packages in which you can take your camel to breakfast, lunch, or dinner. Longer expeditions tour nearby **Rainbow Valley Nature Park** (2,483 hectares), a sublime region of richly colored, broken sandstone gorge. You can camp here on your own, but you'll need to bring a 4WD and your own water. For information about the camel farm and Rainbow Valley tours, check with the tourist bureau or phone (08) 8956-0925. Virginia Camel Farm is open daily 7 a.m.-5 p.m.

Along Ernest Giles Road

About 13 km from the Track (144 km southwest of Alice), follow the signpost to **Henbury Meteorite Craters,** a 16-hectare conservation reserve encompassing 12 separate craters, thought to have been created by a meteor shower 5,000 years ago. The craters range in size from two to 180 meters across, and one is a whopping 15 meters deep! An easy walking track offers explanatory signs. This is another "look but don't touch" site.

Next stop along this road—and probably a welcome one—is **Wallara Ranch,** about 85 km west of the meteor craters and about halfway to Kings Canyon. This rambling local pub is a winner with tourists who stop to soak up the local atmosphere and stock up on supplies. Facilities include moderately priced motel accommodations, a bunkhouse, campsites, a dining room, takeaway, a swimming pool, petrol station, and day tours of the canyon. For information, phone (08) 8956-2901. From Wallara Ranch, you can

take an alternate route 70 km south to the Lasseter Highway or keep going to the canyon, a road's end.

Kings Canyon, often called Australia's Grand Canyon, is a dramatic gorge and escarpment situated 100 km past Wallara Ranch. Now called **Watarrka National Park,** some of the more unusual natural features of this 106,000-hectare area include the **Garden of Eden** palm shelter and the **Lost City,** a strange grouping of weathered outcrops that look like domed houses. A somewhat strenuous walking trail leads to most of the sights, or try the steep climb to the plateau for terrific canyon views. Park facilities include a ranger station and visitor center, plus picnic and camping areas. For information, phone (08) 8956-7460.

Lasseter Highway

You're almost there! **Erldunda Desert Oaks Resort,** at the junction of the Track and Lasseter Highway, offers roadhouse facilities including a range of motel accommodations, a caravan park, campsites, dining room, pub, takeaway, souvenirs, pool, tennis court, petrol station, and tourist information. For information, phone (08) 8956-0984.

Mt. Ebenezer is another roadhouse, 55 km west, owned by the neighboring Imanpa Aboriginal people. Aside from the normal roadhouse features, Mt. Ebenezer also houses a gift shop that displays and sells local artifacts and paintings. For information, phone (08) 8956-2904.

Another 100 km will bring you to the **Curtin Springs** roadhouse, which is also a working cattle station. Founded in 1943, this inn exudes local atmosphere while providing necessary services. For information, phone (08) 8956-2906.

Travel 82 more kilometers west to Yulara, gateway to Ayers Rock and the Olgas.

AYERS ROCK AND THE OLGAS

Uluru National Park (132,566 hectares), by encompassing Ayers Rock and the Olgas, contains one of the world's great natural wonders and one of Australia's top tourist destinations. It is also the heart of Australia—the big red heart.

Uluru National Park encompasses more than 400 plant species, 150 types of birds, and about 75 mammal varieties in a sensitive geological landscape that contrasts drastically from sandy flat plains to those big old rocks. Though Uluru has been returned to its Aboriginal owners, the park was leased to the Australian Nature Conservation Agency and is presently comanaged by that office and the Anangu people.

Blissfully, all the "civilized" trappings are located in **Yulara,** a tourist village built in 1984 specifically to accommodate the hundreds-of-thousands of annual visitors from all over the world. Situated 20 km from the Rock, this complex—a joint government-private sector scheme—features all the comforts any modern-day traveler to a Stone Age site could desire.

Uluru (Ayers Rock)

I would like to be able to spew fluffy prose at you—to say that this incredible rock, of deep spiritual and cultural significance to the Aborigines (who have lived here for at least 10,000 years), is a sacred shrine quite unlike any other. Though that is certainly no lie, it's not the complete truth either; this spectacular monolith is also the site of resorts, facilities, tourist buses, and tourists themselves, decked out in straw sun hats or beer-ad visors and printed T-shirts as they huff and puff their way up the Rock (supporting themselves on the specially installed safety chain). The traditional owners have been pushing, however, to get visitors off their rock and to, perhaps, admire it from a more reverent distance at or around its base.

Ayers Rock (Uluru, to the Aborigines), no matter who's crawling around it, is a pretty breathtaking sight—a 650-million-year-old sandstone behemoth, rising 348 meters above the pancakelike surrounding plain (and it's supposed to be about twice as big *beneath* the surface!). Its dimensions are indeed impressive—8.8 km around

the base, 3.6 km long, and 2.4 km wide—but Uluru's most awe-inspiring feature is the ecstatic glow and haunting colors it exudes at different times of the day (sunrise and sunset are best).

The Rock also features weathered gullies, eerie caves, and Aboriginal carvings and paintings (some 10,000 years old). The public is not permitted access to some declared sacred sites.

If you want to climb The Rock, you are supposed to be in excellent physical condition (a real chuckle once you check out some of the climbers). Also be aware that the higher slopes are often hit by gale-force winds (climbers have died while trying to retrieve a Foster's visor). Check with the park rangers for necessary equipment. Another option is the three- to four-hour walk around the base, which is fringed with caves, waterholes, and various desert vegetation. Admission is $10.

Ayers Rock Observatory, Napala Dr., in Yulara village, is a perfect place to gaze into the clear and astounding outback skies. Optical telescopes and binoculars allow viewing of the southern skies and the Aboriginal legends with which they're associated. Hours are nightly 8:30-11:30 p.m. Admission is $15. For information, phone (08) 8921-8170.

The Olgas

The Olgas (Kata Tjuta, or "Many Heads," to the Aborigines) lie about 27 km to the west and are also part of the protected Uluru National Park. These huge rocks, just as old and once much larger than Ayers Rock, are a jumble of more rounded monoliths, separated by gorges, valleys, and chasms. Many visitors enjoy exploring the Olgas more than the Rock because they have more hidden areas to discover and are a bit less intimidating and less touristed.

A favorite attraction is deep, narrow **Olga Gorge,** which runs between 546-meter-high Mt. Olga and slightly shorter Mt. Wulpa. The Olgas' three main **walking trails** are the two-km track from the carpark to Olga Gorge, the four-km route up to **Kata Tjuta Lookout,** and a four-km circular track around the mysterious **Valley of the Winds,** on the north side. Another option for very fit walk-

AYERS ROCK AND WALKS

ULURU CIRCUIT WALK, 9 km, 4 HRS.

KANTJU GORGE

ULURU—AYERS ROCK

863 m (348 m ABOVE PLAIN)

THE CLIMB, 1.6 km, 2 HRS. RETURN

LIRU WALK, 2 km, 30 MIN. ONE WAY.

RANGER STATION

ABORIGINAL LAND

CONNELLAN AIRPORT

TO ERLDUNDA AND ALICE SPRINGS

LASSETER HWY.

YULARA RESORT

ABORIGINAL LAND

KATA TJUTA—THE OLGAS

SUNSET VIEWING

DOCKER RIVER RD.

SUNSET VIEWING

TO DOCKER RIVER

ULURU NATIONAL PARK

= CAR PARK

ULURU (AYERS ROCK)

ers is the two-km track that joins up with the Valley of the Winds track from Kata Tjuta Lookout. Make sure you carry plenty of water for these excursions. It's also recommended that you check in with the ranger station before exploring the Olgas on your own. Rangers will advise you on accessible areas and necessary equipment.

PRACTICALITIES

Accommodations and Food
The cheapest place you'll find out here is the bunkhouse at **Outback Pioneer Lodge** (tel. 08-8956-2170). Two dorms, each with 40 beds,

run $18 pp. "Budget" cabins are already in the expensive range, as are rooms with small kitchenettes—and shared facilities—at **Spinifex Lodge** (tel. 08-8956-2131). If you're not bothered by room rates almost as high as the Rock, your choices are **Sails in the Desert** (tel. 08-8956-2200) or the **Desert Gardens Hotel** (tel. 08-8956-2100). All the luxuries come with the price tag (in the $200-250 bracket).

Ayers Rock Campground (tel. 08-8956-2055) has campsites and on-site vans, plus a pool. Camping is not allowed anywhere within Uluru National Park.

Both the Sails in the Desert and Desert Gardens offer dining options from snack bars to upscale restaurants. **Ernest Giles Tavern** features both counter and bistro meals. **Outback Pioneer Hotel** has simple fare and takeaways. A **kiosk** at the campground sells a variety of foodstuffs, but there's a better selection at the **supermarket** in the shopping square. **Yulara Coffee Shop** is open daily for snacks, light meals, and takeaways.

Shopping

The **shopping square complex** has a newsagent, supermarket, T-shirt shop, travel agency, and photo processor. Pick up Aboriginal handicrafts and paintings at the **Maruka Arts and Crafts Centre** (owned by the Anangu people), and souvenirs at the **Ininti Store, Ranger Station,** or at the hotel gift shop/galleries. **Mulgara Gallery,** in Sails in the Desert Hotel, features high-quality (and high-priced) arts, crafts, and jewelry.

Services and Information

A **bank, post office, police,** and **fire station** are located in Yulara Village.

The **Visitors Centre,** on Yulara Drive, features informative displays on the area's history, geography, flora, and fauna, and also presents regular slide shows. Literature is available, including walking maps, visitor guides, and *The Yulara Experience* newsletter. Open daily 8 a.m.-9 p.m. For information, phone (08) 8956-2240.

The **ranger station,** at the Rock, also dispenses maps, information, and helpful advice. For information, phone (08) 8956-2299.

A **medical clinic** at the Royal Flying Doctor base, near the police station (tel. 08-8956-2286), is open Mon.-Fri. 9 a.m.-noon and 2-5 p.m., Sat.-Sun. 10-11 a.m.

In emergencies, dial 000, or contact the **police** (tel. 08-8956-2166) or **ambulance** (tel. 08-8956-2286). An emergency alarm is located at the base of the Rock.

TRANSPORTATION

Getting There

Yulara's **Connellan Airport,** six km north of the village, is served by **Ansett** (tel. 13-1300 toll-free), **Qantas** (tel. 13-1313 toll-free), and **Kendell Airlines** (tel. 069-22-0100). Direct flights are available from Adelaide, Alice Springs, Cairns, Sydney, and Perth.

AAT Kings (tel. 08-8956-2171) operates shuttle coaches between the airport and the village for $9. Taxi service, at about the same fare, is available from **Sunworth Taxi Service** (tel. 08-8956-2152).

Greyhound Pioneer Australia (tel. 13-2030 toll-free) operates daily service between Alice Springs and Ayers Rock (450 km). Round-trip day tours cost about $150, and a one-way bus ticket costs around half that. Many agencies offer all-inclusive packages, which include transportation, lodging, and sightseeing.

Holders of bus passes should book ahead as coaches fill up quickly.

Getting Around

It can cost big bucks to rent a car in Yulara—maybe $75-100 per day, including the "remote surcharge." Rental companies include **Avis** (tel. 08-8956-2266), **Budget** (tel. 08-8956-2121), and **Territory Rent-a-Car** (tel. 08-8956-2030). **Sunworth Taxi Service** (tel. 08-8956-2152) also provides service to the Rock.

CLIMBING THE ROCK AND THE OLGAS

Uluru is extremely steep and the climb should not be attempted by any person with a heart condition, high blood pressure, angina, asthma, fear of heights, vertigo, or dizziness. Additionally, strong winds at the top can send both hikers and their possessions aflight. The top of the Rock can be very dangerous, with surfaces prone to sudden collapse into deep ravines. Hikers should be absolutely certain to carry adequate drinking water at all times. A hat, sunblock, and good walking shoes or boots are essential. Don't attempt a climb whenever the temperature is above 38° C (100° F). The best month is July, the worst is January.

For the Olgas (Kata Tjuta), most of the above rules apply, plus be sure to check in with a park ranger before starting out—particularly on that Olga Gorge Track.

Spinifex Lodge (tel. 08-8956-2131) rents bicycles (including safety helmet) for $18 per day and mopeds for $30 per half-day. Current identification and a $50-100 deposit are required.

If you're planning to head out to the Olgas, the road is *miserable!*

Organized Tours

Zillions are available but some of the best are the **ranger-conducted** tours, organized by both the Australian Nature Conservation Agency and the Conservation Commission—and some of these are free. The two-hour **Liru Walk** led by Aboriginal rangers offers a traditional perspective of the land (Tuesday, Thursday, and Saturday 8:30 a.m. summer, 9:30 a.m. winter). See and learn about local flowers and plants with a knowledgeable botanist on the 90-minute **Botanical Tour** (Sunday, Wednesday, and Friday, 3 p.m.),

or take a 90-minute **Mala Walk,** starting from the climb's base, for an introduction to Anangu culture (daily 10 a.m.). Book all of these tours well in advance. For information, contact the Visitor Centre (tel. 08-8956-2240).

Uluru Experience (tel. 1800-80-3174 toll free) offers interesting and informative tours led by geologists, biologists, and other knowledgeable guides.

The **Aboriginal Desert Culture Tour** focuses on bush foods and medicines ($45); the **Uluru Walk** emphasizes the environment, geology, cave paintings, as well as Aboriginal culture ($55, including breakfast).

Flightseeing over the Rock and the Olgas is organized by **Skyport** (tel. 08-8995-62093) and **RockAyer** (tel. 08-8956-2345). Cost is $75-120 pp for the almost-two-hour flight. **Helicopter rides** cost about the same but only last 15 minutes.

THE OLGAS WALK

SUNSET VIEWING

OLGA GORGE WALK, 2 km, 1 HR. RETURN

VALLEY OF THE WINDS WALK, 4 km, 2 HRS. RETURN

LINK TRACK, 2 km, 1 HR. EACH WAY

DOME LOOKOUT WALK, 600 m, 20 MIN. RETURN

= CAR PARK

KATA TJUTA LOOKOUT WALK, 4 km, 2 HRS. RETURN

0   0.5km

MOON

QUEENSLAND
INTRODUCTION

Second largest of the Australian states and twice the size of Texas, Queensland comprises the entire northeast corner of the continent. With 5,000 km of coastline and the magnificent Great Barrier Reef, it's not surprising that almost all of Queensland's attractions are water-oriented. Unless you're looking for snow, Queensland has something for everyone: you can scuba dive on the reef, soak up the rays on a Gold Coast beach, hike through a tropical rainforest, fish for barramundi, or go four-wheel driving through a remote desert national park. Known as the Sunshine State, the beaches, the reef, and the ideal climate attract tourists in droves; a string of cities and towns along the eastern seaboard serve the needs of travelers, some existing for no reason but tourism.

THE LAND

Queensland's most dominant feature is its coastline, the basis for the tourism industry and step-

ping stone for the Great Barrier Reef. The coast is paralleled by the Great Dividing Range, a low ridge of rugged peaks running along the eastern seaboard from the New South Wales border to the tip of Cape York. Along the range sprawl massive plateaus of fertile farming land while to the west lies the outback, a vast and desolate landscape extending to neighboring Northern Territory.

Regions

Aside from the reef, Queensland's most appealing attributes are the beaches, especially those in the southeast of the state. Best-known of the beaches is the Gold Coast, a 30-km stretch of golden sand as beautiful as anywhere in the world and entirely backed by Waikiki-style high-rise resort developments. Northwest of the Gold Coast lies Brisbane, Queensland's capital and third-largest city in Australia. A young and vibrant city, Brisbane lacks the pretensions of its southern cousins. Heading north, beyond the

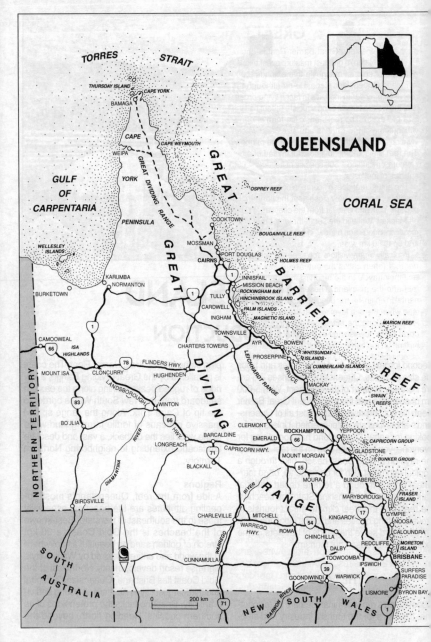

GREAT BARRIER REEF

The awe-inspiring Great Barrier Reef is one of Mother Nature's greatest masterpieces, a kaleidoscope of colorful marinelife that extends 2,000 km along Queensland's coast. And although the reef itself may seem inert, it's in fact a living organism, the world's largest living structure (about half the size of Texas). The reef's basic life-form is **coral**, which comes in all shapes and sizes and whose vivid colors range the full spectrum of the rainbow. The reef is also home to a colorful myriad of other creatures, including 1,500 species of fish and 4,000 species of mollusks.

The actual reef doesn't come in contact with the mainland; it comes very close near the northern tip of Cape York and is as far from the coast as 200 km off Mackay. While in the south the outer reef is almost continuous and narrow, in the north it is broken and up to 80 km wide.

Ironically, many visitors don't see the actual *barrier* reef (often called the outer reef), but instead limit their travels to the resort islands between the reef and the mainland. These islands are **continental** in origin, having been isolated from the mainland when the sea level rose at the end of the last Ice Age. Along the outer reef are more than 300 **coral cays**, low islands of coral debris that have built up on the barrier reef itself. Of the great variety of reef types found off Queensland's coast, three are very distinctive: **fringing** reefs develop around continental islands, **ribbon** reefs are narrow strips on the edge of the Continental Shelf, and **platform** reefs grow on the shelf as oval-shaped lagoons. As well as these common reefs, there's an array of other types, each a different shape due to wave action, currents, and wind.

The reef's allure is undeniable. It's Australia's most popular holiday destination, with resorts on more than 20 islands, and towns such as Airlie Beach exist only to serve reef-bound travelers. But this popularity is also the reef's biggest enemy. The entire reef ecosystem is a delicate balance of nature that has evolved over thousands of years. Its importance is recognized by UNESCO, which has listed the entire reef as a World Heritage Area. Other large parts of the reef are protected by the Great Barrier Reef Marine Park.

Coral Cays

A coral cay is an island composed entirely of debris from the reef. While coral below the water surface is continually growing, dead coral is ground by wave and wind action onto the leeside of the reef, eventually building up above the high tide mark as a sand bank that constantly shifts with wind and water action. As the cay enlarges and becomes more stable, birds begin nesting on its apex. Seeds are brought to the island by nesting birds. Guano helps the seeds germinate, and on some cays up to 30 species of plants thrive. Although cays become more stable as guano cements reef debris and vegetation takes hold, they are always changing shape. Of the Great Barrier Reef's 300 coral cays, 69 are vegetated.

Although the continental islands have fringing reefs, it's around the cays that diving and snorkeling are superior. Just three resort islands are cays—**Lady Elliot, Heron,** and **Green**—the rest are continental islands.

---

beaches of the Sunshine Coast, is Hervey Bay, the center of a large whalewatching industry and gateway to the wilderness of **Fraser Island,** the world's largest sand island.

The Great Barrier Reef, extending from Bundaberg to the northern tip of Queensland, is made up of hundreds of islands. Many are protected as national parks, some are privately owned, and more than 20 have resorts. At the southern end of the reef, you'll find the Bunker and Capricorn Groups, some of the most beautiful island clusters on the entire reef. They are true coral islands; built entirely of reef debris, they sit on the reef itself, surrounded by magnificent coral reefs. More accessible than the cays, the continental islands lie between the mainland and outer reef. One of the most accessible, and with great beaches and a variety of hiking trails, is Great Keppel Island, off Rockhampton. Best-known reef destination is the Whitsundays, 100-odd rugged continental islands rising magnificently from turquoise-colored waters off Proserpine. Townsville, north of the Whitsundays and Australia's largest tropical city, is home to the excellent Great Barrier Reef Wonderland. Cairns, 2,000 km north of Brisbane, is the capital of reef tourism. The city itself has nothing special to offer, but the reef is in close proximity and to the west are magnificent rainforests. The Great Barrier Reef extends beyond the tip of Cape York, but this section is only accessible by boat from Cairns. Although a large part of the state is outback, Queensland also has vast areas of wild and inhospitable land around Cape York Peninsula accessible only by four-wheel drive, while to the west lies Gulf Country, a maze of rivers and streams draining into the Gulf of Carpentaria.

Climate

Of course, in a region spanning 20 degrees of latitude, climatic differences are immense, but all parts of the Sunshine State have a common thread—an abundance of sunny days. Even in Brisbane, in the state's south, daytime temperatures rarely drop below 20° C (68° F). The southern part of the state features ideal weather—summers are not unbearably hot, and winters are mild. The farther north from Brisbane you travel, the more tropical the climate, with rainfall restricted to the Wet (Jan.-March). North of the Tropic of Capricorn, summer conditions can be unbearable for those used to cooler climates, with humid and hot days, punctuated by short and heavy rainfalls in the late afternoon. In the far north of the state, up to two meters of rain can fall in the Wet, with roads cut and land transportation impossible.

HISTORY

Like other Australian states, the European settlement of Queensland began with a penal colony. Explorers sailed north from Sydney Town in the 1820s searching for a possible site. A spot was chosen on Moreton Bay, but the convicts and their guards moved inland to the present site of Brisbane shortly afterward. Free settlers followed in the mid-1930s, but the colony remained part of NSW until 1859 when the state of Queensland was formed. Settlement outside the state's southeast corner was slow. Travel to the north was by boat, and beyond the coastline the land was rugged and inhospitable. Aboriginals had crossed from Indonesia into what is now Queensland 40,000 years before the first Europeans arrived, and as new settlers encroached on their land many bloody battles ensued. Spears were no match for gun-toting Europeans, and the Aborigines were slowly forced to retreat to regions of the state unwanted by Europeans. By the turn of the century, the Aborigines had been completely driven from their land and were forced to live on reserves.

The settlers developed a thriving agricultural base, and while agriculture remains an important part of the economy (the state is a major producer of pineapples, peanuts, sugar, and wheat) Queensland built its modern-day wealth upon

*typical
Queensland pub*

bundant mineral deposits. While NSW and Victoria boomed with 19th-century gold rushes, Queensland's mining industry has only developed this century, with lead, silver, copper, coal, and bauxite the main products.

Tourism is worth more than $10 billion annually to Queensland's economy. Climate and other natural attributes make tourism the single biggest industry, and as many southerners discover the idyllic lifestyle Queenslanders enjoy, they move north. For more than two decades, until 1987, Queensland was ruled by the National Party under the leadership of Sir Joh Bjelke-Peterson, a peanut farmer turned politician whose government was ultraconservative and always controversial.

GOLD COAST AND HINTERLAND

The Gold Coast is Australia's most popular and developed resort area. And although the sun almost always shines and the beaches are among the best in the country, rows of beachfront high-rise development, traffic jams, and crass commercialism mean the place has as many critics as fans. More than four million tourists flock to the Gold Coast annually, creating a year-round carnival atmosphere similar to that found at Miami Beach, Waikiki, or the south of France. The experience of visiting the Gold Coast definitely shouldn't be missed, but allow me to visit the Gold Coast hinterland and Lamington National Park.

The Gold Coast extends 30 km from the New South Wales border to a long sandy spit projecting the wide mouth of Nerang River. The southern end is a long strip of older resorts and residential areas, where suburbs such as Coolangatta, Currumbin, and Burleigh Heads have become one continuous sprawl along the Gold Coast Highway, which skirts the beach. From Miami, the highway heads inland a few blocks, entering a forest of high-rise apartments and massive hotels along a seemingly never-ending strip of neon signs known as Surfers Paradise. This is the center of the action, where scooters vie with towering tour coaches for room on the road, tanned surfers and hordes of sunburnt tourists pound the pavement, and elegant stores with outlets in Paris and New York stand beside fast-food restaurants. Love it or leave it, the Gold Coast is like no other place in the country.

History

In 1870 blocks of land were offered for sale at Southport, at the north end of the Gold Coast, for 10 pounds each, and, at first, developers couldn't find even one buyer. Over the years the lots began to sell, and a town grew on the west bank of the Nerang River. In 1923 a Brisbane developer paid 40 pounds for a block of land on the site that is now Cavill Mall. He built the **Surfers Paradise Hotel,** taking its name from a real estate advertisement. In 1925, when a bridge was built over the Nerang River, carloads of Brisbane people, who up until that time spent their holidays on the beaches of Moreton Bay, flocked to the golden stretches of sand. After WW II, land prices on the coast soared, with developers building beachfront hotels and vast residential suburbs. Sarcastically, a journalist during this time called the strip the Gold Coast, and the name stuck. By the 1960s beachfront land all the way to the New South Wales border was built up, so developers headed inland, to the swamps and wetlands behind what was once sand dunes. Canals were dredged and millions of tons of fill were bulldozed into strips of land, turning nearly every residential block into waterfront property. Development today continues unabated, much of it at the northern end of the Gold Coast, where exclusive resorts and residential estates such as Hope Island and Sanctuary Cove sprawl over reclaimed wetland. The latest trend for developers is security-restricted housing estates; Sovereign Island (known as Griffin Island before developers arrived), right at the tip of Paradise Point, is the most outrageous of these.

SIGHTS AND BEACHES

South Gold Coast

Away from the glitz and gaudiness of Surfers Paradise are quieter stretches of beach and areas of natural bushland. North of where the

Tweed River drains into the ocean, **Coolagatta** spreads over the headland of Point Danger, marking the point where the Queensland/New South Wales border hits the ocean Views from the point extend south along the Tweed Coast and north to Surfers Paradise giving a panoramic view of the Gold Coast. The town beach, **Greenmount,** is relatively protected, making this end of the coast great fo families. North from Coolangatta, Marine Parade hugs the ocean around **Kirra Point,** whe sand has built up alongside two groins, forming what many surfers claim to be one of the world's top-10 waves. Thick swells break over the sandy bottom, spilling over to form tubing wave that break for more than 200 meters. Some the world's best surfers call Kirra home, and they're not in the water when the swell is u there's sure to be 200-odd others.

Currumbin Sanctuary (tel. 07-5534-1266 north of Kirra in an area of native bushland, home to hundreds of Australian native birds a well as kangaroos, koalas, and emus. The santuary started by accident when a local horticu turalist began feeding rainbow lorikeets hone soaked bread to keep them away from his ne tar-bearing flowers. Now it's the tourists wh feed the birds, a daily ritual that is one of th region's most-loved attractions. It's open daily a.m.-5 p.m. Admission is $13 pp. The sanctua is nestled in a strip of bushland that stretches the beach, where Currumbin Creek drains in the ocean. This is another popular surf spo known as the **Alley.** The strip between Cu rumbin and Burleigh Heads is **Palm Beach** where sand has shifted northward in the la 20 years, leaving exposed rock.

Heading north, the next river crossing is **Talle budgera Creek.** At its mouth is 28-hectar **Burleigh Head National Park,** an area coastal bushland surrounded by Gold Coa sprawl. Short trails wind through the park and the foreshore where you'll find columns of vo canic rock. Access is from beyond the Nation Parks and Wildlife Service office (turn right at th first set of traffic lights north of Tallebudger Creek) or along Goodwin St. in downtow Burleigh Heads. Burleigh is another near-perfe barreling right-hand wave that breaks on swel up to three meters. North of Burleigh are **Miam Mermaid Beach,** and **Broadbeach.**

Burleigh Heads

urfers Paradise

urfers Paradise Hotel, for which this area is
amed, has long since disappeared under
aves of development that have turned a one-
m stretch of beach into a jungle of skyscrapers.
he beach at Surfers is particularly wide and
rowded year-round. In winter months long
hadows created by beachfront high-rise creep
cross the sand by early afternoon. **Cavill Mall,**
ie center of the strip, is sandwiched between
ie Gold Coast Highway and the foreshore. In
avill Mall is **Ripley's Believe it or Not!** (tel.
7-5592-0040), a museum of oddities from

STINGERS

Sharks and crocodiles may be Australia's
best-known marine nasties, but the tropical
waters of Queensland have a much less fearsome, yet just as deadly, danger—the box jellyfish, better known in the north as a "stinger."
Found in tropical waters between Nov. and April,
they live mainly around river mouths. However,
it's not recommended to swim anywhere along
the coast or even at many of the islands close to
the mainland during this period (some beaches
and resorts have stinger-free enclosures).

If stung, carefully remove tentacles with
tweezers and douse the wounds liberally with
vinegar. Get to a hospital as quickly as possible.

around the world; open daily 9 a.m.-10 p.m.;
admission adult $9.95, child $5.25.

North of Surfers

Immediately north of Surfers Paradise is **Main
Beach** and **The Spit,** a narrow strip of sand
extending three km to Nerang Head, at the
mouth of the Broadwater. Along Sea World Dr.,
which ends at Nerang Head, is **Fisherman's
Wharf** and **Sea World** theme park. North of
Sea World, development has been restricted
and the dunes retain a resemblance to what
the area to the south would have looked like
last century.

Across the Broadwater from the Spit is
Southport, the Gold Coast's original settlement and still its commercial and administration
center. From Southport, the Gold Coast Highway heads inland to the major theme parks
(see below) and Brisbane while **Marine Parade** continues north through built-up residential estates with romantic names such as **Anglers Paradise, Runaway Bay,** and **Paradise
Point.** West of Paradise Point is a maze of
low-lying swamps around the Coomera River.
Parts of **Hope Island** have been transformed in
the last 10 years with the construction of **Sanctuary Cove,** an up-market residential and resort
complex. **Sanctuary Cove Shuttle Bus** (tel.
07-5573-3777) runs from Surfers Paradise hotels to Sanctuary Cove eight to 10 times daily;
$3 one-way.

South Stradbroke Island

Across the Broadwater from Paradise Point and immediately north of Nerang Head is long and narrow South Stradbroke Island. The *Maranoa,* a historic sailing vessel, departs Fisherman's Wharf daily at 9:30 a.m. for a full-day cruise to South Stradbroke Island. The price, $45 pp, includes morning tea, buffet lunch, on-board entertainment, time to relax on the island, afternoon tea, and accommodation transfers. For bookings call (07) 5529-5777.

RECREATION

Cruises

Tiki Village, at the west end of Cavill Ave. in downtown Surfers Paradise, is the departure point for **Island Queen Cruises** (tel. 07-5592-2332). They depart daily at 10 a.m. and 2:30 p.m. for a two-hour cruise around the canals and into the Broadwater. The fare is $24 pp, which includes hot drinks and light snacks. Other options include a two-hour cruise to Sanctuary Cove ($24 pp; departs daily at 9:45 a.m.) and a full-day cruise to South Stradbroke Island and Sanctuary Cove including a seafood buffet lunch ($49 pp; departs daily at 9:45 a.m.).

Shangri-la Cruises (tel. 07-5591-1800) departs from Fisherman's Wharf on the Spit and offers similar options at the same prices.

Fisherman's Wharf

This marina and shopping complex is the best place on the Gold Coast to indulge in water sports. **Gold Coast Water Sports** (tel. 018-75-9789), based out on the marina, offers a variety of activities including a 10-minute speedboat ride ($35 pp), waterskiing ($30), jet skiing ($50), and parasailing ($50). **Popeye's Boat Hire** (tel. 07-5532-5822), on the same wharf, rents a variety of boats from $20 per hour. Anchored offshore from the marina is **Bungee Downunder** (tel. 07-5531-1103), the world's only floating bungee jump. At just 30 meters, the tower is relatively low, but for $69 it's probably worth it for bungee enthusiasts.

Golf

Golfers migrate to the Gold Coast for its resort courses, some of which are the best in the country. **Parkwood,** four km northwest of Southport on Napper Rd. (tel. 07-5594-6835), is set among native bushland with water hazards on many holes; green fees are $25 and club rental $20. Dotted with thousands of palm trees, **Palm Meadows** is a *very* long course; on Springbrook Rd., west of Surfers Paradise (tel. 07-5594-2450). Hope Island, north of Surfers Paradise, boasts three world-class courses, including two at Sanctuary Cove. The newest course on the Gold Coast is **The Links** on Hope Island (tel. 07-5530-8988). Designed by Peter Thomson, it is styled on a Scottish links course with rolling fairways lined with tussocky grasses. Green fees are $45 and clubs can be rented for $25.

Hooked on Golf (tel. 07-5598-2788) will take you to a different course each day of the week, organize tee times and green fees, and rent clubs.

Other Recreation

Mountain bike touring is popular in the hinterland, with a variety of tours offered from the Gold Coast. Typical of these is **Borderline Bike Adventures** (tel. 07-5545-3412), offering transportation to Lamington National Park, a few hours in the park with a barbecue lunch, then a long ride off the plateau. Departures are Tuesday and Thursday and the cost is $60 pp.

A number of places offer horseback riding, including **Numinbah Valley Adventure Trail** (tel. 07-5533-4137), 23 km southwest of Nerang. The scenic setting makes the three-hour, $2 trip out here well worthwhile.

Hot-air balloon flights are offered by Roger Meadmore (tel. 07-5592-0334). Flights are weather dependent and generally last one hour (a fantastic way to watch the sun rise over the Gold Coast).

Queensland Climbing Centres, 38 Hutchinson St., Burleigh Waters (tel. 07-5593-6919) is a large indoor climbing complex with more than 800 square meters of cracks and overhangs on walls rising 11 meters. Admission for climbers is $10, including basic tuition, but non-climbers can come and watch for free; open daily 10 a.m.-10 p.m.

Theme Parks

Sea World may have the same name as its famous San Diego cousin, but the similarities stop ere. Although there are animal shows, including penguins, sea lions, seals, and dolphins, the mphasis here is on amusement rides, including triple-loop roller coaster, monorail, and water ide park. Admission is adult $32, child $21, nd it's open daily 10 a.m.-5 p.m. Located on e Spit, north of Surfers (tel. 07-5588-2222).

Dreamworld, the most unique of the theme arks, has a Disney-Australian theme. Instead of eing greeted by Mickey and Minnie, Kenny the oala and his friends hang out hugging and ssing and posing for pictures. The 84-hectare ark is divided into 10 theme areas, including um Tree Gully, Rivertown, and Gold Rush ountry. Admission is adult $30, child $19. This ark is located on the Pacific Highway at oomera, 30 km northwest of Surfers toward risbane (tel. 07-5573-1133).

Just south of Dreamworld is the newest of e theme parks, **Movie World,** which opened in 991. Based on the famous Warner Bros. Holwood studio, this park features re-creations the movie sets for *Batman, Gremlins,* and *olice Academy* as well as tours of a studio, a vely Main Street, and a few exhilarating rides. dmission is adult $32, child $21. Open daily 10 m.-5 p.m. (tel. 07-5573-3999).

ntertainment

t last count, the Gold Coast held about 40 ghtclubs, as well as numerous service clubs, a asino, and a handful of live theaters. The folwing clubs are all within a couple of blocks of avill Mall. **Club Cocktails and Dreams,** in the ark shopping center on Orchid Ave., is a longne favorite of backpackers and a younger local owd with a cross section of dance music ayed till 5 a.m. In the same complex is **The arty,** open the same hours. **The Penthouse,** rchid Ave. (tel. 07-5538-1388), is a legendary ace, with each of four stories offering a differnt style of nightlife, including a disco, pool om, and piano bar. **Benson's,** Orchid Ave. el. 07-5538-7600), is popular with the under5s on Friday and Saturday nights, and attracts older crowd the rest of the week.

Surfers Beergarden, upstairs on Cavill Mall, as a real beachside atmosphere, with surfards hanging from the ceiling and old surfg photos adorning the walls. **Beach House avern,** in Iluka Beach Resort at the top end

of Cavill Mall, is another casual place, open from 10 a.m. daily. On the Spit, **Fisherman's Wharf** has an indoor/outdoor beer garden overlooking the Broadwater and often hosts live entertainment in the evening and on Sunday afternoons. **Surfers Paradise Pool Hall,** 51 Cavill Ave. (tel. 07-5592-2585), is open 11 a.m.-11 p.m., and you can bring your own booze.

Conrad Jupiters (tel. 07-5592-1133), Queensland's first (legal) casino, is on Broadbeach Island, part of an artificial canal system three km south of Surfers Paradise. The casino holds just 114 gaming tables but boasts hundreds of video machines and "pokies" (slot machines). Although the casino is open 24 hours and is fairly casual, it's nothing like the glitz and glamour of those in Las Vegas. And as casinos are still a novelty in Australia, don't hold out for any dining or accommodation bargains (standard rooms start at $200). One of the most popular games is **two-up,** an Australian game where punters bet on the outcome of coins tossed in the air. The casino also has bars, restaurants, and an International Showroom where stage productions are performed nightly (for bookings call 07-5592-0067).

ACCOMMODATIONS

Motels, resorts, and caravan parks increase prices dramatically during Christmas school holidays (all of January) and other holiday periods. (Rates at backpacker accommodations remain steady year-round). Outside of Surfers, especially to the south toward Coolangatta, motels often advertise rooms for $35-40 d. The only way to *guarantee* a room is to book ahead, especially during school holidays, and year-round at backpacker lodges. **Accommodation Services** (tel. 07-5592-0067, fax 5592-1804) makes bookings for all standards of accommodations and charges only a small fee for the service.

Motels and Resorts in Surfers
The least expensive motel close to Surfers is **Delilah Motel,** 72 Ferny Ave. (tel. 07-5538-1722), where very basic rooms are $45 s, $50 d. You'll find slightly more expensive but better quality rooms at **Paradise Inn,** 2826 Gold Coast Hwy. (tel. 07-5592-0585); many units have kitchenettes

and there's a pool and laundry. Located in the heart of Surfers is **Trickett Gardens Holiday Inn,** 24 Trickett St. (tel. 07-5539-0988), where each apartment is fully self-contained, complete with laundry, and there's a pool; $80 s or d, rising to $108 at Christmas. Moving up another notch is **Bahia Beachfront Apartments,** 154 Esplanade (tel. 07-5538-3322), one km from Cavill Mall, where each unit is self-contained (request ocean views—from the third floor up); $85-95 s or d. **Iluka Beach Resort Hotel** is centrally located, right opposite the beach and towering above Cavill Mall (tel. 07-5539-9155). Rooms are of a high standard and each has a private balcony; $135-269 s or d. Similarly priced is **Pan Pacific Hotel Gold Coast,** 81 Surf Parade (tel. 07-5592-2250), two km south of Surfers and linked to Conrad Jupiters Casino by monorail. **Gold Coast International Hotel,** Staghorn Ave. (tel. 07-5592-1200 or 1800-07-4020), is a five-star hostelry with a grand lobby and elegantly decorated rooms, many with balconies and ocean views. Rates are $175-195 s or d. **Sheraton Mirage Gold Coast,** Sea World Dr. (tel. 07-5591-1488), sprawls over 30 hectares and is right on the beach and across the road from Sea World. The resort has a tropical feel about it, with lagoons surrounding the units. Rates of $420-590 for a standard room include a buffet breakfast.

Motels South of Surfers
Premium Motel, 1910 Gold Coast Hwy., Miami (tel. 07-5576-3211), has a pool and laundry;

small basic rooms are $39 s or d. **El Ranch** **Motel,** 2125 Gold Coast Hwy., Miami (tel. 07 5572-3655), has a pool, laundry, gas barbe cues, and rooms of a reasonable standard for a low as $25 in the off season.

At Burleigh Heads, **Casino Motel,** 1761 Gol Coast Hwy. (tel. 07-5535-7†33), offers all of th above facilities, and a couple of rooms hav older-style kitchenettes. **Fifth Avenue Mote** also in Burleigh Heads, 1953 Gold Coast Hwy (tel. 07-5535-3588), features rooms of an ex cellent standard and a pleasant pool area awa from highway noise; from $70 s, $75 d.

Tropic Sands on the Beach, 1295 Gol Coast Hwy. (tel. 07-5535-1044), is at the nort end of Palm Beach. Many rooms yield ocea views. The rate of $75 s or d reflects the locatio rather than standard of the rooms.

At the Beach Motel, Gold Coast Hwy. (te 07-5536-3599), is within walking distance c Kirra Beach and, at just $35 s, $40 d, is an ex cellent value. (Don't confuse this place with O the Beach Motel around the corner at Coolar gatta.)

Right on Coolangatta Beach is **Beach Hous** **Seaside Resort,** 52 Marine Parade (tel. 07 5536-5566). Each unit is modern and fully se contained, right down to dishwashers. Eac room has a balcony with water views and ca sleep up to six people; $95-105. Facilities in clude a squash court, half-size tennis cour pool, gym, barbecues, and an arcade with su permarket and choice of restaurants.

Hyatt Regency
Sanctuary Cove

Sanctuary Cove

Hyatt Regency Sanctuary Cove, Manor Circle (tel. 07-5577-1234), is on Hope Island, away from the glitz of Surfers. It's part of a complex spread along the Coomera River and is well suited to golfers as guests have access to the 18-hole **Pines** golf course (otherwise open only to residents). A standard room is $260, while Regency Club rooms at $390 include free booze and breakfast.

Backpacker Accommodations

Without a doubt, the best hostel on the Gold Coast is **Surfers Paradise Backpackers** at 2835 Gold Coast Hwy. (tel. 07-5592-4677), just 100 meters from the beach and one km south of Cavill Mall. Communal facilities, all of the highest standard, include a large pool area, modern kitchen, tennis court, game room with pool table, sauna, outdoor barbecue area, and small gym. All dorm beds are $14 pp, and in the off season a few doubles are offered. **Surf and Sun Backpackers,** Ocean Ave. (tel. 07-592-2363), is on the north side of Surfers one block from the beach. This place has a pool and game room, and each four-bed dorm has a bathroom, TV, and fridge—courtesy of the days when it was a motel; $14 pp. **Surfers Central Backpackers,** 40 Whelan St. (tel. 07-5538-8344), is closest to Cavill Mall, near the Nerang River and just two blocks from the main bus terminal. Beds are $14 pp, $30 d.

Like Surfers Paradise Backpackers, **Trekkers,** 22 White St., Southport (tel. 07-5591-5616), is as good as hostels get, and a bed for one night is just $14 pp, $30 d. The atmosphere here is more relaxed than at hostels in Surfers, and there's a great pool surrounded in greenery, as well as a game room. Staff organize activities most days, including trips to nightclubs.

South of Surfers is **Big Backpacker,** 2623 Gold Coast Hwy. (tel. 07-5538-4633), which is just that—big. It was once a nursing home and is kept immaculately clean. For the budget-conscious it's a steal at just $10 pp, with a few singles at $11 and doubles at $28.

Campgrounds

Main Beach Tourist Park, Main Beach Parade (tel. 07-5581-7722), is the closest campground to Surfers, but tents aren't allowed. The beach is

less than 100 meters away and Surfers is three km south. Powered sites are $13-17, basic cabins $35-40. Pitch a tent and enjoy better facilities at **Broadwater Tourist Park,** on the Gold Coast Hwy. in Southport (tel. 07-5581-7733). Unpowered sites are $10, powered sites $13-18, and cabins $35-45.

South of Surfers, caravan parks are strung out at regular intervals all the way to Coolangatta, and like those above you'll need reservations in January. The best choices are beyond Burleigh Heads. **Tallebudgera Tourist Park,** 1544 Gold Coast Hwy. (tel. 07-5581-7700), is a five-minute walk from the beach and has a pool, laundry, and barbecues. Sites are $10-18.

FOOD

Surfers Paradise

The choice of restaurants in this area of the Gold Coast is staggering, but with millions of tourists to feed, it's not surprising. **Cavill Mall,** the pedestrian thoroughfare linking the Gold Coast Highway to the beach, offers the widest choice of casual eateries, many with outside tables, perfect for people-watching. **Paradise Centre** and **Raptis Plaza,** both off the mall, have food courts, the latter with **Seafood on the Beach,** a good fish and chips joint. Away from the madding crowds is **Cafe on Elkhorn,** a small upmarket place on Elkhorn St. open for breakfast from 7 a.m. and serving hearty lunches from a blackboard for a reasonable $7. **Aroma's,** 27 Orchid Ave., is another popular choice.

Bavarian Steak House, corner Cavill Ave. and Gold Coast Hwy. (tel. 07-5531-7150), is authentically decorated and waitresses don traditional dress; all a bit corny, but it's popular and inexpensive, with lunches from $6.50 and dinners from $11. The **Paddlesteamer,** in the same general area, at 41 Cavill Ave. (tel. 07-5539-0095), is a unique restaurant decked out as the interior of a paddlesteamer, complete with massive waterwheels. Main dishes are around $18, with the menu featuring mostly seafood. Downstairs is the more casual **Lower Deck Saloon,** where prices aren't as steep. Both are open daily noon-2:30 p.m. and from 5:30 p.m. for dinner. For an Aussie experience, head to **Crooked House Restaurant** on the Gold Coast Hwy. northbound at Markwell Ave., six blocks south of Cavill Ave. (tel. 07-5570-1766). The walls and ceilings are strewn with Australian memorabilia and the menu, featuring kangaroo, crocodile, and witchetty grubs, leaves no doubt as to which country you're in. Most meals are $12-18 with the Sunday buffet lunch ($9.95-11.95) a good deal. Open daily from 5:30 p.m.

Without a doubt, the best Mexican in town is at **Mexican Kitchen,** 150 Bundall Rd. (tel. 07-5592-2100), on the west side of the Nerang River. The atmosphere is relaxing, with many tables offering river views, and the food delicious. Lunch is well priced (from $4) and the bar good for pre-dinner drinks, especially Mon.-Fri. 4:30-6:30 p.m. for happy hour.

Danny's, at the river end of Cavill Ave. in Tiki Village (tel. 07-5538-2818), is an elegant Italian restaurant overlooking the Nerang River. Dinner for two (without drinks) will cost about $70-80. Other choices for Italian dining are **Grissini,** 5 Admiralty Dr., Paradise Waters (tel. 07-5532-5788), a casual yet stylish restaurant with a reputation for excellent food, and **Bocconcini,** 3100 Gold Coast Hwy. (tel. 07-5539-9433), an upmarket pizza and pasta place open for lunch Mon.-Fri. and daily for dinner. **La Porte Verte,** 154 Scarborough St., Southport (tel. 07-5591-4669), features provincial French cuisine in an intimate atmosphere; open Tues.-Sat. 6 p.m.-midnight and on Friday for lunch. Definitely worth the splurge.

Far Winds is a revolving restaurant atop Surfers Paradise Travelodge at 2807 Gold Coast Hwy. (tel. 07-5592-9900). For such a fantastic setting, the plain decor is a bit disappointing and buffet-dining is the only option, but the food is good and the views don't come any better.

The Spit
On the Nerang River side of The Spit are three marinas—**Marina Mirage, Mariners Cove,** and **Fisherman's Wharf**—linked by boardwalks running along the waterfront and offering a great variety of dining opportunities. **Grumpy's Barefoot Bar & Grill,** Mariners Cove, is a casual joint with plastic chairs and tables scattered along the wharf (you fill out the check yourself and take it to the cashier), but what may lack in

style is made up for in quality with great fish an chips for $6; Tuesday night features all-you-car eat barbecue ribs and a drink for $10. Upstairs i **Grumpy's Restaurant** (tel. 07-5532-2900), more formal steak and seafood restaurant. Bot are open daily for lunch and dinner. **Zorba's** Mariners Cove (tel. 07-5532-0011), opens u to the marina, with dining indoors and outdoor and belly dancing (not compulsory) and plat smashing Friday and Saturday nights. At Marin Mirage you'll find the casual but elegant **Omero Brothers Seafood Restaurant,** one of the Gol Coast's most popular eateries. Main meals a lunch are $13-18 and at dinner $17-28. Locate in Marina Mirage (tel. 07-5591-5425).

Conrad Jupiters Casino
Nicholson's, in Conrad Jupiters casino (tel. 07 5592-1133), is one of the coast's finest fine dir ing restaurants. Nothing but the best china i used, each table is decorated with colorful o chids, an entire wall is taken up by a glass win rack, and service is impeccable. The menu fea tures dishes from Conrad and Hilton hotel around the world (the restaurant is named fo Conrad Nicholson Hilton, founder of those tw chains), and if you need to ask the price, yo probably can't afford it. If that's the case, th casino has five other restaurants, includin **Prince Albert,** an English-style pub, and **Foo Fantasy,** a buffet restaurant.

South of Surfers
The **Great Khan,** 2488 Gold Coast Hwy., Me maid Beach (tel. 07-5572-9266), is a cavernou Mongolian restaurant; service is fast and eff cient, although impersonal. Main meals start a $11, but for a few bucks more you can indulge i the buffet, along with everyone else.

In Burleigh Heads, it's seafood and mor seafood. **Paragon Seafood Restaurant,** Goodwin Terrace (tel. 07-5535-2300), has ea in and takeaway sections, with fish and chip from $5. For lunch, the **Fish Monger,** on Jame St., is cheaper. Around the corner, on Conne St., are two excellent bakeries. **Burleigh Beac Hotel,** on the Esplanade, has inexpensive lunch es and dinners, with an $8.95 buffet daily 6-p.m. Another good buffet is offered at **Mama' Choice,** 43 Goodwin Terrace (tel. 07-5535 6400), overlooking the beach and with view xtending to Surfers; lunch $10.90, dinner 14.90 and an extra buck will get an all-you-an-drink soft drink. A breakfast buffet is served unday 7:30-10:30 a.m.

In Coolangatta, **Oskar's on the Beach** is an ward-winning restaurant overlooking Green-ount Beach. The eclectic menu features main-seafood, but other meat and vegetarian dishes e also offered. Open daily for lunch and dinner; s on Marine Parade (tel. 07-5536-4621).

TRANSPORTATION

etting There
1e closest international airport to the Gold Coast Brisbane, from where **Coachtrans** (tel. 07-592-5333) runs shuttles every 45 minutes to urfers Paradise for $24 one-way. **Coolangatta irport,** on the NSW/Queensland border, is a usy airport handling domestic flights from south-rn cities. It is served by **Ansett Australia** (tel. 3-1300), **Eastern Australia** (tel. 13-1313), and **antas** (tel. 13-1313). Ansett, Australia, and antas offer Gold Coast packages from Syd-ey starting at $289 pp for airfare and accom-odation. Eastern Australia flies from Brisbane 93 round-trip) and other provincial towns such Ballina and Coffs Harbour. Transfers between is airport and Surfers are $8 one-way.

The main Surfers Paradise **coach terminal** on the corner of Gold Coast Hwy. northbound 1d Beach Rd., two blocks from Cavill Mall and a 3-5 cab ride from all Surfers accommodations. 1e terminal has booking agents for onward trav-, tour operators, lockers, a cafe, car rental agen-es, and an accommodations booking service. All 1ajor bus companies stop at this terminal, in-uding **Greyhound Pioneer** (tel. 13-2030), **Kirk-nds** (tel. 07-5531-7145), and **McCafferty's** el. 07-5538-2700). The fare between Sydney 1d Surfers is $66 one-way, but if you're contin-ng farther north, buy an onward ticket and ask r a free stopover. **Coachtrans** (tel. 07-5538-944) operates buses between Brisbane Transit entre and Surfers at least once hourly ($12) 1d from Brisbane Airport ($24).

The closest rail service to Surfers Paradise is urwillumbah, in northern NSW, from where uses connect to Surfers. Make **Queensland ail** bookings through Surfers Paradise Travel

Centre in Cavill Park Building on Beach Rd. (tel. 07-5539-9088 or 13-2232).

Getting Around
Surfside Buslines (tel. 07-5536-7666) is the Gold Coast's public bus system, serving the length of the coast around the clock. The one-day Rover Pass is $3.55 and a weekly ticket is $24.

Airport Rent-a-Car has offices at Coolan-gatta (tel. 07-5536-6300) and in the coach ter-minal (tel. 07-5538-0700); pick up cars from Coolangatta Airport. Rates for a small car start at $40 per day with 100 free km. **Car-azy Rentals** (tel. 07-5536-8388) has cars from $35 per day with unlimited mileage. All other major rental companies operate on the Gold Coast, including **Avis** (tel. 07-5539-9388), **Budget** (tel. 07-5538-1344), **Hertz** (tel. 07-5538-5366), and **Thrifty** (tel. 07-5538-6511).

Red Back Car Rentals, opposite the coach terminal (tel. 07-5592-1655), rents mopeds for $15 per hour. For mountain bikes, head to **Green Bicycle Rentals,** Birt Ave., Surfers Para-dise (tel. 018-76-6880).

For a cab call (07) 5591-5111.

SERVICES AND INFORMATION

The **post office,** at the beach end of the Para-dise Centre on Cavill Mall, is open Mon.-Fri. 9 a.m.-5 p.m. **Thomas Cook Money Exchange** (tel. 07-5531-7770) is also in the Paradise Cen-tre. An **American Express** office is located at 21 Cavill Ave. (tel. 07-5538-7588).

Gold Coast Hospital is on Nerang St. (tel. 07-5571-8211). You'll find the **24-hour Med-ical Clinic** at 3221 Gold Coast Hwy. (tel. 07-5538-8099), and a **24-hour pharmacy** at 94 Nerang St., Southport (tel. 07-5591-2254).

Gold Coast Tourism operates two informa-tion booths. One is on Cavill Mall (tel. 07-5538-4419); open Mon.-Fri. 8 a.m.-5 p.m., Saturday 9 a.m.-5 p.m., and Sunday 9 a.m.-3.30 p.m. The other is on the ground floor of Beach House Seaside Resort on Marine Parade, Coolangatta (tel. 07-5536-7765). On the north side of Talle-budgera Creek, near Burleigh Heads, is an NPWS office with interesting displays on the ecology of the adjacent national park and infor-

GOLD COAST HINTERLAND

ation on hinterland parks; open daily 9 a.m.-4 m. (tel. 07-5535-3032).

GOLD COAST TO THE HINTERLAND

he heavily forested mountains rising behind e Gold Coast's urban sprawl are one of ueensland's hidden assets. The McPherson ange, which forms the northern and western n of a massive volcano that erupted 20 million ears ago, dominates the scene. To the north is **amborine Mountain,** an isolated plateau with pectacular views across the Gold Coast.

For those without transportation, a variety of ompanies offer tours to both destinations and ill pick up at Brisbane and Gold Coast hotels. o save a few bucks, hire a car from the Gold oast for $40-50 and spend the day exploring n your own.

pringbrook National Park

his 2,950-hectare park protects the Spring- ook Plateau and, in a separate section, the eological wonder of the **Natural Bridge.** The inforests, waterfalls, and lush fern-filled gorges round the park's southern boundary, the New outh Wales/Queensland border, lend just a ste of what's to come farther west in Laming- n National Park. Access to the plateau is 29 n southwest of Mudgeeraba on the Pacific ighway. Along the park access road you'll find campground ($5), park information center pen daily 8 a.m.-4 p.m.), and a number of pic- c areas. Gwongorella picnic area is at Purl- g Brook Falls, a beautiful waterfall that cas- ades into a deep gully.

You can reach the Natural Bridge from the ad that climbs up through the Numinbah Val- y between Nerang and Murwillumbah. Years of ater flowing over the top of an underwater cav- rn eventually wore a hole in it and formed the atural Bridge out of the lip of the cavern's roof. oday a small creek plunges through the hole to a deep pool within the cavern.

LAMINGTON NATIONAL PARK

ense rainforests, hundreds of waterfalls, an xtensive trail system, and excellent accom-

modations combine to make this 20,500-hectare park a great escape from the hustle and bustle of the Gold Coast 80 km to the east.

The Land

Around 20 million years ago, tremendous vol- canic activity created massive changes in the landscape of the far northeastern corner of New South Wales. During the millions of preceding years, erosion broke down the volcanic basalt, leaving a circular rim of rock, with Mt. Warning in the middle. Lamington National Park is perched on the rim's northern edge (which also forms the Queensland/NSW border) from where es- carpments drop hundreds of meters into heavi- ly forested valleys of the caldera. Access to the park is only from the north. Two roads pene- trate the park, both ending at points well north of the rim; at the end of each road is a camping and picnic area. Enter **Binna Burra** from Nerang (55 km) and to **Green Mountains** from Canun- gra (36 km), 22 km west of Nerang.

Flora and Fauna

The park encompasses one of the largest areas of subtropical rainforest in Australia. At higher al- titudes you'll find stands of Antarctic beech trees, including some 2,500 years old, while in the val- leys species such as booyong, carabeen, marara, and strangler figs make up the rainfor- est canopy, with ferns, mosses, and orchids thriving in the moist environment below.

The park is known for its colorful array of birdlife, much of it attracted to areas where visi- tors offer feedings by hand. You'll see crimson rosellas, parrots, and a variety of bower birds around picnic areas while currawongs, bush turkeys, and lyrebirds are commonly seen while hiking.

At dawn and dusk, red-necked pademelons (a species of small wallaby) graze around camp- grounds while brushtail possums, bandicoots, gliders, and a variety of small marsupials can be seen by spotlighting.

Hiking

Naturally, hiking is the most popular activity in the park, with 160 km of trails providing oppor- tunities to explore many of its best features.

The shortest hike at Binna Burra is also the most unique. It is designed for the blind but is just as interesting for sighted people—as long as you wear a blindfold. Also at Binna Burra is the five-km **Caves Circuit**, passing a variety of vegetation including a massive red cedar tree. The 22-km **Border Track** links Binna Burra and Green Mountains facility areas, and many trails branch from it. The best overnight hike is the 55-km **Rainforest Circuit,** which takes three days to complete. It takes in all the best that the eastern section of the park has to offer, culminating in various lookouts at the edge of the escarpment where views extend across the caldera.

At Green Mountains is another **Rainforest Circuit,** this one just 1.4 km. The highlight is a boardwalk, 30 meters above the ground, which passes through the canopy, allowing a perspective usually reserved for birds and possums. Those game enough can continue up 20 meters to a lookout high in a fig tree. Near the end of the trail lies a **botanical garden.** From Green Mountains it is possible to get to the main escarpment and return in one day along a variety of trails, the most interesting of which is 7.6 km one-way and takes in Toolona Falls. **Canungra Creek Circuit** (13 km) is another popular day hike and takes in a number of waterfalls including Box Log Falls and Blue Pool, where you might spot platypuses feeding.

Binna Burra Practicalities

Binna Burra Mountain Lodge (tel. 07-5533-3622) is a rustic accommodation that has operated since 1933. Basic rooms with shared bathrooms are $98-117 pp, while self-contained cabins are $149 pp. Rates include three hot meals, morning and afternoon teas, use of a game room, and daily activities such as guided hikes. Near this lodge is a campground with sites for $7 pp and safari tents at $36 d. Campers have use of modern bathrooms and can eat in the restaurant with advance bookings.

A bus departs Surfers Paradise coach terminal daily at 1:15 p.m. for Binna Burra ($32 round-trip); book through the lodge.

About a kilometer from the end of the road is a **park information center,** open daily 8 a.m.-4 p.m. (tel. 07-5533-3584).

Green Mountains Practicalities

The name O'Reilly is synonymous with Lamington National Park, and has been since 1926 when the family began welcoming guests t what was then a remote mountain hideawa The family originally took up land in 1911, clea ing a large chunk for farming and building guesthouse on a high ridge. When the park wa gazetted in 1917, land remained as private prop erty, surrounded by one of Queensland's to noncoastal attractions. It's not just the scene that makes **O'Reilly's Rainforest Guesthous** (tel. 07-5544-0644) so popular; the family is pa of the experience, welcoming guests upon arriv and always available for information on the par A resident naturalist leads birdwatching expe ditions, nature walks, and 4WD trips. The lodg itself is cosy, with a restaurant, comfortabl lounge area, and tennis court. Rates for th most basic rooms (shared facilities) are $99 p which includes all meals. Rooms with privat bathrooms offer great views and are $145 p The NPWS operates a campground just dow from the lodge, with sites for $7.50; call (07 5544-0634 to make a booking.

All State Scenic Tours (tel. 07-3285-1777 runs daily between Brisbane and Green Moun tains for $16 one-way. Also near the lodge is cafe, grocery store, and **park information cen ter** (tel. 07-5544-0634); it's open Mon.-Fri. 1 3:30 p.m.

TAMBORINE MOUNTAIN

Tamborine isn't a mountain as such, but plateau five km wide, eight km long, and risin 500 meters above the surrounding hinterlanc It's a world apart from the Gold Coast, just 30 kr to the east, with three picturesque mountai communities surrounded by nine small nationa parks. These parks are often referred to as Tam borine National Park but are in fact separate t tles of land. The plateau is a spur of the McPher son Range and is the northernmost extent c lava flow from the Mount Warning Volcanc Much of the plateau has been cleared of origina vegetation, but some small chunks of rainfor est are protected by national parks.

National Parks

Most central of these is **Joalah National Park.** Fc parking, drive to the corner of Geissmann Dr. an Eagle Heights Rd., from where a short trail de cends into a lush rainforest of tree ferns and orchids. The highlight is **Curtis Falls,** where Cedar Creek cascades over an outcrop of basalt into a deep blue pool. **Witches Falls National Park,** located on Tamborine Mountain Rd. just south of the township of North Tamborine, has a trail leading to the falls for which the park is named, passing lookouts where views extend west to the Main Range and south to Lamington National Park. For views north to Brisbane and the Glass House Mountains, head to **The Knoll National Park** at the end of Knoll Rd. (a continuation of Main St., which begins opposite the Visitors Centre). **Palm Grove National Park** features forests of towering palms interspersed with magnificent yellow carabeen trees. To get to this park continue east along Eagle Heights Rd., beyond the roundabout, and then take the first right.

The road up to the mountain from Nerang provides good views of the Gold Coast and Pacific Ocean. Also along this road, and flanking the village of Mount Tamborine, is **Macrozamia Grove National Park,** named for stands of macrozamia palms common in the area.

Thunderbird Park

Nestled below the northern flanks of the plateau in the valley carved by Cedar Creek is Thunderbird Park (tel. 07-5545-1468), which holds the world's largest known deposit of **thunder eggs.** Volcanic in origin, thunder eggs have a hard outer shell protecting a cavity of semiprecious gems such as agate. This particular deposit, formed about 200 million years ago, is exposed as basalt from the Mt. Warning eruptions erodes. For $5 you get a bucket, a spade, and the chance to dig for the eggs. Most people find a few, and there's no real time limit. In a large shed set up in front of the deposit a lapidarist will cut and polish any eggs you find for $2-5 each. Also at Thunderbird Park is bird feeding daily at 3 p.m., an aviary, and mini-golf.

Practicalities

Tamborine Mountain has a wide range of accommodations, including a number of excellent B&Bs. For a basic, bland motel room, **Tall Trees Motel,** 9 Eagle Heights Rd. (tel. 07-5545-1242), should suffice; $50 s, $55 d.

The sprawling **Tamborine Mountain Bed and Breakfast,** built of recycled timber including part of an old bridge, gives an air of rustic elegance. Guests may choose from four rooms spread out from the main house, and take advantage of a large dining/lounge area and extensive verandas overlooking the lush rainforests of Palm Grove National Park; $95 s or d. It's located at 19-23 Witherby Crescent, Eagle Heights (tel. 07-5545-3595). Another comfortable option is **Polish Place,** between Mount Tamborine and North Tamborine at 333 Main Western Rd. (tel. 07-5545-1603). Each self-contained cottage is two stories, with a double bed in the loft, a kitchen, lounge area with TV, and a balcony with westward panoramic views catching the sunset in all its glory. Rates are $85 per unit.

Around the main entrance of Joalah National Park, at the corner of Geissmann Dr. and Eagle Heights Rd., are places offering casual meals, including **Curtis Falls Cafe,** surrounded by lush palms, where Devonshire tea is $4.50 and most main dishes are under $10. Across the road are more cafes and **Squires Inn** (tel. 07-5545-1700), an English-style pub serving lunch and dinner. At Polish Place (see "Accommodations," above), for the price of a coffee you can enjoy the same spectacular views as guests; open daily 10 a.m.-5 p.m. For dinner, don't pass up **Songbirds in the Forest** on Tamborine Mountain Rd. (tel. 07-5545-2563). Tables circle an enclosed courtyard filled with greenery and within view of colorful rosellas feeding nearby. It's open for lunch Tues.-Sun. noon-3 p.m. and for dinner Fri.-Sat. from 6 p.m.

Mount Tamborine Visitors Centre is in Doughty Park, across from the township of North Tamborine (tel. 07-5545-3200); open daily 10 a.m.-3.30 p.m.

MOUNT LINDESAY HIGHWAY

Beaudesert, 35 km west of Tamborine Mountain, is the main town along this highway, the original route between Brisbane and the New England region of New South Wales. On the main street you'll find a small museum and information center. South of town, check out **The Kooralbyn,** a resort that wouldn't look out of place in Cairns or on the Gold Coast. Accommodation is luxurious, but it's the 18-hole championship golf course, tennis courts, and the relaxed setting that attract most people. Rates are reasonable at $90 d for luxurious self-contained villas, rising to $150 s or d in the hotel proper. For reservations call (07) 5544-6222.

Although not as accessible as Lamington, **Mt. Barney National Park** is just as rugged and provides experienced hikers a chance to explore the hinterland away from crowds. The main access to this 11,900-hectare park is west from Rathdowney, then south on Upper Logan Road. Along this road, a hiking trail branches along Barney Creek to Lower Portals, a water-filled gorge 3.7 km from the road. Experienced (and fit) hikers may want to climb 1,360-meter **Mt. Barney.** The trail, which begins from the end of the access road, is steep and often ill-defined. **Mt. Barney Lodge,** also near the end road (tel. 07-5544-3233), is not a lodge but campground, with sites for $10 and hot showers with on-site owners who offer a wealth of information on the adjacent park.

BRISBANE

the last decade and a half Queensland's capital, Brisbane (pronounced "BRIZ-bun"), has own into a dynamic and modern city of more an a million people, many of whom are expates from cooler southern states in search of a sual lifestyle in a modern metropolis. Brisane is Australia's third-largest city and has me to prominence since hosting the 1982 ommonwealth Games and the 1988 World xpo. It sits on the Brisbane River, 33 km upream from Moreton Bay. Sydney is 1,000 km uth; Gladstone, gateway to the southernmost reat Barrier Reef Islands, is 550 km north; airns is 1,710 km north. The city center, reicted by a tight bend of the Brisbane River, ixes modern skyscrapers with some of ueensland's oldest buildings. Brisbane may ck the beauty of Sydney and the culture of elbourne, but scattered across the city are ough sights to keep even the most desperate ef-bound traveler busy for a couple of days.

story

s Sydney's convict population increased, offials looked northward for somewhere to send e worst offenders. In 1824 a penal colony was stablished on Moreton Bay, near the mouth of e Brisbane River. The following year a lack water and hostile natives forced a move upver to the present site of Brisbane's city center. hough *not* the best place to build a city, the te was ideal for convict settlement—a remote cation, surrounded on three sides by a river, d away from the ocean. But when the colony as closed in 1842 and the surrounding land ened to free settlers—who up to this time had ot been allowed anywhere near the colony— risbane Town thrived. From a population of ss than 1,000 in 1846, the town grew to well ver 100,000 by the turn of the century. Graduly convict-built structures were replaced by ermanent sandstone and granite buildings, any of which remain today.

Brisbane was headquarters of South Pacific perations during WW II, a time when thouands of U.S. troops were stationed in the city. etween WW II and the early 1980s, Brisbane's

growth was due to newly discovered mineral wealth elsewhere in the state, but the 1982 Commonwealth Games, 1988 World Expo, and sun-seeking Sydneysiders and Melburnians moving north began a trend of development that continues to this day.

DOWNTOWN SIGHTS

Downtown Brisbane is bordered to the south, east, and west by the **Brisbane River,** with the extensive **Botanic Gardens** in the southern corner and ferry service across the river at various points. **South Bank,** over the Victoria Bridge and within walking distance of downtown, is a good place to park ($4 per day at South Bank Parklands) for a day's sightseeing around the city. City streets are laid out on a grid system, but driving downtown can be confusing as many streets are one-way and feed onto the **Riverside Expressway,** built along the river west of the city center to keep traffic out of downtown. **Queen Street Mall,** one block from Victoria Bridge, is the heart of downtown; it encompasses two blocks and includes a Hilton Hotel, an underground bus terminal, eateries, and the massive $480-million **Myer Shopping Centre.**

Historic Buildings around Queen Street

Brisbane City Council publishes *Heritage Trail* brochures to 10 Brisbane suburbs and downtown, where you'll find the largest concentration of historic buildings. The best place to start a walking tour of downtown is **City Hall,** overlooking King George Square on Ann Street. Completed in 1930, it features a wide facade of Corinthian columns topped by an 85-meterhigh clock tower. Tours of City Hall (adult $6, children free) depart from the foyer Mon.-Fri. at 10 a.m. and 2 p.m. Diagonally opposite City Hall stands the 1889 **Albert Street Uniting Church.** At 261-285 Queen St., beyond the end of the mall, is the 1871 **general post office,** formerly the site of a women's prison. On the second floor is the **GPO Museum,** cataloging

BRISBANE

he history of Brisbane's postal service; it's open Tues.-Fri. 9:30 a.m.-3:30 p.m., and admission is ree. Through the post office arcade and across Elizabeth St. is **Old St. Stephen's Church;** built in 1850, it is Brisbane's oldest church. Next door is **St. Stephen's Cathedral,** built in English Gothic-style and featuring an elaborate facade flanked by two impressive spires.

Historic Sights along George Street

George St. runs parallel to the river and features some of the city's most impressive historic buildings. The **Treasury Building** was constructed in 1886 and was described at the time as "the most splendid public edifice in the Australian colonies." This Italian Renaissance-style building has been totally restored, and behind the colonnaded facade is a casino (see Arts and Entertainment," below). Behind the Treasury is the old **Land Administration Building.** Built in the same flamboyant style and fronted by **Queens Park,** it now serves as the hotel portion of the casino. Across from the park on William St. is the **Commissariat Stores,** one of only two Brisbane buildings dating from the convict era. **Parliament House,** at the end of George St., was built in 1868.

Sciencentre

This hands-on museum features many interactive displays endeavoring to make understanding science both easy and interesting. Admission is $5. Open daily 9 a.m.-5 p.m. It's located at 102 George St. (tel. 07-3220-0166).

SOUTH BANK

South Bank, across the Brisbane River from downtown, was the site of the 1988 World Expo and has since been developed into the city's premier recreation area. Head here to see the **Queensland Cultural Centre,** a sprawling low-rise development that includes the Queensland Museum, Queensland Art Gallery, State Library, and Performing Arts Complex. Adjoining is the **Brisbane Convention and Exhibition Centre** and Conservatorium of Music. Spread out south from here is South Bank Parklands, featuring themed attractions, cafes, and restaurants.

Queensland Museum

Contained on three floors, this museum (tel. 07-3840-7635) showcases the natural and human history of the state through modern and interesting displays. The highlight of the Lower Gallery is 3.6-meter *Acrohc Australis,* the smallest yacht to ever circumnavigate the world. Also on this floor is a realistic panorama of marine mammals, photography display, and a dinosaur skeleton. The next floor features the flora and fauna of Queensland, and a large area is set aside for temporary displays. The upper gallery looks at whales and whaling, with a display cataloging the climatic cycles of western Queensland and relics from Melanesian Culture. The museum is open daily 9 a.m.-5 p.m. and admission is free.

Queensland Art Gallery

In the same building as the museum is the state's largest art gallery (tel. 07-3840-7303), boasting an extensive collection of works by all of Australia's best-known artists. It also hosts national and international touring exhibitions. The gallery is open daily 9 a.m.-5 p.m. and admission is free. Tours are offered Mon.-Fri. at 11 a.m., 1 p.m., and 2 p.m.

South Bank Parklands

Adjacent to the Queensland Cultural Centre and strung out along the river, this 16-hectare park is Brisbane's newest and most popular attraction. Admission is free (except to the themed attractions), making it the perfect place to escape city living. The park's unique feature is the swimming pool; its clear blue waters fringed with palms and a golden sandy beach could be straight out of a five-star resort—and there's even a lifeguard. On the far side of the park, small boats steam up and down a narrow canal, making access to all parts of South Bank easy. South Bank Markets take place Friday night and Saturday and Sunday afternoons.

Gondwana Rainforest Sanctuary is a recreation of a tropical rainforest. A raised boardwalk leads through the sanctuary, allowing a chance to view more than 100 species of native fauna. Admission is adult $9, child $6.50. It's open daily 10 a.m.-5:30 p.m. **Butterfly House** contains an enormous collection of Australian butterflies, as well as many weird and wonderful

DOWNTOWN BRISBANE

VICTORIA PARK GOLF CLUB

0   300 m

VICTORIA

AVE.

PARK

GILCHRIST

GREGORY

TERRACE

SPRING

GREGORY   ST.

SPRING HILL BATHS

BOUNDARY   ST.

HILL

WHARF

ST. PAULS TERRACE

WICKHAM ST.

BALMORAL HOUSE

BRUNSWICK ST.

COFFEE CLUB AND MCWHIRTER'S

ALT. 1

CAFE SOCIETE
GIARDINET
CALIFORNIA

CHINAT

ALBERT PARK INN

WICKHAM TERRACE MOTEL

ALBERT PARK

LEICHARDT

WICKHAM

RIDGE HOTEL

UPPER EDWARD ST.

ANNIE'S SHANDON INN

CENTRAL STATION

RIVER CENT

BRISBANE ARTS THEATRE

PRINCESS ST.

PETRIE

TERRACE

CAXTON

CAXTON HOTEL

PETRIE TERRACE

COUNTESS TERRACE

MARRS TOWNHOUSE

ASTOR MOTEL

SEE DETAIL

CREEK

ST.

ALBERT   ST.

EDWARD   ST.

ANN   ST.

ADELAIDE   ST.

QUEEN   ST.

ELIZABETH   ST.

CHARLOTTE   ST.

MARY   ST.

MARGARET   ST.

ALICE   ST.

TURBOT   ST.

STREET   MALL

GEORGE   ST.

BEAUFORT   HERITAGE HOTEL

POST OFFICE HOT

TRAVELODGE

BRISBANE TRANSIT CENTRE

UNDERGROUND

UPPER ROMA ST.

BRISBANE CITY YHA

ROMA ST.

ALL SEASONS ABBEY HOTEL

NORTH

QUAY

QUAY ST.

RIVERSIDE

EXPRESSWAY

RD.

RIVER

GREY ST.

LIBRARY

MUSEUM AND ART GALLERY

QUEENSLAND CULTURAL CENTRE

SLY FOX TRAVELLERS HOTEL

PERFORMING ARTS COMPLEX

AUGUSTINE'S

PARLIAM HOUSE

MERIVALE

MONTAGUE

BRISBANE

MELBOURNE

GREY ST.

CONVENTION AND EXHIBITION CENTRE

SOUTH

BRISBANE

SOUTH

BANK

SOUTH BANK PARKLANDS

DOCK S

QUEENSLAND MARITIME MUSEU

FORTITUDE VALLEY

E'S PALACE

HARCOURT ST.

KENT ST.

BOWEN ST.

BROWNE ST.

ANNIE ST.

ST.

BRUNSWICK BACKPACKERS

BOWEN ST. BRUNSWICK

BRISBANE HOMESTEAD

LE BRONX AND KOFFIES ESPRESSO BAR

BOWEN TERRACE

SOUTH PACIFIC MOTEL

LANGSHAW ST.

ST.

ST.

NEW FARM

BRISBANE RIVER

BRADFIELD HWY.

GOODWIN ST.

ALT. 1

RYAN'S ON THE RIVER

FERRY ST.

STORY BRIDGE MOTOR INN

OLIMS HOTEL

DOCKSIDE APARTMENT HOTEL

KANGAROO POINT

NIC GARDENS

Y SE

ALT. 1 15

RIVER TERRACE

SOUTHERN CROSS MOTEL

COOK BRIDGE

WALMSLEY ST.

Y RIVER HOTEL

VULTURE ST.

HILLCREST CENTRAL APTS.

DETAIL

BRISBANE TRAVEL CENTRE

ORIENT HOTEL

POST OFFICE SQUARE

CREEK ST.

TURBOT ST.

QUEENSLAND GOVERNMENT TRAVEL CENTRE

GENERAL POST OFFICE

MALL

DEPARTMENT OF ENVIRONMENT AND HERITAGE

ST.

COLES BUILDING

OLD ST. STEPHEN'S CHURCH

ADELAIDE

EDWARD ST.

KING GEORGE SQUARE

ALBERT ST. UNITING CHURCH

METRO ARTS

CARLTON CREST

ANN ST.

CITY HALL

ALBERT

ELIZABETH

CHARLOTTE ST.

MAJESTIC HOTEL

CITY PLAZA

ADELAIDE

QUEEN

MARY ST.

GEORGE ST.

LENNONS HOTEL AND PLAZA

MYER SHOPPING CENTRE

BRISBANE HILTON INTERNATIONAL

GATEWAY HOTEL BRISBANE

NORTH

MLC BUILDING

ELIZABETH ARCADE

BRISBANE BICYCLE HIRE

ST.

GOVINDA'S

QUAY

TREASURY BUILDING/CONRAD TREASURY CASINO

QUEENSLAND ABORIGINAL CREATIONS

RIVERSIDE EXPRESSWAY

LAND ADMINISTRATION BUILDING

BELLEVUE HOTEL

SCIENCENTRE

MARGARET ST.

COMMISSARIAT STORES

MOON

© MOON PUBLICATIONS, INC.

insects. Admission is adult $6.50, child $3.50. Combined with a trip aboard South Ship Ferry (usually adult $5, child $2), a Discovery ticket, for both the above attractions, is adult $18, child $10. In the southern corner of South Bank Parklands is **Our World Environment,** replicating various environments and looking at man's impact upon them. Admission is adult $7, child $5; open daily 9 a.m.-5 p.m.

At the north entrance to the parklands is an information center (tel. 07-3867-2020); open daily 9 a.m.-5:30 p.m.

Queensland Maritime Museum

At the south end of the South Bank Parklands is this riverside museum, on Sidon St. (tel. 07-3844-5361), featuring the WW II frigate HMAS *Diamantina;* maritime memorabilia is also displayed. Admission is adult $4, child $2, and it's open daily 10 a.m.-5 p.m.

PARKS AND GARDENS

City Botanic Gardens

First established as a vegetable garden for the penal colony, 17 hectares of land at the south end of downtown, bordered by the Brisbane River, are now the city's botanic gardens. Part of the gardens' early aim was to grow seedlings for distribution to free settlers, and it wasn't until the early 1980s that the ordered look of today came about. Paved trails lead through the park to an area of rainforest, then to a boardwalk through mangroves, and end at a historic stone cottage that now houses a cafe. Guided tours leave the information desk, opposite the end of Albert St., Tues.-Thurs. at 11 a.m. and 1 p.m.

Mt. Coot-tha Park

This 3,500-hectare park eight km west of downtown provides panoramic views of the city, Moreton and Stradbroke Islands, the Glass House Mountains, and the Gold Coast. Hiking trails crisscross the park and are accessible from Sir Samuel Griffith Dr., which circles the park. One of the most interesting is the Aboriginal Art Trail, a 1.6-km circuit along which all forms of native art—tree carvings, petroglyphs, and pictographs—are represented. At the foot of the mountain you'll find a **botanic garden** featuring

a large dome-shaped greenhouse where a great variety of flora from the tropics thrives; open daily 8:30 a.m.-5 p.m., admission free. The garden is home to the **Sir Thomas Brisbane Planetarium,** combining an observatory, astronomy displays, and the Cosmic Skydome, where special effects re-create the night sky across a 12-meter-wide dome. Show times are: Wed.-Sun. 3:30 p.m. and 7:30 p.m.; Saturday 1:30 p.m., 3:30 p.m., and 7:30 p.m.; and Sunday 1:30 p.m. and 3:30 p.m. Admission is adult $7 child $3.50.

To get to the gardens and lookout, take bus no. 37A from the Ann St. side of King George Square.

Brisbane Forest Park

Few cities the size of Brisbane have an area of virgin bushland as large and as accessible as 28,500-hectare Brisbane Forest Park, which encompasses a large part of **D'Aguilar Range** and extends right to the outer suburb of The Gap. At the park entrance is **Walk-about Creek** (tel. 07-3300-4855), a nature study center for viewing the flora and fauna of a typical subtropical creek, including turtles, snakes, barramundi, and the unique lungfish—which can breathe above the water. It's open Mon.-Fri. 9 a.m.-4:30 p.m., Sat.-Sun. 10 a.m.-4:30 p.m. Admission is a worthwhile $3.50 for adults, $2 for kids.

Northbrook Parkway extends from Walk-about Creek along the highest ridges of the D'Aguilar Range, passing lookouts, picnic areas short hikes, and a small campground in Manorina National Park.

WILDLIFE PARKS

Lone Pine Koala Sanctuary

This wildlife park, 11 km southwest of downtown on Jesmond Rd., Fig Tree Pocket (tel. 07-3378-1366), claims to have the world's largest collection of Australia's most popular native animal, the koala. They currently have 130 of the cuddly little critters, and for an extra $6 you can cuddle one. A variety of other indigenous Australian animals are kept here, including dingos wombats, and a variety of birds including emus Admission is adult $10, child $6; open daily 8:45

a.m.-4:45 p.m. By bus, take no. 518 from the Koala Platform under the Myer Center on Queen Street Mall. **Mirimar Cruises** (tel. 07-3221-0300) departs daily at 11:30 a.m. from North Quay for the sanctuary; $15 round-trip.

Bunya Park Wildlife Sanctuary
Spread over eight hectares 18 km northwest of the city in Eatons Hill (tel. 07-3264-1200), this park boasts the world's second-largest collection of koalas but *doesn't* charge extra for a cuddle. Short shows on the animals are presented four times daily and unusual fauna, including lots of birds and crocodiles, lives here. Admission is adult $9.50, child $5; open daily 9 a.m.-5 p.m. Call Bunya Park for courtesy transfers from downtown hotels.

Alma Park Zoo
This zoo features animals from around the world, as well as many native species, and has five feeding sessions daily, including time spent cuddling koalas. Within the zoo is a cafe and pleasant picnic area. Admission is a bit steep at $13. It's 28 km north of downtown in the suburb of Kallangur; follow signs from Bruce Highway (tel. 07-3204-6566).

OUTDOOR ACTIVITIES

Biking
Brisbane Bicycle Hire, 87 Albert St. (tel. 07-3229-2433), rents mountain bikes for $9 per hour or $20 per day. A good place to head for riding is south along the river to the University of Queensland at St. Lucia.

Swimming
Spring Hill Baths, Torrington St., is a throwback to an earlier era, where swimmers use poolside change rooms. It's open year-round Mon.-Fri. from 6:30 a.m., Sat.-Sun. from 8:30 a.m. Admission is $1.50. The pool at South Bank Parklands is complete with a sandy beach, palm trees, and a lifeguard.

Golfing
The closest golf course to the city is **Victoria Park Golf Club,** on Herston Rd. north of the city (tel. 07-3854-1406). Green fees are $16 for

18 holes and club rentals are $12. The city's other public course is **St. Lucia Golf Links** on Indooroopilly Rd. (tel. 07-3870-3938), along the Brisbane River. (This course was designed by Dr. Alistair Mackenzie, the same bloke who designed Augusta National in Georgia).

Ballooning
Weather permitting, **Lovely Champagne Balloon Flights** (tel. 07-3844-6671) departs at sunrise for a 40-minute trip over the city. The actual departure point varies with the wind direction. The fare is $185 pp, which includes a light breakfast and champagne.

ARTS AND ENTERTAINMENT

Australian Woolshed
Sheep, the backbone of Australia's economy since European settlement, are the stars of this attraction, which showcases the entire woolgrowing industry. During the Ram Show, trained sheep of all breeds strut their stuff on the stage, a shearing exhibition is given, spinning is demonstrated, and sheepdogs show their skills. Shows take place daily at 11 a.m. and 2 p.m.; adult $9, child $4. Other activities take place during the day, including feeding of Australian animals. Before the morning show, billy tea and damper ($2.50) are served and lunch ($6.90-12) is also available. On Friday and Saturday nights there's a barn dance ($28, includes dinner). The woolshed is 13 km northwest of the city center at 148 Samford Rd., Ferny Hills (tel. 07-3351-5366). The closest public transportation is Ferny Hills rail station, an 800-meter walk from the woodshed.

Theater, Music, and Dance
The **Performing Arts Complex** is the premier venue for all performing arts. Within the complex are three theaters—2,000-seat Concert Hall designed to hold a symphony orchestra, 2,000-seat Lyric Theatre for opera, dance, and musical comedy, and 300-seat Cremorne Theatre. Buy tickets in person at the center, or call (07) 3846-4646, or contact any Bass ticketing agency.

  Princess Theatre, 8 Annerley Rd., Woolloongabba (tel. 07-3891-6022), has presented both classical and Australian contemporary works for over 100 years; tickets range $12-24. Other major theaters are **Metro Arts,** 109 Edward St. (tel. 07-3221-1527), for alternative theater and dance works, and **Brisbane Arts Theatre,** 210 Petrie Terrace (tel. 07-3369-2344), home to the city's longest-running amateur theater company.

Cinemas
Alternative films are screened at the **Classic,** 963 Stanley St., East Brisbane (tel. 07-3393-1066); the **Schonell,** University of Queensland, St. Lucia (tel. 07-3371-1879); and **Metro Arts Cinema,** 109 Edward St. (tel. 07-3221-3505).

Casino
In April 1995 one of Brisbane's greatest historic structures, the Treasury Building, opened as **Conrad Treasury Casino.** Don't expect to see flashy neon signs and spectacular shows out front; one of the building's edicts prohibits outside signage. Once inside, though, things are different, with a six-story atrium welcom-

Conrad Treasury Casino

ANDREW HEMPSTEAD

ing gamblers. Games available are roulette, blackjack, baccarat, mini-baccarat, craps, sic bo, big six, and two-up, as well as over 1,000 slot machines. The casino also has a couple of restaurants, cafes, and bars. It's open daily 24 hours. Dress standards apply, including no shorts, tracksuit pants, sports shoes, or collarless shirts. It's on the corner of Queen and George Streets (tel. 07-3306-8888).

Hotels, Bars, and Nightclubs
The **Post Office Hotel,** 38 Edward St. (tel. 07 3221-0072), housed in Brisbane's original post office building, is a bit of a yuppie hangout, but features bands Friday and Saturday nights and Sunday afternoon. Also downtown, the **Majestic Hotel,** 382 George St. (tel. 07-3236-2848), is a casual place with live music some nights. If live music is what you're after, **Metropolis,** on the ground floor of Myer Shopping Centre, hosts bands most nights; cover charge $5-15. Across the river at South Bank Parklands is the **Plough Inn Tavern** (tel. 07-3844-7777), a pleasant place for a beer and meal during the day with live entertainment Fri.-Sunday. **Brunswick Hotel,** 569 Brunswick St., New Farm (tel. 07-3358-1181) has backpacker beer specials Tuesday and Friday nights.

The **Underground,** housed in the old police barracks on Petrie Terrace, Paddington (tel. 07-3236-1511), is the most popular of Brisbane's mainstream nightclubs and has been around since the late 1970s. It's open Wed.-Sun. until 3 a.m. and the cover charge is $5. Another, more stylish, choice is **Someplace Else** in the Sheraton Hotel at 249 Turbot Street. **Margaux's,** suited to the over-30 crowd, is a relaxed nightclub attracting a mature mob. It's open Tues.-Sat. 9 p.m.-3 a.m.; in the Hilton Hotel at 190 Elizabeth St. (tel. 07-3231-3131). A $5 cover charge applies Fri.-Saturday.

Adventurous nightclubbers should head to Fortitude Valley, the center of Brisbane's alternative scene, and to places such as **Site** at 201 Brunswick St. and **Studio 694** at 694 Ann Street.

Jazz, Blues, and Comedy
Brisbane's main jazz venue is the **Jazz and Blues Club** on the first floor of the Travelodge, Roma St., which hosts national and internation-

al acts. The **Caxton Hotel,** 38 Caxton St., Petrie Terrace (tel. 07-3369-5544), features all types of jazz and is most popular Saturday afternoons during jam sessions. The rest of the week it's 60s and '70s music and karaoke in the cocktail bar. **Louis' Jazz Bar,** corner Park Rd. and Coronation Dr., Milton (tel. 07-3368-1200), has live jazz Friday and Saturday from 8 p.m.

For blues, head to the **Orient Hotel** on Ann St. (tel. 07-3839-4625), for live bands most nights (no cover charge).

Comedy venues include the **Laugh Lounge** on Eagle St. Pier (tel. 07-3236-1384) and the intimate **Snug Harbour,** in the Dockside complex, Kangaroo Point (tel. 07-3391-2045).

Festivals and Events
Brisbane Biennial International Music Festival, one of Australia's premier music festivals, features all types of music performed by national and international artists as well as food and wine-tasting daily at South Bank Parklands. The festival takes place over 10 days late May-June every second year (odd years). On the weekend closest to shortest day of the year is another gathering of musicians, this time for the **Winter Solstice Festival** in Davies Park, South Brisbane, featuring folk and blues. The **Warana Festival,** each September, runs for two weeks and has concerts, parades, and other outdoor entertainment.

SHOPPING

Brisbane's shopping mecca is definitely Queen Street Mall, including the Myer Shopping Centre, a five-story department store with 250 specialty shops, an eight-screen cinema, and massive food court.

Paddington, a historic suburb west of downtown, has a great variety of specialty boutiques, antique emporiums, art galleries, and cafes; most of these lie along Given Terrace. In the same area, at 167 Latrobe Terrace, more than 50 antique dealers display wares at **Paddington Antique Center.**

Markets
Each Friday evening and Saturday and Sunday afternoons **South Bank Markets** offer arts, crafts, and clothing at stalls spread along one or two narrow pedestrian streets (on Sunday a real carnival atmosphere prevails). **Riverside Crafts Market,** at the Riverside Centre on Eagle St., operates all day Sunday featuring arts, crafts, street performers, and foodstalls. **Paddy's Markets,** on the corner of Florence and MacQuarie Streets, New Farm, are undercover and feature all sorts of stalls—from handmade crafts to piles of secondhand junk; open daily 9 a.m.-4 p.m.

Australiana
Aboriginal-styled souvenirs are a dime a dozen throughout Australia, but the real thing, handcrafted by native Australians, is a lot harder to find—and also a lot more expensive. **Queensland Aboriginal Creations,** 135 George St. (tel. 07-3224-5730), sells original works by Aboriginal artists throughout the state, including pottery, paintings, and the more traditional bark paintings, weavings, and boomerangs and woomeras. The Supply Store, at the **Australian Woolshed** (see "Arts and Entertainment," above) is the best place for Australian-made souvenirs, including woollen sweaters. For souvenirs to send home, **Australia Post Shop,** in the main post office on Queen St., specializes in gifts designed for posting. For opal, **Quilpie Opal,** Lennons Plaza, 68 Queen St. (tel. 07-3221-7369), is a good place to head—but you'll pay a lot more than out on the opal fields.

HOTEL AND MOTEL ACCOMMODATIONS

Accommodations downtown are limited to those in the moderate to high price range, but immediately north, between Wickham and Gregory Terraces (a 10- to 15-minute walk to Queen Street Mall), is a wide variety of hotels and motels in all price ranges.

Downtown
The **Bellevue Hotel,** 103 George St. (tel. 07-3221-6044 or 1800-77-3097), two blocks from Queen Street Mall, is best the value of all downtown hotels. Views are limited by surrounding high-rises, but the rooms themselves are comfortable and have a tropical feel. Facilities include undercover parking, pool, spa, and restaurant. Standard rooms are $70 s or d, while larger

rooms, some with kitchenettes, are $96. **Gateway Hotel Brisbane,** 85 North Quay (tel. 07-3236-3300), has similar amenities. Some rooms offer river views, and two floors are reserved for non-smokers; $90 s or d. **Lennons Hotel,** 66 Queen St. (tel. 07-3222-3222), is a 20-story hotel right on Queen Street Mall. Facilities include a pool, covered parking, and a restaurant and bar; $96-112 s or d. Another couple of moderately priced options are near the Brisbane Transit Centre, northwest of Queen Street Mall. **Brisbane City Travelodge,** Roma St. (tel. 07-3238-2222), is on top of the Transit Centre, but seems a world away. Rooms aren't too big, but they are well-furnished and many have city views; $95-160 s or d. Across the road is the modern **All Seasons Abbey Hotel,** 160 Roma St. (tel. 07-3236-1444), with a small kitchen and microwave in each room. Also available is a pool, spa, gym, and security parking; all rooms are $130.

A small step up in quality and price is **Carlton Crest,** corner Ann and Roma Streets (tel. 07-3229-9111), overlooking King George Square. Rooms are spacious and elegantly furnished in a heritage style; $150 s or d. **Beaufort Heritage Hotel,** corner Margaret and Edward Streets (tel. 07-3221-1999), is Brisbane's most deluxe hostelry; its 230 rooms, decorated colonial-style with king-size beds, exude a feeling of unpretentious luxury throughout. Rooms are $300 s or d and suites start at $450. The city's other five-star hotels are: **Sheraton Brisbane Hotel & Towers,** 249 Turbot St. (tel. 07-3835-3535), where standard rooms are $200-275 and those on the executive floor, with butler service, private lounge, and a buffet breakfast, are $352; and **Brisbane Hilton International,** 190 Elizabeth St. (tel. 07-3231-3131), on Queen St. Mall, where a 20-story glass-domed atrium separates rooms with city views from those with river views; from $190 s or d.

Spring Hill

Immediately north of downtown, take an easy walk from Queen Street to find a good range of inexpensive hotels and motels. **Annie's Shandon Inn,** 405 Upper Edward St. (tel. 07-3831-8684), dating to 1854, has managers who make an otherwise basic guesthouse feel like home. Rooms with shared bathrooms are $38 s, $48 d, with private bathrooms $48 s, $58 d (all

rates include continental breakfast and use of a laundry). In the same price bracket, but farther from downtown, is **Balmoral House,** 33 Amelia St. (tel. 07-3252-1397), off busy St. Pauls Terrace. Rooms are clean and comfortable and there's a communal kitchen; $28 s, $32 d, or $45 s or d with a private bathroom.

Astor Motel, 193 Wickham Terrace (tel. 07-3831-9522), is close to both Central Station and Brisbane Transit Centre. Rooms are basic; some have a microwave and toaster; $47 s, $53 d. Similar in standard is **Marrs Townhouse,** 391 Wickham Terrace (tel. 07-3831-5388); $55 s, $65 d. A step up in quality is **Wickham Terrace Motel,** 491 Wickham Terrace (tel. 07-3839-9611), with a pool and laundry; $66 s, $72 d.

Ridge Hotel, 189 Leichhardt St. (tel. 07-3831-5000), is a good-value accommodation within easy walking distance of downtown. Rooms are of a high standard and many have views. Standard rooms are $89 s or d; those with kitchens are much larger and sleep four, $109. **Albert Park Inn,** 551 Wickham Terrace (tel. 07-3831-3111), overlooking the park for which it is named, has recently been renovated; $95 s or d.

New Farm

South Pacific Motel, corner Bowen Terrace and Langshaw St. (tel. 07-3358-2366), is in a quiet residential area, west of downtown. Each room has a kitchen and balcony and there's also a pool, barbecue, and laundry. Rates are $59 s, $69 d; great value if you don't mind being a few kilometers from downtown.

Kangaroo Point

The Point, a narrow finger of land formed by a bend of the Brisbane River, is home to the following three motels, all excellent alternatives to those in the city center as they are clustered above a ferry terminal linked to downtown by a regular ferry service. Least expensive of these is **Story Bridge Motor Inn,** 321 Main St. (tel. 07-3393-1433), with a pool and laundry. Standard rooms are $66 s or d, but it's worth paying the extra $5-10 for those with better facilities. Next door is the larger **Olims Hotel,** 355 Main St. (tel. 07-3391-5566), where rooms are $69. **Ryan's on the River,** 269 Main St. (tel. 07-3391-1011), is the pick of the bunch, with 24 rooms on five floors; $75-95 s or d.

On the east side of Kangaroo Point is **Dockside Apartment Hotel,** 44 Ferry St. (tel. 07-3891-6644), comprising self-contained apartments of a very high standard with a tennis court, pool, spa, gym, and marina. Each room has a modern kitchen, dishwasher, and laundry. Rates are $145-195.

Farther south, along the Bradfield Highway, are a few inexpensive options including **Southern Cross Motel,** 721 Main St. (tel. 07-3391-2881); $40 s, $45 d.

South Brisbane

Sly Fox Travellers Hotel, 73 Melbourne St. (tel. 07-3844-0022), is really a backpacker place, with communal facilities, but basic rooms are also available for $32 s, $35 d. Farther south, in the shadow of the Captain Cook Bridge, is **Quality River Plaza Hotel,** 21 Dock St. (tel. 07-3844-4455), a nonsmoking establishment in a good, quiet spot overlooking South Bank Parklands and with a pool and tennis court; rooms are $92 s or d, $110 with a kitchen. A few blocks away is **Hillcrest Central Apartments,** 311 Vulture St. (tel. 07-3846-3000), a small place of 16 large units, each with a well-equipped kitchen and laundry. There's also a tennis court and pool. One-bedroom units are $84, and two-bedroom units, each with a balcony, are $109.

Hamilton

You'll find Brisbane's other main concentration of motels along Kingsford Smith Dr., paralleling the Brisbane River between downtown and Brisbane Airport. **Airport Motel,** 638 Kingsford Smith Dr. (tel. 07-3868-2399), is clean, comfortable, and offers airport transfers; $59 s, $64 d. **Airport International Motel,** 528 Kingsford Smith Dr. (tel. 07-3268-6388), is of a higher standard and has a pool; $72 s, $77 d. The **Powerhouse Boutique Hotel,** on Kingsford Smith Dr. where it crosses the Brisbane River (tel. 07-3862-1800), is a luxurious hotel with all the trimmings. Rooms are $160 s or d.

BACKPACKER ACCOMMODATIONS

Downtown

Brisbane City YHA, 53 Quay St. (tel. 07-3236-1004), is 500 meters from Brisbane Transit Centre and a few blocks farther from the center of town. It has a large communal kitchen, laundry, reading room, cafeteria (dinner $5-7), and a small parking lot. Members pay $14 for a dorm, $17 in a twin room. Nonmembers pay $3-4 extra per night. The easiest way to get onto Quay St. is from Upper Roma Street.

Paddington

A few years ago Paddington had a handful of hostels; now there's just one to recommend, but it's a good one. In a quiet, off-the-main-road location, **Aussie Way,** at 34 Cricket St. (tel. 07-3369-0711), has beds in four-bed dorms; $13 pp.

Spring Hill

Balmoral House, 33 Amelia St. (tel. 07-3252-5892), is a large guesthouse a short walk to the area's restaurants. Recently renovated, it now offers a few backpacker rooms with use of a large kitchen; dorms $10-12, singles $28, doubles $30.

New Farm

Beyond Spring Hill, past Fortitude Valley, in the riverside suburb of New Farm, is the city's greatest concentration of backpacker accommodations. The main route into New Farm is Brunswick St.—check out **Pete's Palace,** no. 515 (tel. 07-3254-1984), and **Brunswick Backpackers,** no. 569 (tel. 07-3254-0400), for adequate but not outstanding dorms for $12. **Brisbane Homestead,** 57 Annie St. (tel. 07-3358-3538), is the pick of the bunch, close to a couple of good cafes and restaurants on Brunswick St. and with excellent facilities including a small pool, laundry, kitchen, and game room. Transfers to the airport and into town can be arranged and tours are offered. Dorms are $12, doubles and twins $30.

West End

Somewhere to Stay, 45 Brighton Rd. (tel. 07-3846-2858), is south of the Brisbane River and just over one km from South Bank Parklands. It's a huge place, with a pool and landscaped barbecue area. Some rooms have a television and balcony. Rates are $11-14 for a dorm, $21-25 s, $28-35 d, and double rooms with bathrooms are $45.

CAMPGROUNDS

Most of Brisbane's caravan parks are full of permanent residents and offer only a few tourist sites. If you don't mind a lack of facilities, head 45 km west to **Manorina National Park,** beyond Mt. Nebo in Brisbane Forest Park. A small and primitive campground here has pit toilets and picnic tables.

South

Dress Circle Mobile Village, 10 Holmead Rd. (tel. 07-3341-6133), in the suburb of Eight Mile Plains, 15 km south of the city on the Logan Freeway, is spread over 15 hectares and has an area set aside for tents; other features are three swimming pools, five laundries, a barbecue area, and nearby public transportation. Unpowered sites are $10, powered sites $17, and cabins $45-60. Further south, in the suburb of Rochedale, is **Gateway Junction Mobile Village,** 200 School Rd. (tel. 07-3341-6333), just south of the Brisbane bypass. Facilities here are also excellent and sites are $17, cabins $50-70. Campgrounds are also located at Coomera, 54 km southeast of Brisbane, and on the north slope of Tamborine Mountain, 81 km south.

North

In the suburb of Apsley, 13 km from downtown along the main route north, are a couple of choices, but tents aren't encouraged. **Caravan Village Brisbane,** 763 Zillmere Rd. (tel. 07-3263-4040), offers powered sites for $15 and excellent cabins for $45-52. **Apsley Acres Caravan Park,** 1420 Gympie Rd. (tel. 07-3263-2668), is another good option, with a few on-site tents for $12 s, $20 d, sites for $15 and cabins $35-45.

DOWNTOWN DINING

Cafes

Scattered along Queen Street Mall, Brisbane's main shopping precinct, are three open-air **Jimmy's on the Mall** cafes. Service is fast and efficient and food fresh. Hot drinks and main meals are expensive, but light snacks such as nachos, sandwiches, and pastries are well-priced; each cafe is open daily 24 hours. **Cafe Mondial,** a trendy cafe off Queen Street Mall, serves a vast array of coffees and cakes. The music can be loud, but the sound is muffled outside at tables spread along the sidewalk.

The nicest place in the city to spend time over a coffee or lunch is **City Gardens Cafe,** an old caretaker's cottage in the botanic gardens south of Alice St. (tel. 07-3229-1554). Brunch is served daily 8-11 a.m. ($5-10) and lunch and afternoon tea are served till 5 p.m. ($4-9).

Other Cheap Eats

Between 11 a.m. and 2 p.m. lunch at the bistro on the ground floor of **Lennons Hotel,** Queen Street Mall, is only $6 (although dishes aren't that hot), which includes a beer or glass of wine.

A bunch of inexpensive restaurants lie along Elizabeth St., between George and Albert Streets. **Govinda's,** 99 Elizabeth St. (tel. 07-3210-0255), is a vegetarian restaurant run by the Hare Krishna; lunch is a good value at $5, and it's also open for dinner Friday. Elizabeth Arcade, 50 meters downhill from this restaurant, has a variety of cafes and retro shops. **The Source Health Foods Cafe** (tel. 07-3221-1569) is one of these. At the end of the arcade is **Tortilla Cantina** (tel. 07-3221-4416), where most dishes are under $10 and there's a lunchtime special for $5; diners have the choice of eating in a courtyard or dimly lit restaurant.

On the ground floor of the Carlton Crest Hotel, on the corner of Ann and Roma Streets, is **Picasso,** a cavernous yet stylish bistro; open daily 7 a.m.-10 p.m.

Fine Dining

Augustine's (tel. 07-3221-9365) is an elegant restaurant in the 1890s Mansions, a row of six terraces at the Parliament House end of George Street. Diners have a choice of eating in the parlor or surrounded by greenery in the courtyard. Main meals start at $20. Closed Sunday. A few of the better hotels have top-floor restaurants, allowing city and mountain views. Of these, **Restaurant Ridge,** 189 Leichhardt St. (tel. 07-3831-5000), features continental cuisine and occasional live entertainment while **Denison's,** 249 Turbot St. (tel. 07-3835-3535), in the Sheraton, is higher, on the 30th floor, and is more formal with main dishes $19-30; open Tues.-Sat. 6:30-10 p.m.

Riverside Centre and Vicinity

The Riverside Centre, on the east side of downtown and linked by ferry to Kangaroo Point accommodations, has a wide variety of restaurants to suit all budgets, including a number of top-end options. **Rivers Cafe & Bar** (tel. 07-3831-4288) has lunches from $8 and, like all restaurants in the center, good views. Around the corner is **Marco's** (tel. 07-3831-5555), a casual yet elegant Italian restaurant specializing in seafood dishes. Next door is one of Brisbane's most acclaimed restaurants, **Michael's** (tel. 07-3832-5522), featuring cuisine from around the world but also specializing in seafood from Queensland waters; main dishes range $20-28; open for lunch Mon.-Fri., dinner Mon.-Saturday. **Friday's** (tel. 07-3832-2122) is a three-part restaurant including an outside grill ($6-20 for main dishes) and a lunchtime buffet ($24).

Along the promenade from the Riverside Centre is **Eagle Street Pier**, another large complex offering a great variety of restaurants. **City Rowers Fish Tavern**, on the second floor (tel. 07-3221-2888), is an open air bistro-style restaurant with great views. Fish-of-the-day specials start at $13, with chicken and beef dishes similarly priced. Also in this complex is **Il Centro** (tel. 07-3221-6090), a modern Italian restaurant with main dishes well-priced at $15-23.

Kookaburra Queen

This wooden paddlewheeler, built using Australian timbers and traditional shipbuilding skills, departs daily from Eagle Street Pier for a variety of dine-aboard river cruises. Devonshire tea cruises depart daily 10 a.m. (also Sunday 3 p.m.) and include live entertainment; $13.90. The Luncheon Cruise departs daily at noon and returns at 2:15 p.m.; cost varies $22-44 depending on the lunch chosen. Dinner cruises depart Mon.-Sat. 7:30 p.m., Sunday 6:30 p.m. and range $22-55. For bookings call (07) 3221-1300.

RESTAURANTS IN OTHER PARTS OF THE CITY

South Bank

South Bank Parklands has about 20 eateries, including a string of fast-food places. **Capt'n Snapper** (tel. 07-3846-4036) is a huge seafood restaurant at the south end of the Parklands. Basic fish and chips from the blackboard menu is $6.95, but many daily specials are also offered, with the Seafood Feast ($16.95) an especially good value. At the back of the restaurant is a takeaway section with a few tables; fish and chips here is $3.95, but tell the cashier to go easy on the spicy salt. Both are open daily for lunch and dinner. Beside Gondwana Rainforest Sanctuary is **Riverside Restaurants,** a complex of three stylish restaurants overlooking the river. **Cafe San Marco** (tel. 07-3846-4334) has a large breakfast for $8, healthy sandwiches from $5, and Mexican dishes $7-9. **Wang Dynasty** (tel. 07-3844-8318) specializes in kangaroo ($14) and crocodile ($20) cooked Asian-style. Upstairs is an elegant Italian restaurant, **Io Ti Amo** (tel. 07-3846-4599).

In the Queensland Cultural Centre (below Victoria Bridge) is **Promenade Cafe,** with tables spread around a pleasant courtyard. All snacks are inexpensive and the coffee excellent; open daily 10 a.m.-5 p.m.

Paddington

One of Brisbane's oldest suburbs, Paddington has a variety of restaurants and cafes, most along Given Terrace, a continuation of Caxton St. from the city. **Sultan's Kitchen,** 163 Given Terrace (tel. 07-3368-2194), is an Indian restaurant with curries ranging $14-18 and a lunchtime buffet for $13. Up the hill, and on the same side of the road, is **King Tut's,** 283 Given Terrace (tel. 07-3369-9775), a trendy cafe with indoor and outdoor tables; open daily 8 a.m.-10:30 p.m. **Sweethearts** is a country-style cafe on the same stretch. At the junction of Given and Latrobe Terraces is **Kookaburra Cafe,** 280 Given Terrace (tel. 07-3369-2400), in a building dating to 1888. Through the years it has seen a variety of uses, but is now an inexpensive cafe featuring pizza and pasta dishes from $5.

Fortitude Valley

Fortitude Valley, north of downtown, is a melting pot of cultures boasting some of the city's better ethnic restaurants, wildest nightclubs, and its most-famous breakfast hangout.

California Cafe, 376 Brunswick St. (tel. 07-3852-1026), is similar in appearance to many other 1950s-style diners, with one major difference—this one was actually around then, when Fortitude Valley was an outlying suburb and speckled laminex tabletops and chrome-colored chairs were de rigueur. It is now Brisbane's oldest cafe, open all day but most popular at breakfast when portions are legendary. Along Brunswick Street Mall are another couple of places open early including **Cafe Societe** and, farther down, **Coffee Club,** with large street-level windows perfect for people-watching. This cafe is part of **McWhirters,** a large emporium with a great food court, a number of small cafes, and trendy boutiques.

Brisbane's **Chinatown** is located between Wickham and Ann Streets, Fortitude Valley. **Universal Noodle Restaurant,** 145 Wickham St. (tel. 07-3854-1168), is one of Chinatown's least expensive eateries; most meals are under $8. At the other end of the scale, in Duncan Street Mall, is **Chinahouse Seafood Restaurant** (tel. 07-3216-0570), where main dishes range $13-20; open daily for lunch and dinner.

For a taste of Europe, head to **Giardinetto,** 366 Brunswick St. (tel. 07-3252-4750), a small Italian restaurant with pastas under $10 and seafood around $15.

New Farm

If you're staying in this quiet part of town, there's no real need to head into the city for a meal as **Le Bronx,** a small, intimate restaurant at 722 Brunswick St. (tel. 07-3358-2088), will suffice. The menu is small, but has something to suit everyone; main dishes start at $10 and all appetizers and desserts are under $9. Open Tues.-Sat. from 6 p.m. (no smoking before 10:30 p.m.). A couple of doors away is **Koffies Espresso Bar,** with indoor and outdoor tables; open 7:30 a.m.-8 p.m.

Newstead

One of Brisbane's most popular places to head for seafood is **Breakfast Creek Wharf Seafood Restaurant,** northeast of town (tel. 07-3252-2451). It's large, seating over 300 diners, both indoors and out and overlooking Breakfast Creek. The main feature is a timber replica of the boat used by early Australian explorer John Oxley, which sits in the middle of the restaurant, and maritime memorabilia fills other parts. The seafood here is always fresh and prepared to

perfection; coral trout and barramundi are especially good ($16). It's open daily noon-2:30 p.m., 6-10 p.m. You can also get takeaway.

For a splurge, **Roseville Restaurant,** 56 Chester St. (tel. 07-3358-1377), a historic Victorian-era house, is worth every cent. Surrounded by immaculate gardens, the house has been totally restored, right down to period stained-glass windows and chandeliers. Service is impeccable and food excellent. It's open daily for lunch and dinner and although an a la carte menu is offered, a better deal is the fixed-price three-course lunch ($25) or dinner ($29).

GETTING THERE

Air

Brisbane Airport is 11 km northeast of downtown. The international and domestic terminals are two km apart and are both younger than 10 years old (a brand-new international terminal opened in September 1995), making the facilities among the most modern and efficient in the country. The international terminal has a currency exchange, bank, restaurant, cafes, and souvenir shop, but no lockers. Both terminals have all major car rental companies. International airlines flying into Brisbane include: **Qantas** (tel. 13-1313); **Air New Zealand** (tel. 13-2476), **British Airways** (tel. 07-3223-3123), and **United Airlines** (tel. 13-1777). **Ansett Australia** (tel. 13-1300), **Qantas** (tel. 13-1313), and **Eastwest** (tel. 13-1313) fly interstate. Regular one-way fares from Brisbane are: Melbourne $353, Sydney $254, Adelaide $470, Darwin $595, and Perth $620. Within the state, **Flightwest** (tel. 13-2392) serves outback destinations, and **Sunstate** (tel. 13-1313) runs up and down the coast.

Skytrans (tel. 07-3236-1000) is a half-hourly bus service that operates daily 6:30 a.m.-8 p.m. between both terminals and Brisbane Transit Centre ($5.40 one-way) and major downtown hotels ($6.50 one-way). A cab between the airport and downtown will run at $13-17, depending on traffic.

Brisbane Transit Centre

This excellent facility, located on Roma St. half a km from downtown and the Brisbane YHA Hostel, is the Brisbane terminus of all long-disance trains and buses. It has a restaurant, banks, lockers, car rental desks, an accommodation booking service, currency exchange, and information center.

Rail

The XPT departs Sydney for Brisbane twice daily with some services requiring a change to coach at Murwillumbah. Either way, the trip takes 14 hours and is economy $98, first class $142.

Queensland's most popular rail trip is up the coast. The Sunlander, Spirit of the Tropics, and Queenslander all make the 32-hour journey to Cairns (economy $123, first class $234) via Townsville (economy $112, first class $218). The Queenslander is more luxurious than other services and has a bar, lounge, and restaurant. The fare to Cairns on this service is $489 one-way including all meals. It departs each Sunday at 10 a.m. and arrives in Cairns 5:15 p.m. Monday. Other services from Brisbane are: Westlander to Charleville (economy $125, first class $190), Spirit of the Outback to Longreach (economy $148, first class $226), and Spirit of Capricorn to Rockhampton (economy $64, first class $103).

The best source of Queensland Rail information is **Brisbane Travel Centre,** 305 Edward St. (tel. 07-3235-1323 or 13-2232).

Bus

All long-distance bus companies have booking offices in the Brisbane Transit Centre and are open daily till at least 6 p.m. **Greyhound Pioneer** (tel. 13-2030) and **McCafferty's** (tel. 07-3236-3033) operate between Sydney and Brisbane for $73 one-way, or $79 with stops at major towns en route. The trip takes 16-19 hours on either the Pacific or New England Highway. Fares from Brisbane to other major destinations include: Bundaberg $44, Rockhampton $62, Airlie Beach $105, Townsville $117, and Cairns $137. Discounts apply for YHA members and seniors, or, if you purchase tickets 15 days in advance, a 50% discount applies. To destinations north of Brisbane, a Greyhound Pioneer Sunseeker Pass, good for six months on the route to Cairns, is a good deal at $154.

Coachtrans (tel. 07-3236-1000) runs regular services from the airport and Brisbane Transit Centre to the Gold Coast; $12 one-way.

GETTING AROUND

Brisbane Transport operates a network of rail, bus, and ferry services throughout the city. For ticketing, the city is divided into five zones, with all downtown falling in Zone 1. Travel on a single sector of this zone is $1.20. For unlimited travel on buses and ferries, a Day Rover is a good deal for $5.50, or $3 for travel 9-3:30 p.m. and after 7 p.m. A Roverlink ticket allows travel on bus, ferry, and rail; $8. For all Brisbane Transport information call 13-1230.

Rail

Citytrains run along an extensive rail network to outer suburbs, daily 4:30 a.m.-1 a.m. They are mostly used by commuters and shoppers. All trains stop at Central Station, on Ann St., and Brisbane Transit Centre, on Roma Street.

Bus

Brisbane Transport operates bus services that radiate from the city center to the suburbs. The terminus of these routes is the bus station beneath the Myer Shopping Centre on Queen Street Mall. There are two main services: **Cityxpress,** with limited stops, and **Citybus,** with multiple stops. The City Circle route runs along Adelaide, Eagle, Alice, and George Streets every five minutes (Mon.-Fri. only).

Ferry

Ferries run along the Brisbane River every 15-30 minutes. The main routes are from the west end of Alice St. to South Bank Parklands and the River Plaza Hotel and from the Riverside Centre to Kangaroo Point and New Farm Point. All routes (except to New Farm Park) fall within Zone 1.

Taxi

For a cab call **Black and White Cab Company** (tel. 13-1008) or **Yellow Cabs** (tel. 07-3391-0191).

Car

Driving in Brisbane isn't as frustrating as other Australian capital cities, although the Riverside Expressway can be confusing at times. Parking stations downtown charge from $4 an hour and $15 per day, with early-bird rates before 9 a.m. A good alternative is underground parking at the Queensland Cultural Centre ($8 per day) or at South Bank Parklands ($4 per day).

Rates for rental cars start at $39 per day with local companies, and rates for multiple days often include unlimited kilometers and insurance. These companies include: **Cut Rate Rentals** (tel. 07-3854-1809), **Delta** (tel. 07-3839-8180), **Aircond** (tel. 07-3216-0303; rates drop to $25 per day over 21 days); and **Penny Wise** (tel. 07-3252-3333). Major car rental companies with outlets in Brisbane are: **Avis** (tel. 07-3252-7111), **Budget** (tel. 07-3252-0151), **Hertz** (tel. 07-3221-6166), **National** (tel. 07-3854-1499), and **Thrifty** (tel. 07-3252-5994).

Tours

Brisbane Transport operates **City Sights Tours** in a tram-on-wheels leaving from the Queen St. side of Post Office Square every half-hour 9 a.m.-4 p.m. Tickets are $12 and are valid all day, allowing you to get on and off at up to 18 stops of interest around the city including Wickham Terrace, Fortitude Valley, Kangaroo Point Ferry, the Maritime Museum, and the Queensland Cultural Centre.

Australian Pacific Tours (tel. 13-1304), **Sunstate** (tel. 07-3236-3355), and **Boomerang Tours** (tel. 07-3236-4163) operate tours of the city and its environs. Fares start at $36 for a half-day tour, which includes admission to a wildlife park.

SERVICES

The **general post office** is at 261 Queen St. and is open Mon.-Fri. 7 a.m.-7 p.m. Another post office operates out of the Brisbane Transit Centre. Cash traveler's checks at all major banks and hotels.

Emergency Services

For all emergencies call 000. **Royal Brisbane Hospital** is on Herston Rd., Herston (tel. 07-3253-8111). **Travellers Medical Service** provides vaccinations for ongoing travel as well as first-aid kits and other travel accessories; it's on the fifth floor, Coles Building, 210 Queen St. (tel. 07-3221-8083).

INFORMATION

Library

Located in the Queensland Cultural Centre on South Bank is the **State Library,** with a large selection of current newspapers from around the world, magazines, audiovisual displays, a collection of historic maps, a research section (tel. 07-3840-7886), and cafe. It's open Mon.-Thurs. 10 a.m.-8 p.m., Fri.-Sun. 10 a.m.-5 p.m. (tel. 07-3840-7666).

Bookstores

Hema Maps, with a wide variety of travel guides and maps, is on the first floor of the MLC Building, 239 George St. (tel. 07-3221-4330). **Billabong Bookshop,** City Plaza, corner of Adelaide and George Streets (tel. 07-3229-2801), specializes in Australiana and carries a wide variety of maps. **Dymocks** has an outlet in Queen Street Mall, and **Angus and Robertson** is located in Post Office Square, Adelaide Street.

Information Centers

A small **information booth** operated by Brisbane City Council is on Queen Street Mall at Albert St. (tel. 07-3229-5918). It's open Mon.-Thurs 8:30 a.m.-5 p.m., Friday 8:30 a.m.-8:30 p.m., and Sat.-Sun. 9 a.m.-5 p.m. **Brisbane Visitors & Convention Bureau** operates information centers at the arrivals level of the international terminal at Brisbane Airport, the foyer of City Hall, and Level 2 of Brisbane Transit Centre on Roma Street. The **Queensland Government Travel Centre,** corner Adelaide and Edward Streets (tel. 07-3221-6111), books tours and attractions throughout the state; open Mon.-Fri. 8:30 a.m.-5 p.m., Saturday 9:30 a.m.-12:30 p.m.

The **Queensland Department of Environment and Heritage,** caretaker of Queensland's national parks, has a great information center at 160 Ann St. (tel. 07-3227-7111); open Mon.-Fri. 8:30 a.m.-5 p.m.

The **RACQ** (Royal Automobile Club of Queensland), beside the post office at 261 Queen St. (tel. 07-3227-8186), is another good source of information, and members of associate motoring clubs—such as AAA—can fill their arms with maps and handy accommodation guides.

TOOWOOMBA AND VICINITY

Once known simply as The Swamp, Toowoomba (pop. 100,000) has grown into one of Queensland's largest regional centers. The city sprawls across the western slopes of the Great Dividing Range, 140 km west of Brisbane. It serves the farming communities of the Darling Downs as well as being home to the University of Southern Queensland. Best known for parks and gardens, tree-lined streets, art galleries, and historic buildings, Toowoomba exudes an air of elegance not usually associated with country towns.

Sights

The **Cobb & Co. Museum,** 27 Lindsay St. (tel. 076-39-1971), boasts Australia's largest collection of horse-drawn vehicles, including many carts and buggies from early last century; admission $2.50. It's open Mon-Fri. 10 a.m.-4 p.m., Sat.-Sun. 1-4 p.m. Across the road is Queens Park, a large area of natural parkland. **Royal Bull's Head Inn** was built in 1847 as a resting stop for people traveling west from Brisbane to the Darling Downs. In its day, it would have gotten a five-star rating as one of the most comfortable stopping houses in Queensland. Although the building has undergone many changes since last century, it retains a historic charm; open Fri.-Sun. 10 a.m.-4 p.m. Admission is $2. You'll find it in the suburb of Drayton, immediately west of the university campus.

From **Picnic Point,** east of downtown at the end of Long St., views extend 360 degrees across the city and to the Great Dividing Range. There's a picnic area, and hiking trails lead down the escarpment. A park of a different type is **Ju Raku En,** a Japanese garden on the campus of

On 1 November 1997 telephone numbers in this section will change. To dial the new number, simply add "46" to all numbers with the area code (076) and add "41" to all numbers with the area code (071). As an example, (076) 12-3456 becomes 4612-3456. The new area code for all numbers in this section will be (07).

the University of Southern Queensland; open daily 7 a.m.-7 p.m. **Toowoomba Bicentennial Water Habitat,** on Mackenzie St., is a re-creation of the wetland environment before the arrival of white man in the area.

Accommodations and Food

Most of Toowoomba's 30-odd hotels and motels lie along Ruthven St. (New England Hwy.) north and south of downtown. **Settlers Inn Hotel,** 633 Ruthven St. (tel. 076-32-3634), is the best in its class, with clean rooms for $18 s, $32 d. **Motel Glenworth,** 1 Margaret St. (tel. 076-38-1799), is inexpensive and handy to downtown; $44 s, $54 d. **Allan Cunningham Motel,** 808 Ruthven St. (tel. 076-35-5466), has large, comfortable rooms with modern conveniences, and a pool; $48 s, $58 d.

Vacy Hall, 135 Russell St. (tel. 076-39-2055), is an elegant home dating to 1883. Lovingly restored, each room has distinctive character and a comfortable brass bed. Standard rooms are $88 s, $112 d, and much larger suites, with a fireplace and veranda, are $124 s, $148 d.

At the other end of the scale is the rather clinical **YWCA Gowrie House,** 112 Mary St. (tel. 076-32-2642). Rooms are clean and bright and tea and coffee are complimentary; $25 s, $35 d, includes a hot breakfast. **Toowoomba Motor Village,** 821 Ruthven St. (tel. 076-35-8186), has great facilities including a barbecue area and laundry; unpowered sites $10, powered sites $14, on-site vans $24, and cabins $28-42.

Dancing Bear Cafe, 1 Scholefield St. (tel. 076-32-6444), is the ubiquitous student hangout—sparsely furnished, notice boards crammed with Wanted to Rent notices, and a motley bunch of students sipping coffee while studying; open daily from 6:30 a.m. **Jacaranda Coffee Shoppe,** in Park House Gallery on Margaret St. (tel. 076-32-8779), is a more relaxed place with lunches served daily and morning and afternoon teas on weekends. **Banjo's** is a family-style steak and seafood restaurant at the corner of Ruthven St. and Hanna Court (tel. 076-36-1033). **Herries House,** 210 Herries St.

Ju Raku En garden

(tel. 076-32-7382), is an Italian restaurant with tables out on a covered veranda or inside around a log fire; open daily for lunch and dinner.

Transportation, Services, and Information

The **coach terminal** is at 28 Neil St. (tel. 076-38-1199). **McCafferty's** has at least two services daily from Brisbane and the Gold Coast to Toowoomba.

Toowoomba Mapping Centre has a wide range of topographical maps and Australiana literature; it's at 185 Herries St. (tel. 076-32-3848). The **Tourist Information Centre** operates out of City Hall on Ruthven St. (tel. 076-39-3797); open daily 9 a.m.-5 p.m.

DARLING DOWNS

This area of far south Queensland, south of Toowoomba and immediately west of the Great Dividing Range, is a vast basin with all watersheds flowing in a southerly direction to form the **Darling River,** which drains into the Murray River and into the Southern Ocean, forming part of Australia's great river system. The especially fertile land provides an ideal environment for a variety of crops and stock. From Brisbane, the most direct access to the Darling Downs is through Ipswich, then southwest along the Cunningham Highway to the region's largest town, Warwick.

National Parks of the Main Range

Traveling west from Brisbane, the coastal plain in which the city lies soon gives way to the Great Dividing Range. This section of the range is protected by an almost continuous strip of national parks that continues southward into New South Wales. The largest is 11,500-hectare **Main Range National Park,** bisected by a road passing through **Cunningham's Gap,** a low pass flanked by peaks rising over 1,100 meters. Apart from panoramic views, this section of the park seems uninspiring; but it is worth getting out at the **The Crest** for one of a number of short hikes. The **Rainforest Circuit** will take only 20 minutes, but this is only the beginning of an extensive trail system on the north side of the road. Off this track a 2.3-km trail leads to Mt. Cordeaux, not really a mountain at all, but a high ridge that comes alive with color in late spring when spear lilies bloom (allow two hours round-trip). On the western flank of the gap is a campground and Park Headquarters (tel. 076-66-1133).

East of the Main Range are four isolated peaks, each protected by a small national park and known wholly as **Moogerah Peaks National Parks.** The summit of each is accessible (784-meter Mt. Moon is the highest), and the cliff faces of **Mt. French** are popular with climbers.

Warwick

Warwick, largest community of the Darling Downs, is 162 km southwest of Brisbane, at the junction of the New England and Cunningham lighways. The city was first settled in 1840, making it Queensland's second-oldest settlement (only Brisbane has been established onger). Many sandstone buildings from this early ra remain, including the courthouse, a number f impressive churches, and **Pringle Cottage,** on Dragon Street. Warwick's biggest drawcard is he **Rose and Rodeo Festival** in October. Events take place throughout the month, culmiating in the rodeo on the last weekend.

Motels in town are of a surprisingly high standard, with **Country Rose Motel,** 2 Palmer Ave., on the road out to Brisbane (tel. 076-61-7700), being an especially good value at $45 s, $50 . **Oasis Caravan Park,** on the New England Hwy. south of town (tel. 076-61-2874), has sites or $10 and on-site vans for $23.

Queen Mary Falls National Park
Located near Killarney, 44 km east of Warwick, his 333-hectare park encompasses two sections of natural bushland on the western slopes f the Great Dividing Range. The falls for which he park is named plunge 40 meters in a narrow bbon of water that cascades photogenically ver an escarpment. You'll find a privately operated campground at the park's entrance, yet within walking distance of the falls; unpowered sites $10, powered sites $12, and a few very asic on-site vans for $22.

Granite Belt
A landscape littered with granite boulders, a legay of volcanic eruptions 200 million years ago, ominates this area, the southernmost part of the tate, where the state border follows the peaks of he Roberts Range. The two national parks are the est places to experience this landscape, and if ou come from the north, you'll pass through **Stanthorpe,** the center of Queensland's wine-roducing area. Other fruits, such as pears, aples, and stone fruits were introduced by tin minrs in the 1870s and now make up the other part f the local economy; in season, roadside stalls re the perfect places to indulge in this local pro-uce. **Happy Valley Homestead,** Glen Lyon Dr. tel. 076-81-3250), four km west of Stanthorpe, eatures a number of cozy cottages scattered round a natural bush setting, while other rooms, with shared facilities, are in the main building. Rates are $60-99 pp including lunch and dinner.

The rugged 11,400-hectare **Girraween National Park,** 40 km south of Stanthorpe, typifies the granite belt. The access road climbs into an area of large granite boulders scattered through deep gullies and high ridges. More than 200 million years of erosion exposed the harder granite boulders, some balanced at impossible angles, looking as if they could roll at the slightest push. At the end of the sealed road are trailheads. The steep **Pyramid Trail** (three km one-way) passes through an area of exceptional beauty, ending at a particularly imposing boulder, deftly balanced on a high ridge. Girraween is Koori for "Place of Many Flowers," and for the flowers alone it is worth visiting the park in spring. The park has two campgrounds, both with hot showers, and there's a visitor center at Castle Rock (tel. 076-84-5157).

Also located on the NSW/Queensland border is 11,200-hectare **Sundown National Park,** known locally as "traprock country" for the ridges and gorges along Severn River. Access from the east is best suited to four-wheel drives (turn off at Ballandean) while from the west a good road leads to Broadwater Camping Area, south of Glenlyon.

Goondiwindi
Meaning "Resting Place for Birds" in the language of the Koori, Goondiwindi is a thriving country town on the MacIntyre River. The river is the lifeblood of the town, allowing agricultural industries such as cotton-growing to thrive. Over 30,000 hectares are irrigated for cotton-growing. MacIntyre Cotton Gin, one of the world's largest, is open for tours April-October. Also in town is an extensive botanic garden and small museum in the old customs house.

WEST FROM TOOWOOMBA

The Warrego Highway, the main route west from Toowoomba, passes through a number of large agricultural towns before ending at Charleville. This is also the most direct route between Brisbane and the Northern Territory.

Jondaryan Woolshed
Jondaryan (pronounced "YON-dar-yan") was once part of one of Queensland's largest cattle stations but has long since been divided into

The daily parade is a highlight of Jondaryan's Australian Heritage Festival.

ANDREW HEMPSTEAD

smaller holdings. The original woodshed, along with other buildings, has been transformed into a heritage theme park featuring a massive collection of steam-powered farm equipment, carriages and buggies, antique tractors, and other pioneering memorabilia. The complex sprawls over 60 hectares, with demonstrations of sheep-shearing, blacksmithing, and agricultural techniques daily. Guided tours of the park depart daily at 1 p.m. and on weekends at 10:30 a.m., 1 p.m., and 3 p.m. Admission is adult $8, child $4, with billy tea and damper an extra $2.50 and full meals starting at $4.50. Travelers can bed down for the night at the old shearer's quarters for $9 pp, and campsites are $8-10. Members of the YHA stay in dorms for just $5.

On the last week of August the woolshed hosts the **Australian Heritage Festival,** when all the machinery is operating and literally thousands of people descend on the place. For more information call (076) 92-2229.

Dalby and West to Charleville

Dalby is a major agricultural center of 5,000, 8 km northwest of Toowoomba on the Warreg Highway. You'll find a large display of antiqu and vintage farm machinery at **Pioneer Park Mu seum** (open daily 10 a.m.-3 p.m.). Also of interes is **Jimbour House;** built in 1876, it is considere one of the finest examples of colonial architec ture in the country. The house, although not ope to the public, is north of Dalby in Jimbour, an the gardens are enjoyable to wander around.

Chinchilla, the first major town west of Dalb is renowned for extensive deposits of petrifie wood.

The largest center along the Warrego High way is **Roma** (pop. 7,000). First settled in th 1860s, Roma has long been associated wit the grazing industry and is also located in a area rich in oil and natural gas. **Easter in th Country,** the town's biggest festival, feature a goat race, rodeo, donkey derby, and rolling-pi throwing contest.

NORTH FROM TOOWOOMBA

Ravensbourne and Crows Nest Falls National Parks

Both these parks are located off the New Eng land Highway, north of Toowoomba. Ravens bourne is a 100-hectare park protecting an are of rainforest similar to that which once covere much of the surrounding area. A short trail lead through a stand of piccabeen palms and alon the access road, east of Hampton, is a picni area. The other park, Crows Nest Falls, is eas of Crows Nest. The falls for which the park i named are one km from the picnic and campin area. Beyond the falls is a lookout over Valley c Diamonds. Further information on both park can be obtained from the NPWS at 158 Hum St., Toowoomba (tel. 076-39-4599).

SOUTH BURNETT

Named for the Burnett River, which drains int the ocean at Bundaberg, this region of the Grea Dividing Range, north of Toowoomba, is a bit ou of the way, neither on the coastal route north nor the highway out west, so it's often bypassed

unya Mountains National Park

rotecting a western spur of the Great Dividing
ange, this 11,700-hectare park featuring lush
ainforests and stands of distinctive bunya pines
well worth a detour. Bunya pines, once com-
on through the mountains of southeast
ueensland, are now confined to this park.
luch of the park is over 1,000 meters above
ea level, creating a climate very different from
urrounding plains. This subtropical environ-
ent promotes rainforest growth including a
anopy of dome-shaped bunya pines and a
reat variety of palms, ferns, orchids, and
ches. The park also boasts a variety of birds,
nd many of the more colorful species, such as
ng parrots and rosellas, can be seen around
cnic areas. At dawn and dusk large numbers of
ed-necked wallabies feed in cleared areas
long the road. The main park facility area is
andabah, where a park information center,
ampground with hot showers, and other acommodations are located. This is also the start-
g point for a variety of trails, including the four-
m scenic circuit that takes in a variety of vege-
ation, a lookout, waterfall, and rock pools.

Other campgrounds lie to the north at West-
cott Plain and Burton's Well, but facilities at
these are more primitive. Not all the mountains
are protected as a national park and a number of
private homes rent by the night or week through
the kiosk (tel. 076-68-3131). They range $55-95
per night, making them excellent values. The
Hunch, one of these, is close to everything,
sleeps nine, and is fully self-contained at $65
per night. The park information center is located
at Dandabah (tel. 076-68-3127).

Kingaroy

Loved by some, hated by others, no one would
argue that Joh Bjelke-Peterson, Australia's best-
known peanut farmer and Queensland premier
for more than 20 years, put his home town of
Kingaroy on the map. More than 35,000 tons
of peanuts are processed annually in town; the
best place to taste this local delicacy is the
peanut van on Kingaroy St. (tel. 071-62-2737).
The **Tourist Information Centre,** Haly St. (tel.
071-62-3199), can arrange tours of local factories; open Mon.-Fri. 9 a.m.-5 p.m., Sat.-Sun. 10
a.m.-2 p.m.

MORETON BAY

or 500,000 years sand, washed down the river
ystems of northern New South Wales, has been
ushed northward by ocean currents and pre-
ailing southerly winds. Some of it is dumped on
e Gold Coast, but most ends up farther north
nd has formed a chain of sand islands east of
risbane. Moreton Bay, protected from the full
rce of the Pacific Ocean by this barrier, is dotted
ith islands, and along the mainland coast are
istoric coastal townships, but massive **North**
tradbroke and **Moreton Islands** are the most
teresting. Although mostly undeveloped, ac-
ess to both islands is inexpensive, with North
tradbroke having a short road system and three
mall towns while Moreton is mostly national
ark, with one small resort on the west coast.

BAYSIDE COMMUNITIES

he Bayside is a stretch of coast extending north
nd south from the mouth of the Brisbane River

for about 40 km. The many seaside towns, once
fishing villages and holiday destinations, are now
really outer suburbs of Brisbane, with Queensland's capital less than an hour's drive west.

The towns of **Wynnum** and **Manly** are immediately south of the Brisbane River. To the
north of Wynnum is **Fort Lytton,** built in 1877 to
defend the mouth of the Brisbane River. Parts of
the fort remain and are open to the public during
daylight hours. In Manly, Cambridge Parade
leads down a steep hill to a large harbor, chock-
full of fishing trawlers, yachts, and motorboats.

Manly Hotel, Cambridge Parade (tel. 07-
3396-8188), is a 1950s-style place with basic
rooms for $35 s, $40 d, and a good outdoor
beer garden overlooking the bay. Opposite, and
overlooking the harbor, is **The Fish Cafe,** with
dine-in and takeaway seafood.

South of Manly is **Cleveland,** departure point
for ferries to North Stradbroke Island. For somewhere to stay, try the **Grand View Hotel,** built in
1851 and completely refurbished in 1992 to its

original glory. It is Queensland's oldest pub; two rooms are available, each decorated in period furnishings. The hotel also has a few bars, including an outside deck overlooking the bay and a restaurant. Located on North St. (tel. 07-3286-1002). On the main road (Old Cleveland Rd.) out to the ferry terminal is **Redlands Tourism** office; open Mon.-Fri. 8:30 a.m.-5 p.m., Sat.-Sun. 9 a.m.-4 p.m.

INNER ISLANDS

St. Helena Island

In the 1860s, when Brisbane's jails were overflowing, it was decided to send the worst prisoners

to this 80-hectare island eight km from the mout of the Brisbane River. Construction was exter sive, with prisoners building two large cell block for themselves, as well as housing for the warders and enough facilities to make the island self-su ficient. After 65 years the prison closed, and muc of the construction material was shipped to th mainland. The stone and brick walls remain, a does Queensland's first tramway, and the islan itself is pleasant (although much altered from it original tree-covered state).

Cat-o-nine-tails is a large catamaran that run from the marina at Manly across to the island few times a week (call 07-3393-3726 to chec times); adult $23, child $13. From the BP Mar na, on the north side of Breakfast Creek, Bris bane, **St. Helena Island Guided Tours** (tel. 07-3260-7944) runs a day tour to the island for the same price.

Coochiemudlo Island

"Coochie," as it's best known, is a small residential island with sandy beaches and many water-based activities, making it a good day trip from the mainland. Within walking distance of the ferry terminal are boat and surf-ski rentals, cafes, and restaurants. Ferries run from Victoria Point (south of Cleveland) every half-hour 6 a.m.-6 p.m.; adult $1.50 one-way, child $1. For details call (07) 3207-8960.

NORTH STRADBROKE ISLAND

According to Captain Cook's 1770 charts, North Stradbroke was once part of a sand island that ran the length of Moreton Bay, with Moreton Island to the north, breaking away first; then in 1896 North and South Stradbroke Islands separated during a storm.

This large island is a great place to escape from the mainland and is good for walking, diving, fishing, and surfing. Although sand is the dominant feature, much of the island is forested, with eucalypts, acacias, and banksias covering the dune system up to 100 meters high. Inland, swamps dominate, and on the island's inaccessible west coast mangroves reign.

Dunwich, the island's first settlement, initially served as a depot for goods bound for Brisbane in 1827, then an Italian mission, and later as a quarantine station. Just north of Dunwich, at One Mile, readable headstones in the cemetery tell a sad story of these early days, when a typhoid outbreak killed 27 people, including the Brisbane doctor sent to treat them. Today the island has three townships and a combined population of a little over 3,000. Settlement is restricted to the island's north end; the rest of the island is remote, inaccessible, and closed to the public due to ongoing mining of mineral sands.

Sights and Recreation

Upon landing, you'll come ashore at **Dunwich,** on the island's west coast. A visitor center is near the waterfront. Part of the original stone wharf built by convicts remains north of the main boat ramp. On Welsby St. is a small **museum.**

From Dunwich, the main road leads northeast to the island's other townships. Another leads east across the island, to **Blue Lake National Park.** A few kilometers out of Dunwich on this road is **Brown Lake,** good for swimming and picnicking, with a nine-hole golf course. The 500-hectare park is best known for the intensely colored lake for which it is named. The lake is fairly shallow—10 meters at its deepest—and is encircled with paperbark trees. The lake is 2.7 km from the road, an easy walk for hikers seeking a refreshing swim.

At the end of the island's other sealed road is **Point Lookout,** Queensland's easternmost point. It's this rocky headland, part of an ancient volcano, upon which the island's sand has built up. From the point, views extend south to the end of the island and on clear days to Mt. Warning. Migrating humpback whales pass under the cape June-November. Surfers and, in calm weather, snorkelers and divers frequent this beach.

Accommodations and Food

Stradbroke Hotel/Motel, Point Lookout (tel. 07-3409-8188), is a modern complex with basic rooms for $50 s, $70 d. Facilities include a pool, barbecue area, restaurant (see below), and bar. An inexpensive option is **Stradbroke Island Guesthouse** on East Coast Rd., just before it descends into Point Lookout (tel. 07-3409-8888). Take advantage of the communal kitchen, free use of water sport equipment, and courtesy pick-ups from Brisbane Transit Centre Monday, Wednesday, and Friday at 2:30 p.m. (book ahead). Singles and doubles are $40 and dorm beds are $15 pp. The local council operates five campgrounds on the island, including one in each of the three towns. Unpowered sites are $5 per night ($6.50 during holidays) and powered sites are $6.50 ($9 during holidays); call (07) 3409-8192 for bookings. At Point Lookout is **Stradbroke Island Carapark** (tel. 07-3409-8127), away from the beach but with a kitchen, kiosk, and laundry; sites are $8-14 and basic cabins are $42 per night.

The best food in town is dished up at the place with the best views, the **Stradbroke Hotel** (tel. 07-3409-8188), better known as "The Straddie." Daily lunch specials in the bistro are about $6 while the restaurant is a little dearer. **Point Lookout Bowls Club** (tel. 07-3409-8182) has inexpensive lunches and dinners. Basic groceries are available from small stores in each town, but prices are high. Also look out for local seafood sold at roadside stands (including delicious crabs).

Transportation, Services, and Information

The mainland departure point for vehicular and passenger services to the island is Cleveland, 35 km east of Brisbane and connected to that city by regular bus and rail services.

The most convenient way of getting to the island without your own vehicle is with **Stradbroke Island Coach Service** (tel. 07-3807-4299). The service includes pick-up from the front of Brisbane Transit Centre and other selected city points, and drop-off at various points on the island. The bus departs from Brisbane Mon.-Fri. at 9:30 a.m. and 4 p.m., and Sat.-Sun. at 7:45 p.m.; $10 one-way, $19 round-trip.

Water taxis are operated by two companies, **Stradbroke Ferries** (tel. 07-3286-2666) and **Stradbroke Flyer** (tel. 07-3286-1964); both depart from Cleveland with hourly services 7 a.m.-7 p.m. The fare is $10 pp round-trip. **Stradbroke Ferries** also runs a vehicular ferry departing Cleveland nine to 11 times daily for Dunwich. The fare for a regular-sized car is $66 round-trip including passengers. The last sailing Mon.-Thurs. and Saturday is 6 p.m., Friday at 8 p.m., and Sunday at 6:30 p.m. In summer you'll need advance bookings.

Stradbroke Island Coach Service (tel. 07-3807-4299) operates regular links between the towns and meets all water taxi arrivals at Dunwich. For a cab call **Stradbroke Taxi Service** (tel. 07-3409-9124); Dunwich to Point Lookout accommodations will be $28. Rent scooters from Stradbroke Island Guesthouse (tel. 07-3409-8888) for $15 an hour and four-wheel drives from Point Lookout Hire (tel. 07-3409-8353) for $110 per day.

Stradbroke Visitors Information Centre is in Dunwich (tel. 07-3409-9555), open daily 9 a.m.-5 p.m. On the mainland, on Old Cleveland Rd., is another information center with island information (open similar hours).

MORETON ISLAND

As sand-mining leases expire, this large sand island north of North Stradbroke Island is slowly reverting to the spectacular and remote wilderness it was before white settlers came. Compared to North Stradbroke, this island is a wilderness, much of it protected by national park, and with no designated roads; it's popular for four-wheel driving and camping. A great little resort sits on the west coast.

The island's east coast is one long beach, almost 40 km long. The island is 185 square km and rises to a height of 280 meters at **Mt. Tempest,** claimed to be the highest coastal sand dune in the world. Behind the ever-changing dune system is coastal heath of banksias, and at lower elevations swamps, while open woodlands dominate and along the west coast mangroves rise from tidal marshes. A lighthouse at the northeastern tip and scattered Koori midddens are the most telling signs of human presence. **Tangalooma Resort** sits on the former site of Queensland's only whaling station, operational 1952-62. Without a four-wheel drive the only way to get around is on foot; from the ferry dock, it's a one-day walk to the island's east coast (14 km one-way) and Mt. Tempest (16 km one-way).

Accommodations

Tangalooma Moreton Island Resort (tel. 07-3268-6333), spread along a palm-fringed beach in the middle of the island's west coast, boasts many activities, including tennis, squash, sailing, diving, snorkeling, and bushwalking. Rooms are furnished with the mild climate and relaxed atmosphere in mind; cane furniture, slate floors, private balconies, and kitchenettes. Rates start at $145 d in the off season, rising to $175 on holidays; rooms with ocean views start at $155 d. A popular deal is the Dolphins in Paradise package, which include transfers, breakfast, and room for $324 pp for five nights. Otherwise transfers are $22 pp one-way by boat, $65 by floatplane.

Camping at designated NPWS campground is $7.50 per night; permits through the NPWS in Brisbane are essential (tel. 07-3227-7111).

Transportation and Tours

Tangalooma Flyer, a high-speed catamaran, transports guests and day-trippers to the resort. It departs from a wharf at the end of Holt St., Eagle Farm (northwest of downtown Brisbane), Tues.-Sun. at 9:30 a.m. returning from Tangalooma at 4 p.m. (except Saturday, 4:30 p.m.) for $25 round-trip. June-Oct. this can be combined with whale-watching ($70, including lunch; Wednesday and Sunday only.). On Friday night there is an extra sailing at 5:30 p.m. for a Dolphin Cruise ($75 pp includes a four-course meal at the resort). Make bookings through the resort (tel. 07-3268-6333). The other way of getting across to the island is aboard *Combie Trader,* a vehicular ferry that departs Scarborough, north of Brisbane, daily except Tuesday for Bulwer on the north end of the island. On Sunday, Monday, and Friday, the boat returns the same day; on other days you'll need to

camp or stay in self-contained units, $60 per night. (call 07-3880-1725 for bookings). Passengers are $20 round-trip, vehicles $90 including passengers. From Bulwer, **Moreton Island Taxi Service** offers drop-offs at campgrounds. The *Combie Trader* offers day tours Monday, Friday, and Sunday, including boat trip, lunch, and a 4WD tour for $55 adult, $35 child.

Sunrover Expeditions (tel. 07-3203-4241 or 1800-07-7353) offers trips emphasizing the island's natural wonders, with a busy itinerary in a four-wheel drive including swimming in Blue Lagoon, visiting the lighthouse, climbing the sand dunes—and tobogganing back down—and snorkeling around a wreck. Rate of $80 pp includes pick-up from Brisbane Transit Centre, boat trip, and lunch. And it really is a full-day trip, departing Monday at 6:30 a.m., Saturday at 5 a.m., and Sunday at 7:30 a.m.

SUNSHINE COAST

The beautiful sandy beaches of the Sunshine Coast extend 70 km between Caloundra, 85 km north of Brisbane, and Rainbow Beach. Along the coastal route you'll find a string of laid-back residential and tourist developments and, most importantly, some of Australia's best beaches. The Sunshine Coast is often compared to the Gold Coast, but it's nowhere near as developed or hectic, with only a couple of pockets of high-rises and long strips of beachfront reserve. That's not to say things aren't going ahead on the Sunshine Coast; population growth runs about 10% annually and each summer hordes of holidaying Australians descend on the beaches. This stretch of coast is also the most northerly on the east coast open to the ocean, and, being so far north, it's T-shirt and shorts weather year-round.

The coastal resort towns of Caloundra, Mooloolaba, Maroochydore, and Coolum form a continuous string of development, while at the north end of the Sunshine Coast Noosa Heads forms the jewel in the crown; a small community with a beautiful national park on the doorstep and chic cafes, stylish boutiques, and luxurious accommodations.

BRISBANE TO CALOUNDRA

Caboolture

This town of 12,000, 40 km north of Brisbane, is a service town for a rich dairy industry. The town's most interesting feature is **Caboolture Historical Village,** a couple of kilometers north of town on the old highway. Historic buildings collected from around southeastern Queensland have been relocated to the site, in a recreation of a bush town. It's open daily 10 a.m.-3 p.m. and admission is $6 pp.

Bribie Island

Where the access road to Caboolture spurs west, another heads east to Bribie Island, linked to the mainland by a bridge spanning Pumicestone Passage. The island is flat and fairly uninspiring. The only development is a smattering of fishing and holiday towns at its southern end, including the town of **Bongaree,** just south of the bridge. Across the island at **Woorim** is a long sandy beach and good camping at **Bribie Island Caravan Park** (tel. 07-3408-1134), across from the beach. Sites are $11-13 per night and cabins $30-42.

Glass House Mountains

This group of bizarrely shaped volcanic peaks dominates the western horizon north of Caboolture. Thirteen in total, the four largest are protected by small national parks. A 22-km forest drive, beginning at Beerburrum and ending at the township of Glass House Mountains, provides access to the base of each, as well as a lookout from where each peak can be recognized from a

The Glass House Mountains are best appreciated from the 22-km forest drive through their midst.

panoramic photo. The easiest peak to ascend is **Mt. Ngungun** (253 meters); allow one hour each way. **Mt. Beerburrum, Mt. Beerwah,** and **Mt. Coonowrin** are for rock climbers only. None of the four parks has camping, and only Mt. Tibrogargan National Park has picnic areas.

CALOUNDRA

While other Sunshine Coast towns have developed on long stretches of sand, Caloundra (pop. 22,000) sprawls over a rocky headland and extends south along the Pumicestone Passage. Within the passage are two safe swimming beaches, Bulcock and Golden, protected from ocean swells by Bribie Island. These safe beaches make Caloundra an ideal destination for families and for those keen on water sports such as fishing, windsurfing, sailing, and swimming. Along Golden Beach, various operators rent water sport equipment during summer months. Right near downtown, at the mouth of the passage, a treed reserve overlooks a wide sandy bank with calm swimming on one side and the roar of the ocean on the other. Aside from the beaches, Caloundra's main attraction is **Queensland Air Museum,** at the airport on the main road into town. About 20 aircraft are on display, along with other aviation relics. It's open Wednesday, Saturday, and Sunday 10 a.m.-4 p.m. (tel. 07-5492-5930).

Accommodation in Caloundra is geared mainly to holidaying families with six caravan parks and dozens of self-contained apartments available. **Rolling Surf Motel,** 10 Levuka Ave. (tel. 07-5491-1300), overlooking all the best beaches, has rooms from $55 s or d, $70 with kitchens. **Caloundra Holiday Resort,** Dicky Beach (tel. 07-5491-3342), has sites for $14-18 and on-site vans for $32.

MOOLOOLABA

This resort town is one of the Sunshine Coast's most pleasant places, with a long stretch of parkland separating a strip of outdoor cafes, restaurants, and boutiques from a glorious beach of golden sand that curves southward from a rocky headland to the mouth of the Mooloola River. The river's course has been much changed through residential canal developments but near its mouth is a busy harbor filled with a colorful collection of pleasure craft and fishing trawlers.

UnderWater World

This three-story complex, incorporating the world's largest oceanarium, is the Sunshine Coast's major commercial attraction. The main aquarium features species from the South Pacific. Other features are: aquariums re-creating river, reef, and swamp ecosystems; a marine mammal cove where seal shows take place five times daily; the Freshwater Billabong with crocodiles, barramundi, and the unique amphibious Queensland lungfish; a seashore display; and audiovisuals on life underwater. The center is open daily 9 a.m.-6 p.m. Admission is adult $15.50, child $8. It's located on Parkyn Parade (tel. 07-5444-8488). Shuttle buses depart daily from Noosa (9 a.m.) and other points along the way for UnderWater World; $9 round-trip.

UnderWater World is part of **The Wharf,** a complex of cafes, restaurants, and souvenir shops spread along the harbor. Also on The Wharf are booking agents for a variety of river cruises, including a one-hour Canal Cruise for $9; call (07) 5444-7477 for bookings.

Practicalities

Central to UnderWater World, the beach, and shops is **River Esplanade Motel,** 73 Brisbane Rd. (tel. 07-5444-3855), where rooms are $39 s, $45 d. Closer to the beach, and with self-contained rooms, is **Sandcastles,** 64 6th Ave. (tel. 07-5443-6700). Each modern unit has a kitchen, laundry, separate living area, and balcony. Rates are $93-120 depending on the view; the penthouses, each with a private rooftop garden, are well-priced at $105-135 s or d. Also central is **Maroochy Beach Park** (tel. 07-5444-1201), unpowered sites are $12, powered sites $15.

For fresh fish and a good serving of chips, head out along Parkyn Parade beyond Under-Water World to **Mooloolaba Fisheries.** Under Sandcastles, **Santesang Cafe,** open all day, is a good place for people-watching. On the corner of Brisbane Rd. and the Esplanade is **Montezuma's** (tel. 07-5444-8444), a large Mexican restaurant where the food is always fresh and main dishes range $10-14; open daily for lunch and dinner.

A small **information booth** outside the Westpac Bank on the Esplanade operates daily 9 a.m.-5 p.m.

MAROOCHYDORE

The coastal strip between Mooloolaba and Maroochydore features some great beaches and surf breaks, but is also very developed. Maroochydore, spread around the braided mouth of the Maroochy River, is the commercial center of the Sunshine Coast. Downtown is an ugly urban sprawl, but the beach is gorgeous. **Cotton Tree Park,** on a sandy spit of land at the end of Alexandra Parade, is an undeveloped area of cotton trees and casuarinas—the perfect place for a picnic.

Accommodations and Food

Maroochydore has a good beachfront caravan park and a number of backpacker hostels, but for other types of accommodations you're better off heading north to Coolum or Noosa or south to Mooloolaba. If you want to stay in town, try **Blue Waters Motel,** 64 6th Ave. (tel. 07-5443-6700), close to the beach and with a pool. Outside holiday periods rooms are $44 s, $49 d. On the north side of the river is **Novotel Twin Waters Resort,** a sprawling complex set around a large lagoon lined with manmade beaches. The resort also boasts one of Australia's best golf courses (call 07-5448-8011 for tee times), free water sports, and an elevated restaurant in the middle of the lagoon. Rooms are large and of a high standard, many with kitchenettes and a spa; rates start at $150 s or d. For bookings call (07) 5448-8000 or (1800) 64-2244.

Suncoast Backpackers, 50 Parker St. (tel. 07-5443-7544), is two blocks from the main drag and a 10-minute walk from the beach. Facilities are good and the hosts are friendly. Dorms are $11-13, doubles $28.

Both the **Sea Breeze Caravan Park,** Melrose Parade (tel. 07-5443-1167), right behind the Tourist Information Centre and backing onto the beach, and **Cotton Tree Caravan Park,** Esplanade (tel. 07-5443-1253), on the riverfront, have unpowered sites for $10 and powered sites for $12 with all the usual facilities. Neither has on-site vans or cabins.

Most of the Sunshine Coast's fast-food outlets lie along Maroochydore's main drag; the **Maroochydore Hotel/Motel,** Duporth Ave. (tel. 07-5443-1999), serves hearty lunches for $4-6 and dinners $8-11.

Transportation, Services, and Information

Travelers flying to the Sunshine Coast land at **Sunshine Coast Airport,** eight km north of Maroochydore. The airport is served by **Sunstate** (tel. 13-1313) from Brisbane ($85 one-way). From the airport, **Airport Bus Service** (tel. 07-5444-7288) heads south ($4 to Maroochydore), and **Henry's Airport Bus Service** (tel. 07-5449-1440) heads north ($7 to Noosa), but if you're staying at a resort transfers should be complimentary.

Sunshine Coast Coaches (tel. 07-3236-1901) operates about 10 buses daily between Brisbane Transit Centre and Maroochydore ($19 one-way), continuing to Noosa while **Sun-air** (tel. 07-5478-2811) links Brisbane Airport to the Sunshine Coast.

Maroochy Information Centre is on the corner of Aerodrome Rd. and 6th Ave., right near the beach (tel. 07-5479-1566). Hours are Mon.-Sat. 9 a.m.-4:30 p.m.

COOLUM

Coolum is usually bypassed for better-known Noosa to the north, but the long beach here is as good as any on the Sunshine Coast. The beach is screened from the main road through Coolum by coastal heath, but many unsealed roads provide access to the ocean.

At the northern end of Coolum an unsealed road spurs east to Stumers Creek, where a picnic and camping area sits alongside a shallow lagoon just a stone's throw from the beach. The western skyline is dominated by 208-meter **Mt. Coolum,** rising gently from the north to a vertical southern face.

Accommodations

Coolum Dreams, 28 Warran Rd. (tel. 07-5446-3868), is the Sunshine Coast's only B&B. Within walking distance of the beach and Hyatt Regency Coolum (see below), it offers clean and comfortable rooms with a large outdoor area and a level of service not available at resort-style accommodations. Rates of $45 s, $70 d include a continental or cooked breakfast.

Set on 140 hectares opposite Coolum Dreams, **Hyatt Regency Coolum** (tel. 07-5446-1234 or 1800-22-2188) is a five-star hostelry modeled on North American spa resorts. Along with one of Australia's top golf courses, sporting facilities include nine tennis courts, squash

courts, a lap pool, aerobics classes, and a jogging track. And while physical activities are promoted, so is relaxation, as guests may take advantage of the pool, jacuzzis, sauna, and a myriad of beauty treatments. Rates start at $240 s or d

NOOSA

At the north end of the Sunshine Coast and 150 km from Brisbane is a conglomeration of com nunities known collectively as Noosa. Best known of these is **Noosa Heads,** which has grown from a 1960s surfing hangout to one of Australia's most stylish resort towns. Yet Noosa manages to offer something for everyone—hiking in an adjacent national park, fishing and boating in a maze of channels around the mouth of the Noosa River, surfing around the headland, swimming and sunbaking at a protected beach, shopping at fashionable boutiques, and dining at various restaurants.

Noosa Heads lies along a short north-facing beach, making it one of only two places along the east coast where resort guests and residents alike have views over a beautiful beach and the ocean while enjoying direct sunshine all day long (the other spot is Wategos Beach, Byron Bay). Sandwiched between this beach, the Noosa River, and a national park, future development is curtailed, forming an exclusive beachfront enclave along just one short street.

Noosa National Park

While tourist and residential development has destroyed most of southeast Queensland's original coastal habitat, an area of 442 hectares around Noosa Heads remains undisturbed, protected as a national park since 1879. It's a beautiful stretch of coast, punctuated by short beaches flanked by rocky headlands and accessed along short hiking trails leading through forests of eucalypt, open meadows, and areas of coastal heath. The popular **Coastal Track** (2.7 km one-way) begins at the end of Park Rd., closely following the coast past Tea Tree Bay, Dolphin Point, and Granite Bay, ending at Hells Gate. It's possible to return along **Tanglewood Track** through an area of rainforest 4.2 km back to the carpark. The park's main entrance is one km east of Noosa Heads along Park Road. A boardwalk also links town to the park. The **Park Information Centre,** at the end of Park Rd. (tel. 07-5447-3243), is open daily 9 a.m.-5 p.m.

From the south, a trail leads into the park from Parkedge Road. For an overview of the entire area, head to the lookout at the end of Viewland Dr. (off Noosa Drive).

Recreation

Swimming, surfing, fishing, and hiking—all the best things at Noosa—are free, but there are also a lot of activities you can pay for. The most worthwhile of these is a cruise on the Noosa River with **Everglades Waterbus Co.** (tel. 07-5447-1878). Cruises depart Harbour Town Marina, Tewantin, daily at 10 a.m. **Noosa Sea Sports,** in Noosa Sound Shopping Centre (tel. 07-5447-3426), rents surfboards and fishing gear.

Accommodations

Hastings Street is *the* place to stay in Noosa, but, naturally, it's not the cheapest and demand for rooms is particularly high throughout summer. During this period, prices also rise dramatically, up to 100% in some cases.

The least expensive beachfront rooms are at **Noosa Court Beach Front Motel,** 55 Hastings St. (tel. 07-5447-4455). Rooms are basic, but each has a private bathroom, small kitchen area, and private balcony with table setting. Rates for beachfront rooms are $95-100 ($130 in summer), while those away from the beach are $70-80 ($80-100 in summer). They also have a two-bedroom suite for a reasonable $160 ($180 in summer). Also on the beach is **Seahaven,** 13 Hastings St. (tel. 07-5447-3422), a modern complex with 46 one- and two-bedroom units, each with a kitchen and balcony. Rates for the smallest rooms (sleeping four) are $160-190 ($220-270 during holidays), and they also have a few small rooms facing the street for $85. The two-bedroom penthouses (sleeping six) are $220 per night and have a private rooftop garden.

Castaways Holiday Motel, David Low Way (tel. 07-5447-3488), is six km south of Noosa and a 200-meter walk through bushland to Sunrise Beach. Facilities are of a high standard, including a pool, barbecue, and laundry; $60 s, $70 d; those with kitchenettes are $80-100. Out on Gympie Terrace, in Noosaville, try **Palm Tree Lodge,** 233 Gympie Terrace (tel. 07-5449-7311), for $45 s, $65 d.

Backpackers have a couple of choices. Closest to Noosa Heads is **Koala Beach Resort,** 44 Noosa Dr., Noosa Junction (tel. 07-5447-3355), a one-km walk from the beach. Facilities include a pool, communal kitchen, cafe, and bikes for rent. Dorms are $12 per night, doubles start at $38. **Noosa Backpackers Resort,** 9 William St. Munna Pt. (tel. 07-5449-

8151), is farther from town but has good facilities. Dorms are $12 pp, doubles $28.

Content Caravan Park, Weyba Rd. (tel. 07-5449-7746), in Noosaville has tent sites for $12, powered sites for $14-16, and on-site vans for $24; book well in advance for school holidays.

Food

Hastings Street is lined with cafes and restaurants, many with tables scattered across the footpath. Most are casual affairs, but prices are often high. Diagonally opposite the information center, **Sandy's Delicatessen** is a good choice for a light breakfast; healthy muffins are $1.50 and breakfasts $4-8. Another popular breakfast spot is **Tea Tree Cafe** in the Sheraton Resort (tel. 07-5449-4787); the large hot and cold buffet is $19.95 pp and from the outside tables you'll catch the morning sun. Another place bathed in sunlight is **Eduardo's** (tel. 07-5447-5875), right on the beach at the front of the Tingirana Motel. Open all day, breakfast dishes range $4-9, lunch and dinner dishes average $11. For great fish and chips (from $6), head to **Saltwater,** at 8 Hastings St. (tel. 07-5447-2234). Next door is **Aqua Bar Cafe** (tel. 07-5447-3237), decorated in typical "Noosa style"— simply furnished with bright pastel colors. The menu features mostly seafood; open daily 11:30 a.m.-10:30 p.m. Another casual place is **Laguna Bay Beach Club,** on the beach side of the Sheraton complex. **Cafe Vespa,** Bay Village, Hastings St. (tel. 07-5447-2473), specializes in pizza from a wood-fired oven ($11.95-14.50 for a large) and has a bar and veranda. **La Plage,** Hastings St. (tel. 07-5447-3308), has a Mediterranean feel and features French cuisine using local seafood. Main meals are $16.50-22.

Noosa's least expensive eatery is **Betty's Burgers,** in the alley linking Hastings St. to Eduardo's; hamburgers start at $1 and you'd be hard pressed to spend more than $5 for lunch. For other cheap eats head to Noosa Junction or Noosaville.

Transportation, Services, and Information

From Brisbane, **Sunstate** (tel. 13-1313) flies to Sunshine Coast Airport at Maroochydore, from where **Henry's Airport Bus Service** (tel. 07-5449-1440) makes connections to Noosa ($7

one-way). **Sun-air** (tel. 07-5478-2811) links Noosa to Brisbane Airport ($19 one-way). **Tewantin Bus Service** (tel. 07-5449-7422) runs frequently between the communities of Noosa and Tewantin and Maroochydore. All major car rental firms have outlets in Noosa. Contact **Sunshine 4WD Hire** (tel. 07-5447-3702) for four-wheel drives ($100-150 per day) or **Noosa Moke Hire** (tel. 07-5447-3777) for mokes ($40-50 per day).

Noosa Information Centre (tel. 07-5447-4988) is at the Hastings St. roundabout; open daily 9 a.m.-5 p.m.

SUNSHINE COAST HINTERLAND

Tropical fruit farms and endless fields of sugar cane dominate the part of the Sunshine Coast hinterland where the Bruce Highway runs through, but it is west of the highway in the Blackall Range where the scenery is most spectacular.

South of Nambour, along the Bruce Highway, are a number of commercial attractions including the **Big Pineapple,** part of a small theme park where you can visit a pineapple plantation and macadamia nut farm, ride a sugarcane train, and take a boat ride through Tomorrow's Harvest. It's six km south of Nambour (tel. 07-5442-1333). North of Nambour, in Yandina, drop by the **Ginger Factory** (tel. 07-5446-7100), the largest such factory in the world. Visitors watch a video, view work areas, and get another opportunity for a ride on a sugarcane train.

Blackall Range and Montville

The Blackall Range rises dramatically west of the Bruce Highway; part of an ancient lava flow, its highest ridge is traversed by a scenic road that passes through the villages of **Maleny, Montville, Flaxton,** and **Mapleton.** The 50-km route through these villages begins at Landsborough, west of Caloundra, and ends in Nambour.

Styled on an English village, Montville is the most developed of the hinterland towns, with an 800-meter strip of tearooms, restaurants and craft shops. Although a couple of artisans have lived in the town for years, it's only re

Montville's relaxed atmosphere and many arts and crafts shops make the town a pleasant detour.

ently that tourism has taken off. Literally dozens of potters, sculptors, glassblowers, weavers, and other artists call Montville home. Also in the village are tearooms, cafes, restaurants, and numerous B&Bs.

Montville Mountain Inn (tel. 07-5442-9499) is a Tudor-style accommodation in the middle of all the action. Rooms are large, many have views, and there's also a pool and tennis court or guest use. Rates are $46 s, $55 d.

Just north of Montville is the turnoff to 353-hectare **Kondalilla National Park,** a remnant of rainforest that once covered the entire Blackall Range. The park's highlight is Kondalilla Falls. Reach a lookout above the falls along a 1.2-km rail from the picnic area. To get a different perspective of the falls, continue one km from the lookout to the valley floor.

NORTH FROM NOOSA

The Bruce Highway stays well inland, passing through the historic gold-mining town of Gympie. The coast is 60 km east of Gympie, but a detour to what is known as the Cooloola Coast, much of it protected by Cooloola National Park, is worthwhile for the colorful sand dunes and lack of crowds.

Gympie

In 1867 Queensland was on the verge of bankruptcy, so when James Nash found gold on the Mary River, the government took more than a passing interest. In the first few years, 15,000 diggers converged on the area. Over four million ounces were taken from the goldfields before operations closed in 1923. The best place to get a feeling of the town's beginnings is at **Gympie Historical Museum,** on the Bruce Hwy. south of town (tel. 07-5482-3995). A number of buildings have been moved to the disused mining site, as has rail rolling stock, horse-drawn buggies, and other pioneer relics. The museum is open daily 9 a.m.-5 p.m. and admission is $4. Adjacent to the museum is **Deep Creek Fossicking Area,** but you need a fossicking license ($5.10), available from the Tourist Information Centre or courthouse, to pan for gold.

Tamworth may be Australia's country music capital, but the **Gympie Muster** is Australia's biggest single country concert, attracting about 30,000 fans to the state forest west of Amamoor for three days of music on the last weekend of August. (Get current information from the Tourist Information Centre.)

Great Eastern Motor Inn, 27 Geordie Rd. (tel. 07-5482-7288), south of town opposite the Tourist Information Centre, has large modern rooms for $55 s, $60 d. Campers should head to **Gympie Caravan Park,** Tin Can Bay Rd. (tel. 07-5486-4555), which has rooms for $38 s, $50 d. **Ace Caravan Park,** Esplanade (tel. 07-5486-4152), has sites for $9-10 and on-site vans for $24.

The **Tourist Information Centre** is adjacent to the fossicking area south of Gympie (tel. 07-5482-5444). In the same building is a **Department of Environment and Heritage** office (tel. 07-5482-4189), good for Fraser Island information and permits. Both offices are open daily 8:30 a.m.-3:30 p.m.

Tin Can Bay

This small fishing town of 7,100, 45 km northwest of Gympie, is spread along a low-lying headland jutting into a maze of channels that make up the protected waters of Tin Can Inlet. Development has taken its toll on the surrounding landscape, with the road into town passing through cleared subdivisions, but once in the town, it won't take long to appreciate the slower pace of life. Commercial fishing is important to the local economy, but the sleepy village is also a popular holiday spot. Follow the main road through town to the end of the headland where a sprawling parking lot takes prime position on the point. **Luxury Afloat** operates yacht and houseboat rentals from the marina. Basic seafaring skills are required for rentals, but the area has nothing like those nasty reefs farther north, and you can explore hundreds of waterways and secluded sandy beaches. Rates start at $150 per day for a 10-meter yacht, rising considerably during holiday periods. For details call (07) 5486-4864.

Sandcastle Motel, Tin Can Bay Rd. (tel. 07-5486-4555), has rooms for $38 s, $50 d. **Ace Caravan Park,** Esplanade (tel. 07-5486-4152), is central and has sites for $12 and on-site vans for $22, but you'll need advance reservations in holiday periods. Overlooking the marina complex on Oyster Parade is **Marina Restaurant** (tel. 07-5486-4400), a casual place with inside and outside tables and a menu featuring local seafood.

Rainbow Beach

As the crow flies, Rainbow Beach is just eight km east of Tin Can Bay, but by road it's closer to 40 km. The village overlooks the long sandy beach of Wide Bay, which extends to Inskip Point, southern gateway to Fraser Island (the town is jammed with four-wheel drive enthusiasts year-round). The beach in front of town is generally safe for swimming, but much of the best scenery is in Cooloola National Park (see below).

Rainbow Beach Hotel/Motel (tel. 07-5486-3125), right on the beach, has rooms of a reasonable standard for $38 s, $45 d. More up market, but worth every dollar, is delightful **Rainbow Shores** (tel. 07-5486-3233), north of town in a forest of eucalypts and with a deserted sandy beach just meters away. Each two-story unit is fully self-contained, with views extending across the beach and to Point Danger as well as back to the landscaped pool area. Rates start at $80 per night for a one-bedroom beach house, rising to $150 for a three-bedroom unit. **Rainbow Beach Holiday Village,** just across the road from the main beach (tel. 07-5486-3222), has sites for $10-12, on-site vans for $25-32, and good units for $45-60; book in advance for the best sites.

The town has a tavern, supermarket, petrol station, a couple of bakeries, and a good fish and chips shop. The **Tourist Information Centre** is on the south side of town (tel. 07-5486-3227).

Cooloola National Park

As wind and rain erode the mountain ranges of northern New South Wales, sediment washes down rivers into the ocean. Prevailing winds and wave action have pushed masses of sand northward, creating a long stretch of sandy coastline and Fraser Island to the north. Over thousands of years, sand has blown off the beach and become entangled in the banksia and she-oak forests along the coast. This has built up, covering whole forests and forming sand dunes more than 200 meters high. One of the park's most famous features is its multicolored sand, which lines many stretches of the coast. A different environment is found in the south of the park, along the Noosa River, where paperbarks, bloodwoods, and low-lying heaths and ferns thrive.

See the most colorful dunes along a two-km walk on the beach from Rainbow Beach. From the dunes, it's possible to continue to **Double Island Point** (10 km one-way), but check tides before setting out. Five km south of Rainbow Beach, an unsealed track leads into the park, ending at a picnic area from where it's a short walk to **Poona Lake,** a body of trapped rainwater tinted brown by tea tree extractions. Cooloola Way is an unsealed route linking Rainbow Beach Rd. to Pomona, just off the Bruce

Hwy. north of Cooroy. Off this road are more unsealed roads, leading to the Noosa River and Lake Cootharaba.

The **Park Information Centre** is in Rainbow Beach (tel. 07-5486-3160); open daily 5:30 a.m.-4:30 p.m.

SUNSHINE COAST TO GLADSTONE

While tourist and residential development has blighted much of Queensland's beautiful coastline, development between the Sunshine Coast and Gladstone is contained in only a couple of areas, and the hinterland is scattered with many thousands of hectares of sugarcane.

The region's main tourist center is Hervey Bay, Australia's whalewatching capital and gateway to magnificent Fraser Island, the world's largest sand island and a paradise for nature lovers and four-wheel drive enthusiasts. The other main population center between the Sunshine Coast and Gladstone is Bundaberg, more famous for its rum distillery than for the thousands of turtles that nest on a nearby beach.

Maryborough

First settled in the 1840s as a port for wool and timber transportation, this historic city of 22,000 sits on the Mary River, a few kilometers inland and halfway between Gympie and Bundaberg. Many buildings from its early era remain, and along with tree-lined streets and Queenslanders, the city has a real sense of country charm. Many impressive historic buildings remain on Wharf St., including restored hotels, a customs house, post office, and courthouse. Also on Wharf St. is **Queens Park** (the perfect place for a picnic), sloping toward the river. **Brennan & Geraghty's Store,** on Lennons St., has operated as a general store for more than 100 years. Traffic down the main street is diverted every Thursday for **Heritage Market Day** and in early April is **Heritage Week.**

Many historic downtown hotels, including the **Criterion** (tel. 071-21-3043), offer accommoda-

On 1 November 1997 telephone numbers in this section will change. To dial the new number, simply add "41" to the old number. As an example, (071) 12-3456 becomes 4112-3456. The new area code will be (07).

tion, or stay in one of the motels strung out along Ferry St., the main route into town from the south. Also on Ferry St. is **Wallace Caravan Park** (tel. 071-21-3970); sites are $9-14, cabins $28.

The **Tourist Information Centre** is at 30 Ferry St. (tel. 071-21-4111); open daily 9 a.m.-5 p.m.

HERVEY BAY

Until a few years ago, the only reason to detour from the main highway to Hervey Bay was to hop aboard a ferry out to Fraser Island, but the development of a whalewatching industry has seen things change quickly. Until the mid-1980s, the shoreline of Hervey Bay was dotted with sleepy settlements off the main tourist route, seemingly a million miles from the hustle and bustle of other east coast resort towns. But in the last decade, shivering southerners discovered Hervey Bay's ideal climate, low land prices, and laid-back atmosphere. What were once five separate towns along the bay are now one long strip of development.

It's difficult to get lost in Hervey Bay. The main road into town from the Bruce Highway ends at **Pialba,** from where the Esplanade heads northwest to the town of **Point Vernon** and east to **Scarness, Torquay,** and **Urangan.** The marina at Urangan is the departure point for whalewatching day trips and foot passengers heading to Fraser Island.

Whalewatching

Between early August and mid-October migrating humpback whales rest in the calm and shallow waters of Platypus Bay, on the west coast of Fraser Island (a one- to two-hour boat trip from Hervey Bay). During migration, whales can be seen at many places along the eastern seaboard, but the waters off Hervey Bay are the only place they stop for any length of time, allowing us humans the privilege of watching them frolic on their rest days. The whales have been following the same

breaching humpback whale

migration pattern for eons, but only recently has anyone except marine biologists shown any great interest in their activity. At last count, 18 operators were running half- and full-day whalewatching trips from the marina at Urangan. Prices range $40-50 pp for a full day on the water, with a lunch, tea and coffee, and running commentary all in- cluded in the price. To make a booking, head to **Fraser Coast Tour Booking Office,** Buccanee Ave., Urangan (tel. 071-25-3287), near where the boats depart. Here, they'll help you decide which boat is best for your needs, away from the hype and confusion of the many other booking offices in town. Bookings can also be made through many accommodations. We had a great day on the medium-sized *Golden Phoenix,* with a cold chicken and salad lunch and, most important, knowledgeable crew.

Throughout the whalewatching season, the **Oceania Project** (tel. 066-85-8128 or 018-40-9178) conducts five-night six-day expeditions viewing whales and dolphins while learning about their lives and the ocean in which they live. The project is involved in long-term re- search on humpback whales, and guests take an active role in collecting data. All meals and accommodation on board are included in the price of $950 pp.

Other Sights

If whalewatching is called off for bad weather, the following commercial attractions may kill a few hours. **Hervey Bay Natureworld,** on the corner of Fairway Dr. and Maryborough Rd., Pialba, features a variety of native fauna, including crocodiles fed daily at 11:30 a.m. The **Great White Shark Expo,** 533 Esplanade (tel. 071-28-9137), operated by Australian shark hunter Vic Hislop, features three frozen great white sharks, up to six meters long. Apart from justifying why they "need" to be killed, the display is interesting, in a gruesome kind of way. Admission is $8; open daily 8 a.m.-6 p.m. Farther along the Esplanade, toward the marina, is **Neptune's Coral Cave,** an aquarium with a variety of reef life. Near the aquarium is **Urangan Pier,** extending over one km into the bay. Originally built for loading sugar, it's now popular with anglers.

Accommodations

Although Hervey Bay has many caravan parks and backpacker lodges, motel accommodation is limited, and getting a room, especially during the whalewatching season, may be difficult. Most motels are spread along the Esplanade, across the road from Hervey Bay. One of the least expensive, **Seven Seas Motel,** 573 Es-

planade, Urangan (tel. 071-28-9699), is $30 s, $40 d, rising to $55 in holiday periods. **Hervey Bay Motel,** 518 Esplanade, Urangan (tel. 071-28-9277), is similarly priced. Part of the marina complex at Urangan is **Great Sandy Straits Marina Resort** (tel. 071-28-9999), comprising luxury two-bedroom fully self-contained units overlooking the marina. Rates are $90-120 s or d, depending on the season.

Koala Backpackers, 408 Esplanade, Torquay (tel. 071-25-3601), is the largest hostel in town. Beds are clean and comfortable and there's also a pool. Dorm beds are $12-13 and double rooms $28. **Beaches Backpackers,** 195 Torquay Terrace, Scarness (tel. 071-24-1322), is away from the bay, but it has a pool and facilities are good; from $12 pp. **Colonial Backpackers,** Boat Harbour Dr., Urangan (tel. 071-25-1844), set among natural bushland, has all the usual facilities and is a short walk from the marina. Dorm beds are $13-15 and twins are $28.

More than 20 caravan parks cater to campers in the Hervey Bay area. **Torquay Caravan Park,** the Esplanade (tel. 071-25-1578), is right on the beach and central to the marina and shopping area of Pialba; unpowered sites $10, powered sites $13. Also in Torquay is **Happy Wanderer Village Caravan Park,** 105 Truro St. (tel. 071-25-1103), with the very best of facilities. Unpowered sites are $11, powered sites $14, and sites with private bathrooms $18. On-site vans are $28 and cabins $35-55.

Food
Service clubs dish out the best bargain meals. **Hervey Bay Sportsmen's Club,** Pier St., Urangan (tel. 071-28-9348), has lunch in the bistro from $4 and dinner from $5. They also offer a small buffet dinner for $10.45, Fri.-Sun. **Hervey Bay Boat Club,** Buccaneer Ave. (tel. 071-28-9643), has a similarly priced bistro and a restaurant with the best views in town. Away from the beach is **Last Resort Tavern,** Boat Harbour Dr., Pialba (tel. 071-24-4111), serving counter lunch and dinner daily in a family atmosphere. **Gringo's,** 449 Esplanade, Torquay (tel. 071-25-1644), is a Mexican restaurant, with most main meals under $10. The best of many seafood restaurants is **Delfino's,** 383 Esplanade, Scarness (tel. 071-24-2466), open daily for dinner with live music on Friday and Saturday nights.

Transportation, Services, and Information
Sunstate (tel. 13-1313) flies daily between Brisbane and Hervey Bay. The airport is on Booral Rd., a $5 cab ride from most accommodations and the marina. All major bus lines operate between Brisbane and Hervey Bay ($30 one-way) and also continue farther north. These buses terminate at **Geldard's Bay Central Coach Terminal,** Central Ave., Pialba (tel. 071-24-4000). **Maryborough Hervey Bay Coaches** (tel. 071-21-3719) operates a regular service along the Esplanade (except Sunday). **Pier One Fruit Market,** 1 Pier St., Urangan (tel. 071-28-9471), rents bikes for $15 per day.

Hervey Bay has no official information center. Instead, there are many privately operated concerns, more interested in selling tours and tacky gifts than handing out information. One exception is **Fraser Coast Tour Booking Office,** Buccaneer Ave., Urangan (tel. 071-25-3287), across the parking lot from the marina. The office produces a handy reference sheet detailing all

whalewatching trips and takes bookings for these trips, as well as for Fraser Island tours and local accommodations (and their fish and chips aren't bad either).

FRASER ISLAND

Fraser Island, 120 km long, 22 km wide and totaling 184,000 hectares in area, is the largest sand island in the world. Apart from a few volcanic outcrops, the island is entirely composed of sand, with Seventy Five Mile Beach, on the island's east coast, one of the world's longest beaches. But the island is more than one great sand dune. Much of the 184,000 hectares is covered in vegetation, including many areas of rainforest and more than 25 species of mammals. Over one-third of the island is protected by **Great Sandy National Park,** and the entire island is listed with UNESCO as a World Heritage Area.

A network of sandy trails, accessible only by four-wheel drive, crisscross the island. If you don't have a four-wheel drive, you'll need to rent from the mainland or jump aboard one of the many tours offered. Access to the island is by barge (for vehicles) or fast catamaran, and once on the island a variety of accommodations are available or, for the self-sufficient, it's possible to camp.

FRASER ISLAND

Many ships were wrecked on Fraser Island after Captain Cook first sighted its east coast in 1770, but, ironically, the island is named for the survivor of a wreck that occurred off Mackay, 300 km north. The tragedy happened in 1836, when the brig *Stirling Castle* sank and the survivors drifted southward, coming ashore on the Great Sandy Island. Although cared for by Kooris, many died on the island before a rescue party could reach them two months later. One of the few survivors was the captain's wife, Eliza Fraser. On return to England she told wild stories of torture and savagery by the island's natives, and, as a mark of her "bravery" in the situation, the name of the island was changed from Great Sandy to Fraser.

FRASER ISLAND

SANDY CAPE

MANANN BEACH.

ROONEY POINT

PLATYPUS BAY

GREAT SANDY NATIONAL PARK

WADDY POINT.

INDIAN HEAD

HERVEY BAY

POINT VERNON

MOON POINT

SCARNESS

PIALBA

URANGAN

TORQUAY

WOODY ISLAND N.P.

CATHEDRAL BEACH

WRECK OF MAHENO

HAPPY VALLEY RESORT

LAKE GARAWONGERA

KINGFISHER BAY RESORT

LAKE McKENZIE

CENTRAL STATION

EURONG BEACH RESORT

LAKE BIRRABEEN

MARYBOROUGH

TO BUNDABERG

GREAT SANDY STRAIT

SEVENTY MILE BEACH

SOUTH PACIFIC OCEAN

MARY RIVER

BRUCE HWY.

HOOK POINT

INSKIP POINT

TO GYMPIE AND BRISBANE

RAINBOW BEACH

TO GYMPIE

DOUBLE ISLAND POINT

0   10 km

History

When Europeans settled the Hervey Bay area in the 1850s, they herded the local Koori over to Fraser Island, using it as a kind of prison. For 30,000 years the island had been a seasonal hunting ground for the natives, who knew it as K'gari, meaning paradise. But their paradise changed quickly and dramatically with the coming of white settlers in the 1800s. As loggers realized the island's potential, the Koori were herded back to the mainland and by 1904 only a small mission of 200 remained.

Part of the island was put aside as a reserve in 1923, but the logging continued. In 1974 a license was granted for a large-scale rutile mining operation, provoking one of the most vicious battles between environmentalists and mining companies that Australia has ever seen. It ended in 1976 with a ban on mining.

In an ironic twist, the island's beauty, which

environmentalists fought so hard to preserve, is now its own worst nightmare—attracting 350,000 visitors annually, up from around 10,000 in 1970.

Exploring the Island
By Four-Wheel Drive

To get the most out of a trip to Fraser Island, you'll need to travel by four-wheel drive, whether in a vehicle rented from the mainland or on a tour. Four-wheel drives can be rented on the island and on the mainland. In Hervey Bay **Aussie Trax,** 56 Boat Harbour Dr., Pialba (tel. 071-24-4433), is among the cheapest, with ex-army Land Rovers for $77 per day (this is one of the few companies allowing one-day rentals). **Bay 4WD Centre,** 114 Boat Harbour Dr. (tel. 071-28-2981), offers small four-wheel drives for $80 per day (seating two) and Land Cruisers (seating five) for $115. Rentals are also possible on the island, and although the cost of barging the vehicle is saved, rates are higher. Small Suzukis at Kingfisher Bay Resort (tel. 071-20-3333) are $150 for a full day. For transportation details see below.

Driving on the island requires a permit ($15 per vehicle). These are available from the Department of Environment and Heritage in Brisbane or Gympie, or the council offices on Tavistock St., Scarness (tel. 071-25-0222).

Exploring the Island on a Tour

For those without the necessary experience to drive off-road vehicles, a tour is the most convenient and enjoyable way to see the island. A great variety of day and overnight island tours operate from Hervey Bay. The tour offered by **Kingfisher Bay Resort** (tel. 071-25-5511) is typical and includes transport to the island, a four-wheel drive along part of Seventy Five Mile Beach, a visit to the wreck of *Maheno,* a peak at the colored sands of Cathedral Beach, and a swim in freshwater lakes. The cost of $58 pp includes morning and afternoon tea and a buffet lunch. It departs Urangan daily at 8:30 a.m. and returns at 5 p.m. **Fraser Venture Day Tours** (tel. 071-25-4444) operates similar tours for a few dollars less. **Sun Safari Tours** (tel. 07-5486-3154) operates from Rainbow Beach Caravan Park, departing daily at 8 a.m., and travels up Seventy Five Mile Beach as far north as Cathe-

dral Beach. Lunch at Eurong Beach Resort included in the price of adult $50, child $25.

Many overnight tours, operated by backpacker lodges in Hervey Bay, cost as little as $80 for three days (not including food and petrol). **Fraser Island Top Tours** (tel. 071-25 3933) offers an overnight tour inclusive of meals transport, and accommodation at Happy Valley Resort for $130 pp.

Accommodations

Kingfisher Bay Resort, the island's largest an most luxurious accommodation, has been de signed to blend with the environment—using Australian timbers—and is spread over 6 hectares of natural bushland. Each of the spa cious hotel rooms has a balcony, TV, and mod ern bathroom. Rates include resort activities ranger-led hikes, and a hot buffet breakfast while other options include whalewatching (i season), island tours ($56 pp), four-wheel driv rental ($150 per day), and scuba diving ($50, in cluding equipment); $180 s or d. The resort als features a general store, petrol supplies, bars bakery, pizzeria, and three restaurants. Ca (071) 20-3333 or (1800) 07-2555 for bookings

A couple of the old logging and sand-minin settlements have accommodations, includin **Happy Valley Resort** (tel. 071-27-9144) on th island's east coast. An overnight stay at thi low-key resort, plus island transfers, day tours and all meals, is $130 pp.

The island has four formal campgrounds (wit drinking water, toilets, and showers), but camp ing is allowed just about anywhere on the is land for $7.50 per site. **Cathedral Beach Resor** (tel. 071-27-9177) is a commercial operatio with campsites for $14.

Transportation,
Services, and Information

Two vehicular ferries run to the island three times daily from River Heads, south of Uran gan. For bookings on the *Fraser Venture* ca (071) 25-4444; on the *Major Dundee* call King fisher Bay Resort at (071) 25-5511. The fare is $50 per vehicle round-trip plus $3 pp. Anothe vehicular ferry is *Fraser II* (tel. 071-25-3933) which departs Urangan twice daily for Moor Point, a remote area of the island's west coast Walk-on passengers on all vehicular barge

ay $10 round-trip. *Kingfisher I,* a passenger
atamaran, jets between Urangan and King-
sher Bay Resort for $25 pp round-trip. Heli-
opter transfers between Hervey Bay and King-
sher Bay Resort are $50 pp; for details contact
kytech at (071) 25-3287.

From Inskip Point, north of Rainbow Beach
see "North from Noosa" under "Sunshine Coast"
arlier in this chapter), *Rainbow Venture* makes
egular crossings to the island's southern point.
he fare is $35 round-trip for a vehicle, including
assengers. Make bookings by calling (07)
486-3154.

Obtain island information and permits from
epartment of Environment and Heritage of-
ces on the mainland. Once on the island, the
ld forestry depot at Central Station has dis-
lays on the island's natural and human history.
you're looking for a book to while away the
ours, try to get hold of Patrick White's *A Fringe
f Leaves,* an intriguing account of Eliza Fraser's
tay on the island. The *Fraser Island Sunmap*
available at most stores, $6) is essential for in-
ependent island exploration.

BUNDABERG

undaberg is a sugarcane-growing center of
0,000, 50 km east of the Bruce Highway and
70 km north of Brisbane. The Burnett River
ows through town, draining into the ocean a
ew kilometers east of the city center by a string of
leepy beachfront settlements. Unlike many other
ane-growing regions, where raw cane is trans-
orted for processing, all parts of production take
lace in Bundaberg, including the distillation of
ustralia's most popular spirit, **Bundaberg Rum.**

Mon Repos Environmental Park
ast of Bundaberg is **Mon Repos Beach,** the
argest and most accessible turtle rookery in
nainland Australia. Four species of turtles nest on
ne beach; loggerhead are the most common,
vith green, flatback, and leatherback turtles also
resent. Between late November and early January, female turtles waddle up the beach after
lark to lay their eggs in the dunes beyond the
each. For two months from mid-January newly
atched turtles emerge from nests to make the
ong trek down the beach and into the water.

Bundaberg's main street

ANDREW HEMPSTEAD

Nearly all activity takes place after dark, with the
most active times being an hour each side of
high tide. When this tide falls between 7 and 9
p.m. the viewing areas can get very crowded.
Access to the beach during nesting periods is
restricted to ranger-led tours that leave from the
park information center behind the beach. For
further details call (071) 59-2628.

Town Sights
The **Bundaberg Rum Distillery** is definitely
the city's number-one attraction. Its connection
to the cane-growing industry is molasses, a
sticky (and smelly) syrup extracted from sugarcane at an adjacent factory. Tours of the distillery include a short video, a walk through all aspects of rum production, and, of course, a drink
of rum. Tours depart four to five times daily and
cost $3 pp. The distillery is on Avenue St., East
Bundaberg (tel. 071-52-4077).

On the same side of town as the distillery is
Schmeider's Cooperage & Craft Centre,
Alexandra St. (tel. 071-52-8573), which displays

BUNDABERG

TO ROSEDALE

KOLAN HWY.

TO MYSTERY
CRATERS AND
GIN GIN

YOUNG ST.

HINKLER AVE.

BERT
HINKLER
MUSEUM

GAVIN ST.

BURNETT   RIVER

ALEXANDRA ST.

AVENUE ST.

BUNDABERG
RUM DISTILLERY

TO MON REPOS
AND OTHER BEACHES

BURNETT   RIVER

HARRIETT ISLAND

SPINNAKER
STONEGRILL
AND BAR

SEE DETAIL

QUAY ST.

WALLA ST.

BOURBONG ST.

BUNDABERG   CREEK

TOURIST INFORMATION
CENTRE

BOURBONG ST.

CREEK

SALTWATER

MARYBOROUGH ST.

WALKER ST.

WALKER ST.

ELLIOTT HEADS RD.

ISIS HWY.

TO MARYBOROUGH

TO ELLIOTT HEADS

DETAIL

QUAY ST.

TANTITHA   ST.

GRAND
HOTEL

ROYAL
MOTEL

PEACOCK GARDEN
AND NUMERO UNO

MATILDA
MOTEL

HOG'S
BREATH CAFE

CITY CENTRE
BACKPACKERS

SUGAR
COUNTRY
MOTOR INN

BOURBONG

STOCKMAN'S CAFE

ST.

WOONGARRA

BAROLIN   ST.

TARGO   ST.

COACH STATION

BINGERA   ST.

BURRUM   ST.

MCLEAN

MARYBOROUGH   ST.

WOODOOOMA

CROFTON   ST.

ELECTRA

BUNDABERG
BACKPACKERS AND
TRAVELLERS LODGE

ST.

ST.

NOON

NOT TO SCALE

he art of making wooden barrels, wood-turn-
ng, pottery, and blacksmithing, as well as selling
wide range of interesting souvenirs. It's open
Mon.-Fri. 9 a.m.-5 p.m., Sat.-Sun. 9 a.m.-3 p.m.

Bert Hinkler, an aviator best known for his
928 solo flight between England and Australia,
was born in Bundaberg. He lived part of his life
n England, and a few years back his English
ouse was transported to Bundaberg and turned
nto a museum featuring his life and feats, in-
luding media reports of his most famous flight.
he museum is open daily 10 a.m.-4 p.m. and
dmission is a worthwhile $3. It's on the road out
o Gin Gin on Young St. (tel. 071-52-0222). On
he same side of the river are **mystery craters,**
f an unknown origin and dated by geologists as
eing about 25 million years old. Admission is $3
nd the site is open daily 8 a.m.-5 p.m.

The beaches east of Bundaberg won't win any
eauty contests, but swimming at them is safe,
nd they are separated by rocky headlands of
olcanic origin, home to interesting marinelife
hriving in rock pools. The best beaches are at
Bargara and farther south at **Elliott Heads.**

Accommodations
Grand Hotel, 89 Bourbong St. (tel. 071-51-
441), has clean and comfortable rooms with
shared facilities for $15 s, $25 d. Handy to the
enter of town is the **Royal Motel,** 155 Bour-
ong St. (tel. 071-51-2201), where basic rooms
re $28 s, $35 d. **Matilda Motel,** 209 Bourbong
St. (tel. 071-51-4717), has rooms of a higher
tandard, as well as a pool and laundry; $38 s,
48 d. The nicest place in town is **Sugar Coun-
ry Motor Inn,** 220 Bourbong St. (tel. 071-53-
166), with large elegantly decorated rooms
nd all modern conveniences; $56 s, $60 d.

Bundaberg's backpacker lodges are geared
mainly to seasonal workers, and if you've got the
orrect visas, lodge staff will help you find work
ruit-picking (Oct.-July). **Bundaberg Backpackers and Travellers Lodge,** corner Targo
nd Crofton Streets (tel. 071-52-2080), right opposite the bus depot, is modern, and being purpose-built has all the usual facilities, including a
pleasant outdoor barbecue area. All beds are
13 pp per night or $85 a week including trans-
portation to crop farms. A little cheaper is **City
Centre Backpackers,** 216 Bourbong St. (tel.
071-51-3501), where dorm beds are $11 and

beds in self-contained motel units with TV and
private facilities are $12.

Turtle Sands Caravan Park, Mon Repos
Beach (tel. 071-59-2340), is right on the beach,
within walking distance of the turtle rookery and
home to many native birds. Sites are $13-15 per
night, on-site vans go for $20-30, cabins $33,
self-contained units $45, and deluxe villas, with
ocean views, are $52.

Food
Stockman's Cafe, 142 Bourbong St. (tel. 071-53-
4774), serves Australian-style meals, including
hearty breakfasts with damper bread for $5. The
rest of the day, it's damper and meat pies. For
counter meals, head to the Grand Hotel, at 89
Bourbong St., where lunchtime specials are just
$2.50 and meals in the beer garden are $5-8.
Peacock Garden, 161 Bourbong St. (tel. 071-52-
5588), is a popular Chinese joint, and a door
away is **Numero Uno,** 167 Bourbong St. (tel.
071-51-3666), a rowdy Italian restaurant where
large servings of pasta are $8-13. The **Hog's
Breath Cafe,** 66 Quay St. (tel. 071-53-5777),
may be American, but its setting in Bundaberg is
true-blue Australian—a restored Queenslander
overlooking the Burnett River. The food's not
cheap, around $13-18 for a main dish, but the
atmosphere is great; open daily for lunch and
dinner. The **Spinnaker Stonegrill and Bar,** Quay
St. (tel. 071-52-8033), specializes in local
seafood, and prices are reasonable, with the outdoor tables having panoramic river views.

A local institution is Sunday lunch at **Bucca
Hotel,** 30 km north of Bundaberg on the road out
to Rosedale (tel. 071-57-8171). The barbecue
costs just $3, including all the salad you can
eat, and kicks off at 1 p.m.

Transportation,
Services, and Information
All northbound trains from Brisbane make stops
at Bundaberg; $43 one-way. The railway sta-
tion is on McLean St., close to downtown. Buses
terminate at the **Coach Station** on Targo Street.
All major bus lines stop at Bundaberg. To make
onward travel arrangements or book local tours,
head to **Stewart and Sons Travel,** in the Coach
Station (tel. 071-52-9700). **Reasonable Rentals**
(tel. 071-51-3058) rents cars from $30 per day
including insurance and unlimited kilometers.

Town of 1770 is a sleepy village overlooking a protected inlet.

The **Tourist Information Centre** is on the main highway into town from the south and is open daily 9 a.m.-5 p.m. (tel. 071-52-2333).

BUNDABERG TO GLADSTONE

Inland Route

A sealed road leading west from Bundaberg to **Gin Gin** on the Bruce Highway is the quickest route north. Southwest of Gin Gin is **Goodnight Scrub National Park,** protecting stands of hoop pine that escaped early logging.

The only worthwhile detour between Gin Gin and Gladstone, 160 km to the north, is **Mount Colosseum National Park,** east of Miriam Vale. This park is mostly undeveloped, with a trail leading to a summit from where the coastline can be seen in all its glory.

Cania Gorge National Park, on the Burnett Highway 123 km west of Gin Gin and 26 km north of Monto, is named for spectacular sandstone cliffs and deep gullies filled with tree ferns

and piccabeen palms. Look for platypuses at dawn and dusk along Three Moon Creek. The park has no campgrounds. **Cania Gorge Caravan Park,** north of the national park (tel. 071-67-8188), has camping and cabins.

Coastal Route

The coast north of Bundaberg is most appealing for its lack of development. A road north from Bundaberg, sealed to Rosedale, has numerous spurs leading to picturesque coastal communities such as **Miara, Norval Park,** and **Rules Beach.** Farther north is **Agnes Water** and **Town of 1770,** named for the year Captain Cook sighted the mainland. The beaches here are the best between the Sunshine Coast and Gladstone, and the view from Round Hill Head is excellent.

North of Agnes Water is 7,830-hectare **Eurimbula National Park,** protecting vegetation that ranges from coastal heath to subtropical rain forests. A primitive campground is located at Bustard Beach, but the access road may be impassable after rain, and you must bring drinking water.

CAPRICORN COAST AND CENTRAL HIGHLANDS

Named for the Tropic of Capricorn, the Capricorn Coast extends between the cities of Gladstone and Rockhampton. For those traveling north it marks the beginning of the 2,000-km **Great Barrier Reef.** Gladstone certainly isn't the most beautiful city in the world, but it is gateway to some of the reef's most beautiful islands, including Heron Island, one of the reef's few coral cays with a resort. A short trip up the Bruce Highway from Gladstone is the tropical city of Rockhampton, gateway to Great Keppel Island, easily accessible to day-trippers and boasting a range of accommodations for all budgets.

West of Rockhampton is the central highlands, a 400-km-long plateau abreast the Great Dividing Range. The main route west is the Capricorn Highway, which passes through the mining towns of Blackwater and Emerald before descending into Queensland's vast outback. South of this highway is spectacular Carnarvon National Park, dissected by a spectacular 30-km gorge.

GLADSTONE

This city, 550 km north of Brisbane, is the mainland gateway for islands of the Capricorn Group, among the most beautiful of all Great Barrier Reef islands. When the giant Comalco company descended on the prosperous provincial town in the 1960s to build the world's largest alumina smelter, Gladstone grew quickly to become an important industrial center and one of Australia's busiest ports. The smelter refines bauxite mined from Weipa, on Cape York Peninsula. To the south of Gladstone, on Boyne Island, the alu-

mina is converted to aluminum. These industries, along with Queensland's biggest power station and the country's sixth busiest port, have transformed Gladstone's coastline into an industrial wasteland.

Curtis and **Facing Islands** lie close to the mainland, linked to Gladstone by a weekend ferry service. Both have campgrounds with limited facilities and at Connor Bluff, a two-km walk from the Curtis Island jetty, is a large rookery where turtles nest Nov.-March.

Practicalities
Rusty Anchor Motor Inn, 167 Goondoon St. (tel. 079-72-2099), has decent rooms for $34 s, $44 d, while **Gladstone Country Club Motor Inn,** corner Far St. and Dawson Hwy. (tel. 079-72-4322), is the flashiest place in town with rooms for $70 s, $80 d.

Sunstate (tel. 13-1313) flies between Gladstone and Brisbane daily. Gladstone is on the main rail line north, and all major bus companies stop in town.

The **Tourist Information Centre** is at 56 Goondoon St. (tel. 079-72-4000); open daily 9 a.m.-5 p.m. The **Department of Environment and Heritage** is in Parklane Plaza on Tank St. (tel. 079-72-6055).

THE BUNKER AND CAPRICORN ISLAND GROUPS

This string of islands lying between 70 and 100 km from the mainland form the southern extent of the Great Barrier Reef. They differ from many of the resort islands farther north, including all the Whitsunday Group, in that they are coral cays, made up entirely of reef debris that has washed up on top of the living reef. Over eons the cays have become vegetated, providing nesting areas for large populations of muttonbirds, black noddy terns, and turtles. Vegetation on all the cays is similar, with the shingly shoreline dominated by the creeper goatsfoot, easily recognizable by

On 1 November 1997 telephone numbers in this section will change. To dial the new number, simply add "49" to the old number. As an example, (079) 12-3456 becomes 4912-3456. The new area code will be (07).

ISLANDS OF THE GREAT BARRIER REEF

ISLAND	GATEWAY	SIZE (HECTARES)	TYPE	WHY GO?	ACCOMMODATIONS	DAY TRIP COST	MODE OF TRANSPORT
Lady Elliot	Bundaberg	42	coral cay	diving, snorkeling	resort	$120-130	plane
Lady Musgrave	Bundaberg/Town of 1770	20	coral cay	snorkeling, beaches	camping	$95-96	boat
Heron	Gladstone	16	coral cay	diving, snorkeling	resort	no day trips	boat
Great Keppel	Rockhampton	1,480	continental	hiking, beaches, resort activities	all types	$20-25	boat/plane
Pumpkin	Rockhampton	6	continental	solitude	cabins	no day trips	
Brampton	Mackay	464	continental	relax, resort activities	resort	$40	boat
Newry	Seaforth	44	continental	low-key, relaxing	camping, cabins	$15	boat
Long	Airlie Beach	1,215	continental	resort activities, relaxation	three resorts	$20	boat
Daydream	Airlie Beach	16	continental	resort activities	resort	$20	boat
South Molle	Airlie Beach	420	continental	resort activities, hiking	resort	$25	boat
Lindeman	Airlie Beach	790	continental	resort activities	resort	$90-130	boat/plane
Hamilton	Airlie Beach	611	continental	resort activities	resort	$35-40	boat
Whitsunday	Airlie Beach	10,800	continental	Whitehaven Beach	camping	$35-69	boat
Hook	Airlie Beach	5,180	continental	snorkeling, diving	lodge, camping	$39-45	boat
Hayman	Airlie Beach	322	continental	to be pampered	resort	no day trips	boat
Magnetic	Townsville	5,030	continental	water sports, hiking	all types	$19	boat
Orpheus	Townsville/Lucinda	1,376	continental	informal yet stylish, snorkeling	resort	no day trips	ferry
Hinchinbrook	Cardwell	39,350	continental	hiking	resort, camping	$45	boat
Dunk	Mission Beach	890	continental	resort activities	resort	$22	boat
Bedarra	Mission Beach	86	continental	exclusive yet relaxed	resort	no day trips	boat
Frankland Islands	Cairns	78	continental	snorkeling, deserted beaches	camping	$98	plane
Green	Cairns	12	coral cay	snorkeling	resort	$29-32	boat
Fitzroy	Cairns	324	continental	fishing, diving	lodge	$27	boat
Lizard	Cairns	1,012	continental	diving, beaches	resort, camping	$275	plane

s light purple flowers. Higher up the beach, sonia, she-oak, and pandanus dominate. But s what's *underwater* that attracts the majority of sitors. Whereas most resort islands to the orth are a two-hour trip away from the reef, e Bunker and Capricorn Groups are right on its oorstep, with the colorful coral and profusion of eef fish a short dive away.

Two of the islands have resorts (because the lands are small, the resorts are low-key, with e emphasis on the natural surroundings), four re open to campers, and six remain uninhabit- d except for thousands of seabirds.

ady Elliot Island

ne of the reef's three coral cays with a resort, is 42-hectare island at the extreme southern nd of the reef is surrounded by a magnificent la- oon. Guano was mined on the island last cen- iry, stripping much of the vegetation, and in 873 a lighthouse, which still stands, was built on e island's west shore to aid northbound ships avigating the beginning of the reef's treacher- us inside channels. Goats, once bred on the is- nd as a source of food for shipwreck survivors, ave been eradicated, and apart from the scar of n airstrip, the island has returned to its original tate. Between October and April tens of thou- ands of seabirds congregate on the island to aise newly hatched chicks, and humpback vhales pass close by on migration routes.

The island's resort is fairly low-key, with rooms urnished for practicality rather than luxury and e emphasis on the island's natural wonders nd surrounding reef. Diving around the island is mong the best and most accessible on the en- re reef. Shore dives are free February, May, nd June, and $25-40 pp per dive at other times f the year. Safari Tent Cabins (very basic, bunk eds; $99 pp), with Reef Units (private facili- es, veranda; $125 pp) and Island Suites (se- luded, lagoon views; $150 pp), in total accom- nodate a maximum of 100 guests. All rates in- lude organized activities and three meals daily. Standby rates are 80% of the full price, giving ou a bed and hot meals from just $80 pp per ight (must be booked less than 48 hours prior o arrival). The only way to get to the island is by ir. The main departure point for the island is Bundaberg ($80 pp round-trip), but transfers an also be made from Hervey Bay or Glad-

stone. For resort and transfer bookings call (071) 53-2485 or (1800) 07-2200; from the United States call (800) 531-9222.

It's possible for day-trippers to visit Lady Elliot Island, but as you must fly in, it's not cheap. The cost from Hervey Bay or Bundaberg, in- cluding snorkeling gear, a guided walk, and lunch, is $120 (the flight only is $99). From Glad- stone, this trip is $130 pp.

Lady Musgrave Island

Just 20 hectares in area, this tiny coral cay is a small part of a massive lagoon, protected from the surrounding ocean by a platform reef ex- posed only at low tide. The island itself is encir- cled by a beach of broken coral that rises to thickly vegetated cover of pisonia. Like Lady Elliot Island to the south, Lady Musgrave was mined for guano and once had a high population of goats but is now totally deserted, save for day-trippers and campers. For those visiting the island, the lagoon is center of most activity, with snorkeling and diving the main attractions; it also provides a safe anchorage for yachties.

Camping on a remote tropical island is many people's idea of the ideal holiday, and Lady Musgrave is the most accessible of the Great Barrier Reef cays for such an adventure, but you'll need to be totally self-sufficient (bring drinking water) and willing to forgo luxuries for a few days, or weeks, or even months if you so choose. Campers require a national parks per- mit ($3 pp per night), and as numbers are limit- ed advance bookings are required; for permits call the Department of Environment and Her- itage in Gladstone (tel. 079-72-6055). **Captain Cook Great Barrier Reef Cruises** (tel. 079- 74-9077) offers camper drop-offs and pick-ups Thursday and Sunday from Town of 1770, north of Bundaberg. The fare is $190 pp round-trip. As well as transfers, this company can organize camping equipment, water containers, and dinghies (great for fishing and snorkeling around the lagoon's outer reaches. **Lady Musgrave Barrier Reef Cruises** (tel. 071-52-9011 or 1800- 07-2110) offers transfers from Bundaberg for $190 round-trip.

Captain Cook Great Barrier Reef Cruises makes day trips to the island Saturday and Sun- day departing Town of 1770 at 8 a.m.; $95 pp. Lady Musgrave Barrier Reef Cruises operates day tours departing Port Bundaberg, 18 km east of Bundaberg, Tuesday, Thursday, Saturday, and Sunday at 8:30 a.m. returning at 6 p.m. The fare is adult $96, child $50, which includes a buffet lunch, snorkeling equipment, glass-bottomed boat tour, and access to an underwater observatory. The trip to the island takes less time from Town of 1770 and more time is spent ashore. Either way, if seas are rough, the journey over will be unpleasant and it may be better flying to Lady Elliot Island (see above) for the day.

Heron Island

A paradise for nature lovers and those who want to escape the regimented formula of other reef resorts, 16-hectare Heron Island is one of the reef's three coral cays with resorts.

Lying in the middle of the Capricorn Group, 80 km northeast of Gladstone and just 30 km from the Continental Shelf, Heron Island sits on the northwest corner of a platform reef nearly 10 km long. The island itself is oval shaped, and just under one km long, but there's enough room for a couple of hundred thousand sea birds as well as a high population of white and gray herons, for which the island is named. Between November and March sea turtles lay their eggs on island, but these animals were not always afforded the security they now enjoy—for much of the 1920s a turtle soup factory operated on the island. The waters around the island are considered among the finest on the entire reef for diving, with the best dive sites in the immediate vicinity of the island.

The resort sprawls over most of the western end of the island, spread among pisonia trees and around two pools, a tennis court, and restaurant complex. Accommodation is inclusive of meals and includes many activities. Rates in the Lodge (shared bathroom) are $140 pp; Heron and Reef Units (private bathroom) are $270 s, $420 d. Point Units are isolated from the rest of the resort and have a terrific beachfront location; $315 s, $510 d. Transfers between Gladstone and the island by catamaran take around two hours each way; $130 round-trip. Helicopter transfers from Gladstone are $354 pp round-trip. When available, standby rates on Heron Island offer considerable savings (usually around $200 pp per day inclusive of

transfers). For resort and transfer bookings ca (079) 78-1488 or 13-2469. In North Americ call (800) 225-9849. It is not possible to vis Heron Island for just the day.

Masthead Island

Unlike other cays at the southern end of th reef, this 65-hectare island was never mine and has had no goats to destroy the native veg etation. Closest of the Capricorn Group to th mainland, it lies 60 km northeast of Gladstone. sits at the northwestern end of a platform ree forming a large lagoon but, unlike Lady Ellio there is no navigitable break in the reef, makin boat landings difficult in rough weather and ar chorage unsafe. Between October and Apr thousands of seabirds nest on the island an Nov.-Jan. loggerhead turtles clamber up th beach to lay their eggs.

Camping on the island is limited to 50 peopl (30 during bird-nesting periods) at any one time and with no scheduled boat service you'll nee to have a flexible schedule to fit in with othe campers (usually groups of 10-20) for trans portation. A number of charter boats go out t the island, but the best chance of getting in wit a group is on *Heron II,* which also transfer guests out to Heron Island. Fares to Masthea are $180 pp round-trip. For bookings call (079 72-5166. For permits, call the Department c Environment and Heritage in Gladstone (tel 079-72-6055).

North West Island

Northwest of Heron Island and 83 km northeas of Gladstone, this 150-hectare coral cay is th largest island of the Capricorn Group and ha been protected as a national park since 1980. I the past it has been mined for guano and, like Heron Island, had a turtle soup factory. Althoug various signs of human history remain, the islan provides an excellent opportunity to escape to a deserted tropical isle. Like other islands of th Bunker and Capricorn groups, it's an importan nesting site for seabirds and has a large gree turtle nesting area.

For camping permits, contact Department o Environment and Heritage in Gladstone (tel 079-72-6055). Boat transfers can be arrange on *Heron II* through Heron Island Resort (tel 079-72-7166); $200 pp from Gladstone.

ryon Island

ust 12 hectares in area, Tryon Island sits on the dge of a massive platform reef a couple of kiloeters beyond North West Island. The island is nged by a shingle beach, and at high tide it kes just 15 minutes to walk around it. Between ctober and May the island is home to thouands of very noisy muttonbirds who come shore to raise chicks. The same camping perit and transportation applies to Tryon as to orth West Island.

ROCKHAMPTON

Best known as "Rocky," this historic city of 55,000 sits on the Fitzroy River 720 km north of Brisbane and is the gateway to Great Keppel Island. The area's first settlers arrived in 1853, and a gold rush 60 km north in 1858 furthered the influx of Europeans. The actual town was established as a river port for the transportation of coal and cattle. Today, Rocky claims to be the Beef Capital of

ROCKHAMPTON

Australia, and with Australia's largest abattoirs on the city's outskirts and one-third of the state's cattle grazing in the region, it's probably true.

Sights

As you enter town from the south, it's impossible to miss The Spire, marking the Tropic of Capricorn (23°26'30"s). Many of Rocky's historic buildings are on Quay St.; *Driving Tour* and *Heritage Walk* brochures detail each and its significance. **Rockhampton City Art Gallery,** Victoria Parade (tel. 079-31-1248), is regarded as one of the state's best provincial galleries; open Mon.-Fri. 10 a.m.-4 p.m., Sat.-Sun. 1:30-4:30 p.m.

On the city's southern outskirts is a **botanic garden** and **zoo.** Established more than 120 years ago, the garden covers 40 hectares and includes a display of palms. Within the botanic garden is a small zoo featuring koalas, kangaroos, crocodiles, cassowaries, emus, and other native animals; no admission charge. To get there, take the first left north of the information center and follow the signs. The grounds are open daily 8 a.m.-5 p.m.

Northeast of downtown **Mt. Archer** rises to an elevation of 604 meters, providing an excellent view of the city and mountains beyond. Frenchville Rd. leads right to the summit. The **Dreamtime Cultural Centre** (tel. 079-36-1655), seven km north of the city at the Yeppoon turnoff, sprawls over 10 hectares of land significant to the local Durambal tribe. The center features a museum, displays of Torres Strait Islander culture, boomerang throwing demonstrations, and explanations of native plant use. Admission is adult $8, child $4. Open daily 10 a.m.-5 p.m. Farther north are a number of limestone cave systems of which two are open to the public. **Cammoo Caves** (tel. 079-34-2774) are open daily for self-guided tours while **Capricorn Caverns** (tel. 079-34-2883) are accessible only on a guided tour.

Accommodations and Food

One of Rocky's most distinctive buildings is the historic **Criterion Hotel** on Quay St. opposite the river (tel. 079-22-1225). Basic rooms are $15 pp while those with private bathrooms are $34 s, $40 d. Motels line the highway north and south of the city. The least expensive are in the suburb of Parkhurst, just north of Yeppoon turnoff. **True**

Blue Motor Inn, Bruce Hwy., Parkhurst (te 079-36-1777), has large clean rooms, a poc and laundry; $38 s, $42 d. Back in the heart town is the nine-story **Country Comfort In** 86 Victoria Parade (tel. 079-27-9933), whe rooms are air-conditioned and have private ba conies; other facilities include a restaurant, ba and laundry; $82 s, $87 d.

Rockhampton YHA Hostel is on the nor side of the river at 60 MacFarlane St. (tel. 07 27-5288). This large hostelry has modern fac ities with dorm beds ranging $12-13 and a fe doubles for $28-30.

North of the Yeppoon turnoff is a rest are where camping is permitted. For more facilitie stay at **Southside Caravan Village,** on th Bruce Hwy. opposite the information center (te 079-27-3013). Facilities are excellent and i clude a pool, kitchen, and small tennis cour Unpowered sites are $13, powered sites $17

Without a doubt, the best place to go for counter lunch is the **Fitzroy Hotel,** 366 East S (tel. 079-27-1355), where a rump steak wi vegetables is just $4. Or try the **Criterion Hote** on the corner of Quay and Fitzroy Streets.

Transportation, Services, and Information

Ansett Australia (tel. 13-1300) and **Qanta** (tel. 13-1313) fly daily between Brisbane an Rocky for $149 one-way, with a cab from th airport to downtown running $7-8.

Queensland Rail's Spirit of Capricorn run daily between Brisbane and Rocky, takin around 10 hours each way and costing $66.9 for an economy-class ticket. For bookings ca 13-2232. All major bus companies stop in tow with fares similar to rail.

Capricorn Coast Information Centre is o the Bruce Hwy. right on the Tropic of Capricorr It's open daily 9 a.m.-5 p.m. (tel. 079-27-2055 For information on nearby national parks, ir cluding those of the central highlands, head t the **Department of Environment and Heritage** on Yeppoon Rd. just off the Bruce Hwy. (te 079-36-0511).

YEPPOON AND VICINITY

Yeppoon, 40 km northeast of Rockhampton may be the largest town on the Capricorn Coast it's still a sleepy seaside resort town. It lies at e north end of a 35-km stretch of coast, which tracts mainly fishermen and families content to njoy a relaxed holiday away from the hustle id bustle of the more commercial coastal areas. ne main road out to the coast is Yeppoon Rd., hich begins five km north of downtown Rocky; a alternative is to take Lakes Creek Rd. out of ocky to **Emu Park,** a small coastal settlement pread over undulating hills overlooking a wide andy beach. On the headland is the **Singing hip,** a 40-meter-high monument to Captain ook. Representing a mast and sail, the hollow pes are pierced to create a musical noise when e wind blows. From Emu Park, the road hugs e coast, passing the community of **Mulambin each** and the turnoff to **Rosslyn Bay,** gate-ay to Great Keppel Island, before ending at eppoon. The effects of the tide at Yeppoon are nazing; as it ebbs, large pools of water are left n the gently sloping beach, and boats moored Fig Tree Creek are left lying on dry mudflats, nly to float again as the tide floods the wide reek bed a few hours later. South of Yeppoon is **Vreck Point** and a lookout affording panoram-views over the Keppel Group.

racticalities

n 1972 Japanese businessman Yohachiro vasaki purchased 8,500 hectares of prime ceanfront land immediately north of Yeppoon. is plans for an international-standard resort ere marred with a decade of controversy, but, fi-nally, **Capricorn International Resort** is now operational, providing accommodation for 800 guests and a myriad of activities, including two 18-hole championship golf courses. The resort is contained on only a small section of the 8,500 hectares, with the rest remaining in its natural state and open for guests to explore on 4WD safaris, nature walks, or on horseback. Originally aimed at the Asian market, many Australians take advantage of low rates and high-standard facilities. Standard rate is $105 s, $110 d while self-contained apartments are $140. Two-night packages, including meals, start at $205 pp, and one night's accommodation, breakfast, and golf is $100 pp. For reservations call (079) 39-5111.

Yeppoon has a number of motels, with **Drift-wood Motel,** 7 Todd Ave. (tel. 079-39-2446), being right on the beach; $40 s, $45 d. **Barrier Reef Backpackers,** 30 Queen St. (tel. 079-39-4702), is an old Queenslander with dorm beds for $12 pp and a few doubles for $26. Staff do pick-ups in Rocky and will also drop guests at Rosslyn Bay Harbour.

Capricorn Coast Information Centre is be-side the big roundabout by Ross Creek (tel. 079-39-4888).

GREAT KEPPEL ISLAND

Great Keppel is a large continental island of 1,480 hectares surrounded by beautiful white beaches and a fringing reef of coral. Most of

Long Beach,
Great Keppel Island

the island is covered in a forest of eucalypts, with casuarinas fringing the beaches and a large area of low-lying wetland on the north side. Not only does ease of access make the island popular, it also has one of the reef's largest and most popular resorts, made famous by the long-running "Get Wrecked on Great Keppel" advertising campaign. If resort-style living isn't your idea of fun, there's also camping in safari-style tents and a backpacker lodge, or just come over for the day.

Hiking

From the north end of an airstrip, a one-km trail climbs to a lookout with spectacular views extending to other islands of the Keppel Group. From the lookout it is two km to the summit of Mt. Wyndham, from where Long Beach can be seen far below and Halfway and Humpy Islands lie immediately south. Other trails lead from the lookout to an old shearing shed and homestead,

to **Leeke's Beach, Wreck Beach,** and a ligh house on the island's remote and rugged we coast.

Accommodations

Set behind a sparkling white palm-fringed bea **Great! Keppel** is a fun-oriented resort with mo activities on offer than any other resort on th Great Barrier Reef—tennis, squash, golf, archer basketball, tandem, skydiving, aqua bikes, scut diving, snorkeling, reef trips, parasailing, ar dancing the night away at a disco—you nam it, the resort has it. Earlier this decade, the reso underwent a $14-million facelift, which include the construction of 60 new units. Facilities now i clude two large pools, a cafe, store, hairdresse and restaurants. Rooms are all basically th same with Garden Units at $148 s, $248 Beachfront Units $186 s, $310 d; and the ne Hillside Units, offering panoramic views, als $186 s, $310 d. These rates include all nonm

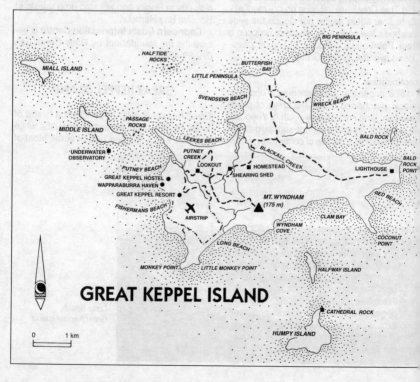

GREAT KEPPEL ISLAND

ized activities and, if you've got any energy
t after the sun has set, free admission to the
ghtclub. The meal package is $60 pp. For book-
s call (079) 39-1744. From North America call
00) 551-2012.

Between Fishermans and Putney Beaches
Wapparaburra Haven (tel. 079-39-1907), of-
ring tent sites ($8 pp), a Tent Village ($12 pp),
d spacious cabins with kitchenettes ($75).
e Tent Village is a series of canvas "tents,"
ch with four bunk beds. Guests have use of a
mmunal kitchen. This complex also has a
all grocery store, cafe, and restaurant. Next
or is **Great Keppel Hostel** (tel. 079-39-4341).
rm beds are $12-14.

ansportation

nstate (tel. 13-1313) flies daily between
ckhampton and the island for $72 each way.
e airline also offers a same-day round-trip
andby fare for $50. Two companies operate
at transfers from Rosslyn Bay Harbour, south
Yeppoon, over to the island. **Keppel Tourist**
rvices (tel. 079-33-6744) departs daily at
15 a.m., 11:30 a.m., and 3:30 p.m., returning
8:15 a.m., 2 p.m., and 4:30 p.m.; $25 round-
p, and for an extra $10 you can either go
omnetting and snorkeling or visit the under-
ter observatory on Middle Island. *Australis*
parts from the main wharf at Rosslyn Bay
arbour daily at 9 a.m. and 11 a.m., returning at
45 a.m. and 4 p.m.; adult $20, child $10, fam-
$50. Book through Rosslyn Bay Kiosk (tel.
79-33-6865).

Keppel Tourist Services (tel. 079-33-6744)
perates the high-speed catamaran *Reefseek-*
to the outer reef Tuesday and Thursday. In-
usive of lunch, snorkeling, and a glass-bot-
med boat ride, the fare is adult $90, child $47.

ther Islands of Keppel Bay

reat Keppel is the largest of 19 islands in Kep-
l Bay. On **Middle Island** is an underwater
servatory. Keppel Tourist Services runs over
the observatory from Great Keppel Island for
10. Another way to visit Middle Island is with
ue Water Sea Kayaking (tel. 079-39-5044),
hich operates a three-hour paddle and snor-
ling excursion from Great Keppel for $30 pp.

North of Great Keppel Island, six-hectare
umpkin Island has five self-contained cab-

ins (sleeping up to six) for $100 per night. For
bookings and transportation details call (079)
39-2431. Camping is permitted on **North Kep-**
pel, Miall, and **Humpy Islands.** You'll need a
permit from the Department of Environment and
Heritage in Rockhampton for camping on any of
these islands. Inquire at Keppel Tourist Services (tel. 079-33-6744) for island transfers.

WEST FROM ROCKHAMPTON

The Capricorn Highway runs west from Rockhampton to the mining towns of **Blackwater**
and **Emerald,** continuing to Longreach in
Queensland's vast outback. The highway also
runs past Carnarvon National Park, south of
Emerald, one of Australia's most spectacular
inland parks.

Mount Morgan

Tourism is about all that keeps this historic gold-
mining town, 38 km southwest of Rockhampton, alive. Gold was first discovered in the area
in 1882, turning out to be among the richest
lodes in the world, with Mt. Morgan Gold Mining
Company extracting over 35 million ounces of
gold in its hundred years of operation. After the
mine closed in the late 1980s, most residents left
town, but it's still an interesting place to visit.
The streets are lined with buildings hinting at
the town's prosperous past. **Mount Morgan**
Museum, 87 Morgan St. (tel. 079-38-2312),
features a good collection of mining memorabilia,
historic photos, and samples of minerals extracted from the mine. It's open Mon.-Sat. 10
a.m.-1 p.m., Sunday 10 a.m.-4 p.m.; admission
$2. **Silver Wattle Tours,** 38 Central St. (tel.
079-38-1081), offers two-hour tours of town
sights, the open-cut mine, and some dinosaur
footprints uncovered during excavation works.
Tours depart daily at 9:30 a.m. and 12:50 p.m.

Blackdown Tableland National Park

This 23,000-hectare park encompasses a large
portion of a plateau rising 600 meters above
the surrounding plains of the central highlands.
Millions of years ago massive forces below the
earth's surface pushed up layers of sedimentary rock, forming a rolling plateau of sandstone.
Over eons, erosion has carved deep gorges,

caves, and crevices along the plateau's escarpment. The plateau is covered in forests of eucalypt, including towering Blackdown stringybark. Where soil is shallow, low heaths dominate, and in spring these areas come alive with color when a profusion of wildflowers bloom.

The plateau was inaccessible until a logging road was cut up its steep slopes in 1971, and a decade later a large part of it was declared a national park. Just beyond the park entrance, trails lead to **Peregrine Lookout** (1.4 km one-way), where views extend for many kilometers north, and **Two Mile Falls** (1.5 km one-way). At **Mimosa Creek** another couple of short trails lead through a deep gorge, and at the end of the access road a five-km trail leads to the rim of a spectacular sandstone gorge.

Mimosa Creek Camping Area has toilets and drinking water; for bookings call the ranger at (079) 86-1964. The park turnoff is 11 km west of Dingo.

The Gemfields

Around 200 km west of Rocky, and just west of Emerald, is the world's most productive sapphire-mining area. Other gems found are amethyst, gold, rubies, diamonds, and zircon. Large companies do a lot of the mining, but during winter months hundreds of amateurs descend on the area, hoping to strike it rich. Most don't, but everyone comes away with a gem of some standard. Before digging, a fossicking license is needed; these are available from the Emerald courthouse. The gemfields are scattered around the towns of **Anakie, Willows, Sapphire,** and **Rubyvale. Gemfields Information Centre,** in Anakie (tel. 079-85-4525), has maps of the region and friendly staff to guide you to the most productive areas. All gemfields towns have caravan parks, each with on-site vans or cabins.

Clermont, 110 km northwest of Emerald, is Queensland's oldest inland tropical town. It exists only to serve workers at **Blair Athol Mine,** a massive open-cut mining operation on the world's largest steaming coal seam.

CARNARVON NATIONAL PARK

A bone-shaking 100 km from the nearest sealed road, and 400 km west of Rockhampton, th park encompasses 251,000 hectares of plateau rising high above the surrounding plain Remarkable **Carnarvon Gorge** is the park major attraction. Almost 30 km long, 250 mete deep, and with innumerable arms, the gor area is a dramatic landscape of sheer-side cliffs, natural bridges, and caves. The gor has been created by **Carnarvon Creek,** lit more than a babbling stream most of the yea but a raging torrent during the Wet. Thousan of years of water erosion have eaten into t multicolored sandstone layers deposited on t bottom of an ocean many millions of years ag

The creek flows year-round, supporting oasis of ferns and mosses that thrive in an ot erwise desolate landscape and attract a su prisingly large number of animals. Forests dry eucalypt dominate higher elevations, wh the lush vegetation of the gorge is mainly tre ferns, cabbage tree palms, orchids, and, alon the creek bed, moss-covered boulders.

The gorge's first human visitors were A originals, who used the many caves as cer monial places, burying their dead among th rocky caves. **Kenniff Cave** is adorned with ea rock art; stencil paintings depict animals an people with boomerangs and shields.

Hiking

The road into the park ends at the entrance the gorge, leaving exploring on foot the only o tion. The main trail leads 9.3 km to **Cathedr Cave,** its lower walls covered in ancient a Along the route side tracks lead to the apt named **Art Gallery** and the park's most ma nificent feature, the **Amphitheatre,** five km fro the visitor center. The final approach is up steel ladder and through a one-meter gap into chasm surrounded by sheer sandstone wa towering more than 100 meters high. An eas walk from the visitor center leads to the **Mos Garden** in Violet Gorge. Here, lush palm mosses, and ferns thrive on the small creek th tumbles down a long ravine.

Practicalities

The campground by the visitor center has toilet drinking water, and cold showers; bookings a essential during holiday periods (tel. 079-8 4505). Just outside the park entrance is **Oasi**

lodge, consisting of individual cabins spread round native bushland. Each has a bathroom, idge, tea- and coffee-making facilities, and a eranda. They also have a lounge, library, and a acked program of activities and guided walks April-Nov. only). Rates, inclusive of all meals, re $150 pp per night, $399 pp for three nights. a the low season (Dec.-March) rates drop to $96 pp per night, $270 for three nights. Flight-west offers a package, including flights between Brisbane and Roma, charter flights between Roma and the lodge, and all-inclusive accommodations for three nights for $859 in high season (tel. 1800-77-7879). For reservations call (079) 84-4503.

hands rock art, Carnarvon Gorge, Queensland

WHITSUNDAY COAST AND ISLANDS

Between Mackay and Bowen lie the Whitsunday Islands, the single most popular destination on the entire reef. Rising magnificently from the turquoise waters that are protected from ocean swells by the outer reef, they are a watery playground for divers and sailors, or those who want to relax at an island resort. They are not true coral islands, but are continental in origin, linked geologically to the mainland.

The Whitsundays are unashamedly tourism oriented, but offer something to suit everyone, whether you want to spend your day hiking along a deserted beach, snorkeling and scuba diving, or participating in resort-style activities (islands close to the mainland are affected by box jellyfish Nov.-March). Of the main group of islands, seven have resorts, with accommodations ranging from rustic lodges to five-star resorts, or you could always camp on an uninhabited island. Day trips to the resort islands start at $20 and many excellent standby deals make island accommodation an excellent value for late arrivals. The islands are the perfect domain for yachties, with many bareboat charter operators renting yachts, or you can sail aboard one of the many maxi-yachts that have retired to islands.

The cane-growing town of Mackay is southern gateway to the Whitsundays and departure point for cruises to Brampton Island. To the north, and east of Proserpine, is Airlie Beach, which exists only to serve tourists heading to the islands. Shute Harbour, 16 km east of Airlie Beach, is the main departure point for island-bound cruise boats.

Cape Palmerston National Park
Accessible only by 4WD, this 7,200-hectare park encompasses an undeveloped stretch of coastline south of Mackay. The landscape is dominated by long stretches of sandy beach separated by grassy headlands and backed by low lying areas of mangroves and swamps. The par is accessed at Ilbilbie, on the Bruce Highway where a rough track parallels the coast past possible campsites on Coconut Beach and ends a the cape itself. Campers must be totally self sufficient. For road conditions call (079) 51-8788

MACKAY

Promoting itself as Sugar Capital of Australia this pleasant tropical city of 60,000 is gateway t the southern islands of the Whitsundays an Eungella National Park. Around seven millio tons of cane are grown and processed in th Mackay region annually. As early as 1875 Mackay had 20 sugar mills crushing cane fo transportation to southern ports. The Pionee River, which flows through town, functioned a a port until the modern **Port of Mackay** wa constructed. At the port is the world's larges sugar terminal, capable of holding 670,000 tor of cane at any one time.

Sights and Beaches
Mackay sprawls south and north of the Pionee River, with commercial center being along th river's south bank. **Victoria Street,** the hea of the city, is a wide boulevard divided by landscaped medium strip dominated by towe ing palms. Many historic buildings dot this pa of the city, including the courthouse (1880) ar police station (1885); *A Heritage Walk in Mac ay,* available at the Tourist Information Centre details the history of these and other building around town. Guided tours of the sugar termin are offered weekdays at 10:15 a.m., and a fe of the sugar mills offer tours during harvest sea son (July-Nov.); for details and all booking contact the Tourist Information Centre (tel. 07 52-2677).

Mackay's best beaches are north of the cit but **Illawong Beach,** at the eastern end Bridge St., is worth seeing at low tide, when it e tends nearly two km out to sea. **Harbour Beac**

On 1 November 1997 telephone numbers in this section will change. To dial the new number, simply add "49" to the old number. As an example, (079) 12-3456 becomes 4912-3456. The new area code will be (07).

Mackay

immediately south of Port of Mackay, has a surf club and palm-filled picnic area with barbecues. Farther north, **Slade Point** and **Eimeo** have reasonable beaches.

Accommodations and Food

Most motels are strung along Nebo Rd. (a continuation of the Bruce Hwy.) south of downtown. **Golden Reef Motel,** 164 Nebo Rd. (tel. 079-57-6572), is one of the least expensive, with rooms at $36 s, $44 d. The excellent **Mackay Motor Inn,** 208 Nebo Rd. (tel. 079-52-2822), has large rooms with comfortable beds, as well as barbecues, laundry, and pool; $42 s, $60 d. Closer to the city, and within walking distance of downtown, is **Paradise Lodge Motel,** 19 Peel St. (tel. 079-51-3644), opposite the bus terminal; $44 s, $48 d.

Backpackers Retreat, 21 Peel St. (tel. 079-51-1115), a distinctive pink building, is just 100 meters from the bus terminal. Facilities are basic but staff are friendly; dorms $12, doubles $30.

On the beach at Illawong is **Beach Tourist Park,** Petrie St. (tel. 079-57-4021), with a large kitchen area, barbecue, pool, and kiosk. Unpowered sites are $12, powered sites $15, on-site vans $28, and cabins $28-42.

Most of Mackay's cafes and restaurants are strung along Victoria St., as are a handful of hotels, many serving counter meals. **Wilkinson's Tavern** (tel. 079-57-2241) serves meals noon-2 p.m. and 6-9 p.m.; most are under $8. Upstairs is a restaurant, with main dishes $9-12.

Mariner Restaurant, 44 Victoria St. (tel. 079-57-3279), has a wide range of Queensland seafood and a huge Saturday night buffet for $35. For something more casual try **Billy Baxter's Cafe** in the Post Office Square on Sydney St. (tel. 079-44-0173).

Transportation, Services, and Information

Ansett (tel. 13-1300) flies nonstop between Brisbane and Mackay, as does **Qantas** (tel. 13-1313); $274 one-way. **Sunstate** (tel. 13-1313) links Mackay to Townsville, Rockhampton, and Gladstone. The airport is on Mackay's southern outskirts. **Queensland Rail** (tel. 13-2232) operates services along the coast. From Brisbane to Mackay costs $100. The railway station is on Boddington Street. All major bus lines stop at **Mackay Bus Terminal,** 500 meters from downtown on Milton Street (tel. 079-51-3088). One-way fares from Mackay include: Brisbane $90, Airlie Beach $26, Townsville $48, and Cairns $70. **Avis, Budget,** and **Hertz** have outlets at the airport.

The **Tourist Information Centre** is three km south of town on the Bruce Hwy. (tel. 079-52-2677). It's open Mon.-Fri. 9 a.m.-5 p.m., Sat.-Sun. 9 a.m.-4 p.m.

ISLANDS OFF MACKAY

Off the coast of Mackay lie 17 islands, part of the Cumberland Islands. Officially they are

VICINITY OF MACKAY

COCKERMOUTH ISLAND

CARLISLE ISLAND

BRAMPTON ISLAND

ST. BEES ISLAND

KESWICK ISLAND

LINNÉ ISLAND

CUMBERLAND GROUP

GOLDSMITH ISLAND

RABBIT ISLAND

ST. HELENS BAY

NEWRY ISLAND

OUTER NEWRY ISLAND

MAUSOLEUM ISLAND

ROCKY ISLAND

PORT NEWRY

SEAFORTH

MT. OSSA

ST. HELENS BEACH

CALEN

CAPE HILLSBOROUGH N.P.

CAPE HILLSBOROUGH

WEDGE ISLAND

SAND BAY

SHOAL POINT

BUCASIA

DOLPHIN HEADS

EIMEO

SLADE POINT

PORT OF MACKAY

HARBOUR BEACH

MACKAY

ILLAWONG BEACH

MACKAY AIRPORT

SANDRINGHAM BAY

DALRYMPLE BAY

BLACK MOUNTAIN (304 m)

PIONEER RIVER

WALKERSTON

MARIAN

MIRANI

FINCH HATTON

EUNGELLA

EUNGELLA NATIONAL PARK

BROKEN RIVER PICNIC AREA

BRUCE HWY.

PEAK DOWNS HWY.

TO EMERALD

55

TO CAPE PALMERSTON N.P. AND ROCKHAMPTON

1

TO AIRLIE BEACH AND TOWNSVILLE

1

O'CONNELL RIVER

0   10 km

nown as the Cumberland Group, one of four roups making up the Cumberland Islands, better known as the Whitsundays. Like the rest of he Whitsundays, islands of the Cumberland Group are continental in origin and were once art of the mainland. The actual Great Barrier Reef lies well beyond the islands and about 00 km from the coast. Apart from Brampton Island, which has an elegant resort, the islands re either privately owned or protected as national parks.

Brampton Island

Brampton, a rugged continental island of 464 ectares, features a deeply indented coastline with seven pretty beaches, each with a fringing oral reef (the best of these are on the island's outh side), while the hilly interior consists of n open forest where gray kangaroos, goanas, and ever-present scrub turkeys can be een. A seven-km trail encircles the island, with two km spur ascending to the summit of 219-neter Brampton Peak.

The Busuttin family, which originally ran sheep n nearby St. Bees Island, planted coconut alms and developed a small resort on a flat ection of the island in 1933. It's now owned by ustralian Resort Companies, who rebuilt the reort in 1985. The emphasis is on rest and reaxation, with no televisions or phones. The each is right at the resort's doorstep, offering all ne usual water sports. The resort caters for 16 people in air-conditioned units. Rates are 197 s, $172 pp d inclusive of all meals and ctivities. For bookings call (07) 3360-2444 or ne resort direct at (079) 51-4499.

Roylen Cruises (tel. 079-55-3066) provides ansportation between Mackay and the island or overnight guests as well as day-trippers; $40 ound-trip. The services depart Port of Mackay aily at 9 a.m. It is also possible to reach the sland on daily flights with Sunstate (tel. 13-313); $70 one-way.

Monday, Wednesday, and Friday, Roylen Cruises continues from Brampton Island to Credlin Reef on the outer reef, where a ponoon is located. The pontoon has a small underwater observatory and provides a base for norkeling, scuba diving, and swimming. The uter reef trip is $90 from Mackay, which inudes a buffet lunch.

Carlisle Island

At low tide a sand bar joins Carlisle Island to Brampton. Protected as a national park, Carlisle is uninhabited, and no tracks delve into its rugged interior. The island has some good beaches and a colorful fringing reef. On the west coast is the hull of *Geelong,* which wrecked in 1888. A small camping area at Southern Bay overlooks the resort on Brampton Island. Campers must be totally self-sufficient and bring their own drinking water. For permits contact the Department of Environment and Heritage on the corner of Wood and River Streets, Mackay (tel. 079-51-8788).

EUNGELLA NATIONAL PARK

An area of rainforest isolated by climatic changes at the end of the last ice age and now supporting species of plants found nowhere else in the country, this 50,800-hectare park (pronounced "YOUNG-gulla") is a world away from the coastal plains immediately to the east. Platypuses are the park's biggest attraction, and it's probably the best place in mainland Australia to view these unique critters.

Access from Mackay is along a road that parallels the Pioneer River up an ever-narrowing valley before climbing steeply to the plateau on which the park lies. From the village of Eungella it's six km south to the Park Information Centre, two campgrounds, and a platypus viewing area. These facilities are contained in a small corner of the park; the rest, north of Eungella, is inaccessible, rising to 1,280 meters at Mt. Dalrymple.

Around 10,000 years ago, at the end of the last ice age, the climate became warmer and drier, and areas of rainforest retreated to higher elevations. Eungella is one such area, now surrounded by open forests of eucalypt. Trees typical of subtropical rainforest—tulip oak, beech, silver quandong, curtain figs, palms, and ferns—all thrive in the environment.

The **platypuses** of Eungella live in the Broken River. They are most active just after dawn and before dusk and best viewed from a platform adjacent to the picnic area. The park boasts many other species of mammals as well as a reported 100 species of birds. One of the park's most interesting animals is the Eungella gastric brooding frog. Eggs are incubated in its stomach, before spitting out the young.

From the Broken River picnic area, the two-km Rainforest Discovery walk passes through typical rainforest environment. The Broken River track branches off this trail, following the river through rainforest to Crediton Creek. Another longer hike is the **Palm Walk Track,** which follows the rim of the escarpment from just south of Eungella township to Broken River (8.3 km one-way.)

Practicalities

The park has two camping areas; both are on the Broken River. Each has toilets, showers, and picnic tables. Open fires are not encouraged; $7.50 per night. For bookings call (079) 58-4552.

Also on the river is **Broken River Mountain Retreat** (tel. 079-58-4528), with self-contained cabins in a setting of native bushland; $48 s or d. **Eungella Chalet Mountain Resort,** in Eungella township (tel. 079-58-4509), is an older establishment perched on the top of the range, with views all the way down the Pioneer Valley. Rooms with a view and shared facilities are $39, rooms with private facilities are $55, and self-contained one-bedroom cabins are $70 s or d. A large grassed beer garden offers tremendous views, as does the restaurant.

No public transportation is available to the park. Tours are offered by a number of operators, including **Platypus Tours Whitsunday.** The $135 pp fare includes transport from Airlie Beach, overnight accommodation at the Chalet, all meals, and guided walks. Departures are Monday and Thursday at 8:30 a.m. For bookings call (079) 46-6922 or drop by any of the Airlie Beach booking agents.

The **Park Information Centre** is beside the Broken River (tel. 079-58-4552). It's open daily 7-8 a.m., 11 a.m.-noon, and 3-3:30 p.m.

NORTH FROM MACKAY

Cape Hillsborough National Park

The diverse habitat and long stretches of beach of this 818-hectare park, 45 km north of Mackay, make it a worthwhile detour from the Bruce Highway. The park access road traverses a large wetland area of mangroves, ending at a beach flanked to the north by a high, rugged headland dropping straight into the ocean. Behind the beach is the visitor center and a grassed picnic area where wallabies feed under the shade of eucalypts. At the very end of the access road is the trailhead for 1.4-km **Hidden Valley Circuit,** passing through littoral rainforest with many palms. At low tide it's possible to walk to **Wedge Island,** off the southern end of the beach. At the opposite end of the beach, a six-km (one-way) trail climbs over the cape to Smalleys Beach.

Behind the beach is a small campground (no showers); $7 per night. At the end of the access road is **Cape Hillsborough Resort** (tel. 079-59-0152). Facilities include a pool, cafe, and laundromat. Unpowered sites are $6, powered sites $10, on-site vans $25, and cabins $35.

Newry Island Group

Newry Island, with a low-key resort, is part of a group of six continental islands that make up **Newry Island Group National Park,** lying close to the mainland around 50 km northwest of Mackay. Each island is rugged and covered in open forests of eucalypts. Koalas (introduced), possums, echidnas, and bandicoots inhabit the islands.

Newry Island Resort (tel. 079-59-0214) is spread along a palm-fringed beach facing Rabbit Island. Walking, fishing, and snorkeling (except Oct.-May, when stingers are present) are a popular activities. Accommodation is in self-contained cabins ($20 pp per night), each with a kitchen and bathroom. The resort has a restaurant and bar, but you'll need supplies from the mainland to be self-sufficient.

Camping is possible on **Rabbit, Outer Newry, Mausoleum,** and **Rocky Islands,** but you'll need to be self-sufficient. To camp, permits from the Department of Environment and Heritage in Mackay (tel. 079-51-8788) are required.

Newry Island Resort provides transfers between the island and Port Newry (a rather fancy name for what is no more than boat ramp), four km north of Seaforth; $15 round-trip. With advance reservations it's possible to make a day trip to the island or arrange drop-offs to other islands of the group.

AIRLIE BEACH AND VICINITY

Airlie Beach, gateway to the Whitsundays, is a bustling resort town 26 km east of Proserpine and 1,130 km north of Brisbane. The town is misnamed—there is no beach, and even the actual departure point for cruises is 15 km beyond the town at **Shute Harbour.** But Airlie Beach is a hive of activity year-round, existing only to serve tourists—both those passing through on their way to an island holiday or those based in town and making day trips to the islands. The short main street is crammed with budget accommodations, restaurants, bou-tiques, and booking agents, but somehow, through all the commercialism and crowds, a relaxed atmosphere prevails.

Conway National Park

This 23,800-hectare park extends south from Airlie Beach to Cape Conway, taking in 50 km of rugged and inaccessible coastline as well as a group of small islands near Shute Harbour. The park is cloaked in subtropical rainforest running right down to the coast, with an extensive swamp of mangroves around the back of Repulse Bay. The road between Airlie Beach and Shute Harbour passes through the park's northern section. From the campground along this

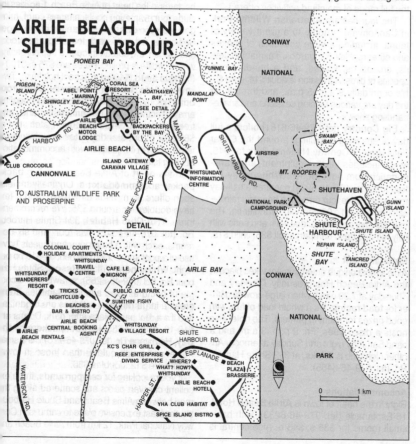

AIRLIE BEACH AND SHUTE HARBOUR

road a trail branches north to **Mt. Rooper,** from where the Whitsunday Islands and Passage provide a spectacular panorama, continuing to Swamp Bay, a round-trip of 6.4 km. Operated by the Department of Environment and Heritage, **Whitsunday Information Centre,** corner Whitsunday and Mandalay Roads (tel. 079-46-7022), is an excellent source of information on all park hikes as well as camping out on the islands. It's open daily 8:30 a.m.-4:30 p.m.

Sights and Recreation

When the weather is inclement, or if you need a break from exploring the islands, head to one of Airlie Beach's many booking agents for details of the full range of mainland activities offered.

The four-hectare **Australian Wildlife Park** in Cannonvale is home to a great variety of fauna, including a huge collection of snakes and other reptiles, kangaroos, Tasmanian devils, crocodiles, koalas, and a hundred-odd species of birds. Admission is adult $14, child $6. It's open daily 9 a.m.-5 p.m., and throughout the day are various feeding sessions and snake-handling shows.

Big Country (tel. 079-46-6181) offers a full day of abseiling (rapelling) around the Cedar Falls area of Conway National Park for $45, which includes lunch, equipment, and transportation from Airlie Beach. **Whitsunday Attractions** (tel. 079-46-6224) operates a half-day four-wheel drive tour through a beautiful rainforest, home to a 1,700-year-old strangler fig. The tour includes an easy guided walk and ends with billy tea and fresh damper; adult $35, child $15.

Entertainment

Airlie's most unique entertainment takes place in the Airlie Beach Hotel (usually Tuesday and Thursday at 7:30 p.m.), when large crowds gather for **toad racing.** It's a whole load of fun, with good prizes for winning punters. The hotel also hosts a disco Tues.-Fri. 9 p.m.-3 a.m. and a band Saturday night and Sunday afternoon. Another nightclub is **Tricks,** at 352 Shute Harbour Rd. (tel. 079-46-6465).

Accommodations

Right in the heart of town is **Airlie Beach Hotel,** 16 Esplanade (tel. 079-46-6233), with basic small rooms for $35 s, $45 d. Also central is

Colonial Court Holiday Apartments, corner Shute Harbour Rd. and Broadwater Ave. (tel 079-46-6180), featuring self-contained units for $45 s, $55 d. **Airlie Beach Motor Lodge,** 6 Lamond St. (tel. 079-46-6418), is another inexpensive option, with rooms for $46 s, $50 d. **Coral Sea Resort,** 25 Ocean View Ave. (tel 079-46-6458), is perched on a headland overlooking Pioneer Bay, a five-minute walk from downtown Airlie Beach. Most rooms have a balcony and ocean views and guests have use of a pool, spa, croquet lawn, private wharf, and restaurant. Rates start at $99 s or d. **Whitsunday Wanderers Resort** (tel. 079-46-6446) is a Polynesian-style complex spread over seven hectares in the heart of Airlie Beach. Facilities include four swimming pools, a tennis court, mini golf, aerobic classes, and an archery range. Self-contained units, each featuring a bathroom and kitchen, are spread through a tropical setting where birdlife is prolific. Rates are $75 s, $100 d (rising to $90 s, $109 d in school holidays). Two km from Airlie Beach in Cannonvale, **Club Crocodile** (tel. 079-46-7155) offers a mind-boggling array of activities, a nightclub, restaurants, and free transfers to Shute Harbour. Rates start at $65 s or d, but standby rates are always offered, often in conjunction with accommodation at Long Island Resort.

In the heart of Airlie Beach are five **backpacker accommodations.** Originally motels, each offers dorm beds for $10-18, and a few have doubles for around $35. We recommend three. **YHA Club Habitat,** 394 Shute Harbour Rd. (tel. 079-46-6312), has four- and six-bed rooms, each with a bathroom, and guests have use of a pool and modern kitchen; $14-18 pp per night. **Whitsunday Village Resort,** Shute Harbour Rd. (tel. 079-46-6266), sprawls over a couple of hectares, and although facilities aren't great, a large range of activities are organized and it's a real party place after dark. Dorms are $10-12, doubles $35-45. **Backpackers by the Bay,** Hermitage Dr. (tel. 079-46-7267), is a small hostel and much quieter than those in town. Dorms are $12, doubles $30.

If you're looking for **campgrounds,** three excellent caravan parks are scattered along the road between Airlie Beach and Shute Harbour, but the least expensive place to camp is in Conway National Park, 12 km from Airlie Beach and our km from Shute Harbour. The campground is small and fills up fast. Sites are $3 pp and there are no hot showers. **Island Gateway Caravan Village,** two km from Airlie Beach toward Shute Harbour (tel. 079-46-6228), has modern bathrooms, a covered kitchen area with basic cooking equipment, a pool, mini-golf, half-court tennis, and movies shown nightly. Unpowered sites are $12, powered sites $16, safari tents $12-8, on-site vans $25, and cabins $35.

Food

Cafe le Mignon (tel. 079-46-7459), beside the parking lot off Shute Harbour Rd., is open daily from 7:30 a.m. with delicious croissants from $4 and healthy sandwiches $3.50-7. For the best fish and chips in town, head to **Sumthin Fishy,** beside the supermarket. On Shute Harbour Rd., **Beaches Bar & Bistro** (tel. 079-46-6244) has a popular bar and inexpensive meals, such as hamburgers and Mexican dishes for $5. **KC's Char Grill,** at the top end of Shute Harbour Rd. (tel. 079-46-6320), is a casual eatery with wooden booths, ceiling fans, and greenery giving it a real tropical ambience. Most meals are charbroiled, with choices including steak, chops, prawns, and delicious racks of lamb; prices range $15-22. Meals are served daily 6 p.m.-2 a.m., and it also opens for Sunday lunch. In Airlie Point Centre is **Spice Island Bistro** (tel. 079-46-6585), an intimate restaurant serving curries from $11.50; the three-course dinner special is good value at $15. Away from the crowds of Shute Harbour Rd. is the large **Beach Plaza Brasserie,** a casual place on the Esplanade and overlooking the bay.

Transportation, Services, and Information

The closest airport to Airlie Beach is in Proserpine. **Qantas** (tel. 13-1313) flies in daily from Brisbane ($199 one-way) and Sydney ($280). If you plan to stay on one of the islands, flying directly to Hamilton Island with **Ansett Australia** (tel. 13-1300) and catching a water taxi to your final destination is less hassle. **Sampson's** (tel. 079-45-2377) meets all Qantas flights and provides bus transfers to Airlie Beach ($11 one-way) and Shute Harbour ($15).

All major bus companies, including **Greyhound Pioneer** (tel. 13-2030) and **McCafferty's** (tel. 079-46-6224), detour from the Bruce Highway to Airlie Beach, terminating in the public carpark off Shute Harbour Road. From Brisbane, the trip takes 15 hours; $105 one-way. Townsville is four hours north; $38 one-way.

Sampson's (tel. 079-45-2377) runs a regular bus service between Proserpine and Shute Harbour, picking up at accommodations en route (when booking day trips to the islands, inquire about free transfers from Airlie Beach accommodations to Shute Harbour).

Between Airlie Beach and Shute Harbour is a short airstrip. It receives no scheduled flights, but a variety of chartered flights leave here for destinations throughout the islands. **Island Air Taxis** (tel. 079-46-9933) offers flightseeing trips around the islands (from $60 pp) and to the outer reef ($100). **Helijet** (tel. 079-46-8249) offers a variety of helicopter joy flights, ranging from a 15-minute flight over a couple of islands ($105 pp) to a three-hour flight to a pontoon on the outer reef ($325).

Avis, Budget, and **National** all have outlets on Shute Harbour Road. Another option for a rental car is **Airlie Beach Rentals,** on Waterson Rd. (tel. 079-46-6110); rates start at $35 half day, $45 full day. For a cab call **Whitsunday Taxi** at (079) 46-6289.

Airlie Beach has no official information center, just a dozen-odd booking agents vying for your business. As each one is a commercial operation, getting general information on the Whitsundays is difficult. **Where? What? How? Whitsunday,** 283 Shute Harbour Rd. (tel. 079-46-5255), has helpful staff who actually find out what you're interested in doing before flogging tours. Staff at **Airlie Beach Central Booking Agent,** beside the public carpark (tel. 079-46-5755), are knowledgeable on the many land-based and adventure-oriented activities in the region. **Whitsunday Travel Centre** is a good source of information on onward bus, rail, and air transportation. It's at 265 Shute Harbour Rd. (tel. 079-46-6224).

WHITSUNDAY ISLANDS

When Capt. James Cook sailed through this area on Whit Sunday, the seventh Sunday after Easter, 1770, he must have been in awe at the beauty of the 100-odd islands crammed within

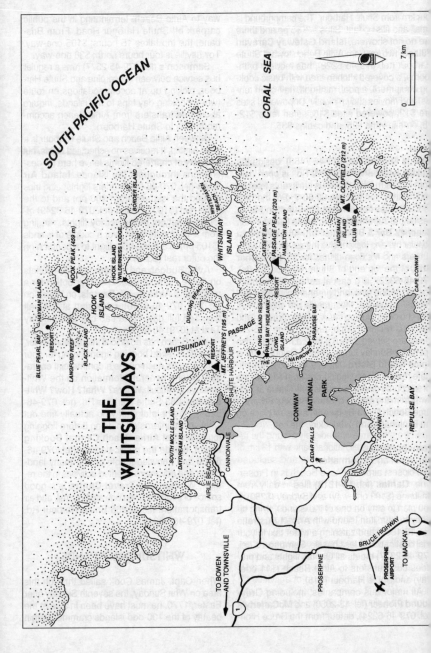

THE WHITSUNDAYS

SOUTH PACIFIC OCEAN

CORAL SEA

7 km

BLUE PEARL BAY
HAYMAN ISLAND
RESORT
LANGFORD REEF
BLACK ISLAND
HOOK PEAK (459 m)
HOOK ISLAND
HOOK ISLAND WILDERNESS LODGE
BORDER ISLAND

WHITSUNDAY ISLAND
WHITEHAVEN BEACH
DUGONG BEACH

CATSEYE BAY
PASSAGE PEAK (230 m)
RESORT
HAMILTON ISLAND

LINDEMAN ISLAND
MT. OLDFIELD (212 m)
CLUB MED

SOUTH MOLLE ISLAND
DAYDREAM ISLAND
WHITSUNDAY
RESORT
MT. JEFFREYS (195 m)
WHITSUNDAY PASSAGE
SHUTE HARBOUR

LONG ISLAND RESORT
PALM BAY HIDEAWAY
LONG ISLAND
THE NARROWS
PARADISE BAY

AIRLIE BEACH
CANNONVALE

CEDAR FALLS

CONWAY NATIONAL PARK

CONWAY

CAPE CONWAY

REPULSE BAY

TO BOWEN AND TOWNSVILLE

PROSERPINE
PROSERPINE AIRPORT

BRUCE HIGHWAY

TO MACKAY

st one degree of latitude. It's the east coast's greatest concentration of islands, each flanked by sandy beaches and fringing coral reefs and ising from magnificent turquoise-colored water. The seven resort islands cater to all budgets, many not as expensive as you'd think, while the rest are uninhabited and protected as national parks. Regular motor launch services link Shute Harbour to the island resorts and a couple of days a week links can also be made from Mackay.

The least-expensive way to book an island holiday in advance is through a travel agent. The packages offered through Ansett Australia (tel. 13-1344) start at $679 for five nights accommodation and return airfares from Sydney. Only during peak holiday periods are resorts running at full occupancy; to fill empty rooms, standby rates are offered, generally two to three days before the empty rooms become available. Savings can be quite considerable, so always ask when making bookings direct through the resort.

The most respected guidebook to the Whitsundays, and definitive reading for yachties, is David Colfelt's *100 Magic Miles of the Great Barrier Reef*.

Long Island

Closest of the resort islands to the mainland, 1,215-hectare Long Island is aptly described by its name. It lies just six km southeast of Shute Harbour, and regular water taxi service links the island's three resorts to the mainland, making a pleasant day trip over smooth waters. Apart from the area immediately around the resorts, the island is all national park, with 13 km of trails leading to high lookouts and secluded coves.

Long Island Resort (tel. 079-46-9400 or 1800-07-5125) is a budget-oriented resort geared toward those looking for action-packed days and to drink and dance the night away. Operated as Happy Bay Resort for 50 years, it was rebuilt in 1984 and has seen various owners and name changes in the time since. Spread around a palm-fringed beach, the large resort is well set up with a wide range of activities offered, a variety of eateries, an outdoor bar, nightclub, and boutique shops. If you don't mind hearing the activities program blasted over the loud-

speaker system all day, it's an enjoyable place to spend a couple of days. Lodge units, with shared bathrooms, are $45 pp per night; Garden units, with private bathrooms, are $65 pp, and Beachfront units are $75 pp. Rates include breakfast and island transfers. No discount is offered for late bookings; instead, if rooms are available, a second night is offered for free. This is currently the Whitsunday's best standby deal, and as there always seems to be vacant rooms, it should be available most of the time.

A 20-minute walk south from Long Island Resort is **Palm Bay Hideaway** (tel. 079-46-9233 or 1800-33-4009), a low-key resort of just 16 free-standing units spread around a pleasant beach area. The relaxed atmosphere appeals to those who want to get away from it all. Water sport equipment, such as catamarans, sailboards, paddle skis, and snorkeling gear, is provided, and there's a small pool, but, for the most part, the guests attracted here spend their days lazing around the beach or relaxing on the hammock and outdoor furniture outside each unit. Rates range $117-153 s, $186-258 d plus meals. Standby rates are often as low as $60 pp per night.

Whitsunday All Over (tel. 079-46-6900) offers transfers for guests and day-trippers to the above resorts for $20 round-trip, which includes bus transfers between Airlie Beach accommodations and Shute Harbour. Departures from Shute Harbour are at 9:15 a.m., returning at 5 p.m.

Like Palm Bay Hideaway, **Paradise Bay,** at the south end of Long Island (tel. 079-46-9777), is a low-key resort. It consists of eight self-contained cabins along a palm-fringed beach backed by steep hills. Rates are $457 pp for five nights and transfers from Shute Harbour. The meal package is $48 pp per day.

Daydream Island

Just 16 hectares in area and only a couple of hundred meters wide, Daydream Island (officially known as West Molle Island) lies four km northeast of Shute Harbour and one km from South Molle Island. The island is best known for a large, moderately priced family-style resort that sprawls over a large part of the island, including the entire southern end. In 1933 the island was bought for 200 pounds and later sold to

Sir Reginald Ansett, who developed a small resort, dismantling it in 1953 to develop Hayman Island. The island lay uninhabited until the 1960s when another resort was developed, and in 1990 the resort of today was constructed.

The resort is best known for an enormous pool from where patrons can swim up to a poolside bar. The island's two beaches are okay (but solitude is hard to find), and snorkeling on the fringing reef is good (stingers are a problem Oct.-May). Guests have use of all nonmotorized water sports equipment, and day-trippers can use one of two pools. Three standards of rooms are available, ranging $180-260 s or d depending on the view. Meal packages are extra, but as the island offers a variety of eateries, it is easier to pay as you go (the nightly dinner buffet is $25 pp). For bookings call Daydream Island Travelodge at (079) 48-8488 or (1800) 07-5040. From North America call (800) 835-7742. Standby rates, when offered, are $77 pp per night inclusive of transfers.

Whitsunday All Over (tel. 079-46-6900) departs Shute Harbour for Daydream Island daily at 9 a.m., returning at 5 p.m.; the fare of $20 round-trip includes bus transfers between Airlie Beach accommodations and Shute Harbour.

South Molle Island

South Molle is a 420-hectare continental island rising gently to 195 meters. Once heavily forested, grazing cattle have cleared much of the island's southern end, but the many hiking trails crisscrossing the island are still interesting. Trails lead to all the island's highest peaks, including Mt. Jeffreys (four km one-way from the resort) and to a couple of secluded beaches at the island's south end (six km one-way). Tourists have been holidaying on South Molle for 60 years, and today **South Molle Island Resort** has grown to be one of the largest resorts of the Whitsundays, with nearly 200 rooms of six configurations. It appeals mainly to families and honeymooners, with a wide range of water sports, a short nine-hole golf course, tennis, and good snorkeling on the fringing reef. The least expensive rooms are $140 pp, inclusive of all meals, activities, and transfers from Hamilton Island or Proserpine Airports. Worth the extra few dollars are the Beachcomber and Polynesian rooms, with ocean views and private bal-

WHAT IS CORAL?

Coral is a polyp, of the same family as the sea anemone and jellyfish. The reef is made up of **hard coral** and **soft coral**. It's the hard coral that is the reef-builder. The polyp secretes a hard calcareous coating that begins as a base, then builds up as a limestone casing into which the polyp can draw itself for protection. The polyp is only two to three millimeters wide; it feeds by capturing floating plankton in tentacles around its mouth.

As the hard corals reproduce, they grow on the limestone skeletons of their predecessors, binding together with secreted limestone and algae to form a solid structure.

Coral is found in various oceans of the world, but the combination of three factors—shallow, warm, and clear water—is needed for a reef to form. The Queensland coast fits these criteria perfectly, although south of Bundaberg water temperature is too cool to allow reef growth. As the sea level rose at the end of the last ice age, low-lying coastal plains were submerged, forming a shallow continental shelf extending up to 300 km from the present-day coastline. This shelf formed the perfect foundation for the coral to form a reef, and it is right on the edge of continental shelf, on the outer reef, that the coral is most spectacular.

conies for $160 pp. The standby rate (book with in 48 hours) is $90 pp. For all bookings ca (079) 46-9433 or (1800) 07-5080. From Nort America call (800) 366-1300.

Whitsunday All Over (tel. 079-46-6900 transfers resort guests from the mainland, a well as taking day-trippers over; departures are daily at 9 a.m. returning at 5 p.m.; $25 round-trip **Seatrek** (tel. 079-46-5255) offers a similar ser vice, or a stop at South Molle can be made a part of a three-island cruise (Daydream an Hook Islands are the others) for $45 pp, incluc ing snorkeling, lunch, and a submarine ride.

Lindeman Island

Home to Australia's first **Club Med** resort, thi 790-hectare island lies at the southern end of th Whitsundays, well away from other resort is lands. It is protected as a national park, wit he resort and airstrip at the south end and thick-y forested ridges dominating the north. Exten-sive grasslands around the island's eastern slopes and 212-meter summit of Mt. Oldfield allow unimpeded views of the beaches below.

Tourists have been coming to the island since the late 1920s, but it wasn't until 1992 that Club Med opened, offering the all-inclusive activity-oriented style that the resort company is known for. Lots of water activities are offered, as well as a large beachfront pool, golf, and tennis. Rates are $260 s, $215 pp d per night; $398 s, $353 pp d for two nights inclusive of air transfers from Airlie Beach or Mackay, all meals, beer and wine, and activities. For reservations call (079) 46-9333 or (1800) 80-1823. From North America call (800) 258-2633.

If you would like to come over to Lindeman Island for just the day, there are three options, but being so far from mainland gateways, it's not cheap. From Shute Harbour, **Whitsunday All Over** (tel. 079-46-6900) departs daily at 7 a.m.; the cost is $100, which includes all resort activities and a buffet lunch. From Mackay, **Roylen Cruises** (tel. 079-55-3066) departs Saturday and Sunday at 9 a.m.; inclusive of meals and booze it's $90 pp. The third alternative is to fly over; the fare is $130 round-trip from either Mackay or Hamilton Island.

Hamilton Island

Hamilton lies in the middle of the Whitsunday Islands, 18 km southeast of Shute Harbour. It's the most developed of the islands, more like a small town than a resort, with high-rise accommodation towers, a 400-berth marina, an endless array of activities, and an international airport capable of handling Boeing 767s. The development of the island was the vision of just one man, Keith Williams (when Williams was at the helm, the resort was known as Williamstown), whose hands-on approach and determination to build a resort like no other in the Whitsundays has become part of Queensland folklore. In the 1970s and '80s when Queensland was ruled by the National Party, changing Hamilton's long-term farming lease to a tourism zoning and getting a megaresort approved in the middle of an UNESCO World Heritage area was met with little opposition. As the high-rise accommodations grew, a bay was dredged for a marina and

a whole hillside dynamited with little government intervention.

Development is on the north end of the island, with the main resort facing Catseye Bay and sprawling over a low ridge to an artificial harbor on the island's west side. The island's south end is scarred by the runway, but the wide eastern peninsula is interesting to explore, with a 15-km hiking trail leading to Passage Peak and a lookout above the resort.

The island can accommodate more than 2,000 guests in three multistory towers and a couple of low-rise lodges along the beachfront. The resort is very activity-oriented, but almost everything is additional to accommodation cost. The least expensive rooms are $195, rising to $335 for a room with a view. Standby rates are $75 pp. For bookings call (079) 46-9999 or (1800) 07-5110.

Until the construction of the island's airport, Proserpine was the gateway to the Whitsundays. Nowadays **Ansett Australia** (tel. 13-1300) flies directly from Brisbane, Sydney, Melbourne, and Cairns to the island. For guests of the resorts on Long, Daydream, and South Molle islands, **Whitsunday All Over** (tel. 079-46-6900) provides transfers from Hamilton Island Airport for $37 round-trip. Lindeman and Hayman Islands operate their own water taxi services. From the Airlie Beach airstrip **Eagle Air** (tel. 079-46-9176) offers charter flights to Hamilton for $35 pp one-way. **Fantasea Cruises** (tel. 079-46-5111) offers boat transfers between the island and Shute Harbour; adult $35, child $17.50. Boats depart Shute Harbour daily at 8:30 a.m. For $39 (child $19.50), island transfers can be combined with a trip to Whitehaven Beach on Whitsunday Island (Tuesday, Thursday, and Sunday only). From Port of Mackay **Roylen Cruises** (tel. 079-55-3066) heads to Hamilton Island Saturday and Sunday departing 9 a.m.; $40 round-trip (a stop is made at Lindeman Island en route).

Whitsunday Island

Largest of the Whitsundays, this 10,800-hectare island is undeveloped and uninhabited. It's most popular with day-trippers who flock to six-km **Whitehaven Beach** on the island's east coast, the longest beach in the group (its pure white sand is almost 99% silica). Rugged topography and long inlets that almost divide it make Whitsunday Island an interesting place to explore. Until the arrival of Europeans in the late 1800s, Aboriginals lived permanently on the island. A sawmill operated at Cid Harbour for many years, but today the entire island is protected as a national park.

Camping is permitted at the south end of Whitehaven Beach, but as there are no facilities or drinking water, you'll need to be totally self-sufficient. A better option for campers is Dugong Beach, on Cid Harbour, where there are toilets, showers, drinking water, and gas barbecues. Most cruise boats do camper drop-offs, including *Whitsunday Explorer III,* whose itinerary includes Cid Harbour on Wednesday and Friday (see below).

Fantasea (tel. 079-46-5111) departs Shute Harbour Tuesday, Thursday, and Sunday at 8:30 a.m. on a cruise taking in Whitehaven Beach and Hamilton Island for $39 pp. For more personal service and an informative commentary *Reef Express* (tel. 079-46-6675) is ideal. This boat departs Abel Point Marina daily at 9 a.m. for Whitehaven Beach, continuing to Hook Island for snorkeling, then returning to Airlie Beach around 5 p.m. This trip is a great value at adult $45, child $23. Similarly priced is *Whitsunday Explorer III* (tel. 079-46-7868); the trip out is slower but lunch is included; departs Tuesday and Thursday only. On Wednesday and Friday this boat heads to Cid Harbour, on the opposite side of the island to Whitehaven Beach. Another option for visiting Whitehaven Beach is aboard a yacht (see "Cruising the Whitsundays," below).

Hook Island

Rugged and remote, 5,180-hectare Hook Island lies 30 km northeast of Shute Harbour and is separated from Whitsunday Island by a narrow channel. The island's fringing reef provides the best diving and snorkeling of all Whitsunday Islands, providing an alternative to more-expensive outer reef diving trips. A small resort and underwater observatory on the southeast coast are the only development on this otherwise uninhabited island.

Hook Island Wilderness Lodge (tel. 079-45-2124 or 1800-07-5080) is a low-key place with basic but adequate accommodations and the only commercial camping on any of the Whitsunday Is-

lands. Snorkeling and scuba diving is good in front of the resort (although visibility can be poor during spring tides), and the resort's dive boat heads out to the reef three times weekly. The resort dive shop rents gear, fills tanks, and operates PADI dive courses. Around a headland from the lodge is an underwater observatory (admission $10), surf-skis for guest use, and basic groceries for sale. Dorm beds are $17-23 pp d; campsites are $8.50 pp, and return transfers $12 pp. At last report, two nights' accommodation and transfers was $37 and five nights' accommodation plus a PADI dive course was $277 pp. Lodge guests and campers may dine in the restaurant (breakfast $5, lunch $3.50-12, dinner $7-12) or cook their own meals in the communal kitchen.

Whitsunday All Over (tel. 079-46-6900) visits its Hook Island Underwater Observatory as part of a three-island day cruise; $45 pp.

Off Hook Island's northwest coast is **Langford Reef,** a popular destination for divers, and **Black Island** (often called Bali Ha'i), where Whitsunday All Over (tel. 079-46-6900) operates a small submarine giving passengers a chance to view a coral reef without getting wet; adult $52, child $26 includes lunch and an hour on Daydream Island.

Hayman Island

Guests at 322-hectare Hayman Island Resort enjoy the absolute best of everything while surrounded by the beauty of one of the best fringing reefs in the Whitsundays. While emphasis at other upmarket island resorts is on natural surroundings, Hayman flatters its guests with facilities and accommodations equal in standard to any of the world's greatest resorts.

In 1985 a planned $25-million facelift turned into a two-year $300 million redevelopment with no expense spared. Highlights include a one-hectare pool featuring both fresh- and saltwater sections separated by narrow walkways, an elegant bar styled on an English gentleman's club, a collection of antiques and artworks, traditional Japanese Garden, palm trees, and 60,000 tons of imported sand that's smoothed over at the end of each day.

The island has excellent scuba diving facilities, including a school, shop, and boat, as well as the following guest activities: windsurfing, sailing, waterskiing, parasailing, tennis, squash, aeroics, and mini-golf. All guest rooms have water views, many with marble bathrooms and air-conditioning. All rates are room-only; transfers, meals, and select activities are extra. Rates start at $375 s or d, rooms along the beach-front start at $500, and suites range $1030-1240. Guests have the choice of dining in one of five restaurants, including the elegant La Fontaine, and enjoying nightly entertainment such as cabaret shows. Access to the island is aboard the 35-meter *Sun Goddess* from Hamilton Island Airport ($200 round-trip). For bookings call (079) 40-1234 or (1800) 07-5175. From North America call (800) 223-6800.

It's not possible to visit the resort on a day trip, but *Illusions,* a 12-meter catamaran, departs Abel Point Marina daily at 9:15 a.m. for Blue Pearl Bay, on the Hayman Island's west coast. This bay has a good stretch of beach and fine snorkeling on the fringing reef; $48 pp, lunch is an extra $6. For bookings call (079) 46-6375.

DAY TRIPS TO THE OUTER REEF

The Whitsundays are Queenland's best known island group, but they lie close to the mainland and well away from actual reef. The closest reefs, which lie 63 km from Shute Harbour, include Bait, Hook, Line, and Sinker (look at a chart to see how they were named). These platform reefs sit at and below water level. There are no islands to explore, no resorts, just a few pontoons moored in strategic positions for the use of day-trippers who come to dive and snorkel at one of the world's great dive sites. Only high-speed motor cruisers can make it from the mainland to the outer reef and back in one day. **Fantasea Cruises** (tel. 079-46-5111) departs Shute Harbour daily at 8:30 a.m. for **Reefworld,** a large pontoon on the outer reef. The pontoon has an underwater observatory, sundeck, restaurant, showers, and plenty of good snorkeling; cost of the cruise is adult $106, senior $80, child $53, family $222. Certified divers pay $140, including gear rental. **Helireef** (tel. 079-46-9102) flies out to Reefworld from Airlie Beach, with snorkeling and lunch for $195 pp. **Eagle Air** (tel. 079-46-9176) offers the least expensive way to see the outer reef, with a one-hour flight over Hayman Island and the reef for $60 pp.

Island resorts offering guests day trips to the outer reef include: Hook, Hayman, Hamilton, Lindeman, and South Molle.

SCUBA DIVING IN THE WHITSUNDAYS

The suspended sediment that gives the waters of the Whitsundays a magnificent color inhibits visibility for divers, so serious divers will want to head to the outer reef. That said, the diversity of coral and fishlife around the islands will not disappoint, and with the islands' fringing reefs protected from the full brunt of the ocean by the outer reef, the waters are relatively calm.

Each of the island resorts caters to divers, with Hook Island Wilderness Lodge being especially good for keen divers and those planning to complete a dive course (package deals offered here are less expensive than staying on the mainland). For those not staying out on the islands, organizing a diving holiday can be problematic. The best diving is on the outer reef, but being more than 60 km from Airlie Beach, it makes for a long and expensive day diving. Numerous operators run to the outer reef (see "Day Trips to the Outer Reef," above), but none caters specifically to divers. **Fantasea Cruises** (tel. 079-46-5111) runs out to Reefworld, on the outer reef, for $140 including lunch, one dive, and equipment.

The Whitsundays' most-respected dive operator is **Reef Enterprise Diving Service,** 386 Shute Harbour Rd. (tel. 079-46-7228 or 1800-62-1133). They offer a two-night diving package including transfers to the outer reef, up to seven dives, all meals, and accommodation on board for $210 pp. Gear rental is $20 per day. This is also the best company to learn to dive with; the basic PADI course is $240 using a pool, and $320 combining two days of shore instruction with two days aboard the *Reef Enterprise.*

CRUISING THE WHITSUNDAYS

Calm waters, sheltered anchorages, uninhabited islands, and an ideal climate make the Whitsundays the prime destination for a sailing holiday, but it is only in the last 15 years that the opportunity to experience the Whitsundays under sail became possible for those without a yacht. The options are a day trip on one of the many racing maxi-yachts that have retired to the Whitsundays, or on a bareboat charter. "Bareboat" is a seafaring term for skippering a rented yacht, and so long as at least one member of the crew can sail it is the perfect way to explore the Whitsundays.

A Day under Sail

Australia's strong ocean-racing traditions date back several decades, and many of the country's fastest yachts spend their retirement days sailing around the Whitsundays with their decks full of tourists. Some examples are *Gretel,* a 20.8-meter maxi that challenged for the America's Cup in the early 1970s; *Apollo,* which won just about every race in the South Pacific including a Sydney-Hobart; and *Ragamuffin,* which won the Sydney-Hobart race three times. These and other yachts depart Shute Harbour daily 8:30-9 a.m., sailing out to Langford Reef (not on the outer reef) or Whitehaven Beach for snorkeling or scuba diving ($40-50 extra) and returning 4-4:30 p.m. Prices range $55-60. Sailing isn't restricted to ex-champions; *On The Edge* is a high-speed catamaran (meaning more time at the destination) sailing to Whitehaven Beach (Monday, Wednesday, Friday, and Sunday) and Hook Island (Tuesday, Thursday, and Sunday); departures are from Abel Point Marina at 9 a.m. The cost is $53 pp; for bookings call (079) 46-5433.

Some operators offer overnight sailing cruises, typically departing 9 a.m. and returning 4 p.m. three days later, with price inclusive of accommodation on board, all meals, and snorkeling equipment for $250-300 pp. Try: **Waltzing Matilda,** a 20-meter ketch; **Pro Sailing,** which has a large fleet and caters to under-35s (bring your own booze); and *Providence,* a timber replica of a gaffed-rigged schooner.

Bareboat Charters

Chartering your own yacht is the ultimate way to enjoy the Whitsundays, although it's not particularly cheap and you'll need at least one crew member proficient at handling the size yacht you intend renting. Local weather and navigational considerations to be taken into effect will be explained before heading out. Most yachts have a hot shower, kitchen, barbecue, music system, and a whole range of other luxuries. Yachts range in size from seven to 15 meters. Each has a recommended crew number, but these are really a maximum—try to crew the boat at least two less. Rates start at $250 per day for the smallest yachts. A 12-meter yacht, perfect for a crew of four, runs $320-400 per day, with discounts for weekly rentals. Most charter operators offer food packs and although convenient, they can really add up ($25-30 pp per day). Two of the most experienced operators are **Queensland Yacht Charters** (tel. 079-46-7400 or 1800-07-5013) and **Whitsunday Rent-a-yacht** (tel. 079-46-9232 or 1800-07-5012).

THE WHITSUNDAYS TO CAIRNS

Once you've managed to drag yourself away from the Whitsundays, it's an easy day's drive 300 km north to Cairns, but along the way are enough distractions to make the trip last at least a few days. This region is the heart of tropical Queensland, dominated by miles of rugged coastline, stately colonial-style buildings, and streets lined with colorful bougainvilleas. The first major center north of Proserpine is Townsville, home to the excellent Great Barrier Reef Wonderland, a living coral reef transposed to the heart of the city. Offshore is Magnetic Island, easily accessible for day-trippers. The reef may be Queensland's favorite holiday destination, but Hinchinbrook Island, halfway between Townsville and Cairns, is another amazing place you shouldn't miss. Lying close to the mainland, it's the world's largest island national park. For the best mainland beaches north of the Sunshine Coast, head to the string of communities along Mission Beach and overlooking Dunk Island,

Bowen

Founded in 1861, this farming and fishing center of wide palm-lined streets dotted with colonial buildings is north Queensland's oldest town. Salt production is also a part of the local economy, with almost 10,000 tons produced annually. Murals along Powell and Williams Streets depict scenes from the town's past, and **Bowen Historical Museum,** 22 Gordon St. (tel. 077-86-2035), displays hundreds of artifacts dating from pre-European days to modern industries. The museum is open Mon.-Fri. 10:30 a.m.-4 p.m., Sunday 10:30 a.m.-12:30 p.m. East of the main street is the coal-loading terminal of **Port Denison** and **Bowen Boat Harbour,** protected

On 1 November 1997 telephone numbers in this section will change. To dial the new number, simply add "47" to all numbers with the area code (077) and add "40" to all numbers with the area code (070). As an example, (077) 12-3456 becomes 4712-3456. The new area code for all numbers in this section will be (07).

from the elements by North Head and an artificial sea wall. Immediately north of Bowen is the long expanse of Queens Beach and rocky **Cape Edgecombe,** indented on its eastern flanks by pretty **Horseshoe Bay,** a narrow cove of sand surrounded by rugged outcrops of granite. At the back of the bay a short trail leads to a lookout high above the beach.

Right downtown, **North Australian Hotel,** 55 Herbert St. (tel. 077-86-1244), has good pub-style rooms with shared bathrooms for $32 s, $38 d. Another inexpensive place to stay is **Barnacles Backpackers,** 16 Gordon St. (tel. 077-86-1245), geared mainly for fruit-pickers. Dorms are $10 pp and doubles are $24. Out at Horseshoe Bay is **Whitsunday Sands Resort** (tel. 077-86-3333). Rooms are fairly basic, and the whole place has seen better days, but the resort has an excellent beachfront location and the price is right; $43 s, $57 d. **Horseshoe Bay Caravan Park** (tel. 077-86-2564), on the same beach, features a heated pool, barbecue area, and kiosk; sites are $12-15, on-site vans $20-23, and cabins $30-55.

A small **information center** in the Town Hall on Gordon St. is open Mon.-Fri. 10 a.m.-noon. South of town, in a rest area on the east side of the road, is an information booth manned by friendly volunteers offering coffee and coconuts to passersby.

Ayr

This town of 8,500 sits on the north bank of the **Burdekin River,** one of Queensland's largest rivers. This is sugarcane country, with one million tons of raw sugar produced annually. **Ayr Nature Display,** corner Wilmington and McKenzie Streets (tel. 077-83-2189), houses 60,000 specimens of small Australian fauna; open daily 8 a.m.-4 p.m.

Bowling Green Bay National Park

Straddling the highway between Ayr and Townsville, this 55,400-hectare park has two distinct sections. East of the highway is Bowling Green Bay, a low-lying area of mangroves protected from prevailing winds and currents by

Cape Bowling Green, a long crescent of land. But it is west of the highway, in a mountainous area dominated by 1,342-meter **Mt. Elliot,** that you'll find the park's accessible attractions. This section of the park protects the southern extent of tropical rainforest in Australia. The high peaks are the source of many watersheds that flow in an easterly direction over granite outcrops and through lushly vegetated gorges. The main access road spurs west from the Bruce Highway 60 km northwest of Ayr and 30 km south of Townsville. The facility area at the end of this road is the trailhead for paths leading up the lower slopes of Mt. Elliot; one, along **Cockatoo Creek,** is eight km one-way (three hours); the other, to **Alligator Falls,** is 11 km one-way (three and a half hours). A campground area has toilets, showers, and barbecues; for bookings call (077) 78-8203.

TOWNSVILLE

Largest tropical city in Australia and Queensland's third-largest city, Townsville (pop. 100,000) lies 1,370 km north of Brisbane and 340 km south of Cairns. It may not be the prettiest place on the coast, but it's home to the excellent Great Barrier Reef Wonderland and is the gateway to Magnetic Island. Townsville was the original capital of reef tourism, especially for North Americans, but the construction of an international airport changed all that, and today, although areas of downtown look a bit rough around the edges, much is being done to spruce the place up. The city sprawls over the delta of the Ross River, with the city center spread along Ross Creek and nestled in the shadow of Castle Hill, a granite massif rising 286 meters from the surrounding plains.

Established by a Sydney businessman in 1864 to serve vast pastoral leases, Townsville grew as a beef and wool center. A rail line completed between Brisbane and Townsville in 1877 and the construction of a line to Mt. Isa in 1929 saw Townsville grow to be Queensland's busiest port.

Great Barrier Reef Wonderland
The Great Barrier Reef may lie 70 km off Townsville's coastline, but modern technology

has brought the reef to the mainland by re-creating its form under artificial conditions. This complex comprises the **Great Barrier Reef Aquarium, Omnimax Theatre,** and **Museum of Tropical Queensland** and serves as the departure point for ferries to Magnetic Island. Without a doubt, the aquarium is the highlight of visit to Townsville. It holds a living reef contained in a tank 38 meters long, 17 meters wide and 4.6 meters deep. All reef conditions are artificially maintained to keep the reef alive. Wave motion, tidal movement, and a farm of algae combine to maintain the natural balance of nutrients while replenishing oxygen within the tank. The aquarium is home to 150 species of coral and 200 species of fish. A transparent walk-through tunnel winds through the main aquarium, allowing visitors to experience life under-water without getting wet. Within the aquarium complex is an interactive display and audiovisual, and information on reef protection.

Another part of Wonderland is the Omnimax Theatre, a cavernous auditorium with a dome roof and seats tilted back for comfortable viewing. For extra clarity, underwater images are shot on film 10 times the normal size; combined with a screen 180-degrees wide, the show gives viewers an awesome experience.

The Queensland Museum operates displays within Wonderland that are related to the natural history of tropics. Displays include those dedicated to the Koori, dinosaurs, and the flora and fauna in the tropics.

A combined ticket to all three attractions is $22. Admission to the aquarium only is $12, the Omnimax Theatre $10, and the museum $3.50 Children are half price. The complex is open daily 9 a.m.-5 p.m. For further information ca (077) 21-2411.

Other Sights
Flinders St. Mall, the commercial center o Townsville, buzzes with activity on weekdays and houses a popular market Sunday. At the east end of the mall is **Flinders St. East,** a strip of historic buildings overlooking Ross Creek. This road continues to a marina and **Sheraton Break water Casino.** One block from Flinders St. Ma is **Townsville Museum,** displaying the region's history through old photographs and memorabilia. It's open daily 9 a.m.-5 p.m. and admission

TO BEACH HOUSE
MOTEL, AQUARIUS ON
THE BEACH, AND
ROWES BAY

SHERATON
■ BREAKWATER CASINO

QUARTERDECK
■ ON THE MARINA

MAGNETIC
ISLAND
FERRIES
TERMINAL

THE STRAND

● Yongala Lodge

FRYER ST.

CRITERION
■ TAVERN

GREAT
BARRIER
REEF
● WONDERLAND

TERRACE

MELTON ST.

FLINDERS ST. EAST

DENHAM ST.

THE
■ MAGNET

● EXCHANGE HOTEL

CREEK

TO SOUTH
TOWNSVILLE

MARITIME
● MUSEUM

● ADVENTURERS RESORT YHA

POST OFFICE

STOKES ST.

WILLS ST.

MALL

FLINDERS ST.

PLUME ST.

● GLOBETROTTERS

◆ TOWNSVILLE TRANSIT CENTRE

PALMER ST.

● TOWNSVILLE
MUSEUM

FISHERMAN'S
■ WHARF

ROSS

DEAN ST.

CACTUS
● JACK'S

● AUSTRALIAN
HOTEL

TO TOWN
LODGE MOTOR INN
AND CASTLE HILL

STANLEY ST.

WALKER ST.

● TOWNSVILLE
TRAVELODGE

OGDEN ST.

MIKE BALL
◆ DIVE
EXPEDITIONS

● CIVIC GUEST
HOUSE INN

BLACKWOOD ST.

STURT ST.

FLINDERS ST.

GREAT
● NORTHERN
HOTEL

■ RAILWAY
STATION

TOWNSVILLE

N

0   200 m

TO CHARTERS
TOWERS
AND CAIRNS

TO AYR AND BOWEN

SIR LESLIE THIESS DR.

KING ST.

BREAKWATER RD.

is $1. It's at 81 Sturt St. (tel. 077-72-5725). Across Ross Creek from downtown is the **Maritime Museum of Townsville,** 42-68 Palmer St. (tel. 077-21-5251). It's only a small facility but worthy of inspection. Admission is $2. Open Mon.-Fri. 10 a.m.-4 p.m., Sat.-Sun. 1-4 p.m.

The **Australian Institute of Marine Science,** at Cape Ferguson (turn off the Bruce Highway 30 km south of Townsville), aims to further biologist's knowledge of marine ecosystems on the reef so that long-term management plans can be put into place. Tours are offered each Friday at 10 a.m.; bookings essential (tel. 077-53-4211).

Parks and Gardens

Sprawling over 27 hectares in the suburb of Mundingburra is **Anderson Park Botanic Gardens.** Many trees featured are unique to the tropics, including a collection endemic to Cape York Peninsula. The highlight of the gardens is a large conservatory housing more than 500 species of tropical rainforest flora. While the park is open all day, the conservatory opens only 9:30-10 a.m., 10:30 a.m.-1 p.m., and 1:30-4:30 p.m.

North of the city, off the coastal road leading to Pallarenda, is **Town Common Environmental Park,** a large expanse of low-lying mangroves and grassland. It's a good place for birdwatching, especially in the morning, when brolgas are often sighted.

Billabong Sanctuary, 17 km south of Townsville (tel. 077-78-8344), is one of North Queensland's largest wildlife parks. Admission is adult $14, child $7. The park is open daily ! a.m.-5 p.m. with feeding times posted on a boar out front.

The Great Barrier Reef beyond Townsville

The most popular destination offshore from Townsville is Magnetic Island (see below), bu like a majority of islands along the coast, it is i long way from the true barrier reef (althougl sections of Magnetic Island boast sections c fringing reef), and swimming is curtailed durin summer by box jellyfish.

Just one Townsville operator, **Pure Pleasur Cruises** (tel. 077-21-3555), offers day trips to th outer reef. Their boats depart Great Barrier Ree Wonderland Tues.-Thurs., Saturday, and Sun day at 9 a.m. for **Kelso Reef** 90 km northeast c Townsville. Once on the reef, there's snorkeling scuba diving, coral viewing, and relaxing on i pontoon. Tour cost is adult $110, child $55 in cluding a buffet lunch.

John Brewer Reef, 74 km northeast o Townsville, was the site of the Barrier Reef Re sort, one of Australia's most controversial an adventurous tourism developments. The shor lived project began in 1988, when the world' only floating hotel—seven stories high, capa ble of accommodating 400 guests, and com plete with restaurants, spas, a tennis court, an a nightclub—was towed into a lagoon on th outer reef. The second part of the project, **Fan tasy Island,** featuring a restaurant, outdoo lounge area, movie theater, and palm-fringe

a bird's-eye view of downtown Townsville

wimming pool, was towed into place two months later. Fantasy Island lasted all of 10 days before a storm sent it to Davy Jones's ocker. Barrier Reef Resort lasted a little longer; racked by monetary problems and low occupancy rates, it was last seen being towed north to Ho Chi Minh City.

Mike Ball Dive Expeditions

One of Australia's premier dive operations, Mike Ball Dive Expeditions is based at 252 Walker St., Townsville (tel. 077-72-3022). The two most popular destinations for dive trips from Townsville are **John Brewer Reef** and the wreck of the *Yongala,* a passenger ship that sank off Cape Bowling Green in 1911 with the loss of 122 lives. Three-day, two-night expeditions out to the *Yongala* depart every Tuesday and Friday at 8 p.m. The tour cost, inclusive of accommodation on board *Watersport*, all meals, and diving, is $416-02 pp. (In bad weather diving the *Yongala* is substituted for John Brewer Reef). A unique feature of Mike Ball's dive program are trips well beyond the outer reef to remote coral reefs where visibility can reach 50 meters. Rates for these seven-day trips range $1947-2802 pp.

At the company's Townsville headquarters is a large and unique complex, with the dive shop built into the side of a training pool. Rates for an open-water PADI course range $359-45.

Arts and Entertainment

The **Criterion Tavern,** corner Strand and King St. (tel. 077-71-2271), comprises a beer garden and nightclub, with bands performing most nights. On Flinders St. East, the wine bar in the Exchange Hotel is a good place for a quiet drink, as is **Quarterdeck on the Marina,** with live music Wed.-Sun. evenings.

Townsville Civic Theatre, 41 Boundary St. (tel. 077-72-2677), hosts performing arts, including drama, orchestral concerts, musicals, and dance. Tickets range $12-40.

Sheraton Breakwater Casino (tel. 077-22-2333) is built on a breakwall that wraps around the harbor. Games offered include roulette, blackjack, craps, keno, and Australia's own two-up. The casino has two bars, a number of eateries, and live jazz Fri.-Sat. nights; open daily 10 a.m.-3 a.m.

Accommodations

Yongala Lodge, 11 Fryer St. (tel. 077-72-4633), a two-story timber building dating to 1884, is named for the *Yongala,* which sank off Townsville in 1911 killing more than 100 people, including the lodge's original owners. Rooms in the main house have been restored while out back are modern motel units. All are $69 s or d. The **Great Northern Hotel,** 496 Flinders St. (tel. 077-76-6191), has typical pub-style rooms with shared facilities and a bar downstairs; $18 s, $30 d.

Town Lodge Motor Inn, 15 Victoria St. (tel. 077-71-2164), is one of the least expensive motels within walking distance of downtown. Facilities include a pool, barbecue, and laundry, and many rooms have a kitchen; $54 s, $59 d. Close to the waterfront is **Beach House Motel,** 66 The Strand (tel. 077-21-1333), a little worse for wear but reasonably priced at $49 s, $55 d. Also on The Strand, at no. 75, is the 14-story **Aquarius on the Beach** (tel. 077-72-4255). All rooms are large and have a kitchen and private balcony with ocean views; $90-115 s or d.

Budget travelers have a few choices. **Adventurers Resort YHA,** 79 Palmer St. (tel. 077-21-1522), is a huge hostel with excellent facilities, including a pool and restaurant; dorm beds are $12-13, while private rooms are $20-22 s, $28-30 d. Another good choice is **Globetrotters,** 45 Palmer St. (tel. 077-71-3242), where a bed in a six-share dorm is $11, singles are $22, and twins are $28. Closer to the city center, and next door to Mike Ball Dive Expeditions, is **Civic Guest House Inn,** 262 Walker St. (tel. 077-71-5381); dorm beds are $11-12 and large doubles are $28.

Rowes Bay Caravan Park, Heatley Parade (tel. 077-71-3576), right opposite the beach, features a pool, barbecue area, and kiosk. Unpowered sites are $12, powered sites $15-20, and cabins range $34-49 per night.

Food

Townsville Travelodge, at the west end of Flinders St. Mall (tel. 077-72-2477), serves an excellent $9.95 buffet breakfast daily 7:30-10:30 a.m.

Townsville may be a big city, but, as always, head to the pubs for hearty and inexpensive meals; try **Great Northern Hotel,** 500 Flinders St., or **Australian Hotel,** on Palmer St., which has a good beer garden. If Townsville can be said to have a trendy street, it would be Flinders St. East, where many of the historic buildings have been converted to restaurants. Downstairs in the **Exchange Hotel** is a wine bar with cheese plates and light snacks offered, while upstairs is **The Balcony** (tel. 077-71-3335), a stylish restaurant with tables inside and out. Once through the massive doors, **The Magnet,** 145 Flinders St. (tel. 077-71-3633), is furnished simply; most pastas are under $10 with seafood only a few dollars extra (try barramundi smothered in mango and macadamia nut sauce; $16.50).

Fisherman's Wharf, Ogden St. (tel. 077-21-1838), is spread out alongside the river. Meals are chosen from a blackboard menu, with small steaks for $8 and pastas a little less. The seafood buffet here is $19.90. It's open Sun.-Fri. for lunch and daily for dinner.

Cactus Jack's, on the south side of Ross Creek, is one of Townsville's most popular restaurants. Featuring all the usual Mexican fare, dishes are large and authentic and range $8-14 for a main dish. It's at 21 Palmer St. (tel. 077-21-1478).

Quarterdeck on the Marina, opposite the casino (tel. 077-22-2333), has seating inside or out on a covered deck over the water. Meals are well-priced with an outside barbecue $7.50-11 each evening. Meals are served daily noon-2 p.m., 6-9 p.m. For a splurge, head to **Melton's,** in the casino (tel. 077-22-2333).

Transportation and Tours

Ansett Australia (tel. 13-1300) and **Qantas** (tel. 13-1313) fly into Townsville from Brisbane ($185 one-way), Sydney ($256), and Cairns ($148) as well as other centers such as Darwin and Alice Springs. **Sunstate** (tel. 13-1313) flies along the Queensland coast and out to Dunk Island. **Flightwest** (tel. 13-2392) operates from Townsville to inland destinations such as Mt. Isa and Longreach. A cab between the airport, seven km southwest of the city, and downtown runs about $9.

Queensland Rail (tel. 13-2232) serves Brisbane and Cairns, stopping at Townsville. From Brisbane, one-way fares on the Sunlander are economy $112, first-class $168, while the more luxurious Queenslander is $433 including meals. Twice weekly the Inlander runs between

Townsville and Mt. Isa; the eight-hour journey i $95 in economy, $192 in a first-class sleeper.

Greyhound Pioneer (tel. 13-2030) and **Mc Cafferty's** (tel. 077-79-5877) have regular ser vices between Townsville and all Queensland' coastal towns. Sample fares from Townsvill are: Brisbane, $117 one-way; Airlie Beach, $38 and Cairns, $40. Regular services head inlan to Mt. Isa ($81 one-way), from where connec tions can be made through to Darwin and Alic Springs. All buses arrive and depart from **Townsville Transit Centre,** Palmer St., wher you'll find accommodation booking agents, lock ers, and a restaurant.

Services and Information

Clothes can be washed at **Southside Laundro mat,** 14 Plume St., South Townsville. **Townsvill General Hospital** is on Eyre St. (tel. 077-81 9211).

In the middle of Flinders St. Mall is a **touris information booth** (tel. 077-21-3660), with friendly staff and handy information sheets de tailing attractions, accommodations, dining, an Magnetic Island practicalities. It's open Mon. Fri. 9 a.m.-5 p.m., Sat.-Sun. 9 a.m.-noon. Th main **Tourist Information Centre** is on th Bruce Hwy. eight km south of the city (not ver convenient if you're arriving from the north o by public transportation). It's open daily 9 a.m. 5 p.m. The **Department of Environment an Heritage** has an information center in Grea Barrier Reef Wonderland (tel. 077-21-2399); it' open Mon.-Sat. 9 a.m.-5 p.m.

MAGNETIC ISLAND

A large continental island lying eight km of Townsville, 5,030-hectare Magnetic Island fea tures white sandy beaches and good bush walking. The atmosphere on the island is re laxed and informal; it's more like an outer suburb of Townsville than a resort island. The island' population is 2,500, most of whom reside in set tlements along the east coast. Southernmos of these is Picnic Bay, where ferries from th mainland dock hourly.

Roughly triangular in shape, the island rises t 497 meters at **Mt. Cook** and extends 11 km a its widest point. About half the island is protect

MAGNETIC ISLAND

...ed by **Magnetic Island National Park.** The park's thickly forested slopes are punctuated with granite outcrops, while granite boulders ...ank many beaches. Birdlife is prolific and sim...lar to that found on coastal mainland of a simi...ar latitude. Rock wallabies are common (look for ...hem on Bright Point), as are koalas (look for ...hem on the Forts hiking trail).

Around the Island

Passenger ferries arrive at **Picnic Bay,** the is...and's largest town, where you'll find shops and ...estaurants, car rental outlets, and accommo...dations. The beach at Picnic Bay has the is...and's only stinger-free enclosure. To the east, ...around Hawkings Point, a steep trail descends ...o **Rocky Bay** and a small secluded beach.

Immediately north of Picnic Bay is **Nelly Bay,** with a number of budget accommodations and residential houses scattered around a low-lying area in the shadow of Mt. Cook. Along the bay is a long beach, scarred at the north end by an ambitious marina development that never came to fruition.

Over the northern headland is **Arcadia,** a small village overlooking two good beaches. Geoffrey Bay, south of the headland, is good for snorkeling on the fringing reef, and at low tide it's possible to take a self-guided walk over the exposed coral. To the north is Alma Bay and a small but picturesque beach. The island's biggest dive operator, **Pleasure Divers** (tel. 077-78-5788), is based in Arcadia Hotel Resort. As well as renting snorkeling equipment

Florence Bay

($6 half-day), they offer certified divers the opportunity to explore various island dive sites ($50-80) and operate PADI open-water dive courses ($249).

Near the north end of the island, the road divides. The right fork leads to three remote beaches, including the island's best beach at **Florence Bay** (good snorkeling at the south end) and, at the end of the road, **Radical Bay.**

The left fork ends at **Horseshoe Bay,** a wide north-facing beach where you can rent a variety of water sport equipment including catamarans, jet skis, aqua bikes, and motor boats. Behind the small township of Horseshoe Bay is **Koala Park Oasis,** a small wildlife park with koala cuddling, koala feeding, and other native animals on display. Admission is adult $7, child $3.50. Open daily 9 a.m.-5 p.m. (tel. 077-78-5260). To the west is **Horseshoe Bay Lagoon Environmental Park,** a good area for viewing abundant and varied birdlife.

Hiking

Trails lead to the island's rugged interior from the east coast, but most are ill-defined and, for some strange reason, traversing them is not encouraged. An easy-to-reach lookout is **The Forts.** The trail begins at the Radical Bay turnoff, climbing steadily to an area of massive granite outcrops inlayed with command posts, lookouts, and gun emplacements used during WW II. The trail is 1.3 km one-way. From the east end of the beach at Horseshoe Bay, a trail climbs

through a forest of dry eucalypt to lovely Baldin Bay and Radical Bay. Longer walks are from Nelly Bay to Arcadia Bay (six km one-way) an Nelly Bay to the summit of Mt. Cook (five kr one-way), but check trail conditions with the De partment of Environment and Heritage at Grea Barrier Reef Wonderland, Townsville (tel. 077 21-2399), before setting out.

Accommodations

Magnetic Island has no upmarket resorts, but sti boasts the widest range of accommodations any Great Barrier Reef island. The listings belov are only a sample of those offered and are liste from the island's south end to its north.

Within walking distance of the ferry terminal i **Picnic Bay Holiday Hotel,** Esplanade (tel. 077 78-5166), with air-conditioned rooms, a pool and beer garden; $45 s or d or $65 with kitchen. For backpackers, **Hideaway Budge Resort,** 32 Picnic St., Picnic Bay (tel. 077-78 5110), offers two-bed dorms for $14 pp, singles for $22, and doubles for $28. Each room is fan cooled and guests have use of a kitchen, bar becue, and pool.

Descending into Nelly Bay, the first accom modation you'll pass is **Beachfront Resort** (tel 077-78-5777), with tent sites for $7 pp, and four and eight-berth cabins for $12-14 pp. This place has a communal kitchen, laundry, and pool, and offers a variety of water sports. In the same price range is **Magnetic Island Tropical Re sort,** 56 Yates St., Nelly Bay (tel. 077-78-5955)

sprawling complex set among native bush-
nd with a pool, spa, bar, game area, and free
ansport to the ferry terminal. Beds in a six-bed
orm are $12 pp and doubles are $38-40. The
land's premier accommodation is **Latitude 19
esort,** Mandalay Ave., Nelly Bay (tel. 077-78-
200), which has a pool, tennis court, and dive
enter; $95 s or d.

Arcadia Hotel Resort, Arcadia (tel. 077-78-
177), has motel-style units, each with a kitchen,
et around a landscaped pool; $55-75 s or d.

Geoff's Place, Horseshoe Bay Rd., Horse-
hoe Bay (tel. 077-78-5577), is well suited for
udget travelers, with many planned activities
nd a party atmosphere. Camping is $6 pp,
orm beds $8-12 pp. Transfers to Picnic Bay
re complimentary.

ood

estaurants and cafes are scattered throughout
he island and each settlement has a grocery
tore. In Picnic Bay Mall, **Green Frog Cafe** has
iews over the bay and is open for breakfast
nd lunch. The hotel in Picnic Bay serves inexensive counter meals.

Over in Nelly Bay, the bistro in **Magnetic Is-
and Tropical Resort,** 56 Yates St. (tel. 077-
8-5955), serves large portions and is open
aily 8 a.m.-8:30 p.m., with all main meals under
10 and a $10 roast served Sunday 6:30-8:30
.m. Dishing up good-quality meals at very rea-
onable prices is **Mexican Munchies** at 37 War-
oys St., Nelly Bay (tel. 077-78-5658).

Banister's Seafood, 22 McCabe Crescent,
rcadia (tel. 077-78-5700), has the best fish
nd chips on the island, either takeaway ($4-
) or eat-in ($9-10); it's open daily 9 a.m.-8:30
.m. **Blue Waters,** in Arcadia Shopping Centre
el. 077-78-5645), is a casual restaurant with tales set among a pleasant garden; open daily
om 6 a.m.

Cotter's on the Beach, in Horseshoe Bay,
pecializes in seafood but also offers beef and
hicken dishes ranging $12-15; call (077) 78-
786 for reservations.

ransportation and Tours

Magnetic Island Ferries (tel. 077-21-1913) de-
arts 13 times daily from a terminal on
ownsville's breakwater for Picnic Bay. The first
leparture is 6:05 a.m. From 8:20 a.m. pick-ups

are also made at Great Barrier Reef Wonderland. The last departure from Picnic Bay is 7:15
p.m., with later services Friday and Saturday
nights. The round-trip fare from Townsville to the
island is adult $19, child $9.50; combined with a
very ordinary island tour the fare is adult $26,
child $13. Pick-ups and drop-offs at Townsville
accommodations are complimentary. **Capricorn
Barge Company** runs two to four times daily
between the island and a boat ramp on Ross
St., South Townsville; $89 per vehicle includes
passengers. For bookings call (077) 72-5422.

Magnetic Island Bus Service (tel. 077-78-
5130) meets all ferries and runs the length of the
island; $7 for an all-day pass or $1.50-3 per
sector. **Magnetic Moke,** Esplanade, Picnic Bay
(tel. 077-78-5377), rents mokes (jeeps) for $39
pp per day including petrol and transfers to the
island.

Services and Information
The tourist information booth in Townsville's
Flinders St. Mall has all the information you'll
need on the island. Once ashore, head to the **Is-
land Travel Centre,** on the foreshore at Picnic
Bay (tel. 077-78-5155); open daily 9 a.m.-5 p.m.

PALM ISLANDS

Located north of Townsville, these 11 continental islands are secluded and, apart from one
island resort, rarely visited by outsiders. Named
by Captain Cook for palm-fringed beaches, the
group has been inhabited by Aborigines for generations and today all but two of the islands are
Aboriginal reserves, including the largest, 5,666-
hectare Great Palm Island, which has a population of 1,400. Those not designated as reserves are Orpheus Island, second-largest of
the group and site of an upmarket resort, and
Pelorus Island, protected as a national park.

Orpheus Island
A long and narrow continental island of 1,376
hectares, Orpheus is rugged and rocky but also
boasts excellent beaches and undisturbed fringing reefs. For the most part, the island is forested and supports a diverse array of birdlife.
James Cook University maintains a small research station at Pioneer Bay.

On the island's west coast, behind a white sandy beach on Hazard Bay is **Orpheus Island Resort.** Geared for those who want to escape (no television or newspapers), the resort is elegant without being pretentious. Accommodation is in stylish beachfront units or six Mediterranean-style villas set on the hillside. Each unit has a queen-size bed and comfortable sitting area. Rates are $390-480 s, $670-770 d per night inclusive of meals. For reservations call (077) 77-7377 or (1800) 07-7167. Within North America, call (800) 448-8355. Transportation to the resort is by floatplane from either Townsville ($260 round-trip) or Cairns ($400); book through the resort.

On the island's west coast are two campgrounds. Campers must be totally self-sufficient and have no access to the resort. Like all other national park islands, permits are required to camp; obtain these from the Department of Environment and Heritage at Great Barrier Reef Wonderland, Townsville (tel. 077-21-2399). For campers, the only transportation is aboard the *Scuba Doo* (tel. 077-77-8220) from Lucinda; $150 pp round-trip.

WEST FROM TOWNSVILLE

The most direct route between Townsville and outback Queensland is along the **Flinders Highway,** which leads southwest from Townsville to the historic mining town of Charters Towers, then west through a dry and desolate piece of country to Mt. Isa, 890 km from the Pacific Ocean.

Ravenswood

Between Charters Towers and Townsville a narrow road leads 40 km south to the once-booming mining town of Ravenswood. Gold was found in the area in 1868 and by the end of the following year a rush was on. Company mining soon took over; equipment capable of crushing huge amounts of ore was brought in, and the town prospered. For a while anyway. The quality of gold was poorer than first thought and in 1912 the original company mine closed. In ensuing years, many companies invested heavily in the area, but today the town is a shadow of its former self. Abandoned mine shafts, equipment

and machinery, and a few remaining building provide a glimpse of past glories.

Charters Towers

This historic town of 9,000, in the Leichhard Range 140 km inland from Townsville, was onc Queensland's second-largest city, with a popu lation exceeding 30,000. Things are a lot quiete in Charters Towers today, but streets lined wit historic buildings and a cool climate make a de tour from the coastal highway worthwhile.

Gold was discovered late last century at nea by Towers Hill by an Aboriginal boy name Jupiter Mosman, who, ironically, was accom panying a group of prospectors. By 1900 th town's population had peaked. By the 1920s the richest lodes of gold had been extracte and the beef industry came to prominence. Mod ern technology made gold mining economical i the 1980s.

Charters Towers' one-time importance is re flected in downtown civic buildings, includin an impressive city hall and stock exchange. Th 1897 **Stock Exchange Arcade,** on Mosma St., has been restored and now houses a sma mining museum; it's open Mon.-Fri. 8:30 a.m.- p.m. and 2-4 p.m.; admission $5. Farther alon Mosman St. is **Zara Clark Folk Museum,** hous ing artifacts and photos from the town's earl est days. Open daily 10 a.m.-3 p.m., admissio $3. It's at 36 Mosman St. (tel. 077-87-4161 **Venus Battery,** five km east of town on Millch ester Rd. (tel. 077-87-2222), was one of dozen of mills used to crush ore during the town' boom period. The battery has been restore and is open for inspection daily 9:30 a.m.-3 p.m with tours at 10 a.m. and 2 p.m.; $3 pp.

Where the Flinders Highway enters town fror the northeast is **Park Motel,** 1 Mosman St. (te 077-87-1022), built as a hotel in 1888. Rooms i the original hotel have been beautifully restored including brass beds and bathtubs; $70 s or c Out back, and spread around a pool, is a string c motel units; $55 s, $63 d. North of town is **Dal rymple Caravan Park** (tel. 077-87-1121), witl good facilities and a saltwater pool. Sites are $10-12, on-site vans $30, and cabins $36-40.

All the pubs serve counter meals, with **Cour House Hotel,** 120 Gill St. (tel. 077-87-1187) offering $4-6 lunches and $6-9 dinners. In the historic Stock Exchange Arcade is **Ye Olde Cof**

ee **Shoppe,** serving sandwiches and light
meals as well as Devonshire teas; open daily
:30 a.m.-5 p.m. For something more substan-
al, try **Lissner's** in the Park Motel (tel. 077-
7-1022). Main dishes range $11-20.

Further information on the town is available at
he **National Trust of Queensland** office in the
tock Exchange Arcade on Mosman Street (tel.
77-87-2374).

Great Basalt Wall

his geological wonder northwest of Charters
owers formed around three million years ago,
when a huge lava flow from violent volcanic ex-
losions cooled to form a "wall" of basalt. Gre-
ory Developmental Rd., linking Charters Tow-
rs to the Gulf Developmental Rd., crosses the
ncient lava flow 44 km north of Charters Tow-
rs. The western end of the flow is protected
y 30,500-hectare **Great Basalt Wall National
Park,** accessible along a rough track spurring off
he Gregory Developmental Rd., 39 km north
f Charters Towers.

Porcupine Gorge National Park

he rolling hills around **Hughenden** seem never-
nding, and the land is so harsh that graziers
re only able to graze one sheep for every three
ectares, but 45 km north of the highway is Por-
upine Gorge, an oasis of lush vegetation sup-
orted by a creek flowing year-round. The grav-
l access road ends suddenly, right on the rim of
he park's main feature, where sheer walls drop
ertically 120 meters. Seeing the creek in the
ry season, it's hard to comprehend the quantity
f water that flows during the Wet, and its power
o carve the canyon in the soft sandstone. A cou-
le of lookouts lie along the gorge rim, but to get
nto the gorge continue north to **The Pyramid,** an
solated outcrop of rock, and descend into the
alley from the parking area. This area is out-
ide the park boundary. Camp here.

TOWNSVILLE TO CARDWELL

From Townsville, it's 110 km north to Ingham,
hen 52 km farther to Cardwell, gateway to
Hinchinbrook Island. Between Townsville and Ingham you'll find two national parks worthy of a
short detour. Southernmost is **Mt. Spec Na-**

tional Park, protecting 10,600 hectares of the
Paluma Range. Camping is permitted at Big
Crystal Creek, west of Paluma township, while at
the top of the range is McClelland's Lookout
and a couple of short hiking trails.

North of Paluma is the turnoff to **Jourama
Falls National Park,** six km west of the Bruce
Highway. The park is named for a waterfall that
cascades down a massive face of granite, 1.5
km from the facility area.

Ingham and Vicinity

The cane-growing town Ingham, 110 km north of
Townsville, holds little of interest, but to the east
and west are interesting detours. To the east
is **Lucinda,** where shallow waters forced the
construction of a six-km-long pier to load bulk
sugar carriers. **Wallaman Falls National Park,**
52 km west of Ingham and just 602 hectares, encompasses a deep gorge through which Stony
Creek drops 300 meters. Camp downstream of
the falls.

Cardwell and Vicinity

Along the entire 1,700 km between Brisbane
and Cairns, Cardwell is the only place where
the Bruce Highway runs right along the coastline,
and even then, it's only for a couple of kilometers. Cardwell holds little of interest, but as gateway to Hinchinbrook Island, staying in town is
often a necessity. **Cardwell Forest Drive** is a
26-km circuit that begins in town and winds
through native forests to a panoramic lookout, a
picnic area, and the trailhead for a couple of
short hikes. North of Cardwell is 6,950-hectare
Edmund Kennedy National Park, an area of
coastal habitat featuring rainforest, swamps,
and long deserted beaches.

Cardwell has a couple of motels, including
Lyndoch Motor Inn, 215 Victoria St. (tel. 070-
66-8500), but the best place to stay is **Kookaburra Caravan Park,** 175 Bruce Hwy. (tel.
070-66-8648), which has excellent facilities including a pool and laundry and free use of golf
clubs (green fees are $7 on the local course),
tennis rackets, bikes, and fishing gear. Camping,
on a shaded grassy area with access to undercover cooking facilities, is $10-12, on-site vans
are $26, cabins are $35, and fully self-contained
villas are $55. Dorm beds (YHA affiliated) are
$12 pp and doubles are $26.

HINCHINBROOK ISLAND

Separated from the mainland by mangrove-choked Hinchinbrook Channel, this magnificent wilderness island rises from the water to over 1,000 meters. The island's west coast is dominated by mangrove flats while on the east coast are 50 km of rugged headlands, secluded bays, and a white sandy beach stretching eight km along Ramsey Bay. Hiking the Thorsborne Trail is the island's biggest attraction, but day trips are also popular and there's a low-key resort at Cape Richards.

The Land
All of the island's 39,350 hectares are protected as a national park. It was once part of the mainland, but after the last ice age, when se levels rose, a high coastal ridge remained as a island. The island's highest peak is **Mt. Bowe** (1,142 meters), Queensland's third highes point, part of a massive spine of granite ex tending the length of the island. On the wester slopes, where rainfall is high, a canopy of trop ical rainforest protects palms, ferns, vines, an figs that extend to mangrove swamps at se level. East of the ridge line, where rainfall i lower and slopes are exposed to high winds dry forests of eucalypt dominate, with patche of rainforest thriving in the gullies. From th middle of the island, a wide, flat peninsul branches northward. On the ocean side is a magnificent stretch of beach backed by six kr of mangrove forests dissected by a maze c shallow channels.

From a visitor's point of view, the most important living creatures to know about are sand [flies], march flies and mosquitoes, all of which [c]an be unbearable. All the usual crocodile and [st]inger warnings are relevant to the island, so [b]eware.

[T]horsborne Trail

[F]ormerly known as the East Coast Trail, this [th]ree- to five-day 30-km bushwalk is one of Aus[tr]alia's premier overnight hikes. The going can [b]e tough, especially after rain when the trail [g]ets very slippery. The trail begins at Ramsey [B]ay (it's most often hiked from north to south), [ac]cessed along a one-km boardwalk from where [sh]allow-draft boats tie up in the mangroves of [M]issionary Bay. Ramsey Bay itself is a mag[ni]ficent stretch of sand (good views from Nina [P]eak), but scenery improves farther south where [th]e trail hugs the coastline, meanders along [s]andy beaches, crosses creeks, passes through [r]ainforest, and climbs to various viewpoints. [A]part from caution at creek crossings and the in[c]essant nuisance of insects, the trail should [p]ose few problems for experienced hikers.

The only way to get on the trail is with a per[m]it; $3 pp per night. For these write: Depart[m]ent of Environment and Heritage, P.O. Box [2]293, Ingham, QLD 4850 (tel. 077-76-1700). [T]his department has an office in Cardwell (down [a] narrow arcade at 79 Victoria St., tel. 070-66-[6]601) for trail information, but permits are ap[p]roved through the Cardwell office and are gen[e]rally snapped up months in advance. If a full [q]uota of hikers is booked on the Thorsborne [T]rail, inquire about permits for travel on only [th]e north section of the trail or camping at Ma[c]ushla Bay or Goold Island, to the north of [H]inchinbrook.

Transportation between trailheads is made [e]asy by two Cardwell companies who offer a [d]rop-off at the trail's north end, boat pick-up [fr]om the trail's southern end to Lucinda, and [c]oach transfers up the Bruce Highway to Card[w]ell for $44 pp. They are **Hinchinbrook Ad[v]entures** (tel. 070-66-8270) and **Hinchinbrook [I]sland Cruises** (tel. 070-66-8539). Both have of[f]ices on Cardwell's main street. Both compa[n]ies can also provide round-trip transfers to the [n]orthern trailhead, Macushla Bay, and Goold [I]sland.

Day Trips to the Island

Hinchinbrook Adventures (tel. 070-66-8270) and **Hinchinbrook Island Cruises** (tel. 070-66-8539) depart daily for the everglades of Missionary Bay, from where it's a short hike along a boardwalk to the sandy beaches of Ramsey Bay. Time is also spent sunbaking and snorkeling at the nearby Brook Islands. Tour cost is adult $45, child $22.50 (snorkeling gear is an extra $10 and lunch $8).

Hinchinbrook Island Resort

Probably least known of the Great Barrier Reef resorts, this low-key development on the tip of Cape Richards emphasizes the natural surroundings and environment-friendly activities such as hiking and snorkeling. Upgraded and expanded in 1989, the resort now caters for 50 guests at a time. Part of the new development includes "treehouses," individual units overlooking Orchid Bay. Meals are all excellent and include a four-course dinner. Rates, which include meals, are $200-265 pp, and child rates are just $90. For resort bookings call (070) 66-8585 or (1800) 77-7021. Transfers are provided by Hinchinbrook Island Cruises (tel. 070-66-8539); $35 round-trip.

MISSION BEACH

Mission Beach, the collective name for a string of coastal communities east of the Bruce Highway between **Tully** (the wettest place in Australia) and **Innisfail,** boasts a 10-km stretch of tropical Queensland's best mainland beaches. You can see islands of the Family Group offshore while immediately behind the coast are rainforests of the UNESCO Wet Tropics World Heritage Area. Resort development is extensive, with motels, backpacker lodges, caravan parks, and restaurants scattered along the beaches.

Without a doubt, the best place for a walk is along the palm-fringed beaches, but inland, in **Tam O'Shanter State Forest,** other opportunities present themselves. Head to Licuala facility area, where a 1.3-km trail leads to an area of rainforest featuring licuala palms; you'll find it on the road linking Tully to the coast. At the north end of the forest, at Lacey Creek, is short trail through an area inhabited by cassowaries.

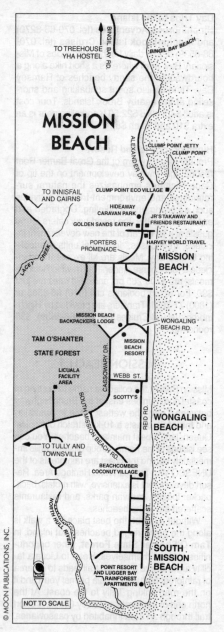

MISSION BEACH

TO TREEHOUSE
YHA HOSTEL

BINGIL BAY RD.

BINGIL BAY BEACH

ALEXANDER DR.

CLUMP POINT JETTY
CLUMP POINT

TO INNISFAIL
AND CAIRNS

CLUMP POINT ECO VILLAGE

HIDEAWAY
CARAVAN PARK

GOLDEN SANDS EATERY

JR'S TAKAWAY AND
FRIENDS RESTAURANT

PORTERS
PROMENADE

HARVEY WORLD TRAVEL

LACEY CREEK

MISSION
BEACH

MISSION BEACH
BACKPACKERS LODGE

WONGALING
BEACH RD.

TAM O'SHANTER
STATE FOREST

MISSION
BEACH
RESORT

CASSOWARY DR.

LICUALA
FACILITY
AREA

WEBB ST.

SCOTTY'S

REID RD.

WONGALING
BEACH

TO TULLY AND
TOWNSVILLE

SOUTH MISSION BEACH RD.

BEACHCOMBER
COCONUT VILLAGE

KENNEDY ST.

NORTH HULL RIVER

SOUTH
MISSION
BEACH

POINT RESORT
AND LUGGER BAY
RAINFOREST
APARTMENTS

NOT TO SCALE

© MOON PUBLICATIONS, INC.

Visiting the Outer Reef from Mission Beach

Two operators run to the outer reef from Clum⋅ Point, at the north end of Mission Beach. **Frien⋅ ship Cruises** departs daily at 8:30 a.m., and ⋅ $55 pp it's one of the cheapest ways to get ⋅ the outer reef anywhere along the coast. But, ⋅ course, there's a downside—it's a slow boat, ta⋅ ing more than two hours to get to the reef. Onc⋅ on the reef, there's snorkeling, a glass-bottome⋅ boat, and a coral cay to sunbake on. For bookin⋅ call (070) 68-7262. The other option is aboa⋅ *Quick Cat* (tel. 070-68-7289), which depar⋅ Clump Point Jetty at 10 a.m. ($110 adult, $5⋅ child). Six hours are spent on the outer reef, wi⋅ the fare including snorkeling, lunch, and a glas⋅ bottomed boat tour. Diving is an extra $45 pp.

Budget Accommodations

Mission Beach has a ton of budget accomme⋅ dations and a few upmarket resorts but n⋅ midrange places—it's either a cheap dorm be⋅ or an $80-a-night room.

Surrounded by lush rainforest, three km we⋅ of Bingil Bay Beach, is **Treehouse YHA Hoste⋅** on Bingil Bay Rd. (tel. 070-68-7137). The com⋅ plex has 46 beds, a pool, large deck area, loung⋅ and kitchen. Rates are $13 pp and camping is $⋅ pp. **Mission Beach Backpackers Lodge,** 2⋅ Wongaling Beach Rd. (tel. 070-68-8317), ju⋅ 200 meters from the beach, is central to th⋅ shops and restaurants of Mission Beach, an⋅ has kitchen and laundry facilities, along wit⋅ meals in an inexpensive cafe. Rates in dorm⋅ are $12-18 pp. **Scotty's** is a family-run back⋅ packer lodge across the road from a great beach⋅ It has a large pool, shaded verandas, and moder⋅ facilities. Dorms are $12-15 pp, doubles $2⋅ and a few rooms have private bathrooms an⋅ air-conditioning for $45. It's at 167 Reid Rd⋅ Wongaling Beach (tel. 070-68-8676).

Hideaway Caravan Park, Porters Prome⋅ nade, Mission Beach (tel. 070-68-7104), ha⋅ great facilities and is only a short walk from th⋅ beach. Sites range $11-15 while cabins are⋅ $36-52. **Beachcomber Coconut Village,** South⋅ Mission Beach (tel. 070-68-8129), equals an⋅ caravan park in the state, with a wide variety ⋅ activities and a beachfront location. Shaded⋅ sites are $12-15, cabins $33-38, and fully self⋅ contained villas $45.

licuala fan palms, Tam O'Shanter State Forest

esort Accommodations

urrounded by rainforest and a short walk rough bushland to the beach is **Clump Point co Village,** Clump Point Rd. (tel. 070-68-7534). ach freestanding bungalow is fully self-con-ined, with a large kitchen, king-size bed, air onditioning, and a television. They are built round a beautifully landscaped pool area and nked to the main restaurant/guest lounge build-g by paths winding through palm-filled gar-ens. Rates are very reasonable at $80 s or d, 85 with a private spa.

Mission Beach Resort is set among 18 ectares of rainforest three blocks from the each. Take advantage of the wide range of porting activities and the pleasant, landscaped ool area. The resort also has four restaurants, nree bars, and live entertainment most nights. ates are $80 s, $90 d; units with kitchenettes are 90 s, $100 d (also inquire about standby rates). 's on Wongaling Beach Rd. (tel. 070-68-8288).

For more upscale lodging, check out the re-sorts at South Mission Beach. The **Point Resort** (tel. 070-68-8154) overlooks Dunk and Bedarra Is-lands and has a large pool and balcony area scat-tered with palms and seating. All units have ocean views and are of the highest standard; $160 s or d. **Lugger Bay Rainforest Apartments** (tel. 070-68-8400) is much the same setup, but on a small-er, more intimate scale, with elegant log units built on poles and catching ocean views. Each has a kitchen, outdoor eating area, spa, and sep-arate sleeping quarters; $225 per night.

Food

A cluster of shops on Porter's Promenade in Mission Beach includes good cafes and restau-rants. **JR's Takeaway** has well-priced seafood; a slab of delicious barramundi, chips, and salad is $9. Next door, **Friends** (tel. 070-68-7107) is a classy seafood restaurant serving meals from $18. Across the road is **Golden Sands Eatery** with a nightly seafood buffet for $19.95.

Transportation

All long-distance bus companies stop at Mis-sion Beach, with four or five services daily mak-ing the detour from the Bruce Highway. All buses stop at Harvey World Travel, Mission Beach (tel. 070-68-7187); the fare to Cairns is $16 one-way, to Townsville $38. **Bazz's Mission Beach Bus Service** (tel. 070-68-7400) runs between the communities of Mission Beach six to eight times daily.

ISLANDS OFF MISSION BEACH

Lying off Mission Beach are 14 islands of the **Family Group.** Most are protected as national parks, and a couple are privately owned. Two of the islands have resorts, including the largest, Dunk, and Bedarra.

Dunk Island

Immortalized by E.J. Banfield in four books, in-cluding his best-known work *Confessions of a Beachcomber,* more has been written about Dunk than any other island on the reef. Ban-field lived on the island for over 25 years, until his death in 1923. His lyrical description of Dunk's flora and fauna and his relationship with the is-land have attracted many to the South Pacific.

The island is five km from the mainland and about 30 km from the outer reef. It is 890 hectares in area, rising steeply to 271-meter Mt. Kootaloo. Apart from a resort, the island has many beaches; the best are on a low-lying spit of sand extending west from the center of the island. Low-lying areas have been cleared, but the island is mostly rugged, and vegetation remains in its natural state, cloaked in a thick cover of tropical rainforest extending right down to the rocky shoreline. Birdlife is prolific.

Walking is one of the island's most popular activities; 13 km of trails crisscross the island including one to the summit of Mt. Kootaloo (1.5 km one-way) and to Coconut Beach (five km one-way), home to a colony of artists. Water sports equipment is available from a kiosk at the beach, but the resort and its facilities are off-limits to day-trippers.

For more than 30 years, Dunk Island has been home to Bruce Arthur, one of the South Pacific's great characters. After a career as a wrestler, which included representing Australia at the 1948 Olympics, he escaped to Dunk, becoming self-sufficient and teaching himself to weave. Over the years, his lifestyle attracted like-minded artists and today a small commune thrives, open to the public Tuesday and Friday mornings ($4 admission).

Dunk Island Resort attracts a variety of holidaymakers but is best suited to those keen to keep active; guests enjoy the two pools, tennis, six holes of golf, archery, trap shooting, horseback riding, and squash as well as all the usual water sports. The resort caters for nearly 400 guests. Rooms set in landscaped gardens are $208 s, $246 d, while those along the beachfront start at $266 s, $444 d. The meal package is $65 pp extra. Children are well looked after, with a petting farm and camping trips offered. For reservations call (070) 68-8199. From North America call (800) 551-2012.

Most resort guests arrive on package tours, with flights included. Otherwise the flight to Dunk Island from Townsville is $107 one-way and from Cairns $97. If you plan to stay at Mission Beach resorts, fly into Dunk Island and catch a water taxi to the mainland.

At last count, four operators ran water taxis between Mission Beach communities and Dunk Island. The trip over takes about 10 minutes.

Dunk Island Bennett's Water Taxi (tel. 070-6 8333) runs six times daily from South Missic Beach; **Dowd's Water Taxi** (tel. 070-68-831 runs seven times daily from Wongaling Beac **Quick Cat** (tel. 070-68-7289) runs once da from Clump Point; and **Dunk Island Cruise** (tel. 070-68-7211) runs twice daily from Clun Point and also offers snorkeling and boomnetti around Bedarra Island ($18). All operato charge $22 round-trip.

Bedarra Island

Lying six km south of Dunk, this 86-hectare islar is home to two resorts, each among the mo exclusive on the reef. It's one of the few Queen land islands best known by its Aboriginal nam although marine charts denote it as Richards I land. The island features great beaches and als has a fine fringing reef. At opposite ends of the i land, and linked by a 1.5-km trail, are two excl sive resorts, **Bedarra Bay** and **Bedarra Hid away,** where guests are guaranteed privacy ar solitude in settings that blend into surroundir rainforest. The Dunk Island Resort mentione above and these two Bedarra Island Resorts a owned by Australian Resorts, but the similaritie end there. Both of the Bedarra Island resor feature 16 split-level villas with sunken baths ar private balconies, a stylish landscaped pool are and a wide range of activities. Rates at both r sorts are all-inclusive (including alcohol); $64 s, $1060 d per night. For Bedarra Hideawa reservations, call (070) 68-8168; for Bedarra Ba call (070) 68-8233. Within North America ca (800) 551-2012. Transport to the island is pr vided for guests by launch from either Missic Beach or the airport on Dunk Island. Day-trij pers are not permitted at either resort.

MISSION BEACH TO CAIRNS

Innisfail, at the confluence of the North an South Johnstone Rivers, is the heart of a ric cane-growing area. The **Australian Sugar Mu seum,** at Mourilyan, south of Innisfail, depicts th industry; open daily 9 a.m.-4:30 p.m.

Wooroonooran National Park

Dozens of creeks, waterfalls, lookouts, and hikin trails are features of this little-known park pro

ecting land west of the Bruce Highway between
Innisfail and Cairns. The Palmerston Section is accessed from Innisfail along the Palmerston Highway, which climbs up the Atherton Tableland.
This section of the park straddles the highway
with two seven-km circuits taking in all the best
natural features. Camping is at Henrietta Creek. In
the park's northern section is **The Boulders** (six
km west of Babinda), starting point for a number of
short trails including one to a lookout above Boulders Gorge and a two-km rainforest circuit. The
Boulders picnic area is also the start of the **Goldfield Trail,** cut through the Bellenden Ker Range
by diggers on their way to a short-lived gold rush.
The trail leads 19 km into the Goldsborough Valley, climbing over the range and descending to the
East Mulgrave River (11 km one-way) and continuing eight km downstream to a campground
accessible by car off the Gillies Highway.

South of Babinda, a road leads eight km west
to **Josephine Falls.** West of the falls is 1,622-
meter **Mt. Bartle Frere,** Queensland's highest
peak. **Bartle Frere Summit Trail** is 7.5 km one-
way, a strenuous but rewarding full-day hike
that should be attempted only by the fit. A softer

option is the climb to Broken Nose (970 meters); four km each way.

Frankland Islands

This beautiful group of continental islands lies 10
km from the coast midway between Innisfail
and Cairns. The combined area of the five islands is less than 80 hectares, and each features
rainforests of casuarinas and sandy beaches
fringed by undisturbed coral reef. Camping is
permitted on **Russell Island,** but you must be totally self-sufficient and obtain permits from the
Department of Environment and Heritage in
Cairns.

The *Frankland Islander II* heads out to the
Frankland Islands daily for five hours of snorkeling, swimming, and sunbaking (usually to
Normanby Island). Coaches pick up passengers from Cairns daily at 8 a.m. for transfers to
the boat, which departs from Deeral Landing
on the Mulgrave River 45 km south of Cairns.
The fare of $98 pp includes all transfers as well
as snorkeling equipment, morning and afternoon tea, and a buffet lunch. For campers, the
round-trip fare to Russell Island is $100 pp.

CAIRNS

Sandwiched between the clear waters of the Great Barrier Reef and lush rainforests of the Atherton Tableland lies Cairns (pronounced "CANS"), tourist capital of far north Queensland and gateway to a myriad of natural wonders. Founded in 1876 as a gateway to western goldfields and growing to become a major sugar port, Cairns has been Australia's fastest-growing resort city for the last 15 years. Wide palm-lined streets, groves of bougainvilleas scattered through parks, and raised whitewashed buildings give Cairns an authentic tropical atmosphere, belying the hustle and bustle of the thriving tourism industry, contained on just a few streets along the bay.

Long a holiday destination for budget-conscious Australians, the construction of five-star resorts, a casino, an international airport, and championship golf courses has broadened the city's appeal. Apart from local fishermen, plantation owners, and Koori, the blend of the international jetsetters, backpackers, four-wheel drive enthusiasts, honeymooners, and holidaying families adds to Cairns unique atmosphere.

Although Cairns is the tourist capital of the far north, it's not the city itself that attracts the visitors, but the proximity to a great variety of natural attractions in the immediate vicinity, including beautiful islands, the outer reef, Atherton Tableland, Port Douglas, the Daintree Rainforest, and Cape Tribulation.

SIGHTS AND RECREATION

Town Sights

The Esplanade, which runs along the shore of Trinity Bay, is the center of the action in Cairns. On one side is a long strip of palm-fringed park

On 1 November 1997 telephone numbers in this section will change. To dial the new number, simply add "40" to the old number. As an example, (070) 12-3456 becomes 4012-3456. The new area code will be (07).

overlooking the calm waters of the bay and o the other a mass of booking agents, cafes, an budget accommodations. At the south end c the Esplanade is **Pier Marketplace,** a larg shopping plaza with boutiques, restaurants wit ocean views, a marina, and markets Saturda and Sunday. Also in the complex is **Underse World** (tel. 070-41-1777). It may not be as e> tensive as Townsville's Great Barrier Reef Wor derland, but tanks display many hundreds c reef creatures, including coral. Admission i adult $12, child $7. Open daily 9 a.m.-9 p.m Pier Marketplace also serves as a departur point for many island and reef trips.

Pier Marketplace is at the mouth of **Trinit Inlet,** a shallow body of water extending thre km into wetlands. Along the mouth of this wa terway are various cruise-departure jetties an Trinity Wharf, the main coach terminal. *Louisa* a small paddlewheeler that departs daily at 1 a.m. and 1 p.m. for a two-and-a-half hour cruis through the inlet and around Admiralty Islanc adult $16, child $6 includes morning or afte noon tea. For bookings, call (070) 31-3065.

At City Place, on Lake Street, is **Cairns Mu seum** (tel. 070-51-5582), displaying Aborigina artifacts, goldfields memorabilia, and phc tographs from the city's earliest days. Admis sion is $2. Open Mon.-Sat. 10 a.m.-3 p.m.

The **Royal Flying Doctor Service** has base in Cairns, serving patients around Queens land's far north, including Cape York. A visitc center at the base is open for hourlong tours a.m.-4:30 p.m.; $5.25. It's at 1 Junction St Edge Hill (tel. 070-53-5687).

Parks and Hiking

A good place to escape the commercialism c Cairns is **Flecker Botanic Gardens** on Collin Ave. west of downtown. Adjoining these ga dens is **Mt. Whitfield Environmental Park** protecting a large chunk of native bushland su rounded by city development. From a parking lc on McDonnel St. (off Collins Ave.) a trail leads t the summit of **Mt. Whitfield** (360 meters), re turning via a different route. The trail is 5.5 kr round-trip, but allow at least three hours to con

CAIRNS

TO AIRPORT, SKYRAIL, ATHERTON TABLELAND, NORTHERN BEACHES, AND PORT DOUGLAS

MT. WHITFIELD ENVIRONMENTAL PARK
TO ROYAL FLYING DOCTOR SERVICE BASE

FLECKER BOTANIC GARDENS

TRINITY BAY

TRINITY INLET

TO PALM ROYALE CAIRNS AND TOWNSVILLE

0   500 m

DETAIL

DAMARI'S
YHA ON THE ESPLANADE
GREEN'S AND MEETING PLACE
END OF THE WORLD NIGHTCLUB
HOSTEL 89
PIER MARKETPLACE AND RADISSON PLAZA HOTEL
BELLVIEW
CARAVELLA'S HOSTEL 77
BARNACLE BILL'S
CAIRNS LEAGUES CLUB
DUNDEE'S
JOHNO'S BLUES BAR
RACQ
GEORGE'S GREEK TAVERNA
WOOLSHED
PACIFIC COAST BUDGET ACCOMMODATION
CAIRNS MUSEUM
CITY PLACE
REEF HOTEL CASINO
GREEN POSSUM BOOKSHOP
RED OCHRE GRILL
ORCHID PLAZA
HILTON INTERNATIONAL
PALM COURT

FLORENCE ST.
LAKE ST.
APLIN ST.
GRAFTON ST.
SHERIDAN ST.
MCLEOD ST.
SHIELDS ST.
SPENCE ST.
ABBOTT ST.
THE ESPLANADE
WHARF ST.

CAIRNS ANGLER MOTEL
HARBOURSIDE HOTEL
FLYING HORSESHOE MOTEL
QUEENSLANDER HOLIDAY APARTMENTS
ADOBE MOTEL
BEL-AIR BACKPACKERS

SEE DETAIL

MARLIN MARINA
GREAT ADVENTURES TERMINAL
TRINITY WHARF

RAILWAY STATION
DEPARTMENT OF ENVIRONMENT AND HERITAGE
POST OFFICE
PLAYPEN INTERNATIONAL
FAR NORTH QUEENSLAND PROMOTION BUREAU

UPTOP DOWNUNDER HOLIDAY LODGE

CAPTAIN ST.
LILY ST.
COOK ST.
DIGGER ST.
SMITH ST.
MCKENZIE ST.
JAMES ST.
SHERIDAN ST.
CHARLES ST.
GATTON ST.
MARTYN ST.
MINNIE ST.
GROVE ST.
SEVERIN ST.
UPWARD ST.
BUCHAN ST.
MULGRAVE RD.
BRUCE HWY.
LAKE ST.
GRAFTON ST.
FLORENCE ST.
BUNDA ST.
SPENCE ST.
HARTLEY ST.

COLLINS AVE.

plete the trail as the going gets tough near the summit. A shorter option is a 1.3-km circuit to a lookout 100 meters above sea level.

A park with a difference is **Cairns Botanical Conservatory,** on the roof of the wing of the Reef Hotel Casino. This massive glasshouse, four stories high, contains a great variety of rainforest vegetation including palms, ferns, and orchids.

River Running

Cairns is base for a number of whitewater rafting companies that run rivers flowing off the Atherton Tableland. You'll encounter the most challenging rapids on the **Tully River,** 140 km south of Cairns; **Raging Thunder** (tel. 070-51-4911) and **R'nR** (tel. 070-51-7777) offer full-day packages including transfers from Cairns, up to five hours on the river, and lunch for $122 pp. If you have only a half day to spare, both companies offer three trips daily on the **Barron River** for $65 pp.

For families, a tamer option is a float down the **Mulgrave River** in a stable inflatable raft; departures are Mon.-Sat. at 1:30 p.m. and include afternoon tea and a visit to a wildlife park for adult $68, child $40. This trip is offered only by Raging Thunder. Also on the Mulgrave River, **Peregrine** (tel. 070-32-2722) offers trips in two-person canoes, the easy pace allowing the chance to view wildlife; adult $80, child $50; family $230 includes lunch.

R'nR offers overnight whitewater rafting expeditions down the **North Johnstone River,** beginning with a helicopter flight into its remote headwaters; the two-day trip is $360 pp, five-day $770.

Other Recreation

Adventure sports are well entrenched in the Cairns scene. Skydiving with **Paul's Parachuting** (tel. 070-35-9666) makes tandem jumps from around 2,700 meters for $198 pp. A more sedate way to view Cairns from the air is with **Raging Thunder** (tel. 070-51-4911), whose hot-air balloons depart daily at dawn; 30 minutes aloft $98, 60 minutes for $160.

Brumby Bob's is a horseback riding outfit operating at Palm Cove north of Cairns (tel. 070-59-1730). Two-hour rides are $45 pp.

A.J. Hackett (tel. 070-31-1119) has two bungee jumping operations around Cairns. On is on the Cook Highway, 15 km north ($89); th other is in the middle of Kuranda Markets ($70 in the Atherton Tablelands (see "Vicinity o Cairns," below).

You'll find a number of excellent golf course in the vicinity of Cairns, but a round of golf isn cheap. **Paradise Palms** (tel. 070-59-1166), on of Australia's top courses, has packages from $190 pp including transfers, club rental, an green fees.

Entertainment

The main center of after-dark entertainment is a old warehouse on the corner of Lake and Hart ley Streets. Inside are three nightspots: **Plaype International,** a cavernous nightclub with liv music Wed.-Sun. ($5 cover charge); **Samuel' Saloon,** a backpacker drinking hole; and **Cour Jester,** a cocktail bar. **End of the World,** corne Abbott and Aplin Streets, is a popular back packer nightclub and also offers inexpensiv meals. **Reno Club International,** Palm Cour Lake St., is divided into a karaoke room an piano bar; open Mon.-Sat. from 8 p.m. **Johno' Blues Bar** features live blues and rock nightl with a cover charge Friday and Saturday. **Night club 1936,** in the Reef Hotel Casino, is theme on New York in 1936 and features a nightl cabaret show as well as an intimate dance floo and separate bar and lounge areas.

The opening of the $210-million **Reef Hote Casino** in the heart of the city has seen Cairns shed its image as a haven for the budget-con scious once and for all. Gaming rooms spraw over two floors, each catering to different level of gambler, with the majority of first-time punter heading to the Main Casino.

HOTEL AND MOTEL ACCOMMODATIONS

A string of backpacker lodges lines Cairns' main commercial strip, the Esplanade, whic runs along the edge of Trinity Bay. In this sam area are high-rise hotels, with most chargin over $100 per night. Sheridan St., running nort from Cairns, has a two-km strip of moderatel priced motels ($50-80). If being close to th main cruise and tour departure points isn't a

iority, head to the northern beaches for acommodations.

expensive

ost among the outdoor tables and booking
gents of the Esplanade is the **Bellview**, 85
splanade (tel. 070-31-4377), a cheap motel
ith a pool, laundry, and air-conditioning. Rooms
e basic; those with shared bathrooms are $27
$32 d; private bathrooms $45-55 d. **Pacific
oast Budget Accommodation** (100 Sheri-
an St., 070-51-1264), a few blocks from the
aterfront, has rooms with shared bathrooms
nd a communal kitchen; $35 s, $42 d.

Adobe Motel, 191 Sheridan St. (tel. 070-51-
511), located in the middle of a long stretch of
otels, has basic but clean rooms for a rea-
onable $45 s, $50 d.

oderate

ying Horseshoe Motel**, 285 Sheridan St. (tel.
70-51-3504), is a friendly place with free airport
nuttles and a pool; $67 s, $77 d. **Cairns Angler
otel**, 287 Lake St. (tel. 070-31-1666), is a
ewer accommodation; each room is air-con-
tioned and features a shower, bath, small
tchenette, and balcony overlooking a large
opical pool area. Rates are $75 s or d.
ueenslander Holiday Apartments**, 22 Digger
t. (tel. 070-51-0122), is a similar setup (al-
ough the pool is smaller). Each balcony has a
ble setting and kitchens are well equipped.
ne-bedroom units are $108, and two-bedroom
nits $135, making them a good deal for families
small groups.

alm Royale Cairns**

way from the hustle and bustle of downtown
airns is Palm Royale Cairns, 7-11 Chester Court
el. 070-32-2700), set on one hectare. The 150
oms surround a large pool area, landscaped to
el like a private beach resort with an outdoor
afe, three pools (one for dive training), and a
pa. Each room has a private balcony with views
ver the pool area and is air-conditioned with
ng-size beds, bath and shower, tea- and coffee-
aking supplies. At the far end of the complex is
olossus, an indoor/outdoor restaurant open
ghtly for dinner. Shuttles run into Cairns every
vo hours. Rates are $130 s or d, $148 for two
ouples while suites are $160 s or d.

Expensive

Harbourside Hotel, 209 Esplanade (tel. 070-51-
8999), is an eight-story hostelry overlooking
Trinity Bay; each modern room has a balcony
with views; $135 s or d, $150 with a kitchenette.
Hilton International Cairns, Wharf St. (tel. 070-
52-1599), is of the high standard associated
with this worldwide chain, and every room has
water views; from $215 s or d. **Radisson Plaza
Hotel** (tel. 070-31-1411) is part of the Pier Marketplace complex, right on the waterfront and
departure point for many day cruises. For guest
use only are an outdoor pool, gym, spa, and
sauna. Rooms start at $200 s or d. (Even if
you're not staying here, check out the amazing
rainforest setting in the lobby.)

More expensive still is Cairns's newest hotel,
the five-star **Reef Hotel Casino** (tel. 070-30-
8888). Each room is luxuriously appointed and
features a spa, interactive entertainment system, and a private balcony. Other hotel facilities include the casino, a rooftop conservatory
filled with plants of the rainforest, a stylish nightclub, restaurants, and bars.

Northern Beaches

On the northern beaches, **Agincourt Beachfront Apartments,** Clifton Beach (tel. 070-55-
3500), has huge units, each with a bedroom,
large living area, private balcony, and kitchen.
Rooms with garden views are $85 per night,
$550 per week; those facing the beach are $98
per night, $650 per week with discounts Nov.-
May. For those in the know, one of North
Queensland's favorite hideaways is **Reef House,**
99 Williams Esplanade, Palm Cove (tel. 070-55-
3633). Secluded from the outside world and featuring Cairns's best beach across the road, tropical surroundings, casual yet elegant rooms, and
unrivaled service, it's a steal at $161 s, $177 d.

BUDGET ACCOMMODATIONS

Backpacker Accommodations

The largest concentration of backpacker places
is along the Esplanade, a location handy to
downtown, cafes and restaurants, and Pier Marketplace. Most lodges are old motels, with as
many beds in each room as possible. **YHA on
the Esplanade,** 93 Esplanade (tel. 070-31-

1919), is one of the better ones, with five-bed dorms, each with a bathroom. Beds are $14-15, with small double rooms for $32. Next door is **Hostel 89,** 89 Esplanade (tel. 070-31-7477); each room is air-conditioned and dorms have a maximum of four beds; $15 pp. **Caravella's Hostel 77,** 77 Esplanade (tel. 070-51-2159), is a large complex but dorms are only $10-11 and doubles with private bathroom are $35.

A few blocks north of the hostels listed above is another bunch, still within easy walking distance of everything. **Bel-air Backpackers,** 157 Esplanade (tel. 070-31-4790), has good facilities; dorms are $12 and doubles a reasonable $24.

Uptop Downunder Holiday Lodge, 164 Spence St. (tel. 070-51-3636), is a friendly place, just over one km from downtown. The kitchen is well equipped and there are two TV rooms, a lounge area, pool, and pool table; dorms $12, doubles $27.

Campgrounds

Cairns has no downtown campgrounds. Closest to the action is **Coles Villa & Caravan Park,** 28 Pease St. (tel. 070-53-7133). All facilities here are of the highest standard; unpowered sites $12, powered sites $15. Also here are large cabins and villas for $42-55. **Cairns Coconut Caravan Resort,** on the Bruce Highway eight km south of downtown (tel. 070-54-6644), also has excellent facilities including a tennis court and saltwater pool. **Ellis Beach Caravan Park** is 32 km north of Cairns (tel. 070-55-3538) and has a great beachfront location.

FOOD

Breakfast

Without a doubt, the best place to head for breakfast is the **Beach Hut** (tel. 070-31-2133), in Pier Marketplace. Its upstairs location allows panoramic views across Trinity Bay. A huge buffet offers plenty of fresh fruit, breakfast cereals, bacon, eggs, some Chinese dishes, and tea and coffee, all for just $6.45; served daily 7-11 a.m. On the Esplanade, the same money will get you bacon and eggs or a croissant and coffee at one of the many sidewalk cafes. **Kipling's,** Orchid Plaza, 79 Abbott St. (tel. 070-31-1886), is an upmarket restaurant best known

for lunch and dinner, but breakfast is also serve (8:30-11:30 a.m.) and is reasonably priced $7-11. **Pacific Flavours Brasserie,** in the Re Hotel Casino, is open daily 24 hours and offe a great variety of breakfast choices.

Cheap Eats

The Esplanade, between Shields and Apl Streets, is a continuous strip of cafes and take aways, many with tables strung out along th footpath. Just around the corner, on Aplin St., **Green's,** a popular spot to head for health sandwiches and burgers. Next door is **Meetin Place,** a small food court with a variety of Asia outlets. On the second floor of Pier Marketplac and overlooking the marina, is a large food cou and a variety of inexpensive restaurants, i cluding the Beach Hut, which has a buffet lunc ($11.45) and dinner ($19.95 or $15.95 before p.m.). **Cairns Leagues Club,** 139 Grafton S (tel. 070-31-1079), has a casual bistro whe you'll get lunch or dinner for under $7.

Australian

With a large proportion of tourists to Cairns con ing from overseas, Australian-style restauran are very popular. The most unique of these **Red Ochre Grill,** 43 Shields St. (tel. 070-5 0100), where all dishes are inspired by Aborig nal food, combining bush tucker with moder cooking styles in a casual atmosphere. **Dun dee's,** 40 Aplin St. (tel. 070-51-0399), feature a menu packed with Australian cuisine, includir emu, crocodile, buffalo, and plenty of loc seafood; open daily from 6 p.m. A more casu Australian-style restaurant, with prices to matc is the **Woolshed,** offering Stockmen's Pie f $6.50 and Shearers Delight (rack of lamb) for $ It's at 24 Shields St. (tel. 070-31-6304).

Other Restaurants

As you can gather from the name, **Barnack Bill's,** 65 Esplanade (tel. 070-51-2241), at th marina end of the Esplanade, specializes seafood, with prawns, lobster, crab, barra mundi, and crocodile all available. Eating her isn't particularly cheap (main dishes $18-27 but a 30% discount is offered on orders take before 6 p.m.; open daily from 5 p.m. Similar priced is one of Cairns's most renowned restau rants, **Kipling's,** upstairs in Orchid Plaza

9 Abbott St. (tel. 070-31-1886). The menu is short but varied and all dishes are served with colorful flair and in a casual atmosphere. Lunch is the most popular time of day for dining here, but the restaurant is also open for breakfast (from 8:30 a.m.) and dinner; dinner main dishes range $15-23. **George's Greek Taverna,** 16 Aplin St. (tel. 070-41-1500), is a stylish place with good food. **Fiesta Cantina,** 96 Lake St. (tel. 070-41-2412), is a trendy Mexican place with most main dishes under $15. **Tamari's,** 171 Lake St. (tel. 070-31-2155), is typically Italian, decorated in red, green, and white, with tables close together and plenty of greenery. Most pizza and pasta dishes are 11-16 with steak and seafood dishes more expensive.

TRANSPORTATION

Getting There

Cairns International Airport is off Captain Cook Dr. north of the city. It is served by the following international airlines: **Qantas** (tel. 1800-7-7767), **Japan Air Lines** (tel. 070-31-2700), **Air New Zealand** (tel. 13-2476), **Garuda** (tel. 070-31-2288), and **Air Niugini** (tel. 13-1380). Qantas has direct flights between Cairns and the west coast of the United States. Facilities at the international terminal include car rental outlets, lockers ($2 per day), shops, showers, a cafe and restaurant, currency exchange, and a tourist information booth. The domestic terminal, a 200-meter walk from international (or a $1 shuttle ride), has similar facilities (no currency exchange) and is served by the following domestic airlines: **Ansett Australia** (tel. 13-1300), **Qantas** (tel. 13-1313), **Sunstate** (tel. 13-1313), and **Flightwest** (tel. 13-2392). The **Airporter** runs between both terminals and downtown; $4.50 one-way (tel. 070-35-9555). A cab between either terminal and downtown runs $11-3. **Coral Coaches** (tel. 070-31-7577) runs north from the airport to Palm Cove ($10 one-way) and Port Douglas ($16.80).

The railway station is located on McLeod St. at Shields St., a part of downtown earmarked for continuing development. The Sunlander, Spirit of the Tropics, and Queenslander all make the 32-hour journey between Brisbane and Cairns

(economy $123, first class $234). The Queenslander is more luxurious than other services and has a bar, lounge, and restaurant. The fare to Cairns on this service is $489 one-way including meals. It departs Brisbane Sunday 10 a.m.

For information on all these services call 13-2232, or if you're in Brisbane drop by **Brisbane Travel Centre** at 305 Edward Street.

All long-distance buses operate from Trinity Wharf, with both major operators, **Greyhound Pioneer** (tel. 13-2030) and **McCafferty's** (tel. 070-51-5899), running five services daily between Brisbane and Cairns. The regular fare between the two cities is $137 one-way, but discounts are offered, including half-price tickets if booked 15 days in advance. Stops are allowed en route for a couple of dollars each.

Getting Around

Local bus companies serve all suburbs of Cairns, with schedules posted at Lake Street Transit on City Place. The most useful of these is the Beach Bus, operated by **Marlin Coast Buslines** (tel. 070-57-7411). This service runs regularly between downtown Cairns and the northern beaches as far as Ellis Beach ($7.80 round-trip). It stops at all beaches on route, including Palm Cove. The **Cairns Explorer** (tel. 070-55-1240) also operates from Lake Street Transit, stopping at nine tourist spots in the vicinity of Cairns. A commentary is given along the way and you may alight and reboard anywhere. Cost is adult $20, child $10.

Major car rental companies are: **Avis** (tel. 070-51-5911), **Budget** (tel. 070-51-9222), **National** (tel. 070-51-4600). **Cairns Rent-a-car** (tel. 070-51-6077) has cars for $51 per day, including unlimited kilometers. The smallest four-wheel drives are $104, with the rate dropping to $91 per day for a week.

For a cab call **Black and White Taxis** at (070) 51-5333.

Tours

The most popular tours from Cairns take in the reef, the hinterland, and rainforest (see "Vicinity of Cairns," below). The major tour companies are **Australian Pacific Tours** (tel. 13-1304), **Cairns Scenic Tours** (tel. 070-32-1381), **Down Under Tours** (tel. 070-33-1355), and **Tropic Wings** (tel. 070-35-3555).

SERVICES AND INFORMATION

The **post office** is on the corner of Grafton and Hartley Streets. **Green Possum Bookshop** is in a small arcade at 55 Grafton St. (tel. 070-51-1344). **Proudmans,** another good bookshop, is in Pier Marketplace.

Cairns has no official information center, but **Far North Queensland Promotion Bureau,** on the corner of Grafton and Hartley Streets (tel. 070-51-3588), is a good source of information on Cairns and surrounding destina-

tions; open Mon.-Fri. 9 a.m.-5 p.m., Saturday a.m.-1 p.m.

The dozen-odd booking agents, most along the Esplanade, offer limited amounts of information, but are really in business to make commissions off booking tours. The **RACQ,** a good source of maps for travel in the far north, is at 112 Sheridan St. (tel. 070-51-4788). For information on the many surrounding national parks and road conditions around the cape, head to the **Department of Environment and Heritage** at 10 McLeod St. (tel. 070-52-3096); open weekdays only.

VICINITY OF CAIRNS

Cairns is an excellent base for day trips to a number of different areas. A great variety of cruises depart daily from Pier Marketplace for Green and Fitzroy Islands, giving day-trippers the chance to experience tropical islands for a reasonable price, as well as to the outer reef. West of Cairns is Atherton Tableland, part of the Wet Tropics World Heritage area, and the small village Kuranda. Along the Captain Cook Highway north of Cairns is Port Douglas, smaller than Cairns, but with its own unique charm and a good access point to the outer reef. North of Port Douglas is the spectacular Daintree Rainforest and, farther north, Cape Tribulation, where rainforest descends right to the ocean.

GREAT BARRIER REEF

Green Island

The appeal of this small 12-hectare island is twofold—it's a coral cay (one of the reef's three true coral islands with resorts), and its location is prime, just 27 km from Cairns. Ringed by a shingle beach of broken coral, the island's interior is thickly vegetated, rising less than two meters

above high-tide level. Declared a national park in 1937 to protect its fragile environment, the island is now, ironically, the most visited site on the entire reef (because of its size there's no escaping the crowds). As well as snorkeling, swimming, and sunbaking, visitors can ride in a semi-submersible or glass-bottomed boat and view the aquariums of Marineland Melanesia.

A hotel was first built on the island in the mid-1960s, but the island didn't come to prominence until August 1994, when five-star **Green Island Resort** opened for business. Although accommodations and facilities are of the highest standard, the unpretentious development blends into the island environment. Rates at the resort are among the most expensive on the reef, and with the amount of day-trippers, solitude can only be found within the resort complex. That said, the pool area is a delightful place to relax and no expense has been spared in furnishing the rooms. Rates of $640 s, $780 d are inclusive of meals. For reservations call (070) 31-3300 or (1800) 67 3366; from the U.S. call (800) 525-4800.

The best deal for day-trippers heading over to Green Island is aboard *Big Cat,* which departs Marlin Marina daily at 9 a.m. The trip over takes 80 minutes, with five hours spent on the island; $32 pp includes snorkeling gear or a glass-bottomed boat trip and lunch is an extra $7. **Great Adventures** (tel. 070-51-0455) runs out to the island on a high-speed catamaran for $29, with snorkeling equipment an extra $5. Other packages offered by this company include a two-hour stop on the island and a trip to the outer reef for $126 plus entry to a

On 1 November 1997 telephone numbers in this section will change. To dial the new number, simply add "40" to the old number. As an example, (070) 12-3456 becomes 4012-3456. The new area code will be (07).

VICINITY OF CAIRNS

island attractions and lunch for $78. Departures are from Great Adventures terminal daily at 9 a.m. Return flights with **Aquaflight Airways** (tel. 070-31-4307) are $80 pp.

Fitzroy Island

This 324-hectare continental island, 23 km east of Cairns, features an inexpensive resort and makes an ideal day trip from Cairns. The beaches are made up of broken coral, making sunbaking unpleasant, but snorkeling on fringing reefs is excellent. Hiking trails lead to Nudie Beach (good snorkeling) and a lookout on the island's eastern extremity, six km from the resort.

The resort is on Welcome Bay, a long stretch of beach flanked by outcrops of large granite boulders. Because of limited resort activities, scuba diving and PADI dive courses attract the most people. Three distinct levels of accommodation are offered, making it one of the few island resorts appealing to all budgets. Beach Bunkhouses have four bunk beds with a shower block and communal kitchen; $26 pp or $90 for the entire room. Beach Cabins have two rooms, bathroom, a balcony, and ceiling fan; $229 s, $320 d, includes breakfast and dinner. Campsites are $10, and unless eating in the resort restaurant, you need to be self-sufficient. For bookings call (070) 51-9588 or (1800) 07-9080.

Sunlover Cruises (tel. 070-31-1055) departs Trinity Wharf daily at 9 a.m. for Fitzroy Island, returning at 4:30 p.m.; $27 round-trip. **Great Adventures** (tel. 070-51-0455) departs the terminal beside Trinity Wharf daily at 8:30 a.m. for $27 with optional extras of snorkeling and scuba diving.

Lizard Island

Northernmost of the resort islands, 1,012-hectare Lizard Island is surrounded by beautiful fringing reefs and some of the best beaches to be found on the entire reef, its upmarket resort a popular spot for divers and game fishing enthusiasts chasing black marlin (Sept.-Nov.). In front of the resort a fringing reef beckons snorkelers, but, immediately south, a platform reef provides a greater array of life. But it's the shoals of the inner reef that scuba divers head to Lizard Island for, including one particular site, the **Cod Hole,** famous for giant potato cod. For resort guests a

day's diving is $105-130 and equipment rental another $50. Although the island is just seve km long, there are some good hiking opport nities, including to the summit of **Cook's Loc** (259 meters), from where Captain Coc searched out a northward passage in 177 Views from this summit are tremendous, e tending 360 degrees.

Lizard Island Lodge is on Anchor Bay, small cove fronted by a wide sandy beach. Th units are very comfortable, with the emphasis c solitude and service, and each is air-conditione Food of the highest standard is served in a di ing area that sprawls along the veranda wi spectacular ocean views. Rates are $520 $860 d inclusive of meals. For bookings ca (070) 60-3999; from North America, call (80 551-2012.

Sheltered in the northern corner of Mrs Wa son's Beach is a national park campground wi toilets, barbecues, and drinking water; $5 p night, book through the Department of Enviror ment and Heritage in Cairns (tel. 070-52-3096 Campers must be self-sufficient as they are de nied access to the resort.

The only scheduled transport to Lizard Is land is from Cairns flying **Sunstate** (tel. 1 1313); $143 one-way. **Reef Air Tours** (tel. 07 35-9530) offers a day trip to the island fron Cairns, with a one-hour flight over the reef, sno keling, and lunch, for $275 pp.

Outer Reef Cruises

One of Cairns's most appealing features is it proximity to the outer reef, which is closer t the mainland off Cairns than at any point far ther south.

The least expensive way to get to the oute reef is aboard **Seastar II,** an 18-meter cruise that holds 40 passengers. Hastings Reef, 5. km northeast of Cairns, is the final destinatior but a stop is also made at Michaelmas Cay $45 pp includes snorkeling and lunch. Depar tures are from Marlin Marina daily at 7:45 a.m (tel. 070-31-4444).

Great Adventures (tel. 070-51-0455 or 180C 07-9080) offers the widest variety of outer ree cruises, all departing from their own termina on Wharf Street. The most popular departs a 8:30 a.m., with two hours spent on Green Is land before speeding out to Norman Reef, 59 kr ortheast of Cairns, where the company has a ontoon, and snorkeling, glass-bottomed boat des, and lunch are included for $126 pp. The 0:30 a.m. departure is a few dollars cheaper, ut no stop on Green Island is made. This company also offers a cruise to Moore Reef, 49 km ast of Cairns, with a stop at Fitzroy Island and e same inclusions for $88 pp. In both cases, ds are half price.

Sunlover Cruises (tel. 070-31-1055) has a ll-day cruise out to Arlington Reef in a large gh-speed catamaran. At the reef is a large ontoon from where submarine tours, glass- ottomed boat cruises, snorkeling, and a buffet nch are offered; adult $108, child $57. This ompany also combines a stopover on Fitzroy land with a trip out to Moore Reef with all the oove inclusions for adult $120, child $60. The rlington Reef cruise, combined with Skyrail nd all transfers, is adult $147, child $73. Both uises depart Trinity Wharf daily at 9 a.m.

Ocean Spirit (tel. 070-31-2920), a luxurious 2-meter sailing catamaran, departs from Mar- n Marina daily at 9 a.m. for Michaelmas Cay, a w coral cay 42 km northeast of Cairns. Once n the island, which is a bird sanctuary, you an snorkel, sunbake, or ride a semi-sub- ersible boat. The fare is adult $120, which in- udes a buffet lunch, pick-ups, and all activi- es (except scuba diving).

The largest operator of reef trips is **Quicksilver** el. 070-31-4299), which operates out of Port ouglas. For Cairns-based tourists, connections Port Douglas with Quicksilver depart Marlin larina daily at 8 a.m. (see "Reef Cruises" under Port Douglas and Vicinity," below).

cuba Diving

ll the above operators offer scuba diving as an xtra, generally $40-65 for certified divers and 50-75 pp for uncertified divers. Diving is also ffered at the three island resorts off Cairns (see bove). At least five Cairns-based companies ffer diving certification courses, but it really pays shop around. You should allow at least four ays and budget $300 for the course.

Tusa Dive (tel. 070-31-1248) is one of the ew operators running day trips to the outer reef pecifically for divers. Trips depart Marlin Mari- a at 8 a.m. Cost is $140 pp for two dives and quipment rental.

Trips aboard ***Rum Runner*** (tel. 070-52-1088 or 1800-80-3183) appeal to experienced divers. The destination on the four-day trip is Holmes Reef, 240 km off the mainland and well beyond the outer reef. Accommodation on board the boat, all meals, and 10-12 dives are included in the fare of $800-850 pp.

One of the Great Barrier Reef's most spec- tacular dive sites is the **Cod Hole**, east of Lizard Island. Officially known as Cormorant Pass, the resident populations of potato cod—which grow up to one meter in length—moray eels, wrasses, and coral trout are all semi-tame and waiting to be fed. **Mike Ball Dive Expeditions** (tel. 070-31- 5484) departs Cairns Friday and Monday at 7:30 a.m. for a three-day trip out to the Cod Hole on *Supersport,* a luxurious 30-meter cata- maran. All-inclusive fare, including flights from Cairns to Lizard Island, is $678-960 pp Jan.- June, $795-1131 July-December.

Flightseeing

Viewing the reef from the air is an unforget- table experience, and in some cases can be combined with a few hours spent lazing on an island. **Reef Air Tours** (tel. 070-35-9530) of- fers a range of inexpensive options, including a 30-minute scenic flight to the outer reef ($45 pp), a 60-minute flight over the reef and as far north as Port Douglas ($85 pp), as well as tours to Lizard Island and Cooktown. **Aquaflight Air- ways** (tel. 070-31-4307) combines flightseeing with reef landings, allowing time to swim and snorkel. Prices range from $80 pp to Green Is- land, $130 pp to Hastings Reef. Departures are from Marlin Marina. **Jayrow** (tel. 070-31- 4214) offers helicopter flights, including 40 min- utes over the reef for $220 pp. A one-way flight to Norman Reef, lunch, glass-bottomed boat tour, snorkeling, and return by high-speed cata- maran is $250 pp.

ATHERTON TABLELAND

This plateau west of Cairns, part of the UN- ESCO Wet Tropics World Heritage Area, fea- tures lush rainforests, waterfalls, and picturesque lakes, away from the crowds and waiting for those who drag themselves from the reef. Ku- randa is as far onto the plateau as many people travel, but it extends 100 km farther south and is all worthy of exploration.

Kuranda Experience

This combination of **Kuranda Scenic Railway, Skyrail,** and **Tjapukai Aboriginal Dance Theatre** is touted as Queensland's most popular mainland attraction.

The railway was completed in 1891, taking five years, and winds from Cairns up the steep escarpment of the plateau to Kuranda with 15 tunnels and 100 curves in 35 km; the final 20 km gains more than 200 meters in elevation and passes through 15 tunnels. A highlight is a photo stop at spectacular Barron Falls. The rail trip begins at Freshwater Railway Station, but most packages pick-up in Cairns; adult $34, child $17.

Skyrail, the world's longest gondola, begins its 7.5-km journey at Caravonica Lakes, west of Cairns, and ends in Kuranda. It traverses virgin rainforest for much of the way

figure from Aboriginal shield design

above the canopy, allowing views of the sea of green below and the ocean beyond. Along the route are several stations; Red Peak, on the edge of the tableland, offers spectacular views across to the Coral Sea; at Barron Falls the mighty Barron River descends into a deep gorge. Also at Barron Falls, the Rainforest Interpretive Centre describes the surrounding environment. The fare is $23 one-way, $39 roundtrip, and accommodation transfers to Caravonica Lakes are an extra $10. Children are half price.

An hourlong **Tjapukai** performance on Kuranda market days proved so popular that the concept was recently expanded into a cultural theme park and relocated to the Skyrail base station at Caravonica Lakes. The dance, spread across four stages, is still the major attraction, but other aspects of Koori culture have been developed, including a traditional village. Shows are held three times daily but the center is open daily 9:30 a.m.-4:30 p.m. Admission is adult $21, child $10.50.

Kuranda Experience, combining the railway, Skyrail, and Tjapukai, is adult $77, child $38.50, which includes accommodation transfers. Book through any agent in Cairns.

Kuranda

The small mountain town of Kuranda, 20 km west of Cairns, is accessed along a winding road, Skyrail, or the scenic railway (see above). Its tree-lined streets shade open-air cafes, boutiques specializing in Australiana, and a few commercial attractions. But it's market for which Kuranda is best known. Held Wed.-Fri. and Sunday, the markets have some great arts and crafts and fresh produce (and also a lot of junk). The markets are spread around Therwine St., but crowds fill the entire town. A good way to escape the market-day masses is to head into **Jumrum Creek Environmental Park,** on the south side of town, or follow Barron Falls Rd. to a spectacular lookout perched on the rim of the Atherton Tableland.

In the middle of the markets is the **Australian Butterfly Sanctuary** (tel. 070-93-7575). The sanctuary has a large outdoor display area, as well as an enclosed aviary. It's open daily 10 a.m.-3 p.m. Admission adult $9.50, child $5. On Coondoo St. is **Kuranda Wildlife Noctarium** (tel. 070-93-7334), where day and night have been artificially reversed for viewing Australia's many nocturnal animals. Admission is adult $8, child $4. Open daily 10 a.m.-4 p.m. with feeding times at 10:30 a.m., 11:30 a.m., 1:15 p.m., and 2:30 p.m.

The only accommodation right in town is **Kuranda Hostel,** 6 Arara St. (tel. 070-93-7355), an old place with dorm beds for $13.50 and a couple of doubles for $30. Just out of town on the road to Mareeba, and a pleasant five-minute walk from Kuranda, is **Kuranda Rainforest Resort** (tel. 070-93-7555 or 1800-80-6996). Set among tropical rainforest, the resort rings a magnificent landscaped pool area. Other facilities include a tennis court, large gym, restaurant, bar, and laundry. Each unit has a balcony and is well furnished; $85 s or d. Scattered around the property are a number of freestanding cedar cabins, each with two bedrooms and a private balcony; $140 s or d. Transfers from Cairns Airport are complimentary. **Kuranda Van Park,** Myola Rd. (tel. 070-93-7316), has sites or $12-14 and a few cabins for $33.

In the Kuranda Settlement complex, opposite the end of Coondoo St., is **Bakehaus** with a delicious array of pies, pastries, and light meals. One of many eateries on Coondoo St. is **Frogs Restaurant** (tel. 070-93-7405), a bright and breezy place with old wooden floors, plenty of greenery, and a few tables on a veranda out back. As well as all the usual cafe fare, seafood is well priced at $10-15 for main dishes.

The most popular way to get to Kuranda from Cairns is aboard **Skyrail** or the **scenic railway** (see "Kuranda Experience," above), but this is not the cheapest way. You can also jump aboard one of **Whitecar Coaches** thrice-daily buses from Tropical Paradise Travel, 25 Spence St.; $7 one-way (tel. 070-51-9533).

Yungaburra and Vicinity

Yungaburra sits in the center of Atherton Tableland, 13 km east of Atherton and 65 km southwest of Cairns. Only 700 people live in Yungaburra, but it has the tableland's best choice of accommodations and restaurants, and is a great base for exploring surrounding sights. Definitely worth the effort to find is the **curtain fig,** a particularly enormous example of a tree that is typical in tropical rainforests. This one is over 15 meters high, having grown along an ancient tree that had fallen against another. After the fallen tree rotted, the curtain fig remained, forming a "sail" of hanging vines. To get there follow the road out of Yungaburra toward Atherton for one km, then head two km south toward Malanda.

East of Yungaburra are two interesting lakes filling the craters of a volcano that erupted 95,000 years ago. **Lake Eacham,** the smaller of the two, has no rivers flowing into it, so it's filled with only rainwater, making it crystal clear. It is encircled by a four-km trail (slippery after rain) and is also good for swimming. **Lake Barrine** has a six-km trail around its circumference and a restaurant overlooking its calm waters. North of Yungaburra is **Lake Tinaroo,** a reservoir that's part of the Barron River hydroelectric

curtain fig

ANDREW HEMPSTEAD

power scheme. To drive around the lake takes at least an hour (60 km) with many rough sections. Along the route are campgrounds (free) and a short nature walk around Lake Euramoo.

In Yungaburra, stay at **Yungaburra Park Motel,** Atherton Rd. (tel. 070-95-3211), where rooms are modern and there's a pleasant outdoor area with barbecue; $44 s, $49 d. At Lake Eacham is a caravan park (tel. 070-95-3730).

Lake Eacham Hotel (tel. 070-95-3515), a classic country pub, serves lunch and dinner. Across the road is **Burra Inn** (tel. 070-95-3657), a more formal eatery with large servings for $16-24.

South from Yungaburra

Malanda, 12 km south of Yungaburra, is home to a large dairy that supplies towns with milk throughout the far north and as far away as Darwin. Right by the road on the town's western outskirts is Malanda Falls, the start of a couple of short hikes and site of a shaded picnic area.

Malanda Falls Caravan Park, between town and the falls (tel. 070-96-5314), has tent sites for $12, on-site vans $28, and cabins $32-40.

Waterfalls tumble off the tableland's higher elevations south of Malanda, and although none are breathtakingly spectacular, each has its own charm, and, chances are, crowds will be minimal. The best are on the **Waterfall Route,** a 24-km drive east of **Millaa Millaa.**

From Millaa Millaa, the Palmerston Highway leads east to Innisfail, 88 km south of Cairns, and the Kennedy Highway leads southwest to the Gulf Developmental Rd., the most direct road link between Cairns and Normanton.

PORT DOUGLAS AND VICINITY

As a sister resort town to Cairns, Port Douglas couldn't be more different. Located on a low spit of land flanked to the east by the magnificent golden sands of Four Mile Beach, the town has one short strip of boutiques, cafes, and restaurants surrounded by a few blocks of residential housing. The four-km road into town from the Captain Cook Highway is lined with palm trees, a subtle sign of the transformation Port Douglas has undergone in the last decade.

Founded in 1877 as a gateway to Hodgkinson goldfields, the town's population peaked late last century at 12,000, but by 1911, after Cairns was chosen as a railhead and tropical cyclones had destroyed most buildings, Port Douglas's short-term destiny was sealed. Things began changing in the mid-1980s, when new resorts, trendy shops, and a million-dollar marina complex breathed life into the sleepy village. Today Port Douglas is a good choice as an alternative to Cairns, retaining its sleepy reputation while providing accommodations for all budgets, having a relaxed tropical feel, and providing easy access to reef destinations.

Sights and Recreation

At the west end of Macrossan St. are the sheltered waters of **Dickson Inlet.** Home to a small fleet of motley-colored fishing vessels just 10 short years ago, the waterway has been transformed by **Marina Mirage,** chock-full of luxurious motor cruisers, where restaurants serve cuisine from around the world, and shops brim with brand names that seem more at home in Paris or New York. The paddlewheeler *Lady Douglas* departs twice daily for a relaxing cruise around Dickson Inlet; $20 pp, which includes a light seafood snack. For bookings call (070) 99-5051. Toward the mouth of the inlet is **Shipwreck Museum** (tel. 070-99-5858), put together by Ben Cropp from the 100 shipwrecks he has discovered off the Australian coastline. Admission is adult $4, child $1.50; open daily 9 a.m.-5 p.m.

Four Mile Beach is a magnificent stretch of sand extending south from Island Point in one unbroken arc. Hidden from the beach by casuarina trees is **Mirage Country Club,** a world-class 18-hole golf course. Green fees are $120; for bookings call (070) 99-5537. The aptly named resort rises like a mirage from a two-hectare swimming pool that surrounds most of the main complex.

On the Port Douglas access road is **Rainforest Habitat** (tel. 070-99-3235), a re-creation of typical rainforest complete with all the creatures you may or may not see in the wild, including crocodiles, cassowaries, and koalas. Entry to the park is steep at adult $16, child $8. Brunch with the Birds, including admission and a hot buffet (8 a.m.-2 p.m.), is adult $30, child $15; park hours are daily 8 a.m.-5 p.m.

Reef Cruises

Port Douglas is home base for **Quicksilver** (tel. 070-99-5500), a large operation with day trips to destinations off Port Douglas, with transfers offered to those based at Cairns. A 37-meter wavepiercer makes daily excursions to **Agincourt Reefs,** a string of reef considered among the most beautiful of those accessible by day-trippers. At the reef is a two-story pontoon, the base for snorkeling, a semi-submersible ride, scuba diving ($80 extra), and helicopter flightseeing ($75). From Port Douglas the fare is $118 (10 a.m. departure), from Cairns $128 (8 a.m. departure).

A more personalized way to view the outer reef is aboard *Aristocat,* a 16-meter high-speed catamaran carrying just 25 passengers. The itinerary includes visiting two reefs, snorkeling, a reef ecology presentation, buffet lunch, morning and afternoon tea, and accommodation pickups. Departures are from Marina Mirage Tuesday, Thursday, and Saturday at 8:30 a.m.; adult

$112, child $60. On Monday, Wednesday, Friday, and Sunday the itinerary is a little different, with less time spent on the reef to allow time for fishing and boomnetting (being pulled behind the boat in a net); adult $124, child $64. For bookings call (070) 99-4544 or (1800) 65-0063.

About halfway between Port Douglas and the outer reef is **Low Isles,** a small coral cay with shingle beaches and a great fringing reef for snorkeling. The cay is thickly vegetated and forms an important bird-breeding area. A lighthouse has operated on the island since 1878. Quicksilver's *Wavedancer,* a 30-meter sailing catamaran, cruises out to Low Isles from Port Douglas daily at 10 a.m. (departures from Cairns at 8 a.m.), with lunch, an informative reef presentation, snorkeling, and a glass-bottomed boat tour included in the fare of adult $82, child $41.50.

Accommodations

Although Port Douglas is best known for its top-end resorts, there are some options for budget travelers, including a few caravan parks and a backpacker lodge. Of the motels, least expensive is **Coconut Grove Motel,** 58 Macrossan St. (tel. 070-99-5124), a friendly place within walking distance of the beach, restaurants, and marina. Facilities include a pool and popular bar/restaurant. Rooms are $50 s or d, a little higher with air-conditioning. **Lazy Lizard Motor Inn,** 121 Davidson St. (tel. 070-99-5900), is a step up in quality and just over one km from downtown; from $75 s or d. On the road into town are a few expensive hotels including **Radisson Royal Palms Resort** (tel. 070-99-5577 or 1800-02-1211), a great value for those who prefer luxurious accommodations; rates start at $150 s or d, and a few rooms cater to physically challenged travelers. As famous for its exiled ex-owner Christopher Skase as its unequaled luxury, **Sheraton Mirage Port Douglas** (tel. 070-99-5888 or 1800-22-2229) features an 18-hole golf course, 10 tennis courts, and a two-hectare pool. Rates start at $400 per night.

Port of Call Lodge, Port St. (tel. 070-99-5422), an associate YHA of the highest standard, has a pool and restaurant. Each four-bed dorm has a bathroom ($15-16 pp) and there are also a few doubles ($30-34). Transfers from Cairns are complimentary.

Four Mile Beach Caravan Park, Barrier St. (tel. 070-98-5281), a pleasant four-km walk from town along the beach, has good facilities; unpowered sites $13, powered sites $15, on-site vans $35, and cabins $50. If this park is full, try those on Davidson St., closer to town but away from the beach.

Food

For a town of just 2,000 residents, Port Douglas has a fabulous array of dining options, most of which are on Macrossan Street. **Cafe Macrossan,** 42 Macrossan St. (tel. 070-99-4372), opens at 9 a.m., and although there's no official breakfast menu, the light meals offered are a great start to the day, especially when enjoyed in the outdoor dining section. Lunch is inexpensive ($6-9) and dinner features local produce, including delicious coral trout. Another good cafe is **Namaste,** 43 Macrossan St. (tel. 070-99-4056), which might be a little cheaper.

Popular for dinner is the restaurant in Coconut Grove Motel, 58 Macrossan St. (tel. 070-99-5124), where three-course meals are under $15 and the small bar has a real tropical ambience. In Marina Mirage, **Fiorelli's** (tel. 070-99-5201) has an extensive menu of classical Italian dishes ranging $13-22 and a well-priced lunchtime blackboard menu. The most elegant of Port Douglas's eateries is **Nautilus Restaurant,** 17 Murphy St. (tel. 070-99-5330), with a menu featuring seafood such as tiger prawns, mud crab, and coral trout.

Transportation

Cairns, and the closest airport, are 60 km south from town, but regular bus and boat connections make travel to Port Douglas easy. **Coral Coaches** (tel. 070-99-5351) operates between Cairns and Port Douglas 10-15 times daily ($27 round-trip), continuing north along the coast to Cooktown. The fare between Cairns and Cooktown is $92 round-trip, with stops in Port Douglas permitted. Tours from Cairns into the Daintree include a stop at Port Douglas on the itinerary.

Quicksilver (tel. 070-99-5500) departs Marlin Marina, Cairns, daily at 8 a.m. in high-speed catamarans, and also pick up passengers in Palm Cove. Primarily designed for day-trippers heading to the outer reef, this service can be used as a transfer to Port Douglas ($16 one-way, $26 round-trip), allowing an inexpensive day trip from Cairns.

Major car rental agencies in Port Douglas include **Avis, Budget,** and **National.** Port Douglas is relatively flat, so biking is a good way to get around; **Aussie Bike Hire,** 79 Davidson St. (tel. 070-99-4444), has mountain bikes for $15 per day.

DAINTREE AND CAPE TRIBULATION

Part of the Wet Tropics World Heritage Area, Daintree and Cape Tribulation National Parks contain an amazing variety of flora and fauna and are among the most beautiful areas of Queensland. Cape Tribulation adjoins the Great Barrier Reef, giving the region the distinction of being the only place on the planet where two UNESCO World Heritage Areas sit side by side. The small sugarcane-growing town of Mossman is gateway to the area. Farther north, a ferry crosses the crocodile-infested Daintree River leading to Cape Tribulation National Park, forested coastline with long stretches of golden beaches. North of the cape, the road is unsealed and passable only in a four-wheel drive.

Mossman and Vicinity
Historic Mossman, 75 km north of Cairns, is Australia's northernmost sugar town. The Mossman River winds through town, emptying into the ocean three km east. On the south side of the river mouth is **Cooya Beach,** where at low tide the beach is over half a km wide. West of Mossman is 56,450-hectare **Daintree National Park,** an area of jagged mountains, steep escarpments, and lush rainforest. Only the park's extreme southern end, where the Mossman River has carved a wide, deep gorge through the rainforest, is accessible. A trail leads along the river, past picnic tables and swimming holes to a couple of photogenic creeks.

In Mossman **Exchange Hotel,** 2 Front St. (tel. 070-98-1410), has basic rooms for $10 pp. One km north of town is **Mossman Caravan Park,** Foxton Ave. (tel. 070-98-1922), with sites for $10-12 and on-site vans $20-25. Out by the gorge is **Silky Oaks Wilderness Lodge** (tel. 070-98-1666), surrounded by virgin rainforest

and home to a variety of orphaned animals. Freestanding bungalows sit throughout the property, each with a tropical ambience and private bathroom, and many have kitchenettes. The friendly owners operate extended tours through Cape York. Rates are $350 per bungalow, which includes breakfast.

Daintree River
For most of the 1980s the Daintree was the focus of international attention as protesters and developers clashed over the fate of rain forest that had changed little since dinosaurs roamed the earth. In 1988 a win for the environmentalists saw the forests incorporated into the Wet Tropics World Heritage Area.

A cruise is the best way to experience the river, and with up to 20 operators, choices are plenty. A variety of wildlife is seen, but crocodiles are the highlight (most often sighted in the winter months). The pick of the bunch is **Daintree Connections** (tel. 070-98-6120 or 1800-65 8833). They offer regular river cruises, departing four times daily from **Daintree Eco Centre,** on the road to Daintree Village, and five times daily from the Daintree ferry. One-hour cruises are adult $12, child $4; 90-minute cruises are adult $20, child $10. This company also operates dawn and dusk cruises (on demand) for small groups, where wildlife viewing is more productive; $25 pp. **Daintree Eco Centre** (tel. 070-98-6120), on the road out to Daintree Village, is a small wildlife park featuring rainforest wildlife, including a crocodile; admission adult $4, child $1.

The tiny settlement of **Daintree Village,** the only community north of Mossman, lies beside the river a few km upstream of the ferry crossing. The short main street is a concentration of tourist shops. The least expensive place to stay is **Daintree View Caravan Park,** right in the center of town (tel. 070-98-6119). Sites are $12 and a few on-site vans are $34 s or d. **Red Mill House,** Stewart St. (tel. 070-98-6169), a B&B has two rooms, with shared bathroom. The gardens are immaculate and there's a pool and spa; $45 s, $55 d includes breakfast. On the road into the village is **Daintree Eco Lodge** (tel. 070-98-6100 or 1800-80-8010). Freestanding bungalows are scattered around the property, each with a balcony boasting spectacular views of surrounding rainforest. All as-

Daintree ferry crossing

ects of the construction and day-to-day lodge operation revolve around the natural surroundings, including a unique restaurant built over a creek and around a tree. Rates are $265 s, $285 d, which includes breakfast and transfers from Cairns for those who require them.

Cape Tribulation National Park

This long and narrow 16,959-hectare park extends between the Daintree and Bloomfield Rivers and from the coastline west to the high peaks of the McDowall Range, rising to 1,374 meters at Thornton Peak. Except after heavy rains, two-wheel-drive vehicles can negotiate the 30 km from Daintree River ferry to Cape Tribulation itself (although many car rental companies prohibit their conventional vehicles traveling north of the Daintree River), but travel north of the cape is four-wheel-drive territory only.

Crossing the Daintree River is made easy by a regular ferry service running every 10 minutes between 6 a.m. and midnight. Ferry charges are car (with passengers) $5 one-way, motor bike $3, pedestrian $1.

Before the road climbs the Alexandra Range, a turnoff to the east leads six km to **Cape Kimberley** and a short beach. From the cape **Snapper Island** is easily identified. In the lee of the cape is **Club Daintree** (tel. 070-90-7500), a campground with a kitchen area, pool, and restaurant. Camping is $10-12, on-site tents $16 d, and cabins start at $32.

Farther north is **Daintree Rainforest Environmental Centre** (tel. 070-98-9171). Admission may seem a little steep (adult $8, child $4), but the self-guided interpretive trail along a raised boardwalk, audiovisual, and other displays will expand your understanding of the surrounding rainforest no end; open daily 9 a.m.-5 p.m.

At the turnoff to Cow Bay is the modern **Cow Bay Hotel** (tel. 070-98-9011), with motel units for $61 s, $72 d including a cooked breakfast. Across the road is **Rainforest Retreat** (tel. 070-98-9101), with dorm beds for $13 and a few basic motel rooms with kitchenettes for $40 s, $60 d. Along the road out to Cow Bay is **Crocodylus Village** (tel. 070-98-9166), a YHA hostel set among tropical rainforest. Accommodation is in large canvas cabins, while the main complex has a restaurant, bar, and swimming pool. Beds are $13-14 or, if you'd prefer some privacy, a few doubles go for $45.

The only national park campground is at **Noah Head,** five km north of the Oliver Creek crossing. Facilities are limited to toilets and drinking water, but the location is magnificent, tucked behind a stretch of golden sand and surrounded by dense rainforest; $5 per site. For bookings call (070) 98-2188.

At the cape itself, a 400-meter boardwalk leads through the rainforest to an elevated lookout where views extend across the beach and bays beyond. Another trail leads over the headland to Myall Beach.

Transportation and Tours

Coral Coaches (tel. 070-31-7577) operates a scheduled bus service between Cairns and Cooktown. Stops are permitted along the route, providing the perfect opportunity to explore the cape without your own vehicle. Three days a week the service travels the coastal route (Tuesday, Thursday, and Saturday) or the inland route (Wednesday, Friday, and Sunday). From Cairns, the round-trip fare to Cape Tribulation is $48 and to Cooktown $92. Transport and accommodation packages offered by Coral Coaches are good value, including one night at Rainforest Retreat, one night at Cooktown Motor Inn, and transport from Cairns for $14 pp.

Jungle Tours (tel. 070-32-2111) operates a four-wheel-drive tour from Cairns taking in Cape Tribulation National Park, a Daintree River cruise, a guided bush walk, Mossman Gorge, and a quick stop in Port Douglas; $78. Departures are daily 7:30 a.m. A similar tour, but with a larger group, is offered by **Tropic Wings** (tel. 070-35-3555), with time also spent at Rainforest Habitat and a barramundi lunch included in the fare of adult $98, child $49.

CAPE YORK PENINSULA

As the population of Australia's east coast continues to mushroom, Cape York Peninsula remains wild and unsettled, one of the world's last great wildernesses. In the Wet (Nov.-April) surface travel is impossible north of Cooktown, but for the rest of the year the Cape is a mecca for four-wheel-drive enthusiasts who trek north for the region's great beauty, the fishing, the adventure, and for the achievement of reaching Australia's northernmost point.

The peninsula extends over 600 km, forming an apex at Cape York and flanked to the east by the Great Barrier Reef and Coral Sea, to the west by the Gulf of Carpentaria, and to the north by Torres Strait. Unchanged for millions of years, the landscape is one of forests, swamps, plains, and rivers, cursed by early explorers and still challenging adventurers today. The Great Dividing Range is the cape's dominant geological feature; on its eastern flanks, rainforests descend right to the ocean, while to the west, swamps and alluvial plains dominate. During the Wet, dozens of rivers flow westward, including the Jardine, just 80 km from the cape, which has the greatest year-round water volume of any Queensland river.

On 1 November 1997 telephone numbers in this section will change. To dial the new number, simply add "40" to the old number. As an example, (070) 12-3456 becomes 4012-3456. The new area code will be (07).

The population of the entire cape is about 20,000. The largest town is Cooktown, 130 km north of Cairns; other major settlements are Coen, halfway up the Cape, Weipa, a bauxite mining center on the gulf, and Bamaga, just south of Cape York.

Organized Tours

Overland tours from Cairns take about seven days to reach Cape York, with the option of returning along the same route, by air, or by sea. One of the well-established operators is **New Look Adventures** (tel. 070-31-7622, or in Sydney call Adventure World at 02-9956-7766). Their 10-day trip includes Cape Tribulation, Quinkan rock art, a tour of Coen, crossing the Jardine River, time at the actual cape, a day and night on Thursday Island, overland back to Weipa, and a flight to Cairns. Rates of $164 pp include three nights' lodge accommodation combined with bush camping, meals, and a transfers. Departures are late May through mid-October. Another established operator is **Oz Tours Safaris** (tel. 070-55-9535), which offers a seven-day four-wheel-drive safari to Cape York with a flight back to Cairns for $1395.

Two companies offer cruises along Cape York Peninsula. **Jardine Shipping** (tel. 070-35-1900 or 1800-81-0634) operates the *Cairns Express*, a 50-meter barge, between Cairns and Thursday Island. Primarily for transporting supplies and vehicles (good for those who only want to drive one-way up the cape), the barge has accommodation for 12 passengers. The boat departs

CAPE YORK PENINSULA

PAPUA NEW GUINEA

TORRES STRAIT

SUE ISLAND

MT. ERNEST ISLAND

THURSDAY ISLAND

HORN ISLAND

CAPE YORK

ALBANY ISLAND

POSSESSION ISLAND

SOMERSET

SEISIA

BAMAGA

USSHER POINT

JARDINE RIVER N.P.

SHELBURNE STATION

HEATHLANDS

WENLOCK RIVER

IRON RANGE N.P.

PORTLAND ROADS

WEIPA

BATAVIA DOWNS

MT. TOZER (545 m)

ARCHER RIVER

ARCHER BEND N.P.

ARCHER RIVER ROADHOUSE

COEN RIVER

ROKEBY N.P.

COEN

PRINCESS CHARLOTTE BAY

CAPE MELVILLE N.P.

LIZARD ISLAND

LAKEFIELD N.P.

GULF OF CARPENTARIA

GREAT DIVIDING RANGE

PENINSULA DEVELOPMENTAL RD.

ALICE RIVER

MITCHELL AND ALICE RIVERS N.P.

LAURA

ENDEAVOUR RIVER N.P.

COOKTOWN

MT. COOK N.P.

BLACK MOUNTAIN N.P.

QUINKAN ROCK ART

LAKELAND

DAINTREE N.P.

TO CAIRNS (4WD ONLY)

TO CAIRNS

CORAL SEA

SOUTH PACIFIC OCEAN

GREAT BARRIER REEF

0   75 km

Cairns Monday 4 p.m., arriving Horn Island Wednesday 10 a.m. and Thursday Island a few hours later, returning to Cairns that same day. The barge is too big to dock at the mainland port of Seisia, and transport must be arranged separately through Seisia Camping Grounds (tel. 070-69-3243) for transport to Horn Island. The Cairns-Horn Island fare is $250 pp one-way, $400 round-trip, including meals. Vehicles cost $600 one-way. The more luxurious option is aboard *Kangaroo Explorer* (tel. 070-55-8188), a 25-meter motorized catamaran designed specially for task. The five-day cruise between Cairns and Thursday Island stops at Cooktown, the Cod Hole, Lizard Island, and Forbes Island with many snorkeling opportunities en route. All rooms feature twin beds, but these can be converted to sleep four. Rates are $1868-2403 June through mid-Oct. ($400 cheaper the rest of the year). Rates include all meals and a one-way flight between Thursday Island and Cairns.

Sunstate (tel. 13-1313) and **Flightwest** (tel. 13-2392) fly between Cairns and Bamaga ($261 one-way) and Thursday Island ($290 one-way). Most operators include these flights in tour prices. **Cape York Air Services** (tel. 070-35-9399), operators of the world's longest mail run, flies to remote cattle stations and communities throughout the peninsula. Routes vary every day, stopping up to a dozen times. The cost is $140-225 pp, and if there's a group of five, a charter flight up the coast to Cape York and lunch on Horn Island costs $485 pp.

COOKTOWN

A small town at the mouth of the Endeavour River, Cooktown's claim to fame as Australia's first European settlement is the main reason for its existence. The town has a real tropical feel, and its many sites of historical significance alone make it a worthwhile destination. It's possible to visit Cooktown and return to Cairns in just one day, but to do the place justice, you should plan to stay overnight.

History
A small cairn beside the Endeavour River and opposite the police station marks the site where Captain Cook and his crew set up camp for

seven weeks in 1770, repairing the *Endeavour* which had been holed on an offshore reef. "Cook's Town" was officially founded 100 years later as a gateway to the Palmer River gold fields, 140 km southwest. Within weeks of the start of the rush, a main street lined with banks, brothels, and hotels had taken shape. Within a year, the population peaked at 30,000, and the settlement had grown to become Queensland's second-largest town. About half the residents were Chinese, and although racial tensions led to rioting, the malaria, typhoid, and dysentery were more deadly. When the gold rush ended, a mass exodus took place. A cyclone in 1907 and the scare of Japanese invasion during WW II just about finished off the town. But in 1970, the bicentenary of Cook's landing saw the quasi ghost town become focus of national media attention, and its future as a tourist destination was assured through the opening of the James Cook Historical Museum.

Sights
James Cook Historical Museum, Helen St. (tel. 070-69-5386), provides glimpses of early life in far north Queensland. One room is devoted to

---

INDEPENDENT TRAVEL TO CAPE YORK

Monsoonal rains make the peninsula inaccessible by road for at least six months of the year, but June-Oct. hundreds of 4WD enthusiasts head up the unsealed **Peninsula Developmental Rd.** with Cape York in their sights. It is a long and rough trip, and much advance preparation is needed. For road conditions, contact the RACQ in Cairns (tel. 070-51-6711). For general touring information, contact the **Far North Queensland Promotions Bureau,** 36 Aplin St., Cairns (tel. 070-51-3588). It is also important to carry a high-frequency radio; to obtain a frequency listing, contact the Royal Flying Doctor Service (tel. 070-53-1952). For travel north of the Jardine River, permits are necessary as the road passes through Aboriginal-owned land. For permits, write: Chairman, Northern Peninsula Reserves, Community Council, Bamaga, QLD 4871.

Cook and his exploration of the area, while other sections are dedicated to the Aborigines, the gold rush, and European and Chinese settlers. The museum is open daily 9:30 a.m.-4 p.m. and admission is $5.

A few monuments around town are worth visiting for their historical significance, including those to Captain Cook and Edmund Kennedy on the road out to the wharf. In the cemetery, at the west end of town, are the graves of many early miners; also buried here is Mary Watson, who was attacked by Aborigines in 1881 while living on Lizard Island. She managed to escape, going to sea in a metal pot and drifting north with her son and a servant. They all died of thirst.

Three very different national parks lie in the vicinity of Cooktown. The closest is **Mt. Cook National Park,** on the southwest outskirts of town; a trail at the end of May St. leads to the 430-meter summit for which the park is named. Across the river from town is **Endeavour River National Park,** accessible only by boat. This park preserves an area of wetland and riverside dunes, unchanged since the botanist on Cook's ship, Joseph Banks, collected plant specimens here in 1770.

South of Cooktown, at the junction of the inland and coastal routes, is **Black Mountain National Park,** protecting a small mountain of granite boulders, the black color coming from a dark green algae that covers them.

Accommodations and Food
Sovereign Hotel Resort, Charlotte St. (tel. 070-69-5400), has a range of rooms; the most basic share facilities; $31 s, $42 d. Apartments with kitchens are $103 s, $114 d. **Cooktown's River of Gold Motel,** corner Hope and Walker Streets (tel. 070-69-5222), has basic but large rooms and a pool and restaurant; $53 s, $64 d.

Cooktown Backpackers, three blocks from the center of town on Charlotte St. (tel. 070-69-5166), features a pool, modern kitchen, and large gardens; rates are $13 pp in the dorm and $20 s, $30 d in private rooms.

On McIvor Rd., a couple of blocks out of town, is **Cooktown Tropical Breeze Caravan Park** (tel. 070-69-5417). Sites are $10.50-13, on-site vans $30, and air-conditioned units $40-54.

Sovereign Hotel Resort, Charlotte St. (tel. 070-69-5400), has inexpensive counter meals and, for something a bit more formal, upstairs is a small restaurant with tables along the balcony; main dishes here range $8.50-17. For fish and chips and other inexpensive meals, **Reef Cafe** on Charlotte St. has takeaway or eat-in.

Transportation and Tours
Flightwest (tel. 13-2392) flies between Cairns and Cooktown daily; $97 one-way. **Reef Air Tours** (tel. 070-35-9530) offers return flights between the two centers, a tour of Cooktown's sights, and lunch at Sovereign Hotel Resort for a reasonable $160 pp.

Coral Coaches (tel. 070-31-7577) departs once daily from Trinity Wharf, Cairns, for Cooktown, traveling the inland and coastal routes on alternate days. The fare is $92 round-trip, but accommodation packages, such as transportation and two nights' accommodation in Cooktown from $113 pp, are excellent deals.

From Cairns, most day tours to Cooktown incorporate a four-wheel-drive trip through Cape Tribulation National Park with a scenic flight, cutting down on travel time considerably. **Oz Tours Safaris** (tel. 070-55-9535) offers the choice of traveling either the inland or coastal route, a town tour, lunch, and one-way air transfers for adult $199, child $159. Two-day tours, taking in both overland routes, range $225-345 depending on the Cooktown accommodation chosen. If you only have a day, and are on a budget, **Strikies Safaris** (tel. 070-99-5599) offers a compromise—traveling from Cairns and back by four-wheel drive, plus a town tour, for just $74—but it's a long day, departing Cairns at 6 a.m. and returning at 9 p.m.

COOKTOWN TO THE CAPE

The only road to Cape York is the 4WD-only **Peninsula Developmental Rd.,** which begins 85 km southwest of Cooktown at the small service town of **Lakeland.**

Quinkan Rock Art
Sprinkled around sandstone escarpments southwest of Laura (turn off 48 km north of Lakeland) are one of the world's largest concentrations of primitive rock art, with hundreds of "galleries" scattered around the area. Of the four galleries

open to the public, **Split Rock,** a 400-meter walk from the parking area, is most accessible while **Guguyalangi** lies 1.2 km farther north along an escarpment. Several pieces of rock art date back 10,000 years, but it's thought that Aborigines inhabited the area much earlier than this. The art depicts mostly animals, painted in colorful ochre colors, along with figures of their religious beliefs. Before entering the sites, you must obtain a permit from the ranger's office in Laura (tel. 070-60-3260). Entry is $3 pp, or take a ranger-led tour for $6 pp. With care, two-wheel drives can make it to the site. **Trezise Bush Guides** (tel. 070-60-3236 or 52-1552) has a longtime association with the rock art and has been instrumental in cataloging and protecting the sites. They offer a one-day trip from Cairns, flying into the area and exploring the sites on foot; $295 pp. They also offer a land-based four-day safari from Cairns; $675 pp.

Quinkan rock art

Laura

Laura, a small community 64 km north of Lakeland, has all necessary services (having a beer under the mango trees outside the pub is almost compulsory). On the last weekend in June Aboriginals from around the cape congregate in town for the **Laura Aboriginal Dance Festival.**

West of town is **Jowalbinna Bush Camp** (tel. 070-60-3236 or in Cairns call 52-1552), operated by the Trezise brothers, who helped catalog the nearby Quinkan rock art. They offer a variety of all-inclusive tours to the camp from Cairns, with the emphasis on hiking, swimming, and Aboriginal art. The two-day safari is $275 pp, three-day $395, and four-day $675 pp.

Lakefield National Park

Immediately north of Laura is the access road to 537,000-hectare Lakefield National Park, most accessible of all the cape's parks. Comprising mostly savannah grasses and open woodlands,

the park also encompasses a 35-km stretch of coast along Princess Charlotte Bay, where salt marshes and mangroves dominate. Through the park flow three major rivers—the Laura, Kennedy, and Normanby—but during the Wet, vast low-lying areas are underwater. In parts of the park this water remains year-round, providing ideal habitat for millions of waterbirds, including storks, jabirus, brolgas, spoonbills, and other species such as black cockatoos and the extremely rare golden-shouldered parrot. Over 18 species of mammals have been recorded in the park; the most commonly sighted are wallabies and kangaroos (look for them grazing in open grassland). Like on the rest of the cape, both species of crocodiles are present, so don't go swimming in deep or murky rivers.

The Peninsula Developmental Rd. skirts the southwest corner of the park, but a much longer, more rugged track heads north from Laura straight through the heart of the park. Campgrounds are scattered throughout the park and permits are required; call the ranger (tel. 070-60-3271) for these and to check road conditions.

Cape Melville National Park

Accessible only by boat, this 42,000-hectare park sits on a remote headland at the northern tip of land extending far east from the peninsula. The park features long sandy beaches linking rocky headlands, and in the west of the park, behind Bathurst Bay, are extensive salt marshes that end abruptly at the Melville Range, similar in composition to Black Mountain, near Cooktown.

To the west, between Bathurst and Princess Charlotte Bays, is the **Flinders Island Group,** comprising several continental islands, including Flinders, Stanley, and Denham, which feature short stretches of sandy beach. Camping on the islands or Cape Melville is by permit only; for these contact the Department of Environment and Heritage in Cairns (tel. 070-52-3096).

Coen

Located on the Coen River and surrounded by rolling hills 245 km north of Laura, this small town is the largest settlement between Cooktown and Cape York. The highlight of Coen's social calendar is the **Annual Picnic Races**, run on a bush racing track each August. Services on the main street include a grocery store, two petrol stations, mechanic, post office, and pub, while on the riverbank north of town are a few campsites.

The first services north of Coen are on the south side of the **Archer River**, 65 km to the north.

Rokeby National Park

Remote Rokeby National Park protects 291,000 hectares between the Coen and Archer Rivers west of the Peninsula Developmental Road. Large elevation changes within the park support many vegetation types, ranging from dense tropical rainforests of the McIlwraith Range to open woodlands of melaleucas on the alluvial plains farther west. The park straddles the Peninsula Developmental Rd., but the only access to the park proper is just north of Coen Airstrip, extending 70 km west to the ranger station at Rokeby. To contact the ranger, call (070) 60-3256.

Archer Bend National Park

Straddling the large Archer River, this 166,000-hectare park is west of Rokeby National Park and is inaccessible to all but the most experienced off-road drivers. The Archer River rises in the McIlwraith Range, near the east coast, and flows across almost the entire peninsula. The river is lined with a luxuriant growth of vine forests and flanked by alluvial plains dotted with swamps and lagoons. High ridges of sandstone form the park's northern and southern boundaries. For more information and road access details contact the ranger at Rokeby National Park (tel. 070-60-3256).

EDMUND KENNEDY

The travels of Edmund Kennedy may not be as well documented as those of Burke and Wills, but his tragic last journey was just as extraordinary, and while Burke and Wills' own ignorance brought about their tragic downfall, it was pen-pushing planners who killed Kennedy. With no experience in tropical travel, Kennedy was placed in charge of an expedition that would become the first to traverse the rugged and inhospitable Cape York Peninsula. On 21 May 1848 Kennedy and his men were put ashore at Rockingham Bay, 900 km from Cape York itself. Although Aboriginals had inhabited the Cape for thousands of years, and passing ships had anchored at various points along the coast, no white man had ever penetrated the region. Things started badly for the Kennedy party, for from the landing site they were hemmed in by a maze of rivers and swamps, and it immediately became obvious to Kennedy that the journey had been planned by officials totally ignorant of the type of country to be traversed. The expedition headed west, to the higher ground of the Great Dividing Range, before any northward progress could be made.

After five months' travel in hellish conditions, and with the Wet upon them, the party stumbled off the Great Dividing Range into Weymouth Bay, three-quarters of the way to their final destination. Inadequate supplies and fatigue led Kennedy to split the party, leaving nine men and most of the horses at the bay. The party split again farther north, leaving just Kennedy and his Aboriginal tracker, Jackey Jackey, to make for the Cape. By mid-December Kennedy was very ill, exhausted, and on the point of starvation, leaning on Jackey Jackey for support and stumbling at every step. Descending to the final river before the rendezvous point with a supply ship, the two realized the severity of their predicament, for the river mouth described on marine charts as having an "inviting shoreline" was in fact the outlet of a swamp many hundreds of square kilometers in area.

Aboriginals had been following the two men for many weeks, and although friendly at times, they were simply biding their time. While resting at a stream, Kennedy was killed by a hail of spears. Using bush skills, Jackey Jackey slunk off, traveling through the swamp to the waiting *Ariel*. Sailing south, no sign was found of the second group left behind, and by the time the ship reached Weymouth Bay, just two of the nine men remained alive.

Iron Range National Park

This 34,600-hectare park, protecting the largest remaining area of tropical lowland rainforest in Australia, extends west from the shoreline of Weymouth Bay to 545-meter Mt. Tozer, the highest point along a ridge of jagged granite summits. Many plant species present in this park are found nowhere else in Australia, yet are common in Papua New Guinea. Much of the park's birdlife is also endemic, including palm cockatoos, green-backed honey eaters, and eclectus parrots.

Access to the park is along a rough 150-km track that spurs off the Peninsula Developmental Rd. 20 km north of the Archer River Crossing. At the end of the road is the small settlement of **Portland Roads** (no services), consisting of a few houses around a palm-fringed beach. A campground is south of Portland Roads. To contact the ranger call (070) 60-7170.

Weipa

Located on the Gulf of Carpentaria and originally the site of an Aboriginal mission established in 1898, Weipa is now a company town of 2,500, existing only to mine the world's largest deposit of bauxite. The mineral occurs around Weipa as red-colored pebbles in layers of clay up to 10 meters deep. Although Dutch explorers were the first to record the red coloring, the true wealth wasn't recognized until the 1950s. After extraction, the bauxite is washed and crushed, then shipped to Gladstone, where it is refined into alumina for use in aluminum products. Since mining began, 130 million tons of bauxite have been mined, but with reserves of 2,000 million tons remaining under lease, Weipa will continue to thrive well into the next century.

There's not really a great deal to do in town. Take to the water at Evan's Landing, either in a rented boat from **Weipa Boat Hire** (tel. 070-69-7495) or on a river cruise with **Weipa River Safaris** (tel. 070-69-7597).

The town has all the services of a similarly sized town, including a supermarket, library, cinema, tennis court, golf course, and swimming pool.

Paxhaven Camping Ground is southwest of Rocky Point, behind Nanum Shopping Centre (tel. 070-69-7871). Facilities include a laundry, hot showers, and barbecue; unpowered sites are $12, powered sites $14.

Flightwest (tel. 13-2392) flies daily between Weipa and Cairns.

Jardine River National Park

Before reaching this magnificent park at the tip of the continent, you must negotiate the **Wenlock River,** 170 km north of the Archer River Roadhouse. The crossing is difficult not only for the river's depth but for its steep banks.

The Jardine River, 155 km north of the Wenlock River, flows year-round from a catchment area of 2,500 square km. Most of its watershed is protected by 235,000-hectare Jardine River National Park, extending east from the Peninsula Developmental Rd. to the Coral Sea and encompassing the northernmost extent of the Great Dividing Range.

In the mid-1980s, a barge service across the Jardine made crossing the cape's most daunting river a whole lot easier. (To the east of the barge is the old crossing point; the river here is nearly one meter deep and 100 meters wide.)

Access to the east coast of the park is possible at a couple of points, through a landscape of wetlands where insectivorous plants such as sundews and pitcher plants thrive. Access to the east coast is 109 km north of the Wenlock River along a track leading to **Shelburne Station** and an area of coast dominated by white silica sand dunes. The other access is 10 km north of the Jardine River to **Ussher Point.** The ranger station is at Heathlands (tel. 070-60-3241).

Bamaga and the Cape

Bamaga (pop. 900), Australia's northernmost settlement, is 35 km north of the Jardine River and just 30 km from Cape York. On the approach into town, just south of the airport, a sign marks the resting place of a DC3 that crashed while attempting to land at Bamaga airstrip during WW II. The town itself has a motel, post office, grocery store, petrol station (closed most weekends), and hospital.

To the north of Bamaga is 510-hectare **Possession Island,** where Captain Cook landed in 1770 and planted a second British flag (the other was at Botany Bay) to complete his goal "possession of the whole east coast."

Halfway between Bamaga and the cape, a road spurs east to the coast and the site of **Somerset,** one of Australia's most remote outosts. It was established in 1864, both as a sign of British occupancy and as a safe haven for sailors shipwrecked in the treacherous Torres Strait. The first posting was given to John Jardine, but it was his son, Frank, who had the most impact on the cape. Placed in charge in 1866, Frank stayed on after the post officially closed 10 years later to marry a Samoan princess, operate a pearling boat, grow coconuts, and even drive a herd of cattle up the cape from Rockhampton. He died in 1919, his wife followed a few years later, and today all that remains of Somerset are their graves, a few coconut trees, and the foundations of a jetty.

If you arrive at the cape on an organized tour, accommodations will have been prebooked and you'll return to Cairns by air from nearby Horn Island, return overland to Weipa for a southern flight, or make the return trip by cruise boat. Having traveled this far north, you may want to spend more time in the area and take a trip over to Thursday Island (see below), but to do so, you'll need to book the following accommodations well in advance. **Punsand Bay Safari Lodge,** 28 km north of Bamaga (tel. 070-69-1722), has safari-style tents for $20 pp and camping is allowed. Just 400 meters from the cape itself is **Pajinka Wilderness Lodge** (tel. 070-69-2100 or 1800-80-2968). Each of the 24 cabins has a bathroom and private balcony. Since the lodge's purchase by local Aborigines in 1993, the Injinoo culture has become part of the activities program, with field trips offered and boats with fishing gear for guest use. Rates are $238 s, $400 d, which includes all meals. A campground has been developed at Seisia, north of Bamaga (tel. 070-69-3243).

Jacky Jacky Airport, nine km southeast of Bamaga, was built during WW II and is now served by **Sunstate** (tel. 13-1313) and **Flightwest** (tel. 13-2392). Book transport to Thursday Island by boat through Seisia Camping Grounds (tel. 070-69-3243).

ISLANDS OF THE TORRES STRAIT

The Torres Strait is a shallow but treacherous body of water between Cape York Peninsula and Papua New Guinea. Until 15,000 years ago, the two pieces of land were joined, but as

the last ice age ended, the sea level rose. Many of the 70-odd islands that dot the strait were the peaks of mountains along the land bridge, while others, to the east, are sandy cays of the Great Barrier Reef. Of the 17 inhabited islands, **Thursday Island,** part of a rugged group of islands northwest of Cape York, has the largest population.

El-Torito, operated by Jardine Shipping (tel. 070-35-1900 or 1800-81-0634), departs Thursday Island every Wednesday on a four-day cruise. The itinerary includes Possession Island, Punsand Bay, historic Somerset, Albany Island (a bastion of Torres Strait heritage and home to a pearl farm), snorkeling on uninhabited Sue Island, and hiking on Mt. Ernest Island. The cost, $1384 pp, includes accommodations and all meals.

History

Torres Strait Islanders are descendants of people who migrated from Polynesia and Melanesia around 2,000 years ago, and are unrelated to the Aborigines of mainland Australia. Violence between tribes dominated the islanders' pre-European lifestyle, when headhunting and cannibalism were rife.

In 1877 the Australian government moved its official northern residence from Somerset to Thursday Island, where pearling had become a major industry, employing up to 1,500 men. In the following years the introduction of Christianity, Japanese bombing raids, and an influx of European bureaucrats caused drastic changes in the islands, and many islanders moved to mainland Australia.

Thursday Island

Rugged Thursday Island (best known as T.I.), just 534 hectares in area and 35 km from Cape York, is no beautiful tropical island, but its interesting history and a laid-back atmosphere make it an appealing, if little-visited, destination. At one time a major pearling center, the island now has a population of 2,500, most of whom live around **Kennedy Bay,** filled with a colorful array of old wooden pearling luggers, aluminum dinghies, yachts, and barges. You'll find most services (a motel, hotels, banks, a supermarket, hospital, post office, motorboat rentals, and a swimming pool) on the island along Douglas St., lined with mango trees. A small museum is housed in the old fort on Green Hill, and the cemetery has some interesting graves, including many hundreds of pearl divers.

Jardine Motel, Victoria Parade (tel. 070-69-1555), is a two-story building across a road from the bay and just 200 meters from the ferry wharf. Rooms have private bathrooms and are air-conditioned; rates are $120 s, $150 d. The only campground, **Traveller's Halt,** is on neighboring Horn Island (tel. 070-69-1304).

Building an airstrip on rugged Thursday Island was never practical, so neighboring Horn Island is used, with ferries meeting all flights; $30 round-trip (if you're not an airline passenger the fare is more reasonable at $5 each way). **Flight west** (tel. 13-2392) and **Sunstate** (tel. 13-1313) have regular flights to Cairns ($290 one-way). **Peddell's Ferry and Tour Bus Service** (tel. 070-69-1551) runs tours around the island and a ferry service to Seisia on the mainland; $35 one-way.

GULF COUNTRY

Queensland's Gulf Country is a remote region of low-lying coastal plains extending hundreds of kilometers inland from the Gulf of Carpentaria. During the Wet, the entire region becomes one huge flooded swamp as a maze of river channels and basins fill with water. The actual coastline is ill-defined, made up of impenetrable tidal flats, mangrove swamps, and, near the Northern Territory border, salt pans. Karumba, on a firm chunk of ground at the mouth of the Norman River, is the only town right on the gulf, with the region's only other settlements being Normanton and Burketown, the former linked to Cloncurry by sealed road and to Cairns by the 700-km unsealed (but passable in two-wheel drive) Gulf Developmental Road. The alternate route west from Cairns is the much longer **Burke Developmental Rd.** (four-wheel drive only), which provides access to Staaten River National Park.

CAIRNS TO NORMANTON VIA THE GULF DEVELOPMENTAL ROAD

Undara Lava Tubes

These fascinating geological features snake for almost 100 km through high country 210 km west of Cairns. They were formed around 190,000 years ago when a stream of lava from a nearby volcano flowed along a dry riverbed. As the outer layer of lava cooled quickly, a molten mass of rock continued flowing underneath. In the time since, layers of sediment, washed off the Great Dividing Range, have covered the tube, and in areas the tube's roof (up to 15 meters high) has collapsed, allowing access, cre-

ating pockets of lush vegetation, and dividing the tube into a row of smaller ones. The tubes are mostly on private property, but a Savannah Guide, based on-site, leads daily tours. Cost for a basic tour is $18 pp, and a half-day tour with lunch is $52 (for bookings call 070-97-1411). The tubes are only a small part of the area's attractions; there's also bushwalking, birdwatching, and flightseeing, and Australia's hottest hot springs are a short drive away.

Undara Experience (tel. 070-97-1411) operates Undara Lava Lodge, a series of railway carriages restored to provide comfortable accommodation; there's also a dining car, lounge car, and reading car. Nightly rates are $96 pp inclusive of meals, or you can camp for $8 pp. Undara Experience offers a variety of packages, including a one-day trip out from Cairns ($92 pp bus, $275 pp plane) and a four-day all-inclusive trip from Cairns ($518 pp bus, $688 plane). **Oz Tours Safaris** (tel. 070-55-9535 or 1800-07-9006) includes Undara in all their trips to the gulf.

The Savannahlander

Forsayth, 40 km south of Georgetown, is the railhead for a line built to Cairns earlier this cen-

> On 1 November 1997 telephone numbers in this section will change. To dial the new number, simply add "40" to all numbers with the area code (070) and add "47" to all numbers with the area code (077). As an example, (070) 12-3456 becomes 4012-3456. The new area code for all numbers in this section will be (07).

ury. A section of rail, between Mt. Surprise and Forsayth, is now used by the Savannahlander, a tourist train operated by Queensland Rail. The trip takes five to six hours and is $35 one-way departs Mt. Surprise Monday and Thursday 2:30 p.m.). For package-tour information, call Queensland Rail (tel. 13-2232).

Cobbold Gorge

Set among the sparsely vegetated gulf savannah, and surrounded by an area rich in gems, this spectacular gorge was discovered by the property owners as recently as 1993. The gorge holds water year-round, its craggy walls shaped by thousands of years of water erosion. A full-day tour, which includes a boat trip into the gorge, a visit to the station and sites of historical significance, and lunch is adult $75, child $30. The gorge cuts through a property 75 km south of Georgetown; for our bookings, call (070) 62-5470.

The Gulflander

This train runs between Croydon, 150 km west of Georgetown, and Normanton along a rail line built late last century to transport supplies to the thriving Croydon goldfields. The train runs Wednesday and Thursday and costs $58 round-trip. For bookings, call (077) 45-1391.

CAIRNS TO NORMANTON VIA THE BURKE DEVELOPMENTAL ROAD

This route is rough in places and should only be attempted by those in four-wheel drives (conventional vehicles can only make it from Cairns as far west as Chillagoe).

Chillagoe-Mungana Caves National Parks

Late last century, Chillagoe, 235 km west of Cairns, was one of Queensland's most productive mining towns, with copper, lead, silver, and gold extracted. Major mining operations ceased in the mid-1940s, but signs of early activity remain, including the ruins of a large smelter. But the height of the area is a string of limestone caves protected by small national parks. The caves are part of a complex geographical structure that also includes limestone pinnacles rising 70 meters. High rainfall has dissolved the limestone surface, and where water has seeped underground ex-

tensive cave systems have formed. Five caves are open to the public; Archway and Pompey caves can be explored independently, while three others, including the most impressive—Royal Arch Cave—can only be visited on a ranger-led hike. To contact the ranger call (070) 94-7163.

Chillagoe Caves Lodge, King St. (tel. 070-94-7106), is a small motel with rooms for $45 s, $55 d. You can also camp here for $8-10.

Staaten River National Park

This large park south of the Burke Developmental Rd. encompasses 470,000 hectares of open woodland, typical of gulf savannah country, as well as a 120-km stretch of the Staaten River. Termite mounds are one of the most distinctive features of the landscape, some up to three meters high, each aligned north-south to minimize heat absorption.

The park has no formed roads, making access difficult. Conceivably, and with permission, you can enter the park through Bulimba or Highbury Stations to the east, or Dorunda Station, which borders the park to the west.

Mitchell and Alice Rivers National Park

Named for the two rivers bordering it, this remote park lies 80 km northwest of Dunbar on the Burke Developmental Road. It features open woodland with small areas of rainforest along permanent rivers. Birdlife is prolific, especially early in the dry season, when large lagoons of water remain. Freshwater and saltwater crocodiles are common, as are feral pigs.

NORMANTON AND VICINITY

With a population of 1,200, Normanton is the largest town in the 120,000-square-km Gulf Country. From Cairns, access is along the Gulf Developmental Rd.; from the south, access is from Cloncurry. By river, the actual gulf lies 40 km beyond Normanton, and 69 km by road. Established in 1867, Normanton grew as a port for copper fields around Cloncurry and, later, as gateway to the Croydon goldfields.

The foot of the gulf is impenetrable, a maze of mangrove swamps, mudflats, and river mouths, but at the mouth of the Norman River is a rare piece of firm ground where the community of

Karumba has been established. It is an important fishing town, a base for prawn and barramundi boats, as well as for holidaying anglers.

Practicalities

Accommodation in Normanton is at the **Albion Hotel,** Haig St. (tel. 077-45-1218), where rooms with private facilities are $45 s, $50 d. **Karumba Lodge Hotel,** Yappar St., Karumba (tel. 077-45-9121), has similarly priced rooms and meals served Tues.-Saturday. You can camp free at Walker's Creek, halfway between the two towns, or at **Normanton Caravan Park** on Brown St. (tel. 077-45-1121); sites cost $10-12, and there are hot showers, a laundry, and barbecue.

Flightwest (tel. 13-2392) flies between Normanton and Cairns, continuing to Karumba and Mornington Island. If you're in Cairns and want to visit the gulf in just one day, contact **Cape York Air Services** (tel. 070-35-9399), which makes a mail run to Normanton every Friday; $225 pp round-trip. **Oz Tours Safaris** (tel. 1800-07-9006) offers a seven-day overland safari from Cairns, taking in all sights along the Gulf Developmental Rd. as well as Lawn Hill Gorge and Burketown, ending at Normanton for a flight back to Cairns. Tours run late April-Oct. and are $1195 pp if camping and $1495 in motels.

BURKETOWN AND VICINITY

The other gulf community worthy of a detour is Burketown, 269 km northeast of the Burke and Wills Roadhouse. In the Wet, Burketown can be isolated for weeks as the surrounding salt pans and savannah grasslands become flooded from inland rainfall. The township has a pub (call 077-45-5104 to book a room) on one side of the road and a few shops on the other.

Lawn Hill National Park

Aboriginals have been coming to Lawn Hill Gorge for at least 20,000 years, and little has changed in this time. It's a magical place, a lush oasis surrounded for hundreds of kilometers by a dry, harsh landscape. The gorge itself is only a small part of the 262,000-hectare park. Water from artesian springs to the west, on the Barkly Tableland, created the gorge and allows tropical vegetation such as palms, ferns, and figs to thrive. Lawn Hill Creek is home to freshwater crocodiles and turtles, and a variety of small mammals and marsupials come from afar to drink its waters. The park's Riversleigh section, straddling the Gregory River in the south of the park and accessible only by four-wheel drive, is the site of important fossil discoveries, some of which are displayed in Mt. Isa.

The park is 400 km from Mt. Isa. To get there, turn off the Barkly Highway 120 km west of Mt. Isa and follow the Burketown Rd. north for 180 km to **Gregory Downs** (rooms, petrol, and food), then cross the Gregory River and head west for 100 km. A primitive camping area has been developed beside Lawn Hill Creek and at **Adel's Grove,** at the park entrance, you'll find a campground with hot showers, barbecues, and basic supplies (tel. 077-48-5502). To contact the park ranger call (077) 48-5572.

OUTBACK QUEENSLAND

While most visitors to Queensland dive on the reef and sun themselves on the beaches, a few

On 1 November 1997 telephone numbers in this section will change. To dial the new number, simply add "46" to all numbers with the area code (076) and add "47" to all numbers with the area code (077). As an example, (076) 12-3456 becomes 4612-3456. The new area code for all numbers in this section will be (07).

venture over the Great Dividing Range and across the tablelands to the outback, an area of endless plains and red-soil desert where towns lie hundreds of kilometers apart, existing only as service centers for road-weary travelers and vast cattle stations. Among this desolate landscape are many surprises—pleasant country towns where hospitality is second nature, and huge national parks protecting all the best natural features.

Outback Queensland is generally regarded as everything west of the **Matilda Highway,** a col

lection of highways 1,700 km long, passing through areas of interest to travelers and also of historical importance. The highway begins on the NSW/Queensland border, about 700 km inland, and makes a long arc around the eastern edge of the outback to Mt. Isa and the Queensland/Northern Territory border. Highways lead westward from the coastal cities of Brisbane (Warrego Highway), Rockhampton (Capricorn Highway), and Townsville (Flinders Highway) to the outback. Travel is best May-October. The rest of the year is stifling hot, and during the Wet roads can be under water for weeks.

MITCHELL HIGHWAY

The Mitchell Highway enters Queensland in the south of the state, 138 km north of Bourke, and parallels the **Warrego River** to Cunnamulla. This highway, and those that continue through to the Gulf of Carpentaria, are promoted as the Matilda Highway.

Cunnamulla

First town north of the border, Cunnamulla sits on the tree-lined banks of the Warrego River. This town of 1,500 is at the western terminus of the rail line used to transport sheep to eastern markets. The small **Bicentennial Museum** on John St. is worth investigating, but little else is. To the west of the town is **Yowah Opal Field,** where opal nuts—opal in a shell of ironstone— are highly sought after.

Charleville

Surrounded by hundreds of thousands of hectares of sheep and cattle stations and 800 km from the coast, Charleville (pop. 3,500) is the hub of southwest Queensland. Reminders of the town's earliest days abound, the most interesting being a Stiger Vortex rainmaker gun. During a terrible drought in 1902 Clement L. Wagge imported six of the guns from Germany, setting them at strategic locations around Charleville. Each was loaded with gunpowder and fired skyward in the hope of creating rain. Two guns imploded, a few horses stampeded, and Mr. Wagge rode out of town the following day—under a cloudless sky. You'll find the remaining gun in Centennial Park, just south of

town. Other highlights in town include the 188 **Queensland National Bank** (open Mon.-Fri. a.m.-4 p.m., Saturday 9 a.m.-noon) and one Queensland's three **Royal Flying Doctor Se vice** bases where a visitor center describes th importance of the service; open Mon.-Fri. 8:3 a.m.-4:30 p.m. (tel. 076-54-1181). East Charleville, the Department of Environment ar Heritage operates a **research station** (tel. 07 54-1255) where you're likely to spot variou species of kangaroos and wallabies grazir among three hectares of native bushland; ope Mon.-Fri. 8:30 a.m.-4:30 p.m.

Charleville Waltzing Matilda Motor In 125 Alfred St. (tel. 076-54-1720), has the lea expensive rooms in town; those with shared f cilities are $29 s, $40 d (the roof of this plae was used as a helipad during flooding in Ap 1990 when the entire town was underwate Of a higher standard is **Warrego Motel,** 75 Wi St. (tel. 076-54-1299), $55 s, $65 d. Campei should head to **Bailey Bar Caravan Park,** 1⁹ King St. (tel. 076-54-1744).

The **Tourist Information Centre** is on Wi St. (tel. 076-54-3057); open daily 9:30 a.m 4:30 p.m.

CHANNEL COUNTRY

In the southwestern corner of the state is ⅋ area known as Channel Country, so named f the mosaic of watercourses that flow through It's either very wet or very dry out here. Summ rains to the north fill the many rivers and cree that flow southwest toward Lake Eyre. The w tercourses divide, rejoin each other, and eve tually dissipate into the soft soils of the far nort eastern corner of South Australia. After exce tionally heavy rains, the whole basin flood creating a massive system of temporary lak that isolate remote stations and flood roads f months.

Diamantina Developmental Road

This 1,350-km road is the main route throug Channel Country, heading west at Charlevi and ending at Mt. Isa. It also provides access the north end of the Birdsville Track.

Quilpie, 210 km west of Charleville, is a cat transportation railhead surrounded by many pi

ıctive opal mines. The next town en route to Mt.
ı is **Windorah,** with a population under 100
ıt enough passing trade to justify a pub, petrol
ımp, and general store. Continuing west, the
ghway passes brilliantly colored red sandhills,
hich rise from the Channel Country like a mi-
ge. Then it's 500 km of gravel to Boulia. It's a
ng trip, the arid landscape broken occasion-
'y by an outcrop of sandstone and the town of
edourie, consisting of just a pub and petrol
ımp. A track heading south from Bedourie
ads to Birdsville. After crossing the Georgina
ıver and passing the small town of Boulia, the
ınd becomes rocky, changing subtly, as the
ad climbs the Isa Highlands to Mt. Isa.

ırdsville

amous for its pub, this is Queensland's most
mote town. It grew from a store established on
e Diamantina River in 1872, the last stop for
ockmen driving cattle southward through the
mpson Desert to Adelaide. Named by a set-
ır's wife for the profusion of birdlife on the river,
ırdsville boasted three hotels, a couple of
ops, and dozens of houses in its heyday.
oday, the population is under 100, but each
eptember more than 5,000 punters descend on
e town for the annual **Birdsville Races,** a col-
ful celebration of everything that outback Ausalia stands for. Needless to say, an amazing
nount of beer is consumed over the week-
nd, much of it in and around the **Birdsville**
otel, right by the airport. This hotel has rooms
r $42 s, $64 d (tel. 076-56-3244).

impson Desert National Park

the extreme west of the state, and accessible
ıly by four-wheel drive, is the enormous one-mil-
ın-hectare Simpson Desert National Park. It
ıcompasses just the northeast corner of a 20-
illion-hectare desert for which the park is
amed. The landscape is barren, featuring waves
: sand dunes, gibber flats, and large areas of
ay plains. The extensive dune system spreads
rough much of the park, typified by dunes up to
5 meters high, spaced 300-400 meters apart,
nd running parallel for up to 70 km. A surpris-
gly large number of life-forms exist in the park—
few species of spinifex, wattle, grevilleas,
nakes, lizards, marsupials, and birds of prey all
rive in this harsh, waterless environment.

Permits are required before entering the park
(available from the Department of Environment
and Heritage in Longreach, tel. 076-58-1761,
or Charleville, tel. 076-54-1255), and you must
also register with the police in Birdsville. The
park has no established camping area, but as
the only formed road leads from Birdsville to
Poeppel Corner (150 km) most people camp
somewhere en route.

CHARLEVILLE TO LONGREACH

Blackall

In 1892, gun-shearer Jack Howe set a new
world record, shearing 321 sheep in less than
eight hours. For blade shearing, the record
stands to this day, and it took until 1950 for a
machine shearer to equal it. A statue of the
great man stands in the main street of Blackall,
a pleasant outback town 300 km north of
Charleville.

Blackwall Woolscour, four km north of town
(tel. 076-57-4637), was where wool was washed
and dried, then sorted, pressed, and transported to eastern ports. Much of the plant remains as
the day it closed, allowing an authentic glimpse
at the industry upon which outback Australia
was built. The complex is open daily 8 a.m.-4
p.m.; admission is adult $5, child $2. Like many
outback towns, Blackall's drinking water is from
artesian bores, and one is located at the
woolscour.

The **Barcoo Hotel,** 95 Shamrock St. (tel.
076-57-4197), is right in the center of town and
has rooms with shared facilities for $35 s, $50 d,
which includes a cooked breakfast. Lunches at
the bar are $4-6 and Friday and Saturday nights
there's a barbecue in the beer garden. **Blackall**
Motel, also on Shamrock St. (tel. 076-57-4611),
has standard rooms for $40 s, $50 d. **Blackall**
Caravan Park, 53 Garden St. (tel. 076-57-
4816), has unpowered sites for $9, powered
sites $11.50, on-site vans $16-22, and cabins
$28-40.

Avington Outback Holiday Station (tel.
076-57-5952) allows guests to enjoy life on a
working cattle station; you can ride horses, round
up sheep, and watch shearers at work, not to
mention cruise on the Barcoo River, golf on a
unique nine-hole course, and play tennis.

Rooms, large and air-conditioned, cost $50 s, $90 d, including meals. To get there, head north out of Blackall for 18 km, then take Avington Rd. for 57 km northwest to the homestead.

Idalia National Park

Located 100 km southwest of Blackall, deep in the Gowan Ranges that form the eastern boundary of Channel Country, is this new 144,000-hectare park. It encompasses the headwaters of the Bulloo River, and although the river is dry for most of the year, a variety of vegetation thrives, including stands of river red gums around low-lying areas. Access is by four-wheel drive only and camping is permitted at Monk's Tank.

Barcaldine

The pleasant town of Barcaldine lies at the junction of the Capricorn and Landsborough Highways, 580 km west of Rockhampton. In 1891 more than 1,000 striking shearers converged on the town, meeting under a big ghost gum outside the railway station to demand higher wages and better working conditions. The following year, union leaders endorsed a candidate for parliament, under the same tree, beginning the formation of the Australian Labor Party. The tree stands today, in mute testimony to the shearers' resolve. The role played by ordinary working Australians, such as shearers, in the development of the country is celebrated at the **Australian Workers Heritage Centre,** which opened in May 1991 on the centenary of the strike. The large complex features a museum, interactive displays, films, historic buildings transported to the site, a seven-story theater where the Australian tribute *Celebration of a Nation* is shown, and extensive landscaped gardens complete with a billabong. Open daily 9 a.m.-5 p.m. On Ash St. (tel. 076-51-1422).

Barcaldine Motel, on the main drag through town (tel. 076-51-1244), has basic rooms for $35 s, $45 d. With nicer rooms and a laundry and pool is **Landsborough Lodge,** also on the highway (tel. 076-51-1100); $55 s, $68 d. **Homestead Caravan Park,** Blackall Rd. (tel. 076-51-1308), has shady sites, a barbecue area where damper meals (with bush tucker) are cooked nightly, and friendly hosts who organize tours to anywhere in the region. Sites are $10-12, on-site vans $28, and small cabins $32.

The **Barcaldine Tourist Information Centre** is on Oak St. (tel. 076-51-1724); open daily a.m.-5 p.m.

LONGREACH

Home to the Australian Stockman's Hall of Fame, Longreach (pop. 4,000) is the largest town in the central west. From Brisbane, it lies 1,232 km to the northwest—a sealed highway spans the whole distance—or 24 hours away on Queensland Rail's Spirit of the Outback.

Longreach began life as a campground for shearers, receiving a boost when a rail line was completed from Rockhampton in 1892. **Qantas** (Queensland and Northern Territory Aerial Services) was born in Longreach. The airline's first flight was made in 1922, and for several years it was headquartered in Longreach.

Australian Stockman's Hall of Fame And Outback Heritage Centre

No one could begrudge the stockmen and others who developed the outback a tribute to their pioneering spirit and never-say-die attitude. And this is it, a magnificent museum dedicated to everything the outback stands for. It opened in 1988, amid much fanfare; even the Queen of England made it to town for the occasion. The architects have combined traditional outback materials with modern design concepts to create a distinct building. The complex comprises a series of corrugated iron half-pipes, overlapping to form one long roof.

Exhibits include those dedicated to shearers, miners, traveling salesmen, women of the outback, and Aboriginals. One display provoked much comment—an 1860s settler's hut. The hut is the size of an average bedroom, but served as a home for one woman and three children, with a stove crammed in one corner and beds taking up most of the rest of the dirt floor. Historical displays are only a part of the Hall of Fame; computers and audiovisual programs help bring the history of the outback to life. The complex also has a gift shop and café. Open daily 9 a.m.-5 p.m. Admission is a worthwhile $15 adult, $7 child, family $35. For further information call (076) 58-2166. Allow at least half a day here.

Other Sights

You'll find the original Qantas hangar at the airport. Plans to build a museum dedicated to the history of the airline are well underway, with the **Qantas Founders Museum Preview Centre** in the Tourist Information Centre offering a taste of what's to come; open daily 9 a.m.-5 p.m.

The **Powerhouse Museum** is on the site of an old power station and remains as it was built in 1921 with many working exhibits. Power was produced by enormous generators, whose engines were cooled by artesian-bore water; open April-Oct. daily 2-5 p.m.

On the Landsborough Highway, east of town, is **Longreach School of Distance Education.** Pupils throughout central Queensland attend lessons broadcast over UHF radios, sending homework by mail and getting together a few times a year. Tours are offered weekdays at 9 a.m., 9:45 a.m., and 10:30 a.m.

Entertainment and Events

Most afternoons, the pioneering spirit of the outback comes alive at **Banjo's Outback Theatre and Pioneer Shearing Shed,** at the end of Kork Rd. (tel. 076-58-2360). Demonstrations of wool shearing, pressing, classing, and spinning take place, with everyone invited to try their hand. A whole lot of bush poetry is read, yarns spun, and light snacks served at the end of it all; $10 pp. Performances are Mon.-Thurs. and Saturday at 2:30 p.m.

The **Outback Muster and Drovers Reunion** brings together stockmen from throughout the outback, and while the old-timers spend the weekend drinking, spinning yarns, bronco-branding, and rough-riding, unique outback sports keep the city slickers occupied. All the action takes place the last week of April. On the third weekend of July **The Diamond Shears,** Australia's most prestigious shearing event, takes place.

Accommodations and Food

Welcome Home Hotel, 128 Eagle St. (tel. 076-58-1361), has air-conditioned rooms with shared bathrooms for $20 s, $35 d. Another inexpensive option is **Swaggies,** 81 Wompoo Rd. (tel. 076-58-3777), a backpacker place with communal kitchen, laundry, and lounge. Beds are $12 pp. **Jumbuck Motel,** Landsbor-

ough Hwy. (tel. 076-58-1799), has a pool, air-conditioned rooms, and a good restaurant; $45 s, $55 d. The best place in town is **Albert Park Motel,** Landsborough Hwy. (tel. 076-58-2411), with a covered pool, sundeck area, and large modern rooms; $56 s, $66 d. The above motels are within 500 meters of both the airport and Hall of Fame. **Gunnadoo Caravan Park,** 12 Thrush Rd. (tel. 076-58-1781), has a pool, barbecue area, and laundry. Sites are $10-12, cabins $45 d.

Along Eagle St. is **Merino Bakery** and a number of cafes open breakfast through dinner. Try the **Star Coffee Shop,** where hearty breakfasts are $6-9. For lunch, all the hotels serve counter meals for under $7. The **R.S.L. Club,** on Duck St., is another option for an inexpensive meal. **Squatters,** Landsborough Hwy. (tel. 076-58-3215), is an Aussie-style restaurant with main dishes ranging $11-16. The Jumbuck Motel also has a restaurant.

Transportation and Tours

Flightwest (tel. 13-2392) serves 36 western Queensland towns, with Longreach the central-western hub. Flights depart Brisbane ($199 one-way) and Townsville daily for Longreach.

A favorite and traditional way to reach Longreach is aboard **Spirit of the Outback,** a twice-weekly rail service between Brisbane and Longreach via Rockhampton. The train departs Brisbane Tuesday and Friday at 7 p.m., with the less-interesting scenery traversed at night and the climb through the Drummond Ranges west of Rockhampton taking place during daylight hours. The train features a themed dining car and bar, and seating to suit all budgets. (It is part of Australian folklore that in 1859, when Queensland was granted statehood, it could only afford a three-foot six-inch gauge rail line, the narrowest in Australia—and you'll come to realize its downside when eating and drinking.) The one-way economy-class fare is $118, economy sleeper $148, and first-class sleeper $226. For bookings call **Queensland Rail** (toll-free 13-2232).

Greyhound Pioneer and **McCafferty's** serve Brisbane daily (16 hours one-way, $77) and Mt. Isa (eight and a half hours, $53) with McCafferty's also running to Rockhampton thrice weekly (nine hours, $51). There's a 50% discount for booking 15 days in advance. All buses stop at Outback Travel Centre, 115 Eagle St. (tel. 076-58-1776).

The major car rental companies with offices in Longreach are **Avis** (tel. 076-58-1799) and **Hertz** (tel. 076-58-1155). For a taxi call **Carolyn's Cabs** at (076) 58-1083.

Outback Aussie Tours (tel. 076-58-3000 or 1800-81-0510) offers a great variety of day and overnight tours. The Outback Longreach Link tour takes in everything there is to do and see in town, including the Stockman's Hall of Fame, a visit to an outlying station, and an evening cruise on the Thompson River. All meals included; $99 pp.

Services and Information

The **post office** is at 100 Eagle Street. For the hospital call (076) 58-1133.

The **Tourist Information Centre** is housed in a replica of the first Qantas booking office in Qantas Park (tel. 076-58-3555); it's open daily 9 a.m.-5 p.m.

LONGREACH TO MOUNT ISA

Winton

Winton may not have a Stockman's Hall of Fame to draw the tourists, but its close ties to the legendary Australian bush poet Banjo Patterson provide the basis for a thriving tourist industry. The town began its life as Pelican Waterhole, with one main street lined with pubs and the usual array of outback businesses. In 1895 Patterson wrote *Waltzing Matilda* after hearing stationhands' recollections of a swagman's suicide in a local billabong. The station owner's wife, Christina MacPherson, sang the words in the North Gregory Hotel on 6 April 1895. Its appeal was immediate, and it soon became Australia's favorite song, recited with pride around the country. The original North Gregory Hotel is long gone. Its replacement, a jewel of 1950s architecture, sits on the main street, and a statue of a not-so-jolly-looking Jolly Swagman stands opposite the pool. The terribly named **Qantilda Museum,** in Pioneer Place, exhibits early Qantas and Waltzing Matilda memorabilia. For those interested, Combo Waterhole, where the swagman took his fatal plunge, is 170 km northwest of Winton, then

five km out of Kynuna. **Matilda Expo,** beside the Kynuna Hotel, catalogs the history of the song, and Richard Magoffin, the bloke who runs the place, will sing the tune for anyone who so desires; open daily 9 a.m.-4 p.m.

North Gregory Hotel, 67 Elderslie St. (tel. 076-57-1375), has rooms for $20 s, $40 d, or stay in **Matilda Motel,** 20 Oondooroo St. (tel. 076-57-1433), which has small but comfortable rooms for $42 s, $47 d. Campers should head to **Matilda Country Caravan Park,** on Chirnside St. (tel. 076-57-1607).

Lark Quarry

While Winton and Longreach provide tourists with a glimpse of the past 100 years, a dry rock area 115 km southwest of Winton provides a look much further back in our history. It's Lark Quarry, site of a dinosaur stampede some 95 million years ago. Today's rocky outcrops and spinifex-studded gullies are much different than they were then, when the landscape was flat and high rainfall ensured lush vegetation. A carnosaur (flesh-eating lizard) walking along a riverbed disrupted a herd of about 200 much smaller animals drinking from a lake and, panic stricken, they stampeded across an area of thick mud. Paleontologists are able to re-create the events of that day incredibly accurately, right down to the fact that the stampeding dinosaurs were moving at 15-30 kilometers per hour. Three areas have been excavated; the largest, covered from the elements, is about 20 meters long, with interpretive boards along its length revealing further details. The site is accessible by two wheel drive, except after rain. **Diamantina Outback Tours** (tel. 076-57-1514) departs Winton daily at 8 a.m. for the quarry and other natural features en route; $75 pp includes lunch.

Diamantina National Park

The road from Winton out to Lark Quarry continues in a southerly direction for 270 km to Windorah, on the Diamantina Developmental Road. Thirty km beyond Lark Quarry, a rough track leads west to Diamantina National Park, encompassing 470,000 hectares of Channel Country on either side of the Diamantina River. Except during the Wet, the river is dry, with just billabongs remaining along its bed. The only vegetation is spinifex and stunted eucalypts. The ark has no facilities and if planning a trip seek dvice from the Department of Environment nd Heritage in Longreach (tel. 076-58-1761).

1cKinlay

nyone who has seen the movie *Crocodile Dundee* will want to stop at this small town of 20, alfway between Winton and Cloncurry. The mall pub here was featured as **Walkabout :reek Hotel** in the movie, and although you're nlikely to see anyone wrestling crocodiles, it's pleasant place to stop for a beer and meal. he hotel has rooms for $30 s, $46 d, and a ew campsites out back (tel. 077-46-8424).

:loncurry

arge lodes of copper were discovered in the ills around Cloncurry in the 1860s and by WW the town was Australia's largest copper pro-ucer. As the mineral-rich Isa Highlands to the vest were developed, interest in Cloncurry

waned. Today abandoned mining claims sur-round this town of 2,500. The town's main claim to fame is as the birthplace of the **Royal Flying Doctor Service.** The service was started by John Flynn (featured on the new $20 note) in 1927, when aircraft were still a novelty and wire-less transmissions through the outback were unheard of. Qantas built him an aircraft, and a Melbourne businessman helped fund the wire-less transmission sets. **John Flynn Place** (tel. 077-42-1251) is a modern complex comprising a museum dedicated to Flynn, an art gallery, and theater; open Mon.-Fri. 7 a.m.-4 p.m., Sat.-Sun. 9 a.m.-3 p.m.

On the east side of town is **Mary Kathleen Memorial Park.** It's home to a couple of civic buildings transported from the uranium-mining town of Mary Kathleen, halfway between Clon-curry and Mt. Isa. The uranium mine was worked 1958-63, when atomic-hungry scientists searched the world for a reli-able source of the mineral. After the mine closed, the town stood empty for many years and was then dismantled. The park's museum houses a mineral col-lection and other historic mem-orabilia; open Mon.-Fri. 7 a.m.-4 p.m., Sat.-Sun. 9 a.m.-3 p.m. (tel. 077-42-1361).

Cloncurry also holds the record for the highest temper-ature ever recorded in Aus-tralia. In 1889 the thermome-ter reached 53.1° C (127.6° F).

North from Cloncurry

Cloncurry marks the end of the Landsborough Highway and the beginning of the Burke De-velopmental Rd., linking Clon-curry to the Gulf of Carpentaria (450 km one-way).

Quamby, the first settlement north of Cloncurry, consists of just a hotel, dominated by a large water tank painted as a can of Fosters.

Northwest of Cloncurry is the Selwyn Range, once home to the fierce Kalkadoon tribe, com-

WALTZING MATILDA

Oh! There once was a swagman camped in a billabong,
Under the shade of a coolabah tree;
And he sang as he looked at his old billy boiling,
"Who'll come a-waltzing matilda with me?
Who'll come a-waltzing matilda, my darling,
Who'll come a-waltzing matilda with me?
Waltzing matilda and leading a water bag—
Who'll come a-waltzing matilda with me?"

Down came a jumbuck to drink at the waterhole,
Up jumped the swagman and grabbed him in glee;
And he sang as he stowed him away in his tucker-bag,
"You'll come a-waltzing matilda with me."

Down came the squatter a-riding his thoroughbred;
Down came policemen—one, two, three.
"Whose is the jumbuck you've got in the tucker-bag?
You'll come a-waltzing matilda with me."

But the swagman, he up and he jumped in the waterhole,
Drowning himself by the coolabah tree;
And his ghost may be heard as it sings in the billabong
"Who'll come a-waltzing matilda with me?"

MOUNT ISA

MILNE BAY RD.

DAVIS RD.

TO CAMOOWEAL
NATIONAL PARK,
LAWN HILL
NATIONAL PARK,
AND TENNANT CREEK

66

ABEL

SMITH PARADE

Riverside Caravan Park

LEICHHARDT RIVER

URQUHART ST.

BARKLY HWY.

WEST ST.

MILES ST.

CAMOOWEAL ST.

ALMA ST.

SIMPSON ST.

SCHOOL OF THE AIR

BARKLY HWY.

BARKLY HOTEL MOTEL

MARIAN ST.

78

CAMPBELL'S TRAVEL

LAUNDROMAT

GRACE ST.

FRANK ASTON
UNDERGROUND MUSEUM

LOOKOUT

TO CLONCURRY
AND TOWNSVILLE

RAILWAY STATION
ROYAL FLYING DOCTOR SERVICE

MT. ISA HOTEL

BURKE & WILLS
ISA RESORT

MARIAN ST.

CORBOULD ST.

MT. ISA TOURIST INFORMATION
AND RIVERSLEIGH FOSSILS
INTERPRETIVE CENTRE

MOUNT ISA
MINES

ISA ST.

CRUSADE
BOOKSHOP

CHURCH ST.

POST OFFICE

TRAVELLERS HAVEN

JOHN MIDDLIN MINING DISPLAY
AND VISITORS CENTRE

CAMOOWEAL ST.

HOSPITAL

PAMELA ST.

SPENCE ST.

EAST ST.

DIAMANTINA DEVELOPMENTAL RD.

4TH AVE.

WALTONS MOTOR
COURT MOTEL

5TH AVE.

TENT HOUSE

4TH AVE.

BUCKLEY AVE.

LEICHHARDT RIVER

19TH AVE.

83

IRISH CLUB

83

23RD AVE.

DIAMANTINA DEVELOPMENTAL RD.
TO BOULIA AND BIRDSVILLE

0   500 m

atants in the bloodiest battle ever fought on Australian soil. During the 1880s, as Europeans settled on traditional hunting grounds, there were many clashes between the two groups. In 1884, a police cavalry charge saw most of the tribe's male population massacred on Battle Mountain. The hotel in Kajabbi (pop. 20), 26 km northwest of the Burke Developmental Rd., is named for the tribe. On Saturday night the pub-ican puts on a barbecue, inevitably followed by a sing-along. The hotel also has rooms, or you can camp (tel. 077-42-5979).

MOUNT ISA AND VICINITY

Best known as The Isa, this outback city of 24,000 is one of the country's great mining towns. Although artesian-bore water allows many gardens to thrive, the city is basically un-appealing, its skyline dominated by the mine and a 270-meter lead-smelter stack. Mount Isa does have one claim to fame: it's the world's largest city in area, at 40,978 square km—and it's in the Guinness Book of Records to prove it. The city exists only because of the mine, but also plays a vital role in reducing the isolation of the outback. It is the world's largest single-mine producer of lead and silver (150,000 tons of lead and 30 tons of silver are extracted annual-ly) and the world's largest underground mine. It is also Australia's largest copper producer, yield-ing 155,000 tons annually. More than 200,000 tons of zinc are also produced here each year.

Mount Isa dates from 1923, when John Campbell Miles, an old-time prospector, found an ore outcrop in an area known as the Isa Highlands, the eastern end of a mineral-rich belt that rises 400 meters above the surrounding landscape. The area may be desolate and un-inviting, but it holds untold wealth. Many mil-lions of years ago, as great forces pushed the land upward, molten intrusions impregnated the sedimentary rock, cooling to form the rich seams of minerals upon which the city grew.

Those who invested in the copper mines around Cloncurry had always banked on a port being established on the Gulf of Carpentaria. But one never eventuated, and by the 1920s, when a rail line was built from Townsville, in-erest in copper had waned. Up until this time,

only small mines were operating farther west. But in 1924 Mount Isa Mines moved into the area, investing enormous sums of money to make mineral extraction viable.

Sights

Mount Isa Mines is across the Leichhardt River from downtown. Touring the mining operation is Mount Isa's main attraction. The three-hour **Underground Mine Tour** requires reservations well in advance. Before heading into the 500 km of tunnels, you are fitted with a hard hat, miner's light, overalls, and boots. These tours depart weekdays 8 a.m. and 11:45 a.m.; $20. Book well ahead by calling (077) 44-2104. The two-hour **Surface Tour** departs daily April-Sept.; $12. **Campbell's Travel** (tel. 077-43-2006) takes bookings for this tour.

John Middlin Mining Display and Visitors Centre, on Church St., has an underground mine mock-up, mineral displays, and large pieces of mining equipment. Also displaying mining exhibits is **Frank Aston Underground Museum** on Shackleton Street. As well as min-ing equipment, there's a replica of a native Kilka-doon camp. It's open March-Nov. 10 a.m.-3 p.m.; $4 admission.

Mt. Isa Tourist Information and Riversleigh Fossils Interpretive Centre, on Marian St. (tel. 077-44-4255), contains displays from River-sleigh, 300 km north of the city. Riversleigh, where limestone beds contain a variety of skele-tons, is one of Australia's most important fossil sites; it's open daily 9 a.m.-5 p.m. Dating from the 1930s, **Tent House,** on 4th Ave., is one of the few remaining examples of early mine-com-pany housing; open April-Sept. Mon.-Fri. 9 a.m.-3 p.m. Other sights worth visiting are **School of the Air,** at Kalkadoon High School on Abel Smith Parade (tours schooldays at 10 a.m. and 11 a.m., tel. 077-43-0255) and the **Royal Flying Doctor Service** on the Barkly Hwy. (tel. 077-43-2800); open weekdays 9 a.m.-5 p.m., Sat.-Sun. 10 a.m.-2 p.m.

Accommodations and Food

Barkly Hotel/Motel, 55 Barkly Hwy. (tel. 077-43-2988), has a few air-conditioned rooms for $35 s, $45 d. Also central is **Walton's Motor Court Motel,** 23 Camooweal St. (tel. 077-43-2377), with a laundry and pool; $40 s, $50 d. If you're willing to spend a few extra dollars, stay at **Burke & Wills Isa Resort,** corner Grace and Camooweal Streets (tel. 077-43-8000), a modern, two-story motel with a swimming pool, gym, spa, and restaurant; rooms here are $85 s, $90 d.

Travellers Haven, corner Spence and Pamela Streets (tel. 077-43-0313), has backpacker accommodations with a communal kitchen, pool, and air-conditioning. It's also only 500 meters from town. Dorm beds are $11, singles $22, doubles $26.

Riverside Caravan Park, 195 West St. (tel. 077-43-3904), is the best of four campgrounds in town, and has a large pool, kitchen with barbecue and refrigerator, and laundry. Unpowered sites $12, powered sites $16, on-site vans $29.

Many of the hotels and clubs serve excellent no-frills meals. The Barkly Hotel/Motel has counter lunches and dinners for $5-8, while **Mt. Isa Hotel,** 19 Miles St., is open for breakfast. More than 60 nationalities converge in Isa, with many clubs reflecting this diversity. The **Irish Club,** Buckley and 19th Streets (tel. 077-43-2577), is one such place, serving buffet lunches and dinners under $12.

Transportation, Services, and Information
Ansett Australia (tel. 13-1300 toll-free), **Flightwest** (tel. 13-2392 toll-free), and **Qantas** (tel. 13-1313 toll-free) fly into Mt. Isa from Brisbane, with Ansett Australia continuing to Alice Springs and Flightwest to Townsville ($207 one-way) and Normanton ($231 one-way).

Queensland Rail's Inlander operates between Townsville and Mt. Isa, departing twice weekly (Sunday and Wednesday 6 p.m.); one-way $95 economy, $125 economy sleeper, and $192 first-class sleeper. For bookings call 13-2232 toll-free.

Greyhound Pioneer and **McCafferty's** have a daily coach service between Townsville and

Mt. Isa ($81 one-way), continuing to Tennant Creek ($68 one-way). Both companies operate a service from Brisbane via Longreach ($12[?] one-way), taking 24 hours.

The major car rental companies in town are **Avis** (tel. 077-43-3733), **Hertz** (tel. 077-43-4142), and **Thrifty** (tel. 077-43-2911).

The **post office** is on the corner of Isa and Camooweal Streets. **City Laundromat** is at 1[?] Miles Street. **Mt. Isa Base Hospital** is at 3[?] Camooweal St. (tel. 077-44-4444).

Crusade Bookshop, 11 Simpson St. (tel. 077-43-3880), carries a good selection of outback literature and a range of topographic maps. The **Tourist Information Centre** is in a large complex on Marian St., between Corbould and Mullan Streets (tel. 077-43-7966). Open Mon.-Fri. 9 a.m.-5 p.m., Sat.-Sun. 10 a.m.-2 p.m.

WEST FROM MOUNT ISA

From Mt. Isa, it's 200 km west to the Queensland/Northern Territory border, then 460 km farther to Tennant Creek, on the Stuart Highway. The only town to speak of is **Camooweal,** just east of the border.

Camooweal Caves National Park
This 13,800-hectare park, north of Camooweal, protects sinkholes formed about 500 million years ago. Further water erosion has created an extensive cave system, with several caves over 200 meters long. With a torch and sturdy footwear anyone can explore the system. Aboveground are plains of Mitchell grass interspersed with stands of dry eucalypt extending to the horizon. At a small billabong which attracts lots of birdlife, is a camping area with toilets. Check road access after rain (tel. 077-43-2055).

SOUTH AUSTRALIA
INTRODUCTION

License plates proclaim it "The Festival State." Border-crossing signs herald it "The Grand Prix State" and, underneath, warn that speeding laws are strictly enforced (those signs, however, don't announce that the Grand Prix's moving to Melbourne in 1996). Fact decrees it the driest state in Australia. And the Tourism Commission banners it—most accurately—"The State of Surprise." The surprises are many, for, dry as most of its 984,200 square kilometers may be, South Australia is definitely not dull.

Flanked by Victoria and New South Wales on the east, by Western Australia on the west, and neatly tucked beneath the Northern Territory, this land has almost as many ripe attractions to pick from as it does grapes growing on its famous vines. Most people have heard about the Barossa and Clare Valleys, famous for fine wines and the warm feelings that go with them; and about Adelaide, the "pretty" capital city, where nearly two-thirds of the state's 1.4 million inhabitants live from one festival to the

next—and, without a doubt, the mere mention of the huge outback part of the state sends shivers down the spines of those who dream of scorching in their boots. Coober Pedy, the opal-mining town so hot that homes and shops are built underground, has also received its share of publicity (though it's often depicted as the end of the earth).

Not so popularized by films, jewels, or wine labels are South Australia's lesser-known gems: Hahndorf, a German settlement where you can pick up streusel on the corner instead of meat pie; Burra, an exquisitely preserved copper center with miners' dugouts, Cornish cottages, and the "monster mine"; Kangaroo Island, abundant in 'roos and other wild-and-woollies, with picnic areas that keep the humans fenced in so the animals can watch *them* eat and perform; the Flinders Ranges, spectacular multicolored rock formations, about 1.6 billion years old, with deep gorges and endlessly changing vistas; the Blue Lake, which is actually gray but turns bright blue at the exact same time each year; Lake Eyre, a (usually) dry salt pan that is Australia's largest lake; and the mighty Murray, the country's most important river, which stretches more than 2,000 kilometers from the Snowy Mountains to Lake Alexandrina.

These, of course, are just a few tidbits to whet your appetite. You will also discover heritage towns with exquisitely crafted sandstone buildings, little sleepy fishing villages, bustling beach resorts, reputed UFO landing sights, and outback tracks to test the heartiest, nerviest, and possibly craziest souls. Naturally, there are some dry spots, but think of them merely as crackers to clear your palate between sips (or gulps) of the sweetest wine.

Most places are easily accessible by a variety of transport. Hop a vintage tram to the beach or catch the Ghan and train it up to the Red Centre. To get around cities, between towns, or across the Nullarbor Plain, hire an air-conditioned luxury car, a 4WD jeep, or use your thumb and feet. Float along the Murray in your own houseboat or sign up for a paddlesteamer cruise. (Incidentally, some of the gurgly ferries-'cross-the-Murray will pang the nostalgic hearts of early 70s travelers who once clutched tattered copies of *Siddhartha* against their searching breasts.)

There is one forthcoming development, however, that may very well turn the State of Surprise into a State of Shock—the Multi-functional Polis, proposed for Adelaide's northwestern suburbs.

The MFP, as it is called, is billed a "city of the future." The 3,500-hectare site will accommodate some very high-tech industries, housing for a hundred thousand people, as well as health, education, and recreation facilities, and it will be financed by Japanese yen. The controversies are many, and politicos, environmentalists, and average citizens continue to form committees. Some of the pros: The MFP will give Australia prestigious international standing while providing a much-needed boost to the ailing economy. Opponents insist that the project will be an environmental nightmare, citing possible seepage of toxic chemicals, higher risk of earthquakes, and death of the all-important mangroves as just a few ramifications of filling in the land. *And* there is fear and consternation that the Japanese may well be using their yen only to satisfy their own cravings.

The project, originally slated for Queensland's Gold Coast area but nixed by that state due to problems with private land acquisitions, was shunted down to Adelaide, the alternate choice (don't ever say second choice—they're touchy about it!).

Amid all the hoopla comes this unique view expressed by South Australia's UFO expert, Colin Norris: "We must stop knocking the Multi-functional Polis because visitors from other galaxies are waiting for it. This is the sort of place that will attract other beings. It's the sort of place they've been waiting for to come to."

So, on that enticing note—welcome, aliens, to South Australia!

CLIMATE

There is good reason why more than 99% of the state's population lives south of the 32nd parallel—it is the only part that isn't hot, harsh, and desolate.

Adelaide is frequently described as having a "Mediterranean-like" climate. The short, mild winters (June-Aug.) average 17° C (63° F). Even with occasional downpours and some very chilly nights, most days are bathed in plenty of sunshine. Summers (Dec.-Feb.) are very dry and range from a warm 29° C (84° F) to a downright hot 38° C (100° F). Autumn (March-May) and especially the spring months (Sept.-Nov.) are delightful times to visit the wine country or plan a bushwalk.

Adelaide's surrounding hills and vineyards are fertile and well irrigated. The southeast corner of the state and Kangaroo Island are cooler and greener yet. And, though snow is a rarity in South Australia, an occasional spatter of white has been sighted atop the Mt. Lofty Ranges.

The outback, which makes up most of the state's northern region, blisters in summer. Searing temperatures of 51° C (124° F) have been recorded in the Oodnadatta area—and that was in the *shade*. The yearly rainfall is less than 25 cm, but an occasional fierce storm can prompt sudden, violent downpours.

In 1989, the Nullarbor Plain actually flooded, even halting the fabled Indian-Pacific train in its tracks! I made the crossing several months after the rains and saw so many pools of water and bits of scrub popping up out of the normally cracked, parched, and stark earth that I feared I was hallucinating multiple oases. Lake Eyre, normally a huge salt pan, has also been getting its fill. For world weather-watchers, these unusual occurrences probably seem all too usual.

HISTORY

There was life before Light—Colonel William Light, that is, the British surveyor general who laid out the site for the capital city.

Thousands of years prior to Britain's colonization of South Australia, small tribes of Aboriginal hunters and gatherers lived a nomadic lifestyle in the environs of what is now Adelaide. Part of the coastline was charted as early as 1627 by Dutch explorer Peter Nuyts, but it was British navigator Matthew Flinders who in 1802 actually became the first white man to fully explore the coast. (Amazingly, American sealers, who established a base on nearby Kangaroo

Island only one year later, stayed right where they were and minded their own business.)

Meanwhile, Charles Sturt, a hotshot who'd been exploring the country's interior, began making his way south along the Murray River, being spit out of its mouth at Lake Alexandrina in 1830. The London tabloids reported the exciting news of his discovery—a rich, fertile riverland. This inspired a fellow named Edward Gibbon Wakefield to come up with a great idea for reducing Britain's unemployment crisis: colonize this bountiful new land and raise much-needed money by selling off parcels. In other words—move in, run out the natives, and start subdividing. Sound familiar? Best yet, they would not need any of those nasty convicts because the settlers, having the "pride of ownership" carrot dangling over their noses, would be motivated to do their own hard labor. To this day, South Australians are pretty haughty about the fact that theirs is the only state in the country that was not begun as a convict colony.

In 1836 the British established their settlement, naming Capt. John Hindmarsh as its first governor. Colonel William Light, responsible for laying out the capital city, called it Adelaide, in honor of King William IV's wife.

The new settlers were supposed to be religious, morally upright, and hardworking. However, as soon as they arrived in "their" new land, the Aboriginal population quickly dwindled. Many were killed by the white men, others died from the diseases the settlers brought, and the remainder were forced out to the hostile territory up north. There were the inevitable squabbles, bickering, red tape, and claims of incompetent government. There was a shortage of labor; bankruptcy loomed. Then in 1842 rich copper deposits were discovered, and South Australia quickly bounced back. Besides the mining boom, crops flourished. Soon Adelaide became an agricultural mecca for wheat, fruits, and wool. Shortly after European refugees settled in the Barossa Valley, bringing with them their considerable talent for winemaking. Though the state's economy is still based mainly on its agricultural products—wine, citrus fruit, merino wool, wheat, barley, and fishing—other important industries include shipbuilding and automobile manufacturing.

A Crown colony in 1842, with its own legislative assembly elected by ballot in 1856, South Australia was made a state of the Commonwealth of Australia in 1901.

The state's staid image has greatly diminished since the advent of the Adelaide Festival of the Arts in 1960, not to mention some rather liberal legislation in the areas of homosexuality, marijuana usage, and Aboriginal land rights.

ADELAIDE

Colonel William Light has practically been beatified for his foresight in planning South Australia's capital city (pop. 1.1 million). The man loved straight lines and broad boulevards. He wanted Adelaide to reflect both simplicity and elegance, and he had a magnificent site on which to realize his vision: a flat plain, centrally located on the southern coastline, with the glorious backdrop of rolling hills and dales and the Mt. Lofty Ranges.

Light designed a one-square-mile central business district composed of grid-patterned streets bisecting at right angles and five perfect city squares interspersed at regular intervals. One of these, Victoria Square, is the designated heart of the city (you'll find the general post office across the street and the central bus station about a block away). Gouger Street, on one perimeter, has not only the bounty-filled Central Market but a bevy of international cuisines and a mini-Chinatown.

*A*pproaching Adelaide from Melbourne, we left the train and were driven in an open carriage over the hills and along their slopes to the city. It was an excursion of an hour or two and the charm of it could not be overstated.

The road wound through gaps and gorges and offered all variety of scenery and prospect—color, color everywhere and the air fine and fresh, the skies blue and not a shred of cloud to mar the downpour of the brilliant sunshine.

And finally the mountain gateway opened, and the immense plain spread out below, stretching away into the dim distance on every hand, soft and delicate and dainty and beautiful.

On its near edge reposed the city; with wide streets compactly built; with fine houses everywhere, embowered in foliage and flowers and with imposing masses of public buildings nobly grouped and architecturally beautiful.

—MARK TWAIN

Running north and south, skirting around Victoria Square, is King William Street, the center for business and commerce and supposedly the widest city street in any Australian capital. (Light named the main thoroughfare after his king, but it was his Queen Adelaide who took the whole city and, eventually, a wine label as well.)

Heading north up King William Street, you'll come to the intersection of Hindley Street on the west and Rundle Mall on the east—same street, but it changes names. Hindley Street is lined with restaurants, discos, and nightclubs, a couple of strip joints, and an adult bookshop or two. This is Adelaide's "racy" quarter, if the occasional street brawl, broken beer bottle, or risqué book jacket justifies the term.

Rundle Mall is the no-cars-allowed main shopping promenade that sports arcades with specialty shops, art galleries, department stores, outdoor cafes, occasional street vendors and buskers, and the much-debated stainless-steel sculpture of an enormous pair of balls. One block farther up King William St., on your right, is the **South Australian Tourism Commission Travel Centre.**

Rundle Street East, an "add-on" of Rundle Mall, is the student sector, replete with grunge and retro shops, alternative everything, the fabulous new East End Market, and an energetic street scene with many outdoor cafes at which to hide behind a tattered copy of Kerouac or Proust.

The city center is bounded in a neat little parcel by broad tree-lined terraces, aptly named North, South, East, and West Terrace. North Terrace, just another block up from the Travel Centre, is where you'll find most of the city's architectural and cultural attractions—Parliament House, the museums, Festival Arts Centre, University of Adelaide, and such. The terraces, in turn, are bordered by expansive parklands with lovely greenbelts, towering eucalyptus trees, picnic areas, and recreation facilities.

The River Torrens, navigated by rowboats, motor launches, and a variety of other putt-putts, separates the business district from North Adelaide, one of the oldest sections of the city. North Adelaide is yet another of Colonel Light's babies—the Chosen Suburb, an exclusive residential grid built around a perfectly regular town square, surrounded by lots of greenery. Melbourne Street, part of the plot, is famed for its too-chic-to-be-believed boutiques and eateries.

Now, don't start thinking that all these well-organized grids and squares mean this is a metropolis full of unimaginative boxes. The architecture is *brilliant* (at least most of it)—luscious stone churches, ornate and filigreed mansions, superb colonial buildings. As in most big cities, however, the old and beautiful structures do sometimes sit beside new and tasteless office locks. But in Adelaide a movement is well underway to preserve as much of the original architecture as possible, or at least to keep the original facades.

Because of its compactness and methodical layout, Adelaide is easy to explore on foot. And, though it lacks the street action of many major cities, the small-town atmosphere and almost pastoral spaciousness make this state capital unique.

You're likely to hear a string of adjectives rattled off whenever Adelaide is mentioned—"calm," "stately," and, occasionally, "staid." The slightly more than one million residents like to think of themselves as sophisticated and infinitely more cultured than those beer-guzzling, telly-watching, footy-fiend louts who inhabit the rest of the country. In Adelaide they drink fine wines, follow the cricket matches, attend the theater, and put on a world-class Festival of the Arts.

Calm, stately, staid? In 1988, Mick Jagger opened his solo world concert tour in Adelaide. Let someone try to grid and square *that* one.

ON THE TERRACE

North Terrace, wedged between the city hustle-bustle and the gentle River Torrens, is Adelaide's historic and cultural heart. This easy walk begins at the corner of West Terrace and North Terrace and ends at the corner of East Terrace. Conveniently, you start off at the **Newmarket Hotel** and finish up at the **Botanic Hotel,** two of Adelaide's most sumptuous pubs, which date back to the late 19th century.

Lion Arts Centre
Many of the Fringe Festival events are held in this old Lions Club building at the corner of Morphett Street. Performance stages, galleries, arts and crafts workshops, and casual eating areas are the core of this vibrantly renovated factory. It is usually open during the daytime for a wander or coffee and a sandwich, otherwise hours depend on scheduled events. For more information, phone (08) 8231-7760.

Holy Trinity Church
The foundation stone for the state's oldest Anglican church, beside the Morphett St. bridge, was laid by Governor Hindmarsh himself in 1838. The present building is actually about 50 years newer, but the original clock still remains.

Adelaide Casino
You can bet that more people cross the threshold of the swanky casino than of the church across the street! Built atop the classic sandstone railway station (still used by commuters) with its majestic colonnades and balconies, the casino offers two floors of gaming tables—roulette, craps, blackjack, baccarat—plus keno, a money wheel, and two-up, an Aussie invention that has something to do with tossing coins in a ring. For those of you who prefer one-armed bandits, you're already out of luck: you'll find

1. St. Peter's Cathedral
2. Light's Vision
3. Adelaide Festival Centre
4. Convention Centre
5. Adelaide Casino (and Railway Station)
6. Parliament House
7. Migration and Settlement Museum
8. State Library
9. Mortlock Library
10. South Australian Museum
11. Art Gallery of South Australia
12. University of Adelaide
13. Royal Adelaide Hospital
14. New Market Hotel
15. Lion Arts Centre
16. Qantas Airways
17. South Australian Tourism Commission Travel Centre
18. Ayers House
19. Hindley St. Restaurant and Entertainment Area
20. Rundle Mall Shopping Area
21. Edmund Wright House
22. general post office
23. Adelaide Town Hall
24. YMCA
25. central bus station
26. Glenelg Tram Terminal
27. Central Market
28. Hilton International Hotel
29. Adelaide Youth Hostel

no poker or slot machines here. High rollers, however, can try to get a pass into the exclusive International Room. Even if you don't gamble, this is a good spot to people-watch. Also, there are five bars and two restaurants, the **Pullman** and the less formal **Carvery.**

Security is tight—photography is not allowed. In addition, a dress code is enforced: dressy or "smart casual." Guards will scrutinize you from head to toe as you cross the marble hall to the entrance, although I'm not at all sure they know what they're looking for—I sashayed in wearing a man's faded tee, a denim mini, and moth-eaten fishnets.

The casino is part of Adelaide Plaza, which also houses the Adelaide Convention Centre and Festival Centre, as well as the Hyatt Regency Hotel. It is open Mon.-Fri. 10 a.m.-4 a.m., Sat.-Sun. 24 hours, closed Christmas Day and Good Friday (when you can probably lay odds that more people are over at the church). Automatic teller machines are on the premises, and visitors under 18 are *not.* For more information, phone (08) 8212-2811.

State History Centre

Sandwiched between the casino and the new Parliament House, South Australia's original Parliament House is one of the state's oldest and most historic buildings. In 1855 it was home to the first Legislative Council. Painstaking renovations were completed in 1980, and it is now the **Constitutional Museum,** which presents audiovisual displays and exhibits depicting the state's history, from Dreamtime to the present. The museum's **House of Assembly** is reputedly the world's oldest surviving chamber of democracy. A bookshop specializes in South Australian history, and there's a relaxing restaurant in the garden courtyard.

New Parliament House, next door, was a 56-year-long construction project, begun in 1883 and completed in 1939. Built out of gray Kapunda marble with high Corinthian columns in neoclassical style, it is a sharp contrast to its simpler predecessor. The public is invited to watch proceedings when Parliament is sitting, and tours are available at various times. For more information, phone (08) 8237-9100.

The State History Centre is open Mon.-Fri. and public holidays 10 a.m.-5 p.m., Sat.-Sun.

noon-5 p.m., closed Christmas Day and Good Friday. Admission is $4. For more information phone (08) 8207-1077.

The Adelaide Festival Centre

On King William Street, just behind the houses of Parliament and banking the River Torrens the Adelaide Festival Centre, built in 1972, is home to the three-week Adelaide Festival of the Arts, held in March of even-numbered years. Ranked as one of the world's top international multi-arts festivals, it draws diverse and big name talents like Eartha Kitt, Yehudi Menuhin, the Royal Shakespeare Company, Japan's Kabuki Theatre, Twyla Tharp, and Mick Jagger. In addition, the Fringe Festival, which takes place simultaneously, presents innovative theatrical productions, performance events, poetry readings, art exhibitions, and a Writers' Week. Fringe events are held at the Lion Arts Centre and a host of other venues around town. The local newspapers' daily listings will keep you informed of when and where.

The Adelaide Festival Centre comprises a 2,000-seat multipurpose theater and concert hall, a drama theater (home to the State Theatre Company), an additional flexible performance space, an open-air amphitheater, a piano bar and two restaurants. A variety of entertainment is presented year-round, including professional productions of successful musicals like *Cats* and *Evita,* chamber orchestra symphonies, and an informal late-night cabaret.

You can tour the Festival Centre Mon.-Fri. 10 a.m.-5 p.m., Saturday 1-5 p.m. Tours depart hourly and the cost is $3, payable at the inquiry counter in the foyer. For more information, phone (08) 8216-8729.

Government House

Back on North Terrace and east across King William Street is the Regency-style official residence of South Australia's governor. The first governor, John Hindmarsh, lived on the same site in 1836, but not in the same house. Governor Hindmarsh lived in a mud hut. It was George Gawler, the second governor (1838-41), who decided it was time to build a more suitable residence and, in 1839, began construction of the east wing. The midsection was added in 1855, and by 1878 the house as you see it was completed.

On either side of Government House are two war memorials: to the west is a bronze infantryman, commemorating South Australians who died in the Boer War; to the east is the National War Memorial, honoring those who died in WW I; plaques along the wall of Government House pay tribute to the dead of WW II.

Royal South Australian Society of Art
Across Kintore St., the Society, founded in 1856, exhibits at least six major members' works per year, its own permanent collection, and works of various individual artists. The archives and reference library are available for research. Hours are Mon.-Fri. 11 a.m.-5 p.m., Sat.-Sun. 2-5 p.m., closed Christmas, New Year's Day, and Easter weekend. Admission is free. For information, phone (08) 8223-4704.

State Library
This place is just a bit confusing: the State Library, which was originally in the old wing, is now in the Angaston white marble building next door; the Mortlock Library, restored to Victorian grandeur, is actually the original state library. To put it another way: the State Library carries all the regular books and overseas newspapers; the Mortlock has all the special collections—memorabilia relating to South Australia, a Historic Treasures Room with Colonel Light's surveying equipment on display, a family history research library, and a cricketing memorabilia collection. Both libraries are open Mon.-Fri. 9:30 a.m.-6 p.m., Wednesday and Friday until 8 p.m., Sat.-Sun. noon-5 p.m., closed public holidays. For information, phone (08) 8207-7200.

Migration and Settlement Museum
Next to the State Library, on Kintore Ave., is Australia's first multicultural museum. The building itself is Adelaide's restored Destitute Asylum. Exhibits and an audiovisual program give a realistic picture of what life was like for the early settlers. You can even visit the dark cells built back in the 1870s after a riot. The bookshop specializes in South Australian history. **Mrs. Gifford's** is a cafe in the courtyard. The museum is open Mon.-Fri. 10 a.m.-5 p.m., Sat.-Sun. and public holidays 1-5 p.m. Closed Good Friday and Christmas Day. Except for special traveling exhibits, admission is free. Guided tours are available. For information, phone (08) 8207-7570.

Police Barracks and Armory
Tucked in a courtyard, near the Migration and Settlement Museum, the small **South Australian Police Museum** displays 1860s law enforcement memorabilia. Open Sat.-Sun. and public holidays 1-5 p.m., closed Christmas Day and Good Friday. Donations are requested. For information, phone (08) 8218-1228.

South Australian Museum
A distinctive North Terrace landmark, with whale skeletons in the front window, this museum is especially noteworthy for its extensive collections of Aboriginal, New Guinean, and Melanesian native artifacts. The museum shop stocks natural history and anthropology books, as well as related gift items. The museum is open daily 10 a.m.-5 p.m., closed Good Friday and Christmas Day. Except for special exhibitions, admission is free. For information, phone (08) 8207-7500.

Art Gallery of South Australia
Next door to the museum, a comprehensive collection of Australian, European, and Asian art is housed in two wings of the gallery. Highlights include examples of Australian impressionists, colonial works (including furniture, silver, and other decorative arts), 20th-century works by important painters like Arthur Boyd, Sir Sidney Nolan, and Russell Drysdale, recent Aboriginal landscapes, and an interesting collection of Southeast Asian ceramics. Changing exhibitions of contemporary art and Australian and international touring shows are also on display. The bookshop has a good collection of art books, periodicals, cards, some jewelry, and other related items. A pleasant coffee shop in the rear sells small cakes and sandwiches. The gallery is open daily 10 a.m.-5 p.m., closed Good Friday and Christmas Day. Admission is free, but there is often a charge for special exhibitions. Tours leave from the front entrance Mon.-Fri. 11 a.m. and 1 p.m., Sat.-Sun. 11 a.m. and 3 p.m. For information, phone (08) 8207-7000.

Museum of Classical Archaeology
The Mitchell Building, a striking Gothic edifice on the **University of Adelaide** campus, is a fitting

site for this collection of Greek, Egyptian, and Etruscan relics—some more than 5,000 years old. The museum, on the first floor, is open Mon.-Fri. noon-3 p.m., closed for two weeks at Christmas. Admission is free. For information, phone (08) 8303-5226. (There are many fine examples of 19th-century architecture on this 10-hectare campus. Of particular interest is castle-like Bonython Hall.)

Ayers House

Across Frome Rd. and opposite the Royal Adelaide Hospital, this former residence of Sir Henry Ayers, former premier of South Australia, is now headquarters of the **National Trust.** Construction on the elegant bluestone manor was begun in 1846 and took 30 years to complete. Carefully preserved and refurnished, Ayers House is a lovely specimen of gracious Victorian living, with special displays of fine silver, crystal, nursery toys, and an early kitchen. You can inspect the house Tues.-Fri. 10 a.m.-4 p.m., Sat.-Sun. and holidays 2-4 p.m., closed Good Friday and Christmas Day. Admission is $4. For information, phone (08) 8223-1655.

OTHER CITY SIGHTS

King William Street

You'll find several more noteworthy attractions as you stroll along King William Street between North Terrace and Victoria Square.

Edmund Wright House, 59 King Williams St., was built in 1876 for the bishop of South Australia. These days the ornate Renaissance-style residence is used for government offices and official functions. Take a peek inside during normal business hours. Free lunchtime music performances are held here every Wednesday during autumn and spring.

The **Telecommunications Museum,** in Electra House at 131 King William St., features working displays and original equipment that trace South Australia's technology from past to present. Open Sun.-Fri. 10:30 a.m.-3:30 p.m., closed Saturday. Admission is free. For information, phone (08) 8225-6601.

Approaching Victoria Square, on the opposite side of the street is **Adelaide Town Hall.** Built in 1863, the freestone facade is carved with the faces of Queen Victoria and Prince Albert. You can take a free one-hour guided tour on Tuesday and Wednesday 2:30 p.m., Thursday at 10:30 a.m. and 2:30 p.m. A two-week advance booking is requested. For information phone (08) 8203-7777.

The post office, across the street, is another fine example of stately colonial architecture. For postal history buffs, the **Postal Museum** next door (on the Franklin St. side) has a reconstructed turn-of-the-century post office, as well as archival philatelic displays. Open Mon.-Fri. 11 a.m.-2 p.m. Admission is free. For information phone (08) 8216-2225.

More Museums and Manors

You can view historic transport vehicles as well as ride on restored trams at the **Australian Electrical Transport Museum** in St. Kilda (about 30 km northwest of the city center). Open Sunday and Wednesday during school holidays, closed Good Friday and Christmas Day. Admission is $4. For information, phone (08) 8261-9110.

Carrick Hill, 46 Carrick Hill Dr., Springfield (a 10-minute drive from the city), was built in 1939 in the fashion of a late Elizabethan-era English manor house. Set on nearly 39 hectares of English gardens and surrounded by native Australian bush, the estate features a superb collection of Australian, English, and French paintings, as well as silver, pewter, and English oak furniture. The grounds also include a sculpture park and picnic area. Devonshire tea is served in the tearooms. The home and grounds are open Wed.-Sun. and public holidays 10 a.m.-5 p.m. closed the month of July. Admission is $6. For information, phone (08) 8379-3886.

Botanic Gardens

The Botanic Gardens sit on 16 hectares near the junction of North and East Terraces. Besides the usual and unusual Australian and exotic species, the Adelaide gardens house Australia's only **Museum of Economic Botany** and the **Tropical Conservatory,** the largest conservatory in the Southern Hemisphere. The museum, housed inside a Grecian-style heritage building, exhibits an array of plants used for commercial, medicinal, and artistic purposes. The conservatory, built with the help of NASA tech-

ADELAIDE AND ENVIRONS

TO PORT WAKEFIELD

OUTER HARBOR

BARKER INLET

PORT RIVER

LADY GOWRIE DR.

VICTORIA RD.

PORT WAKEFIELD RD.

MAIN NORTH RD.

TO BAROSSA VALLEY

LARGS BAY

SEMAPHORE

GLANVILLE

PORT ADELAIDE

BOWER RD.

GRAND JUNCTION RD.

HAMPSTEAD RD.

NORTH EAST RD.

RIVER TORRENS

SOUTH RD.

RAIL LINE TO PORT ADELAIDE

MAIN NORTH RD.

TO ADELAIDE HILLS (BIRDWOOD)

GRANGE

GRANGE RD.

PAYNEHAM RD.

PORTRUSH RD.

HENLEY BEACH

MILITARY RD.

NORTH ADELAIDE

THEBARTON

NORWOOD

HENLEY BEACH RD.

MILE END

ADELAIDE

KENSINGTON

WEST BEACH

ADELAIDE AIRPORT

GREENHILL RD.

EASTWOOD

PARKSIDE

FREWVILLE

GLEN OSMOND RD.

UNLEY RD.

FULLARTON

ANZAC HWY.

KING WILLIAM RD.

GOODWOOD RD.

CROSS RD.

GLENELG TRAMWAY LINE

GLENELG

MORPHETTVILLE

SOMERTON

BRIGHTON RD.

DAWS RD.

TO HAHNDORF

OAKLANDS RD.

BRIGHTON

STURT RD.

SEACLIFF

SEACOMBE RD.

GULF ST. VINCENT

HALLETT COVE CONSERVATION PARK

HALLETT COVE

OCEAN BLVD.

SOUTH RD.

TO THE FLEURIEU PENINSULA

0   2 km

MOON

nology, has been designed to address ecological imbalance and the importance of preserving the rainforests. Built of steel and lens-shaped glass, the building—measuring 100 meters long, 45 meters wide, and 27 meters high—encompasses rainforest plants from Australia, Indonesia, Papua New Guinea, and other nearby Pacific islands. Gardeners will not disturb the growth of any plants (which eventually will number 4,000), allowing leaves and bits of bark to fall and heap on the ground. The workings of a tropical rainforest are clearly explained at two information centers within the conservatory.

The Botanic Gardens are open Mon.-Fri. 7 a.m.-5:30 p.m., Sat.-Sun. and public holidays 9 a.m.-5:30 p.m. (open one hour later in summer). Guided tours leave from the kiosk on Tuesday and Friday at 10:30 a.m. Admission is free. The conservatory is open daily 10 a.m.-4 p.m. Admission is $2.50. The garden complex also features a book and gift shop, and a lakeside restaurant. For information, phone (08) 8228-2311.

Adelaide Zoo

On Frome Rd., next to the Botanic Gardens, the Adelaide Zoo is one of Australia's oldest zoos. Set on the banks of the River Torrens, the animals, birds, and reptiles are contained in grassy moat enclosures, walk-through aviaries (with 1,200 birds), and nocturnal and reptile houses. The zoo is acclaimed for its exhibitions of infrequently seen native animals, such as the yellow-footed rock wallaby (native of the Flinders Ranges), and for its breeding programs of rare species like the Persian leopard, red panda, Prezewalski's horse, ctontop tamarin, pygmy hippopotamus, and other roll-off-your-tongue types. The zoo is open daily 9:30 a.m.-5 p.m., closed Christmas Day. Admission is $8. For information, phone (08) 8267-3255 (ask what the feeding times are for the big cats, seals, bears, penguins, and pelicans).

Other Parks and Gardens

It would be impossible not to stumble onto the many expansive parks that virtually surround this city. **Elder Park,** which fronts the River Torrens, deserves a special mention within this section because it is the departure point for the *Popeye* motor launch, an alternate and cheap

($2) way of traveling between the Festival Centre and the zoo. You can also take a lunch o dinner cruise. For information, phone (08) 8295 4747.

A short ride away aboard the Glenelg tram i **Veale Gardens,** a portion of the South Park lands with lovely flower beds, meanderin streams, fountains, and a conservatory. Fo lowing the terrace east will bring you to **Hime Gardens,** a traditional Japanese garden hor oring Adelaide's sister city.

Wittunga Botanic Garden, Shepherds H Rd., in Blackwood, 14 km southeast of the cit center, and dating from 1901, offers 15 hectare of flowering South Australian, Australian, an African plants, accessed via meandering path ways. Open daily 9 a.m.-5 p.m. For informa tion, phone (08) 8228-2311. **Gamble Cottag Garden,** 296 Main Rd., also in Blackwood, ir tersperses heritage roses with old-fashione perennials and flowering plants and shrubs. Th rear lawn is a delightful picnic area.

North Adelaide

Outstanding architecture and ritzy shops ar the focal points of this exclusive suburb. Lik everywhere else in the city, it's easy to get to— just continue north up King William St., a nic walk across Adelaide Bridge and the River Tor rens (or you can walk up Frome Rd., from th zoo).

If you're coming up King William St., the firs place you'll notice is **St. Peter's Cathedral,** a the corner of Pennington Terrace. It is one of th few churches in the country with twin spires and though the church building itself was bui between 1868 and 1876, the spires and tow ers were not erected until 1902. And here's a fu fact for your almanac—St. Peter's has the fines and heaviest bells in the Southern Hemisphere

Continue west to Montefiore Rd., where ato Montefiore Hill stands **Light's Vision.** A stat ue marks the spot where Colonel William Ligh purportedly started blueprinting his plans for th city. Here you can see his beatific vision throug your own eyes.

Walking about the North Adelaide "grid," you' view many architectural wonders with their gran and fascinating touches. The pricey bluestone mansions are well kept, and most are quite ornat with eye-catching roof lines, iron lace verandas wers, and filigree. Melbourne and O'Connell streets are the "smart" shopping districts, with equally pricey boutiques, restaurants, and hairressing salons, along with some interesting little ubs peppered in between. Many of the commercial buildings are renovated Victorian workers' ottages.

ort Adelaide

ort Adelaide, about 25 minutes from the city enter (buses leave from North Terrace), is outh Australia's first heritage area. The 19th-entury wharf district, an important hub for oastal steamers until World War II, has been reserved as the **Maritime Museum,** spread ver seven historic sites. Main display galleries re inside the **Bond** (1854) and **Free** (1857) tores; **Weman's Building** (1864) is the old ailmaker's shop; the **Lighthouse** (1869), first rected at the entrance to the Port River, was hifted over to South Neptune Island in 1901, nen, in 1986, re-sited to its present location. he **Customs House, police station,** and **ourthouse** complete the museum buildings. ou'll soak up lots of atmosphere just wandering ne streets. Many of the facades, ranging from nodest houses to ornate banks (particularly nose along Lipson St.), have been restored to ld port-days splendor. At **No. 1 Wharf** you can op aboard the *Nelcebee* (1883), an old coastal etch, or the *Yelta* (1949), the last tug to steam n the port. The museum buildings are open ues.-Sun. and daily during school holidays 10 .m.-5 p.m. Admission is $8. For information, hone (08) 8240-0200.

Port Dock Station Railway Museum, also on ipson St., has one of the country's largest collections of locomotives and carriages, as well s lots of memorabilia, an audiovisual theaterette, nd model railways. Go on the weekend when ou can take a ride on one of two different steam rains. A railway cafeteria car houses tearooms. Open Sun.-Fri. and public holidays 10 a.m.-5 .m., Saturday noon-5 p.m. Admission is $6. or information, phone (08) 8341-1690.

Rather planes than trains? The **Historical Aviation Museum,** 11 Mundy St., exhibits various aircraft as well as engines and aero-memorabilia. Open Sat.-Sun. and public holidays 10 .m.-5 p.m. Admission is $3. For information, hone (08) 8264-2199.

If you visit on Sunday, be sure to visit **Port Adelaide Market** in a huge warehouse on Queens Wharf. Junk, junque, and Asian foodstalls are among the offerings. Open 8 a.m.-5 p.m.

Got your sea legs and find the salt air flaring your nostrils? Check at the dock for available cruises.

Glenelg

This is the most popular of Adelaide's suburban beaches. Though not equal to the famed beauties on the east and west coasts, there's water (sometimes blue), sand (at low tide), shark netting (to keep out South Australia's deadly white pointer), a water slide, amusement park, pie carts, and wienie wagons. What more do you want? History? Then you've come to the right place—Glenelg is where South Australia began, the landing place of Governor Hindmarsh and the first settlers back in 1836. Over at the **Patawalonga Boat Haven,** you can climb aboard a replica of the HMS *Buffalo,* from which Captain Hindmarsh stepped ashore and proclaimed South Australia a colony. (Unlike the original, however, this buffalo is fitted with a restaurant, bar, and small museum.) Open daily 10 a.m.-5 p.m. Admission is $2.50. For information, phone (08) 8294-7000.

The **Old Gum Tree,** on MacFarlane St., marks the exact spot where the Union Jack was raised. You can witness a reenactment each year on Proclamation Day, 28 December.

A large shell display, including circa-1930s shell art and crafts, is on exhibit at **Shell Land,** 17 Mary Street. Open Tues.-Sun. 10:30 a.m.-noon and 1-4:30 p.m. For information, phone (08) 8294-5837.

The **Tourist Information Centre,** on the foreshore (tel. 08-8294-5833), provides walking and cycling maps. Open daily, weather permitting, 9 a.m.-5 p.m.

Adelaide's only tram makes a sentimental journey from Victoria Square directly to Jetty Rd., Glenelg's main street, taking approximately 30 minutes. Cost is $2.20 one-way.

Other Options

Favorite local beaches north of Glenelg are West Beach, Henley Beach, Grange, West Lakes, Glanville, Semaphore, and Largs Bay; south of Glenelg (where the surf is decent) are Somerton, Brighton, and Seacliff. Nude bathing is allowed at Maslin Beach, about 40 km south of the city. Between Seacliff and Maslin is **Hallett Cove Conservation Reserve,** where the landscape has been fabulously molded and colored by a glacial movement some 270 million years ago.

At Grange, you can visit **Sturt's Cottage,** where the famous explorer, Capt. Charles Sturt, lived between 1840 and 1853 (when he was home, that is). The house contains his family memorabilia and is furnished in that period's style. Sturt's Murray River campsite has been re-created on the grounds—in case you need some pointers. The home is open Wed.-Sun. and public holidays 1-5 p.m. Admission is $2.50. For information, phone (08) 8356-8185.

Fort Glanville, in Semaphore, was built in 1878 and restored in the 1980s. You can blast your ears out on the third Sunday of each month, 1-5 p.m., when reenactments of rifle drills and cannon firings (two 64-pounders!) are staged. Admission is $3. For information, phone (08) 8242-1978.

For a gentler pursuit, visit **Bower Cottages,** 200 Bower Rd., where you can watch local craftspeople and their works-in-progress. The cottages were built in 1897 to commemorate Queen Victoria's Diamond Jubilee. Open Wed.-Fri. noon-4 p.m., and tours are available. For information, phone (08) 8449-2959.

ACCOMMODATIONS

As in most large cities, accommodations in Adelaide span the spectrum from cheap and basic to ritzy and plush—except here, quite often, the two ends sit side by side and back to back. It's usually easy to find a room unless you arrive at festival time. Keep in mind that the Adelaide Festival of the Arts (first three weeks of March, in even-numbered years) and the spillover from the Barossa Valley Vintage Festival (Easter week, in odd-numbered years) are peak periods. If you plan to attend any of these events, or to be in the Adelaide area at those times, you'd be well advised to book a room *way* in advance.

City Accommodations
Words of caution: If you or your traveling companions are unaccustomed to city noises, you

may not want to bed down on occasionall rowdy Hindley Street. Prices in Adelaide, a might be expected, run somewhat higher than i rural areas.

Inexpensive (under $35): Centrally locate **West's Private Hotel,** 110B Hindley St. (te 08-8231-7575), is cheap ($20 per room), an more of a guesthouse than a hotel. Linen is in cluded, but not much else. Backpackers ar welcome, but women alone should pass on thi one. The **Metropolitan Hotel,** 46 Grote St. (te 08-8231-5471), near Victoria Square, has basi accommodations with shared facilities. Over a the **Plaza Private Hotel,** 85 Hindley St. (tel. 08 8231-6371), rooms come with washbasins. Th Plaza is an old-timer, once nicely kept but no down the tubes. Some of the costlier room ($50) have private facilities. The **Austral Hote** 205 Rundle St. (tel. 08-8223-4660), has clea and simple pub accommodations with shared fa cilities. **The Clarice,** 220 Hutt St. (tel. 08-8223 3560), is both a hotel and motel, near the Eas Terrace side of town. Rooms with shared facil ties start low. It'll cost you $10-20 more to stay i the newer motel wing, with your own showe and toilet.

Moderate ($35-70): Accommodations at **Cit Central Motel,** 23 Hindley St. (tel. 08-8231 4049), have private facilities and include conti nental breakfast. At the corner of Gawler Plac and Flinders St., the **Earl of Zetland Hotel** (te 08-8223-5500) offers good value in pub ac commodations. Rooms are air-conditioned an have private showers and toilets. The pub down stairs puts out a decent buffet spread at lunc (about $6). **Directors Studio Suites,** 25 Gouger St. (tel. 08-8231-3572), offers room apartment-style digs close to the Central Marke Near the Festival Centre and casino, try th **Festival Lodge Motel,** 140 North Terrace (te 08-8212-7877), **The Strathmore,** 129 Nort Terrace (tel. 08-8212-6911), or the **Grosveno Hotel,** 125 North Terrace (tel. 08-8231-2961) This trio is well located and has all the moder amenities. Deluxe rooms at the Grosvenor (th city's former grand dame hotel) can climb a high as $120.

Expensive ($70 and way up): The Man sions, 21 Pulteney St. (tel. 08-8232-0033), is really good deal especially if you're sharing Spacious studios or one-bedroom apartments i

...is circa-1910 building feature cooking facili-...es as well as a rooftop spa and sauna. If you're ... big spender (or you've just hit it big at the casi-...o), Adelaide's two luxury high-rise hotels are ...e **Hilton International,** 233 Victoria Square ...el. 08-8217-0711), peacefully situated over ...e center city square, and the super-glitzy **Hyatt ...egency** (tel. 08-8231-1234) on North Terrace, ...mack dab in the middle of the fun side. Basic ...oubles at either hotel are around $200 and go ...ay up.

...n the Outskirts

... you've got your heart set on staying in lovely ...orth Adelaide, the moderately priced **Princes ...odge Motel,** 73 Lefevre Terrace (tel. 08-8267-...566), on the outer edge of the suburban grid, is ...ur best bet ($35 including continental break-...ast). If you like to spread out, **Greenways ...partments,** 45 King William Rd. (tel. 08-8267-...903), offers one-, two-, and three-bedroom ...ats with cooking facilities and parking. The ...ore deluxe **Adelaide Meridien,** 21 Melbourne ...t. (tel. 08-8267-3033), sits on North Adelaide's ...restigious shopping street. **Adelaide Heritage ...partments** (tel. 08-8272-1355) can book you ... a lovely heritage apartment or cottage—all ...lly equipped, many with fireplaces or spas. ...ates are expensive if you're alone, a great ...eal if you're with one or more companions.

If you're coming in from the southeast, Glen ...smond Rd., which heads straight into the city, ...s Adelaide's motel row. Some good choices ...nclude **Princes Highway Motel,** 199 Glen Os-...nond Rd., Frewville (tel. 08-8379-9253); **Fullar-...on Motor Lodge,** 284 Glen Osmond Rd., ...ullarton (tel. 08-8379-9797); **Sands Motel,** ...98 Glen Osmond Rd., Fullarton (tel. 08-8379-...079); and **Powell's Court,** 2 Glen Osmond ...d., Parkside (tel. 08-8271-7033). (Don't be ...onfused—the suburbs change names fre-...uently along this thoroughfare.) All of these ...notels are in the moderate range. Powell's ...Court has cooking facilities. Just two km from ...ne city, **Parkway Motor Inn,** 204 Greenhill ...d., Eastwood (tel. 08-8271-0451), is well-lo-...ated, has a pool and restaurant, and costs ...lightly more than the others. **Adelaide Her-...tage Apartments** (tel. 08-8272-1355) has two ...ottages in Eastwood, cheaper than the North ...delaide properties.

Glenelg and the Beaches

Glenelg has oodles of places to stay, most at reasonable prices—particularly during off sea-sons, when many of the holiday flats offer at-tractive weekly rates. The tourist office on the foreshore can provide a list of available flats.

St. Vincent Hotel, 28 Jetty Rd. (tel. 08-8294-4377), a cozy, locally popular establishment, has rates of $30-40 per room, and that includes con-tinental breakfast. **Colley Motel Apartments,** 22 Colley Terrace (tel. 08-8295-7535), and the **South Pacific,** 16 Colley Terrace (tel. 08-8194-1352), both opposite Colley Reserve, are good midrange choices for holiday flats. Priced slightly higher, but still excellent value for two or more traveling to-gether, are the holiday flats at **Coral Seaside Units,** 2 South Esplanade (tel. 08-8295-1592), and **La Mancha,** 8 Esplanade (tel. 08-8295-2345). The big ticket in town is the beachfront **Ramada Grand,** Moseley Square (tel. 08-8376-1222), a high-priced high-rise with highfalutin frills.

In Glenelg South, the **Bay Hotel Motel,** 58 Broadway (tel. 08-8294-4244), not far from the beach, has rooms with color television and pri-vate facilities, as does the **Norfolk Motor Inn,** 71 Broadway (tel. 08-8295-6354). Prices at both are moderate.

West Beach and Henley Beach are also packed with holiday flats. In West Beach, try **Cootura Holiday Flats,** 8 West Beach Rd. (tel. 08-8353-3210), **Marineland Village Holiday Villas,** Military Rd. (tel. 08-8353-2655), or **Tui-leries Holiday Apartments,** 13 Military Rd. (tel. 08-8353-3874). A best bet in Henley Beach is **Meleden Villa,** 268 Seaview Rd. (tel. 08-8235-0577), an atmospheric seafront bed and break-fast. Down the way, **Allenby Court,** 405 Seav-iew Rd. (tel. 08-8235-0445), offers fully equipped, two-bedroom holiday flats. Keep in mind that holiday flats are moderately priced but often require minimum stays of two or more nights. Farther north in Semaphore, the **Sema-phore Hotel,** 17 Semaphore Rd. (tel. 08-8449-4662), is your *very* basic pub with shared facili-ties. A better choice is a few doors away at the moderately priced **Federal Hotel,** 25 Sema-phore Rd. (tel. 08-8449-6866).

Hostels

Adelaide's hostels, like everything else in the city, are centrally located and easy to find. Three of the hostels are in the South Terrace district and can be reached by foot or by bus from Pulteney Street). The 50-bed **Adelaide YHA Hostel,** 290 Gilles St. (tel. 08-8223-6007), has a friendly atmosphere and helpful staff. The office is closed Mon.-Sat. 10 a.m.-1 p.m., Sunday 10 a.m.-5:30 p.m., but hostel guests have 24-hour access. The 40-bed **Backpackers Hostel Adelaide** is nearby at 263 Gilles St. (tel. 08-8223-5680) and has two sections: one closes 11 a.m.-3 p.m.; the other section stays open all day but costs a buck more. Office hours are 8-11 a.m. and 3-10 p.m. Both of these hostels have kitchen facilities and lounges where you can meet up with other travelers.

Another hostel, closer to the center of town, is **Backpackers Inn,** 112 Carrington St. (tel. 08-8223-6635). This former pub is run by the same folks at Backpackers Hostel Adelaide and offers both dorm beds and double rooms ($20). **Adelaide City Backpackers,** nearby at 118 Carrington St. (tel. 08-8232-4774), is shabby and best avoided.

Backpack Australia Hostel, 128 Grote St. (tel. 08-8231-0639), makes up for the small dorms with friendly atmosphere, a bar, and inexpensive meals. **East Park Lodge,** 341 Angas St. (tel. 08-8223-1228), is a private family-run hostel, also near the city center. Dorm beds, double rooms, and some meals are available.

Both men and women are welcome at the **YMCA,** 76 Flinders St. (tel. 08-8223-1611), conveniently near Victoria Square and the central bus station. Dorm beds run $11, singles are $18, doubles are priced at $28. Office hours are Mon.-Fri. 9 a.m.-9 p.m., Sat.-Sun. 9 a.m.-noon and 4-8 p.m.

In Glenelg, **Backpackers Beach Headquarters,** 7 Moseley St. (tel. 08-8376-0007), offers home-style accommodations in a heritage building with kitchen, laundry, and even car rental facilities. Dorm beds and some single and double rooms are available.

Homestays

The **South Australian Tourism Commission Travel Centre,** 1 King William St., Adelaide 5000 (tel. 08-8212-1505), will provide you with a list of homestay properties, which include city homes, historic cottages, health resorts, villas, and farms. Prices range from budget to luxury.

Camping

South Australia has a large number of camping facilities, though some accept only caravans, not tents. Most provide powered and unpowered sites, as well as on-site cabins and vans. The state's caravan parks are generally of a very high standard—clean and comfortable. Many have swimming pools, game rooms, and tennis courts. The South Australian Tourism Commission Travel Centre can provide maps and brochures and assist with bookings. The following is a sampling of some of the more convenient and interesting locales.

Adelaide Caravan Park, Bruton St., Hackney (tel. 08-8363-1566), is the nearest park to city attractions. **Brownhill Creek Caravan Park,** Brownhill Creek Rd., Mitcham (tel. 08-8271-4824), set in 120 acres of bushland, is only seven km from Adelaide. **Belair Caravan Park,** Belair National Park (tel. 08-8278-3540), is just 11 km from the city center.

West Beach Caravan Park, Military Rd, West Beach (tel. 08-8356-7654), sits on a good swimming beach and is surrounded by playing fields and golf courses. And, for those of you who want to be near Fort Glanville's big cannons, there's **Adelaide Beachfront Van and Tourist Park,** 349 Military Rd., Semaphore Park (tel. 08-8449-7726), also on the beach.

FOOD

Adelaide does not have the "foody" scene so prevalent in its sister capital cities, Melbourne and Sydney. Though there are some "nouvelle" gourmet establishments sprinkled about, the emphasis here is on casual, outdoor dining—a terrace restaurant along the river, a picnic in the park, takeaways to eat in one of the city squares. Many of the restaurants are licensed, no doubt to keep those famous South Australian wines flowing. Adventurous eaters will often find dishes made from kangaroo meat on the menu—so if you want to try it in some form other than an ole Jumbo Jack, keep your eyes peeled. In fact, this is the only state where it's a common meal selection. If you prefer to pass on the braised 'roo, you'll find plenty of fresh fish and seafood. Especially commendable are King George whiting and the local crayfish (sometimes called lobster).

Most of the ethnic restaurants are on Gouger Street, also home to the Central Market and Chinatown. Noisier dining can be had on Hindley Street, lodged above, between, or beneath the strip joints and sex shops and their accompanying sounds. Rundle Street East is where the fashionable avant garde dine indoors or out in chichi, trendy, and tony establishments; the fashionable old guard usually hangs out on North Adelaide's Melbourne Street. Outdoor cafes on Rundle Mall can fix you up with a caffeine buzz so you don't drop before you shop. Many Adelaide restaurants are closed on Sunday, so plan accordingly.

Moored at Glenelg, this replica of the HMS Buffalo features a restaurant and museum.

Inexpensive

The **Adelaide University** campus has two informal eating places that are popular with students, faculty, and travel types. Both are in the Union Building. The cafeteria, on the ground floor, serves all the typical "uni" fare—sandwiches, apples, weak coffee, a few miscellaneous hot meals. The **Bistro** offers better quality at higher prices, about $5-9 for main dishes. The cafeteria has the customary casual class-in class-out hours; the Bistro is open Mon.-Fri. noon-2:30 p.m. for lunch, 5:30-8:30 p.m. for dinner.

Students and grungers tend to adore **Exeter Hotel,** 246 Rundle St., for both its good-value prices and wine list. Another hot spot for cheap eats is **Bijou,** 208 Hindley Street. Down the street, at 273 Hindley St., **Marcellina Pizza Bar** serves delicious pizzas all night, every night except Sunday. **Al Frescoes,** 260 Rundle St., is a superb late-night cafe, usually packed with Italians eating the Italian food—always a good sign. **Minim's Café,** 199 Hutt St., near the hostels, is popular both for breakfast and burgers. Fifties-style **Ruby's Café,** 255B Rundle St., with changing art exhibitions and a cocktail bar, is famed for its all-day Sunday breakfasts.

Vegetarian travelers will be happy at **Clearlight Café,** 203 Rundle St., with its clean environment and excellent food. The health food store, adjacent, offers a good selection and has a notice board with useful info. Nearby, **Vego and Lovin' It,** 240 Rundle St., is a super-cheap vegan cafe. **Carrots,** 62 Pulteney St., at Hindmarsh Square, is open weekdays for cheap vegetarian fare.

You can get a plain, simple **counter meal** at pubs throughout the city. Usually there's a blackboard outside the door that states meal times (around noon-2 p.m.) and prices (as low as $3). Menus are often bland and occasionally heavy on the grease. Typical choices are fish and chips, chicken schnitzel, and gravy-covered beef and lamb. Some Adelaide pubs now offer more "nouvelle" and international cuisine (which also boosts the prices). Some best bets include: **Old Queen's Arms,** 88 Wright St.; **Hotel Franklin,** 92 Franklin St.; **Austral Hotel,** 205 Rundle St.; and the **Park Tavern,** corner of Hindmarsh Square, at Grenfell Street.

Pick and choose from some of the city's international food centers, where different eateries are positioned around one central dining area. You can mix and match Indian, Thai, Chinese, Australian, and other cuisines for about $5 (more if you get carried away). Centrally positioned food centers are: **Hawker's Corner,** corner of Wright St. and West Terrace; **City Cross Arcade,** off Grenfell St.; **Gallerie of International Cuisine,** Renaissance Tower Center, Rundle Mall; **The Food Affair,** basement level, Gallerie Shopping Centre (between North Terrace and Gawler Place); and the **International Food Plaza,** on Moonta St. next to the Central Market. Most of the foodstalls stay open during shopping hours.

The **Central Market,** between Grote and Gouger Streets (near Victoria Square), is a great spot to put together a meal or a picnic. The many colorful stalls in this historic old building feature fresh fruit and vegetables, meat, bread, cheese, and a variety of other foods. Or you can get a ready-made cheap (under $6) meal at **Malacca Corner,** a restaurant housed inside the market. Market hours are Tuesday 7 a.m.-5:30 p.m., Thursday 11 a.m.-5:30 p.m., Friday 7 a.m.-9 p.m., and Saturday 7 a.m.-1 p.m.

East End Market, on Rundle Street, redeveloped at the site of the original old market, features a huge central food court with stalls selling a delectable array of Asian and continental cuisine, and seating for 200. Fruit, vegetables, meats, cakes, nuts, breads, and other tasty treats are also on sale.

Don't forget about the cafes at the historic sites on **North Terrace.** You can get snacks and simple meals at the Botanic Gardens, Art Gallery, State History Centre, and the Lion Arts Centre.

Moderate

The **Red Ochre Grill,** 129 Gouger St. (tel. 08-8212-7266), is the buzz of the town with its unlikely, but nonetheless successful, marriage of typical outback bush tucker with anything-but-typical gourmet flair. Diners can eat in the swank restaurant, cafe, or outdoors under the vines. Main courses run $13-18. Open Mon.-Fri. lunch, Mon.-Sat. dinner; the cafe is open daily.

Jasmin Indian Restaurant, 31 Hindmarsh Square (tel. 08-8223-7837), has terrific North Indian dishes for about $14. Specialties include tandoori oven dishes and biryani rice plates. Open Tues.-Fri. lunch, Tues.-Sat. dinner.

North Adelaide's **Oxford,** 101 O'Connell St., has been running strong since the 1980s and, in 1995, was South Australia's most awarded restaurant. The fetching cuisine is created from the best and freshest ingredients. The service is dependable and the wine list is outstanding. Open Tues.-Sat. lunch and dinner.

The popular and casual **Boltz Café,** 286 Rundle St. (tel. 08-8232-5234), offers everything the youngish trendsetters could ask for: pseudo-industrial styling, a menu to please most appetites (pizzas, focaccias, curries, salads—in the $10-12 range), live music, and late hours. Open Mon.-Sat. lunch and dinner.

One of my special finds (which I hesitatingly share) is the **Grecian Taverna,** 89 O'Connell

St., North Adelaide (tel. 08-8267-1446). Th intimate restaurant provides beautifully pre sented, delectable Greek specialties in eno mous portions, *plus* it's open for lunch and di ner every day of the week (yes, including Su day). Average cost for main courses is $10.

Expensive

Splurgers should head directly for **Chloe's,** 3 College Rd., Kent Town (tel. 08-8363-1001 comprising several grandly furnished dinin rooms within a stunning restored villa. Class French food and a superb wine list (choose fro a 20,000-bottle cellar!) are standout feature here. Without wine, you can expect to pay abo $50 pp. Book ahead for Mon.-Fri. lunch, Mon Sat. dinner.

Peasant-Mediterranean-turned-flamboyan South-Oz aptly describes **Mezes,** 247 Rundle S (tel. 08-8223-7384). The menu is limited b only in selections—not in imagination. The su roundings are simple, which only makes it mo of a knockout once you taste the food. Plan o spending about $40 pp. Open Friday lunc Tues.-Sun. dinner.

Nediz Tu, 170 Hutt St. (tel. 08-8223-2618 creates exotic and sublime Vietnamese delica cies, in a purifying white room filled with gloriou floral arrangements—a sacred environment f the almost prayer-inducing cuisine. Dinner approximately $40 pp. Open Tues.-Sat. dinne

Jarmers, 297 Kensington Rd., Kensingto Park (tel. 08-8332-2080), just east of the city, another $50-per-header (again, without wine Jarmers presents creative Australian cuisin (watch for that kangaroo!) in an elegant atmos phere for Mon.-Sat. dinner.

For fabulous—and fabulously expensive– hotel restaurants, try **The Grange Restaura and Brasserie,** at the Hilton International (te 08-8217-0711), or **Blake's,** at the Hyatt Re gency (tel. 08-8231-1234).

Late-Night Eats

It's slim pickings for late-night refrigerator raider If you're desperate you might try the **pie cart** which set up outside the post office on Frankli Street and at The Parade, Norwood, every nigh from 6 p.m. until the wee hours. They sell that i famous Adelaide gastronomic *specialité,* th "floater"—an Australian meat pie floating (sort

e a rock) inside a bowl of thick green pea
up, topped with tomato sauce (catsup).

Maybe you'd prefer some harmless pancakes.
he **Pancake Kitchen,** 13 Gilbert Place (tel.
3-8211-7912), on the South Terrace side of
e city grid, is open every day, 24 hours. Also,
n't forget **Marcellina Pizza Bar** on Hindley
treet·(see "Inexpensive," above). And, if you're
essed "correctly," there's always the casino.

For late-night food you're probably best off
cking some tucker in your backpack, satchel,
r motel fridge to tide you over until morning.

ENTERTAINMENT AND EVENTS

delaide has all the usual amusements of a city
s size—cinemas, art galleries, discos, pubs
nd clubs with live music, theater and concert
erformances, plus a couple of extras—the hus-
-bustle casino and a really special festival of
e arts. Newspapers, particularly Thursday's
dvertiser, provide up-to-date information. An-
her good source is the monthly *Adelaide Re-
ew,* with lots of reviews and announcements of
erary, arts, and theatrical happenings. *Rip It Up*
nd *dB,* free local music and street mags, can be
cked up at pubs, clubs, and record stores.
adio SA-FM operates a **club and concert line**
el. 08-8272-1990) or, for jazz venues, try the
azz Line (tel. 08-8303-3755). You can also
ll in at the South Australian Tourism Com-
ission Travel Centre, on King William St. (08-
212-1505), for current entertainment listings
nd booking assistance. And don't forget about
delaide University where, during school ses-
ons, there's always something on.

inemas

you're looking for commercial cinema (with
leases that are ordinarily three to six months
ehind the U.S.), the four-, six- and eight-plexes
e scattered around Hindmarsh Square, Hind-
y St., and Rundle Mall, and on Jetty Rd. in
lenelg. For artier films, try the **Capri,** 141
oodwood Rd., Goodwood (tel. 08-8272-1177),
e **Chelsea,** 275 Kensington Rd., Kensington
el. 08-8431-5080), **Mercury Cinema,** 13 Mor-
hett St. (tel. 08-8410-1934), **New Trak Cine-
a,** 375 Greenhill Rd., Toorak Gardens (tel.
3-8332-8020), or Adelaide University.

The annual **Adelaide Film Event,** held at
the Chelsea from mid-July to mid-Sept., presents a good series of international films (past
programs have included the reconstructed version of *Lawrence of Arabia,* along with *Do The
Right Thing, Jesus of Montreal,* and *Roger and
Me,* and a Glasnost Film Festival). You can either subscribe in advance for a series of tickets,
or purchase a single admission ($12) on the
night of performance, if seats are still available.

Or curl up in front of the telly and watch some
really terrific classic, contemporary, and cutting-
edge films on SBS. Check the newspaper for
times.

Pubs and Clubs
You can do an easy—albeit tacky—pub crawl
along **Hindley Street,** between King William
Street and West Terrace. You'll find mega-dis-
cos at **Jules,** 94 Hindley St., a "real Aussie Pub"
(and a real Aussie meat market), and across
the street at **Rio's,** 111 Hindley St., which also
has a bistro and piano bar and is open 24 hours.

City pubs that regularly feature music are:
Austral Hotel, 205 Rundle St.; **Earl of Aberdeen,** Hindmarsh Square; **Seven Stars Hotel,**
187 Angas St., and, promising "no renovations,
no bullshit," the **Exeter Hotel,** 246 Rundle
Street. Both the Austral and Exeter Hotels are
popular with students and the artsy crowd.

A few of Adelaide's trendiest upmarket musical pubs (where you may well run into renovations and bullshit) are **Bull and Bear Ale
House,** 91 King William St.; **Office Bar and
Bistro,** 110 Pirie St.; **The Oxford,** 101 O'Connell
St., North Adelaide; and, on Melbourne St., also
in North Adelaide, the **Old Lion Hotel.** Still
trendier are the bars and discos housed inside
the **Hilton International** and **Hyatt Regency**
hotels.

You'll pay a cover charge of $4-8 to hear
music in the city pubs; about $12-16 at the big
hotels.

Too-hip-to-be-believed (mainly) dance clubs
are: **Cargo Club,** 213 Hindley St.; **Heaven,** 7
West Terrace, in New Market Hotel; and **Synagogue,** Synagogue Place, off Rundle Street.

Le Rox, 9 Light Square, is a large (two-room),
late-night, groovy, mixed gay club. Also popular
is the perennial **Mars Bar,** 120 Gouger St., with
weekend drag shows.

Serious **winetasters** should not miss the stylish **Universal Wine Bar,** 285 Rundle St., which offers not only an extensive wine list (including many wines-by-the-glass), but winetastings and workshops. **Mecca,** 290 Rundle St., also draws tasters to its bar and bistro.

Beer lovers can sample house-made brews at **Earl of Aberdeen,** Hindmarsh Square; **Old Lion Hotel,** North Adelaide; and **Port Dock Brewery Hotel,** Port Adelaide.

Theater and Concerts

The **Adelaide Festival Centre** is the city's major venue for theater, stage musicals, opera, concerts, and most other performing arts. For information, phone the box office at (08) 8216-8729, Mon.-Sat. 9:30 a.m.-8:30 p.m.; for credit card bookings, phone BASS at 13-1246 in South Australia, or 1800-88-8327 toll-free Australia-wide. The celebrated **Late Show,** in the Centre's Fezbah every Friday night from 11 p.m. until late, features cabaret acts. Free and casual jazz as well as classical and chamber music performances are often held on Sunday afternoon in the Festival Theatre Foyer.

The **Adelaide Symphony Orchestra** and **Australian Chamber Orchestra** perform at the old Adelaide Town Hall on King William Street. For information, phone BASS at the numbers above. BASS also handles bookings for many other events, including Baroque and Renaissance music concerts at St. Peter's Cathedral.

Adelaide has a very active performance and contemporary theater scene. If you don't find what you're looking for at the Festival Centre, check with the Lion Arts Centre (tel. 08-8231-7760). Other good tries are **La Mama,** 4 Crawford Lane, Hindmarsh (tel. 08-8346-4212), a small venue showcasing experimental works, and **Little Theatre,** University of Adelaide (tel. 08-8228-1664), for student productions.

Events

The **Adelaide Festival of the Arts,** the oldest in Australia and one of the best in the world, attracts top international talent. During the first three weeks of March, in even-numbered years, the festival brews such mixes as Shakespearean tragedies with avant-garde performances, Beethoven symphonies with fusion jazz, Yehudi Menuhin with Mick Jagger.

The Fringe Festival, which is often even mo exciting, coincides with the main event. Durir festival time, the city is agog over theater, danc music, and art. Writers' Week attracts a wic array of poets, novelists, playwrights, and jou nalists to swig and tipple as they excerpt and e pound. Make bookings for the festival well advance by writing Adelaide Festival, G.P.C Box 1269, Adelaide, SA 5001 (tel. 08-821 8600).

For information on the **Barossa Valley Vi tage Festival,** contact Barossa Wine ar Tourism Association (tel. 08-8562-1866). F information on the **McLaren Vale Bushing Fe tival,** phone (08) 8323-8999.

SPORTS AND RECREATION

Locals take advantage of the mild weather, go geous parklands, and nearby beaches, ar spend a lot of time outdoors—if not participatir in something themselves, then watching otl ers who are. The parklands, particularly, a full of recreational areas. Meander too long one grassy spot and you'll probably be cor mandeered into a game of soccer or cricke Walkers and joggers will take happily to tr many park pathways with their peaceful vista and gentle climbs. Those of you who are mo interested in a hike or bushwalk, stay tuned f "Hills and Vales," below. For useful info on a most every activity, contact the **Departme of Sport and Recreation,** 11 Hindmars Square (tel. 08-8226-7301). **The Hire Life,** 1 Brebner Dr., Westlakes (tel. 08-8356-1911 rents out just about every type of sports equi ment, including cycles, canoes, windsurfer and rollerblades.

Cycling

Cycling about this nitty-gritty city, and the nir tracks that surround the parklands, is smoo and trouble-free. Rent bikes from **Super E liott,** 200 Rundle St. (tel. 08-8223-3946); A tion Moped Hire,** 400 King William St. (te 08-8211-7060); or **Pulteney Street Cycle 307 Pulteney St. (tel. 08-8223-6678). All ar open Mon.-Saturday. In Glenelg, contact **Bik and Beach Hire,** next to the tourist informa tion office.

cuba Diving

iving is best off Kangaroo Island and the Yorke eninsula, but boat diving isn't bad at Port Noarnga Reef Marine Reserve, 18 km south of delaide, or Aldinga, 43 km south. You'll need roof of diving experience before you can rent quipment. For information, contact the **Scuba ivers Federation of South Australia,** 1 Sturt t. (tel. 13-0666).

wimming

wim along the beaches of Gulf St. Vincent, or p into the **Adelaide Aquatic Centre,** Jeffcott d., North Adelaide (tel. 08-8344-4411), in the orth parklands. The pool's open daily 9 a.m.-5 m. A gym, sauna, and spa are also available.

ennis

oth grass and hard courts, as well as tennis ckets, are available for rent at **Memorial Drive ennis Club,** War Memorial Dr. (tel. 08-8231-371), and **Roseland's Tennis World,** 323 turt Rd., Bedford Park (tel. 08-8231-3033). delaide City Courts are in the parklands.

olf

uests are welcome to tee off at **City of Adeide Golf Links,** Memorial Dr., North Adelaide el. 08-8231-2359). Equipment is available for re.

ailing

delaide's shoreline is fine for sailing. All the ty beaches have yacht clubs, and most welome casual visitors.

kating and Skiing

ou can ice skate round the rink, on either a eginner- or Olympic-size arena, or ski down e 12-meter-high indoor slope (covered in Perasnow, a real snowlike Australian product), **Thebarton Ice Arena,** 23 East Terrace, Thearton (tel. 08-8352-7977). Cost is $8, including kate hire, and both ski and skating instruction is vailable. Hours are Mon.-Fri. 9:30 a.m.-4:30 m., Wednesday and Friday 7-11 p.m., Sat.-un. 12:30-4 p.m. and 7:30-11 p.m.

pectator Sports

delaide Oval, north of the city on King William t., is the main location for **cricket** matches,

the country's favorite summer sport. International and interstate test matches are played Oct.-March.

The big winter sport, **Australian Rules football,** is played—usually on Saturday—at both Adelaide Oval and Football Park, West Lakes. Soccer, rugby, and rugby union are also played during the April-Sept. season.

You can play the ponies or the pups yearround. The **South Australian Jockey Club** conducts meetings at Victoria Park, Morphettville, and Cheltenham; **Adelaide Greyhound Racing Club** is the venue for those flying dogs. Check local newspapers for meeting times.

SHOPPING

It's doubtful you'll ever "shop 'til you drop" in this city, but you will find the basics, maybe a few bargains, and possibly some baubles. **Warning:** Be especially careful when purchasing opals—take your time and shop around for reputable dealers. City shopping hours are generally Mon.-Fri. 8:30 a.m.-5:30 p.m., Saturday 8:30 a.m.-noon, late-night trading Friday until 9 p.m. (late-night trading is held on Thursday in the suburbs).

Rundle Mall, with its branches of arcades, offers standard mall-isms—John Martin's and Myer department stores, specialty shops that are really nothing special, a handful of commercial art galleries, a cinema complex, photo developers, jewelry stores, sandwich shops, a few buskers, and flower carts. **Rundle Street East** is far more exciting, with retro shops, alternative clothing and jewelry, New Age trinkets and nose rings, and black, black, and more black. For bookstores, see "Information," below.

For more chic and boutiques, North Adelaide's exclusive **Melbourne Street** will fill your Louis Vuitton luggage until you make it back to Rodeo Drive.

Markets

For far less sterile shopping, **Central Market,** between Grote and Gouger Streets (near Victoria Square), has colorful stalls stocked with food, produce, flowers, and bazaar items. The **East End Market,** on Rundle Street, has the

ADELAIDE ARCADES

UNDERPASS TO RAILWAY STATION

NORTH TERRACE

STATION ARCADE

BANK ST.

WOODSONS LANE

MILLER'S ARCADE

GRESHAM ST.

SOUTH AUSTRALIAN TOURISM COMMISSION TRAVEL CENTRE

STEPHENS PL.

RUNDLE ARCADE

GAWLER ST.

THE GALLERIE SHOPPING CENTRE

JOHN MARTIN'S PLAZA

RENAISSANCE CENTRE

PULTENEY ST.

PEEL ST.

HINDLEY ST.

KING WILLIAM ST.

SOUTHERN CROSS ARCADE

CITY CROSS

RUNDLE MALL

REGENT ARCADE

RENAISSANCE ARCADE

GAYS ARCADE

ADELAIDE ARCADE

TWIN PLAZA ARCADE

ADELAIDE CITY CENTRE

ARCADE DA COSTA

HINDMARSH SQUARE

CURRIE ST.

GRENFELL ST.

0   100 m

---

same plus bizarre items. **Orange Lane Market,** off The Parade in nearby Norwood, is open Sat.-Mon. for seekers of imported fabrics, retro clothing, antiques, and full-body massages.

The **Brickworks Market,** 36 South Rd., Thebarton, is about three km from the city center. Hundreds of stalls sell everything from food and clothing to arts and crafts to junk and junque. Take the bus from Grenfell and Currie Streets in the city. The market is open Fri.-Sun. 9 a.m.-5 p.m.

Arts and Crafts

Local craftspeople create and sell jewelry, fabric, leather, glass, wood, ceramics, and other handmade wares at the **Jam Factory Craft and Design Centre,** 1 Morphett Street (tel. 08-8410-0727). The gallery features monthly changing exhibitions. Open Mon.-Fri. 9 a.m.-5 p.m., Sat.-Sun. and public holidays 10 a.m.-5 p.m.

Contemporary and traditional Aboriginal arts and crafts are sold and displayed at **Tandanya Aboriginal Cultural Institute,** 253 Grenfell St. (tel. 08-8223-2467). The institute, representing 50 traditional Aboriginal groups of South Australia, also sponsors performing and visual arts and houses a museum. Items for sale include Aboriginal artifacts, T-shirts, backpacks, and

books. Open Mon.-Fri. 10:30 a.m.-5 p.m., Sa Sun. and public holidays noon-5 p.m. Admi sion is $4. **Otherway Aboriginal Arts an Crafts,** 185 Pirie St. (tel. 08-8232-1001), ope ated by Aborigines, also features a good rang of arts and crafts, and all profits are channele back into the community. Open Mon.-Fri. 1 a.m.-5 p.m.

See a broad spectrum of postmodern exhib tions by local and interstate artists, changir every few weeks, at **Union Gallery,** Level Union Building, Adelaide University (tel. 0 8228-5013). Open Mon.-Fri. 10 a.m.-5 p.m.

Chic rustic kitchen accessories made fro recycled wood and environmentally friendly Ka garoo Island swamp gums can be purchase at **D.Lux Homewares,** 238A Rundle St., whi **Bimbo,** a few doors away at 279 Rundle S offers pickings for metal- and wire-lovers.

TRANSPORTATION

Getting There by Air
Qantas, 144 North Terrace (tel. 08-8208-887 or 13-1313 toll-free), is the only internation airline that flies into Adelaide from North Ame ca (and that's with a change of aircraft in Sy

ey); both Qantas and **Singapore Airlines** have onstop service from Singapore; **Garuda Indonesia** flies nonstop from Bali. **British Airways** operates two-stoppers from the United ingdom.

The two major domestic airlines, **Ansett,** 205 ireenhill Rd., Eastwood (08-8208-4101 or 13-300 toll-free), and **Qantas,** 144 North Terrace el. 08-8208-8877 or 13-1313 toll-free), pro-de daily direct and connecting service from Il major Australian cities. Sample fares to or om Adelaide are: Melbourne, $175; Sydney, 260; Brisbane, $320; Perth, $380; Alice prings, $285; Darwin, $365. These prices re-ect the 40% discount accorded international :ket holders, but you can get about the same are by going standby. There are other passes nd discounts available depending upon your ute and length of time traveling. **STA Travel,** 35 Rundle St. (tel. 08-8233-2426), is your best ource for info and bargains.

ietting There by Train

.eswick Railway Terminal, on Railway Ter-ace, near the city center, is the arrival and de-arture point for interstate trains. The **Indian-Pa-ific,** between Sydney and Perth, passes rough both Adelaide and Broken Hill on its vice-weekly run. From Sydney to Adelaide, the 5-hour journey costs $110 economy, $199 conomy sleeper without meals, or $334 first-lass sleeper with meals. From Perth to Adelaide 38 hours), the fare range is $290 economy, -598 economy sleeper without meals, or $932 rst-class sleeper with meals. An alternative om Sydney is the **Speedlink**—an XPT train om Sydney to Albury, a deluxe V/Line coach om Albury to Adelaide. Economy sitting is $95 nd first class is $125. The Speedlink is about ix hours faster than the train.

From Melbourne, the **Overland** departs night-y for the 12-hour overnight journey to Adelaide. ares are $47 economy sitting, $95 first-class sit-ng, $155 first-class sleeper.

The **Ghan** travels once a week between Alice prings and Adelaide (twice weekly April-Jan.). he 20-hour journey costs $145 economy sitting, 249 economy sleeper without meals, or $456 rst-class sleeper with meals. Though the re-urbished Ghan is not nearly as magical as the

original, the trek along the historic Afghan camel-driving route is still quite spine-tingling.

Caper fares provide discounts of up to 30% if tickets are purchased at least seven days in advance. Standby travel, at considerable savings over regular fares, is permitted on some services. For rail information, phone (08) 8231-7699 or 13-2232, toll-free.

Getting There by Bus

Greyhound Pioneer Australia (tel. 08-8233-2777, or 13-2033 toll-free) operates coach services between Adelaide, the other capital cities, and most of the rest of Australia. Major services that operate daily are: Sydney-Adelaide (24 hours), $95; Melbourne-Adelaide (10 hours), $55; Alice Springs-Adelaide (20 hours), $142; Perth-Adelaide (35 hours), $189; Brisbane-Adelaide (34 hours), $155. A number of bus passes are available, allowing unlimited travel for a specified number of days. Some passes need to be purchased outside Australia; others can be issued by STA Travel, YHA Travel, the South Australian Tourism Commission Travel Centre, or the coach company. The **central bus station** is at 111 Franklin St., near Victoria Square. For information, phone (08) 8415-5533.

Getting There by Car

If you're coming to Adelaide by road, the major routes are the coastal **Princes Highway** from Melbourne (929 km), the inland **Western** and **Dukes** Highways from Melbourne (731 km), **Mid-Western** Highway from Sydney (1,414 km), **Sturt Highway** from Sydney (1,418 km), **Barrier Highway** from Sydney (1,666 km), **Stuart Highway** from Darwin (3,026 km), and **Eyre Highway** from Perth (2,691 km). Allow *plenty* of time if you're driving; except for Melbourne, these outback stretches can be risky business for inexperienced motorists.

Getting Around

Warning: Trains, especially late at night, are hotbeds of violence for violent hotheads—it's best to stick to buses or taxis at night.

The **Adelaide Airport Bus** (tel. 08-8381-5311) will whisk you from the airport to center city (six km) every half-hour 7 a.m.-10 p.m., for $4. Taxis charge about $12 for the 25-minute ride.

Adelaide's **TransAdelaide** operates the city's buses, the suburban trains, and its one tram, and prices cover the entire transportation system. Buses run between city and suburbs daily 6 a.m.-11:30 p.m., but there is no service on Sunday morning. Suburban trains serving Glenelg, Port Adelaide, several coastal points, and the Adelaide Hills depart Adelaide Railway Station, North Terrace, daily 5:30 a.m.-midnight (see the "Adelaide Suburban Rail" map). **Circle Line** buses link all the services Mon.-Fri. 7 a.m.-6 p.m. The free **Beeline** bus cruises along King William St., from Victoria Square to the North Terrace Railway Station, every seven minutes Mon.-Thurs. 8 a.m.-6 p.m., Friday 8 a.m.-9 p.m., Saturday 8 a.m.-12:15 p.m. Tickets ($1.80-3.50), priced according to zones, are good for up to two hours on all modes of transport. The **Day Tripper** ticket costs $4.40 and allows unlimited travel within the entire system Mon.-Fri. after 9 a.m., Sat.-Sun. all day. Another money-saver is the **Multitrip** ticket, which gives you 10 rides for the price of seven. Buy tickets and pick up transport maps and timetables at the TransAdelaide Information Bureau, corner of King William and Currie Streets (tel. 08-8210-1000), Mon.-Fri. 9 a.m.-5 p.m., Saturday 9 a.m.-noon.

Taxis are plentiful and can be hired at the airport, railway stations, city center taxi stands, or by phoning direct. Companies include **Adelaide Independent** (tel. 08-8224-6000), **Suburban** (tel. 08-8211-8888), and **United Yellow** (tel. 08-8223-3111).

All the big-name car rental firms are represented in Adelaide, with offices at the airport, the major hotels, and along North Terrace. Several lesser-known and cheaper firms are **Moke Rent-a-Cars** (tel. 08-8352-7044), **Action Rent-a-Car** (tel. 08-8352-7044), **Rent-a-Bug** (tel. 08-8234-0911), and **Hire-a-Hack** (tel. 08-8271-7820). For moped and bicycle rentals, see "Cycling" under "Sports and Recreation," above. Mopeds will run about $28 per day, $8 per hour (be prepared to pay a $50 deposit). Mountain bikes average $20 per day, while 10-speeds are in the $12-14 bracket.

The **Adelaide Explorer Bus** (tel. 08-8212-1505) departs from 18 King William St. daily 9:10 a.m., 10:25 a.m., 12:20 p.m., 1:35 p.m., 2:55 p.m., and 4:10 p.m. (except Christmas Day and Good Friday), for sightseeing trips t eight popular city spots, including Glenelg. On $19 ticket permits you to get on and off at wi so if one place strikes your fancy, you ca spend as much time there as you like, re boarding the bus next time around. Many to operators offer City Sights, Adelaide Hills, M Lofty Ranges, and Adelaide by Night junket Check with the tourist office for the current li of contenders.

Getting Away

Intrastate air carriers include **Kendell Airline August Airlines, Air Kangaroo Islan Whyalia Airlines, Eyre Commuter, Albatros Airlines, Emu Airways, O'Connor Airline Lincoln Airlines,** and **Southern Australia Ai lines.** The smaller carriers will take you to con munities such as Ceduna, Mount Gambier, Po Lincoln, Whyalla, Coober Pedy, Broken Hi Olympic Dam, Woomera, American Rive Kingscote, Parndana, Wudinna, Cummin Tumby Bay, Port Lincoln, Renmark, and Mild ra. Make bookings through Ansett or Qanta or contact the South Australian Tourism Con mission Travel Centre. (see "Getting Around," the On the Road chapter)

The **MV *Philanderer III*** and **MV *Island Na igator*** (tel. 13-1301 toll-free) passenger ferrie operate service from Cape Jervis to Per neshaw, Kangaroo Island. Fares are $32 one way for the one-hour journey. The **K.I. Cor nection** (tel. 08-8384-6860) is a coach servic connecting Adelaide with the Cape Jervis de parture point.

Country trains depart Keswick Railway Te minal for Peterborough, Port Pirie, and Mt. Garr bier. For information, phone (08) 8217-4455.

Aside from the Greyhound Pioneer Australi conglomerate mentioned above under "Gettin There by Bus," several smaller bus companie service the state's country towns, coastal vi lages, and remote stations. The **Country Pas senger Depot,** 101 Franklin St., is next door t the central bus station. For information, phon (08) 8231-4144.

If you're hitching to Melbourne, the bus fror Pulteney St. will take you to Old Toll Gate o Mt. Barker Rd., a good thumb-and-sign post. you're headed far away to Perth, across th

ADELAIDE SUBURBAN RAIL

GAWLER CENTRAL
GAWLER OVAL
GAWLER
EVANSTON
TAMBELIN
KUDLA
MUNNO PARA
SMITHFIELD
BROADMEADOWS
WOMMA
ELIZABETH
PENFIELD
ELIZABETH SOUTH
HILRA
GMH ELIZABETH
NURLUTTA
SALISBURY
CHIDDA
PARAFIELD
PARAFIELD GARDENS
GREENFIELDS
NORTHFIELD
POORAKA
CAVAN
DRY CREEK
TUBE MILLS
KILBURN
ISLINGTON
DUDLEY PARK
OVINGHAM
NORTH ADELAIDE

OUTER HARBOUR
NORTH HAVEN
OSBORNE
MIDLUNGA
TAPEROO
DRAPER
LARGS NORTH
LARGS
PETERHEAD
GLANVILLE
ETHELTON
PORT ADELAIDE
ALBERTON
CHELTENHAM
CHELTENHAM RACECOURSE
HOLDENS
ALBERT PARK
SEATON PARK
E AST GRANGE
GRANGE

ROSEWATER
JUNCTION ROAD
EASTERN PARADE
NORTH ARM ROAD
WINGFIELD

WOODVILLE
WOODVILLE PARK
KILKENNY
WEST CROYDON
CROYDON
BOWDEN

ADELAIDE
MILE END
MILE END GOODS
KESWICK

GLENELG
GLENELG TRAMWAY
GOODWOOD
MILLSWOOD
CLARENCE PARK
UNLEY PARK
EMERSON
EDWARDSTOWN
HAWTHORN
WOODLANDS PARK
MITCHAM
ASCOT PARK
TORRENS PARK
MARION
MITCHELL PARK
OAKLANDS
CHRYSLER PARK
CLAPHAM
WARRADALE
TONSLEY
LYNTON
HOVE
EDEN HILLS
BRIGHTON
COROMANDEL
SEACLIFF
MARINO
MARINO ROCKS
HALLETT COVE
HALLETT COVE BEACH
LONSDALE
CHRISTIE DOWNS
NOARLUNGA CENTRE

BRIDGEWATER
CARRIPOOK
JIBILLA
ALDGATE
MADURTA
HEATHFIELD
MOUNT LOFTY
UPPER STURT
LONG GULLY
NATIONAL PARK
BELAIR
PINERA
GLENALTA
BLACKWOOD

very barren Nullarbor Plain, it's easiest to begin in Port Augusta, at the petrol station nearest to town. Catch the bus from King William St. to Port Wakefield Rd., Gepps Cross, where you can walk to Carvans Petrol Station—your hitching point. Once you get to Port Augusta, be prepared to wait—sometimes days. Try to hit it on Friday night or Saturday morning when the truckies are coming through. **Warning:** Women should *not* hitch alone! **Bigger warning:** Hitching in Australia is illegal, remember?

SERVICES

King William Street is lined with **banks** and other financial institutions. Business hours are Mon.-Thurs. 9:30 a.m.-4 p.m., Friday 9:30 a.m.-5 p.m. When changing traveler's checks, be sure to carry your passport or driver's license for identification. Many city and suburban banking facilities have automatic teller machines that accept international credit cards.

Change money at Thomas Cook, 45 Grenfell St. (tel. 08-8212-3354), or American Express, 13 Grenfell St. (tel. 08-8212-7099).

The **general post office,** 141 King William St., provides the full range of postal services, including a philatelic bureau. Another convenient branch of Australia Post is in Rundle Mall. Hours of operation are Mon.-Fri. 8 a.m.-6 p.m., Saturday 8:30 a.m.-noon.

Just about every hotel, motel, and hostel provides **laundry facilities** for guests. Launderettes are dispersed around the city and suburbs. **Adelaide Launderette,** 152 Sturt St., is open daily 7 a.m.-8 p.m., and provides wash and iron service Mon.-Sat. 8 a.m.-5 p.m.

Stow your bags at any of the hostels, the YMCA residence hotel, the railway station, or central bus station—but not at the airport. The small fee will vary according to how many bags you stash and how long they're left.

Fruit-pickers should have luck finding **casual labor** (during harvest time). Check at wineries in the Barossa and Clare Valleys, as well as the Southern Vales, Riverland, and Coonawarra. The Murray River fruit-bearing districts of Berri, Renmark, and Loxton may also yield seasonal work.

INFORMATION

Bring an extra suitcase for all the literature you' sure to accumulate. Your first stop should b at the **South Australian Tourism Commi sion Travel Centre,** 1 King William St. (tel. 0 8212-1505), where you'll be handed an asso ment of brochures, planners, maps, booklet pamphlets, leaflets, and the like. The center open Mon.-Fri. 9 a.m.-5 p.m., Sat.-Sun. 9 a.m 2 p.m. The **Royal Automobile Association** 41 Hindmarsh Square (tel. 08-8223-4500), an invaluable source for detailed maps (parti ularly of outback areas). They also have a commodations guides and a selection of book available for purchase. If you're a member the American Automobile Association or th U.K.'s RAC and AA, you have full reciproc privileges, but you must show your membe ship card as proof (that's what they say, but I' never been asked).

For literature, maps, and camping and hi ing information on specific parks, contact th **Department of Environment and Natural R sources,** 77 Grenfell St., Adelaide, SA 50C (tel. 08-8207-2000).

The **Disability Information Centre,** 19 Gilles St. (tel. 08-8223-7522), is open Mon-F 9 a.m.-5 p.m.

Adelaide's **YHA** office is at 38 Sturt St. (te 08-8231-5583). Hours are Mon.-Fri. 9:30 a.m 5:30 p.m.

Emergencies

To contact the **police, fire brigade,** or **ambu lance,** phone 000. **Royal Adelaide Hospita** corner of North Terrace and Frome Rd. (tel. 08 8223-0230), is a full-service facility with 24-hou emergency services. Also on Frome Rd. is **Ade laide Dental Hospital** (tel. 08-8223-9211). **Bu den Chemist,** 41 King William St. (tel. 08-823 4701), is open daily 8 a.m.-midnight for you pharmaceutical needs.

Bookstores, Newspapers, and Other Information

Read all about it on North Terrace. The Mortloc Library and bookshops in the museums, his toric sights, and Adelaide University can pr vide inquiring minds with all they want to know about South Australian history, anthropology, archaeology, art, botany, and politics, both past and present.

Two levels of the **Third World Bookshop,** 103 Hindley St., are "literally" crammed with all subjects of secondhand books, radical literature, records, and alternative periodicals. The shop is open daily 9 a.m.-1 a.m.-ish. Another good secondhand bookshop is **O'Connell's,** 23 Gilbert Pl. (tel. 08-8231-5188).

Murphy Sisters Bookshop, 240 The Parade, Norwood (08-8332-7508), specializes in books by, for, and about women, as well as nonsexist and nonracist children's books. This shop is an excellent resource and meeting place for women. Hours are Mon.-Sat. 9 a.m.-5 p.m. Thursday until 8 p.m.), Sunday 1-4 p.m.

Adelaide University Bookshop, on the campus, sells textbooks, plus general fiction, nonfiction, and children's books. The shop is open to the public. For information and hours, phone 08) 8223-4366.

The large mainstream bookshop is **Angus and Robertson,** 112 Rundle Mall, where you'll find an enormous range of titles, including many on Australian and regional topics. **The Mind Field Bookshop,** over on happening Rundle Street (no. 238), features a large selection of Australian fiction and is open late every night.

Psychic sciences, astrology, women's spirituality, health, and healing are some of the selections at **Quantum, The Metaphysical Bookshop,** 113 Melbourne St., North Adelaide. You can also pick up quartz crystals and relaxation

music. Hours are Mon.-Fri. 9 a.m.-6 p.m. (Thursday until 9 p.m.), Saturday 9:30 a.m.-5 p.m., Sunday 1-5 p.m.

The coffee-and-newspaper crowd can choose from the morning *Advertiser* and the *Sunday Mail.*

The Wilderness Society is an Australian conservation group dedicated to addressing important and timely issues, such as preservation of rainforests, harmful effects of logging, and other environmental concerns. They also operate wilderness shops in each state, which sell books, T-shirts, badges, and other "collectibles." In Adelaide, you'll find them at 66 Grote St. (tel. 08-8231-6586). The **Conservation Council of South Australia,** 120 Wakefield St., is another clearinghouse for eco-info and has a bookshop, notice board, and library.

For **women,** the Murphy Sisters Bookshop (see above) is an excellent contact spot. Other resources include: the **Women's Information Switchboard** (tel. 08-8223-1244); the **Women's Studies Resource Centre,** 64 Pennington Terrace, North Adelaide (tel. 08-8267-3633); and **Adelaide Women's Community Health Centre,** also at 64 Pennington Terrace (tel. 08-8267-5366).

South Australia, being the first state to legalize homosexuality, offers a range of hassle-free services. Pick up a copy of the *Adelaide Gay Times* for news on current events, resources, and the club scene. **Lesbian Line** (tel. 08-8223-1982) and **Gay and Lesbian Counseling Service** (tel. 08-8362-3223) can also provide help and information.

HILLS AND VALES

Less than half an hour's drive from grid-and-square Adelaide are rambling hills and rolling vales, secluded hollows and hideaway valleys, nook-and-cranny villages and lush green terrain smothered in wildflowers, delicate orchids, and bold yellow wattle, and bathed in the fragrance of almond, apple, pear, and cherry orchards, and strawberry patches. Euphoric names such as Happy Valley, Tea Tree Gully, Basket Range, Mount Pleasant, and Chain of Ponds will ring in your ears with the distant echo of a near-forgotten, favorite fairy tale.

Adelaide is the perfect base for short excursions into the hills; or do the reverse—nestle into some cozy dell and day trip down to the city.

ADELAIDE HILLS

The hills, part of the Mt. Lofty Ranges, can be explored by a number of meandering scenic routes. There's something for everyone—endless vistas for tourists in buses, scads of secluded picnic spots for lovers and loners, 1,000 kilometers of walking tracks for hikers. One exceptionally pretty itinerary that leads you around and through conservation parks and lookout spots with a bird's-eye view of the city begins at **Windy Point** on Belair Rd. (reached from the city via Fullarton Rd.). Skirt around Upper Sturt Rd. to **Belair National Park,** one of the world's oldest national parks (established 1891). Facilities include tennis courts, football ovals, cricket pitches, a popular golf course, bushwalking tracks, and camping sites. Admission is $3 per vehicle. For information, phone (08) 8278-5477.

Continue along Upper Sturt Rd., cross the South Eastern Freeway, and you'll be on Summit Road. Take the turnoff to **Mt. Lofty,** the ranges' highest point (771 meters). At road's end, a monument pays tribute to Col. Matthew Flinders, and a large lookout area affords a panoramic view of Adelaide and the surrounding hills and plains. Near the summit, **Mt. Lofty Botanic Gardens** covers more than 42 hectares with exotic cool and subalpine plants. The gar-

dens are closed in winter and are most colorfu in autumn. For information, phone (08) 8228 2311.

Cleland Conservation Park, on the slopes o Mt. Lofty, features koalas (cuddling daily 2-4 p.m.), emus, kangaroos, native birds, and othe wildlife, as well as many enticing walking tracks along its 972 hectares of bushland. For infor mation, phone (08) 8339-2444.

Back on Summit Rd., you'll pass pear and apple orchards until you reach **Norton Sum mit,** where there's a restaurant and yet anothe view.

Turning toward the city will bring you into **Mo rialta Conservation Park,** noted for its water falls, deep gorge, and excellent bushwalking Trails lead to the gorge and several waterfalls (and some pretty spectacular views), as we as points like Pretty Corner, Kookaburra Rock and the Giant's Cave. For information, phone (08) 8281-4022.

Magill Rd. runs into Payneham Rd., which leads back to Adelaide. An alternate route is Marble Hill Rd. (turn off before Norton Summit to Montacute, toward the city through Morialta and the **Black Hill** Conservation Parks, then to Payneham Road.

Para Wirra Recreational Park, 40 km north east of Adelaide, is a wooded plateau with steep gullies, kangaroos, birds, spring wildflowers and more good walking trails and picnic areas Admission is $3 per vehicle. For information phone (08) 8280-7048.

Accommodations and Food

See the Adelaide **YHA** for information on its five limited-access hostels in the Mt. Lofty Ranges Advance bookings are required.

Belair National Park (tel. 08-8278-3540 rents campsites, on-site vans, and inexpensiv cabins with cooking facilities. Guestrooms a **Drysdale Cottage,** Debneys Rd., Norton Sum mit (tel. 08-8390-1652), are moderate to ex pensive and include breakfast. **Happy's Nes** Summit Rd., Mt. Lofty, opposite the entranc to Cleland Conservation Park, is a moderatel priced bed and breakfast.

Really big spenders and splurgers should consider a stay at **Mt. Lofty House,** 74 Summit Rd., Crafers (tel. 08-8339-6777). The exquisitely furnished house, built between 1852 and 1858, has sumptuous bedrooms, sitting rooms, and two luscious restaurants. Prices are hefty—$215-430 per double—and the breakfast is light.

You'll find tearooms and pubs tucked cozily away in the hills and valleys. At Norton Summit, the **Scenic Hotel,** hanging onto the hill, is a thrill for meals and drinks.

BIRDWOOD

Once upon a time Birdwood, less than 50 km northeast from Adelaide, was a gold-mining center. Today its claim to fame is the **National Motor Museum,** which displays more than 300 vintage, veteran, and classic motor cars and bikes. Housed inside an 1852 flour mill, the museum is open daily 9 a.m.-5 p.m., closed Christmas Day. Admission is $7. For information, phone (08) 8568-5006.

Cromer Conservation Park, Cromer Rd., has more than 70 species of birds flying around its 50 hectares.

Reached via Lobethal (and the River Torrens Gorge), or through Chain of Ponds and Gumeracha, Birdwood is both a convenient day trip from Adelaide or a stop on the way to the Barossa Valley.

Nearby Sights

The **Toy Factory** of Gumeracha features what is supposedly "the biggest rocking horse in the world" (about six stories high), as well as some nicely crafted wooden toys. The factory, and its coffeehouse, are open daily 9 a.m.-5 p.m., closed Christmas Day. For information, phone (08) 8389-1085.

Cudlee Creek Gorge Wildlife Park, Cudlee Creek (a short detour from Chain of Ponds), boasts a large privately owned wildlife collection, with koalas just dying to be cuddled. The park is open daily 8 a.m.-5 p.m. Admission is $5.50. For information, phone (08) 8389-2206.

Accommodations

The **Gumeracha Hotel,** Albert St., Gumeracha (tel. 08-8389-1001), has the cheapest rooms. In Birdwood, **Birdwood Bed and Breakfast,** 38 Olivedale St. (tel. 08-8568-5444), is a moderately priced cottage with cooking facilities and breakfast ingredients provided. **Gorge Caravan Park,** Gorge Rd., Cudlee Creek (tel. 08-8389-2270), has both campsites and inexpensive cabins.

Transportation

A.B.M. Coachlines (tel. 08-8347-3358) provide twice-daily service, Mon.-Fri., to Birdwood from Adelaide's central bus station. Cost is $3.50 one way.

HAHNDORF

Hahndorf, 20 km southeast from Adelaide, i Australia's oldest surviving German settlemen Founded by East Prussian Lutherans fleein religious persecution in their homeland, the tow is named after Captain Hahn, commander o the ship *Zebra,* which brought them on their ar duous journey. The typically (for its time) nigh marish voyage was fraught with disease, deatl ripped sails, and killer heat; nonetheless th *Zebra* arrived safely at Port Adelaide in 183! Today Hahndorf (pop. 1,300) is a popular da trip from the city, drawing tourists to its histori buildings and well-preserved town to buy slice of streusel and *typisch* folk crafts, to partake o some oldy-worldy charm (albeit on the cutes side). Stop by for a cuppa *kaffee* and you're ap to be greeted with a *"Guten Tag,* mate."

Sights

Hahndorf Academy, 68 Main St., established i 1857 as an educational facility, now functions a the town museum and a showcase for land scape paintings by Sir Hans Heysen, a Hahndc favorite son. The museum is open daily 10 a.m 5 p.m., closed Christmas Day. Admission is $! For information, phone (08) 8388-7250.

This 1860 Bridgewater Mill is the home of Petaluma Winery.

View elaborate timepieces as well as a gigantic cuckoo clock, and buy your own authentic Black Forest cuckoo at the **Antique Clock Museum,** 91 Main Street. Open daily 9 a.m.-5:30 p.m. Admission is $3. For information, phone (08) 8388-7349.

German Model Train Land, 47 Main St., features intricately pieced, imported-from-Germany model trains and villages. Open daily 9 a.m.-5 p.m., closed Christmas Day and Good Friday. Admission is $3. For information, phone (08) 8388-7953.

Nearby Sights

Detour on Mt. Barker Rd. before you get to Hahndorf for an inspection of the 1860 stone **Bridgewater Mill,** restored and transformed into **Petaluma Winery.** View the huge waterwheel, taste the cabernet sauvignon and chardonnay, and have lunch in the cavernous **Granary Restaurant.** Open daily 11 a.m.-5 p.m. For information, phone (08) 8339-3422.

Warrawong Sanctuary, Williams Rd., Mylor, another sidetrack to Hahndorf. See rare and endangered animals on organized dawn, daytime, and nocturnal walks. The property also has a nocturnal observatory and craft and coffee shops. Open by reservation only. For information, phone (08) 8388-5380.

Accommodations and Food

Lochstens, 145 Main St. (tel. 08-8388-7361), has a wide range of accommodations, from on-site caravans to luxury motel units and private chalets. Prices also vary from budget to expensive. **Hahndorf Old Mill Motel and Restaurant,** 98 Main St. (tel. 08-8388-7888), has moderate to expensive rooms with all the creature comforts. **Elderberry,** Old Mt. Barker Rd. (tel. 08-8388-7997), is a one-bedroom cottage with cooking facilities, fireplace, and high-moderate prices.

You can get stick-to-your-bones German food all over town. The **German Arms Hotel,** 50 Main St., dating from 1834, serves pub meals in historic surroundings. Along Main St., **Otto's Bakery, Karl's German Coffee House, Gretchen's Coffee Shop,** and **The German Cake Shop** will keep you going with good coffees and fresh cakes.

Do-it-yourselfers will want to pack the homemade wurst at **Hahndorf Gourmet Foods** and pick the homegrown berries at either the **Berry Farm** on Tischer Rd. (tel. 08-8388-7071) or **Beerenberg Strawberry Farm,** Mt. Barker Rd. (tel. 08-8388-7272).

Events

Hahndorf's big event is the annual mid-January **Schützenfest,** a traditional shooting festival with German folk dancing, entertainment, cuisine, and beer—*lots* of beer.

Transportation

To get to Hahndorf, catch the twice-daily bus from the Franklin Street depot in Adelaide. The ride takes 40 minutes, and the fare is $4. For information and schedules, phone Mount Barker Passenger Service (tel. 08-8391-2977).

THE BAROSSA VALLEY

South Australia's most famous wine district lies in a shallow valley just 29 kilometers long and eight kilometers wide, amid gently rounded hills, icy-cold brooks, neat-as-a-pin grape-staked fields, pseudo chateaus and castles, and authentic Lutheran churches.

Less than an hour's drive north of Adelaide, most of the 50 or so wineries are situated in the 20-kilometer span from Lyndoch to Nuriootpa, with the town of Tanunda in between. Serious connoisseurs or occasional tipplers can follow their noses or their whims to both commercial mega-complexes and family-run boutique wineries for a gargle or a swallow of full-bodied reds, crisp whites, sherries, ports, and sparkling wines.

Two routes will get you to the Barossa—a rather boring, but quicker and more direct road through Gawler, or the longer, winding, picture-postcard way via Birdwood and Torrens Gorge. Assuming that you'll start off on the scenic route and by day's end be wishing for the straight highway with the dividing lines, the following towns have been geographically arranged to reflect that. Also, not all of the wineries have been listed below, only some of the most historical and interesting. Well-placed signposts will lead you to others off the beaten path—it's fun to make a wrong turn here or there, up or down, to make your own vintage discoveries. You can do the Barossa in a day trip from Adelaide, but if your feet get a little wobbly—or you haven't had your fill—consider bedding down for the night at a hostel, guesthouse, or motel along the way.

On 1 February 1997 all telephone numbers in the Barossa Valley will change. In preparation for this, all numbers in this section have been changed to eight digits. To dial a Barossa Valley number before 1 February, simply delete the first two digits of the new number and, if dialing from outside the Barossa Valley, add the area code (085). As an example, (08) 8512-3456 is dialed (085) 12-3456. After 1 February the area code for all numbers in this section will be (08).

History

The Barossa was settled in 1842 by the same persecuted East Prussian Lutherans who arrived on the good ship *Zebra* with Captain Hahn. Their expedition had been funded by Englishman George Fife Angas, one of the original colonizers, in the hopes he was snagging good hardworking folk whose skills would benefit South Australia. The new arrivals who didn't go to Hahndorf followed their pastor, August Kavel, to the Barossa Valley, and put down roots in Lyndoch, Tanunda, Angaston, and Bethany. A few years earlier, the same region had been explored by Silesian mineralogist Johannes Menge, who passed the word that the area, similar to parts of Poland, was a grape-grower's heaven. By the late 1840s the new settlers had planted their vines and were soon turning out vintages ambrosial enough to knock their lederhosen off. At the same time they constructed beautiful stone churches, cottages, and town buildings, which you'll see on your tour of the valley.

The actual name "Barossa" came from German Colonel Light, back in 1837. Twenty-five years earlier he had squared off in a battle at Barrosa, Spain, under the command of Lord Lynedoch. Feeling nostalgic because of the similar-looking terrain, Light named the Barossa "Barrosa" and the town of Lyndoch "Lynedoch."

Springton

You've heard of the old woman who lived in a shoe? Well, pioneer settlers Caroline and Friedrich Herbig lived inside a gigantic hollow gum tree 1855-60. Caroline even bore two of their children there. The **Herbig Gum Tree** is just before Hamiltons Road.

Springton Gallery, Miller St. (tel. 08-8568-2001), has a selection of Australian and international crafts. The gallery, formerly the old settlers store and post office, is open daily except Tuesday 11 a.m.-5 p.m.

For winetastings, check out: **Craneford Wines,** Main St. (tel. 08-8568-2220); **Karl Seppelts Grand Cru Estate,** Ross Dewells Rd. (tel. 08-8568-2374); and **Robert Hamilton Winery,** Hamiltons Rd. (tel. 08-8568-2264). All are open daily.

eyneton

his tiny village was once called "North Rhine" because of its resemblance to the settlers' home-nd. **Henschke Wines** (tel. 08-8564-8223), es-blished 1868, is a small fifth-generation family-n winery with some of the oldest shiraz vines in e region. Specialties are premium red and white ble wines. Hours are Mon.-Fri. 9 a.m.-4:30 m., Saturday 9 a.m.-noon.

ngaston

amed for George Fife Angas, landholder and fi-ncial backer for the *Zebra* voyage, who settled ar the town (pop. 1,950) in 1851. Fife's son ilt **Collingrove Homestead** (tel. 08-8564-061), where family members lived until turn-g it over to the National Trust in 1976. It now rves as a museum for Angas memorabilia, a staurant, and elegant country accommoda-n. Open daily 10 a.m.-5 p.m., closed Christ-as Day and Boxing Day.

Angaston Galleria, 18 Murray St. (tel. 08-564-2648), features local and imported arts d crafts inside a 125-year-old former church ilding. Open Tues.-Sun. and public holidays a.m.-5 p.m.

See how fruits are dried and then buy them -site at **Angas Park Dried Fruit Centre,** 3 rray St. (tel. 08-8564-2052). Open Mon.-Sat. a.m.-5 p.m., Sunday and public holidays 11 m.-5 p.m., closed Christmas Day and Good iday.

Yalumba Winery, Eden Valley Rd. (tel. 08-61-3200), established 1849, is built of An-ston marble and topped with a clock tower. ecialties are premium red and white table nes and champagnes. Open Mon.-Fri. 8:30 m.-5 p.m., Saturday and holidays 10 a.m.-5 m., Sunday noon-5 p.m.

Saltram Winery, Nuriootpa-Angaston Rd. l. 08-8563-8290), founded in 1859, is anoth-old-timer in the Barossa, featuring red and ite table wines and ports. Hours are Mon.-. 9 a.m.-5 p.m., Sat.-Sun. noon-5 p.m., holi-ys 10 a.m.-5 p.m.

uriootpa

ce upon a time this town was an important original bartering center (Nuriootpa trans-es to "A Meeting Place"). After William ulthard, a pioneer settler, laid out his acre in

1854, the town grew around his red-gum-slab hotel. Today, Nuriootpa (pop. 3,200), at the northern end of the Barossa Valley, is the district's commercial heart, with a wide range of facilities, services, and government agencies. Coulthard's hotel is gone, but his home has been preserved and serves as the main information center for the Barossa Valley. Aside from the many clusters of wineries, Nuriootpa has some lovely parks and picnic grounds banking the North Para River, which meanders through town.

Buildings to take note of along Light Pass Rd. are **Immanuel Lutheran Church** (1886), **Luhr's Pioneer German Cottage** (1841), and **Strait Gate Lutheran Church** (1861).

Penfolds Winery, Tanunda Rd. (tel. 08-8562-0389), established in 1812, is a huge commercial complex (particularly after merging with Kaiser Stuhl) specializing in a full range of red and white table wines and fortified wines. This property can store more than 22 million liters of wine! Hours are Mon.-Fri. 9 a.m.-5 p.m., Saturday and holidays 10 a.m.-5 p.m., Sunday 1-5 p.m. Admission is $4.

Elderton Wines, 3 Tanunda Rd. (tel. 08-8562-1058), established 1906, has red and white table wines, sparkling wines, *and* bicycles and mokes for hire. Hours are Mon.-Fri. 8:30 a.m.-5 p.m., Sat.-Sun. 11 a.m.-4:30 p.m.

Wolf Blass Wines (tel. 08-8562-1955), along the Sturt Highway, was only established in 1973, yet practically started out winning Australia's most coveted red-wine prize three years in a row. Specialties are premium red and white table wines and champagne. Hours are Mon.-Fri. 9:15 a.m.-4:30 p.m., Sat.-Sun. and holidays 10 a.m.-4:30 p.m.

Bored with wine? Check out **Tarac Distillers,** Tanunda Rd. (tel. 08-8562-1522), for brandy, rum, gin, bourbon, vodka, whiskey, and tequila. Hours are Mon.-Fri. 8:30 a.m.-4:30 p.m.

Marananga

Gnadenfrei ("Freed by the Grace of God") was the original name given to this little town by its settlers in the 1840s. In 1918, when Germanic names were being changed, it was christened Marananga, Aboriginal for "My Hands."

It's worth making the turn off the main road to see the old schoolhouse, cottages, and splendid

BAROSSA VALLEY

TO RENMARK

TO KEYNETON

KEYNETON RD

ANGASTON RD

KENTON RD

EDEN VALLEY

TO MURRAY BRIDGE

SPRINGTON

HERBIG GUM TREE

KAISERSTUHL
CONSERVATION PARK

HAMILTONS RD

MIRRA WIRRA RD

PENRICE RD

PENRICE

ANGASTON

LIGHT PASS RD

LIGHT PASS RD

COLLINGROVE
HOMESTEAD

VINE VALE RD

MENGLER HILL

SCENIC DR

BETHANY

BAROSSA
NURIOOTPA

TOURIST
INFORMATION
CENTRE

BIEGERSDORF RD

KEV ROHRLACH
COLLECTION

BUNKHAUS
BAROSSA

TANUNDA

MARANANGA

SEPPELTSFIELD

SEPPELTSFIELD
RD

BAROSSA
VALLEY WAY

ROWLAND FLAT

LYNDOCH

SANDY CREEK
CONSERVATION PARK

COCKATOO
VALLEY

SANDY
CREEK

GAWLER

ROSEDALE

NORTH PARA RIVER

STURT HWY

RAILWAY LINE

MAIN NORTH RD

TO THE
MID-NORTH

BAROSSA VALLEY HWY

TO ADELAIDE

ELIZABETH

0   5 km

= WINERY

GREENOCK

14

27

36

35

34

10

30

11

23

29

9

6

8

16

13

2

3

31

32

15

28

24

25

7

19

4

22

26

21

12

17

18

5

33

20

1

1. Barossa Settlers
2. Basedow Wines
3. BernKastel Wines
4. Bethany Wines
5. Burge Family Winemakers
6. Charles Cimicky Wines
7. Charles Melton Wines
8. Chateau Dorien Wines
9. Chateau Yaldara Estate
10. Elderton Wines
11. Gnadenfrei Estate
12. Grant Burge Wines
13. Hardy's Siegersdorf
14. Henschke Wines
15. Heritage Wines
16. High Wycombe Wines
17. Kellermeister Wines
18. Kies Estate Cellars
19. Krondorf Wines
20. Leo Buring Wines
21. Linder McLean Vineyards
    (St. Hallet Wines)
22. Orlando Winery
23. P;enfolds Winery
24. Peter Lehmann Wines
25. Rockford Wines
26. Rovalley Estate
27. Saltram Winery
28. Seppeltsfield Winery
29. Tarac Distillers
30. Tarchalice Wine Co.
31. Tolle Pedare Winery
32. Veritas Winery
33. Wards Gateway Cellar
34. Willows Vineyard
35. Wolf Blass Wines
36. Yalumba Winery

Seppelt, who started off as a tobacco farmer, discovered that his crop was too rank for sale. He experimented with winemaking, and the rest, as they say, is history. And history, as reported in the 1892 *London Gazette,* called Seppelt's cellars and stores "the most modern in the world." Those "modern" buildings have been carefully preserved and make for an interesting tour between sips of red and white table wines, fortified wines, and champagnes. Hours are Mon.-Fri. 9 a.m.-5 p.m., Saturday 10:30 a.m.-4:30 p.m., Sunday 11 a.m.-4 p.m. For information, phone (08) 8562-8028.

Barossa Valley Way

It only takes about five minutes to get from Nuriootpa to Tanunda along this stretch of road, but you'll probably get hung up for hours if you stop at the **Kev Rohrlach Collection** (tel. 08-8563-3407), a private museum of science, transport, and technology. More than 3,000 mechanical exhibits collected by Mr. Rohrlach (a builder) from all over South Australia will amaze, amuse, confound, and confuse you. The transport collection alone includes a maharaja's barouche and the 1955 Australian Grand Prix-winning car. Don't miss it! Hours are daily 10 a.m.-5 p.m. Admission charge is $5.

Tanunda

Established in 1843, Tanunda (pop. 2,860) was the second German settlement in the valley. Many of the traditional early stone buildings line the main avenue, as well as **Langmeil Road,** one of the backstreets. **Goat Square,** site of the first town market, is bordered by original cottages, preserved and classified by the National Trust.

Tanunda is home to four of the valley's most exquisite Lutheran churches: **Langmeil Church,** on the main drag, has Pastor Kavel's remains buried in the adjacent cemetery; **St. John's,** Jane St., is home to life-size wooden statues of Jesus, Moses, and selected apostles; **Tabor Lutheran Church,** north end of Murray St., is notable for its orb-topped spire; **St. Paul's,** corner Murray St. and Basedow Rd., features fine stained glass.

Brauer Biotherapies, 1 Para Rd. (tel. 08-8563-2932), welcomes visitors to its laboratories where homeopathic medicines are concocted.

Gnadenfrei Church, begun in 1857, with additions in 1873 and 1913.

Heritage Wines (tel. 08-8562-2880) is small and new-ish (established 1984), with interesting dry red and white table wines. Hours are daily 11 a.m.-5 p.m.

Seppeltsfield

Take the out-of-place-looking, date-palm-fringed road from Marananga to Seppeltsfield, founded by Silesian migrant Joseph Seppelt in 1851.

Hours are Mon.-Fri. 8:30 a.m.-4 p.m., with guided tours at 2 p.m.

Rather watch performing dogs? You can applaud (or cry over) 25 trained canines at **Norm's Coolie Sheep Dog Performance,** Gomersal Rd. (tel. 08-8563-2198). Show times are Monday, Wednesday, and Saturday 2 p.m. Admission is $6.

The numerous wineries in this area should obliterate both homeopathic remedies and bad dog memories.

Bethany

Bethany was the first German settlement in the Barossa, founded in 1842 by a group of Silesian families. This peaceful, pretty village is still home to old stone houses, cottage gardens, and farmlets, as well as Australia's smallest hotel. The old village common has been transformed into **Bethany Reserve,** a haven for picnickers along bubbling Bethany Creek. The church bells still ring at dusk on Saturday to signal the end of the work week in case anyone forgets. The **Landhaus,** on Bethany Rd. near the railway tracks, claims to be Australia's smallest licensed motel.

BOB RACE

Opposite Bethany Reserve, **Bethany Art Craft Gallery** (tel. 08-8563-2614) is an outlet f handmade textiles, pottery, glass, and woode wares. The gallery is open daily 10 a.m.-5 p.r

Rowland Flat

Commercial winemaking began at Jacobs Cree in 1847 when Johann Gramp planted his fir vines. Nowadays the **Orlando Winery,** whic dominates the town, pays its tribute by carryir an excellent claret with the Jacobs Creek labe The complex is enormous and pretty sterile, b it does offer a very good, educational $1 wine tour. If you visit February through April you'll g to view the grape-crushing process. Red ar white table wines and champagnes are the spe cialties. Hours are Mon.-Fri. 9:30 a.m.-5 p.m Sat.-Sun. and holidays 10 a.m.-4 p.m. For info mation, phone (08) 8521-3140.

Rockford Wines (tel. 08-8563-2720) is c Krondorf Rd., about three km from Rowlar Flat. If you've just been to Orlando, this tiny e tablishment, with its tasting room inside a form stable, may underwhelm you—but the spe tacular vintages won't. Specialties are tradition full-bodied Australian wine styles (premium r gional wines). Hours are daily 11 a.m.-5 p.m.

Lyndoch

Lyndoch (pop. 705), at the southern edge of th valley, was originally settled in 1839 as a farmir community; the first winery was installed in 185 in a converted flour mill. All of the 10 or so wine ies in this district are family-owned. The largest **Chateau Yaldara,** Gomersal Rd. (tel. 08-852 4200), established in 1947 on the remains that same converted flour mill. Besides red ar white table wines, sparkling wines, and port, th "chateau" displays a collection of porcelain ar antiques. Hours are daily 9 a.m.-5 p.m.

Along the Barossa Highway, the **South Au tralian Museum of Mechanical Music** (tel. 08 8524-4014) features antique music boxes, au tomatic accordions, barrel pianos, player o gans, an 1840s musical church, and singin birds. The museum is open daily 9 a.m.-5 p.m closed Christmas Day. Admission is $5.

Cockatoo Valley

Detouring off the Barossa Highway, you'll pas through this small village with a general store (f etrol and provisions), remnants ⁿ goldfields, and an 1870s ᵢiner's cottage (converted ᵢ accommodations). The ᵍ attraction, down the ᵊad, is Barossa Reser-ᵢir (built in 1898) and ᵴ famed **Whispering** **Vall,** a retaining wall ᵢith peculiar acoustics ᵢat enable you to stand ᵢ one side and hear whis-ᵊrs all the way from the ᵊpposite side of the dam.

ᵃwler

ᵃwler (pop. 15,000), founded in ᵌ39, was South Australia's second ᵊuntry town after Port Adelaide. Su-ᵊrb bluestone architecture, dating from ᵊ late 19th and early 20th centuries, is re-ᵊcted in the town hall, post office, and var-ᵢus churches. Other fine buildings are the **ᵢd Telegraph Station** (home of ᵊe National Trust), constructed of ᵊe Tree Hill sandstone, and ᵊmes and fences crafted from ᵊcal limestone.

ballooning over
Barossa Valley vineyards

PRACTICALITIES

ᵊccommodations

ⁿgaston: Barossa Brauhaus Hotel, 41 Mur-ᵃy St. (tel. 08-8564-2014), has both a cozy din-ᵍ room and a saloon bar. Rates are $20 pp in-ᵤding continental breakfast. Historic **Angaston** **ᵊtel,** 59 Murray St. (tel. 08-8564-2428), is ᵊown for the Bacchus mural in its lounge. Both ᵊtels are inexpensive. **Collingrove Home-ᵵead,** Eden Valley Rd. (tel. 08-8564-2061), is ᵊe Angas family ancestral home where guests ᵃn spend the night in converted servants' quar-ᵊrs. Prices are moderate and include conti-ᵊntal breakfast.

Nuriootpa: Barossa Gateway Motel, Kalimna ᵈ. (tel. 08-8562-1033), has plain, inexpensive ᵊoms, and a bed in the hostel section only costs ᵌ10. **Karawatha Guest House,** Greenock Rd. ᵊl. 08-8562-1746), is a much homier environ-ᵊent. Moderately priced rooms include break-

fast. The modern **Vine Inn Hotel/ Motel,** 14 Murray St. (tel. 08-8562-2133), is in the center of town. Rooms run moderate to high and include conti-nental breakfast.

Marananga: The **Hermi-tage of Marananga,** cor-ner Seppeltsfield and Stone-well Roads (tel. 08-8562-2722), features spacious suites overlooking the prop-erty's vineyards. Expensive rates include breakfast in the popular country restaurant.

Seppeltsfield: You have your choice between the comfy, modern, and moderately priced **Holiday Cabins,** Seppeltsfield Rd. (tel. 08-8562-8240), for $41-50 d, or the sumptuous **Lodge,** Main Rd. (tel. 08-8562-8277), where for about $210 you can live in the old Seppelt family digs. (A room with all meals will set you back $360!)

Barossa Way: Barossa Bunk-haus Travellers Cottage, Barossa Hwy. (tel. 08-8562-2260), is a friend-ly backpacker hostel with kitchen facilities, TV room, swimming pool, and bicycle rental. Dorm beds cost $11 per night, and a cot-tage with cooking facilities and fireplace is $30 for two. **Barossa Junction Resort,** Barossa Hwy. (tel. 08-8563-3400), offers motel-style ac-commodations inside converted railway cars, including lounge and dining carriages. Rates, with continental breakfast, are inexpensive to moderate. **Light Pass Farm House,** four km east of the post office (tel. 08-8562-1641), offers expensive cottage accommodations.

Tanunda: Tanunda Hotel, 51 Murray St. (tel. 08-8563-2030), with shared facilities, is inex-pensive and has a restaurant and swimming pool. **Weintal Hotel/Motel,** Murray St. (tel. 08-8563-2303), with bars, a bistro, restaurant, un-derground cellar, tennis courts, swimming pool, and sauna, is moderately priced. In the expen-sive range is rural **Lawley Farm,** Krondorf Rd. (tel. 08-8563-2141), where the farm cottage and barn have been converted into lovely country rooms. Rates include breakfast.

Bethany: The **Landhaus,** Bethany Rd. (tel. 08-8563-2191), may be Australia's smallest licensed motel, but the price is a big $100, including breakfast.

Lyndoch: About 20 km south of Lyndoch, **Kersbrook YHA Hostel,** Roachdale Farm (tel. 08-8389-3185), rents bunks for $7, but there is no public transport to the facility. If you're sharing, **Barossa Country Cottages,** 55 Gilbert St. (tel. 08-8524-4426), is in the moderate range for fully equipped cottage accommodations that include continental breakfast and a community spa. **Chateau Yaldara Estate,** Barossa Valley Hwy. (tel. 08-8524-4268), has a restaurant, swimming pool, and expensive rates.

Cockatoo Valley: The old 1870 **Miner's Cottage,** Goldfields Rd. (tel. 08-8524-6213), has private accommodations comprising a living room with open fireplace, bedroom, and bathroom. Rates are expensive and include continental breakfast.

Gawler: Prasad's Gawler Motel, 1 Main North Rd. (tel. 08-8522-5900), features good rooms, a swimming pool, spa, and sauna. Rates are moderate but double during festival season. **Gawler Arms Hotel,** 102 Murray St. (tel. 08-8522-1856), doesn't have all the fancy amenities, but the moderate prices are steady.

Camping

Barossa Valley Tourist Park, Penrice Rd., Nuriootpa (tel. 08-8562-1404), is a very large park with swimming pool, barbecue, playground, tennis courts, a recreation lake, and reserve. **Tanunda Caravan Park,** Barossa Valley Way, Tanunda (tel. 08-8563-2784), features full-service grass sites in a sheltered setting. **Barossa Caravan Park,** Barossa Valley Hwy., Lyndoch (tel. 08-8524-4262), is fairly plain, but near the Whispering Wall and other hot spots. **Hillier Park,** Hillier Rd., Gawler (tel. 08-8522-2511), has a quiet rural setting, with swimming pool, playground, sheltered picnic and barbecue areas.

Most of the caravan parks offer campsites, onsite vans, and cabins.

Food

You mean you want something besides bread and cheese? You'll easily find tearooms, coffee shops, pub meals, bakeries, and takeaways, as well as some gourmet restaurants with food to match the local wines.

Angaston: Angas Park Dried Fruit Centre, 3 Murray St. (tel. 08-8564-2052), has a wide selection of dried fruit and nuts for your picnic basket. The **Angaston Hotel,** 59 Murray St. (tel. 08-8564-2428), is a favorite for counter meals as well as more expensive a la carte dining. **Barossa Bistro,** 37 Murray St. (tel. 08-8564-2361), is a best bet for upmarket bush tucker. **The Vintners Restaurant,** corner Nuriootpa and Stockwell Roads (tel. 08-8564-2488), is another expensive choice, popular with winemakers so you can be sure of a good menu and exceptional wine list.

Nuriootpa: Family-owned **Linke's Bakery**, 40 Murray St. (tel. 08-8562-1129), has been turning out cakes and breads for more than 5 years. The tearooms serve sandwiches and other lunch items. The dining room at the **Vine Inn Hotel/Motel,** 14 Murray St. (tel. 08-8562-2133), serves standard bistro fare as well as cheap counter meals. Big splurgers hunting interesting game dishes should book at **The Pheasant Farm,** Samuel Rd., off Seppeltsfield Rd. (tel. 08-8562-1286), where menu choices include glazed kangaroo, rabbit-stuffed sausage and, naturally, pheasant. The restaurant is closed during February.

Marananga: Marananga Restaurant, Seppeltsfield Rd. (tel. 08-8562-2888), serves large portions of simple food inside a one-room rustic stone cottage with open beams and a fireplace. Prices are middle-of-the-road.

Tanunda: Stock up on delicious bakery items any day but Sunday at **Apex Bakery,** Elizabeth St. (tel. 08-8563-2483). **Zinfandel Tearooms**, 58 Murray St. (tel. 08-8563-2822), features inexpensive light lunches and cakes. Moderately priced German cuisine is the specialty at **Die Gallerie,** 66 Murray St. (tel. 08-8563-2788), where you eat in the courtyard when it's warm or next to the open fire when it's cold. **Tanunda Hotel,** 51 Murray St. (tel. 08-8563-2030), serves hearty counter meals at reasonable prices. The stylish **1918 Bistro and Grill,** 94 Murray St. (tel. 08-8563-0405), housed in a villa, is known for its regional cuisine and superb wines.

Lyndoch: Get your counter meals at **Lyndoch Hotel,** Gilbert St. (tel. 08-8524-4211). **Lyndoch Bakery,** on Barossa Valley Hwy., offers terrific baked goodies, plus good, moderately priced meals in the adjoining restaurant.

Events

With all that wine around, you can well imagine that denizens of the Barossa Valley are ready to party at the drop of a grape. The big event, of course, is the **Barossa Valley Vintage Festival,** held over Easter week in odd-numbered years. Activities and amusements that fill the valley include grape-picking and -crushing contests, brass bands, maypole dancing, tug-o'-wars, gourmet dinners, arts and crafts exhibitions, and winetastings up the shiraz. For information, phone (08) 8562-1866.

Some other prominent annual events include January's **Oom Pah Festival** in Tanunda (tel. 08-8565-2674), the March **Essenfest** in Tanunda (tel. 08-8563-2211), **Seppeltsfield Balloon Regatta** in May (tel. 08-8389-3195), and **Barossa Classic Gourmet Weekend** also in May (tel. 08-8562-1866). Needless to say all of these events feature a lot of food and grog!

Transportation, Services, and Information

If you're driving, the scenic route can be reached via Chain of Ponds, through Birdwood, to Springton. The direct route is straight up Main North Rd. from Adelaide, through Elizabeth, to Gawler.

Barossa Adelaide Passenger Service (tel. 08-8564-3022) leaves Adelaide's central bus station for Lyndoch, Tanunda, Nuriootpa, and Angaston. Service runs four times Mon.-Fri.,

one time only on Saturday. The fare is about $6 one-way.

Rent bicycles by the day or the hour from the **Bunkhaus,** corner Barossa Valley Hwy. and Nuraip Rd., Nuriootpa (tel. 08-8562-2260); **Elderton Winery,** Nuriootpa (tel. 08-8562-1058); or **Keil's Gift Centre,** 63 Murray St., Tanunda (tel. 08-8563-2177).

Cars can be rented from **BP Service Station,** 8 Murray St., Nuriootpa (tel. 08-8562-3022), or Elderton Winery. Rent mopeds at **Caltex Service Station,** Murray St., Tanunda (tel. 08-8563-2677). Elderton Winery also rents mini-mokes.

Barossa Wine and Tourism Association, 66 Murray St. (inside Coulthard House), Nuriootpa (tel. 08-8562-1866), is the regional information hub for the entire Barossa Valley. You can pick up maps to the vineyards, inquire about guided tours, etc., Mon.-Fri. 8:30 a.m.-5 p.m., Sat.-Sun. and holidays 9:30 a.m.-1:30 p.m. The **Gawler Tourist Association,** Murray St. (tel. 08-8522-6814), is open daily 10 a.m.-4 p.m. (Heritage bus tours of Gawler leave from the tourist office at 10 a.m. every Tuesday.)

For police, medical, and fire **emergencies,** dial 000. **Hospitals** are located at Angaston (tel. 08-8564-2065), Tanunda (tel. 08-8563-2398), and Gawler (tel. 08-8522-1677). **Police stations** are at 61 Murray St., Nuriootpa (tel. 08-8562-1111), and 23 Cowan St., Gawler (tel. 08-8522-1088).

FLEURIEU PENINSULA

The Fleurieu bills itself "South Australia's Holiday Playground." Like the Adelaide Hills and the Barossa Valley, the Fleurieu is easy day-tripping distance south of the city center. Aside from rolling hills, clustered vineyards, and pastoral farmlands, there are beaches—lots of beaches—from the Gulf St. Vincent, around Cape Jervis, along the pounding Southern Ocean, to Encounter Bay and the mouth of the Murray River—beaches to surf at, fish from, swim off, jog along, glide above, sail aside, and sun worship on.

Bushwalkers and nature lovers can explore more than 20 coastal, wetland, and woodland parks inhabited by native birds and animals. Hiking trails are plentiful, particularly within Deep Creek Conservation Park between Cape Jervis and Victor Harbor, where you super-adventurous hikers can hit the Heysen Trail and follow it all the way to the Flinders Ranges. Cape Jervis is also the jumping-off spot for Kangaroo Island, or you can island-hop to Granite Island off Victor Harbor for a glimpse of the fairy penguins, or to Hindmarsh Island, off Goolwa, to boat, fish, or waterski.

Less-sporty travelers will enjoy tasting and tippling at the Wine Coast vineyards (especially noteworthy for reds), admiring early buildings, browsing the many antique shops and crafts cottages, holing up in a secluded cove, or maybe taking the plunge at clothing-optional Maslin Beach.

On 1 February 1997 all telephone numbers with the area code (085) will change. In preparation for this, all (085) numbers in this section have been changed to eight-digit numbers; the first two digits are 85. To dial a number before 1 February, simply delete the first two digits of the new number and, if dialing from outside the area, add the area code (085). For example, (08) 8512-3456 would be (085) 12-3456. After 1 February the area code for all numbers in this section will be (08). **Note:** Numbers in this section with area codes other than (085) have already changed.

History

All the big-name explorers—Sturt, Light, Barker—traversed the Fleurieu, but it was French explorer Nicholas Baudin who, in 1802, named the area for Napoleon's Minister of the Navy Charles Pierre Claret Comte de Fleurieu. In the same year, Baudin "encountered" rival Matthew Flinders at a site that was appropriately named Encounter Bay—the Encounter Coast becoming a natural tangent thereof. Interestingly, neither Baudin nor Flinders spotted the sand-covered mouth of the Murray, Australia's largest river a stone's throw away.

It was at Encounter Bay, in 1837, that South Australia's first whaling station (and first successful industry) was created.

THE WINE COAST

About 20 km south of Adelaide, the Wine Coast stretches from old Reynella, home of Cellar Number One, to Old Willunga, with its own share of historic buildings.

Most of the Fleurieu wineries sprouted in the 1850s when individual farmers harvested small vineyards for their personal use. It was Thomas Hardy who, in 1876, put the area on the map with his purchase of Tintara Vineyards (which subsequently evolved into a dynasty) in McLaren Vale. In the early 1900s, after the all-important London market accepted the Australian wines into their cellars and down their gullets, the local vintners began growing vines with a more serious bent. In 1973, the first annual bushing festival, celebrating the release of the year's vintage, furthered the Wine Coast's popularity. Today the district comprises more than 40 (mostly family-owned) wineries.

Reynella

Old Reynella, at the turnoff from Main South Rd., marks the start of the Wine Drive.

This is the town where John Reynell, South Australia's first commercial winegrower, planted his vines in 1839 and created Cellar Number One (also known as the Old Cave Cellar). See

THE FLEURIEU PENINSULA

MURRAYLANDS

MURRAY RIVER

TAILEM BEND

WELLINGTON

TO MELBOURNE

LAKE ALBERT

LAKE ALEXANDRINA

THE COORONG

MILANG

HINDMARSH ISLAND

MURRAY MOUTH

GOOLWA

SIR RICHARD PENINSULA

VICTOR HARBOR

GRANITE ISLAND

ROSETTA HEAD

ENCOUNTER BAY

NEWLAND C.P.

NEWLAND HEAD

SOUTHERN OCEAN

TO ADELAIDE AND THE HILLS

MT. BARKER

STRATHALBYN

TO ADELAIDE AND THE MID-NORTH

REYNELLA

MORPHETT VALE RD.

ONKAPARINGA RIVER

HACKHAM

OLD NOARLUNGA

MCLAREN VALE

WILLUNGA

KYEEMA C.P.

MT. MAGNIFICENT C.P.

COX SCRUB C.P.

SCOTT C.P.

CURRENCY CREEK

CROWS NEST LOOKOUT

MIDDLETON

PORT ELLIOT

MAIN SOUTH RD.

TO GLENELG

MOANA

PORT NOARLUNGA

MASLIN BEACH

ALDINGA BEACH

SILVER SANDS

SELLICKS BEACH

ALDINGA BAY

O'SULLIVAN BEACH

CHRISTIES BEACH

YUNDI

VICTOR HARBOR RD.

MT. COMPASS

HINDMARSH VALLEY

SPRING MOUNT

INMAN RIVER

WATTLE FLAT

MYPONGA RESERVOIR

MYPONGA

MYPONGA C.P.

MYPONGA BEACH

NORMANVILLE

CARRICKALINGA

YANKALILLA BAY

LADY BAY

RIVER BUNGALA

PARAWA

TUNKALILLA BEACH

PARSONS BEACH

WATIPINGA BEACH

ENCOUNTER BAY

SECOND VALLEY

RAPID BAY

RAPID HEAD

RAPID BAY

DELAMERE

SILVERTON

CAPE JERVIS

MORGANS BEACH

TALISKER C.P.

DEEP CREEK C.P.

TO KANGAROO ISLAND

BACKSTAIRS PASSAGE

GULF ST. VINCENT

FLEURIEU PENINSULA

0   10 km

TO 1

Reynell's original cellar and his home, Chateau Reynell, on the grounds of **Hardy's Reynella Winery,** Reynell Rd. (tel. 08-8381-2266). The winery, established in 1853, is open daily 10 a.m.-4:30 p.m., except Christmas Day and Good Friday.

Reynella's first school, erected in 1858 and since renovated, is on Peach Street.

Morphett Vale

South Australia's first Roman Catholic church, St. Mary's, was built here in 1846. To view other historic buildings, turn off of Main South Rd., at the Noarlunga turnoff, for **Pioneer Village** at Hackham, where they've built a rather hokey re-creation of other old structures, furnished in period style. Hours are Wed.-Sun. 10 a.m.-5 p.m., including public holidays. Admission is $3.

Lakeside Leisure Park, Main South and Brodie Roads, is a 14-hectare hillside park with two lakes, a 700-meter toboggan track, a water slide, horse riding, and—in mini form—railways, miniature golf, and dune buggy rides. Admission is free. Hours are daily 10 a.m.-dusk. For information, phone (08) 8326-0200.

Onkaparinga River Recreation Park, Piggott Range Rd. (tel. 08-8278-5477), is open daily for birdwatching, gum-viewing, and bushwalking (check in with rangers first—some trails are very steep, and flash floods are another potential hazard).

Eat a pork pie, plum pudding, or traditional plowman's lunch at **James Craig Inn,** Main South Rd., Hackham (tel. 08-8384-6944).

Old Noarlunga

This was the oldest concentrated settlement in the southern part of the state. Some of the heritage buildings that remain are **Horseshoe Hotel** (1840), the **market square** (1841), **Horseshoe Mill** (1844), **Church of St. Philip and St. James** (1850), and **Jolly Miller Hotel** (1850).

McLaren Vale

Explore the many surrounding wineries, but pay a special visit to **Hardy's Wines,** Main Rd. (tel. 08-8323-9185), whose purchase by Thomas Hardy in 1876 changed the course of Wine Coast winemaking. (Author's favorite is Hardy's black-bottle-pot-still brandy.) Hardy's is open daily 10 a.m.-4:30 p.m.

Chapel Hill Cellars, Chapel Hill Rd. (tel. 08-8323-8429), formerly the Sir Samuel Way church and school, has a superb stained-glass window, plus excellent dry red and white wines and ports. Hours are daily 11 a.m.-5 p.m.

Luong Rice Winery, Park St. (tel. 08-8323-8156), is Australia's first Chinese rice-winery. **Maxwell Wines,** 26 Kangarilla Rd. (tel. 08-8323-8200), produces both wine and mead (or honey wine). Both wineries are open daily 10 a.m.-5 p.m.

The **World Thru Dolls,** Chalk Hill Rd. (tel. 08-8323-8624), displays antique dolls, portrait figures, nursery rhymes, fairy tales, Bible stories and other toys and dollies. Open Wed.-Fri. 1-4 p.m., Saturday, Sunday, and holidays 1-5 p.m. Admission is $2.50.

You'll need an appointment to visit **Camelot Carriage Complex,** 8 Pethick Rd. (tel. 08-8323-8225), where 40-or-so horse-drawn carriages and related memorabilia (like harnesses and whips) are displayed on a rural property. Admission is $2.50.

Moderately priced **McLaren Vale Motel,** Caffrey St. (tel. 08-8323-8365), has a swimming pool and spa. Bed and breakfasts in the moderate-expensive range include: **McLaren Vale,** 56 Valley View Dr. (tel. 08-8323-9351); **Southern Vales,** 13 Chalk Hill Rd. (tel. 08-8323-8144) and **Samarkand,** Branson Rd. (tel. 08-8323-8756).

Lakeside Caravan Park, Field St. (tel. 08-8323-9255), provides campsites, on-site vans and several cabins.

Quite a few wineries have picnic and barbecue areas, as well as restaurants that feature a winetaster's lunch. **James Haselgrove Wines,** Foggo Rd. (tel. 08-8323-8706), has good meals as does **Oliverhill Wines,** Seaview Rd. (tel. 08-8323-8922), with an Italian winemaker and homemade pasta.

McLaren Vale Bushing Festival (tel. 08-8323-8999), celebrating the release of a new vintage, occurs over several days in October. Activities include tastings, tours, a ball, fairs, toasting and crowning of the Bushing King and Queen, and an Elizabethan feast.

For help, call 000, or **McLaren Vale Hospital** (tel. 08-8323-8606), **police** (tel. 08-8323-8330) or **fire brigade** (tel. 08-8323-8393).

Willunga

Willunga, derived from Willa-unga, Aboriginal for "Place of the Green Trees," was first laid out in 1839. These days the town is one of Ausalia's most important almond-growing regions, with 4,500 acres planted. Several old bluestone buildings preserved by the National Trust include the courthouse and police station, dating from 1855. Many of the roof slates have been quarried locally.

View approximately 1,000 different rose varieties (when in season), all clearly labeled, at the Rose Display Garden, St. Andrews Terrace (tel. 08-8556-2555). Hours are daily during daylight, and tours can be arranged.

If you'd rather smell the horses than the roses, make an appointment to see Arab, Pinto, and Clydesdales at Rondoro Clydesdale Stud, Yundi Rd., Yundi (tel. 08-8556-0234).

Vanessa's Restaurant Motel, 27 High St. (tel. 08-8556-2379), has moderately priced rooms with continental breakfast included. The restaurant is on the expensive side. Willunga House, 1 St. Peters Terrace (tel. 08-8556-2467), offers B&B accommodations (some with fireplaces) in the upper-moderate category.

Rosella Café, Upper High St. (tel. 08-8556-2258), serves light lunches and homemade European cakes. The Salopain Inn, on Old Willunga Rd. before town (tel. 08-8323-8769), features daily lunch in a restored 1861 hotel.

In late July, Willunga celebrates the start of spring with an Almond Blossom Festival.

Conservation Parks

South of Willunga, take the Hope Forest turnoff to Kyeema Conservation Park, which has an active bird population and walking trails, including a special trail that explores park animals' homes.

Also southeast of Willunga, the Yundi turnoff will lead you to Mt. Magnificent Conservation Park, where a portion of the Heysen Trail makes a steep ascent to the top of the mount.

GULF ST. VINCENT BEACHES

Heading south of Adelaide, past Hallet Cove, the first beach you come to is O'Sullivan's, with its breakwater-protected swimming and boating facilities. Next is Christies Beach, a popular family resort with safe swimming, sailing, and reef fishing. Port Noarlunga, circled by steep cliffs and sandhills, features a lovely reef (at low tide), fishing jetty, and the Onkaparinga River Recreation Park, a natural aquatic reserve with many types of waterbirds.

A favorite with surfers is Moana, where you can drive (cautiously!) onto the beach. Moana Beach Tourist Park, on the Esplanade (tel. 08-8327-0677), has on-site vans and campsites. The park has a boat ramp, tennis courts, gymnasium, sauna, and spa.

Maslin Beach, South Australia's first legal nude beach, is exceptionally popular for its, er, scenery and bodysurfing. Be aware that only the 1.5-km southern strip of the beach is clothing-optional (trust me). Maslin Beach Caravan and Camping Ground, 2 Tuit Rd. (tel. 08-8556-6113), rents campsites and on-site vans. Features include swimming pool, tennis court, coin-operated barbecue, and laundry facilities.

Port Willunga is a historic spot with offshore reefs, occasional good surf, scuba diving to the shipwrecked Star of Greece, swimming, and sandy beaches.

Aldinga Beach also has good scuba diving, swimming, and sometimes surfing. Remnant plains scrub, wildflowers, and birdlife are features of Aldinga Scrub Conservation Park, off Cox Road. Walk through the scrub to the beach at Aldinga Holiday Park, Cox Rd. (tel. 08-8556-3444). On-site vans and campsites are available, and there are also five yurtlike cottages and a swimming pool.

There's good fishing from offshore boats at Silver Sands, swimming at Sellicks Beach, and decent surf at sheltered Myponga Beach. Three conservation parks near the town of Myponga are Myponga, nine km southwest, Spring Mount, 13 km southeast, and Nixon-Skinner, behind Myponga Reservoir.

Be careful of the rips at Carrickalinga. A better choice is Normanville, where there's excellent swimming, both jetty and boat fishing, snorkeling on the offshore reef, and paraflying during the summer. A river runs through the Normanville Beach Caravan Park, Jetty Rd. (tel. 08-8558-2038). Rent an on-site van or campsite there, or at Beachside Caravan Park, Willis Dr. (tel. 08-8558-2458).

High Country Trails, Willis Dr., Normanville (tel. 08-8558-2507), organizes horseback rides, from an hour's trot along the beach to three-day pack trips, for learners or experienced riders.

The beaches get pretty rocky from here on out. Try **Lady Bay** for snorkeling, **Second Valley** for boat and jetty fishing, and **Rapid Bay** for excellent scuba diving. (Colonel Light first landed in Rapid Bay.) In Second Valley, **Leonard's Mill** (tel. 08-8598-4184), a restored 1849 stone mill, is open daily for a la carte meals, light snacks, and drinks at indoor or outdoor courtyard bars.

The tiny town of **Delamere,** inland along Main South Rd., has a number of historical buildings including the Uniting Church (1858), rural school (1861), St. James Church (1871), and council offices (1878).

CAPE JERVIS TO VICTOR HARBOR

Rounding the cape, the coast becomes more rugged as the waves of the Southern Ocean pound the shores and branch roads lead through weathered terrain to isolated and occasionally ferocious beaches below.

At the tip of the peninsula, **Cape Jervis** is both the jumping-off point to Kangaroo Island, 13 km across the Backstairs Passage, and the Heysen Trail, which passes through many different conservation parks on its faraway way to the Flinders Ranges. The coastal waters are noted for jetty and deep-sea fishing as well as scuba diving, and the tall cliffs and powerful breezes make it an ideal base for hang gliding. The **Cape Jervis Lighthouse** was in operation from 1871 to 1972. **Old Cape Jervis Station Homestead,** Main Rd. 9 (tel. 08-8598-0233), offers inexpensive B&B accommodations, cheap bunkhouse beds, and a tennis court. **Cape Jervis Tavern Motel,** Main Rd. (tel. 08-8598-0276), has moderate rates that include continental breakfast.

Back on Range Rd., turn into **Talisker Conservation Park,** where you can fossick about the 1862 silver and lead mine. You'll pass through the old mining town of **Silverton** on your way to the park. **Warning:** Watch out for those mine shafts!

Deep Creek Conservation Park is nothing short of spectacular—rugged cliffs form sheer

drops downward to the raging sea, profusions delicate orchids and luxuriant ferns tangle alor cool running streams, native birds and wildlif sweep from steep terrain to secluded cove Accessed from Range Rd., Deep Creek offers number of exciting trails for hikers—everythir from casual strolls to challenging bushwalks. is essential that you check in at park headqua ters before embarking on any of the walks, pa ticularly the strenuous, long-distance Heyse Trail, which is closed outside the conservatio parks in summer. You can also pick up tra maps, camping permits, and other detailed ir formation from the park headquarters, or phon (08) 8552-3677.

Due to powerful rips and changing current only very experienced surfers and strong swim mers should tempt their fate at isolated **Pai sons** and **Waitpinga** Beaches, both part c **Newland Head Conservation Park,** reache from Range Road. The park also has walkin trails and camping facilities. **Rosetta Harbo** on the northern side of the Bluff in Encounte Bay, has good snorkeling and scuba diving.

VICTOR HARBOR

Situated on the shores of Encounter Bay, Victo Harbor (pop. 5,300) is the largest town on th Fleurieu Peninsula. Being a close 83 km from Adelaide makes it exceptionally popular wit city folk who invade the town during summe and school holidays. Two unique natural for mations are the Bluff, a 100-meter-high head land, and—protecting the bay from the Souther Ocean's wild surf—Granite Island, connectee by causeway to the shore.

History

Victor Harbor's whaling stations bustled with activity from 1837 (when the first station wa established) until 1869, attracting both smal and large vessels to its port, making it one of the state's most important export terminals. As suming that Victor Harbor would not only be come *the* river port, but possibly the state capi tal, a railway was built in 1864, linking the towr to Goolwa, at the mouth of the Murray River Unfortunately, big ship owners, scared off by the Southern Ocean's erratic and stormy seas earched for safer spots to drop anchor, and he port soon became obsolete.

ights

he **Museum of Historical Art,** Yankalilla Rd., ree km from Victor Harbor (tel. 08-8552-1546), as a large private collection of shells, rocks, oins, medals, firearms, and miniature cars. pen Sundays and school holidays 1-5 p.m. dmission is $2.

Historic buildings include the **Railway Station, Telegraph Station** (1867), **Newland Memorial Congregational Church** on Victoria St. (1869), and **St. Augustine's Church of England** on Burke St. (1869). The **Victor Harbor Tourist Information Centre,** located in the riginal primary school on Torrens St., will provide maps and direct you.

If you climb to the top of the rather steep **Bluff,** ou'll get a stupendous view of the bay where audin and Flinders had their famous meeting in 802, and below to Rosetta Bay and Whale Haven, where the whaling stations operated.

Ride to **Granite Island** on Australia's only orse-drawn tram. Gentle giant Clydesdales ommute from Victor Harbor to the island daily 0 a.m.-4 p.m. Fare is $2 one-way. Buy tickets t the causeway on the Victor Harbor foreshore. During South Australian school holidays and ood-weather weekends, chairlifts operate to he top of the peak for expansive views of the own and bay. Summertime visitors to the island might spy fairy penguins as they waddle toward their rocky homes each night after dusk.

Urimbirra Wildlife Park, Adelaide Rd., five km from Victor Harbor (tel. 08-8554-6554), is a 6-hectare open-range park with dingoes, crocs there's one named Aunty Jack), koalas, kangaroos, bats, wombats, bettongs, bandicoots, snakes, eels, and a nocturnal house. Hours are daily 10 a.m.-5 p.m. Admission is $6.

Opposite Urimbirra, the one-hectare **Nagawooka Flora Reserve** is planted with almost 1,000 named trees, shrubs, and groundcovers rom all over Australia. The park is open daily during daylight hours.

Safe swimming beaches are on either side of he causeway to Granite Island, along with good snorkeling at **Oliver's Reef** and bodysurfing at **Chiton Rocks,** between Victor Harbor and Port Elliot.

Accommodations

You have a choice of simple guesthouses, motel rooms, or fully equipped holiday flats. Check with the tourist office for long-term selections. If you're visiting during peak periods, book far in advance, and expect rates to increase (and often double).

Anchorage Guest House, 21 Flinders Parade (tel. 08-8552-5970), is a nearly century-old traditional establishment, set right on the sea with terrific views. Inexpensive rates include breakfast. Both the **Grosvenor Hotel,** Ocean St. (tel. 08-8552-1011), and **The Clifton,** 39 Torrens St. (tel. 08-8552-1062), have inexpensive to low-moderate rooms. **Villa Victor,** 59 Victoria St. (tel. 08-8552-4258), charges $45 single, including full breakfast. More luxurious (and expensive) is centrally located **Apollon Motor Inn,** 15 Torrens St. (tel. 08-8552-2777). **Kerjancia Motor Lodge,** 141 Hindmarsh Rd. (tel. 08-8552-2900), also expensive, offers self-contained apartments with a solar pool and spa.

Victor Harbor Holiday Centre, Bay Rd. (tel. 08-8552-1949), has on-site vans, cabins, and campsites, as well as moderately priced motel units with cooking facilities.

Food

You'll find the usual resort town takeaways. **Fine Foods International,** Coral St. (tel. 08-8552-3732), has yummy imported picnic goodies, nuts, dried fruits, and chocolates. **Higgy's Victor Harbor Bakery,** Albert Pl. (tel. 08-8552-3515), bakes fresh pies and pasties and concocts custom-made sandwiches. The **Sub Station,** Ocean St., is another good sandwichmaker, and **South Coast Fish Café,** also on Ocean St., is a good spot for fresh catches. **Anchorage Guest House** serves moderately priced home-style meals in historic surroundings. The **Hotel Crown,** Ocean St., is the cheap pub-meal stop. For finer and costlier meals, try the restaurants at **Apollon Motor Inn, Bayview Motel, Ocean Crest Motel,** or **Whalers Inn.**

Services and Information

Dial 000 for emergencies. **Victor Harbor Hospital** (tel. 08-8552-1066) and **police** (tel. 08-8552-2088) serve the immediate area. For maps and other road information, contact the **Royal Automobile Association** (tel. 08-8552-1033).

PORT ELLIOT

Farther along the Encounter Coast, on Horseshoe Bay, the historic township of Port Elliot (pop. 1,050) attracts body and board surfers to its fabled beaches and tourists to its picturesque shores with views of the Murray mouth and Coorong National Park.

History

Proclaimed a town in 1854—with the opening of South Australia's first iron railway on its inaugural Port Elliot-Goolwa link—Port Elliot was named by Governor Young after his buddy, Sir Charles Elliot. Like neighboring Victor Harbor, Port Elliot did not fare very well as a port. Though the first ship anchored in 1851, and traffic grew to a busy 85 arrivals in 1855, by 1864 seven ships had been sunk and strewn about the bay. So much for Port Elliot—in that same year, another railway link was built to Victor Harbor, and for a short time traffic was redirected.

Sights

Historic structures lining **The Strand** include the **police station** (1853), **courthouse** (1866), **council chamber** (1879), and nearby **St. Jude's Church** (1854). The National Trust has set up a historical display in the **Port Elliot Railway Station,** built in 1911.

For excellent **coastal views,** take the scenic walk from just above Horseshoe Bay and follow the cliffs to Knight's Beach, or look out from **Freeman Knob,** along The Strand at the main Victor Harbor-Goolwa Rd. junction.

West of town, **Boomer Beach** is where experienced bodysurfers come for large, dumping waves. Small, sheltered **Green Bay,** on Freeman Knob, is good for sunbathing, but swimming is dangerous in the rocky bay with its strong riptides. Swimmers will find very good facilities at **Horseshoe Bay,** with small surf at the Commodore Point end. **Middleton Beach,** on the way to Goolwa, is one of the best surfing beaches on the Encounter Coast. **Big Surf Australia,** Main Rd., Middleton (tel. 08-8554-2399), sells bodyboards, swimwear, and accessories, rents quality gear, and is open daily. Flagstaff Hill Rd. leads from central Middleton to another inspiration point, a winery, and a mushroom farm.

Accommodations

Royal Family Hotel, 32 North Terrace (tel. 08 8554-2219), has simple, inexpensive rooms wit shared facilities. Also inexpensive, **Hotel Elliot,** o The Strand by the railway station (tel. 08-8554 2218), has more of a family-type atmosphere Moderately priced **Cavalier Inn Motel,** The Stran (tel. 08-8554-2067), has good views and a swim ming pool. **Thomas Henry's House,** 8 Charteri St. (tel. 08-8554-2003), offers 1930s-style B&B ac commodation at high-moderate rates. If you're staying put, the following spots can set you up i a holiday unit at inexpensive weekly rates: **South Seas Townhouses,** 18 Merrilli Pl. (tel. 08-8554 2029); **Lifeplan,** 4 The Strand (tel. 08-8212-3636) and **Dolphins Court,** Strangways Terrace Horseshoe Bay (tel. 08-8554-2029).

Port Elliot Caravan Park, Horseshoe Ba (tel. 08-8554-2134), has on-site vans, camp sites, and moderately priced cottages. **Middle ton Caravan Park,** Middleton (tel. 08-8554 2383), rents on-site vans and campsites.

Food

Royal Family Hotel and **Hotel Elliot** both serve inexpensive counter meals. **Sitar Indian Restaurant,** The Strand (tel. 08-8554-2144) has moderately priced dinners and takeaways **Arnella Restaurant,** North Terrace, on the mair Victor Harbor-Goolwa Rd., has country-style dinners (lunch, in season, and on Sunday) ir the higher price bracket. And higher yet is the continental cuisine at **Thomas Hardy's Restau rant.**

The **Middleton Fish Shop** (tel. 08-8554 2688) and **Middleton General Store and Pos Office** (tel. 08-8554-2064) are both open daily for takeaway food and snacks.

GOOLWA

Situated where the Murray River meets the grea Southern Ocean, Goolwa (pop. 2,360) draws railway buffs and river rats who come to ride Australia's first iron public railway, to cruise up and down the Murray or around Lake Alexan drina, or to laze away the days by the historic old wharf. Hindmarsh Island, a ferry ride away, sits between the mighty mouth and the entrance to Lake Alexandrina.

History

Prosperous paddlesteamer trade along the Murray River made Goolwa an important port from the mid- to late 1800s. The opening of the railway line to Port Elliot gave the town true, though short-lived, notoriety. Alas, a new line extending all the way to Adelaide and built in the 1880s caused Goolwa's final fizzle as port extraordinaire.

Over on Hindmarsh Island, an obelisk marks the place where Charles Sturt, in 1830, squinted past the sandhills and into the Murray mouth, as did Capt. Collett Barker, another explorer, who must have opened *his* eyes a little too wide before he got speared to death by the natives.

Sights

The **Goolwa Hotel** (1853), Cadell St.; **post office** (1857), Cadell St.; **Corio Hotel** (1857), Railway Terrace; and **police station** (1859), Goolwa Terrace, are some of the old buildings still in use today. (The Goolwa Hotel has a figurehead from the wrecked ship *Mozambique* on its parapet.)

Other historic sights are the **Railway Superintendent's House** (1852), **Railway Horse Stables** (1853), the **Saddlery** (1867), **Town Mechanics Institute** (1868), and **Church of England** (1867), all on Cadell Street.

The **Goolwa National Trust Museum** (1870), Porter St., is housed inside a former blacksmith shop. The museum has many exhibits focusing on Goolwa's early beginnings, including a "Port of Goolwa" room. Hours are Tues.-Thurs., Sat.-Sun., school and public holidays 2-5 p.m. Admission is $1.

Signal Point, The Wharf (tel. 08-8555-3488), opened in 1988 by the illustrious Prince of Wales, is the River Murray Interpretive Center. High-tech computerized displays show what the river was like before the Europeans came as well as the impact of modern industry and development on the important waterway. Climb aboard *Oscar W,* a restored paddlewheeler built in 1908, which sits alongside the wharf. Hours are daily 10 a.m.-5 p.m., except Christmas Day.

The only way to get to **Hindmarsh Island** is by the free 24-hour ferry near the wharf. Walking trails and lookouts enable you to see the Murray mouth on one side and Lake Alexandrina on the other. The Sturt Memorial granite obelisk is about three km from the ferry landing, on the right side of the main road. Boat ramps on the island will launch you into salt or fresh water.

Built between 1935 and 1940, **Goolwa Barrage,** an enormous concrete structure atop a multitude of wooden piles pounded into the riverbed, crosses the lower Murray—from Hindmarsh Island to Sir Richard Peninsula—and separates the salty sea from the fresh river water. A bird blind, off Barrage Rd., lets watchers view the area birdlife.

Currency Creek, an eight-km drive up Cadell St., has an Aboriginal canoe tree alongside the road, picnic areas, and a walking trail that will take you to a waterfall, old copper mine, and short detour to the cemetery.

Goolwa Beach often has big surf, crosscurrents, and some rips—recommended for experienced swimmers only.

Accommodations

Two of the town's oldest buildings, **Goolwa Hotel,** Cadell St. (tel. 08-8555-2012), and **Corio Hotel,** Railway Terrace (tel. 08-8555-2011), have inexpensive rooms with shared facilities. For cheap home-style accommodations, try **Graham's Castle,** corner Castle Ave. and Bradford Rd. (tel. 08-8555-2182).

South Lakes Motel, Barrage Rd. (tel. 08-8555-2194), features moderately priced rooms with kitchenettes, swimming area, and adjacent golf course. Other choices include **Kenmaur House,** Saratoga Dr. (tel. 08-8555-3494), and **Goolwa Cottage,** 3 Hays St. (tel. 08-8555-1021), with slightly higher rates in the heart of the wharf area, which is a "smoke-free zone." For motel-style accommodations, try **Goolwa Central,** 30 Cadell St. (tel. 08-8555-1155), where rates include continental breakfast, a pool, spa, and rec room.

Narnu Pioneer Holiday Farm, Monument Rd., Hindmarsh Island (tel. 08-8555-2002), features self-contained cottages in a rural setting for $50-60 per double, with horse riding and aquatic equipment available.

On-site vans and campsites are available at **Goolwa Camping and Tourist Park,** Kessell Rd. (tel. 08-8555-2144), and campsites only at **Hindmarsh Island Caravan Park,** Madsen St., Hindmarsh Island (tel. 08-8555-2234).

Food

Counter meals and a la carte fare are served daily at both the **Goolwa** and **Corio** Hotels. A coffee shop at **Signal Point** serves light lunches, snacks, and cakes. **South Lakes Motel** has a comparatively pricey restaurant at the water's edge. Otherwise, it's the usual takeaways, chicken joints, and a Chinese restaurant.

Services and Information

The **Goolwa Tourist and Information Centre,** Cadell St. (tel. 08-8555-1144), provides information on all area facilities, as well as maps for historic walking tours. Hours are daily 10 a.m.-4 p.m., closed Christmas Day and Good Friday.

Reach out and touch the **police** (tel. 08-8555-2018), **ambulance** (tel. 08-8552-2111), or **fire brigade** (tel. 08-8555-2000). The **Royal Automobile Association** (tel. 08-8555-2009) will assist with maps and driving-related questions.

STRATHALBYN

Approximately 30 km north of Goolwa, beautiful Strathalbyn (pop. 1,925), a designated heritage township, was settled by Scottish immigrants in 1839. Examples of architecture reflecting Scottish influence are the **Angus Flour Mill** (1852), **20 High Street Crafts** (1854), **London House** (1867), and **Argus House** (1868). **Saint Andrew's Church** (1848), overlooking the river, is one of Australia's most fabled country churches.

The River Angus, which flows through town, is bordered by **Soldiers Memorial Gardens,** a peaceful setting for picnicking, duck-feeding, swan-songing, and gentle strolls. Several Aboriginal canoe trees line the water's edge and gum trees hover above lush lawns and rambling bridges.

Many arts and crafts, antique, and second-hand shops are scattered about the town. A walking-tour book ($1) to Strathalbyn's two shopping areas is available at many locations. You can also pick up tourist literature at 20 High Street Crafts.

Milang, 20 km southeast of Strathalbyn, is another former river port, now used as a launching point for boating, windsurfing, and water-skiing on Lake Alexandrina. **Langhorne Creek,** 60 km northeast from Milang, is a grape- and al-

mond-growing district on the way to **Wellington,** farther east yet, on the banks of the Murray River. Don't miss a ride on the 24-hour free ferry, operating since 1839 (when it was the only access across the river between South Australia and the eastern states).

Accommodations

Two fine old pubs are **Robin Hood Hotel,** 18 High St. (tel. 08-8536-2608), and the **Terminus Hotel,** 17 Rankine St. (tel. 08-8536-2026). Both offer inexpensive rooms with shared facilities.

Strathalbyn Caravan Park, Coronation Rd (tel. 08-8536-3681), has on-site vans and camp-sites.

Food

Both the Robin Hood and Terminus Hotels have reasonably priced counter meals. **Strath Eats,** 10 Dawson St. (tel. 08-8536-3582), dishes up pizza, pasta, chicken, and chips. **Bonnie MacGregor's,** Dawson St. (tel. 08-8536-3535), features gourmet foods and light meals at moderate prices.

Events

The **Penny Farthing Challenge Cup,** held annually in March, is an international event in which more than 30 riders race through the township on pennyfarthings and other vintage bicycles. Accompanying hoopla consists of parades, band performances, barbecues, a pancake brekky, arts and crafts displays, and Scottish street entertainment. For more information, phone (08) 8536-3212.

Services and Information

For **emergencies,** dial 000. For other assistance, phone the **police** (tel. 08-8536-2044), **ambulance** (tel. 08-8536-2333), **fire brigade** (tel. 08-8536-2000), or local **Royal Automobile Association** (tel. 08-8536-2066).

TRANSPORTATION

All buses to the Fleurieu Peninsula depart from Adelaide's Country Passenger Depot, 101 Franklin Street. **Premier Roadlines** (tel. 08-8415-5544) travels the Adelaide-Willunga-Victor

Harbor route three times daily Mon.-Fri., twice daily Saturday and public holidays, once on Sunday. Fare to Victor Harbor is about $12 one-way. **Kangaroo Island Connection** (tel. 08-8231-5959) departs twice daily for Cape Jervis via Aldinga and Normanville. Fare to Cape Jervis is $12 one-way. **Johnson's Motor Service** (tel. 08-8231-5959) provides transportation to Goolwa, twice daily, Mon.-Friday. Fare is $10 one-way. **Mt. Barker Passenger Service** (tel. 08-8391-2977) leaves for Strathalbyn three times daily, Mon.-Friday. Fare is $11 one-way. **TransAdelaide** (tel. 08-8210-1000) serves outer suburbs within the Fleurieu area.

Railway buffs should board the steam-powered **Cockle Train,** which follows the historic Victor Harbor-Goolwa route at least three times daily on school holidays, long weekends, and Sundays. The one-hour-and-45-minute round-trip costs about $12. For information, phone (08) 8231-1707.

The **MV *Philanderer III*** (tel. 13-1301, toll-free from SA) provides ferry service from Cape Jervis to Kangaroo Island up to five times daily for $30 one-way.

Huck Finn-ers and river queens can choose from a variety of Murray River cruises departing from Goolwa. **PS *Mundoo*** makes two-and-a-half-hour paddlesteamer cruises to North Goolwa, Hindmarsh Island, and Currency Creek every Thursday and Saturday at 11:30 a.m. Fare, including bus transfer, is $35. **MV *Aroona*** has a luncheon cruise downstream to the Murray mouth, Tuesday and Saturday, for the same rates. For information, phone Goolwa Cruises (tel. 08-8555-2203).

KANGAROO ISLAND

After Tasmania and Melville (off Darwin's coast), Kangaroo Island (pop. 4,000), approximately 145 km by 60 km, is Australia's third-largest island. Though the climate is temperate, with only rare frosts and highs not usually exceeding 38° C (100° F), the island is at its best (and most crowded) during the summer months.

Dramatic cliffs, sheltered beaches, untamed coastline, untouched scenery, and flourishing wildlife lure tourists to this popular holiday resort, a relatively close 113 km southwest of Adelaide and just a short hop off the Fleurieu Peninsula. Families enjoy swimming and sunning, camping and hiking in their choice of 16 conservation parks. Divers have a grand time exploring the 40-plus ships reported wrecked around the coastal waters, beginning with the *William,* in 1847. Anglers drop their lines from jetties, rocks, and boats, into surf, rivers, and the deep blue sea. Naturalists are enthralled by the plentiful wildlife—kangaroos, natch, plus koalas, seals, fairy penguins, emus, sea lions, echidnas, possums, and an occasional platypus—unscathed by such predators as foxes or dingoes, which are nonexistent on the island. On the western side, you can still see the kin of wild pigs, reputedly set ashore by French explorer Nicholas Baudin as feed for shipwrecked sailors. Besides all the critters, you can tiptoe through more than 700 native wildflower species, and about 150 others brought in from elsewhere in the world.

On 1 February 1997 all telephone numbers on Kangaroo Island will change from five digits to eight digits. In preparation for this, all numbers in this section have been changed to eight digits. To dial a Kangaroo Island number before 1 February, determine what the five-digit number would be using the chart below. If calling from off Kangaroo Island add the area code (0848). After 1 February the area code for all numbers in this section will be (08).

If the new eight digit number is	the five-digit number (valid until 1 February 1997) is
8553-2XXX	22-XXX
8553-3XXX	23-XXX
8553-8XXX	28-XXX
8553-9XXX	29-XXX
8553-1XXX	31-XXX
8553-7XXX	33-XXX
8553-5XXX	35-XXX
8559-2XXX	36-XXX
8559-7XXX	37-XXX
8559-3XXX	93-XXX
8559-6XXX	96-XXX

KANGAROO ISLAND

10 km

✈ = SHIPWRECK

FLEURIEU PENINSULA

CAPE JERVIS

BACKSTAIRS PASSAGE

WILLIAM (1847)

KONA (1916)

PENNESHAW

FRENCHMAN'S ROCK

CHAPMAN RIVER

ANTECHAMBER BAY

CAPE WILLOUGHBY

CAPE HART

CAPE HART C.P.

DUDLEY

PENINGTON BAY

WANDERER (1906)

YOU YANGS (1890)

OSMANLI (1853)

FANNY (1885)

BIRD PROTECTION DIST.

ROBERT BURNS (1908)

GOLDEN HOPE

GEM (1895)

NEPEAN BAY

MEPEAN BAY (1915)

AMERICAN BEACH

AMERICAN RIVER

KINGSCOTE

BROWNLOW

WESTERN COVE

EMU BAY

AIRPORT

PELICAN LAGOON C.P.

FAIRFIELD (1874)

BROTHERS (1916)

MURRAY'S LAGOON

CAPE GANTHEAUME C.P.

CAPE GANTHEAUME

SOUTH COAST RD

PARNDANA

EMU BAY RD

WEST COAST RD

NORTH COAST RD

STOKES BAY

SNELLINGS BEACH

SEAL BAY

SEAL BAY C.P.

LITTLE SAHARA

VIVONNE BAY C.P.

VIVONNE BAY

MONTEBELLO (1905)

SOUTHERN OCEAN

MIMOSA (1884)

WESTERN RIVER COVE

WESTERN RIVER C.P.

PLAYFORD HWY

CAPE TORRENS

CAPE TORRENS C.P.

WEST END HWY

SHACKLE RD

KELLY HILL CAVES

KELLY HILL C.P.

KELLY HILL

CAPE YOUNGHUSBAND

TASMAN (1877)

TREASURE (TROVE) (1876)

INVESTIGATOR STRAIT

HARVE'S RETURN

CAPE FORBIN

MERMAID (1905)

FIDES (1860)

LOCH VENNACHAR (1905)

LARRIKIN LAGOON

FLINDERS CHASE NATIONAL PARK

ROCKY RIVER HEADQUARTERS

REMARKABLE ROCKS

MARS (1855)

EMILY SMITH (1877)

LOCH SLOY (1899)

CAPE DU COUEDIC

DUNCOW (1897)

PORTLAND MARU (1935)

BIRD SANCTUARY

And, if you're into the birds and the bees, keep your eyes and ears perked for crimson rosellas, purple-gaped honeyeaters, ospreys, sea eagles, the rare glossy black cockatoo, and the unique Ligurian honeybee.

Kingscote, on Nepean Bay, is the island's commercial center and the city nearest the airport. Other communities with holiday facilities are American River, Penneshaw, and Parndana. The north coast flaunts calmer waters, with stretches of beach for swimming, sunning, and lazy-day fishing. Dudley Peninsula, along the Backstairs Passage, boasts fairy penguins, pelicans, stunning views, and the Cornwall-style village of Penneshaw. The south coast is the wild side, with sand dunes, crashing waves, and three conservation parks. And Flinders Chase National Park, on the south and west coasts, is Kangaroo Island's spectacular wildlife sanctuary.

History

Not much is known about the Aboriginals who originally inhabited the island; stone tools thought to be more than 10,000 years old are about the only sign of their presence. Anyway, they were long gone by 1802 when Matthew Flinders, voyaging on the *Investigator*, "discovered" Kangaroo Island for himself (and his king). But French explorer Nicholas Baudin was also nosing about, doing some circumnavigating of his own. By the time the two sailors faced off shortly afterward in Encounter Bay, Flinders had named the island—this time in tribute to the many kangaroos he'd seen, instead of for a compatriot—while Baudin had christened the places he'd charted *en français*. Consequently, you'll find French names attached to many island sights, reflecting the French vs. English "tug-of-words."

The island has an American influence also. In 1803, one year after Matthew Flinders had taken the island, a group of American sealers arrived at a site eventually named "American River." Using native pine, they built the *Independence,* South Australia's first boat.

It wasn't until 1836 that the first 400 settlers, sponsored by the South Australian Company, arrived from England aboard the *Duke of York* to formally establish a township at Reeves Point,

north of Kingscote. The lack of fresh water kept this from being a viable colonial settlement and, by 1840, except for a few lingering souls, most of the population had shifted over to the mainland. The fact is, though, that Reeves Point was South Australia's first official European settlement, and the present inhabitants are tremendously proud of that bit of history.

Early industries on the island were yacca gum production, salt mining, and eucalyptus oil distilling (eucalyptus oil was Australia's first export product). Agriculture, however, was in a slump until the 1930s when cobalt and copper were added to the soil. After that, crops flourished and, before long, one-half the island had become productive farmland. Today Kangaroo Island's most vital industries are agriculture, fishing, and tourism.

KINGSCOTE

On the shores of Nepean Bay, Kingscote (pop. 1,450) blends its historical significance with modern-day necessities. Sheer cliffs to the north afford terrific views of the harbor and Western Cove, while cliffs to the south provide a languid drop to the Cygnet River swamp and bird lands. Kingscote is the island's major shipping port and trade center.

Sights

Reeves Point Historic Site is where the *Duke of York* anchored in 1836 and South Australia officially began. You'll find remnants of the first post office, the state's oldest cemetery and, farther north, the state's oldest introduced tree—a mulberry, planted around 1836, that still bears edible fruit! (You can buy jam made from the berries.)

Hope Cottage, the National Trust Museum, on Centenary Ave., is housed in an 1850s building built by two pioneering brothers. Displays include working exhibits, maritime history, family histories, photographs, and early newspapers. Open daily 2-4 p.m., closed mid-July through August. Admission is $2. For information, phone (08) 8553-2151.

St. Alban's Church, built in 1884, is Kingscote's oldest public building. Stained-glass windows, memorials to pioneer families, and graffiti from when the church was used as a school-room are worth seeing.

Memorial Park, on the seafront close to the town center, has memorials to Flinders and the war dead, as well as barbecue and picnic areas for when your nostalgia gives way to hunger pangs.

Fairy penguins parade to their homes at dusk on most nights. Best viewing places are between the swimming pool and jetty, or among rocks near the jetty. At **Bay of Shoals,** see pelicans and other birds fed daily at 4 p.m.

Heritage Walking Trails explore Kingscote's natural history and heritage sights. Pick up maps at the Tourist Information Centre on Dauncey Street. For information, phone (08) 8553-2381.

Family **beaches** with shallow swimming and wading facilities can be found in front of the Ozone Hotel and at Little Brownlow Beach, in front of the Yacht Club. Another spot for safe swimming is the rockbound **seawater pool.**

Accommodations

Be sure to book ahead, especially during school holiday periods. **Kangaroo Island Youth Hostel** (also known as Hillfarm Hostel), Brownlow Beach (tel. 08-8553-2778), has dorm beds for $12 per night, plus bicycle rentals, transportation from Kingscote, and meal service.

Kangaroo Island Holiday Village, 9 Dauncey St. (tel. 08-8553-2225), has self-contained family units with kitchens at moderate prices. **Parade Units,** adjacent to Brownlow Beach (tel. 08-8553-2565), is another decent choice. For a cottage-y experience, try **Nepean Heights Cottage,** 38 Franklin St. (tel. 08-8553-2061).

Slightly higher-priced are the **Island Resort,** Telegraph Rd. (tel. 08-8553-2100), with an indoor heated pool, sauna, and spa, and **Ellison's Seaview Motel,** Chapman Terrace (tel. 08-8553-2030), featuring seafront motel units and guesthouse rooms. **Ozone Seafront Hotel,** the foreshore (tel. 08-8553-2011), at the high end of the moderate range, has great views.

Both **Nepean Bay Caravan Park,** the foreshore, Brownlow Beach (tel. 08-8553-2394), and **Kangaroo Island Caravan Park,** on the Esplanade (tel. 08-8553-2325), rent campsites, on-site vans, and cabins.

Food

Good takeaways are **Pelican Pete's Takeaway Eats,** Main St. (tel. 08-8553-2138), and **Nev's Tucker Box,** 3 Kingscote Terrace (tel. 08-8553-2585). **Port of Call Restaurant,** the foreshore (tel. 08-8553-2834), serves seafood, steak, and pasta in an intimate setting overlooking Nepean Bay. The **Ozone Seafront Hotel** features an a la carte dining room, bistro, and informal coffee shop with meals at all prices.

THE DUDLEY PENINSULA

Kangaroo Island's eastern tip, the Dudley Peninsula, starts as a narrow neck at Pelican Lagoon Conservation Park and white-sand beaches, then rounds northeast to Cornish-influenced Penneshaw, over to rugged Cape Willoughby, south to Cape Hart, and then west to Dudley Conservation Park.

American River

This tiny village, midway between Kingscote and Penneshaw, is named for the American sealers who lived here for four months in 1803. It's a favorite spot for fishermen who come not only for a fresh catch-of-the-day, but for the scenic beauty of gum and she-oak forested hills as they dip to meet the calm waters of Eastern Cove. Try to arrive at the end of August, when the freesias cover every knoll, dell, and pathway with brilliant blossoms.

The nearby aquatic reserve, **Pelican Lagoon Conservation Park,** is abundant with pelicans, swans, and Cape Barren geese.

Linnetts Island Club Resort (tel. 08-8553-7053) has a choice of rooms, suites, villas, or holiday flats, ranging in price from inexpensive to expensive. **American River Motel,** Wattle Ave. (tel. 08-8553-7052), overlooks the American River and has a pool, spa, and sauna. Prices are moderate to expensive and include continental breakfast. Rates are expensive at **Wanderers Rest,** corner Government and Bayview Roads (tel. 08-8553-7140), a guesthouse on a hillside with sweeping views of American River. All of these accommodations have restaurants or dining rooms.

Pennington Bay

Just one kilometer off the Kingscote-to-Penneshaw road, very near American River, Penningon Bay is a popular swimming and surfing beach—but only for the experienced. Otherwise, you can take a hike (more of a climb, actually) to the top of Mt. Thisby for views of both Pelican and Pennington Bays.

Dudley Conservation Park, near Pennington Bay, is one of the island's many wildlife havens where you may see the dama wallaby, Kangaroo Island kangaroo, purple-gaped honeyeater, echidna, and the fairy wren.

Penneshaw

Passing along the sandy-white Island and American Beaches, you'll come to Penneshaw, a Cornish-like hamlet, only 16 km across the Backstairs Passage from mainland South Australia. Tourists are drawn here for the safe bathing beach, excellent fishing off Hog Bay Jetty, and the parade of fairy penguins nesting (returning home each evening) in the cliffs and sandhills near town.

Captain Flinders landed near **Christmas Cove,** also known as "The Basin," in 1802. The granite boulders there had a slightly earlier arrival than the good captain—they were deposited by a glacier more than 200 million years ago.

Frenchman's Rock, at Hog Bay, marks the spot where, in 1803, Captain Baudin, who'd just "encountered" Captain Flinders, came ashore to fill his empty water casks. The two seamen, unaware that their respective countries were waging war, unwittingly became water brothers.

Penneshaw Museum, housed inside the 1922 school, features maritime and other historic and folk exhibits. Hours are Monday, Wednesday, and Saturday 3-5 p.m., daily in January and during Easter. Admission is $1.50. For information, phone (08) 8553-1108.

Hog Bag Jetty, built 1902-09, is not only a famous fishing locale, but home port for the MV *Philanderer III.*

Bookings are essential at **Penneshaw Youth Hostel,** 43 North Terrace (tel. 08-8553-1284, or 1800-01-8258 toll-free), where dorm beds cost $12 per night. Facilities include scooter, bicycle, and boat rentals, kitchen facilities, launderette, swimming beach, nature walks, slide and video presentations, and organized tours of the island.

Tandarra Holiday Lodge, 33 Middle Terrace (tel. 08-8553-1018), offers moderately priced holiday flats and a bunkhouse with $12 beds. **Sorrento Resort** (tel. 08-8553-1028) features modern motel suites, cottages with kitchenettes, and alpine chalets with kitchenettes, ranging moderate-expensive. The resort, set on two acres of seafront gardens, has a safe swimming beach, swimming pool, poolside bar, half-court tennis facilities, spa, and sauna, and offers a variety of island tours.

Penneshaw Caravan Park, Talinga Terrace (tel. 08-8553-1075), with campsites and on-site vans, is opposite a safe beach and close to town.

Condon's Takeaway Foods, 43 North Terrace (tel. 08-8553-1173), serves breakfast, chicken, chips, and rooburgers. You can also buy souvenirs, gas, ice, bait, and tackle, and get your laundry done. The **Old Post Office Restaurant** (tel. 08-8553-1063), in one of Penneshaw's oldest commercial buildings, on the first corner away from the ferry, gives you a choice of a la carte dining or more relaxed (and inexpensive) bistro meals in the enclosed courtyard. It's open every night except Monday.

Antechamber Bay

This long, sweeping stretch of beach meets the ocean, backdropped by the mainland and bisected by Chapman River as it runs into Lashmar Lagoon. Though this area is famous for canoeing and bream fishing, you'll also find hiking tracks leading to bushland, sandhills, and lagoons.

Antechamber Bay Farmhouse (tel. 08-8553-7020) provides inexpensive guest accommodations.

Cape Willoughby

The first flicker of light was emitted from Cape Willoughby Lighthouse (South Australia's first) in 1852. Built of local limestone, the tower measures 27 meters high and sits 73 meters above sea level. Just below the lighthouse the rocky, wild, crashing coastline is aptly named Devil's Kitchen. The lighthouse is open to visitors daily 10 a.m.-4 p.m. For information, phone (08) 8553-2381.

Cape Hart Conservation Park, four km southwest of Cape Willoughby, sports massive granite boulders and sandstone cliffs with drops to the Southern Ocean.

THE SOUTH COAST ROAD

From Kingscote to Flinders Chase National Park, ride the wild side in search of shells, shipwrecks, seals, and scenery, scenery, scenery.

Murray's Lagoon

Kangaroo Island's largest freshwater lagoon is encompassed within **Cape Gantheaume Conservation Park,** a favorite spot for birders. At D'Estrees Bay, on the east side of the park, you can catch fish or collect shells—both line the shores.

Seal Bay

Take the turnoff from South Coast Rd. to **Seal Bay Conservation Park,** a famous breeding colony of rare sea lions whose ancestors escaped the early sealers. Guided tours, led by the National Parks and Wildlife Service, will take you within a few meters of sunbathing sea lions. Tours run regularly year-round, and times are posted just off the road.

Little Sahara

Back on South Coast Rd., the first road on the left (immediately before the bridge) will take you down to Little Sahara desert, where ridge upon ridge of bleached white dunes blend into the surrounding bushland.

Vivonne Bay

The only safe harbor on this side of the coast, Vivonne Bay has a long, curvy beach with dazzling scenery and a variety of activities—beach, boat, and jetty fishing, beachcombing, swimming, picnicking. Students of all ages can take part in the **Outdoor Education Living Classroom,** a series of guided tours to enhance knowledge of the island and its history.

Make inquiries before you take a dip. Normally, safe swimming areas are near the jetty, boat ramp, and Harriet River—other parts of the bay have an undertow.

Correa Cottage (tel. 08-8553-1233) and **Honeymyrtle Cottage** (tel. 08-8559-4279) are available at moderate-expensive rates.

Kelly Hill Conservation Park

The Kelly Hill Conservation Park has an extensive network of limestone ridges, dense mallee,
and a coastal trail that winds its way seaward. Kelly Hill shelters sinkholes, caverns, and cave molded from ornately shaped calcite that cast eerie shadows in the tricky light. The larges cave is open to visitors.

At the park's western boundary and sheltered at each side by ocean reefs and rocky headlands, **Hanson Bay** is another top spot for swimming and fishing.

Continuing along South Coast Rd. you'll soon approach Rocky River Headquarters in Flinders Chase National Park.

FLINDERS CHASE NATIONAL PARK

South Australia's largest national park consists of 73,662 hectares of protected sanctuary for Kangaroo Island's rare and opulent wildlife. Taking up the entire western end of the island, Flinders Chase is a mecca of unspoiled wilderness for friendly kangaroos (the distinctive Kangaroo Island kangaroo has dark, sooty brown fur), emus, Cape Barren geese, koalas, glossy black cockatoos, and possums riding piggy on

"automatic" Cape du Couëdic Lighthouse

eir mothers' backs. The natives are so plenti-
l and friendly that at Rocky River humans pic-
c in enclosed areas while the animals scratch
eir chins and ogle at *them.*

South of Rocky River Headquarters you can
ach the huge, oddly sculpted **Remarkable
ocks,** not to mention **Admiral's Arch,** anoth-
intriguing formation, and **Cape du Couëdic
ghthouse,** an "automatic" opened in 1906.
he island's largest shipwreck, that of the *Port-
nd Maru,* occurred near the cape in 1935.

On the north side of the park, **Cape Borda
ghthouse,** opened in 1858, stands 155 meters
ove the sea. Before radio communication, the
arby cannon was used to signal ships of im-
ending dangers. These days the meteorological
ation, nearby, is a quieter guide—and, no
ubt, preferred by the wildlife inhabitants.

The **Rocky River Headquarters** (tel. 08-
559-7235) will provide you with maps, neces-
ary permits, and all the information you require
r your park visit. Be sure to check in with the
angers before embarking on any lengthy hikes
ong isolated trails. Camping in the park is per-
itted and, if you like, you can spend a night
r two at the Cape du Couëdic and Cape Borda
ghthouses (for a moderate fee). Admission to
e park is $6.50 per vehicle.

THE NORTH COAST ROAD

he West End Highway, which borders the east-
rn edge of Flinders Chase National Park, will
ake you to the Playford Highway, a smooth run
rough grazing country back to Kingscote. The
orth Coast Rd. leaps and jogs off the beaten
ath to smooth beaches, rocky points, snug
oves, and more stunning scenery.

arvey's Return

his rugged, rocky cove, east of Cape Borda,
as once a camp for American sealers. Later,
fter the lighthouse was built, it was used as a
rop-off point for supplies. You can visit the
raves of shipwrecked sailors and lighthouse-
eepers at the nearby cemetery.

ape Torrens Conservation Park

owering cliffs hanging more than 200 meters
bove the sea make this a dazzling spot for

bushwalkers who like trails with drop-dead
views, or for birders in search of the rare glossy
black cockatoo. Be sure to check in with the
rangers at Rocky River Headquarters before
setting out.

Western River Cove

This popular swimming and fishing beach, at
the mouth of the Western River, is a steep descent from **Western River Conservation Park.**
If you don't feel like hitting the beach, the park is
full of stringybark forests, wildlife, and excellent
gorge, water, and valley views from its many
high cliffs.

Snellings Beach

Swim, surf, dive, or fish at this peaceful protected bay, situated at the mouth of the Middle
River (but be careful of the river's hidden snags
and weeds). **Constitution Hill,** above the
beach, affords great views of the area.

Accommodations at **Middle River Homestead** (tel. 08-8553-2357) range moderate-expensive (cheap if you're with several other travelers).

Stokes Bay

Farther east along the coast road, this white
sandy beach draws families to its secluded
shores, reached by walking through a tunnel
within enormous limestone boulders. Though
Stokes Bay is an excellent surf spot and fishing
hole, its special feature is the large rock-enclosed
pool, which provides a safe swimming area.

Paul's Place, between Stokes Bay and Amen
Corner, has horse riding, a large aviary (on the
off chance you haven't seen enough birds in
the wild), and a glass-fronted beehive where
you can get a close-up look at the island's special Ligurian honeybee.

Stokes Bay Holiday House (tel. 08-8559-
6977) provides moderately priced accommodations.

Parndana

You have to head inland, back to the Playford
Highway, if you want to visit this little farming
community.

Though an experimental farm had been set
up in 1938, development was hindered when
the area became a soldiers' settlement during

World War II. Eventually, 174 soldier-settlement farms were established and, in 1950, a government research center was set up on the experimental property. Today, the area is used mainly for sheep and cattle grazing.

For moderately priced holiday house accommodations try **Kelly's Pioneer Bend Homestead,** Pioneer Bend Rd. (tel. 08-8559-2256), or **Coora Cottage,** Wetheralls Rd. (tel. 08-8559-6027). **Gum Valley Resort** (tel. 08-8559-3207) is a B&B in the expensive category.

Emu Bay

In the early 1900s (and up until the 1970s) the town was named Maxwell. Once it was discovered that the bay was both too shallow and too exposed, the port was moved over to Kingscote. Emu Bay is now a top-notch spot for safe swimming and boat or jetty fishing.

TRANSPORTATION

For information on getting to Kangaroo Island by plane or ferry, see "Getting Away" in the "Adelaide" section.

Getting Around

Airport Coach Service (tel. 08-8553-2678) operates a bus from the Kingscote airport into town for $4, and also provides taxi and tour services. **Kangaroo Island Sealink** (tel. 13-1301) runs buses between Penneshaw, American River, and Kingscote, to connect with ferry departures. The Penneshaw and Kangaroo Island youth hostels also provide airport pick-up and some coach services for guests.

If you don't bring a car over with you on the ferry, you can rent one once you arrive. The Kangaroo Island Tourist Information Centre in Kingscote or your accommodation hosts can help you; otherwise, try **Kangaroo Island Car Hire,** corner Telegraph and Franklin Streets (tel. 08-8553-2390), or **Budget,** 76 Dauncey St., Kingscote (tel. 08-8553-3133). Expect to pay $75 and up per day (weekly deals are cheaper). Again, advance bookings are strongly recommended.

Rent bicycles at **Condon's Takeaway** (home of the rooburger), Penneshaw (tel. 08-8553-7173), **Penneshaw Youth Hostel** (tel. 08-8553-1284), or **Wisteria Lodge Motel,** Kingscote (tel.

08-8553-2707); rent scooters at both Condor and the Penneshaw Youth Hostel.

With nearly 1,600 kilometers of roads on the island, only the major highways are sealed. The extensive maze of off-the-beaten-paths range from bush tracks to gravel roads. The combination dust and gravel makes driving at high speed very hazardous. Even the most experienced clists can find road conditions exhausting. Allo plenty of time to cover the distance you expect travel. Except during peak holiday periods, th roads have very little traffic, making it unwise depend on catching a lift. If you're driving, kee your petrol tank full (fill it at Kingscote, Ame can River, Penneshaw, Parndana, and Vivonr Bay, year-round). Bushwalkers must infor rangers before embarking on remote or dange ous trails. And, whether driving, hiking, or c cling, carry plenty of water with you.

For those who'd rather sit back and rela sign up for an organized coach tour. Both you hostels offer an interesting selection of on and two-day jaunts. **Penguin Tours** (tel. 08 8553-2844) departs nightly from Penneshaw and Kingscote for ranger-led observations o penguin lifestyles. Cost is $3.50.

INFORMATION

Kangaroo Island Tourist Information Cer tre, 37 Dauncey St., Kingscote (tel. 08-8553 2381), can help with tours, trails, and treks, an direct you to dive shops and bait stores. Be sur to pick up maps that detail the roads branch ing off main highways. The center is open Mon Fri. 9 a.m.-5 p.m., closed public holidays. (Th public library and council office are in the sam building.)

The information center can also provid brochures, issue permits, and arrange guide tours of the island's many conservation parks Or, contact the **Department of Environmen and Natural Resources** at Murray's Lagoo Headquarters (tel. 08-8553-8233), Seal Ba Conservation Park (tel. 08-8553-8233), Rock River Headquarters (tel. 08-8559-7235), Kell Hill Conservation Park (tel. 08-8559-7231), c Cape Borda (tel. 08-8559-3257). Be sure to pic up a copy of the national park code, and follow all rules to protect the island's sacred wildlife.

Do not fish without first finding out regulations
d acquiring the necessary licenses. The Tourist
ormation Centre can help with these, as well as
commend and organize fishing expeditions.
r more information, phone the **Fisheries Offi-
rs** at 08-8553-2130. At no time is fishing, or
y disturbance of the seabed, permitted at the
lican Lagoon and Seal Bay aquatic reserves.
Most of the island's emergency facilities are

based in Kingscote, though park rangers provide
assistance within their jurisdictions. In the case
of an emergency, call the local ranger station,
dial 000, or, in Kingscote, call the **ambulance**
(tel. 08-8553-2028), **police** (tel. 08-8553-2018),
and/or **fire brigade** (tel. 08-8553-2200).

Island Stationery, 9 Osmond St., Kingscote
(tel. 08-8553-2625), stocks a selection of books
about the island.

THE SOUTHEAST

the map, South Australia's southeast region
esn't appear to be more than a couple of major
ghways along the Adelaide-Melbourne route.
ose "in the know" read between the thick black
es and head straight for the juicy parts—
vamplands and wetlands, bird sanctuaries and
ldlife preserves, sandy dunes and beaches,
wn-away fishing ports (including one marked
a giant walk-in lobster, named Larry), thick-as-
eves pine forests, pastoral farmland, weath-
ed limestone caves, volcanic lakes and craters,
right-regular share of "ye olde" buildings, and
me downright extraordinary red wines.

Aside from bountiful fishing (especially Oct.-
ril, when it's lobster season) and delectable
nes produced from rich *terra rossa,* this area
so sustains timber and farming industries.
ood annual rainfalls yield lush landscapes
d, combined with neighboring western Vic-
ria, this district is known as the Green Triangle.

TAILEM BEND

oth the Dukes and Princes Highways, princi-
al routes between Adelaide and Melbourne,
nverge at Tailem Bend, along with the less-
aveled Ouyen Highway. The inland Dukes
ighway (which becomes Western Highway at
ictoria's border) passes through a lot of flat
rmland and is often referred to as the "boring
ad." The Princes Highway, running along the
past, is the preferred passage, as coastal roads
sually are. If you're not in a rush to get to Mel-
ourne, or if you're not going there at all, you can
ake a complete tour of the southeast by taking
rinces Highway from Tailem Bend to Mt. Gam-
ier; then, detouring north through wine and

cave country, join up with the Dukes Highway at
Keith and loop back to Tailem Bend.

Sights
Tailem Bend's most noteworthy attraction is **Old
Tailem Town,** another one of those authentic
turn-of-the-century villages. The township, five
km north of Tailem Bend, features the usual pioneering cottages, butcher, barber, and bootmaker
shops, emporium, church, one-room schoolhouse, and "real" general store. Old Tailem Town
is open daily 10 a.m.-5 p.m. Admission is $7.
For information, phone (08) 8572-3838.

Accommodations
If you need more time to decide which road to
take, inexpensive **River Bend Motel,** 110
Princes Hwy. (tel. 08-8572-3633), will put you up
for the night. **Westbrook Park River Resort,**
Princes Hwy. (tel. 08-8572-3794), on the banks
of the Murray, has campsites, cabins, and on-
site vans. **Tailem Bend Rivers Edge Caravan
and Tourist Park,** Princes Hwy. (tel. 08-8572-

On 1 February 1997 all telephone numbers in
the southeast will change. In preparation for
this, all numbers in this section have been
changed to eight digits. To dial a southeast
number before 1 February, simply delete the
first two digits of the new number and, if dialing
from outside the southeast, add a zero to the
deleted numbers to get the area code. For example, (08) 8512-3456 would be (085) 12-3456,
and (08) 8712-3456 would be (087) 12-3456.
After 1 February the area code for all numbers
in this section will be (08).

SOUTH AUSTRALIA ~ THE SOUTHEAST

© MOON PUBLICATIONS, INC.

3307), also on the Murray, features a boat ramp and canoes for hire.

MENINGIE

At the northern edge of the Coorong National Park, and the southern side of Lake Albert, Meningie (pop. 900) offers water sports, bird-watching, and easy access to the Coorong. The town is nothing special, but it is a decent place to overnight and stock up on provisions for your Coorong exploration. From Trigg Hill you can look out on Lakes Albert and Alexandrina, which comprise 746 square km of fresh water. **Melaleuca Centre,** 76 Princes Hwy., displays a variety of arts and crafts and also serves as the

Tourist Information Centre. Hours are Mon.-F[ri.] 9 a.m.-5 p.m., Saturday 9 a.m.-12:30 p.m., Su[n]day and public holidays 11 a.m.-3 p.m. For [in]formation, phone (08) 8575-1259.

Accommodations

The motels along Princes Highway are all [in] the inexpensive to low-moderate range. **La[ke] Albert Caravan Park,** Narrung Rd. (tel. 0[8] 8575-1411), offers bike, canoe, and sailboa[t] hire, and a nice lakeside location.

THE COORONG

If you've seen the film *Storm Boy,* the poigna[nt] tale of a boy and his pelican, then you shou[ld] have no trouble visualizing the Coorong, for [it] was filmed here. If you missed the flick, we[ll,] imagine a long, narrow, and shallow saltwater l[a]goon stretching 132 km from the Murray mouth [to] that big lobster Larry's mouth, just north [of] Kingston. Separated from the Southern Ocea[n] by the shimmering sand dunes on Younghu[s]band Peninsula (an average of two km wide), th[e] Coorong is a haven for approximately 400 speci[es]

Pelicans and hundreds of other bird species find sanctuary in the Coorong.

(top left) The Pink Roadhouse is a favorite meeting place for wayward souls.; (top right) Eyre Highway at Nullarbor roadhouse; (bottom) There's no turning back at Gammon Ranges National Park.; (following page) station mailbox near Lyndhurst, South Australia

of birds, including cormorants, terns, shags, ducks, swans, and pelicans. You can get from the Coorong across to the peninsula at Salt Creek during summer months; otherwise there's a year-round road about 75 km south, toward Kingston.

A large Aboriginal tribe lived on the Coorong for thousands of years (the name is derived from "Kurangh," Aboriginal for "Long Neck of Water"), subsisting on fish, seafood, reptiles, birds, kangaroos, and wombats. You'll also come across wells built in the 1800s by Chinese immigrants who landed in Robe and, instead of joining their compatriots who headed for Victoria's goldfields, strayed northward to Adelaide. Australia's first oil well was drilled near Salt Creek in the 1890s, after Coorongite (a derivative of surface algae) was discovered.

In 1966, the Coorong was designated a national park, and since then the National Parks and Wildlife Service has been responsible for its 13,500 hectares, as well as for **Messent Conservation Park,** six km northeast of Salt Creek.

The Coorong is an ideal location for fishing, boating, and hiking. Walking trails are marked throughout the park (try the three-km Lakes Nature Trail at Salt Creek), and during Easter, Christmas, and New Year's holidays rangers lead informative walks. Camping is permitted in the park, but you must obtain a permit first. The **Department of Environment and Natural Resources** has offices at Salt Creek (tel. 08-8575-7014) and Noonameena (tel. 08-8575-1200).

KINGSTON

When you come upon a 17-meter-tall, four-ton, pre-fab lobster named Larry, you've arrived in Kingston (pop. 1,370), "Gateway to the Southern Ports." Larry, presumably the "World's Biggest (fake) Lobster," stands watch over the entrance to this popular fishing port and beach resort. The town was established in 1856 by the Cooke brothers, who had procured government land grants near Maria Creek (so named for the vessel *Maria,* which wrecked near the Cape Jaffa Lighthouse in 1840; the crew and the passengers survived the shipwreck, only to be massacred by Aboriginals after they went ashore). The original jetty was too short and too shallow to make it useful for loading goods and, in 1876, was replaced by another—much longer, sitting in much deeper water—but even that one ceased being practical with the advent of modern roads and railways.

Sights
The **National Trust Museum,** 15 Cooke St., originally a timber mill built in 1872, presents items of local interest, including nautical memorabilia. Hours are daily 3-4 p.m. during school and public holidays. Admission is $2. For information, phone (08) 8767-2114.

Cape Jaffa Lighthouse, moved from its 100-year-old post on Margaret Brock Reef, has been re-erected nearby on Marine Parade and is open to visitors. Other historic buildings are the post office, courthouse, and police station (now an antique shop). Hours are daily 2-5 p.m. during school and public holidays. Admission is $3. For information, phone (08) 8767-2114.

Aside from the Coorong to the north, Kingston is near three other national parks: **Butchers Gap Conservation Park,** six km southwest, off Wyomi Rd., is another natural bird sanctuary where coastal vegetation thrives in the wetlands; part of a former coastal dune, **Mt. Scott Conservation Park,** 20 km east of Kingston, on Keith Rd., has good bushwalks through stringybark forest inhabited by mallee fowl, sugar gliders, and wombats; and **Jip Jip Conservation Park,** 50 km northeast of Kingston, features a variety of wildlife amid big exotically shaped granite boulders. You can also see unusual rock formations much closer to town at the **Granites,** off the highway north of Kingston, along the beach.

The fish are jumping in Kingston; anglers can cast lines from beach, boat, or jetty, either at Kingston or Cape Jaffa, a wee fishing village to the south. The foreshore and Wyomi and Pinks Beaches provide safe swimming, while Lacepede Bay is popular for sailing.

Accommodations
Crown Inn Hotel, Agnes St. (tel. 08-8767-2005), has simple, inexpensive, pub-style rooms. Moderately priced **Bayview Motor Inn,** Marine Parade (tel. 08-8767-2444), is near the jetty on the foreshore. **Kingston Caravan Park,** Marine Parade (tel. 08-8767-2050), is situated on a sand beach. The usual range of campsites, onsite vans, and cabins are offered.

Events

If you're visiting the area in January, you can catch the annual **Yachting Carnival** and Cape Jaffa-to-Kingston race.

Information

Larry, the Big Lobster (tel. 08-8767-2555) is not just another pretty face, but a tourist complex with a bistro, cafeteria, takeaways, souvenir and bottle shops, *and* tourist information. You can also pick up tourist info at **Wood Hut Craft Shop,** Kingston District Hall, Agnes St. (tel. 08-8767-2151). Both places are open daily.

ROBE

In 1802, French explorer Nicholas Baudin cruised this area and bestowed Guichen Bay with its name. The town of Robe (pop. 740) was officially established in 1847, growing to be South Australia's third major port (before the downfall of shipping in 1864). It was used for exporting wool and horses and importing about 15,000 Chinese immigrants. The Chinese, on their way to Victoria's goldfields, had found an ingeniously simple way to avoid the £10-per-head poll tax charged by Victorian officials—they landed in South Australia and quietly made their way across the state line.

Sights

Robe is a peaceful and picturesque village with many historic buildings. The **National Trust Museum,** in the old Customs House (1863), will tell you of the town's early history. Hours are Tues.-Sat. 2-4 p.m. Admission is $1. For information, phone (08) 8768-2419.

From **Beacon Hill,** you can get a great view of Robe, Guichen Bay, and the Southern Ocean. Or look out from the **obelisk,** right or left, to shimmering expanses of coastline.

Little Dip Conservation Park, four km south of Robe, comprises sand dunes, coastal strips, and salt lakes, through which waterbirds and wildlife roam, as can you—along the bushwalking tracks, that is. Rangers lead guided walks during the summer months.

Long Beach, a 17-km stretch of calm white sand along Guichen Bay, is noted for excellent swimming and windsurfing (the National Cham-

pionships were held here in 1989). In the summer, you can drive along the beach and discover your own nook or cranny. Guichen Bay is also popular for sailing.

Anglers can get a bite just about anywhere Crayfish lovers should visit Oct.-April, when the fleet brings in a fresh catch each day.

Events

The Sunday before 1 October is the annual **Blessing of the Fleet.** Afterward, local fishermen invite tourists to join them for a jaunt around the bay.

Accommodations

You'll find all kinds of atmosphere-y accommodations in and around Robe. **Bushland Cabins,** Nora Criena Rd. (tel. 08-8768-2386), has moderately priced units with kitchen facilities The **Caledonian Inn,** Victoria St. (tel. 08-8768-2029), built in 1858, offers newer cottages (moderate) and inexpensive rooms in the restored original section. **Flinders Rest Cottages,** Powell Ave. (tel. 08-8725-2086), in the Long Beach area, rents fully equipped two-bedroom cottages with open fires; also moderately priced.

Or, choose from three caravan parks in the area. **Lakeside Select Caravan Park,** Main Rd. (tel. 08-8768-2193), is on a safe swimming lake. **Long Beach Tourist Park,** the Esplanade (tel. 08-8768-2237), is just 200 meters from the Long Beach water sporting area. **Sea-Vu Caravan Park,** Squire Dr. (tel. 08-8768-2273), is near beaches and attractions. All have camp sites, on-site vans, and cabins.

Information

Robe Historical Interpretation Centre, in the library building on Mundy Terrace (tel. 08-8768-2465), can provide additional tourist information. Hours are Tues.-Fri. 10 a.m.-5 p.m., Saturday 8:30 a.m.-12:30 p.m.

BEACHPORT

Beachport (pop. 410) is another seaside lobster, crayfish, and one-time hustle-bustle port. Set at the northern edge of Rivoli Bay, this former whaling station, established by the Henty brothers in the 1830s, became a township in 1878, the same year a Beachport-Mt. Gambier railway line was built, instantly turning the town into a train-trip-away holiday resort. And, though the trains no longer run, Beachport is still a desirable destination for family excursions.

Sights
If you're coming from Robe, follow the detour to impressive **Woakwine Cutting,** a drainage project constructed by one farmer and his helper in less than three years. You can *ooh* and *aah* from the specially built viewing platform.

See fishing, farming, and whaling displays, as well as local relics, at the **National Trust Museum,** inside the old wool and grain store on Railway Terrace. Hours are Sunday 2-4 p.m. Admission is $2. For information, phone (08) 8735-8013.

Bowman's Scenic Drive, from Foster St. to Wooleys Rocks, takes in terrific views of the town and Lake George on one side, the ocean on the other. You'll find lookout points at Backers Lookout and Salmon Hole.

If you've got a 4WD vehicle you can drive past Wooleys Rocks, along sand dunes, and into **Beachport Conservation Park;** otherwise access is from Railway Terrace North. The park includes tracks through sand dunes and coastal vegetation, and around Wooleys Lake. The eight km drift, accessible only by four-wheelers or two feet, offers safe sailing and windsurfing.

Swimmers will do well around the jetty, scuba divers enjoy the **Back Beach** reef areas, and surfers like a spot known as the **Blowhole.** The **Pool of Siloam,** a very salty (six times more than the sea) lake near Beachport, is thought to be therapeutic.

Accommodations
Beachport Hotel (tel. 08-8735-8003) and **Bombas Hotel** (tel. 08-8735-8333), both on Railway Terrace, have inexpensive pub accommodations. **Beachport Motor Inn,** Railway Terrace (tel. 08-8735-8070), is in the moderate range. Try the Beachport **YHA Hostel,** Beach Rd. (tel. 08-8735-8197), for dorm beds at $8 per night.

Beachport Caravan Park, Beach Rd. (tel. 08-8735-8128), with cabins and on-site vans, is situated on the foreshore with a jetty. **Southern Ocean Tourist Park,** Somerville St. (tel. 08-8735-8153), is close to the beach. It has

open fireplaces, cabins, and campsites. This park is also the local Tourist Information Centre.

MILLICENT

Bordered on the north and southeast by thick, fragrant pine forests, Millicent (pop. 5,075) is big timber country. From Kingston to Millicent, coastal travel is along Alternate Highway 1; it reconnects with the main highway here.

This mini-city, begun in 1870 as a rural community, shifted to a timber center after pines were cultivated in nearby ranges. Sawmills and paper mills soon moved in and were followed by a steady stream of workers (including a large European population).

Sights
Millicent Museum, 1 Mt. Gambier Rd. (tel. 08-8733-3205), is one of the region's most extensive facilities, with natural history and Aboriginal displays, restored horse-drawn vehicles, farm implements, tools, machinery, and a coin-operated waterwheel. The museum also houses **Admella Gallery,** which exhibits and sells local arts and crafts, and which also serves as the Tourist Information Office. Hours are Mon.-Sat. 10 a.m.-4 p.m., Sunday 1-4 p.m. Museum admission is $2.50.

Tantanoola Caves, on Princes Hwy., 21 km from Millicent, are inside a dolomite marine cliff beside the highway. Take one of the hourly guided tours of the single chamber ($4), or sign up for a "wild cave tour" that explores the underground system (by appointment). At the nearby town of Tantanoola, you can view the stuffed carcass of *the* Tantanoola tiger, at—where else?—the **Tantanoola Tiger Hotel.** Load up on brew to go along with all the bull you'll hear about this legendary beast.

If you'd rather climb than cave, coastal **Canunda National Park,** beginning at Southend, 27 km west of Millicent, has a system of huge, wondrous sand dunes for you to sink your feet into. You can also camp here and, in the summer, take informative ranger-guided walks.

Accommodations
Sportsmans Hotel, 72 George St. (tel. 08-8733-2017), has inexpensive rooms, but the facilities are shared. Other motels, all in the inexpensive

to low-moderate range, are **Diplomat Motel,** 51 Mt. Gambier Rd. (tel. 08-8733-2211), **Millicent Motel,** 82 Mt. Gambier Rd. (tel. 08-8733-2655), and **Somerset Hotel Motel,** 2 George St. (tel. 08-8733-2888).

Hillview Caravan Park, Dalton St. (tel. 08-8733-2806), with campsites and cabins, is less than two km from the town center. **Millicent Lakeside Caravan Park,** Park Terrace (tel. 08-8733-3947), also has on-site vans and is adjacent to a swimming lake.

Information

Millicent Tourist Information Centre is at the Millicent Museum. For information on Canunda National Park, contact the **Department of Environment and Natural Resources** at Southend (tel. 08-8735-6053). To sign up for cave walks at **Tantanoola Caves Conservation Park,** phone the park office at (08) 8734-4153.

MOUNT GAMBIER

The volcano has been extinct for 5,000 years, but the city of Mt. Gambier (pop. 20,815), built upon the volcano's slopes and situated about halfway between Adelaide and Melbourne, is a busy commercial center, regarded as the capital of the southeast. The city's big attractions are the many crater lakes. Of these, mysterious **Blue Lake** is the largest, with a circumference of five kilometers. It's so famous that Mt. Gambier is often called the "Blue Lake City." The lake, which is actually gray, mysteriously changes, almost overnight, to an extraordinary blue color each and every November, staying that color until late March, when it gradually reverts to gray. Long believed to be "bottomless," recently echo-sounding equipment dispelled that myth by measuring an 80-meter maximum depth. Blue Lake also supplies Mt. Gambier with its domestic water.

In 1800, Lieutenant James Grant, in the HMS *Lady Nelson,* was sailing along the coast when he sighted two peaks. He named them Mt. Schank (after Admiral Schank, who had invented the *Lady Nelson*'s centerboard keel) and Mt. Gambier (for Lord Gambier of the Royal Navy). Mount Gambier developed as an agricultural township in 1841, when Stephen Henty and his companions, enticed by the rich volcanic soil and appreciable annual rainfalls, built their cottages between Valley and Brownes Lakes and brought their stock to graze on the fertile farmlands. Though agriculture is still im-

ortant, now the city's major source of employ-
ent is the forest industry and the area's six
rge sawmills.

ights

esides Blue Lake, Mt. Gambier's other unique
eature is **Cave Park,** an open cave in the city
enter, surrounded by lovely rose gardens. In
omplete defiance of Mt. Gambier's southern
atitude, two banana trees rise from the cave
nd stretch toward the light. Other caves are
mpherston Cave, with terraced gardens and
icnic grounds, and water-filled **Engelbrecht
ave,** a popular diving spot. Other diving loca-
ons are **Little Blue Lake, Ewens Ponds, Pi-
aninnie Ponds, Three Sisters,** and **Hell Hole.**

Historic buildings near Cave Park are the
ost office, town hall, and **Jens Hotel. Old
ourthouse Museum,** Bay Rd., operated by
e National Trust, displays the original court-
ouse furnishings and other local historic items.
ours are Mon.-Fri. noon-4 p.m., Sat.-Sun. 10
.m.-4 p.m. Admission is $2.50. For informa-
on, phone (08) 8724-1730.

Lewis' Museum, Pick Ave. (across from the
howgrounds), is jam-packed with more than
0,000 Aboriginal, mechanical, industrial, and
storical artifacts. Hours are daily 8 a.m.-4 p.m.
dmission is $4. For information, phone (08)
725-1381.

ccommodations

bout 30 motels and hotels and six caravan
arks are sprawled around the town. Prices for
ouble rooms range from moderate to expen-
ive, but none of the accommodations are ex-
eptional. In this town, a room at the cheap end
hould do you just fine.

The **Jens Hotel,** 40 Commercial St. East (tel.
8-8725-0188), is a beautiful heritage property
ith inexpensive rooms.

Caravan parks with campsites, on-site vans,
nd cabins, include **Blue Lake City Caravan
ark,** Bay Rd. (tel. 08-8725-9856); **Mt. Gam-
ier Central Caravan Park,** 6 Krummel St. (tel.
8-8715-4427); and **Pine Country Caravan
ark,** Port MacDonnell Rd. (tel. 08-8725-1988).

ervices and Information

he **Lady Nelson Tourist and Interpretive
entre,** Jubilee Hwy. East, near the city center

(tel. 08-8724-1730), is a treasure trove of information. Besides the usual brochures and
such, the center arranges all types of accommodations, tours (to sawmills, pumping stations, and dairies), and provides everything you
want to know about the lakes area (including issuing diving permits). It will even prepare a cus-
tomized itinerary. While there, you can view a
full-size replica of HMS *Lady Nelson,* hear Lieutenant Grant (another replica, and *no* competition for Madame Tussaud!) give his spiel, and
watch the volcano erupt in a blaze of neon! The
center is open daily 9 a.m.-5 p.m., closed Christmas Day.

For emergencies, contact **police** (tel. 08-
8725-9333), **Mt. Gambier Hospital** (tel. 08-
8724-2211), or, for road mishaps or info, the
Royal Automobile Association (tel. 08-8725-
4101).

PORT MACDONNELL

South Australia's southernmost port and crayfish
center is Port MacDonnell, 28 km south of Mt.
Gambier. Once a bustling shipping center for
freight being hauled between Adelaide and Melbourne, Port MacDonnell (pop. 650) these days
is a quaint fishing village. On the way to Port
MacDonnell, climb Mount Schank. Follow walking tracks both inside and outside the crater or
just sit back and check out the grandiose view.

Sights

To the west of town, **Cape Northumberland
Lighthouse,** reached by traveling through a
petrified forest, affords a towering view of the
rugged coastline below.

Dingley Dell Conservation Park, two km
west of Port MacDonnell, is the restored 1860s
home of horsey Scottish poet Adam Lindsay
Gordon (he was South Australia's big-time bard).
Picnic on the grounds and soak up some of
Gordon's inspiration.

The large **Old Customs House,** on the foreshore, was built in 1860 to accommodate the
sizable freight loads of the time.

Accommodations

Get an inexpensive room with shared facilities at
Victoria Hotel, 40 Meylin St. (tel. 08-8738-

2213), or anything from on-site vans to fully equipped holiday flats at **Sea View Motel,** 77 Sea Parade (tel. 08-8738-2243).

Services and Information
Gather tourist information at **Port MacDonnell District Council,** Charles St. (tel. 08-8738-2437).

For emergencies, phone the **police** (tel. 08-8738-2216) or the **Royal Automobile Association** (tel. 08-8738-2238).

PENOLA

North of Mt. Gambier, venture through the pine-forested communities of Tarpeena and Nangwarry to this tiny heritage town noted for its beautiful buildings and churches. Penola is also the gateway to the southeastern wine region.

Sights
Many 1850s cottages, built by the town's first settlers, still stand today. The **Penola Heritage Walk,** which departs from the Tourist Information Centre, takes in nearly 30 historic sites around Penola. **Petticoat Lane,** a sort of open-air museum of Penola's early architecture, features a number of traditional buildings, including the former Anglican rectory. Arts and crafts hounds will find galleries and gift shops inside many of the historic sites.

John Riddoch Interpretive Centre, Arthur St., in the former Penola Library and Mechanics Institute, pays tribute to the town's heritage and its most prominent citizens (including John Riddoch). Hours are daily 10 a.m.-4 p.m. For information, phone (08) 8737-2855.

Yallum Park, Old Millicent Rd., Riddoch's personal mansion, built in 1880, depicts the grand style of the upper crust. Hours are by appointment. Admission is $3. For information, phone (08) 8737-2435.

Penola Conservation Park, 10 km west of town, features a signposted interpretive trail into this swampy wildlife sanctuary.

Accommodations
Haywards Royal Oak Hotel, 31 Church St. (tel. 08-8737-2322), offers inexpensive pub rooms with shared facilities. Book a variety of heritage accommodations, at moderate-expensive prices, through **Australian Country Cottages,** 33 Riddoch St. (tel. 08-8737-2250).

Services and Information
Penola Tourist Information Centre, inside the John Riddoch Interpretive Centre, provides maps for scenic drives and heritage walks, and other local information. Hours are daily 10 a.m.-4 p.m., closed Christmas Day and Good Friday.

In emergencies, contact the **police** (tel. 08-8737-2315), **hospital** (tel. 08-8737-2311), **Royal Automobile Association** (tel. 08-8737-2367).

COONAWARRA

It was John Riddoch, Penola mogul, who liked the looks of the grapevines in his Coonawarra Fruit Colony and, subsequently, established the district's first winery. Though the vines of Riddoch's winery, built in 1893, thrived, demand was low. It wasn't until the 1960s that the industry really took off. Today, about 15 wineries in the district, which runs for 16 km north of Penola, are famous for the bold reds produced from the rich *terra rossa.*

Accommodations
Coonawarra offers nothing in the inexpensive category. The most moderately priced cottage accommodations are **Skinner, Redman,** and **The Pickers Hut** (tel. 08-8736-3304 or 8736-3220, for all three).

Chardonnay Lodge, Penola Rd. (tel. 08-8736-3309), is an expensive luxury motel with an art gallery, swimming pool, good restaurant, and complimentary continental breakfast.

Information
For tourist info, see the Penola Tourist Information Centre, above.

NARACOORTE

Proclaimed a town in 1870 (though the first hotel and store were erected in the 1840s), Naracoorte (pop. 4,640) functions mainly as a regional service and commercial center, with lovely old dwellings scattered all about.

ights

the **Sheeps Back Museum** (tel. 08-8762-?518), in the old flour mill on MacDonnell St. and run by the National Trust, traces the history of the wool industry. Hours are daily 10 a.m.-4 m. Admission is $2.

More interesting is the **Naracoorte Museum and Snake Pit,** Smith St. (tel. 08-8762-2059), where more than 100 collections of gemstones, rocks, weapons, butterflies, and other artifacts commingle with venomous snakes and other reptiles lounging about rocks and cacti. Hours re Mon.-Thurs. 10 a.m.-5 p.m., Sat.-Sun. 2-5 .m., closed mid-July through August and on Christmas Day. Admission is $5.

Take a look at **Padthaway Estate,** about 41 m north of Naracoorte, a gracious country manion built in 1882. **Padthaway Conservation ark** boasts stringybark and red gum forests where you can bushwalk or picnic.

Naracoorte Caves Conservation Park, 12 m southeast of town, features about 69 caves long a 25-km expanse of range. Daily tours xplore Alexandra, Blanche, and Victoria Fossil aves, and during holiday periods you can sign p for special wild-caving tours into undeveloped areas (be prepared to climb and crawl). For information and tour bookings, phone (08) 8762-340.

Bool Lagoon, a bit farther south, is a vast nd diverse wetland where you can see about 5 species of birds and other wildlife. Self-guided and organized walking tracks are available. A ird blind and boardwalks, built over the lagoon, allow for excellent birdwatching. For information, phone (08) 8764-7541.

Mary Seymour Conservation Park, near ool Lagoon, is another sanctuary for breeding birds.

ccommodations

Naracoorte Hotel Motel, 73 Ormerod St. (tel. 8-8762-2400), has inexpensive rooms with hared facilities in the older hotel; or, for $20 nore, you can stay in the updated motel section. **Country Roads Motor Inn,** 28 Smith St. (tel. 08-762-3900), is more posh, with rooms in the moderate range. Big splurgers can spring for elegant accommodations at the historic **Padthaway Estate** (tel. 08-8765-5039), where doubles un about $130, including breakfast.

Naracoorte Caravan Park, 81 Park Terrace (tel. 08-8762-2128), is close to the town center and has campsites, on-site vans, and cabins. Camping is permitted at both **Naracoorte Caves** (tel. 08-8762-2340) and **Bool Lagoon** (tel. 08-8764-7541).

Services and Information

The **tourist information office** is at Sheeps Back Museum. In an emergency, call **police** (tel. 08-8762-2066), the **hospital** (tel. 08-8762-2222), or the trusty **Royal Automobile Association** (tel. 08-8762-2247).

BORDERTOWN

Situated 42 km northeast of Padthaway, along the Dukes Highway, Bordertown (pop. 2,320) isn't on but is near the Victorian border, 20 km away. Settled in 1852, along the route of the gold escort from Victoria to Adelaide, the area's rich farmlands produce wine grapes, small seeds, cereals, wool, meat, and vegetable crops. The former Australian Prime Minister Bob Hawke spent his early childhood here. His home has been renovated, and his bust has been bronzed.

Adjacent to Dukes Highway, **Bordertown Wildlife Park** is home to, besides the usual native birds and animals, four specially bred pure white kangaroos.

Accommodations

Several good motels with inexpensive to low-moderate prices line Dukes Highway. **Bordertown Caravan Park,** Penny Terrace (tel. 08-8752-1752), near the town center, is another place to rest your head.

Events

The annual **Camel Racing Festival,** held each November, features camel and donkey races, parachute jumping, various other antics, and camels from every state and territory in Australia.

Services and Information

For tourist information, contact **Bordertown Council Office,** 43 Woolshed St. (tel. 08-8752-1044). For emergency assistance, contact **police** (tel. 08-8752-1355), the **hospital** (tel. 08-8752-1166), or the **Royal Automobile Association** (tel. 08-8752-1270).

KEITH

Keith (pop. 1,190), 46 km northwest of Bordertown, was proclaimed a township in 1889. At one time the region was part of a 90-mile desert, but after zinc and copper were added to the soil, it became profitable grazing and farm land. Most of the old buildings sit along Heritage St., facing the Dukes Highway.

Sights

Peek into the foyer of the **Congregational Church,** on Heritage Street. The 1910 building features four interesting stained-glass windows, made by locals, depicting the pioneering era. Hours are daily 9 a.m.-5 p.m.

Mount Monster Conservation Park, 10 km south of Keith, has spectacular views from the lookout (a signposted walk will guide you) and a variety of vegetation, birds, and wildlife. Mount Monster, and others in a chain of granite outcrops, were islands about 40 million years ago.

Ngarkat Conservation Park, northeast of Keith, is perfect for bushwalks. The 5,000-hectare park is full of native animals and abundant in flora. **Warning:** There are large numbers of beehives in this park.

Situated in the southwest corner 20 km north of Keith, **Mount Rescue Conservation Park** has 28,385 hectares of sand plains and dunes containing rare species of birds and plants.

Accommodations

Keith's only **hotel/motel** and **motor inn** both charge about $50 for a double. **Keith Caravan Park,** Naracoorte Rd. (tel. 08-8755-1957), has campsites and on-site vans.

Services and Information

The **Tourist Information Centre** is inside the old Congregational Church, on Heritage Street.

Hours are daily 9 a.m.-5 p.m. For information phone (08) 8755-1584.

In emergencies, contact **police** (tel. 08-8755-1211), the **hospital** (tel. 08-8755-1757), or **Royal Automobile Association** (tel. 08-8755-1331).

BACK TO TAILEM BEND

Heading back to Tailem Bend, you'll pass through more grazing land. Stop by **Tintara,** 3 km northwest of Keith, which has a nice old post office and homestead (10 km west of town on Woods Well Rd.).

Mount Boothby Conservation Park, 20 km northwest of Tintara, features 4,045 hectares of heath, mallee, pink gum forest, and granite outcrops, where you can picnic or stretch your legs, between farmland scenes.

Watch for **Coonalpyn,** the last dot on the map before Tailem Bend.

TRANSPORTATION

Kendell Airlines (tel. 069-22-0100, or book through Ansett) makes the 50-minute flight from Adelaide to Mt. Gambier, and on to Melbourne several days a week. Fare is $150 one-way from either capital city to Mt. Gambier. The standby fare runs about $25 less. **O'Connor Airlines** (tel. 08-8725-6666, or book through Qantas) makes daily flights from Mt. Gambier to either Adelaide or Melbourne.

Catch **Mt. Gambier Motor Services** (tel. 08-8296-0111) from Adelaide's central bus station to Kingston ($30), Robe ($27), Millicent ($34), or Mt. Gambier ($35), or travel **Greyhound Pioneer Australia** (tel. 08-8233-2797, or 13-2030 toll-free) along Princes Highway to Mt. Gambier ($42).

THE MURRAY RIVER

these parts it's called the "Mighty Murray," nd it conjures up all the romantic images a ighty river should—paddlesteamers plying eir trade, floating casinos and riverboat gam ers, dashing gents and bawdy women, a host rascals, scoundrels, ne'er-do-wells, and free irits, runaways aboard makeshift rafts, and cret trysts along the banks.

Beginning in the Snowy Mountains, travel g along the border between New South Wales nd Victoria, the river gains momentum as it aches South Australia, makes a sharp turn eaward at Northwest Bend, and eventually npties into Lake Alexandrina, where its mighty outh meets the great Southern Ocean. And, ough the Murray has often been called the Mississippi of Australia," and the flavor is much e same, this river—at 2,575 km from source to outh—is less than half the length of its Ameri n counterpart.

Within South Australia's 640-km section, the urray is divided into two districts—the River nd and the Lower Murray. The Riverland in udes the Murray's six locks, bountiful citrus oves, 17,000 hectares of vineyards, and the wns from Renmark to Blanchetown. This, in ct, is Australia's biggest wine-producing re on (yes, *more* than the Barossa, Clare, oonawarra, and even the Hunter Valley, in ew South Wales), noted for high-quality table ines and a variety of other products. The Lower urray spans from below Blanchetown to Mur y Bridge, where you'll encounter more or

chards, large granite outcrops, waterfalls, la goons, and phenomenal birdlife. Throughout the entire Murray area, you'll enjoy abundant sunshine with good fishing, swimming, water skiing, and boating—including both pad dlesteaming and houseboating.

The annual excess flow of the Murray and its tributaries averages only 12.7 mm, the lowest runoff of any major river system, and it takes approximately one month for the Murray flow at Albury to arrive at South Australia. Furthermore— for all you riverphiles—the bed of the Lower Mur ray rests below sea level, thereby making it one of the few rivers on earth to run uphill!

History

In 1824, explorers Hume and Hovell were the first white men to sight the Murray. Six years later, Capt. Charles Sturt steered a whale boat— while a group of soldiers and convicts rowed— some 2,735 km, from the Murrumbidgee and Murray Rivers to the sea and back again. Sturt named the river after Colonial Secretary Sir George Murray, and eventually the Sturt High way, which runs through the Riverland, was named for the brave captain himself.

Lady Augusta and *Mary Ann* were the first pad dlesteamers to navigate the river, making the journey in 1853, from Goolwa to Swan Hill in Vic toria. Until the railway lines were built, river life was a-bustle, with trade being carted to and fro and river towns popping up along the banks (and with them a few rabble-rousers and river rats).

Then, in 1887, up in the Riverland, a fellow named Alfred Deakin, who'd been keeping tabs on irrigation in the California deserts, persuaded Canadians George and William Chaffey (ex perts in the field) to come to Renmark and set up Australia's first irrigation settlement. This pro ject's success led to the high-grade citrus crops and wines produced in the region today.

On 1 February 1997 all telephone numbers in the Murray River area will change. In prepara tion for this, all numbers in this section have been changed to eight digits. To dial a Murray River area number before 1 February, simply delete the first two digits of the new number and, if dialing from outside the Murray River area, add the area code (085). As an exam ple, (08) 8512-3456 would be dialed (085) 12- 3456. After 1 February the area code for all numbers in this section will be (08).

MURRAY BRIDGE

Situated approximately 80 km from Adelaide, Murray Bridge (pop. 16,250) is the state's largest

THE MURRAY RIVER

river town. This city should really be called Murray *Bridges,* since three of them cross the river here. Originally named "Edwards Crossing," the calm waters made this a favored spot for early settlers crossing the river—though at first they floated their wagons from shore to shore atop beer kegs! The road bridge was opened in 1879, followed by the rail bridge in 1927, and the Swanport Bridge—South Australia's longest—in 1979. Dairy farming, chickens, pigs, glasshouse tomatoes, and cereal represent important industries in this region.

Murray Bridge is an ideal spot for water sports, particularly waterskiing between White Sands and Willow Banks. Scads of picnic area and reserves dot the riverfront, affording kic back-and-relax opportunities for the road-wear Or catch the Murray spirit and jump aboard th sternwheeler *Proud Mary* for two- to five-da jaunts.

Sights

Relive local history and heritage at **Captain' Cottage Museum,** Thomas St. (tel. 08-853 0049). Displays of engines, machinery, doll model riverboats, and photos should enlighte you. Hours are Sat.-Sun. and public holiday 10 a.m.-4 p.m. Admission is $2.

Puzzle Park, Jervois Rd. (tel. 08-8532-3709), a fun park with an aquarium, miniature golf ourse, and a 4.5-km maze in which to lose ourself (or perhaps an irritating travel comanion). Hours are daily 10 a.m.-5:30 p.m., osed Christmas Day. Admission is $9.

Butterfly House, next door (tel. 08-8532-366), is the state's only place to prance with live opical species. Hours are daily 10 a.m.-5 p.m. dmission is $4.

ccommodations and Food

you're staying the night, the bare-bones **Balony Private Hotel,** 12 6th Ave. (tel. 08-8532-330), is inexpensive and includes breakfast. so inexpensive, **Motel Greenacres,** Princes wy. East (tel. 08-8532-1090), is a family-owned stablishment five km southeast of the city cener. Some rooms have kitchenettes.

Oval Caravan Park, 4 LeMessurier St. (tel. 8-8532-2588), near the river, has cabins and n-site vans. **Avoca Dell Caravan Park,** Lodon Rd. (tel. 08-8532-2095), on the Murray, has abins and on-site vans, too, but also camptes.

Many **houseboats** are available for weekly entals; inquire at the Tourist Information Centre.

Pick up natural foods, vitamins, herbal teas, nd grains at **Murray Bridge Health Foods,** orner of 7th and 4th Streets. (tel. 08-8532-383). You can get handmade pickled preserves **Cottage Harvest,** Rock Gully Rd. (tel. 08-531-1165), and handmade chocolates at **Cotge Box Chocolates,** Wharf Rd. (tel. 08-8532-055). Both are open daily 10 a.m.-5 p.m.

ransportation, Services, and Information

local bus service operates Mon.-Saturday. or information, phone **Murray Bridge Passenger Service** (tel. 08-8532-2633). There's a xi stand off Bridge Street.

The **Tourist Information Centre** is on Swanort Rd., between South and Mary Terraces el. 08-8532-6660). Hours are Mon.-Fri. 8:30 .m.-4 p.m., Saturday 10 a.m.-3:30 p.m., Sunay and public holidays 10 a.m.-2 p.m., closed hristmas Day.

For emergencies, contact the **police** (tel. 08-532-1888), **fire brigade** (tel. 08-8532-1000), or mbulance (tel. 08-8532-1122). The local ranch of the **Royal Automobile Association**

is on Railway Terrace (tel. 08-8532-1935), and the **hospital** (tel. 08-8532-1333) is at the corner of Swanport Rd. and Monash Terrace.

MANNUM

On your way to Mannum, stop at Mypolonga, eight km north of Murray Bridge on Mannum Road. It's a small farming community comprising both highlands and swamplands. Noted for its well-irrigated orange, apricot, peach, and pear orchards, Mypolonga is another water sport and houseboat haven.

Mannum (pop. 2,000), a wide spot in the river 21 km north of Murray Bridge, is the birthplace of Australia's paddlesteamers. In 1853, Capt. W.R. Randell (who had settled in the district some 10 years earlier) constructed *Mary Ann,* the first steamboat, and the following year sailed it up to Swan Hill in Victoria. In 1854, the busy captain also built Mannum's first house, which, over time, was bought, sold, and transformed into the Mannum Hotel. Subsequent to the *Mary Ann's* inaugural voyage, Mannum became a busy shipbuilding center. Today Mannum is a peaceful community, known for its scenic beauty, rich heritage, and water activities, as well as its designation as new home port for the *Murray Princess.*

Sights

Recreation Reserve (called the "Rec" by locals) lines the banks of the Murray with 350 meters of grassy picnic and barbecue areas, a boat ramp, and scenic lookouts to town, river, and valley.

The National Trust operates **Mannum Museum** (tel. 08-8569-1303) inside the restored 1896 paddlesteamer *Marion.* Moored at Randell's original wharf at Arnold Park, the floating museum contains river relics and other memorabilia. The museum is open daily 9 a.m.-4 p.m., closed Christmas Day. Admission is $2.50.

The **Bird Sanctuary,** on Halidon Rd., is home to ducks, swans, pelicans, and other beautiful waterbirds. Have a look.

Mannum Waterfalls Reserve, 20 km south of town, offers picnic spots and walking tracks, but if you want to see the falls be aware that they flow mainly in the winter.

Accommodations and Food

Stay at Captain Randell's inexpensive home-stead-turned-**Mannum Hotel,** 15 Randell St. (tel. 08-8569-1008), with shared facilities. **Leon-aville,** 69 River Lane (tel. 08-8569-2073), of-fers inexpensive bed and breakfast accommo-dations in an 1883 homestead. **Mannum Motel,** 76 Cliff St. (08-8569-1808), is the expensive choice for standard motel amenities.

Mannum Caravan Park, Purnong Rd. (tel. 08-8569-1402), adjacent to the Bird Sanctuary, has campsites and cabins.

Stroll over to **Kia Marina,** on Younghusband Rd., to check out weekly deals on the many **houseboats** for rent. (P.S. "Younghusband," in a piece of tourist lit, was misprinted "Hunghus-band." A boat, perhaps, docked at the Freudian slip.) Anyway, young and/or hung, the boats are over at the marina.

Riverfront Coffee Spot, 67 Randell St. (tel. 08-8569-1711), is open daily for cappuccino, croissants, cakes, and light meals.

THE MID MURRAYLANDS

The Mid Murraylands comprise the area from Bow Hill in the south (32 km from Mannum) to Swan Reach in the north, from Nildottie in the east to Sedan in the west. Just a 90-minute drive from Adelaide, this district offers lovely scenery and not-so-touristy river action where you can fish and boat in peace or just sit on the banks and float twigs downstream.

There's a stunning **scenic drive** along Younghusband Rd., on the way to Purnong, that takes in lagoons, lakes, stone quarries, and stupendous bird life. **Bow Hill,** before Purnong, is a popular waterskiing spot. **Purnong** is

RULES FOR THE MURRAYLANDS

As part of a "Don't Muck up the Murray" cam-paign, aimed at preserving the river environ-ment, the South Australia Department of Environ-ment and Planning asks that visitors adhere to the following rules:

Protect Water Supplies

Do not bury excrement within 50 meters of the Mur-ray.

Do not use pollutants, like soap, anywhere near the water.

Do not wash plates or utensils within 50 meters of the river.

Camp away from the river bank. Avoid blocking the access of stock or wildlife to the water; they need their water to live.

Respect Farmers, Their Property, and Stock

Leave machinery alone. Windmills, pumps, tractors, and generators are important for a farm's survival. Your in-terference could cause costly or ruinous breakdowns.

Do not frighten or disturb stock. Farm animals are valuable and easily disturbed, and some can injure you. They could be lambing or calving, so

give them a go and keep right away.

Camp away from windmills and pumps and don't interfere with farm water supplies, except in an emergency.

Report vandalism. If you see any acts of vandal-ism, notify the landowner.

Respect and Keep to Roads and Tracks

Fences, gates, roads, and tracks represent impor-tant investments to farmers and property owners, so while you're a guest on their land, be considerate of your respon-sibilities.

Leave gates as you found them.

Avoid damaging fences; use gates and stiles where they are provided.

Keep to existing roads and tracks and do not widen them.

Contact the landowner if you propose to drive off a track or travel across his property.

Avoid vehicle travel when roads are wet.

If you see persons violating or polluting the river, you are asked to phone **River Watch,** the Murray's 24-hour watchdog, at (08) 8582-2700.

DON'T MUCK UP THE MURRAY

slow-going holiday village, but a barrage of river craft float past just the same. Great views can be enjoyed at **Caurnamont Landing,** a base for houseboat rentals. **Walker Flat,** sheltered by tall cliffs, is another location sought out by both waterskiers and waterbirds. Small, rural **Nildottie,** once an old paddlesteamer landing, now bears citrus fruit and vegetable crops. **Big Bend** boasts big river red gums and sandstone cliffs that draw vast numbers of cockatoos to nest.

Surveyed in 1839, **Swan Reach** (pop. 200) is the Mid Murraylands' largest town and halfway point between the Barossa Valley and the Riverland. It's another holiday and water sport mecca. **Punuelroo,** seven km south, is a longtime holiday hot spot, and *not* the place to hit if you want peace and quiet. **Ridley Conservation Park,** five km south of Swan Reach, is where you might glimpse hairy-nosed wombats and the rare striped honeyeater bird. **Swan Reach Conservation Park,** 11 km northwest of Swan Reach, is 1,900 hectares of grasslands, thick mallee, false sandalwood, open woodland, and roaming wildlife, including emus and western gray kangaroos.

Sedan, about 16 km west from Swan Reach Conservation Park, provides facilities for the surrounding farm community. Established in the late 1890s, the town has preserved many of its old buildings. From Sedan, you can take a number of scenic drives. Best is the route that winds from Cambrai through the Marne River Valley—taking in huge river red gums, a granite quarry, a pinnacle of fossils, and a myriad of wildlife—then swings north to Ridley Conservation Park and back to Swan Reach.

Accommodations

Pub-style rooms are inexpensive at **Swan Reach Hotel** (tel. 08-8570-2003). **Yookamurra Sanctuary,** Pipeline Rd. (tel. 08-8562-5011), offers moderately priced bunkhouse accommodations within its delicate woodlands. All meals are included in the rates.

Punyelroo Caravan Park, on the riverbanks (tel. 08-8570-2021), has campsites and on-site vans.

BLANCHETOWN

This popular holiday resort—which begins the Riverland—sits 28 km north of Swan Reach

and 134 km northeast of Adelaide, along the Sturt Highway. Governor R.G. MacDonnell named this town for his wife, Lady Blanche. There were high hopes for Blanchetown, begun in 1855 as an important commercial center and established as a port in 1863, but they fizzled after northerly neighbor Morgan won the much-sought-after railway line. In 1922, construction began here on the complex system of locks and weirs created to control fluctuations of the river's water level. If you stand atop Blanchetown Bridge, you might see a houseboat passing through Lock Number One.

Sights
Brookfield Conservation Park, 11 km west of Blanchetown, features 6,332 hectares of open scrub mallee, mallee box, and yorrell, through which wander red kangaroos, hairy-nosed wombats, fat-tailed dunnarts, and a variety of birds. Don't veer off marked walking trails without checking with the ranger station (three km inside the entrance); some areas are closed due to scientific research on the hairy-nosed wombat.

Trenetas, Old Ferry Landing (tel. 08-8540-5071), a floating sand gallery overlooking the river, exhibits and sells arts and crafts with a sand motif, and also houses a coffee shop. Hours are Tues.-Sat. and public holidays 10 a.m.-8 p.m.

Accommodations
Riverside Caravan and Camping Park (tel. 08-8540-5070) is a quiet riverfront park with a beach, offering campsites, on-site vans, cabins, and canoe-hire.

For **houseboats,** inquire at **Blanchetown** or **Kayandee Moorings.**

Services and Information
In an emergency, contact the **police** (tel. 08-8540-5013), **ambulance** (tel. 08-8541-2444), or local **Royal Automobile Club** (tel. 08-8541-2600).

MORGAN

At one time Morgan (pop. 1,265) was South Australia's second-busiest port (Port Adelaide ranked first). Originally known as "Northwest Bend," "Great Bend," and the "Great Elbow" (this is where the Murray makes its sharp turn), Morgan was officially named after Sir William Morgan by Governor Musgrave in 1878, the same year a railway line was opened. In the good old days Morgan used to have a veritable traffic jam of steamers and barges unloading cargo, which was then transferred by rail to Port Adelaide.

Sights

Reminders of the town's formidable history include the huge wharf, built in 1878, and the heritage buildings along Railway Terrace. **Port of Morgan Historic Museum,** on Railway Terrace, displays original river charts and trading-days artifacts. The 1940s **Pumping Station and Water Filtration Plant,** on Renmark Rd., can be toured on Tuesday 1-3 p.m.

Cross the river by ferry to **White Dam Conservation Park,** in the northwest bend, to view waterbirds in the wetlands or picnic under towering red gums.

Accommodations

Both the **Commercial Hotel** (tel. 08-8540-2107) and **Terminus Hotel Motel** (tel. 08-8540-2006), on historic Railway Terrace, have simple inexpensive accommodations. **Morgan Riverside Caravan Park** (tel. 08-8540-2207) has on-site vans and cabins, with air-conditioning and telly.

Look for **houseboat rentals** along the riverfront.

WAIKERIE

Waikerie (pop. 1,700), reached from Blanchetown along the Sturt Highway, or from Morgan (passing Lock Number Two), is the "Citrus Center of Australia." Founded in 1880 by the Shepherd Brothers, the name "Waikerie" is a derivative of an Aboriginal word meaning "many wings or birds," no doubt because of the abundant colorful birds (and, nowadays, the gliders) hanging around the district's lagoons and riverbanks.

Mild sunny winters and hot temperate summers, combined with modern irrigation, have turned this former desert into a citrus-fruit oasis of more than one million bountiful trees, planted on over 5,000 acres (try to visit in Sept.-Oct when they're in bloom).

Sights

In the center of town is **Waikerie Producers Packing House,** the largest of its kind in Australia. You can arrange for a tour there or at the nearby **Cresta Fruit Juice Factory,** on Virgo Rd. in Cresta.

Pooginook Conservation Park, 12 km northeast of Waikerie, is home to a variety of animal and bird life, in environs ranging from open to dense mallee. **Terrigal Fauna Park** (tel. 08-8541-3414) and **Waikerie Fauna Park** (tel. 08-8541-2077) also afford peeks at local critters. Or, catch your view from atop **Clifftop Lookout,** a short walk from the town center along Goodchild Street.

Accommodations and Food

The centrally located **Waikerie Hotel Motel** McCoy St. (tel. 08-8541-2999), has inexpensive low-to-moderate rates, depending on which section you stay in. The restaurant offers both counter meals and a la carte dining. Air-conditioned on-site vans and cabins are available at **Waikerie Caravan Park,** Ramco Rd. (tel. 08-8541-2651).

Purchase local citrus, dried, and glacé fruits honey, juices, and nonalcoholic wines at **The Orange Tree,** on Sturt Hwy. (tel. 08-8541-2332) A viewing platform looks out over the river and town. Hours are daily 9 a.m.-5 p.m.

Sports and Recreation

Waikerie, sight of the 1974 World Gliding Championships, is the perfect place to soar and spiral the skies. **Waikerie Gliding Club** (tel. 08-8541-2644) offers glider joy flights, as well as instruction.

Services and Information

The **Tourist Information Centre,** 20 McCoy St. (tel. 08-8541-2183), can help with juice queries and other needs. Hours are Mon.-Fri 8:30 a.m.-5:30 p.m., Saturday 8:30-11:30 a.m. closed public holidays.

In emergencies call the **police** (tel. 08-8541-2888) or an **ambulance** (tel. 08-8541-2444) For road service, phone the **Royal Automobile Association** (tel. 08-8541-2900).

BARMERA

Traveling 48 km east of Waikerie, past rural Kingston-on-Murray and the bird refuge at Wachtel Lagoon (part of the Moorook Game Reserve), the Sturt Highway enters Barmera (pop. 1,900), dubbed the Murray's "aquatic playground." Set on the shores of freshwater Lake Bonney, this town draws like flies those who take to the water like fish. Joseph Hawdon discovered the lake while hauling stock overland from New South Wales to Adelaide and named t after his pal Charles Bonney, who was with him. Originally called Barmera by local Aboriginals, the lake's title was transferred to the new township. Besides being a holiday resort, Barmera grows citrus and stone fruits, grapes, and vegetables.

Lake Bonney offers all types of water sports—swimming, fishing, windsurfing, yachting, waterskiing, and speed boating. (In 1964, Englishman Donald Campbell tried to break the world water speed record here.) Or you can picnic, barbecue, and laze around on one of the sandy beaches (Pelican Point, on the western shore, is a nude beach).

Sights

Built in 1859, the Overland Corner Hotel Museum, 19 km from Barmera on Morgan Road, was one of the Riverland's first stone buildings. This was where the weary overlanders and cattle drovers rested themselves and their bullock teams. Restored and run by the National Trust, the museum features pioneer exhibits and area artifacts. Hours are sporadic at the museum, but the pub sticks to its normal schedule. For information, phone (08) 8588-7021.

Country-music fans can view memorabilia at Rocky's Country Music Hall of Fame, Monash Bypass Rd. (tel. 08-8588-3035). Hours are daily 9-11 a.m. and 2-4 p.m. Admission is $2.

At Cobdogla, five km west of town, you can see the world's only operating Humphrey Pump and other historical displays at Cobdogla Irrigation Museum, Trussel Avenue. Admission s $4. For information, phone (08) 8588-2289.

On the other side of Lake Bonney's Nappers Bridge, Loch Luna Game Reserve, set on 1,905 hectares, is another favorite fishing, ca-

noeing, and waterfowl-breeding haunt. There's a picnic area at Lock Number Three, a few kilometers west of the reserve, where you can watch the action.

Accommodations

For lakeshore accommodations, Lake Bonney Caravan Reserve (tel. 08-8588-2234) has everything from on-site vans to holiday flats, all at inexpensive prices. This is a huge family-oriented complex, complete with a gym, sauna, and squash courts. For more resortlike and expensive lodging, head to Barmera Country Club, Hawdon St. (tel. 08-8588-2888), or The Lake Resort, Lakeside Dr. (tel. 08-8588-2555).

Camping is permitted at the Pelican Point nude bathing beach, but there are no facilities. To reach the beach, go three km along Morgan Road and turn right onto Ireland Road.

Recreation and Events

Lake Bonney Aquatic Centre (tel. 08-8588-2679) rents paddleboats, canoes, windsurfers, catamarans, and single and tandem bicycles. The center is open during school holidays and weekends Sept.-May.

Catch the South Australian Country Music Awards, each June on the Queen's Birthday weekend, at the old Bonney Theatre.

Services and Information

For tourist information, drop by Barmera Travel Centre, Barwell Ave. (tel. 08-8588-2289). Hours are Mon.-Fri. 8:30 a.m.-5:30 p.m., Saturday 9-11:30 a.m., Sunday 9 a.m.-4:30 p.m., closed Good Friday.

For emergencies, contact police (tel. 08-8588-2122), fire brigade (tel. 08-8588-2000), ambulance (tel. 08-8588-2501), or Royal Automobile Association (tel. 08-8582-1644). Barmera Hospital (tel. 08-8588-2006) is on Eyre Street.

BERRI

The name is certainly appropriate for this wine and citrus growing district; however, it does not stem from "berry," but from "berri berri," Aboriginal for "wide bend in the river." Established about 1870 as a riverboat refueling stop, Berri (pop.

RESPECT THE RIVER AND ALL OTHER USERS

The Department of Environment and Planning has issued the following warnings to Murray River users:

On the Murray it's important to have consideration for other river users, so please observe all boating and fishing regulations. This includes bag limits and closures, because these are in force to prevent the depletion of fish.

Before boating or swimming, check out the Murray. Get to know its waters. And watch out for snags.

When Swimming

Wear a buoyancy vest. It might look funny but it could save your life.

Don't even think about swimming the width of the Murray. With currents, snags, and power boats you might not make it.

Dive as shallowly as possible, especially if you're not certain of the depth. Steep dives have resulted in back or neck injuries.

Keep clear of busy boating areas. There's a chance the skippers might not see you.

When Boating

Carry all the required safety equipment on board.

Give a wide berth to other boats when overtaking.

Take care when turning and don't turn across the bow of another vessel.

Don't drink and drive. Swimming or driving a motorboat, when drunk, is setting a sure course for disaster. Alcohol, petrol, and water do not mix.

and presents a 10-minute video about the canning and juicing business. Hours are Mon.-Fri. 8:30 a.m.-4:30 p.m., Saturday 9 a.m.-noon, closed on major holidays. For information, phone (08) 8582-1455.

Grant's Super Playground, in the nearby community of Monash, houses more than 180 amusements for kids of all ages. Equipment includes roller coasters, flying foxes, earth-movers, multiple slides, and rotary cones. The park is always open and *free,* though donations are accepted.

The **Riverland Big Orange,** corner of Sturt Hwy. and the Monash bypass, is billed—in the spirit of Larry the Kingston Lobster—as the "Largest (fake) Orange in the World." You can pick up a bag of oranges and get your juices freshly squeezed. There's a small admission fee to the panoramic lookout. Hours are daily 9 a.m.-5 p.m. For information, phone (08) 8582-2999.

Riverland Display Centre, adjacent to the Big Orange, houses a collection of vintage and classic cars, large-scale model airplanes, antique toys and dolls, as well as gem, mineral, and Aboriginal culture displays. Its hours are the same as the Big Orange's. For information, phone (08) 8582-2325.

A Special Place for Jimmy James is a commemorative riverfront walking trail and engraved granite slab dedicated to the esteemed Aborigine. The polished slab contains images of Jimmy's spirit world, and nearby are bronze plaques with statements from admirers.

3,500) is *still* a refueling stop—for wines and juices. The town also sports the customary riverfront parks and water activities. Get your bearings at the lookout tower on Fiedler Street. And, if you're into bronco bulls, pay a visit on Easter Monday for the annual **Berri Rodeo.**

Sights

Berri Estates is reputedly the largest single winery-distillery in Australia—if not the entire Southern Hemisphere; anyway, it's big enough to produce annually seven million liters of premium varietals, bulk, cask, and fortified wines, as well as brandies. The winery is open for tastings Mon.-Fri. 9 a.m.-5:30 p.m., Saturday 9 a.m.-5 p.m. For information, phone (08) 8583-2303.

When you're finished with the hard stuff, **Berrivale Orchards,** on McKay Rd., sells fruit juices, canned fruits, almonds, and gherkins,

Accommodations and Food

Rooms at the **Berri Hotel Motel,** Riverview Dr (tel. 08-8582-1411), are inexpensive to low-moderate, and the pub serves cheap counter meals. **Winkie Holiday Cottages,** Lower Winkie Rd. (tel. 08-8583-2324), runs inexpensive to moderate. You can get a campsite, or on-site

ans and cabins with air-conditioning and television, at **Berri Riverside Caravan Park,**
Riverview Dr. (tel. 08-8582-3723).

If you enjoy fruit, you won't go hungry in these
parts. **Berri Fruit Tree** (tel. 08-8582-1666), on
Sturt Hwy. toward Glossop, sells fresh and dried
fruits, nuts, jams, and honey. Hours are Mon.-Fri.
8 a.m.-5 p.m., Saturday 9-11:30 a.m., Sunday
10 a.m.-2 p.m.

Services and Information
Berri Tourist and Travel Centre, Vaughan
Terrace (tel. 08-8582-1655), can arrange accommodations and provide winery maps and
general information. Hours are Mon.-Fri. 9 a.m.-
5 p.m., Saturday 9-11:30 a.m., closed Christmas Day and Good Friday.

Emergency contacts are: **police** (tel. 08-8582-
2488), **ambulance** (tel. 08-8582-2555), **fire
brigade** (tel. 08-8582-1000), and the **Royal Automobile Association** (tel. 08-8582-2744).

LOXTON

Berri's twin ferries, the main link to Loxton, will
whisk you across the river in one and a half
minutes; from there you pass around Lock
Number Four and Katarapko Island and head
into town. Settled in the 1890s and established
in 1907, Loxton (pop. 7,288) is a picture-postcard township overlooking both the Murray and
a game reserve. Named for William Charles
Loxton, a boundary rider who worked on the
original station property, irrigation methods
turned the area into the same rich grounds as
the rest of the Riverland.

Sights
Loxton's most famous attraction is the **Historical
Village,** a riverfront collection of 25 fully furnished early buildings, including a replica of
William Charles Loxton's pine and pug hut. Early
farm equipment and machinery are also on exhibit. Hours are Mon.-Fri. 10 a.m.-4 p.m., Sat.-
Sun. 10 a.m.-5 p.m. For information, phone (08)
8584-7194.

Penfold's Winery, Berri Rd. (tel. 08-8584-
7236), one of South Australia's largest bulk wineries, specializes in de-alcoholized wines. Hours for
sales and tastings are Mon.-Sat. 10 a.m.-5 p.m.

For easeful entertainment you can check
flood levels on the trunk of **The Tree of Knowledge,** in Lions Park, on the riverfront.

Murray River National Park is home to almost 150 species of birds. You can camp, fish, or
bushwalk through red gum floodplain or explore
horseshoe lagoons and gentle backwaters. **Kai
Kai Nature Trail,** beginning at campsite 20, is a
40-minute walk encompassing a wide variety of
Katarapko Creek birdlife and natural habitat.

Alawoona, 35 km south of Loxton, is the entry
point for mallee country. The 36,815-hectare
Billiatt Conservation Park is home to the western gray kangaroo, hopping mouse, pygmy possum, and many mallee birds, including the endangered mallee fowl and red-lored whistler.

Accommodations and Food
Loxton Hotel Motel, East Terrace (tel. 08-8584-
7266), has both old pub rooms ($35) and newer,
moderately priced river-view motel suites. The
restaurant serves counter meals and offers an a
la carte menu. **Loxton Riverfront Caravan
Park** (tel. 08-8584-7862), on the Murray, has
campsites and on-site vans, plus bicycle and
canoe rentals. A 48-bed hostel is also available.
At **Nadia Host Farm** (tel. 08-8587-4362), 20
minutes from Loxton, you can experience life
on a wheat and sheep farm. Its moderate rates
include breakfast.

East Terrace has decent cafes, as well as a
Chinese restaurant. **Medea Cottage Fruit Train,**
Bookpurnong Rd. (tel. 08-8584-6837), is the
place to buy homemade jams, nuts, and both
fresh and dried fruits. Hours are daily 10:30
a.m.-5:30 p.m.

Getting Around
Rent **trail bikes** from Loxton Motorcycle Hire
Centre, 10 Bookpurnong Terrace (tel. 08-8584-
7698).

Services and Information
Loxton Tourist and Travel, 45 East Terrace
(tel. 08-8584-7919), will assist you with accommodations and tours, as well as canoe, bicycle, or houseboat rentals. Hours are Mon.-Fri. 9
a.m.-5 p.m., Saturday during school holidays
9-11:30 a.m.

For emergency services, contact: **police** (tel.
08-8584-7283), **ambulance** (tel. 08-8584-7565),

or **Royal Automobile Association** (tel. 08-8584-7393).

RENMARK

Renmark (pop. 4,256) sits on a willow-lined Murray River bend, 255 km northeast of Adelaide and very near the Victoria border. Founded in 1887, Renmark is Australia's oldest irrigation district—thanks to Alfred Deakin's idea and the Canadian Chaffey brothers' expertise, the system spurred the Riverland's thriving citrus and wine industry. Ironically, the Chaffey brothers inserted a prohibition clause in their plans for the town's development. In 1897, the British Commonwealth erected the Renmark Hotel, the first hotel to challenge the clause. And we know who won!

Today Renmark is a busy commercial and holiday center, with plenty of wine to taste, houseboats to rent, and arts and crafts galleries to browse.

Paringa, four km east from Renmark, is the location of **Lock Number Five,** and nearby lie the quite wonderful **Headings Cliffs Lookout Tower,** the quite interesting **Lyrup Village** communal growing settlement (dating from 1894), and the quite dumb **Big Tyre.**

Sights

The **PS Industry,** built in 1911, serves as historical museum. Through a coin-in-the-slot operation, you can see how paddlewheels and other engine parts function. Moored on the Murray, between 9th and 10th Streets, the museum is open daily 9 a.m.-5 p.m. Admission is $2. For information, phone (08) 8586-6704.

Olivewood Homestead, Renmark Ave. and 21st St., the original home of Charles Chaffey, now operates as a National Trust museum. Hours are Thurs.-Mon. 10 a.m.-4 p.m., Tuesday 2-4 p.m. Admission is $2.50. For information, phone (08) 8586-6175.

Bredl's Wonderworld of Wildlife, on the Sturt Hwy., five km from town, has pythons, taipans, cobras, boa constrictors, rare yellow anacondas, lizards, alligators, crocs, and other reptiles. Hours are daily 8 a.m.-6 p.m. in summer, 9 a.m.-5:30 p.m. in winter, and there are special snake feedings Sunday 2-3 p.m. Admission is $7. For information, phone (08) 8595-1431.

Accommodations and Food

The historic **Renmark Hotel,** Murray Ave. (tel. 08-8586-6755), has moderately priced rooms and motel units. The hotel features both a bistro and dining room. Prices are high-moderate at **Renmark Country Club,** Sturt Hwy. (tel. 08 8595-1401), and include use of tennis court, swimming pool, spa, and 18-hole grass golf course.

Riverbend Caravan Park, Sturt Hwy. (tel 08-8595-5131), and **Renmark Caravan Park** Patey Dr. (tel. 08-8586-6315), are situated on the riverfront. Both have campsites, on-site vans and cabins for rent.

Rivergrowers Ark Kiosk, Renmark Ave. (tel 08-8586-6705), sells a variety of juices, nuts, honey, jams, chocolates, and fresh and dried fruits—most processed in the factory next door. Hours are Mon.-Fri. 10 a.m.-4 p.m., Saturday 9 a.m.-noon.

Sports and Recreation

Facilities at **Renmark Community Recreation Centre** include indoor tennis, indoor swimming pool, squash courts, weight-training equipment, spa and sauna, a suntan unit, and large multi-purpose stadium for cricket, soccer, netball, badminton, volleyball, basketball, and roller skating. For information, phone (08) 8586-6072.

Shopping

Most of the arts and crafts galleries are situated on or near Renmark Avenue. **Frank Harding's Folklore Gallery,** 117 16th St., features a huge ceiling mural that depicts Australian bushrangers.

Pick up surplus and camping equipment at **Riverland Army Disposals,** Renmark Ave. (tel. 08-8586-6767).

Information

The **Tourist Information Centre,** Murray Ave. (tel. 08-8586-6704), distributes info and rents tandem or single bicycles (there's a good cycling track to Paringa). Hours are Mon.-Fri. 9 a.m.-5 p.m., Saturday 9 a.m.-4 p.m., Sunday and public holidays 10 a.m.-4 p.m., closed Christmas Day.

TRANSPORTATION

Getting There

Southern Australia Airlines flies daily from Adelaide to Renmark and on to Mildura. Book through Ansett (tel. 13-1300).

Murray Bridge Passenger Service (tel. 08-8532-2633) operates daily coaches between Murray Bridge and Adelaide's Franklin Street depot for about $14 one-way. **Stateliner** (tel. 08-8415-5544, or 08-8586-6468 in Renmark) has daily coaches from Adelaide to Blanchetown ($16), Waikerie ($19), Barmera ($21), Berri ($23), Loxton ($26), and Renmark ($26). Many interstate coaches also serve the Lower Murray and Riverland.

River Cruising

Why not feel the river rush through your veins by traveling *on* the Murray, instead of along it? In the Lower Murray, you can rent **houseboats** at Murray Bridge, Mannum, Younghusband, and Purnong; in the Riverland, houseboats are based at Morgan, Waikerie, Loxton, Berri, Paringa, and Renmark. Houseboats are completely self-contained, accommodate four to 10 people, and are capable of traveling six to eight knots. Rental prices depend upon the size of boat, length of rental, and the season you rent it

in—typically about $900 per week (you can get them as low as $600). However, keep in mind that this takes care of both transport and accommodations, as well as cooking facilities—and, if you share the cost with others, it even becomes cheap. At any rate, it will be a delightful and memorable experience, floating along the Murray, in comfort, and at will. Use a little imagination and you may run into Tom Sawyer, Matthew Flinders, or Mr. Lucky.

Book houseboats (*well* in advance) at any South Australian Tourism Commission Travel Centre, or through local Tourist Information Centres. You won't need a boat operator's license, but a driver's license is required.

Or, leave the navigating to someone else. The 18-cabin *Proud Mary* luxury boat departs Murray Bridge for two- to five-day cruises. Cost is $325-700 pp. For information, phone (08) 8231-9472. The 60-cabin paddlesteamer *Murray Princess* departs Mannum for six-night Riverland cruises, at $850 pp. For information, phone (08) 8569-1438. All of the above prices include accommodations and meals.

Get a quick taste of the Murray on a lunch, dinner, or other short sail. Operators offering a wide range of tours (at a wide range of fares) include *Lady Mannum* (tel. 08-8569-1438) from Mannum and MV *Barrangul* (tel. 018-80-4256) from Murray Bridge.

THE MID-NORTH

South Australia's mid-north lies north of the Barossa Valley, west of the Riverland, east of Yorke Peninsula, and just south of the Flinders Ranges. And it is special—touristed, but not *touristy*.

Actually, the mid-north is my favorite part of the state. Burra, the historic copper mining town, was so awesome I dropped my camera, shattering it on the same cobblestone path once used by Cornish miners. Busted Olympus notwithstanding, I instamatically decided to live there for at least six months. And then there's Mintaro, a truly gorgeous heritage town. Down the road is Martindale Hall, a very chic B&B where *Picnic at Hanging Rock* was filmed.

Farther north is Peterborough, a railway junction, where buffs like me—with hearts that chug instead of beat—can all-aboard a narrow-gauge steam train through the mid-north countryside. Port Pirie, along the Spencer Gulf, is a mixture of heritage town, busy seaport, and commercial center.

You have a variety of options for exploring the mid-north. The Clare Valley is a 135-km zip north of Adelaide, along Main North Road.

From Adelaide, the Barrier Highway will lead you (with a couple of detours) to Burra and Peterborough. From Peterborough you turn westward to Jamestown, Gladstone, and Port Pirie, or continue north to the Flinders Ranges. At the junction of the Barrier and Sturt Highways, be sure to take the Kapunda turnoff. The back road,

through Hamilton, Marrabel, and Saddleworth—where you'll reconnect with the Barrier Highway—is one of my favorite day-in-the-country drives.

Highway 1, also from Adelaide, travels to Por Wakefield (where you can cut over to Balaklava) up to Snowtown, Crystal Brook, and Port Pirie then on to Port Augusta and the Eyre Peninsula, or across the Nullarbor to Western Australia

Whichever road you follow, every once in a while veer off the beaten path—this territory is full of little surprises, marked by hand-lettered signposts, European-style back roads, an ornery cow, a stubborn mule, and unusual gusto in the breeze.

KAPUNDA

Located at the northern edge of the Barossa Valley, 75 km from Adelaide, Kapunda (pop 1,620) was the location of South Australia's first significant copper find. An accidental discovery of green copper ore prompted the opening of one of the world's richest copper mines on 32 hectares owned by the Dutton and Bagott families. The mine operated 1844-1912, turning out approximately 14,000 tons of copper, and Kapunda soon grew into the state's largest country town. Though the community now lives off agricultural rather than mining products, many historic buildings, cottages, and churches still stand, and the town retains a lot of its original charm. Particularly stunning is the decorative iron lacework, known as "Kapunda lace," made locally at the turn of the century.

Sights and Events
Kapunda Historical Museum (tel. 08-8566-2657) is in the former Baptist church on Hill Street. Historical exhibits include colonial artifacts, memorabilia, and archival recordings. Hours are Sat.-Thurs. Sept.-May and weekends June-Aug. 1-4 p.m.

The eight-meter-tall bronze sculpture of Map Kernow (Cornish for "Son of Cornwall"), at the south end of town, pays tribute to early Cornish miners.

On 1 February 1997 all telephone numbers in the mid-north will change. In preparation for this, all numbers in this section have been changed to eight digits. To dial a mid-north number before 1 February, simply delete the first two digits of the new number and, if dialing from outside the mid-north, add a zero to the deleted numbers to get the area code. For example, (08) 8512-3456 would be (085) 12-3456, and (08) 8612-3456 would be (086) 12-3456. After 1 February the area code for all numbers in this section will be (08).

SOUTH AUSTRALIA ~ THE MID-NORTH

Take the **Old Kapunda Copper Mine and Walking Trail,** an easy 1.5-km hike through the old mine, for close-up investigation of shafts, tunnels, the open-cut area, the mine chimney, and an early miner's cottage.

The **Heritage Trail** leads to 42 historical buildings along a 10-km route.

The **Celtic Festival,** held the first weekend in April, fills the town's pubs with Celtic, bush, and folk bands and fans.

Accommodations and Food

Refurbished **Sir John Franklin Hotel,** Main St. (tel. 08-8566-2106), has large inexpensive pub-style rooms. Across the street, **Ford House** (tel. 08-8566-2280) is a beautifully renovated B&B with expensive prices ($10 less without breakfast). Excellent a la carte dinners are served at both accommodations, and Sir John Franklin's lively pub also has inexpensive counter meals.

Dutton Park Caravan Park, Baker St. (tel. 08-8566-2094), rents campsites and has a tennis court and playground.

Information

Get maps for both walking trails mentioned above, as well as other information, from **Kapunda Tourist Centre** or Kapunda Historical Society. The tourist center is open daily 10 a.m.-1 p.m., closed Christmas Day and Good Friday. For information, phone (08) 8566-2902.

MINTARO

The entire tiny township of Mintaro (pop. 80) is on the heritage list. Of course, you'll find only a handful of streets, but they're lined with 1850s slate, stone, and wooden colonial structures—influenced by Italian, English, and German hands—constructed of such diverse materials as Baltic pine and Indian cedar. Most buildings incorporate the locally produced fine slate—a specialty of this district—in walls, floors, or fences, and many of the old cottages have been converted into accommodation houses. The town is thought to have been named by Uruguayan mule drivers who stopped there while carting copper ore between Port Wakefield and Burra.

Mintaro sits 130 km from Adelaide and about 14 km from Clare, burrowed amongst gentle hills and rolling pastures. It is a gorgeous, quiet, country village. Go there!

Sights

Robinson's Cottage (tel. 08-8843-9029), a museum inside an original 1851 settler's cottage, features fire engine displays, fire appliances and memorabilia, classic and vintage cars, and other early equipment. Hours are daily 9 a.m.-4:30 p.m., closed Christmas Day.

Reilly's Cottage Gallery (tel. 08-8843-9013) exhibits local and national arts and crafts in a cottage over 120 years old. Hours are Wed.-Sun. 10 a.m.-5 p.m.

Martindale Hall, on the outskirts of Mintaro, is the positively splendid Georgian mansion portrayed as "Appleyard College" in the film *Picnic at Hanging Rock.* A bachelor named Edmund Bowen had the house built in 1879 as an attempt to win the hand of a spoiled rich girl, who promised to marry him if he built her a house as nice as her father's. Martindale Hall (which, in those days, cost the dear sum of £36,000) apparently wasn't up to snuff, for Edmund built the house but then lost the girl! The mansion is open for inspection daily 1-4 p.m., closed Christmas Day. It costs $7 admission, but you can visit the grounds for free.

Accommodations

All Mintaro accommodations are in converted historic digs going for prices that probably have the original inhabitants rolling over in their historic graves. **Pay Office Cottage**, Hill St. (tel. 08-8843-9026), once the cheapest, is now way up there. **Mintaro Hideaway** (tel. 08-8843-9011) and **The Teapot Inn** (tel. 08-8843-9037), both also expensive, include breakfast. **Mintaro Mews** (tel. 08-8843-9011) offers two (yes, expensive) deluxe cottages with breakfast included. And, if you're a romantic or film-crazy, you'll want to stay at the house Edmund built; **Martindale Hall** (tel. 08-8843-9011) will give you a scrumptious room, pamper you with attention, and feed you delectable candlelight dinners. Oddly, this once really expensive spot is now one of the cheapest if you just want a room with breakfast—toss in dinner and the rates double.

THE CLARE VALLEY

The Clare Valley, famous for winemaking since 1851, is a 30-km stretch, 135 km north of Adelaide, nestled within the northern Mount Lofty Ranges. Comprising the surrounding communities of Auburn, Watervale, Sevenhill, and Penwortham, more than 20 wineries—ranging from small boutiques to nationally known brands—take advantage of the district's high rainfall and rich soil to create premium products.

Edward Burton Gleeson founded Clare in 1840, naming the settlement for his native County Clare, Ireland. Only one year later the Hawker brothers set up Bungaree Station, one of Australia's best-known sheep stud farms. The winemaking didn't get going until 1848 when the Jesuits planted vines to produce altar wine, which Sevenhill Cellars still turns out, along with other fine vintages.

You'll find historic buildings, serene roadways, and picturesque scenery throughout the Clare Valley towns, all dating back to the early 1800s—and it's a lot less touristy than the Barossa.

Sights

Historic buildings in **Auburn** include: Miss Mabel Cottage Living (1859), Mechanics Institute (1859), police station and courtroom (1860), St. John's Anglican Church (1862), post office (1862), Stonehurst Gallery and Library (1866), and council chambers (1879).

Stanley Grammar School, Uniting Church of Australia, Watervale Primary School, and the Methodist Church are National Trust buildings in **Watervale.**

Run by the National Trust, the **Old Police Station Museum** (1850), corner Victoria Rd. and West Terrace in Clare (tel. 08-8842-2374), was the valley's first courthouse and police station. Hours are Saturday 10 a.m.-noon, 2-4 p.m., Sunday 2-4 p.m. Admission is $2.

Take a tour of **Bungaree Station,** dating from 1841 when the Hawkers established the famous merino stud farm, and still run by their grandsons! The self-sufficient community has a church, council chambers, school, blacksmith shop, as well as wool shed, stable yard, and shearers quarters, that are still in use. One- to two-hour conducted tours are arranged by appointment only, as the station is still going full-stud. Original knitting patterns and woolen yarns are sold on the premises. For information, phone (08) 8842-2677.

Saint Aloysius Church and Sevenhill Cellars, College Rd., Sevenhill (tel. 08-8843-4222), is where the valley's first vines were planted. Father Aloysius Kranewitter, a young Jesuit priest, chose the site (patterned after the seven hills of Rome) as a cellar for his altar wines. Saint Aloysius Church was begun in 1856 and consecrated in 1875. Besides altar wines, Sevenhill specializes in dry red and white wines, and liqueur Tokay. Hours are Mon.-Fri. 8:30 a.m.-4:30 p.m., Saturday and holidays 9 a.m.-4 p.m., closed Sunday, Christmas Day, New Year's Day, and Good Friday (you know where you can get their wine on *those* days).

Wolta Wolta Homestead (tel. 08-8842-3656) was one of the earliest settler's cottages. Unfortunately, it burned down in 1983's devastating Ash Wednesday fire. The homestead, now restored, features antiques, artworks, history, and memorabilia relating to the Hope family, owners of the property for four generations. Tours are conducted Sat.-Sun. 10 a.m.-4:30 p.m. Admission is $3.

Accommodations and Food

You can stay inexpensively in the shearers' bunkhouse at **Bungaree Station** (tel. 08-8842-2677). Facilities include a large dining hall and modern kitchen. **Clare Valley Cabins** (tel. 08-8842-3917) offers seven two-bedroom self-contained cottages on a large property five km north of Clare. Rates are inexpensive to low-moderate. **Bentley's Hotel Motel**, 191 Main North Rd. (tel. 08-8842-2815), rents moderately priced rooms in both units. **Clare Central Motel**, 325 Main North Rd. (tel. 08-8842-2277), is down the street and runs about $20 more than Bentley's. **Stringy Brae Cottage** (tel. 08-8843-4313) and **Trestrail Cottage** (tel. 08-8842-3794), in Sevenhill, both range high-moderate to expensive and include breakfast ingredients.

Christison Park Caravan Park, Main North Rd. (tel. 08-8842-2724), near Clare, has campsites and on-site vans.

Cheap eats on the main drag are **Clare Valley Café**, **Salad Bowl**, and **Pantry Plus Coffee Shop**. **Bentley's Hotel** serves country-style meals at moderate prices. And more country cookin' is dished up at **Sevenhill Hotel** (tel. 08-8843-4217), for Mon.-Sat. lunch and dinner. **Clare Dragon Restaurant**, 308 Main North Rd. (tel. 08-8842-3644), is both a moderately priced licensed restaurant and an inexpensive takeaway.

Jones Bakery, 269 Main North Rd. (tel. 08-8842-2473), bakes up buns and cakes, pies and pasties. Choose from more than 24 types of breads, as well as pastries and cakes, at **Maurie's Patisserie and Hot Bread Bakery**, 292 Main North Rd. (tel. 08-8842-3523).

Events

Similar to the Barossa event, Clare Valley's **Vintage Festival** happens during Easter of even-numbered years. The **Gourmet Weekend**, held every May, is when connoisseurs sip and sample, and the hungry pig out on a progressive lunch at area wineries.

Recreation

Lakota Ranch (tel. 08-8842-3875) organizes fully escorted horseback rides along the Clare Valley back roads and hills, as well as one-day cattle drives for beginning to advanced riders.

There're good picnicking and leisurely walks at **Pioneer, Christison,** and **Spring Gully** parks.

Information

Clare Valley Tourist Centre, 229 Main North Rd., Clare (tel. 08-8842-2131), has maps of the Clare Valley wineries and other local information. Hours are daily 10 a.m.-4 p.m., closed Christmas Day.

You can get tourist information in Auburn at **Miss Mabel Cottage Living**, St. Vincent St. (tel. 08-8849-2208), Thurs.-Sun. and public holidays 10 a.m.-5 p.m.

BURRA

With the feel and flavor of a down under Bisbee, Arizona, Burra (pop. 2,225) is one of South Australia's most enchanting towns.

Originally, the community was a sheep-grazing area on the brink of bankruptcy. But in 1845, after shepherd William Streair discovered copper, followed by Thomas Pickett's find, the "Monster Mine" was created and Burra blossomed with prosperity. Named "Burra Burra" (Hindi for "Great Great") by Indian coolie shepherds, the district was collectively called "The Burra" and embraced several townships, all named according to their inhabitants' origins—thus Kooringa (Aboriginal), Redruth (Cornish), Aberdeen (Scottish), Hampton (English), and Llywchrr (Welsh).

Though the mine was one rich mother lode, operations ceased in 1877, when it dried up. Agriculture (Burra was declared "Merino Capital of the World" in 1988) and tourism are the local revenue-takers these days. A leisurely 156-km drive from Adelaide, Burra draws visitors to its fascinating streets and dwellings to follow in historic footsteps along the copper trail.

Sights

Just about the whole town can be classified a sight, but you'll need a passport to cross many thresholds. The **Burra Passport** is a rental key, available from the tourist office, that allows you entrance to **Burra Creek Miner's Dugouts, Burra Open Air Museum, Redruth Gaol, Police Lock-up and Stables,** and **Unicorn Brewery Stables.** Cost of the passport is $15 per family or vehicle, plus a $5 deposit.

Also included in the passport's attractions is **Morphett's Enginehouse.** Built in 1858 and reconstructed in 1986, it helped to pump water from the mine. A 30-meter entry tunnel enables visitors to walk into the shaft to view original pump pipes.

Bon Accord Museum, on the site of the original Bon Accord Mine, serves as an interpretive center, with a working forge, five- by six-meter model of the Monster Mine, and tours of the old mine shaft. Hours are Mon.-Fri. 12:30-2:30 p.m., Sat.-Sun. and public holidays 12:30-3:30 p.m. Admission is $3. For information, phone (08) 8892-2056.

Paxton Square Cottages is three rows of 1850s miners' cottages overlooking Burra Creek. The cottages are now visitor accommodations, but **Malowen Lowarth,** furnished as a mine captain's cottage, is open for inspection Saturday 1-3 p.m., Sunday 10:30 a.m.-12:30 p.m. Admission is $3.

If you're into cemeteries, old **Burra Cemetery** is especially nice. If you're into diseases, it will be of interest that most causes of death at the time were typhoid, diphtheria, measles, and consumption.

Market Square Museum consists of a general store, post office, and private home, built 1870-1915. Nearby is the 13-meter ironbark and blue gum **Jinker,** which toted the huge Schneider's engine-house cylinder from Port Adelaide to Burra Mine in 1852. Hours are Saturday 2-4 p.m., Sunday 1-3 p.m., or by arrangement. For information, phone (08) 8892-2154.

Burra Gorge, 18 km east of town, has good walking trails through river gum forests and other scenic bushland.

Accommodations and Food
You can check into a pub for the night, but it's certainly more fun to stay in one of Burra's seeping-with-history heritage dwellings. The tourist center has all the info on these accommodations. The exquisite **Paxton Square Cottages**

(tel. 08-8892-2622), with fully equipped kitchens, cost a very reasonable $40-50 double. **Bon Accord Cottage** (tel. 08-8892-2615), the preserved mine manager's residence, is also available for $75. **Burra View House,** 7 Mount Pleasant Rd. (tel. 08-8892-2648), is a B&B with excellent views and moderate rates. Book all accommodations (especially Paxton Cottages) well in advance.

Reasonably priced places to fill your belly are **Polly's Tearooms** (tel. 08-8892-2544), **Pickett's Pantry** (tel. 08-8892-2530), and the counters at **Burra Hotel** (tel. 08-8892-2389) and **Kooringa Hotel** (tel. 08-8892-2013). **Price's Bakery,** in Market Square, is your stop for homemade soups and fabulous wienies.

Information
Apply for cottage "passports" and load up on brochures at **Burra Tourist Centre,** Market Square (tel. 08-8892-2154). Hours are daily 10 a.m.-4 p.m., closed Christmas Day.

A number of historical books on the area are also sold here (*Discovering Burra* is included with your passport).

TEROWIE

Continuing up the Barrier Highway (be careful of kangaroos) for 63 km north of Burra brings you to Terowie, another historic town and a prominent part of the 1880s railway network. Horse and bullock teams from the surrounding country stations kept up a steady rush hour while loading or unloading produce, supplies, and stock. And, history buffs, get this: Terowie, site of a World War II army bivouac camp, was where Gen. Douglas MacArthur, fresh from his Philippines escape, made his famous "I came out of Bataan and I shall return" statement.

It's a good wander down Main Street, where the original century-old shopfronts reflect times past. **Arid Lands Botanic Garden,** also on Main St., features a large assortment of Australian arid-zone plants and is open daily.

Accommodations and Food
Terowie Hotel (tel. 08-8659-1012) and **Imperial Hotel** (tel. 08-8659-1011), both on Main St., offer inexpensive pub rooms with breakfast in-

cluded. **Terowie Motel,** Barrier Hwy. (tel. 08-8659-1082), also inexpensive, is air conditioned. **Dusty Kitchen,** Main St. (tel. 08-8659-1073), serves meals, snacks, and cakes, daily.

Information

Terowie Information and Souvenir Shop, Main St. (tel. 08-8659-1087), will organize visits to the Terowie Pioneer Gallery and Museum, as well as conducted tours of the town and buildings. Hours are daily 9:30 a.m.-5:30 p.m.

PETERBOROUGH

Turn off the Barrier Highway at Terowie for the 23-km ride into Peterborough—frontier town, historic railway depot, and gateway to the Flinders Ranges. Railway aficionados will thrill to find that Peterborough is one of the world's two known towns where three different rail gauges converge. This is still an important rail center on the Port Pirie-Broken Hill-Sydney main line. Get a good peek at the town (and the tracks) from **Tank Hill Lookout,** at the end of Government Road.

Sights

Don't miss a ride on the steam passenger train, along the narrow-gauge line, from Peterborough to Orroroo (about 38 km). The tourist center has schedules.

Round House Exchange, a unique railway turntable used for rerouting rolling stock, displays historic rail equipment.

Saint Cecelia, the former bishop's residence, is palatially furnished with paintings, antique pianos, polished mahogany, and stained-glass windows within its parlors, ballroom, 10 bedrooms, and library. The coach house now functions as an art center. Moderately priced accommodations are available in the main house, converted stables, coachman's room, or attached artist's studio, and include breakfast. Daily tours 1-4 p.m. are arranged through the tourist center. For information, phone (08) 8651-2849.

The **Gold Battery** once extracted gold from locally mined crushed ore. Guided tours can be arranged. For information, phone (08) 8652-3708.

Information

You can't miss the **Peterborough Tourist Centre** (tel. 08-8651-2708)—it's in a railway carriage along Main Street. Get your steam train tickets here and, if you're headed to the Flinders Ranges, inquire about roads and routes. Hours are daily 9 a.m.-4 p.m., closed Christmas Day, New Year's Day, and Good Friday.

TO PORT PIRIE

Traveling coastward, the back road southwest of Peterborough hooks up with Route 83. At Jamestown, it starts east, leaving Route 83, drops a bit southward at Gladstone, then curves northward, merging with Highway 1, heading to Port Pirie and beyond.

Jamestown

This wool-, wheat-, and barley-producing agricultural community, 44 km from Peterborough, originated back in the 1870s. Its **National Trust Museum** (tel. 08-8665-2036) houses a collection of early memorabilia and historical relics. Hours are Mon.-Sat. 10 a.m.-5 p.m., Sunday 2-4 p.m. Admission is $2.

South Australia's first government forest plantation, **Bundaleer Forest Reserve,** nine km south of Jamestown, affords refreshing walks and picnics. Climb up to the lookout tower and you'll see Mt. Remarkable in the distance.

Gladstone

This pastoral and grazing community, 28 km southwest of Jamestown and adjacent to the Rocky River, also dates back to the 1870s. In 1877, after the railway connected Gladstone to Port Pirie, the community became an important grain collection center. Eventually it became home to South Australia's largest inland silo (which now contains 82,500 tons of grain). At the Gladstone railway yards, you can view one of the world's few places where narrow, standard, and broad gauges are interlaid in one siding.

Experience conditions withstood by "inebriates, debtors and other prisoners" at century-old **Gladstone Gaol** (tel. 08-8662-2068). Some of the "other prisoners" included Italians and Germans interned there during WW II. Hours are Monday, Tuesday, and Friday 1-4 p.m., Sat.-

Sun. and school holidays 10 a.m.-4 p.m. Admission is $3.50.

PORT PIRIE

Port Pirie (pop. 15,114), 210 km from Adelaide, is well-positioned on the eastern side and northern end of Spencer Gulf, shadowed by the Flinders Ranges. As the mid-north's largest center, Port Pirie (named after the colonial workhorse windjammer *John Pirie*) is notable for its enormous lead smelter, capable of producing 280,000 kilograms of silver, 250,000 tons of refined lead, 90,000 tons of sulphuric acid, 45,000 tons of electrolytic zinc, as well as gold, cadmium, copper matte, and antimonial lead alloys—the annual turnout from rich Broken Hill mines.

As the closest port to Broken Hill, the precious metal is railed in and treated at the smelter or exported internationally. Other products shipped from the port are large quantities of wheat and barley.

Obviously industry and shipping get top billing at Port Pirie, yet you'll also discover intriguing old buildings, excellent sports facilities, and a surprising variety of entertainment.

Sights

Port Pirie National Trust Museum, Old Ellen St. (tel. 08-8632-1080), comprises the railway station, customs house, and police station. Displays include historical exhibits, a scale model of the smelters, railway and shipping exhibits, 10,000- to 20,000-year-old diprotodon bones, and a former shunting engine. Hours are Mon.-Sat. 10 a.m.-4 p.m., Sunday 1-4 p.m., closed Christmas Day. Admission is $2.

The historical home **Carn Brae,** 32 Florence St. (tel. 08-8632-1314), belonged to the pioneering Moyles, soft-drink moguls. Aside from fine architecture, collections include turn-of-the-century furnishings, paintings, glassware, and porcelain, as well as more than 2,500 antique and contemporary dolls. Hours are daily 10 a.m.-4 p.m., closed Christmas Day. Admission is $5.

Fishermen's Jetty, with fishing and boat-launching ramps, is either busy or tranquil, depending on the tide. **Solomontown Jetty** provides a safe swimming beach, children's playground along the reserve, and sunbathing area.

Port Davis, 15 km south of Port Pirie off Port Broughton Rd., has both jetty fishing and a boat launch.

Accommodations and Food

Rooms are inexpensive at **International Hotel Motel,** 40 Ellen St. (tel. 08-8632-2422). Moderately priced **Flinders Range Motor Inn,** 151 Main Rd. (tel. 08-8632-3555), offers videos, room service, beer garden, swimming pool, tennis court, and a Saturday night dinner dance. **John Pirie Motor Inn,** Main Rd. (tel. 08-8632-4200), features a swimming pool and room service, with moderate-expensive rates. Both **Port Pirie Caravan Park,** Beach Rd. (tel. 08-8632-4275), and **Range View Caravan Park,** Highway 1 (tel. 08-8634-4221), have campsites and on-site vans.

Hungry? Hope you like Chinese food and fish 'n' chips!

Entertainment and Events

Northern Festival Centre, at Memorial Park, is patterned after the Adelaide Centre. Theater, films, exhibitions, and performances by both visiting and local entertainers are scheduled regularly.

Information

Local details are provided by **Port Pirie Information and Tourism Centre,** 3 Mary Elie St. (tel. 08-8633-0439). Hours are Mon.-Fri. 9 a.m.-5 p.m., Sat.-Sun. 1-4 p.m.

ALONG HIGHWAY ONE

Up Highway 1, beyond Gawler, the coastal road passes picturesque parklands, old copper ports, salty lakes, and sculptural rock formations.

Balaklava

A short 26-km detour east from Port Wakefield, Balaklava (pop. 1,365) was once a rest stop for bullock teams hauling copper ore from Burra to Port Wakefield. Nearby **Rocks Reserve,** with interesting rock formations, is a good picnic spot.

Port Wakefield

Port Wakefield, top of the Gulf St. Vincent, is a one-time copper and wool port with a lovely old wharf. Go bush at **Clinton Conservation Park,** just north of town. Back on Highway 1 and another 30 km north is **Bumbunga Lake,** a huge salt pan covering 3,530 acres. The lake changes color according to the weather—the weather's good if it's blue and unsettled if it's pink. You can tour the processing plant. The scenic drive along Lochiel-Ninnes Road affords a superb view of the inland lakes and countryside.

Snowtown

This primo sheep- and cattle-breeding township, 49 km north of Port Wakefield, was established in the 1840s by early settlers seeking greener pastures. These days Snowtown provides services for surrounding rural communities.

See what's left of **Burunga Gap Township,** 10 km west of Snowtown, established in 1873.

Crystal Brook

Scenic Crystal Brook (pop. 2,100), 52 km north of Snowtown, was declared a township in 1873, though it was named in 1839 by early explorer Edward John Eyre. It's a lovely town with tall river gums, picnic parks, water ponds, and, of course, the crystal brook, which runs from the lower Flinders Ranges to the River Broughton.

Bowman Park, five km east of Crystal Brook, is a peaceful parkland for picnics and play, as well as a mid-north point for the Heysen Trail. The Native Fauna Zone houses crocodiles, koalas, kangaroos, waterfowl, goannas, pythons, eagles, and other critters. Hours are daily 10 a.m.-4 p.m. Admission is $4.50. For information, phone (08) 8636-2116.

Make camp at either **Crystal Brook Caravan Park** (tel. 08-8636-2640) or the 22-bed lodge and tent sites for Heysen Trail trekkers (contact park manager at 08-8636-2116).

TRANSPORTATION

Contact the **Country Passenger Depot** in Adelaide for coaches to Kapunda, Burra, Peterborough, and Port Pirie. For information, phone (08) 8231-4144.

The major transcontinental rail lines stop at Port Pirie and Peterborough on journeys between Adelaide and Perth, Alice Springs and Sydney. For information, phone (08) 8231-7699, or 13-2232 toll-free.

Or *walk!* The **Heysen Trail** passes from Tanunda (in the Barossa), through Burra, Mt. Bryan, Spalding, and Crystal Brook, in the mid-north.

YORKE PENINSULA

Rich fields of golden wheat and barley, moody beaches and sandy coves, wildlife peeking from the bush, fluttering birds, cotton-puff skies, sparkling blue seas, spring wildflower blankets, and Cornish mining settlements, combined with close proximity to Adelaide, make the Yorke Peninsula an attractive holiday getaway. (Either that or travelers miss it altogether, ending up on the Eyre Highway and headed for Western Australia, having lost the whole Yorke in one blink!)

Set between Spencer Gulf and the Gulf St. Vincent, most of the peninsula's parks, beaches, and towns are not more than a two- or three-hour drive from Adelaide. The two sealed highways follow the east coast and midsection of the peninsula, converge at Warooka, and end at Stenhouse Bay in Innes National Park (near the Park Headquarters). Gravel roads and dirt

tracks spur off from the main highways, leading to hideaway beaches, rural communities, and patchwork farmlands. Yet, even on the inland route, you're never more than 25 km from the coast, with beaches to please anglers, divers, surfers, and sunners. So, if you're seeking a destination that lacks in the typical tourist trappings, is user-friendly rather than hard-sell, the Yorke offers a laid-back environment where you can set your own sights. The fishing is good year-round, but it's the spring months (Sept.-Nov.)—when the wildflowers serve up a visual feast of daisies, wattles, orchids, and red flame bush—that are exceptional.

Detour off Highway 1, north of Port Wakefield (about 100 km from Adelaide), along the eastern coast, through the ports of Ardrossan and Edithburgh, down to Innes National Park, where the emus and kangaroos play. Take the scenic

YORKE PENINSULA

TO ADELAIDE

WALLAROO
KADINA
MOONTA BAY
MOONTA
TO PORT AUGUSTA
MOONTA BAY
CLINTON C.P.
PORT
WAKEFIELD
PORT CLINTON
PRICE
SALT
EVAPORATION
PANS
TIDDY
WIDDY BEACH
ARDROSSAN
MAITLAND
ROGUES
POINT
GULF ST. VINCENT
BACK POINT
PINE POINT
WARDANG ISLAND
PORT VICTORIA
URANIA
PORT JULIA
PORT
VINCENT
MINLATON
SPENCER GULF
STANSBURY
BRENTWOOD
WOOL BAY
PORT GILES
HARDWICKE
BAY
COOBOWIE
YORKETOWN
WAROOKA
EDITHBURGH
POINT
TURTON
LAKE
FOWLER
CORNY POINT
LIGHTHOUSE
TROUBRIDGE
ISLAND C.P.
STURT BAY
DALY HEAD
WARRENBEN
C.P.
FORMBY BAY
FOUL BAY
BROWNS BEACH
BUTLERS BEACH
INNES
NATIONAL
PARK
MARION
BAY
MARION BAY
NATIONAL PARK HEADQUARTERS
ETHEL M.
LIGHTHOUSE
CAPE SPENCER
WEST CAPE
INVESTIGATOR STRAIT

0   10 km

1 DEEP LAKE
2 MARION LAKE
3 SNOW LAKE
4 CHAIN OF LAKES

ive around Corny Point, meet the sealed highay at Warooka, pass through the "inland" com-
unities of Minlaton and Maitland, up to the
istoric Copper Triangle towns of Moonta, Ka-
ina, and Wallaroo, to Port Broughton, the sea-
de resort at the Yorke's northern tip.

istory
aptain Matthew Flinders first sighted the Yorke
eninsula in 1802, the year he was exploring
outh Australia's coastline. Sheep farmers,
oking for greener pastures for their stock,
ettled the region in the 1830s, but it was the
859 discovery of copper at Kadina that made
ne Yorke prosper, in addition to providing a
uch-needed boost to South Australia's pre-
arious economy. By 1861, extensive deposits
ere uncovered at Wallaroo and Moonta, and
ne copper rush was on. Cornish (and some
Velsh) miners flocked to the Yorke, bringing
neir picks and shovels and leaving their her-
age and pasties behind. Thus, the Copper
riangle towns of Kadina, Wallaroo, and Moon-
a also became known as "Little Cornwall." A bi-
nnial festival pays tribute to the area's rich
:ornish heritage.

The Yorke's copper mines operated up until
ne 1920s, when declining prices, combined
vith increased labor expenses and interna-
onal competition, prompted closure (Poona
Aine, at Moonta, reopened in 1988). Mines
losed or not, the Yorke was hardly dried up.
he flat plains of Australia's granary are considered one of the world's richest wheat and
barley regions.

Information
For more information on the Yorke Peninsula,
contact **Yorke Peninsula Tourist Information
Centre,** Victoria Square, Kadina 5554 (tel. 08-
8821-2093), or any South Australian Tourism
Commission Travel Centre.

THE COPPER TRIANGLE

The historic Cornish townships of Kadina, Wallaroo, and Moonta are easily reached via the
Kadina turnoff from Highway 1, three km north of
Port Wakefield. Otherwise, if you're exploring
the entire Yorke Peninsula, you'll catch these
towns on your way up the west coast. Most of
the artsy-craftsy galleries are in that "tri-city"
area, so if you're dying for a locally painted landscape, you'll probably find it there.

Kadina
This is the Yorke Peninsula's largest town. As
one-time center of the copper action, Kadina
(pop. 3,500) has a distinctively Cornish atmosphere, reflected in many of the old buildings.

Matta House Museum, 1.5 km south of
Kadina off Moonta Rd., contains many relics
and exhibits pertaining to the good old Matta
Matta mining days, housed in the former mine
manager's home. Hours are Wednesday, Saturday, Sunday, and holidays 2-4:30 p.m. Admission is $2.

The **Banking and Currency Museum,** 3
Graves St. (tel. 08-8821-2906), displays every type
of Australian currency ever issued, as well as other
banking exhibits. The museum also buys and sells
coins, notes, and medals. Hours are Fri.-Wed. 10
a.m.-5 p.m.; closed Good Friday, Christmas Day,
and the month of June. Admission is $2.

A heritage drive leads to **Wallaroo Mines,**
one km west of Kadina, on Wallaroo Road. Signposts lead you on a walking tour of the old site,
where you'll see ruins of the two-story-high engine building and visit places named Jericho
and Jerusalem.

Wombat Hotel, 19 Taylor St. (tel. 08-8821-
1108), has inexpensive pub-style accommodations. **Kadina Village Motel,** 28 Port Rd. (tel.

THE CORNISH PASTY

The pasty was a traditional meal for the miners. Sometimes meat and veggies were
placed at one end, fruit at the other. In all cases,
there was crimping along the top. The crimping
acted as a handle, so the men—hands filthy
from work—could eat their meal and toss away
the "handle." These days the crimped edge is
devoured along with the contents.

The Original Cornish Pasty Recipe
Pasty rolled out like a plate, filled with turmut,
tates an' mait. Doubled up an' baked like fate.
Tha's a Pasty.

08-8821-1920), has slightly higher rates but includes breakfast. **Kadina Caravan and Camping Park,** Lindsay Terrace (tel. 08-8821-2259), has campsites and on-site vans and is close to all facilities.

Food? This is Cornish pasty country—they'll stick to your ribs but won't shrink your pocketbook. Buy 'em anywhere! Try **Cross's Cornish Bakeshop,** 20 Graves St., or **Wallis's Kadina Bakery,** 42 Graves Street. **Dynasty Room,** 4 Goyder St. (tel. 08-8821-2829), offers Chinese, Thai, and Australian cuisine at moderate prices.

For local info, contact the **Tourist Information Centre,** Victoria Square (tel. 08-8821-2093). Hours are Mon.-Fri. 10 a.m.-2 p.m., Sat.-Sun. 9:30 a.m.-1:30 p.m.

In emergencies, contact: **police** (tel. 08-8821-1200), **ambulance** (tel. 08-8821-1029), the local hospital (tel. 08-8821-1544), or **Royal Automobile Association** (tel. 08-8821-1111).

Wallaroo

Wheat and barley are shipped from this busy port (pop. 2,225), but it still doesn't equal the millions of tons of copper ore once trafficked over the jetty to destinations overseas.

Situated 10 km west of Kadina, Wallaroo was originally settled by the Welsh. The **Welsh Chimney Stack,** a Wallaroo landmark, contains 300,000 bricks in its huge square structure. For some reason Welsh masons built square chimney stacks and the Cornish masons made theirs round.

See an extensive pictorial display of sailing ships, exhibits related to the smelting industry, and postal and sporting relics at **Wallaroo Nautical Museum,** Jetty Rd., in the old post office (tel. 08-8823-2366). Hours are Wednesday, Saturday, Sunday, and public and school holidays 2-4 p.m. Admission is $2.

Other heritage buildings include **Harvey's Pumping Station,** the **Institute, General Store,** old **Methodist Church,** and original **Wesleyan Chapel.**

You can safely swim at Wallaroo's sandy beaches. The boating and jetty angling are excellent as well.

Wallaroo Hotel, 26 Alexander St. (tel. 08-8823-2444), is pretty basic, but rooms are only about $25 per double. **Sonbern Lodge Motel,** 18 John Terrace (tel. 08-8823-2291), has mod-

erately priced heritage accommodations, wit rooms in the motel section costing $10 more **Kohler Village,** Heritage Dr. (tel. 08-8823-2531 offers moderate-expensive two-bedroom hol day units with cooking facilities.

Campsites and on-site vans are available a both **Wallaroo North Beach Caravan Park** North Beach (tel. 08-8823-2531), and **Offic Beach Holiday Flats and Caravan Park,** Offic Beach (tel. 08-8823-2722).

Dine on moderately priced local seafood a **The Seafood Corner,** corner Charles Terrac and Irwin St. (tel. 08-8823-2288). For takeawa fresh and smoked fish, crayfish, and prawns, try **& KF Studt,** 35 Owen Terrace (tel. 08-8823 3222).

Moonta

The third point in the Copper Triangle, Moont (pop. 2,200) lies 10 km south of Wallaroo. Moor ta is the nicest of the three mining towns– maybe because it was the richest. The dign fied architecture, from tiny miners' cottages t the Gothic-esque Uniting Church, is a splendi reminder of times past.

After you've explored around town, head fc the nearby mine site to investigate the old build ings and relics. The former schoolhouse, no **Moonta Mines Museum,** is a living history ex hibit where you can experience what condition were like for the miners, many of whom worke the 767-meter-deep Taylor Shaft. The muse um will provide a self-guiding map. **Miner's Cot tage,** adjacent to the museum, is a restore Cornish dwelling, open for public viewing. O weekends you can ride a narrow-gauge touris railway around the mine's complex. Hours ar Wednesday, Sat.-Sun., public and school hol days 1:30-4 p.m. Admission is $1. For informa tion, phone (08) 8825-3422.

Both the **Royal Hotel,** 2 Ryan St. (tel. 08 8825-2108), and the **Cornwall Hotel,** 20 Ryar St. (tel. 08-8825-2304), have inexpensive pul accommodations. **Moonta Bay Caravan Park** Tossell St. (tel. 08-8825-2406), on the fore shore, offers campsites and cabins.

For your Cornish pasty fix, go to **Wither' Moonta Bakery,** 8 George St., or **The Cornish Kitchen,** 14 Ellen St. (tel. 08-8825-3030). Th historic **Cornwall Hotel** serves home-style Aus tralian meals, and the **Shaft Steak House,** Elle

. (tel. 08-8825-2981), specializes, obviously, in
abs of beef.

vents

erneweck Lowender, held in May of every
dd-numbered year, is a festival commemorat-
g the Copper Triangle's Cornish heritage. Ac-
ivities include "A Golya," a Cornish feast with
ancing and drinking, "A Fer Tref," all the fun of
village green fair, "A Fer Kernewek," a Cornish
ir with traditional sports and the crowning of
Cousin Jack" and "Cousin Jenny," and the
orseth ceremony, a gathering of bands from
ornwall and Australia. Aside from Cornish
asties, revelers can sip on Swanky, a special-
brewed ale.

THE EAST COAST

sealed thoroughfare follows the coast to Edith-
urgh, where you either cut inland to Yorke-
wn, Warooka, and Innes National Park, or
ontinue along the coast on mix-or-match grav-
l and dirt roads.

ort Clinton to Ardrossan

ort Clinton, the east coast's northernmost sea-
de resort, has good crabbing beaches and is a
eashell's throw from Clinton Conservation Park.
ort Clinton Caravan Park, on the foreshore
el. 08-8837-7003), has campsites and on-site
ans.

Tiddy Widdy Beach is a good spot for sun-
ing and swimming. **Price Beach** is near a large
alt refinery, harvesting from a vast area of pans
umped full of Gulf St. Vincent seawater.

Ardrossan, about 150 km from Adelaide, is
ot just the largest east coast port, with bulk
rain handling facilities; it's also home of the
ump-jump plough, the particular tool, invented
y Clarence Smith in 1876, that enabled mallee
crubland to be turned into golden wheatfields all
cross the country. The folks over at the
rdrossan District Historical Museum, on
th St., will be delighted to fill you in on more of
e town's history. Hours are Sunday 2:30-4:30
m. Admission is $1. For information, phone
8) 8837-3213.

You can catch a scenic view of Gulf St. Vin-
ent from the **BHP lookout** or trap some crabs
t the jetty.

Royal House Hotel Motel, 1 5th St. (tel. 08-
8837-3007), charges inexpensive rates in the
hotel, $20 more for motel rooms. **Ardrossan
Caravan Park,** Park Terrace (tel. 08-8837-3262),
offers campsites, cabins, and on-site vans.

For emergencies, contact: **police** (tel. 08-
8837-3017), **ambulance** (tel. 08-8837-3295),
or the local **hospital** (tel. 08-8837-3021).

TO EDITHBURGH AND BEYOND

Continuing south, along the coast, you'll pass the
fishing "villagettes" of **Rogues Point, Pine
Point, Black Point,** and **Port Julia.** Divers will
want to check out the shipwrecked *Zanoni,*
about 15 km southeast of Ardrossan.

Port Vincent, set on a sweeping bay 46 km
south of Ardrossan, is an old ketch-landing
place, and a popular swimming, yachting, and
waterskiing resort. The **Port Vincent Fisherman's Retreat,** corner Parsons Rd. and Kemp
St. (tel. 08-8853-7057), offers moderately priced
holiday flats. **Seaside Flats and Caravan Park,**
Minlacowie Rd. (tel. 08-8853-7011), rents inexpensive flats as well as campsites and cabins.

Stansbury, 16 km away, is another sought-
after holiday resort. Originally known as "Oyster
Bay," it still offers some of the state's best oyster
beds. Jetty fishing is also excellent here, and
you'll find a decent selection of tourist facilities.
The units at **Stansbury Villas,** Adelaide Rd.
(tel. 08-8852-4282), are moderately priced self-
contained holiday flats. **Stansbury Holiday
Motel,** Adelaide Rd. (tel. 08-8852-4455), is on
the deluxe side with moderate-expensive rates
(every room has a sea view). Campsites, cabins,
and on-site vans are available at **Stansbury
Caravan Park,** on the foreshore (tel. 08-8852-
4171).

Past **Wool Bay, Port Giles,** and **Coobowie**
lies picturesque **Edithburgh.** A former salt-pro-
ducing township (and the first proclaimed settlement on southern Yorke Peninsula), Edithburgh is celebrated by divers drawn to the many
shipwrecks along its coastline. If you take the
scenic drive up to **Troubridge Hill,** you'll be
able to see part of the shipwreck *Clan Ronald.*

Swimmers will find a rock pool set into a small
cove, while the jetty provides ideal conditions for
anglers. The small **Edithburgh Museum** features maritime displays and artifacts. Hours are

Sunday and public and school holidays 2-4 p.m. Admission is $1.

Take a guided day-tour over to **Troubridge Island** to view fairy penguins and other birds contained within the 14-hectare conservation park. For **Troubridge Island Tours,** contact Chris Johnson, Blanche St., Edithburgh 5583 (tel. 08-8852-6290).

Motel accommodations in Edithburgh are moderately priced. If you plan to stay awhile, you can get a self-contained unit for $160-245 per week at **Ocean View Holiday Flats,** O'Halloran Parade (tel. 08-8852-6029). **Edithburgh House,** Edith St. (tel. 08-8852-6373), offers old-fashioned seaside guesthouse rooms for high-moderate to expensive rates, but they include dinner and breakfast. **Edithburgh Caravan Park,** corner South Terrace and O'Halloran Parade (tel. 08-8852-6056), situated on the foreshore, offers campsites, on-site vans, and cabins.

Venture inland from Edithburgh 16 km to **Yorketown,** one of the peninsula's earliest pastoral settlements. Surrounded by salt lakes where crystal formations decorate the shores, several of the lakes are pink and worth watching at sunset. You'll find inexpensive accommodations at **Melville Hotel Motel,** 1 Minlaton Rd. (tel. 08-8852-1019), or at **Yorke Hotel,** 1 Warooka Rd. (tel. 08-8852-1221), but neither place is really comfy. The motel section at the Melville is probably your best bet. Camping and on-site vans are available at **Yorketown Caravan Park,** Memorial Dr. (tel. 08-8852-1563).

Beyond Edithburgh, the coast road turns to gravel (and occasionally to dirt) as it travels a sparsely populated route along scenic beaches and secluded bays, merging with the sealed highway about 10 km north of Innes National Park.

Hillocks Drive, 16 km east of Marion Bay, is a scenic road leading to **Butlers Beach,** set on a seven-km sea frontage. Privately run by the Butler family, the property has two surf beaches, a number of fishing spots, camping facilities, and a small general store. The property is closed mid-June through mid-August. For information, phone (08) 8854-4002.

INNES NATIONAL PARK

The main entrance to Innes National Park is four km southwest of Marion Bay. Situated at th southernmost tip of the Yorke Peninsula, th spectacular coastal park's 9,141 hectares stretc from Stenhouse Bay on the east coast, arour Cape Spencer, to Browns Beach on the we coast. Just a three-hour drive from Adelaid the park is a favorite with city dwellers who con to surf, fish, dive, and bushwalk.

Big sightseeing attractions are the shipwre *Ethel M,* run aground in 1904 and now disint grating near an isolated cove called The Ga and the old ghost town at **Inneston** (follow th historical markers past the Cape Spenc turnoff).

Clean beaches, crystal-clear water, and cc orful marinelife create a delightful environme for aquatic activities. There's good fishing Chinaman's Beach, Salmon Hole, Pondalow Bay, Browns Beach (terrific for year-roun salmon fishing), Little Browns Beach, and Cap Spencer, and a host of rock fishing spots b tween Pondalowie and Stenhouse Bays (b careful of those wet rocks!).

Bushwalkers can choose from a variety tracks leading through such diverse terrain a low scrub, salt lake flats, coastal dunes, ar rugged cliffs—with a good probability of ru ning into a friendly emu or kangaroo!

Camping is permitted within the park at se eral different areas. The main camping area is Pondalowie Bay, where facilities were recen upgraded.

During Christmas holidays, park rangers co duct guided activities for children and your adults.

For camping permits and other informatio contact **Park Headquarters,** Stenhouse Ba (tel. 08-8854-4044), or the **Warooka Distri Council Office,** Warooka (tel. 08-8854-5055 Admission is $3 per vehicle.

UP THE PENINSULA

Going northward from Innes National Park, th sealed road brushes by **Warrenben Conse vation Park,** 4,061 hectares of dense malle dryland tea-tree vegetation, and native pine The gravel road from Marion Bay sort of wind around the coast, with other gravel or dirt path branching out to the beaches. **Daly Head** is y

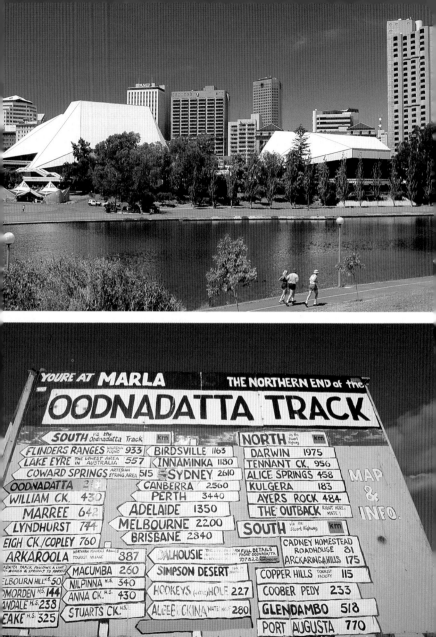

(top) a view from Memorial Drive across River Torrens toward city center
(bottom) a signpost at Marla, northern gateway to the Oodnadatta Track

(top) Point Labatt National Park is home to Australia's only permanent mainland seal colony.
(bottom) Coffin Bay, a fishing and holiday village 45 km west of Port Lincoln

nother special fishing hole, as is **Corny Point**
t the northwestern tip. Corny Point also has a
ghthouse and camping facilities.

At Point Turton, you can either continue zigzag-
ing the beachy back roads to the top of the
eninsula or turn onto the seven-km sealed stretch
at leads back to the main highway at Warooka.

In the tiny township of **Brentwood**, 17 km
orth of Warooka, visit **Brentwood Pottery** (tel.
8-8853-4255) in the old general store/post of-
ce. Rent a **gypsy wagon,** pulled by a gentle
lydesdale, for overnight camping by the sea or
or a longer and leisurely ride around southern
orke Peninsula. Rates run about \$100 per day,
ith a three-day minimum. For information, con-
ct Stansbury Holiday Motel (tel. 08-8852-4455)
r Anthony Honner, Brentwood via Minlaton,
A 5575 (tel. 08-8853-4201). The same peo-
le also arrange farm holidays in moderately
riced self-contained stone cottages.

Minlaton (pop. 900), about 14 km north of
orketown, is referred to as the "Barley Capital of
e World." It's also the home of Capt. Harry But-
r's *Red Devil,* a 1916 monoplane flown by the
oneering aviator during World War I. Ostensibly,
is is the world's only remaining Bristol fighter
ane, and lucky you can see it at the glass-front-
d **Harry Butler Hangar/Museum,** near the town
enter. Nearby, on Main St., the **National Trust
useum** (tel. 08-8853-2127) exhibits photos,
emorabilia, and farming implements, and, at
e corner of Bluff and Maitland Roads, **Jolly's
useum** (tel. 08-8853-2364) features restored
actors and other machinery. **Gum Flat Home-
tead Gallery,** Stansbury Rd. (tel. 08-8853-2287),
vo km east of Minlaton, is an arts-and-crafts
enter with locally made wares for sale.

Rooms are moderately priced at **Minlaton
otel Motel,** 26 Main Rd. (tel. 08-8853-2014).
ent campsites or on-site vans at **Minlaton
aravan Park,** corner Bluff and Maitland Roads
el. 08-8853-2435).

For Minlaton emergencies, contact **police**
el. 08-8853-2100), **ambulance** or local **hos-
ital** (tel. 08-8853-2200), or **Royal Automo-
le Association** (tel. 08-8853-2243).

Turn off at Urania for **Port Victoria,** "last of the
indjammer ports" and now a busy little fishing reort. Sailing and waterskiing are popular around
ardang Island. See relics and curios of the nau-
cal past at **Port Victoria Maritime Museum** (tel.

08-8834-2057). Hours are Sunday and school
holidays 2-4 p.m. Admission is \$1.

Bayview Holiday Flats, 29 Davies Terrace
(tel. 08-8834-2082), offers fully self-contained
units at inexpensive-moderate rates, depending on season. Beachfront **Port Victoria Caravan Park** (tel. 08-8834-2001) has campsites
and on-site vans.

Maitland, the heart of Yorke Peninsula, is
Colonel Light's vision at work again—a modern agricultural center well laid out and surrounded by parklands. View agricultural artifacts and brush up on local history at **Maitland
Museum,** corner Gardiner and Kikerran Streets
(tel. 08-8832-2220). Hours are Sunday and public holidays 2-4 p.m. Admission is \$1.

Maitland Hotel, 33 Robert St. (tel. 08-8832-
2431), "where the beer is cold and the welcome
warm," has inexpensive rooms. The pub serves
good, home-cooked meals. **Eothen Farmhouse**
(tel. 08-8836-3210), near beaches and bush, is
a fully equipped separate home, with kitchen,
lounge, open fires, and high-moderate rates.

Emergency numbers for Maitland are: **police** (tel. 08-8832-2621), **ambulance** and local
hospital (tel. 08-8832-2626).

A 20-km jaunt westward from Maitland brings
you to **Balgowan,** a century-old landing place for
ketches making pick-ups and deliveries for local
farmers. Today it serves as a serene retreat for
fishermen.

Back on the main highway, it's a 35-km drive to
Moonta, lower edge of the Copper Triangle, then
about 60 km more through Kadina to **Port
Broughton,** a seaside resort at the tippy-top of the
peninsula, where there's a safe swimming beach
for children and a good fishing jetty for anglers.

Spend the night at **Port Broughton Hotel,** on
the foreshore (tel. 08-8635-2004). Built in 1888,
this family-style establishment has inexpensive
rooms, with breakfast included. Other facilities
include a main bar, saloon bar, beer garden, large
dining room, a la carte dining room, and bottle
shop. **Main Park,** 2 Broughton St. (tel. 08-8635-
2188), has campsites, on-site vans, and cabins.

Port Broughton Charter Boats, 19 Harvey
St. (tel. 08-8635-2466), offers fishing trips (\$30-
80) or pleasure cruises (\$10, for one hour) in
the Spencer Gulf.

For Port Broughton emergencies, contact:
police (tel. 08-8635-2255), **ambulance** (tel. 08-

8635-2544), the local **hospital** (tel. 08-8635-2282), or **Royal Automobile Association** (tel. 08-8635-2522).

TRANSPORTATION

Premier Roadlines (tel. 08-8415-5544) operates daily service from Adelaide to Kadina, Wallaroo, Moonta, Port Hughes, and Moonta Bay. One-way fare for the three-hour trip to Moonta is $21.

Yorke Peninsula Bus Service (tel. 08-8391 2977) travels daily from Adelaide to Ardrossa ($16), Port Vincent ($20), Edithburgh ($22), an Yorketown ($22).

All coaches depart Adelaide's **Country Pas senger Depot,** 101 Franklin St. (tel. 08-8231 4144).

There is no public transport south of Wa rooka, and if you're hitching road traffic is prett minimal.

EYRE PENINSULA

Wild coastlines with stupendous surf and isolated beaches, round-the-clock steel mills and busy grain terminals, phenomenal rock formations and ancient ranges, gentle sea lion colonies and great white shark breeding grounds are some of the Eyre Peninsula attractions that keep travelers coming (and going).

The peninsula is *wide*, stretching 469 km from Port Augusta in the east, across the Eyre Highway, past the Gawler Ranges, to Ceduna, the last ample outpost before the Nullarbor Plain. Alternate Route 1 (called Lincoln Highway from Port Augusta to Port Lincoln, and Flinders Highway from Port Lincoln to Ceduna) traverses the peninsula, hugging the coast—and its bays, beaches, ports, and parks—along sheltered Spencer Gulf on the east, round the pounding Southern Ocean and the Great Australian Bight. The distance from Port Augusta back up to Ceduna is 668 km. Another option that enables you to see a sizable chunk of this region is to follow the Eyre Highway. If you take this route you can journey into the Gawler Ranges to the north and explore famed Mt. Wudinna Rock along the way, and cut through the center of the peninsula along the Tod Highway (258 km of sheep and cereal scenery) down to Port Lincoln, the adjacent national parks, and the offshore islands. From there, depending on which way you're headed, you can either follow the east coast up to Whyalla (and back to Adelaide or onward to the Northern Territory) or take the west side, skirting round the sea lion colony, passing through Streaky Bay to Ceduna and the great beyond.

History

By now you've surely guessed that super-sailor Capt. Matthew Flinders charted the Eyre Peninsula during his 1802 mega-voyage aboard the *Investigator*. He was not using his own charts, however, but those of Dutch explorer Peter Nuyts, who in 1627 sailed his *Gulden Zeepaard* ("Golden Seahorse") as far as Streaky Bay. Nuyts, more inclined toward trade than homesteading, turned back when he got to the offshore islands now named Nuyts Archipelago.

By the time Flinders arrived, Abel Tasman and Captain Cook had already been there, Tasman circling the country and Cook glimpsing the peninsula's east coast. Flinders did a more thorough examination of the coastline, naming the majority of features after crew and family members, as well as locales around his hometown of Lincolnshire. The peninsula itself was named by Governor Gawler for Edward John Eyre, the explorer who in 1839-40 made a series of frustrating obstacle-fraught overland expeditions, culminating in the first east-west crossing of Australia.

Bountiful golden-grain harvests, iron ore deposits, a thriving steel industry, and an ocean bounty that makes this one of the country's largest commercial fisheries are the region's moneymakers. Port Lincoln and Thevenard, the two biggest seaports—both with road and railway connections—ship a steady flow of cargo worldwide.

Apropos of fish, the white pointer shark breeds around Dangerous Reef, off Port Lincoln's shores, and the underwater scenes in *Jaws* were filmed here.

PORT AUGUSTA

At the head of the Spencer Gulf, bustling Port Augusta (pop. 15,300) is the town at which Highway 1, the Eyre Highway (actually Highway 1 with a change of name and direction), and the

On 1 February 1997 all telephone numbers on the Eyre Peninsula will change. In preparation for this, all numbers in this section have been changed to eight digits. To dial an Eyre Peninsula number before 1 February, simply delete the first two digits of the new number and, if dialing from outside the Eyre Peninsula, add the (086) area code. For example, (08) 8612-3456 would be dialed (086) 12-3456. After 1 February the area code for all numbers in this section will be (08).

Stuart Highway all converge. From this cross-roads, travelers scurry and scamper north to the Flinders Ranges, south to Adelaide, east to Sydney, and west across the Nullarbor, or slightly southwest to the Lincoln Highway and the Eyre Peninsula coast. Besides that, it's on the main railway line used by the Ghan, Trans-Australian, and Indian-Pacific.

Established in 1852, Port Augusta served as a wool port for nearly a century. Today its major functions are transporting goods to and from the isolated outback and generating electricity for much of South Australia.

Sights
Wadlata Outback Centre, 41 Flinders Terrace (tel. 08-8642-4511), features displays, videos,

and models depicting Aboriginal Dreamtime (including a big fiberglass serpent storyteller. Other exhibits highlight the early explorers and the history of electricity and communication. Hours are Mon.-Fri. 9 a.m.-5:30 p.m., Sat.-Su 10 a.m.-4 p.m. Admission is $6.

Homestead Park Pioneer Museum, Els St. (tel. 08-8642-2035), displays pioneer ar facts and machinery. Hours are daily 10 a.m. p.m., closed Christmas Day.

ETSA (Electricity Trust of South Australi Northern Power Station (tel. 08-8642-052 conducts one-hour behind-the-scenes tours of $500 million coal-fired power plant Mon.-Fri. 1 a.m. and 1 p.m. (Strong footwear is advised Turn off Highway 1 at Andy's Truck Stop, 2.5 k east of Port Augusta.

Royal Flying Doctor Service, 4 Vincent St. (tel. 08-8642-2044), provides medical care to outback residents. The center is open for tours Mon.-Fri. 10 a.m.-noon and 1-3 p.m.

School of the Air (tel. 08-8642-2077) offers educational programs to children residing in the outback. Facilities are at Central Primary School at the southern end of Commercial Rd., and tours are conducted Mon.-Fri. 10 a.m., except holidays. Admission is $2.

Accommodations and Food

Augusta Hotel, 1 Loudon Rd. (tel. 08-8642-2701), has inexpensive pub rooms. **Myoora Motel,** 5 Hackett St. (tel. 08-8642-3622), and **Port Augusta East Motel,** Hwy. 1 (tel. 08-8642-2555), both offer comfy rooms at moderate rates. Also moderately priced is centrally located **Flinders Hotel Motel,** 39 Commercial Rd. (tel. 08-8642-2544), with modern conveniences, family units, and good home cookin'.

Both **Shoreline Caravan Park,** Gardiner Ave. (tel. 08-8642-2965), situated on the gulf, and **Big 4 Fauna Caravan Park,** corner of Hwy. 1 and Stokes Terrace (tel. 08-8642-2974), set amidst peacocks and other birds, rent campsites and on-site vans.

Eat at the pubs, where you'll probably catch a live band or DJ disco on weekends. **Ozzie's Coffee Lounge,** 22 Commercial Rd. (tel. 08-8642-2028), in the Port Augusta Mall, serves coffee, croissants, pâté, quiches, and sandwiches. A branch of the **Barnacle Bill Fish 'n' Chippery** sits at 60 Victoria Parade (tel. 08-8641-0000). **Basic Foods,** Commercial St., prepares vegetarian meals. For that 24-hour truckin' experience, stop at **Andy's Truckstop,** Hwy. 1 (tel. 08-8641-0700), 2.5 km east of Port Augusta, where you'll find home-style meals, showers, and a laundromat.

Transportation, Services, and Information

Vehicles can be rented from **Budget,** 16 Young St. (tel. 08-8642-6040), and **Handy Ute and Car Hire,** 46 Stirling Rd. at Mobil Davenport Service Station (tel. 08-8642-4255). **Butler's Outback Safaris,** 3 Prosser St. (tel. 08-8642-2188), is an established company run by Malcolm Butler, who was born in the outback. It's a safe and comfortable way to explore the desolate region north of Port Augusta. Four- to seven-day adventures include transport in air-conditioned 4WD vehicles, all meals, accommodations, and other necessary equipment.

Wadlata Outback Centre, 41 Flinders Terrace (tel. 08-8641-0793), is also home to Port Augusta's Tourist Information Centre. Hours are Mon.-Fri. 9 a.m.-5:30 p.m., Sat.-Sun. 10 a.m.-4 p.m., closed Christmas Day.

For emergencies, dial 000. Other contacts are **Port Augusta Hospital** (tel. 08-8648-5500) and **police** (tel. 08-8648-5020).

WHYALLA

A big-time shipbuilding port until 1978, Whyalla (pop. 26,900) survives today on its round-the-clock steel production and shipments of ore from nearby Iron Knob and Iron Baron. As South Australia's largest provincial city—with a sunny, Mediterranean-style climate—facilities are good, and "pass-through" tourism gives yet another economic boost.

Originally called Hummock Hill by Captain Flinders, the township developed around 1901, after iron ore was discovered at Iron Knob. Trammed from mine to town, the ore was then barged over to the Port Pirie smelters. The flourishing community was renamed in 1914.

Whyalla had two major boom periods—the first in 1938 with the establishment of a blast furnace, and the second in 1958 when BHP Company (still the city's main employer) confirmed plans for building its completely integrated steelworks. In between was the creation of a deepwater port and successful shipyard, memorable days that still tug the hearts of the local old salts.

Sights
Whyalla Maritime Museum, Lincoln Hwy. (tel. 08-8645-8900), is where you can climb aboard Australia's largest landlocked ship, the 650-ton corvette *Whyalla* (a.k.a. HMA *Whyalla* and the *Rip*). Displays inside the Tanderra Building include shipping memorabilia, valuable BHP models, and one of the country's largest model railways. Hours are daily 10 a.m.-4 p.m. Ship tours leave hourly 11 a.m.-3 p.m. (closed footwear mandatory). Admission is $5.

Mount Laura Homestead Museum, Ekblom St., behind Westland Shopping Centre (tel. 08-

8645-9319), is the place to brush up on town history and view restored buildings and machinery. Hours are Sunday, Monday, and Wednesday 2-4 p.m., Friday 10 a.m.-noon. Admission is $1.

BHP Steelworks offers guided tours of the operations, including the blast furnace, steelmaking plant, coke ovens, railway line, and one-kilometer-long rolling mill. Tours last two hours or so and depart from Whyalla Tourist Centre Monday, Wednesday, and Saturday 9:30 a.m. Be sure to wear closed footwear. Admission is $5. For information and bookings, phone (08) 8645-7900.

Hummock Hill Lookout, site of a World War II gun battery, affords a dynamite view of Whyalla, the foreshore, upper Spencer Gulf, Port Bonython, Point Lowly, and the Middleback Ranges. Follow the brown and white "Route 61" (Whyalla Tourist Drive) signs.

Whyalla Wildlife and Reptile Sanctuary, Lincoln Hwy., across from the airport (tel. 08-8645-7044), features koalas, wombats, dingoes, 'roos, emus, deadly snakes, and a walk-through aviary in natural bushland. Hours are daily 10 a.m.-6 p.m. (Nov.-April), 10 a.m.-4:30 p.m. (other months). Admission is $4.50.

Port Bonython, about 10 km north of Whyalla, off the Lincoln Hwy., is the site of the massive SANTOS plant, which distills liquid hydrocarbons that have passed from Moomba through a 659-km underground pipeline. Though you can't tour the facility, you can get a view of operations from along the roadway or shore.

Port Lowly, two km beyond SANTOS, offers beautiful gulf views, a popular summer beach, and the Port Lowly Lighthouse (over 110 years old), which looks out upon playful dolphins that often swim by.

The **Scenic Coastal Drive** is a 20-km combination sealed and gravel road along Spencer Gulf, from Fitzgerald Bay to Point Douglas. Take the marked turnoff before Port Bonython.

The **Whyalla Foreshore** redevelopment provides excellent facilities for swimming, jetty fishing, windsurfing, and picnicking. **Whyalla Marina** has a new four-lane launching ramp for all boating activities.

Murrippi Beach, off Eight Mile Creek Rd., 12 km south of Whyalla, is a legal nude beach (no facilities).

Accommodations and Food

As with most cities this size, you'll find pubs, motels, restaurants, and takeaways—all pretty standard. Most accommodations have their own dining facilities.

Pub rooms are inexpensive at either **Hotel Whyalla,** 9 Darling Terrace (tel. 08-8645-7411) or **Lord Gowrie Hotel,** Gowrie Ave. (tel. 08-8645-8955). **Airport Whyalla Motel,** Lincoln Hwy. (tel. 08-8645-2122), and **Sundowner Hotel Motel,** Lincoln Hwy. (tel. 08-8645-7688), both offer comfortable rooms at low-moderate rates. Campsites, cabins, and on-site vans are available at **Whyalla Foreshore Caravan Park,** Broadbent Terrace (tel. 08-8645-7474).

Entertainment and Recreation

Middleback Theatre, corner Nicolson Ave. and Racecourse Rd. (tel. 08-8645-8022), presents live theater, musical performances and other stage presentations, as well as arts-and-craft exhibitions. You can inspect the theater foyer, its mural, and stained-glass windows Mon.-Fri. a.m.-5 p.m.

Whyalla Recreation and Leisure Centre, off Racecourse Rd. near the junction of Nicolson Ave. (tel. 08-8645-5488), welcomes visitors to use the heated indoor swimming pool, squash courts, gymnasium, weightlifting equipment, sweat track, and volleyball and tennis courts. Equipment is available for rental.

Information

Whyalla Tourist Centre (tel. 08-8645-7900), next to BHP Steelworks on Lincoln Hwy., provides maps, tour bookings, and info on the local bus service (weekdays and Saturday mornings). Hours are Mon.-Fri. 9 a.m.-5 p.m., Saturday 9 a.m.-4 p.m., Sunday and public holidays 10 a.m.-4 p.m. Closed Christmas Day and Good Friday.

TO PORT LINCOLN

From Whyalla, the Lincoln Highway makes a slight inland jag, traveling for a short distance along the iron-ore-rich Middleback Ranges, angling back to the coast (in about 111 km) at Cowell.

Cowell

Set on scenic Franklin Harbour, a protected bay noted for calm waters and great fishing, Cowell (pop. 692) is also famous for its huge jade deposits, discovered in the nearby Minbrie Ranges in 1965, as well as some interesting marble uncovered along with the jade boulders. The area is thought to be the world's largest producer of green and black jade.

Several operators offer mine tours, or you can visit the factory and showroom of **Gemstone Corporation of Australia,** 2nd St. (tel. 08-8629-2111).

Other attractions include the **Franklin Harbour Historical Museum,** in the old post office, and the **Agricultural Museum,** on Lincoln Highway. Both are open by appointment. For information, phone (08) 8629-2032.

Lucky Bay, 16 km north of town, is a popular beach resort with safe swimming, good fishing, and a boat ramp. **Poverty Beach,** just south of town, has good surfing.

Rooms are inexpensive at the **Franklin Harbour Hotel,** 1 Main St. (tel. 08-8629-2015). For moderate rates that include breakfast, **Shultz Farm,** Smith Rd. (tel. 08-8629-2194), offers home-style accommodations on a sheep and grain property overlooking the coast. **Cowell Foreshore Caravan Park** (tel. 08-8629-2307) has campsites, cabins, and on-site vans. Don't miss a taste of the delicious locally harvested oysters.

Obtain local **tourist information** at District Council of Franklin Harbour, 6 Main St. (tel. 08-8629-2019).

Continuing Southward

From Cowell, you can cut inland 42 km to the rural community of **Cleve.** The scenic Cleve-Cowell Hills drive provides great views of the countryside and Spencer Gulf. From Cleve, you can cut southeast 25 km back to the coast at Arno Bay. Or stick to the coastal road and pass along the wide, lovely beaches at **The Knob, Port Gibbon,** and **Point Price Sandhills.**

Arno Bay, halfway point between Whyalla and Port Lincoln, is a tranquil fishing village in winter and a tourist mecca in summer. **Redbanks,** six km north of town, is a designated geological monument of rock pools and just-as-rocky cliffs. **Arno Hotel** (tel. 08-8628-0001),

near the beach, has country-style rooms. Their low rates include breakfast.

Port Neill, 33 km south from Arno Bay and two km off the main highway, is another attractive, clean, safe water sports haven. Check out the blue water and the rolling hills from **Port Neill Lookout,** one km north of town. **Fauser's Museum,** opposite the caravan park (tel. 08-8688-9041), is a private collection of steam and stationary engines, motorcycles, vintage autos, and other relics. Hours are daily 10 a.m.-4 p.m.

Port Neill Hotel, Peake Terrace (tel. 08-8688-9006), has inexpensive rooms. **Henley's Holiday Flats,** Gill St. (tel. 08-8688-9001), are fully self-contained units, also inexpensive. **Port Neill Caravan Park,** Peake Terrace (tel. 08-8688-9067), rents campsites and on-site vans.

If you wait until low tide to visit **Lipson Cove,** another 20 km south, you can walk across to **Lipson Island,** a coastal bird sanctuary.

Tumby Bay shelters fishing and boating waters and is also service center for the surrounding rural townships. **C.L. Alexander National Trust Museum,** corner West Terrace and Lipson Rd. (tel. 08-8688-2574), features local memorabilia in an original wooden schoolhouse. Hours are Friday and Sunday 2:30-4:30 p.m. Admission is $1.

Head to **Island Lookout** to catch a good view of town, bay, and the **Sir Joseph Banks Group of Islands,** 15 km offshore. Named by Captain Flinders for the renowned English botanist, the islands are bird sanctuaries for Cape Barren geese, pied cormorants, eastern reef egrets, crested terns, and many other species. If you don't have your own boat, sign on for a half- or full-day tour with **Sea Jade Charter,** 2 Pfitzner St. (tel. 08-8688-2424).

Seabreeze Hotel, Tumby Terrace (tel. 08-8688-2362), rents inexpensive rooms. **Tumby Bay Motel,** Berryman St. (tel. 08-8688-2311), near the beach, has a swimming pool and is moderately priced. Campsites, cabins, and on-site vans are available at **Tumby Bay Caravan Park,** Tumby Terrace (tel. 08-8688-2208), along the foreshore.

If you don't think you can live without another display of vintage implements, machinery, and artifacts (or if you just want to explore the hill country between Tumby Bay and Port Lincoln), take the 40-km detour to Koppio and the **Koppio Smithy Museum.** Try to get there for the annual

Open Day, when all the machinery is turned on and huffs, puffs, toots, and honks in unison. Hours are Tues.-Sun. 10 a.m.-5 p.m. For information, phone (08) 8684-4243.

Back on the coast, **North Shields,** just 11 km north of Port Lincoln, is home of the **Karlinda Collection,** an amazing amassment of more than 10,000 shells, rocks, minerals, fossils, and other marine curios. It's all housed in the building next to the post office. Hours are daily 9 a.m.-9 p.m. Admission is $1. For information, phone (08) 8684-3500.

You can live cheaply and simply at the historic 1868 **Wheatsheaf Hotel,** Government Rd. (tel. 08-8684-3531), where rates include continental breakfast. The Wheatsheaf serves counter meals in the pub and a la carte in the dining room overlooking Boston Bay.

Heading into Port Lincoln, you will pass through Australia's newest winegrowing region (vines planted in 1984, first harvest in 1987), and the cellars of **Boston Bay Wines.** Specializing in red and white table wines, the vineyard is open Sat.-Sun. and public holidays 11:30 a.m.-4:30 p.m., daily December and January. For information, phone (08) 8684-3600.

PORT LINCOLN

At the Eyre Peninsula's southern edge, Port Lincoln (pop. 12,550) is often referred to as "blue water paradise." Paradise?—not quite, but there *is* plenty of blue water. Boston Bay, stretching from Point Boston to the tip of Port Lincoln National Park, is three times larger than Sydney Harbour. Mild winters and comfortable summers, combined with ideal conditions for boating, fishing, skin diving, and windsurfing (and great white shark breeding!) keep the tourists coming.

Named by Captain Flinders after his home county of Lincolnshire, Port Lincoln was originally set to be South Australia's state capital. A lack of fresh water, along with Colonel Light's decided bent toward Adelaide, caused that plan to be withdrawn. The city didn't fare badly, though. Aside from a healthy tourist industry, Port Lincoln is home to Australia's largest commercial tuna fishing fleet and one of the country's busiest grain terminals.

Sights

Axel Stenross Maritime Museum, Lincoln Hwy. near Shaen St. (tel. 08-8682-3889), features memorabilia from windjammer days, as well as early photos, a working slipway, and a blacksmith shop. Hours are Tuesday, Thursday, Sat.-Sun., and public holidays 1-5 p.m. Admission is $1.50.

A short distance from the maritime museum is the **First Landing Site.** See the freshwater spring that lured the early settlers—it's still bubbling and gurgling through the sand.

Mill Cottage and **Settler's Cottage** museums, located on the grounds of Flinders Park (at Lincoln and Flinders Highways), both display artifacts and historical exhibits of Port Lincoln's early beginnings. Hours for Mill Cottage are Tues.-Sun. 2-4:30 p.m. Admission is $1. Contact Port Lincoln Library to arrange entrance to Settler's Cottage.

Nearby, **Rose-Wal Memorial Shell Museum** (tel. 08-8682-1868), on the grounds of the Old Folks' Home, displays a large and valuable collection of shells and sealife. Hours are daily 2-4:30 p.m. Admission is $1.

Apex Wheelhouse, Hindmarsh St. (tel. 08-8682-2537), across from the caravan park, is a restored tuna boat wheelhouse and interpretive center. Photos, charts, and a color video will brief you on the fishing industry. Hours are daily 9 a.m.-5 p.m.

You'll find excellent lookout points at: **Winter's Hill,** five km northeast of town on Flinders Hwy.; **Puckridge Park,** on Angas St.; and the **Old Mill,** Dorset Pl., an 1846 flour mill (historic both because it's old and because it never operated).

A popular day trip is the cruise to **Boston Island,** a working sheep station, discovered and named by Captain Flinders. Select either the Boston Island Safari (a trip to the island, sightseeing, and historical commentary) or Bay Island Cruise (usually run only if a landing on the island is not possible). Departures are from the jetty at Tasman Terrace. Tours are operated by **Investigator Cruises** and can be booked at the tourist office or Kirton Point Caravan Park.

More daring souls, who'd rather eyeball sharks instead of sheep, can journey to **Dangerous Reef,** "home of the great white shark" and locale for underwater scenes in *Jaws.* You an take a diving charter (good luck) or the *Dangerous Reef Explorer,* a high-speed commuter vessel (travel time about 40 minutes). A safer option for those who left their diving gear at home is a 30- by 12-meter underwater viewing platform with observatory and aquarium (and a dive cage). A large sea lion colony also lives on the reef. For info and bookings, contact the ourist office.

Accommodations and Food

If you plan to stay in a pub, I'm still partial to the old Wheatsheaf in North Shields (see above). Most of the motels are on Lincoln Highway or Tasman Terrace. **First Landing Motel,** 1 Shaen St. near the maritime museum (tel. 08-8682-2919), has moderately priced rooms with our-post beds. **Westward Ho Holiday Flats,** 12 London St. (tel. 08-8682-2425), has fully self-contained units at moderate prices. **San Pan Windinna,** 34 Lincoln Hwy. (tel. 08-8682-513), is a fully equipped beachfront cottage in the expensive category. You can rent an inexpensive cabin or campsite at **Kirton Point Caravan Park,** Hindmarsh St. (tel. 08-8682-2537). And, if you've got the bucks ($175 per week, up, with a minimum of five people and maximum of 12), you can rent all of Boston Island. Tariff includes a six-bedroom home, fishing dinghies, tractor, and trailer. No linen, though—you must bring your own or pay an extra fee. For information, phone Peter Davis (tel. 08-8682-741) or contact the South Australian Tourism Commission Travel Centre.

Tasman Mall has the best cheap eats in own. Aside from that, look to the local pubs for meals and nightlife.

Events

Port Lincoln's big blowout is the annual **Tuarama Festival,** held each January. Festivities include parades, cavalcades, roving musicians, competitions, firework displays, rock concerts, dinner dances, and the crowning of Miss Tuarama.

Information

Port Lincoln Tourist Office, Civic Centre, Tasman Terrace (tel. 08-8682-6666), books tours and accommodations and provides info on bicycle rentals, boat charters, and local coach service. Hours are Mon.-Fri. 9 a.m.-5:30 p.m., Saturday 9 a.m.-noon, Sunday (during holidays) 10 a.m.-noon.

TIP OF THE EYRE

The southernmost edge of the Eyre Peninsula stretches from Lincoln National Park, leaning on Spencer Gulf, to Coffin Bay National Park, jutting into the Great Australian Bight.

Lincoln National Park, 20 km south of Port Lincoln, covers 17,000 hectares with open spaces, rugged cliffs, and peaceful bays. Catch panoramic views of park and town from Stamford Hill. Conventional vehicles can access scenic spots like Surfleet Point, Spalding Cove, Old Donington House, Cape Donington Lighthouse, and Taylor's Landing, but you'll need a 4WD to reach wilderness areas like Memory Cove and Cape Catastrophe. Check with the park ranger (tel. 08-8688-3177) for camping information and road conditions.

You'll need a key and permit ($15 plus $3 deposit) to enter privately owned **Whaler's Way,** a dynamically scenic cliff-top drive at the very tip of the peninsula. Magnificent lookouts, blowholes, caves, sparkling beaches, and roaring surf—as well as a wildlife and bird sanctuary—are some of the features. Get yet another special permit to camp at the Redbanks area. On the road to Whaler's Way, you'll pass **Mikkira Station,** an 1840s sheep station. Pick up keys and permits at Port Lincoln Tourist Office or at service stations. Visits are limited to Sunday and school and public holidays.

Continuing along Flinders Highway, you'll pass **Port Lincoln Fauna Park, Little Swamp, Big Swamp,** and **Wanilla Forest.** Turn off toward Coffin Bay, through **Kellidie Bay Conservation Park** and the **Coffin Bay Lookout,** through the township, and straight into the national park.

Coffin Bay National Park, 46 km from Port Lincoln, is a massive 30,000 hectares of wilderness area, much of it accessible only to bushwalkers and those in four-wheel drives (there are some sealed roads for conventional vehicles). Hike the 25-km **Yangie Trail** to Almonta Beach, Avoid Bay, and Yangie Bay—be careful if swimming: **sharks are common.** The park is particularly spectacular early spring to early summer, when gorgeous wildflowers bloom. Inquire about road conditions and pick up camping permits at the ranger's headquarters, near the park's entrance.

The town of **Coffin Bay** is literally surrounded by parks and offers sheltered waters for fishing, boating, swimming, skin diving, and windsurfing. Normally a teeny township of 350 residents, the population leaps to nearly 10 times that in summer. Oysters cultivated here are renowned across Australia. Pay a visit to **Coffin Bay Oyster Farm,** where the motto is, "Eat fish and live longer, eat Coffin Bay Oysters and love longer."

Holiday flats, ranging from inexpensive to moderately priced, line the Esplanade. **Coffin Bay Caravan Park** (tel. 08-8685-4170) has campsites, cabins, and on-site vans.

Pick up **tourist info,** bus tickets, postage stamps, fishing tackle, and hot roasted chicken at Beachcomber Agencies, the Esplanade (tel. 08-8685-4057).

UP FLINDERS HIGHWAY

Climbing up the peninsula, the highway makes gentle jags inward to pastoral land and country townships, then teases you back to sparkling bays and beaches along the Great Australian Bight.

Turn off at Wangary, 29 km north of Coffin Bay, to **Farm Beach** and Anzac Cove (sometimes called Gallipoli Beach), where the movie *Gallipoli* was filmed. You'll pass Mt. Dutton on the way, a good climb, but get permission first, as the land is privately owned.

Back on Flinders Highway, it's mostly sheep and farm country. At **Coulta,** you can experience farm life for $28 at **Wepowie Farm,** Edilillie Rd. (tel. 08-8687-2063). One- or two-day horseback trips and packhorse treks are offered, as well as customary farm activities. Close by are salty Lake Greenly, with hang gliding at Mt. Greenly, and good surfing at Greenly Beach.

Elliston, 100 km from Coulta, is a small fishing village on Waterloo Bay, where the scenic coastline jumps from rugged cliffs to sheltered inlets. Here you'll find "clogs," fossilized cocoons of the *Leptopius duponti* weevil thought to be

nearly 100,000 years old. **Rocket Site Cottage** on the Esplanade (tel. 08-8687-9028), is a fully equipped cottage at inexpensive-moderate rates. Both **Elliston Caravan Park,** Flinders Hwy. (tel. 08-8687-9061), and **Waterloo Bay Caravan Park,** Beach Terrace (tel. 08-8687-9076), have campsites, cabins, and on-site vans.

Flinders Island, 35 km off the coast of Elliston, is a 3,700-hectare getaway with swimming beaches and picturesque views. Accommodations in either a renovated cottage or shearer's quarters cost about $280 double with a four-night minimum stay. For bookings and air charters ($75 round-trip), phone (08) 8626-1132.

Talia Caves, 40 km north of Elliston, has wonderful limestone caves, gnarly rock formations, and bleached sand dunes to explore. **Venus Bay,** another 22 km north, is a small township popular with small boat and jetty anglers and, increasingly, with surfers. **Needle Eye Lookout** gives a great view of the pounding sea, intriguing rocks and arches, and towering cliffs. Turn off at **Point Labatt,** a designated national park, to view Australia's only permanent mainland colony of sea lions.

Back on Flinders Highway, east of Point Labatt, you'll be able to glimpse **Murphy's Haystacks,** sculptured rock formations rising out of the wheatfields. These huge granite *inselbergs* are reputedly more than 1.5 billion years old.

Streaky Bay, 85 km north of Venus Bay (first sighted in 1627 by Dutch explorer Peter Nuyts) was named by Captain Flinders because of the seaweed streaks coloring the bay. This township (pop. 1,200), another of the myriad picturesque fishing villages, is also a service center for the local agricultural communities. Historical buildings of interest are the **School and Kelsh Pioneer Museum,** full of local artifacts, and **Hospital Cottage,** built in 1864. On Alfred Terrace the **Restored Engine Centre** features a collection of some 60-odd engines, some dating back to the early 1900s. All of the museums are open Tuesday and Friday 2-4 p.m.

Koolangatta Farm, via Piednippie Rd. 25 km from town (tel. 08-8626-1174), offers inexpensive country accommodations that include breakfast ingredients. Even cheaper is **Mulgunyah,** Poochera Rd. (tel. 08-8626-1236).

...lso a cottage on a farm. Breakfast not included ...ut farm activities are. **Streaky Bay Motel,** 7 ...lfred Terrace (tel. 08-8626-1126), features ...oderately priced self-contained units with cook-...ng facilities. Rent a campsite or a cabin at **Streaky Bay Foreshore Tourist Park,** Wells ...t. (tel. 08-8626-1666).

Sheltered **Smoky Bay,** about midway be-...ween Streaky Bay and Ceduna, is a teeny villa-...ette, best known for its annual Easter rodeo.

THE EYRE HIGHWAY

...rom Port Augusta to Ceduna, the Eyre High-...vay (Highway 1) spans 469 km of industrial ...ights, wheat belts, wilderness, and geological ...vonders.

Iron Knob, 68 km west of Port Augusta, is the ...irthplace of Australia's steel industry. Iron ore, ...iscovered here in 1894, is quarried and shipped ...o the Whyalla Steelworks, along with supplies ...rom the neighboring mines of Iron Monarch, ...on Baron, Iron Prince, Iron Queen, and Iron ...Duke (only Iron Knob is open to visitors). Tours ...re available Mon.-Fri. at 10 a.m. and 2 p.m., ...Saturday at 2 p.m. Cost is $3. For information, ...hone (08) 8646-2129.

Iron Knob Mineral & Shell Display, 266 Gill ...t. (tel. 08-8646-2130), features more than 2,000 ...rystals from all over the world and ore speci-...mens from Iron Monarch mine. Hours are daily ...0 a.m.-4 p.m. Admission is $1.

Rooms are inexpensive to low-moderate at ei-...her **Iron Knob Hotel,** Main St. (tel. 08-8646-...2013), or **Iron Knob Motel Roadhouse,** Eyre ...lighway (tel. 08-8646-2058).

Kimba, 89 km from Iron Knob, is the "Gate-...vay to the Gawler Ranges" and, really, not much ...else. If you need a rest, **Kimba Community ...lotel Motel,** High St. (tel. 08-8627-2007), has ...nexpensive rooms ($20 higher in the motel sec-...on) and a bar, bistro, beer garden, and dining ...oom.

At Kimba, turn off onto the winding gravel ...oad that leads through the Gawler Ranges, ...vhere you'll see gentle hills with unique rock ...ormations, varied bird and animal life, and glo-...ious spring wildflowers such as Sturt's desert ...bea, the state flower, which was first sighted ...here in 1839 by Eyre. You can camp at **Mt. Ive**

Station (tel. 08-8648-1817), near Lake Gairdner, in a range of very inexpensive facilities. A large part of the district is privately run, so visitors are asked to stick to the public roads, obtain per-mission before camping or hiking, leave all flora and fauna alone, and take all rubbish with them. Conventional vehicles can access much of the area, but, as in all wilderness and isolated re-gions, check the weather and road conditions regularly. **Gawler Ranges Wilderness Safaris,** P.O. Box 11, Wudinna, SA 5652 (tel. 08-8680-2020), is an experienced operator offering two-to four-day 4WD safaris into the region.

Kyancutta, 89 km from Kimba, sits at the junction of the Eyre and Tod Highways. **Wudin-na,** 13 km farther, is the service center for the surrounding rural community, and the airstrip is used for regular service to and from Adelaide. Travelers stop here en route to see Australia's second-largest granite outcrop, **Mt. Wudinna Rock** (261 meters high), 10 km northeast of town. Other weathered masses in this group are **Polda, Turtle,** and **Little Wudinna Rocks.**

If you need a place to stay in the area, **Gawler Ranges Motel,** Eyre Hwy. (tel. 08-8680-2090), has both moderately priced modern rooms and a caravan park with campsites and on-site vans.

The **Minnipa** area, 38 km northwest of Wudinna, has more granite outcrops. There you'll find the Minnipa-Yardea road, another route into the Gawler Ranges. As you head far-ther east on the Eyre Highway, you'll pass through plains-and-grains country, the town-ships of **Poochera** and **Wirrulla,** and finally into Ceduna.

CEDUNA

On the shores of Murat Bay, and at the junc-tion of the Eyre and Flinders Highways, Ceduna (pop. 2,880) is the last full-service town before the vast reaches of the Nullarbor Plain. As such, its name was quite aptly derived from *chedo-ona,* Aboriginal for "a resting place."

Established as a town in 1901, Ceduna is the business hub of the far west coast and an important regional cereal-growing center (with an airport and regular service to Adelaide). The community began originally at Denial Bay, about 12 km to the west, where cargo ships pulled up close to shore, waited until low tide, then loaded wagons with provisions for the settlers. You can still see the ruins at **McKenzie Landing,** on the road to Davenport Creek. More recently, **Thevenard** (four km from Ceduna) serves as deep-sea port for the area, transporting grain, salt, and gypsum worldwide. (An interesting aside: According to map references in *Gulliver's Travels,* Gulliver encountered those little people of Lilliput on St. Peter and St. Francis Islands, off the coast of Thevenard.)

Aside from being a supply and rest stop for travelers, Ceduna boasts a variety of local beaches for fishing, swimming, boating, and surfing.

Sights

The **Old Schoolhouse National Trust Museum,** Park Terrace (tel. 08-8625-2210), displays historic relics of Ceduna's early days. The **Telecommunication Earth Station** (OTC), 37 km northwest of town, is a global satellite system that channels approximately half of Australia's daily telecommunications with Asia, Africa, and Europe via Indian Ocean satellites. Guided tours of the facility are offered Mon.-Fri. 11 a.m. and 2 p.m. For information, phone (08) 8625-2505.

Accommodations and Food

The hotel section in **Ceduna Community Hotel Motel,** O'Loughlin Terrace (tel. 08-8625-2008), overlooking Murat Bay, is cheapest. Other motels, mostly along Eyre Highway, range from moderate to expensive. (There's not a lot of

choice way out here.) Campsites, cabins, and on-site vans are available at **Ceduna Foreshore Caravan Park,** 5 South Terrace (tel. 08-8625-2290).

Meals are at the pubs, motel dining rooms, coffee lounges, and takeaways, or make your own from the supermarket.

Information

Stop in at **Ceduna Gateway Tourist Centre,** 46 Poynton St. (tel. 08-8625-2780), for local and Eyre Peninsula information. Hours are Mon.-Fri. 9 a.m.-5:30 p.m., Saturday 9 a.m.-2 p.m.

TRANSPORTATION

For air services operating to and about the Eyre Peninsula, contact: **Ansett Australia** (tel. 13-1300 toll-free); **Qantas Airways** (tel. 13-1313 toll-free); **Kendell Airlines** (tel. 069-22-0100); or **Lincoln Airlines** (tel. 1800-01-8234).

Greyhound Pioneer Australia operates daily coach service along the Eyre Highway on the Adelaide-Perth route, with stop-offs at Iron Knob, Kimba, Wudinna, Minnipa, Ceduna, and the Nullarbor. Coaches depart Adelaide's central bus station. For information and bookings, phone 13-2030 toll-free. **Stateliner** coaches serve all west coast towns—on the peninsula and along the highway—from Adelaide. The trip to Port Lincoln (eight hours) costs about $50, and to Ceduna (10 hours), $59. For information and bookings, phone (08) 8415-5544.

CROSSING THE NULLARBOR

Now that the road is sealed, this isn't *quite* the adventure it used to be (we'll get to the authentic outback later). But, sealed highway or not, it is still a long, lonesome (and, sometimes, loathsome) trek across the Nullarbor Plain into Western Australia—480 km from Ceduna to the state line, and another 725 km to Norseman, end of the Eyre Highway, where you either take the high road or the low road another 725 km to Perth.

Nullarbor is Latin for "No Trees," but you'll see some timber, a few saplings, and a bit of scrub along the coastal part of the highway, particularly if you travel after the winter rains. It's the transcontinental railway line, several hundred kilometers north, that traverses the really plain Plains, a span 692 km long and 402 km wide. (By the way, that 478-km chunk of single track is the world's longest stretch of straight railway.)

The usual outback driving rules apply (review the tips in this book). Also, you'll encounter quarantine stations at Ceduna, in South Australia, and Norseman, in Western Australia. Either have a picnic before reaching those two checkpoints or be prepared to surrender plants, fruits, veggies, nuts, grains, wool, animal skins, honey, soil, and even used containers that held these products.

Another thing to remember (or discount altogether) is the time change between Balladonia and Nullarbor. Put your watch back 45 minutes at the border, unless it's daylight saving time—then it increases to three hours. But, all in all,

three hours either way are pretty insignificant when you're smack in the middle of nowhere!

See "Transport" under "The Eyre Peninsula," above, for information on traversing the plain.

History

The Eyre Highway was named for Edward John Eyre, who in 1841 became the first fellow to cross the country from east to west—an agonizing five-month journey in which Eyre's buddy, John Baxter, bit the Nullarbor dust. Following Eyre's dusty footsteps came John and Alexander Forrest, brothers who mapped out much of the overland telegraph route that would connect Perth with Adelaide. In 1877, the eastern and western sections of the telegraph line were linked up at Eucla, and in the 1890s those same bullock and camel tracks that helped build the line were followed by miners on their arduous trip to Western Australia's goldfields. After that, the Nullarbor was crossed by a succession of odd transport—camels, cycles, a 10-horsepower Brush car, a Citroen. In 1941, with the advent of World War II, army engineers commenced construction of the Eyre Highway. Cross-country traffic, at first a trickle in the 1950s, grew (thanks to the Commonwealth Games in Perth) to more than 30 vehicles a day in 1962. The Western Australia section of the highway was sealed in 1969, and the South Australia portion was surfaced seven years later.

Ceduna to Border Village

Penong, 73 km west from Ceduna, is the "Town of 100 Windmills" and a good place to stop for petrol and supplies. Rooms are inexpensive at **Penong Hotel** (tel. 08-8625-1050).

Cactus Beach, 21 km south of Penong, is famous worldwide for its three perfect surfing breaks, "Castles," "Cactus," and "Caves," with both left and right breaks for serious surfers. Other nearby attractions are **Point Sinclair** and **Pink Lake. Fowlers Bay,** on the turnoff to **Nundroo,** is a great fishing hole. **Scott's Bay, Mexican Hat,** and **Cabot's Beach** are popular camel-trekking points. The **Nundroo Hotel**

On 1 February 1997 all telephone numbers on the Nullarbor Plain will change. In preparation for this, all numbers in this section have been changed to eight digits. To dial a Nullarbor Plain number before 1 February, simply delete the first two digits of the new number and, if dialing from outside the Nullarbor, add the (086) area code. For example, (08) 8612-3456 would be dialed (086) 12-3456. After 1 February the area code for all numbers in this section will be (08).

CROSSING THE NULLARBOR

TO PERTH
KALGOORLIE

KAMBALDA

NORSEMAN

FRASER RANGE STATION

NORSEMAN AGRICULTURAL DEPT. CHECKPOINT FOR TRAVELLERS

NEWMAN ROCK

BALLADONIA

OLD TELEGRAPH STATION RUINS

CAIGUNA

COCKLEBIDDY

MADURA

EYRE BIRD OBSERVATORY

W

W W

W

GREAT

TO ALBANY AND PERTH

ESPERANCE

Motel (tel. 08-8625-6120) features moderately priced rooms. You can buy locally made Aboriginal artifacts at **Yalata Roadhouse** (tel. 08-8625-6990), a tourist complex another 51 km along, run by the Yalata Aboriginal Community. Accommodations there are inexpensive and campsites are also available.

From June through October **southern right whales** can be seen during their annual breeding migration along the coastline between Yalata and the border. In 1989, the largest group of these whales to visit the country's shores was spotted just off Yalata Reserve. Permits to enter the land can be obtained at Yalata Roadhouse.

From Nullarbor to the border, you'll pass along sheer coastal cliffs with plunging views of the rugged terrain and the Great Australian Bight. **Nullarbor,** 94 km from Yalata, is adjacent to the original **Nullarbor Homestead.** Rooms in **Nullarbor Hotel-Motel** (tel. 08-8625-6271) are in the moderate price range. The Eyre Highway transects **Nullarbor National Park,** where signs point the way to spectacular lookouts over the Bunda Cliffs, a 200-km stretch from the Head of the Bight almost to the Western Australia border. The area around the Nullarbor is cave land, but

recommended for experienced cavers only **Koonalda Cave** features a collection of Australia's earliest rock engravings. For information and camping permits, phone District Ranger Department of Environment and Natural Resources, Streaky Bay (tel. 08-8625-3144). Permits to enter the area must be obtained from Yalata Roadhouse.

You'll know you've reached **WA/SA Border Village,** 184 km from Nullarbor, when you spot **Rooey II,** a hideous five-meter-tall fiberglass kangaroo. (Climb inside Rooey II's pouch if you're hard up for a photo op.) The signpost with distances to international locales like Paris, London, New York, etc., is another visited site. Rooms are moderate-expensive and campsites are cheap at WA/SA Border Village (tel. 090 39-3474).

To Norseman

In 1887, historic **Eucla,** only 13 km from Border Village, served as an important communications link. Visit the old telegraph station ruins (closed in 1924—the new line runs along the rail line), the town jetty, as well as the nearby cliffs, caves, and blowholes, and the sandhills a

© MOON PUBLICATIONS, INC.

Legend:
W = WATER TANK
★ = SCENIC LOOKOUT
● = REST AREA
▮ = TELEPHONE

0   100 km

Eucla Pass. View gold rush relics at the old School of Mines, Mon.-Fri. 10 a.m.-4 p.m. Admission is $2. **Amber Motor Hotel** (tel. 090-39-3468) has moderately priced rooms (inexpensive in the old hotel section), plus a swimming pool, beer garden, restaurant, bar, and caravan park.

Sixty-six km west from Eucla, **Mundrabilla** is a tiny township with an animal and bird sanctuary along the highway. Rooms at **Mundrabilla Motor Hotel** (tel. 090-39-3465) are moderate, but the adjacent caravan park has inexpensive campsites and cabins.

Ninety-one km along the way, **Madura** once served as a breeding spot for the Indian Army horses. You can still view ruins of the old Madura Roadhouse, located along a track several kilometers from the "new" roadhouse. Moderate-expensive rooms are available at **Madura Pass Oasis Inn** (tel. 090-39-3464), and the adjacent caravan park has campsites.

You can still see the stone ruins of an Aboriginal mission at **Cocklebiddy,** 66 km from Madura. In 1983, a team of French explorers set a world depth record at nearby Cocklebiddy Cave. If you have a four-wheel drive, take the

32-km coastward detour before "town" to **Eyre Bird Observatory** (established in 1977), part of Nuytsland Nature Reserve. Housed inside the 1897 Eyre Telegraph Station, the observatory studies birds, flora, and other fauna. A small museum features old telegraph memorabilia. The observatory also houses a library donated by deceased American millionaire Harold Anderson, who believed a forthcoming nuclear disaster would spare this isolated spot. If you book in advance, you can overnight at the observatory for about $50 (cheaper if you stay longer or have a YHA card) including room and full board. Round-trip transport from Cocklebiddy is about $25. For advance bookings (mandatory), phone (090) 39-3450. In Cocklebiddy, **Wedgetail Inn** (tel. 090-39-3462) has a lounge, pub, dining room, and takeaway. Accommodations are in the moderate to expensive range.

It's another 66 km to **Caiguna,** with service facilities as well as an airstrip used both by charter planes and the Royal Flying Doctors. About 10 km south is the memorial to Eyre's buddy, Baxter, killed in 1841 by angry natives. **John Eyre Motel** (tel. 090-39-3459) has moderate-expensive rates.

The 182-km distance from Caiguna to **Balladonia** is one of the world's longest straight stretches of road. Those rock-hole dams you see just before Balladonia are called **Afghan Rocks,** for the Afghan camel driver who was shot dead for having the audacity to wash his tootsies in the water. **Balladonia Hotel Motel** (tel. 090-39-3453) offers moderately priced rooms, plus a bistro, pub, dining room, and takeaway.

Almost midway between Balladonia and Norseman, **Fraser Range Station** (tel. 090-39-3457) is a family-operated sheep station that dates back to 1864. Pass through in July and you'll be in on the shearing; midwinter through midspring is wildflower season. This YHA associate offers a range of accommodations, including dorm beds ($14 per night) and campsites ($10 per night). If you're traveling by coach phone ahead for pick-up from the nearest Eyre Highway drop-off.

You'll see mine shafts and tailings as you near Norseman, where—depending on your mood—you'll either drop south to the coast or north to the goldfields.

Note: Six-digit phone numbers with the area code (090) will change to eight-digit phone numbers with the (08) area code on 1 April 1998. Add "90" to the existing number to get the new number. For example (090) 12-3456 will become (08) 9012-3456.

THE FLINDERS RANGES

Photographers, painters, bushwalkers, and nature lovers travel to these desert range rock formations for hot shots, divine inspiration, colorful adventure, and a breath of fresh air.

The Flinders Ranges—broken into southern, central, and northern sections—begin to jut between Crystal Brook and Peterborough (about 250 km north of Adelaide), then sweep and arc northward to a point 160 km east of Marree at the edge of the outback.

Thrust up from the sea about 1.6 billion or so years ago, these bent, twisted, buckled, and gorged ranges are best described as earth sculptures. Minerals embedded in the ancient plains and cliffs chameleon along with the sun or moon, the time of year, a turn of your head into delicate pink, salmon, mauve, purple, angry red, and sunshine yellow. These ranges aren't high, but they'll surely make you feel that way!

The scenery varies from woodsy slopes in the temperate south to rugged peaks in the dry north, with Wilpena Pound, the great natural amphitheater in the central region, ranking as the highlight of the Flinders Ranges. Wildflowers (including South Australia's state flower, Sturt's desert pea), wildlife, and birds can be seen throughout the area. In fact, you're likely to spot lots of interesting vegetation and pretty posies, but please help preserve this fragile and beautiful region by leaving your finds intact. As requested by the Royal Automobile Association: "If you must take something home—make it a photograph."

The most popular time to visit is April through October. Summer months are usually very hot and very cold. Rain, at any time of year, can cause flash flooding and render roads impassable. Be sure to follow outback driving regulations and inquire about road and weather conditions along your journey. It is imperative that bushwalkers obtain detailed maps and information from park rangers or Tourist Information Centres before embarking on either a short trail or lengthy trek. Those taking the Heysen Trail should note that the Flinders section is closed 1 Nov.-30 April because of fire restrictions.

The easiest way to reach the Flinders Ranges is via Highway 47 from Port Augusta. The road is sealed to Wilpena Pound, and also up to Lyndhurst (junction of the Strzelecki Track). After that it becomes gravel, dirt, and indescribable. A

On 1 February 1997 all telephone numbers in the Flinders Ranges will change. In preparation for this, all numbers in this section have been changed to eight digits. To dial a Flinders Ranges number before 1 February, simply delete the first two digits of the new number and, if dialing from outside the Flinders Ranges, add the (086) area code. For example, (08) 8612-3456 would be dialed (086) 12-3456. After 1 February the area code for all numbers in this section will be (08).

THE FLINDERS RANGES

TO BIRDSVILLE AND MARREE

STRZELECKI TRACK

TO BIRDSVILLE

FREELING HEIGHTS

MT. GEE

PARALANA SPRINGS

BOLLA BOLLANA

BARRARANNA GORGE

LYNDHURST

ARKAROOLA

GAMMON RANGES NAT'L PARK

MT. AROONA

COPLEY

LEIGH CREEK

BALCANOONA HOMESTEAD (N.P. HEADQUARTERS)

BIG MORO GORGE

LAKE FROME (DRY SALT PAN)

BELTANA

CHAMBERS GORGE

MT. CHAMBERS

LAKE TORRENS (DRY SALT PAN)

PARACHILNA

BLINMAN

FLINDERS RANGES NAT'L PARK

WILPENA

GLASS GORGE

PARACHILNA GORGE

PARACHILNA

BLINMAN

BLINMAN CREEK

GREAT WALL OF CHINA

PARACHILNA CREEK

AROONA HOMESTEAD

AROONA VALLEY

BRACHINA CREEK

YOURAMBULLA CAVE

HAWKER

BRACHINA GORGE

47

KANYAKA

MIDDLE GORGE

BUCKARINGA GORGE

WARREN GORGE

DUTCHMANS STERN C.P.

YARRAH VALE GORGE

QUORN

CARRIETON

PICHI RICHI PASS

PORT AUGUSTA

47

STIRLING NORTH

HORROCK'S PASS

WILMINGTON

ORROROO

1

HANCOCKS LOOKOUT

ALLIGATOR GORGE

MT. REMARKABLE

MAMBRAY CREEK

MAMBRAY CREEK CAMPING AREA

MT. REMARKABLE NATIONAL PARK

MELROSE

56

MURRAY TOWN

WIRRABARA

SPENCER GULF

TELOWIE GORGE C.P.

MAIN NORTH RD. TO ADELAIDE

PORT PIRIE

1

PETERBOROUGH

32

TO CLARE

BUNYEROO GORGE

STOKES HILL LOOKOUT

FLINDERS RANGES N.P. HEADQUARTERS

WILPENA

ST. MARY'S PEAK

WILPENA POUND

ARKAROO ROCK

SACRED CANYON

RAWNSLEY PARK CAMPING CENTRE

56

TO BROKEN HILL

32

N

0   20 km

popular "circle tour" is to start at Port Augusta, pass through Quorn and Hawker to Wilpena, continue northward through Flinders Ranges National Park up to Blinman, swing west to Parachilna, then south back to Hawker.

History
This region is older than the hills—literally.

Captain Matthew Flinders undoubtedly thought he discovered the place when he visited in 1802—after all it was later named after him. Well, try telling that to the Aboriginals. Though you won't find too many of them around anymore. You will find their paintings and rock carvings, some known to be 12,000 years old, scattered about the ranges. (*Please* do not tamper with paintings, carvings, or relics.)

There are a number of historical sites in and around the ranges, mostly old copper- and gold-mining towns, homesteads that served as resting spots for overland teams. They're remnants of the late-1800s wheat farming boom, nipped in the sheaf by bad weather, plagues, and hunger.

SOUTHERN FLINDERS RANGES

You can travel any of several sealed roads from the mid-north to tour the relatively gentler and more accessible southern region.

Telowie Gorge
Located 25 km northeast of Port Pirie, with access off Highway 1, Telowie Gorge (1,946 hectares) is the southernmost park of the Flinders Ranges. Steep red cliffs, open woodlands, spring wattle blossoms, yellow-footed rock wallabies, and prolific birdlife are the main features. There are no facilities and limited camping sites.

Melrose
This one-time copper town, situated at the foot of Mt. Remarkable, is the Flinders Ranges' oldest settlement. These days it's a grazing and wheat- and barley-growing community and a good base for exploring Mt. Remarkable National Park. In fact, a walking trail leads from town all the way to the top of Mt. Remarkable (956 meters). Good views can be had from either the **War Memorial** or **Lookout Hill.**

Historic buildings include the old **police station and courthouse** (now a National Trust museum, open daily 2-5 p.m.), **post office, Jacka's Brewery,** and **Melrose Inn.** Two other oldies built in the 1850s are **North Star Hotel,** Nott St (tel. 08-8666-2110), and **Mt. Remarkable Hotel Motel,** Stuart St. (tel. 08-8666-2119). Both offer inexpensive pub-type accommodations. **Melrose Caravan Park,** Joes Rd. (tel. 08-8666-2060) rents campsites, cabins, and on-site vans.

Mt. Remarkable National Park
Wedged between the Melrose-Wilmington road and the Port Pirie-Port Augusta highway, Mt. Remarkable National Park (8,649 hectares) is known for its dramatic scenery and diverse plant and animal life. The three best places to explore are the somewhat separate Mt. Remarkable (behind Melrose), the narrow Alligator Gorge (accessed one km south of Wilmington), and red gum-lined Mambray Creek (accessed from a branch road about 45 km north of Port Pirie, off Highway 1). Walking trails with plenty of signposts lead to panoramic lookouts and isolated gorges from both Alligator Gorge and Mambrey Creek. Mambray Creek campground is open, except during fire-ban days; bush camping is permitted in some areas. Admission is $3 per vehicle. For information, phone (08) 8634-7086.

Nearby points of interest are: **Hancock's Lookout,** north of the park, at the top of Horrocks Pass; the ghost towns of **Hammond** and **Bruce,** northeast of Wilmington; and, for all you rodeophiles, **Carrieton,** about 25 km northeast of the ghost towns, hosts a nationally known rodeo every October.

Quorn
From 1917 until 1937, Quorn (pop. 1,080) served as an important railway junction on both east-west and north-south transcontinental routes. Not so after a new standard gauge line was built to Marree in 1956, leaving the town to fend for itself. In 1974, after part of the old line was restored to accommodate a steam-powered tourist train, Quorn was back in business—not as the big-time rail depot it used to be but with travelers who want to putt-putt through Pichi Richi Pass. Billed as the "Gateway to the Flinders Ranges," Quorn is about 40 km from Wilmington and a bit farther from Port Augusta.

Quorn's Pichi Richi
Railway takes tourists on
a sentimental journey.

The **Pichi Richi Railway** departs from old Quorn Railway Station for a picturesque two-hour-and-45-minute round-trip journey (about $19) into Pichi Richi Pass, rolling over bridges, along the Pichi Richi River, and through the long-abandoned Pichi Richi township. The train only runs during school holidays and long weekends. Check at the tourist information office or phone (08) 8276-6232 (Adelaide) or (08) 8648-6598 (Quorn) for schedules.

Quorn is full of historic buildings. Aside from the railway station, some of the best examples are the **public school, town hall, National Bank, Bank of Adelaide, courthouse, State Bank, Quorn Mill** (now the local museum), and the **Austral, Grand Junction,** and **Criterion Hotels.** Accommodations in any of the three hotels, all on Railway Terrace, are inexpensive-moderate. You can stay in the old **Quorn Mill,** also on Railway Terrace (tel. 08-8648-6016), which is priced in the high-moderate range, including continental breakfast. **Quorn Caravan Park,** Silo Rd. (tel. 08-8648-6206), offers campsites, on-site vans, and cabins.

Dutchman's Stern Conservation Park (3,532 hectares), five km west of Quorn, has sharp cliffs, steep gorges, and a wide range of plant and bird species (this is the northern limit for Adelaide rosellas, scarlet robins, kookaburras, and the yellow-faced honeyeater). The park has marked walking trails (only pro

bushwalkers should attempt the climb to 800-meter Dutchman's Stern) and a picnic area. Camping is not permitted. For information, phone (08) 8648-6571.

For Quorn emergencies, dial 000, or contact: **police** (tel. 08-8648-6060), **fire brigade** (tel. 08-8648-6000), **ambulance** (tel. 08-8648-6366), **hospital** (tel. 08-8648-6200), or **Royal Automobile Association (RAA)** (tel. 08-8648-6012).

To Hawker
Take your pick: gorges, ruins, or caves. If you take the unsealed road, you'll pass through stunning **Yarrah Vale,** and the **Warren, Buckaringa,** and **Middle Gorges.** Traveling the highway will bring you to **Kanyaka,** remnants of a large sheep station dating back to 1851. Though the station once supported 70 families, all that's left are bricks and pieces of the old stone buildings, and graveyard. Farther along the road, behind a rise, is another group of ruins. Follow the track 1.5 km to **Death Rock Waterhole**—the road's end.

Other **historic ruins** in the area are Wilson, Gordon, Hammond, Saltia, Simmonston, and Willochra. Local information centers sell guidebooks to the sites.

About 10 km south of Hawker and a 30-minute walk from the road, **Yourambulla Cave** features Aboriginal rock drawings and paintings. (Remember—*don't touch!*)

CENTRAL FLINDERS RANGES

At Hawker, you enter the heart of the Flinders and junction of the "Circle Tour" that will take you through the best parts of these ranges.

Hawker
Hawker (pop. 300) is another old railway community, bypassed when the standard gauge was built. Billed as a "typical outback town," Hawker provides tourist facilities for travelers to nearby Wilpena Pound.

Historical buildings worth checking out are the **railway station, Hawker Hotel, Sightseer's Café, post office, Institute Building,** and **Hawker Motors** (tel. 08-8648-4014), formerly the Federal Boot Store, currently a small museum, fuel station, supply shop, and Tourist Information Centre.

Hawker Hotel Motel, corner Elder and Wonoka Terrace (tel. 08-8648-4102), has pub and motel rooms ranging from inexpensive to moderate. **Outback Motel,** 1 Wilpena Rd. (tel. 08-8648-4100), is a modern motel that costs about the same as the Hawker. **Yappala Station,** nine km northwest of Hawker, off Leigh Creek Rd. (tel. 08-8648-4164), provides a variety of accommodations on its working sheep station. A two-night minimum stay is required. **Hawker Caravan Park,** 44 Chace View Terrace (tel. 08-8648-4006), has campsites and on-site vans.

In case of an emergency, call 000. Other emergency numbers are: **police** (tel. 08-8648-4028), **hospital** (tel. 08-8648-4007), and **Royal Automobile Association** (tel. 08-8648-4014).

Wilpena Pound
This natural amphitheater, 55 km north of Hawker and encompassed by the 92,746-hectare Flinders Ranges National Park, is the most popular attraction of the ranges. Once a wheat-farming and sheep-grazing area, this is now a wildlife refuge for many species, particularly kangaroos and spectacular birds ranging from wedge-tailed eagles to colorful parrots. The basin is a grandiose 80 square km, surrounded by a circle of sheer, splintered, multicolored cliffs (the highest point is 1,190-meter **St. Mary's Peak**). Within the circle, however, gentle slopes lead into the vast central plain. Wilpena Pound is

a bushwalker's heaven. Myriad trails guide you along everything from a casual one-hour stroll to a full-day's steep and stony climb. (Be sure to complete a log sheet at the park office, open 24 hours, before embarking on extended walks.) The only access into the pound is through the narrow gorge above **Sliding Rock,** near Wilpena Pound Motel.

The Pound is important in the Aboriginal mythology of the Flinders Ranges (*wilpena* means "a kangaroo skin curled up on its edges"). Tribal drawings, paintings, and carvings can be seen at **Arkaroo Rock,** near Moonarie Gap, and at **Sacred Canyon.** Both areas are about 19 km south of Wilpena (though on different roads).

Other points of interest within Flinders Ranges National Park are the **Bunyeroo** and **Brachina Gorges** and the **Aroona Valley,** where you can see ruins of the old homestead.

The only motel accommodations at the Pound are at expensive **Wilpena Pound Resort** (tel. 08-8648-0004), with pool, bar, and dining room. Tent camping is permitted near the entrance to the Pound for about $10 per night. **Arkaba Station,** 35 km east of the Pound (tel. 08-8232-5454), offers expensive (moderate if sharing) fully equipped cottage accommodations. **Rawnsley Park Camping Centre** (tel. 08-8648-0008), 20 km south of Wilpena, offers campsites, on-site vans, and moderately priced holiday units. For camping within the park, see "Services and Information," below.

To and from Blinman
You'll be traveling on gravel once you leave the Pound. Engaging spots along the 59-km drive to Blinman are **Stokes Hill Lookout** and a long, ironstone-topped rock formation called the **Great Wall of China.**

Blinman (pop. 98), at the northern edge of Flinders Ranges National Park, was a hustle-bustle copper mining town from 1862 until 1890. Old mine machinery and relics are still in evidence, as are a few historic buildings. You can overnight at the 1869 **North Blinman Hotel** (tel. 08-8648-4867), with a pool and inexpensive rates in either the hotel or motel sections. **The Captain's Cottage,** Mine Rd. (tel. 08-8648-4894), is an expensive fully equipped three-bedroom cottage with fireplace. **Blinman Caravan Park,** Mine Rd. (tel. 08-8648-4867), offers campsites.

Heading west to circle back to Hawker, two routes will get you to the highway junction at Parachilna: **Glass Gorge** is slightly out of the way along a dirt road, but the views are terrific, especially when the wild hops are in bloom; the gravel road goes through **Parachilna Gorge,** a tourist village at **Angorichina,** and the spring-ed **Blinman Pools** (near Angorichina, reached from the Parachilna and Blinman Creeks). **An-gorichina Village Camping Area** (tel. 08-8648-1842) rents campsites, cabins, and cottages.

Rejoin the main highway at **Parachilna,** and either go north 70 km to Leigh Creek or south 89 km to Hawker. **Prairie Hotel,** in Parachilna (tel. 08-8648-4895), a "typical bush pub," has mod-erately priced rooms with or without breakfast in-cluded.

About 70 km east of Blinman, along one route to the Northern Flinders Ranges, **Chambers Gorge** features 100 meters of Aboriginal rock carvings on its left wall. **Mount Chambers** (409 meters) provides dynamic views of Lake Frome on one side, Wilpena on the other.

NORTHERN FLINDERS RANGES

Rugged, arid, remote, and exquisite, the north-ern ranges are reached from either Leigh Creek or the Chambers Gorge road.

Leigh Creek

Leigh Creek (pop. 1,635) used to be 13 km north of where it is now. That's right—the whole town just up and moved when the original site was needed for additional coal mining. Beat that for town spirit! Leigh Creek South reopened in 1981 and grass (the kind you mow) has been banned. Like it or not, this is your northern ranges oasis, with shopping facilities, bank, post office, hospital, fuel, auto mechanic, as well as a regional office of the Department of Environment and Natural Resources. **Aroona Dam,** four km west of town, is a popular picnic area.

If you're a coal enthusiast, you'll enjoy looking down at some of the mine workings from the visitor's viewing area, about three km from the turnoff to Leigh Creek Coalfields, on the Hawk-er-to-Marree highway. Free public tours are given March-Oct. and school holidays.

In emergencies, dial 000, the **police** (tel. 08-8675-2004), or the **hospital** (tel. 08-8675-2100).

Arkaroola

Despite the harsh, occasionally hostile environ-ment, Arkaroola's 60,000-hectare sanctuary har-bors a large variety of plants and wildlife. This former mining area was only established as a pri-vately run reserve in 1968. Since then it's been the buzz of naturalists, adventurers, and travel guides.

THE HEYSEN TRAIL

At Arkaroola, see the art gallery, mineral and fossil museum, pioneer cottage, outdoor pastoral museum, and astronomical observatory (tel. 08-8212-1366); viewing is subject to light and weather conditions. Nearby points of interest are the Cornish smelters at **Bolla Bollana,** the dazzling view from **Mt. Painter** (790 meters), waterholes at **Barraranna** and **Nooldoonooldoona,** and **Sitting Bull, Spriggs Nob,** and **The Pinnacles** mountaintops. Radioactive **Paralana Hot Springs,** 27 km north of Arkaroola, is thought to be Australia's last site of volcanic activity, and is also an Aboriginal ceremonial spot.

Gammon Ranges National Park (128,228 hectares) is extremely rugged and isolated territory, accessed only by 4WD vehicles, except for the park headquarters area. Walking trails are not marked, and only very experienced and well-equipped bushwalkers should trek this area. Be sure to notify park rangers of your proposed route. For camping in the park, see "Services and Information," below.

Don't miss **Mt. Gee,** sitting between Mt. Painter and Freeling Heights. It's a crystal mountain, one gigantic mass of crystallized quartz.

Three different motels make up **Arkaroola Tourist Village.** Tariffs range from inexpensive to expensive, and camping sites cost about $15 per night. Book through Arkaroola Travel, 50 Pirie St., Adelaide, SA 5000 (tel. 08-8212-1366) or, on short notice, phone the village direct at (08) 8648-4848.

Even if you're on a tight budget, spring $50 for the 4WD **Ridgetop Tour,** a four-hour adventure up, over, and around absolutely astounding scenery. Book through Arkaroola Tourist Village.

TRANSPORTATION

Augusta Airways (tel. 08-8642-3100) operates scheduled air service between Port Augusta, Adelaide, and Leigh Creek, as well as scenic and charter flights to outback areas.

Stateliner (tel. 08-8415-5544, Adelaide, or 08-8642-5055, Port Augusta) provides coach service to Arkaroola, Beltana, Booleroo Centre, Copley, Hawker, Leigh Creek, Melrose, Murray Town, Mambray Creek, Parachilna, Port Augusta, Port Germein, Peterborough, Quorn,

Wilmington, Wilpena, Wirrabara, and Yunta. Sample fares are: Adelaide-Quorn, $40; Adelaide-Wilpena Pound, $50; Adelaide-Arkaroola, $68. **Greyhound Pioneer Australia** (tel. 08 8642-5055, Port Augusta, or 13-2030 toll-free) offers a Port Augusta-Hawker-Leigh Creek service. The fare to Hawker is about $17, and to Leigh Creek $40.

Bushwalkers *must* carry detailed trail maps and adhere to all warnings. It is mandatory that you check in with park rangers before starting off. Heed rules for outback travel and safety.

Organized Tours

For travelers who'd rather leave rules and regulations in the hands of experienced guides, Flinders Ranges tours are available. Sightsee by air, coach, four-wheel drive, horse, or camel. Any Tourist Information Centre can provide a list of recommended operators. Also inquire locally—often a shopkeeper or motel manager has a tour-guide relative. **Wilpena Pound Resort** and **Rawnsley Park Camping Centre,** at Wilpena Pound, offer many different excursions.

Butler's Outback Safaris (tel. 08-8642-2188) is a well-established company that operates a range of 4WD tours, as does **Flinders Ranges Safaris** (tel. 08-8648-4031). **Arkaba Station** (tel 08-8648-4217) conducts 4WD tag-along tours, as well as nature walks and retreats. **Ecotrek** (tel 08-8383-7198) and **Exploranges** (tel. 08-8294-6530) also offer eco-walks and tours.

Or ride a **camel** (Flinders Ranges Camel Farm, tel. 08-8648-4874), a **horse** (Flinders Rides, tel. 08-8528-2132), or a **motorcycle** (Flinders Ranges Bike Tours, tel. 08-8642-4978).

SERVICES AND INFORMATION

Fuel and **public telephones** are available at the following Flinders Ranges locations: Arkaroola, Beltana, Blinman, Carrieton, Copley, Hawker, Leigh Creek, Mambray Creek, Melrose, Morchard, Murray Town, Orroroo, Parachilna, Peterborough, Port Augusta, Port Germein, Quorn, Rawnsley Park, Wilmington, Wilpena, Wirrabara, and Yunta.

For comprehensive information, contact **Flinders Outback Tourism,** P.O. Box 41, Port Augusta, SA 5700 (tel. 08-8642-2469). This gency also sells detailed maps of the Flinders Ranges and the outback.

Other **regional information centers** are: Melrose Tourist Information Centre, Council Offices, Stuart St., Melrose (tel. 08-8666-2014); Peterborough Tourist Centre, Main St., Peterborough (tel. 08-8651-2708); Port Augusta Tourist Information Centre, 41 Flinders Terrace, Port Augusta (tel. 08-8641-0793); and Quorn Tourist Information Centre, Council Office, 7th St., Quorn (tel. 08-8648-6031). Most motels, caravan parks, and roadhouses also carry tourist information.

Information and **camping permits** for the national and conservation parks within the Flinders Ranges can be obtained from the **Department of Environment and Land Management,** Far North Region, in Hawker (tel. 08-8648-4244).

Contact **park rangers** at Flinders Ranges National Park (tel. 08-8648-0048), Wilpena (tel. 08-8648-0048), Oraparinna (tel. 08-8648-0017), Balcanoona Homestead (tel. 08-8648-4829), and Mambray Creek (tel. 08-8634-7068).

Obtain detailed maps of the **Heysen Trail** from the Department of Recreation, Sport, and Racing, P.O. Box 1865, Adelaide, SA 5001, or at the department's shop at City Centre Arcade, Adelaide (tel. 08-8226-7374). Flinder's area shops, as well as map- and bookstores throughout Australia, sell a range of Ranges maps. Also collect maps and other motoring tips from RAA branches.

Northern Roads Condition Hotline (tel. 1800-11-633) provides up-to-date info on Flinders and outback road conditions.

INTO THE OUTBACK

This region may be as close as you'll ever get to feeling like you're on another planet—one reason being that it's not particularly well-suited to human life.

In 1845, explorer Charles Sturt described the outback as "a country I firmly believe has no parallel on earth's surface" (then he died). And that is precisely why 99% of the state's population lives south of the 32nd parallel. Much of this area is no man's (or woman's) land. Peaceful, open space contrasts with harsh terrain, stony deserts, enormous salt pans, and eerie desolation. Then again, the challenge of surviving the elements is often what attracts travelers in the first place—that and thousands of native birds, fish jumpin' out of desert water-

holes, the search for fiery opals, dry salt lakes, artesian springs, the odd spaceship, and a bunch of odd spaced-out characters.

Encompassing about 60 million hectares, the outback presents a massive frontier to pioneering spirits, some pretty hazardous odds to those who gamble with nature, and breathing space galore for incurable claustrophobes. But pay attention to whose land you're on; vast areas are administered by the Department of Environment and Natural Resources, and others are Aboriginal reserves or part of the military's Woomera Prohibited Area. (Though *you* may feel free out here, the *land* is not!)

Choose from four outback routes. The Stuart Highway, the sealed road connecting Port Augusta with Alice Springs, passes through the Woomera missile test site, Coober Pedy, and the opal-mining district. Oodnadatta Track is the old dirt road that follows the path of the old Ghan railway and overland telegraph lines, eventually meeting up with the Stuart Highway at Marla. Both the Birdsville and Strzelecki Tracks are long, hard treks through remote desert into remote Queensland. Whichever route you take, at some point you'll cross the Dingo Fence, a protective wire stretching more than 3,000 km across central Australia to keep those wild dogs from entering southern pastoral lands. Exceptionally adventurous souls—with a lot of time,

---

On 1 February 1997 all telephone numbers in outback South Australia will change. In preparation for this, all numbers in this section have been changed to eight digits. To dial an outback South Australia number before 1 February, simply delete the first two digits of the new number and, if dialing from outside the outback, add the (086) area code. For example, (08) 8612-3456 would be dialed (086) 12-3456. After 1 February the area code for all numbers in this section will be (08).

OUTBACK TRACKS, TRAILS, AND HIGHWAYS

...oney, and energy—might want to tackle the ...arious "bomb roads" or the Canning Stock ...oute (see the special topics "Bomb Roads" ...nd "Canning Stock Route" in this chapter and ...e Western Australia chapter, respectively).

The best time of year for outback travel is ...pril to September, when the weather is usually ...ild and dry, though early mornings can be frosty ...amping from June through October can be ...ery cold and uncomfortable). Summers, as ...ou'd expect, are scorching infernos when you ...an indeed fry your eggs (and seated body parts) ...top any rock in this hard place. Rains, though in...equent, should be taken quite seriously, par...cularly if you're off the sealed highway. Dirt ...acks can be washed away suddenly, leaving ...ou stranded for what could be a deadly long ...me. But the outback is exquisite after a rain...ll, carpeted with wildflowers and exotic plants.

Make certain both you and your vehicle are ...ell prepared for your journey. Follow outback ...riving rules, inquire about road conditions, carry

detailed maps, keep your car full of petrol and your body full of water.

The first vehicle crossing from Adelaide to Darwin was made in 1908. Since then, historic journeys, in a wide assortment of transport, are still being made. Yours could be next!

ALONG THE STUART HIGHWAY

Woomera and Vicinity

Unless you're desperate for petrol or a quick snack, pass by the ugly little town of **Pimba,** 173 km northwest of Port Augusta. In the 1950s and '60s, Woomera, off the highway a few kilometers from Pimba, was a test site for British experimental rockets. The most famous launching was that of the *Europa,* 1964-70. About those same years NASA ran a deep-space tracking station at nearby Island Lagoon. The testing range and "Narrungar" (the communications station) are controlled by the Australian Defence

---

EQUIPMENT

The Royal Automobile Club suggests you take the following equipment on your outback tour:

Vehicle Equipment
good condition spare wheel
spare tire
jack, jack base
tow rope
fan belt
radiator hose
extra ignition key
fuses, spark plugs
spare bulbs for headlights and tail lights
petrol in jerry cans
engine oil (sufficient for complete change)
container of brake fluid
lubricating spray
insulating tape
epoxy resin putty
tube of silicone rubber gasket
bottle of Bars-Leak
tube of Bostik
two meters of bailing wire
welding wire or copper wire
set of disc brake pads (if fitted)
brass brake-lining rivets
spare air-cleaner element

spare engine oil/fuel filter cartridge
sufficient automatic transmission fluid for a
   complete change

Minimum Tool Kit
hacksaw
hammer
set of box- and open-ended spanners and socket
   spanner set to suit your vehicle
cold chisel
set of screwdrivers
pliers
file
tire pump
wheel chocks
vulcanizing clamp and patches
tire levers
valve key
pressure gauge
jumper cables
two meters of 6.35-mm-inside-diameter
   reinforced fuel-resistant plastic hose
two meters of four-mm low-tension wire

Department. Woomera still serves as a military base, and U.S. personnel continue to be stationed here (and what *stories* people tell about what goes on at this place—spooky doings about spies, satellites, and alien spaceships!).

The **Heritage Museum Centre** at Woomera Village exhibits rockets, weapons, and aircraft. Hours are daily 9 a.m.-5 p.m., March through October. Admission is $3. For information, phone (08) 8673-7042.

For Woomera emergencies, contact: **police** (tel. 08-8673-7244), **ambulance** (tel. 08-8674-3234), **hospital** (tel. 08-8674-3294), or **Royal Automobile Association** (tel. 08-8673-7715).

From Woomera, a detour travels north to newish **Roxby Downs** township, built to house employees at the **Olympic Dam** mines, eight km away. Tours of dam operations depart from the visitor center at 10 a.m. daily.

Andamooka, 30 km east of Roxby Downs, is a small opal-mining site, known for high-quality gems. Claim owners often permit noodling on their claims, but be sure to ask first. You'll see a few dugout homes, as well as **Duke's Bottle Home,** a dwelling built from old beer bottles. **Andamooka Motel** (tel. 08-8672-7186) and **Andamooka Opal Hotel Motel** (tel. 08-8672-7078) both have inexpensive air-conditioned rooms. Campsites and on-site vans are available at **Andamooka Caravan Park** (tel. 08-8672-7117).

For emergencies, contact the **police** (tel. 08-8672-7072) or **ambulance** (tel. 08-8672-7087).

From Roxby Downs, Borefield Rd. (a dirt track) continues north, meeting the Oodnadatta Track near Lake Eyre South.

Back on Stuart Highway, **Glendambo,** 113 km northwest of Woomera, provides tourist facilities. **Glendambo Tourist Centre** (tel. 08-8672-1030) has modern rooms at moderate-expensive rates. The adjacent caravan park offers campsites, on-site vans, and a cheap bunkhouse ($12 beds).

The Stuart Highway continues through part of the gigantic Woomera Prohibited Area, but permits are not necessary. Stay on the road and try not to think about the hush-hush plutonium accident that occurred here in the '50s.

Coober Pedy

Coober Pedy (pop. 2,800), one of the world's leading opal-mining centers, was established in 1915 after a teenage boy discovered a gem while gold prospecting with his father. It's so oppressively hot and dusty that most of the town works, lives, and prays in dugout dwellings underground (Appropriately, the name Coober Pedy is derived from Aboriginal words that, put together, mean "White Man in a Hole.") Lying 254 km northwest of Glendambo, it's a good pit stop (literally); otherwise, this town is better suited to miners (about 40 different nationalities), ants, and movie companies who choose this locale for lunar shots *(Mad Max III)* or drag-queen spectacles *(Priscilla, Queen of the Desert).*

The best spot to noodle (pick through old diggings) is in the "jeweler's shop" area, near Faye's underground house. You don't need a permit unless you're on a pegged claim, and you can use any sort of digging device—otherwise, you must obtain a permit from the Department of Mines and Energy in Adelaide (see the special topic "Do-It-Yourself Mining" in the Introduction chapter).

If you're in the market to buy, beware and shop around (there are more than 30 dealers in town). Highly regarded though expensive outlets are those at the Opal Inn and Desert Cave Motel. You'll find scads of tours to dugout homes and opal outlets (it should be noted that some tour guides double as opal salesmen). Worth investigating are **Old Timer's Mine** (tel. 08-8672-5555), **Umoona Opal Mine and Museum** (tel. 08-8672-5288), and **Crocodile Harry's Underground Home,** on 17 Mile Road.

Opal Inn, Hutchison St. (tel. 08-8672-2054) offers a range of inexpensive-expensive accommodations. Both **Coober Pedy Budget Motel,** corner Oliver and Brewster Streets (tel. 08-8672-5163), and **Umoona Opal Mine,** Hutchison St. (tel. 08-8672-5288), offer cheap basic rooms with communal facilities. **Radeka's Dugout** (tel. 08-8672-5223) has moderately priced motel rooms. The **Underground Motel,** Catacomb Rd. (tel. 08-8672-5324), also in the moderate range, includes breakfast. Luxury digs are $100-plus at the **Desert Cave Motel,** Hutchinson St. (tel. 08-8672-5688).

Rent campsites, on-site vans, or bunkhouse beds at **Oasis Caravan Park,** Hutchison St. (tel. 08-8672-5169), or **Stuart Range Caravan Park,** Hutchison St. and Stuart Hwy. (tel. 08-8672-5179).

Because of Coober Pedy's multinational population, you'll find a wide range of ethnic eating spots. Pub-crawling, as you might imagine, can e rough here—as can the love-hungry miners. Women should be particularly cautious.

For emergencies, contact the **police** (tel. 08-672-5056), hospital (tel. 08-8672-5000), or **Royal Automobile Association (RAA)** (tel. 8-8672-5036).

Breakaways Reserve, 28 km north of Coober Pedy, is a 40-square-km block of low ills featuring a continually changing color landscape, unique flora and fauna, and walking trails.

Marla and Vicinity

The drive to **Cadney Homestead** (tel. 08-8670-994), 153 km north of Coober Pedy, is fairly reary, but the place has expensive homestead accommodations, moderate bunkhouse beds, and cheap campsites. Refuel yourself and your vehicle and either cut east through Arckaringa Hills, Copper Hills, and the Painted Desert to Oodnadatta (160 km), or continue north on the Stuart Highway.

Another featureless 81-km drive brings you to Marla (pop. 240), established in 1978 as a tourist service center. This is also where the highway meets the Ghan railway line. Rooms at **Marla Travellers Rest** (tel. 08-8670-7001) are moderate to expensive; campsites at the caravan park are cheap.

The opal fields at **Mintabie,** 50 km west of Marla (along a gravel road), have proved to be richer than those at Coober Pedy. It's another 65 km to the Northern Territory border, 185 km to teensy Kulgera township, and 464 km to Alice Springs.

ALONG THE OODNADATTA TRACK

Marree to William Creek

Marree (pop. 380), 379 km north of Port Augusta, is the beginning (and ending) point for both the Oodnadatta and Birdsville Tracks. During the 1880s this mini-town was a big depot for camel drivers transporting goods to the outback. (You can still see a couple of leftover date palms and a few Afghani names, as reminders.) Between 1960 and 1980, it was the changing-gauge station for the old Ghan, choo-chooing to

Alice Springs. **Marree Great Northern Hotel,** Main St. (tel. 08-8675-8344), has inexpensive rooms. Campsites and on-site vans are available at **Marree Tourist Park** (tel. 08-8675-8371).

It's 210 km from Marree to William Creek. The track edges along **Lake Eyre South,** where two lookouts adjacent to the roadway afford views of this salt pan, which stretches 185 km north. (This is a baby compared with Lake Eyre North.) A rough piece of track leads to the lakeshore.

At **Stuart Creek** you can view a six-km piece of the original Ghan line, as well as a few preserved sheds, fettler's cottages, and a water tank. The oasis at **Coward Springs,** about 35 km farther north, includes railway ruins, an old plantation (now a bird refuge), some old date palms, and a warm, bubbling pond.

Bubbler and **Blanchecup** are mound springs, six km south of the track (you'll see fences around them), adjacent to Coward Springs. Bubbler is a bubbling pool of fine sand. Blanchecup is deceptively clear and clean-looking, but you have to dip in and out through a muddy, weedy stench. Either of the springs should open every pore in your body; stick your head in and you won't need a facial—or maybe even a shampoo—for years! (You'd pay a fortune for this in Europe!)

Other points of interest are the old **Beresford** railway siding and flowing bore (artesian well), 24 km north of Coward Springs, and, 11 km farther, **Strangways,** the old Overland Telegraph repeater, where there's also a flowing bore (a bare water pipe).

William Creek to Oodnadatta

William Creek, 45 km north of Strangways, is touted as South Australia's (some say the world's) smallest town that lies within one of the state's (if not the world's) largest cattle stations—30,027-square-km Anna Creek. The big thing to do here is hang around the pub, soaking up local color and lore or gawking at other travelers, usually crowded around the pay phone. Basic accommodations at that same **William Creek Hotel** (tel. 08-8670-7880) are inexpensive, and campsites cost just $4 pp.

It's 206 km to Oodnadatta, a journey through gibber (Aboriginal for "stone") plains, ranging in color from sand to charcoal, and in size from pebbles to Frisbees. The gibbers also have a strange reflective quality. Sights along this section of track are **Edwards Creek** ruins and bore (you can take a shower here, but your hair will turn to Brillo), **Warrina Siding** ruin, a memorial to explorer Ernest Giles (in 1876 he crossed from Geraldton, Western Australia, to Peake Telegraph Station, east of the memorial), the **Algebuckina** siding ruin, one of the best old **Ghan railway bridges,** and **Mt. Dutton.**

Oodnadatta (pop. 230) sprang into being in 1891 with the arrival of the railway and then, in the 1980s, came close to disappearing when the rail line was moved and the Stuart Highway was sealed. This true outback town (whose Aboriginal name translates to "Flower of the Mulga") has turned its old railway station into a museum, but the real attraction here is the **Pink Roadhouse,** which serves as social center, petrol stop, supermarket, "Oodnaburger" supplier, mechanic's garage, caravan park, info provider, tour organizer, and travelers' clearinghouse and meeting place. Both campsites and on-site vans are available. The roadhouse is open daily. For information, phone (08) 8670-7822. Rooms at **Transcontinental Hotel** (tel. 08-8670-7804) are inexpensive. **Oodnadatta Caravan Park** (tel. 08-8670-7822) offers campsites, on-site vans, and a rather pricey bunkhaus.

For emergencies, contact the **police** (tel. 08-8670-7805) or **ambulance** (tel. 08-8670-7803).

The Oodnadatta Track continues northwest for 118 km, then turns west. From this junction, it's about 100 km to Marla and the Stuart Highway.

THE BIRDSVILLE TRACK

In the 1880s, the Birdsville Track was created so that stockmen could drive their cattle from the grazing grounds in southwest Queensland to the rail station at Marree, where they were loaded onto a train. This border community kept busy during the days when interstate customs were charged. In 1901, after free trade was instigated, they began to ship the cattle by truck along different routes.

The 517 km from Marree to Birdsville (in Queensland) pass by deserted homesteads and mission ruins, scalding bores and welcoming waterholes, not to mention phenomenal numbers of sandy dunes and rocky plains at the Tirari, Simpson, Sturt Stony, and Strzelecki Deserts. At **Clifton Hills Homestead** the road splits: the inside track, which crosses **Goyder Lagoon,** is closed; the Birdsville goes around it. Seek advice before picking your fork—a wrong decision could be fatal. Also keep in mind that the lagoon is a breeding ground for snakes.

Birdsville, 12 km across the Queensland border, was established in 1882 to serve stockmen headed down the Birdsville Track. Today it caters to travelers following in the stockmen's tracks. Original buildings are the old pub and mission hospital. Even though this is a remote outpost town, after an arduous outback trek Birdsville's simple tourist facilities seem like a limo ride down Rodeo Drive. (See "Birdsville" under "Channel Country" in the "Outback Queensland" section of the Queensland chapter.)

This route is for very well-prepared vehicles and bodies. Check in with police at either Marree or Birdsville, and follow all outback driving rules and local advice.

THE STRZELECKI TRACK

For those with more larceny than cow pie in their souls, who'd rather follow in the bootsteps of outlaws than stockmen, the background on this route has a bit more juice to it.

The Strzelecki Track came into being in 1871 when bushman Henry Radford (a.k.a. Captain Midnight) used it to drive his herds of stolen cattle from Queensland down to the Adelaide markets. (Strzelecki Creek had been named earlier by Charles Sturt, for his fellow explorer Count Strzelecki.) Other drovers, legitimate and otherwise, used the track also, alternating the route a bit around Cooper Creek where there were more watering holes. The track fell into disuse for many years until the Moomba gas fields southwest of Innamincka were established. The Moomba section of this track (from Strzelecki Crossing to Innamincka) is better kept, but the original bit will appeal more to wanna-be rustlers.

Lyndhurst to Innamincka
Starting at Lyndhurst, 193 km north of Hawker and 79 km south of Marree, the Strzelecki Track wends 459 km northeasterly to Innamincka, a

ny service town, then cuts north for 305 km, urning west in Queensland for the 110-km por- on that leads into Birdsville. It's also possible to ross into Queensland from Innamincka and he Arrabury Homestead junction, and to travel 3 km east to Betoota and beyond, instead of ioing west to Birdsville (just keep in mind, you're till a long, long way from "civilization").

Pick up any necessary provisions at Lynd- urst; this is your last fuel stop until Innamincka don't expect a petrol pump at the Moomba gas elds).

Following the northern edge of the Flinders Ranges, you'll pass ruins of several old home- teads, cruise through the Cobbler Desert be- ween Lakes Blanche and Callabonna (inci- entally, **Lake Callabonna** is the site of the fos- ilized diprotodon, the largest known marsupial), nally crossing Strzelecki Creek about 85 km orth of Mt. Hopeless Homestead. From the creek crossing, you must choose either the track hat passes the **Moomba gas fields** (no tourist acilities except a telephone at the security gate) r the old road that goes through **Merty Merty Homestead,** where if you're one of those people vho likes to sprawl across different sides of bor- ers at the same time (and have a photo taken!), ou can drive 109 km southeast to **Cameron Corner,** a coming-together of South Australia, Queensland, and New South Wales.

nnamincka and Beyond

nnamincka, another outpost town a la Birdsville, s also the place where explorers Burke and Wills bit the dust (you can see their legendary **Dig Tree** along Cooper Creek, about 42 km east of the post office). Several historic spots are dotted about this bitsy service town, most of hem memorials to the exploring dead—places vhere bodies were found, moved to, finally buried, where rescue parties set up camp, where he sole survivor was discovered by Aborigi- nes, etc. On Cooper Creek, rock carvings by he Yantrwantas Aboriginal tribe can be seen at the eastern end of Cullyamurra waterhole. Fish can be found inside that very same water- nole as well as the waterholes along the north- vest branch of Cooper Creek.

Find inexpensive accommodations at **In- namincka Trading Post** (tel. 08-8675-9900). Barbecues, dances, and other raves with locals

are usually held weekends at the "upmarket" **Innamincka Motel** (tel. 08-8675-9901).

The **Coongie Lakes,** 112 km northeast of Innamincka, a bird and wildlife refuge, also offers excellent fishing opportunities. It's a long, rough drive from Innamincka to Birdsville, past Cordil- lo Downs and Arrabury Homesteads (no facili- ties) and the ruins of Cadelga Outstation, used in the 1930s by the Royal Geographic Society to observe the transit of Venus.

Again, this is not an out-for-a-Sunday-drive road. Make sure you are well prepared, and check in with police at Lyndhurst.

OUTBACK PARKS

Only the most well-equipped and preinformed travelers should explore the remote, arid out- back parks. Desert park passes must be ob- tained in advance from the Department of En- vironment and Natural Resources. The issuing office will provide you with all necessary rules and regulations.

Lake Eyre National Park

The 1,228,000 hectares of Lake Eyre National Park encompass Lake Eyre North (Australia's largest salt lake), adjacent Tirari Desert, and a desert wilderness conservation area. Lake Eyre, normally a huge dry salt pan, is where, in 1964, Sir Donald Campbell set a world land-speed record (640 kph) in Bluebird, his jet-powered car; when I visited a few years ago, the lake was full of water! Reaching a depth of 16 meters below sea level (where the salt crust measures 230 mm thick), the lake has filled only a few times since European settlement. Smaller salt lakes lie within the duney desert section, and fossil deposits have been discovered at Lake Ngapakaldi, on the far eastern edge.

The park has no facilities. Access is via Mu- loorina Homestead, 90 km north of Marree or, al- ternately, travel six km east of William Creek, then 51 km east to Belt Bay, on the lake's south- west corner.

Elliot Price Conservation Park

Located 105 km northwest of Marree on the southern edge of Lake Eyre North, Elliot Price Conservation Park (64,570 hectares) was the

BOMB ROADS

Bomb roads—offspring of the 1950s, and brain-children of surveyor Len Beadell—were constructed during the Woomera rocket- and Emu A-bomb tests era. Len and his "Gunbarrel Road Construction Party" went to work. The Gunbarrel Highway, Len's first and most well-known feat, was completed in 1958. More than 6,000 km of "road" (really desert tracks, *really* a rocket range) span western South Australia and a chunk of neighboring Western Australia, north of the intercontinental railway line. Some of the roads run east-west, joining up at points with various north-south stretches. Outback adventurers with 4WD vehicles love this desert grid. These are difficult roads. As with all remote Outback travel, make sure your body is healthy, your vehicle is in excellent condition, and that you are well-equipped for breakdowns and emergencies. You will need to carry quite a bit of extra petrol, and permits are required for many of the roads. (Also, be prepared to run into "radioactivity warning" signs!) Detailed information can be obtained from Royal Automobile Club offices.

Gunbarrel Highway: The original Gunbarrel is a very rough, rugged, and desolate stretch running from Victory Downs Homestead, near the junction of the Stuart Highway and Northern Territory and South Australia borders, to Carnegie Homestead (349 km east of Wiluna). Other than the turnoff beyond Giles Meteorological Station to Docker River Aboriginal Community, the Gunbarrel leads to plenty of nowheresville. "Fake imitations," such as the Laverton-Warburton Road and a more "improved" version of the Gunbarrel, will get you from Uluru (Ayers Rock) to Wiluna or Leonora in Western Australia; obtain permits from Central Land Council, Alice Springs (for the Northern Territory section), and Aboriginal Affairs Planning Authority, Perth (for the Western Australia section).

Anne Beadell Highway: Coober Pedy west to Emu (watch the radioactivity warning signs!), across South Australia/Western Australia border, crossing Connie Sue Highway, to Laverton; obtain permits from Defence Support Center (P.O. Box 157, Woomera, SA 5720, tel. 08-8674-3370), Maralinga-Tjarutja Council, or Maralinga Land Council.

Connie Sue Highway: North from Rawlinna railway siding, past Anne Beadell Highway and the Laverton-Warburton Road, to Gunbarrel Highway; obtain permits from Aboriginal Affairs Planning Authority, Perth.

Gary Highway: North from the Gunbarrel Highway (known as Everard Junction) to Canning Stock Route at Well 35—from there heading west, on a mostly unused track, northwest to the Indian Ocean, north of Marble Bar; no permits necessary.

Sandy Blight Junction Road: Between the Gunbarrel Highway, west of Docker River Aboriginal Community, and Sandy Blight Junction, near Kintore Aboriginal Community; obtain permits from Central Land Council, Alice Springs.

Canning-Papunya Road: Alice Springs west, through Papunya, Sandy Blight and Gary junctions, to Canning Stock Route at Well 35; obtain permits from Central Land Council, Alice Springs.

Talawana Track-Windy Corner Road: West on Windy Corner Road at Gary Junction, crossing Canning Stock Route near Well 24, becoming Talawana Track, continuing into Pilbara Region (WA), south of Marble Bar; no permits necessary.

For more information, see the special topic "Canning Stock Route" in the Western Australia chapter.

---

first arid zone reserve. Red kangaroos, grass owls, and low sparse vegetation make the park their home. Hunt Peninsula, within the park, is a long limestone arm reaching into Lake Eyre North. The park has no facilities.

Witjira National Park

Witjira National Park, 120 km north of Oodnadatta, comprises flat hills, salt pans, sandy dunes, desert and gibber plains, and numerous mound, thermal, and hot springs. Formerly Mount Dare Homestead, these 776,900

hectares just became a national park in the 1980s. The most popular attractions here are the 80 or so **Dalhousie Springs,** Australia's largest artesian baths, in which visitors soak and laze away in the bubbles of the tepid waters. This same mineralized bath water originated as rainfall in north Queensland about four million years ago!

Near the springs are ruins and relics of early farming days. After a rain, wildflowers spurt up around the pools. Native birds include brolgas, darters, gibbers, thrush, and cinnamon quail.

A campground is available near the springs. **Mount Dare Homestead** (tel. 08-8670-7835), 70 km northwest of the springs, has accommodations, camping, food, emergency repairs, fuel, and an airstrip.

Simpson Desert Conservation Park

The Simpson Desert Conservation Park is an enormous (692,680 hectares) arid wilderness in the middle of the Simpson Desert. A large bird population, including zebra finches, budgerigars, black kites, and wedge-tailed eagles, shares the land with parallel red sand dunes, salt lakes, gidgi woodlands, and post-rain wildflowers.

The park has no facilities. More-than-adequate provisions, proper equipment, and a first-class 4WD vehicle are essential. Access to the park is via Dalhousie Springs from Oodnadatta, or via Poeppel Corner from Birdsville.

Large areas surrounding Innamincka, including Cooper Creek and the Coongie Lakes, have been declared a regional reserve, as has a huge portion of the Simpson Desert outside of the Witjira National Park and Simpson Desert Conservation Park boundaries.

Travelers who wish to make the hazardous trek across the Simpson Desert should do so only with experienced outback drivers, in top-condition 4WD vehicles, with massive amounts of equipment, provisions, information, and stamina.

TRANSPORTATION

Augusta Airways (tel. 08-8642-3100) operates a "Channel Mail Run" between Port Augusta and Mount Isa (Queensland), with stops in Innamincka and Birdsville on the weekend. This company also offers charter and scenic flights.

For commercial flights between Adelaide, Woomera, Olympic Dam, and Coober Pedy, contact **Ansett** (tel. 13-1300 toll-free), **Qantas** (tel. 13-1313 toll-free), or **Kendell Airlines** (tel. 069-22-0100). Fares run about $150 to Woomera and $250 to Coober Pedy. They are subject to frequent changes.

Stateliner (tel. 08-8415-5544, Adelaide, or 08-8642-5055, Port Augusta) operates frequent coach service from Adelaide and some Flinders Ranges communities to Andamooka, Cadney

Homestead, Coober Pedy, Glendambo, Lyn[e]hurst, Marla, Marree, Olympic Dam, Pimb[a], Roxby Downs, Woomera, and on to Alic[e] Springs. Fares are approximately $50 [to] Woomera, $65 to Marree, $85 to Coober Ped[y.] **Greyhound Pioneer Australia** (tel. 13-203[0] toll-free) provides service to some of the com[-] munities via its express routes.

For **organized tours**, see "Services and I[n]formation" in the "Flinders Ranges" sectio[n] above. Arrangements can be made for fishin[g] and cruising trips along **Cooper Creek**, as we[ll] as other Innamincka area tours. For more in[-] formation, contact **Innamincka Trading Pos[t]** (tel. 08-8675-9900).

SERVICES AND INFORMATION

Fuel and **public telephones** are available a[t] the following outback locations: Andamook[a,] Birdsville, Cadney Homestead, Coober Ped[y,] Glendambo, Innamincka, Kulgera, Lyndhurs[t,] Marla, Marree, Mintabie, Olympic Dam, Oo[d]nadatta, Pimba, Tarcoola, William Creek, an[d] Woomera.

For tourist information, see "Services and I[n]formation" in the "Flinders Ranges" sectio[n] above. Also obtain information at **Coober Ped[y] Tourist Information Centre,** Council Office[,] Hutchison St. (tel. 08-8672-5298). Purchas[e] cards, maps, and local-interest publications a[t] **Underground Books and Gallery** (tel. 08[-] 8672-5558), next to the Desert Cave Motel i[n] Coober Pedy. Additionally, most pubs, motels[,] caravan parks, and roadhouses (particularly th[e] Pink Roadhouse) carry information.

For information on **Desert Park Passes,** abou[t] $50 per vehicle, contact the **Department of En[-] vironment and Natural Resources,** Far North[-] ern Region (tel. 08-8648-4244). Passes can als[o] be purchased at various shops in the area.

FLINDERS RANGES AND OUTBACK RADIO STATIONS

R adio stations that broadcast into the Flinders Ranges and outback are: 5CK 639; 5CL 729; 5AN 891; 5CS 1044; 5AU 1242.

TASMANIA

INTRODUCTION

asmania, Australia's only island state, is sepa-
ted from the mainland by the wild waters of
ass Strait. The island's landscape has few sim-
arities to the rest of Australia and because of its
eenery and mountains is often compared to
ew Zealand. Although small in area, the island
sparsely populated, leaving vast tracts of
ilderness. This is Tasmania's greatest attrac-
on, and much of the island has been dedicated
s national park, including 20% of the island
otected as the Tasmanian Wilderness World
eritage Area. All sorts of outdoor recreation is
ossible, but it is the unparalleled opportunity
r long-distance hiking and whitewater rafting
at attracts the hard-core adventurers. Tasma-
a's history is the most colorful but tragic of all
ates, and while on the mainland progress has
eant the demolition of many historic buildings,
e slower pace of development in Tasmania
as seen dozens of colonial-era buildings saved,
any of which have been converted to B&Bs,
ts and crafts galleries, and restaurants.

For extended coverage of Tasmania, see
Moon Publications' *Tasmania Handbook,* by
Jane King.

THE LAND

Tasmania may not have the size of Western
Australia, the diverse landscapes of Victoria, or
the beaches of Queensland, but what it does
have is sandwiched on an island where no point
is more than 120 km from the ocean, and yet
much of the island is wilderness and seemingly
remote. Most of the population lives along the
east and north coasts, with Hobart, the state's
capital, in the southeast. Water dominates Hobart's layout, and while there are a few high-rise
developments, the many colonial-era buildings
give the city its character. Some of Tasmania's
best-known attractions are on Hobart's doorstep,
including the delightful Huon Valley and the unspoilt beaches of Bruny Island immediately to

TASMANIA

TASMANIAN TIGER *(THYLACINE)*

This large carnivorous marsupial, once widespread throughout Tasmania, has been *officially* extinct since 1936, when the last remaining member of the species died in Hobart Zoo. The demise of the species came about almost entirely through man's doing after the Van Diemen's Land Company put a bounty on the unfortunate animal as its predatory habits were seriously affecting sheep numbers in the northwest of the state. Speculation and debate as to whether the Tasmanian tiger still exists continues to this day. It has been over 65 years since the last wild one was seen (and shot), but the distinctively striped marsupial just may be lurking out there somewhere.

Tasmanian tiger

BOB RACE

historic Launceston, at the headwaters of the Tamar River. The Bass Strait is a treacherous stretch of water that has claimed hundreds of lives, many on board ships that have crashed into the many islands dotting the strait. Two of these, King and Flinders, are populated by a resilient band of Tasmanians who welcome travelers with open arms.

Climate

During winter, Tasmania's southern latitude sees temperatures drop considerably with snowfalls on the higher peaks. Daily maximum temperatures in July are around 10° C (50° F). Summer is more pleasant, with temperatures in the capital averaging about 20° C (68° F). Rainfall along the east and north coasts is fairly consistent year-round, with each month averaging 5.5 cm of precipitation. The interior and west coast are a different story, with some areas receiving over three meters of rain annually.

HISTORY

The first European to sight Tasmania was Dutchman Abel Tasman, who sailed by in 1642, naming the island **Van Diemen's Land.** In the next 140 years a string of European sailors visited Van Diemen's Land, including Capt. James Cook and William Bligh, but all assumed it was part of the mainland. After settlement at Sydney Cove in 1788, shipping in the region became more frequent, with ships sailing between England and Sydney Cove taking a route around the southern tip of Van Diemen's Land. In 1798 Matthew Flinders, captain of the small sloop *Norfolk,* became the first person to circumnavigate Van Diemen's Land, proving that it was in fact an island. He named Bass Strait after fellow explorer and the ship's surgeon George Bass.

e south. East of Hobart is the Tasman Peninula and Port Arthur, site of Australia's harsht penal settlement and now the state's numberme tourist attraction. Along the east coast are eautiful beaches as well as a number of naonal parks, including Maria Island and Freycinet, oth with excellent hiking opportunities. The outhwest of the state is all wilderness and mostinaccessible. Its gateway is Mount Field National Park, which provides day-hikers the ance to experience the alpine environment. the northwest is Franklin-Gordon Wild Rivers ational Park, scene of a lengthy battle in which onservationists blocked the construction of a rdroelectric scheme that would have caused e Gordon River to flood. Strahan, the only town the entire west coast with ocean access, is the eparture point for a variety of river cruises. Best own of Tasmania's national parks is Cradle ountain-Lake St. Clair, in the state's north-cental region, which protects a high alpine area of eep glacial lakes and rugged peaks. The north ast comprises a string of towns and small ies, including Tasmania's second-largest city,

Late in the 1790s, with the population of Sydney Town overflowing, it was decided to establish a second settlement. The site, at the mouth of the Derwent River, Van Diemen's Land, was decided upon in 1804. It wasn't until 1821 that a penal colony was established on the island, first on the west coast, then on Maria Island, and finally, in 1832, at notorious Port Arthur on the Tasman Peninsula. Only the very worst convicts, or those who re-offended once in Australia, were sent to Van Diemen's Land, and the island's notorious reputation grew rapidly. Transportation of convicts was abolished in 1856, and to distance the island from its past, its name was changed to Tasmania, for its European discoverer.

Aboriginal History

European treatment of Aborigines during the last 200 years has been grossly unjust, but it was in Tasmania during the first 30 years of European settlement that the Aboriginals' plight was the most tragic. European settlers fenced off all the best land for farms, and as they encroached upon traditional hunting grounds, the Aboriginals began fighting back. In turn, the settlers hunted and shot down the Aboriginal men as they would animals, kidnapped native children to use as slave labor, and raped and tortured the women. In 1828 Governor Arthur proclaimed a law that gave police the right to shoot Aboriginals on sight. Within a couple of years the entire population had been flushed out from settled districts, and over the following five years the remaining stragglers, numbering less than 200, were transported to Flinders Island to be converted to Christians.

TRANSPORTATION

Getting to Tasmania requires a simple choice—to travel by sea or air. For those with a vehicle, there is but one choice, the *Spirit of Tasmania*, a large ferry service operating between Melbourne and Devonport. Flying is the best option for those with a limited amount of time, and can be inexpensive if booked as part of a package offered by the major airlines.

Getting There by Air

The main gateways are Launceston and Hobart, with most flights originating in Melbourne

SPIRIT OF TASMANIA FARES

	ADULT			VEHICLE		
	HOSTEL	CABIN	UNDER FIVE METERS	UNDER SIX METERS	MOTORCYCLE	BICYCLE
Touring Season (late Jan. to early April, mid-April to mid-Dec.)	$99	$195-325 s, $145-225 pp d	$125	$150	$70	$20
Holiday Season (mid-Dec. to late Jan., early to mid-April)	$120	$210-380 s, $160-280 pp d	$175	$210	$100	$25

All fares quoted are one way; round-trip fares are double. Children under 16 half price. Slight discounts for students and seniors. Separate male and female hostel accommodations. A single supplement of $70-100 applies to private cabins. Book all classes of travel well in advance by calling 13-2010 from Australia or (800) 551-2012 from North America.

and Sydney. **Ansett Australia** (tel. 13-1300) and **Qantas** (tel. 13-1313) have regular flights to Tasmania from major mainland cities. Some sample fares to Hobart are: from Melbourne ($224 one-way), Sydney ($260), and Brisbane $340). Round-trip fares are much cheaper, especially if purchased 14 days in advance. Both major carriers offer inexpensive packages, such as $299-359 (depending on the season) for airfares from Sydney and three nights' accommodations. **Airlines of Tasmania** (tel. 1800-03-0550) flies from Sale and Traralgon, in Victoria's Gippsland, to Launceston and Hobart ($224) via Flinders Island. Their five-night packages are also a good deal, including airfares from the mainland, a two-night stop on Flinders Island, mainland Tasmania accommodations, and a rental car, all for $570-616 pp. **Kendell** (tel. 1800-33-8894) flies between Melbourne and Devonport ($148 one-way) and Burnie ($158). This company also offers packages.

Spirit of Tasmania

This large vehicular ferry operates a regular service across Bass Strait (see the chart "Spirit of Tasmania Fares"). The ship is modern and comfortable, able to accommodate 1,323 passengers and transport 280 cars. More like a cruise ship than a ferry, the ship boasts 10 levels, with three decks of public space that include a variety of restaurants and bars, a swimming pool, sauna, fitness room, disco, video arcade, casino, and visitor center. As the ferry always sails overnight, all fares include accommodations, as well as a buffet dinner and breakfast.

The Spirit of Tasmania departs Port Melbourne every Monday, Wednesday, and Friday

---

at 6 p.m., arriving Devonport 8:30 a.m. the following morning. Return sailings depart Devonport Tuesday, Thursday, and Saturday at 6 p.m., arriving back in Melbourne at 8:30 a.m. the following morning.

Getting Around

Airlines of Tasmania (tel. 1800-03-0550) operates scheduled flights to all major centers and King and Flinders Islands.

Transportation around the island's road system is provided by two bus companies. **Tasmanian Wilderness Transport** (tel. 03-6334-4442) has an extensive timetable, with service to all cities and major towns as well as the most popular national parks. Some routes are served daily, others less regularly and with a limited number of runs April-October. Fares are reasonable with a Wilderness and Highway Pass, valid for unlimited travel: seven days is $99, 14 days $140, and 30 days $179. **Tasmanian Redline Coaches** (tel. 03-6331-3233) offers more daily runs but to fewer destinations, and offers similar passes.

HOBART

Hobart (pop. 200,000), the capital of Tasmania, lies at the mouth of the Derwent River on the island-state's southeast coast. Of Australia's state capitals, only Sydney rivals Hobart for surrounding natural beauty, for behind the city Mt. Wellington, snowcapped during the winter months, rises sharply to an elevation of 1,270 meters, sandwiching the city between the mountains and the water. With less pressure for expansion than other capitals, Hobart has retained

its colonial charm and also has an English feel, not unlike the city of Victoria on Canada's Vancouver Island.

Downtown Hobart surrounds Sullivans Cove, a protected body of water on the Derwent River that is a continuous buzz of activity, from cruise liners to fishing trawlers to, around the New Year, dozens of yachts sailing into the cove upon completion of the Sydney-Hobart Yacht Race. Surrounding the waterfront are dozens

HOBART

of convict-era sandstone buildings, many on Salamanca Place, where a bustling market is held each Saturday.

The Tasman Bridge, spanning the Derwent River north of downtown, links residential suburbs of Rosny, Bellerive, and Howrah to the city center, and also leads northeast to the Tasman Peninsula.

History

With the population of Sydney Town overflowing, the colonial government decided to establish a new settlement in Van Diemen's Land. A settlement was first established at Ridson Cove and a year later, in 1804, moved by the colony's Lieutenant Governor David Collins 10 km downstream. The site was more suitable than Ridson Cove; it was sheltered and had deepwater access, and rainfall was plentiful. A townsite was quickly surveyed, many stone structures built, and in 1812 Hobart Town, popula-

tion 1,000, was declared the capital of Va Diemen's Land. The settlement continued to prosper through the early 1800s, becoming a important shipbuilding and whaling port an by the 1850s rivaling Sydney for commercia importance.

Progress stagnated with the discovery of gol on the mainland, but the 20th century has see Hobart expand greatly, first to the south an north, then, with the completion of the **Tasma Bridge** in 1964, along the eastern bank of th Derwent River. Just 11 years after the comple tion of the Tasman Bridge, tragedy struck whe the iron ore bulk carrier *Lake Illawarra* plowe into the bridge, collapsing two of its massiv support columns, killing 12 people, and sinkin under the weight of the collapsed bridge. It too construction crews two years to rebuild the sha tered bridge, during which time commuters fro the east were forced to either travel across th river by ferry or take a roundabout inland route

DOWNTOWN SIGHTS

The best way to discover Hobart's past is with **Sullivans Cove Walking Tours** (tel. 03-6230-8233), which takes in historic sites around the cove, such as the City Hall, the notorious dockside suburb of Wapping, the laneways off Hunter St., reclaimed Hunter Island, the cellars of the old Customs House (now Parliament House), St. David's Park cemetery, and the site of Hobart's first jail. Tours depart the Tasmanian Travel and Information Centre Monday, Wednesday, and Friday at 9:30 a.m. and Sunday at 10:30 a.m.; adult $8.50, children under 14 free.

Tasmanian Museum and Art Gallery

First-floor displays of this fascinating museum feature Tasmanian fauna, a mineral and gemstone display, sealife found around the Tasmanian coast, and 20th-century Australian art. Displays on the second floor include the story of Tasmanian Aboriginals, a coin collection, "People of the Pacific," the state's maritime history, convict history, and early Australian art. The complex is open daily 10 a.m.-5 p.m. Admission is free. It's at 40 Macquarie St. (tel. 03-6235-0777).

Penitentiary Chapel and Criminal Courts

These attractive redbrick buildings on the corner of Brisbane and Campbell Streets are among the oldest remaining structures in Tasmania. The Penitentiary Chapel, completed in 1835, was used by convicts and warders for compulsory Sunday church services. In 1858 additions were made to the building, and the whole place was converted to criminal courts. The National Trust (tel. 03-6231-0911) offers tours of the chapel, courtrooms, underground passages, graffiti-covered jail cells (the last man hanged in

TO NEW TOWN AND GLENORCHY

TO AIRPORT

DOWNTOWN HOBART

QUEEN'S

TASMAN HIGHWAY

WELLINGTON LODGE

DOMAIN

CAMPBELL

BROOKER

AVENUE

WARWICK ST.

ARGYLE ST.

PENITENTIARY CHAPEL AND CRIMINAL COURTS

ELIZABETH ST.

DERWENT RIVER

DEPARTURE POINT FOR TASMANIAN WILDERNESS TRANSPORT

FOUNTAINSIDE MOTOR INN

THEATRE ROYAL

BLACK PRINCE HOTEL

PATRICK

MURRAY

SEE DETAIL

CITY HALL

HOTEL GRAND CHANCELLOR

BANJO'S BAKERY

CRITERION ST.

HARRINGTON

LA CUISINE / NEW SIDNEY HOTEL

TASMANIAN MUSEUM AND ART GALLERY

MURE'S FISH CENTRE

DRUNKEN ADMIRAL

HUNTER

MACO QUALITY SEAFOOD

MACQUARIE ST.

STATE LIBRARY

TASMANIAN TRAVEL AND INFORMATION CENTRE

WHARF

BRISBANE

MELVILLE

ABC ODEON

FRANKLIN SQUARE

DEAR FRIENDS

SULLIVANS COVE

CENTERTAINMENT

BATHURST

BARRACK

COLLINS

BROOKE ST.

DETAIL

LITTLE BALI

LAND INFORMATION BUREAU

PARLIAMENT HOUSE

BROOKE STREET PIER

LIVERPOOL

ROYAL HOBART HOSPITAL

MACQUARIE

CAFE WHO BAR

SALAMANCA

MALONEY'S HOTEL

WESTSIDE LAUNDROMAT

HOBART MACQUARIE MOTOR INN

ST. DAVID'S PARK

NATIONAL TRUST/ WILDERNESS SOCIETY

PLACE

ELIZABETH STREET MALL

POST OFFICE

COLLINS

HOBART TRANSIT CENTRE

DUKE OF WELLINGTON

ST. HELEN'S PRIVATE HOSPITAL

SALAMANCA INN

KNOPWOOD'S RETREAT/ROUND MIDNIGHT

LENNA OF HOBART

ALABAMA HOTEL

BRUNSWICK HOTEL

METRO SHOP/ HOBART BUS STATION

LIVERPOOL

MONTPELIER

HAMPDEN RD.

RETREAT

BATTERY POINT

TACOS

ELIZABETH

ANGUS AND ROBERTSON

MACQUARIE

VAN DIEMEN'S LAND FOLK MUSEUM

BATTERY POINT BRASSERIE

DA ANGELO RISTORANTE

CENTRAL CITY BACKPACKERS

ST.

DAVEY

SANDY BAY ROAD

ST. IVES HOTEL

MARITIME MUSEUM OF TASMANIA

MURRAY

ST.

COUNTRY COMFORT HADLEYS HOTEL

TO WREST POINT HOTEL CASINO

0   500 m

Australia, in 1968, autographed the wall), solitary cells, and the outdoor execution yard. Tour cost is adult $5, child $2.50. They operate daily 10 a.m.-2 p.m. (tel. 03-6231-0911).

Sullivans Cove

Hobart's main thoroughfare, Elizabeth St., ends to the east at **Franklin Wharf** on Sullivans Cove. The wharf, lined with boats of all sizes and colors, has been Hobart's main tie-up point for shipping since the first settlers arrived in 1804. In the 1800s up to 600 internationally registered ships would visit annually. In times gone by it was the haunt of thirsty seamen, English aristocracy, traveling missionaries, and rowdy whalers, but today things are much quieter. The land around the back of the cove is mostly reclaimed; steps linking Davey and Brooke Streets mark the original extent of water and of the cliff that once surrounded the cove. While commercial use of the cove has changed considerably, it's still a hive of activity with cruise liners, cargo ships, and yachts.

On Brooke Street Pier is **Franklin Wharf Cruise Centre,** operator of a ferry between Sullivans Cove and Bellerive, across the Derwent River from downtown. Ferries operate weekdays only and are $1.60 each way.

BATTERY POINT SIGHTS

This area, a maze of narrow and one-way streets immediately south of downtown, is a great place to wander around exploring one of Australia's greatest concentrations of convict-era architecture. The best source of Battery Point information is the National Trust Shop at 33 Salamanca Place (tel. 03-6223-7371); ask for the *Historic Village Battery Point* brochure (80 cents).

Salamanca Place

This cobbled street lined with Georgian-era sandstone warehouses and bondstores is one of Hobart's best-known landmarks. Built in the 1830s, when Hobart was one of the world's great whaling ports, today the buildings contain arts and crafts shops, art galleries, cafes, and restaurants. Each Saturday between 8 a.m. and 2 p.m. the street comes alive with the sights and smells of bustling **Salamanca Market,** where everything from handcarved Huon pine to candles is sold from colorful streetside stalls

while buskers perform up and down the street. The **National Trust,** preserver of Australia's historic buildings, has its Tasmanian headquarters at 33 Salamanca Place (tel. 03-6223 7371). It's open to the public, with a small gift shop and lots of information on Hobart's oldest buildings. Open Mon.-Fri. 9:30 a.m.-5 p.m., Saturday 9:30 a.m.-1 p.m. Each Saturday at 9:30 a.m. the Trust offers a walking tour of Salamanca Place and Battery Point, ending with a morning tea; $5 pp.

Van Diemen's Land Folk Museum

Housed in **Narryna,** a stately old mansion built in 1836, this museum contains a fascinating collection of household memorabilia dating from the convict era. Each room is authentically decorated, while in the courtyard is the original Hobart Town coat of arms, relics from the whaling era, some old brewing equipment, an anchor salvaged from an 1858 shipwreck, and some horse-drawn buggies. Admission is adult $5, child $2. Open Mon.-Fri. 10 a.m.-5 p.m., Sat.-Sun. 2-5 p.m. It's at 103 Hampden Rd. (tel. 03-6234-2791)

Maritime Museum of Tasmania

This museum is in Secheron House, built in 1831 and considered one of Hobart's finest examples of Georgian architecture. The house contains a large collection of maritime memorabilia, including paintings, photographs, whaling relics, a couple of figureheads, models, and other artifacts from Tasmania's colorful maritime history. Admission is $2. Open daily 10 a.m.-4:30 p.m. Located at the end of Secheron Rd. (tel. 03-6223-5082).

SIGHTS IN OTHER PARTS OF THE CITY

Runnymede House

Built in 1844 for Robert Pitcairn, Hobart Town's first lawyer, this sandstone home has been painstakingly restored and is now surrounded by colorful flower gardens. Later owners, such as Capt. Charles Bayley, who renamed the residence after his ship, made additions, but the house manages to retain its original colonial charm. Admission is adult $5, child $3. Open daily 10 a.m.-4:30 p.m. The house is at 61 Bay Rd., New Town (tel. 03-6278-1269).

Cascade Brewery

This, Australia's oldest brewery, is an impressive building standing southwest of downtown at 140 Cascade Rd., Cascade (tel. 03-6224-1144). Tours take in all elements of the brewing process and include viewing of a small museum. Tours depart Mon.-Fri. at 9:30 a.m. and 1 p.m. (booking essential). The cost is adult $7, child $2.

Taroona

The highlight of Taroona, on the Channel Hwy. 10 km south from downtown, is **Taroona Shot Tower,** the world's only remaining circular sandstone shot tower. Shot was produced by dropping lumps of molten lead from the top of the tower; on the way down it would form a sphere, then hit the water and cool. The tower, which operated between 1870 and 1904, produced award-winning shot. Visitors view a short video, then climb 259 stairs to the top of the tower. Admission is adult $3, child $1.50. Open daily 9 a.m.-5 p.m.

Cadbury Chocolate Factory

Sprawling over 15 hectares, this factory, established in 1921, is Australia's largest confectionery manufacturing plant. Tours are offered Mon.-Fri. at regular intervals between 9 a.m. and 5 p.m.

The tour begins with an audiovisual of Cadbury's history, then it's on to the good stuff— viewing the various chocolate-making processes and doing a bit of quality control. Admission is adult $10, child $5. And, yes, free samples are included in the tour cost. The factory is in the suburb of Claremont 12 km north of downtown. To book a tour call (03) 6249-0333; to inquire about employment call (03) 6249-0111.

Another way to visit the factory is aboard *Derwent Explorer* (tel. 03-6234-9294), on a four-hour cruise departing Brooke Street Pier Mon.-Fri. (departure times vary; call ahead); adult $30, child $14.

PARKS, GARDENS, AND VIEWPOINTS

The **Royal Tasmanian Botanical Gardens** are incorporated in Queen's Domain, on the northern outskirts of downtown. Established in 1818,

the gardens feature a large collection of native Australian species and are noted for colorful floral displays each spring. A conservatory (admission $1 pp) allows a year-round display of some flowering species. The gardens are open daily between 8 a.m. and dusk.

The best city and river views are from the summit of **Mt. Wellington,** which rises immediately west of the city to a lofty elevation of 1,270 meters. A 22-km road passing through the outer suburbs of Cascade and Fern Tree leads right to the summit.

OUTDOOR ACTIVITIES

Biking

If screaming down Mt. Wellington on a mountain bike sounds like fun, **Brakeout Cycling Tours** (tel. 03-6229-1999) offers a 21-km, three-hour-long Summit to Sea downhill experience for $25 pp. Departures are daily and they offer transfers from Hobart accommodations.

Golfing

Royal Hobart Golf Club, at Seven Mile Beach east of the city, is open to members of overseas golf clubs Mon.-Fri. only. Green fees are $30 and club rentals are available. For tee times call (03) 6248-6108.

Wilderness Flightseeing

Two companies offer flightseeing trips from Cambridge Aerodrome, northeast of downtown on the Tasman Highway. **Tas Air** (tel. 03-6248-5088) has a 30-minute flight over Hobart and the Derwent River Estuary for $45 pp (minimum two) and a two-and-a-half-hour flight over Southwest National Park for $135 pp. **Par Avion Wilderness Tours** (tel. 03-6248-5390) has longer tours, including a four-hour trip to the west coast for $130 pp, which includes a cruise on Bathurst Harbour.

ARTS AND ENTERTAINMENT

The best sources of arts and entertainment information are the Friday and Saturday entertainment sections of Hobart's *Mercury* newspaper, where festivals and events, movies, and live music venues are listed. The main booking agent for major shows and events is **Centertainment,** 134 Liverpool St. (tel. 03-6234-5998).

Theater and Music

Theatre Royal, Australia's oldest theater, is a striking sandstone building that hosts Australian and international productions as well as performances by local theater and musical groups. Ticket prices range $10-32. The theater booking office, at 29 Campbell St. (tel. 03-6233-2299), is open Mon.-Fri. 10 a.m.-5 p.m., or book through Centertainment.

For information on the **Tasmanian Symphony Orchestra** (TSO) call (03) 6235-3633 or write TSO Box Office, Box 9994, Hobart, TAS 7001. Most performances are at the ABC Odeon, 167 Liverpool Street.

Cinemas

Village 7 Cinema Complex, 181 Collins St. (tel. 03-6234-7288), is the city's largest cinema center and has double features Friday and Saturday nights starting at 9 p.m.; adult $9. The Australian Film Institute screens locally made films at the **State-A.F.I. Cinema,** 373 Elizabeth St. (tel. 03-6234-6318). Admission to most films is $9.

Casino

Wrest Point Hotel Casino, 410 Sandy Bay Rd., Sandy Bay (tel. 03-6225-0112), was Australia's first (legal) casino; its distinctive white tower overlooking the Derwent River is a city landmark. Gaming facilities are open Mon.-Thurs. 1 p.m.-3 a.m., Fri.-Sat. 1 p.m.-4 a.m., and Sunday noon-3 a.m. Games include roulette, blackjack, poker variations, two-up, keno, and baccarat. As well as providing accommodations and offering many eateries, the casino has a number of bars, nightly live entertainment, and a nightclub.

Hotels, Bars, and Nightclubs

One of the best places in Hobart to enjoy a drink while soaking up some colonial atmosphere is **Knopwood's Retreat,** at 39 Salamanca Place (tel. 03-6223-5808). Located in the heart of Hobart's historic precinct, this bar with its casual Victorian atmosphere attracts an eclectic array of patrons, who range from visiting dignitaries to local artisans. Opened in 1829 as a drinking hole for thirsty seamen, the bar has come a long way in the time since, now offering over 100 beers and a great variety of Tasmanian wines.

St. Ives Hotel, 86 Sandy Bay Rd., Sandy Bay (tel. 03-6223-3655), has bands playing Friday and Saturday nights from 10 p.m., Sunday afternoon from 3 p.m. Other pubs with live weekend entertainment include the **Theatre Royal Hotel,** 31 Campbell St. (tel. 03-6234-6925), and **Duke of Wellington,** 192 Macquarie St. (tel. 03-6223-5206), with bands most nights covering popular rock songs. **Maloney's Hotel,** 87 Macquarie St. (tel. 03-6234-4790), has several bars, a DJ, light show, and dance floor. Admission charged only Friday and Saturday nights. Above Knopwood's Retreat is **Round Midnight,** 39 Salamanca Place (tel. 03-6223-2491), a local favorite for dancing the night away; open Tues.-Sat. 9 p.m.-4 a.m. **Wrest Point Hotel Casino** has a number of different bars and a stylish nightclub.

Jazz

Cafe Who Bar, 251 Liverpool St. (tel. 03-6231-2744), has a variety of music performed Tues.-Sat., but it's most often jazz; small admission charge. If cruising along the Derwent River enjoying the sounds of Dixieland jazz is your idea of good entertainment, consider a **Sunday Showboat Cruise,** departing Brooke Street Pier each Sunday at 2 p.m.; $15 pp. Book at (03) 6223-1914.

SHOPPING

Most downtown shops are open Mon.-Fri. 9 a.m.-5 p.m. (until 9 p.m. Friday), Saturday 9 a.m.-noon. The main shopping precinct is Elizabeth Street Mall, in the heart of downtown, but for the most interesting selection of Tasmanian arts and crafts head to **Salamanca Place** or Battery Point. Some of the best shopping experiences on Salamanca Place can be had at the **Handmark Gallery, Spinning Wheel, National Trust Shop,** and **Wilderness Society Shop.** Don't miss **Salamanca Market** each Saturday morning, when an amazing array of items are on offer at over 200 colorful stalls set along the street.

FESTIVALS AND EVENTS

Sullivans Cove is busy year-round, but for the finish of the **Sydney-Hobart Yacht Race**, between 28 December and 2 January, the harbor, and in fact the whole city, buzzes, as hundreds of yachties celebrate the completion of Australia's most famous yacht race. In conjunction with the race, Hobart hosts the **Taste of Tasmania Food Festival**, when an old waterfront in front of Salamanca Place is chockablock with stalls of samplings from local cafes, restaurants, and wineries.

The first week of April, **Heritage Week**, hosted by the National Trust, offers the opportunity to visit many of Hobart's historic buildings at a reduced cost, with tours and daily entertainment at some venues.

ACCOMMODATIONS

Downtown Hotels and Motels
Downtown Hobart has a number of inexpensive hotels, but most have seen better days. Pick of the bunch is **Alabama Hotel**, 72 Liverpool St. (tel. 03-6234-3737); $28 s, $44 d. In the same general area is **Brunswick Hotel**, 67 Liverpool St. (tel. 03-6234-4981), with rooms for $33 s, $50 d. The **Black Prince Hotel**, 145 Elizabeth St. (tel. 03-6234-3501), one km north of downtown, has clean and comfortable rooms with shared facilities for $45 s, $60 d, including breakfast. **Wellington Lodge**, 7 Scott St., Glebe (tel. 03-6231-0614), is a restored Victorian-era house one km north of downtown. Five guest rooms are offered; one has a private bathroom while the others have shared facilities. Rates are $50-65 s, $65-80 d.

Good value among downtown motels is **Fountainside Motor Inn**, corner Brooker Ave. and Liverpool St. (tel. 03-6234-2911), which has large well-equipped rooms from $49 s, $59 d. **Hobart Macquarie Motor Inn**, 167 Macquarie St. (tel. 03-6234-4422), has rooms of a good standard, as well as a heated pool, spa, and laundry, for $70 s, $79 d. More central, and a little more expensive, is **Country Comfort Hadleys Hotel**, 34 Murray St. (tel. 03-6223-4355), where rooms start at $85 s or d.

The **Salamanca Inn,** 10 Gladstone St. (tel. 03-6223-3300), comprises one-bedroom self-contained apartments 200 meters from Salamanca Place. Each apartment is well appointed and has a full kitchen and in-house movies, while guests have use of a laundry service, indoor pool, and restaurant. Rates are $164-280 s or d. On Battery Point, and just around the corner from Salamanca Place, is **Lenna of Hobart,** 20 Runnymede St. (tel. 03-6232-3900), a grand old sandstone mansion dating from 1874. Rooms are spacious and elegantly furnished, and each has a private bathroom. Rooms with mountain views are $140 s or d; those with harbor views are $160. **Hotel Grand Chancellor,** 1 Davey St. (tel. 03-6235-4535), overlooking the harbor, is Hobart's most prestigious accommodation. Many rooms have water views, and all are luxuriously equipped. Guest facilities include a heated indoor pool, health club, restaurant, bistro, and bar. Rates start at $230 s or d.

Hotels and Motels in Other Parts of the City
Staying at **Wrest Point Hotel Casino**, 410 Sandy Bay Rd. (tel. 03-6221-1750), south of downtown, isn't cheap, but there are a few price options. Most rooms are in the tower. These feature panoramic views, tea- and coffee-making facilities, fridge, large lounge area, and a spacious bedroom with king-size bed. Rates range $198-340 s or d, depending on the view. Motor Inn rooms, with river or garden views, are older and start at $100 s or d. In the same part of the city is **Regent Park Apartments,** 17 Regent St., Sandy Bay (tel. 03-6223-3200). These luxurious units, each with a well-equipped kitchen and laundry facilities, are great value at $89-114 s, $99-149 d.

In New Town, a few km north of downtown along Hwy. 1, the best-value choice of accommodations is **Hobart Tower Motel**, 300 Park St. (tel. 03-6228-0166), where clean and comfortable rooms are $46 s, $54 d. Farther north, six km northwest of downtown, is **Martin Cash Motor Lodge,** 238 Main Rd., Glenorchy (tel. 03-6272-5044), featuring rooms of a good standard for $75 s, $85 d.

Across the Tasman Bridge from Hobart, motels are scattered through most suburbs, and although they are less expensive than those downtown, you'll need your own transportation. A good choice on this side of the bridge is **Lindisfarne Motor Inn,** 103 East Derwent Hwy. (tel. 03-6243-8666); $50 s, $60 d.

Pines Resort, 20 km east of Hobart on Seven Mile Beach (tel. 03-6248-6222), is a good choice for those who have their own transportation and want to be on the beach. The resort comprises self-contained two-bedroom units spread around sprawling grounds; $115-125 s or d.

B&Bs
The luxurious **Islington Elegant Private Hotel,** built in 1845, is a beautiful old colonial home in a quiet residential area two km southwest of downtown at 321 Davey St. (tel. 03-6223-3900). Each of the eight rooms is spacious and tastefully decorated. Guests relax in a large downstairs lounge area, and large French doors open to a garden. A continental breakfast is served in a bright sunny room overlooking the swimming pool. Rates are $75 s, $130 d for a standard room and $95 s, $150 d for a Grand Room. **Corinda,** 17 Glebe St., Glebe (tel. 03-6234-1590), is a restored 1880 Victorian mansion with mountain and city views. Accommodation is in an upstairs attic room or in a couple of 1850s cottages out back that were formerly servants' quarters. Rates start at $140 s or d.

In Taroona, along the coastal highway between downtown and Kingston, is **Hillgrove Colonial Accommodation,** 269 Channel Hwy. (tel. 03-6227-9043), in a stunning location across from the Shot Tower. The original Georgian-era cottage has been greatly expanded, and the entire lower floor has been converted to a suite with stunning river views from the balcony. The suite has a kitchen and breakfast provisions are included in the rate of $70 s, $90 d.

Backpacker Lodges
Hobart's main YHA accommodation is **Adelphi Court,** three km north of downtown at 17 Stoke St., New Town (tel. 03-6228-4829). It's a large complex centered around a courtyard. Facilities include a communal kitchen, dining room, laundry, lounge, outdoor barbecue area, and bike rentals (half day $12, full day $20). Members of the YHA pay $12-15 pp for a dorm bed, $16-19 pp twin, and $32 for sole use of a room. Nonmembers pay around $3 pp extra per night.

The office is open daily 7:30 a.m.-10:30 p.m The Airport Shuttle offers a discounted fare of $6 pp to the hostel. In the suburb of Bellerive across the Derwent River from downtown, is **Bellerive YHA Hostel,** 52 King St. (tel. 03-6244-2552), an old stone schoolhouse dating from the 1860s. Dorm beds here are $10 pp.

Central City Backpackers, 138 Collins St (tel. 03-6224-2404), is right downtown in the Imperial Mansions (enter from the Imperial Arcade). This friendly place features a modern kitcher and comfortable lounge area. Rates are $12-14 pp in a dormitory and $18 pp in a twin or double room. Also central is **Transit Centre Backpackers,** 199 Collins St. (tel. 03-6231-2400) above the Transit Centre. Dorm beds are $12 pp and there are a few double rooms for $35.

Campgrounds
The closest camping to the city center is **Sandy Bay Caravan Park,** 1 Peel St., Sandy Bay (tel 03-6225-1264), on a hillside overlooking the Derwent River four km south of downtown. Facilities include hot showers, a kitchen, and a laundry. Unpowered sites are $12, powered sites $14, self-contained on-site vans $32, and cabins start at $55.

On the opposite side of the city, nine km north of downtown, is **Treasure Island Caravan Park** 671 Main Rd., Berriedale (tel. 03-6249-2379). All facilities are of the highest standard and there are cooking facilities for campers. Sites are $12-15, on-site vans $32, and cabins $46-50. To get to the park from the highway, take the Berriedale East exit.

FOOD

Cheap Eats
Elizabeth Street boasts a number of inexpensive eateries, including many in the **Cat and Fiddle Arcade** food court, where you'll find pasta, seafood, souvlaki, pizza, fruit salad, and baked goods. Like most of Hobart, it's closed Sunday Also on Elizabeth St. is **Banjo's Bakery,** 103 Elizabeth St. (tel. 03-6234-1999), serving an array of delicious breads, pastries, rolls, and Devonshire teas. **Lipscombe Larder City,** at the north end of Elizabeth St. Mall (tel. 03-6234-3758), offers gourmet sandwiches and hot foods

eat in-house or take away. **La Cuisine,** 85 athurst St. (tel. 03-6231-1274), is a trendy little afe offering healthy lunches for about $5-7.

For a pub meal, head to **New Sydney Hotel,** 7 Bathurst St. (tel. 03-6234-4516), where daily unch specials average $6 and dinner $8.

eafood
unter St., running along the waterfront on the pposite side of Sullivans Cove to Salamanca lace, is home to the **Drunken Admiral,** 17 unter St. (tel. 03-6234-1903), decorated with naritime memorabilia and renowned for a wide ariety of seafood. Start with oysters, cooked ur different ways, or the legendary Fish Market :howder ($7.50), then dive into the fish stew, nade with everything available at the markets nat morning ($17). Open daily for dinner only, 6-1 p.m. Also on Hunter St. is **Maco Quality eafood Takeaway,** offering fresh seafood ooked to order; a juicy chunk of Australia's evally is $3.50 and a large serving of hot chips ; $1.50. They have a few tables (50 cents xtra), but if the sun's out, you're better off find-ng a spot along the waterfront.

On the docks in front of downtown is three-tory **Mures Fish Centre,** with eateries to suit all udgets: **Fishmongers,** selling fresh fish, shell-sh, and smoked fish (perfect if you have cook-ng facilities at your accommodation); **Fish Fac-ory,** selling Tasmanian gourmet smoked fish nd other seafood products; a **bistro** serving eafood dishes under $10; and **Upper Deck lestaurant** (tel. 03-6231-1999), featuring great arbor views and offering a three-course lunch or $18.50 pp and dinner for $25.

\sian and European Restaurants
.ittle Bali, 84A Harrington St. (tel. 03-6234-426), is a small place offering inexpensive In-onesian dishes weekdays at lunch and week-nds for dinner. Most main meals are under 10 and you'd be doing well to spend $18 pp for nree courses. Most of the other Asian restau-ants are at the north end of downtown along :lizabeth Street. One of these is **Vanidol's,** -53 Elizabeth St. (tel. 03-6234-9307), which pecializes in Indian and Thai food; most main ishes are under $12.

For excellent Italian food and a buzzing at-nosphere, try **Marti Zucco,** 364 Elizabeth St.

(tel. 03-6234-9611), featuring freshly prepared pizza and pastas for $9.50-15.

Upmarket
In recent years **Dear Friends,** 8 Brooke St. (tel. 03-6223-2646), has been consistently voted Tasmania's best restaurant. The set-ting is elegant, and the walls are adorned with stylish works by Tasmanian artists. The chef is best known for his preparation of local pro-duce, with salmon and King Island beef the favorite choices. Main courses range $15-21. It's open Mon.-Fri. for lunch and Mon.-Sat. for dinner.

Salamanca Place
Delicious food can be found at most times of the day and during the early evening hours at one of the many interesting eateries lining Sala-manca Place, immediately south of the city cen-ter. One of the most unusual places is **Mr Wooby's,** behind 65 Salamanca Place (tel. 03-6234-3466), named for an early Hobart mer-chant who late last century ran a sweets stall on the wharf. The food offered is hearty and inex-pensive (under $15 for three courses), but it's the homey atmosphere that attracts most visitors, many of whom come only to sip coffee. It's closed Sunday. The **Cove Food Hall,** 27 Sala-manca Place (tel. 03-6223-7511), with dining inside and out, has an array of delicious deli-style foods and daily specials served 7:30 a.m.-6 p.m. (until 4 p.m. on Sunday). **Tea House Restaurant,** 33 Salamanca Place (tel. 03-6224-8700), offers the cuisine of Malaysia, Singa-pore, Thailand, Indonesia, and China in a smart Oriental atmosphere. All main dishes are under $16. Open Wed.-Sun. for lunch and Tues.-Sun-day for dinner.

The first warehouse built on Salamanca Place, and still with bare sandstone walls, is now the **Ball and Chain Restaurant,** 87 Sala-manca Place (tel. 03-6223-2655). Charcoal-grilled steak for $18-20 is the specialty, but those who don't eat beef have plenty to choose from. It's open Mon.-Sat. for lunch and daily for dinner. Next door, at no. 89, is one of Salamanca Place's trendiest eateries, **Panache Cafe Restaurant** (tel. 03-6224-2929), attracting a well-dressed clients who come for freshly pre-pared pasta dishes.

Other Battery Point Restaurants

Also on Battery Point is **Tacos,** 41 Hampden Rd. (tel. 03-6223-5297), a stylish Mexican joint with authentic southern dishes at reasonable prices; most main dishes are $12-16. In an old post office a little farther along the same road is **Battery Point Brasserie,** 59 Hampden Rd. (tel. 03-6223-3186). Local game is featured heavily on the menu, and for these you pay a reasonable $12-18. It's open Mon.-Sat. 6:30 p.m.-midnight. **Da Angelo Ristorante,** 47 Hampden Rd. (tel. 03-6223-7011), has delicious pizza from $6.50 and daily blackboard pasta specials for $10-12. This place is extremely popular, both for the food and the great atmosphere, so advance bookings are necessary.

Wrest Point Hotel Casino

The casino, at 410 Sandy Bay Rd., Sandy Bay (tel. 03-6225-0112), has three eateries. The 24-hour **Coffee Shop** offers a lot more than coffee, with a daily breakfast buffet ($11.50 pp), a lunch buffet Mon.-Sat. ($16.90; $25 for Sunday brunch), and a daily dinner buffet ($25). The **Asian Restaurant** is open for dinner Tues.-Sat. with main meals from $13.50 and desserts from $5.50. Atop the casino tower is **The Point Revolving Restaurant,** offering 360-degree views of Hobart and surrounds from every table (a full revolution takes one hour). At lunch, appetizers are all $7, main meals $14, and desserts $5. Dinner is more formal, with a set four-course meal for $47.50—or choose from the a la carte menu where main seafood and local game dishes range $23-30. On Sunday, a buffet breakfast is offered for $14.95 pp.

Moorilla Estate Restaurant and Winery

On the Derwent River nine km north of downtown, this complex comprises a winetasting room and restaurant. The restaurant, open for lunch daily noon-2:30 p.m., has seating indoors and out (most tables have views of the vineyard) and a menu that changes with the season. Appetizers are $4-6 and main meals range $14-17. Try the Grapepickers Lunch, a sample of many local produces, for $18.50. Tasting the latest wine releases costs $5, which includes a sampling of Tasmanian cheeses. Open daily 9 a.m.-5 p.m. It's at 655 Main Rd., Berriedale (tel. 03-6249-2949).

TRANSPORTATION

Getting to Hobart from mainland Australia means flying with **Ansett Australia** (tel. 13 1300) or **Qantas** (tel. 13-1313) or taking the ferry *Spirit of Tasmania* (tel. 13-2010) across Bass Strait and connecting with an across-island bus service. For details on all the above services, as well as air and bus service throughout the state, see "Transportation" under "Introduction," above.

Air

Hobart Airport is on the Tasman Hwy. 19 km northeast of downtown. Within the main terminal is a cafe, information boards, Ansett Australia and Qantas reservation desks, and Avis, Budget, and Thrifty car rental desks. Tasmanian Redline Coaches (tel. 03-6231-3233) operates an **airport shuttle** that meets all incoming flights and leaves the city one hour prior to most departures. The fare is $6.50 each way. A cab between the airport and downtown runs about $20. Parking at the airport is a reasonable $5 per day.

Sample airfares from Hobart are: Melbourne ($224 one-way), Sydney ($260), and Brisbane ($340), but both Ansett Australia and Qantas offer cheaper fares for advanced bookings and airfare and accommodation packages from as little as $300.

From Hobart by Coach

Hobart Transit Centre, at 199 Collins St., is the terminus of all buses operated by **Tasmanian Redline Coaches** (tel. 03-6231-3233). This company offers scheduled services throughout the state, sightseeing tours, and an airport shuttle. The terminal is also used by the **Convict Country Bus Service** (tel. 03-6234-4567), departing weekdays at 7:40 a.m. for Port Arthur. The other major carrier, with services to all major national parks and most tourist centers, is **Tasmanian Wilderness Transport** (tel. 03-6334-4442 or 1800-03-0620), with departures from 4 Liverpool Street.

Getting Around Hobart by Bus

City buses go just about everywhere throughout the city; services to suburbs in the south and west depart from Franklin Square while those to the north and east depart from Hobart Bus Station at the corner of Macquarie and Elizabeth Streets. Fares are $1.30 per ride or $10 for an all-day ticket. For all public bus information, head to the **Metro Shop,** in the Hobart Bus Station (tel. 03-6233-4232). It's open Mon.-Fri. 8 a.m.-5:15 p.m., Saturday 8:30 a.m.-12:30 p.m.

Taxi

Hobart's two main cab companies are **Taxi Combined Services** (tel. 13-2227) and **City Cabs** (tel. 13-1008). A cab anywhere around downtown is under $5; from downtown to the casino will run about $6, and to the airport is about $20.

Car Rental

All major car rental companies have offices in Hobart, including **Avis** (tel. 1800-22-5533), **Budget** (tel. 13-2727), **Hertz** (tel. 13-3039), and **Thrifty** (tel. 1800-65-2008). There's lots of competition for business, with vouchers in many tourist brochures, standby rates, and lots of drop-off locations. Independent agencies will offer better rates, but cars are often older models. These agencies include **Advance** (tel. 03-6224-0822), **Bargain Car Rentals** (tel. 03-6234-6959), **Metro Auto Rentals** (tel. 03-6234-3717), and **U-Drive Tasmania** (tel. 03-6231-1077).

City Tours

Half-day tours of the city and to the summit of Mt. Wellington are offered by **Hobart Sightseeing Tours** (tel. 03-6231-3511); adult $23, child $15. Similarly priced are tours offered by **Hobart Coaches** (tel. 03-6234-4077).

SERVICES

The **general post office** is right in the heart of downtown on the corner of Elizabeth and Macquarie Streets. Traveler's checks can be cashed at banks and most major hotels; for checks not in Australian currency a fee or commission will be charged. Automatic teller machines are located at most Hobart banks, but once you're outside the capital these machines become few and far between, so plan ahead.

Most central of Hobart's laundromats is **Westside Laundromat,** on the corner of Goulburn and Molle Streets; open daily.

Emergency Services

For medical emergencies call 000 or one of the following hospitals: **Royal Hobart Hospital,** 48 Liverpool St. (tel. 03-6238-8308), or **St. Helen's Private Hospital,** 186 Macquarie St. (tel. 03-6221-6444).

INFORMATION

The **State Library of Tasmania** is at 91 Murray St. (tel. 03-6233-8011). One whole section is devoted to "Tasmaniana." The library is open Mon.-Fri. 9:30 a.m.-5 p.m. For a large selection of books, including many Australian travel guides, head to **Angus and Robertson,** 98 Collins St. (tel. 03-6234-4288). The **Commonwealth Government Bookshop** is at 31 Criterion St., opposite YHA Tasmania (tel. 03-6234-1403). Another good spot for Tasmanian literature is the **Wilderness Society Shop** at 33 Salamanca Place (tel. 03-6234-9370).

The **Tasmanian Travel and Information Centre,** at 20 Davey St. (tel. 03-6230-8233), provides information on the city as well as the rest of the state. Staff can make transportation and accommodation bookings throughout Tasmania. It's open Mon.-Fri. 8:30 a.m.-5:15 p.m., Sat.-Sun. 9 a.m.-4 p.m.

The **Land Information Bureau,** operated by the Department of Environment and Land Management, caretaker of Tasmania's parks, is at 134 Macquarie St. (tel. 03-6233-8011).

SOUTH FROM HOBART

Before setting out north from Hobart to Port Arthur and the famous national parks, consider spending a day or two exploring the rugged landscape south of the capital, driving through the apple orchards of the Huon Valley to Cockle Creek, gateway to the vast wilderness of Southwest National Park, or traveling by ferry over to Bruny Island, a sparsely populated island with ample opportunities for exploration.

Kingston

The most direct route south from Hobart is the Huon Highway, but if you're heading out to Bruny Island take the Channel Highway through Kingston to Kettering. The highlight of Kingston is the headquarters of the **Australia Antarctic Division**, on the Channel Hwy. (tel. 03-6232-3209). This center is the base for Australian expeditions heading to Antarctica and provides support services for field stations. Within the complex, a display room open to the public features the history of Australian involvement in Antarctica through photos, maps, and relics. Admission is free and it's open daily 9 a.m.-5 p.m.

BRUNY ISLAND

Lying off the coast immediately south of Hobart, and separated from the mainland by D'Entrecasteaux Channel, this elongated island is almost cut in two by a long isthmus of sand. The island's two halves are very different. In the north, where the passenger-and-vehicle ferry from Kettering docks, the landscape is relatively flat, while in the south the terrain is hilly and almost mountainous with long stretches of beach and rugged headlands along the coast. In 1642 Abel Tasman became the first European to record the island, but it wasn't until 1792, when French Admiral Bruny D'Entrecasteaux charted Tasmania's southwest coast, that it was named. Today, the island's main drawcards are long stretches of golden sand, opportunities for hiking along the beaches and headlands, and abundant birdlife.

Island Sights

Heading south from the ferry terminal, the island's main road passes **Camel Tracks** (tel. 03-6260-6335), which offers camel rides (except Friday) out to Big Lagoon ($22 pp) and along the beach ($38). From Great Bay, the road south traverses a narrow isthmus and **Bruny Island Neck Game Reserve.** Within the reserve is a platform to view the prolific birdlife, including muttonbirds (Sept.-April) and fairy penguins (Sept.-February). Beyond the isthmus are the island's two main communities, **Alonnah** and **Lunawanna.** From Lunawanna, an unsealed road continues south to **Labillardiere State Reserve,** on Great Taylors Bay, where there are a number of short walks. Facing the wild Tasman Sea, on the southern shore of Adventure Bay, is the **Bligh Museum** (tel. 03-6293-1117), named for Captain Bligh of *Bounty* fame, who visited the island in the 1788. Constructed of bricks salvaged from a nearby convict-built church, this small museum catalogs the island's history. Admission is $2.50. Open daily except Wednesday 10 a.m.-3 p.m.

Accommodations

At Dennes Point on the island's northern tip is **House Sofia,** Nebraska Rd. (tel. 03-6260-6277), a rambling old house offering beds in various configurations for $40 pp, which includes three delicious meals served in a spacious timber dining room. Book well in advance. At the southern end of Adventure Bay are two caravan parks. Best of these is **Adventure Bay Caravan Park** (tel. 03-6293-1270), with sites for $10-13 and on-site vans and cabins for $30-40. Camping is also possible at Neck Beach, on the isthmus, and in the south at Cloudy Bay and Jetty Beach.

Transportation, Services, and Information

Ferries to Bruny Island depart Kettering nine times daily between 7:15 a.m. and 6:30 p.m. The crossing takes 10-15 minutes. The fare for a vehicle under five meters is $18 round-trip ($23 on Friday afternoon, Saturday, Sunday, and all public holidays). Bicycles are $3 round rip. Foot passengers travel free of charge. For more information call Bruny Island Ferry Service at (03) 6233-5313.

Before heading over to Bruny Island, visit Bruny D'Entrecasteaux Visitor Centre in Kettering (tel. 03-6267-4494) and pick up a copy of the *Bruny Island* brochure ($2). Open Mon.-Sat. 9 a.m.-5 p.m. In Hobart, visit the Land Information Bureau at 134 Macquarie St. (tel. 03-6233-3011) for information on island reserves.

HUON VALLEY TO THE END OF THE ROAD

The lush Huon Valley, south of Hobart, is dominated by apple orchards. To find out more about the industry, stop by the **Huon Valley Apple and Heritage Museum,** near Grove (tel. 03-6266-4345), which displays 500 different types of apples—all grown in a nearby orchard—along with an antique apple corer and peeler, apple-picking equipment and graders, and other apple-growing memorabilia. Admission is adult $3, child $1.50. Open daily 9 a.m.-5 p.m. (closed July).

Huonville

This picturesque town (pop. 1,600) on the Huon River 48 km south of Hobart is the hub of the Huon Valley. The river, discovered by Bruny D'Entrecasteaux in 1792, was to provide easy access to the valley, which was blessed with large supplies of Huon pine, a softwood good for construction. The most popular form of recreation in Huonville is the 40-minute jet-boat ride with **Huon River Jet Boats** (tel. 03-6264-1838), which runs over four sets of exciting rapids; adult $34, child $18. A place you may, or may not, want to visit is **German Train World,** 183 Main Rd. (tel. 03-6264-2116), featuring around 30 working scale models of German trains that run through a model of typical German countryside. Admission adult $4, child $2. Open in summer 9:30 a.m.-4 p.m., shorter hours the rest of the year.

Accommodation in Huonville is limited to the ugly **Grand Hotel** right downtown at 2 Main Rd. (tel. 03-6264-1004), where rooms with shared facilities are $25 s, $35 d, and **Budget Holiday Villas,** 183 Main Rd. (tel. 03-6264-1847), where the two self-contained units are $65 each. A

much better option is **Franklin Lodge,** a few km south of town (tel. 03-6266-3506). This two-story colonial-era guesthouse features rooms of the highest standard for $75 s, $90 d, including a continental breakfast.

With river views, **Huon Manor Bistro,** corner of Main Rd. and Short St. (tel. 03-6264-1311), is one of the better places in town for a meal. The menu is varied and wine can be ordered by the glass. At lunch, when eating at the outdoor tables is popular, main meals start at $6.50, while in the evening they range $11-16.50. Closed Sunday and Monday.

Geeveston

South of Huonville is Geeveston, center of a large timber industry and gateway to the rugged Hartz Mountains to the west. A highlight of a visit to town is the **Esperance Forest and Heritage Centre,** on Church St. (tel. 03-6297-1836). Displays incorporate the entire history of southwestern Tasmania's forestry through to modern management techniques. Admission is adult $4, child $2. In the same complex is an information center (with maps of surrounding forest drives) and an arts and crafts outlet. Hiking trails leading from the information center take you through various forest environments and to a lookout high above the rainforest canopy. Open daily 10 a.m.-4 p.m.

Queens Inn Teahouse, Church St. (tel. 03-6297-1834), offers a range of delicious meals in a delightful atmosphere; on colder days the staff will stoke the fireplace. Open daily 10 a.m.-5 p.m.

Hartz Mountains National Park

Making up only a tiny portion of the Tasmanian Wilderness World Heritage Area, and adjacent to the vast wilderness of Southwest National Park, this small 7,226-hectare park 25 km west of Geeveston boasts many good hikes and, unlike most of the World Heritage Area, is easily accessible. The park's rugged landscape was carved by glaciers, with extremes in weather finishing the job. The rugged snowcapped peaks rise above deep gorges and plateaus of alpine heathland. Within the park are short but strenuous hikes, the most spectacular ending atop mountain ridges. All hiking trails are well defined and geographical features signposted. The most popular trail leads to the 1,255-meter summit of **Hartz**

Peak. From the trailhead to the summit takes about two hours each way, but there are many tempting detours to be made, including to **Lakes Esperance, Osborne,** and **Hartz.**

The park's only facility area is at **Waratah Lookout,** where there are picnic facilities. The park has no campground. For further information, contact the Land Information Bureau in Hobart at (03) 6233-8011.

Dover

The small port of Dover, on the Huon Hwy. 25 km south of Geeveston, developed around the logging of Huon pine, which was processed in town, then transported to East Asian and European markets. Today, the town's main industry is the farming of Atlantic salmon.

As Dover is a popular tourist spot, there are a number of accommodations. Pick of the bunch is **Driftwood Cottages,** Bay View Rd. (tel. 03-6298-1441), with outstanding views of Esperance Bay. The units are modern, each featuring interior furnishings in a different native timber. Rates are $80 s, $98 d. On Main Rd., and also overlooking Esperance Bay, is **Dover Hotel** (tel. 03-6298-1210). Rooms are basic, and many share bathrooms, but the location is right and within the complex is a bar and restaurant. Rates start at $22 pp, with breakfast included $30. Another inexpensive option is **White Cliffs Backpacker Hostel,** Bay View Rd. (tel. 03-6298-1180), a large place with panoramic water views. Facilities include a lounge and game room, communal kitchen, and laundry. Double rooms are $36 and dorm beds are $13 pp. **Dover Beachside Caravan Park** (tel. 03-6298-1301) has an absolute waterfront location and a good grassed area set aside for tent campers. Sites range $8-10 and on-site vans are $28.

Hastings Caves and Vicinity

South of Dover and 10 km west of the Huon Highway is Hastings Caves State Reserve (tel. 03-6298-3209), which protects a number of caves including the magnificent **Newdegate Cave,** alive with formations that have evolved

through thousands of years of water seeping through the dolomite bedrock. Tours of this cave (45 minutes) are offered four to six times daily adult $8, child $4.

On the road leading to the caves are thermal springs that bubble out of the ground a about 28° C (82° F). A pool area has been developed around them. Admission is adult $6 child $1.50. The pool is open Oct.-March daily 9 a.m.-6 p.m. and April-Sept. daily 9 a.m.-5 p.m.

Continuing South

Beyond **Southport** the road turns to gravel and makes a detour around Southport Bay to Lune River and ends 30 km farther south at Cockle Creek, Australia's southernmost point accessible by vehicle.

The 16-km **Ida Bay Railway** (tel. 03-6298-3110) departs Lune River in summer daily at 10:30 a.m., noon, 1:30 p.m., and 3 p.m. (Sunday only the rest of the year) for Deep Hole Bay and a delightful little beach. The round-trip fare is adult $10, child $5. Immediately south of town is **Lune River Cottage** (tel. 03-6298-3107), offering comfortable accommodations in five rooms; $30 s, $56 d, includes breakfast. Lune River also has a YHA hostel (tel. 03-6298-3163), but it's a bit rough around the edges. Camping free of charge is possible at **Gilliams** and **Finns Beaches,** farther south.

Walking opportunities present themselves at Cockle Creek. One of the shorter trails leads to Fishers Point, northeast of Cockle Creek and an easy 40-minute walk from the end of the road. Hiking along the final section of the 170-km South West Track is also rewarding, with the first section, to South Cape Bay (seven km one-way), taking about two hours.

Southwest National Park

The massive wilderness protected by this 605,000-hectare park is accessible on foot from Cockle Creek or by road west from Hobart. For further information on the park see "Southwest National Park" under "Southwestern Tasmania," below.

TASMANIA'S EAST COAST AND THE MIDLANDS

Tasmania's east coast is blessed with some of the state's best beaches, but before rushing north for swimming and sunbaking, plan to make a detour to Tasmania's most-visited attraction, Port Arthur, on the Tasman Peninsula, site of a penal colony built to contain convicts who had re-offended upon arriving in Australia. The road north from the Tasman Peninsula makes a wide loop inland before passing offshore Maria Island, also formerly penal settlement. One of Tasmania's premier natural features is the Freycinet Peninsula, protected as a national park and accessible only on foot. North of the peninsula is a string of seaside resort towns, including Bicheno, and a great inland wilderness. For those with limited time, the inland route between Hobart and Launceston, through the midlands, is interesting for some of Tasmania's best-preserved historic towns.

HOBART TO PORT ARTHUR

The main highway along the east coast, the Tasman Highway, begins in downtown Hobart, crosses the Tasman Bridge and continues past the airport to a long causeway spanning the wide mouth of the Coal River. The causeway, built in 1866, shortened the trip along the coast considerably, cutting out a long inland detour through Richmond. At the end of the causeway is **Sorell,** an agricultural service center of 3,000. From Sorell, it's 42 km along the Arthur Highway to Dunalley, gateway to the Forestier and Tasman Peninsulas. An alternate route east follows the coastline of Frederick Henry Bay through Dodges Ferry and along the mouth of the Carlton River. A side road over the river leads eight km to **Primrose Sands Coastal Reserve.** From the top of the protected dune system, the panorama extends along a magnificent beach and over Frederick Henry Bay to Green Head on the Tasman Peninsula.

Copping
If you are traveling to the Tasman Peninsula along the more direct Tasman Highway, take time to stop at the **Colonial Convict Exhibition,** in Copping, featuring an eclectic collection of convict-era relics, much of it from the Tasman Peninsula. Admission $6. Open daily 9 a.m.-5 p.m.

Forestier Peninsula
This wide peninsula is more like an island, joined to the mainland by an isthmus at Dunalley. The Tasman Highway runs across the peninsula, under the shadow of 319-meter Mt. Forestier, and over **Eaglehawk Neck,** a narrow isthmus linking the peninsula to Tasman Peninsula. The seaward side of this link is the long curve of **Pirates Bay.** At the bay's northern end is the **Tessellated Pavement,** a stretch of vertically cracked sandstone beds that have further eroded to form an intriguing natural mosaic. Search out the abundant marinelife in adjacent rock pools at low tide. **Eaglehawk Neck Backpackers** (tel. 03-6250-3248) is a great little place featuring two cabins, each with a kitchen and living room. The friendly owners are a great source of information on outdoor recreation in the region. Beds are $13 pp per night, or you can pitch a tent for $4 pp.

Pirates Bay to Port Arthur
Over the narrow bridge linking the two peninsulas a road spurs southeast to a number of natural geologic formations, the result of relentless wave action into the soft sandstone. From north to south, they are: **Tasman Blowhole, Tasman Arch,** and **Devil's Kitchen.**

The first town beyond Eaglehawk Neck is **Taranna,** terminus of Australia's first railway. The railway was built to transport convicts and supplies across the peninsula to Port Arthur, saving a hazardous journey by ship around the coast. **Tasmanian Devil Park** (tel. 03-6250-

TASMAN PENINSULA

TO SORELL AND HOBART

ARTHUR HWY

RIVER

WIELANGTA FOREST DRIVE

TO TRIABUNNA

COPPING

CARLTON

DODGES FERRY

PRIMROSE SANDS COASTAL RESERVE

DUNALLEY

FREDERICK

MT. FORESTIER (319 m)

FORESTIER

HENRY

GREEN HEAD

LIME BAY

BAY

PENINSULA

ABEL TASMAN

FOREST

COAL MINES HISTORIC SITE

ARTHUR HWY

RESERVE

SALTWATER RIVER

EAGLEHAWK NECK

TESSELLATED PAVEMENT

PIRATES BAY

TASMAN BLOWHOLE

TASMAN ARCH

DEVIL'S KITCHEN

ABEL TASMAN

TARANNA

FOREST

ROARING BEACH

TASMAN

NUBEENA

RESERVE

PENINSULA

FORTESCUE BAY

WHITE BEACH

CAPE HAUY

PORT ARTHUR

CAPE PILLAR

PALMERS LOOKOUT

STATE

CAPE RAOUL STATE RESERVE

REMARKABLE CAVE

RESERVE

0   10 km

MOON

CAPE PILLAR

MAINGON BAY

TASMAN ISLAND

CAPE RAOUL

230), on the site of an old Aboriginal camp site, features Tasmanian animals, including the park's namesake, kangaroos, wallabies, and wombats, and a variety of birds. Admission is a bit steep at adult $8, child 4, especially if you miss feeding time (daily 10 and 11 a.m.). Open daily a.m.-5 p.m. **Norfolk Bay Convict Station** (tel. 03-6250-3487) is a historic building now operating as a B&B. It's right on the waterfront, with a private jetty and wide veranda. Rates are $70 s, $100 d.

Port Arthur penal settlement

PORT ARTHUR

While the grounds of Port Arthur are now quiet, between 1830 and 1877 this penal settlement was one of the country's most-feared places. Since its closure, time has taken its toll on the convict-built stone-and-timber structures, with only 30 of about 260 buildings remaining. But, instead of an air of desolation and hopelessness that the convicts must of felt, the crumbling stone walls rising from neatly trimmed grass and a backdrop of a picturesque bay give the place an intriguing feel of peacefulness.

History

In 1830, with overcrowding in Hobart Town a serious problem, Governor Arthur chose to send the worst convicts to the Tasman Peninsula, where escape was nearly impossible. To keep would-be escapees on the peninsula a pack of savage dogs was placed across the isthmus of land at Eaglehawk Neck, and rumors circulated about surrounding shark-infested waters. Port Arthur grew to become the British Empire's largest prison, but it evolved into more than a holding yard for wayward souls. At one time 43 various trades were operating in the bustling colony, making Port Arthur almost self-sufficient. A telegraph system allowed almost-instant communications with Hobart.

In 1853, after transport to Australia ceased, only convicts from within Australia were sent to Port Arthur. Over the following years, many inmates received either pardons, allowing them to become free settlers, or tickets of leave, allowing them to work for a wage. As the years wore on, remaining Port Arthur convicts reached their twilight years and, in 1877, Port Arthur closed. In the following years, when the peninsula opened up to free settlers, bushfires all

Port Arthur

A CONVICT'S LIFE AT PORT ARTHUR

In the half-century that Port Arthur served as a penal settlement about 12,500 of Australia's worst convicts served time at the prison. Those sent to Port Arthur were generally hardened criminals who had re-offended upon arriving in Australia. The worst of these convicts spent their days in chains, building stone structures and roads. Until 1848, those who offended *again* were subjected to a flogging. These took place on Sunday, after a compulsory church service, and with the other convicts watching.

After flogging was abolished in 1848 a new form of punishment was devised: solitary confinement in the Model Prison. Convicts feared it more than a good flogging. Upon being sent to the Model Prison convicts were stripped of their identity, their name replaced by a number. They were confined to a tiny cell 23 hours of every day, permitted one hour of exercise daily in the confines of a walled yard while wearing a head mask, banned from talking, and fed a diet of bread and water.

but destroyed the town and convict ruins. To rid the peninsula of its convict stigma the old settlement was renamed Carnarvon, but as the need to preserve the country's convict past overtook any desire to cover up an unsavory history, restoration began and its former name was reinstated. Port Arthur is now Tasmania's most popular attraction.

Visiting the Site

Spread over 40 hectares that slope gently to Mason Cove, Port Arthur is visited by about 200,000 visitors annually (more than half Tasmania's total number of visitors), many whom visit on an organized day trip from Hobart. Upon arrival, the first stop should be the Information Office (tel. 03-6250-2363), at the end of the park access road. Before exploring the grounds, it's a good idea to view the audiovisual presented regularly in the Asylum, built for the mentally ill in 1867 and now also containing a museum. Take one of the guided tours (free with admission) that depart regularly through the day or wander around at your own pace

with one of the many information sheets avai able. Admission is adult $12.50, senior $1C child $6. The site is open daily 9 a.m.-5 p.m After hours, no admission is charged, but there is no access to the many buildings ope through daylight hours. Within the grounds ar cafes and restaurants as well as souveni shops and a couple of outlets selling the work of local artisans.

Isle of the Dead, a small offshore island, wa the burial grounds for convicts and free settlers c Port Arthur. Cruises out to the island depart the wharf immediately east of the Information Office daily at noon and 4:30 p.m. Cost is $5 pp.

After Dark Entertainment

Not all the action at Port Arthur takes place dur ing the hours of daylight. In the years since the penal colony closed, many ghostly apparition. have been reported around the grounds. His toric Ghost Tours, departing nightly at 8:3 p.m. (9:30 p.m. during daylight saving) from th Information Office, allow you the opportunity to maybe, view the apparitions. Adult $7.50, chil $3.50. Make bookings at the Information Office or by calling (03) 6250-2539.

Another form of entertainment is to view the original version of *For the Term of his Natura Life,* based on convict life at Port Arthur. The film is screened nightly in the Broad Arrow Tea House, on the historic site (tel. 03-6250-2242) Admission is $5. The film is also screened on in house televisions for guests of the Port Arthu Motor Inn.

Accommodations

Port Arthur is an easy day trip from Hobart, bu the Tasman Peninsula has enough attractions to keep you busy for two or even three days. A few peninsula townships have accommoda tions, and right at Port Arthur there are a couple of choices. Closest to the historic site is Por Arthur Motor Inn, overlooking the site (tel. 03-6250-2101). Rooms are pricey, at $80 s, $9C d, but comfortable, and there's a restaurant.

The grandly named Port Arthur Holiday World, about 700 meters from the historic site (tel. 03-6250-2262), overlooks delightful Stewarts Bay. Accommodations are in attractive self-contained log cabins scattered through native bush. Rates are a reasonable $90-140 per night depending on cabin size. These cabins are a reat deal and therefore advance reservations ill be needed. **Fox & Hounds Resort,** two km orth of Port Arthur (tel. 03-6250-2217), has otel rooms from $80 and self-contained villas ith cooking facilities for $110.

On the same road as Port Arthur Motor Inn, nd overlooking the historic site, is **Port Arthur 'HA Hostel** (tel. 03-6250-2311), a mustard- olored two-story historic building complete with reaking hallways and steep stairwells leading to ark rooms. Rates are $12 pp.

The expansive **Port Arthur Caravan and :abin Park** is out on Garden Pt., two km from 'ort Arthur (tel. 03-6250-2340). The park is well naintained, and facilities, including two kitchens, arbecues, kiosk, and laundry, are excellent. ent sites are $11, powered sites $12 ($18 with rivate bathroom), and cabins $50. Also offered re dorm beds for $13 pp. A coastal walking 'ack links the campground to Port Arthur His- oric Site; 40 minutes each way.

Food

Vithin the historic site are a number of eateries, ncluding **Frances Langford Tearooms,** in a tone structure built originally as policemen's ving quarters. Light lunches and Devonshire eas are served daily 10 a.m.-5 p.m. **Kelley's,** at 'ort Arthur Holiday World (tel. 03-6250-2666), is n a spectacular log building with seating in- loors or out on a covered deck. Tasmanian eafood is the specialty, with main dishes start- ng at $17, which includes salad, chips, and reshly baked bread. The restaurant in the **Port Arthur Motor Inn** (tel. 03-6250-2101) has ex- ansive views across the historic site and a typ- cal motel restaurant-style menu, and is priced accordingly. Dinner plates average $16.

Transportation

The only way to visit Port Arthur from Hobart and return the same day is on an organized our. The best of these are run by **Hobart Sight- seeing Tours** (tel. 03-6231-3511) and **Gray- ine** (tel. 03-6234-4077). Tours cost $33-49 de- ending on inclusions, and pick-ups at Hobart accommodations are complimentary. **Hobart :oaches** (tel. 03-6234-4077) runs once a day Mon.-Fri. between Hobart and Port Arthur; $11 each way. **Peninsula Coach Service** (tel. 03- 5250-3186) runs from the Hobart Transit Centre

to Port Arthur and also makes drops at the hos- tel; $9 each way. **Convict Country Bus Service** transports passengers and mail between Ho- bart and Port Arthur. Buses depart the Tas- manian Redline Coaches depot in Hobart at Mon.-Fri. at 7:40 a.m.; $9 each way. Book at (03) 6234-4567.

OTHER SIGHTS ON THE TASMAN PENINSULA

Fortescue Bay and Vicinity

This deep coastal indent lies on the east coast of an arm of the Tasman Peninsula 20 km east of Port Arthur. It's a beautiful place: clear water lap- ping against a beach of golden sand and backed by towering eucalypts. A campground lies in the bay's protected southern corner; cost is $6 pp, which includes one wheelbarrow filled with fire- wood. **Cape Hauy** is a pleasant walk from the campground; allow two hours each way. South of the bay is **Cape Pillar State Reserve,** a tract of wilderness reached only on foot. The track out to Cape Pillar is 16 km each way, too far to return in one day, but perfect for an overnight hike.

Remarkable Cave

South from Port Arthur, the main road passes a golf course, then skirts the shore of Safety Bay before cutting across a narrow neck of land to scenic Basket Bay, where sheer cliffs drop into the ocean. A steep path leads down to sea level where at low tide Remarkable Cave is exposed. From the road into the cave, a two-km side road leads to **Palmers Lookout,** comprising well- manicured gardens and a barbecue area. Views from the lookout extend to Port Arthur, the Isle of the Dead, and across Maingon Bay to Tasman Island Lighthouse.

Port Arthur to Saltwater River

From Port Arthur, the road westbound cuts across a wide section of the peninsula to **Nubeena.** Coastal access is possible along hik- ing trails in **Cape Raoul State Reserve** and at **White Beach,** where there's a caravan park (tel. 03-6250-2142) fronting a nice sandy beach. Beyond Nubeena a gravel road leads to **Roar- ing Beach,** a windswept stretch of sand that catches all the swell.

When Port Arthur was a penal colony many other convict outposts were scattered around the Tasman Peninsula. The most important of these was beyond Saltwater River at Plunkett Point, where coal was discovered in 1833. It's now preserved as 214-hectare **Coal Mines Historic Site.** In typical colonial fashion, when a coal deposit was discovered, Governor Arthur requested that a convict with coal-mining experience examine the site for its mining potential. Deeming it good, gangs of convicts were sent to begin mining. At peak production, around 50 tons of coal were excavated daily and loaded directly onto ships bound for Hobart Town. Like Port Arthur, fire and vandalism have taken their toll on the site.

At **Lime Bay,** beyond the mining area, is a pleasant campground set behind a sandy beach and among boulders and trees.

TASMAN PENINSULA TO TRIABUNNA

To continue north from the Tasman Peninsula along sealed road entails a detour inland, back through Sorell. The alternative is **Wielangta Forest Drive,** a winding gravel road spurring off the main highway west of Copping. First stop should be the **Wielangta Forest,** where a one-km (round-trip) trail leads through a forest of towering eucalypts. The trailhead is south of Robertson Bridge, one of the state's longest log bridges. As the road climbs from the forest, the panorama of the coastline and offshore Maria Island come into view. After crossing Sandspit River, the road forks. Take the eastern option, which parallels the coast and passes access tracks to numerous beaches. **Spring Beach** is particularly scenic and is a popular surfing spot.

Triabunna

On the far reaches of Spring Bay, this small village was established in the 1800s as a mainland base for shipping supplies and convicts to offshore Maria Island (see below), and is today home to a small fleet of cray, abalone, and scallop boats. On the town's main street is the **Pioneer and Working Horse Museum,** 5 Vicary St. (tel. 03-6257-3197), with interesting displays

and many working relics from Tasmania's pas? Admission is $4 and it's open daily 9 a.m.-5 p.m

Surrounded by pastureland, **Triabunna YH Hostel,** Spencer St. (tel. 03-6257-3439), acros? Maclaines Creek from the center of town, is pic turesque. Facilities are basic but comfortable Dorm beds are $9 pp. **Tandara Motor Inn,** o the north side of town (tel. 03-6257-3333), has pool, barbecue, and laundry; $50 s, $55 d.

MARIA ISLAND NATIONAL PARK

This hourglass-shaped island, 15 km east of the mainland, is protected as national park. Th island is much altered from its original state an has seen a tumultuous history, but, still, it re mains an excellent destination ideal for explo ration on foot. The island can be visited as a day trip or an overnight excursion for those pre pared to camp or stay in rustic dorm-style ac commodations. Transport to the island is on a ferry (foot passengers only) that departs regu larly from south of Triabunna.

The island is 20 km from north to south and about 13 km at its widest point. A narrow isthmus of sand, pushed above sea level by wind an wave action, is the island's most interesting nat ural feature. This narrow strip of sand links wha around 10,000 years ago would have been two separate islands, which in turn were part o mainland Tasmania many millions of years ago

While some species of larger mammals such as wombats, echidnas, and pademelons are native to the island, others such as the Foreste kangaroo and Bennett's wallaby were intro duced in the 1960s when the island was firs declared a wildlife reserve. Maria Island is good for birdwatching enthusiasts; some of the more interesting species present include the alba tross, gannet, muttonbird, and Japanese snipe Like the mammal population, some bird species have been introduced, including the Cape Bar ren goose, first introduced to the island in 1968

History

Maria Island was the site of Tasmania's sec ond penal colony, established in 1825 at Dar lington, on a bay in the northwest. The settle ment was short-lived, closing seven years later then reopening for a few years in the 1840s. In

convict-built barn, Maria Island

884 Italian entrepreneur Diego Bernacchi arrived on the island, setting up winegrowing and silk industries. He renovated many of the deserted convict buildings, and with grand expectations renamed the settlement San Diego. Business for Bernacchi started well enough, but by the end of the century he left the island, returning after WW I to use the island's abundant limestone deposits to establish a cement works. A wildlife reserve was first established in the 1960s, and in 1972 the entire 9,672-hectare island was declared a national park.

Buildings from the convict era remain in varying states of disrepair, some having been restored as accommodations and to serve park staff. Historic Tours, operated by park staff, depart the Commissariat Store daily at 2 p.m. (pre-register before 1:45 p.m.).

Hiking
The island offers many hiking opportunities, and those staying on the island overnight have the chance to explore farther afield. One of the most popular short hikes is to the **Fossil Cliffs** (two km each way), where hundreds of ancient shell fragments are embedded in a cliff face. A hike of a similar distance is to the **Painted Cliffs,** a sandstone headland sharply eroded and covered in colorful patterns left by iron and magnesium oxides.

Beyond the Fossil Cliffs, a moderately steep trail continues a farther steep two km to the summit of **Bishop and Clerk Mountain,** at the north end of a high ridge. From this peak, views extend north to the Freycinet Peninsula. Farther south along this ridge is the island's highest peak, **Mt. Maria** (709 meters). From Darlington, this peak is eight km each way (allow five to six hours for the round-trip), with the final ascent up a scree slope. The walk to the sandy isthmus is 12 km each way, making the return trip to Darlington a long day hike. At the isthmus are two campgrounds; these provide a good base for exploring the island's southern reaches.

Accommodations
Accommodation on the island is in convict-built structures converted to bunkhouses. These are often booked out by groups, so call ahead to reserve a bed. Bunk beds are $8 pp per night and private rooms range $20-40. All rooms are sparse; you must bring your own linen or sleeping bag, lantern or flashlight (no electricity), and cooking utensils and camp stove. A nearby campground has toilets, fresh water, and gas barbecues (bring change for these); sites are $3 pp. No supplies are available on the island. For all bookings and further information call the park ranger at (03) 6257-1420.

If you'd prefer to stay on the mainland, visiting the island for just the day, consider staying at **Eastcoaster Resort** (tel. 03-6257-1172), right at the ferry terminal. This large holiday resort features indoor and outdoor pools, a tennis court, squash, golf, spa and sauna, bar, and restaurant. Standard rooms, each with a kitchen and comfortable furnishings, are $90 s or d (less in the off season).

Transportation, Services, and Information
The 15-km crossing of the Mercury Passage takes about 20 minutes aboard the *Eastcoaster*

Express (tel. 03-6257-1589), operated by the Eastcoaster Resort. The fare is adult $16 round-trip ($19 with camping gear), kids $10. A bike or kayak is an additional $3. Departure times vary with the season and weather conditions, but there are generally at least four sailings daily; call ahead for details of the current timetable.

Built in 1825, the sturdy **Commissariat Store** now serves as a **park information center.** The center features a large relief map of the island and a photography display of island highlights. Between December and Easter the center is open daily 9:30 a.m.-4:30 p.m. At other times of the year, it's open weekends only. To contact the ranger call (03) 6257-1420.

SWANSEA

The small town of Swansea (pop. 500) over-looks the protected waters of Great Oyster Bay 140 km north of Hobart. It's along a stretch of coast popular with holidaymakers. The area was first settled in 1821, and Swansea grew as a rural service center. The oldest remaining build-ing in Swansea is Morris Store, built in 1834. The highlight of a visit to town is **Swansea Bark Mill,** on the Tasman Hwy. north of town (tel. 03-6257-8382). Built in 1885, the mill crushed bark to extract the tannic acid that was then used in the tanning of leather. Admission adult $5, child $2.75. Open daily 9 a.m.-5 p.m. In the same complex is Wattle Bark Wine and Wool Centre, selling wine and sheepskin products, and Miller's Pantry, open daily for lunch. A **museum** is housed in the 1860 Swansea School House, on Franklin Street. It features many relics from the town's past, but the highlight is an oversized bil-liards table dating from 1860 ($2 a game). Ad-mission to the museum is $3.

Accommodations and Food

Although Swansea has a couple of motels, a better choice would be to stay in one of the many historic accommodations. **Oyster Bay Guest House,** 10 Franklin St. (tel. 03-6257-8110), dating from 1836, is one of Swansea's oldest buildings. Guests have a choice of 10 simple but well-furnished rooms, while down-stairs there's a small guest lounge with fire-place, and a popular restaurant. Rates start at $45 s with shared facilities, and the doubl rooms, which open to a veranda and spectacu lar views, are $85. All rates include a cooke breakfast. Another good choice is two-stor **Schouten House,** 1 Waterloo Rd. (tel. 03-625 8564), which offers spacious rooms with pr vate bathrooms for $90-118 s or d, including cooked breakfast. **Central Swansea Back packers,** 20 Franklin St. (tel. 03-6257-8399 is a rambling old house that dates from 186 Views from the wide front veranda extend acros the bay, and inside there are a number of con fortable living areas. Rates start at $12 pp pe night. Also overlooking the bay is **Swanse Caravan Park and Holiday Village,** Shaw S (tel. 03-6257-8177), with a beach frontage. Fa cilities include a heated pool, lounge room kitchen, barbecue area, and laundry. Tent sites right on the beach, are $12, powered sites ar $15, and cabins range $35-60.

For its size, Swansea has a surprising numbe of eateries. One of the most popular is **Mag gie's Coffee Lounge,** on Franklin Street. Th **Old Swan Inn,** 1 Franklin St. (tel. 03-6257 8102), offers counter meals Mon.-Sat. noon- p.m. and daily 6:15-8:15 p.m. **Shy Albatros Restaurant,** in the Oyster Bay Guest House a 10 Franklin St. (tel. 03-6257-8110), is open fo dinner Tues.-Sat. nights. The menu feature mostly pasta ($8-12), with daily specials, usuall steak, chicken, and seafood dishes ($16-18.50,

FREYCINET NATIONAL PARK

This magnificent park protects an elongated penin sula that juts southward from Tasmania's eas coast. The park is undeveloped and penetrate only partway by road. This leaves the rest of th park to be explored on foot, including famou **Wineglass Bay,** a stretch of golden sand flanke by rugged peaks of granite. The park encom passes 10,100 hectares, extending the length o the peninsula from the small town of **Coles Bay** 205 km north of Hobart. In the north is the Haz ards, a steep rocky ridge. This part of the park i separated from the southern end of the peninsu la by an isthmus flanked by Wineglass Bay in th east and Hazards Beach in the west. Across th isthmus is another range of mountains, dominat ed by 620-meter **Mt. Freycinet.** Off the peninsu

FREYCINET NATIONAL PARK

's southern extremity is **Schouten Island,** also art of the park.

Around 50 million years ago massive forces eep below the earth's surface thrust sections of asmania skyward. One section was the Freyinet Peninsula. In the time that has elapsed ince, erosion has worn the mountaintops to heir present level. When sea levels rose around 0,000 years ago they cut the peninsula in two laces, creating two islands. Sand has since uilt up south of the Hazards, forming a penin-ula, but Schouten Island remains separated.

The park features diverse habitats, ranging om low shrublands in exposed areas to forests of eucalypt and profusions of orchids in pro-tected gullies. Wildlife is plentiful throughout the park, with dawn and dusk the best times for viewing resident fauna. Commonly sighted are a variety of possums, Tasmanian devils, pademel-ons, Bennett's wallabies, wombats, sugar-glid-ers, and quolls.

Sights and Hikes

The park's only access road ends at Parsons Cove, five km south of Coles Bay. This road passes a couple of beautiful spots including **Honeymoon Bay,** a sandy beach flanked by rocky headlands. The road out to Cape Tourville skirts **Sleepy Bay,** a pleasant stretch of sand with rock ledges at either end that are perfect for exploration at low tide. For the more adventur-ous, it's possible to climb 331-meter **Mt. Par-sons** in about an hour.

Freycinet's best-known feature, **Wineglass Bay,** is a popular destination with day-hikers. The hike starts with a gentle climb to a low pass of the Hazards, where the panorama of the bay unfolds in all its glory. From the lookout, the trail descends to the golden sands of the bay, perfect for a day's sunbaking and swimming. At the beach's southern end are the remains of a cutter that wrecked on the peninsula in 1885. The trek between the parking lot and Wineglass Bay takes 60-90 minutes each way. A good alternative to returning along the same route is taking the Isthmus Track from Wine-glass Bay across to Hazards Bay, returning to the parking lot on the Hazards Beach Track. The entire circuit is just over nine km; allow three hours without stops. For experienced hik-ers, it is possible to complete the **Peninsula Track** in one long day, but most will find it more comfortable to extend the trip to two days, camping at Cooks Beach. The high point of this trek is 579-meter Mt. Graham, from where views extend west across Great Oyster Bay and south to Schouten Island.

Accommodations and Food

A campground is on the park access road, and six other backcountry campgrounds are scat-tered through the park. **Freycinet Lodge** (tel. 03-6257-0101) comprises 32 comfortable cab-ins designed to blend into the environment. Guests have use of a tennis court, recreation room, and laundry. Rates start at $130 s or d, $160 with a spa bath, and include use of all facilities and the services of a naturalist who leads short interpretive hikes in the vicinity of the lodge.

Coles Bay has no motels, but **Coles Bay Caravan Park** (tel. 03-6257-0100) has backpacker beds for $14 pp and a few on-site vans for $30. Campsites here are $11-13. Also in Coles Bay is a general store selling basic groceries and camping supplies, but the only place open for regular meals is the restaurant in **Freycinet Lodge**, where main dishes range $13-22.

Transportation, Services, and Information

Getting to the park by public transport is possible but time-consuming. From Hobart, you'll need to get yourself to Bicheno aboard either a **Tasmanian Redline Coaches** or **Hobart Coaches** service, then jump aboard one of the **Bicheno Coach Services** buses (tel. 03-6357-0293), with two daily connections to Coles Bay. Between Monday and Friday this company offers transport (on demand) between Coles Bay (departs 9:40 a.m.) and the national park; $2 round-trip; book ahead. The **Swansea-Coles Bay ferry** sails daily from Swansea Jetty to Coles Bay; $9 each way, $15 round-trip. Book through Central Swansea Backpackers (tel. 03-6257-8399).

The **ranger station,** at the park entrance, is open in summer daily 8:30 a.m.-5 p.m. and the rest of the year daily 9 a.m.-noon. Park entry is $8 per vehicle. Available at the ranger station is *Freycinet Map and Notes* ($8), good for those planning extensive hiking. To contact the ranger or any of his friendly staff call (03) 6257-0107.

BICHENO

As early as 1800, sealers and whalers used the natural harbor around which Bicheno now lies as shelter from rough seas. No permanent settlement was established until 1854, when the bay was used as a port for loading coal mined nearby. In the time since, Bicheno (pop. 700) has grown to become one of Tasmania's busiest holiday towns, with tourism, along with fishing, most important to the local economy.

Sights

One of the greatest joys in Bicheno is explorin the town's natural surroundings, walking alor the waterfront south to a blowhole and to Cou lands Bay. From **Freycinet Lookout,** west town, views extend south to the high peaks Freycinet National Park. At low tide it's possibl to walk over to **Diamond Island** where a color of fairy penguins has their burrows. Back i town is the **Sea Life Centre** (tel. 03-6375-1121 with a motley collection of marinelife, includin crayfish and seahorses. Also on display is a re stored ketch. Admission is a bit steep at $ Open daily 9 a.m.-5 p.m.

Accommodations and Food

Accommodation outside of the caravan park is limited to a few motels. Pick of the bunch is th **Wintersun Motel,** 35 Gordon St. (tel. 03-637 1225), north of downtown, which has standar rooms for $35 s, $50 d. Closer to the center town is **Silver Sands Resort,** Burgess St. (te 03-6375-1266), with basic but clean and com fortable rooms, many with ocean views, for $5 s, $75 d. **Bicheno Cabin and Tourist Park,** Champ St. (tel. 03-6375-1117), is a large camp ground with sites for $10.50-12.50 and goo cabins for $65-70.

Transportation

Both **Tasmanian Redline Coaches** (tel. 03 6231-3233) and **Hobart Coaches** (tel. 03-6234 4077) have one service a day between Hoba and Bicheno ($18.80 each way) Mon.-Fri. only Redline has a service between Bicheno an Launceston via Campbell Town for $19.10.

NORTH FROM BICHENO

Douglas-Apsley National Park

North of Bicheno the Tasman Highway closel follows the coastline, with 16,080-hectare Doug las-Apsley National Park, a vast tract of undis turbed forest, west of the highway. The par only came into being in 1989, and hiking an camping facilities are limited. The park is name for two main watersheds that rise in the wes of the park, flowing eastward through dee gorges where pockets of rainforest thrive. Ac cess at the Douglas River includes a couple c hort trails, including one leading to a deep qua-colored waterhole. Above the main water-ole are smaller pools and good views of the Douglas River Valley. Near the trailhead is a ampground with basic facilities. The other park ccess is along a gravel road north of Seymour.

St. Marys

At the headwaters of the South Esk River sys-em and 10 km inland is St. Marys, lying in the hadow of the Mt. Nicholas Range.

The town developed as the eastern terminus of a rail line and is still today an important trans-portation hub, as it lies at the intersection of he Tasman Highway and the A4, which fol-ows the South Esk River to **Fingal,** a coal-mining town, and links up to the busy Midlands Highway.

St. Marys Hotel, Main St. (tel. 03-6372-2181), has inexpensive rooms (from $18 s, $32 d) and serves good pub-style counter meals. The other accommodation option is **St. Marys YHA Hos-el** (also known as Seaview Farm Lodge), on German Town Rd. eight km north of town (tel. 03-6372-2341). The location, on a sheep farm with panoramic coastal views, is magnificent. Dorm beds are $9 pp, and there are a few units or $20 s or d.

Scamander

This small resort town at the mouth of the Sca-mander River halfway between St. Marys and St. Helens is on a picturesque stretch of coast. The town features many delightful beaches and dream fishing in the river. A good place to stay is **Scamander Kookaburra Caravan Park,** right on the beach one km north of town (tel. 03-6372-5121). Sites are $8-10 and the few basic on-site vans are $25. **Scamander Beach Re-sort** (tel. 03-6372-5255) is beside the mouth of the Scamander River, making it a good base for walking, river and beach swimming, or fish-ng. Rates are $75 s or d, but standby rates can be as low as $48.

St. Helens and Vicinity

Although away from the ocean beaches, St. Helens (pop. 1,200) is a popular coastal resort at the head of narrow Georges Bay. Established as a whaling station in the 1830s, the local econo-my still relies heavily on the ocean's renewable

resources, and today St. Helens boasts the state's largest fishing fleet. The town itself has lit-tle of interest, and the best beaches are east of town along Georges Bay. **St. Helen's Histo-ry Room,** 61 Cecilia St. (tel. 03-6376-1744), features the local history with lots of photos and an audiovisual. South of town, the road contin-ues beyond the airport to **St. Helen's Point,** winding past some decent sandy beaches and the Peron Dunes. From the end of the road a short trail leads past a rocky point to **Beerbarrel Beach.** The road along the north side of Georges Bay leads to **Humbug Point State Recreation Area,** passing good beaches at Binalong Bay. Within the recreation area are many good day-use areas and beachfront camp-ing at Dora Point and Moulting Bay (bring drink-ing water from St. Helens). The coastline within the recreation area comprises many short stretches of pristine beach as well as protected coves perfect for exploring on foot.

St. Helens has a variety of inexpensive lodg-ings, and although there is a caravan park, campers should head out to Humbug Point (de-scribed above). The least expensive place to stay in town is **St. Helens Hotel/Motel,** 49 Ce-cilia St. (tel. 03-6376-1133), where rooms start at $25 s, $45 d. Also central is the comfortable **Artnor Lodge** at 71 Cecilia St. (tel. 03-6376-1234). Rooms with shared facilities are $35 s, $50 d; private facilities $45 s, $60 d. All rates in-clude breakfast. **Warrawee** (tel. 03-6376-1987) is an old guesthouse on a few hectares over-looking Georges Bay south of town. Rates start at $40 s, $65 d, including a cooked breakfast. For a feed, head to **Captain's Catch.** A small **in-formation center** is at 20 Cecilia St. (tel. 03-6376-1329).

West from St. Helens

From St. Helens the highway veers inland, fol-lowing the George River through rolling hills to a high pass before descending to plains that slope gently to Bass Strait. In **Pyengana,** just off the highway 24 km west of St. Helens, is **Healey Pyengana Cheese Factory** (tel. 03-6373-6157), a great spot for cheese lovers to sample deli-cious cheddar cheeses made the traditional way from pasteurized milk and salt. The factory is open daily 9 a.m.-6 p.m. While in town don't miss the picturesque **Pub in the Paddock** (tel.

03-6373-6121), complete with a resident beer-drinking pig. Rooms are $35 and inexpensive counter meals are served through the day. Beyond Pyengana is 90-meter-high **St. Columbia Falls,** with a flow of 200,000 liters per minute in the Wet. The falls can be seen from the road, but from the parking lot a short trail leads to the valley floor for a different angle of the falls.

At **Weldborough Pass Scenic Reserve** is a 15-minute **rainforest walk,** with interpretive boards describing common species of the local flora and fauna communities. To the north, in Weldborough itself, is the whitewashed **Weldborough Hotel** (tel. 03-6354-2223), proclaiming itself "the worst pub in Tasmania."

Derby

Sandwiched between a steep hill and the Cascade River, Derby, in the far northeast of the state, flourished after the discovery of tin in 1874. Today, much of the architecture from the mining era remains, with rows of miner's cottages surrounded by well-kept gardens. Payable tin had been found throughout the northeast, with many leases taken up by the Briseis Tin and General Mining Company. At the time, the Briseis Mine was the Southern Hemisphere's largest open-cut tin mine, with 120 tons of the mineral extracted each month. On 4 April 1929, after 30 years of production, heavy rainfalls collapsed a dam wall at the mine workings, releasing 3,000 million liters of water into the already flooded Cascade River. The disaster destroyed much of the mine workings and part of Derby, leaving 14 dead. The mine reopened a few years later, but never at its former capacity, and in 1948 it closed for good.

Derby Tin Mine Centre Museum, in an old schoolhouse, catalogs the history of local mining, including the famous Briseis Mine, through relics, historical records, and photographs. Within the grounds is a re-creation of a shantytown featuring old Derby buildings such as a cottage, store, butcher shop, mines office, the original blacksmith's shop, and jail. You can also pan for tin and gemstones and feed rainbow trout. Admission is a worthwhile $4. A popular annual event is the **Derby River Derby,** held on the third Saturday of every October. The event attracts hundreds of competitors to run a five-km

route down the river on homemade watercraft. Many competitors never reach the finish line, but those who do can win prizes in a multitude of divisions, including one class for boats holding up to 24 people.

Derby's only accommodation is the **Dorset Hotel** (tel. 03-6354-2360), which has basic rooms for $28 s, $45 d, including breakfast. The pub also does counter meals, or grab a light snack at the museum tearooms.

Mt. William National Park

This spectacular coastal park of 13,899 hectares lies in the far northeastern corner of the state. It protects long stretches of unspoilt beach rising to a low mountain range that forms the park's western border. The park provides an important sanctuary for the Forester kangaroo, Tasmania's largest mammal. Their preferred habitat is open areas of high grasses, and for this reason several large areas of developed pasture have been incorporated into the park and are maintained in this condition to support the species. Also present in the park are Bennett's wallabies, wombats, and echidnas. Over 100 species of birds are also present, including kookaburras and honeyeaters.

Southern access to the park is along a road that traverses some spectacular scenery, passing beautiful **Picnic Point Beach** and ending at **Eddystone Point Lighthouse,** from where views extend north along the park's best beaches to the Furneaux Group islands. Northern access to the park is along a 23-km road east from Gladstone. Within the park, this road forks. The right fork leads to a great campground at **Stumpy's Bay.** Also along this road, south of the bay, is a short trail to the summit of 216-meter **Mount William.** Views from this peak, the park's highest point, are panoramic, extending across the park and the entire northeastern corner of Tasmania. The left fork leads you to a group of holiday shacks and a campground at **Musselroe Bay** at the park's northern tip.

The nearest services are in **Ansons Bay,** a small village south of the park with petrol and a general store selling groceries, fishing tackle, and hot food. Gladstone, in the north, has similar services. To contact the park ranger call (03) 6357-2108.

THE MIDLANDS: HOBART TO LAUNCESTON

The 200-km route between Tasmania's two largest cities was established in 1825, before which all supplies between the two centers had been transported by sea. In the early days of the overland route, with bushrangers roaming the bush robbing travelers, garrison stations were established to protect travelers. Many of these stations grew into townships, and today they boast an amazing array of historic buildings. What's more, early settlers planted English trees to ease homesickness, giving the midlands a distinctive English feel.

Richmond

With over 50 buildings dating from the first half of last century, Richmond, 30 km north of Hobart, is a classic example of an 1800s town. As the population of Hobart Town expanded, exploration inland commenced, and one of the first spots chosen for settlement was Richmond, in the Coal River Valley, on the route between Hobart and Port Arthur. Today, Richmond's best-known feature is a convict-built bridge dating from 1823. **Richmond Gaol** (tel. 03-6260-2127), built about the same time, housed convicts engaged in local construction projects. Within the solid structure are displays of convicts and the penal system under which they were held. Admission is $2.50. It's open daily 10 a.m.-5 p.m. Other historic land-

marks include the 1834 **St. John's Church,** Australia's oldest Catholic church; the 1825 **courthouse;** and **Richmond Arms Hotel,** built in 1888. **Old Hobart Town,** on Bridge St. (tel. 03-6262-2502), is a scaled down model of Hobart, built from the original plans. Admission adult $4.50, child $2.50. Open daily 9 a.m.-5 p.m.

Richmond is an easy day trip from Hobart, and many tour operators head out there. The other public transportation option is with **Hobart Coaches** (tel. 03-6234-4077), which runs out to Richmond four times daily (except Sat.-Sun.) for $6 round-trip.

Oatlands

Of all Tasmania's historic townships, none has the concentration of convict-era buildings that Oatlands does. The town straddles the Jordan River, 85 km north of Hobart, and was established as a garrison station on the route between Hobart and Launceston. Many historically important buildings have plaques detailing their history and past tenants. Along the main street alone sit 87 historic sandstone buildings, including many dating from the 1820s. The town's dominant structure is **Callington Mill,** a steam-powered windmill built in 1837. The craftsmanship is amazing. The tower is 15 meters high, each sandstone block cut to a different size to create a conical taper. The building fell into disrepair at the turn of the century, but at peak production it was capable of grinding enough wheat to produce up to a ton of flour per hour. Admission to

Richmond Bridge

the mill and an adjacent cottage and stables is $2. It's open daily 9 a.m.-5 p.m.

Midlands Hotel, 91 High St. (tel. 03-6254-1103), has basic but spotlessly clean rooms with shared facilities for $35. Opposite is **Oatlands Lodge,** 92 High St. (tel. 03-6254-1444), a rambling old guesthouse with four rooms of a high standard for $65 s, $85 d, inclusive of a cooked breakfast. South of Oatlands on a picturesque creek is **Commandant's Cottage,** Jericho (tel. 03-6254-4115), built in 1839 to house the superintendent of a road-building gang. Today it provides accommodation for travelers. Each room in the cottage has its own charming character, with slate floors, comfortable beds, and a fully-equipped kitchen with breakfast provisions. Nearby is a creek where platypuses are sometimes sighted. The cottage takes only one booking per night, so if you're a couple or family, you get the whole place to yourselves; $80 d, $20 each extra person.

The **Midlands Hotel** serves good counter meals daily noon-1:30 p.m. and 6-7:30 p.m. Across the road is **Delegans Tearooms and Takeaway,** with hamburgers from $3 and seafood baskets for $5.50.

Ross

Established in 1812 to protect travelers from bushrangers, this picturesque town on the Macquarie River 120 km north of Hobart is one of Tasmania's rural gems. The tree-lined streets are dotted with beautiful old buildings (the best way to get around is on foot). The dominant feature of Ross is the convict-built bridge spanning the Macquarie River. A convict stonemason, Daniel Herbert, left his mark on the bridge by way of over 150 carvings, and in return he was granted a pardon. The bridge, along with three historic churches, is floodlit at night. One of the most colorful features of Australia's convict past is the many Female Factories, where settlers were encouraged to use the labor of female convicts for household chores and pardoned convicts were able to chose a wife. The Female Factory in Ross operated between 1847 and 1855. It was destroyed soon after, but foundations and the original staff quarters remain. To get there take Church St. out of town, turn left onto Bridge St., then right onto Bond Street. Across the road from the site, and along the

gravel path following the old stone wall, is **Ross Original Cemetery,** with readable gravestones dating from 1840. The **Tasmanian Wool Centre** on Church St. (tel. 03-6381-5466), has interesting displays on the Tasmanian wool industry and woolen articles (not cheap) for sale. Within the center is a small museum cataloging the history of Ross and the importance of the wool industry in the town's growth; museum admission is $4. If you want to know more about Ross and, in particular, the carvings on Ross Bridge, contact Tim Johnson who, dressed in appropriate period costume complete with top hat, operates a guided tour around the village from $25 for two (tel. 03-6381-5354).

Least expensive of the town's accommodations is **Ross Caravan Park,** Bridge St. (tel. 03-6381-5462), in a beautiful shaded spot beside Ross Bridge. Park facilities are adequate. The park has resident possums and ducks, and if you're lucky, you'll see the platypuses in the river. Tent sites are $8 and powered sites $10. Also within the park are five small cabins (supply your own linen) with limited cooking facilities for $20. Local Tim Johnson has restored five cottages scattered around town. Each has its own charm and contains an album telling the story of the cottage and its restoration. Typical is **Captain Samuel's Cottage,** built in 1830. It features a large living area and bathroom, modern kitchen and opens to a veranda and a garden that extends down to the river. Call ahead for reservations and directions at (03) 6381-5354. Built in 1832, **Elms Inn,** Church St. (tel. 03-6381-5246), is an attractive sandstone guesthouse with four upstairs guest rooms. Rates are $55 s, $65 d, including breakfast. The other accommodation is **Man-O-Ross Hotel,** on the corner of Church and Bridge Streets (tel. 03-6381-5240); $35 s, $48 d.

As well as providing accommodations, Man-O-Ross Hotel has a delightful shaded beer garden and restaurant. Prices start at $8.50 for main meals, and on Sunday night there's a barbecue for adult $10.50, child $5. This hotel also serves cooked breakfasts 8-9:30 a.m. for $10 pp. **Old Ross General Store** has a variety of light snacks and a small tearoom out the back.

Campbell Town and Vicinity

Like Ross, 12 km to the south, this picturesque village was established as a garrison station in he early 1820s. The highway runs right through he center of town and over a fine old bridge cross the Elizabeth River. One of the town's ldest and most attractive buildings is **Fox unters Return,** built as an inn in 1829. Acommodations in town include **Powells Hotel,** 18 High St. (tel. 03-6381-1161), with basic ooms for $30 s, $40 d, and **The Gables,** 35 ligh St. (tel. 03-6381-1347), with comfortable ooms with shared facilities for $79.

East of Campbell Town, about halfway out o the coast, is **Lake Leake,** a popular trout-shing and boating spot. **Lake Leake Chalet** el. 03-6381-1329) has basic rooms with shared acilities for $25 s, $40 d, which includes a light reakfast. Counter meals in the bar are $8-12. In the lakeshore is a primitive campground; $3 er night.

ongford

irst settled in 1813, Longford, 28 km south of auncceston, is one of northern Tasmania's old-st towns. The main street is lined with Geor-ian-era buildings. The historic property **Wool-ners** has been in the same family for seven enerations, with the main house having been ved in since 1819. Typical of the era is the

exposed timber framework filled in with bricks and white-washed. The interior is complete with furnishings from around the turn of the century, including shutters to keep bushrangers out. In the grounds is an old timber windmill, pumphouse, the original cottage, stables and barns, blacksmith's shop, a barn full of antique cars and machinery, and a superb little church with its original Huon pine pews. Woolmers is open daily for two-hour tours throughout the day ($12.50 pp); for bookings call (03) 6391-1251.

Brickendon, Wellington St. (tel. 03-6391-1251), is an 1830s house with two historic cot-tages renovated to accommodate visitors. The cottages are spacious and feature a kitchen, separate bedrooms, private garden, and a living area with fireplace. Both are $120 per night. Or check in at the **Racecourse Inn,** 114 Marlbor-ough St. (tel. 03-6391-2352). If you're looking for a counter meal, head to the **Checkered Flag Bistro** at the Country Club Hotel on Wellington Street. For about $8-10 you can choose from a blackboard menu with a large variety of main dishes. Also in Longford is **James Service Store,** a delightful old-fashioned store with some tempting gourmet fare.

SOUTHWESTERN TASMANIA

This region is accessed from the **Lyell Highway,** which follows the Derwent River from Hobart then crosses a mountainous region to end on the west coast. It's a stretch of highway just 300 km long, but it provides various access points to the Tasmanian Wilderness World Heritage Area, worthy of as much time as you can afford. The World Heritage Area encompasses five national parks, of which three are accessed along the Lyell Highway. Closest to Hobart is Mt. Field National Park, a highland area of mountains with one of Tasmania's two downhill ski resorts (no accommodations). Farther west is Southwest National Park, a massive expanse of wilderness that extends from the mountainous area around Lake Pedder to the inhospitable coastline of the state's extreme south. Adjacent and to the north is Franklin-Gordon Wild Rivers National Park, a wilderness area best known for its narrow escape from flooding that would have been caused by a proposed hydroelectric scheme in the late 1970s.

NEW NORFOLK

This historic town of 6,000, on the Derwent River 34 km west of Hobart, was named for the area's earliest settlers, who were relocated from Norfolk Island in 1807. The first party comprised 34 islanders, and in the following year another 500 arrived, leaving Norfolk Island uninhabited. By the 1860s many local farmers were growing hops—the flavoring and preservative used in beer—an industry that continued for most of this century. Hop-growing has been phased out in the valley, but many signs of the industry remain, including distinctive rows of stately poplars, planted as windbreaks to protect the hops from wind damage.

Sights
One of Tasmania's oldest buildings, **Old Colony Inn,** was built of brick and mud in 1815 to store hops. In later years a second story was added, and it was converted to a residence. Today, the ground floor is an intriguing museum storing

enormous bellows, assorted balls and chains, horseshoes, old bicycles, a collection of lamps, and all sorts of interesting historical items. Admission $1.50. It's at 21 Montagu St. (tel. 03-6261-2731).

Behind Old Colony Inn a trail leads along the Derwent River to the confluence with the Lachlan River. Across the Lachlan River is **Oast House** (tel. 03-6261-1030), part of the former Tynwald hop-growing property. Built as a hop drying kiln, the Oast House is now a museum dedicated to the industry, with walk-in kilns, some great old photos, and hop-growing implements on display. An interesting art gallery is upstairs. Admission is $3.50. It's open daily 9:30 a.m.-5 p.m. Back in the center of town are many other historic buildings, including **St. Matthew's Church of England** (1823), one of Australia's oldest churches; **Willow Court** (1830), once a hospital for convicts; and **Old Watch House Gaol** (1838), built of locally quarried sandstone.

On 21 April 1864 a container of trout roe arrived in Tasmania after a 90-day journey from London. The hatchlings formed the breeding stock for the first trout released in streams across southern Australia and New Zealand. The **Salmon Ponds,** 11 km west of New Norfolk (tel. 03-6261-1614), the site of the original breeding program, has been developed into a museum displaying the process. Admission is $3.50 and it's open daily 9 a.m.-5 p.m.

Accommodations
Bush Inn, 49 Montagu St. (tel. 03-6261-2256) has the cheapest rooms in town, and has been serving travelers since way back in 1815. Rates are $28 s, $48 d, which includes breakfast. At the **Old Colony Inn,** on Montagu St. (tel. 03-6261-2731), accommodation is offered in a small cottage with a private balcony overlooking the inner courtyard; $70-75 d, includes a full breakfast. Dating from the 1830s, **Tynwald-Willow Bend Estate,** Lyell Hwy. (tel. 03-6261-2667) is a stunning building that was built for a local hop farmer. The home is magnificent, featuring wrought-iron lacework and surrounded by well manicured gardens. Five rooms have been re

tored for guests, and each is furnished with
ntiques. A pool, tennis court, old-fashioned
ounge room, laundry, and restaurant are other
eatures. Rates are $95 s, $118 d, including
reakfast. Also on the grounds is The Granary,
self-contained cottage dating from 1822; $122
er night.

New Norfolk Caravan Park, the Esplanade
el. 03-6261-1268), on the river and a short
valk from the center of town, has good facili-
es (coin-operated showers). Sites are $8-12,
n-site vans $30, and cabins $40.

ood

ush Inn, 49 Montagu St. (tel. 03-6261-1075),
as a dining room out back with river views.
rices are a little higher than your average pub
eal, but quality is good. Main dishes range
9.50-12. It's open daily for lunch and dinner. For
n English-style meal head to **Old Colony Inn,**
lso on Montagu St. (tel. 03-6261-2731). The
estaurant at **Tynwald** (tel. 03-6261-2667) is a
ttle more formal. Main dishes range $17-21.
)pen nightly.

MOUNT FIELD NATIONAL PARK

agged peaks, a string of glacial lakes, lush rain-
orests, and one of the state's two downhill ski
reas are features of this 16,977-hectare park 73
m west of Hobart. Its proximity to the capital
nakes the park a popular day trip, but some day
ikes and a range of accommodations make an
vernight stay almost compulsory.

he Land
he land encompassed by the park is general-
v of a high elevation. The lowest elevations
re around the facility area, which is only 180
neters above sea level. The park's central sec-
on is a high plateau, flanked by high peaks, in-
luding 1,434-meter **Mt. Field West.** The cen-
al plateau is dotted with deep lakes of glacial
rigin. In fact, most of the park's dominant fea-
ures are glacial in origin. Ice covered this region
s recently as 15,000 years ago and upon re-
eating left a variety of easy-to-recognize scars.
road River Valley is typical; as a glacier flowed
own the valley, then retreated as tempera-
ures warmed, it ground away the valley walls,

scraping away protruding ridges and forming
a U-shaped valley. At the head of the valley is
Lake Seal, a massive basin carved by the same
glacier. Glaciers have long since melted, but
erosion continues. Russell Falls, near the park
entrance, is a good example of the process.
Water rushing down Russell Falls Creek has
carved steep walls into the mudstone behind
the falls, washing the sediment downstream to
build up somewhere else.

Like all of Tasmania's mountain parks, weather conditions in Mt. Field are very dynamic, and
the old cliche of four seasons in one day is very
apt. Snow and sleet can fall at any time of year,
and the park experiences more overcast than
clear days.

Flora and Fauna
As the park is near the center of the state, it
has flora from both the east and west side of
the island. As well, abrupt elevation changes
make defining the various vegetation zones
easy. At lower elevations, such as around the facility area, are forests of eucalypt with swamp
gum, which grows up to 100 meters high. Also
dogwood, stringybarks, and white gums grow
in the area. In gullies and other sheltered areas
grow Antarctic beech and sassafras. Subalpine
forests, dominated by colorful snow gums and
areas of low heath, grow up to an elevation of
800 meters. On the plateau, where drainage is
poor, dead and dying plant matter has formed
extensive bogs, which, after time, have become
overgrown with low-growing heath plants. The
only larger species at high elevations are
conifers, generally twisted and stunted by harsh
weather conditions.

The variety of habitat provides a home for diverse species of fauna, but few larger mammals are within the park. The marsupials, such
as Bennett's wallabies and pademelons, feed at
dawn and dusk while bandicoots and potoroos
only feed at night. Possums are widespread
through the park, but again, they are only active
at night. Echidnas and platypuses are also present; look for the latter at dusk in quiet reaches of
Russell Falls Creek.

Sights and Hikes
Little exertion is needed to reach **Russell Falls.**
Just a couple hundred meters from the facility

area (the trail begins opposite park headquarters), they are one of the most beautiful waterfalls in Tasmania. The trail to the falls passes through a variety of lush vegetation, emerging at the falls, which cascade over five tiers before plunging 40 meters into a fern-lined pool below.

From the facility area on the park's eastern boundary, a winding road climbs steadily through an ever-changing forest to the central plateau and ends at **Lake Dobson,** the trailhead for a number of challenging hikes. The first hike along the road, five km from the facility area, is **Lyrebird Nature Walk,** just 15 minutes round-trip. The forested landscape changes dramatically as the road ascends over a ridge and onto the plateau, almost treeless and strewn with moss-covered boulders. Immediately to the right upon reaching the plateau is a parking lot for a number of trails, including to **Seagar's Lookout** (1.7 km; allow 30 minutes each way) and the summit of 1,270-meter **Mt. Field East** (four km; allow two hours each way), along a trail that passes two alpine lakes. Back on the road, beyond these trailheads, is **Lake Fenton,** encircled by stunted eucalypts. At Lake Dobson is a map of all trails and a self-registration booth. **Pandani Grove Nature Walk** (2.4 km; 40 minutes round-trip) leads around picturesque Lake Dobson and through a stand of ancient pencil pine. Most serious hikers will want to head farther afield to destinations such as **Twisted Tarn** (six km; two and a half hours each way). The ascent of the park's highest peak, 1,434-meter **Mt. Field West** (10 km; four hours each way), should only be attempted on a clear day. The going can be tough.

Mount Mawson Ski Area

Although Tasmania's southern latitude should mean ample snowfall, that is not the case, and when it does snow, conditions are often atrocious. That said, Tasmanian skiers are a hardy bunch, and as the closest downhill skiing to Hobart, this small ski area overlooking Lake Dobson is very popular. The area has three tows, ski rental, and instructors. From the Lake Dobson parking lot to the lifts is a 30-minute walk. For ski conditions, call (03) 6288-1319.

As well as downhill skiers, wintertime attracts those keen on cross-country skiing, tobogganing, snow trekking, and ice skating.

Accommodations

Russell Falls Holiday Cottages, just beyon the park gate (tel. 03-6288-1198), comprise rustic but spacious four- and six-berth cabin with a kitchen in each. Rates are a reasonabl $35 s, $50 d; advance bookings are a goo idea. Each of the three **Lake Dobson Cabins** 15 km beyond the park gate, has six bunks, wood heater, running water, toilets, and fire wood (bring your own stove). The cost is $10 pp Book through the park ranger (tel. 03-6288 1149) and collect the key from him upon arriva at the park entrance.

Outside the park, in the small village of **Na tional Park,** are two more options. **Nationa Park Hotel** (tel. 03-6288-1103) has basic room with shared facilities for $30 s, $50 d, includin breakfast. Across the road is **National Par YHA Hostel** (tel. 03-6288-1369), where dorr beds are $10.

The **campground,** close to the park entrance has a variety of sites, including some right by th river. Facilities include hot showers, laundry and a cooking shelter with two barbecues. Fire wood is supplied, but you're better off with you own stove. Nonpowered sites are $5 pp an powered sites are an extra $1 pp. No booking are taken for holiday periods; the rest of th year call (03) 6288-1149 to reserve a site. Dur ing the night, nocturnal wildlife abounds aroun the campground, so zip up your tent and seal a food containers.

Other Practicalities

Tasmanian Wilderness Transport (tel. 03 6334-4442) operates a bus service betwee the park (the pick-up point is outside the kiosk and Hobart for $25 one-way, $45 round-trip. I summer buses depart Hobart daily at 8:30 a.m with service Monday, Wednesday, and Saturda the rest of the year.

Basic groceries are available at the **Par Kiosk** (open daily 8:30 a.m.-6 p.m.), but it' best to stock up on supplies before heading t the park. **National Park Hotel** serves meal but closes early. At Westerway, four km eas of the park entrance, tire chains can be rente from the service station, while other shops se groceries, stove fuel, and takeaway food.

The **Visitor Centre,** at the park entrance, ha displays of the park's natural history and infor nation sheets on the most popular hikes. It's open daily 8:30 a.m.-5 p.m. To contact the ranger, call (03) 6288-1149. A 1:50,000 topographical map is available from the Visitor Centre, or pick one up from any Tasmap Sales Centre.

SOUTHWEST NATIONAL PARK

Encompassing the entire southwestern corner of Tasmania, this 605,000-hectare park is a vast wilderness of mountain ranges and river systems along an almost-inaccessible stretch of coast. And while Mt. Field and Cradle Mountain-Lake St. Clair National Parks may have a concentration of natural wonders, the joy of this park comes from the opportunity to experience a real wilderness area and, for those experienced in backcountry travel, attempt long-distance hikes. The park also makes up a significant section of the Tasmanian Wilderness World Heritage Area, which includes Franklin-Gordon Wild Rivers National Park immediately to the north. The main park access is 42 km west of the Mt. Field National Park turnoff. From this point Scotts Peak Rd. leads south along **Lake Pedder** to campgrounds and trailheads for a variety of hikes, while Gordon River Rd. leads west to **Strathgordon.** Apart from the motel at Strathgordon the park has no services. Maydena is the last fuel stop.

Scotts Peak Road

This gravel road leads south from Junction Hill and ends at the southern reaches of Lake Ped-

der, where there are camping and hiking opportunities. Near the beginning of the road on the right is **Creepy Crawly Nature Trail,** a one-km circuit through rainforest. Around 10 km south is the trailhead for a seven-km (one-way) trek to the summit of 1,425-meter **Mt. Anne;** allow 10 hours for the round-trip.

At earth-filled Edgar Dam, a farther 10 km south and past a fantastic lookout, is **Edgar Campground,** while a farther four km is **Huon Campground.** Both campgrounds have toilets, drinking water, and firewood. The road dead-ends at **Red Knoll Lookout,** where views extend north across the lake and south to the jagged Arthur Range.

Port Davey/South Coast Tracks

Southwest National Park is best known for its longer hikes, including the combination of these two trails, which link the shore of Lake Pedder to the southern tip of Tasmania, a 170-km trek that takes 10-18 days, depending on how many side trips you make. It's possible to walk each trail separately, but this requires an air charter through Melaleuca. **Par Avion** (tel. 03-6248-5390) and **Tasair** (tel. 03-6248-5088) provide this service and can also fly in food drops for those attempting the complete hike.

The trails can be hiked in either direction, but the most popular section is the South Coast Track from Melaleuca to Cockle Creek. The Port Davey Track, which begins from Huon Campground at the end of Scotts Peak Rd., traverses a remote valley along the back of the jagged Arthur Range

taking in the remote southern coastline along the South Coast Track to Lost World Plateau before descending along Spring Creek to Bathurst Narrows, 62 km from the trailhead. This deep channel is the outlet for Bathurst Harbour. On each side of the crossing point is a small dinghy. It is imperative to leave one on each side after crossing (which will entail multiple crossings and some simple common sense). From Joan Point, on the south side of the narrows, it's 14 km to Melaleuca, site of a small mining operation, an airstrip, and the only huts along the track. From Melaleuca, the coast is an easy day's hike through open plains of buttongrass. The trail then parallels the coast, descending to sandy bays, heading inland to cross the larger rivers, and climbing to a number of lookouts before ending at Cockle Creek, 87 km from Melaleuca.

Hikers do not need permits but should check trail conditions with the ranger (tel. 03-6288-1283) and register with the Tasmanian police.

Strathgordon

Established to serve workers on a nearby hydro-electric scheme, Strathgordon is a good base when visiting nearby Gordon Dam and trout fishing in the area. The settlement lies on an isthmus of land between Lake Gordon and Lake Pedder in the north of the park, and 33 km west of Junction Hill. Accommodation is provided at **Lake Pedder Chalet** (tel. 03-6280-1166), a large complex of 75 rooms right on the lake. Rooms are only basic (they originally housed workers) but have bathrooms. Guest facilities include heated indoor pool, sports center, tennis courts, squash, sauna, boat rental, barbecue area, laundry, restaurant, and bar. Rates range $50-85 s or d, depending on the season.

Beyond Strathgordon, the road ends at **Gordon Dam Lookout,** where there's a visitor center and picnic area.

LAKE COUNTRY AND VICINITY

Lake Country, the southern section of Tasmania's central plateau, forms the headwaters for dozens of rivers that flow in a southwesterly direction to the Derwent River. The vast volume of water flowing through these watersheds is harnessed by a string of hydroelectric projects that supply just under 10% of Australia's total electricity demands.

Hamilton

The rural town of Hamilton lies on the River Clyde 70 km northwest of Hobart. The area was settled soon after New Norfolk had been established and was destined to become Tasmania's capital—except barges were unable to travel far enough up the Derwent River. So instead, the village became a transportation hub for the rich agricultural districts of the central plateau. Many convict-built structures remain, including **Glen Clyde House,** built as a private residence in 1840 and now an excellent gallery, full of Tasmanian arts and crafts. It's on Grace St. (tel. 03-6286-3276) and is open daily 9:30 a.m.-5 p.m.

The **Old School House,** Lyell Hwy. (tel. 03-6286-3292), was built in 1856 for the town's ever-growing population of school-age children. After being saved from bulldozers in the 1970s, it's been restored and converted to a comfortable accommodation. In the schoolhouse is a double room furnished with antiques, while in the garden is a self-contained cottage. Both are $95 per night including breakfast.

Bothwell

Bothwell is on the east bank of the River Clyde 30 km upstream of Hamilton. Once an important cattle and sheep center, the town is now a sleepy center of 800. The earliest settlers were Scottish, and their legacy is excellent trout-fishing in the surrounding streams and rivers. For trout fishing gear and hints on all the best spots, head to **Crown Tackle Shop** (tel. 03-6259-5508). They can also arrange guides. Over 50 historic buildings line Bothwell's wide streets. The best way to appreciate them is by following the *Let's Browse Bothwell* brochure, available at the council building. Bothwell also boasts Australia's oldest golf course, with unique fenced-off greens to prevent grazing sheep from spoiling the grass.

If you fancy staying in your own little country hideaway, consider **Birch Cottage,** on Elizabeth St. (tel. 03-6259-5502). Rooms are small but comfortable and well-furnished. Rates are $55 s, $85 d. **Bothwell Grange,** Alexander St (tel. 03-6259-5556), is a large two-story sandstone building dating from 1836. Owned by two friendly Brits, it has eight guest rooms, each with a bathroom. Rates are a reasonable $62 s, $74 d. **Bothwell Caravan Park** is just a small grassed area behind the public toilet building on Market Place, but it's peaceful and pleasant, and costs only $2.50 for unpowered sites and $6 for powered. Dating from 1829, the **Castle Hotel,** Patrick St. (tel. 03-6259-5502), serves lunch daily, dinner Friday and Saturday, and cold beer all the time.

Hamilton to Derwent Bridge

This 100-km stretch of the Lyell Highway parallels the Derwent River and passes through small towns and by many river access points. Along this section of the river are seven large power stations.

North of **Ouse** and at the north end of Wayatinah Lagoon is **Wayatinah Power Station,** and off an access road beyond the power station is a campground with tennis, pool, and a golf course. Sites are $7. The next town north is **Tarraleah,** built for hydroelectric workers. Visitors are welcome at the power station; it's north of town and very ugly.

A signposted road 19 km from Tarraleah spurs northeast from the highway to a private road that leads to **London Lakes Fly-Fishing Lodge** (tel. 03-6289-1159). The lodge caters specifically to fly-fishing enthusiasts (it hosted the 1988 World Fly-fishing Championships), but its remote setting on a private estate of 2,000 hectares appeals to varying interests. The lodge is rustic but comfortable, and with only five rooms, service is personal. Rates include accommodations, three excellent meals, and use of all lodge facilities. Fully guided, the rate ranges $450-680 pp per night, depending on the season (Nov.-March is high season); nonguided, but with all equipment provided, rates range $245-340. Nonanglers pay $185-260.

Derwent Bridge

This small service center, 165 km northwest of Hobart, is the southern gateway to Cradle Mountain-Lake St. Clair National Park. Although the park's most famous features are accessed from the north (see "Cradle Mountain-Lake St. Clair National Park" under "Northwestern Tasmania" later in this chapter), Lake St. Clair is just up the road from Derwent Bridge. A cruise boat operates on the lake, accessing easy day hikes and picking up adventurers who have completed the Overland Track from Cradle Valley.

Immediately west of the Lake St. Clair turnoff is **Derwent Bridge Hotel** (tel. 03-6289-1144), a large wooden complex with rooms, a restaurant, and bar. Rooms are basic but comfortable. Rates are $35-45 s, $55-75 d, depending on facilities. Backpacker accommodation is $15 pp. None of the rooms have cooking facilities, but the restaurant is inexpensive and open for all meals.

FRANKLIN-GORDON WILD RIVERS NATIONAL PARK

Declared in 1981, this 440,000-hectare park protects the entire watershed of the untamed Franklin River. On the western side of the park tributaries flow south into the Franklin from the Cheyne Range, 1,400 meters above sea level and running along the southern boundary of Cradle Mountain-Lake St. Clair National Park.

JANE KING

Nelson Falls, Franklin-Gordon Wild Rivers National Park

Fed by a heavy annual rainfall of over 300 cm, the river is in turn the major tributary of the mighty Gordon River, Tasmania's largest river. The river parallels a 20-km stretch of the Lyell Highway, but for the most part it flows through a wild and totally inaccessible region of the state. The Lyell Highway is the only road to traverse the park, offering you a chance to experience a dramatic mountain landscape dominated by rugged peaks and valleys of ancient forest.

The 1981 discovery of stone tools in a cave on the Lower Franklin confirmed a long-held theory that during the last ice age Tasmania was the earth's most southerly point of human occupation. Escaped convicts from a penal colony on Macquarie Harbour were the first Europeans to venture into the area. The first recorded crossing between Hobart and the west coast was in 1840, but it wasn't until 1932 that a road was completed, and as recently as 1974 that it was sealed. The 1970s brought worldwide attention to the Franklin River with conservationists fighting to save it from flooding from the construction of the Gordon-Lower Franklin Dam. They eventually won, having the park declared in 1981 and incorporated in the Tasmanian Wilderness World Heritage Area two years later.

Park Highlights

The park's eastern boundary is eight km west of Derwent Bridge and beyond Lake King William.

Just inside the park boundary is 800-meter-high King William Saddle, marking the divide of the Derwent and Gordon river systems, which flow to the east and west coasts respectively. Continuing west, the road passes through open fields of buttongrass before a sudden change of scenery sees the road enter the dense rainforest of the Surprise Valley. In this valley is **Franklin River Nature Trail,** where an information board details attractions along the Lyell Highway. The one-km (25 minutes round-trip) nature trail follows the banks of the Franklin and Surprise Rivers. Although it's only a short trail, the feeling is one of total wilderness, and the roar of the river drowns out any traffic noise.

Frenchman's Cap, an impressive massif of quartzite, is visible from several lookouts along the Lyell Highway, but to reach its summit entails a three- to five-day trek. From the highway it's 27 km to the summit and an elevation gain of just over 1,000 meters, with some sections of muddy plains and others of rough slopes of scree. The most exciting section of the entire hike is crossing the Franklin River aboard either a swing bridge or flying fox. From the highway, the river is an easy 15-minute walk.

Donnaghy's Hill, six km west of the trailhead for Frenchman's Cap Walking Track, is 400 meters from the highway (40 minutes round-trip) and provides panoramic views of the wilderness to the south. A farther four km west, the highway crosses the **Collingwood River,** put-in point for

trackies on the summit of Frenchman's Cap, Franklin-Gordon Wild Rivers National Park

Franklin River rafters. Continuing west, the highway passes through a picturesque valley backed by the rugged Raglan Range to the south. **Nelson Falls** is an easy 10-minute (each way) walk from the highway. The trail passes through a rainforest of lush ferns and colorful leatherwood trees before emerging at the falls, a spectacular cascade of water over a sandstone ledge.

The park has no information center and the only facility is primitive camping by the Collingwood River. To contact the ranger, call (03) 6471-7122.

Running the Franklin River

Symbolizing a victory for conservationists against the overwhelming tide of human encroachment, this wild river is Australia's premier whitewater rafting destination. But it certainly isn't a trip for the fainthearted. The 10- to 14-day trip entails wilderness travel and should only be attempted by experienced rafters or under the leadership of a qualified guide.

The river's headwaters are shallow, so the preferred put-in point is where the Lyell Highway crosses the Collingwood River. Most of the fearsome rapids—including Churn, Cauldron, and Thunderush—are on the upper half of the river. Once beyond Frenchman's Cap, the river is quieter and passes alongside some Aboriginal caves before it drains into the Gordon River, just over 120 km from the Lyell Highway.

Peregrine (tel. 03-6231-0977) operates a variety of trips down the river. These range from a five-day easy float starting halfway down the river (from $1020 pp) to running the entire river in over 13 days ($1800). Trips run Nov.-April. If you plan to run the river independently, contact the **Department of Parks, Wildlife, and Heritage** in Queenstown (tel. 03-6471-2511). From Heritage Landing, on the Lower Gordon River, arrange pick-ups with **Gordon River Cruises** (tel. 03-6471-7317) or **Wilderness Air** (tel. 03-6471-7280).

TASMANIA'S REMOTE WEST COAST

Tasmania's west coast is dominated by wilderness. Steep mountains rise from deep gorges, rainforests descend to raging rivers, and the coastline itself is accessible in only a couple of spots. But it's also a region of stark contrasts, one that boasts the wonders of the UNESCO Tasmanian Wilderness World Heritage Area alongside a bizarre landscape resulting from years of humanity's exploitative use of the environment's natural resources.

QUEENSTOWN

The mining town of Queenstown (pop. 3,000) lies on the Queen River, 260 km west of Hobart. Surrounding the town is a landscape like no other place in the country. But the panorama is certainly no natural beauty—it's all humanity's doing (or undoing). The barren but colorful surroundings are due to a combination of factors, but all relate directly to the town's famous **Mt. Lyell Copper Mine.** Over a period of 73 years smelters from the mine gave off dense clouds of sulphur-laden smoke. Rich in mineral content, the clouds settled on the surrounding hills, destroying vegetation for kilometers in all directions. It was a vicious cycle—as new growth on the land cleared to feed the smelters was killed off by the sulphurous clouds, soil was washed away by heavy rainfall, leaving surrounding hills barren and impregnated with sulphur. During this same period about 1.5 million tons of mine tailings were dumped into the Queen River annually and washed into the King River, eventually draining into Macquarie Harbour. Consequently, the lower King River is ecologically dead, and a two-km-square delta is a solid mass of gray sludge. All the doom and gloom aside, a visit to Queenstown is fascinating, for it gives visitors the chance to understand humanity's everchanging attitude to the environment. The best way to get an overview of the entire area, including the bare hills and township, is by catching a chairlift that ends at a viewpoint high above an old silica quarry.

Sights

Don't miss **Galley Museum,** on the corner of Driffield and Sticht Streets, which gives an insight to Queenstown's industrial past. Originally the Imperial Hotel, it contains an eclectic collection of local memorabilia spread over two floors. Displays include the story of Aboriginal habitation, the development of Queenstown and Strahan, the region's geology, and the development of mining processes over the last 100 years. Admission is $3. It's open in summer 10 a.m.-5:30 p.m. (shorter hours the rest of the year). Across the road is **Miner's Siding,** dedicated to local miners and their work. Their story, along with that of Queenstown, is told through copper sculptures, but the centerpiece is a steam locomotive designed to traverse the gradient of a steep rail line constructed to transport copper from Queenstown to Strahan.

Lyell Tours

These tours operate from Western Arts and Crafts at 1 Driffield St. across from the Empire Hotel (tel. 03-6471-2388). The most popular tour takes in Mt. Lyell Copper Mine (surface tour), a drive through the famous bare hills while a story of current mine development and its revitalization unfolds; adult $9.50, child $5.50. This tour is offered several times a day, every day. Other tours include a visit to the face of the working mine ($36 pp) and a 4WD adventure along the historic Kelly Basin rail line to the Bird River Valley (adult $55, child $35, includes a light meal).

Lake Burbury

Lake Burbury, east of Queenstown, is crossed by the Lyell Highway but can also be accessed along a road south from Queenstown. After crossing the King River, where a massive power station harnesses redirected water from the King River, this road climbs the western slopes of the West Coast Range, passing through a section of cool-temperate rainforest that features leatherwood, myrtle, celery-topped pine, and sassafras. At the range's summit, the jagged peak of **Mt. Jukes** (1,168 meters) is easily iden-

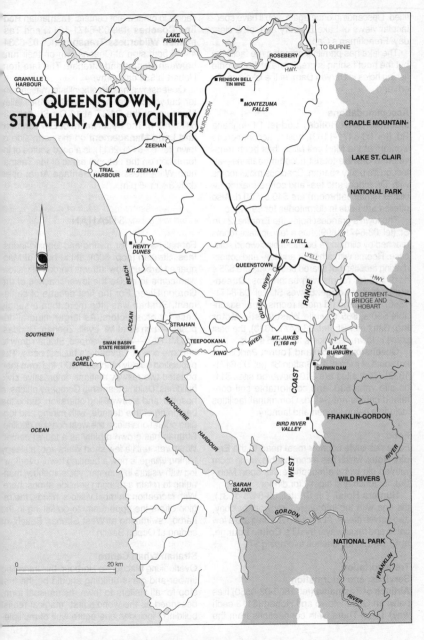

QUEENSTOWN, STRAHAN, AND VICINITY

LAKE PIEMAN

ROSEBERY

TO BURNIE

HWY.

GRANVILLE HARBOUR

RENISON BELL TIN MINE

MONTEZUMA FALLS

CRADLE MOUNTAIN-

LAKE ST. CLAIR

NATIONAL PARK

MURCHISON

ZEEHAN

TRIAL HARBOUR

MT. ZEEHAN

MT. LYELL

LYELL

QUEENSTOWN

HWY.

TO DERWENT BRIDGE AND HOBART

HENTY DUNES

QUEEN RIVER

MT. LYELL

RANGE

SOUTHERN

BEACH

OCEAN

STRAHAN

TEEPOOKANA

KING RIVER

RIVER

MT. JUKES (1,168 m)

LAKE BURBURY

WEST COAST RANGE

SWAN BASIN STATE RESERVE

CAPE SORELL

DARWIN DAM

OCEAN

MACQUARIE HARBOUR

BIRD RIVER VALLEY

FRANKLIN-GORDON

WILD RIVERS

SARAH ISLAND

GORDON RIVER

FRANKLIN RIVER

WEST COAST

NATIONAL PARK

RIVER

0   20 km

tified. Descending once again, you'll have spectacular views of Lake Burbury and, on a clear day, Frenchman's Cap.

The lake has primitive camping (no facilities) but the trout fishing is great; one of the favorite fishing holes is **Darwin Dam,** at the lake's southern end.

Accommodations
Mountain View Holiday Lodge, 1 Penghana Rd. (tel. 03-6471-1163), built to accommodate workers at the Mt. Lyell Mine, has been renovated to provide tourist accommodations—although it's pretty spartan. Spacious motel rooms with TV, fridge, and tea- and coffee-making facilities (small bathroom) are $40 s, $50 d. Also offered are beds in dormitories for $9-12 pp.

The town's grandest hotel, the **Empire,** 2 Orr St. (tel. 03-6471-1699), has a few upstairs rooms reached by climbing a beautiful blackwood staircase. Rooms with a heater and tea- and coffee-making facilities but shared bathrooms are $35 s or d, $45 for rooms with bathrooms. **Queenstown Motor Lodge,** Bowes St. (tel. 03-6471-1866), has standard motel rooms for a reasonable $50 s, $65 d, while **Westcoaster Motor Inn,** Batchelor St. (tel. 03-6471-1033), the best place in town, has rooms for $105 s or d.

Queenstown Cabin and Tourist Park is two km south of town at 19 Grafton St. (tel. 03-6471-1332). Tent sites are $10, powered sites $11, on-site vans $30, and comfortable self-contained cabins are $45 d. Communal facilities include a camp kitchen and laundry.

Food
For a pub-style counter meal head to the **Empire Hotel,** which has a comfortable dining room with an old-world atmosphere. It's open Mon.-Sat. for lunch and nightly for dinner.

Hunters Hotel, Orr St. (tel. 03-6471-1531), the one with the impressive ironwork balcony, also serves meals. Along the main drag are a few cafes and takeaways: try **JJ's Coffee Lounge,** at 13 Orr St., for lunches averaging $7.

Transportation, Services, and Information
Airlines of Tasmania (tel. 1800-03-0550) flies between Queenstown and Hobart ($113 each way) Tues.-Thurs. with connections from the capital to other major centers. **Tasmanian Redline Coaches** (tel. 03-6471-1011) and **Tasmanian Wilderness Transport** (tel. 03-6334 4442) both stop at Queenstown on their runs between Hobart and Strahan. The fare from Hobart is $35 each way.

Queenstown has no official information center, but you can get information from the Galley Museum, or the RACT at 18 Orr St. (tel. 03 6471-1974). The **Department of Environment and Land Management** on the north side of town (tel. 03-6471-2511), is a good source of information on the national parks of the Tasmanian Wilderness World Heritage Area; open daily 8 a.m.-5 p.m.

STRAHAN

Formally a port for mining and logging industries, Strahan (pop. 600), at the head of Macquarie Harbour, now attracts hordes of visitors who come to cruise the lower reaches of the Gordon River. For the first decade of settlement, Strahan was little more than a supply base for prospectors. As larger mineral deposits—such as at Mt. Lyell, Zeehan, Dundas, and Mt. Reid—were developed, Strahan grew to become one of Tasmania's busiest ports. The population quickly reached 1,500; the town then boasted two railway stations, impressive civic buildings, Union Steamship Company offices, a hospital, and a sawmilling operation. Since the beginning of this decade, with mining and logging operations along the west coast in decline, Strahan has grown rapidly as a tourist center. What was, until a few short years ago, a sleepy fishing village is now a bustling town, overflowing with visitors in summer, yet, somehow, managing to retain a relaxing seaside atmosphere. With recreation on most visitors' minds, the region offers the opportunity to go fishing in the harbor, swimming at West Strahan Beach, or surfing at Ocean Beach.

Strahan Wharf Centre
Overlooking Macquarie Harbour, this intriguing timber-and-glass building should be the first stop for all visitors to town. Its unusual form, described as the world's first "magical realist building," includes one entire wall of multiple-

aned glass supported by roughly hewn poles of celery-topped pine, a wood featured throughout the interior. In the foyer, where a massive Huon pine desk is located, are seven mural scenes describing western Tasmania's human history. Beyond the information desk is a museum cataloging southwestern Tasmania's entire natural and human history. From the sounds and sight of a rushing waterfall upon entering the museum, to the lifestyle of Aboriginals, to the story of conflicts between conservationists and developers, the complex gives an excellent overview of the west coast. Admission to the exhibition section of the center is a worthwhile adult $4.50, child $3. The complex is open Dec.-April daily 10 a.m.-8 p.m. and May-Nov. daily 10 a.m.-6 p.m.

Adjoining the complex is an outdoor amphitheater where the play *The Ship that Never Was,* detailing the plight of Sarah Island convicts, is performed throughout summer; adult $7.50, child $5. For more information call (03) 6471-7488.

Scenic Drives
Teepookana, on the King River south of Strahan, was the site of a thriving logging industry early this century. From Strahan, the road south out to Teepookana passes Lettes Bay, where the Mt. Lyell Company built a small holiday village for workers, and passes through paddocks that once supported the dairy herds that provided the mining communities with fresh milk. At Teepookana, a rusting iron bridge is the major remnant of this once-bustling township.

A gravel track off the road out to Ocean Beach heads south through **Swan Basin State Reserve,** where a steep trail to a lookout and picturesque picnic area are located. From here the road continues south through a lush forest of pine plantations to **Macquarie Head Camping Ground;** $5 per night. Beyond the campground is a long sandy beach, with views across the narrow mouth of Macquarie Harbour to the white, cross-topped lighthouse on Cape Sorell. From this point you can continue on foot to the southern end of Ocean Beach. At the end of the access road to Ocean Beach, west of Strahan, is a muttonbird colony that comes alive Nov.-April when thousands of birds return to their burrows from a day's feeding at sea.

Between Strahan and Zeehan lie the **Henty Dunes.** An access road in their midst leads to a picnic area, where you can scramble up the dunes to the 360-degree views on the highest ridges.

Gordon River Cruises
Strahan has two companies competing for your cruising dollars. The main destination for both is the lower reaches of the Gordon River, part of the Tasmanian Wilderness World Heritage Area, but both companies include interesting stops en route. One of these is Sarah Island, site of a remote and brutal penal settlement at the beginning of the 1800s. Another interesting stop is made at Heritage Landing, where a raised boardwalk leads through coastal rainforest. **Gordon River Cruises** (tel. 03-6471-7187) has a full-day cruise departing Strahan Wharf daily at 9 a.m. for $60 and a half-day cruise for $42 (includes meals). They also have an evening cruise 6-8:30 p.m. for $40 pp including a crayfish dinner. **World Heritage Cruises** (tel. 03-6471-7174) is a smaller and more personal operation. Their cruises run daily 9 a.m.-4:30 p.m.; adult $36, child $16 (no meals included).

Wild Rivers Jet (tel. 03-6471-7174; book at the office on Strahan Wharf) operates 50-minute jet-boat rides up the King River for $33 pp. **Wilderness Air** (tel. 03-6471-7280) has a 90-minute flightseeing trip taking in the Gordon and Franklin Rivers and Frenchman's Cap for adult $95, child $60.

Accommodations
Right downtown is **Hamers Hotel** (tel. 03-6471-7191), part of a complex that includes a bakery, cafe, restaurant, bar, and laundry. Upstairs rooms are basic and have shared facilities, but views across Macquarie Harbour are good; $45 s, $55 d, which includes breakfast at the bakery. Terrace Rooms are of a higher standard, have private facilities, and water views; $75-100 s or d. The hotel also operates **Strahan Village Cottages,** nearby. Cottages are small but well furnished. Rates are $99-115 s or d, $120-130 with a spa. On the northwest outskirts of town is **Strahan Lodge,** Harvey St. (tel. 03-6471-7142), a simple yet comfortable accommodation. Rooms have shared facilities, and there's a spa, barbecue area, and indoor pool; $30 s, $45 d.

Strahan's most luxurious accommodation is **Franklin Manor,** on the Esplanade (tel. 03-6471-7311). Built in 1889, the mansion has 14 guest rooms, each with bathroom, and a few have private spas. Guests have use of a comfortable lounge with a large fireplace. Rates of $80-140 s, $90-150 d include breakfast, and an extra $35 pp will get you a three-course dinner.

Near the turnoff to Ocean Beach, and a 10-minute walk from town, is **Strahan YHA Hostel** (tel. 03-6471-7255). Beds in the dormitories are $12-14 pp. Three small A-frame cabins for $35 s or d are also offered.

Strahan Caravan Park, west of town on Innes St. (tel. 03-6471-7239), is across the road from the beach. Grassy tent sites are $10, powered sites $12. Between this park and downtown is **Strahan Cabin Park** (tel. 03-6471-7442), providing self-contained cabins with cooking facilities for $45-60.

Food

If you feel like fish and chips, there's no option but **West Coast Fishmobile,** beside the wharf. Their takeaway meals include locally caught fish, salmon burgers, crayfish salad, scallops (in season—April), and fish fingers for the kids. Prices range $2.50-8.50 and it's open daily until 8:30 p.m. Another place for an inexpensive feed is **Strahan Bakehouse,** the Esplanade, offering pies, pastries, and sandwiches along with freshly brewed coffee. Between 6 and 9 p.m. pizza and pasta are also offered. **Hamers Grill,** in Hamers Hotel, features Tasmanian specialties such as crayfish, scallops, and oysters. Lunch prices start at $4.50, rising to $25 for a crayfish salad. Dinner is more of the same, but a little more expensive. **Regatta Point Tavern** (tel. 03-6471-7103) is another popular spot for a casual meal.

Transportation, Services, and Information

Airlines of Tasmania (tel. 1800-03-0550) flies between Strahan and Hobart Tues.-Thurs. for $113 each way. **Tasmanian Wilderness Transport** (tel. 03-6334-4442) departs Hobart every Saturday at 8:30 a.m. for Strahan, with a one-hour stopover at Lake St. Clair; $40 one-way, $75 round-trip. This company also offers a service between Strahan and north coast towns each Saturday, departing Launceston at 8:30 a.m. and Devonport at 10:30 a.m. for $40 one-way, $70 round-trip. **Tasmanian Redline Coaches** (tel. 03-6431-3233) operates a direct service between Hobart and Strahan Mon.-Sat (departs Hobart 8:30 a.m.) for a similar price.

The old Customs House Building contains the **post office,** a **Commonwealth Bank** agency, and **Department of Environment and Land Management** office (tel. 03-6471-7122) which incorporates a World Heritage Area Visitors Centre. The latter is open daily 8 a.m.-5 p.m. A board outside lists all local activities.

ZEEHAN AND VICINITY

Sailing along Tasmania's west coast in 1642 Abel Tasman recorded a peak he named for his ship, *Zeehan.* Over 200 years later, with the discovery of a silver and lead deposit immediately north, a township developed. The mineral wealth attracted thousands of workers, and in 1910 Zeehan's population peaked at 10,000. From this time onward the town's fortunes took a nosedive, and it wasn't until the 1970s and the re-opening of the Renison Bell Tin Mine that the economy stabilized.

Zeehan's main street is lined with attractive turn-of-the-century buildings. One of these, the 1902 School of Mines building, is now **West Coast Pioneers Memorial Museum** (tel. 03-6471-6225). Browsing through the museum's many galleries, which include a large mineral collection, historic photos, the re-creation of an underground mine, old maps, and relics from the west coast penal colonies, can easily take a couple of hours. The museum is open daily 8:30 a.m.-5 p.m., and don't forget to drop a $2 donation for admission into the miner's wheelbarrow (made from Huon pine).

Tasmania's west coast is remote in the truest sense of the word, with only a half dozen access points along its entire length. Two of these, **Trial Harbour** and **Granville Harbour,** are west of Zeehan; neither has services.

Practicalities

The town's best-value accommodation is **Treasure Island West Coast Caravan Park,** on Hurst St. one km northeast of town (tel. 03-6471-6633). Small caravans with cooking facilities and bathrooms are $36 while cabins range

$46-50. For campers, pitching a tent will cost $11 and powered sites are $14. Right down-town is **Hotel Cecil** (tel. 03-6471-6221), where rooms have shared facilities and are $35 s, $40 d. On the south side of town is **Heemskirk Motor Hotel** (tel. 03-6471-6107), with a high

standard of rooms for $75. This hotel is the place to grab a counter meal; lunches are about $6 and dinners range $7-12.50.

Tasmanian Redline Coaches stops in Zee-han Mon.-Sat. on the route between Strahan and Devonport.

NORTHWESTERN TASMANIA

While most of Tasmania's best-known sights are bunched around Hobart and scattered through the interior, northwestern Tasmania, facing the wild waters of Bass Strait, is also worth exploring. The main routes through the area are the Murchison Highway and the Bass Highway, which follows the coast closely for over 80 km. Bass Highway's western terminus is the west coast, where a couple of small com-munities cling to the rugged coastline. West-ernmost of the towns facing Bass Strait is Stan-ey, nestled below a distinctive lump of land known as the Nut, and port for the surrounding rural area. East of Stanley are Wynyard, Burnie, and Penguin, which are great bases for ex-ploring the more remote areas of coastline or just relaxing on the beaches. Largest of the north coast towns is Devonport, where the pas-senger and vehicle ferry *Spirit of Tasmania* from mainland Australia docks. From Devon-port you can reach **Cradle Mountain-Lake St. Clair National Park,** 161,000 hectares of stun-ning topography.

MURCHISON HIGHWAY AND VICINITY

This highway links Tasmania's west and north coasts, although access to the actual ocean is limited. Northeast of Zeehan the Murchison Highway passes Renison Bell Tin Mine and the trailhead for a five-km hike to **Montezuma Falls,** considered one of Tasmania's most pho-togenic waterfalls. Farther east, on an arm of manmade Lake Pieman, is **Rosebery,** an old mining town with a tumultuous history. Although the town has little of interest the surrounding landscape of rolling hills and forests of leather-wood is picturesque. **Tullah,** north of Rose-

bery, was established as a mining town and now functions as a service center for workers on nearby hydroelectric schemes.

To the West Coast
Halfway between Rosebery and Wynyard a road branches west, dead ending at Corinna on the Pieman River. The first town along this route is **Waratah,** founded in 1871 after the discovery of a rich tin deposit on the slopes of nearby 784-meter Mt. Bischoff. Mining began in earnest in 1888, and for a time it was the world's richest tin mine. Some turn-of-the-century buildings re-main along the main street, including the court-house, which now houses a museum. Adjacent to the museum is a replica of an old miner's hut.

West of Waratah the road passes two mining towns, each existing to serve mine workers and their families, before turning to gravel and ending at **Corinna** on the Pieman River. It was the dis-covery of gold in 1881 that first brought settlers to this remote part of the state, and although the rush was shortlived, it was particularly rich, with the largest nugget found weighing 243 ounces. The area's only formal tourist activity is a cruise along the Pieman River aboard *Arcadia II*. De-partures are daily at 10:30 a.m. Accommodation in town is at **Pieman Retreat** (tel. 03-6446-1170), which has cabins for $50-80 per night (supply your own linen) and tent sites for $3 pp.

Hellyer Gorge
Carved by the Hellyer River, this impressive gorge is accessed by a one-km trail (15 min-utes each way) that starts on the west side of the highway where it crosses the river. The trail passes through a lush rainforest of ferns, sas-safras, giant myrtle, blackwood, and leather-wood. Across the road from the trailhead is a great little picnic area.

STANLEY

In 1825 the Van Diemen's Land Company was granted a large tract of land in northwestern Tasmania, establishing its headquarters at Highfield and developing a port facility at nearby Stanley. As the importance of Highfield diminished, Stanley grew in stature. Today the town boasts a population of about 600. Stanley is nestled in the shadow of a massive knob of basalt that rises from the ocean. Geologists think it formed about 12 million years ago when a mass of molten rock spewed from a crack in the earth's surface, cooling to form basalt. Named Circular Head by early explorers, the landmark is better known today as, simply, the **Nut.** Along the Nut's southern flanks is a large port facility and a breakwall that protects a colorful fleet of fishing vessels. At the base of the Nut (on Browns Rd.) is a parking lot from where a trail leads up to the summit, 143 meters above sea level. Another option for reaching the summit is to ride the **chairlift;** adult $5.50, child $3.50. Once at the top, there's a three-km circuit trail dotted with interpretive signs. One of the trail highlights is a rookery of shearwaters that nest Nov.-March. The extremely rare peregrine falcon is occasionally sighted on the Nut.

Town Sights

Plough Inn, 35 Church St. (tel. 03-6458-1226), dating from 1840, was a licensed hotel for a couple of decades in the mid-1800s. A few rooms have been restored, each decorated with furnishings you'd expect in an inn from this period. Admission is $4.50. Open daily 9:30 a.m.-5 p.m. Also on Church St. is the **Discovery Centre Folk Museum,** cataloging Stanley's early history through photographs as well as having relics from shipwrecks and mineral and shell displays. Admission is $2, and it's open daily 10 a.m.-4 p.m. (closed in winter). Those interested in the history of Australian politics may want to visit **Lyon's Cottage,** a bluestone building preserved as the birthplace of Joseph A. Lyons, prime minister of Australia between 1932 and his death in 1939. Open for inspection daily 10 a.m.-4 p.m.

Highfield Historic Site

At Greenhills, six km from Stanley, is Highfield, the original Tasmanian headquarters of the Van Diemen's Land Company. Granted 250,000 acres, this British stock company was instrumental in the northwest's settlement. The company's massive business empire functioned almost as a separate colony, with ships sailing directly between England and Highfield and developing whole towns to service their workers. The Highfield property remains much as it would have looked in the mid-1800s, with many original buildings still standing and an interesting array of farm machinery scattered around the grounds. The main residence has been extensively restored, and a self-guided tour takes you through each room, with detailed descriptions of all displays. Admission to the site is $2 pp and it's open daily 10 a.m.-4:45 p.m. To visit the house is an additional $4 pp.

Accommodations and Food

Stanley Motel and Holiday Units, Dovecote Rd. (tel. 03-6458-1300), is one km west of town. Basic motel rooms start at $55 d, those with spas are $75. The self-contained units are older but have great ocean views, making them good value at $65-75. **Harbour Masters Colonial Accommodation,** 42 Alexander Terrace (tel. 03-6458-1209), is a comfortable three-bedroom house dating from about 1860 with views extending across the beach to the ocean. Rates are $85 d, which includes the use of a kitchen stocked with breakfast provisions. Across from Highfield Historic Site is **Anthony's at Highfield** (tel. 03-6458-1245), a spacious accommodation with clean and bright rooms, ocean views, and a kitchen stocked with breakfast provisions. Rooms start at $80 d. **Stanley Caravan Park,** right at the waterfront on Wharf Rd. (tel. 03-6458-1266), is a large place with plenty of good campsites and cabins with water views. The camper kitchen features stoves and a fridge. Tent sites are $9, powered sites $11, on-site vans $30, and cabins $50. Book ahead in summer. Within this caravan park is **Stanley YHA Hostel,** which has all the usual facilities; $10 pp.

Stanley has a few good restaurants specializing in local seafood. Pick of the bunch is **Julie and Patrick's,** 2 Alexander Terrace (tel. 03-6458-1103), featuring oysters, crayfish, and seafood crepes. Main dishes average $15. Open daily from 6 p.m. Below this restaurant is a seafood takeaway and bakery. For a filling counter meal, head to the popular **Union Hotel** on Church St. (tel. 03-6458-1161). This places really comes alive on Friday night when bands crank up the pace and seemingly half the town crams in. Part of the same complex is **Hursey Seafood,** which features two massive tanks, one filled with a variety of fish, the other with crays. They sell fresh seafood, perfect if you have access to a kitchen, or they'll cook it for you. Open daily 9 a.m.-6 p.m.

THE REMOTE NORTHWEST CORNER

The Bass Highway extends 65 km west from Stanley to a remote stretch of coast accessible in only a couple of spots. Just out of Stanley is **Smithton,** an administrative center for the surrounding farming region. South of Smithton, on the road to Edith Creek, is **Allendale Gardens,** featuring two hectares of pleasant gardens crisscrossed with walking trails. Admission $5. Open Sept. to mid-May 9 a.m.-5 p.m.

Marrawah

This small seaside community at the end of the Bass Highway is Tasmania's westernmost town. It comprises little more than a hotel and general store, but beyond is **Green Point,** one of Tasmania's premier surfing spots.

Arthur Pieman Protected Area

The small community of **Arthur River,** 14 km south of Marrawah, lies at the north end of 100,000-hectare Arthur Pieman Protected Area. Between Marrawah and Arthur River are various access points to the wild coastline, but access roads are rough. The protected area encompasses a 90-km stretch of the coast and features a diverse landscape of rocky headlands, dune systems, and rivers rolling down westward from the Norfolk Range. The best way to explore the river is on an **Arthur River Cruise** aboard a beautiful old timber boat. The cruise penetrates around 14 km upstream, passing rainforest to Turk's Landing where a barbecue lunch is served. The trip lasts about five hours and is a reasonable adult $35, child $15. For bookings, call (03) 6457-1158. The coastal scenery out by Gardiner Point, at the mouth of the Arthur River, is quite spectacular, with water

from the river flowing headlong into the ocean. From Arthur River, a road continues south, with many sidetracks leading to the ocean. Around Couta Rocks, 18 km south of Arthur River, the scenery is especially spectacular. Farther south are the remains of **Balfour,** a once-thriving copper-mining town that slid into oblivion after the mine closed in 1916.

The only accommodation in the area is **Arthur River Holiday Units** (tel. 03-6457-1288), comprising comfortable self-contained units for $60-70 and a few backpacker dormitories with beds for $20 pp.

STANLEY TO BURNIE

Rocky Cape National Park

Protecting a rugged stretch of coastline where the Bass Highway makes an inland detour east of Stanley, this 3,064-hectare park features sheltered beaches flanked by rocky headlands. The main entry is from the east, but another access road dead-ends out on Rocky Cape, the park's westernmost point. From the end of this road a short trail descends to **North Cave,** once used by Aboriginals as shelter.

Access west from Boat Harbour leads to the golden sands of **Sisters Beach.** Near the end of the road is a fork. The road to the left leads to 10-hectare **Birdland Nature Park,** where a short hiking trail passes through various local habitats to a lookout where views extend over Sisters Beach. Admission is $2.50. Open daily 9 a.m.-5 p.m. Several trails begin from the end of the sealed road. The most enjoyable is east along the beach, returning via an inland trail; allow 90 minutes round-trip. Another trail (two km round-trip) leads through a dense grove of coastal banksia. The Anniversary Bay Circuit, taking about two and a half hours to complete, heads to a hidden coastal beach, with sidetracks to a lookout and waterfall. The trail between Sisters Beach and Rocky Cape is 11 km each way (allow three and a half hours each way), with the option to return along an inland route. Beyond the trailheads for the above hikes a rough gravel road continues west, providing access to the beach at various points. The park has no campgrounds; the only facilities are at a shaded picnic area beside Sisters Creek.

Boat Harbour Beach

Along the main road into Rocky Cape National Park the road branches right to Boat Harbour Beach, one of Tasmania's most beautiful stretches of sand. Behind the beach is a pleasant holiday village with all facilities. **Boat Harbour Beach Resort,** Esplanade (tel. 03-6445-1107), with coastal and ocean views, a pool, spa, and sauna, has rooms for $55 s, $75 d. **Country Garden Cottages** (tel. 03-6445-1233) comprises cozy timber cottages surrounded by well-manicured gardens. Each has a separate bedroom, kitchen, and living area. Rates are $60-70 per cottage with breakfast hampers an extra $3-6 pp. Across from the beach is **Boat Harbour Beach Caravan Park,** with coin-operated showers, a general store, a laundry, and grassed tent sites. Sites are $8-11, on-site vans $30. **Harbour Restaurant** (tel. 03-6445-1371) specializes in seafood, with dinners averaging $18. Open Tues.-Sat. for lunch and dinner. Next door is **Harbour Shoppe,** a takeaway joint serving great hamburgers.

Wynyard and Vicinity

Although Wynyard itself has little of interest, this commercial center of 4,800 is a good base for exploring the surrounding coastal habitats. Immediately west of town is **Table Cape,** a magnificent plateau of green fields that drop dramatically into the ocean. On the cape itself is **Fossil Bluff,** best viewed at low tide. Also out on the cape is a lighthouse dating from 1888 and a lookout with views extending back to Wynyard and the valley in which it lies.

Leisure Ville Caravan Park, 145 Scenic Drive (tel. 03-6442-2291), three km west of town, is a great place to stay, with a shell-covered beach across the road and views of Table Cape. Facilities include an indoor heated pool, spa, barbecues, and laundry. Sites are $10-17, on-site vans $32, and cabins $48-50. **Wynyard YHA Hostel,** 36 Dodgin St. (tel. 03-6442-2013), is a small house one block from downtown. Beds are $10-12 per night. For a little more style, there's **Alexandria Guesthouse,** an old homestead out on Table Cape that dates from 1908. Each of the four rooms has a bathroom while guests have use of a pool, barbecue, and laundry. Rates of $65 s, $80 d include a cooked breakfast. For bookings call (03) 6442-2094.

Grab a meal at the **Federal Hotel,** 82 Goldie St. (tel. 03-6442-2056), open daily for lunch and dinner; main dishes average $10. **Seaview Diner,** on the Esplanade one km east of downtown (tel. 03-6442-8727), offers breakfasts from $4 and hamburgers and fish and chips from $3.50. Desserts, made on the premises, are very good. Open daily 9 a.m.-9 p.m.

BURNIE

Burnie (pop. 21,000) is a bustling service and tourist center on the shore of Emu Bay 20 km east of Wynyard and 326 km northwest of Hobart. It is an important industrial center, with Amcor, Australia's largest papermaker, having a mill in town. The town's port is an intregral part of all local industry. Constructed as a single wharf in 1827 to move ore from Waratah onto ships bound for the mainland, it has grown to be Australia's fifth-largest containerport.

Sights

On Wilmot St., one block from the Bass Hwy. the **Civic Centre Precinct** features the Pioneer Village Museum, an information center, a library, and an art gallery. **Pioneer Village Museum** is a replica of an 1890s street, complete with a blacksmith's shop, printer, bakery, and bootmaker. Also part of the museum is a collection of historic wedding gowns and photography and map displays. Admission is adult $4, child $2. Open Mon.-Fri. 9 a.m.-5 p.m., Sat.-Sun. 1:30-4:30 p.m. In the same complex is the **Regional Art Gallery;** open the same hours as the museum and with free admission.

Burnie Park, along Shorewell Creek off North Terrace, is a pleasant spread of parkland with a few caged animals. Also within the park is **Burnie Inn.** This small inn, Burnie's oldest building, dates from 1847 and is open daily except Tuesday 10:30 a.m.-3:30 p.m.

Lactos Cheese Factory, on Old Surrey Rd (off Bass Hwy. east of downtown), has a Tasting and Sales Room open Mon.-Fri. 9 a.m.-5 p.m. Sat.-Sun. 10 a.m.-4 p.m. Meals served here are remarkably inexpensive, with a filling Farmer's Lunch only $5.50 and a chunk of delicious cheesecake a tempting $2.

Accommodations and Food

In summer, finding somewhere to stay in Burnie can be difficult; even the caravan parks require advance bookings. Best value of all accommodations is **Treasure Island Caravan Park,** on the Bass Hwy. three km west of town (tel. 03-6431-1925). Self-contained units are $54, cabins start at $44, and campsites range $10-13. Otherwise try the very basic **Hillside Inn,** 20 Edwards St. (tel. 03-6431-3222), southeast of downtown; $40 s, $60 d. The flashiest place in town, and priced accordingly, is **Innkeepers Voyager Motor Inn** at 9 North Terrace (tel. 03-6431-4866); $119-130 s or d.

Rose's on the Park Cafe, in the historic Burnie Inn (Burnie Park), is open for morning and afternoon teas and lunch. For a good quality counter meal, head to the **Beach Hotel,** on the corner of Wilson St. and North Terrace. The seafood here is delicious; daily specials are about $13. Across the road, in the Innkeepers Voyager Motor Inn, is **Terrace Cafe,** with water views and main meals from as little as $7.50. For a more formal meal, **Wellers Inn,** 36 Queens St. (tel. 03-6431-1088), is the place to go. This restaurant specializes in seafood (from $15), but chicken and beef dishes are also offered. **Alto Restaurant,** Wilmot St. (tel. 03-6431-7718), has a wide range of Italian dishes, with meals averaging around $12. Open Mon.-Sat. for lunch and dinner. (Also, see the Lactose Cheese Factory in the "Sights" section above.)

Transportation, Services, and Information

Burnie Airport is a $19 cab fare west of town at Wynyard. This is the closest Tasmanian airport to the mainland (apart, of course, from those on King and Flinders Islands), and fares start at $154 one-way from Melbourne. **Kendell** (tel. 13-1300) flies this route daily. From this airport **Airlines of Tasmania** (tel. 1800-03-0550) flies to other state centers. **Tasmanian Redline Coaches** (tel. 03-6331-3233) and **Hobart Coaches** (tel. 1800-03-0620) have regular services between Burnie and Devonport, with Redline continuing two days a week to Stanley.

The **Tasmanian Travel and Information Centre,** right downtown in the Civic Centre Precinct (tel. 03-6434-6105), has information on not only Burnie but the entire northwest, and staff will help find overnight accommodations.

The center is open Mon.-Fri. 9 a.m.-5 p.m., Saturday 9 a.m.-noon.

BURNIE TO DEVONPORT

Penguin

Named for the colonies of fairy penguins that were once common along the north coast, this small town of 3,000 is spread along picturesque bays and backed by rolling hills of forest. The penguin population has all but been wiped out in the immediate vicinity of town, but Nov.-March, if you're lucky, you may sight the odd bird at dusk near the caravan park. Organized penguin viewing is at Penguin Point at dusk; adult $5, child $2. Call ahead at (03) 6437-2570.

Beachfront Lodge, 64 Main St. (tel. 03-6437-2672), right in the center of town, has four high-standard rooms from $40 s, $55 d, including a light breakfast.

Penguin to Ulverstone
Via the Inland Route

The coastal townships of Penguin and Ulverstone lie 12 km apart via a coastal road, but a far more interesting route detours inland through the Gunns Plains. **Gunns Plains Hop Farm,** on Gunns Plains Rd. (tel. 03-6429-1366), offers guided tours in summer Mon.-Sat. 10 a.m.-4 p.m.; adult $4.50, child $1.

At the end of a beautiful valley southwest of Gunns Plains, **Gunns Plains State Reserve** protects a small system of limestone caverns. Tours of the caves depart daily 10 a.m.-4 p.m. on the hour; adult $6, child $3. For details call (03) 6429-1388.

Beyond Gunns Plains and alongside the Leven River is 40-hectare **Wings Farm Park,** Winduss Rd. (tel. 03-6429-1335). This large campground is in a great rural location with camping on a grassed area or in shade along the river. Tent sites are a bargain at $6, powered sites are $8.50, and self-contained cabins with river views are $45.

Ulverstone

Straddling the wide mouth of the Leven River, this bustling town of 10,000 is in the heart of a rich agricultural district. Like Penguin to the west, the town is a popular holiday spot with loads of facilities and many nearby beaches and headlands to explore. The aptly named **Ocean View Guest House,** 1 Victoria St. (tel. 03-6425-5401), is in a great location right across from the beach. Rooms are clean and comfortable and a bargain at $35 s, $55 d, including breakfast. Also good value is **Ulverstone Motor Lodge,** 2 Tasman Parade (tel. 03-6425-1599), west of downtown, where rooms are $50 s, $55 d.

DEVONPORT

In 1890 settlements on the east and west banks of the Mersey River united to become the town of Devonport. Today this industrial town is a port for the mainland ferry, *Spirit of Tasmania,* and is northwestern Tasmania's largest town. Devonport's main attractions are all within walking distance of each other, with a hiking trail following the west bank of the Mersey River from downtown to the river mouth and out to Mersey Bluff.

Mersey Bluff
On this magnificent headland immediately north of downtown is Devonport's top attraction, **Tiagarra,** an Aboriginal culture and arts center. The entire history of Tasmanian Aboriginals, from 23,000 years ago when they crossed a land bridge from mainland Australia and developed their own unique culture, to their undignified fate 150 years ago, is detailed. From the center, a trail leads along the coast to Tasmania's most accessible concentration of native rock art, with about 240 engravings. Admission is adult $2.50, child $1. Open daily 9 a.m.-4 p.m. For more information call (03) 6424-8250.

Other Sights
The **Tasmanian Maritime and Folk Museum,** at the north end of Victoria Parade, is open daily except Monday 1:30-4:30 p.m. (shorter hours in winter). It contains a collection of maritime memorabilia, including model ships, a Lloyd's Register of Ships, relics from the whaling era, a historical display of the Bass Strait Ferry, old diving gear, and a full listing of all the wretched souls deported on the First and Second Fleets. Admission is a worthwhile $2.

In the old Baptist Church at 45-47 Stewart St. (tel. 03-6424-8296) is **Devonport Gallery and Art Centre,** featuring works by Tasmanian artists. Open Mon.-Sat. 10 a.m.-5 p.m., Sunday 2-5 p.m.

Home Hill, 77 Middle Rd. (tel. 03-6424-3028), a large whitewashed home, was built in 1916 for former prime minister Joseph A. Lyons, who ran Australia between 1932 and 1939. A guided tour of the property is $5. Farther west, where the Bass Hwy. crosses the Don River, is **Don River Railway and Museum** (tel. 03-6424-6335). The museum features Tasmania's largest collection of steam locomotives and carriages as well as offering the opportunity to ride an old train that operates daily 11 a.m.-4 p.m., adult $6, child $3. Admission to the museum is $2 pp.

Accommodations
The most popular travelers' accommodation in Devonport is **River View Lodge,** 18 Victoria Parade (tel. 03-6424-7357), across the road from the Mersey River and a short walk from downtown. Each room is well decorated and has a television; some have bathrooms. Communal areas include a lounge with woodstove, dining room, laundry, and outdoor barbecue area. Rates are a reasonable $45-55 s, $55-65 d, which includes a delicious hot breakfast. **Mac Wright House YHA Hostel,** 155 Middle Rd. (tel. 03-6424-5696), is beyond Home Hill historic house, just over two km southwest of downtown. It's a friendly place, with a spacious living area and well-equipped kitchen. Beds are from $11 pp.

Motel accommodation in Devonport is limited. The least expensive option is **Edgewater Motor Inn,** 2 Thomas St. (tel. 03-6427-8441), close to the ferry terminal and a short hop by commuter ferry from downtown. The exterior isn't particularly appealing, but the rates are only $44 s, $54 d. **Innkeepers Gateway Motor Inn,** 16 Fenton St. (tel. 03-6424-4922), is also not attractive, but is central to downtown and offers a high standard of facilities; from $90 s, $98 d.

One of a row of tiny cottages, **Turton Cottage,** 28 Turton St. (tel. 03-6424-1560), features a comfortable living room complete with piano, a kitchen stocked with breakfast provisions, and a bedroom with a high four-poster bed. Out back is a pleasant veranda with seating and a wood-fired barbecue. Rates are $100 s or d. Book ahead.

MERSEY BLUFF

DEVONPORT

TIAGARRA

MERSEY BLUFF
CARAVAN PARK

BASS
STRAIT

BEACH RD.   BLUFF   RD.

BAY VIEW HOLIDAY
VILAGE

TASMANIAN MARITIME AND
FOLK MUSEUM

VICTORIA

NORTH

CAROLINE

ST.

FENTON

ST.

JAMES

ST.

ABEL TASMAN
CARAVAN PARK

ST.

GEORGE

ST.

WRIGHT

TARLETON

DAVID

MARY

ST.

RIVER VIEW
LODGE

BROOKE

ST.

NICHOLLS

GUNN

WILLIAM

PARADE

CHURCH

THOMAS

ST.

RONALD

PARKER

INNKEEPERS GATEWAY
MOTOR INN

EDGEWATER MOTOR
INN

MURRAY

CAROLINE

ROOKE STREET
MALL

OLDAKER

BACKPACKER'S
BARN

ROOKE

DEVONPORT
SHOWCASE

FERRY TERMINAL

STEPHEN
ST.

ST.

BEST

ST.

FORMBY HOTEL

DOUGLAS

DEVONPORT GALLERY
AND ART CENTRE

STEWART

SILKY APPLE
RESTAURANT

JOHN

ST.

STEELE

ST.

TORQUAY

RD.

MERSEY

TASMAN

FORBES

ROOKE

RIVER

FORMBY

VALLEY

MIDDLE

ROAD

ROAD

HIGHWAY

TO AIRPORT AND
LAUNCESTON

TO
DON RIVER RAILWAY AND MUSEUM
AND ULVERSTONE

BASS

HOME HILL

ROAD

MIDDLE

MAC WRIGHT HOUSE
YHA HOSTEL

NOT TO SCALE

On a windswept headland north of downtown is **Mersey Bluff Caravan Park** (tel. 03-6424-8655), with brilliant coastal views from an absolute waterfront location two km from downtown. Unpowered sites are $12, powered sites $13.50, on-site vans $34, and self-contained cabins $44. Facilities include a kitchen, barbecue, and laundry. **Abel Tasman Caravan Park** at 6 Wright St. on the east side of the river (tel. 03-6427-8794) has a pleasing parkside location a stone's throw from where the waters of the Mersey River drain into Bass Strait. This park offers plenty of flat grassy sites, showers (20 cents), and a large laundry room, as well as a shop with hot food takeaways. Tent sites are $8, powered sites $10, on-site vans with cooking facilities and television from $30 d, and self-contained cabins range $46-52. On the east side of the Mersey River are three more caravan parks. Best of these is **Bay View Holiday Village,** 2 Caroline St. (tel. 03-6427-0499), along the rocky shoreline of Bass Strait. Sites are $7-11, and excellent cabins, complete with bathrooms and kitchens, are $38-45.

Food

For a quick meal, head to the pedestrian mall on Rooke St., where there are plenty of choices. For breakfast try **Banjo's,** a bakery on the mall open from 6 a.m. serving bacon and eggs for $3.60-4.60. The rest of the day, Devonshire tea is $3 and there's the usual choice of pies, cakes, and pastries. **Formby Hotel,** 82 Formby Rd. (tel. 03-6424-1601), right downtown and with river views, offers the Formby Feast, a choice of three main courses plus an all-you-can-eat salad and dessert bar for $12.95. Open daily for lunch and dinner. The best Chinese food in town is dished up at **Silky Apple Restaurant,** 33 King St. (tel. 03-6424-4148); main dishes average $13. Part of this restaurant is a takeaway section where lunch is $4.50 and dinner $7.50. **Rialto Restaurant,** 159 Rooke St. (tel. 03-6424-6793), features stylish decor and an Italian-influenced menu; soups are $4-6, antipasti $6.90-8.50, and most main pasta meals $11 (minimum $15 pp). Open Mon.-Fri. for lunch and daily for dinner. **Dangerous Liaisons,** 28 Forbes St. (tel. 03-6424-6431), is an old redbrick house popular for everything from a light lunch or cappuccino to a pre-theater drink in the intimate wine ba. Open Tues.-Fri. for lunch and dinner and Sa urday for dinner only.

Transportation, Services, and Information

Devonport is the terminus of *Spirit of Tasma nia,* the passenger and vehicle ferry linking Tas mania to mainland Australia. The timetable i fairly straightforward. The ferry departs Me bourne every Monday, Wednesday, and Frida at 6 p.m. (check-in time is 3:30 p.m.), arriving i Devonport the following morning at 8:30 a.m Every Tuesday, Thursday, and Sunday th timetable is reversed, with the ferry departin Devonport at 6 p.m. (check-in time is 3:30 p.m and arriving in Melbourne approximately 14 an a half hours later. The ferry terminal is across th Mersey River from downtown. The ticket office i open Mon.-Sat. 8 a.m.-6 p.m. All passengers, in cluding those with vehicles, should make rese vations well in advance. For these, call 13-201 anywhere in Australia.

For those who arrive in Devonport withou transportation, there are a few options. The eas iest way to travel between the terminal an downtown is aboard a small commuter ferr that crosses the Mersey River every 15 mir utes; $1.20 each way. A shuttle bus also run into town from the terminal. On the upstairs leve of the terminal are desks for the following ca rental agencies: Avis, Budget, Colonial, Hertz and Thrifty. Cars should reserved well in ad vance; book through any mainland office.

Tasmanian Wilderness Transport (tel. 03 6334-4442) and **Tasmanian Redline Coache** (tel. 03-6331-3233) depart the terminal for des tinations throughout the state soon after th ferry arrives. Sample one-way fares from De vonport are: Launceston $18, Hobart $29, Cra dle Mountain $30, and Strahan $40.

Devonport's **Pardoe Airport** is seven kr east of town on the road out to Port Sorell. It i served by **Kendell** (tel. 13-1300), Southern Aus tralia Airlines (tel. 13-1313), and **Airlines o Tasmania** (tel. 1800-03-0550). An airport shut tle (tel. 03-6424-9112) meets all flights; $5 eac way. At the airport are a few car rental desks, bu again, reserve a car well in advance. **Bass Flight Services** (tel. 03-6427-9777) offers flight seeing starting at $50 pp for a quick run alon e coast, but the opportunities are unlimited, ith flights also over Cradle Mountain and along e remote west coast.

Backpacker's Barn, 10 Edwards St. (tel. 03-424-3628), has a good range of camping and ackcountry equipment. It's open Mon.-Fri. and aturday morning. The **Tasmanian Travel and nformation Centre** is in Devonport Showcase t 5 Best St. (tel. 03-6424-4466); open Mon.-ri. 9 a.m.-5 p.m., Sat.-Sun. 9 a.m.-4 p.m. In e same complex is a **Travel Centre,** for tour nd accommodations bookings throughout the tate. It's open Mon.-Fri. 9 a.m.-5 p.m., Saturday a.m.-noon.

DEVONPORT
TO CRADLE MOUNTAIN

heffield and Vicinity

ounded in 1886 after gold was discovered in e area, Sheffield nestles among rolling hills lanketed in lush green farmland with the south-rn horizon dominated by 1,231-meter Mt. oland. Since 1986 Sheffield has become nown as "Town of Murals," and you'll see why ruising down the main street (even the local ilet block is decorated). The town has 33 mu-ls in total, most created by local artists and epicting the history, geography, wildlife, and eople of north-central Tasmania. The **Kentish luseum,** 93 Main St. (tel. 03-6491-1861), with isplays on the nearby Mersey-Forth hydro-lectric scheme and the world's first self-serve etrol pump, is open Mon.-Fri. 1-3 p.m. and in ummer Sat.-Sun. 2-4 p.m. Admission by do-ation. Pottery shoppers shouldn't miss **No /here Else Pottery,** also on the main street el. 03-6491-1952), which sells a great variety of nusual pieces.

The best-value accommodation in the Shef-eld area is **Paradise Cottage,** on Jeffrey's Rd. ve km south of town (tel. 03-6491-1613). It's on 30-hectare farm in the shadow of towering It. Roland. The cottage is divided into two ooms; both are spacious and open to an out-oor area with stunning views. Rates are $30-45 , $45-60 d. Another bed and breakfast-style ccommodation is **Tanglewood,** 25 High St. el. 03-6491-1854), just west of the post office. ooms are comfortable and good value at $60 s,

$75 d. The other option is **Sheffield Caravan Park** at 63 High St. (tel. 03-6491-1366), where sites are $8-10 and basic on-site vans are $25 (coin-operated showers).

Best of the bunch of cafes along the main street is **Red Rose Cafe,** open daily from 7:30 a.m. Across the road is **High Country Bakehouse,** which has delicious bread rolls and a choice of fillings for only $2.

The best source of town information is **Diversity Gallery,** at 34 Main Street (tel. 03-6491-1613), which screens an audiovisual on the murals. Open Mon.-Sat. 9 a.m.-5:30 p.m., Sunday 12:30-5 p.m.

Silver Ridge Retreat

This magnificent accommodation is on Rysavy Rd. 11 km south of Sheffield (tel. 03-6491-1727). It comprises self-contained, fully equipped, two-bedroom timber cottages, each with a log fire and comfortable lounge area. The property over-looks a working farm with the distinct Mt. Roland as a backdrop. Other features include an in-door heated swimming pool, a resident family of platypuses, lounge bar, and a restaurant serving delicious home-style meals. Cottages are $135 d or $150 for the luxury of a private spa with mountain views.

Gowrie Park

Gowrie Park was established as the construction base for the massive Mersey-Forth hydroelectric scheme, which was completed in 1973. The de-velopment comprises seven power stations, seven large dams, and three major tunnels, all of which combine to harness power from the flow of four rivers over an area of 2,070 square kilo-meters. At the time of construction 2,500 work-ers were accommodated in the settlement, but upon completion, most buildings were removed, leaving only an assortment of structures to house administrative and mechanical concerns. Hiking trails allow you the opportunity to explore the natural surroundings, although most peo-ple will want to push on farther into the moun-tains. One hike worth considering is to the sum-mit of Mt. Roland, a leisurely six-hour round-trip. The best sources of trail information are the hosts of the backpacker lodge (see below) or the book *Family Walks in Northwest Tasmania* by Jan Hardy and Bert Elfin.

Part of the remaining workers' quarters has been converted to **Mt. Roland Backpackers Accommodation** (tel. 03-6491-1385), with spacious communal facilities including a kitchen, dining room, living room, and laundry; from $12 pp. Also in the complex is **Weindorfer's Restaurant.** The menu features something to suit everyone, with main meals starting at $8.80. It's open Oct.-May daily from 10 a.m., but you'll need reservations for dinner.

CRADLE MOUNTAIN-LAKE ST. CLAIR NATIONAL PARK

Of Tasmania's many wilderness areas, the mountainous terrain encompassed by this 161,000-hectare park is generally accepted as the most spectacular, while also being relatively accessible. Not only is the region protected as a national park, but it's also an integral part of the Tasmanian Wilderness World Heritage Area. Park topography is varied and complex but can be basically divided into three regions. In the north is a high treeless plateau broken by deep glacial lakes and the ridge upon which 1,545-meter Cradle Mountain sits. The park's central portion is also high, an area of heathland surrounded by jagged peaks, including Tasmania's highest peak, 1,617-meter **Mt. Ossa.** In the south is the Du Cane Range, whose watershed flows eastward to **Lake St. Clair.**

The park's main facility area is the Cradle Valley, in the north of the park. By road, this valley is 85 km south of Devonport and 284 km northwest of Hobart.

The Land

Present park landforms are a result of glacial activity some 20,000 years ago, but it was many millions of years before that the mountains themselves were formed. Ice was first involved in the mountain-making process 290 million years ago when the region was covered in a sheet of ice, which, when melted, exposed a massive river plain upon which layers of sediment were deposited over time. Massive upward thrusts around 160 million years ago formed a mountain range that subsequent ice ages and wind and water erosion have sculpted to its present form. Glaciation in Tasmania ended 14,000 years

ago. In the 10,000 years preceding that time vast areas of the state's western portion were covered in a sheet of ice. As the ice retreated the high valleys, it gouged massive U-shaped valleys, rounded off mountaintops, and left moraines of rock to form natural dams.

Weather conditions within the park are unpredictable; even the most beautiful sunny morning can turn into a howling gale and driving sleet within hours. Almost three meters of precipitation falls annually, and the park averages rain on 275 days of every year. This figure doesn't take into account overcast days; these account for another two out of every 10 days. On average just 32 days a year are sunny.

Flora and Fauna

Due to extreme elevation differences within the park, you'll encounter a great variety of plant species. In the valleys cool-temperate rainforest thrives. These areas are dominated by Antarctic beech with an understory of mosses, ferns and lichens. Eucalypts are found away from the damp valley floors, but it's above the treeline that the real survivors of the plant kingdom are found. At higher elevations glacial forces have scraped the bedrock almost bare of soil while freezing winds and heavy winter snows prohibit growth more than a meter or so above the ground.

Since the coming of Europeans, the state's most famous animal, the Tasmanian tiger, has been wiped out from the Cradle Valley (as well as the rest of Australia). The country's largest carnivorous mammal, the Tasmanian devil, remains in the area, but there's nothing to fear as this shy creature prefers animal carcasses to *Homo sapiens.* Mammals most likely to be seen by casual observers include the Bennett's wallaby, pademelons, and possums. The platypus and echidna, the world's only two monotremes, are also common in the park. Many smaller animals once prolific across Australia are now confined to remote areas of Tasmania, such as this park. One of these is the Tasmanian mountain shrimp, a relic of Gondwana that has remained relatively unchanged over millions of years.

History

Aboriginals used the Cradle Valley on their nomadic travels for many hundreds of years before

CRADLE MOUNTAIN-LAKE ST. CLAIR NATIONAL PARK

TO LAUNCESTON

TO DEVONPORT

CAMPGROUND

AIRSTRIP

VISITOR CENTRE

CRADLE MOUNTAIN LODGE

PINE CREEK

CRADLE VALLEY

LEMONTHYME LODGE

WALDHEIM HUTS

CRATER LAKE

DOVE LAKE

CRADLE MTN. (1,545 m)

FORTH RIVER

MERSEY RIVER

LAKE MACKINTOSH

OVERLAND RIVER

LAKE ROWALLAN

CRADLE MOUNTAIN-

PELION GAP

MT. OSSA (1,617 m)

WALLS OF JERUSALEM

LAKE MURCHISON

MURCHISON

TRACK

DU CANE RANGE

LAKE ST. CLAIR

NATIONAL PARK

RIVER

PINE VALLEY

NATIONAL PARK

QUEENSTOWN

CHEYNE RANGE

LAKE ST. CLAIR

LAKE BURBURY

LYELL

CYNTHIA BAY

DERWENT BRIDGE

TO HOBART

FRANKLIN-GORDON WILD RIVERS

HWY

LAKE KING WILLIAMS

0   10 km

NATIONAL PARK

the arrival of Europeans. During the European push to eradicate Tasmania's native population, one of the last remaining families hid in the valley, evading capture until 1842. Throughout the 1800s, the region was visited by surveyors, prospectors, loggers, and cattlemen. It wasn't until this century, though, that the region was appreciated for more than its resources. In 1912 Austrian Gustav Weindorfer built Waldheim, a rustic chalet, in the Cradle Valley. His enthusiasm for the mountains brought guests back year after year, and in 1921 he first proposed a sanctuary. At first two reserves were set aside, then, in 1947, they were combined to create Cradle Mountain-Lake St. Clair National Park.

Day Hiking

Tracks lead along the east and west shores of **Dove Lake** but never meet. The **Truganini Track** traverses the lake's eastern shore, passing Suicide Rock and many quartzite beaches. To the end of the trail is two km (40 minutes each way).

Across the lake, a trail passes through the **Ballroom Forest,** an enchanting area of rainforest, and ends near a waterfall on Plateau Creek; two km (40 minutes each way). From the waterfall the trail climbs steeply to the plateau from which Cradle Mountain rises, and it's possible to follow the ridge west to Kitchen Hut for a summit climb or east to the Lake Rodway Track. From Dove Lake, the **Lake Rodway Track** (six

km each way) passes the Twisted Lakes 2. km from the trailhead. This part of the park is good place to get a feeling for hiking in an alpin area without being too exposed to the element

One of the most popular destinations for da hikers is **Crater Lake,** 1.8 km from Waldhein The lake was misnamed; it is not a crater at a but, in fact, was formed by glacial action. Fro the lake's boatshed, Marion's Lookout (1,22 meters) is a steep 45-minute scramble.

The summit of Cradle Mountain is a popula destination for fit hikers, but check the foreca before attempting the climb. From the trailhea at Waldheim, the track gains around 700 meter in elevation, following the Overland Track t Kitchen Hut (five km) before making the fin. leg-burning ascent to the 1,545-meter summit farther 1.3 km). Allow six hours for the round-tri

Overland Track

One of Australia's most famous hikes, this 80-k five- to eight-day trail traverses a great variety terrain to link Cradle Valley to Cynthia Bay on th shore of Lake St. Clair. It can be completed b anyone of a reasonable level of fitness—if yo don't feel competent attempting the trip by you self, a number of companies offer fully guide adventures. It can be hiked in either direction but north to south is most popular.

The track officially begins at Waldheim, the passes Crater Lake before ascending to an e posed plateau and the beautiful Waterfall Valle a good overnight stop. From there the trail co

Cradle Mountain,
Dove Lake, and
Suicide Rock

nues through an area of heathland exposed to the elements, then climbs to a ridge before descending to deep blue Lake Windermere, another overnight stop. Continuing south, the trail passes through a forest of eucalypt, re-emerging into open heathland, then, after two km, descends to Frog Flats and the Forth River, which crossed via a bridge. The next overnight stop Pelion Hut, a basic accommodation 2.4 km beyond the bridge. Some of the track's most spectacular vistas are at Pelion Gap, 2.8 km beyond the hut. From this pass, it is possible to climb 1,617-meter **Mt. Ossa,** Tasmania's highest point (five km each way; allow three hours round-trip). From Pelion Gap, the main track descends to Pinestone Creek and Kia-ora Hut. Along the Overland Track 2.8 km south of his hut is a 500-meter trail to Hartnett Falls, where the Mersey River plunges over a rocky edge into a deep pool below. From the Mersey River Valley, the main track climbs steadily to Du Cane Gap before descending two km to Windy Ridge Hut. From this hut it's only 12 km to Lake St. Clair, but most hikers make the overnight detour up Pine Valley, where there's an array of unusual geological features, such as the Acropolis, a ridge of intriguing columns, and the Labyrinth, a high plateau of small lakes. From Pine Valley Hut, Lake St. Clair is a soggy nine km south. From the hut at Narcissus Bay, the Maclair (tel. 03-6289-1137) transports hikers out to civilization at Cynthia Bay. The trip is made twice daily, with times posted on the hut wall. The trip is $13 one-way. To continue on boot to Cynthia Bay is a farther 19 km.

Weather conditions in the mountains can deteriorate quickly, but the region is less prone to unpleasant weather in summer. Still, being in alpine area, the weather is unpredictable year-round. Although the huts en route are open to anyone, they fill early, so it is imperative to bring a tent and sleeping bag. Warm clothing, hiking boots, and a cooking stove are also necessary. A 1:100,000 scale topographical map has been produced especially for the Overland Track; it can be purchased at most outdoor shops or at Cradle Mountain Lodge. All hikers attempting the Overland Track must register with a park ranger ($10 pp); this fee can be paid at either end of the trail. To contact the ranger in advance, call (03) 6492-1133.

Craclair Tours (tel. 03-6424-7833) operates an eight-day guided hike along the Overland Track. The pace is leisurely, with the option of climbing peaks en route or resting. Rates range $895-980, which includes camping equipment, all meals, and transportation to and from Devonport. These tours run Oct.-April.

The more luxurious option is with **Cradle Huts** (tel. 03-6331-2006). This company operates the same style of trip but with overnight accommodations in magnificent timber huts, each with hot showers, hot meals, comfortable beds, and a relaxing lounge area. This trek includes a boat trip across Cynthia Lake, shortening the trail by 20 km. Cost of the six-day trip is $1250 pp, which includes transportation to and from Launceston.

Cradle Mountain Lodge and other Accommodations

For those who want to experience the beauty of the Tasmanian wilderness while staying in a luxurious accommodation, you can't go past this stately two-story lodge surrounded by magnificent mountain scenery. The most popular rooms are the Pencil Pine Cabins, each with a potbelly stove, bath, and shower; $140 s or d, $180 with a private spa. Upstairs in the main lodge are basic rooms, each with two bunk beds and a double bed, tea- and coffee-making facilities, and shared bathrooms. These rooms are $85 s or d. Facilities in the lodge include a large comfortable lounge, two bars, and a dining room open for all meals (reservations necessary for dinner). For accommodation bookings, call (03) 6492-1303 or (1800) 03-0377. In the United States, call (800) 225-9849.

Dove Lake

The least expensive place to stay in the area is **Cradle Mountain Campground,** two km north of the Visitor Centre and a 40-minute walk to Cradle Mountain Lodge. The campground is large, and sites have lots of privacy. Facilities include showers, toilets, laundry sinks, covered cooking shelter, and kiosk. Camping fees are $8 pp per night. Within the campground are bunkhouses with bunk beds and heaters (no cooking facilities). Guests must also supply their own linen. Rates are $22 pp or an entire bunkhouse is $60. The campground office is open in summer 8:30-11:30 a.m. and 12:30-7 p.m. Only during holidays and summer weekends are reservations necessary (tel. 03-6492-1133). Within the park, eight km south of the Visitor Centre, are the **Waldheim Huts.** The huts sleep four to eight people and are fairly basic; each has a gas stove, cooking utensils, cutlery, crockery, table, and heater, but no linen. Facilities are shared. Rates are similar to the bunkhouses and should be booked through the Visitor Centre.

Outside the park, off the road to Launceston, is remote **Lemonthyme Lodge** (tel. 03-6492-1112), a wilderness retreat set on 43 hectares. The main lodge is a stunning log structure with four adjacent self-contained cabins nestled among the trees. Rooms in the main lodge are rustic and have shared facilities; $75-85 s or d. The cabins are spacious and more comfortable. Each has a separate bedroom, large living area with a log fire, and kitchen. These are $130 s or d. In the main lodge is a cavernous dining area with timber tables and chairs, comfortable lounge area with a fireplace, bar, barbecue area, and large deck with bush views. All meals are available and are reasonably priced. As well as for guests, 7 p.m. is feeding time for local wildlife, which congregates outside the lodge.

**Transportation,
Services, and Information**
Tasmanian Wilderness Transport (tel. 03-6334-4442) operates a daily bus service (May-Oct. Tuesday, Thursday, and Saturday only) to the park from Devonport ($30 each way; $55 round-trip) and Launceston ($35 each way; $65 round-trip). On Saturday the service continues from the Cradle Valley to Strahan ($35 each way; $65 round-trip), returning the following day.

Between December and Easter, Tasmania Wilderness Transport operates a shuttle bu along the Cradle Valley and to Dove Lake. One way fares are $5. From Cynthia Bay, at th south end of the Overland Track, Tasmania Wilderness Transport runs to Hobart ($35 one way; $65 round-trip), Launceston, and Devo port (both $45 each way; $80 round-trip) dai during summer.

Maxwell's (tel. 03-6292-1400) runs a ta between Derwent Bridge and Cynthia Bay; $ each way.

Viewing the park's rugged topography fro above is an awesome experience. Flightsee ing with **Seair Adventure Charters** (tel. 0: 6492-1132) is $65 pp for 25 minutes and $95 f 50 minutes; heli-sightseeing starts at $75 pp.

Cradle Mountain Visitor Centre (tel. 0: 6492-1133) is just inside the park boundary, in a area of lush rainforest above Pencil Pine Cree Inside the attractive building are displays we worth viewing, including a three-dimension model of the park, a photographic display, and a audiovisual. It's open year-round daily 8 a.m.- p.m. From the center, a 500-meter boardwa leads through rainforest to Pencil Pine Falls.

The **ranger station** at Cynthia Bay (tel. 0: 6289-1172) is another source of information.

CRADLE MOUNTAIN
TO LAUNCESTON

To get to Launceston from Cradle Valley, tak the first turnoff at Moina. The winding eastwa road skirts the base of the great central platea upon which Walls of Jerusalem National Pa lies. The road has spectacular views of the Grea Western Tiers and descends through the lus Mersey River Valley and an area of farmlan to the plains, beyond which lies Launceston.

Walls of Jerusalem National Park
When talking of north-central Tasmania, it Cradle Mountain-Lake St. Clair National Pa that is thought of, but immediately east, an part of the Tasmania Wilderness World Her tage Area, is the fabulous and remote scenery 51,800-hectare Walls of Jerusalem Nationa Park. The park is part of the central plateau dotted with a maze of shallow lakes and su

ounded by a natural amphitheater of rugged peaks rising to 1,500 meters. Access is from the north, along an unsealed road that hugs the eastern bank of Lake Rowallan. The road ends at the park boundary. From this point a few trails begin, but most serious hikers will want to explore their own routes and ascend surrounding mountain ranges. There are no designated campgrounds within the park. For further park information, call (03) 6363-5182. **Tasmanian Wilderness Transport** (tel. 03-6334-4442) departs Launceston each Tuesday and Friday at :30 a.m. for the park, with return services Sunday only; $40 each way, $75 round-trip.

Mersey River Cave Systems

Along the Mersey River and its tributaries west of Mole Creek is extensive karst terrain, which comprises a limestone bedrock that has been eroded by underground waterflow to create complex cave systems extending many kilometers. Two caves are open to the public. Westernmost is **King Solomon Caves,** part of a state reserve on the road to Liena. Tours of this cave system depart from the ticket office, a five-minute walk from the road, six times daily between 10:30 a.m. and 4 p.m. The tour costs adult $8, child $4. Equally spectacular, **Marakoopa Caves,** nine km from the King Solomon turnoff, is known for its glowworms. Tour times and costs are the same as for King Solomon Cave. If you plan on visiting both, buy a combined ticket for adult $12, child $6.

Halfway between the caves and Mole Creek is **Mole Creek Caravan Park** (tel. 03-6363-150). Facilities are basic, but it's in a great little spot, spread along Sassafras Creek and surrounded by forested hills. Sites are $5-8.

Mole Creek

Lying in the shadow of the Great Western Tiers, Mole Creek has a picturesque location and some good accommodations (see "Mersey River Cave Systems," above, for camping). Important to the local economy is leatherwood honey. The leatherwood tree is confined to damp areas of the state, and here in the Mersey River Valley it thrives. The honey is produced Jan.-April, and during these months you can watch the process in the local factory; open Mon.-Fri. 8 a.m.-4 p.m.

Mole Creek's biggest attraction is the large **Trowunna Wildlife Park,** several km east of town. It features a range of native animals, including many species casual observers are unlikely to see in the wild. Featured are the koalas (not native to Tasmania), waterfowl, raptors, lizards, wombats, tiger snakes, Tasmanian devils, and potoroos. The noctarium contains those animals most active at night, such as possums, Eastern bettongs, spotted-tail quolls, and sugar gliders. Kangaroos and wallabies hop throughout the park and raucous cockatoos make themselves known among the trees. Also at the park are a restaurant serving typical Aussie fare, like damper and billy tea ($6), and a shop selling some interesting pieces of pottery. Admission to the park is adult $7.50, child $3.50. It's open daily 9 a.m.-5 p.m.

Rooms at **Mole Creek Hotel** (tel. 03-6363-1102) have shared facilities and are only $20 s, $35 d. Breakfast is a few dollars extra. **Mole Creek Guest House,** a few hundred meters west of the hotel (tel. 03-6363-1399), has five tastefully decorated rooms, which although basic are comfortable; $30 s, $50 d ($60 with bathroom), including breakfast provisions. Downstairs is **Laurelberry Tearooms,** a pleasant place for a meal, with lunch specials for about $7.50 and dinner $10-12.50. Meals are also available at Mole Creek Hotel, but no orders are taken after 7:30 p.m.

Deloraine

Midway between Devonport and Launceston, Deloraine features many buildings from the mid-1800s and a fabulous backdrop of the Great Western Tiers. The town has a wide range of accommodations, making it a good base for exploring nearby natural attractions. Worth visiting, **Bowerbank Mill,** two km east of town (tel. 03-6362-2628), houses a gallery chock-full of art from all mediums. It's open daily 9 a.m.-5:30 p.m.

Historic **Bush Inn Hotel,** Bass Hwy. (tel. 03-6362-2365), has very basic rooms for $15 pp, including breakfast. The other inexpensive option is **Highview Lodge,** a YHA hostel at 8 Blake St. (tel. 03-6362-2996). Facilities are clean and modern, and a spacious deck takes full advantage of the mountain vista. Dorm beds are $12-14. **Deloraine Apex Caravan Park,** 51 West Parade (tel. 03-6362-2345), has riverside sites for $8-10 but no vans or cabins. Originally a hospital, the atmosphere at **Arcoona,** East Barrack St. (tel. 03-6362-3443), couldn't be more different today. It's been restored to an upmarket B&B, with four spacious and comfortable rooms, each with a bathroom. Also available for guest use is a laundry, barbecue area, and dining room. Rates are $82 s, $110 d, including breakfast. Another good option for those who enjoy historic accommodations are the two cottages at **Bowerbank Mill,** two km east of town (tel. 03-6362-2628); $110-120 s or d.

Deloraine Hotel, Emu Bay Rd. (tel. 03-6362-2022), serves meals for $7-12, while the **Bush Inn Hotel,** Bass Hwy. (tel. 03-6362-2365), has a dinner buffet for $10 and live entertainment on weekends. **Sullivans Take-away Restaurant,** 17 West Parade (tel. 03-6362-3264), is a popular local hangout dishing up no-frills meals at good prices; open daily from 8 a.m. Next door to the Deloraine Hotel is **Bonney's Inn** (tel. 03-6362-2122), built in 1830, open for morning tea ($3-6.50), lunch ($4.50-11), and dinner ($11-14.50). Closed Sunday and Monday.

Deloraine Visitor Information Centre, 29 West Church St. (tel. 03-6362-2046), is open daily 7 a.m.-6 p.m.

Westbury

With grand plans for a city, this historic town was first settled in 1828. Many original buildings remain, including **White House,** on the corner of Adelaide and King Streets (tel. 03-6393-

1171), which dates from 1841. The main hous contains a collection of 17th- and 18th-centur furniture and other artifacts from the era Around the inner courtyard are several restore buildings, including a bakehouse (which fea tures an enormous wood-fired, cast-iron oven selling breads and cakes, the bakery is open t the public Wed.-Sun. 9 a.m.-5 p.m.), stable and a garage full of vintage cars, horse-draw carriages, and a collection of 1860s bicycle The complex is open Tues.-Thurs. and Sat Sun. 10 a.m.-4 p.m. (closed winter); admis sion is $5. Also in town is **Westbury Minera and Gem Stone Display,** 61 Main Rd. (te 03-6393-1688), the largest private gemston collection in Australia. Admission $2. Ope daily 9 a.m.-5 p.m. Next door is **Pearn's Stea World** (tel. 03-6397-3313), a collection c steam-powered farm machinery. It's open th same hours as the gem display and admissio is $3.

Egmont, 922 Birralee Rd. (tel. 03-639 1164), in the same family since 1838, is a his toric home renovated to a guesthouse. Su rounded in gardens, the house features a larg fireplace, country kitchen and dining area, an plenty of rooms and halls to explore. Rates f the entire house are a reasonable $75, which ir cludes breakfast provisions. The other alterna tive is the old **Westbury Hotel** in the center c town (tel. 03-6393-1151); $28 s, $42 d. Thi hotel also offers inexpensive counter meals.

LAUNCESTON AND VICINITY

aunceston, a small city 200 km north of Hobart, lies at the head of the **Tamar River,** a tidal waterway extending 50 km from Bass Strait. The city sprawls around the confluence of two rivers, the North Esk and South Esk, which merge to form the Tamar River. From this confluence, and the city of Launceston, the river flows northwestward to Bass Strait through the wide Tamar Valley, dotted with orchards, wineries, and various accommodations. Flanking the river mouth are rugged Asbestos Range National Park and historic George Town, settled in 1804.

Launceston was founded in 1805, making it Australia's third-oldest city. Earlier attempts at settlement along the Tamar River had proved unsuccessful, but the ideal location, along with rich mineral deposits farther inland, saw the settlement grow to become one of Australia's wealthiest mining towns and to develop as Tasmania's major industrial center. Today, the city has a population of 67,000, making it Tasmania's second-largest city.

LAUNCESTON SIGHTS

Launceston is a colorful city, featuring many gardens, a friendly atmosphere, and plenty of opportunities for exploring on foot.

Cataract Gorge

This spectacular gorge on Launceston's western outskirts was formed through a combination of a powerful earthquake 40 million years ago and erosion caused by the flow of the South Esk River. The gorge is protected by a reserve through which many hiking trails have been cut, but the gorge itself is most spectacular. From Kings Bridge, trails lead along both sides of the gorge to First Basin, a deep pool of water, where you'll find the **Interpretation Centre** (open Mon.-Fri. 9 a.m.-4 p.m., Sat.-Sun. till 4:40 p.m.), a swimming pool, tearooms, and a restaurant. A 300-meter-long chairlift spans the gorge, ending at an area called **Cliff Grounds,** which is alive with trees, ferns, exotic plants, and grassy lawns.

Tickets for the chairlift are adult $4, child $2.50. One of the best ways to escape the crowds is to head out along the 2.3-km trail along the south side of the gorge to **Duck Reach,** site of an old power station.

Off Gorge Rd., which leads into the reserve's north end, is a road leading to **Freelands Lookout Reserve,** which has a good view of the Tamar River and surrounding landscape.

Penny Royal World

This large complex, beside Kings Bridge and opposite the north end of Cataract Gorge, recreates life in the mid-1800s through working displays, a watermill, gunpowder museum, cornmill, and candy factory. Other action is on the water, including an old sloop, barges, and *Lady Stelfox,* a paddlesteamer that cruises along the Tamar River. Admission is a steep $19.50, child $9.50, but it's possible to take the river cruise only for about $6.50. Also on site is a cafe, restaurant, and gift shop.

The park is open daily 9 a.m.-4:30 p.m. For more information call (03) 6331-6699. Show your admission tickets at the adjacent Penny Royal Watermill Motel for a 25% accommodation discount.

Other Town Sights

Downtown Launceston features many historic buildings and areas of parkland, and a **tram tour,** with an informative commentary, is the best way to view them; $15 pp.

The main displays at **Queen Victoria Museum and Art Gallery,** housed in a large building on Wellington St. (tel. 03-6331-6777), include Tasmania's all-important mineral deposits, Launceston's interesting geology, the state's unique flora and fauna, and a collection of Chinese treasures. The Art Gallery contains a fabulous collection of colonial art. Admission to both is free. They are open Mon.-Sat. 10 a.m.-5 p.m., Sunday 2 p.m.-5 p.m. Within the same complex is **Launceston Planetarium,** featuring astronomical displays and a changing program of events. It's open Tues.-Sat. at 2 p.m. and 3 p.m.; admission is adult $3, child $2.

LAUNCESTON

RAVENSWOOD

ST. LEONARD

RD.

RD.

TO BEN LOMOND N.P.

HOBBLERS BRIDGE

RIVER

TAMAR

ESK

RIVER

NORTH

ESK

RIVER

TAMAR

HENRY

ELPHIN

CRES.

RACECOURSE

ABBOTT

ST.

CLARENCE

HIGH

ST.

ST.

ARTHUR

MULGRAVE

ST.

MARY

ST.

CANNING

ST.

CLEVELAND

DETAIL

TAMAR

ST.

GEORGE

ST.

CAMERON

ST.

ST. JOHN

ST.

CHARLES

ST.

WELLINGTON

ST.

FREDERICK

YORK

ST.

MARGARET

ST.

ELIZABETH

PATERSON

BRISBANE

ST.

ST.

ST.

ST.

- Batman Fawkner Inn
- Novotel Launceston
- Post Office
- Konditorei Cafe Manfred
- Bus Depot
- O'Keefes Hotel
- Launceston City Backpackers / Hard Times Cafe
- Wilderness Society Shop
- Tasmanian Travel and Information Centre
- Petrarch's Launceston Bookshop
- Community History Museum
- Civic Square / Henty House
- Queen Victoria Museum and Art Gallery

SEE DETAIL

INVERMAY

RD.

EAST

TAMAR

HWY.

LINDSAY

ST.

FORSTER

ST.

INVERMAY

ST.

TAMAR

ST.

BRISBANE

CIMITIERE

ST.

YORK

ST.

GEORGE

ST.

ST. JOHN

CHARLES

WELLINGTON

BATHURST

ST.

MARGARET

ST.

HILLSIDE

CRES.

BROXHAM

RD.

GRANVILLE

ST.

WILHELMINA AVE.

BROXHAM ST.

HOWICK

ST.

ST.

GLEN

DHU

ST.

THISTLE

ST.

WELLINGTON

ST.

TO AIRPORT, WESTBURY AND HOBART

- Sportsman's Hall Hotel
- Penny Royal Watermill Motel
- Ritches Mill Art Centre
- Penny Royal World
- Centennial Motel
- Launceston City Youth Hostel
- Treasure Island Caravan Park

TO EAST TAMAR VALLEY: GEORGE TOWN AND LILYDALE

TAMAR

RIVER

WEST

TAMAR

HWY.

TREVALLYN

RD.

BALD

HILL

RD.

GORGE

RD.

TO BEACONSFIELD AND WEST TAMAR VALLEY

FREELANDS LOOKOUT RESERVE

CLIFF GROUNDS

GORGE RESTAURANT

CATARACT

GORGE

CHAIRLIFT

FIRST BASIN

BASIN

SOUTH

ESK

RIVER

TREVALLYN STATE RECREATION AREA

TO DUCK REACH

0   0.4 km

TO AIRPORT, WESTBURY AND HOBART

If you're interested in local history, the **Community History Museum,** corner of Cimitiere and St. John Streets (tel. 03-6337-1391), is the place to head. It's in a building built back in 1842 and formerly used as a trading center for grains, wine, and spirits. Admission is $1. It's open Mon.-Sat. 10 a.m.-4 p.m., Sunday 2 p.m.-4 p.m.

Housed in another historic building is **Ritchies Mill Art Centre,** at 2 Bridge Rd. (tel. 03-6331-1422). Originally a mill, it now houses galleries and studios and a great little cafe. It's open daily 9 a.m.-5 p.m.

Trevallyn State Recreation Area

This 450-hectare heavily forested park immediately west of downtown is bordered on three sides by the Esk River, and is most easily accessed from the Tamar Highway. Beyond the park gate (locked nightly at 8:30 p.m.) is an information center, the starting point for several short walks, including to a lookout (100 meters) and to Trevallyn Dam (1.3 km). The dam is a popular windsurfing spot, while within the park you can go horseback riding and hang gliding down a cable ($7 per ride).

PRACTICALITIES

Accommodations

Sportsman's Hall Hotel, 252 Charles St. (tel. 03-6331-3968), is a historic pub in a quiet area a few blocks from downtown. Rates are $28 s, $40 d, which includes breakfast. **Batman Fawkner Inn,** 35 Cameron St. (tel. 03-6331-7222), dates from 1822 and oozes colonial charm. (Check out the prints in the lobby, including those of the hotel's namesakes, John Batman, founder of Melbourne, and John Pascoe Fawkner, the hotel's original landlord). Rates range $40-50 s, $70-80 d, and for a few bucks extra you'll get a light breakfast.

Penny Royal Watermill Motel, 147 Paterson St. (tel. 03-6331-6699), is in a historic watermill building dating from 1825. Rooms are decorated in old-English style; from $79 s, $94 d, including breakfast. The six-story **Novotel Launceston,** 29 Cameron St. (tel. 03-6334-3434), right downtown, is one of the city's tallest buildings and also its finest hotel. For the standard of rooms, the rates of $140 s or d are reasonable.

The Shambles, at 129 Balfour St. (tel. 03-6334-2231), is one section of various historic accommodations that share a lovely garden. The Shambles is a row of small, comfortable, attached cottages, each individually decorated with huge old fireplaces, high four-poster beds, claw-footed baths, lots of intriguing objects from the past, and theme-related curios and knick-knacks, yet all the modern conveniences you'd expect. Ample breakfast provisions are included in the price of $105 s, $125 d. Built in 1870, the two-story **Old Bakery Inn,** 270 York St. (tel. 03-6331-7900), has a good standard of rooms, each with private facilities, for just $89 s, $93 d.

Launceston City Youth Hostel (not a YHA), a large backpacker accommodation with 100 beds, is at 36 Thistle St., two km south of downtown (tel. 03-6344-9779). The hostel is not particularly inviting, but it offers a wide range of guest facilities, including a spacious living area, fully equipped kitchen, lockers, and bathrooms with coin-operated showers. Dorm beds are $11 pp, with discounts for stays over three nights. The owners have backpacking equipment and mountain bikes for rent (10- and 12-speed bikes are $12 per day or $65 per week). Another inexpensive choice is **Launceston City Backpackers,** 139 George St. (tel. 03-6334-2327). Dorms are $14 and there are a few doubles for $30.

Launceston has one campground, **Treasure Island Caravan Park,** 94 Glen Dhu St. (tel. 03-6344-2600), a noisy place right beside the main route into town from the south and two km from downtown. Sites are $12-15, on-site vans $32, and cabins with good cooking facilities $50.

Food

Konditorei Cafe Manfred, 95 George St. (tel. 03-6334-2490), has German-style cakes and pastries, including excellent apple strudel. For a casual snack or meal with water views, you can't go past **Ripples Cafe** in Ritchies Mill Art Centre on Bridge Rd. (tel. 03-6331-2433). Meals start at $3 and the coffee isn't bad either.

O'Keefes Hotel, 124 George St. (tel. 03-6331-4015), is a popular local hangout offering an inexpensive blackboard menu that includes delicious beer-battered fish ($8). Open daily for lunch and dinner. Another place for a pub meal, if you don't mind the stuffed animals overhead, is **Centennial Hotel** on the corner of Balfour and Bathurst Streets (tel. 03-6331-2184). The daily two-course special is good value at $7.

Owl's Nest Restaurant, 147 Paterson St. (tel. 03-6331-6699), part of Penny Royal Watermill Motel, is a cozy restaurant with old stone walls and dark timber furniture, giving it a real colonial atmosphere. Local produce is featured on the menu, where main dishes range $14.50-16.50. On the same property is an English-style pub. **Hard Times Cafe,** 135 George St. (tel. 03-6334-1387), is a popular lunchtime hangout with great tomato and lentil soup ($3.50) and nachos ($6.50). It's open for dinner nightly and lunch in summer only. The **Gorge Restaurant,** on the northwest side of Cataract Gorge (tel. 03-6331-3330), takes advantage of the surrounding natural beauty with outdoor seating (and peacocks). It's open for lunch and dinner Tues.-Sat. and for lunch on Sunday only.

Avenue Brasserie, in the Novotel Launceston at 29 Cameron St. (tel. 03-6334-3434), is open daily for a buffet breakfast ($12-16.50) and buffet lunch Mon.-Thurs. ($14.50). Dinner is also all-you-can-eat ($24), with Saturday including seafood ($29), and Sunday a carvery ($21). For a Chinese buffet, try the **Golden Sea Dragon** on the corner of Bathurst and Canning Streets (tel. 03-6331-7728); $16.50.

Lawrence Street Brasserie, 20 Lawrence St. (tel. 03-6331-9991), features Mediterranean cuisine using Tasmanian produce. Other stylish restaurants are **Cucina Simpatica Cafe,** corner Margaret and Frederick Streets (tel. 03-6334-3177), featuring local seafood, and **Fee and Me,** 190 Charles St. (tel. 03-6331-3195), housed in a grand mansion dating from 1835.

Transportation, Services, and Information

Launceston is a major gateway for airlines from mainland Australia (see "Transportation" under "Introduction" at the beginning of this chapter), while **Airlines of Tasmania** (tel. 1800-03-0550) links the city to other state centers such as Hobart ($76 one-way) and Burnie ($88). **Tasmanian Redline Coaches** operates an airport shuttle for $6 each way. To book this service call (03) 6331-3900. A cab between the airport and downtown runs about $18. Tasmanian Redline Coaches also operates bus services between

Launceston and Devonport ($11.80 one-way Burnie ($15.80), St. Marys ($13.40), and Ho bart ($17). The **depot** is at 112 George St. (te 03-6331-3233). To top the monopoly off, Tas manian Redline Coaches also offers tours the city for $23 pp; for these, call (03) 6331 9177. The other bus company serving the city i **Tasmanian Wilderness Transport** (tel. 03 6334-4442). Sample fares from Launceston are Cradle Mountain $35 each way, $65 round-trip Strahan $40 each way, $75 round-trip; an Bicheno $30 each way, $55 round-trip.

Metro (tel. 03-6331-9911) runs a local bu service, with a $2.60 day pass for unlimite travel Mon.-Fri. 9 a.m.-4:30 p.m., after 6 p.m and all weekend. All major car rental companie have outlets in Launceston, but for somethin cheaper call **Apple Car Rentals** (tel. 03-6343 3780). **Rent-a-cycle,** at Launceston City Yout Hostel (tel. 03-6344-9779), has mountain bike from $12 per day.

The **post office,** on St. John Street oppo site Civic Square, is a grand old building. **Pe trarch's Launceston Bookshop** is in Quadrar Mall on Brisbane St. (tel. 03-6331-8837). Th best source of local and state information i **Tasmanian Travel and Information Centre** corner St. John and Paterson Streets (tel. 03 6336-3122). For accommodation bookings, ca this office at (03) 6336-3133. It's open Mon. Fri. 9 a.m.-5 p.m., Sat.-Sun. 9 a.m.-noon. Fc adventure travel information, head to th **Wilderness Society Shop,** 174 Charles S (tel. 03-6334-2499).

The offices for the **Department of Environ ment and Land Management** are in Hent House on Civic Square (tel. 03-6336-2339).

TAMAR VALLEY

The wide Tamar River extends over 60 km in land from Bass Strait to Launceston. It is crosse by a bridge in just one place, 20 km from th mouth, making a round-trip along both sides c the valley possible with a short detour to wil Asbestos National Park. The valley is Tasma nia's premier wine-producing area, with vine yards on both sides of the river. Many roadside stalls sell local produce, and arts-and-crafts out lets abound.

Launceston to Beaconsfield

From Launceston the highway through West Tamar passes open farmland with plenty of river views. The first township north of Launceston is **Legana.** A good alternative to staying in the city, **Legana Tourist Caravan Park** (tel. 03-330-1714), has a large grassed area for tents, and clean, modern facilities. Sites range $10-12, and there are a few cabins for $35. North of Legana is **Grindelwald,** a Swiss-style residential and resort complex complete with a man-made lake, golf course, accommodations, and restaurants. Accommodation in self-contained chalets is $140, while motel rooms are slightly less expensive. For bookings, call (03) 6330-799.

Beyond this complex is **Strathlynn Wine Centre,** part of Pipers Brook Vineyard. It's open for tastings daily 10 a.m.-5 p.m. Also nearby is **St. Matthias Vineyard,** with tastings also and similar hours.

Waterbird Haven Trust, 17 km from Launceston, is a marshy area along the Tamar River protected as a bird sanctuary. Within the reserve is a massive walk-through aviary, a display of geese, and a variety of other caged birds. Admission is $4. It's open daily between 9 a.m. and dusk. To book a guided tour, call ahead tel. 03-6394-4087).

The next stop heading north should be **Rosevears Waterfront Tavern** (tel. 03-6394-4074), a historic hotel and microbrewery first licensed in 1831 (look for original brickwork in the public bar). Meals are served at lunch and dinner, but don't expect any bargains; most start at $10.

Back out on the main road is **Brady's Lookout,** a vantage point used by the bushranger Matthew Brady. For many years, this area was the haunt of Brady and his gang. They also evaded capture in remote **Notley Gorge State Reserve,** accessed from southwest of Exeter. The reserve escaped logging because of its inaccessibility, the same reason Brady found it an excellent hideout.

The area surrounding the village of **Deviot** is dotted with more vineyards while to the north is **Batman Bridge,** the only span across the Tamar River. It is a cable-stayed bridge, dominated by a 100-meter-high steel-frame tower.

Beaconsfield and Farther North

Founded to serve a nearby gold mine, this small town is best known for **Grubb Shaft Gold Museum** (tel. 03-6383-1473), on the site of Tasmania's largest gold mine, from which 849,913 ounces of the precious metal were extracted before its closure in 1914. Today it's a tourist attraction, with working models, exhibits and photographic displays, domestic displays, and a re-created mine office depicting life at the turn of the century. Admission is a worthy $3 and it's open daily 10 a.m.-4 p.m.

North of Beaconsfield is the aptly named **Beauty Point,** a great little spot overlooking the Tamar River. Stay at **Astra Motel** (tel. 03-6383-4375), with river views and an extensive rose garden. Rates are great value at $35 s, $45 d.

To the north is **Greens Beach,** a typically picturesque end-of-the-road village with a great stretch of sandy beach, golf course, tennis, and a variety of accommodations. **Greens Beach Caravan Park,** a stone's throw from the beach (tel. 03-6383-9222), has tent sites for $7-12.

Asbestos Range National Park

This 4,281-hectare park extends along the coast between Greens Beach, at the mouth of the Tamar River, and beautiful Bakers Beach, opposite Port Sorell. It features long sandy beaches and rocky headlands backed by extensive dune and lagoon systems. Behind these is the Asbestos Range, providing challenging hiking and some spectacular lookouts. The park was declared as recently as 1976, and yet wildlife populations are high and the magical feeling of an unspoilt wilderness area prevails.

The park's main feature, its namesake, was thrust skyward around 600 million years ago and slowly eroded to its present height of about 400 meters since. Between the range and Bass Strait are layers of gravel and sand, pushed inland by wind and water to form the low coastal topography. The park's flora is extremely hardy. Climatic extremes, a lack of fresh water and decent soil, and salt-laden winds allow only a few species to survive. Early settlers drained swampland behind the dune systems to create pastures for grazing cattle. The introduced species are long gone, native species abound. The best time for viewing park wildlife is dusk; species you'll most likely spot are brush-tailed possums, pademelons, Bennett's wallabies, wombats, and Tasmanian devils.

Access to the park is from Beaconsfield, with the road joining the coast at **Badger Beach.** The beach is a beautiful golden-yellow color and is deserted at all but the busiest times of year. Along this beach after heavy storms, sand is often washed away, revealing the roots of ancient she-oaks dating from the last ice age when Tasmania was linked to the mainland. Farther west, around Badger Head, is Bakers Beach and the main facility areas.

Starting at the park information center, the Springlawn Nature Walk leads along the edge of a lagoon (where towering melaleucas sit with their roots submerged in the water), through typical coastal heathland, and past various water ecosystems that attract abundant waterbirds. A more challenging trail is to **Archer's Knob** (two km each way), with its panoramic coastal vistas.

Within the park are four campgrounds; each has pit toilets, bore water, and a limited amount of firewood. All sites are $4 pp. The small information center features a three-dimensional model of the park and boards detailing ranger-led activities. It's open daily 9 a.m.-5 p.m. (tel. 03-6428-6277).

George Town

In 1804 Col. William Paterson came ashore with 180 convicts to found George Town, northern Tasmania's first settlement. Today the town has a population of about 5,000, and although the streets are lined with many historic buildings, most local attractions lie farther north, toward Low Head. In town is **The Grove,** 25 Cimitiere St. (tel. 03-6482-1336), an elegant stone house dating from 1829. It's open daily 9 a.m.-5 p.m., with regular (and short) tours for $3 pp. **Mount George Scenic Lookout,** accessed along a road spurring west from the information center, allows views over the entire area.

The least-expensive place to stay in town is the **Travellers Hostel** (YHA), 4 Elizabeth St. (tel. 03-6382-1399), across from the Pier Hotel and bus depot. All the usual facilities are provided; rates are $12 for dorms or $40 in a family room. Another inexpensive option is

Nanna's Cottage, a small, cozy, self-containe cottage in the grounds of The Grove at 25 Cim tiere St. (tel. 03-6382-1336). Rates are $5C 65 s or d. **Central Court Motel,** Main Rd. (te 03-6382-2155), has basic self-contained unit from $55. More expensive, but of a higher star dard and with river views, is **Pier Hotel** at Elizabeth St. (tel. 03-6382-1300). Facilities ar shared but are clean and modern. Rates ar $80-90 s or d. This hotel has an exceller restaurant with a casual and friendly atmc sphere. **Ned's Takeaway** has good hamburg ers and chips (about $6).

Entering George Town from the south, you pass a small **information center** (tel. 03-6382 1700) run by friendly volunteers who seem t know everything that's happening in town. It' open daily 11 a.m.-4 p.m.

Low Head and Vicinity

Low Head is a narrow finger of land at the mout of the Tamar River. On the river side of th headland is **Port of Launceston Authority' Pilot Station,** manned since 1805, and althoug operation equipment has changed considerabl in that time, its function is basically the same– to guide shipping through the treacherous mout of the Tamar River. Within the complex is a va riety of buildings, including some convict-bui structures dating from 1835. One of the oldes buildings on the site, originally built as accom modation for the pilots, now houses an inter esting collection of maritime memorabilia, in cluding old navigational lights, compasses barometers, maps, historic prints, and a collec tion of 19th-century log books. Admission is $. and it's open daily 8 a.m.-6 p.m. (tel. 03-6382 1143).

Toward Low Head itself, past a row of state ly colonial-era houses, is a **penguin walk a Low Head Coastal Reserve.** The track is ope year-round, but the birds are most active Oct. Jan. at dusk. At the end of the road is **Low Hea Lighthouse** and stunning river and ocean views

Beach Pines Holiday Village, in a protecte hollow on the ocean side of Low Head (tel. 03 6382-2602), is a short walk from the beach anc features a good range of facilities. Tent sites are $8-14.50 and self-contained timber cabins are $55.

NORTHEAST OF LAUNCESTON

rom Launceston two roads lead through hilly
errain to **Scottsdale,** an agriculture center and
ie gateway to the remote northeast tip of Tas-
iania. The longer of the two routes passes
irough **Lilydale** on the way. Just north of this
iwn, Lilydale Falls Reserve has a short trail
eading to the falls, a picnic area with barbe-
ues, and free camping.

ridestowe Estate Lavender Farm
he bright purple fields of this farm, north of
labowla on the road between Lilydale and
icottsdale, are in stark contrast to the sur-
iunding native bush. You can tour the farm
ind buy an assortment of lavender products
ind souvenirs. Admission is $3 during the flow-
iring season (January), and it's open daily 9
.m.-5 p.m. (closed weekends in winter). Call
)3) 6352-8182 for more details.

icottsdale
iurrounded by rolling hills and backed by a re-
iote mountainous wilderness, this town is an
mportant agricultural center of 5,000. The main
ireet is lined with buildings dating from the turn
f the century. At 46 King St. is **Anabel's of
icottsdale** (tel. 03-6352-3277), with three
ioms for overnight accommodation. Each room
ias a bathroom and cooking facilities. Rates
ire $85 s or d. In the same complex is a taste-
illy decorated restaurant open for dinner daily
rom 6:30 p.m. Also in town is **Lalla Appleshed
eahouse** (tel. 03-6334-4517), in an attractive
ild building. It has pottery, crafts, stained glass,
iatercolors, scarves, jams, and preserves for
iale. They offer morning and afternoon tea and
light lunch menu.

iridport and Farther East
his popular seaside holiday village lies on An-
lerson Bay, 20 km north of Scottsdale. The
iad into town follows the foreshore, passing a
itty and a colorful assortment of fishing boats.
here's not much to see, but it's a relaxing place
i hangout when visiting the couple of wildlife re-
ierves in the area.

The least expensive place to stay is **Bridport
iackpackers** across the road from the estuary at

47 Main St. (tel. 03-6356-1585). Dorm beds are
$12 pp and doubles are $30. Facilities include a
kitchen with water views and a laundry, and
guests can rent bikes for $8 per day. **Bridairre
Bed and Breakfast,** Frances St. (tel. 03-6356-
1438), offers small, clean rooms on the lower
floor of a home. Communal bathrooms and living
room; $39 s, $59 d. A little farther out of town, on
Ada St. (tel. 03-6356-1873), is **Platypus Park
Farm Chalets,** surrounded by open fields and
native bushland. The rooms are self-contained
and quite comfortable. Rates are $80 s or d.

East of Bridport, a sealed road leads 65 km to
Tomahawk, a remote village on **Ringarooma
Bay.** The bay's eastern arm is protected by a
narrow reserve. Access is only possible at a
few spots, including the outlet of Ringarooma
River. Accommodation is at **Tomahawk Caravan Park** (tel. 03-6355-2268).

BEN LOMOND NATIONAL PARK

Located 50 km southeast of Launceston, this
16,527-hectare park encompasses the magnificent Ben Lomond Range, which rises dramatically to a height of 1,573 meters at Legges Tor.
The park is best known for its ski slopes, but in
summer the scenery is equally spectacular, especially along the hiking trail to the summit of
Legges Tor. The display of alpine wildflowers
each spring is magnificent, while at lower elevations forests of eucalypt dominate.

From the turnoff at the North Esk River it's
eight km to the park gate and 18 km to the end
of the road. The road is unsealed and all uphill,
getting progressively steeper as you ascend.
The summit track is four km each way (allow
three hours round-trip) but is ill-defined in places.
Another track leads across the lunar-like landscape to **Ladder Lookout** for views to the valley
below. The park has no official trails, but on the
back of the park map are distances between
prominent landmarks.

In the village is **Ben Lomond Creek Inn** (tel.
03-6372-2444), offering accommodations year-
round, meals in a cozy restaurant, and drinks at
the bar. Rooms are sparse and rates aren't
cheap at $105 s, $120 d, including meals. The
park has no campgrounds (see below for an
alternative). For park information, call the ranger

at (03) 6390-6279. For ski area information, call **Ben Lomond Ski Rentals** (tel. 03-6331-1312). When the ski area is open **Tasmanian Wilderness Transport** (tel. 03-6334-4442) operates transfers from Paddy Palin, at 59 Brisbane St., Launceston, to the mountain; $25 round-trip.

From the turnoff to the park, the road continues eastward to the coast. Near Upper Blessington are great views of Ben Lomond Range to the south. Farther east is **Griffin Camping Area,** a pleasant grassed area beside the South Esk River where views extend west to the Ben Lomond Range.

BASS STRAIT ISLANDS

About 12,000 years ago, as the sea level rose at the end of the last ice age, the land link between Tasmania and mainland Australia was broken, leaving the high peaks of the link as rugged islands dotted through the waters of Bass Strait. Of the strait's 120 islands, most of which are barren outcrops of rock, just two—King and Flinders—are populated. King and Flinders Islands are magical places, with rugged headlands separated by unspoilt beaches and coastlines alive with large populations of marine mammals and sea birds, and, in the case of Flinders Island, opportunities for hiking the high peaks of Strzelecki National Park. The two islands are very different. King Island is dominated by lush green farmland and renowned for culinary delights such as cheese, seafood, and honey. Flinders is renowned for its adventure opportunities and long beaches. Both are delightful destinations, different from anywhere else in the country, and little known, even to mainland Australians.

Both islands are well equipped for travelers, with a range of accommodations and restaurants, air links to both Tasmania and the mainland, and rental cars. The least-expensive way to visit them is on an all-inclusive package from **Airlines of Tasmania** (tel. 1800-03-0550).

History

The idyllic lifestyle of today's Bass Strait islanders belies a wild and bloody history of shipwrecks, kidnapping, and the massacre of almost all the islands' seals. George Bass, who became the first European to record the fact that Tasmania was separated from mainland Australia, told of an abundance of seals in the strait. Sealers descended on the area in the hundreds. Dumped on the islands by unscrupulous employers, they lived in temporary camps with often-inadequate provisions and

worked long hours in the harshest weather conditions. Seal oil and skins were to become Australia's first export; by 1800 25,000 skins a year were being transported to England. As seal numbers declined, most sealers moved back to the mainland; those remaining on the islands lived a rough and reckless life, a lifestyle that attracted many escaped convicts and rogues.

The discovery of Bass Strait had cut 1,000 km from the main shipping route between England and Sydney, but the advantages of the shorter journey were overshadowed by Bass Strait's treacherous waters. *Sydney Cove,* bound for Sydney Town with 7,000 gallons of spirits, became the first ship to be wrecked when it went aground in 1797 en route from England. During one month in 1835, Bass Strait claimed 358 lives when the convict ships *George III* and *Neva* wrecked (in a cruel twist of fate, some survivors from the *Neva* died of alcohol poisoning after salvaging pans of whisky). The region's worst disaster occurred a decade later when the *Cataraqui,* filled with British immigrants, crashed into a reef on King Island's west coast, killing all but nine of the 425 people aboard. Shipwrecks were so much a part of life in Bass Strait that the islanders came to rely on their cargo for survival.

The islands entered this century much different from the last. Residents now live a more sedate lifestyle, relying heavily on high rainfall to keep agriculture concerns profitable. Until 1990, scheelite, a tungsten-bearing ore used for hardening steel, was mined on King Island.

KING ISLAND

Lying off the northwestern tip of Tasmania, rugged King Island has been the setting for some of Australia's most tragic maritime disas-

KING ISLAND

CAPE WICKHAM

YELLOW ROCK BEACH

LAVINIA POINT

REEKARA

ELEPHANT RIVER

LOORANA

ING ISLAND DAIRIES

SEA

ELEPHANT

SEA ELEPHANT BAY

NARACOOPA

CURRIE

PEGARA

LYMWOOD

GRASSY HARBOUR

SURPRISE BAY

STOKES POINT

0   20 km

...ers, but today it's best known for gourmet foods such as creamy brie cheese, fresh seafood, and juicy beef. The island is 55 km long and 22 km wide, but its contrasts are staggering, ranging from long sandy beaches flanked by rugged headlands to lush fields filled with herds of dairy cows. **Currie,** on the west coast and with a population of 900, is the island's main settlement. At **Surprise Bay,** south of Currie, is a forest of calcified plantlife. On the southeast coast is **Grassy Harbour,** which has undergone major upheaval since the scheelite mine, the only reason for

the town's existence, closed in 1990. Formerly known as Grassy, the settlement was built purely to serve miners and their families. The mine had a turbulent history, its fortunes fluctuating with world tungsten prices. After its closure most miners and their families moved from the island, leaving a town complete with swimming pool, tennis courts, and golf course, deserted. Recently, a group of local businessmen banded together and bought the whole town, securing its future against demolition. Look for the penguin rookery at the end of the town's breakwall. To the north, past a honey farm, is the small east coast community of **Naracoopa,** on beautiful Sea Elephant Bay. The north end of the island is more remote, with a narrow road leading to **Cape Wickham,** where a lighthouse has been guiding ships since 1861. Other roads from Currie end at secluded bays, such as Yellow Rock Beach, where a wreck is visible.

Accommodations and Food

King Island Colonial Lodge, 13 Main St. (tel. 03-6462-1245), right in the heart of Currie, has six rooms with shared facilities and a laundry. It is also the departure point for island tours. Rates are $40 s, $50 d, which includes a light breakfast. Also right in town is **Parer's King Island Hotel,** Main St. (tel. 03-6462-1633), a modern place where rooms have bathrooms. A bar, bistro, and restaurant are on the premises; $65 s, $90 d. A rental car makes access to other accommodations possible, including **King Island Gem Accommodation,** two km north of Currie (tel. 03-6462-1260). On-site vans ($40 s or d) and two-story A-frame units ($70 s or d) are self-contained, allowing you to sample home-cooked King Island produce without the cost of eating at a restaurant. Also here are a few motel units for $60 s, $80 d. Over at Naracoopa is **Rocky Glen Retreat** (tel. 03-6461-1103), a series of chalets set among landscaped gardens and right by a long stretch of beautiful beach; $55 s, $80 d.

For many, a highlight of a visit to King Island will be sampling the local fare. The best place to start a culinary tour is **King Island Dairies,** north of Currie (tel. 03-6462-1348), for creamy brie cheeses. In Currie, **King Island Seafoods** (tel. 03-6461-1528) has crayfish in season. For a light meal or just coffee and home-cooked cakes, head to **Nautilus Coffee Lounge,** on Edward St., Currie (tel. 03-6462-1868). For the best range of local produce, try the following restaurants: **Fishbowl Restaurant** (tel. 03-6462-1288), overlooking the ocean at the Boomerang Motel, open nightly from 6 p.m.; one of the three eateries in Parer's King Island Hotel; or, over in Naracoopa, **Golden Spoon Restaurant,** Lovers Lane (tel. 03-6461-1103).

Transportation, Services, and Information
Airlines of Tasmania (tel. 03-6391-8755 or 1800-03-0550) flies from various points in Tasmania to King Island, including from Launceston ($110 one-way) and Hobart ($191). They also fly to the island from Sale ($224), in Victoria's Gippsland. This airline offers packages from Launceston for $279 pp, inclusive of return flight, two nights' accommodation, and car rental. From mainland Australia, **Kendell Airlines** (tel. 03-6462-1322 or 13-1300) flies daily from the domestic terminal at Melbourne Airport to King Island. The regular one-way fare is $132, advance purchase fares start at $173 round-trip, but, again, a package is the way to go—from $279 pp for flights, three nights' accommodation, most meals, and three-day tours.

If a rental car isn't included in your package, **Howell's Auto Rent** (tel. 03-6462-1282) has small sedans for $57-63 per day including unlimited kilometers. **Top Tours** (tel. 03-6462-1245) offers three-day tours, each taking in a different part of the island; $50 pp includes lunch.

King Island Tourist and Information Centre is at 13 Main Rd., Currie (tel. 03-6462-1245).

FLINDERS ISLAND

Flinders Island is the largest of the **Furneaux Archipelago,** a group of 70 islands that lie off Tasmania's northeastern tip. This island has only one-third of King Island's population and is better suited to those looking for a more active holiday, with camping, birdwatching, hiking, fishing, and scuba diving all possible. This island also features endless stretches of unspoilt beach and a national park.

The final chapter of one of Australia's most appalling events, the massacre of Tasmania's Aborigines, took place on Flinders Island. Be-

tween 1829 and 1934 George Robinso brought the few Aborigines who had surviv Tasmanian massacres to the island and es tablished **Wybalenna,** a community where the were to be trained in the ways of Christianit Within a few years, over half died, unable t cope with the ways of the white settlers an losing the will to live. All that remains of th community is a chapel, the only building in Tas mania associated with early Aborigines, and cemetery. The site is Settlement Point, halfwa up the west coast and north of the airport. Als on the point is a **muttonbird rookery,** with a observation platform for easy viewing. To th west is **Emita Historical Museum,** chock-full o relics from the strait's early history, includin many items salvaged from shipwrecks. It's ope Sat.-Sun. and daily during holidays 1-5 p.n Farther north is **Killiecrankie Bay** where Ki liecrankie diamonds (clear topaz) are occa sionally found.

Whitemark, south of the airstrip, is the com mercial center of the island and has all se vices. At Adelaide Bay, on the south coast, i **Lady Barron,** the island's only other settlemer and home to a fleet of fishing vessels. The is land's southern peaks are protected by 4,215 hectare **Strzelecki National Park,** which als encompasses a pristine stretch of coastline The hike to the summit of 756-meter Mt. Strze lecki is seven km each way (allow four to fiv hours round-trip).

Accommodations and Food

As with King Island, most visitors to Flinders Is land arrive as part of an all-inclusive packag tour (see below), which will include options fo the many cottages scattered around the island On Bluff Rd., Whitemark, is **Flinders Islan Cabin Park** (tel. 03-6359-2188), where self contained cabins are good value at $25 s, $40 d Between Whitemark and the airport is **Bluf House** (tel. 03-6359-2034), a B&B with bed for $33 pp. At Emita is **Greenglades Hos Farm,** Fairhaven Rd. (tel. 03-6359-8506), a small guesthouse with two rooms, a lounge and laundry; rates here are $60 pp, which in cludes meals. The island's largest accommo dation is **Furneaux Tavern,** in Lady Barron (te 03-6359-3521). Rooms here are $59 s, $78 d. A **Trousers Point,** beside Strzelecki Nationa

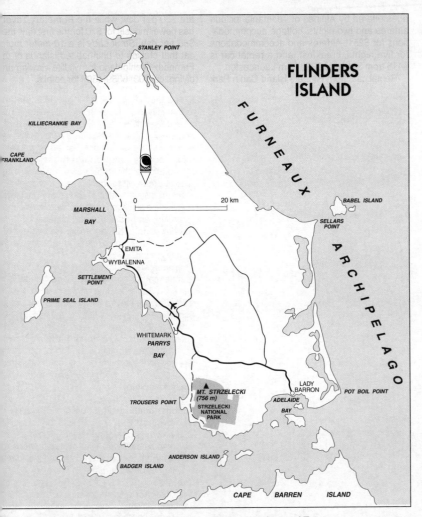

FLINDERS ISLAND

STANLEY POINT

KILLIECRANKIE BAY

CAPE FRANKLAND

F U R N E A U X

MARSHALL BAY

0   20 km

BABEL ISLAND

SELLARS POINT

EMITA
WYBALENNA

SETTLEMENT POINT

PRIME SEAL ISLAND

A R C H I P E L A G O

WHITEMARK
PARRYS BAY

▲ MT. STRZELECKI
(756 m)
STRZELECKI NATIONAL PARK

LADY BARRON

POT BOIL POINT

ADELAIDE BAY

TROUSERS POINT

ANDERSON ISLAND

BADGER ISLAND

CAPE   BARREN   ISLAND

Park, is a picturesque campground under a stand of she-oaks. Facilities include toilets, fireplaces, and drinking water. It's possible to camp elsewhere on the island, including Stanley Point on the north tip.

Whitemark and Lady Barron have shops selling groceries. Otherwise eat at **Shearwater Restaurant** in the Furneaux Tavern (tel. 03-6359-3521), where views extend over Adelaide Bay.

Transportation and Tours
Airlines of Tasmania (tel. 03-6391-8755 or 1800-03-0550) flies between Hobart and Flinders Island five days a week ($191 each way). From Launceston the fare is $110 each way. Flights to Flinders Island also originate from Sale, in Victoria's Gippsland, for $130. To save up to 50% on all these fares book a round-trip flight more than 14 days in advance. Pack-

ages offered by Airlines of Tasmania include airfares and two nights' cottage accommodations for $251. Airfares and accommodations for five nights, breakfast, and a rental car is $415 from Sale and $399 from Launceston.

Rental cars from Flinders Island Cabin Park are $50 per day, while the Furneaux Tavern has newer models for $70 for the first day, then $65 per day. *Strait Lady* is a 10-meter motor cat that cruises to uninhabited islands of the Furneaux Archipelago for wildlife viewing and diving; call (03) 6359-4507 for details.

VICTORIA

THE LAND

Occupying just three percent of Australia (similar in size to Great Britain) and smallest of the mainland states, Victoria is a package of welcome surprises. To the north, separated by the Murray River, is New South Wales; to the west is South Australia; and to the south is 1,300 km of rugged coastline, which gets the full brunt of unpredictable weather from Bass Strait and the Southern Ocean. Victoria has the most diverse landscape of any state; within the confines of these borders are wild ocean beaches, a desert-like landscape in the west, snow-covered peaks in the east, forests filled with unique Australian flora and fauna, and cities steeped in gold-rush history.

Regions

Melbourne is very central to the state's attractions; all parts of the state can be reached within a day's drive. Immediately north of the capital are the goldfield towns of Ballarat and Bendigo. The Great Ocean Road, which follows the coastline southwest of Melbourne, is one of the world's great ocean drives. In the west of the state are the Grampians, a spectacular outcrop of mountains with some of the state's best hiking and wildlife-viewing. The mighty Murray River originates in the east of the state and flows westward; along its banks are the charming towns of Mildura, Swan Hill, and Echuca, which originated as inland ports. Some of Victoria's most spectacular scenery is found in the High Country, the southern extent of the Great Dividing Range. These mountains are protected by Alpine National Park and provide endless opportunity for exploration, whether on foot, horseback, or a 4WD day trip. And yes, Australia *does* have snow; this part of the state is dotted with ski resorts. The coastal Princes Highway provides an alternative route between Melbourne and Sydney and detours can easily be made to Phillip Island, home to a large population of penguins, and Wilsons Promontory, southernmost point of mainland Australia.

Climate

Victoria, and Melbourne in particular, has a reputation among those living in the northern states

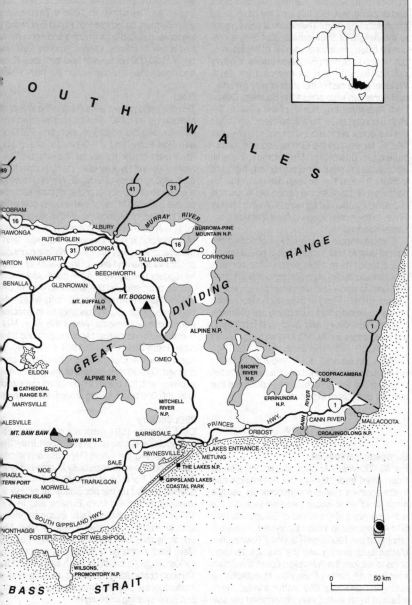

© MOON PUBLICATIONS, INC.

for inclement weather, namely overcast skies and drizzling rain. But this isn't the case, or so the statisticians claim. Their records prove, much to the delight of southerners, that Sydney receives twice the annual rainfall of Melbourne, but, whereas Sydney has short bursts of heavy rain, Melbourne can be overcast for days. Weather in the rest of the state is very dynamic; cold fronts can whip across the Southern Ocean from Antarctica any month of the year. In the High Country, snow falls June-Sept. and often flurries occur a month either side (snow also falls as far west as the Grampians and, on occasion, in downtown Melbourne). Rainfall throughout the state is not particularly high, but is more frequent in coastal areas. In the far northwest of the state, the desert-like landscape is drastically affected by rainfall. As the Murray River, to the north, floods, it flows through a series of floodplains.

Climate should play a role in choosing the time of year to visit Victoria but is not as important a factor as in other parts of the country. (You should avoid summer school holidays—mid-Dec. to Jan.—as everywhere is crowded.) Summer (Dec.-Feb.) is the only season when ocean swimming and sunbaking are pleasant. Spring (Sept.-Nov.) and autumn (March-May) are good times for touring and walking. Winter (June-Aug.) sees the crowds head to High Country ski resorts, but, compared to North America, winters are mild and there is no better time explore the goldfields or experience the culinary delights of Melbourne.

HISTORY

European Settlement

For 40,000 years Aboriginals, known also as Koori, lived freely throughout Australia; those in the southeast lived a seminomadic lifestyle throughout what would become Victoria, but within 50 years of the arrival of Europeans, only 500 Aboriginals in Victoria survived. At the beginning of the 1800s, with Sydney Town's population overflowing and the French sending ships to explore the Australian coast, the British sent a small party of convicts to establish a colony in Port Phillip Bay. Within a year, due to a lack of fresh water, they abandoned the settlement and sailed for Van Diemen's Land, now known as Tasmania. In 1835 a Tasmanian John Batman, sailed into Port Phillip Bay searching for land suitable for grazing and agriculture. For a few blankets, knives, and trinkets, he bought 250,000 hectares of land from local Koori and established a settlement on the Yarra River.

Gold

Ten thousand people were living in the vicinity of Melbourne by 1840. Towns had been established along the coastline, including Portland and Port Fairy, and a few remote sheep stations were scattered across the interior. Gold rushes west of Sydney drew many people from the fledgling colony of Victoria. Wanting to avoid a collapse of the city, a group of businessmen posted a reward to anyone who found gold within 100 miles of Melbourne. Within weeks gold had been discovered at Warrandyte, northwest of Melbourne, and by the end of that year, 1851 massive gold strikes had been made throughout central Victoria and tens of thousands of hopeful diggers had flocked to the goldfields. Immigrants from around the world arrived in the colony; Melbourne boomed, and what had begun as rough shanty towns grew to become permanent settlements. About this time, Melbourne businessmen set about separating from New South Wales, and in 1851 a new colony, named for the Queen of England, was proclaimed. By 1860 the biggest of the gold rushes was over and the colony's population stabilized with 600,000 people living in Melbourne alone.

20th Century

On 1 January 1901 Australia was federated and Victoria became a state. Apart from the 1920s, during the Great Depression, Victoria continued to boom, especially in times of high wool prices. For most of this century, immigration policies topped up the population; after WW II immigrants arrived from Europe and in the 1970s from Southeast Asia. Property prices shot skyward in the 1980s, but by 1990 the economy recessed and Victoria was hit particularly hard. A change of government in the early 1990s brought a breath of fresh air to the state. Through cost-cutting measures and aggressive marketing, the state has managed a turnaround and is prospering once again.

MELBOURNE

A blend of impressive Victorian-era buildings, modern skyscrapers, tree-lined avenues, large areas of parkland, and trams trundling the streets of downtown combine to make Melbourne (pronounced "MEL-bun") one of the world's great cities to visit (a 1990 U.S. survey declared Melbourne to be the "world's most livable city"). Sydneysiders see their southern relatives as conservative and dull, while Melburnians see themselves as refined and culturally inclined. Indeed, Melbourne is often called "The East Australian City."

Melbourne is the capital of Victoria, and with a population of 2,900,000 it is Australia's second largest city. In area, Melbourne is one of the world's largest cities, extending 100 km from north to south and 80 km from east to west. It sprawls over coastal plains around Port Phillip Bay, a massive body of water indented into the coastline of Victoria. Whereas Sydney lies around a beautiful natural harbor, Melbourne has no such natural feature, just the sluggish Yarra River winding through it. Its dirty brown color is not man's doing, but due to suspended clay sediment.

Downtown Melbourne is spread along the Yarra River a couple of km from Port Phillip Bay. North of the river are, traditionally, working-class suburbs such as Richmond and Collingwood, while to the south are middle- and upper-class suburbs such as South Yarra, Kew, and, on an elevated area west of downtown, Toorak, one of Australia's most expensive addresses and *definitely* the most expensive away from water.

The city boasts an air of distinctive tradition, making it hard to believe that just 150 years ago it was an expanse of savannah grassland. Through a short, nonconvict past, Melbourne flourished as a cultural center, supportive of music and the performing arts, as well as being the home of many distinguished artists, sophisticated shopping precincts, and fine dining restaurants. Not all Melbourne's culture revolves around the visual and performing arts. There's also sporting culture. One of the world's great sporting venues, the **Melbourne Cricket Ground,** is the scene of cricket matches all summer. Few cities have proclaimed a public holiday for a three-minute horse race, in this case the **Melbourne Cup.** But it is Victoria's own code of football, **Aussie Rules,** that has the most fanatical following.

History

The European history of Melbourne began in 1835 when John Batman and a group of pastoralists from northern Tasmania established a settlement beside the Yarra River. For the first 50 years, Melbourne's only link to the outside world was by sea, and in 1883 a rail link was completed with Sydney.

Upon separation from New South Wales in 1851, Melbourne was declared capital of the newly named Victoria. That same year, gold was discovered in Victoria and the city boomed, its population doubling to 46,000 within 12 months, and, by the end of the decade, its population had eclipsed that of Sydney. The gold rush attracted businesses that based themselves in the gateway city, and by the 1880s Melbourne had become the financial capital of Australia. As the gold rush ended, public land was set aside for diggers, encouraging them to remain in the Melbourne district. By late last century Melbourne's economy had become strongly linked to Victoria's pastoral hinterland, where sheep and cattle stations had been established. The large population in Melbourne formed a base for the business and manufacturing industry that continues to thrive today. It was during this period that much of Melbourne's impressive architecture dates, a time when Melbourne was the South Pacific's most important city, attracting travelers, writers, and adventurous aristocrats from around the world.

In 1901, when the Australian colonies were federated, Melbourne was proclaimed the seat of federal parliament and remained temporary capital until 1927 when parliament moved to Canberra. After WW II, Melbourne's British origins were slowly diluted as immigration policies changed, bringing large numbers of Italians, Greeks, Turks, and other Europeans into Aus-

MELBOURNE

TRAMS AND CARS: A DANGEROUS COMBINATION

Traveling by tram is one of the true joys of Melbourne, but driving on the roads with them is a different matter. A special road rule has been developed to allow trams to travel more freely through the city. Sure, if you've lived all your life in Melbourne, it seems straightforward, but to visiting drivers it can be confusing. It applies at intersections marked by a black-and-white sign hanging from cables. When turning *right,* you must pull to the *left* and wait for the lights of the street you're turning into to turn green. Also, trams can only be overtaken on the *left,* and you must always stop behind a tram when it stops.

ralia. To this day, Melbourne remains the world's second-largest Greek city and has the largest population of Italians outside Italy.

DOWNTOWN SIGHTS

Swanston Street
A ferry service that once connected Swanston St. to the south side of the Yarra River saw this street become downtown's main thoroughfare, with many historic buildings constructed along its length. The street is now closed to vehicular traffic—only trams and pedestrians travel the route. At the Yarra River-end of the street is **Flinders St. Railway Station,** a long domed building that has been the transportation hub of Melbourne for most of this century. Diagonally opposite is **St. Paul's Cathedral,** sections of which date from 1880; open daily 7 a.m.-6 p.m. Across the road is **Young and Jackson's Hotel.** Built in 1861, the hotel is best known for *Chloe,* a painting of a nude woman, which hung in the public bar for 80 years before being moved to the upstairs restaurant. One block north is **City Square,** currently undergoing redevelopment and home to a statue of the hapless Burke and Wills. Diagonally opposite is the 1932 **Manchester Unity Building,** one of Melbourne's first high-rise buildings and home to the city's oldest escalator. Next to the Manchester Unity

Building is the **Capitol Building,** designed by Walter Burley Griffin. The original facade has been replaced, but, inside, the Capitol Theatre is considered one of the world's greatest theaters (now showing Chinese language films only). Opposite is **Town Hall,** built in 1890.

Four blocks north, two very different buildings face each other. On the east side of Swanston St. is the **State Library,** sections of which date to 1854. Its classical facade leads into a cavernous foyer and the famous domed reading room. Opposite the library is **Melbourne Central,** an ultramodern retail complex and 55-story office tower.

Museum of Victoria
A new state museum is currently under construction on the south bank of the Yarra River. For the time being the collection is housed in the State Library building on Swanston St., with the main entrance being on La Trobe St. (tel. 03-9669-9888). Because of limited space, only a fraction of the museum's collection is displayed, but it's still a worthwhile attraction. On the Ground Level is an exhibition of underwater creatures, and on the larger Levels One and Two is the stuffed body of Phar Lap, Australia's most famous racing horse, an exhibition of the history of Australian wine, relics from Koori culture, and a display of Australia's unique flora and fauna. Admission is adult $5, child $2.50. Open daily 10 a.m.-5 p.m.

In the museum is a **planetarium** with shows Mon.-Fri. at 3 p.m., Sat.-Sun. hourly noon-3 p.m. Admission is adult $3, child $1.50.

Old Melbourne Gaol
When troopers finally captured Australia's most infamous bushranger Ned Kelly, it was in this jail that he was held and hanged. It was completed in 1858, and in its 90-year history over 100 souls were hanged. Today, it's open to the public, a good place for those with a fascination with Australia's convict history to view morbid relics such as death masks and gallows. Other displays include documents cataloging the small crimes that condemned people to a life in a penal colony and a grim collection of memorabilia that allows a glimpse at life behind bars. The platform from where Ned and others were hanged is on display, as is his bullet-dented armor and death

DOWNTOWN MELBOURNE

FITZROY GARDENS

■ COOK'S COTTAGE

TREASURY GARDENS

PARLIAMENT GARDENS

CARLTON GARDENS

AUSTRALIAN GALLERY OF SPORT AND OLYMPIC MUSEUM

MELBOURNE CRICKET GROUND (M.C.G.)

NATIONAL TENNIS CENTRE

YARRA RIVER

KINGS DOMAIN

ROYAL BOTANIC GARDENS

SYDNEY MYER MUSIC BOWL

TO NATIONAL HERBARIUM

TO RICHMOND

TO ST KILDA

■ CITY SQUARE

FLINDERS ST STATION

SOUTHGATE
MELBOURNE CONCERT HALL
THEATRES BUILDING
VICTORIAN ARTS CENTRE
NATIONAL GALLERY OF VICTORIA

SOUTHBANK

■ YOUNG AND JACKSON'S HOTEL

■ SHERLOCK HOLMES

■ LE MERIDIEN HOTEL
● GRAINSTORE TAVERN

SEE "DOWNTOWN MELBOURNE DETAIL" MAP

QUEEN VICTORIA MARKET

FLAGSTAFF GARDENS

■ LAZAR
■ HANABISHI

● RIALTO TOWER
● V-LINE TRAVEL CENTRE
● TERRACE
● PACIFIC INN

TO ARDEN MOTEL
● FLAGSTAFF CITY MOTOR INN

TO MELBOURNE AIRPORT

HOTEL ENTERPRIZE
● BANKS HOTEL

SPENCER ST STATION

■ WORLD TRADE CENTRE

POLLY WOODSIDE MARITIME PARK

YARRA RIVER

GRIMES BRIDGE RD.

0   250 m

WESTGATE FWY.

LORIMER ST.

mask. Admission is $6, $2.80 for children. Open daily 9:30 a.m.-4:30 p.m. Located on Russell St., one block north of the Museum of Victoria tel. 03-9663-7228).

Chinatown

The colorful sights and aromatic smells of Chinatown are marked by an ornate gateway across Little Bourke St. at Swanston Street. This part of town was a focus for the Chinese since the gold rush, and the streetscape has changed little since. The **Chinese Museum,** in Cohen Place, depicts the history of Chinese in Australia and the racism and persecution they encountered on the goldfields. Admission is $3 and it's open Sun.-Thurs. noon-5 p.m. (tel. 03-9662-2888).

Parliament House

One of Melbourne's oldest buildings, Parliament House lies in an area known as the Parliamentary Precinct, set aside by early town planners for various civic buildings, parks, and a treasury. The

Parliament House

precinct is located east of Spring St., with the impressive facade of Parliament House facing Spring Street. Construction started in 1856, at a time when the gold rush was injecting untold wealth into the colony of Victoria. Various additions were made to the building during its early years, but a dome that was part of the original plan still hasn't been completed. The interior of the building is also impressive, and on days when parliament isn't sitting tours are offered hourly 10 a.m.-3 p.m.; call (03) 9651-8362 for bookings.

Behind Parliament House are a few blocks of historic buildings, including churches and the **Commonwealth Building,** used 1901-27 when Melbourne was the temporary national capital. Beside Parliament House is the **Old Treasury,** its size and formidable appearance testimony to the vast wealth the goldfields produced; open daily 9 a.m.-5 p.m. with tours at 1 and 3 p.m. (tel. 03-9651-2233).

Windsor Hotel

Across from Parliament House is Australia's only remaining Victorian-era hotel. Built in 1883, it features a distinctive facade, and in the foyer, all the opulence you'd expect, with the original elevators now serving as phone booths.

Collins Street

Prestigious Collins St. is lined with 19th-century buildings housing some of Melbourne's most exclusive shops as well as restaurants and cafes, interspersed with modern buildings such as 35-story Regent Melbourne. The street's east end has the fashionable boutiques while west of Swanston St. is home to bankers and stockbrokers. Between Exhibition and Swanston Streets are three historic churches; the oldest, **Collins St. Baptist Church,** dates from 1862 (open Mon.-Fri. 11 a.m.-2 p.m.). At 162 Collins St. is **Georges,** Melbourne's most exclusive department store. Between Swanston and Elizabeth Streets is **Block Arcade,** a stylish arcade of shops built in 1892 and styled on the Galleria Vittorio Emmanuel in Milan, Italy. It features shopfronts with high windows, mosaic floors, marble columns, and high vaulted ceilings.

The many historic buildings of the financial district are dwarfed by **Rialto Tower,** a modern 55-story office tower (tallest building in the Southern Hemisphere). On the top floor is a viewing

THERRY ST.

YWCA
FAMILY
HOTEL

MAC'S HOTEL

McCAFFERTY'S
COACH
TERMINAL

OLD MELBOURNE GAOL

RUSSELL

SWANSTON

FRANKLIN   ST.

TOAD HALL

ELIZABETH

QUEEN

LITTLE LA TROBE ST.

INDIA
HOUSE

ST.

MUSEUM OF VICTORIA

ST.

STATE LIBRARY

LA TROBE

MUSEUM
RAILWAY
STATION

MELBOURNE CENTRAL

ST.

FLIGHT CENTRE

DOWNTOWN
MELBOURNE
DETAIL

LONSDALE

RUBY RED

TSINDOS
THE GREEK'S
RESTAURANT

KING'S
WOK

SUPPER
INN

THE LOUNGE

KUN
MING

LITTLE

LONSDALE

ST.

MYER DEPARTMENT
STORE

ONG
INTERNATIONAL
FOOD COURT

SWANSTON

HORSE & HOUND TAVERN

BOWYANGS
TRAVEL
BOOKS

BOURKE

TRAVELLER'S
MEDICAL CLINIC

GENERAL
POST
OFFICE

INFORMATION BOOTH

CAMPARI BISTRO

LITTLE

ST.

QUEEN

ST.

ELIZABETH

BOURKE

0   100 m

DAVID JONES

GOPAL'S

ABORIGINAL
HANDCRAFTS

ST.

N
MOON

VICTORIA
TOURISM
CENTRE

COLLINS

MET
SHOP

ST.

BLOCK ARCADE

CITY
SQUARE
MOTEL

LITTLE

COLLINS   ST.

CARLTON GARDENS

VICTORIA PARADE

LA TROBE

EXHIBITION ST.

LONSDALE ST.

LITTLE

SPRING ST.

ALBERT ST.

PARLIAMENT GARDENS

PARLIAMENT ST.

NICHOLSON ST.

LONSDALE

■ COMEDY THEATRE

■ LUCATTINI'S

■ CHINESE MUSEUM
● NEW CHATEAU HOTEL

■ PRINCESS THEATRE

BOURKE

■ LITTLE MALAYSIA

■ STALACTITES
TOKI SUSHI BAR

LITTLE

● BRYSON HOTEL

LE MONDE
METRO ●

PARLIAMENT HOUSE

■ SHARK FIN HOUSE
● PELLEGRINI'S
FLORENTINO CELLAR BAR

BOURKE

■ ABORIGINAL GALLERY OF DREAMING

WINDSOR HOTEL ●

● ITALIAN WAITERS' RESTAURANT

PARLIAMENT STATION

APPY WORLD

● WONG SHING KEE
● CITY SCENE BACKPACKERS

CITY CENTRE PRIVATE HOTEL

● BACKPACKERS CITY INN

COLLINS

CAFE ALCASTON

OLD TREASURY

LITTLE

RUSSELL ST.

■ MIETTA'S

ST.

● REGENT MELBOURNE

SPRING ST.

● VICTORIA HOTEL

COLLINS

EXHIBITION

COLLINS PLACE

LANE

WN HALL
GEORGE'S ●
COLLINS ST. ✝ BAPTIST CHURCH

■ HYATT FOOD COURT

HENAEUM

FLINDERS

■ CITY SQUARE

FLINDERS ST.

© MOON PUBLICATIONS, INC.

deck; open daily Mon.-Fri. 11 a.m.-11 p.m., Sat.-Sun. 10 a.m.-11 p.m. Admission is adult $6, child $3.50, which includes a 38-second lift ride, use of telescopes, and viewing of a historic display.

Victorian Arts Centre

On the south side of the Yarra River, this complex comprises two main buildings, the **Theatres Building** and distinctive circular **Melbourne Concert Hall,** which are linked by landscaped walkways. On the first floor of the Concert Hall, which hosts major events year-round, is **Performing Arts Museum** (tel. 03-9684-8263). Exhibitions change regularly but feature all aspects of the arts. Admission is adult $5, child $3.50, and it's open Mon.-Fri. 11 a.m.-5 p.m., Sat.-Sun. noon-5 p.m.

National Gallery of Victoria

As Australia's premier art gallery, this facility displays about 70,000 works of art from around the world. It was built in the late 1960s, part of an arts precinct that includes the Victorian Arts Centre and Victorian College of Arts. Out front is *Angel,* a colorful and distinctive sculpture by Deborah Halpern. The gallery has collections of art from all eras of Australian history, including works by prominent Aboriginal artists, Arthur Streeton, Tom Roberts, Arthur Boyd, and Sir Sidney Nolan. Picasso, Monet, Rembrandt, and Turner are featured in international galleries, while in the courtyard are works by sculptor Henry Moore. The gallery is open daily 10 a.m.-5 p.m. On Monday only two floors are open, but admission is free. On other days, admission is adult $4.50, child $2 (tel. 03-9685-0203).

Southgate

This riverfront complex sits on the Yarra River opposite Flinders St. Station and beside Melbourne Concert Hall and is linked to downtown by a footbridge across the river. Three-story Southgate houses a food court, restaurants, and boutiques. On the first floor is **AustraliaGate SensorVision Theatre,** a unique complex where the movie *Experience Australia* is screened with the help of a huge video screen, the latest audio technology, a range of smells piped into the theater, and computer-controlled temperature and humidity changes. The idea is to experience as many aspects of life in Australia as possible, including the Dreamtime, a convict ship, early settlers, the goldfields, bushfire, rainforest, life on a beach, and Australians at war. The show runs 50 minutes, running hourly 11:30 a.m.-4:30 p.m. Tickets are a worthwhile $6 for adults, $3.50 for children (tel. 03-9690-9800).

Polly Woodside Maritime Park

Polly Woodside, an Irish-built ship dating to 1885, spent her working life sailing between Europe and South America before ending her working life as a coal hulk in Port of Melbourne. Restoration began in 1972, and she now sits in dry dock on the south side of the Yarra River, downstream from Southgate. One of only six ships worldwide to be awarded an International Heritage Medal for excellence in restoration, it is part of an ever-growing museum with a small lighthouse, an old pumphouse, and other maritime memorabilia. Admission is adult $7, child $4. Open daily 10 a.m.-4 p.m. (tel. 03-9699-9760).

PARKS AND GARDENS

Kings Domain

Bordered by the Yarra River, St. Kilda Rd., Domain Rd., and Anderson St., Kings Domain is one of Melbourne's finest chunks of parkland. The southeast corner is the **Royal Botanic Gardens,** encompassing 36 hectares and containing over 11,000 plants from Australia and around the world. It is a peaceful place to spend an hour or so, with many lakes attracting waterfowl and a lakeside cafe serving Devonshire teas (daily 9 a.m.-5 p.m.). A visitor center is in the **National Herbarium,** on Birdwood Avenue. The herbarium was established in 1853 to help the general public with plant identification. Open daily 10 a.m.-5 p.m. (tel. 03-9655-2341). Toward the city is the **Shrine of Remembrance,** built for the memory of Victorians killed in WW I; from its lofty perch views extend to the city. **Governor La Trobe's Cottage,** on Birdwood Ave., is the original governor's residence, a far cry from the new Government House, built in 1872 and open for tours Monday, Wednesday, and Saturday; call (03) 9654-4562 for times. The original cottage is open to the public Monday and Wednesday 10 a.m.-4 p.m. and Sat.-Sun. 11 a.m.-4 p.m. Admission is adult $3.50, child $1.80.

Carlton Gardens

These gardens are on the northeast corner of downtown, encompassing the **Royal Exhibition Building,** built for the 1880 Great Exhibition and still in use today.

Fitzroy Gardens

Fitzroy Gardens date to 1857, and are laid out in the design of Great Britain's flag, the Union Jack. They feature tree-lined avenues, colorful flower displays, and a fern-filled gully. **Cook's Cottage,** in a corner of the park, was the English home of Capt. James Cook's parents. It was dismantled and rebuilt in the gardens in 1934. The interior is furnished with period antiques, and a small part of the cottage is devoted to the life of their famous son. Admission is $2 and it's open daily 9 a.m.-5 p.m.

Yarra Park and the Melbourne Cricket Ground

Yarra Park, a sprawling area east of downtown, is home to the Melbourne Cricket Ground (M.C.G.), one of the world's great sporting fields; the **National Tennis Centre,** home to the Australian Open; and a variety of other sporting fields. The M.C.G. oozes tradition; its cavernous hallways lead to rooms full of sporting relics. In 1858 the first official game of Australian Rules Football was played on a field where the carpark now stands, and in 1877 Australia met England in the first test match between the two countries. The ground also hosted athletic events of the 1956 Summer Olympic Games.

At the main entrance to the M.C.G., off Wellington Parade, is the **Australian Gallery of Sport and Olympic Museum,** dedicated to sport-loving Australians. It has three levels chock-full of memorabilia, including the original Australian Rules Football rules and displays cataloging the history of 10 sports. Other areas of the M.C.G. are open to the public, but you must take a tour to view them, including change rooms, Members Hall, Long Room, and a hallway filled with paintings of various sporting scenes. A combined ticket is adult $7, child $5. Open daily 10 a.m.-4 p.m. with tours on the hour. For further details call (03) 9657-8864. The M.C.G. is a 10-minute walk from Flinders St. Station, or jump aboard tram no. 48 or 75.

Linked by a footbridge to the M.C.G., the National Tennis Centre was built in 1988 and is the premier such facility in the country, with an enormous retractable roof. April-Sept. tours are offered Wed.-Fri. at 11 a.m., noon, and 1:30 p.m. Tour cost is $3 for adults, $1.50 for kids. For bookings call (03) 9655-1234.

Yarra Bend Park

The Yarra River flows through Melbourne's northeast suburbs and for much of the way is lined by parkland and golf courses. Yarra Bend Park, in the suburb of Collingwood, is one of the most popular expanses, home to a variety of birds, with a large area of native bushland. Also in the park is **Riverside Boathouse,** with canoes for rent and light snacks served in an 1860s building.

SIGHTS NORTH OF DOWNTOWN

Queen Victoria Market

A mecca for shoppers, this market has operated on the same site since 1878 and is today an integral part of many Melburnians' weekly shopping trips. Some buildings are over 100 years old but most of the action is under long open-walled sheds where you can buy just about anything you'll ever need. Market days are Tuesday and Thurs.-Sun., and the best time to go is the morning. To get there from downtown take tram no. 55 up William St. or any tram up Elizabeth Street.

Melbourne University

Victoria's premier higher education facility is in the suburb of Carlton, one km north of downtown. The campus is made up of buildings that span a century. **Percy Grainger Museum** catalogs the life of the museum's namesake, a life-long traveler with an eccentric interest in folk music. Admission is free. Open daily 10 a.m.-4 p.m. Also on campus is the **University Gallery,** a small gallery of Australian art, and the **Sir Ian Potter Gallery,** featuring temporary exhibitions of contemporary art. Both are open Wed.-Sat. noon-5 p.m.

Royal Melbourne Zoo

Established in 1861, this is one of the world's great zoos (and third oldest), boasting a collection of 3,000 animals in "natural" surroundings. And, as far as zoos go, cages are spacious and viewing easy. The collection of Australian fauna is extensive and includes a platypusary, where one of the world's most unusual animals is on display, and underwater viewing of fur seals. Other highlights include gorillas in a rainforest setting as well as bears and snow leopards. The zoo has a good souvenir shop, two restaurants, and a cafe. Admission is adult $11.50, child $6. Open daily 9 a.m.-5 p.m. with free guided tours offered throughout the day. Located on Elliot Ave., Parkville (tel. 03-9285-9300). To get there by tram, take no. 55 or 56 north on William St., or on Sunday no. 68 on Elizabeth Street.

Heide Art Gallery

Set among parkland extending to the banks of the Yarra River, this place was originally the home of John and Sunday Reed, whose 1930s patronage of famous Australian artists such as Sir Sidney Nolan and Albert Tucker, combined with a web of sexual intrigue between the artists and patrons, saw the house become the scene of change in Australian contemporary art. It now houses a large collection of art from that era and is open Tues.-Fri. 10 a.m.-5 p.m., Sat.-Sun. noon-5 p.m. Admission $2. It is located at 7 Templestowe Rd., Bulleen (tel. 03-9850-1500). Take bus no. 203 to get there.

THE DANDENONGS

When Melburnians want to escape from the rat race, this is where they come, a world away from the city, but just 40 km east of downtown. Early settlers cleared large tracts of the Dandenongs, and although hordes of visitors flock to the many parks and villages, the area has managed to retain its original charm. Early settlers established many gardens, planting English trees to make them feel at home, building stone churches, and, in later years, developing guesthouses. Access is easiest with your own transport (take South Eastern Frwy., turning north on Ferntree Gully Rd. in the suburb of Notting Hill), or take the train to Belgrave Station. From Upper Ferntree Gully, **Mount Dandenong Tourist Rd.** winds through the center of the range, passing quaint villages and public gardens, including **The Rhododendron Gardens**

in Olinda (tel. 03-9751-1980). This 40-hectare garden features thousands of rhododendron and azaleas, with a three-km path leading through the colorful gardens (best Sept.-Dec.) Admission is adult $5.50, kids free. Open daily 10 a.m.-4:30 p.m. Take a train to Upper Ferntree Gully, then bus no. 698.

William Ricketts Sanctuary, in Mt. Dandenong, is an amazing collection of clay sculptures inspired by the Koori of central Australia. Sculptures are spread throughout the six-hectare property, among towering mountain ash, fern filled gullies, and waterfalls. Admission is $5 and it's open daily 10 a.m.-4:30 p.m.

Dandenong Ranges National Park

For most of this century the Victorian government has been buying back land in the Dandenongs and protecting it as a national park. Currently, the park encompasses 1,920 hectares in three distinct sections. The Mt. Dandenong Tourist Rd. provides access to the park's many picnic areas, lookouts, and hiking trails. The Ferntree Gully section is accessed from the beginning of the Mt. Dandenong Tourist Rd., from where a three-km hiking trail leads into the park. East of the tourist road is Sherwood Forest Section, home to a population of lyrebirds.

Puffing Billy

A restored steam train, Puffing Billy has been chugging along a scenic 13 km of track between Belgrave and Emerald Lake for 90 years. Originally built to provide a link between Melbourne and the mountains, it is now run for the tourists, with open-sided carriages allowing views of the lush forest. The round-trip takes a little over two hours, but allow time at the lake, which has a picnic area, paddle boats, and a model railway. The fare is adult $13, child $8.50. To get to Belgrave, take a train from Flinders St. Station. Call (03) 9754-6800 for the Puffing Billy timetable.

SIGHTS SOUTH OF DOWNTOWN

Como House

Built in 1840, Como House overlooks the Yarra River in South Yarra. The original house was a single-story residence, with later owners exanding it to the grandeur evident today. Landscaped gardens and interior restoration make his house one of the finest places to view early Melbourne life. Open daily 10 a.m.-5 p.m.; admission is adult $6.60, child $3.30. To get there from downtown, take tram no. 30 to stop 30 and walk down Como Avenue.

St. Kilda

Late last century, St. Kilda, south of downtown on Port Phillip Bay, was a seaside resort popular with day-trippers wanting to escape the crowded streets of downtown Melbourne. First they came by horse and cart, then a tram line was built, opening the suburb up to everyone. People would flock to the beach, the swimming baths, the foreshore fun parks, and the hotels and restaurants. By the turn of the century, St. Kilda was home to many of Melbourne's wealthiest citizens. For most of this century, though, the suburb was in decline, but has undergone a dramatic facelift in the last 5 years, its brothels and drug dens replaced with fashionable boutiques, stylish cafes, and many fine restaurants. Most of the action is on Fitzroy St., which ends at the foreshore, at a large strip of coastal park where **St. Kilda Pier** juts into the bay. South of the pier is the familiar laughing face of **Luna Park,** a fun park dating to 1912. It's free to wander around the park, or you buy a ticket for unlimited rides for half a day; adult $14, child $11. Call (03) 9534-4654 for hours.

WILLIAMSTOWN AND VICINITY

South of where the Yarra River drains slowly into Port Phillip Bay is the suburb of Williamstown, Victoria's first port and at one time destined to become state capital. Until the Yarra River was dredged and the Port of Melbourne developed, it was Melbourne's major port, the base for Victorian customs and immigration, and had large dockyards extending to the mouth of the river. **Nelson Place** is the main road through Williamstown, running along the foreshore and lined on one side with historic buildings, many constructed of locally quarried bluestone. Restaurants, cafes, and antique shops line the street and at 5 Electra St. is a small

This bluestone lighthouse dates to the days when Williamstown was an important port.

ANDREW HEMPSTEAD

museum of maritime relics and artifacts from Williamstown's earliest days; open Sunday 2-5 p.m. At Gem Pier **HMAS *Castlemaine,*** a mine sweeper built at Williamstown in 1842, now operates as a museum; open Sat.-Sun. noon-5 p.m. Admission adult $2.50, child $1.50 (tel. 03-9397-2363).

Williamstown is a 20-minute drive from downtown, or take a ferry from Southgate; $10 one-way, $18 return; call (03) 9397-2255 for times.

Scienceworks

This museum combines science and technology with a hands-on approach. Kids love it, but all ages can enjoy the old machinery, displays explaining the principles of light, sound, movement, and centrifugal force, interactive exhibits, and other temporary displays. To get there by public transport, take the train to Spotswood Station, then walk 700 meters down Craig Street. It's at 2 Booker St. (tel. 03-9392-4800).

OUTDOOR ACTIVITIES AND SPECTATOR SPORTS

Canoeing and Boating

The Yarra River certainly isn't one of the world's most beautiful waterways, but many sections are good for flatwater canoeing. For something more adventurous than a river cruise, canoes and small boats can be rented at **Riverside Boathouse,** in Yarra Bend Park northeast of the city (tel. 03-9853-8707). Boats can also be rented at **St. Kilda Boat Hire,** on the pier at St. Kilda (tel. 03-9534-2491), and **Williamstown Boat Hire** (tel. 03-9397-7312). **Note:** Check weather forecasts before heading out on Port Phillip Bay.

Swimming

Melbourne City Baths, corner Swanston St. and Victoria Parade (tel. 03-9663-5888), at the top end of downtown, has a 25-meter indoor pool and other facilities including a gym, spas, and saunas. Admission is $5. Open Mon.-Fri. 6:15 a.m.-10 p.m., Sat.-Sun. 8 a.m.-6 p.m.

Golfing

Melbourne is blessed with a number of Australia's top golf courses along a strip southeast of the city known as the "sand belt." They include **Huntingdale, Kingston Heath, Metropolitan,** and **Royal Melbourne,** ranked as the world's sixth-best course by *Golf* magazine. All these courses are private, and unless you're a member of an equally prestigious club, getting a game is difficult.

Melbourne has around 100 other courses, with **Yarra Bend** (tel. 03-9481-3729) considered one of the country's finest public courses. Closer to the city, you'll find courses in Royal Park (tel. 03-9387-1326) and Albert Park (tel. 03-9510-5588). Green fees at these courses average $12-20 and all have club rentals.

The **Australian Masters,** held each February at Huntingdale, is a permanent fixture on the calender of many of the world's top golfers. For tickets call (03) 9696-2022.

Tennis

Except when major tournaments are in progress the public can rent courts Mon.-Fri. 7 a.m.-11 p.m., Sat.-Sun. 9 a.m.-6 p.m., at the **National Tennis Centre,** in Flinders Park, southeast of downtown off Batman Avenue. Court charge range $14-32 per hour, or for $75 per hour you can play on Court One; call (03) 9655-1244 for bookings. For information on the many other courts around Melbourne, call the Tennis Association of Victoria (tel. 03-9510-3137).

The **Australian Open,** one of the tennis world's four Grand Slam tournaments, attracts the world's best male and female players each January. For tickets call (03) 9655-1277.

Australian Rules

Best known as Aussie Rules, this unique sport has a fanatical following in Melbourne, which is both the birthplace and center of the sport. The game combines kicking with running, marking (catching the ball, often by leaping in the air), and passing. Each team has 18 men, with the ultimate goal to kick the ball through the opposing team's goal posts. Six points are awarded for a goal kicked through the central post and one point through posts either side. Because of its pace, and often rough tactics, Aussie Rules is a great game to watch, especially when surrounded by 40,000 fanatical fans. The season runs early March through Sept., with the Grand Final held on the last Saturday of September at the M.C.G. in front of a crowd of 100,000.

Cricket

Each summer, cricket can be seen on parks and grounds throughout the city, but the biggest crowds are drawn to the Melbourne Cricket Ground where international tests and one-day matches are held among the world's leading cricket nations. For dates and ticket prices call (03) 9650-3001.

Horse Racing

On the first Tuesday in November the entire country stops for the **Melbourne Cup,** Australia's richest horse race. For many Australians it is the only day of the year they make a wager, and then for a few minutes they crowd around radios and television sets for the famous two-mile race. It is held at Flemington Racecourse and is part of the monthlong Spring Racing Carnival. For ticketing details call (03) 9863-7375.

ARTS AND ENTERTAINMENT

Art Galleries
The National Gallery of Victoria in the Victorian Arts Centre (see "Downtown Sights," above) is the city's premier gallery, but there are many commercial galleries open to the public. One of the most interesting is **Montsalvat,** an artist's colony established by Justus Jorgensen in the 1930s on Hillcrest Ave., Eltham (tel. 03-9439-7771). The grounds are interesting, with work in a variety of mediums for view and sale. Open daily 9 a.m.-5 p.m.; admission is adult $2, child 50 cents. **Meat Market Craft Centre,** 42 Courtney St., North Melbourne (tel. 03-9329-9966), is a former meat market converted for craftspeople to work and display their wares. Materials worked with include wood, clay, metal, textiles, leather, and glass. The market is open Tues.-Sun., but the craftspeople only work weekdays.

Theater
The cultural center of the city is the **Victorian Arts Centre,** on St. Kilda Rd. south of downtown. It comprises three theaters—State, Playhouse, and George Fairfax—and the Melbourne Concert Hall. The State Theatre seats over 2,000 people on three levels and is capable of staging opera, ballet, and musical comedy productions. The Playhouse seats 888 and is home to the Melbourne Theatre Company. Ticket prices are dependent on the production, but range $30-73. "An Evening at the Victorian Arts Centre" includes a show, dinner, and a tour of the center; cost is $71-126 pp. For bookings call (03) 9684-8484.

Built in 1886, **Princess Theatre,** 163 Spring St. (tel. 03-9639-0022), is Melbourne's oldest theater; its impressive marble staircase and intricate plaster ceiling signify days gone by. It was restored for the opening of *Les Miserables* and today offers short runs of big musicals; ticket prices range $20-60. Another historic theater is the **Athenaeum,** 188 Collins St. (tel. 03-9650-3504), built in 1884 and opened as a theater in 1924. Performances vary greatly, but are often Shakespeare; tickets are $16-40. The **Comedy Theatre,** 240 Exhibition St. (tel. 03-9662-2222), opened as a comedy venue but is now home to musicals and plays. Tickets

range $30-44. The **Malthouse,** 113 Sturt St., South Melbourne (tel. 03-9685-5111), is a new complex featuring Australian contemporary theater performed by the Playbox Theatre Centre. Tickets range $6-30. **La Mama,** 205 Faraday St., Carlton (tel. 03-9347-6142), is a tiny theater company performing new and innovative works by Australian writers.

Music and Dance
The **Australian Opera Company** performs at the State Theatre in the Victorian Arts Centre on St. Kilda Road. Tickets start at $40. The State Theatre is also home to the **Victoria State Opera** and the **Australian Ballet Company.**

The 2,677-seat **Melbourne Concert Hall,** part of the Victorian Arts Centre, is home to both the **Melbourne Symphony Orchestra** and **State Orchestra of Victoria.** This venue is renowned for excellent acoustics, aided by massive glass shells suspended above the stage. Tickets are $35-40. The **Sidney Myer Music Bowl,** Kings Domain (tel. 03-9684-8360), is used for opera, jazz, and ballet performances in the summer months.

Cinemas
The city's largest cinemas are around the intersection of Bourke and Russell Streets. They include a **Greater Union, Hoyts,** and **Village.** Carlton has a few cinemas, such as **Nova,** 380 Lygon St. (tel. 03-9347-5331), and **Carlton Moviehouse,** 235 Faraday St. (tel. 03-9347-8909), that feature alternative and foreign films. In St. Kilda, the **Astor,** corner Chapel St. and Dandenong Rd. (tel. 03-9510-1414), has more of the same as does **Valhalla,** 89 High St. (tel. 03-9482-2001).

Pubs, Bars, and Taverns
Built in 1853, **Young and Jackson's Hotel,** corner Flinders and Swanston Streets (tel. 03-9650-3884), is one of the city's oldest pubs. The much-admired *Chloe,* a painting of a nude woman, adorned the walls of the bar for 100 years before being moved upstairs, but the public bar is still a good place to have a beer. **Mac's Hotel,** 34 Franklin St. (tel. 03-9663-6855), dates from the same year and was originally the terminus for gold escorts, with a special lockup provided for the gold.

For an English atmosphere head to **Horse & Hound Tavern,** 221 Queen St. (tel. 03-9670-8488), or **Sherlock Holmes,** 415 Collins St. (tel. 03-9629-1146), both popular lunchtime hangouts and open daily till midnight. The **Cricketers Bar,** in the Windsor Hotel on Spring St., combines the feel of an elegant English pub with cricketing memorabilia. **Le Monde** is a trendy bar/cafe that stays open 24 hours; it's at 18 Bourke St. (tel. 03-9663-7804).

The old **Esplanade Hotel,** overlooking Port Phillip Bay in St. Kilda, is beginning to look out of place as the suburb goes upmarket, but it is one of the city's best live music venues, with bands performing nightly. In the city, **Grainstore Tavern,** 46 King St. (tel. 03-9614-3570), is another popular venue. North of downtown, **Jimmy Watson's,** Lygon St., is a wine bar that has been around for years.

Nightclubs

Melbourne boasts the largest number of night clubs of any Australian city. The **Metro,** 2 Bourke St., is a three-level nightclub in an ol theater building. It has eight bars and is th largest nightclub in the Southern Hemisphere **Grainstore Tavern,** on King St., has live band and a disco most nights. **The Lounge,** 24 Swanston St., is one of downtown's trendies dance clubs. **Bobby McGees,** Bryson Hote 186 Exhibition St. (tel. 03-9639-0630), is popu lar with under-25s after 10 p.m., but 5-7 p.m. attracts all ages for free light snacks and tw drinks for the price of one (Mon.-Fri. only). **Laza** 240 King St. (tel. 03-9602-1822), is a three-leve converted warehouse that attracts well-dresse dancers prepared to pay high prices for cock tails. It's open Wed.-Sun. with a band on Fr day night. **Monsoon's,** in the Grand Hyatt a

---

MELBOURNE FESTIVALS AND EVENTS

Summer

Christmas is celebrated with **Carols by Candlelight** at the Myer Music Bowl, when 30,000 people sing their hearts out along with some of the country's top entertainers. For tickets call Bass (tel. 03-9529-3544). The **New Year** is ushered in with partying on the streets and, the following day, an international cricket test match at the Melbourne Cricket Ground. Later that same month is the **Summer Music Festival,** offering a daily program of a wide variety of music in the Victorian Arts Centre. February is a busy month. **Chinese New Year Festival** sees celebrations through Chinatown. **St. Kilda Festival,** a week-long celebration of food, music, sports, and art displays, takes place through St. Kilda. The **Melbourne Food and Wine Festival** has events in the hearts of Carlton, South Yarra, and St. Kilda.

Autumn

Moomba, supposedly meaning "Getting Together and Having Fun," features 10 days of events through downtown Melbourne, with an amusement park and displays set up along the Yarra Valley. The finale is Sunday. The **Dragon Boat Festival** on the Yarra River commemorates the death of Qu Yuan, a Chinese poet who threw himself into a river as a

protest against political corruption, and his friends, who set out in boats, thrashing the water with oars and beating drums to keep away the monsters. The city's largest ethnic gathering is **Antipodean Festival,** promoting the culture of Greece through art, music, and food. April is the **International Comedy Festival,** with performances by acts from around the world at all the city's comedy venues.

Winter

The only event of note in winter is the **Melbourne International Film Festival,** held each June. It has been part of the calender for nearly 50 years and screens some of the world's most innovative contemporary films.

Spring

In September the country comes to the city for the **Royal Melbourne Show,** a large agricultural fair with wood chopping, show jumping, and equestrian events. The **Melbourne International Festival of the Arts,** in October, is a 17-day extravaganza of performing arts featuring writers, artists, singers, musicians, and dancing from around the world. In October, at the Royal Melbourne Showgrounds, **Oktoberfest** is held in the tradition of its famous Bavarian origins.

Dragon Boat Races, Moomba Festival

val (see the special topic "Melbourne Festivals and Events"), Melbourne has many comedy options. The **Last Laugh,** 64 Smith St., Collingwood (tel. 03-9419-8600), has local and international acts nightly. Generally, dinner is served 7:30 p.m. and the show commences at 9 p.m. Tickets are $19-39, or to see the show only is $10-22. Upstairs is **Le Joke,** a smaller venue open Fri.-Sat. nights (showtime 8:30 p.m.). The **Waiting Room** in the Esplanade Hotel, St. Kilda, is another comedy venue.

SHOPPING

The main shopping area is right downtown, with the best places to browse and buy being the large department stores and plazas. **Myer** is the world's fifth largest department store, with 12 floors of shopping pleasures, including a great Food Emporium on the ground floor; the main entrance faces Bourke St. Mall. **Daimaru,** Australia's only international department store, is part of the Melbourne Central on La Trobe Street. Other large department stores are **David Jones** at 310 Bourke St., spanning two blocks, and **George's,** 162 Collins St., for old-fashioned luxury.

Block Arcade is a stylish shopping arcade running between Collins and Little Collins Streets. Farther up the hill, **Royal Arcade** links Little Collins and Bourke Streets. **Australia on Collins** is a modern, stylish arcade.

Markets

The city's largest is **Queen Victoria Market,** between Elizabeth and William Streets north of downtown. It encompasses a few blocks, offering rows and rows of just about everything imaginable, including food from around the country, furniture, clothing, giftware, kitchenware, and souvenirs. The market is open Tuesday and Thursday 6 a.m.-2 p.m., Friday 6 a.m.-6 p.m., Saturday 6 a.m.-1 p.m., and Sunday 9 a.m.-4 p.m. Other major markets the one on **St. Kilda Esplanade** every Sunday, and **South Melbourne Market** on the corner of Hopkins and Leeds Streets Thurs.-Saturday.

Australiana

Aboriginal Handcrafts, 9th Floor, 125-133 Swanston St. (tel. 03-9650-4717), sells authentic

23 Collins St. (tel. 03-9657-1234), attracts a similar crowd, but in a more intimate atmosphere. Cover charge is $8-15, and a strict dress code is enforced.

Jazz, Folk, and Comedy
Limerick Arms Hotel, 364 Clarendon St., South Melbourne (tel. 03-9690-2626), has live jazz on Thursday and Sunday nights; cover charge $5-10. Downtown, **Ruby Red** (9 Drewery Lane) is a popular jazz venue, and on Sunday afternoons **Beaconsfield Hotel** (341 Beaconsfield Parade, St. Kilda) has live jazz. If you're around in January, the **Montsalvat Jazz Festival,** at an artist's colony northeast of downtown, shouldn't be missed.

The Melbourne Folk Club hosts performances at **Brunswick East Hotel,** Lygon St., Brunswick. Closer to town, in North Melbourne, **Dan O'Connell Hotel,** 225 Canning St., has live folk music Wed.-Sat. nights (no cover charge).

Besides the **International Comedy Festi-**

Aboriginal art, but it's not cheap. Artifacts include bark paintings, carvings, boomerangs, woomeras, and didgeridoos; open Mon.-Friday. **Aboriginal Gallery of Dreaming** (73-77 Bourke St.) is another good place to check out. **Yarrandoo Souvenirs and Native Art,** in Collins Place at 45 Collins St., has a huge range of Australiana souvenirs, although most of the less-expensive Aboriginal work isn't authentic.

Thomas Cook, 60 Hoddle St., Abbotsford (tel. 03-9417-7555), is the place to head for Australian clothing such as an Akubra hat or a Driza-bone coat.

HOTEL AND MOTEL ACCOMMODATIONS

Downtown—Budget and Moderate

Many of the oldest downtown hotels have been refurbished (or demolished) in recent years, so finding a cheapie is difficult. If you're on a budget consider staying outside the city center, as public transport to downtown is efficient.

City Centre Private Hotel, 22 Little Collins St. (tel. 03-9654-5401), looks dowdy from the street, but rooms are clean and each floor has a communal kitchen; $34 s, $50 d. Rooms with shared facilities at **Hotel Enterprize,** 44 Spencer St. (tel. 03-9629-6991), are similarly priced, and rates include breakfast and parking. Nicer rooms here, with private facilities, are $79 s, $89 d. **Terrace Pacific Inn,** 16 Spencer St. (tel. 03-9621-3333), is a new hotel across from Spencer St. Railway Station and the casino, and is a 10-minute walk to downtown. Rooms with shared facilities are $49 s or d, while rooms with private facilities are $79-99. Most central of the budget hotels is **Victoria Hotel,** half a block from Swanston Walk at 215 Little Collins St. (tel. 03-9653-0441). It is a rambling old place, with over 500 rooms. Those with shared facilities are $38 s, $50 d; those with bathrooms are $75 s, $99 d.

City Square Motel, 67 Swanston St. (tel. 03-9654-7011), just a block from Flinders St. Station and right on the main shopping strip, has rooms that aren't particularly special and cost $63 s, $79 d. Once one of Melbourne's grand hotels, **New Chateau Hotel,** 131 Lonsdale St. (tel. 03-9663-3161), is slowly losing its stars, but rates are coming down accordingly, and it's good

value now at $85 s, $125 d. Rooms are large each has a balcony, and the place has all th services of the more expensive places. Park ing is $10 per day. On the corner of Spence St. and Flinders Lane is **Banks Hotel** (tel. 0. 9629-4111), recently restored and as friend as any of the downtown accommodations. Fa cilities include a pool, sauna, gym, restauran bar, and laundry. Rates are $105-195 s or d. little farther out, but good value, is **Arden Mote** 15 Arden St. (tel. 03-9329-7211), which ha large, basic rooms for $65 s, $68 d. Priced th same, and a little closer to downtown, **Flagstaff City Motor Inn,** 45 Dudley St. (te 03-9329-5788).

Downtown—Expensive

Melbourne has a good choice of internationa class accommodations downtown, and whil most are fully booked during the week, whe the businesspeople have gone home for th weekend rooms are easy to come by *and* th rates are reduced, often drastically.

The grand lady of Melbourne is the **Wind sor Hotel,** 103 Spring St. (tel. 03-9653-0653 one of Australia's grandest hostelries. Built i 1883, the imposing Victorian facade, complet with top-hatted doormen, is a Melbourne inst tution. Inside, the foyer and Grand Dining Room exude opulence of a bygone era, with marbl floors and mahogany furniture. Standard room are $320 s or d, while suites, much larger an with balconies, start at $400 s or d.

Bryson Hotel, 186 Exhibition St. (tel. 0. 9662-0511), has well-decorated rooms, eac with a view, and there's an outdoor pool; $195 or d. If you're into paying over $200 for a roon the **Regent Melbourne,** 25 Collins St. (tel. 0. 9653-0000), is a good choice. The lobby is be hind an elegant shopping mall, away from th street, and the hotel takes up the top 15 floors a 50-story building, ensuring excellent views Room furnishings are of the highest standards. restaurant and cafe are on the 35th floor, as is gym, spa, and sauna. Rates are from $240 s d but weekend packages are considerably lowe

North Melbourne and Carlton

North of the city center, the suburbs of Nort Melbourne and Carlton have a wide range c accommodations, with plenty of public trans rt running downtown. One of the closest to ty center is **North Motalodge,** 113 Flemington d. (tel. 03-9329-7433), for $63 s, $69 d. **Old elbourne Hotel,** 5-17 Flemington Rd. (tel. 03-329-9344), is a large hostelry built around a ourtyard. Rooms have recently been renovated and facilities include a pool, restaurant, and ar; rooms start at $104-131 s or d. **Marco Polo n,** corner Flemington Rd. and Harker St. (tel. 3-9329-1788), has spacious rooms, a laundry, nd pool; $90 s, $98 d. Farther up Flemington d., at no. 94, is **Park Squire Motor Inn** (tel. 03-329-6077), within walking distance of the zoo nd good value at $68 s or d. **City Gardens oliday Apartments,** 335 Abbotsford St. (tel. 3-9320-6600), are spread over one hectare, ade up of two-story townhouses. All rooms e fully self-contained; many even have dish- ashers, and rooms are serviced weekly. The nallest studios are $118, one-bedroom units 128, and two-bedroom units $137.

Downtowner on Lygon Motel, 66 Lygon St. el. 03-9663-5555), is in the suburb of Carlton nd has decent-sized rooms for $109 s or d. Of slightly higher standard is **Townhouse Hotel,**)1 Swanston St. (tel. 03-9347-7811), a modern ve-story place with a pool and sauna; $129 s or **Lygon Quest Lodgings,** 700 Lygon St. (tel. 3-9345-3888), is made up of 33 self-contained oartments, each with laundry and cooking fa- lities. They range $130-190, depending on ze.

Around the junction of Royal Parade and Park t. is another group of motels. Least expensive **Princes Park Motor Inn,** right at this junc- on (tel. 03-9388-1000), where each room has a balcony; $73 s, $78 d.

ast Melbourne
eorgian Court Guest House, 21 George St. el. 03-9419-6353), built in 1870, has an au- entic historic atmosphere, with antiques scat- red throughout. Rooms are fairly basic, but ach has a TV and tea- and coffee-making fa- lities. Rates in rooms with shared facilities are 60 s, $70 d, with larger rooms going for $80 s, 90 d. All rates include breakfast. Another option **Magnolia Court,** 101 Powlett St. (tel. 03-419-4222), located on a quiet street among ther historic terraces. Part of the property dates om 1858 and has been restored to its former

glory. These rooms are $110 s, $120 d, while rooms in the newer wing are less expensive. Breakfast is the only meal served here, and the managers enjoy helping guests organize itin- eraries.

South Yarra
South Yarra is a stylish suburb where many of the original buildings have been restored and boutiques and cafes line the streets. It's also only a five-minute train or tram trip to down- town. **Domain Motel,** 52 Darling St. (tel. 03-9866-3701), is a short walk to public trans- portation and has rooms of a reasonable stan- dard for $58 s, $64 d. **Tilba Hotel,** 30 West Toorak Rd. (tel. 03-9867-8844), was once a pri- vate residence, and a bit of refurbishment has transformed it into a stylish and elegant ac- commodation that attracts an eclectic collec- tion of guests. Rooms are decorated with an- tiques, and each has a bathtub. The hotel's many alcoves have lounge chairs, while classi- cal music is piped in throughout the hotel. Rates are $125-170 s or d and include breakfast. Book well in advance.

Hotel Como, 630 Chapel St. (tel. 03-9824-0400), features the best of everything. Each room has ultramodern furnishings, most with views, and downstairs is Maxim's, one of Mel- bourne's best restaurants; rates start at $275 s or d (weekend packages provide a better deal).

St. Kilda and Other Bayside Suburbs
The bayside suburb of St. Kilda has Melbourne's best range of backpacker accommodations, but also boasts a wide range of motels, including many cheapies not quite up to scratch. **Cabana Court Motel,** 46 Park St. (tel. 03-9534-0771), is an exception for the price, and each room has a small kitchen; $65 s, $69 d. **Novotel Bayside Melbourne,** 16 the Esplanade (tel. 03-9525-5522), a modern and luxurious hotel, overlooks Port Phillip Bay. Rates are $130 s or d, and rooms with kitchens are $170. The **Kingsgrove,** 44 Fitzroy St. (tel. 03-9536-3000), is a small place with 24 self-contained apartments, each with a well-equipped kitchen and modern living area; from $78 s or d for a one-bedroom unit, $130 for a two-bedroom unit that sleeps four.

To the west of St. Kilda is Albert Park and a number of good accommodation choices. Built in

1888, **Hotel Victoria,** 123 Beaconsfield Parade (tel. 03-9690-3666), is a classic Victorian building with unbroken views across Port Phillip Bay. The hotel has only 30 rooms, 20 with shared facilities ($45 s, $50 d) and 10 spacious corner rooms with fantastic views and private bathrooms ($150 s or d).

On the other side of Albert Park is the recently renovated **Travelodge,** corner St. Kilda Rd. and Park Street (tel. 03-9699-4833), where rooms range $130-190.

BACKPACKER ACCOMMODATIONS

Most of the best backpacker lodges are in St. Kilda, while Melbourne's two YHAs are in North Melbourne. Right downtown are a few possibilities, but their standards are generally not as high as in the suburbs.

Downtown
City Scene Backpackers, 131 Bourke St. (tel. 03-9650-9918), is one of Melbourne's newer places. It is small and friendly, with a communal kitchen and TV room, and sits right opposite a major movie complex. Dorms are $13, twins and doubles $17 pp. Another good option is **Toad Hall,** 441 Elizabeth St. (tel. 03-9600-9010), close to major bus terminals and Museum Station. It has all the usual facilities, as well as a courtyard with barbecue. Beds in the dormitory are $15, singles $25, doubles $50. One block north is the **YWCA Family Hotel,** 489 Elizabeth St. (tel. 03-9329-5188), part of a complex where guests have use of a pool, gym, and fitness classes. Beds are $16.50 and private rooms are $46 s, $58 d. Very central, but a bit rough around the edges, is **Backpackers City Inn,** upstairs in the Carlton Hotel, 197 Bourke St. (tel. 03-9650-2734). Meals are available downstairs, and there's a communal kitchen, game room, and laundry; $12 pp, $25 s, $35 d.

North of Downtown
Queensberry Hill YHA Hostel, 78 Howard St., North Melbourne (tel. 03-9329-8599), is as good as any city backpacker accommodation you're likely to find. It opened in August 1991, everything is new, the kitchens are large and modern, and many rooms have private bathrooms. On

the roof is a large patio with city views. The hotel is very safety-conscious, with security parking and a small locker beside every bed. Other facilities include a currency exchange, laundry and travel agency, and guests have free use of bikes. A cafeteria serves meals all day, with breakfast around $5 and dinners under $ Rates are $14-20 for members ($3 extra for nonmembers). Singles are $45-52, doubles $5 58. The hostel is one km from North Melbourne Station and about 1.5 km from downtown. A bit farther out is the much smaller **Chapman S Hostel,** 76 Chapman St. (tel. 03-9328-3595 also affiliated with the YHA. It is also older, with dorms $13, and a few twin beds for $16 pp.

In the suburb of Preston is **The Terrace,** 41 Murray Rd. (tel. 03-9470-1006), a classic Victorian terrace in a quiet residential area. There plenty of room to move, with many shops nea by, a tennis court, game room, and spa. Dorm here are $12.

St. Kilda
This suburb, south of downtown and on Po Phillip Bay, has the city's largest concentratic of backpacker accommodations, many located within a block of busy Fitzroy Street. Most popular is **Enfield House,** 2 Enfield St. (tel. 03-953- 8159 or 1800-03-2635), an old boardinghous with 20 four-bed dorms ($12) and a few single ($16) and doubles ($28). Within 200 meters Enfield House is a cluster of five hostels; nor are particularly good, but beds are general just $10, or less, per night. Try similarly price **Coffee Palace Backpackers,** 24 Grey St. (te 03-9534-5283), and **Kookaburra Cottage,** 5 Jackson St. (tel. 03-9534-5457).

Olembia, 700 meters from Fitzroy St., 9 Barkly St. (tel. 03-9537-1412), has a relaxe atmosphere and friendly staff. Rooms are oka but all communal facilities are excellent. Dorm are $14, and the few singles and doubles ar $30 and $50 respectively.

CAMPGROUNDS

North
The closest campground to the city center the excellent **Melbourne Big 4 Holiday Park** 265 Elizabeth St. (tel. 03-9354-3533), nine k

north in the suburb of Coburg East. The tenting area is shaded and grassy, with a covered kitchen. Other facilities include a pool, recreation room, and laundry. Unpowered sites are $14, powered sites $16.50, sites with a bathroom $21, small on-site vans $34, and self-contained cabins $39.50-52. Northeast of the city, in the suburb of Doncaster, is **Crystal Brook Holiday Centre,** 182 Warrandyte Rd. (tel. 03-9844-8637), not really suited to tent camping. Sites are $16, on-site vans $30, and well-equipped cabins are $45-60.

Southeast

Heading toward Phillip Island, the closest campground to downtown is in Chelsea Heights, 32 km southeast of downtown, where you'll find **Blue Gum Caravan Park,** Wells Rd. (tel. 03-9772-8436). It has excellent facilities including a pool, tennis court, and barbecues; tent sites $10, powered sites $12, cabins $26-48. A farther 5 km toward Phillip Island, in the small town of Beaconsfield, is **Blue Gum Eastside Caravan Park,** Brunt Rd. (tel. 03-9707-2753), which has basic facilities and a few powered sites for $12.

West

Coming into Melbourne from Ballarat, **Bacchus Marsh Caravan Park,** 54 km west of the city, is just off the main freeway and has sites for $10-12 and cabins for $30-45 (tel. 03-5367-2775). South of Bacchus Marsh is Brisbane Ranges National Park, which has a basic campground.

DOWNTOWN DINING

Melbourne is regarded as Australia's culinary capital, and with over 3,000 restaurants featuring food from 70 countries, it would be hard for anyone to disagree. Melburnians take their dining seriously; at least a dozen food and wine festivals are scattered through the year, and, at last count, there were three books guiding diners to the best restaurants on offer.

Cafes and Food Courts

Melbourne has literally hundreds of cafes, and while some come and go, the reputations of many have remained high for years. **Pellerini's,** 66 Bourke St. (tel. 03-9662-1885), has

been wooing coffee lovers for decades. The clientele may have changed looks over the years, but they still come, drinking espresso coffee and enjoying inexpensive Italian meals, such as pasta from $5; open daily 8 a.m.-11:30 p.m. In the same part of town, toward Parliament House, is **Le Monde,** 18 Bourke St. (tel. 03-9663-7804), a trendy cafe attracting an eclectic mix of patrons, especially during the early hours of the morning. They also offer light Italian meals and a selection of delicious cakes. Downtown also has a few upmarket cafes, including **Cafe Rialto,** in Le Meridien Hotel at 495 Collins St., and **Cafe Alcaston** in a historic building at 2 Collins St. (tel. 03-9650-9387). At the **Lounge,** in the Windsor Hotel, 103 Spring St. (tel. 03-9653-0653), a grand afternoon tea is served Mon.-Sat. 3:15-5:30 p.m.; $20 pp.

Many downtown shopping plazas have a food court on the ground floor, featuring cuisine from all parts of the world for $5-8. The **Hyatt Food Court,** 127 Collins St., has the widest variety of choices, is open 7:30 a.m.-midnight, and has a certain amount of class. Under the Myer Department Store is **Myer's Wonderful World of Food,** on Little Bourke St., with an eclectic mix of foods from around the world.

Chinese

Before hightailing it to Chinatown, consider a meal at **King's Wok,** 247 Lonsdale St. (tel. 03-9663-3072), a small restaurant serving authentic Chinese dishes at very good prices. Soups are all under $4, and for $6 you've got a choice of just about everything except seafood. Chinatown itself is centered along Little Bourke St., between Spring and Swanston Streets. **Kun Ming,** 212 Little Bourke St. (tel. 03-9663-1851), won't win any interior design awards, but the food is delicious, and with soups under $2 and main dishes from $5.50 you can't go wrong; open Mon.-Sat. noon-3 p.m., 5-10 p.m., and Sunday 5-9 p.m. Moving up the street, **Supper Inn,** 15 Celestial Ave. (tel. 03-9663-4759), upstairs along a narrow alleyway (and easy to miss), has an extensive menu and large servings that will satisfy everyone's Chinese cravings. **Shark Fin House,** 131 Little Bourke St. (tel. 03-9663-1555), is one of the few restaurants featuring *yum cha* during the week. It's a huge place, three stories of trolley-wheeling waiters offering around 50

Chinatown, on Little Bourke St., is a good place to head for a cheap meal.

dishes; open daily 11:30 a.m.-3 p.m., 5:30-11 p.m.

Some Chinatown restaurants don't open for lunch, but instead stay open all hours of the night. Off Little Bourke St. is **Happy World,** 141 Russell St. (tel. 03-9663-3341), a little worse for wear but with excellent food. **Wong Shing Kee,** 166 Russell St. (tel. 03-9663-1346), is a casual place with more of the same.

Other Asian Restaurants
Gopal's, 139 Swanston St. (tel. 03-9650-1578), by Little Collins St., is a small vegetarian cafe operated by the Hare Krishna. Servings aren't enormous, but most dishes are under $4, with some main dishes as low as $1.50. A three-course meal, with a drink, is $6. **India House,** 401 Swanston St. (tel. 03-9663-5858), is another cheapie. The atmosphere is quiet and relaxed and most dishes are under $7. At the top end of Chinatown is **Little Malaysia,** 26 Liverpool St. (tel. 03-9662-1678), a large place where service is

fast and efficient and a three-course meal is under $20 per head. **Ong International Food Court** is good for a lunchtime meal, with cuisine from throughout Asia; it's at 265 Little Bourke Street.

Japanese restaurants are, on the whole, more expensive than other Asian places, but a few inexpensive options are scattered around downtown. **Toki Sushi Bar,** 230 Russell St. (tel. 03-9663-8118), has sushi for $15. **Hanabishi,** 187 King St. (tel. 03-9670-1167), is a stylish restaurant, popular with the lunch time crowd; closed Sunday.

Greek
Lonsdale St. is the Greek center of downtown and as Melbourne is the world's third-largest Greek city, naturally there are lots of Greek dining choices. **Tsindos the Greek's Restaurant,** 197 Lonsdale St. (tel. 03-9663-3194), features a variety of grills (from $9) and mezze platters to start, a plate full of dips, cheeses, and cold vegetables. On Friday and Saturday nights after 8:30 p.m., they have live entertainment. **Stalactites,** 177 Lonsdale St. (tel. 03-9663-3316), has an offering of basic Greek dishes in a bland setting, but the price is right, the portions good, and it's open daily 24 hours.

Italian
Campari Bistro, 25 Hardware St. (tel. 03-9670-3813), is a typical Italian restaurant—always busy and great for people-watching. Pasta, starting at $10 for a main dish, is cooked to perfection. **Italian Waiters' Restaurant,** 20 Meyers Place (tel. 03-9650-1508), is noted among Melburnians for exceptional food, good prices (all main dishes are under $15), and healthy portions; open Mon.-Sat. until midnight. **Amiconi,** 359 Victoria St. (tel. 03-9328-3710), is a classy yet inexpensive Italian bistro about one km west of downtown. **Florentino Cellar Bar,** 80 Bourke St. (tel. 03-9662-1811), looks more expensive than it actually is, with daily lunchtime specials for $6 and dinner $11-15. **Lucattini's,** 22 Punch Lane (tel. 03-9662-2883), is at the Parliament House end of Chinatown and features traditional Italian dishes ranging $14-20 (less at lunch); closed Sunday.

French
Mietta's, 7 Alfred Place (tel. 03-9654-2366), located just off Collins St., is one of Melbourne's

finest restaurants. The building has been restored to its Victorian glory and is furnished with period antiques. Food is of the highest standard, averaging $25 for main dishes. Of note is the fixed-price lunch, good value at $18 pp; closed Sunday. Downstairs is a lounge that stays open till 3 a.m., and light meals range $8-16. **Le Restaurant,** 25 Collins St. (tel. 03-9653-0000), on the 35th floor of the Regent Melbourne, is one of the city's most renowned upmarket restaurants. The views are fabulous, service excellent, ambience sophisticated, and, it goes without saying, expensive.

Colonial Tramcar Restaurant

In this unique restaurant, housed in one of Melbourne's familiar trams, diners are whisked around the streets while enjoying fine food in an elegant atmosphere. The tram was built in 1927 and has since been restored to the height of luxury with comfortable velvet seating, brass lamps, and silver service. The menu changes regularly, but is generally five courses, with a choice of main dishes. Lunch (1-3 p.m.) is $60, early dinner (5:45-7:15 p.m.) $50, and dinner (8:35-11:30 p.m.) $75 Mon.-Fri., $85 weekends. Departures are from the National Gallery of Victoria, Southbank Boulevard just off St. Kilda Rd.; for reservations, call (03) 9696-4000.

Other Downtown Restaurants

Crystal chandeliers, marble floors, and imposing stained-glass domes create an atmosphere of absolute Victorian luxury in the **Grand Dining Room** of the Windsor Hotel, 103 Spring St. (tel. 03-9653-0653). The service is impeccable, with white-gloved waiters tending to your every need and serving food of the highest quality. The fixed-price dinner is $55.

Southgate, on the south side of the Yarra River, has a wide range of eateries, including a large food court. Many of the restaurants in the complex overlook the river and have tables inside and out. A good choice is **Akvavit** (tel. 03-9699-9947), which has a lunch buffet for $15 and a dinner buffet for $27. **Walter's Wine Bar** (tel. 03-9690-9211) has light meals from $6 to accompany a huge variety of wines by the glass, while the more substantial dishes run $16-19. Next door to Southbank, in the Melbourne Concert Hall, is **Treble Clef** (tel. 03-9684-8264),

serving breakfast ($5.50-9.50), lunch, and dinner. The menu is varied, pleasing all tastes. The pizza ($12.70-13.50) is especially good as is the antipasto main meal ($14.70).

DINING IN THE SUBURBS

Carlton

Carlton has been home to a large population of Italians since late last century, with many using their cooking expertise to operate restaurants. The restaurants were centered along Lygon St., and although the style of them has changed considerably, Carlton is still the center of Italian culture in Melbourne, with many Italian-style coffee shops and pasta houses.

Toto's, 101 Lygon St. (tel. 03-9347-5974), is a legendary pizza place that claims to be Australia's original pizzeria (operating since the mid-1960s). It's always busy, and noisy, but the pizza is great and priced right. Open daily noon-1 a.m. **Pasta Veloce,** 181 Lygon St. (tel. 03-9347-4273), is a no-frills pasta house where everything is cooked to perfection. Huge plates of pasta start at $10, $14 with meat or seafood sauces; open daily noon-midnight. A couple of doors away, **Nyonya,** 191 Lygon St. (tel. 03-9347-8511), serves inexpensive Malaysian meals in a bright and airy atmosphere, not unlike the Italian restaurants that surround it. Curries start at $6 while most other main dishes are under $10. **La Spaghettata,** 238 Lygon St. (tel. 03-9663-6102), is a casual eatery with tables inside and out. All pasta is made on the premises, with a blackboard menu offering choices under $15 and mouthwatering Italian desserts for about $5; open daily noon-3 p.m., 5-11 p.m. **Papa Gino's,** 221 Lygon St. (tel. 03-9347-5758), is the place to head for gigantic servings at reasonable prices (pastas average $12).

Farther north, on Rathdowne St., are many more choices. At **Carlton Curry House,** 204 Rathdowne St. (tel. 03-9347-9632), a favorite of students, takeaway is the main trade, but there are a few worn-looking tables in the back. **La Porchetta,** 392 Rathdowne St. (tel. 03-9347-8906), is one of Carlton's least expensive restaurants, with nothing over $8, including the large pizzas. This, naturally, attracts droves of students from the nearby university.

The majority of Carlton's restaurants are within two km of downtown; take tram no. 1, 15, 21, or 22 north along Swanston Street.

Fitzroy

While Carlton is predominantly Italian, Fitzroy, immediately to the east, features cuisine from around the world. Dozens of trendy restaurants are interspersed with shops selling weird and wonderful gifts, retro clothing, antiques, books, and crystal balls. In just three blocks of Brunswick St., you'll find cuisine ranging from African to Caribbean, while Johnston St. has a concentration of Spanish restaurants.

Annick's, 153 Brunswick St. (tel. 03-9419-3007), is a popular French restaurant, with main dishes $13-18. **Thai Thani,** 293 Brunswick St. (tel. 03-9419-6463), is a small, dimly lit restaurant where diners have the choice of eating Thai-style, sitting on the floor, or at a table. Appetizers range $4-7 and all main meals are under $14. Open Mon.-Sat. 6 p.m.-midnight.

Along Johnston St. the tastes of Spain dominate. The pick of the bunch is **Carmen,** 74 Johnston St. (tel. 03-9417-4794), always packed to the rafters, usually by Spanish locals. Outside is a cook-your-own barbecue and most nights flamenco is performed. Open Mon.-Sat. noon-1 a.m.

Back on Brunswick St. **Rhumbaralla's,** 342 Brunswick St. (tel. 03-9417-5652), is a microcosm of Fitzroy, attracting an eclectic array of patrons with a varied and inexpensive menu. **Baker's Cafe,** 384 Brunswick St. (tel. 03-9419-7437), is much more intimate but attracts the same sort of crowd. Pastas cost about $8, and coffee and cake is under $5; open daily 7 a.m.-10 p.m. **Ambrosia,** 363 Brunswick St. (tel. 03-9417-7415), is the only Greek restaurant in Fitzroy. It has an authentic Mediterranean feel, with a menu of traditional Greek cuisine; expect to pay about $25 for three courses.

Richmond

East of downtown, this suburb has always been a bastion of Greek culture, but in recent years, as new Australians arrive from Southeast Asia, Victoria St. has turned into a Vietnamese shopping area, gaining the nickname "Little Saigon" along the way. In most cases, emphasis in Vietnamese restaurants isn't on decor, but for an adventurous meal at an affordable price, Victoria St. is a good place to head. **Victoria,** 311 Victoria St. (tel. 03-9427-0337), is a popular place, always crowded and offering Vietnamese and Thai dishes. The big bowls of soup ($4.50-6) could just about make a main meal. **Van Doi,** 120 Victoria St. (tel. 03-9428-3264), toward the city, is cheaper and has set menus under $10 for dinner, not to mention some delicious seafood choices.

Rajdoot, 142 Bridge Rd. (tel. 03-9427-1118) is a small, inexpensive Indian restaurant with a large tandoor oven churning out delicious dishes (most under $12); open for lunch Tues.-Fri. and daily for dinner.

Vlado's, 61 Bridge Rd. (tel. 03-9428-5833), is one of Melbourne's premier steakhouses, with mouthwatering cuts of beef grilled to perfection. The three-course set menu is $50 pp; closed Sunday. This is the perfect place for a splurge if you're staying at nearby Georgian Court Guest House.

Running parallel to Bridge Rd., and to the south, is Swan St., with distinctive-sounding Greek music wafting from the restaurants. **Salona,** 260 Swan St. (tel. 03-9429-1460), is a good place to head for fresh seafood cooked Greek-style, for $14. Most other dishes are under $10.

South Yarra, Toorak, and Prahran

Toorak Rd. and Chapel St. are the two main shopping and dining strips in South Yarra, offering restaurants with a wide variety of cuisine and the chance to mix a shopping expedition with lunch. From South Yarra, Toorak Rd. continues east to the stylish suburb of Toorak, which boasts many elegant bistros, while Chapel St. leads south to more restaurants and the excellent **Prahran Markets,** a great place to stock up on fresh fruit and vegetables.

Mitton's, 10 Murphy St. (tel. 03-9867-3605) is a good breakfast hangout, with an extensive menu, and gourmet sandwiches served till closing at 7 p.m. **Barolo Bistro,** 74 Toorak Rd. (tel. 03-9866-2744), which has a large courtyard, is enjoyable on a sunny day or clear summer night. Pastas average $10; open daily 9 a.m.-midnight. Of the dozen or so Italian restaurants and bistros along this strip, try **Tamani,** 156 Toorak Rd. (tel. 03-9866-2575), for pasta cooked to perfection for under $12. **Pieroni,** 172 Toorak Rd. (tel. 03-9827-7833), is the place for a splurge.

Up in Toorak, **Minootz,** 436 Toorak Rd. (tel. 03-9826-9121), looks a lot more expensive than it is. Cuisine is Italian and under $10 for lunch main dishes, or just relax with a coffee and enjoy the stylish ambience.

The first stop walking down Chapel St. from Toorak Rd. should be at **Caffe e Cucina,** 581 Chapel St. (tel. 03-9827-4139)—if you can get a table, that is (expect a wait at lunch). Most main dishes are under $14, with pastas around $11. The wine and beer are also reasonably priced. **Ankara,** 310 Chapel St. (tel. 03-9529-4940), is one of Melbourne's few Turkish restaurants. All the entree dips are around $5 and no main dish is over $10, including combination kabob and grill.

St. Kilda and Other Bayside Suburbs

Melbourne's lively seaside suburb of St. Kilda has an eclectic mix of eateries spread along fashionable Fitzroy St., which links St. Kilda Rd. to the bay. Most cafes and trendy bars are at the bay end of the street. **Topolino's,** 87 Fitzroy St. (tel. 03-9534-4856), has legendary pasta (from $8) and pizza (from $6) and is busiest early in the evening. Open daily from noon until at least 4:30 a.m., **Angelucci's on Fitzroy,** 43 Fitzroy St. (tel. 03-9525-3133), has great seats for people-watching, if that's your thing, or you can dine in the stylish area around the rear courtyard. **Jean-Jacques by the Sea,** 40 Jacka Blvd. (tel. 03-9534-8221), is an informal seafood restaurant overlooking Port Phillip Bay whose dishes have a French emphasis. Main dishes start at $18, or stick to the two-course fixed-price lunch or dinner for $25, or $37.50 for three courses. Away from the main restaurant is a takeaway section where fish and chips will set you back $6.

Scheherezade, 99 Acland St. (tel. 03-9534-722), is typical of many Acland Street restaurants: well-priced, serving healthy portions, and low-key—a world away from busy Fitzroy Street.

A day trip to the bayside suburb of Brighton can be complemented with dinner at **Anou Thai,** 56 Bay St., Brighton (tel. 03-9596-5407), one of Melbourne's better Thai restaurants, with authentically prepared dishes from $11.

GETTING THERE

Air

Melbourne Airport is 20 km northwest of downtown in the suburb of Tullamarine. It serves both international and domestic flights, and after a $190 million redevelopment project completed early in 1996, it's Australia's most modern and efficient airport. Around 11 million travelers pass through the airport annually, of which about 17% are traveling internationally. On the arrivals level there is no real information center, but a few motels have courtesy phones. The major car rental companies have service desks, there's a currency exchange, and lockers are $4 per day. **Sky Plaza,** on the departures level, has a food court, bar, restaurant, a variety of touristy shops, a post office, and the ubiquitous duty-free shop for international travelers, who must also pay departure tax of $27. Around 20 international airlines fly into Melbourne, including **Qantas** (tel. 13-1313), **United Airlines** (tel. 13-1777), **Air New Zealand** (tel. 13-2476), and **British Airways** (tel. 03-9603-1133). **Ansett Australia** (tel. 13-1300), **Eastern** (tel. 13-1313), **Kendell** (tel. 13-1300), and **Southern Australian** (tel. 13-1313) are the domestic airlines that fly to Melbourne. Standard one-way fares from Melbourne are: Hobart $234, Sydney $234, Brisbane $353, Cairns $540, Adelaide $221, Perth $528, and Darwin $600. Advance purchase tickets are generally around 50% of this price, and even lower if bought in conjunction with an incoming international ticket.

Transfers between the airport and downtown are offered by **Skybus** (tel. 03-9335-3066), which runs half-hourly, daily 6 a.m.-7:30 p.m. The main downtown drop-off is Bay 30 in the coach terminal at Spencer St. Station. The fare is $8.50 one-way, $13 round-trip. A cab between the airport and downtown runs about $20-28, depending on the traffic. A less expensive option is bus 478 or 479, which depart hourly from the arrivals terminal for Moonee Ponds Junction, from where you transfer to a tram for downtown; $3.20 one-way.

Rail

The main interstate services are the XPT from Sydney and the Overland from Adelaide. **V/Line** operates all rail services throughout the state and offers regular service between Melbourne and Ballarat ($11.60 one-way), Warrnambool ($28.80), Mildura ($46), and Albury ($33). All long-distance trains arrive and depart from Spencer St. Station. Special fares are offered year-round, including the Super Saver, a saving of 40% for travel Tues.-Thursday. For all bookings call 13-2232 or drop by the **V/Line Travel Centre**, 589 Collins Street.

Bus

Melbourne has two long-distance bus terminals. **Greyhound Pioneer** (tel. 13-2030) arrives and departs from a terminal next to the Spencer St. Station, while **McCafferty's** (tel. 03-9670-2533) uses a terminal on the corner of Franklin and Swanston Streets. Competition between the major companies is fierce; the best deals are the various travel passes offered by each. From Melbourne, standard sector fares are: Sydney $40; Brisbane $100; Cairns $200; and Alice Springs $185.

Ferry

Port Melbourne is the main departure point for ferries between mainland Australia and Tasmania. For details see "Transportation" in the "Introduction" of the Tasmania chapter.

GETTING AROUND

The Met

Known collectively as the Met, trams, trains, and buses make up an excellent system of public transportation from throughout the inner city to all major sights and outlying suburbs. One ticket covers all three forms of transportation, which have three fare zones. Most of the city falls within Zone 1: $1.40 per sector (one ride within a zone), $2.10 for three hours of unlimited travel, $4 for an all-day ticket, and $17.30 for a weekly ticket.

Tram routes cover the inner city, with many heading into the suburbs; all lines are served every eight to 15 minutes. The City Circle tram route is for the tourists. It runs along Flinders, Spring, and Nicholson Streets, Victoria Parade, La Trobe St., and Spencer St. with the driver giving a running commentary. It is burgundy-colored and runs daily 10 a.m.-6 p.m. Best of all it's free.

Flinders St. Station, on the City Loop rail line that encircles downtown, is the main city terminal. Trains service the outlying suburbs and places such as the Dandenong Ranges.

Taxi

Cab prices in Melbourne are comparable to those in other Australian cities, and the cabs are particularly useful after midnight when all public transportation stops. The flag charge is $2.60, then 68 cents per kilometer. Midnight to 6 a.m., the flag charge is $3.60 and the kilometer rate is 85 cents. A good place to look for taxis is outside Flinders St. or Spencer St. Stations. The main companies are **Arrow Taxi Service** (tel. 03-9417-1111), **Embassy Taxis** (tel. 03-9320-0320), and **Silver Top Taxi Service** (tel. 03-9345-3455).

Car

There are three very good reasons for not driving in downtown Melbourne: high parking charges, a strange road rule (see the special topic "Trams and Cars: A Dangerous Combination"), and, the biggest obstacle, trams. Parking charges average $4 per hour, with all-day rates offered before 9 a.m.

If the above hasn't dissuaded you from city driving, or you need a car to explore outlying areas, expect to pay from $35 per day to rent an older car and from $60 per day to rent from the larger car rental chains. Main companies are **Avis** (tel. 1800-22-5533), **Budget** (tel. 13-2727), **Dollar** (tel. 1800-65-8658), **Hertz** (tel. 13-1918), **National** (tel. 03-9329-5000), and **Thrifty** (tel. 03-9663-5200). Backpackers staying in St. Kilda may want to try **Y-Not** (tel. 03-9525-5900) for car rentals.

Bicycle

Bike paths wind through much of the city, including along the Yarra River, around Port Phillip Bay, and along Moonee Ponds Creek. **Hang Ten Bike Maps,** a set of three, cover these and other major paths and are available from outdoor shops. **Bicycle Rental** (tel. 03-9801-2156) is located under the Princes Bridge on the south side of the Yarra River. Mountain bikes are $10 per hour and $25 per day. **St. Kilda Cycles**

Trams make travel through the city enjoyable.

11 Carlisle St. (tel. 03-9534-3074), is similarly priced.

Ferry
The bayside suburb of Williamstown is linked by ferry to downtown Melbourne and St. Kilda on Saturday and Sunday. The boat leaves the World Trade Centre, downtown Melbourne, at 10 a.m. for Williamstown, and for the rest of the day runs between St. Kilda and Williamstown. The fare from either departure point is $8 return. For information call (03) 9397-2255.

Tours
City Explorer (tel. 03-9650-1511) is a double-decker bus that makes a continuous loop starting from Flinders St. Station, stopping at all major tourist sights. It runs on the hour 10 a.m.-4 p.m.; adult $15, child $8. Several companies offer sightseeing tours of Melbourne, including **Grayline** (tel. 03-9654-7700), **Great Sights** (tel. 03-9650-5488), and **Melbourne Day Tours** (tel. 13-1304). Typically, they pick up passengers at major hotels. The tours usually include downtown sights, the Dandenong Ranges, and a cruise on the Yarra River. Each company has a basic three- to four-hour tour for $35-40, with a river cruise included for around $50, and a full-day tour taking in city sights and Penguin Parade on Phillip Island for $78-92. **Melbourne River Tours** (tel. 03-9650-2055) departs regularly from Princes Bridge for a cruise along the Yarra River for $11-26.

SERVICES

The **general post office** is on the corner of Bourke and Elizabeth Streets and is open Mon.-Fri. 8:15 a.m.-5:30 p.m. Traveler's checks can be cashed at all banks and major hotels, but remember, if your checks aren't in Australian currency you'll be charged a fee or commission.

Kodak, 1-19 Hoddle St. (tel. 03-9483-1011), processes slide film in 24 hours.

The **Flight Centre,** 317 Swanston St. (tel. 03-9663-1304), is the place to start looking for onward airline tickets. Also check the travel section in Saturday's *Age* newspaper.

Downtown has no self-service laundromats, but most hostels and hotels offer a laundry service. **Brown Gouge Dry Cleaners** is in Flinders St. Station (tel. 03-9614-3342).

Emergency and Support Services
For medical emergencies call 000 or one of the following hospitals: **Royal Melbourne Hospital,** Grattan St., Parkville (tel. 03-9342-7000); **St. Vincents Hospital,** Victoria Parade, Fitzroy (tel. 03-9288-2211); **Alfred Hospital,** Commercial Rd., Prahran (tel. 03-9276-2000); or **Royal Women's Hospital,** Grattan St., Carlton (tel. 03-9344-2000). Private medical clinics are an alternative for nonemergency cases. A good option is **Fitzroy Central Clinic,** 117 Brunswick St., Fitzroy (tel. 03-9419-3488). **Traveller's Aid Support Centre,** 169 Swanston St. (tel. 03-

9654-2600), assists travelers with nonmedical problems, offering advice, showers, toilets, and light snacks. For onward travel **Traveller's Medical Clinic,** 2nd Floor, 393 Little Bourke St. (tel. 03-9602-5788), advises on vaccinations and infectious diseases, and sells medical kits; open Mon.-Fri. 8:30 a.m.-5:30 p.m.

INFORMATION

Libraries
The **State Library,** much of which dates to last century, is an impressive domed building on Swanston Street. The cavernous **reading room** makes for a great rainy day hangout. Open Mon.-Sat. 9 a.m.-6 p.m.

Bookstores
The main bookshop chains—**Collins, Angus and Robertson** and **Dymocks**—all have outlets scattered throughout downtown and in major shopping centers. **Bowyangs Travel Books,** 372 Little Bourke Street (tel. 03-9670-4383),

specializes in travel books as well as a variety of accessories such as maps.

Information Centers
Melbourne City Council runs a small **information booth** in the Bourke St. Mall. It's open Mon.-Thurs. 9 a.m.-5 p.m., Friday 9 a.m.-7 p.m. and Sat.-Sun. 10 a.m.-4 p.m. The **Victorian Tourism Centre,** run by the Royal Automobile Club of Victoria, is at 230 Collins St. (tel. 03-9650-1522). It is a good source of general tourism information about the state and can make bookings. Members of the RACV and many overseas motoring clubs (show your membership card) get free maps and accommodation discounts; open Mon.-Fri. 9:15 a.m.-5:15 p.m. Saturday 9 a.m.-noon. The **Met Shop,** 103 Elizabeth St. (tel. 03-9617-0900), has information on the public transport system.

The **Department of Conservation and Natural Resources** (DC&NR), which looks after the state's national parks, has an information center at 240 Victoria Parade, East Melbourne (tel. 03-9412-4011).

GOLDFIELDS

n early 1851, when gold was discovered near Bathurst, New South Wales, people from around the country and as far away as California descended on the area. For the newly established city of Melbourne, the exodus of people from Victoria caused a massive problem, and so a handsome reward was offered to anyone who found gold within 100 miles of Melbourne. Within weeks, gold had been discovered at Warrandyte near Clunes, and with thousands of diggers swarming over every river and stream in the region, many more strikes occurred. The most important strike was made in September 1851, near Ballarat, which grew to become inland Victoria's largest city and one of the world's richest gold-bearing areas. Town populations grew quickly, with often as many as 30,000 diggers living in deplorable conditions in cities of canvas. Ballarat and Bendigo are gracious reminders of this prosperous past, and still thrive today while other towns, such as Maldon, Clunes, Talbot, and Moliagul are a shadow of their former selves and diggings such as Amherst have slipped into oblivion, completely.

MELBOURNE TO THE GOLDFIELDS

Organ Pipes National Park
A few years ago the main feature of this 85-hectare park, 25 km northwest of Melbourne along the Calder Highway, was part of a privately owned farm and overgrown with noxious weeds. When the weeds were killed a group of 20-meter basalt columns were exposed. They formed when lava from a volcano cooled quickly upon coming into contact with an ancient river. Native vegetation has been restored and today the park is a pleasant place for a short walk and picnic lunch. The **Park Information Centre** (tel. 03-9651-3038) is open daily 8:30 a.m.-4:30 p.m. (the park is locked outside these hours).

Sunbury
Sunbury, originally a stopping point for those heading to the goldfields, is the birthplace of cricket's best-known trophy. **Rupertswood,** a 50-room mansion on the outskirts of town, was the scene of a social cricket match held in late 1882 between a team of touring English cricketers and a motley bunch of locals—who apparently got thrashed. As a joke, the locals burnt part of the cricket stumps and presented the ashes in an urn to the captain of the English team. Today **The Ashes** is a five-match series between Australia and England, and the original ashes are presented to the winner.

On the main road through town in a restored courthouse is **Sunbury Tourist Information Centre** (tel. 03-9744-2291); open daily 9 a.m.-5 p.m. In the grounds of the police station, next door, is a relocated jail, dating to the gold rush.

Macedon Ranges
The Macedon Ranges rise to the northeast of the Calder Highway, around 65 km from Melbourne. The highest peak is **Mount Macedon** (1,013 meters), an extinct volcano. A road leads right to the summit, where views extend southeast to Melbourne. The surrounding area, serviced by the small townships of **Macedon** and **Mt. Macedon,** is a popular retreat for Melburnians, where pleasant gardens, tearooms, and guesthouses are scattered about.

Hanging Rock
This unique geological feature, known as a *mamelon,* was formed as lava spewing from a vent in the earth's crust solidified quickly, forming a large rounded hillock that stands above the surrounding plains. Scientific explanations aside, the rock is best known as the setting for Australian author Joan Lindsay's novel, *Picnic at Hanging Rock* about the disappearance of a group of schoolgirls. The area around Hanging Rock is a reserve, with trails leading to the 710-meter summit and other landmarks named for bushranger Mad Dog Morgan, who used the rock as a refuge. Also in the reserve are tearooms, a picnic area with barbecues, and a racecourse, where "picnic" races are held each New Year's and Australia Days. Admission is $5 per car.

GOLDFIELDS

Wombat Ranges

The most direct route between Melbourne and Ballarat is the Western Freeway, passing through the historic town of **Bacchus Marsh.** North of Bacchus Marsh are the Wombat Ranges and **Lerderderg Gorge State Park,** named for a spectacular gorge through which trails were cut by gold diggers. The park has four basic campgrounds and some good hiking, but you'll need a map from the DC&NR on the main street of Bacchus Marsh to find your way around. To the north and east of the park is **Wombat State Forest,** accessible through **Blackwood** and **Trentham.** The road through these towns from Bacchus Marsh continues north to Daylesford (see below).

Brisbane Ranges National Park

A springtime display of over 400 different species of wildflowers is this park's main attraction. The 7,517-hectare park is not on the way to anywhere else, so a detour is required either south from Bacchus Marsh or north from Geelong, to reach the facility area at **Anakie Gorge.** The gorge was created over millions of years, as water from Stony Creek eroded the soft sandstone and igneous bedrock. A hiking trail links two picnic areas (three km one-way), crossing Stony Creek a number of times. The park has a large population of koalas, often seen lounging in eucalypts along the gorge. Facilities at **Boar Gully Campground,** in the north of the park on Thompsons Rd., include pit toilets

icnic tables, and drinking water. No firewood is
vailable, so bring a stove. For park informa-
on call (03) 5284-1230.

BALLARAT

Vith a population of 70,000, Ballarat is Victoria's
argest inland city. Formerly one of Australia's
chest goldfields, Ballarat maintains an air of
legance with many fine examples of Victorian
rchitecture and distinctive lace ironwork, ex-

tensive gardens, one of the country's best
provincial art galleries, and Sovereign Hill, a reconstructed gold-mining township. "Eureka" was
the cry in 1851, when gold was discovered in the
area, but three years later Eureka became synonymous with Ballarat for a more somber reason, that of the Eureka Stockade, Australia's
most famous political uprising.

Early History and the First Gold Strikes
Before the arrival of white people, the hills and
valleys where Ballarat now lies were occupied by

BALLARAT

DOWNTOWN BALLARAT

the Wathurung tribe, who camped on the banks of Lake Wendouree (Ballarat is Aboriginal for "Resting Place"). When gold was first discovered there was no crazy rush, but within two years, in 1853, 20,000 miners from all parts of the world had converged on the shallow diggings. Within five years, 100 million ounces of gold had been extracted, including the **Welcome Nugget,** weighing 68,956 ounces, unearthed on Bakery Hill.

The Eureka Stockade

The goldfields were a great equalizer. No matter what a man's background or how wealthy he was, the amount of gold he found was dependent on how hard and long he toiled. As miner numbers swelled, the quantity of easily found al-

luvial gold began diminishing, and the inequalit between the diggers and political power widened. The miners had no powers to purchas crown land, nor could they vote, but their mail grievance was the licensing system, whereb they paid 30 shillings per month for the right to di for gold. Not only did they feel the fee was un necessary, it was administered by the police many of whom were exconvicts, and as they re ceived half of each fine they were often brutal i their chase for licenses. The catalyst for the re bellion was when James Bently, owner of the Eureka Hotel, was honorably discharged on murder charge against one of the diggers. O 17 October 1854, 5,000 miners gathered out side the hotel and burnt it down. Under the lead ership of Peter Lalor they proceeded to burn a

[ed. 1]

WESTERN 🐝🐝 AUSTRALIA

No. 911

Fee—One Pound

Yilgarn Goldfield.

MINER'S RIGHT.

Issued to *Patrick Hannan*

under the provisions of "The Goldfields Act, 1886," to be in force until

10th August 1894

Date of issue 11 Aug, 1893

[Not Transferable]

R. Hedden *Warden.*

he licenses, then stood under a blue flag adorned with the Southern Cross and pledged to fight their arrest. A rough-and-ready stockade was built around the Eureka Claim. Early on 3 December 1854 over 300 police charged the compound, quickly overpowering the undisciplined diggers and killing 25 of them in the process. The diggers had paid a price, but ultimately they achieved their goal—the aftermath was a Miner's Right (license), costing one pound a year and allowing diggers to cultivate their own land and vote for members of the Legislative Assembly. All rebels were acquitted, except the editor of the Ballarat Times, whose articles on police brutality led to a six-month jail term.

But the diggers' joy was shortlived. As alluvial deposits dried out, larger companies, capable of extracting lodes of gold deep below the surface, moved in. The last of the company mines closed in 1918, but the city has continued to prosper as the center of a large merino wool district, by the farming of a variety of crops, and as an important inland transportation hub.

Sovereign Hill

Sovereign Hill, once one of Victoria's richest goldfields, is now a 25-hectare reconstructed gold-mining village where visitors can wander through period buildings, watch working exhibits, and observe craftsmen at work. It is one of the best such historical parks in Australia, and it's easy to spend at least five or six hours wandering through. Along the township's main street is a hotel, blacksmith's shop, bank, bakery, and a variety of other businesses, all with workers dressed in period costume and acting out their parts. At the back of the main street is Red Hill

Gully diggings, site of the original claim. Most of the equipment is original, right down to the mine shaft, and for a small fee you can pan for your own gold. Also represented are the Chinese who lived in a tent village on a slight rise behind Red Hill Gully diggings. The period 1860-1918, when large companies dominated the local mining industry, is displayed through a mine tour, associated buildings, and a museum. Guided tours are offered of the museum, diggings, and Chinese Village, while a shuttle bus tour (small fee) takes in the diggings and township.

Many shops are open for business, selling the goods they did in the 1850s—the post office handles mail, Waterloo Store sells gold, drinks, and snacks, and meals are available at stores throughout the grounds.

The park is open daily 9:30 a.m.-5 p.m. and admission is adult $15, child $11. For more information call (03) 5331-1944. Ballarat Transit's route 9 and 10 depart Curtis St. twice an hour for Sovereign Hill.

Blood on the Southern Cross is a nightly spectacular of light and sound that re-creates events that led to the Eureka Stockade. It takes place across the entire park and definitely shouldn't be missed. Showtimes vary, but it's usually an hour after dusk. Tickets are adult $17, child $8, but packages are available that include dinner, accommodation, or daytime park admission.

Museums

Across the road from the entrance to Sovereign Hill is the **Gold Museum,** built on the mullock heaps of early mining activity. The museum features imaginative displays, including one on the Eureka Stockade, as well as some gold nuggets. Admission is included in the Sovereign Hill ticket or separate admission is adult $3.50, child $1.50.

The **Eureka Exhibition** is on Eureka St., opposite the site where all the action took place. Here, details of the rebellion, its causes, and its aftermath are displayed. For what it is, admission is steep—adult $4, child $2. Open daily 9 a.m.-5 p.m. (tel. 03-5331-5822).

Lydiard Street is lined with historic buildings.

Eureka Museum is contained in the 1856 **Montrose Cottage,** Ballarat's only remaining bluestone miner's cottage. It is meticulously furnished in the period style and has extensive gardens, great for relaxing when the sun's out. Admission is adult $4, child $2. Open daily 9:30 a.m.-5 p.m. Located at 111 Eureka St. (tel. 03-5332-2554).

The only non-gold-related museum in town is **Ballarat Aviation Museum,** at the municipal airport northwest of town on the Sunraysia Hwy. (tel. 03-5339-5016). The museum houses a collection of vintage aircraft and is open Sat.-Sun. 1-5 p.m. Admission is adult $5, child $2.

Lydiard Street
Lydiard St., which crosses Ballarat's main drag (Sturt St.) just west of the information center, has been designated a historic precinct, thereby protecting the many fine Victorian buildings along its length. Many buildings function today as they did when first built, including the **George Hotel, Tawana Lodge, Ballarat Fine Art Gallery,** and **Her Majesty's Theatre.** Just off Lydiard St., on Sturt St., is the magnificent **Town Hall,** built in 1870.

The Ballarat Fine Art Gallery is one of Australia's premier provincial galleries. Most work is Australian, including paintings by artists Sir Sidney Nolan, Russell Drysdale, and Tom Roberts. One room is devoted to the works of the Lindsay family, who once lived just north of Ballarat. Also on display is the original Eureka flag, or at

least remnants of it. Admission is adult $3, chil $1.50. Open Tues.-Fri. 10:30 a.m.-4:30 p.m. and weekends 12:30-4:30 p.m. Located at 40 Lydiard St. (tel. 03-5331-5622).

Commercial Attractions
Kryal Castle, a replica of a medieval castle, is the most popular of Ballarat's commercial attractions. Features include jousting, hangings and medieval reenactments. Admission is adult $11, child $8.50. The castle is on Forbes Rd. eight km southeast of Ballarat (tel. 03-5334 7388).

Ballarat Wildlife and Reptile Park is on York St., East Ballarat (tel. 03-5333-5933). Highlights include the Tropical Reptile House, a koala show daily at 11 a.m., and Tasmanian devil feeding a 2:30 p.m. Admission is adult $7, child $3.50 Open daily 9 a.m.-5:30 p.m.

Recreation
Originally a large swamp, **Lake Wendouree** near the center of town, and its surrounding parks and gardens are popular with joggers and cyclists. The 40-hectare **Botanic Gardens,** or the western shore, were first planted in the 1850s and are well maintained. Within the grounds is the cottage of poet Adam Lindsay Gorden. **Wendouree Parade** encircles the lake and features many Victorian buildings. **Midlands Golf Club** has an 18-hole championship golf course open to the public; located on Heinz Lane (tel. 03-5332-6965).

Festivals and Events

Ballarat Rainbow Festival, held the last weekend of January in the School of Mines building, features workshops and displays aimed at improving lifestyles through alternative methods. Ballarat's largest celebration is the **Begonia Festival,** in mid-March. Many thousands of people converge on the Botanic Gardens for 10 days of floral displays, arts and crafts stalls, music, and a street parade. Later that same month is the **Eureka Jazz Festival.** There's an agricultural show in November and **Eureka Commemorations** in December. Call the Ballarat Tourist Information Centre for dates (tel. 03-5332-2694).

Antiques and Galleries

Ballarat has an astonishing number of antique emporiums and art galleries. Many of the pieces for sale were brought to the area by those on the goldfields who struck it rich, and it is these items that command the highest prices. The **Antiques and Collectables Centre,** in the old Mining Exchange building at 12 Lydiard St. (tel. 03-5331-7996), is the largest, boasting more than 60 stands. **McGarry's Trading Post,** at 811 Sturt St., has a good selection of unrestored pieces and some great examples of early Australian furniture.

Accommodations

Unfortunately, the grand old hotels that feature so prominently in most country towns are often not so grand on the inside. But here in Ballarat a number have been restored to their former glory, offering guests a taste of the luxury afforded to those who struck it rich during the gold rush. **Craig's Royal Hotel,** 10 Lydiard St. (tel. 03-5331-1377), is the best of these. Rooms of varying standards are available; the most basic, with shared facilities, are $45 s, $50 d, while those with private bathrooms start at $80 s or d. Cheaper hotels are the **Criterion Hotel,** 18 Doveton St. (tel. 03-5331-1451), where rates are $25 s, $40 d, which includes breakfast, and **Tawana Lodge,** 128 Lydiard St. (tel. 03-5331-3461), adjacent to the railway station; $25-48 s, $39-53 d.

Ambassador Motel, 1759 Sturt St. (tel. 03-5334-1505), is a good-value motel with lots of facilities and large rooms for $54 s, $60 d.

One of the most impressive bed and breakfasts is **Ballarat Terrace,** at 229 Lydiard St. (tel. 03-5333-2216), within walking distance of downtown. It is a Victorian-style terrace, with cast-iron balcony, antique furnishings, a relaxing guest room and rooms with private bathrooms; $75 s, $110 d.

Sovereign Hill's **Government Camp** allows you to stay within the grounds of the park, but it is a long way from the city. Rates for members of Hostelling International are $12.50-15, a few bucks extra for nonmembers, with motel-style rooms also available. For bookings call (03) 5333-3409.

More central is **Ballarat Backpackers,** in the old Bridge Mall Inn at 92 Bridge St. Mall (tel. 03-5331-3192). A bar operates downstairs but rooms are relatively quiet; facilities include a large kitchen, pool room, and jukebox; beds are $13 per night.

The closest campground to the center of town is **Goldfields Caravan Park** on Clayton St. (tel. 03-5332-7888). Sites are $11-14 and on-site vans start at $28. Of the half-dozen other parks, **A Welcome Stranger Caravan Park,** east of town at 263 Scott Parade (tel. 03-5332-6818), has the best facilities.

Food and Entertainment

L'Espresso, 417 Sturt St. (tel. 03-5333-1789), is one of many cafes in downtown Ballarat; it has a good range of coffees and a few outdoor tables. The **Old Dispensary,** 205 Dana St. (tel. 03-5332-1822), built in 1902, dispenses just coffee now, and is also an art gallery. Head to **Eureka Pizza,** at 316 Sturt St. (tel. 03-5331-3682), for plenty of pastas and pizza; most dishes are under $10. **Rustic Reflections,** 429 Main Rd. (tel. 03-5332-4922), at Sovereign Hill, is a bit corny, as you'll gather from the swagman out front; they have Aussie-style meals for around $10. For an inexpensive pub meal, head to the Criterion Hotel at Doveton Street. **Porter's,** corner Mair and Peel Streets (tel. 03-5331-4320), is an old pub that has been renovated into a restaurant. The menu is varied, diners have a choice of two sizes of main meals, and service is excellent. Open for lunch Tues.-Fri., dinner Tues.-Saturday.

One of Ballarat's better upmarket restaurants is **Alibis,** 10 Camp St. (tel. 03-5331-6680), open for dinner only Tues.-Saturday. It is housed in a bluestone building dating to the 1850s and has a small but varied menu, including mouthwatering rack of lamb.

George Hotel, 27 Lydiard St., is a popular student drinking hole, and **Hot Gossip,** 102 Dana St., is the hottest nightclub in town.

Transportation, Services, and Information

The railway station is on Lydiard St. (tel. 03-5337-8565). **V/Line** trains run daily between Ballarat and Melbourne ($12.80 one-way) and west to Stawell ($14.80) and Mildura ($44). V/Line buses leave from the railway station for Geelong ($9 one-way), Hamilton ($22.80), and Bendigo ($16.80). **Ballarat Coachlines** (tel. 03-5333-4660) operates a shuttle service between Ballarat and Melbourne International Airport three to five times daily; $20 one-way. The depot is at 202 Lydiard St., right beside the railway station.

Ballarat Transit has two terminals on Bridge St. Mall and routes that take in all major sights (tel. 03-5331-7777). For **Ballarat Taxis** call (03) 5331-3355.

The **post office** is on the corner of Sturt and Lydiard Streets. The **DC&NR** is on the corner of Doveton and Mair Streets (tel. 03-5333-6782). **Ballarat Base Hospital** is on Sturt St. (tel. 03-5320-4000).

If you're keen to do some gold panning, head to **E.E. Day & Sons,** 822 Howitt St. (tel. 03-5339-2211), which rents and sells gold-mining equipment, including metal detectors.

Ballarat Tourist Information Centre is right in the heart of town at 39 Sturt St. (tel. 03-5332-2694); open Mon.-Fri. 9 a.m.-5 p.m., Sat.-Sun. 10 a.m.-4 p.m.

NORTH OF BALLARAT

The area north of Ballarat is rich with gold-mining history, and, although the populations have dwindled, the area's towns retain elegant buildings and historic charm.

Creswick

At one time Creswick, 18 km north of Ballarat, had a population of over 25,000 diggers, most attracted by the discovery of gold in 1852. Today

Creswick is a quiet highway town of 2,500 with many historic buildings lining the main street and evidence of diggings all around. On Albert St. is a small **historical museum,** open Sunday 1:30-4:30 p.m., and two km north along the road to Clunes is **Australasian Mines,** site of what was, at the time, Australia's worst mine disaster—Mine No. 2 flooded, killing 22 men.

Since the 1880s, Creswick has been the center of a large forest industry, with the **School of Forestry** (tel. 03-5345-2100) working toward re-establishing the area's natural vegetation.

Clunes

Clunes, 20 km northwest of Creswick, was the site of one of Victoria's first gold rushes. When gold was first discovered a few thousand diggers pitched their tents on the banks of Creswick's Creek, but their interests were soon diverted. The gold that was in the area lay in quartz reefs, deep below the surface, and required large operations to successfully extract it. So in 1856 the Port Phillip Company set up a large-scale operation. By the 1860s and 1870s many impressive buildings had been constructed along **Fraser St.,** including the **Town Hall** (1873) and the **Post and Telegraph Office** (1879), and on other streets bluestone churches began to appear. **Clunes Museum,** 36 Fraser St. (tel. 03-5345-3592), is the best place to begin your visit; open daily during school holidays 11 a.m.-4:30 p.m., and at other times during the year, Saturday only 10 a.m.-4:30 p.m. Walking tour brochures to Clunes (40 cents) and the many other towns dotting the area are available there.

Keebles of Clunes, 114 Bailey St. (tel. 03-5345-3220), was built as the Telegraph Hotel in 1863 and has been restored to provide six comfortable rooms, each with private bathrooms. Other facilities include a guest lounge with log fire, game room, and library. Rates are $85 s, $130 for bed and breakfast; dinner is also available.

Tuki Trout Farm

East of Clunes and eight km north of Smeaton is Tuki Trout Farm (tel. 03-5345-6233), where you can go trout fishing in an artificial reservoir, then have your catch filleted and served up with a delicious array of salads for $15 pp.

Talbot and Vicinity

With a population optimistically stated as 350, Talbot's deserted streets and surrounding open fields seem a world away from Ballarat, yet during the height of the gold rush 30,000 diggers lived in a city of canvas tents around workings along Back Creek.

Permanent buildings, constructed in the 1860s, still exist in varying states of disrepair, providing a glimpse into life on the goldfields. One that has been restored is the **Bull and Mouth Hotel** (tel. 03-5463-2325), which has been converted to an accommodation and restaurant. Rooms are in modern heritage-style cottages and start at $75 s or d. The restaurant is open for dinner Thurs.-Sun. and serves a variety of country-style meals; main dishes start at $15.

Amherst was a thriving center during the gold rush, but the years have taken their toll—many buildings have been taken apart for their materials and bushfires in 1985 destroyed most of those that were left. The town's streets are still discernible, many with extensive basalt culverts, as are some foundations. But the best way to appreciate the town's one-time importance is by walking through the cemetery—it's huge. Amherst is four km northwest of Talbot on the road to Avoca.

Maryborough

Maryborough, 10 km north from Amherst, is a thriving agricultural center of 8,000 on the Pyrenees Highway. Gold was discovered in the nearby White Hills in 1854, and within six months 25,000 diggers had converged on the area. Fine examples of Victorian architecture are a legacy of the town's one-time prosperity, including the railway station (some say it was designed for Melbourne but somehow was built in Maryborough), Bull and Mouth Hotel, and Town Hall. If you're in the area during the Sept.-Oct. school holidays, don't miss the **Golden Wattle Festival,** where highlights include the Australian Gumleaf Playing Championship and a birdcalling competition.

Wattle Grove Motel, 65 Derby Rd. (tel. 03-5461-1877), is the least-expensive motel in town at $38 s, $44 d, but **Eany Farm** is more comfortable, and rates of $30 s, $50 d include a hearty country-style breakfast. It's 10 km southeast of Maryborough (tel. 03-5464-7267). **Golden Coun-**

try Caratel, 134 Park Rd. (tel. 03-5461-2344), has a number of self-contained units for $52 s, $62 d, and tent and caravan sites start at $12.

The old lantern room on the platform of the Maryborough railway station is now **Twains,** a delightful little restaurant, where main meals range $8-13 (tel. 03-5460-4062).

Maryborough Tourist Information Centre is on the corner of Tuaggra and Alma Streets (tel. 03-5461-2643); open daily 10 a.m.-5 p.m.

Avoca and Nearby Wineries

Avoca is a small agricultural center at the junction of the Sunraysia and Pyrenees Highways, 70 km northwest of Ballarat. To the west is the spectacular Pyrenees Range, named by Major Thomas Mitchell in 1836 for the Pyrenees Mountains in western Europe, but they bear little resemblance to them—the highest point is **Mt. Avoca,** just 762 meters high. Still, the area has strong connections to France through a number of renowned vineyards. In the early 1960s, Remy Martin, famed for its brandy, established Chateau Remy Winery seven km west of Avoca and produces sparkling wines. Chateau Remy has extensive gardens and is open to the public for tasting (tel. 03-5465-3202). Just to the south of Chateau Remy is **Mt. Avoca Vineyard,** which produces some of the region's most successful wines; open daily 10 a.m.-5 p.m. (tel. 03-5465-3282).

Warrenmang is best known for its red wines but also boasts a renowned restaurant and 14 colonial-style timber cottages dotted among towering eucalypts. Its bed and breakfast is $99 d ($189 d Sat.-Sun. dinner included). The elegant restaurant has impressive views over the surrounding vineyards to the mountains beyond. To get there, take the Sunraysia Highway northwest from Avoca and turn off to Moonambel and follow the Warrenmang signs (tel. 03-5467-2233). Back in town, **Avoca Caravan Park,** Liebig St. (tel. 03-5465-3073), has a tranquil setting by the river; $10 for tents, and on-site vans are $28 d.

The Golden Triangle

Within the area bounded by Inglewood, Wedderburn, and Dunolly, 90% of the world's largest gold nuggets have been found, including the 2,293-ounce **Welcome Stranger,** the largest chunk of gold ever found. The Welcome Stranger was found by John Deason and

Richard Oates in 1869 near the small hamlet of Moliagul; now a cairn marks the site of the find. **Dunolly,** south of Moliagul, has a small museum full of gold-mining memorabilia including the anvil on which the Welcome Stranger was unceremoniously cut up—so that it would fit on the scales! The museum is open 1:30-5 p.m., daily during school holidays, and Sunday only the rest of the year.

From Dunolly, the most interesting route to the northern tip of the Golden Triangle is northeast through almost-a-ghost-town **Wanyarra,** to **Tarnagulla,** which boasts some fine examples of Victorian architecture, then onto **Bridgewater,** a town of 1,500 on the Calder Highway.

Just northwest is **Inglewood,** center of a large eucalyptus oil industry that started shortly after the gold rush ended. That's not to say there's no gold left—in 1980 a 952-ounce nugget was found in the old schoolyard. West of Inglewood is **Kooyoora State Park** (3,500 hectares), where Captain Melville, the gentleman bushranger, had a hideout, living in a series of large overhangs and using a rocky ledge as a lookout point to detect troopers.

Farther up the Calder Highway is **Wedderburn,** worth visiting for the **Christmas Reef Mine,** five km west of town. The mine is owned and operated by two Aussie characters, Doug and Anne McGuire, who encourage you to visit their working mine while they search for the elusive reef of gold. Admission is adult $5, child $3. Ask for directions from the classic old **General Store Museum** (open daily) on High Street.

SPA COUNTRY

The twin towns of Daylesford and Hepburn Springs are surrounded by Australia's largest concentration of mineral springs. Signs of the prosperity bought by the gold rush are abundantly clear, but it is the springs themselves that are the main attraction.

Daylesford

The Wombat Flat Diggings grew around Lake Daylesford after the discovery of gold there by John Egan in August 1851. The tent city gradually grew more permanent and underwent a name change from Wombat to Daylesford. As the gold rush ended, the soothing qualities of the mineral springs grew in reputation, attracting the wealthy from Melbourne, creating a need for grand guesthouses and other facilities that the wealthy demanded. Today the town has a population of 2,500, many of whom are Melburnians who have escaped to the idyllic lifestyle the town provides.

Apart from wandering along the main street and admiring the many arts-and-crafts shops, you can head to **Wombat Hill Botanic Garden,** off Central Springs Road. Also, **Central Highlands Tourist Railway** operates between the station on Fraser St. and the small community of Musk. The self-propelled diesel passenger cars are restored versions of those used earlier this century. Trains depart Sunday on the hour 10 a.m.-3 p.m. Adults are $5 return, children $3. For details call (03) 5348-3503.

As has been the tradition for over 100 years, the most popular accommodations in Daylesford are self-contained cottages. **Acacia Cottage,** 33 Vincent St. N (tel. 03-5348-2444), is a small miner's cottage with two bedrooms, a colonial-style kitchen, and many antiques. It costs $65-95 per night. Overlooking Lake Daylesford is **Ambleside Bed and Breakfast,** 15 Leggatt St. (tel. 03-5348-2691), a historic house carefully renovated to retain a Victorian ambience; rates start at $95 d. **Jubilee Lake Caravan Park** (tel. 03-5348-2186) is on the shores of the eponymous lake, three km south of town. Sites are $9-11 and on-site vans start at $30.

Daylesford boasts a number of gourmet eateries and delis—one that shouldn't be missed for fine chocolates and a delicious array of light meals is **Sweet Decadence,** on Vincent Street. At 77 Vincent Street is **The Food Gallery** (tel. 03-5348-1677), a French-Italian bistro dishing up homemade meals and picnic hampers to go; open daily 9 a.m.-6 p.m. **Lake House** is regarded as one of country-Victoria's finest weekend getaways. The luxurious accommodation here may be a little more than most budgets allow ($230-270 d, includes dinner, bed, and breakfast), but the licensed restaurant overlooking Lake Daylesford is open to the public and features continental cuisine starting at $20 for main dishes and a three-course dinner on Saturday night for $54 pp. The lodge is on King St. (tel. 03-5348-3329).

The closest railway station to Daylesford is Woodend, from where the fare to Melbourne is 11.40 one-way. Daily buses connect Daylesford and Woodend, departing and arriving from garage at 45 Vincent St.; $3.60 one-way.

Spa Centre Tourist Centre is at 49 Vincent St. (tel. 03-5348-3707); open daily 9 a.m.-5 p.m.

Hepburn Springs

Diggers who came to the Hepburn Springs area were predominantly of Swiss-Italian descent and, as the gold began running out, they saw value in the mineral springs. **Hepburn Springs Reserve** was established in 1865, and soon after a pavilion for bathers was constructed. Today the reserve is an idyllic place to relax; each of four main springs contains water of a different chemical composition—magnesium, soda, iron, and sulphur—and each is obtainable from iron hand-pumps scattered throughout the reserve. Also in the reserve is **Hepburn Springs Spa Complex,** where the health-giving properties of the water have attracted generations of Melburnians. Admission to the pool and indoor spa is $7, 20 minutes in a spa is $15, and massages are also available; open Mon.-Fri. 10 a.m.-8 p.m., Sat.-Sun. 9 a.m.-8 p.m. (tel. 03-5348-2034).

Numerous hiking trails crisscross the area around Hepburn Springs, including one that begins at the end of Blowhole Rd. and follows Sailors Creek though **Brace's Flat** to the Mistletoe Mine and **Tipperary Spring.**

For accommodation, **The Springs,** 124 Main Rd. (tel. 03-5348-2202), has pub-style rooms with shared facilities for $50 s, $60 d, and a number of motel units out the back starting at $90 s or d (all rates include a cooked breakfast). Another inexpensive place to stay is **Liberty House,** 20 Mineral Springs Crescent (tel. 03-5348-2809), opposite Mineral Springs Reserve; $40 s, $80 d. The upmarket **Perini Country House,** 4 8th St. (tel. 03-5348-2579), is an English-style house set in extensive and well-manicured gardens overlooking Doctor's Gully. Each room has a private bathroom and possesses distinctive charm. Rates start at $115 d, which includes a sumptuous breakfast. At the other end of the scale is **Springs Caravan Park,** Forest Ave. (tel. 03-5348-3161), where tent sites are $8 and on-site vans $25.

Springs Cosy Corner Cafe, 10th St. (tel. 03-5348-3825), is the only casual dining in Hepburn Springs, although many of the guesthouses offer formal dinners with advance bookings.

A shuttle bus runs hourly between Spa Centre Tourist Centre in Daylesford and Hepburn Springs (Mon.-Fri. only).

Trentham and Vicinity

Trentham is a picturesque hamlet nestled in the middle of the densely forested Wombat Ranges east of Daylesford. Although many buildings lining Trentham's main street date to the gold rush, it is the surrounding bush that's the drawcard here. Casual prospectors still find gold in the surrounding hills, and many trails used by the old diggers are today used as hiking tracks. The 50-km **Wombat Forest Drive** is a scenic route through the hills with many lookouts, mineral springs, and other points of interest. It starts in Daylesford and heads east through Lyonville and Trentham, then south to Blackwood, where a renowned four-hectare botanic garden is located. North of Trentham you'll find **Trentham Falls** cascading over a wide rock ledge into a deep pool below.

Kyneton

Kyneton's main street is one of the best-preserved examples of a Victorian streetscape in the country. Today many of the buildings house specialty shops. There's a small Russian museum in Walkden's General Store and a collection of old brewing equipment in the Royal George Hotel. An old bank, at 67 Piper St., houses **Kyneton Museum,** which has recently been renovated and features a replica of a settler's cottage and a vast collection of colonial memorabilia. Open Wednesday, Saturday, and Sunday noon-4:30 p.m.

CASTLEMAINE AND VICINITY

While Bendigo and Ballarat survived and thrived on company mining, Castlemaine was less fortunate. Gold was discovered in the area in late 1851, and subsequent diggings became known as Mt. Alexander. At first, the promise of gold produced the largest of the early rushes, and as the wealth continued Castlemaine saw itself as a sister city to Bendigo. Businessmen built accordingly. By the time alluvial gold began running out, streets had been laid out and a large market building, banks, civic buildings, and a theater had been constructed.

Today, the city of 7,500, 119 km northwest of Melbourne, is the center of a fruit-growing and farming district, its excellent examples of Victorian architecture a lasting legacy of the short-lived gold rush.

One of Australia's favorite beers, Castlemaine XXXX, was first brewed here in 1859, but the brewery moved to Queensland in 1887 and is now the preferred *drop* in that northern state.

Sights

Castlemaine Market, built in 1862, is now a museum with mining artifacts and an audiovisual display of the town's history; open daily 10 a.m.-5 p.m. Dignified homes from last century are scattered throughout town, but one of special note is **Buda Historic Home,** built by local silversmith Ernest Leviny. The house and surrounding gardens are open daily 10 a.m.-5 p.m., and admission is adult $4, child $2; located at 42 Hunter St. (tel. 03-5472-1032). Other worthy sights are botanic gardens (one of the state's oldest), on Walker St., and **Castlemaine Art Gallery,** on Lyttleton St., which boasts a fine collection of colonial paintings.

Accommodations and Food

Built in 1854, **Broadoaks,** 31 Gingell St. (tel. 03-5470-5827), was the last home of Robert O'Hara Burke, of Burke and Wills fame. The home features antique brass beds and a comfortable lounge with log fire, and a hearty country-style breakfast is served each morning. Rooms begin at $65. Another historical accommodation is **Ellimatta,** 233 Barker St. (tel. 03-5472-4454), a gold-rush-era hotel with rooms furnished in period-style; $65 s, $100 d. **Botanic Gardens Caravan Park,** Walker St. (tel. 03-5472-1125), beside the botanic gardens, has tent sites from $8.50 and on-site vans for $26-32.

Theatre Royal, 28 Hargreaves St. (tel. 03-5472-1196), is a historic theater that functions as a cinema and restaurant. Meals average about $12, but three-course meal-and-movie deals

are often offered weeknights. For a casual meal or light snack, **Tog's Place,** 58 Lyttleton St. (tel. 03-5470-5090), has a unique style and serves delicious gourmet sandwiches.

Transportation, Services, and Information

The railway station is on Kennedy St. (tel. 03-5472-4205). **V/Line** trains run daily to Melbourne ($14.80 one-way) and Bendigo ($3.60), while buses depart from the station for Ballarat ($12.80 one-way).

Castlemaine Tourist Information Centre (tel. 03-5472-2480) is on the main route into town from Melbourne (Pyrenees Hwy.); open school holidays and weekends only, 10 a.m.-5 p.m.

Maldon

Of all the goldfields' towns, Maldon, 20 km northwest of Castlemaine, remains as well preserved an example of a gold-rush town as any other. At one time 20,000 diggers lived in and around Maldon; now the population is less than 2,000, but the hotels, theaters, and civic buildings remain. In fact virtually every building on the main street is recognized by the National Trust as being of "historical importance." Many of the shops now house specialty gift shops and antique emporiums—adding to the old-world charm.

Off Parkin's Reef Rd., two km south of town, is **Carman's Tunnel,** a 600-meter-long tunnel cut through solid rock over a period of two years in the 1880s. The result of this immense effort was a paltry $300 worth of gold. Tunnel tours take place Sat.-Sun., daily during school holidays, 1-4:30 p.m.; $2 for adults, 50 cents for children. For bookings, call (03) 5472-2656. To the north of the tunnel is **Mt. Tarrengower,** where a lookout gives you tremendous views of the surrounding countryside.

BENDIGO

Like Ballarat, Bendigo, 140 km north of Melbourne, is a grand and prosperous city founded on the wealth of gold. The mines around Bendigo were among the richest in Australia; their legacy is streets lined with extravagant Victorian-era architecture.

BENDIGO

TO JOSS HOUSE
AND
WHITE HILLS CEMETERY

TO
LAKE WEEROONA
AND
ECHUCA

GOLDEN DRAGON
MUSEUM

BENDIGO CENTRAL
MOTOR LODGE

TO
FORTUNA VILLA
AND
EAGLEHAWK

LOOKOUT

ROSALIND PARK

DUDLEY
HOUSE

CAPITOL
THEATRE

BENDIGO
ART GALLERY

CLOGS

HOUSE OF
KHONG

TO
TRAMWAY
MUSEUM

POST
OFFICE

SHAMROCK
HOTEL

METROPOLITAN
HOTEL

OLD CROWN
HOTEL

DC&NR

TOURIST INFORMATION
CENTRE

CITY CENTRE
MOTEL

MULLY'S CAFE

TO
NANGA GNULLE
AND
HEATHCOTE

SACRED HEART
CATHEDRAL

CITY FAMILY
HOTEL

CAFE
CUMBERLAND

JOLLY
PUDDLER

MATILDA'S

TO
CENTRAL CITY CARAVAN PARK
AND
CASTLEMAINE

CENTRAL DEBORAH
GOLD MINE

RAILWAY
STATION

MOON

NOT TO SCALE

History

In 1851 gold was discovered at Ravenswood. The tens of thousands who descended on the diggings spread out over claims that totaled 360 square km. With so much activity, alluvial gold quickly ran out and the diggers moved to a newly discovered field, **Sandhurst,** as Bendigo was then known. As surface gold ran out, companies moved in to extract gold located in reefs of quartz. By the mid-1860s reef mining was in full swing, and it is from this period that Bendigo's more impressive buildings date.

Sights

Named for the gold-bearing reef of quartz that it was sunk to mine, 500-meter-deep **Central Deborah Gold Mine** was the last on the Bendigo field to close. It reopened in 1972, this time for tourists. The mine remains much as it was when it closed, although a replacement poppet head from the rich Sheepshead Line Mine is now in place. A tour takes in displays of mining memorabilia and a talk, then it's on with a hard hat and light to descend 60 meters underground and experience what life as a miner was like and how the gold was extracted. Open daily 9 a.m.-5 p.m. and tour cost is adult $11, child $5.50. The mine is at 76 Violet St. (tel. 03-5443-8322). **Golden Link,** a tourist-oriented facility with a cafe, information center, and parking lot has been developed at Central Deborah Gold Mine. It's also the terminus for **Bendigo Talking Tram,** a vintage tram that runs through town to all the sights. Trams run hourly 9:30 a.m.-5:30 p.m. The fare is $6 pp, which includes admission to a tramway museum along the route.

The Bendigo diggings attracted a large contingent of Chinese diggers, whose hard work often yielded better results than other diggers, causing widespread resentment. Bridge St. was the original **China Town,** and a few reminders of their colorful culture remain. **Golden Dragon Museum,** 9 Bridge St. (tel. 03-5441-5044), has a large collection of Chinese artifacts in a modern setting with the highlight being 100-meter-long **Sun Loong,** the world's longest ceremonial dragon. Admission is adult $5, child $2.50. Open daily 9:30 a.m.-5:30 p.m.

The **Joss House,** one of four Chinese places of worship that once dotted Bendigo, was built in 1864. It's painted bright red, a traditional Chinese color, and the front entrance is guarded by a pair of mythical beasts. Inside are a variety of paintings, embroidered banners, and Chinese lanterns. Admission is adult $3, child $1. Open daily 10 a.m.-5 p.m.; on Finn St., north of the rail line. **White Hills Cemetery,** farther along Finn St., has a Chinese section with a traditional prayer oven where mourners burnt money in respect for the deceased.

Pall Mall, Bendigo's main street, is lined with impressive Victorian-era buildings that mirror the wealth the goldfields produced. Along View St. are the restored **Capitol Theatre, Dudley House,** home to the historical society, and **Bendigo Art Gallery.** At 42 View St., the latter is one of the state's finest regional galleries (open Mon.-Fri. 10 a.m.-5 p.m., Sat.-Sun. 2-5 p.m.). Behind these buildings is **Rosalind Park,** site of some of Bendigo's later gold rushes. Sign of the actual mining has disappeared under landscaped gardens, but a few outcrops of quartz remain. At a high point of the park is a poppet head, which once sat above the shaft of Bendigo's richest mine, Garden Gully United.

Panoramic views from the tower extend 360 degrees. The **Shamrock Hotel,** corner Pall Mall and Williamson St., is a classic example of elegant goldfields architecture. The structure is four stories high and has an impressive balcony lined with iron lace, a cavernous ballroom, and an elegant foyer. Tours of the hotel are offered Sat.-Sun. at 2:30 p.m. (for bookings call 03-5447-1383). Rooms are available (see "Accommodations," below), or drop by for a beer anytime the bar is open. **Sacred Heart Cathedral,** on the corner of Mackenzie and Wattle Streets, is one of many grand churches that dot the city. Parts of the sandstone and granite structure date to 1897 and its spire stands 86 meters tall.

Fortuna Villa, Chum St. (tel. 03-5442-0222) was the 1860s home of George Lansell, one of Bendigo's wealthiest residents. His mansion, at one time the largest in Australia, is open for tours Sunday at 1 p.m.

Eaglehawk, seven km northwest of the city center, was the site of a gold rush in 1852. Now part of city sprawl, many buildings there date to the 1860s.

Festivals and Events

Each year during **Easter Fair,** the dragon Sun Loong, all 100 meters of him, is paraded through the streets of Bendigo (with the help of 100 attendants). The parade takes place Easter Monday, but the preceding week is packed with events, including free street entertainment, theater, and kids' activities. The other major annual event, which, surprisingly, attracts just as many people, is the **Classic Cars—National Swap Meet,** when up to 30,000 enthusiasts descend on the showgrounds on the second weekend of November.

Accommodations

The grand **Shamrock Hotel,** corner Pall Mall and Williamson St. (tel. 03-5443-0333), has rooms for travelers, and slowly they are being refurnished to their former glory. Those with shared facilities are $45 s, $50 d; those with private facilities are $60 s, $65 d. **Old Crown Hotel,** 238 Hargreaves St. (tel. 03-5441-6888), has pub-style rooms of a reasonable standard for $25 s, $40 d, including breakfast. A well-priced and central motel is **City Centre Motel,**

6 Forest St. (tel. 03-5443-2077), 200 meters orthwest of Pall Mall; rates are $39 s, $47 d. **endigo Central Motor Lodge,** 181 View St. el. 03-5443-9388), has good rooms, a pool, undry, and barbecue area; $39 s, $49 d. Opposite Lake Weeroona, on the Midland Highay, is a string of motels, including **Tea House Motor Inn** (tel. 03-5441-7111), good value at 47 s, $57 d, and **Julie-Anna Inn** (tel. 03-5442-855), which has large well-furnished rooms et around a pool and landscaped courtyard for 80 s, $95 d.

Nanga Gnulle, east of downtown at 40 Harley St. (tel. 03-5443-7891), is a uniquely uilt bed and breakfast set among a hectare of andscaped gardens. It's built with mud bricks, ecycled bricks, and railway sleepers, but still is tylish with large elegantly furnished rooms; 110 d including breakfast; dinner is $34 pp.

Bendigo's only backpacker accommodation s **Central City Caravan Park,** 362 High St. el. 03-5443-6937), which has six bunk rooms f four beds for $10 pp. Although over two km outh of downtown, this park is closest to the atractions. Powered and unpowered sites are 10-14, on-site vans $30, and cabins $42-50.

Food

Bendigo's hotels are the best place to head for an inexpensive meal. **City Family Hotel,** 41 High St., has decent-sized counter lunches for around $5. Try the **Metropolitan Hotel,** corner Bull and Hargreaves Streets for a bit more style. **Cafe Cumberland,** in the Cumberland Hotel, 56 Williamson St. (tel. 03-5443-4665), has a pleasant setting overlooking the street from a second-story balcony. Sandwiches are $3-7, pasta is $7-10, or a huge serving of Nachos Supreme is just $7. You can also relax with just a coffee and cake or dessert. Open Tues.-Saturday. Located in the 1887 National Bank building is **Mully's Cafe,** 32 Pall Mall (tel. 03-5441-8566), open for light, inexpensive meals, and with a gallery upstairs. Open daily 10 a.m.-5 p.m. and for dinner Friday and Saturday. **Clogs,** 106 Pall Mall (tel. 03-5443-0077), is a modern bistro-style restaurant where you can stop for just coffee or a full meal. Pizza and pasta is around $8, with other main dishes $11-16.50. **House of Khong,** 200 Hargreaves St. (tel. 03-5443-5656), is a good, inexpensive Chinese

restaurant, with a buffet lunch weekdays for $9. **Matilda's,** corner High and Don Streets (tel. 03-5441-4088), is an Aussie-style restaurant with reliable-quality meals $11-14.50, a good lunchtime buffet for $7.95, and all-you-can-eat ice cream for $2.25. At the other end of the scale is the **Jolly Puddler,** 101 Williamson St. (tel. 03-5443-9859), an intimate restaurant with main dishes from $15.

**Transportation,
Services, and Information**

V/Line (tel. 03-5440-2765) has regular rail services between Melbourne and Bendigo; $19.40 one-way. The station is on Railway Place, off Mitchell Street. V/Line buses from Bendigo head to Castlemaine ($3.60 one-way), Ballarat ($16.80), Echuca ($5.20), and Mildura ($44). **Bendigo Associated Taxis** can be contacted at (03) 5443-0777.

The **post office** is on Pall Mall, opposite the end of Williamson Street. The **DC&NR** is at 31 Mackenzie St. (tel. 03-5444-6666). **Bendigo Tourist Information Centre** is on the corner of High and Mitchell Streets (tel. 03-5441-5244); open daily 10 a.m.-4 p.m.

VICINITY OF BENDIGO

Whipstick State Park

Now protected as a state park, this area north of Bendigo saw its share of diggers, and still produces small amounts of alluvial gold to amateur prospectors who try their luck. The 2,300-hectare park was established to protect an area of whipstick mallee, a hardy and distinctive plant unique to the area. Near the park entrance is **Hartland's Eucalyptus Farm** (tel. 03-5448-8270), which has been producing eucalyptus oil for over 100 years. Open daily (tours Sunday only; $3) 10:30 a.m.-4 p.m.

Heathcote

Heathcote is a historic gold-mining town of 1,900, located 47 km east of Bendigo on the McIvor Highway, an alternate route between Melbourne and Bendigo. In 1853, at the height of the gold rush, 30,000 diggers lived in the town. Now a few old buildings remain along the main street. On the south side of town, to the west of the highway, is **Pink Cliffs Reserve,** an area of erosion caused by sluicing operations. On the east side of the highway, a 10-minute hike from the end of Barrack St. leads to a lookout with views across town. The area is noted for man, fine wineries, including **Heathcote Winery,** 18 High St. (tel. 03-5433-2595), in a historic build ing right in the center of town.

GREAT OCEAN ROAD

"A tourist road comparable to that in California . . ." was the claim when it was first proposed to carve a road into coastal cliffs between Torquay and Apollo Bay. And after driving the route, few would disagree with the comparison. Officially, the Great Ocean Road extends between Anglesea and Apollo Bay, but generally the entire coastal highway from Geelong to Warrnambool is considered part of the road. The road has three distinct sections—the **Surf Coast,** from Geelong to Apollo Bay, the lush, green world of the **Otway Ranges,** and the **Shipwreck Coast,** from Princetown to Warrnambool. The road's most famous landmarks are the spectacular rock formations, such as the Twelve

Apostles, of **Port Campbell National Park,** bu the entire road is a smorgasbord of history scenery, surfing, and shipwrecks.

If you don't have a car, it's difficult to sam ple the entire smorgasbord. **V/Line** has no direc bus or train service along the Great Ocean Road, but V/Line trains run daily between Mel bourne and Geelong and Melbourne and Warr nambool (see "Geelong," below, and "Warr nambool," under "Victoria's Southwest Coast, later in this chapter); V/Line buses run from Geelong to as far as Apollo Bay and, on Frida only, continue to Warrnambool. From Melbourne one-way fares are: Lorne $20.40, Apollo Ba $25, and Warrnambool $44.

Melbourne to Geelong

The easiest way to head southwest from downtown Melbourne is on the Westgate Frwy., which crosses the 2.7-km **Westgate Bridge** southwest of the city center and passes through 75 km of industrial sprawl, ending at Geelong. The only worthwhile detour is **You Yangs Regional Park,** a 2,025-hectare reserve surrounding volcanic intrusions (You Yangs translates from Koori to mean "Big Mountain in the Middle of the Plain"). The park's highest point is 348-meter **Flinders Peak,** accessible along a 1.6-km (one-way) trail. A longer trail circumnavigates the peak and provides more great views. A visitor center at the entrance is open daily 8:30 a.m.-4:30 p.m. (tel. 03-5282-3356).

GEELONG

With a population of 130,000, Geelong is Victoria's second-largest city. The Princes Highway bypasses the main commercial center, but if you have the time, some parts of what at first seems like just a massive industrial and residential sprawl are worth exploring.

The original settlement was established in the 1830s, mainly to service surrounding grazing land. The town boomed during the gold rushes of the 1850s, and as western Victoria was opened to settlers, Geelong's role as a major port for shipping grain and wheat increased.

National Wool Museum

This excellent museum is housed in the National Wool Centre, an 1855 bluestone building used as a woolstore for over 100 years. Displays catalog the history of wool-growing, traditionally one of Australia's major industries, through a re-creation of a shearing shed. Other points of interest include displays showing the many breeds of sheep and the uses of each wool class, a short audiovisual in which shearers relate stories from the sheds, and a variety of machinery that classes, presses, and dispatches wool. The top floor was originally the sales room, and on display now are bales of wool ready for inspection by buyers. On the first floor, in the large foyer area, are shops selling wool and other Australiana products, and an information center. The complex is open daily 9 a.m.-

National Wool Centre, Geelong

ANDREW HEMPSTEAD

5 p.m. with admission to the museum adult $7, child $3.50. Located at 26 Moorabool St. (tel. 03-5226-4660).

Other Sights

The city has over 100 buildings classified by the National Trust, many of which are downtown and covered in the brochure *City of Geelong Heritage Trail,* available at local information centers.

Built in 1854, **Balmoral Gallery,** on Aberdeen St. west of downtown, and overlooking Moorabool River, has been restored with period furniture. Admission is $1. Open daily 10 a.m.-5:30 p.m. For a wider range of paintings (mostly Australian), head to **Geelong Art Gallery** at Little Malop St. (tel. 03-5229-3645). Works of many well-known Australian artists as well as touring exhibitions are its highlights. Admission adult $3, child $1. Open Tues.-Fri. 10 a.m.-5 p.m., Sat.-Sun. 1-5 p.m.

A small part of a larger reserve, **Geelong Botanic Gardens,** a few blocks from downtown, was first planted in 1850. Within the gardens is a timber cottage dating to 1838 and a tearoom open daily 10:30 a.m.-3:30 p.m. The main reserve extends to the shore of Corio Bay and **Eastern Beach,** a pleasant sandy area backed by formed gardens. Rent boats and aqua bikes in summer at the beach (tel. 03-5243-4306).

Accommodations

Motels line the main routes into Geelong. One of the most central, **Kangaroo Motel,** 16 the Esplanade S (tel. 03-5221-4022), also has a restaurant; $40 s, $50 d. Northwest of downtown on Ballarat Rd. (Midland Hwy.) and right opposite Geelong Golf Club is **Parkwood Motel** (tel. 03-5278-5477), where rooms are $38 s, $48 d. A little more upmarket is **Innkeepers Motor Inn,** 9 Aberdeen St. (tel. 03-5221-2177), for $59 s, $69 d.

Geelong YHA Hostel is a small establishment in a residential area 10 blocks from downtown. All the usual facilities are available and beds cost only $8 pp (tel. 03-5221-6583).

On Barrabool Rd., alongside the Barwon River southwest of the city center, are three caravan parks.

Food

Inexpensive and casual eateries are spread along Little Malop and Moorabool Streets. If you've just spent a few hours in the National Wool Museum, **Lamby's Bar and Bistro** (tel. 03-5223-2392), in the National Wool Centre's basement, is an enjoyable place for a meal or just a drink. Roast of the day is $10, but a wide selection of other dishes and lighter meals start at $6.50. The **Hill Grill,** 228 Moorabool St. (tel. 03-5221-3388), is another casual place with most dishes $5-10, but it's very popular later in the evening and gets rather noisy. **Le Parisien,** 16 the Esplanade (tel. 03-5229-3110), is a classy French restaurant with an extensive menu and many local wines. Another more formal establishment is **Tousson,** located in a two-story heritage building at 310 Moorabool St. (tel. 03-5221-1375).

Transportation, Services, and Information

V/Line operates hourly train services to Geelong from Melbourne ($7.60 one-way); the station is on Fenwick St. (tel. 03-5226-6526).

McHarry's Bus Line (tel. 03-5223-2111) rur daily around the Bellarine Peninsula and ▉ Torquay from Geelong.

The main source of information is **Cori▉ Tourist Information Centre** on the Princes Hwy., seven km north of the city. It's a good in formation source, not only for Geelong, but fe the entire Great Ocean Road; open daily 1 a.m.-4 p.m. (tel. 03-5275-5797). Also, the Na tional Wool Museum has a good deal c brochures, as well as books for sale. Th **DC&NR** office is at the corner of Fenwick an Little Malop Streets (tel. 03-5226-4667).

BELLARINE PENINSULA

The Bellarine Peninsula, a wide thumb of lan▉ extends into Port Phillip Bay southeast of Gee long. A popular holiday destination for Melbu nians, it has great fishing, scuba diving, an▉ some protected beaches. The peninsula's mai access is along the Bellarine Highway, whic ends at the historic seaport of Queenscliff. regularly scheduled car and passenger ferr plies the narrow opening to Port Phillip Bay linking Queenscliff to Sorrento on the Morninç ton Peninsula, making a 200-km round-the-ba excursion possible.

On the peninsula's northern tip is the sma township of **Portarlington.** The massive three tiered flour mill there dates to the 1850s and i open for inspection Sunday 2-5 p.m. **Portar lington Public Reserve** has the state's larges campground with 1,250 sites ranging $16-2 (tel. 03-5259-2764).

Queenscliff

The settlement of Queenscliff grew from a pilo station set up to guide ships heading through th treacherous waters between the Bellarine an▉ Mornington Peninsulas. In the 1880s the tow became popular with those who struck it ric▉ on the goldfields. Many buildings from that era have been restored and the seaside holiday vil lage atmosphere remains. A fort, built in 1870 t▉ repel a perceived Russian invasion, overlook▉ the bay. It's open for tours Mon.-Fri. at 2 p.m and Sat.-Sun. at 1 and 3 p.m. The tour cost of $2 also includes admission to Victoria's only blac▉ lighthouse.

During summer plenty of tourist-orientated activities happen in and around town. The most popular of these is **Bellarine Tourist Railway** (tel. 03-5258-2069), which runs between Queenscliff and Drysdale every Sunday at 10:30 a.m. and 2:40 p.m. Round-trip fare is adult $10, child $5. North from the main pier, on Weeroona Parade, is **Marine Studies Centre** (tel. 03-5258-3344), which operates a program of cruises and activities, such as swimming with seals, throughout summer. Next door is **Queenscliff Maritime Centre** (tel. 03-5258-3440), housing displays of the area's shipping history. Open Sat.-Sun. and daily during school holidays 10:30 a.m.-4:30 p.m. On the same street is **Bellarine Bike Hire** (tel. 03-5258-1747), and over the narrow bridge, on Swan Island, is **Queenscliff Golf Club** (tel. 03-5252-1951).

For a seaside holiday resort, Queenscliff is surprisingly free of motels, but there are many good alternatives. The grandest place to stay in Queenscliff is **Vue Grand** (tel. 03-5258-1544). This historic hotel overlooking the heads has been extensively restored with all modern facilities, an elegant dining room, and simple but well-furnished rooms. Rates for bed and breakfast are $105 s, $180 d, but often midweek packages including dinner are offered. In the same central area, and from the same era, is the large **Ozone Hotel** (tel. 03-5258-1011), where rooms with shared facilities are $50 s, $85 d including breakfast. **Queenscliff Inn,** 59 Hesse St. (tel. 03-5258-3737), is an Edwardian guesthouse with a relaxing atmosphere; private rooms are $45 s, $70-85 d, and dorm beds are $20 pp; all rates include breakfast. The closest camping to town is **Recreation Reserve Camping Area,** along the foreshore. Sites are $14-22. **Beacon Resort Caravan Park,** toward Point Lonsdale, is more modern and has better facilities. Sites here are $15-22 and cabins are $36-45.

Casual eateries are spread along Hesse Street. None stand out, although the **Ozone Hotel,** 42 Gellibrand St. (tel. 03-5258-1931), has good bar meals from $6 and a larger menu in the Boat Bar, decorated with historical photographs. More formal are **Miettas** in the Queenscliff Hotel (tel. 03-5258-1066) and the elegant dining room in Vue Grand.

McHarry's Bus Line (tel. 03-5223-2111) has a regular service between Geelong and Queenscliff. *Peninsula Princess* (tel. 03-5258-3244) is a car and passenger ferry making six to 12 trips daily from Queenscliff to Sorrento on the Mornington Peninsula. Fares vary with the season but are, in high season (summer), $32 for a car and $70 for the average motorhome. Adults are an extra $3, children $2 (double that for passengers without a car); no reservations taken.

Queenscliff to Torquay

Point Lonsdale, another popular summer resort, is linked to Queenscliff by a long sandy beach. From the lighthouse on the headland, views extend to Mornington Peninsula, and, if you're lucky, you'll be able to see ships negotiate the treacherous waters of "The Rip."

In 1835, when a group of Europeans, the first to visit the area for over 30 years, were preparing to establish a settlement on Port Phillip Bay, they were amazed to come across a white man. He was William Buckley, an escaped convict who had spent 30 years in the area, much of this time in a cave below the lighthouse.

West of Point Lonsdale are the seaside resort communities of **Ocean Grove** and **Barwon Heads.** Both have good beaches, fishing, and scuba diving. Barwon Heads has a great golf course; call (03) 5254-2302 for tee times.

TORQUAY

Surf City

Outside of Hawaii, few towns in the world can claim surfing as their major industry. But Torquay (tor-KEY) can. With a population of 5,000, Torquay lies 90 km southwest of Melbourne. All the town's beaches and reefs have waves for all surfers, but it's **Bells Beach,** southwest of town, which is most famous. In 1949, when Vic Tantau and Owen Yateman first surfed the waves at Bells Beach, they would have had little idea that surfing would hold the key to Torquay's future. Its large swells from the Southern Ocean and sandy shallows strewn with reefs form consistently perfect waves. Surfers from around the world gather here to ride the long right-handed wave at Bells and other sublime ripples at nearby points such as **Winkipop.** But it is Eastertime's **Bells Surfing Classic,** the world's longest running professional surfing competition, that draws the biggest crowd.

Surfing now plays an important role in Torquay's economy. Two surf-clothing companies, **Quiksilver** and **Rip Curl,** were started by local surfers and are today world leaders in innovative surfwear. Both have factory outlets in Torquay, along with a dozen other surf-related companies, in **Surf Coast Plaza,** on Surf Coast Highway. Also here is **Surfworld Australia** (tel. 03-5261-4606), Australia's only surfing museum. The museum delves into surfing's roots, from the styles and attitudes of Australia's earliest boardriders to today's top professionals, through audiovisuals and hands-on interactive displays. Open daily 9 a.m.-5 p.m.; admission adult $5, child $2.50.

If you feel like surfing, **No Limitz,** in Surf Coast Plaza (tel. 03-5261-6106), rents boards and wetsuits.

Accommodations

The best value of Torquay's three motels is **Surf City Motel,** 35 The Esplanade (tel. 03-5261-3492), where the large rooms are loaded with modern facilities and the beach is only a short walk away; from $68 s, $79 d. The heritage-style **Freshwater Green Country House** is a more relaxing alternative, and only slightly more expensive. Each luxuriously appointed room has a private entry. As well, guests have use of a large lounge area with open fire (complete with homemade cakes, tea, and coffee) and the elevated spa. Located at 2265 Hendy Main Rd. (tel. 03-5261-3366) in the township of Bellbrae, west of Torquay.

Bernell Caravan Park, Surf Coast Hwy. (tel. 03-5261-2493), is the pick of Torquay's four campgrounds; sites start at $17 and cabins are $39-88.

Food

Without a doubt, **Mussels,** corner Boston and Pearl Streets (tel. 03-5261-6198), is the best place in Torquay for fish and chips. The fish is always super-fresh and fried in a light batter, and the chips (about $4) are cooked to perfection. For the extra hungry the Classic Ocean Fish Pack ($6.90) would fulfill even the most voracious appetite. Gilbert St. is the main shopping strip, with a large supermarket, bakery, butcher, and a few cafes. **Yummy Yoghurt,** at the bottom end of Gilbert St., is a popular local hangout for light, healthy snacks, and, judging by the comments scribbled on the walls, many professional surfers think so too.

TORQUAY TO WARRNAMBOOL

Before a road connected the string of towns between Torquay and Apollo Bay, the only coastal access was rough tracks over the Otway Ranges from farmlands of southern Victoria. As servicemen returned from WW I they were offered work constructing a coastal road. The vast undertaking commenced in 1919, taking three years to reach Eastern View, where the commemorative arch is located. It took another 1 years to complete, but was still only a rough and dusty one-way track between steep cliff and the raging ocean. One journalist of the time noted that ". . . it was beauty, but at present there is too much thrill in it." Over the years the road has been sealed, and many of the more dangerous bends eliminated.

Anglesea

Point Roadknight juts into Bass Strait just south of Anglesea, protecting a long, curved bay where the holiday town of Anglesea lies. The town straddles **Anglesea River,** which cuts deeply through the hills of the hinterland. At the river's delta is **Coogoorah Nature Park,** an area offering nature walks, safe canoeing, fishing, barbecues, and an adventure playground. **Anglesea Golf Course** is home to a large population of kangaroos that freely roam the course. The course is open to the public and green fees are $20; located on a hill above town off Noble St (tel. 03-5263-1582).

The 70-year-old timber **Debonair Guest house & Motel,** Great Ocean Rd. (tel. 03-5263-1440), is the best value accommodation in town It has a restaurant, pool, tennis court, and laundry, but rooms are very basic; $44 s, $54 d. Another cheapie is **Ocean Rd. Motel,** 4 Noble St (tel. 03-5263-1364), with rooms for $35 s, $45 d **Anglesea Family Caravan Park** is close to both the ocean and river mouth. It has sites for $12 and great little wooden cabins for $45 s or d. Located on Cameron Rd. (tel. 03-5263-1583).

Diana's Riverbank Restaurant, 113 Great Ocean Rd. (tel. 03-5263-2500), in a small cottage by the river, has a small but varied menu; main meals start at $13. For bistro meals head **Anglesea Hotel,** just off the main road at 1 Church Crescent (tel. 03-5263-1210).

Aireys Inlet

Aireys Inlet, a seaside holiday town, has the forest-covered hills of Angahook-Lorne State Park as a backdrop. The town grew as the turn-around point of Melbourne's Cobb & Co. coach service, and in later years, after **Split Point Lighthouse** was constructed in 1891, many wooden holiday cottages sprang up around the protected inlet. Most of the older houses were destroyed by ravaging Ash Wednesday bushfires in 1983, and the town has since been rebuilt. Although the lighthouse isn't open to the public, the point on which it sits is the start of many coastal walks. Behind the lighthouse is **Lighthouse Keepers Inn** (tel. 03-5289-6306). These historic cottages are self-contained and spread through a well-manicured garden. All the old lighthouse outbuildings have been put to use—the old stone stables are now a cafe where lunch and afternoon teas are served daily 10 a.m.-6 p.m.

Lorne and Vicinity

For most of the year Lorne, at the mouth of the Erskine River, is a quiet seaside town, but each summer hordes of Melburnians descend on the town; accommodation is at a premium, the roads are jammed with cars, and the footpaths and beaches are crammed with people. The town developed early this century, housing timber cutters working in the surrounding forest, and has grown into a popular holiday getaway. On the main street, opposite the Commonwealth Bank, is a display of historical photos from the days of the Great Ocean Road's construction.

Behind town is **Angahook-Lorne State Park.** This hilly 22,000-hectare park traps a large amount of rainfall, which enables it to support lush forests of ferns and blue gums. Most of the park's 50 km of walking trails follow tramways built by timber cutters. From Lorne there are two main access roads into the park along which the network of walking trails begin. For details of these, picnic areas, and campgrounds head to the DC&NR office in Lorne, located at 56 Polwarth Rd. (tel. 03-5289-1732).

The **Grand Pacific Hotel,** Great Ocean Rd. (tel. 03-5289-1609), may not be that grand anymore, but views from many of the rooms are stunning; from $55 s, $65 d. **Motel Kalimna** is on the same high hill overlooking the ocean and has a tennis court, pool, restaurant, and bar. The rooms are plain but spacious and each has a balcony; $64 s, $74 d (tel. 03-5289-1407). **Erskine House,** at the other end of town, is a 1930s guesthouse with rooms starting at $40 s, $80 d including breakfast; located at 136 Mountjoy Parade (tel. 03-5289-1209). A short stroll from downtown and the beach, **Great Ocean Road Backpackers,** Erskine Ave. (tel. 03-5289-1809), is a number of modern timber cottages set among native bushland. Dorm beds are $15-18 pp. **Erskine River Caravan Park** is located in town, right by the river, and has tent sites from $12 and cabins for $35. A lot quieter, but three km south of town, is **Cumberland River Reserve,** in a pleasant bush setting. The Lorne Foreshore Committee (tel. 03-5289-1382) takes booking for these campgrounds, or you can stay in one of seven camping areas in the surrounding state park.

Finding a place to eat in Lorne is easy enough; finding a table during summer is a different matter. Some eateries, such as **The Arab,** Great Ocean Rd. (tel. 03-5289-1435), have been around for decades and have become institutions, while others come and go with the summer crowds. **The Seafood Restaurant** (tel. 03-5289-1119), below the Grand Pacific Hotel, has stunning views of the bay and forested hills beyond. This stylish eatery is fairly casual, but expensive; open daily for breakfast, lunch, and dinner. Also on the pier is a cooperative selling fresh seafood.

Lorne Information Centre, 144 Mountjoy Parade (tel. 03-5289-2709), has a small amount of information on the town but mainly functions as a booking agency for accommodations; open daily 9 a.m.-5 p.m.

Lorne to Apollo Bay

Between these two townships, the Great Ocean Road is at its most spectacular as it hugs the ocean, backed by steep cliffs on one side and the powerful Southern Ocean on the other.

Along the route are a number of small settlements, sandy beaches, gravel roads heading inland, and lookouts.

Just beyond Kennett River is **Whitecrest** (tel. 03-5237-0228), a luxurious accommodation on a gentle slope overlooking the ocean. Each unit is split-level, with a large dining, kitchen, and lounge area, opening to a private balcony on one level and the comfortable double bed on the other. Rates range $65-125 s or d.

Apollo Bay

The long curving beach around Apollo Bay is the setting of a picturesque fishing town of the same name. The wide beach in front of the township is lined with cypress trees, and the bay's protected waters are perfect for swimming. The bay was named after the schooner *Apollo,* which carried wool from Port Fairy to Melbourne in the 1840s. In those days Point Bunbury, which protects the bay from heavy swells, was the site of a whaling station, a far cry from the grassy fairways of today's Apollo Bay Golf Course, one of the most picturesque courses in Victoria. The treacherous sea off Apollo Bay has claimed several large ships. Relics from these wrecks, as well as other local memorabilia, are housed in a small museum located in an old cable station on the Great Ocean Rd.; open Sat.-Sun., and daily during school holidays, 2-5 p.m.

If you plan on spending $70-100 on accommodation in Apollo Bay, don't think of staying anywhere but **Seafarers.** Set on eight hectares of land that slope gently to the ocean, it offers rooms with amazing ocean views, enjoyed from within glass-fronted ocean aspects and private balconies. Each has a kitchen and some have fireplaces. The property even boasts a trout pond—the perfect chance to catch dinner. Located three km east of town (tel. 03-5237-6507). Very central **Apollo Bay Motel,** Moore St. (tel. 03-5237-6492), has well-furnished rooms for $60 s, $70 d. In front is **Apollo Bay Hotel** (tel. 03-5237-6250), where motel-style rooms are slightly cheaper. **Waratah Caravan Park,** 7 Noel St. (tel. 03-5237-6562), has reasonable campsites for $13 and basic on-site vans for $31.

Otway National Park

The **Otway Ranges** rise west of Lorne and run parallel to the coast, branching south to Cape Otway and west to the vicinity of Lavers H[?] The 12,750-hectare Otway National Park pr[?] tects the southern arm of the range, where [?] ends at a rugged peninsula of sandstone cli[?] and sandy beaches. The backdrop for this spe[?] tacular coastline is of luxuriant blue gum, gre[?] gum, and towering mountain ash forests, whic[?] form a dense canopy protecting an understory [?] ferns and pockets of cool-temperate rainfores[?] Over 250 species of birds and 45 species [?] mammals have been recorded in the park. C[?] particular interest are the birds that visit the pa[?] while migrating, including the Japanese snip[?] and fluttering shearwater from Eurasia. Th[?] main access road into the park leads 15 k[?] from the Great Ocean Rd. to Cape Otway.

Sailors kept well clear of the treacherous Cap[?] Otway until 1848, when a lighthouse was bu[?] on the remote headland. The stone structur[?] stands to this day, in testimony to the quality [?] convict labor. The lighthouse grounds are ope[?] Tuesday, Thursday, Saturday, and Sunday, wit[?] tours offered hourly; adult $5, child $2. At othe[?] times you can't get to the cape, but a track lead[?] along the cliff to some impressive ocean views[?] The first turnoff from the Melbourne side of th[?] park leads to **Shelly Beach Picnic Area** fro[?] where a trail leads down to the mouth of the Ellio[?] River, providing access to the rugged coast.

Within the park are two campgrounds, eac[?] with basic facilities and fresh water. The one a[?] Blanket Bay is sheltered from southerly wind[?] and is near a sandy beach. For park informa[?] tion and to book camping sites drop by th[?] DC&NR office in Apollo Bay, corner of Cartwrigh[?] and Nelson Streets (tel. 03-5237-6889). The[?] only other accommodation on the cape is avail[?] able in the assistant lightkeeper's sandston[?] cottages, built in the 1850s and still retainin[?] their historic charm. Rates in the one-bedroor[?] cottages are $40-50 during the week and $55-6[?] on weekends, while the entire four-bedroor[?] house starts at $100 per night. For reservation[?] call (03) 5237-9240.

Johanna

Johanna is a windswept coastal community c[?] holiday cottages spread haphazardly along the[?] Johanna River and protected from the brunt o[?] Southern Ocean storms by scrub-covered sand[?] dunes. The shifting sand bars of Johanna's beach[?]

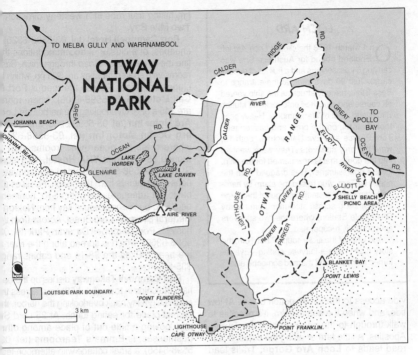

OTWAY NATIONAL PARK

TO MELBA GULLY AND WARRNAMBOOL

JOHANNA BEACH

JOHANNA BEACH

GREAT OCEAN RD.

GLENAIRE

LAKE HORDEN

LAKE CRAVEN

AIRE RIVER

CALDER RIDGE RD.

CALDER RIVER

CALDER RD.

RIVER

RANGES

OTWAY

LIGHTHOUSE RD.

PARKER RIVER

PARKER RIVER RD.

GREAT OCEAN RD.

ELLIOTT RIVER RD.

ELLIOTT RD.

SHELLY BEACH PICNIC AREA

BLANKET BAY

POINT LEWIS

POINT FLINDERS

= OUTSIDE PARK BOUNDARY

0   3 km

LIGHTHOUSE CAPE OTWAY

POINT FRANKLIN

TO APOLLO BAY

GREAT OCEAN RD.

re famous among surfers for the heavy waves that consistently roll onto shore. You'll want to check the weather forecast before setting up camp at the semi-official campground behind the beach—it's unprotected from the wind.

Melba Gully

Located southwest of the hilltop community of Lavers Hill, this grove is part of a 65-hectare park that protects an area of lush tree ferns, covered by a canopy of myrtle, beech, and eucalypt. A short nature walk leads through this green wonderland to the cleverly named **Big Tree,** a 300-year-old messmate eucalypt measuring an incredible 27 meters in circumference. The park is also known for **glowworms,** best seen on tours offered by park staff each evening during summer school holidays.

tree fern

Port Campbell National Park

From **Princetown** to Peterborough, at the mouth of the Curdies River, the Great Ocean Road passes through 1,750-hectare Port Campbell National Park, a narrow strip of coast that is among the most photographed in the country. The relentless power of the Southern Ocean has carved innumerable gorges, arches, caves, and a large number of offshore stacks along limestone cliffs rising from the ocean.

Traveling from the east, the first of these dramatic formations is also the most photographed—the **Twelve Apostles.** The offshore stacks were once part of the headland, but as wave action eroded softer parts of the rock, they became separated from the mainland and, one day, will succumb completely to the power of the ocean. Just east of the Apostles is **Gibson's Steps,** cut into the cliffs by early settlers to pro-

LOCH ARD

On 1 March 1878 the clipper *Loch Ard* left England bound for Australia. She was carrying 54 passengers and a hull full of general cargo. Just 90 days later, at the entrance to Bass Strait, tragedy struck as the ship veered off course and smashed onto rocks off Mutton Bird Island, east of Warrnambool. Heavy seas took their toll on the crew and passengers; Tom Pearce and Eva Carmichael, both 18, were the only survivors. They were washed into the gorge that is now named for the ship. Eva, a non-swimmer, was dragged from the ocean by Tom, who raised the alarm by heroically climbing the steep cliffs out of the gorge and stumbling across stockmen from nearby Glenample Station, where the two survivors subsequently recuperated.

And what of the lucky couple? For Tom, the story didn't have a fairytale ending—Eva returned to Ireland and married someone else.

vide access to the sandy beach below. At low tide, and when the sea is calm, it's possible to walk through to the beach behind the Twelve Apostles. A little farther along the coast, a side road leads to **Loch Ard Gorge.** Trails lead around the gorge to a small cemetery and then down to the beach.

Port Campbell

Port Campbell is a small township at the back of a protected harbor, the only spot along this stretch of coast where boats can be safely moored. The town was established as a base for sealers and whalers and has grown into a service center for the masses of tourists traveling the Great Ocean Road. Along Lord St., the main drag through town, are motels, cafes, takeaways, and other service shops. **Loch Ard Shipwreck Museum,** Lord St. (tel. 03-5598-6463), has an interesting array of treasures salvaged from shipwrecks along the coast and details of five major wrecks and subsequent salvage operations; open in summer daily 9 a.m.-5 p.m. **Olde Hall Gallery,** just down the road, has more of the same, as well as local arts and crafts for sale (closed Tuesday and Friday). From the beach at the back of the harbor a 2.6-

km hiking trail runs in a westerly direction **Two Mile Bay.**

Port Campbell Hotel (tel. 03-5598-6320) cheapest of a cluster of accommodations th line the Great Ocean Road through town. Bas rooms with shared facilities are $25 pp, which i cludes breakfast. Across the road is **Port** **Call Motel** (tel. 03-5598-6206), where room are $45 s or d. Overlooking the harbor are **Loc Ard Motor Inn** (tel. 03-5598-6238) and **Sout ern Ocean Motor Inn** (tel. 03-5598-6231 where rates for ocean-view rooms start around $84. **Tregea YHA Hostel,** 18 Trege St. (tel. 03-5598-6379), is a partially renovate house 200 meters from the beach. Facilities a basic but adequate; members $10, nonmer bers $11; book and collect a key from **Nelson General Store** on Lord Street. Across from th hostel is **Port Campbell Caravan Park** (tel. 0: 5598-6369), which is spread along the river ' the beach. Sites are $8-14 and cabins rang $35-50.

Port Campbell Takeaway dishes up the be fish and chips in town ($4-4.50), and across th road is a grassy bank overlooking the harbor, th perfect place for eating lunch. At 25 Lord St and looking a little out of place among othe businesses, is **Emma's Tearooms** (tel. 0: 5598-6458), a small cottage with afternoon tea from $4 and main meals from $9; reservation essential in the evening. For finer dining **Napier's** (tel. 03-5598-6231), in the Souther Ocean Motor Inn, is recommended and ove looks the harbor.

The Port Campbell Caravan Park operates variety of tours including: along the coast ($25 to a local wildlife park ($25), and an evenin trip to the glowworms of Melba Gully ($15). Fc details call (03) 5598-6369.

The **Park Information Centre,** Morris St. (te 03-5598-6382), has displays on the park's fa mous natural features along with relics fron various shipwrecks, including an anchor sal vaged from the ill-fated *Loch Ard.* The 12-minute audiovisual is also worthwhile. Open daily a.m.-5 p.m.

London Bridge and Vicinity

Another of Port Campbell National Park's fa mous natural features is **London Bridge,** wes of Port Campbell. On 15 January 1990, the

andward arch of London Bridge collapsed into
he sea, forming another offshore stack and
eaving two rather surprised tourists wondering
now to get off. Just to the east is **The Arch**
and to the west, **The Grotto** and **Bay of Is-**
ands.

At the mouth of Curdies Inlet, and marking the
western boundary of Port Campbell National Park,
is the windswept fishing and holiday village of
Peterborough, which has good fishing in a protected inlet, a nine-hole golf course along the cliff
edge, and camping in a small reserve by the river.

VICTORIA'S SOUTHWEST COAST

For ships sailing between England and Australia in the 19th century, sailing along Victoria's
southwest coast and negotiating Bass Strait
was the first hazardous navigation they had to
do after Cape Horn, and many wrecked. A lighthouse constructed on Cape Otway in 1848 did
little to alleviate the problem—ships hugging
the coast looking for the light more often than not
ended up on the rocks. Although time has ravaged many of the wrecks, coastal communities
still have strong ties to their maritime heritage.
Warrnambool has the excellent Flagstaff Hill
Maritime Museum, and to the west is the quiet
fishing town of Port Fairy. West of Port Fairy
and the deepwater port city of Portland are the
long sandy beaches of Discovery Bay, into
which the Glenelg River flows, protected in its
lower reaches by Lower Glenelg National Park,
which offers the perfect opportunity for a wilderness canoe adventure.

WARRNAMBOOL AND VICINITY

Since 1802, when the French navigator Nicholas
Baudin noted the site as suitable for a lighthouse and as having a sheltered harbor, Warrnambool's links to the ocean have been strong.
The bay was originally settled as a sealing and
whaling station but grew as an important transportation link with the wool and grain industry of
Victoria's western district. The city has since
grown to be one of Victoria's largest coastal
cities, yet retains much of its historic charm and
laid-back, holiday atmosphere.

Flagstaff Hill Maritime Museum
Flagstaff Hill, overlooking Lady Bay, is a recreation of a 19th-century port and definitely
shouldn't be missed. Once inside the grounds, it
takes little imagination to feel you've stepped

back in time. The complex catalogs Australia's
entire seafaring history and is continually expanding, with additional relics salvaged from
shipwrecks displayed each year. Some of the
buildings are original, including the lighthouse
and lightkeeper's cottage. Fortifications and cannons, put in place in 1887 to fend off a perceived
Russian invasion, are in their original position.
The other buildings have been constructed using
authentic materials and methods. Many of the
shops and storehouses are open, and hundreds
of items salvaged from shipwrecks are spread
throughout the grounds, including a large and
colorful porcelain peacock that was en route to
Melbourne from London aboard the ill-fated *Loch*
Ard. Many smaller pieces are displayed in a
small shipwreck museum. Watch a movie in the
village's theater; all are seafaring classics. The
village fronts a small lake where two restored
ships float. Also within the grounds are various
gift shops, a restaurant, and a bar. The complex is open daily 9 a.m.-5 p.m., and admission
is adult $9.50, child $4. Located on Merri St. (tel.
03-5564-7841).

Other Sights
Warrnambool's main natural attraction is the
wild Southern Ocean. **Lady Bay** (Warrnambool
Bay) is sheltered and has safe swimming off
Pertobe Rd., which begins near Flagstaff Hill
and heads past a cluster of campgrounds and
picnic areas to a breakwall, which provides protection for a fleet of fishing boats. The wall is
popular for fishing and provides a panoramic
view of the city and beaches to the east.
    Mahogany Walking Track, a 22-km (one-
way) trail linking Warrnambool to Port Fairy, is
well marked and can be accessed from various
points, enabling walkers to do just one section of
it. The trail is named for a mysterious mahogany
ship reported to be hidden under shifting sand

WARRNAMBOOL

TO TOWER HILL AND PORT FAIRY

RAGLAN PARADE

FITZROY RD.

BOTANIC RD.

COLONIAL VILLAGE MOTEL

MORTLAKE RD.

MOORE ST.

CYPRESS DRIVE

LAVA ST.
KOROIT ST.
TIMOR ST.

HYLAND ST.

WELLINGTON ST.
YOUNGER ST.

MERRI RIVER

FAIRY ST.
MERRI ST.
KEPLER ST.
LIEBIG ST.
BANYAN ST.

TOURIST INFORMATION CENTRE

SEE DETAIL

TO ALLANSFORD CHEESEWORLD AND GREAT OCEAN RD.

RAGLAN PARADE (PRINCES HWY.)

WARRNAMBOOL GOLF CLUB

RAILWAY STATION

OLDE MARITIME MOTOR INN

NICHOLSON ST.

FLAXMAN ST.

HOPKINS RIVER

MAHOGANY

WALKING TRACK

LAKE PERTOBE

LAKE PERTOBE ADVENTURE PLAYGROUND

PERTOBE RD.

MAHOGANY SHIP RESTAURANT

SURFSIDE HOLIDAY PARK

FLAGSTAFF HILL MARITIME MUSEUM

HOPKINS POINT RD.

LADY BAY

LOGANS BEACH RD.

LOGANS BEACH

SOUTHERN OCEAN

MERRI ISLAND
MIDDLE ISLAND

BREAKWALL

0   1 km

DETAIL

HOTEL WARRNAMBOOL

KOROIT ST.

ROYAL HOTEL

TIMOR ST.

FAIRY ST.
KEPLER ST.

LAUNDROMAT

GOOD FOOD DELI

LIEBIG ST.

GALLERY NIGHTCLUB

SHAZ SUES

COLLINS BOOKSELLERS

AMARANTS

WHALERS INN

POST OFFICE

PERFORMING ARTS CENTER

WARRNAMBOOL ART GALLERY

---

dunes. If you stumble across it, you will rewrite Australia's history, as many historians believe it predates the discovery of Australia by Captain Cook by 250 years.

Warrnambool Art Gallery, 165 Timor St. (tel. 03-5564-7832), features a large collection of Australian works, from colonial to contemporary, including Thomas Clark's "The Mahogany Ship." Admission is $2.50. The gallery is open Tues.-Fri. 10 a.m.-4 p.m. and weekends noon-5 p.m.

Allansford Cheeseworld, 10 km east of Warrnambool (tel. 03-5565-1209), is a large cheese-tasting and restaurant complex. The center is open Mon.-Sat. and admission is free.

Recreation and Events

The 18-hole **Warrnambool Golf Course** is o Younger St. (tel. 03-5562-2108). **Cypress Drive** on Moore St., is a multi-use facility with tenni courts and a nine-hole golf course; $3 all day **Lake Pertobe Adventure Playground,** on Pe tobe Rd., rents kayaks, canoes, and paddle boats, and has a maze, and small lakes stocke with fish; open holidays and weekends.

The **Wunta Festival,** held each February, ce ebrates the town's close ties to the ocean with wine and seafood fair, whaleboat race, and mus concert. The **May Racing Carnival** features Aus tralia's longest horse race, a 5.5-km steeplechase

SOUTHERN RIGHT WHALE

Five species of right whales *(Balaenidae)* are found in the world's oceans, but they were hunted to near-extinction last century. They were easy to hunt—a slow swimmer, preferring shallow water to breed, and floating when killed—and had a high yield of baleen; hence the name, southern *right* whale. Today, although the species has been protected for over 60 years, fewer than 2,000 survive worldwide.

Although their population is not dramatically increasing, a small number migrate to the waters around Warrnambool to bear their young. They occasionally arrive as early as May, but are most often seen July-October. At **Logans Beach,** across the Hopkins River from Warrnambool, a viewing platform allows you to view the whales. Bring binoculars—they stay well away from shore.

BOB RACE

Accommodations

None of the hotels in Warrnambool's downtown core are particularly appealing, but if you're looking for a cheap and central place to stay try **Royal Hotel,** corner Timor and Fairy Streets (tel. 03-5562-2063), for $15 pp, including a self-serve breakfast, or **Hotel Warrnambool,** corner Koroit and Kepler Streets (tel. 03-5562-2377), for $30 s, $50-60 d. The best of 20-odd motels is **Olde Maritime Motor Inn,** corner Banyan and Merri Streets (tel. 03-5561-1415), which is very central, has large well-furnished rooms, and is a reasonable $65-120 s, $75-120 d. A good standby is **Colonial Village Motel,** 31 Mortlake Rd. (tel. 03-5562-455), a couple of km from downtown. It has limited cooking facilities in each room and a tennis court, barbecue, and laundry; $40-65 s, $46-85 d.

Surfside Holiday Park (tel. 03-5561-2611) is a sprawling campground spread out behind the dunes of Lady Bay's main swimming beach and is one km from town. The park has all the usual facilities with sites $19 in summer and $12-15 during the rest of the year—a bit rich considering they also have coin-operated show-

ers. The cabins there are of a high quality and range $45-80.

Food and Entertainment

A huge range of eateries is on Liebig St., between Koroit and Timor Streets. **Whalers Inn,** 53 Liebig St. (tel. 03-5562-8391), is an old pub that has had its insides ripped out, literally, giving it a bright airy feeling around an indoor courtyard. At lunch and dinner, bistro-style meals start at $5, with the salad bar an extra $2. The **Royal Hotel,** corner of Timor and Fairy Streets (tel. 03-5562-2063), is another hotel with good meals—the buffet runs every lunch and dinner and costs $10. **Shaz Sues,** 92 Liebig St. (tel. 03-5562-0367), serves wholesome meals from $2.50 and aptly named Doorstop Sandwiches from $5. Across the road is **Good Food Deli,** serving similar meals. A good choice for more substantial fare is **Amarants,** 158 Timor St. (tel. 03-5561-3833). It offers a variety of pastas (around $8) as well as steak and seafood; open Mon.-Sat. from 6 p.m. The **Mahogany Ship,** Merri St. (tel. 03-5561-1833), has tremendous views over Flagstaff Hill Maritime Museum and Lady Bay. The bar serves light, simple meals for up to $10, while the more formal restaurant is more expensive.

Gallery Nightclub, 214 Timor St. (tel. 03-5562-0741), is the town's only nightspot and hosts live bands or disco Wed.-Sunday. The beer garden there is popular on Sunday. The Mahogany Ship (see above) also has occasional live music but is a great place to have a drink at any time. Warrnambool also has a **performing arts center** on Timor St. (tel. 03-5564-7904).

Transportation, Services, and Information

Trains run daily between Melbourne and Warrnambool ($31.80 one-way) terminating at the V/Line station on Merri St. (tel. 03-5564-7166). From there buses head west to Port Fairy ($3.60 one-way), Portland ($11.40), and into South

Australia; north to Ballarat ($16.80); and, on Friday only, east along the coast to Apollo Bay ($19.40). For a cab call **Warrnambool Taxis** (tel. 03-5561-1114).

At 234 Timor St. there's a **laundromat** open daily till 10 p.m. **Collins Booksellers,** 99 Liebig St. (tel. 03-5562-4272), has a large selection of Australiana literature, or for local material head to the gift shop at Flagstaff Hill.

Warrnambool Tourist Information Centre, 600 Raglan Parade (tel. 03-5564-7837), is open in summer daily 9 a.m.-5 p.m., daily 10 a.m.-4 p.m. the rest of the year. Ask about their interesting audiovisual display on southern right whales. *Warrnambool Visitors Handbook* (free) is an excellent resource listing everything there is to do, see, and eat in town.

Tower Hill

Tower Hill, about midway between Warrnambool and Port Fairy, is Victoria's largest and most recent volcano. The rim of the crater is only slightly higher than the surrounding farmland, but inside is a system of lakes, wetlands, and plenty of native flora and fauna. Early settlers devastated the crater's vegetation and most animals within its walls. In 1961 the crater was declared a **state game reserve,** and since then 250,000 native trees have been planted and many native animals re-introduced. On the loop road that encircles one lake, you have a good chance of seeing emus, kangaroos, wombats, and echidnas. Along the way are many lookouts, a bird-hide, picnic areas, and the **Natural History Centre;** open daily 9:30 a.m.-4:30 p.m. (tel. 03-5565-9202).

PORT FAIRY

One of Victoria's oldest ports, Port Fairy is home to a large fishing fleet and maintains the historic atmosphere of an old seaport. Port Fairy originated as a whaling and sealing station in the 1830s, but as whale and seal numbers became depleted, the population turned to fishing and farming for a livelihood. By 1860 over 2,000 people lived in the area, making the town one of the largest in rural Victoria.

Port Fairy's Victorian character has been preserved. More than 50 buildings date from that era, and seamen's bluestone cottages are scattered among veranda-fronted civic buildings. Many of the pubs still retain their charm, including the **Caledonian Hotel,** where the still-unfinished rooms show how workers there left for the goldfields in a great hurry.

Sights

Along the **Moyne River,** which separates the center of town from the beach, is a long boardwalk where fishing boats and pleasure cruisers tie up. An old wooden footbridge crosses the river farther upstream and leads to safe swimming at Port Fairy Beach. The **History Walk** passes many of the National Trust-classified buildings; on each a plaque provides a brief history; brochures available at the information center will get you on your way. One place open to the public is the historic **Mott's Cottage** at 5 Sackville Street. It was built as a boardinghouse and is now refurnished in the Victorian style; open daily (except Tuesday) 10 a.m.-4 p.m. A small **museum** at 24 Bank St. has a good collection of local seafaring memorabilia. Open daily during school holidays 2-5 p.m., Wednesday, Saturday, and Sunday only the rest of the year. At the south end of Port Fairy Bay is **Battery Hill,** where, like other coastal settlements the town fortified itself against a Russian invasion; now only cannons remain.

Griffiths Island, across the Moyne River from Battery Hill, was once a whaling station but is now a wildlife reserve. The island is riddled with the nesting burrows of short-tailed shearwaters (commonly known as muttonbirds), which arrive to nest there in late September, lay eggs in January, and leave for Alaska in April. During their time on the island they feed in the ocean returning in the evening and providing a spectacular sight best appreciated from the island's viewing platform.

Port Fairy Folk Festival

This is Australia's largest folk festival, attracting national and international acts and, of course thousands of festival goers who descend on Port Fairy for the three-day Labour Day weekend in March. As well as musical performances enjoy the food festival, craft fair, parade, buskers and folk circus. For details and ticket reservations call (03) 5568-2227.

Accommodations

Of the 30-odd hotels that once graced Port Fairy's streets, only four of the originals remain. Each offers rooms of varying standards. **Star of the West Hotel,** Bank St. (tel. 03-5568-1715), has backpacker-style rooms for $12 pp. Of a higher standard is **Caledonian Hotel,** Bank St. (tel. 03-5568-1044), where rooms are $45 s, $55 d. Across the road from the bustle of Moyne River is **Merrijig Inn,** 1 Campbell St. (tel. 03-5568-2324), built in 1842 to house the travelers of last century. Each of the five rooms is tastefully decorated and has a private bathroom. Downstairs is a large lounge area with log fires and a conservatory that opens to a garden. The inn also has a restaurant and cozy bar. Rooms are $70 s, $90 d. **Hanley House,** 14 Sackville St. (tel. 03-5568-2709), is another historic home, this one built in the 1850s for the family of a local newspaper owner. The house has only three rooms, each with a log fire; $55 s, $85 d, which includes a cooked breakfast. **Seacombe House Motor Inn,** 22 Sackville St. (tel. 03-5568-1082), was built in 1847 and has basic rooms for $30 s, $40 d. Some modern motel-style rooms are tacked onto the side for $75 s, $80 d, and scattered through the grounds are bluestone cottages dating to 1853 for $130 s or d per night.

Port Fairy YHA, 8 Cox St. (tel. 03-5568-2468), is in an 1844 building, with dorm beds in the main house and a more modern addition out back. The hostel also has bikes and canoes for hire; dorm beds are $10 for members, $13 for nonmembers.

Gardens Reserve Caravan Park, 111 Griffiths St. (tel. 03-5568-1060), is the closest camping area to town and is only 100 meters from the beach. Tent sites are $10-12 and cabins start at $50.

Food

Belfast Bakery and Tearooms, on the main street, bakes delicious pies, pastries, and cakes. It has a number of tables for sit-down meals; open Mon.-Sat. 8:30 a.m.-5:30 p.m. **Lunch On Bank,** 20 Bank St. (tel. 03-5568-2642), is in the former town hall and serves simple bistro meals at reasonable prices. For bar meals try the **Caledonian Hotel** at 41 Bank Street. They have a wide selection of chicken and meat dishes starting at just $6, with soups for $2.

Merrijig Inn, 1 Campbell St. (tel. 03-5568-2324), has a great little restaurant furnished with Victorian-era antiques; main meals range $12-18. It's open daily in summer, and only on weekends the rest of the year, from 6 p.m. **Dublin House Inn,** 57 Bank St. (tel. 03-5568-1822), is another historic building with a restaurant, although a little more formal than the Merrijig Inn.

Transportation, Services, and Information

V/Line buses run daily from Port Fairy to the rail station in Warrnambool ($3.60), from where there are regular train connections to Melbourne. Buses also run west to Portland ($7.60), continuing into South Australia.

The **Tourist Information Centre** is on Bank St. (tel. 03-5568-2682); open in summer daily 9 a.m.-4 p.m.

PORTLAND

This industrial city of 11,500 is south of the Princes Highway, 265 km west of Melbourne. It's on the leeward side of a massive peninsula along which breakwalls have been constructed, providing protection for shipping. **Portland Port,** the only deepwater port between Melbourne and Adelaide, and a $2-billion **aluminum smelter** dominate the landscape.

A shore-based whaling station was established here in 1828, but it wasn't until the Henty family came ashore in 1834 that a permanent settlement developed, one year before the official settlement of Melbourne, making Portland Victoria's first permanent settlement. Throughout the city's commercial and urban development over 200 National Trust-listed buildings have survived.

Town Sights

A walking trail brochure, available from the Tourist Information Centre, is the easiest way to discover the historic buildings scattered around the city center. One of the few open to the public is the **Steam Packet Inn,** at 33 Bentinck Street. Completed in 1841, it functioned as a hotel, often of ill-repute, for much of the last century and is now one of Victoria's oldest buildings. The inn is open Thursday and Sunday 2-4 p.m., and admission is

$2. **Burswood,** 15 Cape Nelson Rd. (tel. 03-5523-4686), was built in 1850 for the city's first permanent resident, Edward Henty, and is surrounded by immaculate gardens, looking much as they did in Henty's days. The gardens are open daily 10 a.m.-5 p.m., and admission is $3. On Cliff St. are **botanic gardens,** developed in the 1850s, with hundreds of species of trees and shrubs from throughout the world. Also here is a historic bluestone cottage (open Sunday 1:30-3:30 p.m.).

Other Sights

A redeeming feature of Portland's industrial sprawl is that the coastal foreshore south and west of the city is protected from development. At **Point Danger,** the site of the aluminum smelter, a 2.2-km wheelchair-accessible nature walk has been developed. Farther west, directly offshore, is **St. Lawrence Rock,** home to a colony of over 5,000 Australasian gannets. Cape Nelson Rd. (Bentinck St. through town) leads to **Cape Nelson State Park,** where the lighthouse, built in 1883, is open for tours Tuesday and Thursday. Back at the intersection of Cape Nelson Rd. and Scenic Drive is the trailhead for a three-km walk through coastal scrub to a spectacular cliff lookout. Scenic Drive will take you to a number of barbecue areas and tracks that lead to the ocean.

Still farther west, along Bridgewater Rd., is the wide sandy beach of **Bridgewater Bay,** home to a colorful array of holiday cottages and the only surf club in the vicinity of Portland. At the beach's western end is the trailhead of a two-hour hike along the rocks and up a hill to a lookout, where seals and whales (Sept.-April) can be seen.

Bridgewater Rd. continues past the beach and climbs to a lookout where a short but rough trail leads to a **petrified forest.** The actual trees are long gone but a layer of stone formed around the trunks, slowly filling the trunks as the organic matter rotted, leaving "casts" of what scientists believe are moonah trees.

Accommodations

Mac's Hotel, 41 Bentinck St. (tel. 03-5523-2188), is right downtown and has basic pub rooms for $20 s, $30 d, and motel-style units next door for slightly higher rates. **Portland Inn,** 4 Percy St. (tel. 03-5523-2985), a two-story timber house built in the 1840s, has well-appointed rooms for

$45 s, $65 d, which includes a cooked breakfast and lunch. **Burswood,** 15 Cape Nelson Rd. (tel. 03-5523-4686), is the homestead built for Portland's first settler, Edward Henty, but has been extensively refurbished; $75 s, $95 d.

Of Portland's six caravan parks, **Centenary Caravan Park** is most central; tent sites $12-14 and cabins $42-50. **Henty Bay Caravan Park,** Dutton Way (tel. 03-5523-3716), is just north of town but has an excellent location, and the tent sites are set among native bush.

Food

On Julia St., which links the main drag to the waterfront, are many eateries worth checking out. There's an excellent bakery on one side of the road and opposite is **Pino's Pizza House** (tel. 03-5521-7388), which offers a wide selection of Italian dishes under $10. A little farther down the hill, in a historic commercial building, is **Shanty Bistro,** an old-world-style English pub with a simple blackboard menu and dishes averaging $10. Upstairs, with a similar atmosphere, is the more formal **Old Bond Store** (tel. 03-5523-3485). **Top of the Town** is a Lebanese restaurant on the corner of Julia and Percy Streets (tel. 03-5521-7469). The atmosphere is casual and the food and service impeccable.

Transportation, Services, and Information

Buses to Portland stop at the corner of Henty and Percy Streets. They run daily to Port Fairy ($7.60) and Warrnambool ($10.40) and west to South Australia. For bookings call **V/Line** at (03) 5525-0020.

The **Tourist Information Centre** is in a bluestone watchhouse built in 1850 on Cliff St. (tel. 03-5523-2671). Open Mon.-Fri. 9:30 a.m.-4:30 p.m., Sat.-Sun. 10 a.m.-3 p.m. The **DC&NR** is housed in offices on Julia St.; they have information on all state and national parks in this part of the state (tel. 03-5523-3232).

FAR SOUTHWEST COAST

Mount Richmond National Park

Mount Richmond, 23 km west of Portland, is an extinct volcano that erupted around two million years ago. Over the years sand from Discovery Bay has blown in and around the crater, covering all evidence of volcanic activity. The major clue to the mountain's origin is the lack of creeks and lakes—as quickly as it falls, rain soaks into the sandy and porous ground, settling only in low areas where swamps are formed. The park may only be 1,700 hectares, but, still, 450 species of plants have been recorded, including 50 species of orchids. This varied vegetation provides an ideal habitat for a variety of mammals, including eastern gray kangaroos, koalas, red-necked wallabies, and the rare **southern potoroo,** one of the smallest members of the kangaroo family.

From the picnic area along the main access road, short trails traverse the park's varied topography. It's a very short walk to the summit of Mt. Richmond (229 meters), where there are 360-degree views of Lady Julia Percy Island, Discovery Bay, and the Grampians. The two-km **Benwerrin Nature Walk** is a self-guided walk through a variety of vegetation.

Discovery Bay Coastal Park

The beach, dune system, wetlands, and coastal heathlands between Cape Bridgewater and Nelson, on the South Australia border, are protected by this narrow strip of park. The park has no "sights" as such, but spending time walking along the totally deserted beach (especially during the all-too-frequent storms) or exploring the wetland communities behind the high dunes is an enchanting experience. For those with more time, and the experience, the **Great South West Walk** loop may be worth considering. It begins from the Tourist Information Centre in Portland and makes a 250-km circuit along the coast, through Lower Glenelg National Park to South Australia and back to Portland. Of course it's possible to do sections of the track but 12-15 days should be allowed for the entire length. Along the route are 16 campsites, each with fresh water, toilets, and fireplaces. Car access and camping is possible at **Swan Lake,** 34 km from Portland, where grassy sites are a short walk from the lake and beach. Farther west, at **Lake Mombeong,** is another camping area.

Lower Glenelg National Park

The deep gorges, lush forest, and spectacular limestone caves of this 27,300-hectare park are in stark contrast to the windswept beaches of Discovery Bay immediately to the south. The park protects the final 40 km of the **Glenelg River,** which begins its journey in the Grampians and drains into the ocean at Nelson, a small fishing and holiday village at the west end of Discovery Bay. The river meanders through the park carving a gorge up to 50 meters deep into the limestone bedrock. The park's highlight is **Princess Margaret Rose Cave,** one of 60 known caves within the park. The caves formed when rainwater drained through the soft rock, eating away at the limestone over tens of thousands of years. Tours of the Princess Margaret Rose Cave are offered at various intervals daily, except Friday, and admission is adult $5, child $3. The short **River View Nature Walk** begins at the cave's entrance and winds through various sights relevant to the cave system before ending at a couple of lookouts high above the Glenelg River. The caves are only one small corner of the park; a network of unsealed roads both north and south of the river make exploration easy; on the south side, a road leads into the park from Nelson and follows the river for over 15 km. Along this road are a number of established campgrounds and picnic facilities. Farther east, off the road to Dartmoor, is picturesque **Pritchards Campground.** The **Park Information Centre** (tel. 08-8738-4051) is located at Princess Margaret Rose Caves; open daily except Tuesday 9 a.m.-4:30 p.m. The caves are a long way from the rest of the park, especially if coming from the north or east, so pick up information from the DC&NR in Portland (tel. 03-5523-3232).

Nelson

Nelson is a picturesque holiday and fishing village of 200 located at the mouth of the Glenelg River, just a few km east of the South Australia border. The main services overlook a sharp bend in the river, where a colorful array of boatsheds line up, fishers putter along in small aluminum boats, families picnic, and black swans feed among the river's reedy banks. From the west side of the river, the *Endeavour* cruises upriver into the national park and to Princess Margaret Rose Cave. Cruises depart daily at 9:30 a.m. and 1 p.m.; adult $12, child $6. For bookings call (08) 8738-4191. **Nelson Boat Hire,** just below the general store (tel. 08-8738-4048), rents canoes ($10 per hour) and small motor boats ($30 per hour). A road through town leads along the shallow inlet to a carpark where trails lead to the estuary and across dunes to an ocean beach. Accommoda-

tion choices are the **Nelson Hotel** (tel. 08-8738-4011), $15 s, $30 d; and the **Black Wattle Motel**, on the highway west of the Glenelg River (tel 08-8738-4008), $38 s, $48 d.

flint pick

WESTERN VICTORIA

The ancient landscape of western Victoria is a world apart from the rest of the state. Parts of this arid land were settled as recently as the 1920s, and vast sections, set aside as national parks, will never be settled.

In the southwest is the city of Hamilton and the ancient volcanoes of Mt. Eccles and Mt. Napier, which have lava flows, lava caves, and craters for all to explore. The Grampians, north of Hamilton and rising over 1,000 meters above the surrounding plains, are an oasis of lush forests, waterfalls, and spectacular rock formations and home to a staggering variety of flora and fauna. For rock climbers, Mt. Arapiles, west of Horsham, is a mecca. To the north is Little Desert National Park, home of the intriguing mallee fowl and a number of national parks protecting vast tracts of mallee scrub, a low-growing and hardy eucalypt that has frustrated settlers for generations. The state's northern border is the Murray River, one of Australia's largest rivers, lined with historic towns such as Mildura and Swan Hill.

HAMILTON AND VICINITY

Hamilton (pop. 11,500) lies 290 km west of Melbourne and 80 km north of the coastal city of Portland. It has grown as a service center for one of the world's richest wool-growing areas, surrounded to the south by distinct volcanic features and to the north by the Grampians.

Town Sights

Although the fiberglass **Big Woolbales** is a pretty tacky idea, displays within the gaudy exterior will give you a good idea of the wool-growing industry, the various strains of wool, how it is best preserved, and an insight into the quintessential Aussie working nomad—the shearer. The center is located two km west of town along the road out to Coleraine. Admission is adult $4, child $2. Open Mon.-Fri. 9 a.m.-5 p.m., Sat.-Sun. 10 a.m.-4 p.m. A lot less commercial are the expansive **botanical gardens,** on French St., which were first planted in 1870. **Hamilton**

Art Gallery, Brown St. (tel. 03-5573-0460), is one of Victoria's premier provincial galleries, featuring 19th-century Australian paintings; closed Monday.

Hamilton was the birthplace of **Sir Reginald Ansett,** founder of one of Australia's most successful transportation empires. The company's first hanger is the base for **Sir Reginald Ansett Transport Museum,** a small showcase of company memorabilia, including a Fokker Universal, similar to the one used on Ansett's 1936 inaugural flight. Open daily 10 a.m.-4 p.m. Admission $2; located on Ballarat Rd., east of town (tel. 03-5571-2767).

Accommodations and Food

For basic but adequate pub rooms, **Grand Central Hotel,** 141 Gray St. (tel. 03-5572-2899), should suffice; rates are $29 s, $44 d, which includes a hearty cooked breakfast. Of the motels, **Lenwin on the Lake Motor Inn,** 2 Riley St. (tel. 03-5571-2733), is one of the best priced; $44 s, $52 d. **Goldsmith Motel,** 30 Goldsmith St. (tel. 03-5572-4347), has larger, more modern rooms for only $58 s, $66 d.

Takeaways and restaurants are in Hamilton's main commercial center, along Gray and Thompson Streets. **Gilly's,** on Gray St. (tel. 03-

---

THE GOLDEN BALE

Hamilton's claim as "Wool Capital of the World" may seem a little fanciful, especially to New Zealanders, but early in 1995 local grower Ian Appledore sold a bale of wool for more than $1 million (around $10,300 per kilogram), the most expensive bale of wool ever produced. Known as the "Golden Bale," it was transported under armed guard to a scouring plant in New South Wales before being whisked off to Japan for processing. Not every bale raises prices this high; this ultrafine wool, a specialty of the area, is garnered from sheep that are hand-fed, live indoors, and wear plastic coats.

5571-9111), is a casual restaurant serving up decent portions for $5-7 and is popular with the lunchtime business crowd. Sandwiched between fast-food joints on Coleraine Rd. is **Stirring Pot Restaurant,** 212 Coleraine Rd. (tel. 03-5572-2535), located in an 1880 residence with antique furnishings and an authentic colonial feel; main meals are $12-18.

Transportation, Services, and Information

Passenger trains no longer run to Hamilton, but the old station is the arrival and departure point for **V/Line** (tel. 03-5573-0665) buses to Melbourne ($36.40 one-way) and Mt. Gambier in South Australia ($16.80).

The **Tourist Information Centre** is just off Thompson St. on Lonsdale St. (tel. 03-5572-3746) and is open daily 9 a.m.-5 p.m. The **post office** is nearby in the commercial center along Gray and Thompson Streets.

Mount Napier State Park

Mount Napier, 15 km south of Hamilton, last erupted around 7,000 years ago. The summit of the cone is 447 meters above sea level, making it an easily identifiable landmark on the surrounding volcanic plain. A trail leads to the summit and into the shallow crater, but the most unique aspect of the area is **Byaduk Caves** (turn east off the Port Fairy Rd. 12 km south of Hamilton—just before the village of North Byaduk). These lava caves, or "tubes," were formed when molten lava from Mt. Napier cooled on the outside but continued to flow on the inside. The area is riddled with volcanic rock and is totally undeveloped (ask for a Caves Map at the Tourist Information Centre in Hamilton). The easiest cave to access is **Harman No. 1,** 200 meters south of the gate at the end of the road. This cave is about 70 meters long but is very dark and damp—you'll need a torch or lantern to get to the end. From this cave, the ancient lava flow zigzags toward the Mt. Napier, first to the east, to **Bridge Cave** (you'll need a rope to get into this one), then south to the large **Church Cave** and other smaller openings.

Mount Eccles National Park

West of the small town of MacArthur, this 5,470-hectare park protects a lava field where major eruptions occurred as recently as 7,000 years ago. Mount Eccles first erupted 20,000 years ago; this and two subsequent eruptions formed the three main craters that now hold the deep blue waters of **Lake Surprise.** Lava flowed from the volcano in all directions, with one canal flowing into the ocean and under the sea, forming flat-topped Lady Julia Percy Island. The two-km **Crater Rim Nature Walk** starts and ends at the main carpark and takes in most features of the area including a small lava cave, a lava canal, and views of the tranquil lake below. Another trail descends into the crater and circles the lake.

Near the main carpark is a **campground** with fireplaces, picnic tables, and toilets; $7 per night. Also here is an information center explaining the park's intriguing natural history (tel. 03-5576-1014).

WESTERN HIGHWAY

The Western Highway is the quickest route between Melbourne and the Grampians and is also the main route between Melbourne and Adelaide. After passing through Ballarat (see "Gallarat," under "Goldfields," above) it passes through an area known as the Wimmera, named by early explorer Major Thomas Mitchell, who misspelt woomera, a Koori implement designed for longer spear throwing.

Ararat and Vicinity

Named by the area's first permanent settler, who likened his journey out west to that of Noah and his ark, Ararat has grown into a thriving service center for the surrounding wheat, wool, and wine industries.

West of town is the abandoned **Lanton Lead Mine,** where displays relate the area's Chinese heritage. Behind the botanic garden on Vincent St. is a bluestone jail, which dates to 1858. It was used for over 100 years and one time was a home for the criminally insane. Admission is adult $5, child $2; open public holidays and every Sunday. **Langi Ghiran State Park,** east of town, is an intriguing area of granite boulders scattered among a native forest, dominated by a 922-meter peak that the park is named for.

If you're looking for a place to stay, try **Chalambar Motel,** two km north of town (tel. 03-

5352-2430). It's pretty old, but rooms are only $30 s, $34 d. Ararat also has a caravan park and the **Caffe Dominica,** 291 Barkly St. (tel. 03-5352-1002), an 1890s mansion converted into three eateries—a cafe, bistro, and formal dining room.

Ararat Tourist Information Centre, corner Vincent and Barkly Streets (tel. 03-5352-2181), is open Mon.-Fri. 9 a.m.-5 p.m.

Great Western

Midway between Ararat and Stawell is the small town of Great Western, birthplace of Australian sparkling wine and home of **Seppelt Great Western,** established in the 1860s and now part of one of Australia's largest wine companies. The tradition of sparkling wine dates to the gold rush, when a French champagne maker was convinced by local businessmen to quit the goldfields and use his expertise to make wine. Tours of Seppelt's include descending to the "drives," underground tunnels dug by early miners and later used to store maturing wines. The winery is open Mon.-Sat. 9 a.m.-5 p.m., Sunday noon-4 p.m., with four tours daily (tel. 03-5356-2202). Also known for sparkling wine is **Best's Great Western** (tel. 03-5356-2250), established in 1866. The tasting room here is a classic old stable built of red gum in 1870.

Stawell

Each Easter Stawell's population of 6,000 swells to over 20,000 for the running of the **Stawell Gift,** Australia's most prestigious, and the world's richest, professional running race. The beginnings of the event date to the gold rush, when diggers loved a bit of a wager and competition to get their minds off the toil of mining and breaking the land. The inaugural event was held in 1878; the original medal, photographs, video footage, and other memorabilia are housed in the **Hall of Fame** at Stawell Athletic Club on Main Street. The race meeting takes place over three days of Easter in Central Park, but it's the 120-meter handicapped dash on Easter Monday that is the big one.

Historic downtown Stawell has been bypassed by the highway, where a bunch of strip motels vie for business with advertised rates generally less than $50. For a bit of a splurge, stay at **Clovelly House,** a Victorian-era home built in 1872. The house is surrounded by well-tended gardens and has been extensively restored, losing none of its original charm. Each of the two bedrooms has a log fire and private bathroom, and a delicious cooked breakfast is included in the rates; $70 s, $90 d. Located at 7 Clifton Ave. (tel. 03-5358-2986).

Stawell Tourist Information Centre is on the Western Hwy. (tel. 03-5358-2314) and can make accommodation bookings in the Grampians; open Mon.-Fri. 9 a.m.-5 p.m., Sat.-Sun. 10 a.m.-4 p.m.

GRAMPIANS NATIONAL PARK

The Grampians is a spectacular mountain range rising high above surrounding plains 260 km west of Melbourne. The 167,000 hectares protected as a national park encompass a spectacularly diverse landscape like no other in Victoria—one of lofty viewpoints, powerful waterfalls, lush valleys, and an amazing array of flora and fauna that includes over 1,000 species of wildflowers. To Koori, the mountains were known as **Gariwerd,** a sacred place where many Dreamtime myths originated and ceremonial gatherings took place; over 100 rock-art sites attest to these early human visitors. Today's visitors are a different breed of humans, and to cater to them hotels, restaurants, and souvenir shops have been developed, most at **Halls Gap,** on the park's eastern boundary.

The Land

The Grampians comprise four main ranges, each around 100 km long and running roughly north to south. Around 400 million years ago, tremendous upheavals forced layers of sandstone and granite upward, tilting great slabs to form parallel ridges, each with a steep cliff on one side and a gentle slope on the other. For millions of years the mountains were an island, surrounded by the raging waters of the Southern Ocean, which started the never-ending process of erosion. Since the water level dropped, wind and water have eroded the weaker rock, creating the weathered look of today.

The Grampians' combination of high mountains and long valleys surrounded by low plains creates a climate of its own. Rainfall in the Grampians is higher than the surrounding plains,

and often mist hangs in the valleys until late morning. In winter, snow is not uncommon at higher elevations, but rarely does it lie on the ground for longer than a day or two.

Flora and Fauna

The high peaks and deep valleys of the Grampians provide diverse habitats, ranging from fern-filled gullies to stands of stringybarks and forests of red gum. Some plants, such as the skeleton fork fern, are found nowhere else in the world. Spring is a magical time within the park; hundreds of species of wildflowers bloom, including 100 species of orchids alone.

Wildlife in the park is prolific, with nearly 40% of the state's mammal species having been recorded in the park. Easiest to spot are koalas (around Halls Gap and in tall eucalypts along the valley) and kangaroos (Zumstein Recreation Area, an open field near MacKenzie Falls). The dense native woodland habitat throughout the valleys provides shelter for rare species of mammals, including brush-tailed rock wallabies. The diverse habitat also provides a home for over 200 species of birds, including raucous gang-gang cockatoos, often seen feeding around Halls Gap, and endangered peregrine falcons, which nest in high sandstone cliffs.

Sights and Short Hikes

Easily accessible and interesting natural features are located within close proximity of Halls Gap and along Mt. Victory Rd. toward Wartook

in the northern Grampians. The **Wonderland Range,** immediately west of Halls Gap, is one of the most popular parts of the park for hiking, mainly because of the number of interesting short walks. Of these, the **Pinnacle,** a panoramic viewpoint, is most worthwhile. The easiest access is from Sundial Picnic Area (two km one-way); tracks also lead to the summit from Wonderland carpark (2.6 km one-way) and Halls Gap (five km one-way), although these two have considerably more elevation gain. Around a dozen other hikes crisscross this area, leading to viewpoints, waterfalls, and lushly vegetated gullies. **Boroka Lookout** is a lofty perch with views across to Lake Bellfield, Major Mitchell Plateau, and the plains beyond. The lookout access road branches off Mt. Victory Rd. eight km from Halls Gap. Farther along Mt. Victory Rd. is **Reid Lookout,** where you can see Serra Range and Victoria Valley to the south and Wartook Reservoir and Mt. Difficult to the north. From the carpark, a 900-meter trail leads through dense tea tree bushes to **The Balconies,** also colorfully known as **Jaws of Death,** a series of sandstone ledges, a scene that is featured on the cover of just about every Grampians brochure you're likely to see. A short, steep trail (lots of steps) leads down to beautiful **MacKenzie Falls,** one km off Mt. Victory Rd., which cascade over a wide rock ledge. **Zumstein Recreation Area,** with a picnic area and lots of kangaroos, is three km downstream on foot from MacKenzie Falls, or a little longer by road.

Grampians National Park is full of pleasant surprises, including many small waterfalls.

Rock-art sites are scattered throughout the Grampians; many are inaccessible, and those that can be easily reached are protected by wire fences. Southeast of Mt. Zero, in the far north of the park, are **Ngamadjidj** ("The Cave of Ghosts") and **Gulgurn Manja** ("Flat Rock"). **Bunjil** (the spirit creator), the area's best known painting, is in the Black Range outside the park; it's located south of Stawell along Old Moyston Road.

Longer Hikes

An excellent bushwalk from Halls Gap leads to Mackeys Peak, then along a high ridge to Pinnacle, down to Wonderland carpark, and along Stoney Creek past the Elephants Hide, on back to town. Although only 10 km round-trip, this strenuous hike takes over five hours.

At the southern end of the park, in the Serra Range, is **Mt. Abrupt** (827 meters), a single peak where there is a 360-degree panoramic view. The summit is accessible via a steep, winding track from Mt. Abrupt Road. Allow two hours one-way to complete this very steep hike.

Mt. Sturgeon (594 meters), a little farther south, is also climbable, with an easy gradient at first and most of the elevation gain being made in the final two km; 3.6 km one-way.

The park's most popular overnight hike is up to and across **Major Mitchell Plateau.** This two-day 28-km hike begins 21 km south of Halls Gap, at Stockyard Creek. The trail climbs onto the plateau, past various camping sites to the park's highest peak, Mt. William (1,167 meters), before following an old fire road back to the main road, six km from Stockyard Creek.

Check trail conditions with park staff before setting out on any hike, and, if you'll be around for a few days, grab a copy of *50 Walks In The Grampians,* available at the souvenir shop in Halls Gap.

Camping

Dotted around the park, and accessible by road, are 15 camping areas, each with drinking water, pit toilets, and fireplaces. Sites are first-come first-served and cost $7 per night, plus a once-only park-use fee of $6.50.

Halls Gap Caravan Park (tel. 03-5356-4251) is a commercial campground smack in the middle of Halls Gap. Sites are fairly close together, but the complex is surrounded by magnificent forests and is rarely full. Facilities include hot showers and a laundry. Sites are $10-12, on-site vans $30, cabins $35. Similarly priced is **Halls Gap Lakeside Caravan Park** (tel. 03-5356-4281), south of Halls Gap, and **Happy Wanderer Holiday Resort** (tel. 03-5383-6210), in the northern Grampians.

Other Accommodations

Halls Gap Motel (tel. 03-5356-4209) is close to the center of town and has basic rooms for $45 s, $55 d. Behind the town's main group of shops is **Pinnacle Holiday Lodge** (tel. 03-5356-4249), where some rooms have kitchenettes; from $65 s or d. Of the self-contained holiday flats, **Kingsway,** one km south of town (tel. 03-5356-4202), is the least expensive at $30-50 per unit. Much nicer is **Grampians View Holiday Cottages** (tel. 03-5356-4210). Each stone cottage has two bedrooms, kitchenette with microwave, washing machine, log fire, TV and video, and a veranda. They are great value at $63-80, but you'll need advance reservations. South of Wartook, in northern Grampians, is **Emu Holiday Park** (tel. 03-5383-6304), situated on 16 hectares of natural bushland with a lake, golf driving range, bush tennis court, and some short nature walks; on-site vans ($28-30), cabins ($35-46), and two-bedroom cottages ($52).

In the middle of Halls Gap is the old-fashioned **Mountain Grand Guest House** (tel. 03-5356-4232). Established in 1945, the rambling building has many modern features, such as central heating, in each of the well-appointed rooms. A large lounge area overlooks the extensive gardens and beyond to the mountains. Bed and breakfast is $50-75 s, $75-85 d, with dinner packages being around $15 extra pp.

Halls Gap YHA Hostel is located in a bush setting one km north of town on Buckler Road. This small hostel has adequate cooking facilities and separate male and female dorms; members $10, nonmembers $13. The fee is collected nightly or call (03) 5356-6221 for reservations.

Food

Along the main drag through Halls Gap are fast food eateries, restaurants, and a supermarket. In a new complex alongside Stony Creek is a butcher, bakery, ice creamery (serving large waffle cones), and the **Flying Emu,** a cafe overlooking the creek. Try the Flying Emu's big breakfasts, for $5-8 from 8:30 a.m. daily, or head to the bakery, grab a meat pie, cream bun, and flavored milk for under $5, and sit on the grassy bank or in the small gazebo overlooking the creek. **Ralphy's** is a family restaurant in a basic, boring setting with main dishes averaging $8. The **Golden Phoenix,** a Chinese restaurant, is similarly priced.

For a great evening meal there is no real reason to eat anywhere but **Kookaburra Restaurant,** 200 meters south of the post office (tel. 03-5356-4222). The building was once a cow shed, but has since been brick-veneered and decorated in a charming modern-colonial style with lace curtains and rustic furniture. Over the years the food here has gained a solid reputation, without being priced too high (main dishes are $11-18), using local game and produce. This place gets really busy so reserve in advance by phone or, as a message on the window says, slide a note under the door.

Across the road, in Mountain Grand Guest House, a casual bistro-style restaurant also serves excellent food.

Transportation, Services, and Information
The only public transportation into the park is the daily **V/Line** bus service between Stawell and Halls Gap ($6.30 one-way). Stawell is on a main V/Line rail link to Melbourne; $29.40 one-way. The YHA hostel offers guests a pick-up service from Stawell on demand.

Sandlants operates coach service around the Wonderland Range loop road ($5-8, depending how far you go), dropping off and picking up at designated spots. Once a daily service, it now—at last report—runs only Wednesday and Sunday so call (03) 5356-9342 to confirm the latest timetable.

Halls Gap has a petrol station, post office, cinema, and all the souvenir shops associated with tourist areas. **Brambuk Living Cultural Centre,** located in an intriguing building 2.6 km south of Halls Gap, displays the history and culture of the Koori who have inhabited the Grampians—or Gariwerd, as they call it—for thousands of years. The stone and timber used in the building came from the immediate surroundings, and the distinctive curved roof is designed to complement the landscape. Exhibitions catalog the Koori lifestyle, their persecution by early whites, and their current culture. Open daily 10 a.m.-5 p.m. Admission is adult $3.50, child $2.50 (tel. 03-5356-4452).

In front of the center is the **Park Information Centre,** with interesting displays on the park's natural and human history; a film is shown, and there's plenty of literature on the park. Open daily 9 a.m.-4:45 p.m. (tel. 03-5356-4381).

HORSHAM AND VICINITY

Horsham lies at the junction of the Henty, Western, and Wimmera Highways, 300 km northwest of Melbourne. The city itself doesn't have a great deal to offer tourists, but nearby are some interesting natural features, and the Grampians are only a one hour's drive south.

Horsham
This city of 13,000 began as a crossing point on the Wimmera River and has grown into the Wimmera's largest commercial center. At the southern end of Firebrace St. are **botanic gardens** and a trail that leads to a small river island. Also of interest in town is the **Wool Factory,** Golf Course Rd. (tel. 03-5382-0333), where ultrafine wool is processed. Tours of the complex are conducted four times daily; adult $4, child $2. **Horsham Art Gallery** houses a collection of Australian art bequeathed by Mack Jost, including works by Sir Sidney Nolan; located at 80 Wilson St. (tel. 03-5382-5575). Open Tues.-Fri. 10 a.m.-5 p.m. and Saturday 1-4:30 p.m.

Mark Twain once stayed at the **White Hart Hotel,** 55 Firebrace St. (tel. 03-5382-1231), where rates are $25 s, $35 d, but that doesn't really make it much better than the other hotels downtown or the scores of motels on all roads leading into the city. **Westlander Motor Inn** is three km south of town along the Western Hwy. (tel. 03-5382-0191); rooms are large and adequately furnished, and there's an indoor pool, laundry, and gymnasium; rates are $45 s, $56 d. **Glynlea Motel** (tel. 03-5382-0145) is along the same stretch of road and is a little cheaper. **Horsham Caravan Park** has a good riverfront location at the end of Firebrace St. and has a ton of facilities including cooktops. Tent and powered sites are $8-12 and on-site vans are $30 (tel. 03-5382-3476).

Olde World Connexion, 37 O'Callaghans Parade (tel. 03-5382-6509), is an old-fashioned tearoom decorated with an array of antiques. Morning and afternoon teas range $4-7 and are served daily 10 a.m.-5:30 p.m.

Murtoa and Minyip

These two small towns are in the middle of an extremely rich grain-growing area northeast of Horsham. Murtoa's **Water Tower Museum** is located in a large, brick water tower and is open Sunday 2-5 p.m. The colonial streetscape of Minyip may be more recognizable to the English and Australians as **Coopers Crossing,** home of the television drama series *The Flying Doctors.*

Mount Arapiles

Rising abruptly from the plains west of Horsham, this 369-meter peak, within 5,060-hectare **Mt. Arapiles-Tooan State Park,** is one of Aus-

Mt. Arapiles is one of Australia's climbing hot spots.

ANDREW HEMPSTEAD

tralia's few internationally renowned rock climbing sites. Rock climbing is only just beginning to gain wide appeal in the country, and with artificial climbing walls springing up everywhere, Mt. Arapiles will undoubtedly become a hive of activity. The small town of **Natimuk,** eight km east of the mountain, has already become home to a number of hard-core climbers, fostering a climbing shop and a couple of guiding companies. Climbing takes place on the quartz and sandstone cliffs of Mt. Arapiles, two km along Centenary Park Road. Over 2,000 routes have been attempted, ranging from beginner to expert.

For experienced climbers, all necessary gear and route information can be gained from **Arapiles Mountain Shop,** 69 Main St. (tel. 03-5387-1529). **The Climbing Company,** 117 Main St. (tel. 03-5387-1329), offers weekend instruction courses for beginners for $150 pp.

At the base of the mountain, in Centenary Park, is a campground. All summer it is packed with a colorful array of climbers; if you don't know the difference between a cramp and a crampon, you probably won't fit in; $7 per night. Back in Natimuk, the **National Hotel** (tel. 03-5387-1300) has basic rooms for $25 pp, including breakfast.

If climbing isn't your game, two very steep but short hiking trails lead to the summit ridge from Centenary Park, or you can drive to the summit along a sealed road from the Wimmera Highway.

Little Desert National Park

Little Desert isn't a desert at all, but 132,000 hectares of semi-arid land stretching from the Wimmera River to the South Australia border. Each spring many of the park's 650-plus species of native plants produce brilliantly colored wildflowers. In 1955 a small chunk of land was set aside to protect the rare **mallee fowl;** hectares have been added to it ever since, with today's park divided into three main "blocks." The central and western blocks are the most recent additions. These parts of the park are also the most remote, accessible only by 4WD, and have no facilities.

Camping is at **Horseshoe Bend,** on the western bank of the Wimmera River south from Dimboola, where the self-guided **Pomponderoo Hill Nature Walk** introduces hikers to the park's nvironment. South of Kiata, on the Western lighway, is another campground and nature valk (one km return). Both campgrounds have it toilets, drinking water, fireplaces; $6 per night. for more information, or if you plan to explore he central and western blocks of the park, conact the DC&NR in Horsham, 21 McLachlan St. tel. 03-5381-1255), or in Nhill, 6 Victoria St. tel. 03-5391-1275).

THE MALLEE

Since the 1880s, when the first white settlers began arriving, the far northwestern corner of Victoria has been known as, simply, "the mallee." t is a semi-arid area, bounded to the north and east by the Murray River and to the west by the South Australian border, and is often described as "Victoria's Outback." Mallee is a hardy and squat eucalypt, with leathery leaves and gnarled, chunky root systems. Clearing mallee was a nightmare for early settlers, and inventions such as the stump-jump plough and the mallee scrub oller did little to make the job easier. Today, over two-thirds of the land remains virgin mallee scrub, with the only cleared areas generally within 20 km of rail lines. To experience the real mallee, you'll need to leave the main highways and drive headlong into the national parks. From Melbourne, the most direct route into the mallee s the **Calder Highway,** which passes through Ouyen, the region's largest town, before ending at Mildura, on the Murray River.

Wyperfeld National Park

Wyperfeld, at 366,000 hectares, is the largest of the mallee parks and is also the most popular. The park's landscape is one of mallee scrub and open heathland, with a string of dry lakes lying along **Outlet Creek** and the southeast area of the park being the most accessible. Southeast of the park is Lake Albacutya. On the rare occasions that water from the Grampians fills this lake, Outlet Creek and its lakebeds act as an overflow. Only twice this century—the last time was in 1974—has this happened.

More than 450 species of plants are native to the park. In the lakebeds and sand dunes near of the campground distinct plant communities can be seen, including river red gums and, every spring, colorful displays of wildflowers. Fauna is plentiful, with western gray kangaroos and emus coming around the campgrounds. The park's birdlife is a major draw with an array of cockatoos, parrots, and galahs always in residence.

The facility area is centered around Outlet Creek (30 km west of Hopetoun, on the Henty Hwy., then 20 km north). The park information center (tel. 03-5395-7221) has both literature on the mallee parks and displays detailing Outlet Creek's life-cycle. The 15-km Eastern Lookout Drive, beginning from the information center, provides an introduction to the park, and the lookout allows a good view of the mallee scrub. Of the many hiking trails around the Outlet Creek area (get details at the park information center), we found **Desert Walk Circuit** the most interesting because it traverses a variety of habitat and provides a good view of the system of dry lake beds. It begins 600 meters along Nine Mile Square Track, five km south of the campground (allow two hours round-trip).

The campground has pit toilets, picnic tables, and fireplaces spread around a wide open area opposite the park information center. Water is not always available, so, to be safe, bring your own.

West of Outlet Creek the park is unaffected by humans. It is a vast area that extends west to Murrayville-Nhill Rd., with only the 4WD **Milmed Rock Track** penetrating the scrub. Between the Murrayville-Nhill Rd. and South Australia is an even more remote tract of land, 113,500 hectare **Big Desert Wilderness,** where the only access is on foot.

Ouyen

Sixty years ago, dozens of towns dotted the mallee. Today only a few remain; those that survive do so because of their position on a main highway. Ouyen (OY-en) is one such town. It's at the junction of the Mallee and Sunraysia Highways and is within an hour's drive of all three mallee parks. The town itself has little of interest, although walking down the main street is like stepping back in time (the bakery even still uses real cream).

On Rowe St., opposite the rail line, is **Victoria Hotel** (tel. 03-5092-1550), a rambling old bush pub with small-town atmosphere. Rooms are basic, with shared facilities, and are $26 s, $40 d, which includes breakfast. **Ouyen Motel,** on the Calder Hwy. (tel. 03-5092-1397), is another option; $48 s, $50 d.

Murray-Sunset National Park

This 633,000-hectare park, northwest of Ouyen, extends to South Australia and is mostly undeveloped. The park was just dedicated in July 1991, so many maps still label the roadless tract of land as **Sunset Country.** Visitor facilities are at **Pink Lakes,** in the south of the park.

The "pink" of the four lakes is formed from an algae that secretes a reddish-orange pigment into the water. During summer, the water in the lakes often evaporates, leaving a thick crust of pink-colored salt behind. Salt was mined commercially at the lakes until the 1950s, but no signs of the small operation remain. The four Pink Lakes are close together and linked by walking trails.

A campground is at the southern end of Lake Crosbie, the perfect place to view a famous Pink Lakes' sunset. Facilities include picnic tables, pit toilets, and fireplaces. Drinking water is also available, but bring your own to be safe. Access to the Pink Lakes is north from Linga, 60 km west of Ouyen.

Lindsay Island is in the part of the park north of the Sturt Highway. This low-lying Murray River island is ringed by river red gums and hosts a wide variety of flora and fauna. A couple of areas have been set aside for camping, but there are no facilities. Access to the island is along a poorly marked road that branches north off the Sturt Highway around 40 km west of Cullulleraine. For park details call (03) 5092-1322.

Hattah-Kulkyne National Park

The Hattah Lakes, east of the Calder Highway, is a tranquil waterway lined with towering river red gums and an oasis to a variety of wildlife. For all intents and purposes, the park extends to the Murray River, for a total area just under 50,000 hectares, although officially a strip along the river is **Murray-Kulkyne Regional Park.** The significance of both parks was recognized by UNESCO, and in 1982 they were listed as a World Biosphere Reserve. The lakes are only filled when the Murray River floods, but, often, water remains for years. Official park literature states "western gray kangaroos are abundant."

This is a bit of an Aussie understatement; in the 1980s 'roos were in plague proportions, degrading the land through sheer numbers. Old timers call the park "The Kangaroo Paddock" and have done so for as long as anyone can remember. Over 200 bird species have been recorded in the park; naturally the best bird watching area is around the lakes, where you can also see emus.

You can get to the park from a place marked on maps as Hattah, a once-thriving town, where just a roadhouse remains. **Hattah Nature Drive** begins from the Park Information Centre. Along the six-km route are numbered pegs corresponding to those in a brochure. Near the park entrance is a 1.2-km nature trail, but walking around any of the lakes is interesting.

A campground, just beyond the Park Information Centre, has basic facilities and drinking water is generally available. The Park Information Centre has some interesting boards describing the park's landscape; daily 8:30 a.m.-4:30 p.m. (tel. 03-5029-3253).

Red Cliffs

Red Cliffs is a northern mallee town on the Calder Highway 20 km south of Mildura. Opposite the Tourist Information Centre is **Big Lizzie,** a massive steam-powered tractor built in Melbourne in 1915. The original idea was to use it to transport wool from sheep stations in outback NSW. With a top speed of just one mph, it took two years to reach the Murray River from Melbourne. Unfortunately, no one considered how Big Lizzie would cross the Murray River—and she never did. Big Lizzie was used for clearing mallee scrub for a few years, before finding its final resting place. **Lindemans,** Australia's largest winery, is located south of Red Cliffs along Karadul Rd.; tours aren't offered but the sheer size of the structure and surrounding vineyards is worth a look. The cellars are open daily 9 a.m.-5 p.m. Red cliffs, for which the town is named, stand east of town on the bank of the Murray River.

MILDURA AND VICINITY

In the far northwest corner of the state, on the southern bank of the Murray River, is Mildura, a

MILDURA

VICTORIA

OLD MILDURA HOMESTEAD

0   500 m

TO BURONGA AND
WENTWORTH

RIO VISTA AND
REGIONAL
ART GALLERY

NEW
SOUTH
WALES

20

TO GOLDEN RIVER ZOO
AND BIG 4
GOLDEN RIVER

MILDURA COUNTRY
CLUB MOTEL

MILDURA
RAILWAY
STATION

BURONGA
BOATMAN

MILDURA WHARF
PSYCHE BEND PUMP

RIVER

VICTORIA

SEE DETAIL

KAR-RAMA
MOTOR INN

DC & NR

MID CITY
PLANTATION MOTEL

MILDURA
WORKINGMAN'S CLUB

TO RIVERSIDE
GOLF CLUB

ROSEMONT GUEST HOUSE

HUMPTY'S
WORLD

TO RED CLIFFS,
MELBOURNE,
AND ADELAIDE

20

DETAIL

LANGTREE

SEVENTH

MILDURA
GRAND
HOTEL
RESORT

RENDEZVOUS

SUNRAYSIA TOURISM
INFORMATION CENTRE

AUSTRALIAN DRIED
FRUITS ASSOCIATION

CITRUS SHOP

DEAKIN

EIGHTH

MADDEN

---

surprisingly large city of 20,000—an oasis, surrounded in all directions by an arid, desert-like
landscape. Mildura is primarily an agricultural
town; complex irrigation systems support what
seems like endless vineyards, fruit orchards, and
olive groves. Two Canadians, the Chaffey brothers, developed an irrigation scheme on the river in
the late 1880s, and it is from their foundations
that the city prospers. Tourism is also a major
part of the local economy. **Sunraysia,** as the area
is known, promotes long sunny days and a ton of
commercial attractions as a major drawcard.

River Cruises

Riverboat cruises are what will interest most people visiting Mildura. Each of the operating riverboats was used on the Murray when it served as
a major transportation route. All cruises depart
from Mildura Wharf at the end of Deakin Avenue.
The *Melbourne* is the best known and departs
daily except Saturday at 10:50 a.m. and 1:50 p.m.
for a two- to four-hour river trip; adult $15, child $6.
The faster *Rothbury,* operated by the same company, runs downstream to the zoo Wednesday
(adult $28, child $14) and upstream to Trentham

paddlesteamer, Mildura

Estate Winery Thursday ($30 adult, $15 child). For reservations on either of the above boats call (03) 5023-2200. *Showboat Avoca* operates a daily lunchtime cruise for adult $15, child $6; with lunch the fare is adult $23, child $10. On Thursday evening the *Showboat* has a Night Cruise and Carvery for adult $32, child $9. On Saturday evening the atmosphere is more formal, with a three-course dinner and dancing; adult $32, child $24. For bookings call (03) 5021-1166.

Town Sights
Along the riverfront is a stretch of parkland and pleasant picnic areas. Downstream from Mildura Wharf is **Old Mildura Homestead** and a small heritage park. The homestead, really just a cottage, was the first home of the town's founders, the Chaffeys. Admission is $1 and it's open daily 10 a.m.-4 p.m. On the riverbank, overlooking Mildura Wharf, is **Psyche Bend Pump,** an imposing brick building that was built by the Chaffey brothers to pump water into their irrigation system. Another legacy of the Chaffeys'

is **Rio Vista,** once an imposing homestead, now a museum depicting the late 1800s throug rooms set up as they would have been in tha period. Open Mon.-Fri. 9 a.m.-5 p.m., Sat.-Sun 2-4:30 p.m. Located at 199 Cureton Ave. (te 03-5023-3733). Adjoining the homestead is **Mil dura Regional Art Gallery,** boasting a fine co lection of Australian works.

Commercial Attractions
Golden River Zoo, four km northwest of tow on Flora Ave. (tel. 03-5023-5540), is mainl aimed at kids, with many hands-on animal feec ing sessions throughout the day. Admission i adult $8.50, child $4, and it's open daily 9 a.m. 5 p.m. **Orange World** (tel. 03-5023-5197), se on a working orchard, is eight km north of Mil dura in Buronga. A one-hour tour on a tractor-le cart gives an interesting insight into the citrus in dustry. Tours depart daily at 10:30 a.m. and 2:30 p.m.; closed Friday. A place you may wan to take kids is **Humpty's World,** Cureton Ave (tel. 03-5023-1429), which boasts the world': largest Humpty Dumpty.

Recreation, Festivals, and Events
Buronga Boatman, opposite Mildura Whar (tel. 03-5023-5874), hires canoes and kayaks from $8 an hour; summer only. **Riverside Gol Club,** off Etiwanda Ave. (tel. 03-5023-1560), is a picturesque course alongside the Murray; club rentals are available and green fees are $12 For a different perspective of town, **Cameron Balloon Flights,** 167 7th St. (tel. 03-5021-2876) has hot-air balloon flights for $100-120 pp.

Held in early January is **Siesta Fiesta,** which you'd probably have to live in town to appreciate in April there are various skiing, rowing, and boating races on the river; July sees a hot-air ballooning championship; **Country Music Week** is held during September school holidays; and **Mildura Jazz and Wine Festival** takes place early October. Call the Sunraysia Tourism Information Centre (tel. 03-5021-4424).

Accommodations
The only decent hotel in Mildura has recently been renovated to **Mildura Grand Hotel Resort,** 7th St. (tel. 03-5023-0511). The building itself is impressive—of a Spanish mission design and housing a casino. But the rooms are

asic; $55 s, $77 d. There are about 20 other hotels in town, many well priced. Try **Kar-rama Motor Inn,** 153 Deakin Ave. (tel. 03-5023-4221), or rooms starting at $37 s, $41 d; **Mid City Plantation Motel,** 145 Deakin Ave. (tel. 03-5023-0317), which has large rooms and a nice pool area for $40 s, $44 d; or **Mildura Country Club Motel,** 12th St. (tel. 03-5023-3966), beside the golf course and with its own putting green; $65 s or d.

Staying in a houseboat is a unique and practical way to spend a couple of days in the Mildura area. Over 20 companies keep a whole range of boat sizes, and guests need no boating experience. Most boats have a minimum of three nights' rental and begin at $90 per day or a small two-bedroom boat. For details call the Houseboat Holiday Hotline (tel. 1800-80-9152).

Rosemont Guest House, 154 Madden Ave. tel. 03-5023-1535), is an associate YHA, with clean kitchens, a good lounge area, and private rooms for $15-19 s, $35-38 d, including breakfast.

Mildura has over 20 caravan parks, of which three are clustered together southwest of city limits on the Calder Highway. Campgrounds on the river are nicer, but farther from Mildura; try **Big 4 Golden River,** Flora Ave. (tel. 03-5021-2299), where sites are $12 and cabins $30.

Food and Drink

Mildura is the perfect place to stock up on fresh fruit, wine, and dried fruit. Roadside stalls are the best places to pick up citrus fruits (oranges are generally around 10 cents each). On Deakin Ave., beside Sunraysia Tourism, is the **Australian Dried Fruits Association,** which has a large choice of dried fruits for sale as well as a cafe that serves Devonshire teas and healthy lunches. On the same street is the **Citrus Shop.** Both are open Mon.-Fri. 9 a.m.-5:30 p.m., Saturday 9 a.m.-12 p.m.

In the city center, along a pedestrian mall on Langtree Ave., are many cafes and casual restaurants. **Rendezvous,** 34 Langtree Ave. (tel. 03-5023-1571), is a classy place that combines a cafe, bistro, and restaurant under one roof. The bistro is fairly casual and main dishes are $10-12 while the restaurant is only slightly more expensive; open for lunch Mon.-Fri. and for dinner Mon.-Saturday. Mildura Grand Hotel

Resort, 7th St. (tel. 03-5023-0511), has four eateries of which the **Grand Bistro** has the most variety. **Mildura Workingman's Club,** Deakin Ave. (tel. 03-5023-0531), is a nondescript redbrick building included in the *Guinness Book of Records* for its bar—at 91 meters it is the longest in the world.

Transportation, Services, and Information

Southern Australia Airlines (tel. 03-5022-2444) flies daily between Mildura and Adelaide ($110 one-way), Melbourne ($157), and Broken Hill ($98). The railway station is close to the center of town on 7th St. (tel. 03-5023-9001). **V/Line** trains run four times weekly between Melbourne and Mildura ($50.60 one-way). V/Line buses run on days of no rail service and are the same price. The bus depot is at 100 7th Street. V/Line **Murraylink** buses run along the Murray River to Echuca ($34.80) and Albury-Wodonga ($50.70). The three national bus lines pass through Mildura daily, heading to Melbourne ($42 one-way), Adelaide ($42), and Sydney ($89). **Mildura Bus Lines** (tel. 03-5023-0274) runs a regular Mon.-Sat. service around town. For a cab call **Mildura Taxis** (tel. 03-5023-0033).

Sunraysia Tourism Information Centre is at 41 Deakin Ave. (tel. 03-5021-4424). They can book accommodations and all tours. Open Mon.-Fri. 9 a.m.-5 p.m., Sat.-Sun. 10 a.m.-4 p.m. The **DC&NR,** a good source of information on mallee national parks, is at 253 11th St. (tel. 03-5027-3624).

Wentworth

Wentworth is 30 km west of Mildura at the confluence of two of Australia's largest rivers—the Murray and Darling. The town may be smaller than Mildura, but more historic buildings remain, and it, favorably, lacks commercialism. Highlights of Wentworth are: **Perry Sandhills, Sunraysia Oasis Botanical Gardens, Wentworth Gaol,** and Australia's only monument to a tractor. The information center is in the craft shop on Adams St. (tel. 03-5027-3624).

Southwest to Swan Hill

Upstream of Mildura the Murray River winds its way through the mallee scrub, with the main road access being River Rd. in Hattah-Kulkyne

National Park. The most direct route from Mildura to Swan Hill is through NSW to Robinvale, located on a long U-shaped curve in the river, then along the Murray Valley Highway.

SWAN HILL

The peaceful Murray River town of Swan Hill (pop. 9,500) is located halfway between Mildura and Echuca and is 365 km north of Melbourne. The town was named by Major Thomas Mitchell, who visited the area in 1836 and, so the story goes, couldn't get to sleep for the noise of swans. Although a couple of homesteads were established in the 1840s, it wasn't until 1853, when the first paddlesteamers arrived, that a town was established.

Sights

Swan Hill's major attraction is **Swan Hill Pioneer Settlement,** a re-creation of an 1800s river town. Once inside the impressive entrance—a large riverboat—you enter 2.6 hectares of living history. The main street is lined with businesses of the day—a general store, bakery, blacksmith, and so on, with workers plying their trades. Around the settlement are many horse-drawn carts and buggies, old cars, and farm machinery. The *Pyap* plies the river, departing from the park daily at 10:30 a.m. and 2:30 p.m. ($6). Admission is adult $9, child $5. Open daily 8:30 a.m.-5 p.m. Located right in the middle of town (tel. 03-5032-1092).

The two original homesteads still stand, and both are open to the public. **Murray Downs Homestead,** two km east of town (tel. 03-5032-1225), is on a 4,000-hectare working farm. The mansion and English-style gardens have remained as they were when built, with much of the original furniture still in place. Also on the property is a small animal park and tearooms. Admission is $6, which includes a one-hour tour. Open Tues.-Sun. 9 a.m.-4:30 p.m. The other homestead, **Tyntynder,** is 17 km north of town along the Murray Valley Hwy. (tel. 03-5037-6506). This property also has delightful gardens. The house itself is private property, but a small museum has many articles of interest. Admission is $6. Open Sun.-Fri. 9 a.m.-4:30 p.m.

Opposite Settlement Park is **Swan Hill Regional Art Gallery,** with mostly contemporary art. The only other point of interest in Swan Hill is the **Military Museum** at 400 Campbell St. (tel. 03-5032-4382). It contains a huge range of military memorabilia. Entry is $4.50 pp. Open Mon.-Sat. 9 a.m.-5 p.m., Sunday 9 a.m.-noon.

Accommodations

The **Commercial Hotel,** 91 Campbell St. (tel. 03-5032-1214), has basic, clean rooms with shared facilities for $20 pp, including breakfast. **Paddlesteamer Holiday Resort,** Murray Valley Hwy. (tel. 03-5032-2151), is three km south of town; rooms are large and have lots of facilities. The resort also has a communal cooking area and pool. Rates are $40 s, $50 d. **Swan Hill's Resort Motor Inn,** 405 Campbell St. (tel. 03-5032-2726), has a great landscaped pool area, and the rooms are as modern as they come in Swan Hill; $69 s, $80 d.

Riverside Caravan Park, Monash Dr. (tel. 03-5032-1494), has shaded sites and is right on the river central to town. Sites are $10-12, on-site vans are $26, and cabins start at $36.

Food

For good and inexpensive tucker, head for the Commercial Hotel, where bistro meals are $3-6 at lunch and $5-9 at dinner; located at 91 Campbell Street. **Carriages,** at Pioneer Motor Inn, 421 Campbell St. (tel. 03-5032-2017), is located in a couple of old train carriages that have been converted to a restaurant. One carriage is formal, the other more casual, with prices to match. At Swan Hill Pioneer Settlement, the largest paddlesteamer ever to work the Murray has been converted to a fun restaurant with a menu that features Aussie tucker such as witchetty grubs, kangaroo, and Murray cod.

Transportation, Services, and Information

V/Line trains run daily between Melbourne and Swan Hill ($40.60 one-way). The station is in the center of town on Curlewis Avenue. V/Line's Murraylink bus service runs daily to Mildura ($27.20) and Echuca ($21.80).

Swan Hill Tourist Information Centre is at 306 Campbell St. (tel. 03-5032-3033 or 1800-625-5373); open Mon.-Fri. 9 a.m.-5 p.m., Saturday 10 a.m.-1 p.m.

CENTRAL VICTORIA: MELBOURNE TO THE MURRAY

THE HUME HIGHWAY: MELBOURNE TO BENALLA

The Hume Highway, linking Melbourne and Sydney, is one of Australia's busiest highways. What was originally an 1850s wagon track between Sydney and the Victorian goldfields is today a four-lane divided freeway. The buses that link Melbourne and Sydney make stops in many of the towns in between.

Euroa

Euroa National Bank was held up by the Kelly Gang in December 1878, and that is Euroa's main claim to fame. The town is bypassed by the Hume Highway; roadhouses and petrol stations remain along the short access roads into town, and the main street is lined with many historic red brick buildings. **Euroa Historical Society Museum,** in an old hotel on Kirkland St., is open Sunday 2-4 p.m. **Seven Creeks Run** is a touristy wool-growing complex housed in an old shearing shed one km north of Euroa.

Benalla

Benalla (pop. 9,000) straddles the Broken River, just off the Hume Hwy. 200 km northeast of Melbourne. Although many of the older buildings have been knocked down, the town retains much of its original character and is a pleasant stopover along the otherwise boring highway. Benalla grew from a crossing point on the Broken River, and as travelers moved between goldfields it grew in importance. In 1871, at just 16, Ned Kelly stood trial in Benalla court for assaulting and robbing a Chinese trader. Ned came back to Benalla in 1877, this time charged with riding a horse on the footpath and being drunk. He escaped temporarily but was recaptured, and further charges were added. The **Costume and Pioneer Museum,** Mair St. (tel. 03-5762-1749), houses some pieces of Kelly memorabilia, including the witness box that Ned came to know so well. Also on display is the door of the Benalla lockup upon which Joe Byrne—a member of the Kelly Gang—had his dead body slung up and photographed. The museum also contains period costumes, underwear from the 1850s, and an 1870 artificial leg. Open daily 10 a.m.-5 p.m. The colorful **botanical gardens** and **Benalla Art Gallery** (tel. 03-5762-5140) are together on the west bank of the river. The gallery houses an impressive collection of colonial and contemporary art in an equally impressive building overlooking Broken River. Admission is $2. Open daily 10 a.m.-5 p.m.

Broken River Hotel, 39 Bridge St. (tel. 03-5762-2014), has clean rooms for $20 s, $32 d, which includes do-it-yourself breakfast ingredients. Of the many motels, **Rose City Motor Inn,** corner Midland Hwy. and Faithful St. (tel. 03-5762-2611), is a good cheapie; $35 s, $45 d. More modern and with facilities such as a restaurant, pool, and larger rooms is **Glider City Motel,** corner Old Sydney Rd. and Witt St. (tel. 03-5762-3399), where rooms are a reasonable $55 s, $65 d. **Motor Village Caravan Park** (tel. 03-5762-3434) is on Winton Rd., three km northwest of town; sites are $8-12 per night.

Hide's Bakery, on Bridge St., serves a variety of delicious pies and pastries and has tables both inside and out. For something more substantial **Victoria Hotel,** 2 Carrier St., has counter meals from $4. **Georgina's,** 100 Bridge St. (tel. 03-5762-1334), is a small country-style restaurant in a building that dates from the 1880s; the menu is short and varied, with main dishes ranging $11-18. Open for dinner Tues.-Sun. 6-10 p.m.

The **Tourist Information Centre** is in the same complex as the museum on Mair St. (tel. 03-5762-1749); open daily 10 a.m.-5 p.m.

GLENROWAN

The sight of Ned Kelly suited in a coat of crude heavy armor fighting off police with all guns

NED KELLY

Australian bushrangers were similar to the outlaws of the American West, but while Jesse James and his contemporaries held up the odd bank and robbed a couple of trains, Australian bushrangers would capture whole towns, bail up the townsfolk and keep them amused with stories of life on the run, forcing the local publican to supply free booze to all comers; then they'd rob the local bank and ride out of town. Australia's best-known bushranger, Ned Kelly, is also the country's greatest folk hero; his life on the run is retold in song, literature, and film.

Ned Kelly was born to poor Irish parents who'd been transported to Australia in the 1840s. Ned, his brother Dan, and four sisters grew up in a rough slab hut near Greta in the foothills of the High Country, surrounded by families of similar circumstances. The boys began duffing (cattle stealing) at an early age, and, in 1871, at 16, Ned was arrested for the first time.

In March 1878, a warrant was issued for the arrest of Dan Kelly. When a constable arrived on his doorstep to serve it, a scuffle ensued, and the policeman was shot and wounded. Ned and Dan, accompanied by close friends Steve Hart and Joe Byrne, fled to the Wombat Ranges, evading police for six months. At Stringybark Creek, on 25 October 1878, the gang stumbled upon the camp of a search party. In a fierce gun battle, constables Kennedy, Scanlon, and Lonigan were killed by Ned; it would be the point of no return in the young outlaws' lives. Public opinion toward the gang was divided—poorer folk sympathized with their predicament, while the well-off saw them as cold-blooded murderers.

A £500 reward was placed on the gang; instead of persuading their sympathizers to turn them in, it spurred Ned on to more daring exploits. Their reputation for boldness grew, especially after they visited a homestead outside Euroa, bailing up over 30 staff and passersby, demanding that the women of the house cook a feast for everyone—then they robbed the local bank the following morning. The most daring escapade occurred just over the New South Wales border, in Jerilderie, in February 1879. After locking the town's policemen in their own cells, the gang spent the weekend living it up in town. They robbed the bank first thing Monday morning and left with a display of horseback-riding skills down the main street, much to the amusement of cheering townsfolk.

On 27 June 1880, the gang took over Glenrowan Inn. By this time, the reward for their capture had been increased to £8000 an amazing amount of money for the time, and Joe Byrne had murdered his best friend, Aaron Sherritt, as a suspected police informer. They planned to derail a special train filled with police called from Melbourne to flush them out of hiding. Over two days, the gang bailed up over 60 people, allowing them free grog from the hotel, and even ran an athletic competition between themselves and the townsfolk. After tricking Ned into going home with his "sick" sister, the local schoolmaster flagged down the special train before it reached the vandalized rail line. The police aboard alighted and surrounded the hotel, but were met by a volley of gunfire and the shouted words "You can't hurt us!" The Kelly Gang was prepared, having made crude armor from quarter-inch iron to protect their heads, chests, and backs. Ned laughed as he was pummeled with gunfire, but a few shots in the legs and arms brought him down. The shootout continued into the night; Joe Byrne was killed early on, the wounded Ned was captured, and the hotel burnt to the ground with the two remaining outlaws inside. Ned Kelly, the only surviving gang member, was tried in Beechworth, and on 11 November 1880, at 26, he was hanged on the gallows at Melbourne Gaol. His mother's final words, "mind you die like a Kelly, Ned!" became part of Australian folklore.

---

blazing is an image that has become part of Australia's folklore. That final showdown took place at Glenrowan, less than two hours on horseback from Kelly's childhood home of Greta. The small township seems to accept its place in Australia's history with a good deal of ambivalence; apart from Kelly commercialism along the old Hume Highway, there is little evidence of Glenrowan's most famous visitor. The Kelly Gang was the last of the real bushrangers, and as recently as the 1950s there were folks around town who could remember the gang's last stand. Many descendants of Kelly sympathizers still live in the area, but the only people who enjoy talking of the Kelly Gang are those who are cashing in on the name along the main drag.

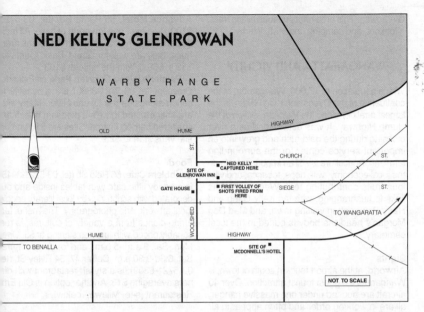

NED KELLY'S GLENROWAN

WARBY RANGE
STATE PARK

OLD   HUME   HIGHWAY

ST.

CHURCH   ST.

■ NED KELLY
CAPTURED HERE
SITE OF
GLENROWAN INN

GATE HOUSE ■   ■ FIRST VOLLEY OF   SIEGE   ST.
SHOTS FIRED FROM
HERE

TO WANGARATTA

WOOLSHED

HUME   HIGHWAY

TO BENALLA

SITE OF
MCDONNELL'S HOTEL ■

NOT TO SCALE

Sights

Unfortunately all buildings relevant to the Kelly Gang's last stand have long since gone, including the Glenrowan Inn, which was destroyed on the night of the siege and never rebuilt. Six small stone obelisks provide the only reminders of that fateful night. Each is numbered, but to make searching them out more rewarding, you should read some Kelly Gang literature. On the main street is **Ned Kelly Memorial Museum,** which has various memorabilia in a small room and a replica of the Kelly homestead out back; admission $2. Open daily 9 a.m.-5 p.m. A little farther up the road, past a seven-meter statue of Ned, is **Glenrowan Tourist Centre,** where *Ned Kelly's Last Stand,* a computerized audiovisual, is shown. The theater spans four rooms, each depicting a chapter in Ned's life. Through modern technology, the historic scenes are brought to life, but for adult $12.50 and child $6, it's a bit expensive. Each show lasts 40 minutes; screened daily 9:30 a.m.-4:30 p.m.

Practicalities

The only place to stay in town is **Glenrowan Kelly Country Motel** (tel. 03-5766-2202), where the rooms are $42 s, $49 d. Over the rail line and two km north is **Glenrowan Bushland Caravan Park** (tel. 03-5766-2288). It's in a natural bush setting with basic but adequate facilities. Sites are $10-12 and on-site vans a reasonable $22 s or d. **Glenrowan Hotel,** a pleasant escape from the busy main street, has good bar meals.

If you can get past the gun-toting bushranger in front of **Billy Tea Rooms** (tel. 03-5766-2496), you'll get some good tucker, such as the Ned Kelly pie and chips, or scones and endless coffee for $3.95. A three-course meal with damper is $11.95.

Also along the main street are several souvenir shops, a post office, and an antique shop.

Warby Range State Park

This park encompasses a low range of granite outcrops that extend for 30 km north from Glenrowan. The park's highest point, **Mt. Glenrowan** (410 meters), overlooks the town and would have provided a good lookout point for the Kelly Gang. A four-km (one-way) trail leads to the summit from Taminick Rd., five km beyond the caravan park. The north section of the park is best accessed from Wangandry Rd., 18 km north of

Glenrowan. This area offers various hiking trails, a lookout, and camping under Mt. Warby.

WANGARATTA AND VICINITY

With a population of 17,000, Wangaratta, at the confluence of the Ovens and King Rivers, is the largest rural city along the Victorian section of the Hume Highway. It was established as a river crossing during the gold rush and grew into an important service center for the surrounding farmland. Agriculture is still an important factor in the local economy, with hops, tobacco, and various fruits contributing to it. Wangaratta has links to bushranging, with the Kelly Gang and Harry Power often visiting town, and Mad Dog Morgan's headless body is buried in the local cemetery.

Sights

Airworld, at the airport four km south of town, is Wangaratta's biggest tourist attraction. Over 40 aircraft are housed under one massive hangar; all are in working order and often appear in air shows around the country, but, for the most part, they remain here, offering a good opportunity for aircraft buffs to get a close-up view of the world's largest collection of operational civil aircraft. Open daily 9 a.m.-5 p.m. Admission is adult $6, child $4 (tel. 03-5721-8788).

Head to the information center, south of downtown on the Hume Highway, for a brochure describing the many buildings of historical importance along Faithfull, Reid, and Ford Streets, some of which date to the 1850s. A small museum is housed in the Old Fire Station on Ford St., but it's only open Sunday. Also at the information center is **House in Miniature,** a house built to one-sixth scale by a Mrs. Gay Stell, who spent 10 years on the project; she used only a Stanley knife, a small saw, and file. Admission is $2.

Accommodations

Pinsent Hotel, 30 Reid St. (tel. 03-5721-2183), is very central and has basic rooms with shared facilities for $25 s, $40 d, which includes a small breakfast. Least expensive of the motels is **Billabong Motel,** 12 Chisholm St. (tel. 03-5721-2353), which has good-sized rooms for $30 s, $45 d. (Chisholm St. is at the southeast end of Reid Street.) At the other end of the scale is

Advance Motel, 55 Parfitt Rd. (tel. 03-572 9100), just over one km north of town. All faci ties are modern and, although the rooms arer huge, they are well-furnished. Basic rooms a $59 s, $69 d, with the suite at $103.

Painter's Island Caravan Park, off Pinkertc Crescent (tel. 03-5721-3380), is in a beautiful l cation alongside the Ovens River. Many site are shaded, and there's a pleasant beach ar sheltered barbecue area. Sites are $10 and o site vans start at $25.

Food

Scribblers Cafe, 66 Reid St. (tel. 03-5721-3945 is a trendy little cafe with tables inside and ou decorated with scribblings by local literary peopl local artwork, and photography. The menu, fea turing dishes from a variety of cultures, is rea sonably priced with lunches starting at $5. Ope Mon.-Sat. 9 a.m.-5 p.m., and for dinner Thurs Sat. 6:30-9:30 p.m. **Cellar 47,** 54 Ryley St. (te 03-5721-6309), is a stylish restaurant with din ners averaging $16. Another option is Old Em Restaurant (see "Milawa," below).

Transportation, Services, and Information

Trains run daily between Melbourne and War garatta ($27.20 one-way). The station is on No ton St., off Docker St., west of town (tel. 03 5721-3641). **V/Line** buses also use this station running daily to Beechworth ($4.20 one-way and Bright ($4.20). **Avis** has an office at 4 Parfitt Rd. (tel. 03-5722-1223). For a cab ca (03) 5721-8888.

Wangaratta Tourist Information Centre i on the Hume Hwy. at the corner of Handley St on the south side of town (tel. 03-5721-5711 open daily 9 a.m.-3 p.m. The **DC&NR** is on For St. (tel. 03-5721-5022).

Milawa

Milawa, 18 km southeast of Wangaratta, can b an expensive detour if you're a lover of gourme foods. The small township is home to the famou **Brown Brothers Winery,** Milawa Cheese Co., a number of good restaurants, and an excellen bakery—all in a town where the population i 250. The Brown family has been producing win at Milawa since 1889, and its operation ha grown to become one of Australia's best-know and largest wineries. The large winetasting area

as a huge range of wines (including some released only at the winery) and a small historical
display. Winetasting is daily 9 a.m.-5 p.m., till 8
p.m. during the ski season. Also here is the **Epi-
curean Center,** an open, well-lit restaurant with
casual atmosphere. Main dishes start at $10
and all are served with wine. For bookings call
03) 5720-5500.

On the opposite side of Milawa is **Milawa
Cheese Co.** (tel. 03-5727-3588), producer of
specialty cheeses. Tastings are held daily 9
a.m.-5 p.m. and the cheese is $29 a kilo. The
Old Emu, a restaurant on Milawa's wide main
street, is housed in a building of handmade
bricks dating to 1861. Morning and afternoon
teas and lunch are served daily 10 a.m.-5 p.m.
tel. 03-5727-3410).

Eldorado

The reefs of gold at Eldorado, 22 km east of
Wangaratta, were 100 meters below the surface, needing larger-scale commercial operations to extract. In the 1930s, when a massive
dredge was put in place, extraction became viable. Eventually mining costs overcame the
company and, in 1955, it closed. The dredge
remains in Eldorado, the largest such one in
the Southern Hemisphere.

Eldorado Museum is open Sunday 2-5 p.m.
Opposite the museum is **Gemstone Caravan
Park** (tel. 03-5725-1745), with sites $7.50-11,
on-site vans for $21, and cabins from $33.
McEvoy Tavern (tel. 03-5725-1612), purported
to be Victoria's smallest hotel, has information on
the area and lots of good, cold beer.

East from Eldorado an unpaved road follows
Reedy Creek to the charming town of Beechworth. This little-used stretch of road traverses
an area known last century as **Woolshed Valley.** It was once home to many Kelly sympathizers and littered with caves used by the gang
as hideouts; little has changed in the valley since
those days. Trout fishing in Reedy Creek is
good and there are places you could camp.

Chiltern

Gold was discovered in Chiltern in 1855 and
mined with a varying degree of success until
early this century. The streetscape of this small
town, midway between Wangaratta and Albury,
has changed little over the last 100 years and
has been used as a set for a number of movies.

The main street is lined with historical redbrick
buildings, many protected by the National Trust.
Some have been partly restored while others
exist in varying states of disrepair. Some of the
buildings are open to the public.

The **Athenaeum Library** was built in 1866
and is open on weekends, as is **Dows Pharmacy,** the **Federal Standard Newspaper Office,** and **Lakeview House,** childhood home of
Australian author Henry Handel Richardson.
The **Famous Grapevine Old World Attraction** (tel. 03-5726-1395) is on the main street
in the Star Hotel and Theatre. Part of the complex, the Grapevine Museum (open daily 9 a.m.-
5 p.m.), has a display of antique furniture, but a
grapevine in the courtyard is the highlight. It
was planted in 1867 and now has a base circumference of 1.7 meters, with vines covering
an area of 72 square meters.

Lake Anderson Caravan Park (tel. 03-5726-
1298) is located on the lake, only a short walk
from town. Shady tent sites are $10, powered
sites $12, and on-site vans $25-30.

Along the main street are antique shops, tearooms, and the **Telegraph Hotel,** which serves
bar meals daily noon-2 p.m. and 6-9 p.m. The
Mulberry Tree Restaurant, 28 Conness St. (tel.
03-5726-1277), is in the Bank of Australia building.
Lunch and afternoon tea are served daily and
Thurs.-Sat. an a la carte dinner menu is offered.

Chiltern Regional Park

This 4,500-hectare park protects various areas of
historical importance and one of Victoria's largest
stands of box-ironbark. The park straddles the
Hume Highway north and east of Chiltern.
Chiltern Historic Drive, on the north side of the
highway, begins on the road to Rutherglen. Along
this well-signposted route are the remains of the
Indigo Goldfields, once home to thousands of
diggers. The Magenta Mine, farther along the
route, is also interesting to explore.

SHEPPARTON AND
THE GOULBURN VALLEY

Shepparton (pop. 26,000) is the largest town in
the Goulburn Valley, the state's richest agricultural region. It's at the confluence of the Goulburn and Broken Rivers and is best known for its
canneries, but also has a couple of good mu-

seums and galleries where the work of local artisans is displayed.

Sights

Shepparton Art Gallery houses an ample collection of paintings, including works by two great Australian artists—Boyd and Streeton. It's beside Town Hall on Welsford St. (tel. 03-5821-6352); open Tues.-Fri. 1-5 p.m. and Sat.-Sun. 2-5 p.m. Also on Welsford St., at High St., is **Shepparton Historical Museum,** housed in the 1873 courthouse; open Sunday only, 1-4 p.m. **Shepparton International Village,** Parkside Dr. (tel. 03-5822-1026), is hyped up in all the tourist literature but doesn't seem to be that special; it's a series of pavilions, each representing a different country, connected by paths that wind around the pleasant gardens. Admission is adult $5, child $1. Open daily 9:30 a.m.-4:30 p.m.

Accommodations

The least expensive place to stay is **Victoria Hotel,** corner Fryers and Wyndham Streets (tel. 03-5821-9955), where basic pub rooms are $19 s, $30 d, and the more-modern motel units are $32 s, $40 d. **Shepparton Motel,** three km east of town (tel. 03-5821-3866), is the least expensive of a dozen motels; $32 s, $40 d. **Shepparton Golf Club Motel,** Golf Links Dr. (tel. 03-5821-2155), is six km northwest of town. Rooms are basic and box-like but overlook a golf course; $40 s, $48 d. **Belltower Motor Inn,** 587 Wyndham St. (tel. 03-5821-8755), is of a higher standard and is more central; $53 s, $58 d. A little farther out is **Parklake Motor Inn,** 481 Wyndham St. (tel. 03-5821-5822), the classiest place in town, with an indoor pool, spa, gym, and restaurant; $75 s, $85 d.

Victoria Lake Caravan Park (tel. 03-5821-5431) is right beside the Tourist Information Centre and backs onto a lake. Tent sites are $10 and on-site vans $30.

Food

Fryers Street Cafe, 96 Fryers St. (tel. 03-5822-2181), has a country atmosphere, with no rush to move on. Breakfast and lunch menus are displayed on a blackboard, and the coffees are delicious; open Mon.-Sat. 9 a.m.-5 p.m. **Higgins Bakery** on Wyndham St. is also good.

Quarterdeck Cafe doesn't have as much at mosphere but overlooks Victoria Lake. **Tuscany's Restaurant,** 125 Fryers St. (tel. 03 5831-1058), is in a renovated redbrick church with stained glass windows, high ceilings, and a unusual (for a church) purple color scheme. Th menu is varied, averaging $12 for lunch an slightly higher for dinner.

Transportation, Services, and Information

V/Line trains run daily between Melbourne an Shepparton ($21.50 one-way). The railway sta tion is on Purcell St. (tel. 03-5820-2405). V/Lin buses depart from here for Albury ($25.40 one way), Benalla ($6.40), and Bendigo ($13.60).

Shepparton Transit (tel. 03-5831-2150) run buses on five routes, each originating from Maude Street. For a cab call (03) 5821-4466.

Shepparton Tourist Information Centre i south of town on Wyndham St. (tel. 03-5832 9870); open daily 9 a.m.-5 p.m.

Kyabram

This farming center of 6,000, 35 km west o Shepparton, is home to **Kyabram Fauna Par** (tel. 03-5852-2883). The park houses Australian native fauna; many species wander around th grounds and are very tame. Admission is adul $5, child $2.50, and it's open daily 10 a.m.-(p.m.

Murchison

This small town, southwest of Shepparton on the Goulburn River, was the impact point for a meteorite in 1969. The meteorite has long since gone but a **Meteorite Information Display** ir town will tell you all about it.

Longleat Winery, south of Murchison, has a pleasant barbeque area shaded by towering eucalypts—the perfect place for lunch with a bottle of their renowned red wine.

Rushworth and Whroo Historic Reserve

Rushworth, in the hills southwest of Murchison was a resting place for diggers traveling between Bendigo and Beechworth, but by the mid-1880s gold had been found in many places around the settlement. The gold lasted only long enough for some classic bluestone buildings to be erected along the main street.

Alluvial gold was found south of Rushworth at
Whroo (pronounced as simply "ROO"), but it
wasn't until large companies began mining
quartz reefs that the settlement gained a permanent look. By the turn of this century gold
began running out and today Whroo is a shadow
of its former self. Most buildings have been dismantled, but the old mine shafts, some foundations, and a cemetery remain. A short trail
leads into the open-cut Balaclava Mine where
other relics lie.

ECHUCA

For 50 years Echuca was the largest and most
important of the Murray River towns, part of a
transportation network that extended along the
Murray to South Australia, the Darling River to
outback NSW, and rail to Melbourne.

The town of Echuca was founded in 1853 by
exconvict Harry Hopwood, who settled in the
area and started a ferry service across the river.

With the gold rush in full swing, business thrived, so he built the Bridge Hotel. When he died, in 1869, Echuca had grown to become the largest inland port in the Southern Hemisphere and, in later years, a major railhead from Melbourne.

Port of Echuca

History lives on at Echuca; the riverfront area looks much the same as it did in the days of paddlesteamers. There may not be as many buildings along the riverfront as there once were, and the red gum wharf that stretched over a kilometer has been partly dismantled, but everything is original, not set up like so many other historic

parks. A "passport" (adult $4.80, child $2.50) allows entry to the Star and Bridge Hotels and the wharf. Tickets are available at the **Star Hotel**, where there's a paddlesteamer display and the exit is a tunnel under the hotel, dug in the days of prohibition. At the wharf, the railway station houses some large vehicles and the cargo shed has a display of life on the river. Moored alongside the wharf is PS *Pevensey* (used in the miniseries *All the Rivers Run*—in fact, most of the series was shot in and around the port area) and PS *Adelaide.* The **Bridge Hotel** has another historic display. This was the hotel built by the enterprising Harry Hopwood. Whenever trade at the bar

Port of Echuca

vas slow, his ferry service would close due to mechanical problems." Open daily 9:15 a.m.-5).m. (tel. 03-5482-4248).

Other Sights

Downstream from the port is **Red Gum Works,** a historic working sawmill where woodturners and blacksmiths make traditional kitchen and household wares; open daily 9 a.m.-5 p.m. (tel. 03-5482-5711). Near the Star Hotel is **Sharp's Magic Movie House and Penny Arcade** (tel. 03-5482-2361), Australia's largest collection of restored penny arcade machines. Admission is adult $6.50, child $3.50. Open daily 9 a.m.-5 p.m. Also near the riverfront, at 57 Murray Esplanade, is **Coach House Carriage Museum** (tel. 03-5482-5244), with a large collection of horse-drawn vehicles and carriage rides around town (Sat.-Sun. only); admission adult $4, child $2.

The historic courthouse on Dickson St. is home of **Njernda Aboriginal Cultural Centre,** which houses an interesting collection of Koori artifacts and a resource center with videos. Admission is adult $2.50, child $1. Open Tues.-Sun. 10 a.m.-4 p.m. (tel. 03-5482-3904). Also in Dickson Street is **Echuca Historical Museum,** in the old police station; open Sat.-Sun. 1-5 p.m.

Recreation, Festivals, and Events

Paddlesteamers operate on the river and a trip on one is a good way to immerse yourself in local history. PS *Pride of the Murray* (tel. 03-5482-5244) and PS *Canberra* (tel. 03-5482-2711) were both built in the early 19th century and cruise the river daily from Paddle Steamer Wharf. One-hour cruises are adult $7, child $3. PS *Emmylou* (tel. 03-5482-3801), as well as doing one-hour cruises, is the only wood-fired steamer in the world offering overnight accommodation; two-night weekend cruises are $400 pp, including all meals.

Echuca Boat and Canoe Hire (tel. 03-5480-6208) rents canoes ($10-12 an hour) and motor boats ($20), and can provide transport upstream for full-day and overnight float trips; located at Victoria Park, downstream from Port of Echuca.

On the first June long weekend is a **Steam, Horse, and Vintage Rally** that brings together vintage and veteran cars, steam engines, and plenty of horse power. The year's other major event is the **Rich River Festival,** held the third week of October; events include a parade of paddlesteamers, arts and crafts displays, and the Henry Hopwood Ball.

Accommodations

Echuca has a wide range of accommodations, including a number of comfortable B&Bs. **Murray House,** 55 Francis St. (tel. 03-5482-4944), is a historic house decorated with period antiques and surrounded by a charming English-style garden; rates are $80 s, $100 d, which includes a hearty breakfast; dinner is also available. Similarly priced is **River Gallery Inn,** 578 High St. (tel. 03-5480-6902).

The hotels in town aren't the accommodation bargain they are elsewhere; **American Hotel,** 239 Hare St. (tel. 03-5482-5044), has basic rooms for $30 s, $40 d, including breakfast. The decent **Steam Packet Motel** is housed in a historic 1860s building. Its rooms, some overlooking the river, are $56 s, $68 d; located on Murray Esplanade at Leslie St. (tel. 03-5482-

3411). **Big River Motel,** 317 High St. (tel. 03-5482-2522), is a centrally located budget motel; $42 a, $55 d. **Caledonian Hotel/Motel,** 110 Hare St. (tel. 03-5482-2100), is a restored hotel with high-standard units, each with modern facilities, some with spas; $45 s, $70 d.

Closest camping to town is at **Echuca Caravan Park,** Crofton St. (tel. 03-5482-2157), which is right alongside the river in a setting replete with trees. Sites are $10, on-site vans $28, and cabins $40.

Echuca Riverboat YHA Hostel, 103 Mitchell St. (tel. 03-5480-6522), a 10-minute walk from town, is run by a friendly host with plenty of information on the area. Dorm accommodation is members $10, nonmembers $13.

Food

A good place for lunch is **Wistaria Tea Rooms** at 51 Murray Esplanade (tel. 03-5482-4210). Built in the 1880s as a private residence, it is surrounded in colorful gardens. Light lunches are served, but the morning and afternoon teas are the specialty (from $4); open daily 10 a.m.-5 p.m. For more substantial meals, **Bridge Hotel,** Hopwood Place (tel. 03-5482-2247), is a good choice. **Riverside Restaurant,** 101 Murray Esplanade (tel. 03-5482-5133), overlooks the river and has a shaded veranda—perfect for lunch or dinner on those warmer evenings. The menu features mainly local game and produce with main dishes starting at around $12. **Fiori,** 205 Pakenham St. (tel. 03-5482-6688), is a casual yet stylish Italian restaurant that many locals swear by.

Transportation, Services, and Information

From Melbourne, **V/Line** operates trains as far north as Bendigo, from where buses continue to Echuca ($25 one-way); the terminal is in the old railway station on Sturt St. (tel. 03-5482-3589). From Echuca buses run west to Swan Hill ($21.80 one-way) and Mildura ($34.80), and east to Wodonga ($29.10).

V/Line offers a variety of day trips to Echuca from Melbourne that include a cruise on a paddlesteamer. Call (03) 9619-5000 for details. Other companies offering Echuca day tours are: **AAT Kings** (tel. 03-9650-1244, Thursday and Saturday) and **Australian Pacific Tours** (tel. 03-9654-7700, Wednesday and Sunday).

Housed in the historic Customs House **Echuca Tourist Information Centre** at 2 Lesl St. (tel. 03-5482-4525); open Mon.-Fri. 9 a.m.-p.m., Sat.-Sun. 10 a.m.-4 p.m.

ALONG THE MURRAY FROM ECHUCA TO WODONGA

Barmah State Park

This 30,000-hectare park along a 100-km stretc of the Murray River contains the world's large and oldest red gum forest. The forest floor wa once part of a vast inland lake and still toda acts as a natural flood control for the river. N just the number, but the sheer size of the re gums—as high as 40 meters—is staggering Within the forest are many hiking trails, camp grounds, and wildlife such as kangaroos, koalas and platypuses. During the Wet many trails ar flooded, and the only way to get around is b canoe or boat. This is also the best time to vie the 200 species of birds present. Tours throug the park are offered on *Kingfisher* (tel. 03-5866 2702), a flat-bottomed boat. The two-hour cruis leaves four times weekly and costs $15 pp.

The park's only facilities are a basic camp ground and **Dharnya Visitor Centre** (tel. 03 5869-3302). Built of red gum, the latter house artifacts relating to the local Yorta Yorta Koo and has general park information. Access t the forest is from the small town of Barmah, 3 km east of Echuca.

Ulupna Island

East of Barmah State Park is Barmah Stat *Forest.* You can get there through the park, bu it's easier to take the gravel road that lies one kn west of **Strathmerton.** The sign says Ulupn Island. Continue to the end of the road and tak the left fork. Most of the island is cleared, but thi section is home to a colony of koalas. They are hard to spot at first, but as your eyes become ac customed to spotting the furry little critters, thei numbers become apparent. Although there are no facilities on the island, it's a wonderful spot t camp.

Cobram and Yarrawonga

Cobram and its NSW counterpart, Barooga, are the center of a stretch of the Murray River popu-ar with families for the sandy beaches and ourist facilities that have sprung up around 1em.

Yarrawonga is on the banks of Lake Mulvala, an artificial lake used for irrigation. The .ady Murray (tel. 03-5744-2005) cruises the iver daily with a lunchtime cruise for only $12. 3uilt in 1842, **Byramine Homestead** was the 1ome of the area's first white settlers. Admission s adult $4, child $2, and it's open daily 10 a.m.-:30 p.m. Located 15 km west of Yarrawonga tel. 03-5748-4258).

Rutherglen

This small town of 2,000 people and many historic buildings, 46 km east of Yarrawonga and 40 km north of Wangaratta, is the hub of Victoria's oest-known wine area. The Rutherglen region is renowned for its fortified wines, but each of the lozen-odd wineries has its own specialties.

Walkabout Cellars, 84 Main St. (tel. 060-32-9784), stocks local wines and is a good source of tourist information. The brochure *The Winemakers of Rutherglen* (available at all local vineries) covers all local wineries and makes t easy to decide which direction to head. Walkabout Cellars also rents bikes for $15 per day—he perfect way to get from one winery to the next. One of the original wineries is **Fairfield Vineyard,** 13 km east of Rutherglen (tel. 060-32-9381). The original homestead, built in the 1880s, still stands and is open for tours. Best known for its reds, this winery still uses original equipment; open Mon.-Sat. 10 a.m.-5 p.m., Sunday noon-5 p.m. **Campbell's Winery,** two km west of Rutherglen (tel. 060-32-9458), is another well-established winery renowned for fortified wines. This place has a self-guided tour

and small museum. Open daily 9 a.m.-5 p.m.

The classic old **Victoria Hotel,** 90 Main St. (tel. 060-32-8610), was built in the days of the gold rush, and although the rooms haven't changed much since, they are clean and the beds comfortable; $22 s, $36 d. **Mount Ophir** is the homestead of a former vineyard owner and has been refurnished to an excellent upmarket B&B. Rates are $106 d, with dinner available.

Both pubs in town serve good bar meals. The **Shamrock** (tel. 060-32-8439) is a historic two-story building on Main Street. The menu is small, but the chef does an excellent job, with daily specials usually being local game.

Wodonga

Wodonga is talked about in the same breath as Albury, its twin town on the NSW-side of the Murray River border. Wodonga, the smaller of the two with a population of around 28,000, has grown steadily since a rail line from Melbourne arrived in 1873. It has also had strong links to the military since 1943, including being home for a time to the famed Australian war heroes the Rats of Tobruk. The **RAA Ordinance Corps Museum** is on the base, four km southeast of Wodonga; open Tues.-Sun. 10 a.m.-4 p.m.

Two good sources of information are the **DC&NR** office, in the local TAFE College at 1 McKoy St., off Moorefield Park Dr. (which is off Melbourne Dr., tel. 060-55-6111), and **Gateway Tourist Centre,** on the east side of the Hume Hwy., halfway between Wodonga and Albury. The latter has a ton of information on both Victoria and NSW destinations, and offers local arts and crafts for sale and a roaring log fire during winter. Open daily 9 a.m.-5 p.m. (tel. 060-41-3875).

HIGH COUNTRY

In world terms, the Great Dividing Range isn't particularly high; in fact, no Victorian peak reaches over 2,000 meters; but the High Country is spectacular, encompassing a vast section of northeastern Victoria that offers steep-sided valleys covered in forests of gnarled and stunted snow gums, cascading mountain streams, and high plateaus above the treeline with views extending many hundreds of kilometers.

Although most of the region is very remote, a number of roads penetrate the region, leading from the valley floor to ski villages perched among the mountain peaks. The most direct access is along the Hume Freeway, from where access roads spur east into the mountains. But a more picturesque alternative is through the Yarra Valley to Healesville and Marysville, from where it's only a short drive around massive Lake Eildon to Mansfield, a classic High Country town surrounded in rolling hills. East of Mansfield is Mt. Buller, one of four High Country ski resorts. The others are farther north: head to Mt. Buffalo for the relaxed atmosphere, Mt. Hotham for the expert skiing, and Falls Creek for all the style of an upmarket European resort. Another major gateway to the High Country is Beechworth, one of Australia's best-preserved goldrush towns.

Alpine National Park

This 6,460-square-km park was proclaimed in 1989, providing an important advancement in the protection of Australia's alpine region. The park extends from the Latrobe Valley, in Gippsland, along the Great Dividing Range to the New South Wales border and Kosciusko National Park. The park provides opportunities for a great variety of recreational pursuits, including hiking, fishing, camping, horseback riding, and, in winter, downhill and cross-country skiing. The most spectacular part of the park is above the treeline, where views extend hundreds of kilometers. The main access to the park is east from Mansfield and south from Bright and Mount Beauty to the **Bogong High Plains.**

Alpine Walking Track

This 400-km trail was in place before proclamation of the park. It extends from Walhalla, near Baw Baw National Park, to Cowombat on the NSW border and can be walked in 30 days. Attempting the entire length of the trail requires much planning and backcountry experience, but many short sections can be hiked in a day, and as the trail crosses six highways, access is easy.

For details on the Alpine National Park and Alpine Walking Track, call (03) 5772-1633.

MELBOURNE TO THE HIGH COUNTRY VIA THE YARRA VALLEY

The most direct route to the High Country ski resorts and the towns of Mansfield, Beechworth, and Mt. Beauty is the Hume Freeway, but by detouring along the Yarra Valley you'll pass a number of interesting towns.

Healesville

Healesville, 61 km from Melbourne, is best known for **Healesville Wildlife Sanctuary,** one of the best showcases of Australian fauna in the country. The park grew from a plot of native bushland used for a study of Australian marsupials in 1929 and remains, for the most part, in its natural state—although the density of animals has increased. A trail winds its way through the sanctuary, passing wetlands, aviaries, various large enclosures, and a nocturnal creekside habitat. Park staff give informative talks and there are animal feeding sessions a couple of times a day. Other facilities include picnic tables, a barbecue area, cafe, and souvenir shop. Admission is adult $10, child $5. Open daily 9 a.m.-5 p.m. Located on Badger Creek Rd. (tel. 03-5962-4022).

Close to the wildlife park are **Sanctuary House Motel** (tel. 03-5962-5148) and **Ashgrove Caravan Park** (tel. 03-5962-4398).

Yarra Valley-Healesville Tourist Information Centre is on the north side of Healesville at Kinglake Rd. (tel. 03-5962-2600); open daily 10 a.m.-5 p.m.

Kinglake National Park and Vicinity

This 11,430-hectare park is made up of three separate sections of the Kinglake Ranges (an arm of the Great Dividing Range), each surrounded by cleared farmland. Central to the three sections is the small township of Kinglake, 33 km northwest of Healesville. In the park's western section, near Masons Falls, are short hikes and a park office (tel. 03-5786-5328). Camping is at **The Gums,** in the northern section (accessible along Eucalyptus Rd., northeast of Kinglake). Sites are secluded and nearby trails lead along Hirts Creek and to the summit of Andrews Hill (661 meters), the park's highest peak.

Toolangi, 16 km east of Kinglake, along the road to Healesville, was once the home to poet C.J. Dennis, who wrote "The Sentimental Bloke." Gardens developed around his property, **Arden,** are open to the public, and Devonshire teas are served on weekends. Also in Toolangi is the **Forest Discovery Centre,** a uniquely shaped building set among a towering eucalypts. Interpretive displays inside explain forest environments and humanity's role in protecting them. Open daily 10 a.m.-5 p.m.; admission $2.

Marysville

For the early part of this century, when Melburnians went on their honeymoons, they went to Marysville. The many guesthouses, tearooms, and specialty shops remain, and it's still a popular spot for weekend getaways, surrounded by forested hills and with nearby gardens, valleys, and streams adding to the beauty. At 84 meters, **Steavenson Falls,** four km from town, is the highest of any waterfall in the state; it's floodlit daily until midnight. In winter Marysville is the gateway to **Lake Mountain,** an excellent cross-country skiing facility 21 km to the east (see the special topic "Victoria's Ski Resorts").

Marylands Country House is one of the original guesthouses, having been completed in 1928, 27 years before the township got electricity. Everything about the original house was done on the grandest scale. Built as a country resort with all modern facilities, today it retains much of its original elegance. Rates are $85 pp, which includes breakfast and a three-course dinner; located on Falls Rd. (tel. 03-5963-3204). In a more modern setting—and with a swimming pool, spa, sauna, and large lounge area with library—is **Nanda Binya Lodge,** one km from the center of town along Woods Point Rd (tel. 03-5963-3433). Rates are a reasonable $38 s, $58 d, for bed and breakfast. Marysville also has a couple of moderately-priced motels and a caravan park by the river (tel. 03-5963-3443).

Cathedral Range State Park

North of Marysville is this 3,550-hectare park named for the impressive cliffs that dominate the eastern skyline as you travel along the Maroondah Highway. Access is limited to gravel roads at the north and south ends of the park and a variety of signposted hiking trails heading of into the relatively remote wilderness. The park's five camping areas each have pit toilets, a water source, and not much else. Further information is available from the **DC&NR** on Lye St. in Marysville (tel. 03-5963-3379).

Lake Eildon

Water from this reservoir is used to irrigate surrounding farmland and the Goulburn Valley, but the lake itself offers many opportunities for water-based activities, which center mostly around the small town of **Eildon.** On the lake's western shore is **Fraser National Park,** 17 km beyond Alexandra. The park access road climbs a low, bare hill before descending into a native forest of eucalypts. The lakeshore isn't particularly pretty, but areas of the park once used for grazing are slowly being regenerated, providing the habitat for koalas, possums, wombats, and a large population of gray kangaroos. For birdwatching, the best part of the park is Candlebark Gully Nature Walk, beginning from Candlebark Campground. Scattered around the shoreline are three campgrounds with great facilities, including showers at Coller Bay and Candlebark (book in summer at 03-5772-1293). The park entrance fee is $3 per day.

Eildon grew from a settlement for hydroelectric workers and is now an accommodation center for holidayers. Worth stopping at is **Snobs Creek Freshwater Fisheries Research Station,** six km southwest of town (tel. 03-5774-2208). A visitor center within this large hatchery complex has displays on the important role hatcheries have in maintaining stocks of fish in

Jamieson church

Victoria's inland waterways. Admission is adult $3.50, child $1.75. Open daily 10 a.m.-4:30 p.m.

The shortest route from Eildon to Mansfield is around the lake's northwestern arm, but the eastern route is more interesting. That road, around 100 km to Mansfield, forms the southern boundary of **Eildon State Park,** which runs right down to Lake Eildon.

Jamieson and Woods Point Road

Only a short distance from the southeastern arm of Lake Eildon, the historic gold-mining town of Jamieson lies at the confluence of the Goulburn and Jamieson Rivers, surrounded by rolling hills. Decent gold strikes were made throughout the area, and many buildings from the gold-rush era remain, including a courthouse and church. The **Court House Hotel** (tel. 03-5777-0503) has motel-style rooms ($20 pp) and a restaurant.

Southeast from Jamieson, an unsealed road winds its way through a valley littered with evidence of early mining operations to Woods Point, then spurs west to Marysville. If you've got a full tank of petrol, it is possible to continue south to the Latrobe Valley.

MANSFIELD AND VICINITY

Located 185 km northeast of Melbourne, Mansfield is one of the main gateways to the High Country. As land in the Goulburn Valley was

settled, graziers began looking farther afield, eventually setting up pastoral leases in the remote valley in which Mansfield lies. There's not a lot to see and do in the actual town, but with plenty of tourist facilities it makes an excellent base for exploring the nearby alpine areas, and in winter at nearby Mt. Buller ski lifts crank up on some of Australia's best slopes.

Those interested in following the trail of the bushrangers may want to wander up to the cemetery at the end of Highett Street. While Ned and his gang were treated as folk heroes elsewhere in Victoria, the headstones on the graves of three murdered policemen here tell a different story. In the middle of the roundabout back in town is another memorial to the troopers.

Accommodations

Mansfield Hotel, 86 High St. (tel. 03-5775-2101), has basic pub rooms, with breakfast thrown in for $25 pp. Also at the budget end of the scale is **Mansfield Backpackers Inn,** 122 High St. (tel. 03-5775-1800), which offers good clean dorm accommodation (some double rooms) with a modern kitchen, laundry, and barbecue area. Rates are $15 pp ($20 pp in winter). If you're just after a standard motel room, a few places in Mansfield, Merrijig, and up at Mt. Buller are open year-round, but remember prices rise dramatically during the ski season (in winter make bookings through Mt. Buller Central Reservations, tel. 1800-03-9049). **Alzburg Inn Resort,** 39 Malcolm St., Mansfield (tel. 03-5775-

2367), is spread out around a 100-year-old convent and has a large pool, tennis court, and restaurant. Off-season rates (summer) start at $68 s or d, with a two-night adventure package offered for $185 pp. In town, **Alpine Country Cottages,** 5 the Parade (tel. 03-5775-1694), comprises small self-contained cottages set in pleasant gardens; rates are $90 per cottage. Toward Mt. Buller is the upmarket **Pinnacle Valley Resort** (tel. 03-5777-5788), spread out over a picturesque property with a small lake. Rooms are modern and facilities include a restaurant with stunning views, game room, gym, tennis courts, horse riding, and mountain bikes.

Food

Bon Appetit, 39 High St. (tel. 03-5775-2951), serves healthy breakfasts and deli-style lunches daily 7:30 a.m.-5 p.m. On either side are bakeries. Across the road is **Witch's Brew Cafe,** 28 High St. (tel. 03-5775-2623), famous for its eerie decorations, or head to the light, bright **Collopy Street Cafe,** 24 High St. (tel. 03-5775-1081). The town's finest restaurant is **Grants of Mansfield,** Mt. Buller Rd. (tel. 03-5775-2963), located in a classic federation home; European dishes start at $15. Up on Mt. Buller, the **Arlberg Hotel** has an inexpensive bistro and a more formal restaurant, a couple of places that stay open year-round (tel. 03-5777-6260).

Transportation, Services, and Information

Mansfield Bus Depot is in the center of town on High St. (tel. 03-5775-2606). **V/Line** operates daily services between Melbourne and Mansfield ($25 one-way). **Benalla Bus Lines** links Mansfield with Benalla Monday and Thursday ($7 one-way). Staff at the depot can organize transportation beyond Mansfield and operate 4WD tours into the High Country.

Legendary Country Tourist Information Centre is in an old railway station on the Melbourne side of Mansfield; open daily 10 a.m.-4 p.m. (tel. 03-5775-1464).

Merrijig and the Surrounding High Country

Beyond Mansfield, the highway passes through the small town of Merrijig, which hosts a big rodeo each Labour Day weekend (March), then parallels the Delatite River and climbs into the High Country. The ski resort of **Mt. Buller** (see the special topic "Victoria's Ski Resorts"), 4 km east of Mansfield, only opens lifts on special occasions in summer, but with the newly opened Australian Alpine Institute attracting more summer visitors, the lifts may operate more frequently. The institute offers a variety of short courses that, although designed for learning, are a fantastic way to experience the High Country. For details call (03) 5777-6450. If you want to commune with nature, walking trails lie throughout the resort's village area, and the area around Mt. Stirling is less developed. Much of the movie *Man From Snowy River* was filmed up here and **Craig's Hut,** part of the original set, is the destination of a popular four km (one-way) hike along a rough 4WD track. **Mansfield Mountain Safaris** offers 4WD tours from Mansfield up to the hut ($49 pp), as well as full-day and overnight tours (from $150 pp). They are based at the Mansfield Bus Depot (tel. 03-5775-2606). For a horse-powered High Country expedition **Stoney's Bluff and Beyond Trail Rides** offer a full-day ride into the wilderness for $75 pp including lunch; based at Stockyard Creek, along the Howqua Track on the Mt. Buller side of Merrijig (tel. 03-5775-2212).

Stringybark Creek

This small creek flowing through an undistinguished valley of the Wombat Ranges north of Mansfield is synonymous with the Kelly Gang, claimed by some to be the place where Australia lost its innocence. On 25 October 1878 four troopers set off from Mansfield in search of the Kelly gang; through relatives and friends the gang learned the whereabouts of troopers and stormed their camp, killing three officers with the fourth managing to escape to raise the alarm. It didn't take long for Australia's biggest manhunt to get underway, concluding with a fiery showdown at Glenrowan. The massacre site is marked by a small plaque implanted in a large eucalypt. To get there from Mansfield take the first left through town signposted to **Tolmie.** Beyond Tolmie, a gravel road spurs northwest (left) to Tatong (along this part of the route are two primitive campgrounds); the Kelly tree is signposted 11 km from Tolmie. Near the tree is a pleasant picnic area.

Headstones dotted around the High Country are about the only reminders of the days of bushrangers. This one and two others in Mansfield Cemetery mark the resting places of police shot by Ned Kelly at Stringybark Creek.

In Tolmie, the **Rose & Oak Inn** (tel. 03-5776-2389) serves beer and bar meals and across the road is a petrol pump and general store with a hand-drawn map of the area.

The road out to Stringybark Creek continues north to Benalla, and the sealed road through Tolmie continues north to Wangaratta through the King Valley.

OVENS VALLEY

Gold diggers, then graziers and farmers, settled this wide valley through which the **Ovens River** flows in a northwesterly direction from Mt. Hotham through Wangaratta before it drains into the Murray River. Along the valley floor are the towns of Myrtleford and Bright, gateways, re-

spectively, to the spectacular granite slabs of Mt. Buffalo National Park and, in winter, some of Australia's steepest ski slopes at Mt. Hotham.

Mount Buffalo National Park

Towering 1,000 meters above the surrounding plains, this 31,000-hectare park protects a plateau that, from a distance, early explorers likened to a buffalo. The impressive landscape of strange-looking tors alone makes the long and winding 30-km drive from the Ovens Valley worthwhile. The park also produces a dazzling display of wildflowers each spring and boasts impressive waterfalls, a picturesque lake, some of Australia's most challenging rock climbing, and, in winter, downhill skiing.

The plateau was formed around 300 million years ago when forces beneath the earth's crust pushed a molten mass through sedimentary rock, forming a plateau three times its present height. Through eons, wind and water have eroded the plateau to its present height. In many places the granite has cracked, with huge chunks falling away leaving the sheer cliffs.

Summer temperatures in the park average 10° C (about 20° F) cooler than the valley below. Only a few species of plants survive in this harsh subalpine environment; snow gum and alpine ash dominate, while areas with little soil and water support dry heath, grasses, and mosses. The presence of larger mammals is limited by surrounding cliffs, but the park does have populations of wombats and swamp wallabies. Over 100 species of reptiles and 130 species of birds have been recorded, including superb lyrebirds and a variety of cockatoos.

From **Porepunkah,** six km northwest of Bright, the access road passes the park gate ($6 per car) and climbs past scenic viewpoints to the plateau and **Lake Catani.** View Point Nature Walk begins from the lake and passes through a variety of plant communities (four km round-trip). From the lake, the road continues climbing to Dingo Dell, a downhill and cross-country skiing area (see the special topic "Victoria's Ski Resorts"), past a field stacked with towering granite rock stacks, including the impressive Cathedral, and onto **Cresta Valley,** where the main skiing area and an information center are located.

The campground at Lake Catani has excellent facilities, including showers. Reservations are

ANDREW HEMPSTEAD

Mount Buffalo National Park

needed only during public and school holidays (tel. 03-5755-1466). Within the park are two guesthouses, both offering year-round accommodations. **Tatra Inn** (tel. 03-5755-1988) is a modern lodge located at the end of the main access road, right by the main downhill skiing area. Off-season discounts aren't as steep here as other ski resorts, mainly because the area is so popular during summer. Dorm beds are $54 pp, double rooms $65 pp, rising to $73 and $95 pp respectively in the ski season. All rates include three cooked meals. Away from the action but with historic charm is **Mt. Buffalo Chalet** (tel. 03-5755-1500). This grand old chalet overlooks a spectacular gorge, with the Buckland Valley far below and the horizon lined with Victoria's highest peaks. Rooms have recently been renovated, without losing any of their original charm. But with tennis, a swimming pool, cricket, croquet, a gym, and the wonders of the park, you won't want to spend long in your room. Rates start at $89 pp for rooms with shared facilities, and rooms with a view range $119-127

pp; all rates include a cooked breakfast, picnic lunch, and a three-course dinner in the Grand Dining Room. Nonguests can dine at the chalet with advance reservations.

Park Headquarters, on the main access road, is open daily 8:15-8:30 a.m. and 4-4:30 p.m.; at other times information is available at the Tatra Inn, where a booth is staffed daily 1:30-2:30 p.m.

Bright

This picturesque town of 2,000, spread out along the banks of the Ovens River, is at the crossroads of the High Country, a center of activities during summer and a good base for trips to the three major ski resorts in winter. After a gold rush in the nearby Buckland Valley, many diggers decided to settle in the area, and the town of Bright developed.

Lining the main thoroughfare are rows of elms, poplars, and chestnuts, which turn brilliant shades of orange and red each fall. Around town are a variety of walks, and a small museum is in the railway station (open Tuesday, Thursday, and Sunday 2-4 p.m.). **Wandiligong Valley,** immediately south of Bright, is today a far cry from the 1860s, when thousands of diggers lived in shanty towns along Morses Creek. Self-guided walks lead along the creek and through buildings that have survived the ravages of time.

Like all High Country towns, emphasis in Bright is on outdoor recreation. **Bright Sports Centre,** 47 Gavan St. (tel. 03-5755-1339), rents mountain bikes for $6 an hour or $21 a day. For guided horseback riding, **Bright High Country Safaris,** on the road over to Mt. Beauty (tel. 03-5755-1896), has rides for all ability levels, including three- and five-day expeditions for around $90 pp per day. Mount Buffalo is a popular launch site for experienced hang gliders, but for first-timers, the **Eagle School of Hang Gliding** offers a two-day introductory course for $300 pp; contact the information center for details.

Bright Alps Guesthouse, 83 Delany Ave. (tel. 03-5755-1197), is an inexpensive accommodation. Rooms have shared facilities and there's also a lounge and dining area. Rates are $25 s, $48 d, including breakfast. **Bright Central Motel,** 2 Ireland St. (tel. 03-5755-1074), has good, basic rooms from $30 s, $50 d, as oes **Ovens Valley Motor Inn,** two km west of own (tel. 03-5755-2022). **Bright Caravan Park,** Cherry Ave. (tel. 03-5755-1141), is spread out along the banks of Morses Creek. Tent sites are $10, powered sites $12, and on-site vans 25. Within the grounds is **Bright Youth Hostel,** a modern structure built for the recent World Hang Gliding Championships. Each dorm has our beds and a private bathroom, with rooms nked by a covered walkway to the main building, where a modern kitchen and comfortable ounge with an open fire are located. Rates are 14 pp.

The Alpine Hotel, a restored pub on Anderson St., has an extensive bistro menu, available at the bar or in the lounge. For a more relaxed atmosphere, **Hummingbird Coffee Shop,** Starr Rd. (tel. 03-5755-1830), is open daily 10 a.m.-5 p.m., serving healthy lunches and Devonshire teas. **Liquid Am-bar,** 8 Anderson St. tel. 03-5755-2318), is a funky kind of place with all meals under $10. A little more stylish is **Rebekka's at Bright,** 98 Gavan St. (tel. 03-5750-251). It's a restored house with dining areas in our rooms, each with a fireplace, and summer dining in an outdoor courtyard; open daily from 5:30 p.m.

V/Line buses connect Bright with Wangaratta (daily except Saturday); $9 one-way.

Bright Tourist Information Centre is in a small park on the main drag through town (tel. 03-5755-2275). It's open daily 10 a.m.-4 p.m.

Harrietville to Hotham

Like Bright, Harrietville, 25 km to the southeast, is a gold-rush town. It is the gateway to Mt. Hotham ski area, a steep, 41-km drive away. East of Harrietville is **Mt. Feathertop;** at 1,923 meters it's Victoria's second-highest peak. It stands apart from the main range, making it all the more impressive. The hike to the summit is pretty steep, but is easy if tackled as an overnight trip. The trailhead is one km down a gravel road at the bridge just before own. From the carpark, it is nine km (four hours) to a hut and primitive campground. From here it's three steep km to the summit. You can return to the valley floor along the same route or by climbing the summit track for one km, then following a track that spurs left, passing another hut and ending on the Ovens High-

way, four km north of Harrietville. A number of topographical maps cover the mountain; the best seems to be *Feathertop-Hotham Divide* (Algona Guides), available at outdoor shops in Bright and Harrietville.

Beyond Harrietville the highway climbs steeply to a ridge above Mt. Hotham Ski Area (see the special topic "Victoria's Ski Resorts"). Not much happens up here in summer, although the road continues to the resort community of **Dinner Plain,** in Alpine National Park, and onto **Omeo** on the Omeo Highway.

MOUNT BEAUTY AND BEYOND

Nestled below **Mt. Bogong** (1,986 meters), the state's highest peak, the township of Mt. Beauty makes an excellent base for exploring the surrounding High Country. It lies at the end of the Kiewa Valley, separated from the Ovens Valley by a forested ridge and bounded to the south by Bogong High Plains. A winding 40-km road links Mt. Beauty to Bright, or the township can be approached from the north along the Kiewa Valley Highway. The town is relatively new, having been built in the 1940s for workers on the Kiewa Hydro Electric Scheme.

Bogong Horseback Adventures retains the original form of High Country transportation with half- and full-day rides starting from stables on Mountain Creek Rd. in Tawonga. December through April, overnight packhorse adventures are offered, starting at $450 for three days (tel. 03-5754-4849). **Cranky Charlie** (tel. 03-5754-4227) rents mountain bikes for $15 per day. For the less energetic, green fees at the short but challenging 18-hole **Mt. Beauty Golf Course** are $10 ($25 per week); Snow Gum Motel (tel. 03-5754-4508) has club rentals.

Mount Beauty Practicalities

The cheapest accommodations are in Mt. Beauty's twin town of Tawonga South and, farther north, in Tawonga. **Bogong Hotel,** in Tawonga (tel. 03-5754-4482), has clean rooms for just $25 s, $45 d, including breakfast. **Bogong Resort,** on Mountain Creek Rd. (tel. 03-5754-4247), is an excellent facility with summer rates starting at $42 s, $55 d. In Mt. Beauty itself **Snow Gum Motel,** on the Kiewa Valley Hwy.

VICTORIA'S SKI RESORTS

Victoria has five downhill ski resorts and three areas set aside for cross-country skiing. Each downhill resort has on-snow accommodation, and this should be booked well in advance. Roads to resorts are very steep, and chains must be carried at all times (grab them from all gateway towns). Although the resorts are owned privately, each is managed by the Alpine Resorts Commission, which collects a toll of $8-16 per *every* car using resort access roads (the fee increases in winter). This fee, plus chain hire ($15-20 per day), equipment hire ($21-40 per day), and lift tickets ($30-54 per day), makes for an expensive outing. But skiing above the treeline, among stunted snow gums and great outcrops of granite, is an experience that Northern Hemisphere skiers won't forget in a hurry. Ways to cut down costs are by taking an all-inclusive package from Melbourne, or staying off the mountain. The closest snowfield to Melbourne is **Mt. Donna Buang,** near Healesville, where "Sightseeing Snow" is the main attraction.

Mount Baw Baw
This 25-hectare ski area with a vertical drop of 140 meters is located in Baw Baw National Park, 178 km east of Melbourne. It has eight lifts and is best suited to beginners and families. **Mt. Baw Baw Hostel** (tel. 03-5165-1129) is open daily during the season and rates are $26 for members, $31 for nonmembers, with three meals an extra $10. Otherwise, call **Baw Baw Bookings** at (03) 9879-7809 for other options and current transportation links. Lift tickets are $37 for adults, $20 for kids, and the entry fee for cars is $14. For more information call (03) 5165-1136 or, for a recorded message, call (03) 5165-1126.

On the southern end of the same plateau is **Mount St. Gwinear** (tel. 03-5165-3481), a cross-country ski area with marked tracks, a kiosk, and ski rentals. Entry is $6 per car per day.

Lake Mountain
Australia's premier cross-country skiing area, Lake Mountain is 22 km west of Marysville at the top of the Yarra Valley and has over 40 km of groomed trails. All trails are groomed daily and marked according to degree of difficulty. Facilities include ski hire, kiosk and cafe, information center (tel. 03-5963-3288),

and snow camping. You'll be charged $10 per car plus a trail fee of $5 pp. The closest accommodation is in Marysville, from where **Fallon's Bus Service** (tel. 03-5772-1796) runs a weekend shuttle to the mountain.

Mount Buller
Mount Buller is Victoria's largest ski resort. It's located 240 km from Melbourne, 47 km beyond the town of Mansfield, which provides inexpensive accommodation alternatives to the mountain. This place gets busy on weekends, but has an extensive snowmaking system, ensuring most of the mountain remains open, even in years of poor snowfall. The resort covers 160 hectares and is served by 26 lifts. The village itself, with fantastic views across the High Country, has dozens of accommodations, an ice-skating rink, and night skiing on Wednesday and Saturday. Lift tickets are $54 for adults, $27 for children, and those under five and over 70 ski free. Gate entry fees are $14 per car. For accommodation call Mt. Buller Central Reservations at (1800) 03-9049. The **Kooroora Hotel** (tel. 03-5777-6050) is one of the mountain's least expensive places to stay at $50 pp, including breakfast. For resort information, call (03) 5777-6052, or for a snow report, (03) 5777-6067. Transportation to the village is operated by **V/Line** from Melbourne ($38.50 one-way). If you're only up for the day, there's no need to park near the village; lift tickets can be bought at the base of the Horse Hill chairlift.

Mount Stirling
This cross-country skiing area is 40 km from Mansfield along the same access road as Mt. Buller. It has 60 km of groomed trails, some through forests of snow gums, others above the treeline. After heavy snowfall, it's possible to ski between Mt. Stirling and Mt. Buller. Facilities include a ski school, rentals, cafe, and information center. The daily trail fee is $5 pp and car entry fee is $8. For information and snow reports call (03) 5777-6067.

Mount Buffalo
This resort may lack the hype of other areas, but the location, atop a massive plateau of granite surrounded by spectacular High Country scenery, makes up for a lack of challenging runs. Cresta Valley, with

five lifts, is the main downhill area, with 27 hectares and a vertical drop of 157 meters. Throughout the park are some good cross-country skiing runs. Accommodation is at the on-slope **Tatra Inn** (tel. 03-5755-1988) or **Mt. Buffalo Chalet** (tel. 03-5755-1500). Lift tickets are adults $30, children $15, and gate entry fee is $9 per car. The area is not served by public transportation, but if you're booked at either of the lodges, transportation from Wangaratta can be arranged. For snow reports, call (03) 5755-1216.

Mount Hotham

The issue of which Australian ski resort has the most challenging slopes is always contentious, but Mount Hotham's name is always mentioned. The slopes are higher than others and more open to the elements, but, at 1,750 meters, snowfall is high. The makeup of the resort is also different—the beginners area is around the summit of Mt. Hotham, while more difficult runs drop away from the village into a tree-filled valley. The resort has eight lifts scattered over an area of 43 hectares and has a vertical drop of 428 meters. The village is tuned more to accommodating skiers rather than après-ski entertainment. Lift tickets are adult $45, child $23. The entry fee for cars is $15 per day. Accommodation in the village and nearby Dinner Plain can be booked through **Ski-com** (tel. 03-5759-3522) or **Mt. Hotham Accom-modation Service** (tel. 03-5759-3636). **Trekset Snow Services** (tel. 03-9370-9055) serves the mountain with a bus service from Melbourne each weekend and serves communities at the base of the mountain daily. For resort information, call (03) 5759-3508. For snow reports, call (0055) 32-002.

Falls Creek

A long 375-km drive from Melbourne, Falls Creek is one of Victoria's largest ski resorts. It is located on the Bogong High Plains, at the end of Kiewa Valley. Its 22 lifts are spread over two distinct areas, covering an area of 145 hectares; the vertical drop is 267 meters. The resort is the most upmarket in Victoria, and the village boasts a lively nightlife. Lift tickets are $54 for adults, $27 for children, and the entry fee is $14 per car. On-mountain accommodation starts at around $100 pp per night in the high season and can be booked through **Falls Creek Chamber of Commerce** at (03) 5754-4718. To lower costs, plan to stay at Mt. Beauty, on the valley floor. **Pyles Coaches** (tel. 03-5754-4024) operates a Fri.-Sun. bus service between Melbourne and Falls Creek ($49 one-way) and a daily service from Albury ($22). The bus line also operates a frequent shuttle from Mt. Beauty up to the slopes ($12 one-way). For resort information, call 5758-3280; for snow reports, call (0055) 32-003.

tel. 03-5754-4508), has rooms of an excellent standard for $45 d, 55 d. Between Mt. Beauty and Tawonga South is **Mt. Beauty Holiday Centre** (tel. 03-5754-4396), offering camping sites for $10-18, self-contained cabins for $30-50 d, and European yurts for $80 per night.

The main shopping precinct has a couple of supermarkets, but there's nowhere to recommend for a meal—try the golf club.

Pyle's Coaches operates a winter-only bus service from Albury and Melbourne to Falls Creek and in summer offers a variety of 4WD trips onto the Bogong High Plains. Rates are $45-65 pp for a full-day trip (tel. 03-5754-4024). This depot, on the main road into Mt. Beauty, is also the agent for Budget rental cars and the office of Falls Creek Chamber of Commerce; open daily 9 a.m.-4 p.m. The **Australian High Country Visitor Centre,** toward Mt. Beauty, is another source of information (tel. 03-5754-3172).

Bogong

From Mt. Beauty, the road begins a steady ascent through a forest of eucalypt to the Bogong High Plains. En route is the small hamlet of Bogong, built to house workers on the nearby hydroelectric scheme. It is set around manmade **Lake Guy,** where canoes can be rented. The general store can arrange accommodations and has details of hiking in the area.

Falls Creek and Bogong High Plains

Falls Creek, as well as being one of Australia's top ski resorts (see the special topic "Victoria's Ski Resorts"), is a great summer destination with a variety of outdoor activities possible when it's not covered in snow (late Nov.-April). The village is located on Bogong High Plains, a plateau of low tussocky grasses, an alpine environment easily enjoyed by all levels of fitness. Surrounding the plains are steep-sided valleys filled with gnarled snow gums, and the odd isolated peak, such as Mt. Bogong, a huge chunk of granite separated from the main range. The village is the center of most organized outdoor recreation, but experienced bushwalkers will find plenty to do in the more remote areas of the High Plains. The 85-km (five- to six-day) **Bogong High Plains Circuit** takes in the best of the High Country; beginning and ending at the village of Bogong, it makes a wide circuit around Falls Creek village and includes a summit-climb of Mt. Bogong. It is also possible to walk only sections of this trail, including from above Falls Creek back to the village. Topographical maps and more details are available from the **DC&NR** on the Kiewa Valley Hwy. in Tawonga South (tel. 03-5754-4693). Rangers at the DC&NR operate various walks and talks in Alpine National Park through summer.

One of Falls Creek's chairlifts operates for sightseeing, Christmas through January and at Eastertime. It operates 11 a.m.-3 p.m. and costs $8 for unlimited rides; call (03) 5758-3280 for details. During this same period **Bogong Horseback Adventures** (tel. 03-5754-4849) operates horseback riding trips from corrals set up at the village. **Alpine Nature Rambles** has short guided hikes through the high country each afternoon (tel. 03-5758-3492).

A few of the ski lodges are open through summer and offer some great accommodation deals. Best of the bunch is **Pretty Valley Lodge** (tel. 03-5758-3210), where the rate of $67 pp per day includes three meals, use of mountain bikes, canoes, tennis facilities, and pool area. **Trackers** (tel. 03-5758-3346) is also open year-round and is one of the best lodges on the mountain; rates there are $75 pp per day, including meals. **Snowland,** part of the base facilities, sells groceries and booze and has a small cafe open daily 10 a.m.-4 p.m.

BEECHWORTH

Of all historic gold-mining towns in the country, none are as well-preserved and picturesque as Beechworth, nestled in the foothills of the High Country, 37 km east of the Hume Highway and 270 km northeast of Melbourne. The wide tree-lined streets are dotted with National Trust-classified buildings, antique emporiums, excellent museums, good restaurants, and plenty of reasonably priced accommodations. Beechworth's attractions extend beyond town limits; in the surrounding area are the remains of the various gold rushes.

Town Sights
Named for Capt. Robert O'Hara Burke, police superintendent of Beechworth until becoming lost on the ill-fated Burke and Wills expedition across Australia, the **Burke Museum** is a definite must-see while in Beechworth. Main features include a replica of an 1860s streetscape with 16 shops, a good collection of gold-rush-era photographs, and Kelly Gang memorabilia

Beechworth

BEECHWORTH

BEECHWORTH

BEECHWORTH HISTORIC PARK

TO WOOLSHED FALLS, RUTHERGLEN, AND YACKANDANDAH

SYDNEY RD.

GORGE RD.

KARS ST.

CAMP ST.

WILLIAM ST.

FINCH ST.

LOCH ST.

VICTORIA PARK

M. B. HISTORIC CELLARS

POWDER MAGAZINE

FOXGLOVES GUEST HOUSE

CARRIAGE MOTOR INN

BURKE MUSEUM

ROSE COTTAGE

BEECHWORTH PRISON

FINCHES OF BEECHWORTH

BEECHWORTH BOOK SHOP

TOWN HALL

COURTHOUSE

DC&NR

CHURCH ST.

THE BANK

PARLOUR AND PANTRY

BEECHWORTH BAKERY

ROCK CAVERN

STAR HOTEL

TANSWELL'S COMMERCIAL HOTEL

HOTEL NICHOLAS

FORD ST.

HIGH ST.

ALBERT ST.

CARRIAGE MUSEUM

RAILWAY AVE.

LAKE SAMBELL CARAVAN PARK

LAKE SAMBELL

0   500 m

TO WANGARATTA

Admission is adult $2, child $1. Open daily 9 a.m.-4:30 p.m. Located on Loch St. (access is easiest through the gardens of Town Hall, tel. 03-5728-1420).

Ford Street has the best examples of gold rush-era architecture with most buildings still in use. The **courthouse,** across from Town Hall, was where Ned Kelly made a court appearance for the triple murder at Stringybark Creek. The courthouse is open daily 10 a.m.-4 p.m., and admission is $2. Across the road, at the back of Town Hall, is the dingy cell in which Ned was held while awaiting trail; admission 20 cents.

Beyond the courthouse is **Victoria Park** and **Beechworth Prison,** built in 1859. Farther along Ford St., **Gorge Rd.** leads off to the west, eventually looping back to town. The road has numerous scenic views, and the **powder magazine,** a stone building built to store blasting materials, is open daily 10 a.m.-noon and 1-4 p.m.; admission $1. **M.B. Historic Cellars,** on the corner of William and Last Streets, is below a hundred-year-old brewery. The cellar is set up as a small brewing museum that includes a large collection of interesting bottles. Admission is $2. The **Carriage Museum,** located in a goods shed on Railway Ave., houses about 20 horse-drawn carriages, buggies, and even an old bus. Open daily 10 a.m.-4 p.m. (closed noon-1 p.m. weekdays). Admission is $1.50.

Beechworth Historic Park

While buildings from the gold rush era line the streets of Beechworth, signs of the 15,000 diggers in the valleys below are just about non-existent. Much of the activity, which followed the 1852 gold discovery in Spring Creek, took place directly below town, between Gorge Rd. and Woolshed Falls. The area has been declared a historic park and is crisscrossed with hiking trails. Along Gorge Rd. trails start from Ingram's Rock, One Tree Hill, and the powder magazine, dropping steeply into the valley below, but you really need the brochure *Discovering Beechworth Historic Park on Foot* ($1), from the DC&NR, to find your way around.

Woolshed Falls, five km north of town, is also part of the park. This was the hub of the goldfields, home to thousands of diggers, and a hive of activity for over 20 years. Today, little evidence of this frenzied period remains. A 1.2-km trail loops around Spring Creek, along which many miners lived, ending back near the carpark at Woolshed Falls. It is also possible to walk from town to the falls (six km one-way), crossing Sheep Station Creek, where Aaron Sherritt, a police informer who brought about the downfall of the Kelly Gang, was gunned down by Joe Byrne, a member of the gang.

Accommodations

The **Star Hotel,** 59 Ford St. (tel. 03-5728-1425), is a classic two-story pub built in 1864. Although run as a hotel, it offers the only backpacker accommodation in town; dorm beds are $15 pp, and doubles are $40. Other facilities include a communal kitchen and lounge area; breakfast is available for an extra $4-6. **Tanswell's Commercial Hotel,** 55 Ford St. (tel. 03-5728-1480), is of the same era and has undergone extensive restorations, with the lounge area and dining room retaining their original grandeur; $25 s, $40 d.

Beechworth has a few decent motels, such as **Carriage Motor Inn,** 54 Sydney Rd. (tel. 03-5728-1301), with rooms for $44 s, $49 d, but you'd be better off staying in one of the many B&Bs, which have more character. **Rose Cottage,** 42 Camp St. (tel. 03-5728-1069), was built in 1876 and after being fully restored maintains an authentic atmosphere from the gold rush era. Each room is decorated with antiques and has tea and coffee supplies, while the relaxing guest lounge has a log fire; $60 s, $85 d. **Foxgloves Guest House,** 21 Loch St. (tel. 03-5728-1322), directly opposite the Burke Museum, is another restored cottage with rooms for $70 s, $100 d. Moving up in price is **Kinross,** 34 Loch St. (tel. 03-5728-2351), built in 1858. This lodging is more luxurious than the others. Each room is large and has a fireplace and private bathroom; rates are $110 s, $135 d. **Finches of Beechworth,** 3 Finch St. (tel. 03-5728-2655), is another historic B&Bs—this one surrounded by an amazing garden. Rates are $150 d.

Lake Sambell Caravan Park is a couple of kilometers from town on Jarvis Rd. (tel. 03-5728-1421). Sites are $11 and on-site vans $28.

Food

Beechworth Bakery is the center of much activity each morning. It has a great range of pies, pastries, and cakes to be consumed at tables inside, outside, upstairs, and downstairs. **Parlour & Pantry,** 69 Ford St. (tel. 03-5728-2575), has an old-world atmosphere. Within a historic shop it houses a gourmet deli, coffee shop, and restaurant. You can also buy picnic hampers from $10 pp. **Hotel Nicholas,** 1 Camp St. (tel. 03-5728-1051), has a bistro open daily for lunch and dinner. Inexpensive bar meals are available from **Tanswell's Commercial Hotel,** also on Ford Street. One of the few formal dining rooms in Beechworth is **The Bank,** at 56 Ford St. (tel. 03-5728-2223). The main foyer of this historic building has been converted to an upmarket dining room with a small but varied menu; main meals range $14-16.50.

Transportation, Services, and Information

Beechworth has no bus depot; buses stop outside the post office. Service between Beechworth and Wangaratta runs twice daily weekdays and once on Sunday; $4.20 one-way and $31.80 for the train/bus combination from Melbourne.

Minibus tours of the town can be booked through Rock Cavern (corner of Ford and Camp

Streets (tel. 03-5728-1374)). They run around 90 minutes and depart daily 12:30 and 3:30 p.m.

Beechworth Book Shop, 31 Camp St. (tel. 03-5728-2611), carries a good range of new books, including many on the area's history, as well as a couple of shelves of secondhand literature.

Rock Cavern, corner Ford and Camp Streets (tel. 03-5728-1374), is meant to be the town's main Tourist Information Centre, but unless you're booking a tour or willing to pay $2 for the displays, they're not usually much help; open daily 10 a.m.-5 p.m. The **DC&NR** has some excellent displays and literature on Beechworth Historic Park and some interesting maps of the area; on Ford Street, next to the courthouse; open Mon.-Thurs. 9 a.m.-12:45 p.m., Friday 8:30 a.m.-4:30 p.m. (tel. 03-5728-1501).

OMEO HIGHWAY AND THE NORTHERN HIGH COUNTRY

Yackandandah

Once on the main wagon route between Sydney and Melbourne, this well-preserved town looks much as it did in the days of the gold rush. In 1852 gold was discovered in a nearby creek, but, by the time a permanent settlement was established, the gold had run out. Today, along a street lined with deciduous trees, the sturdy redbrick civic buildings and original shopfronts remain, housing antique emporiums, tearooms, a bakery, and shops good for general browsing. The **Bank Museum** houses displays focusing on the history of the town; open Sunday and daily during school holidays noon-4 p.m.

Star Hotel (tel. 060-27-1493) has rooms from $21 pp, and there's a caravan park down by the river, but most people visit the town as a day trip from Beechworth, 30 km away.

Tallangatta

Tallangatta is a small town that sits on the Murray Valley Highway, which parallels Lake Hume before traversing the remote northern corner of the state. The original townsite had to be moved when the Mitta Mitta River was dammed in the 1950s. The town's layout is very symmetrical, with shops and other services surrounding a semicircular park, all of which overlook the man-

made lake. The streetscape of Old Tallangatta can be seen when water levels are low; located seven km east of town.

Omeo Highway

This is the major route through the High Country. It begins east of Tallangatta and winds its way south for 300 spectacular km to Bairnsdale on the Princes Highway. The first community along the route from Tallangatta is **Mitta Mitta,** a historic gold-mining center, from where a gravel road leads southeast to **Lake Dartmouth** in Alpine National Park.

Around 170 km from Tallangatta is the remote town of **Omeo** (pop. 580). The town has a wild history; when gold was discovered, diggers flocked to the region, and being so remote it took many years for the police to establish a post. Traces of gold can be found by panning in Livingstone Creek and a number of historic buildings remain in town. It's also a base for skiers heading to Mt. Hotham, one hour's drive west. The original courthouse and log jail still stand, and a small museum opens during school holidays. **Golden Age Hotel** (tel. 03-5159-1344) has basic rooms for $25 pp, while **Holston Tourist Park** (tel. 03-5159-1351) has sites from $9 and on-site vans for $28. **Octagon Bookshop** (tel. 03-5159-1411) serves as an information center and is open Thurs.-Tues. 10 a.m.-5:30 p.m.

Burrowa-Pine Mountain National Park

Access to this remote 18,400-hectare park, located in the far northeastern corner of the state, is north from Cudgewa on the Murray Valley Highway between Tallangatta and Corryong. Two massive outcrops of volcanic rock are the park's main features, with Mount Burrowa rising to 1,300 meters. Along Falls Rd., near the park's entrance, is a picnic area from where a two-km (one-way) trail leads to Bluff Falls. Beyond the picnic area is a small campground. For further information on the park, call (060) 55-6111.

Corryong

"In Memory of The Man From Snowy River Jack Riley Buried Here 16th July 1914." These simple words adorn the grave of Australia's most famous horseman, buried in the Corryong cemetery. The valleys and mountains around

Corryong were the haunt of horsemen like Jack Riley, and many others, who earned a living using their skills to round up wild horses. Riley's fame grew from a poem written by Banjo Patterson, who stayed in his mountain hut and listened to him recall a ride down an impossibly steep slope near Tom Groggin. It was from this encounter that Patterson's immortal poem, "The Man From Snowy River," was written. It has since been made into one of Australia's most successful movies. The **Man From Snowy River Folk Museum,** Hansen St. (tel. 060-76-1253), is about life in the High Country, rather than about Riley himself. It also displays an interesting collection of old snow skis. It's open daily 10 a.m.-noon and 2-4 p.m. (except June-Aug.) and admission is a worthy $2. **Corryong High Country Festival,** held each March, features a Stockman's Muster, poetry

night, bush dancing, a market, and, the highlight, a horseback ride from Tom Groggin down into Corryong.

Alpine Gateway Lodge, 96 Hansen St. (tel. 060-76-1269), has basic accommodations in a renovated house for $34.50 s, $51.50 d. **Corryong Country Inn,** 7 Towong Rd. (tel. 060-76-1333), is a little nicer and has the best restaurant in town; $54 s, $66 d. At the west end of town, the caravan park (tel. 060-76-1152), has plenty of room for tents and vans, and on-site vans are only $20 d. Apart from the restaurant in Corryong Country Inn, there's a bakery on the main drag, and **Crystal Cafe,** at the top end of town, is open daily 8:30 a.m.-8:30 p.m.

The news agency has some information on the area and the library has a large map on its side wall. The **DC&NR** office is at 8 Jardine St. (tel. 060-76-1655).

SOUTHEAST FROM MELBOURNE

MORNINGTON PENINSULA

Mornington Peninsula is a cusp of land extending south from Melbourne, around the eastern shore of Port Phillip Bay, and coming to an apex at Point Nepean, a couple of km from the Bellarine Peninsula on the opposite side of the bay. The bay side of the peninsula is lined with a string of holiday towns and safe sandy beaches. At the other extreme is the peninsula's southern coast, battered for eons by the wild Southern Ocean. The wave-eroded cliffs are dotted with sandy beaches. Many ships have wrecked along this stretch of coast, and the pounding surf has claimed many lives, including that of Australian prime minister Harold Holt, who drowned in 1967 while swimming at Cheviot Beach.

The peninsula has long been a favorite getaway for Victorian holidaymakers and towns such as Frankston and Mornington have become part of Melbourne's urban sprawl.

Arthur's Seat State Park
Arthur's Seat, the highest peak on the peninsula, is a granite massif that rises 305 meters. The surrounding park contains natural bushland and mature gardens. Near the summit is **Seawinds Botanical Garden,** from where views extend across Port Phillip Bay to Melbourne. A chairlift to the summit runs Sept.-April daily 9 a.m.-5 p.m. and weekends only the rest of the year. The park is well signposted south of Dromana, off Morning Peninsula Freeway.

Sorrento
This historic port faces the quiet waters of Port Phillip Bay along the narrow western tip of Mornington Peninsula. It was the site of Victoria's first permanent European settlement, abandoned after just one year due to a lack of fresh water. All that remains are a few graves, but at the site of the settlement, east of Sorrento, just off Point Nepean Rd., is a display center (open Sat.-Sun. and school holidays 1-4:30 p.m.). Sorrento itself has historic buildings dating to the 1870s and a small museum on Melbourne Rd. that's open Sunday 1:30-4:30 p.m.

South Channel Fort, six km from Sorrento, is an island constructed in 1888 as a garrison to protect Melbourne from the threat of warships entering Port Phillip Bay. It was manned during the two world wars but is now in a state of disrepair, with the public only recently allowed access. The island has become a nesting ground for birds. Many tours are offered to the island, some of which include low-lying **Mud Island,** a wildlife reserve.

Carmel B&B, 142 Ocean Beach Rd. (tel. 03-5984-3512), is a classic limestone cottage in the center of town. The four rooms have shared facilities, $60 s, $90 d. **Motel Saltair,** corner Melbourne and Bowen Roads (tel. 03-5984-1356), has rooms for $35 s, $45 d. For backpackers, purpose-built **Bell's Hostel,** 5 Miranda St. (tel. 03-5984-4323), has modern facilities; $13 pp. Campgrounds are spread along the entire length of the peninsula; closest to Sorrento is **Sorrento Foreshore Reserve,** west of town (tel. 03-5984-2797), where sites are $10-15 per night (coin-operated showers).

Ocean Beach Rd. is lined with eateries, including two bakeries and a number of cafes. **Just Fine Food,** 23 Ocean Beach Rd. (tel. 03-5984-4666), open daily 7 a.m.-5 p.m., serves hearty breakfasts and healthy lunches. **Koonya Hotel,** 1 the Esplanade (tel. 03-5984-2281), has the best bistro of three hotels, with views across the bay and an outdoor dining area. **Smokehouse,** 182 Ocean Beach Rd. (tel. 03-5984-1246), is a casual yet stylish pizza and pasta place—but you'll need a booking on weekends.

Trains from Melbourne run as far as Frankston, from where **Portsea Passenger Service** (tel. 03-5986-5666) runs every couple of hours to Sorrento ($4.90 one-way) and onto Portsea. Sorrento is also the terminus of ferries from Queenscliff on the Bellarine Peninsula. Ferries run six times daily and cost $5 for adults and $30 for cars. For details call (03) 5258-3244.

Sorrento Tourist Information Centre is at 155 Ocean Beach Rd. (tel. 03-5984-0777).

Portsea

Portsea, the westernmost community on the peninsula, has an air of elegance about it, with many large mansions overlooking the bay. The beach here is safe for swimming, and keen anglers stand shoulder to shoulder on the long wooden pier in the busy months of summer. Accommodation is more expensive here than the rest of the peninsula, with rooms at the Portsea Hotel being $80 d. **Delgany Country House Hotel,** Point Nepean Rd. (tel. 03-5984-4000), is one of the state's grandest and most luxurious accommodations. The main building is a turreted limestone castle set in over five hectares of immaculately manicured gardens. Every last touch is aimed at making guests feel like king of the castle, and, if you drag yourself away from the award-winning restaurant, you'll find a large saltwater swimming pool and tennis courts. Weekday rates start at $200 d. The restaurant here, **Two Faces** (tel. 03-5984-4000), is open to nonguests, with the set two-course lunch a steal at $25 per head and dinner at $65.

Point Nepean National Park

Over 100 years of military occupation has been a blessing in disguise for the western portion of Mornington Peninsula. While the rest of the peninsula has been, for the most part, heavily developed, this area has remained relatively unscathed. When the army moved out in 1988, the DC&NR moved in, declaring the area a national park. The park not only encompasses the point for which it is named, but extends eastward along a narrow coastal strip to Cape Schanck. Entry to the western portion of the park is regulated, with this part open only weekends and school holidays, and only a certain number of people allowed in each of those days ($7 pp). Access to the many walks is by tractor-drawn trailers, which shuttle visitors to trailheads.

At the back of Portsea is a patrolled surf beach and, to the west, unusual rock formations such as Sphinx Rock and London Bridge. Access to the coastal strip of the park is unrestricted, with access roads leading through heath-covered dunes to the beach. Interconnecting trails lead along the coast and the entire strip of coast is 28 km. The southernmost tip of the park is **Cape Schanck,** where there's a lighthouse and walking track to **Bushranger**

Bay. Access to this part of the park is south from Rosebud on Boneo Road. For park information call (03) 5984-4276.

Western Port and French Island

The sheltered waters fringed by the mostly undeveloped coast of Western Port are a stark contrast to the frenzied activity a half-hour's drive away on the other side of Mornington Peninsula. With no reliable source of fresh water, settlement around this body of water was slow, although the towns of **Flinders, Somers,** and **Hastings** have grown to become popular seaside holiday towns. Flinders has a picturesque harbor, filled with fishing boats, pleasure crafts, and views extending to Phillip Island.

In the middle of Western Port is French Island, formerly a prison farm, and undeveloped except for a smattering of houses and shops around **Tankerton,** the island's only community. The 180-square-km island is low-lying; **Mt. Wellington** (96 meters) is the highest point. Half the island is a state park, in which koalas, potoroos, more than 200 species of birds, and 500 species of plants have been recorded. **Tortoise Head Lodge** (tel. 03-5980-1234) is the island's only accommodation. Rates are $95 pp, including three meals. **French Island Ferry** runs from Stony Point, south of Hastings, across to Tankerton; $7 one-way (tel. 03-5979-3722). Many of the island's attractions can be reached on foot, but a mountain bike is a good way to get around.

PHILLIP ISLAND

Linked to the mainland by bridge, this 10,000-hectare island is at the mouth of Western Port and 135 km by road from Melbourne. The island is one of Victoria's major tourist destinations, most famous for the nightly **Penguin Parade,** when thousands of fairy penguins march from the water and cross the sand to nesting grounds. Long sandy beaches, rugged coastal landscapes, large populations of koalas and seals, good fishing and surfing, and the sleepy towns of Cowes, Rhyll, and Newhaven also combine to make the island so popular.

Members of the Bunurong tribe lived on the island up to 40,000 years ago, but their nomadic lifestyle meant they lived on the island only seasonally. George Bass landed on the island's north shore in 1798, and sealers and whalers lived in shanties around the protected northern coastline for much of the early 1800s, but it wasn't until 1842, when the McHaffie family leased the entire island, that the first permanent settlement developed. The major crop was chicory, a beet-like vegetable that was ground to make a coffee substitute. A bridge to the mainland was constructed in 1940, creating a boom in tourism that continues to this day. Cowes, on the protected northern shore, is the island's largest town.

Newhaven and Vicinity

The motorist's gateway to Phillip Island is the small fishing town of Newhaven. Once on the island, the first stop should be **Phillip Island Information Centre,** one km west of the bridge; open daily 10 a.m.-5 p.m. (tel. 03-5956-7447). The center is a complete source of island information, and staff can book various attractions (including the Penguin Parade) and accommodations. If you're planning to view most of the commercial attractions, purchase an **Island Passport,** valid for 12 months.

Diagonally opposite the information center is

PHILLIP ISLAND

PENGUIN PARADE

Like clockwork, shortly after sunset every night of the year, fairy penguins (also called little penguins) leave the water after a day's fishing and march to their burrows at the back of **Summerland Beach.** Their timing is incredible; as soon as the sun sets below the horizon, small groups, which have congregated in the shallows, head up the beach. In early summer the spectacle is heightened by the squealing of chicks waiting to be fed. The viewing areas, reached by elevated boardwalks, line a strip of sand, and in peak season up to 4,000 people will be there. On a bluff above the beach is **Penguin Parade Visitor Centre,** featuring a simulated underwater environment, an audiovisual, and a souvenir shop. The center is open daily from 10 a.m. and is busiest an hour before sunset. Admission to the center and for viewing the penguins is adult $7, child $3; just to the center it's $2.50 and $1, respectively (tel. 03-5956-8300).

the **Australian Dairy Centre** (tel. 03-5956-7583), which houses the country's largest collection of dairy farming memorabilia as well as a realistic replica of an 1892 cheese factory, horse-drawn milk carts from various eras, some ice-cream-making equipment, and a small factory where specialty cheeses and candies are produced. Admission is adult $2.50, child $1. Open in summer daily 10 a.m.-6 p.m. (closed Monday and Tuesday mornings the rest of the year).

Just beyond the dairy center, a narrow road leads north to historic **Churchill Island,** site of Victoria's first permanent building, which was constructed in 1801. The building is gone, but nearby is a stone cottage dating to 1874 and some old farm machinery. Various short walks lead around and across the island; allow two hours to walk around the shoreline; admission to the island is adult $5, child $2. Open daily 10 a.m.-4.30 p.m.

Cape Woolamai and Vicinity
At 109 meters above sea level, Cape Woolamai is a natural landmark on an island that is generally less than 30 meters above sea level. The cape is at the end of a narrow isthmus sep-

arating the surfing beach of **Woolamai** from the protected waters of **Cleeland Bight.** From **Woolamai Surf Lifesaving Club** a three-km (round-trip) hiking trail leads to the summit of the cape and around cliffs where a number of muttonbird (short-tailed shearwater) rookeries are located.

Six km west of the Woolamai Rd. turnoff, Phillip Island Rd. divides; the right fork leads to the island's largest town, Cowes, and the left fork (Back Beach Rd.) leads to the island's western extremity. A few kilometers along Back Beach Rd. is a **motor racing circuit.** Australian Grand Prix were held on Phillip Island 1928-35 along public roads. This circuit was built in 1956 and hosts the Australian Motorcycle Grand Prix each year (except 1991-95 when it moved to NSW). Beyond the circuit, Pyramid Rd. leads south to **Pyramid Rock,** where pyramid-shaped basalt columns rise from the ocean.

The Nobbies
West of Summerland Beach the rugged and deeply indented coastline continues to Phillip Island's western tip, The Nobbies, and **Seal Rocks,** home to Australia's largest colony of southern fur seals. An elevated boardwalk meanders around the point and to a blowhole that struts its stuff when the swell is up. The road out to the cape is closed after sunset. Seal numbers are highest during the breeding season (Oct.-Dec.), but after close-up viewing of penguins, the seals are a disappointment from the mainland—the colony is nearly two km offshore, and viewing with the coin-in-the-slot telescopes doesn't do them justice. **Bay Connections** (tel. 03-5678-5642) has summer cruises from Cowes out to the seals for adult $28, child $16.

Rhyll
Rhyll was the landing point of George Bass in 1798; a monument on Fishermans Point in the small fishing community of Rhyll marks the site. Along Rhyll Inlet are extensive mudflats that can be observed at low tide. In town is a small **Maritime Museum.**

Koala Conservation Centre
Although Phillip Island has always been considered a good place for viewing koalas, they are not native to the island, and until the develop-

ment of this center, their population was in serious decline. They were introduced to the island in 1870, and by the 1930s only 1,000 remained in Victoria, most of which were on Phillip Island. Koalas can be seen in various reserves around Cowes, but this center has the highest density. It's open daily from 9 a.m. to sunset, and admission is adult $2.50, child $1. For more information call (03) 5952-1307.

Other Commercial Attractions

To appease the masses, a variety of attractions have been developed on the island. **Phillip Island Wildlife Park,** one km south of Cowes (tel. 03-5952-2038), is the most worthwhile of these, with 16 hectares of native animals and birds. Admission is adult $7, child $3.50; open daily 9 a.m. to dusk. Opposite the Koala Conservation Centre is **A Maze 'N Things** (tel. 03-5952-2283), comprising a maze and mini-golf course. **Indy Go Carts** (tel. 03-5952-3888) is out by the Motor Racing Circuit. **Grumpy's Waterslide and Crazy Golf** (tel. 03-5952-3060) is in Cowes. Back on the mainland, just north of the Phillip Island bridge, is **Wildlife Wonderland** (tel. 03-5678-2222), a first-class wildlife park. Many displays are indoors, making it an ideal rainy-day destination. Admission is adult $7.90, child $3.90.

Recreation and Tours

Boats can be rented from **Western Port Rent-a-boat,** opposite the boat ramp at 14 Beach St.,

Rhyll (tel. 03-5956-9238). From Rhyll, many fishing spots along the island's north shore can be accessed by these boats—or just throw a line in from the many jetties and rock walls around the island.

The best surfing is at **Woolamai Beach,** where there's a surf shop with board rentals. **Cowes Golf Club** is an 18-hole course on Settlement Rd., just to the east of Cowes; for tee times call (03) 5952-2141.

Bay Connections offers a variety of cruises departing from Cowes Foreshore. In January cruises depart at least three times daily, with fewer sailings the rest of the year. The most popular trips are Seal Rocks Voyage (adult $28, child $16), French Island Tour (adult $30, child $18), and Evening Shearwater Cruise (adult $16, child $10). From Cowes, they operate a drop-off service to French Island and Stony Point, on the mainland. For details, drop by the rotunda on the waterfront in Cowes, or call (03) 5678-5642.

Also based at the rotunda is **Island Harley Tours** (tel. 03-5956-7551); a five-minute spin is $7, with full-island tours lasting up to 40 minutes costing $35.

Phillip Island Air (tel. 03-5956-7316) offers tours ranging from a 10-minute flight around Cape Woolamai ($30 pp) to a 40-minute flight over Western Port ($75 pp). They also operate charters, including to King and Flinders Islands.

Nobbies, Phillip Island

Accommodations

Even with more than 20 hotels and motels on the island, getting a room in summer entails booking well ahead. Phillip Island Information Centre (tel. 03-5956-7447) can make advance bookings.

Isle of Wight Hotel, the Esplanade (tel. 03-5952-2301), has a great location—right opposite the waterfront in downtown Cowes. Rooms in the hotel are $30 s, $35 d, and slightly higher in the motel out back. With more facilities, including a heated pool, is **Coachman Motel,** 51 Chapel St. (tel. 03-5952-1098); $53 s or d.

Castle Inn by the Sea, 7 Steele St. (tel. 03-5952-1228), is a luxurious B&B a short stroll from Cowes and the waterfront. Each room has a bathroom and private deck, and rates include a delicious three-course breakfast; $45-60 s or d. On the other side of the island is **Cliff Top House,** Marlin St. (tel. 03-5952-1033), which overlooks spectacular coastline and is only a short walk from sandy Smiths Beach. The house features well-appointed guest rooms, a lounge with fireplace, and a snooker room; $80 s, $120 d.

Amaroo Caravan Park, 97 Church St., Cowes (tel. 03-5952-2548), is part of a large caravan park one block from the main street, with cooking facilities, well-priced meals, and a bar. The park also has a swimming pool, runs day trips, and organizes pick-ups from Melbourne hostels. Dorm beds are $15 pp, tent sites $10, powered sites $12, and on-site vans start at $30 d. Over a dozen other caravan parks are on the island, including **Anchor Belle Holiday Park,** 272 Church St., Cowes (tel. 03-5952-2258), and **Koala World Caravan Park,** opposite the Koala Conservation Centre (tel. 03-5952-2283).

Food

Most restaurants and takeaways are along Thompson Ave. and the Esplanade, both in Cowes. Many of these specialize in seafood, including **Fishbizz** on the Esplanade, which has takeout fish and chips from $4, and upmarket seafood restaurants such as **The Jetty,** also on the Esplanade (tel. 03-5952-2060), which has a rustic atmosphere and sea views. Head to **Dutchies Stonegrill,** 1 Vista Place, Cape Woolamai (tel. 03-5956-6000), for inexpensive dishes grilled on red-hot stones, served while still being cooked; open nightly Tues.-Sunday. Another elegant restaurant is **Banfields,** 192 Thompson Ave., Cowes (tel. 03-5952-2088), furnished in a colonial-Australian style and specializing in seafood and steaks.

Transportation, Services, and Information

Scheduled flights between Phillip Island and the mainland ceased in early 1995, but it is possible they may recommence in the future; call **Phillip Island Air** (tel. 03-5956-7316) to check.

From Melbourne, there is no direct bus or train transportation to the island. From Dandenong Station, a short train trip from Melbourne, **V/Line** buses run daily to Cowes; $12.80 one-way. **Amaroo Park Backpackers** offers complimentary shuttles twice a week for their guests from Queensberry Hill Hostel in Melbourne. By boat, **Bay Connections** (tel. 03-5678-5642) links Cowes to San Remo ($9 one-way) and Stony Point ($9 one-way) on Mornington Peninsula.

Phillip Island Information Centre is just over the bridge from the mainland and has a great deal of information on all attractions, sights, and accommodations; open daily 9 a.m.-5 p.m. (tel. 03-5956-7447).

GIPPSLAND

Gippsland, southeast of Melbourne, extends from the rugged Great Dividing Range south to the wildly beautiful coastline of Bass Strait.

The **Princes Highway,** a coastal route between Melbourne and Sydney, passes through the Latrobe Valley, Victoria's industrial and farming heartland. An alternative route east is the longer **Bass Highway,** which takes you through coastal holiday towns. Both routes lead to Wilsons Promontory, a rugged peninsula surrounded by steep cliffs, white sandy beaches, and slabs of granite that rise many hundreds of meters above sea level.

For thousands of years, waves bending around Wilsons Promontory have deposited sand along the shore of East Gippsland, forming a beach 140 km long and enclosing a vast stretch of lagoons known as Gippsland Lakes, perfect for boating and fishing. This complex lake system is breached at only one place, the holiday playground of Lakes Entrance, 314 km from Melbourne.

WEST GIPPSLAND AND THE LATROBE VALLEY

The predominantly industrial Latrobe Valley has some of the world's largest known deposits of brown coal, the fuel for the power stations that supply most of Victoria's electricity. The main route through the valley is the Princes Highway. To the north and south of the route are areas of natural bushland and many small towns dotting the hills.

Warragul, Moe, and Erica

Westernmost town in the valley is Warragul, a center of 13,000 serving the surrounding dairy farms. South of Warragul are pick-your-own farms and villages filled with antique emporiums, arts and crafts shops, and tearooms.

With a population of 20,000, Moe is the largest of the Latrobe Valley towns and serves surrounding industrial and agricultural regions. **Old Gippstown Pioneer Township** (tel. 03-5127-3082) is Moe's main attraction. It is a re-

creation of a late-1800s Gippsland town. Most buildings are original and have been moved to the park. The staff dresses in period costume and many of the "businesses" have working displays, giving the place an air of authenticity. The park is open daily 9 a.m.-5 p.m. and admission is adult $7, child $3. It's on the Princes Highway at the western end of town. **City of Moe Jazz Festival** is held each June long weekend and is one of Australia's largest provincial gatherings of jazz musicians and admirers.

Erica is a small timber milling town 26 km north of Moe. The local hotel has memorabilia from the town's earliest beginnings, and a small museum catalogs the history of a rail line that once ran between Erica and Walhalla.

Baw Baw National Park

This 13,300-hectare park encompasses a granite plateau extending south from the Great Dividing Range, its highest peak being **Mt. St. Phillack,** at 1,566 meters. The plateau's extensive subalpine vegetation comes alive with wildflowers each spring, and the steep-sided gullies running off the main plateau support Antarctic beech and stands of mountain ash at lower elevations.

The main access to the park is from the south, along a picturesque road extending 40 km north from Moe. This road traverses only a small part of the park, but from it gravel roads lead into more remote areas. The **Alpine Walking Track,** which begins in Walhalla (see below), follows the main plateau through the heart of the park and can be hiked in sections. From Mt. Erica carpark, **Beech Gully Nature Walk** (one km round-trip) begins, as does a trail leading to the summit of Mt. Erica (four km one-way). Campgrounds are at Eastern Tyers and Aberfeldy River; both are well signposted. On the park's western boundary is a small downhill ski resort open late June-Sept. (see the special topic "Victoria's Ski Resorts" in the "High Country" section). During summer, a hiking trail opens to Mt. St. Phillack and a hostel (tel. 03-5165-1129) that's open weekends; $10-15 pp.

Walhalla

Walhalla may be West Gippsland's smallest town, but it is also the most interesting. It's located 46 km north of Moe, along a road that winds through rolling hills and into the foothills of the Great Dividing Range. The 1880s saw Walhalla grow to become one of Victoria's richest gold-mining towns, and **Long Tunnel Mine** the most profitable mine in the state, producing nearly one million ounces of gold. At the mine entrance is a small museum open daily during school holidays and on weekends; tours of the mine shaft are offered at 1:30 p.m. and cost $4 pp (tel. 03-5165-6242). Along the main street are a number of restored shops surrounded by hills dotted with timber miners' cottages, an interesting cemetery beside the creek, and an old cricket ground.

A rather unusual guesthouse is the **Old Hospital** (tel. 03-5165-6246), which is exactly that. The rooms have shared facilities and are $40 pp, which includes a hot breakfast. Otherwise, camp along the creek.

Morwell and Vicinity

Now a service town for a power station, pulp mills, and an open-cut coal mine, Morwell was originally little more than a supply point for diggers working goldfields to the north. The **Generation Victoria Visitors Centre** (tel. 03-5135-3415) has displays on the local nonrenewable resource industry, with tours of the power station and mine offered weekdays 9 a.m.-3 p.m. On the same road as the Visitors Centre is **Latrobe Regional Gallery**, 138 Commercial Rd. (tel. 03-5134-1364); open Tues.-Fri. 10 a.m.-5 p.m., Sunday 1:30-4:30 p.m.

At just 410 hectares, **Morwell National Park** is only a remnant of the great forests that once covered the slopes of the **Strzelecki Ranges.** The mountain gray gum and blackwood eucalypt forests are best appreciated from Fosters Gully Nature Walk, which begins from the main facility area off Jumbuk Road. The park has a picnic area with drinking water, but no camping.

Traralgon, east of Morwell, is another industrial center, and is home to the Southern Hemisphere's largest power station, Loy Yang; worth driving through to appreciate its enormity. On Franklin St., **Ryans Hotel** has been extensively refurbished and serves tasty and inexpensive bar meals daily noon-2 p.m. and 6-9 p.m.

Sale

Sale is a modern town of 14,000 at the junction of the Princes and South Gippsland Highways, at the eastern end of the Latrobe Valley. The town developed through river links to the Gippsland Lakes and is now a service center for surrounding agricultural areas and offshore oil platforms. On the Princes Hwy. is **Central Gippsland Information Centre** (tel. 03-5144-1108), with displays explaining the workings of oil rigs; open daily 9 a.m.-5 p.m.

SOUTH GIPPSLAND

The **Bass Highway** between Phillip Island and Wilsons Promontory is a scenic, but longer, alternative to the South Gippsland Highway to the north. The road follows an inland route, but you'll find many opportunities to head to the wild coastline of Bass Strait.

To the north of the highway are the **Strzelecki Ranges** and the scenic town of **Mirboo North,** home to Gippsland's only brewery. Mirboo is also a stopping point along the **Grand Ridge Road,** a spectacular 140-km mountain drive between the South Gippsland Highway, west of Korumburra, and Tarra-Bulga National Park.

Wonthaggi

Wonthaggi's main attraction is the **State Coal Mine,** southeast of town along Billson St. (tel. 03-5672-3053). The grounds are dotted with mine buildings and a small museum, but the highlight of a visit here is an underground tour, usually led by an ex-miner. Tours are conducted daily 10 a.m.-3:30 p.m.; adult $4, child $2. Also look for the enormous pair of whale jawbones outside the hotel on Murray Street.

Bunurong Marine Park

The most scenic route east from Wonthaggi is along the coast. From downtown Wonthaggi head southeast, past the State Coal Mine, to **Cape Paterson.** From here the road hugs 14 km of coastline, passing a number of sandy beaches, rocky headlands, caves, and intertidal rock platforms; there are plenty of opportunities for swimming, snorkeling, and walking.

nverloch to Wilsons Promontory

nverloch is a small seaside town at the eastern extremity of Bunurong Marine Park. Nearby beaches are somewhat protected from the elements by Cape Paterson to the west and Cape Liptrap to the east. To cater to the holiday rush, here's a number of caravan parks and motels.

East of Inverloch, the Bass Highway follows Anderson Inlet before heading inland and across to Fish Creek and onto Wilsons Promontory. An interesting detour is to head south to **Tarwin Lower,** popular with fishermen for its location on he Tarwin River. Country music fans may want o check out Tarwin Lower Hotel (tel. 03-5663-5211) on Sunday afternoon when local and interstate country music bands perform for free.

Venus Bay, on the seaward side of Anderson nlet, is the starting point for a three-km (one-way) trek through low banksia heathland to Point Smythe, opposite Inverloch.

The road south from Tarwin Lower passes 38-hectare **Bald Hills Wetland Reserve,** where a short trail leads to a bird hide and ends at **Cape Liptrap Lighthouse.** From this cape, you can see Wilsons Promontory. In the right swell, the reef below the lighthouse is a legendary surf break.

East of the cape is **Waratah Bay,** a large body of water with a few small communities, each with a scattering of permanent residences and holiday cottages. **Walkerville North** and **Walkerville South** are both at the end of one-way roads and have protected sandy beaches, and a walking track links the two. The community of **Sandy Point** is farther around the bay and has a pleasant caravan park.

WILSONS PROMONTORY NATIONAL PARK

"The Prom," as it's best known, is a rugged peninsula whose coastline of spectacular granite outcrops and white sandy beaches juts into Bass Strait, forming the southernmost point of mainland Australia. The entire peninsula (49,000 hectares) was declared a national park in 1905; the signs of earlier attempts at settlement have all but disappeared. Even though the park is one of the most popular in Australia, the masses tend to congregate at **Tidal River,** where the park information center, all accommodations, and a cafe are located.

The Land

Wilsons Promontory is a massif of granite, formed around 350 million years ago as molten rock from deep below the earth's crust was pushed upward and, as it cooled, folded and wrinkled into the mountains and valleys that exist today. At that time, the promontory was part of a chain of mountains linking Tasmania to the mainland. Near the end of the last ice age, around 12,000 years ago, the link was severed, and what is now Wilsons Promontory became an island, similar in makeup to the rocky islands of Bass Strait. Over time, drifting sand filled the gap between the rocky outcrop and mainland, forming a low and narrow isthmus between the two. When the molten mass of rock originally cooled, it did so slowly, forming crystals such as garnets, rubies, and sapphires. Iron is also present; the iron-stained granite boulders that line Tidal River, in particular, are a photographer's delight.

Flora and Fauna

More than 700 species of plants have been recorded on the peninsula, many otherwise found only in Tasmania. Higher elevations are dominated by forests of eucalypt, with the protected, east-facing slopes interspersed with temperate rainforests and the more exposed slopes supporting only stunted eucalypt and banksia. Corner Inlet, in the north of the park, has the world's southernmost mangrove swamp.

Tidal River is well known for its population of rosellas, which seem to know just who has food scraps for the taking, foraging the grounds in front of the cafe and posing on visitors' shoulders for photographs. Possums and wallabies have also become tame around the campground area, while bandicoots, quolls, koalas, echidnas, and platypuses are sighted in more remote areas of the park.

Hiking

Many short trails lead from the park's main road to beautiful sandy beaches on the west coast. From the campground, a footbridge over Tidal River accesses easy trails to the north, including **Pillar Point** (1.6 km one-way), from where there are excellent coastal views, and **Squeaky Beach**

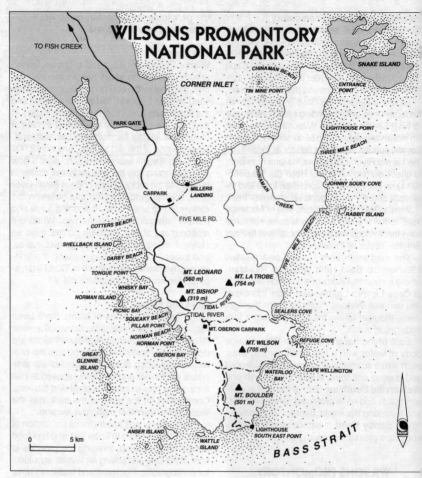

**WILSONS PROMONTORY
NATIONAL PARK**

TO FISH CREEK

CORNER INLET

SNAKE ISLAND

CHINAMAN BEACH

TIN MINE POINT

ENTRANCE POINT

PARK GATE

LIGHTHOUSE POINT

THREE MILE BEACH

CARPARK

MILLERS LANDING

JOHNNY SOUEY COVE

FIVE MILE RD.

CHINAMAN CREEK

RABBIT ISLAND

COTTERS BEACH

SHELLBACK ISLAND

DARBY BEACH

FIVE MILE BEACH

TONGUE POINT

MT. LEONARD
(560 m)

MT. LA TROBE
(754 m)

WHISKY BAY

MT. BISHOP
(319 m)

NORMAN ISLAND

TIDAL RIVER

PICNIC BAY

SEALERS COVE

SQUEAKY BEACH

TIDAL RIVER

PILLAR POINT

MT. OBERON CARPARK

NORMAN BEACH

MT. WILSON
(705 m)

REFUGE COVE

NORMAN POINT

OBERON BAY

GREAT GLENNIE ISLAND

CAPE WELLINGTON

WATERLOO BAY

MT. BOULDER
(501 m)

ANSER ISLAND

LIGHTHOUSE
SOUTH EAST POINT

WATTLE ISLAND

BASS STRAIT

0   5 km

NOON

(two km one-way). At the north end of Squeaky Beach, a trail continues through low heathland vegetation to Picnic and Whisky Bays.

About four km north of Tidal River, along the main road, is the trailhead for **Lilly Pilly Gully Nature Walk** (five km round-trip), which traverses heathland vegetation before suddenly descending into a temperate rainforest. From the cleared area above the rainforest, the trail climbs steeply, and a short spur leads to Mt. Bishop (319 meters), although returning along the original trail from the rainforest is much easier.

Of the few overnight hikes, the one to **South East Point** will bring the most satisfaction, as it is the southernmost point of land on mainland Australia. Along the most direct route, from the Mt. Oberon carpark, the point is 18.4 km one-way, but worthwhile options for the return trip are possible via Oberon or Waterloo Bays, where the white sand and deeply forested backdrop create a beautiful landscape.

Options for hiking in the north section of the park are less varied, but crowds are thinner. From the carpark at the end of Five Mile Rd., 21 km from Tidal River, a two-km track leads through groves of banksias to Millers Landing on Corner Inlet. Other trails from this carpark require an overnight stay at one of the many back-country campgrounds.

Practicalities

All services are located at **Tidal River,** 30 km from the park gate (where national park staff issue park-use tickets; $6 per car). The large campground at Tidal River is excellent. Sites are well spaced, allowing a certain amount of privacy, especially on the Norman Beach side of the campground, and hot showers are available. All sites are $6.50 per night. Scattered throughout the Tidal River area are a number of different sized huts and cabins. Motor huts sleep two to six and have basic cooking facilities, but bathroom facilities are shared with campers; $34 per night. The flats are larger and self-con-

These impressive boulders, beside Tidal River, mark the beginning of trails leading to some beautiful beaches.

tained; Sept.-April a minimum of seven nights must be booked, from $325, while the rest of the year it's more flexible—weekends are $102.50, Mon.-Fri. $143.50. With 300,000 visitors a year, demand is high for all park accommodations; chances of getting a hut or cabin without advance reservations are slim, but a number of campsites are reserved each day for out-of-state and overseas visitors. For all bookings call (03) 5680-9555.

At the campground entrance is a cafe and grocery store with petrol. Also here is the **Park Information Centre** (tel. 03-5680-9555). The excellent displays give an insight into the park's natural and human history, and the staff issue permits for camping at Tidal River in the backcountry; open daily 8:30 a.m.-4:30 p.m. Behind the store is a small cinema; tickets are $7.50 (tel. 03-5680-8512).

TARRA TERRITORY

Foster and Vicinity

Foster, on the South Gippsland Highway, was established in the 1860s after gold was found in the surrounding hills. Today, this sleepy rural community of 1,100 is a major gateway to Wilsons Promontory and a pleasant stop for those traveling the Gippsland Highway. **Foster Museum,** open each Sunday and daily during school holidays, is in an old post office and boasts a collection of relics from the gold-mining era. Across the road is Stockyard Creek and a shady park with barbecues.

Stockyard Creek Cottage, McGlead's Rd. (tel. 03-5682-2493), two km west of Foster, is a large self-contained cottage on a small self-sufficient farm. The cottage has two bedrooms, kitchen, laundry, log fire, and a veranda overlooking a lush valley, all for only $50 per night.

North of Wilsons Promontory and the South Gippsland Highway are the Strzelecki Ranges, rounded hills covered in a canopy of cool temperate rainforest. **Grand Ridge Road** traverses the ridge of the range, beginning between Warragul and Korumburra and ending east of Tarra-Bulga National Park, north of Yarram. For most of the way, this spectacular road is unsealed. It's well signposted.

Tarra-Bulga National Park

Beautiful Tarra-Bulga National Park is only 1,520 hectares, but within its boundaries are deep, fern-filled gorges, many stands of towering mountain ash, and a healthy population of lyrebirds. Two-km **Fern Gully Nature Walk** begins from the Park Information Centre, in the north of the park, just off Grand Ridge Rd., and crosses a high suspension bridge. The park has no campgrounds.

Port Albert

As miners flooded the goldfields of Omeo and Walhalla it was through Port Albert that they arrived. Many buildings from this era remain, including **Port Albert Hotel,** which has held its liquor license for over 150 years. The narrow spit of land on which the town sits is surrounded by protected waters, perfect for exploring in one of the boats for hire on the waterfront. In the maze of sandy-bottomed channels, fishing for snapper (Oct.-May), whiting, and flathead is excellent. On the road into town, west of the roundabout, is two-km **Old Port Trail,** which follows the shoreline, passing foundations of the town's bygone buildings.

   Seabank Caravan Park (tel. 03-5183-2315) is four km north of the town, or, in town, is **Port Albert Hotel** (tel. 03-5183-2212), where motel-style units are $50 s or d, and meals at the bistro average $9.

GIPPSLAND LAKES

Gippsland Lakes is one of Australia's largest inland waterways. The three main lakes—King, Victoria, and Wellington—are fed by a number of High Country watersheds and drain into the ocean at the same place, Lakes Entrance.

   Until 12,000 years ago, the entire area was a vast bay, then, as the sea level rose at the end of the last ice age, the land link between mainland Australia and Tasmania was broken. Prevailing wind and swell from the Southern Ocean deposited millions of tons of sediment east of Wilsons Promontory, forming a long ridge of sand and, eventually, enclosing the bay. Ninety Mile Beach separates these shallow lakes from the ocean and extends from the protected inlets north of Wilsons Promontory to Lakes Entrance.

The lakes are undeveloped, although small fishing villages dot the shore of Lake King.

Ninety Mile Beach

This endless stretch of white sandy beach and scrub-covered sand dunes backed by shallow lakes is part of **Gippsland Lakes Coastal Park.** A 30-km stretch of road between **Seaspray** and **Golden Beach** provides the easiest access to the beach, ocean, and innumerable camping and beach-walking opportunities. The main access to the area is from Longford, south of Sale on the South Gippsland Highway. The small townships of Seaspray and Loch Sport have caravan parks and general stores.

The Lakes National Park

This 2,380-hectare park protects Sperm Bay Head Peninsula, a low-lying area of coastal heath, separated from Ninety Mile Beach by a shallow channel. To get there, take the access road from Golden Beach.

   Since 1890, when a channel was dredged through Ninety Mile Beach to the ocean, the increased salinity of the water has killed vegetation along the lakeshore, but, inland, are well-preserved examples of coastal vegetation, and the area has a large wildlife population, including eastern gray kangaroos (look for them around the picnic area at Point Wilson), swamp wallabies, wombats, possums, sugar gliders, and echidnas.

   Short walks begin and end at Point Wilson, including the Dolomite Walking Track, which passes through a dense forest of melaleucas to Pelican Point.

   Rotamah Island, between Sperm Whale Head Peninsula and Ninety Mile Beach, is also part of the park. The Royal Australasian Ornithologists Union operates an observatory on the island. A converted old farmhouse has basic dorms and double rooms, with a kitchen, lounge and library. Birdwatching is the island's main drawcard, but wildlife viewing, beachcombing, fishing, and hiking bring people out, too. The daily rate is $60 pp, which includes three meals. For further information, write to Rotamah Island Bird Observatory, P.O. Box 75, Paynesville VIC 3880 (tel. 03-5156-6398).

   The national park's only other facilities are primitive campsites at Emu Bight (Loch Sport as the closest commercial campground) and a ark information center at the park's entrance tel. 03-5146-0278); open Mon.-Fri. 8 a.m.-4 p.m.

Bairnsdale

Bairnsdale is a major agricultural service center of 11,000 located on the Mitchell River. A museum on MacArthur St., an interesting church beside McDonalds, and a boardwalk across a wetland reserve, just beyond the museum, are about the only sights in town, but Bairnsdale's location on the Princes Highway makes it an ideal spot to spend the night.

The **Commercial Hotel,** on Main St. (tel. 03-5152-3031), has basic rooms for only $15 pp, including breakfast. **Bairnsdale Backpackers Hostel,** 119 Macleod St. (tel. 03-5152-5097), is one block from Main St. and a short walk from the railway station; beds are $12-15 pp. At the other end of the scale is **Riversleigh Country Hotel,** 1 Nicholson St. (tel. 03-5152-6966), a restored Victorian-era hotel with rooms for $74, $84 d. This hotel also has a fine restaurant with main dishes beginning at $17.50.

Between McDonalds and St. Mary's Church, at 240 Main St., is an **information center** (tel. 03-5152-3234); open Mon.-Fri. 9 a.m.-5 p.m., Sat.-Sun. 10 a.m.-4 p.m.

Mitchell River National Park

Located 42 km northwest of Bairnsdale, this 1,900-hectare park features spectacular Mitchell River Gorge and **Den of Nargun,** a small cave that Koori believed was home to a half-stone creature that dragged people to their deaths. Within the park are two distinct vegetation zones—the river gullies, home to warm-temperate rainforest, and the higher elevations, where vegetation is sparse. The gorge is popular with whitewater-rafting enthusiasts, and hiking and camping is also possible. For park information call (03) 5152-6211.

Paynesville

South of Bairnsdale, on the bank of a channel that links Lake King and Lake Victoria, is this small community of 1,800, with a commercial fishing fleet, holiday cottages, and a car and passenger ferry that plies the 200-meter-wide channel to **Raymond Island,** an isolated spot with a number of short walks.

North of Paynesville the silt-laden Mitchell River flows into Lake King. Over hundreds of years, the river's silt has been banked up at its mouth, forming twin fingers of land that protrude over nine km into Lake King. A gravel road extends along the southern finger all the way to the end, to a popular fishing spot.

LAKES ENTRANCE AND VICINITY

For 20 years people struggled to cut a permanent entrance to the ocean from the Gippsland Lakes, but it took a wild storm on 14 June 1889 to make the final break. When the area was first settled, a natural opening occurred east of the present entrance, but it was often unnavigable. Even today, the opening has to be continually dredged to make the often-rough crossing safe. Once fishermen and coastal shipping had a permanent entrance, a community quickly grew. Today Lakes Entrance (pop. 5,500) has grown into a bustling holiday center on a spit of land between the Mitchell River's Cunningham and North Arms.

Sights and Recreation

Being one of Victoria's main holiday playgrounds, Lakes Entrance has a ton of tourist-oriented attractions, most of which are spread along the Esplanade.

For views of the lakes, town, and ocean, head to **Jemmy's Point Lookout,** at the west end of town over North Arm bridge. A footbridge opposite the end of Myer St. crosses Cunningham Arm, connecting the town to scrub-covered dunes and Ninety Mile Beach. From the bridge the lakes' entrance, for which the town is named, is 2.3 km (one-way) away.

The best way to explore the lake system is on a cruise operated by **Peels Tourist & Ferry Service,** based on Post Office Jetty (tel. 03-5155-1246). Cruise timetables vary with the season. *Thunderbird* is their largest boat and is most popular for the longer cruises around Lake Victoria ($16-19). *Bluebird* does shorter trips to Metung ($13) and a lake fishing trip ($14). *Stormbird* does a luncheon cruise, allowing two hours at the small tourist town of Metung ($22, includes lunch). **Victor Hireboats,** based on Marine Parade (tel. 03-5155-1888), has motor boats to rent from $15 per hour.

Sea Shell Museum, claimed to be the largest of its type in Australia, is at 125 the Esplanade (tel. 03-5155-1538).

Accommodations

There's certainly no lack of accommodations here, but finding a vacant room in January will pose a problem. **Blue Horizon Motel,** Princes Hwy. (tel. 03-5155-1216), has large modern rooms from $38 s, $40 d, but it's three km from the center of town. More central, and more expensive, are **Sherwood Lodge,** 151 Esplanade (tel. 03-5155-1444), with smart rooms, a pool, and laundry for $55 s, $59 d, and **Bamboo Motor Inn,** 167 Esplanade (tel. 03-5155-1551), for $50 s, $58 d. In Metung, on Metung Rd., is **Terrazas del Lago** (tel. 03-5156-2666), a series of two- to five-bedroom villas overlooking Bancroft Bay, with two heated pools and a spa. Each villa is totally self-contained and has a balcony with outdoor furniture and a barbecue. Rates start at $65 d.

Of the 20 caravan parks in town, **Silver Sands Caravan Park,** 33 Myer St. (tel. 03 5155-2343), is most central, but has crowded sites. Sites are $14-19 and on-site vans start at $25. **Lakes Main Caravan Park,** 7 Willis St (tel. 03-5155-2365), is similarly priced and includes **Lakes Entrance Hostel,** with dorms from $10 pp and doubles from $12 pp. Other facilities include indoor and outdoor kitchens a laundry, and TV room.

Food

Along the Esplanade is a profusion of pizzerias, fish and chips joints, and takeaways, but one place you shouldn't miss is **Lakes Entrance Bakery.** "The best bakery in Victoria," we exulted after eating there. Regular salad and meat rolls are huge ($3.50), but the foccacia bread topped with chicken, mango chutney, and delicious salad ($5.20) is better. Meat pies are also delicious and start at $1.70, but it's worth investing an extra 50 cents in the chunky beef. The

est way to finish is with a splendid cream bun
eal cream) and a cappuccino. Tables are inside
r out, and it's open daily 7:30 a.m.-5 p.m. A
tle farther along the Esplanade is **Sea Fare,** a
ourmet fish and chips shop with a large, bright-
colored blackboard that makes decisions eas-
r; expect to pay $4.50 for fish of the day and
hips. Also serving fish, but at the expensive
nd of the scale, is **Skippers,** 481 Esplanade
el. 03-5155-3551), where main seafood dishes
tart at $16; open daily from 6 p.m. and for lunch
uring school holidays. **Out of the Blue Float-
ng Restaurant** (tel. 03-5155-1400) is exactly
hat—a barge moored on Cunningham Arm,
ith a restaurant serving moderately priced
teak and seafood dishes.

Fresh prawns are often sold directly from
oats moored in the inlet (from $20 per kilo-
ram), and a wide variety of seafood is sold at
he co-op on Bullock Island.

**ransportation,
ervices, and Information**
uses run daily between Lakes Entrance and

Bairnsdale ($6.40 one-way), where **V/Line** trains
run to Melbourne. During school holidays and
four days a week the rest of the year, buses
continue east along the Princes Highway to Mallacoota and New South Wales.

Lakes Entrance Tourist Information Centre
has a ton of information on the area and can
book many of the accommodations and cruises.
Its location, on the corner of the Princes Hwy.
and Marine Parade, makes it a short walk from
downtown (tel. 03-5155-1966); open daily 9
a.m.-5 p.m. **DC&NR** is at 233 the Esplanade
(tel. 03-5155-1539).

Lake Tyers
Lake Tyers, 12 km east of Lakes Entrance, is a
series of flooded valleys that extend far inland,
unlike the lagoons to the west. The township is
behind scrub-covered sand dunes, and access
to the lake is nearby. The beaches at **Red Bluff**
are popular with surfers, and fishing in the lake
is excellent. The small settlement has three caravan parks, a couple of stores, and summer
cruises on the lake.

WILDERNESS COAST

Traveling east from Lakes Entrance, the scenery changes dramatically. Gone are the farms and holiday townships of Gippsland; this is the remote corner of the state, a region never cleared for agriculture (although logging now plays an important role in the local economy), with vast tracts of forest and coastline preserved as national parks (here you'll find three of Victoria's least-visited national parks). The two most interesting coastal areas to explore are Cape Conran and Croajingolong National Park, both spectacular landscapes of beaches, inlets, rocky headlands, and some of the world's highest sand dunes.

LAKES ENTRANCE TO CANN RIVER

Orbost

Orbost is on the banks of the Snowy River, 50 km east of Lakes Entrance. It is mainly a service center for the local logging industry, but the excellent **Rainforest Centre,** 6 Browning St. (tel. 03-5161-1375), is definitely worth stopping for. The best-known rainforests are those in tropical and subtropical environments, but a large proportion of Australia's remaining rainforest is temperate, and is in Victoria. Three types of temperate rainforest—warm, cool, and dry—all thrive in the far east of the state. The center was developed to enhance understanding of these forests; this is done through displays, an audiovisual, and landscaped gardens established in an old quarry out back. The center also has information on Wilderness Coast national parks and is open daily 9 a.m.-5 p.m.

Across the road from the center is **Netherbyre Art and Gemstone Gallery** (tel. 03-5154-2064). The operators are keen geologists who spend the winter months fossicking in various parts of Australia to add to their already impressive collection.

On the corner of Nicholson and Clarke Streets is **Slab Hut Information Centre** (tel. 03-5154-2424). The structure was built in 1872 by an early settler on the Snowy River and moved to its present site 10 years ago.

Marlo

Watching the small fishing boats cruising aroun the quiet waters in front of Marlo, 15 km south east of Orbost, it's hard to believe that 140 kr upstream this body of water is a raging, ice-fe torrent whose main source is Mt. Kosciusko Australia's highest mountain. The river flow into a shallow lagoon, separated from the ocea by sand dunes, and breaks though at one place a channel that is constantly moving. The Snow Mountains Scheme, which channels the rive into hydroelectric stations and then inland t the Murrumbidgee Irrigation Area, takes ove two trillion liters of water from the river annually but this works in Marlo's favor—the low-lyin areas around the river mouth are less prone t flooding and, as water flow is regulated, drougl is also. The town's population is only slightl higher than 300, but that seems to be enough fo a cinema and two caravan parks. Fishing in th river estuary is great, especially from the jetty **French Narrows,** east of Marlo, has a larg population of birdlife and a small footbridge pro viding access to ocean beaches.

Across the Snowy River from Marlo is **Co ringle Slips Campground,** accessible fror Newmerella, four km west of Orbost. The camp ground is spread out along the estuary, but ge ting to the ocean is easy. Facilities include pit to lets, barbecues, and a limited supply of drinkin water (best to bring your own); $7.50 per nigh

Cape Conran

From Marlo, the road continues east to Cap Conran, skirting a wide open beach with plent of access points for swimming, surfing, and su fishing. The cape is totally undeveloped, a de lightful place to experience the remote coasta environment.

Cape Conran Nature Trail begins from th end of Cape Conran Rd. and traverses coasta vegetation of tree palms and banksias to **Join ers Channel** (2.5 km one-way). From the chan nel, it's an easy half-hour scramble around rock to the cape itself. If you don't feel that energetic West Cape Rd. leads to a point just before th cape. Some longer walks, including a 1.6-kr rack to Yeerung River Estuary, start on Yeerung Road. **Pearl Point** is 13 km past the river (allow eight hours round-trip) and can be reached along the beach or an inland service road. A shorter hiking option would be to **Dock Inlet**, seven km one-way) from the Yeerung River, a landlocked lagoon of tannin-colored fresh water supporting a wide variety of waterfowl.

Banksia Bluff Camping Area, on Yeerung Rd., has over 100 sites, each semiprivate and with easy access to East Cape Beach. Facilities nclude pit toilets, bush showers, and a few barbecues (bring drinking water). Sites are $5-13 depending on the season. Farther along Yeerung Rd. is a collection of cabins made from local timbers. Each self-contained cabin sleeps four to six in basic bunk accommodations. Rates vary with the season but are generally $45-60 per night. To book campsites or cabins call (03) 5154-8438.

Lind National Park

This 1,365-hectare park between Orbost and Cann River protects one of Australia's few areas of warm-temperate rainforest and is home to a variety of interesting fauna, including wombats, possums, dingos, and lyrebirds. The park, for the most part, is undeveloped. Euchre Valley Nature Drive, part of the old Princes Highway, passes through the heart of the park and has a picnic area at Growlers Creek (listen for lyrebirds along the track that begins here).

Cann River and Vicinity

This small highway town at the junction of the Princes and Cann Valley Highways has a pub, petrol station, grocery store, and cafe—everything you'll need before heading into surrounding national parks. On the main road through town is a **DC&NR** office, with tons of useful information on all parks and current road conditions posted out the front; open daily in summer 10 a.m.-4 p.m., the rest of the year Mon.-Fri. 10 a.m.-3 p.m. **Nulluak Gundji Cultural Centre** has various displays on the significance of the area to the local Koori community, but it doesn't seem to be open very often. Located just north of town on the Cann Valley Highway.

Mountainous **Alfred National Park** is 20 km east of Cann River. The park protects areas of warm-temperate and subtropical rainforests but has no facilities or trails.

CROAJINGOLONG NATIONAL PARK

Beautiful unspoiled beaches, remnants of ancient forests, some of the world's highest sand dunes, and Mallacoota Inlet make this 100-km stretch of coastline one of Victoria's undiscovered jewels. The park's deeply indented coastline is a legacy of ancient river courses that changed with the onset of the ice age. Because of its undisturbed rivers, lakes, and inlets; the many rare plants species and endangered fauna; the varied vegetation, ranging from coastal heathland

lace monitor,
Croajingolong
National Park

CROAJINGOLONG NATIONAL PARK

to rainforests; and its sand dunes, UNESCO designated the park a Biosphere Reserve in 1983. For further protection, as human encroachment continues, two adjacent chunks of land have been declared wilderness areas.

Birdlife throughout the park is prolific; over 250 species have been recorded, including raucous black cockatoos, the rare ground parrot, colorful lyrebirds, and eagles and hawks. Of all the fauna, none is as unusual as the prehistoric-looking **lace monitor,** a member of the goanna family, which grows to lengths exceeding two meters.

Sights and Hikes

The conditions of access roads into the park vary greatly, from excellent to unpassable—the DC&NR office in Cann River keeps updated bulletins on conditions (see "Cann River and Vicinity," above). From Cann River, Tamboon Rd., which becomes Pat Hicks Rd., leads to the mouth of the **Thurra River** and along the foreshore to **Point Hicks,** the first point of mainland Australia sighted by Captain Cook's 1770 expedition.

The park's sand dunes are the highest this side of Namibia, Africa. Two distinct types of

dune occur—"relic" (well-vegetated and stable and "mobile" (constantly moving and changin shape). From Thurra River Campground, a two km trail leads through coastal banksia heath land to the dunes. To experience the most spec tacular of the mobile dunes, hang a right where the trail first enters the dunes, traverse along low ridge, and the panorama of dunes soon be comes apparent below.

Other access roads from the Princes Highwa lead to **Sydenham Inlet** and **Wingan Inlet** where there's a 30-minute self-guided nature walk. For experienced hikers, a coastal track leads 63 km from the township of Mallacoota to the Thurra River. The park also encompass es much of Mallacoota Inlet, considered one c Victoria's premier fishing grounds (see below)

Practicalities

Campgrounds within the park are at Tamboon Inlet, Thurra River, Wingan Inlet, and Shipwreck Creek; each has basic facilities, and you shoul bring drinking water. All sites are $8. Furthe information is available from the DC&NR in Mal lacoota (tel. 03-5158-0219) or Cann River (tel 03-5158-6351).

MALLACOOTA

The laid-back holiday and fishing town of Mallacoota (pop. 800) is on Mallacoota Inlet, just over 500 km east of Melbourne. The township itself holds little of interest, but the inlet's great fishing, boating, and birdwatching, its easy access to surf beaches, and the surrounding Croajingolong National Park make Mallacoota the ideal place to spend a couple of days.

The best way to explore the many islands, coves, and beaches of the inlet is by boat. **Rankin's Hire Cruisers** (tel. 03-5158-0555) is based on a small jetty just around from the main wharf. A full-day hire is $50, plus $50 bond; this allows enough time to reach an eastern arm of the inlet, where an early settlement was located. Also on this side of the inlet, the **Spotted Dog Gold Mine** operated for 25 years, and although not much is left, the DC&NR have set up a self-guided interpretive walk around the site. Farther around the shoreline is **Lake View Hotel,** built in 1882. Poet Henry Lawson stayed at the hotel in 1910 and was inspired to write "Mallacoota Bar."

The *Loch Ard* is an old timber ferry that runs cruises around the inlet. The five-hour Gipsy Point Cruise costs adult $16, child $6, and the four-hour National Parks Explorer Cruise is adult $14, child $7. Book at the wharf or Mallacoota Hotel (tel. 03-5158-0455). Rankin's Cruisers operates the modern *Discovery* on a full-day trip to some remote parts of the inlet (usually Tuesday, Friday, and Sunday); adult $30, child $20, includes a barbecue lunch. Book at 43 Maurice Ave. (tel. 03-5158-0555).

To experience the coastal environment, allow two to three hours for the **Mallacoota Walking Track,** which begins from the roundabout in the center of town and heads out to Bastion Point, along the beach, and back to town through coastal heathland.

Practicalities

Of the many accommodations, **Mallacoota Hotel** has the most reasonably priced rooms, with singles from $40 and doubles from $50. **Adobe Mudbrick Flats,** 17 Karbeethong Hill Ave. (tel. 03-5158-0329), consisting of a collection of mud-brick one- and two-bedroom cottages scattered through a pleasant bush setting, is also home to a wide variety of animals. Summer rates start at $59 per night, but the rest of the year from $38.

Mallacoota Hotel serves moderately priced meals noon-2 p.m. and 6-9 p.m. The other option is **Tide Seafood Bistro** on Maurice Ave. (tel. 03-5158-0552).

Note: What this place needs is a decent information center. The two places on the main street that have Information Centre signs out front seem more interested in selling real estate and boat trips; you may have more luck at the DC&NR office on the corner of Buckland St. and Allan Dr.; open weekdays 10:30 a.m.-3:30 p.m. (tel. 03-5158-0219).

THREE REMOTE NATIONAL PARKS

Snowy River National Park

Straddling the Snowy River, this 95,300-hectare park is a remote wilderness encompassing deep gorges, vast eucalypt forests, and spectacular waterfalls. The vegetation varies, with cool-temperate rainforests, stands of gray gum, alpine ash, native pine, and mallee scrub. Whitewater-rafting enthusiasts are drawn to the park for the challenge of tackling the Snowy River, especially the section between Mackillop's Bridge and a point to the east of Buchan. The four-day float is really an experts-only trip, but **Peregrine** (tel. 03-9602-3066) and **World Expeditions** (tel. 03-9670-8400) offer guided trips down the river for all levels of expertise.

Access to the park is along two main roads, both originating from Orbost; one passes through Buchan, the other is the Bonang Highway, to the east. Along the park's northern border, these roads are linked by **Mackillop's Rd.,** along which the park's limited camping and picnic facilities are located. At **Mackillop's Bridge,** a 250-meter span over Deddick River, are sandy beaches with good swimming, **Snowy River Nature Track,** which traverses a dry forest and flood plain, and a campground. West of the bridge is **Little River Gorge** and a lookout. For park information call (03) 5154-6222.

Errinundra National Park

This 25,600-hectare park encompasses Errinundra Plateau and protects Victoria's largest cool-temperate rainforest, a verdant place with trees up to 400 years old. Other parts of the park feature wet eucalypt forests of shining gum, which protects an understory for rainforest, creating an ideal habitat for a diverse variety of birds and mammals. Easiest access to the park is from 58 km east of Orbost at Lind National Park, but access is also possible from the Bonang Highway north of Orbost. The only official campground is at Frosty Hollow. For park information call (03) 5154-6222.

Coopracambra National Park

A rugged landscape, lack of facilities, and remote location make this 38,800-hectare park one of the state's least visited. It is located on the NSW border, east of the Cann Valley Highway. The park's most distinct feature is a spectacular sandstone gorge carved by the Genoa River. This is accessible along the only road that passes through the center of the park. The other dominant geological features are the granite peaks of **Mt. Kaye, Mt. Denmarsh,** and **Mt. Coopracambra,** all visible from the Cann Valley Highway. **Beehive Creek,** two km east of the highway, is a pleasant spot where water cascades into deep pools. The park has no official campgrounds; the closest accommodations are in Cann River or Genoa. For park information call (03) 5154-6222.

WESTERN AUSTRALIA
INTRODUCTION

Western Australia is the country's "sexy" state—a land of rising pinnacles and deep cuts that come in all shapes and sizes; the fabulous sea with its ebb and flow of wave upon endless wave; the veritable orgy of this state's famous wildflowers, blossoming from well-pollinated pouches of fertile seeds. Fact is, WA (as the Aussies call it) is not mere organic lust, but the makings for some down-and-dirty wanderlust.

THE LAND

Western Australia is not merely big, it is humongous. Its 2.5 million square kilometers, taking up about one-third of the Australian continent and boasting an area more than triple the size of little ol' Texas, comprise the harsh, desolate expanses of the Great Sandy, Gibson, and Great Victoria Deserts, sandwiched like dry toast between the Kimberley Plateau and the Nullarbor Plain. Yet within all this space dwell a mere 1.5

million inhabitants (approximately 10% of the country's total population), most of them in or around Perth, the relaxed and youthful state capital, or along the southwest coastal sections.

Western Australia is divided into eight regions: the south coast, famed for its wineries, beach resorts, and surfer and sailor havens; the southwest (or Great Southern), boasting more swimming, surfing, and wave-pounded coastlines, as well as forests, wildflowers, coves, and capes; the wheatlands, notable not only for the obvious grain and wheat fields, but for its unusual rock formations; the goldfields, with its street of "sin" and "pound their chest" miners; the midwest, with more wildflowers, coastal hideaways, and the port city of Geraldton; the Gascoyne, with sights ranging from tame dolphins at Monkey Mia to relatively unknown Mount Augustus, the world's largest monocline; the Pilbara, famed for rich iron ore mines, stunning landscapes, fishing villages, and big-ship Port Hedland; and the remote Kimberley, a rugged

© MOON PUBLICATIONS, INC.

land of cattle stations, eyeball-popping gorges, Wolfe Creek meteorite crater, the beehive-ish Bungle Bungle Ranges, and the old pearling port of Broome with its mini-Chinatown and maxi-dinosaur footprints.

It probably goes without saying that distances between Western Australia's sights and cities are vast and not always easily accessible, so plan your itinerary and your timetable carefully. However, it is this very remoteness and the consequent self-reliance of which Western Australians—particularly the residents of Perth—are so proud. Chances are, unless you are a surfer or a sailor, you didn't even know Western Australia existed until the Americans won back the America's Cup at Fremantle in 1987. The U.S. recaptured the cup, but WA managed to keep luring visitors not just to the site of the "victory" in Fremantle but also up the coast, down the coast, into the interior, and especially to the Kimberley, where adventurous and pioneering spirits can explore deserts, fertile plains, beehive mounds, and lots of gorges and chasms.

Wildflowers

An astounding 8,000 species of wildflowers burst from Western Australia's soil, many of them in and around Perth, from Kalbarri on the midwest coast to Albany in the southwest, and interspersed throughout the wheatlands. The "season" runs from early August into early November, following the rainy months of May, June, and July. Some of the more extraordinary flora include 150 types of ground orchids (including a fully underground orchid), the largest known mistletoe, grass trees (blackboys), several black-flower plants, trigger plants that have neuromuscular-type reflexes, and 80 different types of carnivorous plants.

CLIMATE

Perth reputedly has the best climate of any Australian city—"best" meaning sunny with mild temperatures and low humidity. Summer months (Dec.-Feb.) range from a low 17° C (63° F) to a high of 29° C (84° F). Winter (June-Aug.) sees lows of 9° C (48° F), highs of 18° C (64° F), and about 16.6 cm of rainfall per month.

The northern part of the state is similar in climate to the Northern Territory's Top End, experiencing both wet and dry seasons as well as intense heat and humidity. You will be more comfortable traveling this region in the winter months; besides, many areas are closed during the Wet due to impassable roads and other weather-provoked conditions. Winter is also the best time to traverse the state's desert areas. Though nights can be freezing, it still beats the summertime average of 40° C (104° F).

Make sure when you're on those roads less traveled that you check with local police or the Automobile Association for the latest road and weather conditions, and that you and your vehicle are prepared for breakdowns and other emergencies. There will *not* be a McDonald's around the next bend.

HISTORY

In 1616 Dutchman Dirk Hartog and his fellow sailors rowed ashore from their vessel the *Eendracht,* making them the first acknowledged Europeans to land on Western Australia's coast. Between then and 1699 so many Dutchmen, traveling around South Africa on their way to Indonesia, sighted or alighted upon the shores that the region was dubbed "New Holland."

Buccaneer William Dampier landed near Broome in 1688, then again in 1699, but his findings went ignored by the British, who were none too impressed with his description of the area. Though Sydney was settled in 1788, the British showed little interest in extending their boundaries for another 38 years, when two important events took place: Matthew Flinders sailing round Australia in 1801 concluded that the east coast and New Holland were one and the same continent; and Britain got wind that the French, who'd been stirring about the local waters, might be planning to colonize. The usual barrage of dispatches, reports, and proposals were bandied about until, in 1826, Major Edmund Lockyer arrived from Sydney with a band of convicts and soldiers to settle a small penal colony at King George Sound (now Albany).

Shortly afterward, Capt. James Stirling was dispatched by the governor of New South Wales to check out the Swan River region, already partially surveyed by the French, leading to the settlement of both Perth and Fremantle in 1829.

The new settlers soon became discouraged. The sandy soil rendered farming terrible and many of the newcomers scurried back to the east coast. Eventually the remaining colonists discovered fertile land at Guildford, between the Swan and Helena Rivers, and began planting crops and raising livestock. Aside from devastating floods and droughts, there were occasional face-offs with local Aborginals who, a mite miffed with the settlers for stealing their traditional lands, murdering their kinfolk, and contaminating them with heretofore unknown diseases, directed an occasional spear and ripped off the odd beast.

In 1850, the settlers were given a new lease on life when those workhorse convicts were brought in to build roads and bridges that would create vital links and replace the ferries thus far used to transport goods to and from Guildford. By the 1870s the area north of Perth was opened to grazing, followed by the eastern wheatlands, and cattle ranching up in the Kimberley region, but it was the 1892 gold rushes at Coolgardie and Kalgoorlie that helped the colony finally prosper and increase its population.

Western Australia achieved self-government status in 1890 but was left to fall by the wayside by the rest of the country during the Depression. This prompted a move in 1933 to secede from Australia, an effort knocked down by the British Parliament, then laid to rest during the subsequent postwar Good Times, though rumblings and grumblings of secession are still occasionally heard. Today's Western Australia is the wealthiest state in the country, thriving on the Pilbara's incredibly rich iron-ore deposits, productive farm and winegrowing districts, and the tourism boom of Broome and the Kimberley.

PERTH

Western Australia may well be the sexy state, but Perth—its sunny capital city—can be described either as pant-a-second foreplay or a half-snoring lover. It depends on your (or *my*) perspective, of course.

Isolated on the southwestern corner of the Australian continent, Perth is closer to Indonesia than to either Sydney or Melbourne. Nonetheless, this laid-back metropolis outdid its sister cities by once boasting the most millionaires in the country (though many of these are now bankrupt) as well as the fastest-growing population (in numbers, that is, not in age; approximately one-half of Perth's 1.8 million residents are, well, if not younger than springtime, at least basking in the summery sun).

As with the 1890s gold rush inland, the rich mineral deposits of the northern Pilbara region in the 1970s have filtered enormous wealth into the city, and this shows no evidence of slowing. Add to that local entrepreneurs, such as Alan Bond of America's Cup fame, who have managed to wheel and deal megabucks from the east coast and other sources, parlaying them into an incredible variety of national and international conglomerates, resorts, and other enterprises (not all of which have done too well—and that goes for Big Boy Bond, too).

Sitting on the banks of the Swan River (named in 1697 by Dutch navigators for its resident black swans), Perth was settled by Capt. James Stirling and his colonists in 1829 and declared a city in 1856. In 1962, Perth achieved worldwide attention when just about every light in town was turned on for orbiting astronaut John Glenn, thus tagging it the "city of lights." Perth was "put on the map" again in 1980, when America's Skylab satellite smashed to smithereens over the eastern desert and, of course, in 1987, when the America's Cup was held in neighboring Fremantle. Perth today is a relaxed beach- and boat-loving center of commerce, surrounded by a gorgeous coastline, striking wildflower meadows, and fertile vineyards and farmlands.

On 1 May 1997 all Perth telephone numbers will change. To dial the new number, simply add a 9 to the old number and change the area code to (08). For example, (09) 123-4567 will become (08) 9123-4567.

PERTH

EAST PERTH

HAIG PARK

WELLINGTON
SQUARE

GLOUCESTER PARK
TROTTING GROUND

NELSON AVE.

QUEENS
GARDENS

W.A.C.A.
OVAL

ROYAL PERTH
HOSPITAL

YMCA JEWELL
HOUSE

PERTH MINT

ROYAL
AUTOMOBILE
CLUB

TRANSPERTH
DEPOT

LANGLEY
PARK

RIVERSIDE DR.

TERRACE RD.

ADELAIDE TERRACE

GODERICH ST.

MOORE ST.

WATERLOO CRESCENT

PLAIN ST.

BENNETT ST.

HILL ST.

HEIRISSON
ISLAND

CAUSEWAY

RIVER

TO GUILDFORD ROAD

EAST PERTH
TERMINAL

CLAISEBROOK
STATION

SUMMERS ST.

WEST PARADE

BULWER ST.

LORD ST.

EDWARD ST.

53

51

65

65

5

5

TO THE GREAT
EASTERN
HIGHWAY

TO
ALBANY HIGHWAY

© MOON PUBLICATIONS, INC.

Compact and laid out in grids, Perth is a great city to get around in, particularly if you have no car—it's easy to walk just about anywhere. Both the bus and metropolitan railway stations are on Wellington St. just a few blocks from the city center, as are the general post office and Tourist Information Centre. Parallel to Wellington St., heading south, are Murray and Hay Streets, the main shopping district; then comes St. George's Terrace, the major business street. Beyond St. George's Terrace is the Swan River and Barrack Street Jetty (with many of the big high-rise hotels sandwiched in between), and Kings Park sits at the west edge of town. North of the railway tracks is the suburb of Northbridge, home to many of the backpacker hostels, inexpensive ethnic eateries, chic cafes, and the Perth Cultural Centre.

Many books and brochures liken this city to California's San Diego or some place on the Mediterranean—the perfect blend of pant-a-second and half-a-snore.

ST. GEORGE'S TERRACE

This tour of the city's main business thoroughfare—a mix of glitzy modern banks and office buildings interspersed with historic structures—begins on the west side of Victoria Avenue and continues westward to Barracks Archway, then covers the north side of the street returning back to the government buildings.

Perth Concert Hall

Adjacent to Government House, this elaborate space with four foyers and two exhibition halls is the city's premier venue for folk music, orchestra recitals, and other year-round musical performances by both national and international artists. For information, phone (09) 325-9944.

Government House

This Gothic-revival-style residence complete with turrets and arches (a la the Tower of London), built between 1859 and 1864 at a cost of $30,000, still serves as the official home to the governor of Western Australia, as well as to visiting royalty. The public is welcome to visit the surrounding expansive gardens during special celebrations.

Council House

On the other side of Government House, Perth's civic administration center, opened by HRH Queen Elizabeth in 1963, houses five levels of offices, a circular council chamber, councillors' dining room, a large reception area, and a free public library. Hours are Mon.-Fri. 9 a.m.-4 p.m (ground floor only). Guided tours are available Mon.-Fri. at 10:30 a.m. and 2:30 p.m. Admission is free. For information, phone (09) 425-3333.

Supreme Court

Just below Government House, the Supreme Court complex (Francis Burt Law Centre) includes the **Old Court House,** one of the city's oldest surviving colonial buildings (erected in 1836 with a few rear additions made in 1905) with many original details still intact. Presently serving as a legal history museum, the Old Court House includes a replica of an early legal office and related objects. An audiovisual presentation depicts the history of the law and the WA legal profession. The surrounding **Supreme Court Gardens,** sheltered by Norfolk Island pines, are a popular brown bag lunch spot for city workers. The **Barrack Street Jetty,** ferry and riverboat departure point, is just beyond the gardens.

The Old Court House hours are Tuesday and Thursday 10 a.m.-2 p.m. Admission is free. For information, phone (09) 325-4787.

Alan Green Conservatory

Continuing west across Barrack St. along the green lawns of the Esplanade, you'll see this pyramid-shaped conservatory, which houses a wide range of exotic tropical and semitropical plants within its controlled environment. Hours are Mon.-Sat. 10 a.m.-4 p.m., Sunday and public holidays noon-4 p.m. Admission is free. For information, phone (09) 425-3333.

R and I Tower

Head north on William St. back to St. George's Terrace. The R and I Tower, at the corner, is home to both the beautifully restored, ornate old **Palace Hotel** (currently used as banking chambers) and Alan Bond's astounding collection of impressionist paintings (which may have been confiscated or sold off by the time you get there). For information, phone (09) 320-6206.

Old Perth Boys' School

Pointing west again, and situated along St. George's Terrace between William and Mill Streets, this former government school (built in 1854) resembles a medieval church with its quarried limestone, steeply pitched gable roof, and Gothic windows. Several additions were constructed in 1860, 1865, and 1876. The building presently serves as headquarters for the National Trust of Western Australia. Hours are Mon.-Fri. 9 a.m.-5 p.m. Admission is free. For information, phone (09) 321-6088.

Barracks Archway

At the western end of St. George's Terrace where it branches off and becomes Malcolm Street), the three-story Tudor-style archway, built in 1863-66 of Flemish bond brickwork, stands as a memorial to WA's early pioneers and is all that remains of the old Pensioners Barracks, which were demolished in 1966. The archway fronts **Parliament House,** which is open for conducted tours on weekdays. For information, phone (09) 222-7222.

The Cloisters

Between King and Milligan Streets on the north side of St. George's Terrace, the snappy brick Cloisters, established in 1858, was WA's first boys' secondary school.

His Majesty's Theatre

Turn north on King St. to see this restored Edwardian building—frequently referred to as "gracious"—a venue for ballet, opera, and theater performances. For information, phone (09) 322-2929.

London Court

Back on St. George's Terrace, beyond William St., the London Court Arcade, built in 1937, is a great bit of Aussie kitsch. Running all the way to Hay Street Mall, the *very* mock-Tudor laneway, the brainchild of hit-it-rich gold miner Claude de Bernales, features sublimely silly details like medieval clocks with mechanical jousting knights. The clock at the Hay Street end is a mini-Big Ben.

Town Hall

Walk a short distance along the Mall to Barrack Street. Perth Town Hall, on the southeast corner,

was constructed by convicts to resemble an English market. Check out the tower—still visible is a piece of hangman's rope carved in the stone. The tower windows are built in the shape of reversed broad arrowheads—a symbol meaning "convict-built."

St. George's Cathedral

Reached from Cathedral Ave., off St. George's Terrace, this was the site of Perth's first church, constructed of timber and rush in 1829, then replaced by a stone building that served worshippers until 1841. The foundation stone for the present cathedral was laid in 1880.

The Deanery

At the corner of St. George's Terrace and Pier St., the Deanery, which currently functions as Anglican church offices, was built in the late 1850s as a residence for the first Anglican dean of Perth and ranks among WA's few remaining houses from that period.

OTHER CITY SIGHTS

Perth Cultural Centre

Cross the railway tracks at Horseshoe Bridge to reach Northbridge, site of the Perth Cultural Centre, a "mall" comprising several buildings, including the Art Gallery of Western Australia and the Western Australian Museum.

Closest to Horseshoe Bridge, the **Art Gallery of Western Australia** exhibits contemporary and traditional Australian and European paintings and sculpture, including a collection of Aboriginal paintings and crafts (with informative pamphlets). Hours are daily 10 a.m.-5 p.m., closed Good Friday and Christmas Day. Admission is free. Free guided tours are offered Tues.-Fri. at noon. For information, phone (09) 328-7233.

On the corner of the Mall and Beaufort St., the **Western Australian Museum** is centered on the **Old Gaol,** a restored, convict-built Georgian stone courthouse and jail that served its purpose from 1856 to 1889 (the grounds were used for a number of public executions). Now serving as a museum, exhibitions feature WA historical and cultural memorabilia, including household items, political records, early mementos, a collection of meteorites (one weighs 11 tons!), a 25-meter blue whale skeleton, plus an outstanding Aboriginal gallery. Hours are Mon.-Fri. 10:30 a.m.-5 p.m., Sat.-Sun. 1-5 p.m., closed Christmas Day and Good Friday. Admission is free. For information, phone (09) 328-4411.

More Museums

The **Mineral Museum of Western Australia,** 100 Plain St. East (in Mineral House), features rocks, minerals, and special displays related to mining and geology. Hours are Mon.-Fri. 8 a.m.-5 p.m. Admission is free. For information, phone (09) 222-3333.

Perth's oldest **fire station,** corner Irwin and Murray Streets, serves as a museum depicting WA's firefighting techniques and machinery from 1901 to the present day. Hours are Mon.-Thurs. 10 a.m.-3 p.m. Admission is free. For information, phone (09) 323-9468.

At the northeast edge of the city, at the junction of Lord and Bulwer Streets, the **Army Museum of Western Australia** houses uniforms, badges, medals, and other military items ranging from the colonial period to the present. Hours are Sunday and Thursday 1-4:30 p.m. A donation is requested. For information, phone (09) 227-9269.

Scitech Discovery Centre

At the corner of Railway Parade and Sutherland St., Scitech features entertaining hands-on experiments (for kids of all ages) on high-tech equipment. Hours are Mon.-Fri. 10 a.m.-5 p.m., Saturday 10 a.m.-9 p.m., Sunday 10 a.m.-6 p.m. Admission is $10. For information, phone (09) 481-6295.

It's a Small World

See a huge museum collection of little things—miniature cars, rooms, trains, et cetera—located at 12 Parliament Place, West Perth. Hours are Sun.-Fri. 10 a.m.-5 p.m., Saturday 2-5 p.m. Admission is $4. For information, phone (09) 322-2020.

Old Mill

Perth's first flour mill, built in 1835, is at the southern end of the Narrows Bridge and displays many pioneering relics. Hours are Monday, Wednesday, and Thursday 1-5 p.m., Sat.-Sun. noon-4 p.m. A donation is requested. For information, phone (09) 382-4144.

Perth Mint

Dating from 1899, the mint still produces gold, silver, and platinum bullion coins. Displays include various coins, including a one-kg nugget coin. Located at 310 Hay Street. Hours are Mon.-Fri. 9 a.m.-4 p.m., Saturday 9 a.m.-1 p.m. Admission is free (no place to put any more coins?). For information, phone (09) 421-7277.

Perth Zoo

Across the Swan River (and beyond the Old Mill), at 20 Labouchere Rd., South Perth, the zoo is easily reached by bus or ferry from the city center. Noteworthy attractions include the great ape complex, nocturnal house, wallaby park, great cat enclosure, gibbon lake, walk-through aviary, and the Conservation Discovery Centre. Hours are daily 10 a.m.-5 p.m. Admission is $6. For information, phone (09) 367-7988.

Parks and Gardens

Kings Park, at the west edge of the city, is Perth's park supreme—even though bushfires in 1989 burned nearly half of it. A short drive or easy walk from city center, its nearly 400 hectares consist mostly of natural bushland as well as a five-hectare **botanic garden** (noted for its spring wildflowers), natural trails, picnic areas, and paths for walking, jogging, and cycling. You'll catch some terrific views of the city, river, and surrounding countryside from various perches and lookouts—especially from **Mount Eliza,** the park's most prominent knoll. Free guided tours are available. For information, phone (09) 321-4801.

On the eastern edge of the city, **Queens Garden,** corner Hay and Plain Streets, is a quiet English-style park with a water garden. **Hyde Park,** corner William and Vincent Streets, North Perth, caters to families with its adventure playground and to birdwatchers with its ornamental lake. **Lake Monger,** in the close-by suburb of Wembley, is a popular spot for watching those seductive black swans, as well as wild ducks and other birdlife.

Beaches

Pick and choose from any of Perth's well-known beaches. For calm, Swan River swimming

PERTH BEACHES AND SUBURBS

INDIAN OCEAN

SORRENTO BEACH

NORTH BEACH

TRIGG ISLAND BEACH

SCARBOROUGH BEACH

CITY BEACH

SWANBOURNE

SWANBOURNE BEACH

NORTH COTTESLOE BEACH

COTTESLOE BEACH

MOSMAN PARK

NORTH FREMANTLE

FREMANTLE

MITCHELL FREEWAY

WEST COAST HWY.

SCARBOROUGH BEACH RD.

LAKE MONGER

LEEDERVILLE

JOLIMENT

WEST PERTH

NORTH PERTH

SUBIACO

NORTHBRIDGE

PERTH CITY

EAST PERTH

CLAREMONT

STUBBS TERRACE

STIRLING HWY.

CRAWLEY

MOUNTS BAY RD.

SOUTH PERTH

PEPPERMINT GROVE

SWAN RIVER

CANNING HWY.

LEACH HWY.

KWINANA FREEWAY

COMO

SHEPPERTON RD.

VICTORIA PARK

GREAT EASTERN HWY.

GUILDFORD RD.

BREARLEY AVE.

WEST SWAN HWY.

CAVERSHAM

GUILDFORD

PERTH INTERNATIONAL AIRPORT
DOMESTIC TERMINAL

INTERNATIONAL TERMINAL

MORRIS MILLER DR.

TONKIN HWY.

ALBANY HWY.

BULL CREEK

CANNING VALE

GOSNELLS

ARMADALE

0   2 km

noon

beaches, try **Crawley, Peppermint Grove,** and **Como.** If you'd rather tackle the surf, head for the beaches along the Indian Ocean—best bets are **Cottesloe, City Beach** (site of many national surfing contests), **Scarborough,** and **Trigg Island.** If you're looking for surf *and* you forgot your bathers, **Swanbourne** (north of Cottesloe) is a popular nude beach. Almost all beaches can be easily reached by bus.

SUBURBAN SIGHTS

Claremont Museum
Housed within one of WA's oldest buildings (constructed by convicts in 1861-62), the museum's displays depict early settlement, convict and farming life, as well as replicas of bootmaker and barber shops. Located at 66 Victoria Ave., Claremont. Hours are Tues.-Thurs. and Sunday 1-4 p.m., daily 2-5 p.m. during school holidays. Admission is $2. For information, phone (09) 386-3352.

Museum of W.A. Sport
Inside the Superdrome, trophies and other memorabilia recall the good and not-so-good moments of Western Australian sports figures. It's on Stephenson Ave. in Mt. Claremont. Hours are daily 8 a.m.-8 p.m. Admission is free. For information, phone (09) 387-8542.

Museum of Childhood
Two buildings contain dolls (wax, wooden, and bisque), toys, photographs, literature, clothing, furniture, and other curios and playthings (almost 20,000 items) associated with WA's pioneer children. Located at 160 Hamersley Rd., Subiaco. Hours are Mon.-Fri. 10 a.m.-3 p.m., Sunday 2-5 p.m. Admission is $2.50. For information, phone (09) 381-1103.

Aviation Museum
Exhibits depicting the history of civil and military aviation from the origins up to the present (with an emphasis on WA) feature historic aircraft (such as the Lancaster heavy bomber and the Spitfire fighter), uniforms, medals, models, photos, and other aero-memorabilia. The museum is on Bull Creek Dr. in Bull Creek. Hours are daily 11 a.m.-4 p.m., closed Christmas Day

and Good Friday. Admission is $4.50. For information, phone (09) 332-7205.

Swan Brewery
Tour WA's famed brewery and guzzle or sip some of the "homegrown" brews such as Swan Lager, Swan Draught, and Emu. Located at 25 Vaile Rd., Canning Vale. Tours last 90 minutes to two hours and are available Mon.-Thursday. Advance reservations are necessary. For information, phone (09) 350-0222.

Cohunu Wildlife Park
Visit the Southern Hemisphere's largest aviary (on Mills Rd. in Gosnells) and see native animals in a "natural" environment. This is also the spot to have your photo taken with a koala (400 tame kangaroos and photo-loving koalas are "natural?"). Hours are daily 10 a.m.-5 p.m. Admission is $7.50. For information, phone (09) 390-6090.

Elizabethan Village
Full-size re-creations of Shakespeare's birthplace and Anne Hathaway's cottage are furnished with 500-year-old antiques. The village is on Canns Rd. in Armadale. Hours are Mon.-Fri. 10 a.m.-4 p.m., Sat.-Sun. 10 a.m.-5 p.m. Admission is $5. For information, phone (09) 399-3166.

Pioneer World
This working model of a 19th-century gold miners' village allows visitors to pan for their own gold nuggets, filings, and dust (30-minute limit). Other attractions include working craftsmen, sing-alongs, silent movies, vaudeville shows, and other entertainment. Located at junction of South West and Albany Highways, Armadale. Hours are daily 10 a.m.-5 p.m. Admission is $8.50. For information, phone (09) 399-5322.

ACCOMMODATIONS

Perth's varied accommodations are as conveniently located as everything else in town. Older, cheaper hotels and some hostels are clustered in and around the city center, while others are just across the railway tracks in Northbridge. South Perth and several of the closer suburbs also provide motel and holiday-flat units. Big spenders will find no shortage of luxury hotels.

most of which are between St. George's Terrace and the Swan River.

Optimism over Perth's tourism boom in conjunction with the America's Cup—and its accompanying groupies—saw upmarket accommodations increase by several thousand rooms. Many of these hotels have since experienced low occupancy, so it may be possible to strike a good deal on rates. Campgrounds and caravan parks are scattered 10-20 km from town.

As with all Australian cities and tourist centers, it's advisable to book rooms in advance. If you arrive without a reservation, contact the **Western Australia Tourist Centre,** Forrest Chase, corner of Wellington St. (tel. 09-483-1111).

Inexpensive (Under $35)

Jewell House, 180 Goderich St. (tel. 09-325-8488), is a YMCA-run establishment with clean, but basic, rooms. The reception office is open 24 hours, and guests have use of two TV rooms and a laundry room. Meals, weekly rates, and free baggage storage are available. The well-recommended **Downtowner Lodge,** 63 Hill St. (tel. 09-325-6973), opposite the Perth Mint, has 12 clean, quiet rooms, plus TV lounge and laundry facilities. The **Court Hotel,** 50 Beaufort St. (tel. 09-328-5292), offers inexpensive rooms near the Perth Cultural Centre.

Farther beyond the Cultural Centre, **Cheviot Lodge,** 30 Bulwer St. (tel. 09-227-6817), features modern kitchen and bathroom facilities, TV and game room, a laundry room, and free pick-up service from the bus station. **Mountway Holiday Units,** 36 Mount St. (tel. 09-321-8307), close to Kings Park, offers self-contained one-bedroom flats with cooking facilities, full-size bathtubs, and TVs.

Moderate ($35-70)

Make advance reservations for **The Adelphi,** 130A Mounts Bay Rd. (tel. 09-322-4666), situated at the base of Kings Park bluff. Rooms are bright and cheery (upper levels feature Swan River views) and have air-conditioning, TVs, phones, and cooking facilities. Another popular choice is **City Waters Lodge,** 118 Terrace Rd. (tel. 09-325-1566), also with kitchens, phones, TVs, air-conditioning, and off-street parking.

Perth Riverview Holiday Apartments, 42 Mount St. (tel. 09-321-8963), close to both Kings Park and city center, offers clean rooms in a good neighborhood, with all the conveniences of the other self-contained flats. **Airways Hotel,** 195 Adelaide Terrace (tel. 09-323-7799), located near the deluxe hotels, has many different sizes of rooms with cooking facilities, plus a restaurant on the premises.

Also on the "good side" of town, with Swan River views, is the **New Esplanade Hotel,** 18 the Esplanade (tel. 09-325-2000), with room service, restaurant, bar, and a less-expensive "travelers' wing." **Miss Maud European Hotel,** 97 Murray St. (tel. 09-325-3900), is a small, friendly, centrally located establishment with Scandinavian decor, adjacent restaurant, and bakery. Breakfast is included in the rates.

Expensive ($70 and Way Up)

As you might imagine, with all the millionaires and money around, there is no shortage of luxury hotels in this city. Most are centrally located (i.e., near the banks) and all of them have the customary amenities such as restaurants, bars, room service, shops, health clubs, and the like. The **Parmelia Hilton,** Mill St. (tel. 09-322-3622), is considered one of the best. Public rooms are beautifully decorated with antiques and other artwork, and guest rooms have either river or city views. The **Sheraton Perth,** 207 Adelaide Terrace (tel. 09-325-0501), is another hefty-price winner with terrific views, well-decorated guest rooms, and a superb formal dining room.

Chateau Commodore, 417 Hay St. (tel. 09-325-0461), one of the city's older hotels, is a local favorite, and cheaper than the name brands above. Though the decor is somewhat . . . robust, the rooms are large and some have balconies with views. The Chateau is also cheaper than the others. For those who like their action packed, **Burswood Island Resort,** Great Eastern Hwy., Victoria Park (tel. 09-362-7777), has a full-on 24-hour casino (largest in the Southern Hemisphere), plus an 18-hole golf course and beautifully decorated rooms with city or river views.

Hostels

Most of Perth's hostels and backpacker accommodations are easy walks from the bus and rail stations. Dorm beds average $9-14 per night.

The city's three **YHA hostels** are busy establishments, all situated in Northbridge. The closest hostel is 87-bed **Northbridge-Francis St. YHA Hostel,** 42 Francis St. (tel. 09-328-7794), corner of William and Francis Streets, past the Perth Cultural Centre. Around the corner, **Britannia YHA Hostel,** 253 William St. (tel. 09-328-6121), offers 145 beds. Both sites have a communal kitchen, laundry, rec room, and bicycle hire. **YHA Perth City Hostel,** with 48 beds, is at 60 Newcastle St. (tel. 09-328-1135), about a 15-minute walk from the city center.

Backpackers Perth Inn, 194 Brisbane St. (tel. 09-328-9958), has clean, spacious rooms in a renovated colonial house with gardens. **Budget Backpackers' International,** 342 Newcastle St. (tel. 09-328-9468), and **North Lodge,** 225 Beaufort St. (tel. 09-227-7588), are other choices with communal lounges and kitchens.

Males and females are segregated in the two-houser **Perth Travellers Lodge,** 156 Aberdeen St. (tel. 09-328-6667). Other possibilities on the same street are **Aberdeen Lodge,** 79 Aberdeen St. (tel. 09-227-6137), with four-bed dorms; **12.01 Central,** corner of Aberdeen and Fitzgerald Streets (tel. 09-227-1201), with a deli and cafe below; and **Backpackers International,** corner of Aberdeen and Lake Streets (tel. 09-227-9977).

Travelers of both sexes are welcome to mix and mingle with residents and retirees at the main **YMCA** facility in the city center at 119 Murray St. (tel. 09-325-7627). They're pretty basic accommodations, but the weekly rates are a good deal. The renovated **Grand YWCA Central,** 379 Wellington St. (tel. 09-221-2682), offers varied accommodations and $15 bunk beds, along with a restaurant and cafe.

Camping

The following campgrounds and caravan parks fall within 20 km of the city and offer both on-site vans and campsites: **Central Caravan Park,** 38 Central Ave., Redcliffe (tel. 09-277-5696); **Kenlorn Caravan Park,** 229 Welshpool Rd., Queens Park (tel. 09-458-2604); **Caversham Caravan Park,** Benara Rd., Caversham (tel. 09-279-6700); **Careniup Caravan Park,** 467 North Beach Rd., Gwelup (tel. 09-447-6665); **Starhaven Caravan Park,** 18 Pearl Parade, Scarborough (tel. 09-341-1770); **Kingsway Car-** **avan Park,** corner Kingsway and Wanneroo Rd., Landsdale (tel. 09-409-9267); **Perth Tourist Caravan Park,** 319 Hale Rd., Forrestfield (tel. 09-453-6677); **Forrestfield Caravan Park,** 351 Hawtin Rd., Forrestfield (tel. 09-453-6378); **Guildford Caravan Park,** 372 West Swan Rd., Guildford (tel. 09-274-2828); and **Orange Grove Caravan Park,** 19 Kelvin Rd., Orange Grove (tel. 09-453-6226).

FOOD

Perth is hardly a culinary tour de force like Melbourne, but those millionaires do like to eat. About 700 restaurants dot the city, including many ethnic establishments along William Street in Northbridge, coffee shops and cafes in the city center, and high-priced gourmet dining rooms in hotels or spattered about the inner suburbs. Fresh, local seafood tops many of the menus.

Inexpensive

The cheapest—and perhaps tastiest—places to eat at are the foodstalls and halls, where you can do a budget-type graze of many different types of food for less than a greasy spoon takeaway. One of the best choices is **Down Under Food Hall,** near William St., downstairs in the Hay Street Mall. Select from a variety of ethnic goodies such as Indian, Indonesian, Chinese, and Mexican. Hours are Mon.-Wed. 8 a.m.-7 p.m., Thurs.-Sat. 8 a.m.-9 p.m. Nearby, but a bit more expensive, is **Carillon Food Hall,** in Carillon Arcade, also on Hay Street Mall. Hours are Mon.-Sat. 8 a.m.-9 p.m. In Northbridge, try **Northbridge Pavilion,** corner Lake and James Streets, **Victoria Gardens,** on Aberdeen St. overlooking Russell Square, or the two Asian halls on James Street.

Fast Eddy's, corner Hay and Milligan Streets, is a 24-hour burger joint. **Magic Apple,** 445 Hay St., features healthy salads, smoothies, and sandwiches. Another health-style lunch spot is **Granary Wholefoods,** 37 Barrack St. (downstairs), with a good range of vegetarian selections. Down the way, **Mr. Samurai,** 83 Barrack St., is a top choice for cheap Japanese specialties.

Northbridge is packed with ethnic restaurants, many of them inexpensive. Take your tummy for a walk along William Street and you'll never go hungry—**Hare Krishna Food for Life** is just one of your options.

A local favorite for beachside breakfast is **North Cott Café,** 149 Marine Parade, Cottlesloe.

Moderate

Kings Park Garden Restaurant, with city and river views, is a delightful spot for lunch and morning or afternoon teas. Dinner, with live music, is in the expensive range. For those not-to-be-missed yuppie lunches, infiltrate **Moon and Sixpence Bar,** 300 Murray St., or **44 King Street,** around the corner. And don't miss the oh-so-cool **Frostbites Bar and Grill,** 397 Murray Street.

Super Italian fare is served at **Mamma Maria's,** 105 Aberdeen Street. Other pasta feasts line Aberdeen St., including **Café Navona, La Luna Café,** and **Aberdino's.**

In Subiaco, **Bar Bzar,** corner of Railway Rd. and Rokeby St., is rife with wanna-be-but-never-will Bohemians. The **Witch's Cauldron,** 89 Rokeby St., casts its spell with killer garlic prawns and other potent concoctions.

Suburban Leederville is becoming another see-and-be-seen haunt. Cruise Oxford St., between Aberdeen and Vincent Streets, for everything from rock 'n' roll pizza to postwar Vietnamese.

Expensive

Inquire about dress codes and reserve tables well ahead, especially for weekends and holiday periods. **Fraser's,** in Kings Park (tel. 09-481-7100), is a two-level, river-and-city view establishment, with fresh, flavorful contemporary cuisine. Open daily for lunch and dinner.

Searching for a top-notch, noisy, crowded, chic, imaginative, 24-hour brasserie with great cakes and a wonderful wine list? Choose from a cast of one: **Oriel,** 480 Hay St., Subiaco (tel. 09-382-1886).

Perugino, 77 Outram St., West Perth (tel. 09-321-5420), is considered Perth's best Italian restaurant. Regional specialties are prepared with fresh ingredients and fresh imagination. Recently renovated, the garden setting lures locals involved in romantic encounters, important business, or pure self-indulgence. Open Mon.-Fri. lunch, Mon.-Sat. dinner.

And, for one of the best French restaurants, the prizewinner is **Pierre's,** 8 Outram St., West Perth (tel. 09-322-7648). Pierre's is elegant, formal, and very expensive. This magnificently restored colonial residence offers scrumptious cuisine and—naturally—a fabulous wine list. Open Mon.-Fri. lunch, nightly dinner.

In Northbridge, **Choi's Inn,** 68 Roe St. (tel. 09-328-6350), is a friendly, casual Chinese establishment that serves traditional Cantonese and fiery Sichuan meals. Advance orders are necessary for the beggar's chicken and Peking duck. Open daily for lunch and dinner.

ENTERTAINMENT AND EVENTS

Much of Perth's entertainment scene is geared toward its vibrant, young (or young at heart) residents, with Northbridge being the major gathering spot. Check local newspapers, particularly the lift-out entertainment guide in Thursday's *West Australian* newspaper for current listings of arts and cultural events. For gig info, pick up a copy of *X-Press,* the free weekly music mag, at any record shop and many other locations. The *Westside Observer,* free at Arcane Bookshop (212 William St.), has lists of gay and lesbian entertainment venues.

Cinemas

Perth has the usual round of commercial cinema complexes, with most of the flicks appearing months after their U.S. debut. Movie houses that show more arty and/or cerebral films are the **Lumiere,** in the Perth Entertainment Centre; **Cinema Paradiso,** 164 James St., Northbridge; and the **Astor,** corner of Beaufort and Walcott Streets, Mt. Lawley.

There's a two-level wraparound **Omni Theater** at the corner of Railway Parade and Sutherland St., West Perth (tel. 09-481-6481).

Pubs and Clubs

Plentiful clubs, pubs, and discos feature live music most nights of the week. Northbridge is the prime area for contemporary and casual venues ($4-8), while discos and nightclubs in the big hotels cater to the yup-and-coming ($10-15).

Catch live music in Northbridge at **Brass Monkey Tavern,** 209 William St.; **Aberdeen**

Hotel, 84 Aberdeen St.; and **The Lone Star,** corner of Beaufort and Newcastle Streets (travelers' night is Wednesday). **Aqua,** 232 William St., is a favorite late-night spot (Thursday is Latin American night) popular with the hip set. For pure dance, **St. James' Nightclub,** 139 James St., is a huge club with four bars, playing retro and mainstream tunes to a bebopping young crowd.

Exit Nightclub, 187 Stirling St., has split-levels and split-styles (techno, rap, and hip-hop), appealing to sophisticates who like to pretend they're not.

In Leederville, **Hip-E Club,** corner of Newcastle and Oxford Streets, spins the tunes of the '60s and '70s to the never-were hippie set (Tuesday is backpackers' night).

Perth has the usual round of hot discos with cold meat inspectors. Fashion victims might try **Brannigan's,** Irwin St., in the Perth International Hotel; **Geremiah's,** Milligan St., in the Orchard Hotel; **The Loft,** 237 Hay St.; or **Club Rumours,** 418 Murray Street.

For good old drinkin' pubs, try **Sherwood's Tavern,** 77 St. George's Terrace; **Milligan's,** 205 James St.; and the **Northbridge Hotel,** 198 Brisbane Street.

The Casino
Burswood Island Resort, WA's first casino, features more than 140 gaming tables, including roulette, baccarat, blackjack, craps, and Australia's own two-up. Restaurants, bars, and a cabaret are also part of this luxury resort complex on the banks of the Swan River, near the city. Open 24 hours a day except Christmas Day and Good Friday. For information, phone (09) 362-7777.

Theater, Dance, and Concerts
The stunning **His Majesty's Theatre,** 825 Hay St. (tel. 09-322-2929), is home not just to many of Perth's theatrical productions but also to the **West Australian Ballet Company** and the **West Australian Opera Company.** Modern and traditional ballets are performed in February, May, June, and October, while the operatic season (April, August, and November) features classical works and operettas.

The **Playhouse Theatre,** 3 Pier St. (tel. 09-325-3500), is headquarters of the **Western Aus-**tralian **Theatre Company,** which presents a number of classical and contemporary plays throughout the year. Other good local theaters include: **Dolphin Theatre,** University of Western Australia, Crawley (tel. 09-380-2432); **Regal Theatre,** 474 Hay St., Subiaco (tel. 09-381-1557); **Subiaco** and **Hole in the Wall,** 180 Hamersley Rd., Subiaco (tel. 09-381-2733).

Perth Entertainment Centre, on Wellington near Milligan St., is where the big-name rock concerts and other major events are held. You can't miss the **Betts & Betts Walk of Fame** out front—a walkway of celebrities' autographed footprints. For information, phone (09) 322-4766.

Folk music, orchestra recitals, and more "mellow" concerts are performed at **Perth Concert Hall,** 5 St. George's Terrace (tel. 09-325-9944). In summer, the band shell in the **Supreme Court Gardens** presents a variety of live music.

Schedules for almost every entertainment event are advertised in the lift-out entertainment guide in Thursday's *West Australian.*

BOCS is the state's major ticket booking agency for everything from concerts and ballet to theater and sporting events. For information, phone (09) 484-1133, or stop by the outlet at the Western Australia Tourist Centre, on Forrest Place.

Theme Parks
Adventure World, 179 Progress Dr., Bibra Lake, is a family-oriented entertainment complex with an amusement park, native animals, waterways, and parklands. Hours are daily Sept.-May, and school holidays, 10 a.m.-5 p.m. Admission is $18, children $15. For information, phone (09) 417-9666.

Travel through an underground acrylic tunnel to view approximately 5,000 species of underwater life (such as starfish, crustaceans, and a small Port Jackson shark) at **Underwater World,** Hillary's Boat Harbour, West Coast Highway. Other attractions include Microworld, where you can watch sea horses, shellfish, and anemones through a video camera, and Touch Pool, where you can feel the creatures. There's also a gift shop, and an underwater cafe that looks out on the Indian Ocean. Hours are daily 9 a.m.-5 p.m. Admission is $14. For information, phone (09) 447-7500.

Events

The city's big extravaganza is the annual **Festival of Perth** held in February and March. The festival showcases international and national big-name talents, as well as local joes, with a program roster that includes music, theater, dance, film, visual and literary arts, and a host of outdoor activities. For information, contact the University of Western Australia, Mounts Bay Rd., Crawley (tel. 09-386-7977).

SPORTS AND RECREATION

Great weather, great beaches, great park—it means Perth offers all types of land and water sports and year-round recreational opportunities. Call or drop by the **Western Australia Tourist Centre** on Forrest Place for information on spectator and participant sports throughout the state.

Diving

A few scattered, centuries-old shipwrecks offshore should make things interesting for divers. Contact **Perth Diving Academy,** 281 Wanneroo Rd., Nollamara (tel. 09-344-1562), or the **Australasian Diving Centre,** 259 Stirling Hwy., Claremont (tel. 09-384-3966).

Fishing

You'll luck out on the catch of the day at many coastal ports, particularly Fremantle, as well as along the Swan River banks. The prized fish in these parts is the blue marlin. Charter boats are available (check the Yellow Pages).

Swimming Pools

Not happy with the ocean or the river? A freshwater swimming pool is located at the **Superdrome,** Stephenson Ave., Mt. Claremont (tel. 09-441-8222).

Sporting Facilities

Tennis: Fees are reasonable at public tennis courts within metropolitan and suburban parks. For sites and details, contact **Tennis West** (tel. 09-472-1195).

Golf: Select from one of the city's many public golf courses after consulting with the **Western Australia Golf Association** (tel. 09-474-1005) or the tourist office. Some of Perth's country clubs are on the snooty side (but what else is new?).

Other Participant Sports

Yachties should head straight for the tourism office. **Catamarans** and **windsurfers** are available for hire at the Coode Street Jetty, South Perth (tel. 09-367-2988). They are popular on weekends and holidays, so book ahead. Depending on weather conditions, you can **parasail** on weekends at the South Perth foreshore. For information, contact **Flying High Parasailing** (tel. 09-446-1835).

Bushwalkers, cyclists, and **joggers** will find excellent trails throughout Kings Park and along the Swan River. The tourist office has maps and brochures, or contact the **Ministry of Sport and Recreation** (tel. 09-387-9700).

Spectator Sports

Aussie Rules football is the prime winter spectator sport, with games played every Saturday afternoon March through September, at various league grounds throughout the city. For information, phone the **Western Australia Football League** (tel. 09-381-5599). In summer months, **cricket** is the buzz, with Sheffield Shield, Test, and one-day cricket played at the W.A.C.A. (Western Australia Cricket Association) grounds in Nelson Crescent, East Perth. For information, phone **W.A.C.A.** (tel. 09-325-9800).

Other spectator sports include **rugby, soccer, basketball, baseball,** and **hockey.** Watch for details of all matches and sporting events in the Sports section of the Friday and Saturday newspapers.

Racing is a big-time favorite of Western Australians. For schedules and locales of **horse, trotting,** and **greyhound** racing, watch the Sports section of the morning newspapers. For **motor racing,** contact the W.A. Sporting Car Club (tel. 09-381-4432). For **motorcycle racing,** phone the Motorcycle Racing Club of W.A. (tel. 09-409-1002). On Friday nights throughout spring and summer months, the **RAS Showground** in Claremont hosts thriller speedcar and motorcycle races. Look for details in Thursday's *West Australian.*

SHOPPING

Perth's main shopping district is the pedestrians-only Hay Street Mall and Murray Street Mall, both running parallel between William and Barrack Streets, and the many arcades that branch off to St. George's Terrace and Wellington Street. Major department stores are located here, as are Woolworth, Coles, scads of boutiques, specialty shops, bookshops, schlock and dime stores, cinemas, coffee lounges, and all kinds of general merchandise. King Street, a few blocks away, within the past few years has nosed its way into the shopping mecca with some choice galleries and funky shops. Customary shopping hours are Mon.-Fri. 9 a.m.-5:30 p.m., Thursday until 9 p.m., and Saturday 9 a.m.-noon.

Markets

Colorful, bargain-filled markets offering a wide range of merchandise are: **Subiaco Market,** near Subiaco Railway Station, at Roberts and Rokeby Roads (Thurs.-Sun. 8 a.m.-6 p.m.); **Canning Vale Market,** corner of Bannister and Ranford Roads (Sunday 7 a.m.-4 p.m.); and **Midland Sunday Market,** 284 Great Eastern Hwy. (Sunday 8 a.m.-4 p.m.).

Crafts

For **Aboriginal handicrafts,** don't miss the **Creative Native,** 32 King St. (tel. 09-322-3398), with its excellent range of traditional and contemporary handmade Aboriginal art, including carved emu eggs and boomerangs.

Crafts Council Gallery, Wellington St., at the railway station (tel. 09-325-2799), exhibits crafts by leading Western Australians and also provides listings of other craft shops and outlets.

For items constructed from native jarrah and grass tree wood, visit **Contempo Gallery,** 329 Murray St. (tel. 09-322-2306).

Other Shops

How about gems and money? See gems before they're turned into rings, pendants, and key chains at **Perth Lapidary Centre,** 58 Pier St. (tel. 09-325-2954). Purchase proof-issue coins, commemoratives and banknotes, coin jewelry,

and books related to coin collecting and Western Australia's pioneering prospectors at **The Perth Mint,** 310 Hay St. (tel. 09-421-7277).

Record collectors and purveyors of the local *muso* scene will groove at **78 Records,** 884 Hay Street. On the way to or from, you'll be faced with enough retro and grunge wear for all your nights on this town.

TRANSPORTATION

Getting There by Air

If you're coming from Europe, Africa, or Southeast Asia, Perth will most likely be your Australian gateway city. **International carriers** include Qantas, Air New Zealand, United Airlines, British Airways, South African Airways, Garuda Indonesia, Malaysian Airlines, Thai Airways, Singapore Airlines, and Japan Air Lines.

Domestic carriers that serve Perth from other Australian states are Ansett (tel. 13-1300 toll-free) and **Qantas** (tel. 13-1313 toll-free). For up-to-date prices and cheapest deals, consult the **Britannia YHA,** 253 William St., Northbridge (tel. 09-328-6121), or **STA,** 100 James St., Northbridge (tel. 09-227-7569). Inquire into moneysaving **passes** before you leave home (or enter the country).

Perth International Airport is about 16 km northeast of the city center, and the separate **domestic terminal** is about 10 km closer. Moneychanging and other customary big-city facilities are available.

The **Perth Airport Bus** (tel. 09-250-2838), a private shuttle, meets all incoming flights and drops passengers off at city airline offices and major hotels. Fare is $7 international, $6 domestic. Several **Transperth** city buses operate between the domestic airport and city center. Services run daily, every 40-50 minutes 6 a.m.-10 p.m., less frequently on Saturday, not at all on Sunday. William St., between St. George's Terrace and the Esplanade, is the main pick-up and drop-off spot. Fare is $2. **Taxis** are readily available and the 25-minute ride to city center should cost $15-20.

Getting There by Train

Interstate trains arrive into and depart from the **East Perth Railway Terminal,** West Parade.

The fabled **Indian-Pacific** runs between Perth and Sydney. The 64-hour, three-night journey passes through Broken Hill and Adelaide and crosses the Nullarbor Plain on the world's longest straight stretch of railway line. Trains depart Sydney on Monday and Thursday, and Perth on Monday and Friday. One-way fares are: $932, first-class berth with meals; $598, economy berth with meals; and $290, economy seat. The Indian-Pacific is included in the **Austrailpass** (except the eight-day Austrail Flexi-Pass), which must be purchased outside the country.

For information and bookings, phone **Rail Australia** (tel. 13-2232 toll-free) or **Westrail** (tel. 09-326-2813 or 13-2232 toll-free).

Contact Westrail for bookings on the Prospector (six times weekly Perth-Kalgoorlie, $58) and the Australind (daily Perth-Bunbury, $35). The Australind departs from the Central Railway Station, Wellington St., next to the bus station.

Getting There by Bus

Greyhound Pioneer Australia (tel. 13-2030 toll-free) serves Perth daily from other Australian states. Routes from the east coast usually travel via Adelaide, while the Darwin-to-Perth coaches journey across the Top End and down the west coast. Sample fares are: Sydney-Adelaide-Perth (61 hours), $310; Adelaide-Perth (37 hours), $189; Darwin-Perth (59 hours), $347. Inquire about stopover privileges and special passes for overseas visitors.

Getting There by Car

Western Australia is long, far, and wide. Sealed roads, suitable for conventional vehicles, are: Eyre and Great Eastern Highways from Adelaide (2,697 km); Eyre, South Coast, and South Western Highways from Adelaide (3,212 km); Stuart, Victoria, Great Northern, North West Coastal, and Brand Highways from Darwin (4,379 km); and Stuart, Victoria, and Great Northern Highways from Darwin (4,253 km). Make sure your vehicle and body are prepared for the arduous trek.

Though roadhouse facilities are available along the major byways, distances between them can be vast. The road from Ayers Rock is unsealed all the way to the goldfields region, where it connects with the big highways. Carry plenty of spare everything, even passengers to share the *very* long—and often boring—drive and expensive petrol costs. Also see "Crossing the Nullarbor," in the South Australia chapter.

Hitching

It's fairly cheap—and a lot less exhausting—to take the bus or share a ride (check the YHA bulletin boards). Waits of several days are not uncommon, plus who knows where you'll be waiting. There are some creepy stories about hitchhiking out there! Some friends once picked up a haggard old guy—who looked as if he hadn't eaten for a year—from the edge of the Nullarbor and the middle of nowhere. He drove with them about 100 km even deeper into nowhere, said, "This is where I get out," and wandered off into the proverbial sunset. I'm sure that story has one of the better endings!

If you're dead set on thumbing it, hop a train to Midland if you're headed north or east, or Armadale if your direction is south. Women should be especially careful, and preferably travel with a male companion (or a pit bull).

Getting Around on Buses and Trains

Transperth, the metropolitan transit district, operates five free City Clipper buses approximately every 20 minutes Mon.-Fri. 7 a.m.-6 p.m. Routes are color-coded and circle the city center, covering most tourist attractions. The Yellow Clipper, around the central city, also runs on Saturday morning. Other buses connect the business center with suburban areas, and though not free, they're still good deals. Tickets, good for two hours from the time of issue, range $1.50-2.50, depending on the number of zones you travel. Going to Fremantle, for example, you'll go through only two zones and it's about 20 km away! Even sweeter, tickets are interchangeable on all Transperth buses, trains, and ferries.

If you're sticking around for a while, you might want to consider a **multirider ticket,** which gives you 10 trips for the price of nine. Buses operate Mon.-Fri. 6 a.m.-11:30 p.m., less frequently on weekends and public holidays.

Obtain maps, schedules, tickets, and other information from Transperth Information Services, Perth Central Bus Station, Wellington St. (tel. 13-1213 toll-free), or at the City Bus Port, Mounts Bay Rd., at the bottom of William Street.

Even more convenient is the Transperth information office in the Plaza Arcade, off the Hay Street Mall. Hours are Mon.-Fri. 6:30 a.m.-8 p.m., Saturday 8 a.m.-5 p.m.

Taxis

Meter-operated taxis can be hailed on city streets, plucked from taxi ranks around the central business district and Fremantle, or hired by phoning **Swan Taxis** (tel. 09-322-0111) or **Black and White Taxis** (tel. 09-333-3333). Taxis for **disabled passengers** are available Mon.-Fri. 8 a.m.-4:30 p.m. For information, phone (09) 333-3377. Cab fare begins at $2.20 plus 70 cents per km, rising to a base charge of $3.70 6 p.m.-6 a.m.

Car Rentals

The big-name rental car companies are located at both the domestic and international airports and in the city center. Charges range $50-90, depending on size—some include unlimited kilometers while others give only the first 100-150 km for a free allowance. For information, contact **Avis** (tel. 09-325-7677), **Hertz** (tel. 09-321-7777), or **Budget** (tel. 09-322-1100).

Rent heartier vehicles for outback travel from **South Perth Four Wheel Drive Rentals,** 80 Canning Hwy., Victoria Park (tel. 09-362-5444).

Plenty of other companies are listed in the phone book, but be cautious: sometimes the bigger companies can afford to give the better deals, particularly if you book your car from outside Australia. Get tips from the YHA hostels or STA office in Northbridge.

Bicycles

Excellent trails and climate make Perth an ideal city for cycling. Rent bicycles for $10 per day from the YHA on Francis St. or from **Rideway Cycle Hire,** on the western side of the causeway (tel. 09-354-2393). A guaranteed buy-back scheme is offered at **WA Bicycle Disposal Centre,** 47 Bennett St., East Perth (tel. 09-325-1176).

Ferries

Transperth ferries depart from the Barrack Street Jetty to Mends Street Jetty, across the Swan River in South Perth, daily 6:45 a.m.-7:15 p.m. One-way fare is under $1. Contact Transperth Information Services, Perth Central Bus Station, Wellington St. (tel. 13-1213 toll-free), for details. (Don't forget—your two-hour bus ticket is good on this ferry.)

For **Rottnest Island** ferries, contact **Boat Torque** (tel. 09-221-5844) or **Oceanic Cruises** (tel. 09-430-5127).

Tours

The Western Australia Tourist Centre can help you plan and book organized tours within the city and state. Prices vary $20-120 and include such destinations as wildflower-viewing sites (Aug.-Nov.), Swan Valley, the Darling Ranges, Wave Rock, Monkey Mia, Mt. Augustus, and Yanchep National Park. Longer three- to four-day treks up and down the coast average $400-550. Again, first check with YHA and STA for the best deals with, possibly, more simpatico companions.

City Sights coach tours run about $18 for a half day, $10 for the **Perth Tram** (actually a bus in drag), which makes 90-minute commentator-assisted trips around the city sights. The tram operates daily 9:30 a.m.-6:30 p.m. Pickup point is at 124 Murray St. (near Barrack St.).

Free guided **walking tours** of Kings Park are available April-October. For information, phone (09) 321-4801. A three-hour **Perth and Beyond** tour takes in the city as well as the park. For information, phone (09) 483-2601.

All **boat cruises** leave from Barrack Street Jetty. The bargain of the lot is Transperth's MV *Countess II,* which departs at 2 p.m. daily except Saturday, on a three-hour upstream Swan River cruise. Fare is $12. For information, phone (09) 425-2651. Both **Boat Torque** (tel. 09-221-5844) and **Captain Cook Cruises** (tel. 09-325-3341) operate scenic cruises including Swan River journeys, winery visits, and lunch and dinner extravaganzas.

Whalewatching cruises are offered by various operators, including **Boat Torque** (tel. 09-246-1039), **Oceanic Cruises** (tel. 09-430-5127), and **Mills Charters** (tel. 09-401-0833). **Rockingham Dolphins** (tel. 09-527-1803) departs Magles Bay for two-hour dolphin sightings.

Westrail offers a variety of rail excursions lasting from one day to one week, covering everything from coastal resorts and timber forests to wildflowers and goldfields. For information and bookings, contact the Western Australia Tourist Centre, or Westrail (tel. 09-326-2813 or 13-2232).

And, who would want to miss the free 90-minute tour of **Swan Brewery**? Tours depart Mon.-Wed. 10 a.m. and 2:30 p.m., Thursday 2:30 p.m. only. For bookings, phone (09) 350-0650.

Getting Away

Ansett (tel. 13-1300 toll-free) schedules regular services between Perth and many WA communities including Broome, Derby, Kununurra, Port Hedland, Newman, Exmouth, Carnarvon, Geraldton, and Kalgoorlie.

Skywest (tel. 09-334-2288, or book through Ansett, tel. 13-1300) flies from Perth to Albany, Esperance, Kalgoorlie, Geraldton, Cue, Meekatharra, Wiluna, and other communities. **Western Airlines** (tel. 09-277-4022) links Perth with Geraldton, Kalbarri, Useless Loop, and Monkey Mia.

For Rottnest Island Service, contact **Rottnest Airlines** (tel. 09-277-4198).

Transperth (tel. 13-1213 toll-free) operates frequent rail service between the city center and Fremantle, Midland, Armadale, and points in between. Trains run less often on weekends and public holidays.

SERVICES

Branches of all the major national **banks** are on or about St. George's Terrace, along with the ubiquitous automatic teller machines. You'll find **Bank of America Australia** at 28 the Esplanade (tel. 09-322-7555). Banking hours are Mon.-Thurs. 9:30 a.m.-4 p.m., Friday 9:30 a.m.-5 p.m.

The **general post office**, 3 Forrest Place (tel. 09-326-5211), between the railway station and Hay Street Mall, is open for all postal services Mon.-Fri. 8 a.m.-6 p.m., Saturday 9 a.m.-noon.

For migrant information (employment, permits, etc.), see the **Immigration Office**, 12 St. George's Terrace (tel. 09-220-2311).

Some countries with Perth-based consulates are **United States,** 16 St. George's Terrace (tel. 09-221-1177); **Canada,** 44 St. George's Terrace (tel. 09-322-7930); **United Kingdom,** 95 St. George's Terrace (tel. 09-322-3200); **New Zealand,** 16 St. George's Terrace (tel. 09-325-7877); and **Germany,** 16 St. George's Terrace (tel. 09-325-8851). Don't ask about France.

INFORMATION

As with all of Australia's capital cities, the state tourist office is chockablock with information, accommodations, and tour bookings. The **Western Australia Tourist Centre** (also known as WATC) is on Forrest Place, at the corner of Wellington Street and across from the railway station. Hours are Mon.-Fri. 8:30 a.m.-5:30 p.m., Saturday 9-1 p.m. For information, phone (09) 483-1111. A **Perth City Tourist Booth** is located along Hay Street Mall.

The **ACROD Access Committee,** 189 Royal St., East Perth (tel. 09-222-2961), provides **disabled visitors** with helpful brochures and information on accommodations, restaurants, theaters, and recreational areas within the state. **Paraquad** (tel. 09-381-0173) has info on accessible accommodations.

To obtain maps and touring advice, call in at the **Royal Automobile Club of W.A.** (RAC or RACWA), 228 Adelaide Terrace (tel. 09-421-4444). The bookshop has a good section of travel books, literature, and maps (many are free if you have proof of membership with a reciprocal club in another country). For an even broader range of maps, call into the **Perth Map Centre,** 891 Hay St. (tel. 09-322-5733).

The **library** is at the Perth Cultural Centre, James St. (tel. 09-427-3111).

In an emergency, dial 000 to summon **fire, police,** and **ambulance** services. **Royal Perth Hospital,** Victoria Square (tel. 09-224-2244), maintains a 24-hour emergency room. For relief from killer toothaches, go to **Perth Dental Hospital,** 196 Goderich St. (tel. 09-325-3452).

Bookstores and Newspapers

Angus and Robertson, 199 Murray St. and 625 Hay St., is the large commercial reading outlet. Another good shop is **Down to Earth Books,** 874 Hay Street. We love **Arcane Bookshop,** 212 William St., Northbridge (big selection of alternative literature, gay and lesbian sections, and poetry), and ditto for **New Editions,** South Terrace, Fremantle (with a cafe for real bookshop lovers).

The *West Australian* is the Mon.-Sat. paper, while the *Sunday Times* finishes the weekend. **Plaza Newsagency,** in the Plaza Arcade off Hay Street Mall, sells national and international newspapers, as do some of the large hotels.

VICINITY OF PERTH

Even though this megastate spans a third of the continent, you can still manage to get to some pretty interesting places in the course of a day or two.

FREMANTLE

You've heard of Fremantle—site of the 1987 America's Cup race where Kevin Parry lost the yachties' prized petunia to San Diego's Dennis Connor. Believe it or not, Fremantle actually existed *before* then—and has continued since.

Perth's port district (pop. 25,000), called "Freo" by the locals, sits 19 km southwest of Perth, where the Swan River kisses the Indian Ocean. Founded along with Perth in 1829, the city was named for Capt. Charles Howe Fremantle, who claimed Australia's west coast for the British Crown. The settlement was practically dormant until those hardworking convicts were brought in to construct many of the town's buildings—including their own jail.

Though Fremantle is a modern port, much of the old district with its 19th-century buildings and shop fronts has been preserved and—thanks to the Cup race—spruced up and painted, at least within the last decade. It's an easy stroll, a popular tourist town of historical sites, art galleries, and sidewalk cafes. The place is—dare I say it—"picturesque, charming, and quaint."

Historical Sights
If you arrive by train, you'll begin your tour at **Fremantle Railway Station,** Victoria Quay, opened in 1907 to serve the harbor. Check out the cluster of black swans on the building's facade, as well as the **memorial water trough** in the park out front, which commemorates the death of two outback explorers (who died of thirst).

The **Round House** (1831) at Arthur Head, west end of High St., actually has 12 sides and is WA's oldest remaining public building. Now roofless and empty, this was originally the colony's first jail, site of its first hanging, and later a "holding tank" for Aborigines being shipped to Rottnest Island. Hours are daily 10 a.m.-5 p.m. Admission is free.

The convict-built **Western Australian Maritime Museum** (1850), corner of Cliff St. and Marine Terrace, was once a commissariat store. Exhibits include relics from 17th-century Dutch ships wrecked off the coastline. One highlight is the ongoing reconstruction of the 1629 *Batavia* hull, a process that visitors can view as conservationists work. Hours are Mon.-Thurs. 10:30 a.m.-5 p.m., Fri.-Sun. 1-5 p.m. Admission is by donation.

Following Marine Terrace back toward town, you'll pass the **Old Court House** on your left and a statue of **C.Y. O'Connor** (he's the bloke who built the artificial harbor here in the 1860s) off to the right. Continue on Marine Terrace, turning left at Essex Street, which, as you cross South Terrace, becomes Henderson Street.

Fremantle Markets, on the corner, date from 1897. Reactivated in the mid-'70s (wasn't everything?), this is still the area's most lively weekly market. Approximately 170 stalls offer fruit, veggies, arts, crafts, and other market kitsch, bargains, and buskers. Shopping hours are Friday 9 a.m.-9 p.m., Saturday 9 a.m.-5 p.m., Sunday and public holidays 10 a.m.-5 p.m.

The **Sail and Anchor** pub, across Henderson St., is a restored 1903 building that served as "command post" during the America's Cup trials and also houses a brewery (sheer coincidence no doubt). This one-time site of the old Freemason's Hotel has housed pubs since the 1850s. Next to the markets, on South Terrace, **Scots Presbyterian Church** also dates from the 19th century.

On 1 April 1997 all phone numbers with the (096) area code will change. To dial the new number, simply add a 96 to the old number and change the area code to (08). For example, (096) 12-3456 will become (08) 9612-3456. On 1 May 1997 all telephone numbers with the (09) area code will change. To dial the new number, simply add a 9 to the old number and change the area code to (08). For example, (09) 123-4567 will become (08) 9123-4567.

VICINITY OF PERTH

The **Warders' Quarters** (1851), near the corner of William St., are stone terraces built by convicts to house their keepers at Fremantle Prison. The grim **Fremantle Prison**, on The Terrace off Fairburn St., was also constructed by convicts between 1851-59 and was used as a lock-up until 1991, and a tourist attraction ever since. A museum next to the prison gates depicts prison history and features prison memorabilia and other articles of bondage. Hours are daily 10 a.m.-6 p.m., closed Christmas Day and Good Friday. Admission is $10—and you're free to leave whenever you like.

Going left at William St., it's a two-block walk to St. John's Square. **Fremantle Town Hall** (1887), past the information center, is an elegant structure opened in conjunction with Queen Victoria's Jubilee. Opposite the Town Hall, on

William St., the **Federal Hotel** is another atmospheric pub that dates from 1887. **St. John's Anglican Church** (1881), next door, is a stone structure that took three years to complete.

Old **St. Patrick's Church** sits at the corner of Adelaide and Quarry Streets. **Proclamation Tree,** across Quarry St., is a Moreton Bay fig tree planted around the turn of the century. On the opposite side of Adelaide St., the **Old Fremantle Boys' School** used to be guess what.

Fremantle Museum and Arts Centre, corner of Ord and Finnerty Streets in Fremantle Park, served as the local lunatic asylum between 1861-65, a women's home (i.e., old ladies) in the early 1900s, and the 1942 headquarters for American forces stationed in Western Australia. After a 13-year restoration, the Gothic-esque sandstone building reopened in 1972 as a museum and art center featuring changing exhibitions (with an emphasis on Western Australian artists), a museum wing with displays and mementos of Fremantle's history, a lecture room, and cloistered courtyard used for music and theatrical performances and crafts fairs. Museum hours are Thurs.-Sun. 1-5 p.m. Arts center hours are daily 10 a.m.-5 p.m., Wednesday 7-9 p.m. Admission to both wings is free. For information, phone (09) 335-8211, museum, or (09) 335-8244, arts center.

One block south, at the corner of Ord and Ellen Streets, **Samson House** (1888) was and still is associated with a prominent Fremantle family (name of Samson). Contained within are historic photographs, antique furnishings, and a 20-meter-deep, in-house well. Hours are Sunday and Thursday 1-5 p.m. Guided tours are available.

Other Sights

Down in the B Shed, at Victoria Quay, **Historic Boat Shed Museum** features a wide range of vessels, including the America's Cup winner *Australia II* and a full-size replica of the *Endeavour,* the ship in which Capt. James Cook "discovered" Australia. Hours are daily 1-5 p.m. Admission is free.

Fremantle Wharves and Passenger Terminal, accessible by car, is usually filled with assorted ships from all over the world—free entertainment for boat lovers of all ages.

Up Mews Road toward the Esplanade, **Fremantle Crocodile Park** is home to more than 200 fresh- and saltwater crocs, living as they might in their Kimberley homeland. Viewing is from the safety of a raised metal walkway, enclosed with a tall chainlink fence. Education tours and a film document crocodile history and explain how the Aussie crocs were saved from extinction. Hours are daily 10 a.m.-5 p.m. Admission is $8. For information, phone (09) 430-5388.

Eyeball the terrific view of Fremantle Harbour from the **Observation Tower** of Fremantle

"Freo" hosted the 1987 America's Cup

Port Authority, 1 Cliff Street. Tours, departing the foyer, are available Mon.-Fri. at 2:30 p.m.

If you're into gas and electricity, you can study its local history at the **Energy Museum,** 12 Parry Street. Hours are Mon.-Fri. 12:30-4:30 p.m., Sat.-Sun. 1-4:30 p.m. Admission is free.

Arts and Crafts

Fremantle is filled with artisans, and their wares are on display and for sale in converted boat sheds, warehouses, and historic buildings and markets throughout town.

Bannister Street Craftworks, 8 Bannister St., is a converted warehouse that houses studios representing pottery, stained glass, fabric printing, leatherwork, woodwork, weaving, and gold- and silversmithing. Hours are Tues.-Sat. 10 a.m.-5 p.m. Sunday and public holidays 12:30-5:30 p.m.

Bather's Beach Gallery and Potters Workshop, Mews Rd., Bather's Beach, features the work of 20-or-so Western Australian artists, including renowned potter Joan Campbell. Hours are Mon.-Fri. 10 a.m.-5 p.m., Sat.-Sun. 11 a.m.-5 p.m.

A Shed Cafe and Gallery, Victoria Quay (next to B Shed, of course), has been transformed into an arts and crafts venue and atmospheric cafe. Hours are daily 10 a.m.-5 p.m.

Accommodations

Inexpensive pub accommodations are available at the **Newport Hotel,** 2 South Terrace (tel. 09-335-2428). The **Norfolk Hotel,** 47 South Terrace (tel. 09-335-5405), and the **Fremantle Hotel,** 6 High St. (tel. 09-430-4300), both historic beauties, are moderately priced pub offerings.

The huge 200-room **Ocean View Lodge,** 100 Hampton Rd. (tel. 09-336-2962), features a variety of inexpensive rooms, good weekly deals, and a pool, gym, sauna, and billiard room.

Studios and one-bedroom apartments are costly at the river-view **Tradewinds Hotel,** 66 Canning Hwy., East Fremantle (tel. 09-339-

266). The **Fremantle Esplanade,** 46 Marine Terrace (tel. 09-430-4000), represents the big splurge ($150-290 per night), with all the goodies that come with big bucks.

Dorm beds are available at **Bundi Kudja Homestead,** 96 Hampton Rd. (tel. 09-335-8467). This former nurse's quarters also has cheap rooms, plus kitchens, a video lounge, and game room.

Fremantle Village Caravan Park, corner of Cockburn and Rockingham Roads (tel. 09-430-4866), a couple kilometers from town, has campsites and cabins.

Homestays can be arranged, at a variety of rates, through **Fremantle Homestays** (tel. 09-319-1256).

Food
You'll find plenty of reasonably priced pub meals and ethnic eateries in Fremantle, but fresh fish and seafood are the local specialties.

Lombardo's, Mews Rd., Fishing Boat Harbour, is a waterfront complex with everything from takeaway fish and chips stalls and outdoor cafes to bistros and fine restaurants.

South Terrace is another popular area lined with cappuccino bars and sidewalk cafes. One of Fremantle's ranking favorites is **Old Papa's,** 33 South Terrace, which serves coffee, cakes, and pasta dishes on a terrace overlooking the street. If there's a long wait, try the **Mexican Kitchen** next door, or—if you have your heart set on Italian—**Pizza Bella Roma** across the street. If you have your heart set on being *seen* eating Italian, **Gino's,** 1 South Terrace, is a good bet. And, at 64 South Terrace, the historic **Sail and Anchor Hotel** has an enjoyable brasserie and an ever more enjoyable brewery (this was the first Australian on-site brewery, hopping the way for the boutique-beer industry).

The best breakfasts are at **Pisa Café,** 1 High St., and the **Round House Café,** also on High Street. **Vung Tau,** 19 High St., serves up Vietnamese and vegetarian dishes.

The **Upmarket Food Centre,** Henderson St., across from the market, is full of mostly Asian chow-down stalls. Hours are Thurs.-Sun. noon-9 p.m. Be prepared for long lines on market days.

The **Left Bank,** 15 Riverside Rd., East Fremantle, in a colonial mansion on the Swan Riverbank, is *the* trendy, upmarket, hip, cool spot in

town. Runner-up is the **Surf Club,** on the beachfront, at North Fremantle. Both places house expensive restaurants and cheap-ish cafes.

Entertainment
High Street and South Terrace are where you'll find most of the live bands and a disco or two. Try **West End Hotel** and the **Orient,** both on High Street, both with bands at high volume. **Seaview Tavern** and **Newport Arms** are two frontrunner band venues on South Terrace.

Catch techno, house, rap, and dance music into the wee hours at **Metropolis,** 58 South Terrace. **Fly By Night Musicians Club,** Parry St., draws the reggae, blues, and folk crowd. **Harbourside Tavern,** 4 Beach St., features local bands most weekends.

Transportation, Services, and Information
Frequent bus and train service connect Perth with Fremantle. **Transperth buses** (tel. 13-2213 toll-free), traveling various routes, depart from St. George's Terrace, while trains (traveling only one route) leave from Perth Central Station.

Captain Cook Cruises (tel. 09-325-3341) provides daily ferry service from Perth ($12). In addition, some Rottnest Island ferries make a stop at Fremantle. For information, phone **Oceanic Cruises** (tel. 09-430-5127) or **Boat Torque Cruises** (tel. 09-430-7644).

For **bicycle rentals,** contact **Captain Munchies,** 2 Beach St. (tel. 09-339-6633), or **Fleet Cycles** (tel. 09-430-5414). The **Fremantle Tram,** like the Perth Tram, makes frequent tours (with accompanying commentary) around the local sights. Cost is $7. A harbor tour ($7) and Top of the Port tour ($10) are also available. For information, phone (09) 339-8719.

Pick up info, brochures, and walking tour maps at the **Fremantle Information Centre,** Kings Square, in the Town Hall. Hours are Mon.-Fri. 9 a.m.-5 p.m., Saturday 9 a.m.-1 p.m., Sunday 10 a.m.-3 p.m. For information, phone (09) 430-2346.

ROTTNEST ISLAND

This sandy island resort—affectionately known as "Rotto"—lies just 19 km off the Fremantle coast and is a favorite day excursion and holiday destination for Perth residents drawn to its bleached beaches, turquoise waters, and activities (or inactivity).

Rottnest translates to "Rat's Nest," a name bestowed upon it by Dutch mariner Willem de Vlamingh. Landing there in 1696, Willem mistook the native quokkas—a type of small marsupial—for a bunch of big, old rats. These days the quokkas are a protected species and one of the island's big tourist attractions.

Originally used as a prison settlement for mainland Aborigines back in 1838, the prison was vacated in 1903, and 14 years later it became a getaway spot for society—and still is today. Thomson Bay is the main resort area of this tiny 11-km-long, five-km-wide island, and is one of the few shady spots. The rest of the landscape consists of sparse vegetation, a few low hills, some shallow salt lakes, plenty of white-sand beaches, and secluded rocky bays. Add to that the surrounding reef, protected lagoons, and some 12 shipwrecks to explore.

Sights

Get your bearings at **Rottnest Museum,** located at the main settlement. Exhibits and memorabilia cover convict history, wildlife, and shipwrecks. Walking-tour leaflets, including info and directions around the remaining convict-built buildings, are available. Hours are daily 10 a.m.-1:30 p.m. and 2:30-4:30 p.m. Dec.-Feb., daily 11 a.m.-1:30 p.m. and 2:30-4 p.m. other months. For information, phone (09) 372-9752.

Vlamingh Lookout, via Digby Dr., offers panoramic views of the island, surrounding ocean, and Gordon Lake. **Oliver Hill,** via Digby Dr., offers yet another dynamic island view and a leftover artillery battery.

Constructed of locally quarried limestone, **Rottnest Lighthouse,** Wadjemup Hill, in the center of the island, dates back to the mid-1800s. **Bathurst Lighthouse,** Gem Rd., Bathurst Point, the second of Rotto's lighthouses, was built in 1900.

Located in the island center east and northeast of the jetty are the small **salt lakes**—Government House, Serpentine, Herschell, Baghdad, Pink, and Garden Lakes. You'll see those quokkas (relatives of the wallaby) at the **Quokka Colony,** between Government House and Herschell Lakes. This lot—used to having their faces stuffed by tourists—is quite tame.

Best **swimming beaches** include **Parakee Bay,** at the northernmost tip of the island, and **The Basin,** north of the main settlement. **Wes End,** the westernmost point on the island, is popular (and crowded) with hopeful **fishers Shipwreck** sights are signposted along a marked trail around the island; however, snorkelers will need a boat to reach most of them (Boats, and snorkeling and fishing gear, can be hired on the island.)

Accommodations and Food

If you want to make Rotto more than a day trip keep in mind that accommodations must be booked way in advance, particularly during holidays and summer months when the Perthos descend en masse. For information on rates and bookings, phone **Rottnest Island Authority** (tel. 09-372-9729).

Accommodations are concentrated around the Thomson Bay settlement and comprise cabins, hotel and motel rooms, a hostel, and campground. Due to a water shortage, showers a Rotto accommodations are saltwater; bring salt water shampoo and soap with you as it's more expensive on the island.

Moderately priced **Rottnest Hotel** (tel. 09 292-5011) overlooks the main beach and is Rotto's gathering spot. Built in 1864 as the summer residence of Western Australian governors it was reopened as a hotel in 1953. **Rottnest Island Authority Cottages** (tel. 09-372-9729 sleep four to eight people, at a cost of $175 675 per week.

Kingston Barracks Youth Hostel (tel. 09 372-9780), about one km from the ferry terminal is in a former 1936 barracks and still looks the part. Facilities include a lounge and kitchen, bu hot water is scarce. Beds cost $13-16.

Campsites, tents, and cabins are available at **Thomson Camping Areas** (tel. 09-372 9737).

Food is relatively expensive, as on mos tourist-type islands—even at the general store and fast-food center. **Rottnest Hotel** serves moderately priced steaks and salads in a casual environment, while another section offers fine dining. The **Rottnest Island Lodge** has a similar setup: the restaurant is a la carte and expensive; the bar section features inexpensive all-you-can-eat midweek meals. Buy fresh read and yummy baked goodies at the **Rottest Island Bakery.**

Transportation, Services, and Information
Rottnest Airlines (tel. 09-277-4198) flies daily from Perth for about $45 round-trip. A shuttle bus takes you from Rottnest Airport to the main wharf area.

Boat Torque Cruises operates a daily ferry service to the island aboard its *Star Flyte,* departing from Perth's Barrack Street Jetty and from Fremantle. Fare is $42 round-trip from Perth, $25 round-trip from Fremantle. *Sea Raider III* departs daily from Hillarys Boat Harbour, north of Perth. For information and bookings, phone (09) 430-7644.

White Dolphin Cruises, operated by Boat Torque, and **Oceanic Cruises** (tel. 09-430-0127), travel between Fremantle and Rottnest Island. Fare is $12-15, extended stay fares are $20-25 (Oceanic Cruises is cheapest for now anyway—watch for continuing price wars).

No cars are allowed on the island. Most visitors rely on bicycles—a round-the-island bike path covers 26 kilometers. Bring your own cycle on the ferry (an extra $5) or rent one from **Rottnest Bike Hire,** behind the Rottnest Hotel (tel. 09-372-9722). Rates run $10 per day.

Bus service is available during summer months, and bus tours around the island are available most months. Check with the tourist information office for schedules and bookings. *Underwater Explorer* takes passengers on 45-minute boat tours over primitive corals, marine-fe, and shipwrecks. Departures are from the main jetty. Fare is $12. For information, phone (09) 221-5844.

Tourist information and walking and cycling maps are available at the **Tourist Information Centre,** at the end of the main jetty (tel. 09-372-9729). Hours are daily 9 a.m.-4 p.m.

Dial 000 to request **emergency assistance** or contact **Rottnest Medical Centre** (tel. 09-372-9727).

YANCHEP NATIONAL PARK

Only 51 km north of Perth, Yanchep National Park is a 2,799-hectare, family-oriented coastal wonderland with bushland, caves, walking trails, a wildlife sanctuary, boating lake, swimming pool, golf course, footie ovals (football fields), limestone gorges, fauna exhibits, aviaries, a beer garden, and a museum. Despite all these attractions, 90% of the park has been maintained in its natural state.

Of the numerous caves set in the limestone hills, **Crystal Cave,** open to the public, features an underground stream in the main grotto, good examples of stalactites and stalagmites, and "fantasy lighting." Guided tours are offered several times daily.

Another favorite activity is the **Yanjidi Trail,** a 28-km walk through the Loch McNess wetlands, a refuge for waterfowl and other birds (and the Loch McNess monster?). Signs along the path—which follows the tracks used by the local Yaberoo Aborigines—explain the wetland ecology.

To reach Yanchep, follow the West Coast Highway north out of town, or catch a daily Transperth bus from Perth Central Bus Station. Admission is $5 per vehicle, or $2 per bus passenger.

Other Sights
Traveling the West Coast Highway from Perth, you'll pass through **Wanneroo,** another popular wine-producing area and a fast-growing artsy-craftsy-touristy center. The **Gumnut Factory,** 30 Prindiville Dr., Wangara Centre (tel. 09-409-6699), manufactures all types of gumnut creations and *you,* folks, can watch it happen. Don't miss Gumnutland, a model village with more than 30 handcrafted buildings, working railways, roads, and mini gumnut people—all crafted from timber, flowers, and gumnuts. Hours are daily 9 a.m.-5 p.m. Admission is $1.

If you're passing through Wanneroo on the weekend, stop at the **market** in the carpark at the corner of Prindiville Dr. and Ismail St., where 200 stalls offer a wide range of goods for sale.

Wineries offering tastings are **Bonannella Wines,** 96 Pinjar Rd. (tel. 09-405-1084), and **Paul Conti Wines,** 529 Wanneroo Rd. (tel. 09-409-9160).

And then there's **Wild Kingdom Wildlife Park,** also on Two Rocks Rd. (tel. 09-561-1399), with wombats, dingoes, foxes, and other animals, as well as birdlife. Hours are daily 9:30 a.m.-5 p.m., closed Christmas Day. Admission is $3.

Accommodations

The **Yanchep Lagoon Lodge,** 11 Nautical Court (tel. 09-561-1033), at Yanchep Lagoon, has moderately priced guesthouse accommodations. **Club Capricorn,** Two Rocks Rd. (tel. 09-561-1106), is an expensive beachfront resort with lodge and chalet accommodations, plus restaurant, swimming pools, and tennis courts.

Information

For info on **Yanchep National Park,** phone (09) 561-1661. In **Wanneroo,** the Tourist Information Centre is at 935 Wanneroo Rd. (tel. 09-405-4678).

THE DARLING RANGE

This range, full of wooded hills, valleys, and dams, runs east of Perth and parallel to the coastline. It's a popular picnic, bushwalking, and weekend-away place for Perth dwellers, particularly from September to November when an astounding assortment of more than 4,000 wildflower species are in bloom. You can take a number of different roads as far and flung as you like; one easy, close-to-Perth route is to catch Kalamunda Rd. from South Guildford, to Kalamunda sights, then pick up Mundaring Weir Rd., meeting the Great Eastern Highway back into Perth. Transperth buses journey to the range on a variety of routes.

Sights

For some great coastal plain and city lights views, negotiate three kilometers of sharp hairpin and hair-raising turns on the one-way **Zig Zag Road** (formerly a railway line). Signs are posted off Kalamunda Road, Gooseberry Hill. You can also reach steep, 33-hectare Gooseberry Hill via Gooseberry Hill Rd., Williams Rd., or Lascelles Parade.

Stirk Park and Cottage, 9A Headingly Rd., Kalamunda, is a restored 1881 cottage surrounded by a public reserve with scenic walks and waterways, an ornamental lake, model boat pond, and bowling greens. Hours are daily 9 a.m.-9 p.m. The cottage is open Sunday 1:30-4:30 p.m.

History Village, corner Railway and Williams Roads, Kalamunda, is a museum on the site of

the old railway station, plus the original state school building, post office, and a settler's cottage, transported to the site. Memorabilia and displays illustrate the area's early history. Hours are Thurs.-Sat. 9 a.m.-noon, Sunday 2-4:30 p.m. Admission is $1.

Kalamunda National Park, via Kalamunda Rd., offers 375 hectares of forest scenery, granite boulder outcrops, seasonal wildflowers, wildlife, and birdlife. Visitors must carry their own water in hot weather.

Mundaring Weir, Mundaring Weir Rd., Mundaring, is the reservoir that provides water for the goldfields towns more than 500 km away. The **C.Y. O'Connor Museum,** named for the engineer who devised this system, features displays and exhibits relating to the complicated water system. Museum hours are Monday, Wednesday, Thursday, Friday, and public holidays 10:30 a.m.-3 p.m., Saturday 1-4 p.m., Sunday noon-5 p.m.

John Forrest National Park, reached via the Great Eastern Highway, consists of 1,577 hectares of open forest and woodland, spring wildflowers, city and coastal views, and scenic walking trails. Western Australia's first national park was declared in 1895 and named for Lord John Forrest, the state's premier 1890-1901.

Accommodations

Travellers Rest, 885 Great Eastern Hwy. (tel. 09-295-2950), offers moderately priced holiday units with cooking facilities, a pool, and continental breakfast included. Expensive **Mundaring Weir Hotel,** Mundaring Weir Rd. (tel. 09-295-1106), is a popular getaway for Perth runaways.

The YHA operates a **hostel** at Mundaring on Mundaring Weir Rd. (tel. 09-295-1809), offering dorm beds for $10 per night.

Campsites are available at Mundaring Caravan Park, Great Eastern Hwy. (tel. 09-295-1125).

SWAN VALLEY

The good news is that the scenic, fertile Swan Valley and its 20 or so wineries are a mere 20 km northeast of Perth—an easy car ride or river cruise away. The bad news is that the area is so

(previous page) hiking in Hancock Gorge, Karijini (Hamersley Range) National Park
(top) a sunset camel ride, Cable Beach, Broome
(bottom) Sun Pictures is one of Australia's few remaining open-air cinemas.

close to the city and the city is expanding so rapidly that many of the rural communities are blending into urban-ity. The Swan River meanders the wide valley set at the foot of the Darling Range—a patchwork mix of small farms and award-winning wineries, stretching from Perth through historic Guildford to the Upper Swan, passing a number of interesting sights along the way.

Sights

The 1830 **Tranby House**, Johnson Rd., Maylands, is Western Australia's oldest inhabited property. Hours are Mon.-Sat. 2-5 p.m., Sunday 11 a.m.-1 p.m. and 2-5 p.m. Admission is $2.50. View nearly 30 locomotives (including steam, diesel, and electric), antique carriages, and other railway memorabilia, photos, and artifacts at the **Rail Transport Museum,** 136 Railway Parade, Bassendean (300 meters east of Ashfield Railway Station). Steam train tours are available May-October. Hours are Sunday and public holidays 1-5 p.m., Wednesday 1-4 p.m. during school holidays. Admission is $3. For information, phone (09) 279-7189.

In Guildford, situated at the rear of the historic 1840 Rose and Crown Hotel, 105 Swan St., the private **Hall Collection** consists of 40,000 antique and nostalgic artifacts, including porcelain, paintings, glass, copper work, cameras, musical instruments, toys, and kitchen items. Hours are Tues.-Sun. 10 a.m.-4:30 p.m. Admission is $3. For information, phone (09) 279-6542.

Woodbridge House, 3rd Ave., Guildford, is the National Trust-restored 1885 residence of Perth personality extraordinaire Charles Harper. Hours are daily except Wednesday 1-4 p.m., Sunday 11 a.m.-1 p.m. and 2-5 p.m. Admission is $2. For information, phone (09) 274-2432.

The **Historic Gaol and Settlers Cottage,** Meadow St., Guildford, exhibits period furnishings and clothing, blacksmithing tools and equipment, and bric-a-brac. Hours are 2-5 p.m. March to mid-December. Admission is $1. For information, phone (09) 279-1248.

Other 19th-century Guildford buildings are **St. Matthew's Church,** in Stirling Square, and the jail, corner of Swan and Meadow Streets. See local pottery at **Guildford Potters,** 105 Swan Street. Hours are daily 10 a.m.-3 p.m.

Caversham Wildlife Park and Zoo, corner of Arthur Rd. and Cranleigh St., West Swan, is a wildlife park featuring Australian and imported animals and birds. Hours are daily 10 a.m.-5 p.m. Admission is $4.50. For information, phone (09) 274-2202.

Gomboc Gallery, James Rd., Middle Swan, displays paintings, sculptures, and graphics by Western Australian artists. Hours are Wed.-Sun. and public holidays 10 a.m.-5 p.m.

Wineries

Swan Valley vineyards are sprinkled along the river, from the Guildford area to Upper Swan. Though vines were first planted in the 1830s, it's the Middle Swan district (with its more recent plantings) that is responsible for much of the high production. Most of the wineries welcome visitors for divine tastings.

Olive Farm Winery, 77 Great Eastern Hwy., South Guildford (tel. 09-277-2989), named for the olive trees planted along with the vines, is the region's oldest winery. Hours are Mon.-Fri. 10 a.m.-5:30 p.m., Saturday and public holidays 9 a.m.-3 p.m.

Some of the valley's renowned wineries include: **Houghton Wines,** Dale Rd., Middle Swan (tel. 09-274-5100); **Jane Brook Estate Wines,** Toodyay Rd. (tel. 09-274-1432); **Sandalford Wines,** corner West Swan and Middle Swan Roads, Caversham (tel. 09-274-5922); **Twin Hill Wines,** Great Northern Hwy., Baskerville (tel. 09-296-4272); and **Westfield Wines,** Memorial Ave., Baskerville (tel. 09-269-4356).

For maps and information about all of the wineries plus other Swan Valley attractions, stop into the Western Australia Tourist Centre in Perth or the **Swan Valley Tourism Association,** Great Eastern Hwy., Midland (under the Town Hall clocktower), or phone (09) 274-1522.

Transportation

Transperth buses and trains depart regularly for the Swan Valley. Trains stop at Guildford, then go on to the valley's gateway town of Midland. Buses travel all the way to Upper Swan along Middle Swan Road. For information, phone Transperth (tel. 13-2213 toll-free).

If you're traveling by car (30-40 minutes' drive), take Guildford Road or the Great Eastern Highway to Midland, then turn onto the Great Northern Highway through the valley's center.

AVON VALLEY

Homesick English settlers fell in love with this lush, hilly valley, which reminded them of their very own Avon—hence the name. Rainfall-green in winter and parched-sun brown in summer, this rural land, settled only one year after Perth, follows the course of the Avon River (an east- and southward branch of the Swan), running through the historic towns of Toodyay, Northam, and York.

Toodyay

Say "Two Jay," otherwise you'll be ignored—or worse. Toodyay (pop. 560) sits at the bend where the Avon River turns from east to south, and is the smallest of the river towns. There was an earlier Toodyay settled in the 1830s, some eight km downstream; today's Toodyay—established in 1860 as Newcastle—was rechristened in 1910. The National Trust declared the town "historic" in 1980, and some 13 buildings have been classified as worthy of preservation.

Connors Mill, corner of Stirling Terrace and Piessa St., contains a steam engine, 1941 generator, and the **Moondyne Gallery,** which recounts the story of infamous bushranger Joseph Bolitho Jones (a.k.a. Moondyne Joe). Hours are Mon.-Sat. 9 a.m.-5 p.m., Sunday and public holidays 10 a.m.-5 p.m. Admission is $1.

Trace the lives (and deaths) of 1800s pioneers and convicts at the **Old Gaol Museum and Police Station,** Clinton Street. The Old Gaol, an early stone and shingle-roofed structure, includes original cells. Hours are Mon.-Fri. 11 a.m.-3 p.m., Saturday 1-4 p.m., Sunday and public holidays 11 a.m.-4 p.m. Admission is $2.

White Gum Flower Farm, Sandplain Rd., features commercially grown wildflowers amid 283 hectares of white gum timberland. Hours are Wed.-Sun. 10 a.m.-4 p.m. Closed Christmas Day through March.

Avon Valley National Park, via Toodyay Rd. (make a left at Morangyup Rd. and follow posted signs), is a beautifully scenic 4,377-hectare park with valleys, slopes, woodlands, and open forest.

Northam

Believe it or not, Northam (pop. 6,800) is not only the largest Avon Valley town, but WA's second-largest inland center (it's on the railway line to Kalgoorlie), notable for its black swans, white swans, and the whitewater Avon Descent Race.

See the **Avon Valley Arts Society,** 33 Wellington St., which comprises two historic structures—the Old Post Office (1892) and the Old Girls School (1877). The art center sells locally made arts and crafts. Hours are Tues.-Fri. 9 a.m.-4 p.m., Sat.-Mon. 10 a.m.-4 p.m.

The **Old Railway Station,** Fitzgerald St. West, contains early 1900s appliances and railway relics, plus renovated carriages and an old steam train. Hours are Sunday 10 a.m.-4 p.m. Admission is $2.

Other historic sights are **Pioneer Graves,** Goomalling Rd.; **Morby Cottage** (1836), Avon Dr.; the **police station** (1866) and **courthouse** (1896), both on Wellington St.; **St. John's Church** (1890), Wellington St.; **St. Saviour's Church** (1862), Toodyay Road; and **Presbyterian Church** (1908), Duke Street (present home of the Link Theatre).

Near Northam, at Irishtown, **Buckland House** (1874) is one of the state's most stately homes. The restoration, and collections of antique furnishings, paintings, and silver, are worth a peek. Hours are Mon.-Wed. and Sat.-Sun. 10 a.m.-5 p.m. Closed Christmas Day through February. Admission is $4. For information, phone (096) 22-1130.

York

Settled in 1830, this one-time commercial center for the Avon Valley declined when the railway passed it by in 1894, and it reverted to an agricultural community. In the 1970s, York (pop. 1,140) was rediscovered for its architectural delights and reputedly has more original buildings than any other town in Western Australia.

Avon Terrace, the main street, features buildings reflecting architectural styles ranging from the 1860s to the turn of the century. The **Old Police Station** complex comprises the old courthouse, troopers' cottage, stables, and cell blocks. Hours are Mon.-Fri. 11 a.m.-3 p.m., Sat.-Sun. and public holidays 10 a.m.-4 p.m. The **Post Office Museum** illustrates York's postal history beginning from 1840. Phone (096) 41-1301 to arrange admittance. Car lovers can rev their engines at the **Motor Museum,** where more than 100 veteran, vintage, classic, and racing vehicles are on display. Hours are daily 10 a.m.-5 p.m., closed Christmas Day and Good Friday. Admission is $6.

Trace printing history through commentary and demonstrations on a century-old letter press at **Sandalwood Press.** Hours are Tues.-Thurs. and Sat.-Sun. 1-3 p.m.

The **Art Gallery,** Avon Terrace, exhibits locally crafted jarrah furniture, paintings, and stained glass. Hours are Sun-Fri. 10 a.m.-4 p.m., Saturday 10 a.m.-1 p.m. The **Doll Museum,** also on Avon Terrace, features more than 1,000 doll babies representing all nationalities. Hours are Sat.-Sun. 10 a.m.-noon and 1-3 p.m.

One of York's oldest buildings is the **Residency Museum,** Brook Street. In a structure dating back to 1842, the museum displays photographs and artifacts of the town's early days. Hours are Tues.-Thurs. and school and public holidays 1-3 p.m., Sat.-Sun. 1-5 p.m.

Balladong Farm, 5 Parker Rd., outside York on the way to Beverley, has been restored by the National Trust to show visitors what farm life was like in the 19th century. Displays include original breeds of stock and farm machinery, plus demonstrations of blacksmithing, milking, and wool spinning. Hours are Tues.-Sun. 10 a.m.-5 p.m. Guided tours can be arranged. For information, phone (096) 41-1279. Admission is $5.

Accommodations

Toodyay: Avondown Inn, 44 Stirling Terrace (tel. 09-574-2995), a one-time convent, offers inexpensive rooms. For inexpensive pub rooms, try either the **Victoria Hotel** (tel. 09-574-2206) or the **Freemasons Hotel** (tel. 09-574-2201). Both are on Stirling Terrace. **Appleton House,** Julimar Rd. (tel. 09-574-2622), is a moderately priced, colonial-style B&B nestled in the hills. Campsites and on-site vans are available at both **Toodyay Caravan Park,** Railway Rd. (tel. 09-574-2612), and **Broadgrounds Park,** Stirlingia Dr. (tel. 09-574-2534). **Avon Valley National Park** (tel. 09-574-2540), 35 km west of Toodyay, has campsites with limited facilities.

Northam: Find basic pub rooms at **Avon Bridge Hotel,** Fitzgerald St. (tel. 096-22-1023), or the **Grand Hotel,** Fitzgerald St. (tel. 096-22-1024). **Buckland** country mansion, Buckland Rd., Irishtown (tel. 096-22-1130), offers stately—

and expensive—accommodations in two upstairs rooms. The mansion is closed Christmas Day through February. **Mortlock Caravan Park,** Great Eastern Hwy. (tel. 096-22-1620), has campsites and on-site vans.

York: Opposite the railway station, the **YHA Hostel,** 3 Brook St. (tel. 096 41-1372), features dorm beds in a converted hospital for $11 per night. The **Castle Hotel,** Avon Terrace (tel. 096-41-1007), is the recommended pub. Moderately priced **Hillside Homestead,** Forrest Rd. (tel. 096-41-1065), a classified historic site, is an Edwardian residence with B&B accommodations, swimming pool, tennis court, and bicycles included in the price. Campsites and on-site vans can be rented at **Mt. Bakewell Resort and Caravan Gardens,** 8th Rd. (tel. 096-41-1421).

Events

Avon Valley has about a dozen noteworthy events. Toodyay's **Moondyne Festival,** held annually in April, is a celebration of the colonial past including mock shoot-em-up holdups, jail breaks, coppers and convicts, plus an array of other fun sports and games.

The **Avon Descent Race,** begun at Northam each year on the first August weekend (when the river is full), features 800 or so canoeists in a fast-paced and furiously paddled whitewater race to Perth—a distance of 133 kilometers. The cheering crowds partying on the banks are just as much fun to watch—and join.

Other popular draws are October's **Jazz Festival** and the **Vintage and Veteran Car Race** in August.

Transportation, Services, and Information

Westrail operates buses to Northam and York, departing Perth every morning. Fare is about $12 one-way.

The Prospector rail service, also operated by Westrail, calls at Toodyay and Northam on its daily run to Kalgoorlie. Fares are a buck or two more than the bus. For information, schedules, and bookings, phone (09) 326-2813 or 13-2232 toll-free.

It's about an hour-and-some's drive from Perth to any of the Avon Valley towns, and the distance between each of them averages 30 kilometers. The two main valley roads branch from Midland. Choose either the Great Eastern

Highway to Northam and York or the Toodyay Road to Toodyay. If you're returning to Perth, take one route going and the other coming back.

In Toodyay, the **Tourist Bureau** is on Stirling Terrace, in Connors Mill. Hours are Mon.-Sat. 9 a.m.-5 p.m., Sunday and public holidays 10 a.m.-5 p.m. For information, phone (09) 574-2435.

The **Northam Tourist Bureau,** 138 Fitzgerald St., is open Mon.-Fri. 9 a.m.-5 p.m., Sat.-Sun. and public holidays 10 a.m.-4 p.m. For information, phone (096) 22-2100. **York Tourist Bureau,** 105 Avon Terrace, is open Mon.-Fri. 9 a.m.-5 p.m., Sat.-Sun. 9 a.m.-4 p.m. For information, phone (096) 41-1301.

THE SOUTH COAST

Below Fremantle the coastal road to Augusta, down in the southwest corner, passes nickel smelters, seaside resorts, industrial towns, established vineyards, and superb beaches (including WA's best surfing spot). The inland route takes in some good bushwalking trails, dams, waterfalls, and a historic structure or two.

TO BUNBURY

Rockingham

Facing the Indian Ocean, Warnbo Sound, and Shoalwater Bay, Rockingham (pop. 25,000), 47 km south of Perth, once a major seaport 1872-1908—before Fremantle grabbed the honors), is now a favored holiday resort.

Rockingham Museum, corner Flinders Lane and Kent St., is a social history museum with memorabilia related to the district's early settlers. Hours are Tues.-Thurs. and Saturday 1-4:30 p.m., Sunday 10 a.m.-4:30 p.m. Admission is $1.

Safe **swimming beaches** are at the Foreshore Reserve, Rockingham Rd., and Point Peron, at the southern end of Cockburn Sound. Point Peron is favored by photographers who click with the superb sunsets.) Daily ferry service will transport you to **Penguin Island,** a colony of fairy penguins, and to **Seal Island,** with a colony of guess what.

A good Sunday **market** is held on Flinders Lane, 9 a.m.-4 p.m.

Good-value **accommodations** are offered at **CWA Rockingham,** 108 Parkin St. (tel. 09-527-

On 1 April 1997 all phone numbers with the (097) area code will change. To dial the new number, simply add a 97 to the old number and change the area code to (08). For example, (097) 12-3456 will become (08) 9712-3456. On 1 May 1997 all telephone numbers with the (09) area code will change. To dial the new number, simply add a 9 to the old number and change the area code to (08). For example, (09) 123-4567 will become (08) 9123-4567.

9560). Two units house six to eight people. **Rockingham Ocean Clipper,** Patterson Rd. (tel. 09-527-8000), is a moderately priced hotel with room service, pool, and TVs. Campsites and on-site vans are available at **Lakeside Caravan Park,** Mandurah Rd. (tel. 09-524-1182), and **Rockingham Palm Beach Holiday Village,** 37 Fisher St. (tel. 09-527-1515).

Yachties should note that the annual **Cockburn Sound Regatta,** WA's largest, takes place here between Christmas and New Year's.

For local info (including ferry schedules), see the **Tourist Bureau,** 43 Kent St. (tel. 09-592-3464). Hours are Mon.-Fri. 9 a.m.-4:30 p.m., Sat.-Sun. 10 a.m.-4 p.m.

Transperth buses will get you there from Perth or Fremantle. For information, phone 13-2213 toll-free.

Mandurah

Another 29 km south will bring you to Mandurah (pop. 11,000), one more beat-the-heat spot, situated at the entrance of Peel Inlet and at the mouth of Harvey Estuary (where dolphins are occasionally sighted).

Hall's Cottage, on Leighton Rd., built in the early 1830s, is the local history museum. Hours are Sunday 1-4 p.m. Admission is $1.

Other historic structures are: **Christ Church** (1871), Scholl St. and Pinjarra Rd.; **Cooper's Cottage** (1845), Mandurah Terrace, near the bridge; **Eacott Cottage** (1842), Gibla St.; **Allandale** (1913), Estuary Rd., Dawesville (south of town); and **Hardy's Cottage** (built from local materials), Estuary Rd., Dawesville.

Kerryelle's Unique Collectors Museum, Gordon Rd. (tel. 09-581-7615), exhibits collections of gemstones, seashells, coins, banknotes, stamps, old bottles, dolls, and model cars. Hours are Tues.-Fri. 10 a.m.-4 p.m., Sat.-Sun. 10 a.m.-5 p.m. **House of Dunnies,** Henry Rd., Melrose Beach (15 km south), features handcrafted folk dunnies (that means outhouses—a real Australian art form). **Threlfall Galleries,** Old Coast Rd. (tel. 09-534-2704), houses a collection of paintings and sketches depicting the local history. Hours are daily May-Aug. 9:30 a.m.-4 p.m.

THE SOUTH COAST

Estuary Drive, a detour from the Old Coast Road, is the scenic route to Peel Inlet and Harvey Estuary, weaving through bushland and picnic spots. The **Foreshore Reserve,** in central Mandurah, is home to Slim Jim, Australia's tallest cotton palm. About 60 years old, Jim stands 39-plus meters high.

Marapana Wildlife World, Paganoni Rd. (tel. 09-537-1404), is WA's first drive-through deer park and kangaroo sanctuary. Other wild things include donkeys, emus, and cockatoos. Visitors can feed the animals (food provided). Hours are daily 10 a.m.-5 p.m. Admission is $5.

See a large variety of Australian birds in natural bushland and water settings at **Western Rosella Bird Park,** Old Pinjarra Rd. (tel. 09-535-2104). Hours are daily 9:30 a.m.-5 p.m., closed Good Friday and Christmas Day. Admission is $4.

Brighton Hotel, Mandurah Terrace (tel. 09-535-1242), has inexpensive pub rooms and counter meals. Also centrally located, the **Crabshell,** Gibson St. (tel. 09-535-5577), has motel rooms in the low-moderate range, plus air-conditioning, TVs, and a saltwater pool. The **Albatross Guesthouse,** 26 Hall St. (tel. 09-581-5597), offers moderately priced B&B accommodations.

Some of the many camping and on-site van facilities are: **Peninsula Caravan Park,** Ormsby Terrace, at the entrance to Peel Inlet (tel. 09-535-2792); **Belvedere Caravan Park,** 153 Mandurah Terrace (tel. 535-1213); **Dawesville Caravan Park,** Old Coast Rd., Dawesville (tel. 09-582-1417); and **Timbertop Caravan Park,** Peel St. (tel. 09-535-1292).

For tourist info, contact **Mandurah Tourist Bureau,** 5 Pinjarra Rd. (tel. 09-535-1155). Hours are Mon.-Sat. 9 a.m.-5 p.m., Sunday 9 a.m.-4 p.m.

Transperth (tel. 13-2213 toll-free) and **Westrail** (tel. 09-326-2813 or 13-2232 toll-free) provide bus service from Perth and Fremantle to Mandurah.

Yalgorup National Park

About halfway between Mandurah and Bunbury, on a narrow coastal strip that includes Lake Clifton and Lake Preston, Yalgorup contains 11,545 hectares of heath, woodland, smaller lakes, interesting geological formations, and diverse bird- and wildlife (some birds migrate, visa-free, each year from the Soviet Union). Preston Beach, accessed through the park, offers good swimming and fishing. For information, phone (097) 39-1067.

Warning: Tiger snakes are known to inhabit the paperbark swamps and sedge lands; additionally, the lakes are salty—be sure to carry fresh water on long bushwalks during summer.

Australind

The name is a contraction of Australia-India, derived from an 1840s plan to colonize the area and breed horses for the Indian army. The ambitious venture never got off the ground, but the name sure stuck.

Located on the eastern bank of Leschenault Inlet, Australind (pop. 2,900), along with neighboring Bunbury, is famed for blue manna crabs—thousands of which are caught in the inlet each season.

The **Gemstone and Rock Museum,** 267 Old Coast Rd. (tel. 097-97-1241), contains displays of Bunbury agates and other Australian gemstones, natural crystals, as well as Aboriginal, Native American, and English stone artifacts, *and* a cactus garden. Hours are Tues.-Thurs. and Sat.-Sun. 10 a.m.-5 p.m. Admission is $1.

St. Nicholas' Church (1860), Paris Rd., is supposedly the smallest church (four by seven meters) in Western Australia—though the expanding congregation necessitated building a large adjacent edifice (circa 1987). **Henton Cottage** (1840), also on Paris Rd., once the Prince of Wales Hotel, is now an arts and crafts center.

The **scenic drive,** skirting the estuary, leads to crabbing and picnicking sites, while the **Collie River** offers recreational swimming, boating, and fishing.

Leschenault, 14 Old Coast Rd. (tel. 097-97-1352), on the estuary, is a moderately priced B&B with two guest rooms, TV lounge, and a pool. Campsites and on-site vans are available at **Leschenault Inlet Caravan Park,** Scenic Dr. (tel. 097-97-1095).

Most Bunbury-bound coaches from Perth call in at Australind.

The Inland Route

The South Western Highway runs from Perth, some 20 km inland, until it merges with the Old Coast Road at Bunbury. Various roads crisscross between the two highways, allowing travelers to venture inland through pine and jarrah forests or coastward en route.

Serpentine National Park (635 hectares), 52 km south of Perth on the western edge of Darling Scarp, consists of lots of hills with steep gullies, granite outcrops and slopes, and the Serpentine River flowing through the middle. The park's most popular facility is its natural rock pool, ideal for swimming. Steep trails make bushwalking difficult, and rock climbing is not recommended. Admission is $4 per vehicle, $2 per bus passenger. For information, phone (09) 525-2128.

Pinjarra (pop. 1,340), 86 km south of Perth, was settled by farmers in 1830, making it one of WA's oldest towns. Located on the estuary, this agricultural and timber-producing township features a number of historic structures. **Hotham Valley Tourist Railway** operates steam train journeys Aug.-Oct. on the preserved 1913 railway line between Pinjarra and the timber community of **Dwellingup.** Fares are $25-30. For information, phone (09) 221-4444.

Waroona, 25 km south of Dwellingup, is the turnoff for Yalgorup National Park and Preston Beach. **Waroona Dam,** on Scarp Rd., is a power-boating, waterskiing, and fishing area.

In 1916, the state's first controlled irrigation scheme was built at **Harvey** (pop. 2,480), 28 km beyond Waroona. If you drive out to **Harvey Weir,** three km east off Weir Rd., you can still see some of the workers' campsites. The 20-meter-tall **Big Orange** houses a small zoo, a miniature train, arts and crafts, and fruit and veggies.

BUNBURY

Located 180 km south of Perth, on Koombana Bay, Bunbury (pop. 22,000) wears many hats—port, resort, industrial town, gateway to the southwest, and blue-manna-crab-lovers' paradise.

Sights

King Cottage Museum, 77 Forrest Ave., was built in the 1880s with bricks made from clay dug on the property. Examine pioneer memorabilia Sat.-Sun. 2-4 p.m. Admission is $2.

Other early structures are **St. Mark's Church** (1842), corner Flynn Rd. and Charterhouse St., and **St. Patrick's Cathedral** (1921), Parkfield Street—that spire, however, is a 1960s contribution. The **Cathedral Church of St. Boniface,** corner Parkfield and Cross Streets, though only about 25 years old, is impressive for its interior built from native blackbutt wood.

The **Old Convent of Mercy** (1860s), Wittenoom St., has been turned into city and regional art galleries and a community arts complex. Hours are daily 10 a.m.-5 p.m.

The **Boyanup Transport Museum,** South Western Hwy., Coombana Bay (20 minutes from Bunbury), houses the Leschenault Lady and Koombana Queen, two of Australia's oldest steam trains. Hours are daily 10 a.m.-4 p.m. For information, phone (097) 31-5250.

Catch some great views from: **Boulter Heights,** Withers Crescent; the **Lighthouse,** Apex Dr. off Malcom St.; **Marleston Hill Lookout Tower,** Apex Dr.; and along **Ocean Drive,** which follows the coastline for eight kilometers.

Big Swamp Bird Park, Prince Phillip Dr. (tel. 097-21-8380), has a walk-in aviary with 2,000 birds, a wildlife and waterfowl wetland, and a penguin pool and cave. Hours are Wed.-Fri. 1-5 p.m., Sat.-Sun. and holidays 10 a.m.-5 p.m.

On Koombana Beach, the **Bunbury Dolphin Trust** is a mini-Monkey Mia, where visitors can interact with playful bottlenose dolphins. Established in 1989, the dolphins "went public" shortly thereafter, and regularly come for feedings in the Inner Harbour—a flag signals their (and the tourists) arrival.

Accommodations and Food
Prince of Wales, Stephen St. (tel. 097-21-2016), has inexpensive pub rooms. **Clifton Beach Motel,** 2 Molloy St. (tel. 097-21-4300), and **Admiral Motor Inn,** 56 Spencer St. (tel. 097-21-7322), offer moderate rates and modern facilities. The **Lord Forrest,** Symmons St. (tel. 097-21-9966), is Bunbury's big and expensive luxury hotel.

YHA operates **The Residency Retreat Hostel,** corner of Stirling and Moore Streets (tel. 097-91-2621). This lovely restored 1895 building offers $13 dorm beds. **Bunbury Backpackers,** 22 Wittenoom St. (tel. 097-21-3359), offers hostel accommodations for $12 per night—free transport to the dolphin site is included.

Grab campsites and on-site vans at: **Bunbury Village Caravan Park,** corner Bussel Hwy. and Washington Ave. (tel. 097-95-7100) **Waterloo,** South Western Hwy. (tel. 097-25-4434); or **Punchbowl Caravan Park,** Ocean Dr. (tel. 097-21-4761).

For **food,** check out the numerous cafes around the town center, as well as the **International Food Hall,** on Symmons St., and the **Centrepoint** shopping center.

Memories of the Bond Store, on Victoria St., is a good local haunt, as is nearby **Drooly's** for pizza. Also on Victoria St., for Chinese food choose from the **Golden Flower** and the **Friendship.**

Try the counter meals—and the many beers on tap—at the **Rose Hotel** on Wellington Street Meatheads can pig out at **Lump of Rump,** 119 Beach Rd., and foodies can do their nouvelle number at **Louisa's,** 15 Clifton Street.

Transportation, Services, and Information
South West Coachlines (tel. 09-324-2333) operates a daily Perth-Bunbury service, continuing to Busselton. **Westrail** (tel. 09-326-2813 or 13-2232 toll-free) also provides daily service. Cost is $17.

Westrail's train Australind makes the trip twice a day for about the same fare as the bus. **Westrail Coaches** meet the train at Bunbury and go on to Busselton and Margaret River. Augusta is the last stop.

Bunbury City Transit (tel. 097-91-1955) covers the area from Australind to the north and south down to Gelorup.

Tourist info can be obtained at the **Bunbury Tourist Bureau,** Carmody Place, in the old railway station (tel. 097-21-7922). Hours are Mon.-Fri. 8:30 a.m.-5 p.m., Saturday 9 a.m.-4 p.m. Sunday 9:30 a.m.-4:30 p.m., public holidays 10 a.m.-3 p.m.

FARTHER SOUTH

Busselton and Vicinity
Sheltered by Geographe Bay, Busselton (pop. 6,470) is a peaceful seaside resort not unlike Bunbury, 49 km to the north—a lazy place to

fish, crab, and have beachy fun. It's also close to Yallingup, which some say is Australia's very best surfing beach.

The **jetty**, two km long, used to be the longest wooden jetty in the Southern Hemisphere until 1978, when Cyclone Alby shortened its act. At the corner of Queen and Albert Streets, see the Ballarat, a timber-hauling locomotive and WA's first engine. Other historic sights are: **Wonnerup House and Old School** (1859), Layman Rd., Wonnerup; **Newtown House** (1851), Bussell Hwy., Vasse; and **St. Mary's Church of England** (1843), Queen St., the oldest stone church in the state.

The **Old Court House**, 4 Queen St., now completely restored, houses an art gallery, information center, book and craft shops, coffee shop, and artists' studios. Hours are Tues.-Sat. 10 a.m.-4 p.m. The **Old Butter Factory** (it's not "Ye Olde," but it has the same flavor), Peel Terrace, features 16 rooms of early pioneer furnishings, clothing, and artifacts, plus machinery and working models. Hours are Wed.-Mon. 2-5 p.m. Admission is $2. **Bunyip Craft Centre**, Bunyip Rd., Wonnerup, exhibits the wares of more than 150 craftspeople. Hours are Wed.-Mon. 10 a.m.-4 p.m.

The **Oceanarium**, Geographe Bay Rd. near the jetty, displays local fish, including a white pointer shark and stingrays. Hours are daily 9 a.m.-9 p.m. Dec.-March, 9 a.m.-3 p.m. April-November. Admission is $2.

Slightly north of Busselton, **State Tuart Forest**, Bussell Hwy. between Capel and the Sabina River, is the world's only natural tuart forest. Some trees are estimated to be 300-400 years old.

Dunsborough, 24 km west of Busselton, is a pretty holiday town. For an impressive view of the Indian Ocean, continue another 13 km to **Cape Naturaliste Lighthouse** at the tip of Geographe Bay.

Yallingup Beach, eight km southwest of Dunsborough, is surf heaven according to national and international sources. Each November, the **Margaret River Surfing Classic** draws champions from around the world. Pick up a copy of the *Down Under Surf Guide* at the Dunsborough tourist office. It's full of information on wave and swell sizes and wind direction—and it's free.

Follow Caves Road. **Yallingup Cave**, off Caves Rd. north of Yallingup, a limestone cave discovered in 1899, is highlighted with stalactites, stalagmites, pillars, columns, flowstone, cave crystals, helictites, and straws. Hours are daily 9:30 a.m.-3:30 p.m. For information, phone (097) 55-2152.

Accommodations: In Busselton, the **Geographe**, 28 West St. (tel. 097-52-1451), and **Villa Carlotta**, 110 Adelaide St. (tel. 097-54-2026), are inexpensive B&B guesthouses. **Motel Busselton**, 90 Bussell Hwy. (tel. 097-52-1908), offers inexpensive motel rooms but is often heavily booked.

Broadwater Resort, corner of Bussell Hwy. and Holgate Rd. (tel. 097-54-1633), offers one- or two-bedroom apartments in the expensive range.

This area has many caravan parks offering campsites and on-site vans. Some suggestions are: **Mandalay Caravan Park**, Bussell Hwy. (tel. 097-52-1328); **Acacia Caravan Park**, Bussell Hwy. (tel. 097-55-4034); and **Busselton Caravan Park**, 163 Bussell Hwy. (tel. 097-52-1175).

Hostel accommodations in the Dunsborough area are available at **YHA**, 285 Geographe Bay Rd., Quindalup, two km south of Dunsborough (tel. 097-55-3107). Canoes, sailboards, and bicycles can be hired. Beds are $14. Campsites and on-site vans are offered at **Yallingup Beach Caravan Park**, Valley Rd. (tel. 097-55-2164), and **Caves Caravan Park**, corner of Caves and Yallingup Beach Roads (tel. 097-55-2196).

Information: For information about the Busselton area, contact the **Busselton Tourist Bureau**, Southern Dr. (in the civic center), Busselton (tel. 097-52-1350), or the **Dunsborough Tourist Centre**, Naturaliste Terrace, Dunsborough (tel. 097-55-3517). Both are open Mon.-Fri. 9 a.m.-5 p.m., Sat.-Sun. 10 a.m.-4 p.m.

Margaret River

Midway between Yallingup and Margaret River, along Caves Road, is a cluster of wineries, with several more sprinkled around the Margaret River valley. Indeed, Margaret River (pop. 800), tiny though it may be, has come into its own as a winegrowing district that's giving the Swan Valley a run for the grapestakes. **Leeuwin Estate, Cape Mentelle,** and **Sandalford** wineries are just a few of the delectable labels, now numbering about 35 in this region.

A tourist-oriented township, 47 km south of Busselton, situated on its eponym, Margaret River is enticingly close to pounding surf beaches and calm swimming bays.

The **Old Settlement Craft Village,** on the banks of the Margaret River, depicts 1920s settlement life with period farm buildings and machinery, along with crafts studios with gift items for sale. Hours are daily 9 a.m.-5 p.m., closed Christmas Day. For information, phone (097) 57-2775.

View displays of seashells at **Bellview Shell Museum,** Bussell Highway. Hours are daily 8 a.m.-6 p.m. Interesting buildings include **St. Thomas More Catholic Church,** Mitchell St., and the **Greek Chapel,** Wallcliffe Road.

Set in bushland, **Eagle's Heritage,** Boodjidup Rd. (tel. 097-57-2960), boasts the largest collection of Australia's birds of prey. Hours are daily 10 a.m.-5 p.m. Admission is $4.50.

The **Marron Farm,** Wickham Rd. (tel. 097-57-6279), 11 km south of town, produces thousands of the chestnut-like marron, which can be seen in their various stages of development. Swimming and picnic facilities are provided. Hours are daily 10 a.m.-4 p.m. Guided tours are available several times each day.

Popular **Prevally Park,** south of the river mouth, 10 km west of town, is known to have powerful surf. Follow Caves Rd. south through the lovely **Boranup Karri Forest.**

Mammoth Cave, 21 km south of Margaret River off Caves Rd., is noted for its fossil remains (including skeletons of Tasmanian tigers) and huge stalactites. **Lake Cave,** a few kilometers farther south, reached via a natural winding staircase down into a vast crater, contains an underground lake. The big bonanza, however, is **Jewel Cave,** eight km before Augusta on Caves Road. Western Australia's largest tourist cave features one of the world's longest straws (5.9 meters long and more than 3,000 years old), as well as gigantic pillars, grotesque formations, and a mysterious underground river. All caves are open daily except Christmas, with guided tours available several times a day.

Accommodations and Food: As with most wine regions, B&Bs are staked almost as often as the grapes. Some of the many choices are: **Margaret River B&B,** 28 Fearn St. (tel. 097-

57-2118); **Margaret House,** Devon Dr. (tel. 097-57-2692); and **Croft Guesthouse,** 54 Wallcliffe Rd. (tel. 097-57-2845).

The YHA **Margaret River Lodge,** 220 Railway Terrace (tel. 097-57-2532), offers dorm and bunkhouse accommodations for $11 per night, plus use of a swimming pool and TV lounge with open fireplace.

For campsites and on-site vans, contact **Margaret River Caravan Park,** 36 Station Rd. (tel. 097-57-2180), or **Riverview Caravan Park,** 8 Willmott Ave. (tel. 097-57-2270).

For cheap pub food, try the **Settler's Tavern,** Bussell Highway. The **1885 Inn,** on Farrelly St., has continental cuisine, superb regional wines, and expensive prices. For everything in between, you'll find a host of diners and cafes along Bussell Highway.

Or pick your own strawberries (Oct.-April), raspberries, boysenberries (Dec.-Jan.), and kiwi fruit (May-Aug.) at **Berry Farm Cottage,** Bessell Rd. (tel. 097-575-5054). Jams and wine are available for purchase. Hours are daily 10 a.m.-4:30 p.m.

Information: Winery maps and other tourist information are available at **Margaret River Tourist Bureau,** corner Tunbridge Rd. and Bussell Hwy., Margaret River (tel. 097-57-2911). Hours are daily 9 a.m.-5 p.m.

Augusta

Situated near Australia's southwestern tip, Augusta (pop. 470) sits 320 km from Perth and is WA's third-oldest settlement. Blue waters and white beaches, surfing and swimming sites keep holidaymakers happy.

The **Augusta Historical Museum,** Blackwood Ave., displays early shipping relics and historical exhibits. Hours are daily 10 a.m.-noon and 2-4 p.m. summer, 10 a.m.-noon winter. Admission is $1.

Hillview Lookout, Golf Links Rd. off Caves Rd., affords panoramic views and a directional plate to help you pick out nearby landmarks. **Cape Leeuwin Lighthouse,** at the end of Cape Leeuwin Rd., marks the junction of the Indian and Southern Oceans and functions as an important meteorological station. Open to visitors daily 9:30 a.m.-3:30 p.m. Admision is $3.

Nearby, see the waterwheel, built in 1895 to provide water for lighthouse builders, now encrusted in salt deposits.

Accommodations: Inexpensive holiday flats with kitchen facilities are offered at **Calypso,** Ellis St. (tel. 097-58-1944). **Augusta Hotel Motel,** Blackwood Ave. (tel. 097-58-1944), has moderately priced hotel rooms but expensive motel units.

The **YHA,** corner Bussell Hwy. and Blackwood Ave. (tel. 097-58-1433), has one cottage, which accommodates 11 warm bodies. Beds run $10 per night.

Doonbanks Caravan Park, Blackwood Ave. (tel. 097-58-1517), features a riverfront location with campsites and on-site vans.

The **Augusta Hotel,** Blackwood Ave., offers an a la carte food-service area, as well as the usual counter-meal setup. **Squirrels,** next door, has a good selection of sandwiches and burgers. And, for sheer romance (or more tourist kitsch), head over to the **Last Café Before Antartica,** on Albany Terrace, and gawk at the intercourse between Flinders Bay and the Blackwood River.

Information: Augusta Information Centre, 70 Blackwood Ave., Augusta (tel. 097-58-1695), assists with local inquiries. Hours are Mon.-Fri. 8:30 a.m.-5 p.m., Sat.-Sun. 8:30 a.m.-1 p.m. (open weekends only in winter months).

Transportation
Daily buses operate between Perth and the Busselton/Margaret River/Augusta region. For information and bookings, contact **South West Coachlines** (tel. 09-324-2333) or **Westrail** (tel. 09-326-2813 or 13-2232 toll-free).

THE SOUTHWEST

A few different routes will take you through Western Australia's southwest to the coastal region, known as the "Great Southern," with glorious beaches, rugged ranges, capes and parks, holiday resorts, and historic settlements. The South Western Highway travels inland from Bunbury, meeting the coast (and the South Coast Highway) at Walpole. The Albany Highway runs *way* inland in a southeasterly direction from Perth, connecting with the coastal highway at Albany. Other itineraries include the Great Southern Highway from Perth, Vasse Highway (from Busselton), the Brockman Highway (north of Augusta), and the Muirs Highway (between Manjimup and Mount Barker).

THE SOUTH WESTERN HIGHWAY

Leaving Bunbury, you'll journey into **Donnybrook,** the center of Western Australia's oldest apple-growing region, where Granny Smith is queen of the crop (try to make this trip in late October when it's apple blossom time). Many artsy-craftsy shops and studios permeate this area. Farther along the landscape gives way to rolling hills, pine plantations, jarrah and karri forests, and—eventually—the big, blue sea.

One particularly scenic detour is the stretch from Balingup, 29 km beyond Donnybrook, to **Nannup,** an old timber town on the Vasse Highway. The narrow, winding, 45-km drive crosses, then follows, the Blackwood River.

Westrail buses serve South Western Highway towns and most Vasse Highway communities several times each week. **South West Coachlines** also travels into some areas.

Bridgetown
Settled in 1857, Bridgetown (pop. 1,520) is a peaceful little community 95 km south of Bunbury in the heart of jarrah land. Visit **Bridgedale,** 1 Hampton St., the town's oldest house, built in the 1860s and restored by the National Trust. Hours are Wed.-Sat. and Monday 2-5 p.m., Sunday 11 a.m.-1 p.m. and 2-5 p.m.

The **Brierly Jigsaw Gallery,** Hampton St., is supposedly the country's only public jigsaw gallery. The collection includes puzzles from all over the world and visitors are invited to go to pieces over unfinished works. Hours are Thurs.-

On 1 April 1997 all telephone numbers in this section will change. To dial the new number, simply add the last two digits of the existing area code to the old number. As an example, (098) 12-3456 becomes 9812-3456. The new area code will be (08).

Mon. 10 a.m.-4 p.m. Admission is $2.

Good bushwalking and picnic spots are at **Bridgetown Jarrah Park** on Brockman Highway and **Blackwood River Park** at the southern edge of town.

Carnaby Butterflies and Beetles, Bridge St., is 31 km northeast in Boyup Brook. The collection contains many rare specimens and is reputed to be the largest outside of the British Natural History Museum. Hours are daily 10 a.m.-4 p.m.

The **Bridgetown Hotel,** 38 Hampton St. (tel. 097-61-1030), offers inexpensive pub rooms with breakfast included. **Riverwood House,** South Western Hwy. (tel. 097-61-1862), is a moderately priced, no-smoking-allowed B&B. Campsites and on-site vans are available at **Bridgetown Caravan Park,** South Western Hwy. (tel. 097-61-1053).

Pick up tourist info at the **Bridgetown Tourist Bureau,** Hampton St. (tel. 097-61-1740). Hours are daily 9 a.m.-5 p.m.

Manjimup

You can't miss that fact the Manjimup (pop. 4,150), 37 km from Bridgetown, is the gateway to the Tall Timber Country—timber arches signal your arrival at both edges of town. Karri trees, more than a century old, are abundant here.

Bone up on the local timber industry at **Timber Park,** corner Rose and Edwards Streets. The complex houses Timber Park Gallery, Bunnings' Age of Steam Museum (WA's only timber museum), displays of vintage machinery and implements, and other attractions. For a close-up look at the industry, put on a pair of sturdy shoes and visit the **Bunnings Diamond Mill,**

THE SOUTHWEST

© MOON PUBLICATIONS, INC.

252 = TOURIST DRIVE

0   50 km

Eastbourne Road. Tours are available Monday, Wednesday, and Friday at 1:30 and 3 p.m.

Seven kilometers down Seven Day Road, **Fonty's Pool,** once used to irrigate veggies, has been converted into a much-used swimming pool.

King Jarrah, three km along Perup Rd., is a 1,200-year-old tree with nearby walking trails. **Diamond Tree Tower,** 10 km south of town, sports a fire lookout atop a 51-meter karri tree and is usually crawling with tourists.

A bit of log and decking is all that remains of **One Tree Bridge** on Graphite Rd., 22 km from town. A couple of kilometers from the bridge stand **The Four Aces,** 300- to 400-year-old giant karri trees.

Manjimup Caravan Park, Mottram St. (tel. 097-71-2093), has campsites and on-site vans, as well as a bunkhouse with dorm-type accom-

modations. **Fonty's Pool Caravan Park,** Seven Day Rd. (tel. 097-71-2105), is another option.

The **Tourist Bureau,** in Timber Park, provides local information. Hours are daily 9 a.m.-5 p.m., closed Christmas Day and Good Friday. For information, phone (097) 77-1083.

Pemberton

Set amid luscious karri forests, Pemberton (pop. 870) is reached via the Vasse Highway turnoff, 15 km south of Manjimup, or along the Vasse Highway from Nannup (76 km).

The **Pioneer Museum,** Brockman St., houses records, photos, and machinery from the early forestry settlement. Hours are daily 9 a.m.-5 p.m. Admission is $1.

Restored **Brockman Saw Pit,** on the Pemberton-Northcliffe road, depicts lumber-cutting methods of bygone days. The **Pemberton**

Sawmill, conversely, is highly automated and one of the largest in the Southern Hemisphere. The Tourist Bureau can arrange tours.

Follow the signs to **Gloucester Tree** off Brockman St., the world's highest fire lookout tree. The view from up top is great, but don't attempt the dizzying 60-meter climb unless you're in good shape and vertigo-free!

The **Rainbow and Tramway Trails** were the original 91-mm gauge railways that transported karri logs to the sawmill back in the 1920s. Sights along the Rainbow Trail include **Big Brook Arboretum** and **Big Brook Dam** (popular for fishing, canoeing, and sailboarding). Take a four-hour forest ride across rivers, streams, and old wooden bridges on the 1907 replica **Pemberton Tramway.** Fares are $12 to Warren River, $18 to Northcliffe. For bookings and information, phone (097) 76-1322.

Other pretty spots around Pemberton are **Beedelup Falls,** off Vasse Hwy., and the **Walk Through Karri,** in Beedelup National Park (this 400-year-old tree has a hole you can stand inside). **Warren National Park** also contains huge karri trees.

Trout lovers and fishers might want to visit **King Trout Farm,** Northcliffe Rd., or **Treenbrook Downs Trout Farm,** Old Vasse Highway. Both offer fishing gear rentals and cooking facilities. See how the fish you've just eaten breed at the **Trout Hatchery,** Pumphill Road (tel. 097-76-1044). Hours are daily 9 a.m.-noon and 1-4 p.m. Admission is $1.

Shops that sell local timber crafts are **Fine Woodcraft,** Dickinson St.; **Outpost Art and Crafts,** Brockman St.; **Warren River Arts and Crafts,** 63 Jamieson St.; and **Woodcraftsman's Studio,** Lot 6, Jamieson Street.

Moderately priced accommodations in town are available at **Gloucester Motel,** Ellis St. (tel. 097-76-1266), and **Tammeron Motor Lodge,** Widdeson St. (tel. 097-76-1019). **Pump Hill Farm,** Pump Hill Rd. (tel. 097-76-1379), offers mud-brick cottages, with fireplaces and cooking facilities, in the expensive range.

The **YHA Hostel,** Pimelea Rd. (tel. 097-76-1153), sits in the middle of the state forest, about 10 km northwest of town. Dorm beds run $10 per night.

Campsites with limited facilities are offered at **Pemberton Forest Camp** and **Warren National Park.** For information, phone (097) 76-1200.

Tourist information is available at **Pemberton Tourist Centre,** Brockman St. (tel. 097-76-1133). Hours are daily 9 a.m.-5 p.m.

Beyond Pemberton

Northcliffe, 28 km southeast of Pemberton, features more virgin karri forests. **Northcliffe Forest Park,** adjacent to town, is an ideal place to bushwalk, especially when the wildflowers are in bloom (Sept.-Nov.). The park is also home to the twin and hollow-butt karri trees. The **Pioneer Museum,** Wheatley Coast Rd., displays early settlement artifacts. Hours are daily May-Aug. 10 a.m.-2 p.m. Admission is $1.

Keep going another 27 km to reach **Windy Harbour,** a relatively deserted coastal beach popular with rock climbers for its huge D'Entrecasteaux Cliffs. Limited **camping** facilities (summer only, with a three-day maximum) are available at **Windy Harbour Camping Area** (tel. 097-76-7056).

Walpole/Nornalup

This coastal region with luscious bays, coves, and forests is reached via the South Western Highway, 119 km southeast of Manjimup. It marks the beginning of the South Coast Highway and the Rainbow Coast.

Walpole and Nornalup are two townships at either edge of **Walpole Nornalup National Park,** 18,116 hectares of bushwalking trails, eucalyptus forests, desolate beaches, and diverse bird- and wildlife. **Valley of the Giants** is a scenic drive through tingle and karri tree forests, three km east of Nornalup. Check out the view or stop for a picnic along **Knoll Drive,** also three km east of Nornalup in the park.

There's good fishing at **Walpole/Nornalup inlets, Mandalay Beach,** and on the **Frankland River. Deep River,** 36 km northwest of Walpole, is favored by canoeing enthusiasts.

Tinglewood Homestead, Walpole (tel. 098-40-1035), has moderately priced B&B accommodations. Book ahead for dorm beds at the **Dingo Flat YHA Hostel,** Dingo Flat Rd. off Valley of the Giants Rd. (tel. 098-40-8073). Beds are $6 per night (the property is on a cattle and sheep station). Campsites, on-site vans, cottages, and cabins are available at **Rest Point**

Tourist Centre, Walpole Inlet (tel. 098-40-1032).

For tourist information, contact **Walpole Tourist Bureau,** Pioneer Cottage, Pioneer Park (tel. 098-40-1111).

Denmark

No, this is not a Danish settlement. Denmark (pop. 985), 66 km east of Nornalup, was named for Dr. Alexandra Denmark, an 1800s naval physician. It's a favorite of surfers and hippies. Located on the Denmark River, recreational opportunities include surfing, swimming, fishing, waterskiing, bushwalking, and a couple of wineries.

In town, the **Denmark Gallery,** 27 Strickland St., sells and exhibits local arts and crafts. **Groundrey Wines,** 11 North St. (tel. 098-48-1525), housed within a converted 1928 butter factory, features local crafts as well as wine sales and tasting. Hours are Mon.-Sat. 10 a.m.-4:30 p.m., Sunday 11 a.m.-4:30 p.m.

Wilson Inlet is the local windsurfing, fishing, boating, and waterskiing haven, while **Ocean Beach** is favored by surfers.

The **Fauna Sanctuary,** Ocean Beach Rd. adjacent to the caravan park, shelters a variety of marsupials, including endangered—and unexplainable—species such as the tammar, woillie, darma, agile, and bettong. Hours are Tues.-Thurs. and Sat.-Sun. 2:30-4:30 p.m.

Best ocean and countryside views are from **Mount Shadford Scenic Drive** off South Coast Hwy., along North St. to Mt. Shadford Road. **William Bay National Park,** 15 km west of town, eight km off South Coast Hwy., offers close-up views of rocks and reefs.

Denmark sports a wide range of holiday accommodations. **Denmark Guesthouse,** 31 South Coast Hwy. (tel. 098-48-1477), offers inexpensive rooms with shared facilities. **Gum Grove Chalets,** Ocean Beach Rd. (tel. 48-1378), and **Riverbend Chalets,** E. River Rd. (tel. 098-48-1107), have moderately priced, self-contained accommodations.

The **YHA Hostel** is at **Wilson Inlet Holiday Park,** Ocean Beach Rd. (tel. 098-48-1267). Beds cost $10 and facilities include a tennis court and boat hire. Book ahead.

Campsites and on-site vans are available at **Rivermouth Caravan Park,** Inlet Dr. (tel. 098-48-1262), and **Rudgyard Beach Holiday Park,** Rudgyard Rd. (tel. 098-48-1169).

The **Tiger and Snake,** beneath Denmark Guesthouse, serves Indian and Chinese dishes (judging by the name, you might want to check on ingredients when ordering). **Blue Wren Café,** on South Coast Hwy., and **Mary Rose,** on North St., are other possibilities, along with **Scoundrel's Brasserie,** along the river.

If you visit in December, January, or on Easter Saturday, drop by the annual **Arts and Crafts Market Days,** along the Denmark River, where all kinds of goodies are for sale.

For tourist information, contact **Denmark Tourist Bureau,** Strickland St. (tel. 098-48-1265). Hours are daily 9 a.m.-5 p.m.

ALONG THE ALBANY HIGHWAY

From Perth, the Albany Highway passes through a hodgepodge of timber, sheep-farming, and mixed agricultural districts and small service towns. En route, **Williams, Arthur River,** and **Kojonup** are smattered with assorted historic buildings, crafts galleries, picnic areas, and simple accommodations. **Cranbrook** is an access point for Stirling Range National Park. Turn off at **Kendenup** to see the site of WA's very first gold find.

Mount Barker

Though the local industries are mainly sheep and cattle grazing, Mount Barker (pop. 1,520), some 359 km southeast of Perth, is also known for its wine production. Eyeball panoramic views of the area from atop the 168-meter-high TV tower on **Mount Barker Hill.**

The **Old Police Station,** Albany Hwy., built by convicts in 1867, has been preserved as a museum with period furnishings and pioneer artifacts.

Mount Barker Tourist Bureau, 57 Lowood Rd. (tel. 098-51-1163), provides local information and maps to the wineries. Hours are Mon.-Fri. 9 a.m.-5 p.m., Saturday 9 a.m.-2 p.m., Sunday 10 a.m.-2 p.m., closed Christmas Day.

The Stirlings and the Porongurups

Sounds like the guest list for an amusing country weekend, doesn't it? Nope—these are two mountain ranges (and national parks) that rise dramatically from the surrounding flat, agricultural plains. Both parks are close enough to Albany for a day outing.

Stirling Range National Park (115,671 hectares)—about 66 km long and 18 km wide—is filled with mountains, valleys, cliffs, delicate wildflowers, eucalyptus forests, rare plants, profuse bird- and wildlife, and moody mountain views. **Bluff Knoll** (1,073 meters) is WA's third-highest peak, and the park's most popular climb, followed by **Toolbrunup** (1,052 meters) and **Ellen Peak** (1,012 meters and a *hard* trek). You must obtain permission from the ranger on duty before embarking on any climb. If you don't feel like walking, a scenic drive will take you through the center of the park. For more information, phone (098) 27-9230.

Closer to Albany, **Porongurup National Park** (2,401 hectares) features karri forests, excellent birdwatching, panoramic views, easy walking tracks, and some of the world's oldest rock. The best bushwalks are to **Castle Rock** (570 meters), **Hayward's Peak** (610 meters), **Devil's Slide** (671 meters), **Nancy Peak** (662 meters), and **Morgan's View** (662 meters). For information, phone (098) 53-1095.

Campsites with limited facilities are available at Stirling Range National Park (tel. 098-27-9278). The **YHA**, Bluff Knoll turnoff (tel. 098-27-9229), has $12-per-night dorm beds in eight chalets. Campsites and on-site vans are also available at **Stirling Range Caravan Park**, Chester Pass Rd., South Borden (tel. 098-27-9229).

At Porongurup, **Karribank Guest House**, Main St. (tel. 098-53-1022), offers inexpensive rooms plus swimming pool, tennis court, and golf course. Adjacent to Karribank, **Porongurup Caravan Park**, Main St. (tel. 098-53-1057), rents campsites and on-site vans.

ALBANY

Albany (pop. 16,320) is Western Australia's oldest settlement and, because of its superb Princess Royal Harbour, it remained the state's principal port for years. Since its creation in 1826 as a military outpost to ward off French colonists, Albany (called Frederickstown until 1832) has served as both a whaling port and coaling station. Situated 409 km southeast of Perth, this town is presently known as the Great Southern's commercial center as well as a tourist resort.

Historical Sights

Albany has preserved a number of its colonial buildings; most are on or around York St., Stirling Terrace, and the harbor foreshores.

The **Residency Museum**, Residency Rd., sits on the exact site where Major Edmund Lockyer and his merry band of convicts landed in 1826. Built in 1850, the museum was formerly the local magistrate's home and a naval training facility. Exhibits concern regional history, geography, and environment. Hours are daily 10 a.m.-5 p.m., For information, phone (098) 41-4844.

Explore a full-scale replica of Lockyer's brig *Amity*, Port Rd., near the museum. You can go below deck and imagine how some 45 men and accompanying livestock survived in the cramped quarters. Hours are daily 9 a.m.-5 p.m., closed Christmas Day. For information, phone (098) 41-6885.

The one-time convict-hiring depot and **Old Gaol** (1851) in Stirling Terrace now serves as a museum with WW I and II relics, pioneer tools and equipment, and Aboriginal artifacts. Hours are daily 10 a.m.-4:15 p.m., closed Christmas Day and Good Friday. For information, phone (098) 41-1401.

The restored **post office** (1870), Stirling Terrace, once housed the customs and bond store, court, holding cells, magistrate's and jury rooms. These days it comprises an Inter-Colonial Communications Museum and a restaurant. Hours are daily 10 a.m.-5 p.m.

Constructed of wattle and daub, **Patrick Taylor Cottage** (1832), Duke St., is thought to be Albany's oldest building. The cottage contains thousands of items, including early costumes, old clocks, and kitchenware. Hours are daily 2-4:15 p.m. Admission is $2. For information, phone (098) 41-6174.

Strawberry Hill Farmhouse, Middleton Beach Rd., built in 1836, is WA's oldest farm. Originally the private home for the government resident, the two-story stone house has been restored by the National Trust. You can take tea in the adjoining miner's cottage. Hours are daily 10 a.m.-5 p.m., closed during June. Admission is $2.50. For information, phone (098) 41-3735.

Other historic structures include: **St. John's Church of England** (1848), York St., the first church consecrated in Western Australia; **Albany Town Hall** (1888), refurbished in 1983 and converted into the Albany Town Theatre;

Vancouver Arts Centre (1880s), used for regular arts and crafts exhibitions; and **Princess Royal Fortress** (1893).

Other Sights

Dog Rock, a huge granite outcrop near the corner of Middleton Road and Young Street, resembles the head of a big dog.

Emu Point, where Oyster Harbour enters the sea, is a favorite place for boating, swimming, and windsurfing. Other good swimming sites are **Middleton Beach, Ellen Cove,** and **Jimmy Newell's Harbour,** south of town.

Mount Clarence offers the best views plus a recast of the original Desert Mounted Corps memorial erected at Suez in 1932 (Gallipoli, remember?). You can see bullet marks in the granite blocks, transported from Suez. **Mount Melville** and **Marine Drive Lookout** offer other wide-eye panoramas.

On the coast, 21 km south of Albany, **Torndirrup National Park** affords a number of spectacular sights including the blowholes, Natural Bridge, and The Gap. To reach the park, follow Frenchman Bay Road.

At the end of Frenchman Bay Rd., **Whaleworld,** the former whaling station responsible for taking up to 850 whales each season (until operations ceased in 1978), now serves as a museum. Have a whale of a time learning the history of Albany's oldest industry. Hours are daily 9 a.m.-5 p.m. Admission is $4.50. For information, phone (098) 44-4021.

Two Peoples Bay, 24 km east of Albany along Two Peoples Bay Rd., features more pretty beaches and a nature reserve that protects a small colony of noisy scrub birds. Believed to be extinct, the birds were rediscovered in 1961. Other nearby attractions are **Two Peoples Marron Farm,** Two Peoples Bay Rd., and **Valley Ponds Trout Farm,** Gull Rock Road.

Accommodations and Food

Colonial Guesthouse, 136 Brunswick Rd. (tel. 098-41-3704), and **Middleton Beach Guesthouse,** 18 Adelaide Crescent (tel. 098-41-1295), are inexpensive B&Bs.

Moderately priced motels are: **Travel Inn,** 191 Albany Hwy. (tel. 098-41-4144); **Friendly Motel,** 234 Albany Hwy. (tel. 098-41-2200); and the **Albany International Motel,** 270 Albany Hwy. (tel. 098-41-7399). Heaps of others are scattered around town and along Albany Highway. The best and most expensive ($160-230) hotel is **The Esplanade,** Middleton Beach (tel. 098-42-1711), with views to everywhere and the usual mega-plethora of amenities.

The **Albany YHA Hostel,** 49 Duke St. (tel. 098-41-3949), offers communal facilities and dorm beds for $11 per night, but fills up quickly.

You'll find many caravan parks to choose from. Some offering both campsites and on-site vans are **Mount Melville Caravan Park,** 22 Wellington St. (tel. 098-41-4616); **Middleton Beach Caravan Park,** Flinders Parade, Middleton Beach (tel. 098-41-3593); **Panorama Caravan Park,** Frenchman Bay Rd. (tel. 098-44-4031); and **Emu Beach Caravan Park,** Medcalfe Parade, Emu Point (tel. 098-44-1147).

Looking for food? Stirling Terrace is filled with fill-you-up eateries. For burgers, pancakes, and other light meals, try **Dylan's on the Terrace,** 82 Stirling Terrace. **Kooka's,** at 204 Stirling Terrace (tel. 098-41-5889), offers excellent fresh and nouvelle-ish cuisine in a colonial cottage with a kookaburra theme. Meals are in the expensive range and reservations are advised. The **Post Restaurant,** 33 Stirling Terrace, in the old post office, features moderately priced seafood specialties and cook-your-own steaks in a colonial atmosphere.

For Asian fare try **Lemon Grass Thai,** 370 Middleton Rd.; **Three Plenties** Chinese restaurant, York St.; or **The Melting Pot,** 338 Middleton Road.

Transportation, Services, and Information

Ansett (tel. 13-1300 toll-free) and **Skywest** (book through Ansett) operate daily flights from Perth Airport to Albany (about $150).

Westrail (tel. 09-326-2813 or 13-2232 toll-free) provides daily coach service from Perth ($35) and travels to Denmark four times each week ($45).

If you're driving, the Albany Highway from Perth (409 km) should get you here in under five hours. The South Western and South Coast Highways from Bunbury (402 km, not counting detours) will take about the same time.

Love's Bus Service, the local transport company, travels weekdays and Saturday mornings to points along the Albany Highway, as well as to Middleton Beach, Spencer Park, and Emu Point.

Rental cars are available from **Avis** (tel. 098-42-2833), **Budget** (tel. 098-41-2299), and **Albany Car Rentals** (tel. 098-41-7077). Rates are about $50 per day with unlimited kilometers.

Contact the **Albany YHA Hostel** for bicycle hire outfits (about $10 per day) and cheap tours into the Stirling Ranges or up and down the coast ($15-30). The **Tourist Bureau** can also arrange local tours.

For a free copy of *Albany Experience,* a local mini-guide, or for other info, contact the **Albany Tourist Bureau,** corner York St. and Peels Place (tel. 098-41-1088). Hours are Mon.-Fri. 8:30 a.m.-5:30 p.m., Sat.-Sun. and public holidays 9 a.m.-5 p.m.

Pick up street maps and other road info at the **Royal Automobile Club,** 110 Albany Hwy. (tel. 098-42-1210).

THE WESTERN BIGHT

From Albany to Esperance, the South Coast Highway teases its way along the western end of the Great Australian Bight—a 480-km odyssey through capes and parks, bays and beaches.

Out of Albany

Turn off at Boxwood Hill, 117 km northeast of Albany, and veer coastward another 63 km to **Bremer Bay,** a popular location for fishing, boating, waterskiing, and scuba diving.

Back on South Coast Highway, **Jerramungup** is about 60 km north of Boxwood Hill. The **Military Museum,** on the highway (tel. 098-35-1119), features a large privately owned collection of fighting memorabilia, including vehicles, badges, medals, guns, and swords. Hours are Mon.-Fri. 10 a.m.-3 p.m., Sat.-Sun. 10 a.m.-1 p.m. Admission is $2.

Ravensthorpe

A former gold and copper mining town, Ravensthorpe (pop. 330) is 114 km northeast of Jerramungup.

Cocanarup Homestead, classified as a historical site by the National Trust, is made up of several century-old stone buildings. The early 1900s **Dance Cottage Museum** is home to the local historical society's memorabilia collection. The old smelter sits three km from town, while

ruins of a baked-out bakery and a played-out gold mine can be explored at **Kundip,** some 20 km farther. If you want to check out the **Ravensthorpe Range** at the northern end of Foater Road, beware of the old mine shafts in that area!

Ravensthorpe Motel, junction Hopetoun and Esperance Roads (tel. 098-38-1053), and **Palace Motor Hotel** (tel. 098-38-1005) both offer inexpensive to moderate accommodations. Campsites are available at **Ravensthorpe Caravan Park,** Morgan St. (tel. 098-38-1050).

Local info can be obtained at the **Ravensthorpe Tourist Information Centre,** Morgan St. (tel. 098-38-1001). Hours are Mon.-Fri. 8:30 a.m.-5 p.m.

Below and Beyond Ravensthorpe

Hopetoun, situated on the coast 50 km south of Ravensthorpe, offers more secluded bays, beaches, inlets, and fishing holes. Whales can often be seen near these shores in August and September.

Fitzgerald River National Park, accessed either from Hopetoun, Jerramungup, or Bremer Bay, features 240,000 hectares of sand plain, river valleys, narrow gorges, rugged ranges, coastal cliffs, sandy beaches, visible wildlife, and approximately 1,350 species of wildflowers and native plants. Check in with a ranger before you go bushwalking, and be sure to carry plenty of water. Swimmers should be aware of dangerous coastal rips. Some park areas are restricted at certain times of the year. For information, phone (098) 35-5043.

Stokes National Park (10,667 hectares), reached via gravel roads off the South Coast Highway east of Young River, is a coastal region for bushwalking, ocean fishing, inlet swimming, and birdwatching (seals have been sighted, too). Facilities are limited and you must carry your own water. For information, phone (098) 76-8541.

ESPERANCE

Beautifully situated across from the Archipelago of the Recherche, 730 km southeast of Perth, versatile Esperance (pop. 6,375) wears three hats—seaport, seaside resort, and agricultural center.

Named for the French frigate *L'Esperance* in 1772, the town was settled in 1863 when the Dempster brothers arrived with their families after an overland trek. Some 30 years later, with the advent of gold exploration, Esperance boomed as a port, then faltered again when the gold rush rushed out. Then, shortly after World War II *and* after a lot of research, it was discovered that trace elements were missing from the surrounding soil, which prohibited agriculture. The situation was remedied and voila—a rich agro-center and grain-loading port.

Sights

Esperance Municipal Museum, James St., features early machinery, tools, furnishings, and—best of all—a big Skylab display (Esperance was the lucky spot where Skylab decided to fall to earth in 1979). The museum park also houses **Craft Village,** where you can buy locally produced arts and crafts. Hours are daily 1:30-4:30 p.m. Admission is $2. For information, phone (090) 71-1579.

Local crustaceans, fish, other marinelife, and shells are on view at **George's Oceanarium,** the Esplanade. Hours are Tues.-Sun. 10 a.m.-4 p.m., Sept.-May. For information, phone (090) 71-2940.

The original **Dempster Homestead,** Dempster and Emily Streets, is privately owned and can be admired only from the road.

The **Australian Parrot Farm,** Fisheries Rd., Yarrumun, exhibits parrots, pheasants, guinea fowl, and peafowl, plus a collection of more than 2,000 vintage bottles. Hours are daily 9 a.m.-5 p.m. For information, phone (090) 76-1284.

Salt-tolerant algae and saline are what makes **Pink Lake** pink—and sometimes purple. Some years, as much as 500,000 tons of salt are dredged from the lake, which is three km out of town along Pink Lake Road.

Twilight Beach Scenic Drive leads from town up to Observatory Point and Lookout, then to Pink Lake. **Rotary Lookout,** on Wireless Hill, affords yet another town-and-bay vista.

Twilight Cove, near the town center, is a good, safe swimming and fishing beach.

Islands and Parks

The **Archipelago of the Recherche,** also known as the Bay of Isles, comprises approximately 100 islands with sandy beaches, turquoise waters, plentiful waterbirds, and seal and penguin colonies. The MV *Cape Le Grand II* makes scenic two-hour cruises of the archipelago, or the MV *Sea Lion* will take you over to Woody Island—a wildlife sanctuary—for a five-hour picnic trip (January, February, and major holidays). For information, phone (090) 71-1772.

Cape Le Grand National Park (31,390 hectares), 48 km southeast of Esperance, has some dynamite coastal scenery. Sand plains, freshwater pools, swamps, and massive granite outcrops (Mt. Le Grand, 353 meters, is the highest) make up the remaining terrain—home to birds, reptiles, gray kangaroos, possums, and bandicoots. A marked 15-km walking trail will lead you along the coast from Cape Le Grand to Rossiter Bay. Come September through November, when the wildflowers are in bloom. For information, phone (090) 71-3733.

Cape Arid National Park (279,415 hectares), 125 km east of Esperance, can be reached by conventional vehicle, but tracks within the park are suitable only for four-wheel-drive (weather permitting). Cape Arid also features splendid coastal scenery, granite outcrops, and excellent lookouts as well as diverse fauna. You must obtain permission from a park ranger before rock climbing; swimmers should be wary of rips. Cape *Arid* also translates as *bring your own water*. For information, phone (090) 75-0055.

Accommodations and Food

Pink Lake Lodge, 85 Pink Lake Rd. (tel. 090-71-2075), offers inexpensive rooms.

Moderately priced, self-contained holiday flats are available at **Captain Huon,** 5 the Esplanade (tel. 090-71-2383); **Esperance All Seasons,** 73 the Esplanade (tel. 090-71-2257); and **Esperance Beachfront Resort,** 19 the Esplanade (tel. 090-71-2513).

The **Watersedge YHA Hostel,** Goldfields Rd. (tel. 090-71-1040), is two km east of the town center. Eight dorm and two twin rooms accommodate 110 happy hostelers. Dorm beds cost $11 per night. **Wirraway House Esperance Backpackers,** 14 Emily St. (tel. 090-71-4724), is a new hostel with dorm beds for $12 per night and inexpensive double rooms.

Rent a campsite or on-site van at **Bather's Paradise Caravan Park,** corner Westmacott and Chaplin Streets (tel. 090-71-1014); **Bush-**

lands Holiday Village, Collier Rd. (tel. 090-71-1346); **Esperance Bay Caravan Park,** corner the Esplanade and Harbour Rd. (tel. 090-71-2237); or **Pink Lake Caravan Park,** Pink Lake Rd. (tel. 090-71-2424). Campsites with limited facilities are offered at both Cape Le Grand and Cape Arid National Parks.

Numerous coffee shops, cafes, and fish-and-chip shops provide belly stuffers. **Spice of Life,** Andrew St., leans toward the vegetarian appetite. **Ollie's on the Esplanade** is open daily, early morning to late night, and offers a variety of choices.

Transportation, Services, and Information
Ansett (tel. 13-1300 toll-free) and Skywest (phone Ansett for bookings) fly daily from Perth to Esperance ($190), and **Goldfields Air Services** (tel. 090-93-2116) makes a once-a-week trip from Kalgoorlie via Norseman ($140).

Three times each week the Prospector Perth-Kalgoorlie train connects with a Westrail coach to Esperance. If you'd rather take the bus all the way, Westrail coaches also depart Perth for Esperance three times a week. For information, phone (09) 326-2813 or 13-2232 toll-free.

The YHA hostel rents **bicycles** for $10 per day.

If you're heading up to the goldfields region, take the Coolgardie-Esperance Highway north out of town, straight up to Coolgardie (375 km north of Esperance and 39 km southwest of Kalgoorlie), or turn onto the Eyre Highway at Norseman (207 km) for the eastward trek across the Nullarbor Plain (see "Crossing the Nullarbor," in the South Australia chapter).

For tourist and tour information, contact the **Esperance Tourist Bureau,** Dempster Street, in Museum Village (tel. 090-71-2330). Hours are daily 9 a.m.-5 p.m.

THE WHEATLANDS

Don't be put off by the boring name—this agricultural heartland, stretching from Perth to Coolgardie and north of Albany to the Great Eastern Highway, has some wild rock formations, Aboriginal rock carvings, and worth-a-stop historical sights.

YORK TO HYDEN

Beginning at the Avon Valley, weave and wind your way through side ways and byways to various wheatlands attractions, ending at the simply *awesome* Wave Rock.

The Yoting-Kellerberrin Road, beyond the small wheaty township of Quairading (166 km east of Perth), accesses both **Kokerbin Rock,** with caves, a lookout, and a scenic drive, and **Mount Stirling,** a huge granite outcrop often climbed for the view.

Bruce Rock, 77 km east of Quairading, is another noteworthy outcrop. **Bruce Rock Museum,** 24 Johnson St., contains pioneering items. Hours are daily 10 a.m.-4 p.m. Admission is $2.

Situated 68 km southwest of Bruce Rock, **Corrigin** (pop. 840) dates back to the 1880s. The **Pioneer Museum,** corner of Kunjin Rd. and Kirkwood St., displays early machinery and pioneering memorabilia. Hours are daily 10 a.m.-4 p.m. Admission is $2.

Locally produced handicrafts can be purchased at the **Craft Cottage,** Walton Street. Hours are Mon.-Fri. 10 a.m.-5 p.m., Saturday 9:30-11:30 a.m.

Gorge Rock, 23 km southeast of Corrigin, is a swimming area created from a dammed gorge. **Jilakin Rock,** 50 km southeast, through Kulin, is a gray granite monolith overlooking a 1,214-hectare lake surrounded by bushland.

Wave Rock, three km outside Hyden and 108 km southeast of Corrigin, is the destination of most wheatland travelers. This enormous 50-meter-high granite rock formation—shaped by wind and rain—is estimated to be 2.7 billion years old. It resembles a huge curling wave made even more distinctive by vertical bands of color on its sloping face. A marked track will lead you around the base of Wave Rock over to **Hippo's Yawn,** another unique outcrop. **Bates Cave,** 21 km northwest of Hyden, features Aboriginal hand paintings.

Inexpensive accommodations in Hyden are offered at **Dieps B&B,** 17 Clayton St. (tel. 098-80-5179). **Hyden Hotel,** 2 Lynch St. (tel. 098-80-5052), is in the moderate range. Campsites are available at **Wave Rock Caravan Park,** Wave Rock (tel. 098-80-5022).

The **Hyden Tourist Information Centre** is on Lynch St. (tel. 098-80-5182). Hours are daily 10 a.m.-4 p.m.

THE GREAT SOUTHERN HIGHWAY

Situated on the Avon River, 66 km south of York, **Beverley** is known for its **Aeronautical Museum,** Vincent St., with displays of aviation equipment, model airplanes, and the *Silver Centenary,* WA's first privately made airplane. Hours are daily 10 a.m.-4 p.m. For information, phone (096) 46-1555.

Historical buildings include **St. Paul's Church** (1862), Avon Dr., **St. John's in the Wilderness** (1895), Dale-Beverley Rd., and Beverley's oldest surviving building (now a museum), **Dead Finish** (1872), 138 Vincent Street.

Narrogin (pop. 5,000), 137 km south of Beverley, is the commercial hub of this district. The **Court House Museum,** Norseman Rd., gives insight into early industry and society. Hours are Tuesday, Friday, and Sunday 2-4:30 p.m.

Albert Facey's Homestead, on the road between Wickepin and Nomans Lake, was built by the colorful character of the same name. Facey's autobiography, *A Fortunate Life,* later

On 1 April 1997 all telephone numbers in this section will change. To dial the new number, simply add the last two digits of the existing area code to the old number. As an example, (090) 12-3456 becomes 9012-3456. The new area code will be (08).

THE WHEATLANDS

became a TV miniseries. The homestead is open Mon.-Fri. 9 a.m.-5 p.m. Admission is $2.50.

Attractions around **Wagin,** 50 km down the highway, include the **Giant Ram Tourist Park** (the ram is 15 meters long and seven meters high and called the "Largest (fake) Ram in the Southern Hemisphere"), **Wagin Historical Village,** and nearby **Mount Latham,** for rock climbing and bushwalking. **Puntapin Rock** is another large, intriguing rock formation. **Lake Dumbleyung,** 39 km east of Wagin, is the spot where Donald Campbell broke the world water speed record in 1964. Around a portion of the lake is a nature reserve with varied birdlife, a scenic drive, and a lookout point.

Settled in the 1840s, **Katanning** (pop. 4,415) mixes a bit of history with modern services. The **Old Mill** (1889), Main St., houses early machinery, equipment, and a crafts shop. Hours are Mon.-Fri. 10 a.m.-4 p.m., Saturday 10 a.m.-noon. Admission is $1.

The Great Southern Highway joins the Albany Highway 85 km south of Katanning.

THE GREAT EASTERN HIGHWAY

The 500-km stretch from Northam to Kalgoorlie is also known as the Goldfields Heritage Trail and follows the original 1860s route established by surveyor Charles Hunt.

Meckering, a little rural town 133 km east of Perth, was severely damaged in a 1968 earthquake. Though the town was immediately rebuilt, you can see mementos of the destruction at the tourist center gazebo.

The Municipal Museum at **Cunderdin,** 24 km east, displays assorted vintage farm machinery, tractors, photos, and other relics. Hours are daily 10 a.m.-4 p.m. Admission is $2. Cunderin Hill itself puts on a good spring wildflower show.

Kellerberrin, another 47 km eastward, is one of the route's oldest settlements. The **District**

Museum, Leake and Bedford Streets (tel. 090-45-4006), displays yet more early implements. Open by appointment. Kellerberrin Hill, north of the post office, is a good viewing spot. You can also turn off here for Mount Stirling and Kokerbin Rock.

Situated on both the Perth-Kalgoorlie railway line and the Great Eastern Highway, **Merredin** (pop. 3,520) represents the commercial center for this region. The **Old Railway Station** on the highway is a group of four 1920s buildings that now serve as a museum and arts center. Hours are Mon.-Fri. 9 a.m.-3 p.m., Sat.-Sun. and school holidays 10 a.m.-4 p.m. Admission is $2. Two walks that start off from the railway station are **Merredin Peak Heritage Trail,** an easy jaunt around the town's historic buildings, and a longer (six km) hike around the peak. **Burracoppin Rock,** 24 km east of Merredin, is a large rock outcrop popular with picnickers.

Merredin Oasis Hotel, 8 Great Eastern Hwy. (tel. 090-41-1133), has moderately priced, air-conditioned rooms with TVs, as well as a swim-ming pool. Campsites and on-site vans are available at **Merredin Caravan Park,** Great Eastern Hwy. (tel. 090-41-1535).

Western Australia's gold rush began in 1887 at **Southern Cross,** 109 km east of Merredin. Though the fever quickly moved east to Coolgardie and Kalgoorlie, Southern Cross (pop. 800) still retains its wide streets and historic buildings. **Yilgarn History Museum** (1892), Antares St., was originally the Mining Registrar's Office, then the town courthouse. Exhibits trace the town's early settlement and include mineral displays. Hours are Mon.-Sat. 9 a.m.-noon and 1:30-4 p.m., Sunday 1:30-4 p.m.

Other turn-of-the-century buildings are the **Forrester's Resource Centre** and **Lisignolis Shop,** both on Antares Street. **Wimmera Hill,** site of WA's first major gold discovery, offers good views of the area.

Southern Cross marks the end of the wheatlands and the beginning of the 188-km desert stretch to Coolgardie and the goldfields region.

THE GOLDFIELDS

Western Australia's goldfields are hot, flat, and extremely arid, punctuated with deserted outposts, preserved ghost towns, and its semi-thriving hub, Kalgoorlie. The streets are wide, shoot-'em-out affairs (made that way so camel trains could turn around easily), and many of the buildings exude the wealth and opulence associated with gold frenzy. Try to ignore the cranes, conveyers, and tailings dumps and envision the Golden Mile's hundred mines all flourishing simultaneously.

History
Until that 1887 gold strike in Southern Cross, Western Australia received merely poor-relative status from the eastern colonies. But what brings relatives flocking faster than gold? Though the Southern Cross find quickly ran dry,

in 1892 prospector Arthur Bayley (acting on a hot tip given by a man he'd saved from death) staked a claim at Bayley's Reward, a huge gold reef about three kilometers east of Coolgardie. By 1900, the town's population soared to 15,000, dropping considerably by 1905 when the rush rushed elsewhere. Bayley's Reward, however, continued to produce gold until 1963.

In 1893, Irish prospectors Paddy Hannan, Tom Flannigan, and Dan Shea found gold near the site of the present Mount Charlotte Mine. Though surface gold soon ran out, a bigger and deeper find was discovered along the Golden Mile (reputedly the world's richest square mile of gold-bearing earth), prompting companies and diggers to go underground. At one time, the Golden Mile boasted more than 100 working mines.

One enormous problem was the lack of water, or the pollution of what water there was: miners were dropping like flies from thirst and disease. Engineer C.Y. O'Connor came up with the perfect invention—a 563-km wood and pitch water pipe from Mundaring Weir, near Perth, to Kalgoorlie. Mocked and taunted by ignorant disbelievers, O'Connor nonetheless persevered with his pipeline. Unfortunately, three days after

On 1 April 1997 all telephone numbers with the (090) area code will change. To dial the new number, simply add 90 to the old number. The new area code will be (08). For example, (090) 12-3456 will become (08) 9012-3456.

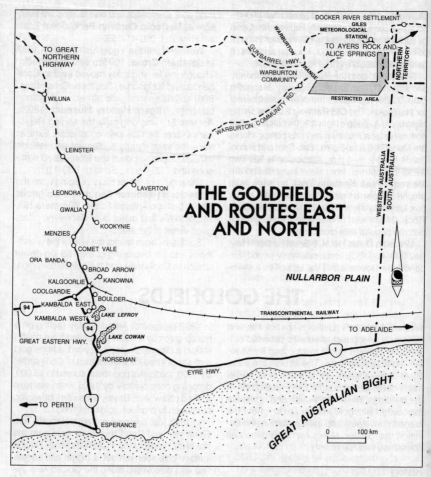

THE GOLDFIELDS
AND ROUTES EAST
AND NORTH

the water pumps were started and there was still nary a trickle, the despondent O'Connor shot himself to death—not realizing the water would take two weeks to travel such a distance. Dead or not, he'd solved the problem. By 1903 water began filling Kalgoorlie's new reservoir.

KALGOORLIE

"Queen of the Golden Mile," Kalgoorlie (pop. 20,000) sits 596 km east of Perth at the end of

the Goldfields Heritage Trail. Kalgoorlie goldfields continued to produce during the lean 1920s, ebbing and falling during depression and war. Just as the mines were faltering economically (Mount Charlotte Mine is the only big operation), the 1960s nickel boom brought renewed prosperity—and tourism—to town.

Sights

Kalgoorlie's biggest tourist attraction is **Hannan's North Tourist Mine,** Boulder Block Rd., Fimiston (on the Golden Mile). See mining memorabilia and the inner (or under) workings. Visitors can take a 30-minute surface tour, 90-minute underground tour, or both. Tours depart several times daily and cost about $14 each, though you can explore the surface displays on your own, for free. For information, phone (090) 91-4074.

Learn the history and development of WA's eastern goldfields at the **Museum of the Goldfields,** 22 Outridge Terrace—look for the Ivanhoe mine headframe. Check out the exhibits and the underground gold vault, then ride the elevator to a viewing platform on the headframe for a miner's-eye view. The museum encompasses the teensy **British Arms Hotel,** supposedly the narrowest pub in Australia. Hours are daily 10 a.m.-4:30 p.m., closed Good Friday and Christmas Day. Admission is free. For information, phone (090) 21-8533.

The **W.A. School of Mines and Mineral Museum,** Egan St., features displays of minerals, meteorites, gold nuggets, and gemstones. Hours are Mon.-Fri. 9 a.m.-4 p.m. For information, phone (090) 22-0109.

The 1903 **Town Hall,** Hannan St., houses historical memorabilia and an art gallery. Outside the building, a bronze statue of Paddy Hannan holding his waterbag doubles as a drinking fountain. Hours are Mon.-Fri. 9 a.m.-5 p.m. For information, phone (090) 21-2544.

Other architectural delights on Hannan St. are the **post office** and the **Exchange Hotel.**

Paddy Hannan's Tree, Outridge Terrace, near the head of Hannan St., marks the spot where Paddy found Kalgoorlie's first gold back in 1893.

Mount Charlotte Reservoir off Park St., near the end of Hannan St., is where C.Y. O'Connor ended his pipeline. The lookout gives a good town view.

Hammond Park, Lyall St., Lamington, is a flora and fauna reserve with tame emus and kangaroos and a detailed model of a Bavarian castle. Hours are daily 9 a.m.-5 p.m.

The **Arboretum,** adjacent to Hammond Park, features a marked walking trail to individual trees and a variety of birdlife.

Illegal and Legal

Amsterdam it ain't, but Hay Street is lined with brothels, a la Dutch treat, where costumed ladies of the night beckon the menfolk passing by. Though officialdom turns its eagle eye from this long-practiced local activity, it is not actually legal.

The **Two Up School,** Broad Arrow Rd., six km north of Kalgoorlie, is Australia's only legalized bush two-up school. This famous Aussie gambling game has been played in Kalgoorlie since the beginning of the gold rush. Hours are Mon.-Sat. 1:30 p.m.-dark, Sunday 11 a.m.-dark. Closed on race days and the mine's payday. Don't bring alcohol and don't come if you're under 18 years old. For information, phone (090) 21-1413.

Accommodations

Would you want to stay anywhere but one of the classic old pubs? Find inexpensive to moderate rooms at the **Exchange Hotel,** Hannan St. (tel. 090-21-2833); **York Hotel,** Hannan St. (tel. 090-21-2337); **Palace Hotel,** Hannan St. (tel. 090-21-2788); and **Surrey House,** 9 Boulder Rd. (tel. 090-21-1340). The **Star and Garter,** 497 Hannan St. (tel. 090-21-3004), has motel rooms in the expensive range, TVs, and a swimming pool.

Campsites and on-site vans are available at **Golden Village Caravan Park,** Hay St. (tel. 090-21-4162); **Goldminer Tourist Caravan Park,** Great Eastern Hwy. (tel. 090-21-3713); and **Prospector Tourist Park,** Great Eastern Hwy. (tel. 090-21-2524).

Food

All of the pubs serve filling counter meals at reasonable prices. Hannan St. is lined with taverns and eateries. The **Palace, Exchange,** and **York Hotels** are especially recommended. **Matteo's,** 113 Hannan St., makes up good pizzas, and the **Victoria Café** is a popular local breakfast spot. The **Broccoli Forest Health Food Store and Kitchen,** at the top end of Hannan St., serves eat-in or takeaway vegetarian meals and stocks bulk nuts, fruits, grains, and other natural foods.

If you've just hit gold, reserve a table at the very expensive **Amalfi,** 409 Hannan St. (tel. 090-21-3088). This long-established Italian restaurant is famous for its scaloppine.

Kalgoorlie brews its own beer, aptly named **Hannan's.**

Shopping

Got that gold fever? You can buy prospecting supplies and metal detectors at **International Lapidary,** 67 Hannan St. (tel. 090-21-3017), or rent equipment through the tourist office.

Transportation, Services, and Information

Both **Ansett** (tel. 13-1300 toll free) and **Skywest** (book through Ansett) fly to Kalgoorlie daily from Perth ($225). **Goldfields Air Services** (tel. 090-93-2116) does the Esperance-Norseman-Kalgoorlie route every Tuesday ($135).

Greyhound Pioneer Australia (tel. 13-2030 toll-free) stops in Kal en route to the capital cities ($75 from Perth); **Westrail** (tel. 090-21-2023) operates three times weekly between Kal and Esperance ($32); and **Kalgoorlie Express** (tel. 09-328-9199) does a twice-a-week run between Kalgoorlie and Perth, venturing into northern towns.

The Indian-Pacific and Trans-Australian trains both stop at Kalgoorlie on their way to and from Perth several times each week. The Prospector leaves East Perth Rail Terminal every day for the eight-hour trip ($60, including a meal). For information and bookings, phone Westrail (tel. 09-326-2813 or 13-2232 toll-free)—book this one ahead.

The local **bus** operates regular runs between Kalgoorlie and Boulder for $1 each way. The Tourist Centre has timetables.

Taxis are available 24 hours a day; a ride between the town and the airport is about $10. For bookings, phone (090) 21-2177.

All of the major car rental firms are at Kalgoorlie Airport.

Bicycles can be hired for $12 per day from **Johnston Cycles,** 76 Boulder St. (tel. 090-21-1157).

Goldrush Tours, Palace Chambers, Maritana St. (tel. 090-21-2954), offers guided tours and excursions including town tours, gold detector tours, ghost towns, and in-season wildflowers.

Tour the local **Royal Flying Doctor** base, 56 Piccadilly St., Mon.-Fri. at 2:30 p.m. For information, phone (090) 21-2899.

For local information and tour bookings, contact **Kalgoorlie-Boulder Tourist Centre,** 250 Hannan St., Kalgoorlie (tel. 090-21-1966). Hours are Mon.-Fri. 8:30 a.m.-5 p.m., Sat.-Sun. 9 a.m.-5 p.m.

A branch of the **Royal Automobile Club** is at the corner of Hannan and Porter Streets. For information, phone (090) 21-1511.

For **emergencies,** phone 000 or the **Kalgoorlie Regional Hospital** (tel. 090-21-2222).

VICINITY OF KALGOORLIE

Looking for gold? It's still out there. Grab a metal detector and join other weekend prospectors, but be sure you're well prepared—carry water, spare parts, and good maps. Check in with the Tourist Centre and Royal Automobile Club before venturing out into this rugged, remote region. Both Boulder and Coolgardie are popular pit stops. Good luck.

Boulder

Boulder (pop. 5,600) is actually a satellite town of Kalgoorlie, built during the boom to service the Golden Mile. Boulder Block pubs used to see nonstop action, but, alas, the town is much quieter these days.

The **Boulder Town Hall,** on Burt St., features an ornate clocktower and an exhibition of works by local artists. Next door, the **Goldfields War Museum** houses military artifacts and vehicles but—as of press time—was closed for renovations. For information, phone (090) 93-1083.

The 1897 Boulder City Railway Station is home to the **Eastern Goldfields Historical Society** and its historical and pioneering exhibits. Hours are daily 9-11:30 a.m.

The **Cornwall Hotel,** on Hopkins St., is another gorgeous old grand dame.

The **Rattler** tourist train departs daily from Boulder City Railway Station for a one-hour, commentary-accompanied journey of the entire Golden Mile. This is the train that originally linked Kalgoorlie with Boulder. Fare is $10. Departures are daily 10 a.m., Sunday and holidays 10 a.m. and noon. For information and bookings, phone (090) 21-7077.

Coolgardie

You won't find the frenzied boom town of 1892. Settled into ghost-town retirement, Coolgardie (pop. 900), 40 km southwest of Kalgoorlie, is still a popular stopping place for gold-era aficionados. You'll easily get a sense of what this town was like in its glory just by the size of the streets and structures.

Details of Coolgardie's history can be gleaned from the 150 markers placed about town, which recount the original use of each building. An index to the markers is posted near the **Goldfields Exhibition** on Bayley Street. The exhibition relives Coolgardie's not-so-humble beginnings and includes goldfields memorabilia and a 35-minute video. Hours are daily 10 a.m.-5 p.m., closed Christmas Day. Admission is $2.50. For information, phone (090) 26-6090.

The **Old Railway Station,** Woodward St., serves as a transport museum and features a display of Modesto Varischetti's rescue. The name doesn't ring a bell? In 1907, Modesto became trapped by floodwaters while 300 meters underground and was rescued by divers some 10 days later. Hours are daily 9 a.m.-5 p.m., closed Thursday afternoon and Christmas Day. **Ben Prior's Open Air Museum,** Bailey St., is an amazing assortment of gold-boom junque sitting by the edge of the road. Open daily.

Warden Finnerty's House, Hunt St., belonged to the gold rush rule maker. Hours are Tuesday 1-4 p.m. and Sunday 10 a.m.-noon. Admission is $2.

Before jails were built, prisoners were chained to the **Gaol Tree,** on Hunt St., over the old railway bridge. The attached leg irons are replicas. **Bayley's Reward,** Kalgoorlie Rd., is the site of Coolgardie's first gold find. **Coolgardie Cemetery,** Great Eastern Hwy., west of town, has some interesting old graves and headstones, including those of a few Afghan camel drivers.

Learn the history of camels in the goldfields and take a ride yourself at the **Camel Farm,** Great Eastern Highway. Hours are daily 9 a.m.-5 p.m. Admission is $2 (rides are $2.50). For information, phone (090) 26-6159.

Queen Victoria Rock Nature Reserve, Queen Victoria Rock Rd., is a huge rock surrounded by woodlands, with a walking trail across the rock and up to the summit. You might be able to sight the "freckled duck," one of the world's rarest waterfowl, at **Rowles Lagoon,** Bonnie Vale Road. Rock climbing is popular at **Cave Hill Nature Reserve,** Sunday Soak Track. **Burra Rock Nature Reserve,** Burra Rock Rd., offers rock exploration, swimming, and wide views.

Pick up tourist info at the **Coolgardie Tourist Bureau,** 62 Bayley St. (tel. 090-26-6090). Hours are daily 9 a.m.-5 p.m.

The **Denver City Hotel,** Bayley St. (tel. 090-26-6031), and the **Railway Lodge,** Bayley St. (tel. 090-26-6166), two of the beautiful original hotels, offer inexpensive pub rooms. The **Coolgardie Motor Inn,** Great Eastern Hwy. (tel. 090-26-6002), has moderate prices and a swimming pool.

The **YHA Hostel,** 56 Gnarlbine Rd. (tel. 090-26-6051), has dorm beds for $11 per night.

Campsites and on-site vans are available at **Coolgardie Caravan Park,** Bayley St. (tel. 090-26-6009).

The **Coolgardie Motel** has a passable restaurant, but the **Premier Café,** Bayley St., is a step higher. For counter lunches, try the **Denver City Hotel.**

All of the interstate coaches stop in Coolgardie on the way to and from Kalgoorlie. **Bonnie Vale Station,** 12 km away, is a stop for Kalgoorlie-bound trains.

Kambalda

Kambalda, 55 km south of Kalgoorlie, was originally a gold-mining town called Red Hill (1897-1906). Regaining new importance—and a new name—when nickel was discovered in 1966, Kambalda continues to exist as a major mining center of the region. Situated on the shores of saltwater Lake Lefroy, Kambalda is a popular spot for weekend land yachting.

Red Hill Lookout offers vantage points of the town, lake, and surrounding countryside. **John Hill View Point** will give you a vantage point of the mine and slime dump.

Pick up permits to visit the mines at **Kambalda Tourist Bureau,** Irish Mulga Dr., Kambalda West (tel. 090-21-1446). Hours are Mon.-Fri. 9 a.m.-5 p.m.

Norseman

Often called the "eastern gate to the western state," Norseman (pop. 1,900) sits at the western end of the Eyre Highway and is a major junction for travelers heading east across the Nullarbor Plain, south to Esperance (207 km) and the Rainbow Coast, or north to Coolgardie (also 207 km) and on to Perth. Since 1892, the Dundas Goldfields have been yielding gold from their super-rich quartz reef.

CANNING STOCK ROUTE

This old stock route, spanning 1,750 km from Wiluna to Halls Creek in Western Australia, is the harshest, lengthiest, most difficult (and probably most expensive) 4WD journey in Australia.

In the early 1900s pastoralists in the Kimberley region had become desperate for an overland route by which to move their livestock down south to the monied meat-eaters in the goldfields. An outbreak of cattle tick had banned all ship transport around the coast—the southern graziers were taking no chances that it would spread to their land. Another discovery was that the nasty little ticks would simply and conveniently die during a trip through the sizzling desert.

In 1906, after the Kimberley boys pressured the government and put up some of the bucks, Alfred Canning, surveyor extraordinaire, was hired to make a preliminary exploration. His report was favorable—he could sink 54 wells approximately 20 km apart. Canning and his construction party went to work, completing the route between March 1908 and April 1910. The first stock trod by in 1911. In 1958 the route was abandoned with the introduction of road trains. As of 1995, the four-wheelers are still trying to keep on track.

In 1929, a team led by William Albert Snell refurbished the wells up to No. 35 and Alfred Canning (retired by then) finished the job. Fear of a Japanese invasion of Australia's north spurred another refurbishment in 1942—just in case citizens and livestock had to flee the area.

In their prime, the wells each possessed a hand-operated windlass, two buckets, a whip-pole for water-hauling, and a galvanized steel trough for cattle-watering. Unfortunately, since 1958 the wells have been desecrated by termites, rust, and fires; some retain only a bit of wood, ironwork, and the odd bucket.

Warning: This is an extremely arduous journey, requiring major preparations, a top-notch 4WD vehicle, permits from pastoralists, two-way radio transceivors, a *lot* of fuel, and other provisions. There is no help along the way. Travelers—increasingly—die on this journey. It should only be undertaken late April until early October, with June through August being the best months.

The Royal Automobile Club puts out an excellent map and can provide you with information, but even their literature carries red-ink warnings.

A collection of gold-rush tools and other items is on display at the **Historical and Geological Museum,** Battery Road. Hours are Mon.-Fri. 10 a.m.-4 p.m. Admission is $2. For information, phone (090) 39-1593.

Mount Jimberlana, seven km east of town, is an estimated 550 million years old—one of the oldest geological areas in the world. A walking trail to the summit takes about 30 minutes each way and affords great views of the hills, salt lakes, and mine operations. The **Heritage Trail**—dating from the turn-of-the-century—leads through bushland to **Dundas Rocks,** a popular picnic and bushwalk site 24 km south of Norseman.

If you want to try your luck fossicking in the **Western Gemstone Area,** first pick up a permit ($10) at the tourist bureau. The main gemstones to be found are moss agate, moss opalite, chrysophase, and jasper. Or, if you're more inclined toward panning for gold, get a permit for the **Gold Lease.**

Norseman Tourist Bureau is on Roberts St. (tel. 090-39-1071). Hours are daily 9 a.m.-5

p.m. Free conducted tours of the mine workings depart the tourist bureau Mon.-Fri. at 10 a.m. and 1 p.m. Cost is $5.

On Robert St., the **Norseman Hotel** (tel. 090-39-1023) and **Railway Hotel** (tel. 090-39-1115) both offer inexpensive rooms. The **Norseman Eyre Motel,** Robert St. (tel. 090-39-1130), is in the expensive range. Campsites and on-site vans are available at **Gateway Caravan Park** (tel. 090-39-1500), on Prinsep Street.

Goldfields Air Services (tel. 090-93-2116) can put down in Norseman on its Kalgoorlie-to-Esperance service. All of the interstate coaches stop in Norseman on the way to and from Kalgoorlie.

NORTH OF KALGOORLIE

Be prepared for long, lonely stretches with no services or facilities. The road is sealed only up to Leonora, 237 km north of Kalgoorlie, and from Leonora to Leinster (131 km north) and Laverton (124 km northeast). This region of

CANNING STOCK ROUTE

INDIAN OCEAN

KIMBERLEY

TO DARWIN →

HALLS CREEK

TANAMI TRACK

GREAT NORTHERN HWY.

GREAT SANDY DESERT

LAKE GREGORY

PORT HEDLAND

LAKE WAUKARLYCARLY

PERCIVAL LAKES

LAKE DORA

STOCK RTE.

LAKE DISAPPOINTMENT

GIBSON DESERT

PILBARA

NORTHERN HWY.

GREAT

WESTERN

AUSTRALIA

CANNING

GUNBARREL HWY.

LAKE CARNEGIE

0   200 km

MEEKATHARRA

WILUNA

TO PERTH

TO KALGOORLIE

GREAT VICTORIA DESERT

---

once-bustling gold towns harbors few reminders of the glory days (and *far* fewer residents).

Kanowna, 22 km along a dirt road northeast of Kalgoorlie, used to be filled with hotels, churches, and about 12,000 residents, but all that remains is the old railway station.

On the sealed road, **Broad Arrow** has held onto one turn-of-the-century hotel. The 1911 Ora Banda Hotel, along the dirt road west of Broad Arrow, has been restored since its 1960s movie

debut in *The Nickel Queen*. Stone ruins are all that's left of **Comet Vale,** on the highway beyond Lake Goongarrie. **Menzies,** 132 km north of Kalgoorlie, managed to keep a number of buildings, including the Town Hall and Old Railway Station. The **Grand Hotel,** with its large rooms and wide verandas, lives on at **Kookynie,** 25 km along a dirt stretch east of the main road.

Forging northward another 105 km will bring you to **Leonora** (pop. 525) and its twin town

Gwalia. After gold was discovered in 1896, the Sons of Gwalia Mine claimed its fame as the largest underground mine outside the Golden Mile. And who do you suppose the mine's first manager was? Herbert Hoover—future president of the United States. Small world. Though the mine closed in 1963, much of it remains intact, as do many of the original structures. To get a feel for the place, see a historical display at the Gwalia Mine office or walk the one-kilometer-long **Gwalia Heritage Trail.** Present-day Leonora serves as an administrative center for renewed gold, copper, and nickel mining operations.

Turn-of-the-century, gold-boom life was *wild* at **Laverton** (pop. 875), 124 km northeast of Leonora, until the gold (and the town) died out in the early 1900s. The 1970s Poseidon nickel boom—and the huge Windarra Mine—have considerably revived Laverton, often used by visitors as a base from which to explore surrounding ghost towns and gold mines.

North of Leonora, the sealed road ends 131 km away at Leinster, another nickel-producing town. Following the unsurfaced road 166 km northwest will take you to **Wiluna** (a has-been 1930s arsenic-mining community), and then to **Meekatharra** (183 km west), on the Great

Northern Highway between Port Hedland an Perth.

The sealed portion of the **Warburton Community Road** to Ayers Rock (1,033 km north east) ends at Laverton. If you intend to trave this route, make sure you have a well-equippe 4WD or conventional vehicle with good ground clearance (the road is not suitable for caravans or trailers). You will also need permits to enter Aboriginal lands en route (see the special topi "Permits," in the On the Road chapter) and enough fuel for a 600-km stretch. Check on cur rent road conditions at the Laverton Shire Council and notify police of your intended departure and arrival times. Due to intense heat, travel is *not* recommended Nov.-March. Fuel, food, sup plies, and camping facilities are available a **Warburton Roadhouse,** 692 km from Leonora

The road joins 45 km of the Gunbarrel High way near Giles Meteorological Station (230 km northeast of Warburton), crosses the Norther Territory border at Docker River Settlement bringing you to Uluru (Ayers Rock) and Yulara another 233 km east. When you reach the bor der, you'll see the memorial plaque to Harold Lasseter (of Lasseter's Folly fame), who claimed to have found a magnificent gold reef out there and died trying to find it again.

THE NORTH COAST

The northern part of Western Australia has undergone so much expansion that, in 1976, the Brand Highway was opened to smooth the way or travelers who had previously relied on the Midlands Road up to Dongara (80 km longer and with many more stops). Above Geraldton he Brand becomes the North West Coastal Highway, linking with the Great Northern Highway from Port Hedland to Broome and through the Kimberley. Collectively, all of these roadways are still Highway 1, the sealed route that circles Australia.

It's a 1,780-km journey from Perth to Port Hedland, passing through the state's midwest, Gascoyne, and Pilbara regions. The coastal road only really becomes coastal as it nears the Midlands Road junction; until then it runs about 40 km inland. Both the inland and coastal highways are *hot* during summer months.

PERTH TO GERALDTON

The Brand Highway cuts into the Great Northern Highway 55 km northeast of Perth. It's 150 km to the turnoff for Cervantes (pop. 240), a fishing town established in 1962, and the closest town to **Nambung National Park.** A spectacular site within the park is The Pinnacles, calcified spires of widely varying shades, sizes, and shapes, scattered eerily amid 400 hectares of yellow and ochre sand. Some of the long-eroded formations are thought to be 30,000 years old. Several lookouts over the desert and coast can be accessed via a 500-meter walking trail. The best time for Pinnacle viewing is sundown. Day tours depart Cervantes Service Station daily at 1 p.m. For information, phone (096) 52-7041.

On 1 April 1997 all telephone numbers in this section will change. To dial the new number, simply add the last two digits of the existing area code to the old number. As an example, (096) 12-3456 becomes 9612-3456. The new area code will be (08).

For park and Pinnacle information, contact the **Department of Conservation and Land Management** (tel. 096-52-7043).

Warning: Bushwalkers should be wary of **kangaroo ticks**—use the appropriate repellent.

To reach **Jurien,** a tiny rock lobster port on a sheltered bay, follow the side track 50 km north of Cervantes. **Drovers Cave National Park,** six km east of Jurien, has some good bushwalks, but all of the numerous caves have been locked up.

Greenhead, 56 km north of Jurien via the gravel Jurien Road or the sealed Brand Highway, features safe swimming, skin diving, and all kinds of fishing. **Leeman,** a short distance away, is also a relaxed fishing village.

Dongara (pop. 1,155) and neighboring **Port Denison** are holiday resorts and crayfish ports that touch the coast 359 km north of Perth. **Royal Steam Roller Flour Mill,** Walldeck St., is part of a restored village that includes the 1870 Old Dongara Police Station and Tourist Information Centre. Hours are Mon.-Fri. 9 a.m.-5 p.m., Sat.-Sun. 10 a.m.-2 p.m. The 1870 **Russ Cottage,** Port Leander Dr., is furnished with period items. Hours are Sunday and public holidays 2-4 p.m. Admission is $1.

The National Trust has classified a number of stone buildings at **Greenough,** an 1850s wheat-farming hamlet 41 km north of Dongara. The **Pioneer Museum,** Wonga Park, will fill you in on local folklore. Hours are Sat.-Thurs. 10 a.m.-4 p.m.

Midlands Road

The old Midlands Road begins 30 km farther up the Great Northern Highway, past the Brand Highway turnoff. This is well worth the drive in spring when the wildflowers put on a stupendous show.

At **Coorow,** you can detour 12 km west along Greenhead Road to Perth Basin, one of the world's deepest sedimentary basins. **Yarra Yarra Lakes,** between Carnamah and Three Springs, is a salty lake system with some wild color variations (red, green, and blue), plus prolific birdlife. Climb to the top of **Mingenew Hill** for excellent east and west views of the Irwin Valley.

THE NORTH COAST AND
THE GREAT NORTHERN HIGHWAY

BROOME

TO THE KIMBERLEY

SANDFIRE
ROADHOUSE

GREAT

INDIAN OCEAN

DAMPIER ARCHIPELAGO

PORT HEDLAND

GOLDSWORTHY

KARRATHA
DAMPIER
POINT SAMSON
WICKHAM
WHIM CREEK

MARBLE BAR

ROEBOURNE

MOUNT HERBERT
PYTHON POOL

NORTH WEST CAPE
VLAMING HEAD

RED HILL

MILLSTREAM-
CHICHESTER
NATIONAL PARK

THE PILBARA

EXMOUTH

MOUNT BROCKMAN

WITTENOOM

CAPE RANGE
NATIONAL PARK

WITTENOOM GORGE

NINGALOO

TOM PRICE

KARIJINI (HAMERSLEY RANGE)
NATIONAL PARK

MOUNT MEHARRY

CORAL BAY

PARABURDOO

NEWMAN

TROPIC OF CAPRICORN

MINILYA ROADHOUSE

ROCKY POOL

MOUNT AUGUSTUS

GASCOYNE JUNCTION

MT. AUGUSTUS
NATIONAL PARK

CARNARVON

GASCOYNE RIVER

SHARK BAY

DENHAM SOUND

MONKEY MIA

HAMELIN POOL

DENHAM
NANGA

OVERLANDER ROADHOUSE

HAMELIN

MEEKATHARRA

GANTHEAUME BAY

KALBARRI
NATIONAL PARK

CUE

TO THE GOLDFIELDS

SANDSTONE

KALBARRI

PORT GREGORY

MOUNT MAGNET

HORROCKS

NORTHAMPTON

MULLEWA

GERALDTON

DONGARA

THREE SPRINGS

CARNAMAH

GREENHEAD

YARRA YARRA LAKES

WUBIN

JURIEN

CERVANTES

NAMBUNG NATIONAL PARK
(AND THE PINNACLES)

NEW NORCIA

INDIAN OCEAN

BRAND HWY

PERTH

0   150 km

(previous page) embracing boabs
(above) Masonic Lodge, built 1909, Murchison District

Wildflower Way

One more alternate route to Geraldton is Wildflower Way, which runs parallel to the Midlands Road beginning at Wubin, off the Great Northern Highway, and continuing 222 km to Mullewa, where you hook up to Highway 123 west. **Mullewa** (pop. 918), a sheep and wheat farming township, features a number of historical and natural sights. It should go without saying that Wildflower Way is a springtime bloom-a-thon that will knock your petals off.

GERALDTON

Established in 1849 as a major seaport for the Murchison lead mines (and later the Murchison Goldfields), Geraldton (pop. 20,895) is the major town of WA's midwest region. Situated 424 km north of Perth, it is a leading winter holiday resort renowned for its crayfish and rock lobster industry.

Sights

View 17th- and 18th-century Dutch shipwreck artifacts at **Geraldton Museum,** Marine Terrace. Other displays relate to the district's cultural and natural heritage. Hours are Mon.-Sat. 10 a.m.-5 p.m., Sunday 1-5 p.m., closed Christmas Day and Good Friday. For information, phone (099) 21-5080.

Monsignor John Hawes, both a priest and architect, was responsible for the California mission-style **St. Francis Xavier Cathedral,** Cathedral Avenue. Building commenced in 1916 but was not completed until 1938.

The Hermitage, Cathedral Ave., was built to be Monsignor John Hawes's retirement home. Hours are by appointment only. For information, phone (099) 21-3999.

The Geraldton Historical Society headquarters is at the **Lighthouse Keeper's Cottage,** Point Moore Road. In continuous operation since 1878, the 35-meter-high lighthouse is banded in red and white stripes. Hours are Thursday 10 a.m.-4 p.m. For information, phone (099) 21-3999.

Geraldton Art Gallery, corner Durlacher St. and Chapman Rd., exhibits work by regional artists. Hours are Mon.-Sat. 10 a.m.-5 p.m., Sunday 1:30-4:30 p.m., closed Christmas Day and Good Friday. For information, phone (099) 21-3999.

Mount Tarcoola, Sydney St., and **Separation Point Lookout,** Willcock Dr., both offer expansive views.

Most of the local beaches offer safe swimming. Lifeguards patrol **Mahomets Beach** on summer weekends.

Accommodations

Marine Terrace is the main drag for oldie-but-goodie seaside guesthouses with inexpensive lodging. Suggestions: **Sun City Guesthouse,** 184 Marine Terrace (tel. 099-21-2205), and **Grantown Guesthouse,** 172 Marine Terrace (tel. 099-21-3275).

The **Mariner Motor Hotel,** 298 Chapman Rd. (tel. 099-21-2544), offers inexpensive rooms. **Geraldton's Ocean West,** corner Hadda Way and Willcock Dr., Mahomets Beach (tel. 099-21-1047), has moderately priced, self-contained cottages with TVs and cooking facilities. Motels in the same price range include **Hacienda Motel,** Durlacher St. (tel. 099-21-2155), and **Club Sun City Resort,** 137 Cathedral Ave. (tel. 099-21-6111). **Hospitality Inn,** 169 Cathedral Ave. (tel. 099-21-1422), and **Quality Inn,** Brand Hwy. (tel. 099-21-2455), are the two chain representatives with the representative high rates.

The **YHA Peninsula Backpackers Hostel,** 311 Marine Terrace (tel. 099-21-4770), has eight rooms for 50 people. Dorm beds run $12 per night. More $12 beds are available at **Batavia Backpackers,** corner of Chapman Rd. and Bayly St. (tel. 099-64-3001).

Campsites and on-site vans are available at: **Separation Point Caravan Park,** corner Portway and Separation Way (tel. 099-21-2763); **Sun City Caravan Park,** Bosley St., Sunset Beach (tel. 099-38-1655); and **Belair Gardens Caravan Park,** Willcock Dr., Point Moore (tel. 099-21-1997).

Food

Marine Terrace is also the location for takeaways, cafes, pubs, cake shops, pizza places, and Chinese restaurants. Geraldton, in fact, ranks high on the list of fast-food heavens. Put together a good international meal at the **Cuisine Connection** food hall, on Durlacher Street—Australia, Thailand, Italy, China, and India are all well represented. The **Boatshed,** on Marine Terrace, has excellent seafood, albeit at higher prices.

Transportation, Services, and Information

Both **Ansett** (tel. 13-1300 toll-free) and **Skywest** (book through Ansett) fly between Perth and Geraldton ($160). **Western Airlines** (tel. 09-277-4022) wings a Perth-Geraldton-Kalbarri-Useless Loop-Denham route three times a week ($140).

Westrail (tel. 09-326-2813 or 13-2232 toll-free) and **Greyhound Pioneer Australia** (tel. 13-2030 toll-free) both provide regular coach service to and from Perth. Fare is in the $50 range. Northbound buses travel Highway 1 en route to Broome and Darwin. The coach terminal is in the same building as the tourist bureau.

A **local bus** provides service to neighboring communities. For information, phone (099) 21-1034.

Avis, Budget, and Hertz have Geraldton agencies, but the best rates (from $35 per day) are at **Batavia Coast Hire Cars,** 25 Marine Terrace (tel. 099-21-2767). Hire bicycles for $10 per day from **Wheel Nuts Bicycle Hire,** Chapman Rd. (tel. 099-21-6600).

Batavia Tours (tel. 099-23-1006) operates day trips to Monkey Mia and other nearby areas.

The **Geraldton Tourist Bureau,** Chapman Rd. (in the Bill Sewell Community Recreation Centre), provides local and statewide information, as well as coach, tour, and accommodations bookings. Hours are daily 9 a.m.-5 p.m., closed Christmas Day and Good Friday. For information, phone (099) 21-3999.

FARTHER NORTH

Beyond Geraldton

Leaving Geraldton, the Brand Highway metamorphoses into the North West Coastal Highway. **Northampton** (pop. 750), 50 km north, was a favorite Aboriginal site until lead and copper mines were established in the 1840s. Today the community prospers from the surrounding farmlands. Constructed of local sandstone, **Chiverton House Folk Museum** (1868-75), North West Coastal Hwy., houses a collection of early machinery and memorabilia. Hours are Thurs.-Sun. 10 a.m.-noon and 2-4 p.m. For information, phone (099) 34-1215.

Horrocks Beach, 22 km west of Northampton, features a reef surrounding its five-km swimming beach, as well as good fishing (kingfish, whiting, herring, skippy, tailor, and rock lobster). The **Bowes River** turnoff, four km south of Horrocks, is the location for a number of ancient Aboriginal cave paintings. Bowes River is another jumpin' fishing spot.

Port Gregory, 43 km northwest of Northampton, is the midwest coast's oldest port, and nearby **Lynton** is a former convict-labor hiring depot. Though the town is defunct, many of the old ruins can still be seen.

From Lynton, follow Yerina Springs Rd. north, then turn east on Ogilvie West Rd. to **Hutt River Province,** where self-appointed "Prince Leonard" is ruler. Having seceded from the Australian Commonwealth in 1970, Prince Leonard's kingdom rakes in revenue off special stamps, money, souvenir items, tearooms, a swimming pool, and other tourist snares.

Kalbarri

Situated where the Murchison River meets the Indian Ocean, Kalbarri (pop. 820) is a holiday resort famous for its gorgeous gorges and terrific fishing. This is also the area where the Dutch ship *Zuytdorp* was wrecked, *and* the long-ago home of a 400-million-year-old, two-meter-long scorpion known as the eurypterid.

Kalbarri National Park (186,096 hectares) features awesome sandstone cliffs and banded-in-red gorge walls (formed 400-500 million years ago). The fossil tracks of prevertebrate marine creatures have been located in the sandstone. The park also harbors a wide variety of wildlife and flora; try to come during the spring wildflower season. **Ross Graham** and **Hawk's Head** lookouts provide dynamic gorge views. A 35-km scenic drive leads to **The Loop** and **Z Bend,** two other spectacular viewing perches. Park facilities include short and long walking trails as well as picnic sites. Carry your own drinking water. For information, phone (099) 37-1140.

Jake's Corner, a few kilometers south of Kalbarri, has some of WA's best surfing breaks. **Red Bluff,** just south, is where you can see tracks left by the ancient eurypterid (possibly the first creature to have walked on land) and explore frozen, tearlike threads of rock and other intriguing formations (also thought to be 400 million years old).

Rainbow Jungle, Red Bluff Rd., is lush with palms, ferns, tropical plants, rare and tropical birds, and fish. Open Tues.-Sun. 10 a.m.-5 p.m. Admission is $4. For information, phone (099) 37-1248. **Fantasyland,** Grey St., combines collections of dolls, marinelife, fossils, and gemstones. Every morning at 8:45 a.m., the proprietor feeds pelicans on the foreshore opposite. Hours are Sun.-Fri. 9 a.m.-noon and 1:30-5 p.m., Saturday 9 a.m.-noon. Admission is $3.50. For information, phone (099) 37-1062.

Sailboats, canoes, surf cats, and pedal boats can be hired at **Kalbarri Boat Hire** (tel. 099-37-1245), on the foreshore across from Murchison Caravan Park. **Kalbarri Sports and Dive,** Grey St. (tel. 099-37-1126), hires diving equipment and offers instruction.

Av-er-est, Mortimer St. (tel. 099-37-1101), offers inexpensive weekly rates on self-contained holiday units with TVs and cooking facilities. Holiday units in the moderate range include **Kalbarri Reef Villas,** Coles St. (tel. 099-37-1165), and **Sunsea Villas,** Grey St. (tel. 099-37-1187). Campsites and on-site vans are rented at **Kalbarri Tudor Caravan Park,** Porter St. (tel. 099-37-1077); **Murchison Caravan Park,** Grey St. (tel. 099-37-1005); and **Red Bluff Caravan Park,** Red Bluff (tel. 099-37-1080).

Western Airlines (tel. 09-277-4022) provides service between Kalbarri and Perth three times

a week ($155). **Westrail** (tel. 09-326-2813 or 13-2232 toll-free) operates bus service three times a week, in each direction ($60). A shuttle connects with **Greyhound Pioneer Australia** (tel. 13-2030 toll-free) on its thrice-weekly runs along the North West Coastal Highway.

Rent bicycles at **Murchison Cycle Hire,** Porter St. (tel. 099-37-1105), for about $10 per day. For local tours (including a cruise up the Murchison River on the *River Queen*) contact **Kalbarri Travel Service,** Grey St. (tel. 099-37-1104).

AROUND SHARK BAY

The Overlander Roadhouse (179 km north of Kalbarri) marks the turnoff from the North West Coastal Highway to Shark Bay, site of the first European landing on Australian soil (Dutchman Dirk Hartog in 1616).

Stromatolites, among the world's oldest living fossils, can be seen in **Hamelin Bay's** clear, shallow waters. **Shell Beach,** near Nanga via Denham Rd., is created from billions of minute shells packed about 20 meters deep. Actual shell "blocks" (compacted by nature) have been constructed by locals along the Shark Bay foreshore. **Freshwater Camp,** Nanga's pioneer homestead, features the usual relics.

DOLPHIN ETIQUETTE

Please—Monkey Mia is *not* a dolphin Disneyland. These babies are not trained for your pleasure. When you're wading with the dolphins observe the following rules:

• wade about knee-deep

• wait until the dolphins approach you

• never touch, or put anything into, the blowhole

• don't touch the head, dorsal fin, or tail (pat gently along the side of the body)

• do not scare the dolphins with loud noises

• don't try to swim with the dolphins, and don't reach over them for any reason

• check with rangers before feeding—the dolphins are fussy about their food

• If a dolphin gives you a fish, don't give it back. Accept it and say "thank you."

one of the
untrained
dolphins at
Monkey Mia

MARK MORRIS

One-time pearling port **Denham,** 48 km northwest of Nanga, sits on the west side of Peron Peninsula (just above the 26th parallel) and is Australia's westernmost town. Sightseeing **cruises** and fishing trips depart Denham Jetty. For cruise bookings and information on other local tours, contact **Shark Bay Tourist Information Centre,** 83 Knight St. (tel. 099-48-1253). Hire **bicycles** ($10 per day) at **Shark Bay Recreation Centre** (tel. 099-48-1218).

Well-posted signs lead to **Monkey Mia,** one of the country's—and the world's—most unusual natural attractions, 25 km northeast of Denham. Since 1964, when a woman from one of the area's fishing camps began the practice, dolphins have regularly come up to these shores to be hand-fed by rangers and throngs of visitors. These sweet mammals will accept only whole fish, not any that have been gutted or gilled. Obey rangers' instructions on feeding and petting. There is no set feeding time—the dolphins are free to come and go as they please. An information center provides educational exhibits and videos on dolphin behavior. Fresh fish are sold for your feeding pleasure. Hours are daily 8:30 a.m.-4:30 p.m. Admission is $3. For information, phone (099) 48-1366.

Bay Lodge, 109 Knight Terrace, Denham (tel. 099-48-1278), is a YHA associate. Backpacker accommodations run $12 per night, while self-contained holiday units are in the moderate range. Other moderately priced, self-contained units are **Denham Villas,** 4 Durlacher St. (tel. 099-48-1264), and **Hartog Holiday Villas,** Denham-Hamelin Rd. (tel. 099-48-1323). **Heritage Resort Hotel,** Knight Terrace (tel. 099-48-1133), with deluxe facilities, is the expensive choice. **Shark Bay Accommodation Service** (tel. 099-48-1323) manages a variety of holiday flats and cottages.

Campsites and on-site vans are available at **Denham Seaside Caravan Park,** Knight Terrace (tel. 099-48-1242); **Shark Bay Caravan Park,** Spaven Way, off Durlacher St. (tel. 099-48-1387); **Blue Dolphin Caravan Park,** Hamelin Rd. (tel. 099-48-1385); and **Monkey Mia Dolphin Resort** (tel. 099-48-1320).

Local restaurants offer the usual counter meal and takeaway fare. The **Old Pearler Restaurant,** Knight Terrace, Denham (tel. 099-48-1373), is built out of shell blocks. Food is on the upmarket side and reservations are recommended. The **Shark Bay Hotel** is your counter-meal stop.

Western Airlines (tel. 09-277-4022) operates a Perth-Denham service three times a week. Fare is $190 one-way.

Greyhound Pioneer Australia (tel. 13-2030 toll-free) will drop you at the Overlander three times a week ($125); from there, a Denham Tourist Centre shuttle will transport you to to Denham and Shark Bay ($25).

Hired cars cost about $80 per day from **Budget** (tel. 099-48-1247) and **Shark Bay Hire Cars** (tel. 099-48-1203), both in Denham.

A local bus departs Denham for daily forays to Monkey Mia. Check with the tourist office for fares and schedules.

Dolphin Express Hovercraft (tel. 099-41-1146) will whisk you from Carnarvon to Monkey Mia—$90 round-trip for the 90-minute journey, and you're almost sure to see dolphins en route.

CARNARVON

Positioned at the mouth of the Gascoyne River, Carnarvon (pop. 5,050) is known as the tropical gateway to the north. This seaside commercial center is famed for its tropical fruit plantations (particularly bananas) and its mile-long jetty, beloved by fishers. This was also the spot about which Capt. Dirk Hartog and various other explorers said such lousy things, but post-jetty, big-banana Carnarvon has redeemed itself. After all, the place can't be all bad if the fish come up to the foreshore to be hand-fed.

Carnarvon Museum, Robinson St., features historic displays and a shell collection. Hours are Mon.-Fri. 9 a.m.-5 p.m., Sat.-Sun. 9 a.m.-noon and 2-5 p.m. For information, phone (099) 41-1146. Other local relics—including a whale bone arch—can be seen at **Pioneer Park,** Olivia Terrace.

Ponder trial plantings of tropical fruits and winter veggies at **Gascoyne Research Station,** South River Rd., North Carnarvon. Hours are Mon.-Fri. 8 a.m.-5 p.m. For information, phone (099) 41-8103.

Check with the Tourist Bureau for directions to the former **NASA Tracking Station** (closed in 1975).

Pelican Point is a good swimming and fishing site, just five kilometers from town. Other top fishing spots include Dwyer's Leap and Prawn Jetty Beach.

Practicalities

Old-ish, cheap pub-hotels are: Gascoyne Hotel, Olivia Terrace (tel. 099-41-1412); Port Hotel, Robinson St. (tel. 099-41-1704); and the Carnarvon Hotel, Olivia Terrace (tel. 099-41-1181). The Outcamp, 16 Olivia Terrace (tel. 099-41-2421), is a wonderful B&B that doesn't cost much more than the old pubs.

Both Carnarvon Close, 96 Robinson St. (tel. 099-41-1317), and Carnarvon Beach Holiday Resort, Pelican Point Rd. (tel. 099-41-2226), offer moderately priced, self-contained holiday units.

The YHA Backpackers Paradise, Robinson St. (tel. 099-41-2966), has beds for $12 per night—and only two beds per room! Weekly rates are an even bigger bargain. Carnarvon Backpacker's, 46 Olivia Terrace (tel. 099-41-1095), has communal facilities, is centrally located, and also charges $12 per night.

Among the numerous caravan parks offering campsites and on-site vans are Plantation Caravan Park, Robinson St. (tel. 099-41-8100); Carnarvon Caravan Park, Robinson St. (tel. 099-41-8101); and Startrek Caravan Park, North West Coastal Hwy. (tel. 099-41-8153).

The Gascoyne, Port, and Carnarvon Hotels all have similar counter meals at reasonable prices. Robinson Street is the food strip: fish and chips, pizza, and the ubiquitous coffee lounge.

Tel-O-Mac, 280 Robinson St. (tel. 090-41-1873), sells fishing, camping, and diving gear. Rosco's Sports Shop, 11 Robinson St. (tel. 090-41-1385), rents diving equipment.

For local information, including tours and fishing charters, contact Carnarvon District Tourist Bureau, 6 Robinson St. (tel. 099-41-1146). Hours are daily 9 a.m.-5 p.m.

Daily Perth-Carnarvon flights are operated by Ansett (tel. 13-1300 toll free)—about $250 one-way from Perth, but many special deals are available. Carnarvon is a regular stop on the north-south Greyhound Pioneer Australia route (tel. 13-2030 toll-free), and is also served by Westliner (tel. 09-250-3318). Fare is around $100.

Rent bicycles from Rosco's Sports Shop for about $9 per day.

VICINITY OF CARNARVON

Oyster-picking and crayfishing are specialties at the Blowholes, 70 km north of Carnarvon, via Pt. Quobba Road. Salt headed for Japan is loaded at Cave Cuvier, a deep natural port some 30 km north of the Blowholes.

Rocky Pool is a deep, freshwater swimming pool on Gascoyne Junction Rd., 55 km inland. Gascoyne Junction, another 122 km east, is a gateway to the rugged Kennedy Range, full of wildlife, Aboriginal caves, rock paintings, and semiprecious gemstones. Gascoyne Junction Hotel, constructed of corrugated iron, is a famous old bush pub.

Mount Augustus, a 289-km gravel drive from Gascoyne Junction, is the world's largest monocline, measuring 717 meters above the surrounding plain (1,105 meters above sea level), and it remains one of Australia's best-kept secrets. Mount Augustus National Park, only just proclaimed in 1989, is also noted for Aboriginal rock paintings and unusual flora and fauna. Coach tours and scenic flights operate out of Carnarvon. Mount Augustus Station Tourist Resort (tel. 099-43-0527), at the foot of the rock, offers campsites and moderately priced units.

CONTINUING NORTH

The Ningaloo Reef

You'll be able to view everything from humpback whales to egg-laying turtles around this mini-Great Barrier Reef, one of the world's major reef systems. Running 260 kilometers along the North West Cape from Exmouth to Amherst Point, Ningaloo Reef—far more accessible than Queensland's Great Barrier—is fast becoming a snorkeling, scuba diving, fishing, and boat-trip mecca. Get there before the developers do!

Also, environmentalists are concerned about this region, now that the North West Cape region is heavy into offshore drilling. State legislation in 1994 decreed drilling in the fragile marine park to be off-limits, but since when does local government usurp the power of oil interests?

The turnoff from North West Coastal Highway is just past the Minilya Roadhouse, 142 km north of Carnarvon.

Coral Bay, 78 km from the roadhouse (you'll cross the Tropic of Capricorn about midway), is the main entry point to **Ningaloo Marine Park,** just meters offshore. The reef covers more than 5,000 square kilometers of the Indian Ocean, is made up of almost 200 types of coral, and shelters incredibly diverse marinelife—from teensy tropical fish to scary-looking whale sharks—in its crystal waters. Five shipwrecks around Ningaloo Station provide additional fun for divers. Sign up for a tour aboard the *Sub-Sea Explorer Coral Viewer* (tel. 099-42-5955), a semisubmersible viewing craft, or contact **Bay View Caravan Park** (tel. 099-42-5932) for a glass-bottomed boat cruise. **Coral Dive** (tel. 099-42-5940) runs a full program of diving courses and rents necessary equipment. For game and deep-sea fishing charters, contact **Coral Cruiser** (tel. 099-42-5900) or **Norstar** (tel. 099-42-5940).

At Coral Bay, **Bayview Holiday Village Caravan Park** (tel. 099-42-5932) offers campsites, cabins, chalets, and on-site vans. Rates run from inexpensive to moderate. Self-contained holiday units are in the expensive bracket at **Coral Bay Lodge** (tel. 099-42-5932), but facilities include tennis courts and hired boats.

You'll need a 4WD to access most of **Cape Range National Park** and its 50,831 hectares of coastal scenery, limestone rocks, and gorges. Marked bushwalking trails lead to some of the gorges and lookout points. **Lightfoot Heritage Trail** is a seven-km walk through rugged limestone formations. First-come, first-served campsites are available at selected locations. Come April-Oct. for best weather. For information, phone (099) 49-1676.

Exmouth

Exmouth (pop. 2,590), at the tip of the peninsula and 155 km north of Coral Bay, is also popular for fishing, diving, and other beach activities. The town was founded, however, as late as the 1960s to service and house personnel at the joint U.S./Australian naval base at the top of the North West Cape. Used as an Allied base known as "Potshot" during WW II, the facility has ostensibly been used to maintain interna-

tional contact with U.S. Navy vessels (including submarines) via 13 very low frequency radio transmitters. If the oil tycoons have their way, proceeding with offshore drilling around Ningaloo Marine Park, Exmouth may soon become their "company town."

Take steep **Lighthouse Drive** for panoramic views of the reef, cape, and communication towers.

Norcape Lodge Resort, Truscott Crescent (tel. 099-49-1334), offers lodge accommodations, family apartments, motel rooms, and campsites in every price range. For other campsites and on-site vans, contact: **Exmouth Cape Tourist Village,** corner Truscott Crescent and Murat Rd. (tel. 099-49-1101); **Lighthouse Caravan Park,** Vlaming Head (tel. 099-49-1478); or **Exmouth Accommodation and Caravan Park,** Yardie Creek Homestead (tel. 099-49-1389).

For reef dives and equipment hire, contact **Q Dive Exmouth Sales Hire and Service** (tel. 099-49-1662) or **Neilsen Diving** (tel. 099-49-1201).

Collect tourist information and book reef or fishing tours at **Exmouth Tourist Bureau,** Thew St. (tel. 099-49-1176). Hours are daily 9 a.m.-5 p.m.

Ansett (tel. 13-1300 toll-free) flies every day except Saturday between Perth and Exmouth ($325).

Several-times-weekly Perth-Exmouth bus service is provided by **Greyhound Pioneer Australia** (tel. 13-2030 toll-free) and **Westliner** (tel. 09-250-3318). Fare is around $150.

Avis (tel. 099-49-1014) and **Budget** (tel. 099-49-1052) rent cars for about $65 per day. Hire **bicycles** at Norcape Lodge (tel. 099-49-1334) or Exmouth Squash Centre (tel. 099-49-1149). Rates are $9 per day.

THE PILBARA COAST

The coastal portion of the Pilbara region is a cluster of early pioneering towns that are getting fat off their own natural resources and the rich inland mines. The Burup Peninsula area harbors some 10,000 ancient Aboriginal petroglyphs, most depicting the wildlife of the time.

Karratha (pop. 8,400), on Nickol Bay about 530 km northeast of Minilya Roadhouse, was established mainly because of the Hamersley Iron Project. Additional growth can be attributed to the Woodside Petroleum Project, which has developed a gigantic natural gas reserve on the North West Shelf. The **Woodside LNG Visitors' Centre** (tel. 091-83-8100) will acquaint you with the project—at least one side of it. Hours are Mon.-Fri. 9 a.m.-4:30 p.m. during winter months.

The 3.5-km **Jaburara Heritage Trail,** beginning at the water tanks, will lead you to Aboriginal carvings, grinding stones, shellfish middens, and taboo spiritual sites.

Up the road, **Dampier** (pop. 2,500) was built in the 1960s to serve as port facility for Hamersley Iron. The **Dampier Archipelago,** which the town faces, has a more exciting history of shipwrecks, whaling, and pearling. Boating and fishing these waters (with reefs containing more than 200 species of living coral) are primary pastimes.

Roebourne (pop. 1,700), 32 km southeast of Karratha, is known as "Gateway to the Pilbara." Established in 1864 along with the gold and copper mines, Roebourne is the oldest town in the northwest, as evidenced by its many remaining early stone buildings.

Aiming toward Cape Lambert, **Cossack,** the northwest's first port, once known as Tien Tsin Harbour, also has preserved its beautiful stone buildings. Nearby, **Wickham** is another iron ore company town. **Point Samson,** though modernized, is still a lovely little fishing village.

Accommodations in this area are on the expensive side. **King Bay Holiday Village,** the Esplanade, Dampier (tel. 091-83-1440), a YHA associate, is still in the moderate-expensive range. **Victoria Hotel,** Roe St., Roebourne (tel. 091-82-1001), has moderately priced pub rooms, and the least expensive motel is **Samson Accommodation,** Samson Rd., Point Samson (tel. 091-87-1052). Campsites and on-site vans, probably your best bet, are available at **Karratha Caravan Park,** Mooligum Rd., Karratha (tel. 091-85-1012); **Harding River Caravan Park,** De Grey St., Roebourne (tel. 091-82-1063); and **Solveig Caravan Park,** Samson Rd., Point Samson (tel. 091-87-1414).

Forget the shopping center food and go to Point Samson for fresh fish and chips and other seafood. **Moby's Kitchen** specializes in fresh local seafood in a garden setting overlooking the ocean, plus offers takeaways.

For Roebourne area tourist information, contact **Karratha and Districts Tourist Office,** Karratha Rd. (tel. 091-44-4600); **Dampier Community Association,** the Esplanade, in King Bay Holiday Village (tel. 091-83-1440); or **Roebourne Tourist Bureau,** Roe St., Roebourne (tel. 091-82-1060).

Ansett (tel. 13-1300 toll-free) flies daily to Karratha from Perth. For bus info, contact **Greyhound Pioneer Australia** (tel. 13-2030 toll-free) or **Westliner** (tel. 09-250-3318). Fare is about $120 from Perth.

Vicinity of Roebourne

Traveling 60 km inland on the Wittenoom Road will bring you to **Python Pool,** a former oasis for Afghan camel drivers *and* for the area's many pythons.

Millstream-Chichester National Park (199,710 hectares), 60 km farther, is an odd contrast to its semiarid surroundings, with natural springs, permanent river pools, lily ponds, and groves of date palms (thought to have been brought by the camel drivers). Carry your own food and water, and be prepared for heavy rain and rough roads. Camping is allowed in designated facilities. For information, phone (091) 84-5144.

Back on the North West Coastal Highway, 78 km east of Roebourne, the 1887 **Whim Creek Hotel** was a rowdy outback pub, built to serve the Whim Well Copper Mine. Historic photos are on display and today's brew is on tap.

Port Hedland

Established originally as a service center for the surrounding cattle stations, Port Hedland (pop. 11,200), 1,762 km from Perth, is now the major deepwater port for the megabuck Pilbara iron ore industry—visited by some of the world's biggest ships. By tonnage, it is Australia's biggest port. The entire town and **South Hedland,** its satellite, live and breathe for those rich inland mines. And, as if those miners aren't salty enough, the real stuff is produced a few kilometers away where huge salt dunes encrust the landscape.

Pretty Pool, behind Cooke Point Caravan Park, is a favorite spot for fishing and shell collecting. Wear sturdy shoes if you want to walk on the reef at low tide—these waters are full of venomous stonefish.

For the most part, Port Hedland accommodations are comparatively high in price. **Pier Hotel,** the Esplanade (tel. 091-73-1488), in the upper-moderate range, is the best deal, and next best is **The Esplanade,** corner of Anderson St. (tel. 091-73-1798).

Port Hedland Backpackers Hostel, 20 Richardson St. (tel. 091-73-2198), offers dorm beds for $12 per night.

Campsites and on-site vans are available at **South Hedland Caravan Park,** Hamilton Rd., South Hedland (tel. 091-72-1197); **Dixon's Port Hedland Caravan Park,** opposite the airport (tel. 091-72-2525); and **Cooke Point Ocean Beach Caravan Park,** Athol St. (tel. 091-73-1271).

Food is the usual coffee lounge, pub, and supermarket put-togethers. The **Hedland Hotel,** corner Lukis and McGregor, does the best counter meals. The **Coral Trout** has excellent fish in both its restaurant and takeaway section.

For local information and tour bookings, contact **Port Hedland Tourist Centre,** 13 Wedge St. (tel. 091-73-1711). Hours are daily 9 a.m.-5 p.m.

Port Hedland Airport is an international gateway. **Garuda** provides service between Port Hedland and Bali.

Ansett (tel. 13-1300 toll-free) operates daily flights to Port Hedland from Perth ($375). Frequent flights serve Broome, Derby, and Darwin. **Greyhound Pioneer Australia** (tel. 13-2030 toll-free) and **Westliner** (tel. 09-250-3318) make regular runs between Perth and Port Hedland ($125); to Broome ($58); and to Darwin ($185).

Avis, Budget, and **Hertz** have agencies at Port Hedland Airport, and a taxi into town runs about $15. **Hedland Bus Lines** (tel. 091-72-1394) operates Mon.-Sat. between Port Hedland and South Hedland.

The Backpackers Hostel has **bicycles** for hire.

THE GREAT NORTHERN HIGHWAY

Though the coastal route to Port Hedland is more interesting, the inland Great Northern Highway is actually more direct. From Perth, the highway travels northeast through the midwest and Pilbara regions, veers coastward at Newman, meeting up with the North West Coastal Highway 42 km south of Port Hedland.

Perth to the Pilbara

Up the highway, 132 km northeast of Perth, **New Norcia** is a strange contrast to other country towns. Founded in 1846 by Benedictine monks who came to inflict their gospel on the Aborigines, the Spanish village-esque monastic community consists of the monastery, church, old mill, jail, hotel, and the original boarding schools (now used as a Catholic college). The Benedictine monks still live and work there, much as they used to. The **Museum and Art Gallery** relates the town's history and also houses a **Tourist Information Centre.** Hours are daily 10 a.m.-4:30 p.m., closed Christmas Day and Good Friday. For information, phone (096) 54-8056.

Mount Magnet, Cue, and **Meekatharra**—560, 640, and 760 kilometers respectively from Perth—are old Murchison River goldfields. Gold is still being mined at Mount Magnet. Nearby **ghost towns** include Austin (20 km south of Cue), Cuddingwarra (10 km west), Pinnacles (24 km east), Reedys (60 km northeast), and Tuckanarra (40 km north).

Prospecting for gold is still popular at **Sandstone,** 158 km east of Mount Magnet, which is also surrounded by a myriad of abandoned mining settlements. From Meekatharra, it's 183 km of unsealed road to Wiluna where the road turns south to Kalgoorlie, 534 km away (with the 166-km Wiluna-Leinster portion unsealed).

The Pilbara

This region encompasses 510,335 square km of isolated territory, rugged ranges, deep gorges, gigantic mining operations, company towns, and enormous wealth. Come see men and their ultra-big monsters rip the earth apart and extract its riches, then cart it off to Port Hedland for worldwide shipment.

More than 100,000 tons of iron ore are produced daily at **Newman,** 422 km north of Meekatharra, then shipped via private railway to Port Hedland and the big blue yonder. **Mount Newman Mining Company** operates free tours of its Mount Whaleback Mine (the world's largest open-cut mine). Tours depart Mon.-Fri., except public holidays, at 8:30 a.m. and 1:30 p.m. For information and bookings, phone (091) 75-1511.

Karijini National Park (formerly Hamersley Range National Park) is reached via unsealed road off the Great Northern Highway, 180 km west of Newman. The 617,606-hectare park encompasses spectacular gorges, stony watercourses, and permanent pools, as well as Mount Meharry (1,245 meters), Western Australia's highest mountain. Campsites with limited facilities are available. For information, phone (091) 89-8157.

I'll tell you the truth: I have not been to Wittenoom and I am *not* going—ever. And I'm not going to advise anyone else to go, either. Yes, I *know* it is the heart of the Pilbara, and that it sits at the mouth of the breathtaking Wittenoom Gorge. However, in this instance, the word "breathtaking" is given a whole new meaning: asbestos. Wittenoom mined blue asbestos 1937-66, when the mine closed and the population dropped from 1,500 down to 60. The fact is, microscopic asbestos fibers are still present in the Wittenoom tailings dumps and in the landfill used in and about town, and the place continues to be a health risk. (An aside: A friend of mine who previously was unable to conceive immediately hatched twins after a visit to Wittenoom—and she was traveling *alone*.)

Tom Price, WA's highest town, at 747 meters, and **Paraburdoo,** on the edge of the Hamersley Range, are two other company towns south of Wittenoom that rail their ore production over to Dampier. Continuing along the Wittenoom Road (Highway 136) will take you to the North West Coastal Highway.

Another off-the-beaten path from Newman is along unsealed Highway 138. **Marble Bar** (pop. 357), 306 km north, is reputedly Australia's hottest place. It was hot gold-wise, too, with more than two million ounces produced since an 1891 discovery. The town was named for the Marble Bar, Australia's only jasper bar, easiest seen where it crosses the Coongan River, 1 km west of town. You're not allowed to chip at it, but you can get a sample at the jasper deposit on the road to Comet Mine. The **Comet Mine,** 10 km south of town, is still operating and features a souvenir shop with beautiful rocks, including the regional Pilbara jade. This whole area offers superb fossicking.

Goldsworthy, almost at the coast, was the Pilbara's first iron ore town, and it thrived until mining shifted eastward to **Shay Gap.** Both towns took the brunt of Cyclone Enid when it hit in 1980.

As the Great Northern Highway merges with the North West Coastal Highway, south of Port Hedland, it remains the Great Northern Highway throughout the Kimberley region and almost to the Northern Territory border. It's 610 km from Port Hedland up to Broome. **Eighty Mile Beach** and several roadhouses are the diversions along the way.

THE KIMBERLEY

This is it, my nouveau-pioneer readers—the last outpost, the frontier for which Daniel Boone would give the coonskin off his cap for the chance to explore. Even with phones, faxes, and the sealed highway, this 350,000-square-km region is remote and rugged, and *was* sparsely traveled until it hit the cover of *National Geo-*

graphic and prime-timed its way onto the "must-be-seen" travel circuit.

Though an 1885 gold find at Hall's Gap provided the first lure to this isolated area, it was soon supplanted by cattle ranching, and—thanks to the successful Ord River Irrigation Scheme—tropical fruit production for both domestic and worldwide markets.

The Kimberley is a magical haven of desert ranges, outback stations, tropical forests, raging rivers, national parks, and more, more, more. The weather is a big drawback, however. It's best to travel here April to September, during the dry season. At other times of the year, not only do temperatures swelter above 40° C (104° F),

On 1 April 1997 all telephone numbers with the (091) area code will change. To dial the new number, simply add 91 to the old number. The new area code will be (08). For example, (091) 12-3456 will become (08) 9112-3456.

THE KIMBERLEY

TIMOR SEA

JOSEPH
BONAPARTE
GULF

INDIAN OCEAN

KALUMBURU
MISSION

DRYSDALE RIVER
NATIONAL PARK

DRYSDALE RIVER
HOMESTEAD

HOME VALLEY

WYNDHAM

ORD R.

HIDDEN
VALLEY
NATIONAL
PARK

IVANHOE

THE
GROTTO

KUNUNURRA

CAMBRIDGE GULF

EL QUESTRO

LAKE ARGYLE
TOURIST VILLAGE

BARNETT
RIVER
GORGE

GIBB RD.

GIBB R.

CAPE
LEVEQUE

MANNING
GORGE

MT. BARNETT

MT. ELIZABETH
STATION

MT.
BARNETT
STATION

PENTECOST
DOWNS

ARGYLE
DIAMOND MINE

LAKE
ARGYLE

TO
STUART HIGHWAY
AND DARWIN

DURACK R.

LOMBADINA
MISSION

NAPIER
RANGE

KING

ISDELL
GORGE

ADCOCK
GORGE

TURKEY CREEK

BEAGLE BAY
MISSION

KING
SOUND

LENNARD
RIVER GORGE

LEOPOLD

MT.
BUCHANAN

LENNARD R.

DERBY

WINDJANA GORGE
NATIONAL PARK

TUNNEL CREEK
NATIONAL PARK

RANGES

MT. MAHONY

PURNULULU
(BUNGLE BUNGLE)
NATIONAL PARK

CAPE
LEVEQUE
RD.

OSCAR
PLATEAU

OSCAR RANGE

BROOKING GORGE

BROOKING SPRINGS

DUNCAN RD.

BROOME

FITZROY RIVER

GEIKE GORGE
NATIONAL PARK

HALLS CREEK

OLD HALLS CREEK

TO PORT HEDLAND

FITZROY CROSSING

GREAT NORTHERN HWY.

WESTERN AUSTRALIA
NORTHERN TERRITORY

WOLFE CREEK
CRATER
NATIONAL PARK

TANAMI TRACK

CARRANYA

0   100 km

---

but the very wet Wet swells rivers, floods roads, leaves settlements stranded, blackens tempers, and renders attractions inaccessible. Also common are bone-biting cold nights, May to July. You'll need a well-equipped 4WD for off-highway exploration.

BROOME

As the "Gateway to the Kimberley," Broome (pop. 3,670) is one of the hottest (in both temperature and popularity) destinations in the country. Situated 2,353 km northeast of Perth, this dusty, cosmopolitan town is filled with boab trees, red dust, and oodles of character (and characters).

Pearls before swine—or at least cattle—certainly held true here. Beginning in the 1880s, the gung-ho pearling industry provided work for about 400 luggers (boats) and 3,000 men, contributing 80% of the world's mother-of-pearl until the advent of plastics. Now only a few luggers remain, in conjunction with newly established cultured pearl farming. But there's beef—and *plenty* of it as Broome's modern meatpacking industry is capable of processing some 40,000 head of cattle each season.

Though the Japanese targeted Broome during WW II, evidence of damage by both sides can be seen in the wrecked carcasses of Allied flying boats in Roebuck Bay and the Japanese plane engines mounted near the Continental Hotel.

The Asian pearlers contributed to Broome's rich cultural mix, mini-Chinatown, and atmospheric appeal for a new breed of travelers—backpackers, frontrunners, and high-lifers.

Chinatown

Bounded by Carnarvon St. and Dampier Terrace, Short St., and Napier Terrace, "Chinatown" basically refers to Broome's older section—once alive with saloons, billiard parlors, boardinghouses, and pearling sheds—now lined with restaurants, souvenir shops, and ubiquitous pearl purveyors.

The **Roebuck Bay Hotel** is *rowdy* most nights and weekends. Live bands play in the beer garden most Saturday afternoons, and you won't want to miss those arm wrestling and wet T-shirt contests!

Dating from 1916, **Sun Pictures,** near the corner of Short and Carnarvon Streets, is one of Australia's few remaining open-air cinemas. Regular screenings of not-terribly-old releases are shown nightly. For program information, phone (091) 92-1677.

The glass-encased model of a **Chinese temple** sits on Dampier Terrace, near Short Street.

Other Sights

The **Broome Historical Society Museum,** Saville St. (in the old customs house), presents pearling-era items, historical displays, and a shell collection. Hours are Mon.-Fri. 10 a.m.-4 p.m., Sat.-Sun. 10 a.m.-1 p.m. Admission is $2. For information, phone (091) 92-2075.

The **Courthouse,** Frederick St., offers another sweep at Broome's past. Hours are Mon.-Fri. 9 a.m.-noon and 1-4 p.m.

Horrie Miller (founder of Ansett WA) displays his Wackett aircraft outside the **Library and Art Gallery,** corner Mary and Hammersley Streets.

The marble headstones with Japanese inscriptions and a commemorative column are the most interesting at the **cemetery** on Ann Street.

Buccaneer Rock, at the entrance to Dampier Creek, commemorates the visit by Capt. William Dampier and the *Roebuck*.

The **Golden Staircase to the Moon** is an effect created by the full moon's reflection off the ocean bed during low tides. Check with the tourist bureau for dates and best vantage points.

Sights near Broome

Popular **Cable Beach,** six km from town on Gantheaume Bay, is a white-sand and turquoise stretch for surfing, swimming, and sunning (nude, beyond the rock at the northern edge). Stingers invade these shores during summer months.

See some 500 crocs, ranging from babies to six-meter-long adults, at **Broome Crocodile Park,** Cable Beach Rd., Cable Beach. Primarily a research center, the farm also presents tours and video screenings. Hours are daily 10 a.m.-5 p.m. Admission is $9. For information, phone (091) 92-1489.

Dinosaur footprints, 130 million years old, are visible at low tide at Gantheaume Point, seven km south of Broome, at the end of Cable Beach. If you're not able to see the real thing, cement casts are displayed near the beacon on the cliff. **Anastasia's Pool,** a manmade rock pool north of Gantheaume Point, fills up at high tide for those who want to take a dip.

Pearl Coast Aquarium, Port Dr., eight km from town at the deepwater port, supplies aquariums worldwide with local tropical fish. A pearling display explains modern farming techniques. Hours are daily 10 a.m.-5 p.m. For information, phone (091) 92-2443.

Birdwatchers can view more than 200 species of their feathered friends at the **Broome Bird Observatory,** 18 km east of town on Roebuck Bay. Hours are Tues.-Sun. 8 a.m.-noon and 2-5 p.m. For information, phone (091) 93-5600.

Cape Leveque Road, from Broome to Cape Leveque Lighthouse, spans a distance of around 200 km. Sights along the way include the Beagle Bay and Lombadina Aboriginal communities and their beautiful churches, plus another at One Arm Point, beyond Cape Leveque Lighthouse. Only the churches and souvenir shops welcome travelers.

Accommodations

The tourist influx has, unfortunately, driven accommodation rates way up. It's best to book ahead, especially during Australian school holidays.

Forrest House, 59 Forrest St. (tel. 091-93-5067), is a moderately priced guesthouse with breakfast included in the tariff. **Kimberley Holiday Home,** Herbert St. (tel. 091-92-1134), offers self-contained holiday units with cooking facilities in the upper-moderate range.

Both the **Continental Hotel,** Weld St. (tel. 091-92-1002), and **Roebuck Bay Hotel/Motel,** Carnarvon St. (tel. 091-92-1221), have air-conditioning, TVs, and swimming pools, and are expensive. **Cable Beach Club,** Cable Beach Rd. (tel. 091-92-0400), with bungalows, suites, and studio units, is super-posh and super-expensive.

The YHA operates two **hostels: The Last Resort,** 2 Bagot St. (tel. 091-93-5000), and the more sedate **Ocean Lodge,** Cable Beach Rd. (tel. 091-93-7700).

Campsites are located at **Broome Vacation Village,** Port Dr. (tel. 091-92-1057); **Cable Beach Caravan Park,** Millington Rd. (tel. 091-92-2066); **Roebuck Bay Caravan Park,** Walcott St. (tel. 091-92-1366); and **Broome Caravan Park,** Great Northern Hwy. (tel. 091-92-1776).

Food

The sometimes-too-lively **Roebuck Bay Hotel** in Chinatown serves a good range of counter meals for lunch and dinner, and higher-brow fare in its restaurant section.

For Chinese in Chinatown, try **Wing's** on Napier Terrace and **Murray's Asian Affair** on Dampier Terrace. **Chin's Chinese Restaurant,** Hamersley St., offers Asian specialties at moderate prices, plus takeaways.

The **Tea House,** Saville St., serves a good variety of Thai-style seafood. **Charters,** in the Mangrove Hotel, has a wonderful reputation for its seafood specialties.

Weld Street Bistro in the Continental Hotel offers daily changing menus, with emphasis on seafood, in the moderate-and-up price range.

For your splurge in fine dining, Broome's best is the **Club Restaurant** at Cable Beach Club, where only fresh ingredients are used. For reservations (required) phone (091) 92-2505. **Lord Mac's** is a more casual spot to watch the hot sun slip away over a cold beer.

Shopping

Absolutely scads of shops will be happy to sell you **pearl jewelry** at expensive prices. Some high-quality (and high-priced) outlets are: Paspaley Pearling, Short St.; Linney's, Dampier Terrace; and the Pearl Emporium, Dampier Terrace.

Transportation and Tours

Ansett (tel. 13-1300 toll-free) offers scheduled service from Perth ($470) and Darwin ($350). The local Ansett office is on the corner of Barker and Weld Streets (tel. 091-93-5444).

Greyhound Pioneer Australia (tel. 13-2030 toll-free) operates regular bus service to Broome from Perth ($190) and Darwin ($170). The local office is at **Broome Travel,** Hamersley St. (tel. 091-92-1561).

Broome Coachlines runs buses between Broome and Cable Beach. For schedules and information, phone (091) 92-1068.

Major car rental firms are represented at the airport, with prices beginning at about $60 per day. You might get a better deal at **Topless Rentals,** Hunter St. (tel. 091-93-5017), or **Woody's,** Napier Terrace (tel. 091-92-1791).

Broome is an easy town for cycling. **Broome Cycle Centre,** at Checkpoint Service Station, corner of Hamersley St. and Napier Terrace (tel. 091-92-1702), rents bicycles for $8 per day, with a break for weekly rentals.

Many local and extended tours depart Broome. For example, you can take a glorious twilight cruise aboard a yacht, a pseudo-lugger, or on *The Dampier*—an authentic pearl lugger. Cost is around $50, including beer or wine. Book this and other tours through the tourist office.

Kimberley Hovercraft will take you for a one-hour glide over Roebuck Bay for $50. For information, phone (091) 93-5025.

Inquire at the tourist office for the latest on bushwalks, 4WD safaris, and Harley rides.

Services and Information

For tourist information and local tour bookings, contact **Broome Tourist Bureau,** corner Great Northern Hwy. and Bagot St. (tel. 091-92-2222). Hours are daily April-Nov. 9 a.m.-5 p.m., and in other months, Mon.-Fri. 9 a.m.-5 p.m., Sat.-Sun. 9 a.m.-1 p.m.

Broome Hospital, Anne St. (tel. 091-92-1401), has a casualty department.

DERBY

Broome may be the "Gateway to the Kimberley," but Derby (pop. 3,000)—at the heart of many scenic attractions—has been dubbed "Gateway to the Gorges." Situated on the King Sound shore 220 km northeast of Broome, this port town was lively during the 1880s gold boom, until it, too, went the cattle route. More recently oil, diamonds, and, of course, tourism have played an important role in the town's development as both an administrative center and a base for travel to some of WA's most stunning gorges.

Sights

The **Derby Cultural Centre,** Clarendon St., exhibits Aboriginal artifacts, local arts and crafts, Jowlaenga sandstone, and a palm tree botanic garden. Hours are Mon.-Wed. and Friday 10 a.m.-4 p.m., Thursday 1-7 p.m., Saturday 8 a.m.-noon. For information, phone (091) 91-1733.

At the corner of Loch and Elder Streets, the 1920s **Wharfinger's House,** built for the harbormaster, typifies tropical architecture.

The original **Old Derby Gaol,** dating from the 1880s, is situated next to the modern-day Derby Police Station.

The present **jetty,** constructed in 1963-64 to replace the original 1885 wooden structure, is used mainly for fishing or observing the tidal movements (tides up to 11 meters give this the highest tidal range of any wharf in the Southern Hemisphere).

Visitors are welcome to see outback medical care in action (or about-to-be action) at the Kimberley headquarters of the **Royal Flying Doctor Service,** 60 Clarendon Street. For information, phone (091) 91-1211.

Estimated to be 1,000 years old, the hollow **Boab Prison Tree,** seven km south of town, was used as an overnight "holding cell" for prisoners on their way to Derby.

Pigeon Heritage Trail details the adventures of an Aboriginal outlaw and folk hero named Pigeon who was shot and killed in 1887, following a three-year standoff with police and white settlers. The self-guiding tour is presented in two stages—one from Derby, the other from Windjana Gorge. The tourist bureau provides brochures.

Events

The annual two-week **Boab Festival** in late June and early July presents a rodeo, mardi gras, street parties, arts and crafts exhibits, and mud football.

Accommodations and Food

West Kimberley Lodge, corner Sutherland and Stanwell (tel. 091-91-1031), and **Spinifex Hotel,** Clarendon St. (tel. 091-91-1233), offer inexpensive guesthouse lodging. On the moderate side is **Derby Boab Inn,** Loch St. (tel. 091-91-1044). **King Sound Tourist Hotel,** Delewarr St. (tel. 091-93-1044) is the expensive choice.

Aboriginal Hostels Ltd., 233 Villiers St. (tel. 091-91-1867), has $10 beds and cheap meals.

Derby Caravan Park, Rowan St. (tel. 091-91-1022), has campsites and on-site vans.

The **Spinifex Hotel,** Clarendon St., and the **Derby Boab Inn** both serve moderately priced counter meals. **Lwoy's,** on Loch St., offers a Chinese fix, and **Wharf's Restaurant,** on the jetty, specializes in seafood.

Transportation, Services, and Information

Daily flights from Perth ($450) or Darwin ($300) are operated by **Ansett** (tel. 13-1300 toll-free). The local Ansett office is at 14 Loch St. (tel. 091-91-1266).

Greyhound Pioneer Australia (tel. 13-2030 toll-free) and **Westliner** (tel. 09-250-3318) run buses to Derby from Broome ($25), Port Hedland ($80), Perth ($200), and Darwin ($150).

Cars can be rented through Avis or Hertz, and begin at $70 per day.

The tourist bureau can arrange scenic flights to Koolan and Cockatoo Islands, as well as to some of the other Buccaneer Archipelago islands, but they start from $100 pp, with a four-person minimum. **Buccaneer Sea Safaris** (tel. 091-91-1991) will cruise you along the Kimberley coast.

Walking maps, tourist literature, and tour bookings are available at **Derby Tourist Bureau,** Clarendon St. (tel. 091-91-1426). Hours are Mon.-Fri. 8:30 a.m.-4:30 p.m., Saturday 8:30-11:30 a.m.

For emergencies, dial 000, the **police** (tel. 091-91-1444), **hospital** (tel. 091-93-3333), or **Royal Automobile Club** agency (tel. 091-91-1256).

GIBB ROAD

This 705-km back road is used primarily to transport beef from the Kimberley's huge cattle stations to ports at Derby and Wyndham. It's also the most direct route over to Wyndham with convenient, if not always easy, access to the majestic gorge country and—for the well-prepared adventurer—to places where no one else has ever set foot! Although it's possible for conventional vehicles in excellent condition to negotiate this harsh road (a combination of bitumen, gravel, and natural earth, marked with some very large pits and pocks), a 4WD is advisable. Make this trip only April-Nov., and carry plenty of extra supplies. Petrol is available approximately midway at Mount Barnett Station.

The road to Windjana and Tunnel Creek Gorges shoots off Gibb Rd. 120 km east of Derby. **Windjana Gorge** features awesome multicolored cliffs that rise 90 meters above the Lennard River (which rages during the Wet, trickling down to a few pools during the dry season). **Windjana Gorge National Park** (2,134 hectares), part of the Napier Ranges, is home to a variety of native fauna—including crocodiles. Campsites with limited facilities are available May-October. For information, phone (091) 91-5121.

Pigeon's first victim, Constable Richardson, was killed at **Lillmooloora Police Station,** a couple of kilometers beyond Windjana Gorge.

Aptly named **Tunnel Creek,** about 35 km south, has cut a 750-meter-long tunnel through the Oscar Range. A central shaft exposes natural light. During the dry season, the tunnel can be explored, but bring a torch or lantern, be ready for a short wade through cold water, and watch out for flying foxes. Aboriginal cave paintings can be seen near the tunnel's north end. From Tunnel Creek, it's 68 km to the Great Northern Highway and another 37 km to the roadhouse services at Fitzroy Crossing.

Back on Gibb Road, you'll mosey along the foothills of the King Leopold Ranges, a rugged area of tall granite outcrops, then you'll pass through Ingliss Gap to the top of the range before dipping down to the Broome Valley. Along the way are sidetracks to **Lennard River Gorge, Isdell Gorge,** and **Adcock Gorge.**

Replenish petrol (no LPG) and other supplies at **Mount Barnett Station,** 308 km east of Derby, on the banks of the Barnett River. Campsites with limited facilities are available. For information, phone (091) 91-7007. **Manning Gorge,** on Mount Barnett Station, offers swimming, fishing, and a two-km walking trail to a waterfall.

Forging onward, the turnoff to **Barnett River Gorge** is another 22 km. Moderately priced accommodations and cheap campsites are available at **Mount Elizabeth Station** (tel. 091-91-4644), 30 km off Gibb Road. The station also operates 4WD tours and scenic flights.

You must know where you are going, what you are doing, and—probably not a bad idea—who you are doing it with before adventuring onto **Kalumburu Road.** This extremely isolated, rough, and rocky road is often closed. **Drysdale River Homestead,** 66 km from the Gibb-Kalumburu Road junction, is the last information center and service point. From there on out, you're on your own—*really* on your own. Many of the attractions, such as Mitchell Plateau and Drysdale River National Park, can be reached only by foot. And, if you do make it to **Kalumburu,** at the end of the 276-km haul, you'll discover that Kalumburu Mission is an Aboriginal reserve, requiring an entry permit (see the special topic "Permits," in the On the Road chapter).

The next pit stop along Gibb Rd. is **Jack's** (or, sometimes, Joe's) **Waterhole** on the Durack River, a popular swimming, fishing, and camping stop. **Durack River Homestead** (tel. 091-61-4324) has moderately priced accommodations with all meals included. Four-wheel-drive tours of the region depart from here daily.

Home Valley Homestead (tel. 091-61-4322) is 56 km beyond Jack's (or Joe's). Accommodations, camping, and local tours are available here also. **El Questro Homestead** (tel. 091-61-4320), on the Pentecost River, has a fully self-contained stone cottage that accommodates six people, and a riverside camping area—it has been pushing for the yuppie/trendy clientele. This is the last facility on Gibb Road. It's 33 km to the junction of the Great Northern and Victoria Highways, where you go north to Wyndham or continue east to Kununurra.

THE GREAT NORTHERN HIGHWAY

Fitzroy Crossing and Vicinity

From Derby, it's 214 km to the gravel road north to Windjana Gorge and Tunnel Creek National Parks, and another 42 km to Fitzroy Crossing (pop. 430) on the Fitzroy River. Basically a cattle town, this little township is enjoying the fruits of Kimberley's popularity, providing services to travelers either about to cross the river or stranded because of the Wet's floods, and giving access to **Geikie Gorge National Park** (3,136 hectares), 21 km northeast. The 14-km-long gorge cuts through a fossilized "barrier reef" dating from the Devonian period some 350 million years ago, and fossil deposits can be seen in the limestone cliffs. The park is filled with interesting vegetation and abundant wildlife including sawfish and stingers (usually found only near the sea), freshwater crocodiles, kangaroos, and wallabies. The park is open April-Nov. (depending on the river's level). Boat tours of the gorge depart daily at 9:30 a.m. and 2 p.m.

The historic 1890s **Crossing Inn** (oldest pub in the Kimberley), near Brooking Creek (tel. 091-91-5080), offers moderately priced B&B rooms and plenty of local color.

Darlngunaya Backpackers, in the old post office on Geikie Gorge Rd. (tel. 091-91-5140), although four km from town, has $10 dorm beds.

During the dry season, campsites with limited facilities are available within the park; in Fitzroy Crossing, try the **Fitzroy River Lodge Caravan Park** (tel. 091-91-5141), **Fitzroy Crossing Caravan Park** (tel. 091-91-5080), or **Tarunda Caravan Park** (tel. 091-91-5004).

Brooking Gorge is also close to Fitzroy Crossing, but inquire first at Brooking Springs Station both for directions and permission to cross the privately owned land.

Fitzroy Crossing Information Centre is at Fitzroy River Lodge, Great Northern Hwy. (tel. 091-91-5141).

Halls Creek and Vicinity

The turnoff to Tanami Track is 272 km beyond Fitzroy Crossing and 16 km before Halls Creek—then it's another 114 km of unsealed road south to **Wolfe Creek Crater National Park** (1,460 hectares). Discovered in 1947 (but probably dating back a couple million years), the crater measures 835 meters wide and 50 meters deep and is the second-largest meteorite crater in the world. The road is usually accessible May-Nov., but check at Halls Creek for current conditions. **Carranya Station** (tel. 091-68-8927), seven km south of the crater, provides limited supplies and camping facilities.

Western Australia's first gold rush took place in 1885 at **Halls Creek** (pop. 1,000), although the gold dried up just a few years later. Now the center of the vast East Kimberley beef lands, you can still see crumbling reminders of the old gold days at the town's original site, 15 km away along Duncan Road. **Mount Bradley Mine** off Duncan Rd. is one of the region's original mines (some shafts are still open—and deep—so take care when walking around). You can still see the rusting machinery left behind at the **Ruby Queen Mine,** abandoned in the 1970s.

Good local swimming and picnic spots are at **Caroline Pool, Sawpit Gorge,** and **Palm Springs. China Wall,** on the way to old Halls Creek, is a natural white-quartz formation that resembles a mini-Great Wall of China.

Moderately priced, basic cabin accommodations with air-conditioning are available at **Shell Roadhouse,** 31 McDonald St. (tel. 091-68-6060). Lodging in the expensive range is offered at the **Kimberley Hotel,** Roberta Ave. (tel. 091-68-6101)—though there's a cheap backpacker section—and **Halls Creek Motel,** Great Northern Hwy. (tel. 091-68-6001). **Halls Creek Caravan Park,** Robert Ave. (tel. 091-68-6169), has campsites and on-site vans.

Fresh bread is baked Mon.-Sat. at **Halls Creek Bakery,** Great Northern Highway. The **Kimberley Hotel** has the usual counter meals and a higher-quality bistro (the bar here has a readily apparent black/white border).

Halls Creek Information Centre, Great Northern Hwy. (tel. 091-68-6262), is open May-Sept.; info is also available at the shire office, Thomas St. (tel. 091-68-6007). In emergencies, dial 000, or the **police** (tel. 091-68-6002) and **hospital** (tel. 091-68-6002).

One of Australia's greatest natural wonders is the 208,000-hectare **Purnululu National Park** (formerly Bungle Bungle National Park), with its amazing tiger-striped rock formations banded with black lichen and orange silica, plus thousands of low, domed, beehive-appearing peaks. Though Purnululu was only "discovered" in 1983, the place was no secret to the Kidja Aboriginals—and now no secret to tourists who may well turn this area into the next Uluru (Ayers Rock). Vegetation is composed of everything from the Bungle Bungle fan palm to spinifex and eucalpyts. Access to the park (a *very* rough 55 km from the Great Northern Hwy., 108 km from Halls Creek) is difficult, limited only to 4WDs with good clearance, and only during April-October. Check on road and weather conditions beforehand. Daytime temperatures can be extreme and water must be carried.

Hikes can be taken to **Echidna Chasm** in the north, **Cathedral Gorge** in the south, and **Piccaninny Gorge,** an intense 18-km round-trip. Entrance fee is $20 per vehicle. Because of the fragile ecology and travel difficulty, many visitors choose to take a scenic flight (departing from either Halls Creek or Kununurra) over the park—inquire at both tourist offices. **Camping** is permitted at Belburn Creek. For information, phone the **Department of Conservation and Land Management,** P.O. Box 242, Kununurra, WA 6743 (tel. 091-68-0200).

The Great Northern Highway calls into **Turkey Creek Roadhouse** (tel. 091-68-7882), 53 km north of the Purnululu turnoff. The roadhouse offers petrol, overnight accommodations, and 4WD Bungle Bungle tours.

Sorry, folks, they won't let you into the **Argyle Diamond Mine** up the road from Turkey Creek unless you fly in on an air tour from Kununurra (about the same cost as a small diamond). Discovered in 1979, this is supposedly the world's largest diamond deposit. Its annual production of 30 million carats includes white, champagne, and cognac diamonds, as well as rare and valuable pink diamonds.

From Turkey Creek, it's 151 km to the Great Northern and Victoria Highways junction, from where you proceed north to Wyndham or east to Kununurra.

WYNDHAM

Western Australia's northernmost port welcomes you with a 20-meter-long concrete "Big Croc" sculpture at the town's entrance—a replica of the salties that inhabit its waters. Situated on Cambridge Gulf, at the end of the Great Northern Highway, Wyndham (pop. 1,500) is nicknamed the "top town in the West." During the Halls Creek gold rush days the town prospered, then declined, made a comeback in 1919 when the Meatworks was established, then fizzled again after a 1985 fire closed the plant down. Today it survives mostly on tourism and as a service center for surrounding pastoral and Aboriginal communities.

Sights
What do you think about a spot called **Blood Drain Crocodile Lookout?** Located on the gulf side of the Meatworks complex, the adjacent creek once was used as a blood drain. Well, guess who came for dinner? And about 20 of them at a time! Since the Meatworks closed and the blood stopped flowing, fewer crocs dropped by until feeding began in 1987. Inquire at the Tourist Information Centre for feeding times and tide charts (they eat an hour before the full tide).

Five Rivers Lookout, at the top of the Bastion Range, offers magnificent views of the Forrest, Pentecost, Durack, King, and Ord Rivers, as well as the port, Meatworks, surrounding gulf, and mudflats. Sunrise and sunset are the best viewing times.

Three Mile Valley, a miniature East Kimberley Range, is reached via Five Rivers Road. Rough gorges, splintered rocks, clear pools, and colorful vegetation closely duplicate the larger range. Walking trails lead to good sites.

Aboriginal rock paintings depicting spiritual figures and animals are located on the road to Moochalabra Dam. Built to provide the town's water supply, the dam is also a good picnic spot and fishing hole.

The **Grotto,** a rockbound waterhole off the Wyndham-Kununurra Road, is a favorite swimming spot. **Prison Tree,** King River Rd., is a huge boab tree lock-up dating back to the 1890s.

Pay your respects to the historic dead at the **Gully, Bend,** or **Afghan** cemeteries.

Accommodations
It's sparse pickings up here. Least expensive motel units are at **Wyndham Roadhouse,** Great Northern Hwy. (tel. 091-61-1290). Accommodations in the moderate-expensive bracket are **Wyndham Town Hotel,** 19 O'Donnell St. (tel.

LOOKALIKES

The vicinity of Kununurra is inundated with lookalike rock formations:

- **Shark Fin Tree,** on Parker Road, looks like . . .
- **City of Ruins,** Weaber Plains Road, looks like . . .
- **Zebra rocks,** in the East Kimberleys, near Kununurra, look like . . .
- **Sleeping Buddha,** along the Ord River on Victoria Highway, looks like . . .
- **Elephant Rock,** an end-on view of the Sleeping Buddha, looks like . . .
- **Sleeping Mummy** looks like **Sleeping Buddha** looks like **Elephant Rock** looks like . . . *you?*

091-61-1003), and **Wyndham Community Club,** Great Northern Hwy. (tel. 091-61-1130). **Three Mile Caravan Park,** Baker St. (tel. 091-61-1064), offers campsites and on-site vans.

Transportation, Services, and Information

Ansett (tel. 13-1300 toll-free) has a daily Perth-Kununurra flight ($570 one-way), or from Darwin ($200).

From Kununurra, **I.J. and S.A. Thorley** (tel. 091-61-1201) provides daily coach transport to Wyndham. Fare is $25 one-way.

Rental cars begin at about $70 per day and are available at Branko BP Motors, Great Northern Hwy. (tel. 091-61-1305).

Wyndham Tourist Information Centre, O'-Donnell St. (in the Old Port Post Office), provides tourist literature, including a brochure detailing the heritage trail. For information, phone (091) 61-1054. Hours are daily 8 a.m.-5 p.m.

For emergencies, dial 000, the **police** (tel. 091-61-1055), **hospital** (tel. 091-61-1104), or local **Royal Automobile Club** (tel. 091-61-1305).

KUNUNURRA

Where were *you* in the sixties? Kununurra (pop. 2,100) was just being born as center of the Ord River Scheme, the Kimberley region's successful irrigation project. Then, in 1979, it was a double whammy when the world's largest diamond deposit was discovered south of town at Smoke Creek. Surrounded by water, natural attractions, birds, and wildlife, Kununurra is a travelers' stopover en route west to Broome (1,057 km) or east to Darwin (825 km).

Sights

Pandanun Palms Wildlife Park, Packsaddle Plains Rd., is a still-developing wildlife park with a range of native animals and birds. Hours are daily 8 a.m.-6 p.m. Admission is $2. For information, phone (091) 68-1114.

The **Zebra Rock Gallery** features displays of this unusual striped rock found only near Kununurra. Hours are daily 8 a.m.-6 p.m. For information, phone (091) 68-1114.

Collections of Aboriginal artifacts are displayed and sold at **Waringarri Aboriginal Arts,** Speargrass Road. This Aboriginal-run outlet offers boomerangs, didgeridoos, paintings, spears, fighting sticks, and many more crafts. Postcards, books, and music are also for sale. Hours are Mon.-Fri. 9 a.m.-5 p.m. For information, phone (091) 68-2212.

Kelly's Knob, near the town center, is a 191-meter-high viewpoint over the town, Ord River, and surrounding farmlands.

Adjacent to town, artificial **Lake Kununurra** has a wealth of wildlife and vegetation both on the lake and in the wetlands. Boat cruises are available.

The town fishing hole is **Ivanhoe Crossing,** a permanent waterfall on the Ord River near the Ivanhoe Station Homestead.

Hidden Valley National Park (1,817 hectares) near town is termed a "mini-Bungle Bungle." Features of this 300 million-year-old region include scenic gorges, rugged sandstone hills, Aboriginal rock art, abundant birdlife, and short walking trails.

Created by the Ord River dam, **Lake Argyle,** 72 km south of Kununurra along Parker Rd., contains nine times the water of Sydney Harbour. Rugged islands—which used to be mountain peaks—support a large number of birds and wildlife. Watch for Aboriginal rock paintings during the drive in. Boat cruises on Lake Argyle depart daily.

Moved from its original Lake Argyle site, the reconstructed **Argyle Homestead Museum,** Parker Rd., provides the history of early settlers' lives. Hours are daily 9 a.m.-4 p.m.

Accommodations

Seasons up here mean as much to travelers as to Aborigines when it comes to accommodation rates—there can be a wide variation. If you come during low (inferno-hot) season, you might well get an inexpensive deal at a "better" place.

Ranging moderate-expensive are **Country Club Hotel,** Coolibah Dr. (tel. 091-68-1024); **Kimberly Court,** corner of River Fig Ave. and Erythrina St. (tel. 091-68-1411); and **Hotel Kununurra,** Messmate Way (tel. 091-68-1344). And that shining beacon—the **Quality Inn**—is located on Duncan Hwy. (tel. 091-64-2622). **Lake Argyle Inn and Tourist Village,** Parker Rd. (tel. 091-68-7360), offers expensive rooms and cheap campsites.

Choose from three **hostels: Desert Inn Backpackers** (most popular), Tristania St. (tel. 091-68-2702); **Kununurra Backpackers,** 112 Nutwood Crescent (tel. 091-68-1711); and the YHA associate **Raintree Lodge,** Coolibah Dr., at the Uniting Church (tel. 091-68-1372). Dorm beds range $10-12.

Campsites are available at **Hidden Valley Caravan Park,** Weaber Plains Rd. (tel. 091-68-1790); **Kimberleyland Holiday Park,** Duncan Hwy. (tel. 091-68-1280); **Town Caravan Park** (on-site vans, too), Bloodwood Dr. (tel. 091-68-1763); and **Kona Lakeside Caravan Park** (tel. 091-68-1031), a bit out of town, but worth it for its lakeside location and prolific bird population.

Food

Gulliver's Tavern, corner of Konkerberry Dr. and Cotton Tree Ave., is a local drinking hole that also serves counter meals as well as more upmarket dinners in the dining room.

The **Kununurra Hotel** is another counter-meal establishment. A decent Chinese restaurant is housed inside the **Country Club Hotel** on Coolibah Drive.

Snackers might try **Three Star Café,** Banksia St.; the **Salad Bowl,** Coolibah Dr.; or **Valentines Pizza,** on Cottontree Avenue.

Transportation, Services, and Information

Ansett (tel. 13-1300 toll-free) has a daily Perth-Kununurra flight ($570 one-way), as well as flights from Broome ($250) or from Darwin ($200). Ansett's local office is in the Charlie Carter shopping mall (tel. 091-68-1444).

Greyhound Pioneer Australia (tel. 13-2030 toll-free) stops through on the Darwin-Perth route.

For **bicycle rentals** ($10 per day), inquire at any of the hostels or at the Visitors' Centre.

Rental cars start at $70 per day and are available from **Avis,** Bandicoot Dr. (tel. 091-68-1258), and **Hertz,** Poinciana St. (tel. 091-68-1257).

A full range of **tours** depart from Kununurra to surrounding sights. Book with the Visitors' Centre or the YHA Hostel (you'll get a discount if you're staying there). Just a few choices include the increasingly popular Purnululu scenic flights, horseback treks through the Kimberley Ranges, Ord River cruises, Lake Argyle cruises, and an extensive range of 4WD safaris and coach excursions.

From Kununurra, it's 513 km along the Victoria Highway to Katherine, junction of the Victoria and Stuart Highways. Proceeding 321 km north on the Stuart Highway (also called the Track) will bring you into Darwin—a kangaroo hop from Indonesia.

For information on local attractions and tours, contact **Kununurra Visitors' Centre,** Coolibah Dr. (tel. 091-68-1177). Hours are daily 8 a.m.-5 p.m.

For emergencies, dial 000, the **police** (tel. 091-69-1122), **hospital** (tel. 091-68-1522), or **Royal Automobile Club** (tel. 091-68-2236).

GLOSSARY

You only *think* they speak English down here. They don't—they speak "Strine" (Australian). Also, they do *not* parlez français. Here is one linguistic idiosyncracy that will make beaucoup de fou: "ballet" is pronounced "bal-ette," "filet" is "fill-ette," "gourmet" is "gor-mette," and picturesque" is "picture-skew." Another point to remember: Many words are shortened by adding "y" or "ie" to them (e.g., brekkie for breakfast, telly for television), and an "o'" is often attached to the end of someone's name (as in "Johno" or "Bozo").

abo—derogatory term for "Aborigine," best avoided

amber fluid—beer

Anzac—Australia and New Zealand Army Corps

arvo—afternoon

avago—have a go, give it a try (also, **avagoyermug**)

back o'Bourke—in the middle of nowhere (also **back of beyond**)

banana bender—a Queenslander

banker—a nearly overflowing river

barbie—put another shrimp on the . . .

barra—barramundi

barrack—to cheer on or root for a team

bathers—bathing suit (also **cozzie**)

battler—one who struggles

beaut or beauty—great, wonderful

bikies—motorcyclists

billabong—pond or waterhole in an otherwise dry riverbed

billy—a tin can with a wire handle used for fixing "billy tea" over a campfire

bitumen—a sealed or surfaced road

black stump—the back o'Bourke begins at the black stump

bloke—a man

blowies—blow flies

bludger—a nonworking person who parasites off another's resources

bluey—swag

bonnet—the hood of a car

bonzer—terrific

boomer—huge

boomerang—curved flat wood used as an Aboriginal hunting tool

boot—the trunk of a car

booze bus—the Breathalyzer police van

bottle shop—liquor store

brolly—umbrella

bruss—Central Oz Aboriginal for mate or brother

Buckley's—no chance

bull bar—extra-large front bumper protection from road animals

bungarra—a large goanna, especially Gould's goanna—an Aboriginal food source

bunyip—mythical swampland bush spirit

bush—the country, forest, or outback (almost anyplace outside the city)

bushrangers—Wild West-type outlaws (though some were good guys)

bush tucker—outback grub au naturel

bushwhackers—hicks

BYO—bring your own (booze); a restaurant that permits patrons to bring their own liquor

camp draft—rodeo, Australian-style

carn—rallying cry at football games (e.g., "carn the Magpies")

cheeky—sarcastic, insolent, rude

chook—chicken

chunder—vomit

cobber—old-timer's term for "mate"

cocky—a farmer

come good—turn out okay

compo—compensation, such as worker's compo

cooee—originally an Aboriginal shouting-distance greeting, i.e. "you hoo"

corroboree—an Aboriginal meeting, usually with song, dance, and ceremonies

counter meal—pub food

cozzies—swimming garb

crook—sick

crow eater—a South Australian

cut lunch—sandwiches

dag, daggy—a nerd, or nerdlike (actually the dirty wool lump on a sheep's bottom)

damper—bush bread cooked in a camp pot

dekko—to take a look at

dero—derelict

didgeridoo—Aboriginal men's wind instrument

digger—several meanings: a miner; soldier or veteran; old timer

dill—idiot

dilly bag—Aboriginal woven-grass carrying bag

dingo—a wild yellow dog

dinkum—honest, true (also **fair dinkum**)

dinky-di—genuine

Dog Fence—the world's longest, installed to protect southeastern Australia from dingoes

donk—automobile engine

don't come the raw prawn—don't fool me!

drongo—a stupid or worthless person

duco—automobile paint

duffing—cattle-stealing

dunny—an outhouse

earbash—nonstop chatter

Esky—popular brand of portable ice chest

fair go—an equal opportunity

fall pregnant—to get pregnant

financial—to be in good monetary condition

flat out—busy

footy—football

footpath—sidewalk

fossicking—gem- or rockhounding

galah—a fool or idiot (also a noisy parrot)

garbo—trash collector

g'day—good day

gibber—stony desert

good on ya—good for you, well done

good oil—good information or ideas

grazier—big-time sheep or cattle farmer

The Green—The Wet, in the Kimberley

homestead—station owner or manager's residence

hoon—a jerk or noisy rabble-rouser

Hughie—sometimes God, sometimes just surf and rain God

hump—to carry something

humpy—temporary bark hut used by Aborigines

icy pole—popsicle or ice cream on a stick

jackeroo—male ranch hand

jillaroo—female ranch hand

joey—pouch-riding baby kangaroo or wallaby

journo—a journalist

jumbuck—sheep

jumper—a sweater

Kiwi—a New Zealander

knackered—extremely tired

knock—to criticize

knockers—those who knock others (down)

Koori—Aborigine from southeastern Australia

lay by—lay away (to hold something in a store or shop)

lollies—candy

loo—toilet

mad as a cut snake—*really* crazy or crazy mad

manchester—household linen items

mate—friend or casual aquaintance

matilda—swag

milk bar—the corner shop or convenience store

milko—milkman

moke—also mini-moke; a jeep

mozzies—mosquitoes

mud map—rough hand-drawn map

mulga—the bush

Murri—Aborigine (usually Queensland)

muster—round up sheep or cattle

never never—way out in the outback

new Australians—newer immigrants (usually non-British descendants)

no worries—no problem

nought—zero

nulla-nulla—Aborigines' wooden club

ocker—a brash, rude Aussie

offsider—an assistant

on the piss—out drinking

O-S—overseas

outback—Australia's—and one of the world's—most remote regions

OYO—Own Your Own (flat, condo, apartment)
Oz—Australia

paddock—a fenced-in area for livestock
pastoralist—bigger big-time than a grazier
perve—to lust after
piss—beer
pissed—drunk
pissed off—irritated
plonk—rot-gut wine
pokies—poker or slot machines
pom—an English person
postie—a mail person

Queenslander—a house, usually built off the ground, constructed to maximize natural cooling

randy—horny
rapt—*really* pleased or enraptured
ratbag—mild rebuke for an eccentric or trouble-stirrer
ratshit—lousy
reckon—"I reckon that randy, ratshit ocker will push the milko down the loo."
rego—car registration
ridji didge—the genuine article (also "ridgy didge")
right—okay ("She'll be right, mate.")
ripper—good, great, terrific
road train—a semi with several trailers
rollies—roll-your-own ciggies
ropable—intensely angry or fiery-tempered
rubbish—garbage (also, to tease)
rug rat—toddler

sandgroper—a Western Australian
sandshoes—sneakers
see ya later—maybe you will, maybe you won't
shanty—typically, an unlicensed pub in goldmining enclaves
sheila—archaic term for "girl"
she'll be right—no problem
shoot through—leave *fast*
shout—to treat or buy a round of drinks ("It's your shout.")
sickie—a day off work (often not having anything to do with sickness)
singlet—sleeveless T-shirt

smoko—tea break
snag—sausage
spunk, spunky—good-looking ("He's a spunk")
station—a large ranch or farm
stickybeak—nosy or curious person
stinger—box jellyfish
stuffed—exhausted, beat
sunbake—sunbathe
super—superannuation, pension
surfies—surfers
swag—bedroll containing your possessions (often carried over your shoulder)
swagman—a swag-toting itinerant worker
sweets—dessert

ta—thank you
tacker—toddler
takeaway—takeout, fast food
tall poppies—successful people, often cut down
taxi rank—taxi stand
tea—dinner, supper, evening meal
terra nullius—the outrageously racist claim of the Australian government that no one had lived on the continent before 1788
thingo—you know, a *thing* (a-ma-bobby)
true blue—honest, real, dinkum
tucker—food, grub
two-up—Aussie gambling game

uni—university
ute—pickup truck

waddy—Aborigines' wooden club
wag—to cut school
walkabout—a long walk away from civilization
waltzing matilda—old term for a swagman
watch house—police station holding cell
weatherboard—wooden dwelling
whinge—whine or complain
willy-willy—dust storm
wobbly—shaky behavior
wowser—a tightass, prude

yabber—jabber, chat, yak yak
yahoo—loud, ill-mannered person
Yank—an American
yarn—a story or tale
yobbo—an unmannered, brash person

BOOKLIST

The majority of books listed can be purchased at either chain or independent bookshops in Australia, and many are available in the United States. Australian embassies and consulates often house libraries with a wide range of reference and reading matter. The most comprehensive collections are found at the Australian High Commission (London), the Australian Embassy (Washington, D.C.), and the Australian Consulate (New York). International Specialized Book Services (5804 N.E. Hassalo St., Portland, OR 97213-3644; tel. 800-547-7734 or 503-287-3093) stocks many Australian titles, including university press publications and maps.

ABORIGINAL CULTURE, HISTORY, AND STUDIES

Berndt, Ronald, and Catherine Berndt. *The Speaking Land: Myth and Story in Aboriginal Australia.* Penguin, 1989. Nearly 200 myths from a variety of Aboriginal societies and cultures are compiled in this first-of-a-kind anthology.

Broome, Richard. *Aboriginal Australians.* Allen and Unwin, 1982. A black response to the white invasion spanning 1788-1980.

Dixon, R.M.W. and Martin Duwell, eds. *The Honey-Ant Men's Love Song & Other Aboriginal Song Poems.* University of Queensland Press.

Edwards, W.H. *An Introduction to Aboriginal Societies.* Social Science Press, 1988. Though mainly a college text, this volume is an excellent introduction to Aboriginal economic, social, religious, and political organization and values.

ABORIGINAL WRITINGS

Davis, Jack, Stephen Muecke, Mudrooroo Narogin, and Adam Shoemaker, eds. *Paperbark: A Collection of Black Australian Writing.* University of Queensland Press, 1989. More than 40 black authors have contributed oral literature, poetry, drama, novellas, and other literary forms.

Gilbert, Kevin, ed. *Inside Black Australia: An Anthology of Aboriginal Poetry.* Penguin, 1988. Diverse voices from riverbanks, universities, jail cells, urban ghettoes, campfires, and reserves.

Headon, David, ed. *North of the Ten Commandments.* This anthology of Northern Territory writings is filled with insights and discoveries from a wide range of contributors.

Morgan, Sally. *My Place.* Fremantle Arts Centre Press, 1987. A powerful and poignant autobiography that traces three generations of Aborigines.

Narogin, Mudrooroo. *Master of the Ghost Dreaming.* HarperCollins, 1993. In this book by the first Aboriginal novelist, Jangamuttuk, the custodian of the Ghost Dreaming, uses his shamanist powers to will his tribal people to their land.

Narogin, Mudrooroo. *Wild Cat Falling.* HarperCollins, 1993 (orig. 1964). The first novel ever published by an Aboriginal writer, this is the study of an Aboriginal youth who is convicted of petty theft, jailed, and then plunked back out into society.

Narogin, Mudrooroo. *Wildcat Screaming.* HarperCollins, 1993. This satirical sequel to *Wild Cat Falling,* written 27 years later by Australia's most prolific Aboriginal author, sees our fellow back in jail.

Neidjie, Bill, Stephen Davis, and Allan Fox. *Australia's Kakadu Man.* Bill Neidjie, one of the last of the Kakadu tribe, passes along some of his people's ancient wisdom through text and color photos.

Nunukul, Oodgeroo. *My People.* Jacaranda-Wiley, 1981. Oodgeroo was formerly known as Kath Walker. This provocative book of poems is now in its third edition.

Nunukul, Oodgeroo. *Stradbroke Dreamtime.* HarperCollins, 1993. The Aboriginal author has penned a two-part book: the first half is a childhood memoir, the second contains Aboriginal folklore tales.

ART AND PHOTOGRAPHY

Bachman, Bill. *Local Colour.* Odyssey, 1994. A hardback coffee-table edition with 354 exquisite and unique photographs. Bachman, king of outback photography, supplies his own insightful and humorous text, supplemented by that of award-winning Western Australian author Tim Winton.

Bachman, Bill. *Off the Road Again.* Lothian, 1989. A terrific compendium of both quirky and mystical outback photos.

Coleman, Peter. *Bruce Beresford: Instincts of the Heart.* Angus and Robertson, 1993. An in-depth study of the Aussie director with film credits such as *Driving Miss Daisy, Tender Mercies,* and *Breaker Morant.*

Granville, James. *Australia the Beautiful.* Weldons, 1983. This glossy volume of photography and text will take you on a pictorial journey of the continent and its inhabitants.

Isaacs, Jennifer, ed. *Aboriginality: Contemporary Aboriginal Paintings and Prints.* University of Queensland Press, 1992. This lavish, revised edition showcases 25 contemporary artists committed to expressing their cultural heritage in a variety of vibrant works.

Isaacs, Jennifer. *Australian Aboriginal Paintings.* Weldons, 1989. A selection of traditional canvas and bark paintings from tribes of Arnhem Land and the western desert regions, including translated information from the artists.

Spencer, Sir Walter Baldwin. *The Aboriginal Photographs of Baldwin Spencer.* Viking, 1987. A coffee-table edition of the widely acclaimed Aboriginal photos, taken by Sir Walter 1894-1927, on expedition in northern and central Australia.

AUSTRALIAN CLASSICS

Baynton, Barbara. *Bush Studies.* Angus and Robertson. A female view of bush life told through a collection of stories.

Clarke, Marcus. *For the Term of His Natural Life.* HarperCollins/Angus and Robertson. An Australian literary classic depicting the gruesome life inside a penal colony.

Clark, Manning. *A Short History of Australia.* Penguin, 1987. The acclaimed historian's abridged and accessible version of his five-volume *A History of Australia.*

Franklin, Miles. *My Brilliant Career.* HarperCollins/Angus and Robertson. The novel-turned-film of a smarty-pants young woman coming of age in turn-of-the-century outback Australia.

Herbert, Xavier. *Capricornia.* HarperCollins/Angus and Robertson, 1977. Originally published in 1938, this elaborate saga portrays the mistreatment of half-castes in Australia's north.

Stowe, Randolph. *The Merry-Go-Round in the Sea.* Penguin. A classic story, against a World War II backdrop, of a young bloke coming of age in outback Western Australia.

BUSH BALLADS AND YARNS

Edwards, Ron. *The Wealthy Dog.* Rams Skull Press. Classic Australian yarn-spinning—a genre of its own, akin to the "tall tale."

Lawson, Henry. *The Best of Henry Lawson.* Angus and Robertson. Bush ballads and poems from one of the country's most famous balladeers and poets.

Paterson, A.B. "Banjo." *Collected Verse.* Harper-Collins. A selection of bush ballads and poems from the country's *most* famous balladeer and poet.

Semmler, Clement, ed. *Banjo Paterson.* University of Queensland Press. A collection of classic works—many depicting outback characters—by Andrew Barton "Banjo" Paterson of *Man from Snowy River* fame.

FICTION, LITERATURE, AND SOME HYPE

Bryson, John. *Evil Angels.* Bantam. Saga of the 1980s Lindy Chamberlain trial and media event, in which she swore her baby was carried off by a dingo from an Uluru (Ayers Rock) campground. Ultimately tried, convicted, then released, Lindy's story is *still* being bandied about. (Besides, she was played by Meryl Streep in the movie version.)

Facey, A.B. *A Fortunate Life.* Penguin, 1988. An Australian best-seller, written by Bert Facey (published when he was 87 years old), describing the "ordinary" life of this extraordinary man.

Flood, Tom. *Oceana Fine.* Allen and Unwin, 1989. An award-winning fantasy/thriller/whodunit novel set in Marvel Loch, Western Australia—a place of myth and mystery.

Keneally, Thomas. *The Chant of Jimmy Blacksmith.* Penguin. A very disturbing and brutal account of the inner psyche and outer workings of an Aboriginal criminal.

McCullough, Colleen. *The Thorn Birds.* Avon Books. Be-still-my-heart saga (and miniseries), set in Western Australia, of lusty forbidden love between priest and parishioner.

Morgan, Marlo. *Mutant Message Down Under.* HarperCollins, 1994. The unlikely tale of a middle-aged Missouri woman "chosen" by a small Aboriginal tribe to become privy to their culture, dreams, and way of life—all in the span of four months. Oh *pleeease!* Originally, this self-published book was sold as fact but the Harper-Collins edition sensibly carries an ass-covering disclaimer and catalogs the work as fiction.

Pritchard, Katharine Susannah. *Coonardoo.* HarperCollins/Angus and Robertson, 1975. This story of interracial love between a white station owner and his Aboriginal housekeeper was hot stuff in 1929 when it was first published.

Shute, Nevil. *A Town Like Alice.* Published in 1950, *Alice* was the first widely read outback-themed novel. *In the West* (1953) and *Beyond the Black Stump* (1956) were other outback-based Shute follow-ups.

White, Patrick. *The Aunt's Story,* Penguin, 1948.

White, Patrick. *The Tree of Man.* Penguin, 1955.

White, Patrick. *Voss.* Penguin, 1957. Australia's Nobel prize-winner portrays outback life, hardships, and characters in his heavy epic works.

Winton, Tim. *Cloudstreet.* Graywolf. The superb Mr. Winton spins an engaging tale of two families sharing a household in postwar Perth.

Wongar, B. *The Last Pack of Dingoes.* Angus and Robertson, 1993. Aboriginal and non-Aboriginal cultural differences exposed through clever short stories which combine an intriguing blend of political critique with mythological beliefs.

Wongar, B. *The Track to Bralgu.* HarperCollins, 1993. An enlightening though hardly upbeat short-story collection depicting the Aborigines' trials and tribulations.

GENERAL INTEREST

Antipodes. American Association of Australian Literary Studies (190 6th Ave., Brooklyn, NY 11217). A twice-yearly Australian literary journal featuring Aussie poetry, fiction, essays, book reviews, and literary scene updates.

BP Touring Atlas of Australia. Viking O'Neil, 1990. This large-format, fully indexed road atlas contains easy-to-read maps, including key maps and capital city maps.

Dunstan, Keith. *The Amber Nectar.* Viking O'Neil, 1987. A book celebrating the brewing and imbibing of Australian beer.

Goodwin, Ken, and Alan Lawson, eds. *The MacMillan Anthology of Australian Literature.* MacMillan, 1990. Thematically organized sketches, narratives, speeches, poems, and historical and biographical material.

Hirst, Robin. *Pocket Guide to the Southern Skies.* Dynamo Press, 1985. Get your bearings on the Southern Cross, Magellan's Clouds, and other phenomena of the southern skies.

Johansen, Lenie. *The Dinkum Dictionary: A Ripper Guide to Aussie English.* Viking O'Neil, 1988. More than 16,000 entries of slang, usage, and Aussie vernacular.

King, Jane. *Tasmania Handbook*. Chico, CA: Moon Publications, 1997.

Mayo, Oliver. *The Wines of Australia*. Faber and Faber. Tipple over Aussie-made vintages and their vintners.

Saunders, R. *Prehistoric Aussiegami: Paperfolding Dinosaurs*. Lothian Publishing, 1992. Lots of diagrams and illustrations guide you through your creation of dinkum Aussie origami dinosaurs.

Warren, Mark. *Atlas of Australian Surfing*. HarperCollins. Good guide to riding Australia's famous waves.

You Can Draw a Kangaroo. Australian Government Publishing Service. A step-by-step how-to paperback—fun for kids as well as adults tempted by those "try-to-draw" matchbook advertisements.

HISTORY

Aitchison, Ray. *The Americans in Australia*. AE-Press, 1986. Americans have exerted considerable influence in Australia.

Cannon, Michael. *Who Killed the Koories?* Heinemann Australia. A no-bedtime-lullaby of the violent clash between inland-bound settlers and Aborigines in 1840s New South Wales.

Grant, Joan, ed. *The Australopedia*. McPhee Gribble/Penguin Books, 1988. Informative descriptions for young readers about the workings of Australia after 200 years of civilization.

Gunn, Aeneas. *We of the Never Never*. Random Century Australia, 1987. This turn-of-the-century account of outback pioneer life and Aboriginal encounters is an Australian classic.

Hawke, Stephen. *Noonkabah*. Fremantle Arts Press. A former Premier's son relates the early 1980s headlock between Aborigines and the Labor Party over oil exploration near Fitzroy Crossing.

Hughes, Robert. *The Fatal Shore*. Collins, 1986. The best-seller that traces the country's convict origins, beginning with the 1788 arrival of the First Fleet.

Isaacs, Jennifer. *Pioneer Women of the Bush and Outback*. Weldons, 1990. Learn how ordinary bush and country women coped with daily life and hardships beginning from the last century onward.

Pilger, John. *A Secret Country*. Knopf. Read all about Aboriginal maltreatment, racism, British nuclear experiments, and other political and social dirt—spewed forth by a genuine-born Aussie bloke.

Rajkowski, Pamela. *In the Tracks of the Camelmen*. Angus and Robertson, 1987. The lowdown on some of outback Australia's most intriguing pioneers.

Rosser, Bill. *Up Rode the Troopers: The Black Police in Queensland and Dreamtime Nightmares*. University of Queensland Press. Nineteenth-century Queensland's dispersion methods for ridding the land of Aborigines, along with reasons why the indigenous people had little chance of resistance.

Sherington, Geoffrey. *Australia's Immigrants, 1788-1988*. Allen and Unwin, 1990. This recently revised volume explores the role migration has played in Australian society.

Webby, Elizabeth. *Colonial Voices*. University of Queensland Press, 1989. An anthology with glimpses of 19th-century historical events as well as daily life.

Whitlock, Gillian and David Carter, eds. *Images of Australia*. University of Queensland Press. This introductory guide to Australian studies includes historical development, Aboriginal culture, muliculturism, bush legends and suburban lifestyles.

NATURAL HISTORY

Bush Dwellers of Australia. Australian Government Publishing Service. A second edition with color shots of critters you're apt to encounter out bush.

Cogger, Harold G. *Reptiles and Amphibians of Australia*. More than 800 species are featured in photos and line drawings.

Dangerous Australians: The Complete Guide to Australia's Most Deadly Creatures. Bay Books, 1986. Read up on venomous and dangerous wildlife, creepies, and crawlies.

Ellis, G., and S. Cohen. *Outdoor Traveler's Guide: Australia.* HarperCollins/Angus and Robertson, 1988. This descriptive guide—containing many color photos and maps—embraces Australia's geography, vegetation, wildlife, parks, and natural areas.

Flood, Josephine. *The Riches of Ancient Australia.* University of Queensland Press Australia. Follow the continent's prehistoric heritage in this book complete with maps, photos, and drawings.

Longhurst, Peter. *Bush Strokes.* Bay Books, 1987. A full-color portfolio of 20 native outback animals, combined with informative text.

MacKness, Brian. *Prehistoric Australia.* Golden Press, 1987. Catch up on four billion years of the continent's evolution.

Phillips, Bill. *Koalas: The Little Australians We'd All Hate to Lose.* Australian Government Publishing Service. Learn more about the koala and its fragile existence.

Slater, Peter. *The Birdwatcher's Notebook.* Weldons, 1989. A field notebook with useful sighting charts, birdwatching techniques, bird characteristics, and much more birding info.

Triggs, Barbara. *The Wombat: Common Wombats in Australia.* The New South Wales University Press. Wombats, wombats, and more wombats: One-third of this book is photographs.

Webb, G. and C. Manolis. *Australian Freshwater Crocodiles.*

Webb. G. and C. Manolis. *Australian Saltwater Crocodiles.* G. Webb Pty. Ltd. Both 33-page texts feature color photos of fascinating and terrifying crocs.

TRAVEL INSPIRATIONS

Chatwin, Bruce. *The Songlines.* Viking, 1987. In this superb account, the author chronicles his life with central Australian Aborigines and helps to demystify some of the cultural complexities.

Davidson, Robyn. *Tracks.* Allen and Unwin 1982. An interesting tale of a determined woman who walks alone with her camels from Alice Springs to the Western Australia coast

Hawthorne, Susan and Klein, Renate, eds. *Australia for Women: Travel and Culture.* Spinifex Press, 1994. Rural and urban Aboriginal and Australian women share their culture and experiences in this unique compendium specifically for women travelers.

Stewart, D., ed. *Burnum Burnum's Aboriginal Australia, a Traveler's Guide.* Angus and Robertson, 1988. A large hardback volume that sets you exploring the country from an Aboriginal viewpoint.

INDEX

Italicized page numbers indicate information in charts, illustrations, maps, photos, or special topics.

ABOUT THE AUTHORS

Marael Johnson has been exploring and writing about Australia since 1983. She has freelanced as an area editor, researcher, and writer for many Fodor's Travel Guides (specifically in the Australia, New Zealand, and South Pacific regions) and has reviewed Australia's hotels and resorts for *Star Service Worldwide Hotel Guide*. She is the author of *Outback Australia Handbook* (Moon Publications, in its second edition)—winner of a Society of American Travel Writers' Lowell Thomas Award, *San Diego Agenda* (Fielding Worldwide, Inc.), *Why Stop? A Guide to California Roadside Historical Markers* and *Why Stop? A Guide to Louisiana Roadside Historical Markers* (Gulf Publishing Co). She is co-author of Fielding's Hawaii and Bahamas guides and contributing author to Microsoft's *Automap* and Fielding's *World's Most Dangerous Places*. She is an active member of the National Writer's Union and the Society of American Travel Writers. The author is currently working on Moon's *Louisiana Handbook*.

Since beginning work for Moon Publications, Australians Andrew Hempstead and Nadina Purdon have worked on Moon Handbooks to Alaska, British Columbia, and New Zealand. They are also the authors of *Alberta and the Northwest Territories Handbook*. For *Australia Handbook* they researched and wrote the chapters on New South Wales, Victoria, Tasmania, and Queensland.

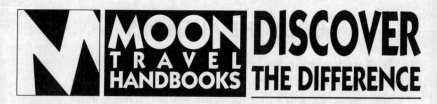

MOON TRAVEL HANDBOOKS DISCOVER THE DIFFERENCE

Moon Travel Handbooks provide focused, comprehensive coverage of distinct destinations all over the world. Our goal is to give travelers all the background and practical information they'll need for an extraordinary travel experience.

Every Handbook begins with an in-depth essay about the land, the people, their history, art, politics, and social concerns—an entire bookcase of cultural insight and introductory information in one portable volume. We also provide accurate, up-to-date coverage of all the practicalities: language, currency, transportation, accommodations, food, and entertainment. And Moon's maps are legendary, covering not only cities and highways, but parks and trails that are often difficult to find in other sources.

Below are highlights of Moon's Asia and Pacific Travel Handbook series. Our complete list of Handbooks covering North America and Hawaii, Mexico, Central America and the Caribbean, and Asia and the Pacific, are listed on the order form on the accompanying pages. To purchase Moon Travel Handbooks, please check your local bookstore or order by phone: (800) 345-5473 Monday-Friday 8 a.m.-5 p.m. PST.

MOON OVER ASIA
THE ASIA AND THE PACIFIC TRAVEL HANDBOOK SERIES

> "Moon guides are wittily written and warmly personal; what's more, they present a vivid, often raw vision of Asia without promotional overtones. They also touch on such topics as official corruption and racism, none of which rate a mention in the bone-dry, air-brushed, dry-cleaned version of Asia written up in the big U.S. guidebooks."
>
> —*Far Eastern Economic Review*

AUSTRALIA HANDBOOK
by Marael Johnson, Andrew Hempstead, and Nadina Purdon, 913 pages, **$21.95**
Explore the "land down under" with Moon's *Australia Handbook*, providing comprehensive coverage of outdoor recreation, the hottest sights, and detailed travel practicalities.

BALI HANDBOOK
by Bill Dalton, 800 pages, **$19.95**
"This book is for the in-depth traveler, interested in history and art, willing to experiment with language and food and become immersed in the culture of Bali."

— *Great Expeditions*

NEPAL HANDBOOK
by Kerry Moran, 428 pages, **$18.95**
Winner: Lowell Thomas Gold Award, Society of American
Travel Writers
"This is an excellent guidebook, exploring every aspect of the
country the visitor is likely to want to know about with both wit
and authority."

—*South China Morning Post*

NEW ZEALAND HANDBOOK
by Jane King, 544 pages, **$19.95**
"Far and away the best guide to New Zealand."

—*The Atlantic*

OUTBACK AUSTRALIA HANDBOOK
by Marael Johnson, 432 pages, **$18.95**
Winner: Lowell Thomas Silver Award, Society of American
Travel Writers
"Well designed, easy to read, and funny"

—*Buzzworm*

PAKISTAN HANDBOOK
by Isobel Shaw, 660 pages, **$22.50**
Pakistan Handbook guides travelers from the heights of the
Karakorams to the bazaars of Karachi, from sacred mosques in
Sind to the ceasefire line of Azad Kashmir. Includes a detailed
trekking guide with several itineraries for long and short treks
across the Hindu Kush, Karakoram, and Himalaya.

PHILIPPINES HANDBOOK
by Peter Harper and Laurie Fullerton, 638 pages, **$17.95**
"The most comprehensive travel guide done on the Philippines.
Excellent work."

—*Pacific Stars & Stripes*

PRACTICAL NOMAD
by Edward Hasbrouck, 200 pages, **$13.95**
The Practical Nomad is a planning guide for travelers considering
extended, multistop international trips, including around-the-world
journeys. This how-to handbook features essential information on
understanding airfares and ticketing, working with a travel agent,
and handling required documentation such as passports and
visas.

ROAD TRIP USA by Jamie Jensen, 800 pages, **$22.50**
Road Trip USA is a comprehensive travel guide to the "blue
highways" that crisscross America between and beyond the
interstates. This guide provides 11 cross-country, non-interstate
routes, many of which intersect, allowing travelers to create their
own driving adventure.

PERIPLUS TRAVEL MAPS

Periplus Travel Maps are a necessity for traveling in Southeast Asia. Each map is designed for maximum clarity and utility, combining several views and insets of the area. Transportation information, street indexes, and descriptions of major sites are included in each map. The result is a single map with all the vital information needed to get where you're going. No other maps come close to providing the detail or comprehensive coverage of Asian travel destinations. All maps are updated yearly and produced with digital technology using the latest survey information. **$7.95**

Periplus Travel Maps are available
to the following areas:

Bali	**Kuala Lumpur**
Bandung/W. Java	**Ko Samui/S. Thailand**
Bangkok/C. Thailand	**Lombok**
Batam/Bintan	**N. Sumatra**
Cambodia	**Penang**
Chiangmai/N. Thailand	**Phuket/S. Thailand**
Hong Kong	**Sabah**
Indonesia	**Sarawak**
Jakarta	**Singapore**
E. Java	**Vietnam**
Java	**Yogyakarta/C. Java**

MOONBELT

A new concept in moneybelts. Made of heavy-duty Cordura nylon, the Moonbelt offers maximum protection for your money and important papers. This pouch, designed for all-weather comfort, slips under your shirt or waistband, rendering it virtually undetectable and inaccessible to pickpockets. It features a one-inch high-test quick-release buckle so there's no more fumbling around for the strap or repeated adjustments. This handy plastic buckle opens and closes with a touch, but won't come undone until you want it to. Moonbelts accommodate traveler's checks, passports, cash, photos, etc. Size 5 x 9 inches. Available in black only. **$8.95**

Travel Matters

Travel Matters is Moon Publications' free newsletter, loaded with specially commissioned travel articles and essays that get at the heart of the travel experience. Every issue includes:

Feature Stories covering a wide array of travel and cultural topics about destinations on and off the beaten path. Past feature stories in *Travel Matters* include Mexican professional wrestling, traveling to the Moon, and why Germans get six weeks vacation and Americans don't.

Transportation tips covering all forms of transportation by land, sea, and air. Transportation topics covered recently have included driving through Baja California, new Eurail passes, trekking in Tibet, and biking through Asia.

Health Matters, by Dirk Schroeder, author of *Staying Healthy in Asia, Africa, and Latin America,* focusing on the most recent medical findings that affect travelers. Learn about hepatitis A and B, critical travel supplies, and how to avoid common ailments.

Book and Multimedia Reviews providing informed assessments of the latest travel titles, series, and support materials. Recent reviews include The Rough Guide to *World Music, Passage to Vietnam* CD-ROM, and *I Should Have Stayed Home: The Worst Trips of Great Writers.*

The Internet page, which provides updates on Moon's WWW site, online discussions, and other travel resources available in cyberspace. A wide range of topics have been covered in this column including how to go online without going crazy, the Great Burma Debate, and details on Moon's *Road Trip USA* project.

Fellow Traveler, a reader question and answer column for travelers written by an international travel agent and world traveler.

To receive a free subscription to *Travel Matters,* call (800) 345-5473, e-mail us at travel@moon.com, or write to us at:

Moon Publications
P.O. Box 3040
Chico, CA 95927-3040

Please note: Subscribers who live outside of the United States will be charged $7 per year for shipping and handling.

MOON TRAVEL HANDBOOKS

NORTH AMERICA AND HAWAII

Alaska-Yukon Handbook (0161) $14.95
Alberta and the Northwest Territories Handbook (0676) $17.95
Arizona Traveler's Handbook (0714). $17.95
Atlantic Canada Handbook (0072) $17.95
Big Island of Hawaii Handbook (0064). $13.95
British Columbia Handbook (0145). $15.95
Colorado Handbook (0447) $18.95
Georgia Handbook (0390) $17.95
Hawaii Handbook (0005). $19.95
Honolulu-Waikiki Handbook (0587) $14.95
Idaho Handbook (0617). $14.95
Kauai Handbook (0013) $13.95
Maui Handbook (0579) $14.95
Montana Handbook (0498). $17.95
Nevada Handbook (0641) $16.95
New Mexico Handbook (0153). $14.95
Northern California Handbook (3840) $19.95
Oregon Handbook (0102) $16.95
Road Trip USA (0366). $22.50
Texas Handbook (0633) $17.95
Utah Handbook (0684) $16.95
Washington Handbook (0455). $18.95
Wyoming Handbook (3980) $14.95

ASIA AND THE PACIFIC

Australia Handbook (0722) $21.95
Bali Handbook (0730). $19.95
Bangkok Handbook (0595) $13.95
Fiji Islands Handbook (0382) $13.95
Hong Kong Handbook (0560) $15.95
Indonesia Handbook (0625). $25.00
Japan Handbook (3700) $22.50
Micronesia Handbook (0773) $14.95
Nepal Handbook (0412) $18.95
New Zealand Handbook (0331) $19.95
Outback Australia Handbook (0471). $18.95
Pakistan Handbook (0692). $22.50
Philippines Handbook (0048) $17.95

Southeast Asia Handbook (0021). $21.95
South Pacific Handbook (0404). $22.95
Tahiti-Polynesia Handbook (0374) $13.95
Thailand Handbook (0420). $19.95
Tibet Handbook (3905) $30.00
Vietnam, Cambodia & Laos Handbook (0293) $18.95

MEXICO

Baja Handbook (0528) $15.95
Cabo Handbook (0285). $14.95
Cancún Handbook (0501) $13.95
Central Mexico Handbook (0234). $15.95
Mexico Handbook (0315). $21.95
Northern Mexico Handbook (0226). $16.95
Pacific Mexico Handbook (0323) $16.95
Puerto Vallarta Handbook (0250) $14.95
Yucatán Peninsula Handbook (0242) $15.95

CENTRAL AMERICA AND THE CARIBBEAN

Belize Handbook (0307) $15.95
Caribbean Handbook (0277). $16.95
Costa Rica Handbook (0358) $18.95
Jamaica Handbook (0706) $15.95

INTERNATIONAL

Egypt Handbook (3891) $18.95
Moon Handbook (0668). $10.00
Moscow-St. Petersburg Handbook (3913) $13.95
Staying Healthy in Asia, Africa, and Latin America (0269) . . . $11.95
The Practical Nomad (0765) $13.95

PERIPLUS TRAVEL MAPS
All maps $7.95 each

Bali	Jakarta	Phuket/S. Thailand
Bandung/W. Java	E. Java	Sabah
Bangkok/C. Thailand	Java	Sarawak
Batam/Bintan	Kuala Lumpur	Singapore
Cambodia	Ko Samui/S. Thailand	Vietnam
Chiangmai/N. Thailand	Lombok	Yogyakarta/C. Java
Hong Kong	N. Sumatra	
Indonesia	Penang	

WHERE TO BUY MOON TRAVEL HANDBOOKS

BOOKSTORES AND LIBRARIES: Moon Travel Handbooks are sold worldwide. Please contact our sales manager for a list of wholesalers and distributors in your area.

TRAVELERS: We would like to have Moon Travel Handbooks available throughout the world. Please ask your bookstore to write or call us for ordering information. If your bookstore will not order our guides for you, please contact us for a free catalogue.

> **Moon Publications, Inc.**
> **P.O. Box 3040**
> **Chico, CA 95927-3040 U.S.A.**
> **tel.: (800) 345-5473**
> **fax: (916) 345-6751**
> **e-mail: travel@moon.com**

IMPORTANT ORDERING INFORMATION

PRICES: All prices are subject to change. We always ship the most current edition. We will let you know if there is a price increase on the book you order.

SHIPPING AND HANDLING OPTIONS: Domestic UPS or USPS first class (allow 10 working days for delivery): $3.50 for the first item, 50 cents for each additional item.

EXCEPTIONS: *Tibet Handbook, Mexico Handbook,* and *Indonesia Handbook* shipping $4.50; $1.00 for each additional *Tibet Handbook, Mexico Handbook,* or *Indonesia Handbook.*

Moonbelt shipping is $1.50 for one, 50 cents for each additional belt.

Add $2.00 for same-day handling.

UPS 2nd Day Air or Printed Airmail requires a special quote.

International Surface Bookrate 8-12 weeks delivery: $3.00 for the first item, $1.00 for each additional item. Note: Moon Publications cannot guarantee international surface bookrate shipping. Moon recommends sending international orders via air mail, which requires a special quote.

FOREIGN ORDERS: Orders that originate outside the U.S.A. must be paid for with an international money order, a check in U.S. currency drawn on a major U.S. bank based in the U.S.A., or Visa or MasterCard.

TELEPHONE ORDERS: We accept Visa or MasterCard payments. Minimum order is US$15. Call in your order: (800) 345-5473, 8 a.m.-5 p.m. Pacific standard time.

ORDER FORM

Prices are subject to change without notice. Be sure to call (800) 345-5473 for current prices and editions or for the name of the bookstore nearest you that carries Moon Travel Handbooks • 8 a.m.–5 p.m. PST. (See important ordering information on preceding page.)

Name: _____ Date: _____

Street: _____

City: _____ Daytime Phone: _____

State or Country: _____ Zip Code: _____

QUANTITY	TITLE	PRICE

Taxable Total_____

Sales Tax (7.25%) for California Residents_____

Shipping & Handling_____

TOTAL_____

Ship: ☐ UPS (no P.O. Boxes)   ☐ 1st class   ☐ International surface mail

Ship to: ☐ address above   ☐ other _____

Make checks payable to: **MOON PUBLICATIONS, INC.**, P.O. Box 3040, Chico, CA 95927-3040 U.S.A. We accept Visa and MasterCard. **To Order**: Call in your Visa or MasterCard number, or send a written order with your Visa or MasterCard number and expiration date clearly written.

Card Number: ☐ **Visa**   ☐ **MasterCard**

☐☐☐☐ ☐☐☐☐ ☐☐☐☐ ☐☐☐☐

Exact Name on Card: _____

Expiration date: _____

Signature: _____

THE METRIC SYSTEM

1 inch = 2.54 centimeters (cm)
1 foot = .304 meters (m)
1 mile = 1.6093 kilometers (km)
1 km = .6124 miles
1 fathom = 1.8288 m
1 chain = 20.1168 m
1 furlong = 201.168 m
1 acre = .4047 hectares
1 sq km = 100 hectares
1 sq mile = 2.59 square km
1 ounce = 28.35 grams
1 pound = .4536 kilograms
1 short ton = .90718 metric ton
1 short ton = 2000 pounds
1 long ton = 1.016 metric tons
1 long ton = 2240 pounds
1 metric ton = 1000 kilograms
1 quart = .94635 liters
1 US gallon = 3.7854 liters
1 Imperial gallon = 4.5459 liters
1 nautical mile = 1.852 km

To compute celsius temperatures, subtract 32 from Fahrenheit and divide by 1.8. To go the other way, multiply celsius by 1.8 and add 32.